HALSBURY'S
Laws of England

FIFTH EDITION
2014

Volume 97A

This is volume 97A of the Fifth Edition of Halsbury's Laws of England, containing the title TRADE MARKS AND TRADE NAMES.

The title TRADE MARKS AND TRADE NAMES replaces the Fourth Edition title TRADE MARKS AND TRADE NAMES, contained in vol 48 (2007 Reissue).

The Fourth Edition volume 48 (2007 Reissue) may now be archived.

For a full list of volumes comprised in a current set of Halsbury's Laws of England please see overleaf.

Fifth Edition volumes:

1 (2008), 2 (2008), 3 (2011), 4 (2011), 5 (2013), 6 (2011), 7 (2008), 8 (2010), 9 (2012), 10 (2012), 11 (2009), 12 (2009), 13 (2009), 14 (2009), 15 (2009), 16 (2011), 17 (2011), 18 (2009), 19 (2011), 21 (2011), 22 (2012), 23 (2013), 24 (2010), 25 (2010), 26 (2010), 27 (2010), 28 (2010), 30 (2012), 31 (2012), 32 (2012), 33 (2013), 34 (2011), 35 (2011), 36 (2011), 37 (2013), 38 (2013), 38A (2013), 39 (2009), 40 (2009), 41 (2009), 42 (2011), 43 (2011), 44 (2011), 45 (2010), 46 (2010), 48 (2008), 49 (2008), 50 (2008), 51 (2013), 52 (2009), 53 (2009), 54 (2008), 55 (2012), 56 (2011), 57 (2012), 60 (2011), 61 (2010), 62 (2012), 63 (2012), 64 (2012), 65 (2008), 66 (2009), 67 (2008), 68 (2008), 69 (2009), 70 (2012), 71 (2013), 72 (2009), 73 (2009), 74 (2011), 75 (2013), 76 (2013), 77 (2010), 78 (2010), 79 (2008), 80 (2013), 81 (2010), 82 (2010), 83 (2010), 84 (2013), 84A (2013), 85 (2012), 86 (2013), 87 (2012), 88 (2012), 88A (2013), 89 (2011), 90 (2011), 91 (2012), 92 (2010), 93 (2008), 94 (2008), 95 (2013), 96 (2012), 97 (2010), 97A (2014), 98 (2013), 99 (2012), 100 (2009), 101 (2009), 102 (2010), 103 (2010)

Fourth Edition volumes (bold figures represent reissues):

1(1) (2001 Reissue), **8(1)** (2003 Reissue), **8(2)**, **12(1)**, **16(2)**, **17(2)**, **23(1)**, **23(2)**, 24, **39(1B)**, 51, 52

Additional Materials:

Housing (*Housing Benefit*) containing vol **22** (2006 Reissue) paras 140–186; *Sentencing and Disposition of Offenders* (*Release and Recall of Prisoners*) containing vol **92** (2010) paras 761–820; *Tort* (*Conversion and Wrongful Interference with Goods*) containing vol **45(2)** (Reissue) paras 542–686

Fourth and Fifth Edition volumes:

2013 Consolidated Index (A–E), 2013 Consolidated Index (F–O), 2013 Consolidated Index (P–Z), 2014 Consolidated Table of Statutes, 2014 Consolidated Table of Statutory Instruments, etc, 2014 Consolidated Table of Cases (A–G), 2014 Consolidated Table of Cases (H–Q), 2014 Consolidated Table of Cases (R–Z, ECJ Cases)

Updating and ancillary materials:

2013 Annual Cumulative Supplement; Monthly Current Service; Annual Abridgments 1974–2012

January 2014

HALSBURY'S
Laws of England

FIFTH EDITION

LORD MACKAY OF CLASHFERN
Lord High Chancellor of Great Britain
1987–97

Volume 97A

2014

 LexisNexis®

Members of the LexisNexis Group worldwide

United Kingdom	LexisNexis, a Division of Reed Elsevier (UK) Ltd, Lexis House, 30 Farringdon Street, LONDON, EC4A 4HH, and London House, 20–22 East London Street, EDINBURGH, EH7 4BQ
Australia	LexisNexis Butterworths, Chatswood, New South Wales
Austria	LexisNexis Verlag ARD Orac GmbH & Co KG, Vienna
Benelux	LexisNexis Benelux, Amsterdam
Canada	LexisNexis Canada, Markham, Ontario
China	LexisNexis China, Beijing and Shanghai
France	LexisNexis SA, Paris
Germany	LexisNexis GmbH, Dusseldorf
Hong Kong	LexisNexis Hong Kong, Hong Kong
India	LexisNexis India, New Delhi
Italy	Giuffrè Editore, Milan
Japan	LexisNexis Japan, Tokyo
Malaysia	Malayan Law Journal Sdn Bhd, Kuala Lumpur
New Zealand	LexisNexis NZ Ltd, Wellington
Poland	Wydawnictwo Prawnicze LexisNexis Sp, Warsaw
Singapore	LexisNexis Singapore, Singapore
South Africa	LexisNexis Butterworths, Durban
USA	LexisNexis, Dayton, Ohio

FIRST EDITION	*Published in 31 volumes between 1907 and 1917*
SECOND EDITION	*Published in 37 volumes between 1931 and 1942*
THIRD EDITION	*Published in 43 volumes between 1952 and 1964*
FOURTH EDITION	*Published in 56 volumes between 1973 and 1987, with reissues between 1988 and 2008*
FIFTH EDITION	*Commenced in 2008*

A CIP Catalogue record for this book is available from the British Library.

ISBN 13 (complete set, standard binding): 9781405734394

ISBN 13: 9781405790345

ISBN 978-1-4057-9034-5

9 781405 790345

Typeset by Letterpart Limited, Caterham on the Hill, Surrey CR3 5XL
Printed and bound by CPI Group (UK) Ltd, Croydon, CR0 4YY
Visit LexisNexis at www.lexisnexis.co.uk

Editor in Chief

THE RIGHT HONOURABLE

LORD MACKAY OF CLASHFERN

LORD HIGH CHANCELLOR OF GREAT BRITAIN

1987–97

TRADE MARKS AND TRADE NAMES

Consultant Editor

SIR RICHARD ARNOLD

one of the Justices of Her Majesty's High Court of Justice

The law stated in this volume is in general that in force on 1 December 2013, although subsequent changes have been included wherever possible.

Any future updating material will be found in the Current Service and annual Cumulative Supplement to Halsbury's Laws of England.

TABLE OF CONTENTS

HOW TO USE HALSBURY'S LAWS OF ENGLAND

Volumes

Each text volume of Halsbury's Laws of England contains the law on the titles contained in it as at a date stated at the front of the volume (the operative date).

Information contained in Halsbury's Laws of England may be accessed in several ways.

First, by using the tables of contents.

Each volume contains both a general Table of Contents, and a specific Table of Contents for each title contained in it. From these tables you will be directed to the relevant part of the work.

Readers should note that the current arrangement of titles can be found in the Current Service.

Secondly, by using tables of statutes, statutory instruments, cases or other materials.

If you know the name of the Act, statutory instrument or case with which your research is concerned, you should consult the Consolidated Tables of statutes, cases and so on (published as separate volumes) which will direct you to the relevant volume and paragraph. The Consolidated Tables will indicate if the volume referred to is a Fifth Edition volume.

(Each individual text volume also includes tables of those materials used as authority in that volume.)

Thirdly, by using the indexes.

If you are uncertain of the general subject area of your research, you should go to the Consolidated Index (published as separate volumes) for reference to the relevant volume(s) and paragraph(s). The Consolidated Index will indicate if the volume referred to is a Fifth Edition volume.

(Each individual text volume also includes an index to the material contained therein.)

Additional Materials

The reorganisation of the title scheme of Halsbury's Laws for the Fifth Edition means that from time to time Fourth Edition volumes will be *partially* replaced by Fifth Edition volumes.

In certain instances an Additional Materials softbound book will be issued, in which will be reproduced material which has not yet been replaced by a Fifth Edition title. This will enable users to remove specific Fourth Edition volumes from the shelf and save valuable space pending the replacement of that material in the Fifth Edition. These softbound books are supplied to volumes subscribers free of charge. They continue to form part of the set of Halsbury's Laws Fourth Edition Reissue, and will be updated by the annual Cumulative Supplement and monthly Noter-Up in the usual way.

Updating publications

The text volumes of Halsbury's Laws should be used in conjunction with the annual Cumulative Supplement and the monthly Noter-Up.

The annual Cumulative Supplement

The Supplement gives details of all changes between the operative date of the text volume and the operative date of the Supplement. It is arranged in the same volume, title and paragraph order as the text volumes. Developments affecting particular points of law are noted to the relevant paragraph(s) of the text volumes. As from the commencement of the Fifth Edition, the Supplement will clearly distinguish between Fourth and Fifth Edition titles.

For narrative treatment of material noted in the Cumulative Supplement, go to the Annual Abridgment volume for the relevant year.

Destination Tables

In certain titles in the annual *Cumulative Supplement*, reference is made to Destination Tables showing the destination of consolidated legislation. Those Destination Tables are to be found either at the end of the titles within the annual *Cumulative Supplement*, or in a separate *Destination Tables* booklet provided from time to time with the *Cumulative Supplement*.

The Noter-Up

The Noter-Up is contained in the Current Service Noter-Up booklet, issued monthly and noting changes since the publication of the annual Cumulative Supplement. Also arranged in the same volume, title and paragraph order as the text volumes, the Noter-Up follows the style of the Cumulative Supplement. As from the commencement of the Fifth Edition, the Noter-Up will clearly distinguish between Fourth and Fifth Edition titles.

For narrative treatment of material noted in the Noter-Up, go to the relevant Monthly Review.

REFERENCES AND ABBREVIATIONS

ACT	Australian Capital Territory
A-G	Attorney General
Admin	Administrative Court
Admlty	Admiralty Court
Adv-Gen	Advocate General
affd	affirmed
affg	affirming
Alta	Alberta
App	Appendix
art	article
Aust	Australia
B	Baron
BC	British Columbia
C	Command Paper (of a series published before 1900)
c	chapter number of an Act
CA	Court of Appeal
CAC	Central Arbitration Committee
CA in Ch	Court of Appeal in Chancery
CB	Chief Baron
CCA	Court of Criminal Appeal
CCR	County Court Rules 1981 (SI 1981/1687) as subsequently amended
CCR	Court for Crown Cases Reserved
C-MAC	Courts-Martial Appeal Court
CO	Crown Office
COD	Crown Office Digest
CPR	Civil Procedure Rules 1998 (SI 1998/3132) as subsequently amended (see the Civil Court Practice)
Can	Canada
Cd	Command Paper (of the series published 1900–18)
Cf	compare
Ch	Chancery Division
ch	chapter
cl	clause

Cm	Command Paper (of the series published 1986 to date)
Cmd	Command Paper (of the series published 1919–56)
Cmnd	Command Paper (of the series published 1956–86)
Comm	Commercial Court
Comr	Commissioner
Court Forms (2nd Edn)	Atkin's Encyclopaedia of Court Forms in Civil Proceedings, 2nd Edn. See note 2 post.
Court Funds Rules 1987	Court Funds Rules 1987 (SI 1987/821) as subsequently amended
CrimPR	Criminal Procedure Rules 2010 (SI 2010/60) as subsequently amended
DC	Divisional Court
DPP	Director of Public Prosecutions
EAT	Employment Appeal Tribunal
EC	European Community
ECJ	Court of Justice of the European Community
EComHR	European Commission of Human Rights
ECSC	European Coal and Steel Community
ECtHR Rules of Court	Rules of Court of the European Court of Human Rights
EEC	European Economic Community
EFTA	European Free Trade Association
EWCA Civ	Official neutral citation for judgments of the Court of Appeal (Civil Division)
EWCA Crim	Official neutral citation for judgments of the Court of Appeal (Criminal Division)
EWHC	Official neutral citation for judgments of the High Court
Edn	Edition
Euratom	European Atomic Energy Community
Ex Ch	Court of Exchequer Chamber
ex p	ex parte
Fam	Family Division
Fed	Federal
Forms & Precedents (5th Edn)	Encyclopaedia of Forms and Precedents other than Court Forms, 5th Edn. See note 2 post.
GLC	Greater London Council
HC	High Court
HC	House of Commons
HK	Hong Kong
HL	House of Lords

IAT	Immigration Appeal Tribunal
ILM	International Legal Materials
INLR	Immigration and Nationality Law Reports
IRC	Inland Revenue Commissioners
Ind	India
Int Rels	International Relations
Ir	Ireland
J	Justice
JA	Judge of Appeal
Kan	Kansas
LA	Lord Advocate
LC	Lord Chancellor
LCC	London County Council
LCJ	Lord Chief Justice
LJ	Lord Justice of Appeal
LoN	League of Nations
MR	Master of the Rolls
Man	Manitoba
n	note
NB	New Brunswick
NI	Northern Ireland
NS	Nova Scotia
NSW	New South Wales
NY	New York
NZ	New Zealand
OHIM	Office for Harmonisation in the Internal Market
OJ	The Official Journal of the European Community published by the Office for Official Publications of the European Community
Ont	Ontario
P	President
PC	Judicial Committee of the Privy Council
PEI	Prince Edward Island
Pat	Patents Court
q	question
QB	Queen's Bench Division
QBD	Queen's Bench Division of the High Court
Qld	Queensland
Que	Quebec
r	rule
RDC	Rural District Council
RPC	Restrictive Practices Court

RSC	Rules of the Supreme Court 1965 (SI 1965/1776) as subsequently amended
reg	regulation
Res	Resolution
revsd	reversed
Rly	Railway
s	section
SA	South Africa
S Aust	South Australia
SC	Supreme Court
SI	Statutory Instruments published by authority
SR & O	Statutory Rules and Orders published by authority
SR & O Rev 1904	Revised Edition comprising all Public and General Statutory Rules and Orders in force on 31 December 1903
SR & O Rev 1948	Revised Edition comprising all Public and General Statutory Rules and Orders and Statutory Instruments in force on 31 December 1948
SRNI	Statutory Rules of Northern Ireland
STI	Simon's Tax Intelligence (1973–1995); Simon's Weekly Tax Intelligence (1996-current)
Sask	Saskatchewan
Sch	Schedule
Sess	Session
Sing	Singapore
TCC	Technology and Construction Court
TS	Treaty Series
Tanz	Tanzania
Tas	Tasmania
UDC	Urban District Council
UKHL	Official neutral citation for judgments of the House of Lords
UKPC	Official neutral citation for judgments of the Privy Council
UN	United Nations
V-C	Vice-Chancellor
Vict	Victoria
W Aust	Western Australia
Zimb	Zimbabwe

NOTE 1. A general list of the abbreviations of law reports and other sources used in this work can be found at the beginning of the Consolidated Table of Cases.

NOTE 2. Where references are made to other publications, the volume number precedes and the page number follows the name of the publication; eg the reference '12 Forms & Precedents (5th Edn) 44' refers to volume 12 of the Encyclopaedia of Forms and Precedents, page 44.

NOTE 3. An English statute is cited by short title or, where there is no short title, by regnal year and chapter number together with the name by which it is commonly known or a description of its subject matter and date. In the case of a foreign statute, the mode of citation generally follows the style of citation in use in the country concerned with the addition, where necessary, of the name of the country in parentheses.

NOTE 4. A statutory instrument is cited by short title, if any, followed by the year and number, or, if unnumbered, the date.

TABLE OF STATUTES

TABLE OF STATUTORY INSTRUMENTS

TABLE OF CIVIL PROCEDURE

Civil Procedure Rules 1998, SI 1998/3132 (CPR)

Practice Directions supplementing CPR

Other Practice Directions

TABLE OF EUROPEAN
UNION LEGISLATION

TABLE OF CONVENTIONS ETC

TABLE OF COMMAND PAPERS

TABLE OF CASES

I

Decisions of the European Court of Justice are listed below numerically. These decisions are also included in the preceding alphabetical list.

TRADE MARKS AND TRADE NAMES

1. INTRODUCTION TO TRADE MARKS ETC

1. Scope of title and historical background. This title deals primarily with registered trade marks[1] and passing off[2]. Registered trade marks can be either United Kingdom registered trade marks, or Community trade marks[3] which are applied for in respect of, and have effect throughout, the territory of the European Union. In addition, protection can be obtained[4] for a protected international trade mark (UK)[5], and this protection is for almost all purposes equivalent to a United Kingdom registration. This title also deals with statutory marks of various kinds, hallmarking and similar matters.

In early times trade and industry were concentrated in London and other large towns where the merchants and craftsmen organised themselves into guilds. Many guilds were established as corporations either by statute or by charter[6] and the trade and craft of these were supervised under byelaws. Those statutes and byelaws contained provisions for the allocation and use of trade marks[7]. Sometimes the use of trade marks was made compulsory to avoid deceit[8]. With the onset of the industrial revolution the guilds lost control over manufacturers, and as commerce grew, the courts responded to commercial need by developing both the common law tort of passing off and, in equity, a specialised form of property in a trade mark which had been put into public use[9].

Both because litigation was expensive and because there was a need for greater certainty as to what trade marks were already the property of others, trade mark registration was introduced by the Trade Marks Registration Act 1875. That Act created the register of trade marks[10] and set the basic structure[11] for all successive legislation[12] until the mainly new law embodied in the Trade Marks Act 1994. The Trade Marks Registration Act 1875 provided that registration of a trade mark should be deemed to be equivalent to public use of the mark concerned[13]. That Act also provided that no proceedings for infringement of a trade mark could be brought unless and until the mark had been registered[14]. A general law concerning the use of false trade descriptions was introduced and the common law tort of passing off continued to develop.

In 1994 much of the law of registered trade marks within the United Kingdom was revised in order to bring its substantive provisions into line with a harmonised European Community approach[15], and subsequently the right to obtain Community trade marks was introduced by EC Regulation[16]. Today the main branches of the law, so far as private rights are concerned, are United Kingdom and Community registered trade marks, and passing off. So far as public rights are concerned, the matters are now covered by the Trade Descriptions Act 1968 and later legislation. This title does not cover the law relating to false trade descriptions, which more properly fits with the general law of consumer protection[17].

1   As to the meaning of 'registered trade mark' see PARA 111.
2   As to passing off see PARA 287 et seq.
3   As to Community trade marks see PARA 159 et seq.
4   Ie under the Madrid Protocol via the International Bureau of the World Intellectual Property Organisation at Geneva: see PARA 11 et seq. As to the Madrid Protocol see PARA 8.
5   As to the meaning of 'protected international trade mark (UK)' see PARA 12 note 8.
6   As to the development of guilds see CORPORATIONS vol 24 (2010) PARA 507 et seq.
7   However, the legal validity of such provisions was not always upheld by the courts: see *Blanchard v Hill* (1742) 2 Atk 484, 26 ER 692, where the Court of Chancery rejected a claim for an injunction to protect the 'Mogul' mark for playing cards based on the provisions of a charter which the court held to amount to the grant of an illegal monopoly.
8   Eg those relating to gold and silver.

9 The history of this form of property is described in detail in *Berlei (UK) Ltd v Bali Brassiere Co Inc* [1969] 2 All ER 812, [1969] 1 WLR 1306, [1969] RPC 472, HL; and *General Electric Co v General Electric Co Ltd* [1972] 2 All ER 507 at 518–520, [1972] 1 WLR 729 at 742–743, sub nom *GE Trade Mark Ltd* [1973] RPC 297 at 325–327, HL, per Lord Diplock.

10 See the Trade Marks Registration Act 1875 s 1 (repealed).

11 A considerable number of embellishments were, however, added over the years.

12 Ie the Trade Marks Registration Amendment Act 1876, the Trade Marks Registration Extension Act 1877, the Patents, Designs and Trade Marks Act 1883, the Patents, Designs and Trade Marks Act 1888, the Trade Marks Act 1905, the Trade Marks Act 1919, the Trade Marks (Amendment) Act 1937, the Trade Marks Act 1938 and the Trade Marks (Amendment) Act 1984. All those Acts have been repealed.

13 See the Trade Marks Registration Act 1875 s 2 (repealed).

14 See the Trade Marks Registration Act 1875 s 1 (repealed). This provision has been re-enacted ever since and is now contained in the Trade Marks Act 1994 s 2(2): see PARA 398. But for this provision it might be argued that the equitable trade mark could co-exist with registered trade marks. Unregistered marks in use can affect the registrability of later marks: see PARA 61.

15 Ie by the Trade Marks Act 1994, passed principally to give effect to Council Directive (EC) 89/104 (OJ L40, 11.2.89, p 1) to approximate the laws of the member states relating to trade marks (the latter since replaced by European Parliament and Council Directive (EC) 2008/95 (OJ L299, 8.11.2008, p 25)): see PARA 5.

16 Ie by Council Regulation (EC) 40/94 (OJ L11, 14.1.94, p 1) on the Community trademark (since repealed and replaced by Council Regulation (EC) 207/2009 (OJ L78, 24.3.2009, p 1)): see PARA 159 et seq.

17 See CONSUMER PROTECTION vol 21 (2011) PARA 401 et seq.

2. REGISTERED TRADE MARKS IN THE UNITED KINGDOM

(1) LEGISLATION AND INTERNATIONAL BACKGROUND

(i) Domestic Legislation

2. The Trade Marks Act 1994 and its interpretation. Domestic legislation relating to trade marks is mainly contained in the Trade Marks Act 1994. That Act repealed[1] all previous legislation[2] relating to trade marks. Its stated purpose[3] is: (1) to make new provision for registered trade marks[4], implementing the Trade Marks Directive[5]; (2) to make provision in connection with the Community Trade Mark Regulation[6]; (3) to give effect to the Madrid Protocol[7] and to certain provisions of the Paris Convention[8]; and (4) for connected purposes. In addition it has been amended to give effect to certain provisions of the Agreement on Trade-Related Aspects of Intellectual Property Rights ('TRIPs')[9]. The Trade Marks Act 1994 is not stated to be an amending Act. Many of its main provisions are derived from provisions of the Trade Marks Directive, both the mandatory and most of the optional provisions. Where such provisions fall to be implemented by the registrar[10], the Trade Marks Directive is binding upon him[11]. In any event, the relevant provisions of the Trade Marks Act 1994 must be construed so far as possible in accordance with the Trade Marks Directive[12]. Furthermore, both the Trade Marks Act 1994 and the Trade Marks Directive must so far as possible be construed in accordance with the relevant provisions of TRIPs[13]. Other provisions of the Trade Marks Act 1994 are not derived from that Directive and so will fall to be construed in accordance with the normal rules of statutory interpretation[14]. In appropriate cases concerning domestic provisions it may be legitimate to refer to Hansard[15] or the White Paper[16] which preceded the passing of the Act.

1   Ie except for certain administrative provisions contained in the Patents and Designs Act 1907 relating to arrangements for the setting up of the Intellectual Property Office ('IPO') and the appointment of staff: see ss 62–64; and **PATENTS AND REGISTERED DESIGNS** vol 79 (2008) PARAS 575, 577, 579. As to the Intellectual Property Office (an operating name of the Patent Office) see PARA 16 note 2.

2   Ie the Trade Marks Act 1938.

3   See the long title to the Trade Marks Act 1994. As to the status of long titles see **STATUTES AND LEGISLATIVE PROCESS** vol 96 (2012) PARA 670.

4   As to the meaning of 'registered trade mark' see PARA 111.

5   Ie Council Directive (EEC) 89/104 (OJ L40, 11.2.89, p 1) to approximate the laws of the member states relating to trade marks (replaced by European Parliament and Council Directive (EC) 2008/95 (OJ L299, 8.11.2008, p 25)): see PARA 5.

6   Ie Council Regulation (EC) 40/94 (OJ L11, 14.1.94, p 1) on the Community trade mark (repealed and replaced by Council Regulation (EC) 207/2009 (OJ L78, 24.3.2009, p 1)): see PARA 159.

7   Ie the Protocol relating to the Madrid Agreement Concerning the International Registration of Marks (Madrid, 27 June 1989; Cmnd 1601): see PARA 8.

8   Ie the International Convention for the Protection of Industrial Property (Paris, 20 March 1883) (the 'Paris Convention'), as revised (Stockholm, 14 July 1967 to 13 January 1968; TS 61 (1970); Cmnd 4431). As to the Paris Convention see PARA 6.

9   The Patents and Trade Marks (World Trade Organisation) Regulations 1999, SI 1999/1899, Pt IV amended the Trade Marks Act 1994 in order to give effect to certain provisions of the Agreement on Trade-Related Aspects of Intellectual Property Rights (OJ L336, 23.12.94, p 214). This Agreement comprises Annex 1C to the Agreement Establishing the World Trade

Organisation (Marrakesh, 15 April 1994; Cm 2556–2559; Cm 2561–2569; Cm 2571–2574). It was ratified by the United Kingdom on 15 September 1994 and entered into force on 1 January 1996: see PARA 7.

10 As to the registrar see PARA 19.

11 *MISTER LONG Trade Mark* [1998] RPC 401, Appointed Person; *Nettec Solutions Ltd's Trade Mark Application* [2003] RPC 308, Appointed Person; *Sensornet Ltd's Trade Mark Application* [2007] RPC 185, Appointed Person; *CITYBOND Trade Mark* [2007] RPC 301, Appointed Person.

12 See PARA 5 note 3.

13 Case C-53/96 *Hermès International Société en commandite par actions, Paris v FHT Marketing Choice BV* [1998] ECR I-3603, [1999] RPC 107, [1998] All ER (D) 275, ECJ; Joined Cases C-300/98 and C-392/98 *Parfums Christian Dior SA v TUK Consultancy BV* [2000] ECR I-11307, ECJ; Case C-89/99 *Schieving-Nijstad vof v Groeneveld* [2001] ECR I-5851, [2002] IP & T 353, ECJ; Case C-49/02 *Heidelberger Bauchemie GmbH* [2004] ECR I-6152; Case C-245/02 *Anheuser-Busch Inc v Budejovicky Budvar NP* [2004] ECR I-10989, [2007] All ER (EC) 40, [2007] IP & T 348, [2004] All ER (D) 271 (Nov), ECJ; Case C-431/05 *Merck Genéricos – Produtos Farmacêuticos Lda v Merck & Co Inc* [2007] ECR I-7001. As to TRIPs see PARA 7.

14 As to the rules of statutory interpretation see STATUTES AND LEGISLATIVE PROCESS vol 96 (2012) PARA 1078 et seq.

15 Reference to parliamentary materials is allowed where: (1) legislation is ambiguous or obscure or the literal meaning leads to an absurdity; (2) the material relied on consists of statements by a minister or other promoter of the Bill which leads to the enactment of the legislation together, if necessary, with such other parliamentary material as is necessary to understand such statements and their effect; and (3) the statements relied on are clear: *Pepper (Inspector of Taxes) v Hart* [1993] AC 593, [1993] 1 All ER 42, HL; *R v Secretary of State for the Environment, Transport and the Regions, ex p Spath Holme Ltd* [2001] 2 AC 349, [2001] 1 All ER 195, HL; *Wilson v First County Trust (No 2)* [2003] UKHL 40, [2004] 1 AC 816, [2003] 4 All ER 97; and see STATUTES AND LEGISLATIVE PROCESS vol 96 (2012) PARA 1081. It is not, however, appropriate to refer to Hansard or the White Paper to construe a provision of the Trade Marks Act 1994 which derives from EEC Council Directive 89/104 (OJ L40, 11.2.89, p 1): *British Sugar plc v James Robertson & Sons Ltd* [1996] RPC 281, [1996–97] ETMR 118.

For proceedings in the House of Lords prior to the passing of the Trade Marks Act 1994 see 550 HL Official Report (5th series), col 749 (2nd Reading, 6 December 1993), Committee Stage (13–20 January 1994); 552 HL Official Report (5th series), col 728 (Report, 24 February 1994); 553 HL Official Report (5th series), col 69 (3rd Reading, 14 March 1994); and 556 HL Official Report (5th series), col 2105 (Commons' amendments, 15 July 1994). For proceedings in the House of Commons prior to the passing of the Trade Marks Act 1994 see 241 HC Official Report (6th series), col 658 (2nd Reading, 18 April 1994); HC Official Report, SC B (Trade Marks Bill) (Committee, 17 May 1994); 245 HC Official Report (6th series), col 78 (remaining stages, 20 June 1994).

16 Ie *Reform of Trade Marks Law* (Cm 1203).

3. Territorial scope. The Trade Marks Act 1994 extends to England and Wales, Scotland and Northern Ireland[1]; and it also extends to the Isle of Man, subject to such exceptions and modifications as Her Majesty may specify by Order in Council[2].

For the purposes of the Act, the territorial waters of the United Kingdom[3] are treated as part of the United Kingdom[4]; and that Act applies to things done in the United Kingdom sector of the continental shelf[5] on a structure or vessel which is present there for purposes directly connected with the exploration of the sea bed or subsoil or the exploitation of their natural resources as it applies to things done in the United Kingdom[6].

A trade mark registered in the United Kingdom is property situated there even though it is the mark of a foreign owner[7].

1 Trade Marks Act 1994 s 108(1).

2 Trade Marks Act 1994 s 108(2). Under this power, the Trade Marks (Isle of Man) Order 2013, SI 2013/2601 has been made. Subject to that Order in Council, references in the Trade Marks Act 1994 to the United Kingdom are to be construed as including the Isle of Man (s 108(2)).

'United Kingdom' means Great Britain and Northern Ireland: Interpretation Act 1978 s 5, Sch 1. 'Great Britain' means England, Scotland and Wales: Union with Scotland Act 1706, preamble art I; Interpretation Act 1978 s 22(1), Sch 2 para 5(a). Neither the Channel Islands nor the Isle of Man are within the United Kingdom. See further CONSTITUTIONAL LAW AND HUMAN RIGHTS vol 8(2) (Reissue) PARA 3.

3 As to the territorial waters of the United Kingdom see the Territorial Sea Act 1987 s 1; and INTERNATIONAL RELATIONS LAW vol 61 (2010) PARA 123 et seq.

4 Trade Marks Act 1994 s 107(1).

5 For these purposes, 'the United Kingdom sector of the continental shelf' means the area designated by Order in Council under the Continental Shelf Act 1964 s 1(7) (see ENERGY AND CLIMATE CHANGE vol 44 (2011) PARA 1040): Trade Marks Act 1994 s 107(3).

6 Trade Marks Act 1994 s 107(2).

7 See eg *RJ Reuter Co Ltd v Mulhens* [1954] Ch 50 at 95–96, [1953] 2 All ER 1160 at 1183, 70 RPC 235 at 257, CA, per Romer LJ; *Adrema Werke Maschinenbau GmbH v Custodian of Enemy Property and Administrator of German Enemy Property* [1957] RPC 49 at 56, CA, per Lord Evershed MR, and at 59 per Jenkins LJ. It is presumed that the same applies to protected international trade marks (UK) (see PARA 11 et seq).

4. Commencement, savings and transitional provisions. All the provisions of the Trade Marks Act 1994 came into force on 31 October 1994[1]. Existing trade marks[2] registered under the old law[3] were transferred to the register kept under the Trade Marks Act 1994 and have effect[4] as if registered under that Act[5]. Applications for registration of trade marks which were pending[6] on 31 October 1994 must be dealt with under the old law[7], unless the applicant opts to convert the pending application into an application under the Act[8]. Marks registered as a series under the Trade Marks Act 1938[9] continue to be so registered in the new register[10]. The former system of association of marks[11] is not continued by the Trade Marks Act 1994[12]. Under that Act there is no system for imposing conditions upon registration so that any conditions imposed upon trade marks already registered on 31 October 1994 ceased to have effect on that date[13]. A disclaimer or limitation in place on the former register in relation to an existing registered mark immediately before 31 October 1994 was transferred to the new register[14]. Activities which were lawful under the Trade Marks Act 1938 are protected under the Trade Marks Act 1994[15].

1 Trade Marks Act 1994 s 109(1); Trade Marks Act 1994 (Commencement) Order 1994, SI 1994/2550, art 2. Different days might, however, be appointed for different provisions and different purposes: Trade Marks Act 1994 s 109(1). For transitional provisions generally see s 105, Sch 3.

2 For these purposes, 'existing registered mark' means a trade mark, certification trade mark or service mark registered under the Trade Marks Act 1938 immediately before 31 October 1994: Trade Marks Act 1994 Sch 3 para 1(1).

3 For these purposes, 'the old law' means the Trade Marks Act 1938 and any other enactment or rule of law applying to existing registered marks immediately before 31 October 1994: Trade Marks Act 1994 Sch 3 para 1(1).

4 Ie subject to the provisions of the Trade Marks Act 1994 Sch 3.

5 See the Trade Marks Act 1994 Sch 3 para 2; and PARA 21.

6 For these purposes, an application is to be treated as pending on 31 October 1994 if it was made but not finally determined before that date (Trade Marks Act 1994 Sch 3 para 1(2)(a)); and the date on which it was made is to be taken to be the date of filing under the Trade Marks Act 1938 (Trade Marks Act 1994 Sch 3 para 1(2)(b)).

7 See the Trade Marks Act 1994 Sch 3 para 10; and PARA 345 note 5.

8 See the Trade Marks Act 1994 Sch 3 para 11; and PARA 345 note 5.

9 Ie under the Trade Marks Act 1938 s 21(2) (repealed).

10 See the Trade Marks Act 1994 Sch 3 para 2(2); and PARA 21 note 16.

11 Ie under the Trade Marks Act 1938 s 23 (repealed).

12 See the Trade Marks Act 1994 Sch 3 para 2(3); and PARA 21 note 17.

13 See the Trade Marks Act 1994 Sch 3 para 3(1); and PARA 21 note 14.

14 See the Trade Marks Act 1994 Sch 3 para 3(2); and PARA 21 note 14.
15 See the Trade Marks Act 1994 Sch 3 para 4(2); and PARA 81.

(ii) International Legislation

5. The Trade Marks Directive. The Trade Marks Act 1994 was passed[1] (inter alia) to implement the Trade Marks Directive[2]. The main provisions of the Act are closely modelled on provisions, both mandatory and optional, of that Directive. Accordingly it is a principle of EU law that the Trade Marks Act 1994 must be construed, so far as possible, to be in accordance with that Directive[3]. That may in turn involve questions of interpretation of that Directive. Such questions can be, and in appropriate cases are, referred to the European Court of Justice[4]. Although the 'Statements for Entry in the Minutes of the Council Meeting at which the Directive is adopted' apparently prepared by the European Council and Commission have been published by the Office for Harmonisation in the Internal Market[5], it seems clear that those statements cannot be used in construing the Directive[6], particularly since the adoption of the Directive was, as stated in the recitals, in co-operation with the European Parliament and the Economic and Social Committee, both of which bodies were not parties to the entries in the minutes.

The purposes of the Directive are, as is usual, set out in the recitals. The main purpose is not comprehensive harmonisation of the whole field of trade mark law; it is limited to approximating those national provisions of law which most directly affect the functioning of the internal market[7]. Many procedural matters are left to member states[8], and the right to protect trade marks acquired through use is preserved to the member states[9].

The provisions of the Directive correspond closely to the substantive provisions of the Community Trade Mark Regulation[10].

1 See the long title to the Trade Marks Act 1994. As to the status of long titles see STATUTES AND LEGISLATIVE PROCESS vol 96 (2012) PARA 670.
2 Ie Council Directive (EEC) 89/104 (OJ L40, 11.2.89, p 1) to approximate the laws of the member states relating to trade marks, now replaced by European Parliament and Council Directive (EC) 2008/95 (OJ L299, 8.11.2008, p 25) (Codified version).
3 See Case C-106/89 *Marleasing SA v La Comercial Internacional de Alimentación SA* [1990] ECR I-4135, [1992] 1 CMLR 305, ECJ; and also *Litster v Forth Dry Dock and Engineering Co Ltd* [1990] 1 AC 546, [1989] 1 All ER 1134, HL; Cases C-397/01 to C-403/01 *Pfeiffer v Deutsches Rotes Kreuz, Kreisverband Waldshut eV* [2004] ECR I-8835, [2005] ICR 1307,, ECJ; *Revenue and Customs Comrs v IDT Card Services Ireland Ltd* EWCA Civ 29, [2006] STC 1252; *Vodafone 2 v Revenue and Customs Comrs* [2009] EWCA Civ 446, [2010] Ch 77, [2009] STC 1480.
4 Cases in which questions of interpretation of the Directive have been referred to the European Court of Justice by English courts include: *Scandecor Development AB v Scandecor Marketing AB* [2001] UKHL 21, [2001] 2 CMLR 645, [2002] FSR 122 (questions referred to European Court of Justice but case settled prior to ruling); Joined Cases C-414/99 to C-416/99 *Zino Davidoff SA v A & G Imports Ltd* [2002] Ch 109, [2001] ECR I-8691, ECJ; Case C-143/00 *Boehringer Ingelheim KG v Swingward Ltd* [2003] Ch 27, [2002] ECR I-3759, ECJ; Case C-299/99 *Koninklijke Philips Electronics NV v Remington Consumer Products Ltd* [2003] Ch 159, [2002] ECR I-5475, ECJ; Case C-206/01 *Arsenal Football Club plc v Reed* [2003] Ch 454, [2002] ECR I-10273, ECJ; Case C-259/02 *La Mer Technology Inc v Laboratoires Goemar SA* [2004] ECR I-1159, [2004] FSR 785, ECJ; Case C-404/02 *Nichols plc v Registrar of Trade Marks* [2005] All ER (EC) 1, [2004] ECR I-8499, ECJ; Case C-353/03 *Société des Produits Nestlé SA v Mars UK Ltd* [2006] All ER (EC) 348, [2005] ECR I-6135, ECJ; Case C-259/04 *Emanuel v Continental Shelf 128 Ltd* [2006] ECR I-3089, [2006] IP & T 887, sub nom *Elizabeth Florence Emanuel v Continental Shelf 128 Ltd* [2006] ETMR 56, ECJ; Case C-533/06 *O2 Holdings Ltd v Hutchison 3G UK Ltd* [2008] ECR I-4231, [2008] 3 CMLR 397 (interpretation of Directive 89/104 art 5(1)(b) in context of comparative advertising);

Case-323/09 *Interflora Inc v Marks & Spencer plc* [2011] ECR I-8625, [2013] All ER (EC) 519, [2011] IP & T 888, ECJ (whether key word advertising on internet in accordance with Council Directive (EEC) 89/104 (OJ L40, 11.2.89, p 1) art 5(1)(a), (2), 9(1)(a),(c) (see now European Parliament and Council Directive (EC) 2008/95 (OJ L299, 8.11.2008, p 25) arts 5, 9) (see also *Interflora Inc v Marks and Spencer plc* [2013] EWHC 1291 (Ch), [2013] ETMR 35, [2013] All ER (D) 238 (May); and PARAS 58 notes 9, 22, 68 note 9, 69 note 3); Case C-324/09 *L'Oreal SA v eBay International AG*, [2012] All ER (EC) 501, [2011] IP & T 819, ECJ, (interpretation of Council Directive (EEC) 89/104 (OJ L40, 11.2.89, p 1) arts 5, 6, 7 (see now European Parliament and Council Directive (EC) 2008/95 (OJ L299, 8.11.2008, p 25) arts 5, 6, 7) in context of online market place via websites) (see also *L'Oréal SA v eBay International AG* [2009] EWHC 1094 (Ch), [2009] RPC 693, [2010] IP & T 95); Case C-487/07 *L'Oreal SA v Bellure NV* [2009] ECR I-5185, [2010] All ER (EC) 28, ECJ (interpretation of Council Directive (EEC) 89/104 (OJ L40, 11.2.89, p 1) art 5 (see now European Parliament and Council Directive (EC) 2008/95 (OJ L299, 8.11.2008, p 25) art 5) in the context of comparative advertising); Case C-482/09 *Budejovicky Budvar, narodni podnik v Anheuser Busch Inc* [2011] ECR I-8701, [2012] RPC 247, ECJ (interpretation of Council Directive (EEC) 89/104 (OJ L40, 11.2.89, p 1) arts 4(1)(a), 9(1) (see now European Parliament and Council Directive (EC) 2008/95 (OJ L299, 8.11.2008, p 25) arts 4(1)(a), 9(1)) in the context of registration of two identical marks designating identical goods); Case C-307/10 *Chartered Institute of Patent Attorneys v Registrar of Trade Marks* [2013] RPC 313, [2012] IP & T 650, ECJ; (clarity and precision with which goods and services must be identified under the Directive); Case C-252/12 *Specsavers International Healthcare Ltd v Asda Stores Ltd* [2013] ECR I-0000, [2013] ETMR 46, (2013) Times, 1 October, ECJ (interpretation of Council Regulation (EC) 207/2009 (OJ L78, 24.3.2009, p 1) arts 9(1)(b),(c), 15(1), 51(1)(a)).

5 OJ OHIM 5/96 p 606. As to the Office for Harmonisation in the Internal Market see PARA 163 et seq.

6 Case C-245/02 *Anheuser-Busch Inc v Budejovicky Budvar NP* [2004] ECR I-10989, [2007] IP & T 348, [2004] All ER (D) 271 (Nov), ECJ. The true meaning of rules of EC law can be derived only from those rules themselves, having regard to their context; the meaning cannot be affected by a statement by the member states inserted in the minutes of the EC Council meeting relating to the adoption of the act in question: Case 237/84 *Re Business Transfer Directive, EC Commission v Belgium* [1986] ECR 1247 at 1256, [1988] 2 CMLR 865 at 873, ECJ; Case C-292/89 *R v Immigration Appeal Tribunal, ex p Antonissen* [1991] ECR I-745, [1991] 2 CMLR 373, ECJ; Case C-306/89 *Re Transport Workers, EC Commission v Greece* [1991] ECR I-5863, [1994] 1 CMLR 803, ECJ; Joined Cases C-197/94 and C-252/94 *Société Bautiaa v Directeur Service Fiscaux des Landes* [1996] ECR I-505, ECJ. See also *Wagamama Ltd v City Centre Restaurants plc* [1995] FSR 713, [1996] ETMR 23; Case R 46/1992–2 *Giacomelli Sport SpA's Application* [2000] ETMR 277, OHIM Board of Appeal.

7 See Council Directive (EEC) 89/104 (OJ L40, 11.2.89, p 1) 3rd recital; and European Parliament and Council Directive (EC) 2008/95 (OJ L299, 8.11.2008, p 25) 4th recital.

8 Member states remain free to fix the provisions of procedure concerning the registration, the revocation and the invalidity of trade marks acquired by registration; they can e g determine the form of trade mark registration and invalidity procedures, decide whether earlier rights should be invoked either in the registration procedure or in the invalidity procedure or in both and, if they allow earlier rights to be invoked in the registration procedure, have an opposition procedure or an ex officio examination procedure or both; member states remain free to determine the effects of revocation or invalidity of trade marks: see Council Directive (EEC) 89/104 (OJ L40, 11.2.89, p 1) 5th recital; and European Parliament and Council Directive (EC) 2008/95 (OJ L299, 8.11.2008, p 25) 6th recital.

9 See Council Directive (EEC) 89/104 (OJ L40, 11.2.89, p 1) 4th recital; and European Parliament and Council Directive (EC) 2008/95 (OJ L299, 8.11.2008, p 25) 5th recital. In the case of the United Kingdom such unregistered marks are protected under the law of passing off (as to which see PARA 287 et seq). The Trade Marks Directive takes unregistered marks into account only in regard to the relationship between them and trade marks acquired by registration: See Council Directive (EEC) 89/104 (OJ L40, 11.2.89, p 1) 4th recital; and now European Parliament and Council Directive (EC) 2008/95 (OJ L299, 8.11.2008, p 25) 5th recital.

10 Ie Council Regulation (EC) 40/94 (OJ L11, 14.1.94, p. 1) on the Community Trade Mark (repealed and replaced by Council Regulation (EC) 207/2009 (OJ L78, 24.3.2009, p 1): see PARA 159 et seq.

6.   The Paris Convention. Under the International Convention for the Protection of Industrial Property (the 'Paris Convention')[1] the countries

('Convention countries')[2] acceding to it formed themselves into a union for the protection of industrial property[3]. Most countries are now members of the union. The basis of the union is equal treatment of the nationals and residents of the Convention countries. The Paris Convention is not itself part of either domestic or EU law, though it may be referred to in accordance with general principles[4]. The Trade Marks Act 1994 does, however, implement a number of provisions of the Paris Convention, namely:

(1) the recognition of priority in Convention countries based on a first application in one Convention country[5];

(2) the protection of well known trade marks[6];

(3) controls on the registration of flags, armorial bearings, hallmarks or official signs of Convention countries or of international intergovernmental organisations[7];

(4) the protection by means of a right to an injunction in respect of the matters mentioned in head (3) above[8]; and

(5) measures to prevent an agent of a person in a Convention country from registering or holding a mark of which that person is the owner[9].

The Secretary of State[10] may by order make such amendments of the Trade Marks Act 1994, and rules made under it, as appear to him to be appropriate in consequence of any revision or amendment of the Paris Convention on or after 31 October 1994[11].

1 Ie the International Convention for the Protection of Industrial Property (Paris, 20 March 1883) (the 'Paris Convention'), as revised (Stockholm, 14 July 1967 to 13 January 1968; TS 61 (1970); Cmnd 4431). As to the Convention see PATENTS AND REGISTERED DESIGNS vol 79 (2008) PARA 652. For the purposes of the Trade Marks Act 1994, 'the Paris Convention' means the Paris Convention for the Protection of Industrial Property of 20 March 1883, as revised or amended from time to time: Trade Marks Act 1994 s 55(1)(a) (amended by SI 1999/1899). The text of the Convention is available from the World Intellectual Property Organisation ('WIPO') or on its website, accessible at the date at which this volume states the law at www.wipo.int.

2 For the purposes of the Trade Marks Act 1994, a 'Convention country' means a country, other than the United Kingdom, which is a party to the Paris Convention or to the WTO Agreement: Trade Marks Act 1994 s 55(1)(b) (amended by SI 2006/1028). As to the meaning of 'United Kingdom' see PARA 3 note 2. As to the WTO Agreement see PARA 7.

3 'Property' covers patents, utility models, industrial designs, trade marks, service marks, trade names, indications of source or appellations of origin, and the repression of unfair competition: see the International Convention for the Protection of Industrial Property art 1(2). The term is to be understood in its broadest sense: see art 1(3), (4). Broadly speaking, the Convention relates to all forms of intellectual property save for copyright.

4 See INTERNATIONAL RELATIONS LAW vol 61 (2010) PARA 12 et seq.

5 See the Trade Marks Act 1994 s 35; and PARA 360.

6 See the Trade Marks Act 1994 s 56; and PARA 136.

7 See the Trade Marks Act 1994 ss 57–59; and PARAS 51–52, 470–471.

8 See the Trade Marks Act 1994 ss 57(6), 58(4); and PARAS 470–471.

9 See the Trade Marks Act 1994 s 60; and PARA 137.

10 As to the Secretary of State see PARA 16.

11 Trade Marks Act 1994 s 55(2) (amended by SI 1999/1899). Any such order must be made by statutory instrument which is subject to annulment in pursuance of a resolution of either House of Parliament: Trade Marks Act 1994 s 55(3). At the date at which this volume states the law no such order had been made.

7. The WTO Agreement and TRIPs. The Agreement establishing the World Trade Organisation ('the WTO Agreement') was signed at Marrakesh on 15 April 1994[1]. That Agreement consisted of a series of individual agreements dealing with different subject matters, one of which was the Agreement on Trade-Related Aspects of Intellectual Property Rights, commonly known as 'TRIPs'[2]. The overall purpose of TRIPs is to reduce distortions and impediments to international trade arising from excessive discrepancies in national rules protecting intellectual property[3]. To that end, it contains provisions designed to lay down minimum standards concerning the availability, scope and use of intellectual property rights including trade marks[4], together with minimum procedural standards for enforcement of intellectual property rights[5]. The WTO Agreement has been declared to be an EU Treaty for the purposes of the European Communities Act 1972[6], and the European Court of Justice has held itself to have jurisdiction to interpret at least some aspects of TRIPs[7].

TRIPs requires its members to give effect inter se to most of the substantive provisions of the Paris Convention[8], including those relating to trade marks[9]. In some respects, it expands the effect of those provisions. TRIPs requires that the protection of well known marks provided for under the Paris Convention is to apply to marks for services as well as to trade marks for goods[10]. Effect has been given to this extension of protection for well known marks in United Kingdom domestic law[11]. TRIPs also requires that the protection of well known marks is to extend to goods or services which are not similar to those in respect of which the trade mark is registered, provided that the use of the trade mark would indicate a connection and there is a likelihood of damage[12]; however, it does not appear that effect has been given to this provision in United Kingdom domestic law[13].

The Secretary of State[14] may by order make such amendments of the Trade Marks Act 1994, and rules made under it, as appear to him to be appropriate in consequence of any revision or amendment of the WTO Agreement (including TRIPs) on or after 31 October 1994[15].

1   See the Agreement establishing the World Trade Organisation (Marrakesh, 15 April 1994; Cm 2557). The Agreement is commonly referred to, and is abbreviated in the text of the statute, as 'the WTO Agreement'. Most countries in the world have acceded to the WTO Agreement. For the purposes of the Trade Marks Act 1994, 'the WTO Agreement' means that Agreement: see the Trade Marks Act 1994 s 55(1)(aa) (added by SI 1999/1899).

2   See the Agreement on Trade-Related Aspects of Intellectual Property Rights ('TRIPs') (1994) (Cm 2557). The text of TRIPs is available from the World Trade Organisation ('WTO') or on its website, accessible at the date at which this volume states the law at www.wto.org.

3   Agreement on Trade-Related Aspects of Intellectual Property Rights preamble.

4   The Agreement on Trade-Related Aspects of Intellectual Property Rights arts 15–21 defines what kinds of signs member states must treat as protectable subject matter for trade mark registration, defines in broad terms the exclusive right which flows from registration and the minimum term of protection, allows cancellation for non-use only if an uninterrupted period of at least three years has elapsed, and prevents member states from unjustifiably encumbering the use of a trade mark in the course of trade or granting compulsory licences of trade marks.

5   Agreement on Trade-Related Aspects of Intellectual Property Rights Pt III. Articles 42–49 provide for civil and administrative procedures and remedies, including injunctions (art 44), damages (art 45) and seizure of infringing goods (art 46). Article 50 requires that the judicial authorities be given power to order prompt and effective provisional measures (such as temporary or interim injunctions). Articles 51–60 provide for customs seizures of infringing goods. Article 61 requires the member states to provide for criminal procedures and penalties to be applied at least in cases of wilful trademark counterfeiting on a commercial scale.

6   See the European Communities (Definition of Treaties) (The Agreement Establishing the World Trade Organisation) Order 1995, SI 1995/265 (amended by SI 2011/1043).

7   Case C-53/96 *Hermès International Société en commandite par actions, Paris v FHT Marketing Choice BV* [1998] ECR I-3603, [1999] RPC 107, [1998] All ER (D) 275, ECJ.

8   Ie the International Convention for the Protection of Industrial Property (Paris, 20 March 1883) (the 'Paris Convention'), as revised (Stockholm, 14 July 1967 to 13 January 1968; TS 61 (1970); Cmnd 4431). As to the Paris Convention see PARA 6.

9   The Agreement on Trade-Related Aspects of Intellectual Property Rights art 2(1) requires members to comply with the Paris Convention arts 1–12, 19.

10 The Agreement on Trade-Related Aspects of Intellectual Property Rights art 16(2) requires that the Paris Convention art 6 bis (which provides for the protection of well known marks) is to apply mutatis mutandis to services: see PARA 136.

11 See the Patents and Trade Marks (World Trade Organisation) Regulations 1999, SI 1999/1899, reg 13(4) (made under the European Communities Act 1972 s 2(2)), which amends the Trade Marks Act 1994 s 56(1) and (2) by adding a reference to the WTO Agreement after the reference to the Paris Convention. Thus the Trade Marks Act 1994 s 56 (see PARA 136) on the protection of well-known marks will apply to marks for services upon which protection is conferred by TRIPs art 16(2), as well as to marks for goods which are protected by the Paris Convention art 6 bis as it applied in the absence of TRIPs. The Patents and Trade Marks (World Trade Organisation) Regulations 1999, SI 1999/1899, reg 14(1) contains a transitional provision protecting persons who continue a bona fide use of a trade mark begun before 1 January 1996. Corresponding amendments are made by reg 13(1) to the Trade Marks Act 1994 s 6(1)(c) (see PARA 54), so conferring on the owner of a well known service mark protected under TRIPs the right to object to someone else attempting to register an identical or similar mark: see PARAS 54–56, 136.

12 Agreement on Trade-Related Aspects of Intellectual Property Rights art 16(3).

13 The Trade Marks Act 1994 s 56(2) (see PARA 136) gives the proprietor of the well known mark the right to restrain use in relation to identical or similar goods or services. The Patents and Trade Marks (World Trade Organisation) Regulations 1999, SI 1999/1899, reg 13, while inserting a reference to the WTO Agreement (see note 11), has not amended the wording of the provision to extend its scope to goods or services which are not similar. It may be arguable, however, that an effect of the WTO Agreement having been defined as an EU Treaty (see note 6) is that some of its provisions could enjoy direct effect within the domestic law of the United Kingdom by virtue of the European Communities Act 1972 s 2(1); in which case, TRIPs art 16(3) might be construed as having such direct effect.

14 As to the Secretary of State see PARA 16.

15 Trade Marks Act 1994 s 55(2) (amended by SI 1999/1899). Any such order must be made by statutory instrument which is subject to annulment in pursuance of a resolution of either House of Parliament: Trade Marks Act 1994 s 55(3). At the date at which this volume states the law no such order had been made.

8. The Madrid Agreement and the Madrid Protocol. The Madrid Agreement Concerning the International Registration of Marks[1] provides for a system by which a mark registered in one country may be deposited with an international bureau[2] and will take effect, subject to prior rights, in other countries which are parties to the Madrid Agreement. An application so made is called an 'international application' and a mark so registered an 'international registration'. The United Kingdom[3] is not a party to the Madrid Agreement, but is a party to the Protocol to the Madrid Agreement[4]. The parties to the Protocol, even where they are not party to the Madrid Agreement, are members of the same union of which countries party to the Madrid Agreement are members[5].

The Secretary of State[6] may by order make such provision as he thinks fit for giving effect in the United Kingdom to the provisions of the Madrid Protocol[7]. Provision may in particular be made with respect to:

(1) the making of applications for international registrations by way of the Intellectual Property Office ('IPO')[8] as office of origin[9];

(2) the procedures to be followed where the basic United Kingdom application or registration fails or ceases to be in force[10];

(3) the procedures to be followed where the IPO receives from the International Bureau[11] a request for extension of protection to the United Kingdom[12];

(4) the effects of a successful request for extension of protection to the United Kingdom[13];

(5) the transformation of an application for an international registration, or an international registration, into a national application for registration[14];

(6)   the communication of information to the International Bureau[15];
(7)   the payment of fees and amounts prescribed in respect of applications for international registrations, extensions of protection and renewals[16]. Without prejudice to the generality of the above provisions, provision may be made by regulations applying, in relation to an international trade mark (UK)[17], the statutory provisions relating to the remedy for groundless threats of infringement proceedings[18], the importation of infringing goods, material or articles[19], and offences[20].

1   Ie the Madrid Agreement Concerning the International Registration of Marks (Madrid, 14 April 1891; TS 71 (1970); Cmnd 4437), as revised at Stockholm in 1967 and as amended in 1979.
2   This bureau is known as the International Bureau of the World Intellectual Property Organisation ('WIPO') and is based in Geneva. There were international bureaux provided for under WIPO's predecessors (the Paris Convention for the Protection of Industrial Property and the Berne Convention for Literary and Artistic Works). Those two bureaux were united in 1983 and functioned under various names until 1970 when they were replaced by the International Bureau of Intellectual Property (usually designated as 'the International Bureau') by virtue of the WIPO Convention (ie the Convention establishing the Word Intellectual Property Organisation (Stockholm, 14 July 1967 to 13 January 1968; TS 52 (1970); Cmnd 4408); the Convention was ratified by the United Kingdom on 26 February 1969). The International Bureau is the secretariat or administration of WIPO. For more information generally see the WIPO website, accessible at the date at which this volume states the law at www.wipo.int.
3   As to the meaning of 'United Kingdom' see PARA 3 note 2.
4   Ie the Protocol relating to the Madrid Agreement Concerning the International Registration of Marks (Madrid, 27 June 1989; Cm 1601), as amended in 2006. The Protocol was also published with the parallel text of the Madrid Agreement Concerning the International Registration of Marks by WIPO in 1990. The Madrid Agreement itself has, however, still not been ratified by the United Kingdom. The text of both the Madrid Agreement and the Protocol is available from WIPO or on its website (see note 2).
5   Protocol relating to the Madrid Agreement Concerning the International Registration of Marks art 1. The European Community (now the European Union) has also acceded to the Madrid Protocol: see Council Regulation (EC) 40/94 (OJ L11, 14.1.94, p 1) on the Community trade mark, arts 140–156 (added by Council Regulation (EC) 1992/2003 (OJ L296, 14.11.03, p.1)) (see now Council Regulation (EC) 207/2009 (OJ L78, 24.3.2009, p 1) arts 145–161); Council Decision (EC) 2003/793 (OJ L296, 14.11.03, p 20) approving the accession of the European Community to the Protocol relating to the Madrid Agreement concerning the international registration of marks, adopted at Madrid on 27 June 1989. See note 17; and PARA 159.
6   As to the Secretary of State see PARA 16.
7   Trade Marks Act 1994 s 54(1). For these purposes, 'the Madrid Protocol' means the Protocol relating to the Madrid Agreement concerning the International Registration of Marks, adopted at Madrid on 27 June 1980 (see note 4): Trade Marks Act 1994 s 53.
        Under this power, the Secretary of State has made the Trade Marks (International Registration) Order 2008, SI 2008/2206 (amended by SI 2009/2464; SI 2010/32; SI 2013/445; and SI 2013/2237), which came into force on 1 October 2008. See further PARA 11 et seq. See also the Community Trade Mark Regulations 2006, SI 2006/1027; and PARA 160 note 8.
8   As to the Intellectual Property Office (an operating name of the Patent Office) see PARA 16 note 2.
9   Trade Marks Act 1994 s 54(2)(a).
10 Trade Marks Act 1994 s 54(2)(b).
11 For these purposes, 'the International Bureau' means the International Bureau of the World Intellectual Property Organisation (see note 2): Protocol relating to the Madrid Agreement Concerning the International Registration of Marks art 2(1); definition applied by the Trade Marks Act 1994 s 53.
12 Trade Marks Act 1994 s 54(2)(c).
13 Trade Marks Act 1994 s 54(2)(d).
14 Trade Marks Act 1994 s 54(2)(e).
15 Trade Marks Act 1994 s 54(2)(f).
16 Trade Marks Act 1994 s 54(2)(g). An order under s 54 must be made by statutory instrument which is subject to annulment in pursuance of a resolution of either House of Parliament:

s 54(4). As to orders made under s 54 see the Trade Marks (International Registration) Order 2008, SI 2008/2206 (amended by SI 2009/2464; SI 2010/32; SI 2013/445; and SI 2013/2237) and PARA 11 et seq.

17 For these purposes, 'international trade mark (UK)' means a trade mark which is entitled to protection in the United Kingdom under the Madrid Protocol and 'international trade mark (EC)' means a trade mark which is entitled to protection in the European Union under the Madrid Protocol: Trade Marks Act 1994 s 53 (amended by SI 2004/2332; and SI 2011/1043).

18 Ie the Trade Marks Act 1994 s 21: see PARAS 107–109.

19 Ie the Trade Marks Act 1994 ss 89–91: see PARAS 132–135.

20 Trade Marks Act 1994 s 54(3). The provisions so specified in relation to offences are s 92 (see PARAS 124–127), s 93 (see PARA 129), s 95 (see PARA 131) and s 96 (supplementary provisions relating to summary proceedings in Scotland): s 54(3).

9. The Trademark Law Treaty and the Singapore Treaty on the Law of Trademarks. The Trademark Law Treaty ('TLT')[1] was adopted under the auspices of the World Intellectual Property Organisation ('WIPO')[2]. Its aim is to make national and regional trade mark registration systems more user-friendly by simplifying and harmonising procedures during the phases of application, changes after registration and renewal[3]. The Singapore Treaty on the Law of Trademarks[4] was also adopted under the auspices of WIPO, and is a revision of the TLT. Its aim is similar to that of the TLT, but it has a wider scope of application and addresses new developments in the field of communication technology, as well as making procedural changes[5].

1 Ie the Trademark Law Treaty (Geneva, 27 October 1994; TS 76 (1996); Cm 3348). The text of the treaty is available from WIPO or on its website, accessible at the date at which this volume states the law at www.wipo.int.

2 See PARA 8 text and note 2.

3 The United Kingdom has ratified the Trademark Law Treaty, but the Trade Marks Act 1994 contains no express reference to it.

4 Ie the Singapore Treaty on the Law of Trademarks (Singapore, 27 March 2006). The text of the treaty is available from WIPO or on its website (see note 1).

   The Singapore Treaty enters into force when it has been ratified by ten eligible states or intergovernmental organisations: art 28. This happened on 16 March 2009 ten such states having ratified it. The United Kingdom ratified the Treaty on 21 March 2012.

5 The United Kingdom has ratified the Trademark Law Treaty, but the Trade Marks Act 1994 contains no express reference to it. As to the meaning of 'United Kingdom' see PARA 3 note 2.

10. The Nice Agreement. The Nice Agreement[1] establishes an International Classification of goods and services for the purposes of registering trade marks. The International Classification consists of a list of classes (currently 34 for goods and 11 for services) and an alphabetical list of goods and services allocating them to classes (currently comprising some 11,000 items). Both lists are from time to time amended and supplemented by a Committee of Experts on which all contracting states are represented[2].

1 Ie the Nice Agreement Concerning the International Classification of Goods and Services for the Purposes of the Registration of Marks (Nice, 15 June 1957; Misc 16 (1977); Cmnd 6898), revised at Stockholm on 14 July 1967 and at Geneva on 13 May 1977 and amended on 28 September 1979.

2 The tenth edition of the International Classification entered into force on 1 January 2013. This is given effect in the United Kingdom by the Trade Marks Rules 2008, SI 2008/1797, r 7(2): see PARA 352. Copies of the International Classification are available from the World Intellectual Property Organisation and from its website, accessible at the date at which this volume states the law at www.wipo.int. The International Classification is also known as the Nice Classification: see also PARA 352.

(iii) International Trade Marks

11. International registration of trade marks. In order for the United Kingdom[1] to participate in the system of international registration of trade marks in accordance with the Madrid Protocol[2], it has been necessary to make provision in domestic law for two main aspects of the system, namely: (1) outgoing international applications, that is, applications for international protection which are based upon a United Kingdom registered trade mark or a trade mark application filed in the United Kingdom; and (2) the legal effects within the United Kingdom of international trade marks which receive protection here and for the domestic procedures by which such protection is conferred. Provision has been made in the domestic law of the United Kingdom for both these aspects by the Trade Marks (International Protection) Order 2008[3]. The international aspects of the trade mark registration process, that is the procedures operated by the International Bureau[4] including the maintenance of and the making of entries in the international register, are governed directly by the Madrid Protocol and by the Common Regulations[5].

1   As to the meaning of 'United Kingdom' see PARAS 3 note 2.
2   As to the Madrid Protocol see PARA 8.
3   See the Trade Marks (International Registration) Order 2008, SI 2008/2206 (amended by SI 2009/2464; SI 2010/32; and SI 2013/445), made under the Trade Marks Act 1994 s 54. See further PARA 12 et seq.
4   Ie the International Bureau of the World Intellectual Property Organisation ('WIPO'): see PARA 8 text and note 2.

5   Ie the Common Regulations under the Madrid Agreement Concerning the International Registration of Marks and the Protocol Relating to that Agreement, adopted by the Assembly of the Madrid Union with effect from 1 April 1996, as amended with effect from 1 April 2004. The text of the Common Regulations is available from WIPO or on its website, accessible at the date at which this volume states the law at www.wipo.int.

12. International trade marks (UK). An international registration[1] which is the subject of a request for extension[2] is entitled to protection subject to the provisions of the Trade Marks Act 1994, the Trade Marks (Relative Grounds) Order 2007[3] and the Trade Marks Rules 2008[4] as applied by the Trade Marks (International Registration) Order 2008[5] if the particulars of the request for extension were contained in an application for registration of a trade mark under the Trade Marks Act 1994 and such application would satisfy the requirements of the Act (including any imposed by the Trade Mark Rules 2008)[6].

Subject to what is said below[7], a protected international trade mark (UK)[8] must be treated as if it were a trade mark registered under the Trade Marks Act 1994 and the holder must have the same rights and remedies but must be subject to the same conditions as the proprietor of a registered trade mark[9].

The provisions of the Trade Marks Act 1994 (with some exceptions[10]), the Trade Marks (Relative Grounds) Order 2007[11] and the Trade Marks Rules 2008[12] (with some exceptions[13]) apply to international trade marks (UK) and requests for extension with the following modifications:

(1)   references to a registered trade mark include references to a protected international trade mark (UK);

(2)   references to a proprietor of a registered trade mark include references to the holder of a protected international trade mark (UK);

(3)   references to an application for registration of a trade mark include references to a request for extension;

(4)   references to an applicant for registration include references to the holder of an international registration in respect of which a request for extension has been made;

(5)   references to registration of a trade mark include the conferring of protection on an international registration which is the subject of a request for extension;

(6)   references to the goods or services for which a trade mark is registered include references to the goods or services in respect of which a protected international trade mark (UK) confers protection;

(7)   references to the publication of the application include references to the publication of the notice of details of the international registration in the Journal;

(8)   references to the register are to the supplementary register[14];

(9)   certain further modifications[15]; and

(10) such further modifications as the context requires for the purpose of giving effect to those provisions as applied by the Trade Marks (International Registration) Order 2008[16].

1   'International registration' means a registration of a trade mark in the International Register; and the 'International Register' means the register of trade marks maintained by the International Bureau for the purposes of the Madrid Protocol (see PARA 8): Trade Marks (International Registration) Order 2008, SI 2008/2206, art 2. As to the International Bureau see PARA 8.

2   'Request for extension' means a request for an extension of protection to the United Kingdom under the Madrid Protocol art 3*ter* (1) or (2) (see PARA 8) which has been notified by the International Bureau: Trade Marks (International Registration) Order 2008, SI 2008/2206, art 2.

3   Ie the Trade Marks (Relative Grounds) Order 2007, SI 2007/1976: see also PARAS 64, 103, 354, 378, 441.

4   Ie the Trade Marks Rules 2008, SI 2008/1797: see PARA 334 et seq.

5   Ie the Trade Marks (International Registration) Order 2008, SI 2008/2206.

6   Trade Marks (International Registration) Order 2008, SI 2008/2206, art 3(1).

7   See the Trade Marks (International Registration) Order 2008, SI 2008/2206, art 3(3); and heads (1)–(10) in the text.

8   'Protected international trade mark (UK)' means an international registration which is the subject of a request for extension and which is protected in accordance with the Trade Marks Act 1994 s 38 as modified by Sch 2 para 6 (see note 15) and references to 'protection' and 'protected' are construed accordingly: Trade Marks (International Registration) Order 2008, SI 2008/2206, art 2.

9   Trade Marks (International Registration) Order 2008, SI 2008/2206, art 3(2).

10 Ie except those listed in the Trade Marks (International Registration) Order 2008, SI 2008/2206, art 3(3), Sch 1 Pt 1, ie the Trade Marks Act 1994 s 24(2)(b) (assignment or other transmission in relation to use of the trade mark in a particular manner or locality) (see PARA 113); s 32(1), (2) and (4) (application for registration) (see PARA 345); s 33(1) (date of filing) (see PARA 348); s 34 (classification of trade marks) (see PARA 351); s 39(2) (withdrawal, restriction or amendment of application) (see PARA 357); s 40 (registration) (see PARAS 23, 370); s 41 (registration: supplementary provisions) (see PARAS 346, 349); s 42 (duration of registration) (see PARA 31); s 43 (renewal of registration) (see PARAS 31, 32); s 44 (alteration of registered trade mark) (see PARAS 106, 375); s 45 (surrender of registered trade mark) (see PARA 377); s 64(4) (change of name and address by proprietor or licensee) (see PARA 29); s 65 (adaptation of entries to new classification) (see PARA 374); s 79 (fees) (see PARA 18); s 94 (falsification of register) (see PARA 130).

11 See note 3.

12 See note 4.

13 Ie except those listed in the Trade Marks (International Registration) Order 2008, SI 2008/2206, art 3(3), Sch 1 Pt 2 ie the Trade Marks Rules 2008, SI 2008/1797, r 6 (claim to priority) (see PARA 360); r 8 (application may relate to more than one class and shall specify the class (Form TM31C)) (see PARA 353); r 9 (determination of classification) (see PARA 353); r 12(4)(a) (failure to provide an address for service) (see PARA 340); r 13 (deficiencies in application) (see PARA

345); r 46 (form of register) (see PARA 21); r 47 (entry in register of particulars of registered trade marks (Form TM24)) (see PARA 21); r 56 (request for information; s 67(1) (Form TM31C)) (see PARA 372).

14 'Supplementary register' means the register of international trade marks (UK) required to be maintained under the Trade Marks Act 1994 s 63 as modified by Sch 2 para 8 (see note 15): Trade Marks (International Registration) Order 2008, SI 2008/2206, art 2.

15 Ie the modifications set out in the Trade Marks (International Registration) Order 2008, SI 2008/2206, art 3(3)(i), Sch 2 (amended by SI 2009/2464; and SI 2013/445): see below.

The provisions modified are the Trade Marks Act 1994 s 25 (registration of transactions affecting registered trade mark) (see PARAS 114, 118) (Trade Marks (International Registration) Order 2008, SI 2008/2206, Sch 2 para 1(1), (2), (3), (4), (5), (6)); the Trade Marks Act 1994 s 33 (date of filing) (see PARA 348) (Trade Marks (International Registration) Order 2008, SI 2008/2206, Sch 2 para 2); the Trade Marks Act 1994 s 35(5) (claim to priority of convention application) (see PARA 360) (Trade Marks (International Registration) Order 2008, SI 2008/2206, Sch 2 para 3); the Trade Marks Act 1994 s 37 (examination of application) (see PARAS 355, 363) (Trade Marks (International Registration) Order 2008, SI 2008/2206, Sch 2 para 4); the Trade Marks Act 1994 s 38(2) (publication, opposition proceedings and observations) (see PARA 366) (Trade Marks (International Registration) Order 2008, SI 2008/2206, Sch 2 para 5); the Trade Marks Act 1994 ss 38A, 38B (ie added by way of modification) (see PARAS 355, 366, 371 respectively) (Trade Marks (International Registration) Order 2008, SI 2008/2206, Sch 2 para 6 (amended by SI 2013/445); the Trade Marks Act 1994 s 39 (withdrawal, restriction or amendment of application) (see PARA 356) (Trade Marks (International Registration) Order 2008, SI 2008/2206, Sch 2 para 7 (amended by SI 2009/2464)); the Trade Marks Act 1994 s 63 (the register) (see PARAS 19, 21) (Trade Marks (International Registration) Order 2008, SI 2008/2206, Sch 2 para 8(1), (2), (3), (4)); the Trade Marks Act 1994 s 67(2)(a) (information about applications and registered trade marks) (see PARA 372) (Trade Marks (International Registration) Order 2008, SI 2008/2206, Sch 2 para 9). As to calculation of time periods in regard to the Trade Marks (International Registration) Order 2008, SI 2008/2206, Sch 2 para 6 (see above) see Tribunal Practice Notice (TPN 1/2013), available from the Intellectual Property Office ('IPO') website, accessible at the date at which this volume states the law at www.ipo.gov.uk. As to the Intellectual Property Office (an operating name of the Patent Office) see PARA 16 note 2.

16 Trade Marks (International Registration) Order 2008, SI 2008/2206, art 3(3).

13. International applications originating in the United Kingdom. There are a number of provisions[1] applying in relation to the making of applications for international registration[2] by way of the Intellectual Property Office ('IPO')[3] as office or origin[4].

An applicant for the registration of a trade mark, or the proprietor of a registered trade mark, may[5] apply by way of the IPO as office of origin for the international registration of the trade mark[6]. For these purposes an applicant is (1) a British citizen, a British overseas territories citizen, a British overseas citizen, a British subject or a British protected person[7]; (2) an individual domiciled in the United Kingdom[8]; (3) a body incorporated under the law of a part of the United Kingdom; or (4) a person who has a real and effective industrial or commercial establishment in the United Kingdom[9].

Where the registrar has reasonable doubts about whether an applicant is eligible, the registrar must inform the applicant of the reason for those doubts; and may require that applicant to file evidence in support of his eligibility[10]. Where the registrar has no doubts or is satisfied as to the applicant's eligibility; and the particulars appearing in the application for an international registration correspond with the particulars at that time in the basic application[11] or, as the case may be, the basic registration[12], the registrar must submit the application to the International Bureau[13].

Where the registrar submits an application to the International Bureau[14] and the basic application or basic registration is terminated[15], where, before the end of the relevant period[16], a basic application or basic registration is terminated, the registrar must request that the International Bureau cancel the international registration[17].

A basic application is terminated where it is (a) not accepted; (b) refused; or (c) withdrawn (including deemed as such)[18]. A basic registration is terminated where the rights in the registered trade mark cease to have effect[19].

Where a basic application or basic registration is terminated in respect of some only of the goods or services for which the trade mark is registered (or is sought to be registered), the request must relate only to those goods and services[20].

If during the relevant period[21] the registrar becomes aware of proceedings which may result in the termination of the basic application or basic registration, the registrar must notify the International Bureau accordingly, stating that no final decision has been made[22]. On completion of these proceedings[23] the registrar must promptly notify the International Bureau of their outcome[24].

Where the registrar submits an application to the International Bureau[25] and the basic application is divided into two or more applications; or two or more basic applications or basic registrations are merged into a single application or registration[26], where, before the end of the relevant period[27], a basic application is divided or two or more basic applications or basic registrations are merged, the registrar must notify the International Bureau and must indicate (i) the number of the international registration or, where the mark has not been registered, the number of the basic application; (ii) the name of the applicant or the holder of the relevant trade mark; and (iii) the number of each application resulting from the division or the number of the application or registration resulting from the merger[28].

1   See the Trade Marks (International Registration) Order 2008, SI 2008/2206, art 4, Sch 3.

2   As to the meaning of 'international registration' see PARA 12 note 1. 'International application' means an application by way of the Intellectual Property Office (see note 3) as office of origin to the International Bureau for registration of a trade mark in the International Register: Trade Marks (International Registration) Order 2008, SI 2008/2206, art 2. As to the International Bureau see PARA 8. As to the meaning of 'International Register' see PARA 12 note 1.

3   As to the Intellectual Property Office (an operating name of the Patent Office) see PARA 16 note 2. See also PARA 8 text and note 8.

4   Trade Marks (International Registration) Order 2008, SI 2008/2206, art 4.

5   Ie subject to the provisions of the Trade Marks (International Registration) Order 2008, SI 2008/2206, Sch 3 para 1.

6   Trade Marks (International Registration) Order 2008, SI 2008/2206, Sch 3 para 1(1).

7   As to British citizens and citizenship see BRITISH NATIONALITY vol 4 (2011) PARAS 406, 421–444; as to British overseas territories citizens and citizenship see BRITISH NATIONALITY vol 4 (2011) PARAS 406, 445–458; as to British overseas citizens see BRITISH NATIONALITY vol 4 (2011) PARAS 406, 459–463; as to British subjects see BRITISH NATIONALITY vol 4 (2011) PARAS 407, 469–474; and as to British protected persons see BRITISH NATIONALITY vol 4 (2011) PARAS 408, 476–480.

8   As to the meaning of 'United Kingdom' see PARA 3 note 2.

9   Trade Marks (International Registration) Order 2008, SI 2008/2206, Sch 3 para 1(2).

10 Trade Marks (International Registration) Order 2008, SI 2008/2206, Sch 3 para 1(3). As to the registrar see PARA 19.

11 For these purposes, 'basic application' means an application for registration of a trade mark in the United Kingdom in respect of which application is made for international registration: Trade Marks (International Registration) Order 2008, SI 2008/2206, Sch 3 para 1(5)(a).

12 For these purposes, 'basic registration' means a trade mark registered in the United Kingdom in respect of which application is made for international registration: Trade Marks (International Registration) Order 2008, SI 2008/2206, Sch 3 para 1(5)(b).

13 Trade Marks (International Registration) Order 2008, SI 2008/2206, Sch 3 para 1(4).

14 Ie in accordance with the Trade Marks (International Registration) Order 2008, SI 2008/2206, Sch 3 para 1: see the text and notes 1–13.
15 Trade Marks (International Registration) Order 2008, SI 2008/2206, Sch 3 para 2(1).
16 For these purposes, the 'relevant period' is the period of five years beginning immediately after the date of the international registration: Trade Marks (International Registration) Order 2008, SI 2008/2206, Sch 3 para 2(6) (amended by SI 2013/445). 'Date of the international registration' means the date of the international registration under the Madrid Protocol art 3(4) (see PARA 8): Trade Marks (International Registration) Order 2008, SI 2008/2206, art 2. As to calculation of time periods in regard to Sch 3 paras 2(6), 3(3) see Tribunal Practice Notice 1/2013, available from the Intellectual Property Office ('IPO') website, accessible at the date at which this volume states the law at www.ipo.gov.uk. See note 3.
17 Trade Marks (International Registration) Order 2008, SI 2008/2206, Sch 3 para 2(2).
18 Trade Marks (International Registration) Order 2008, SI 2008/2206, Sch 3 para 2(3).
19 Trade Marks (International Registration) Order 2008, SI 2008/2206, Sch 3 para 2(4).
20 Trade Marks (International Registration) Order 2008, SI 2008/2206, Sch 3 para 2(5).
21 See note 16.
22 Trade Marks (International Registration) Order 2008, SI 2008/2206, Sch 3 para 2(7).
23 Ie the proceedings referred to in the Trade Marks (International Registration) Order 2008, SI 2008/2206, Sch 3 para 2(7).
24 Trade Marks (International Registration) Order 2008, SI 2008/2206, Sch 3 para 2(8).
25 See note 14.
26 Trade Marks (International Registration) Order 2008, SI 2008/2206, Sch 3 para 3(1).
27 For these purposes, the 'relevant period' is the period of five years beginning immediately after the date of the international registration: Trade Marks (International Registration) Order 2008, SI 2008/2206, Sch 3 para 3(3) (amended by SI 2013/445). See note 16.
28 Trade Marks (International Registration) Order 2008, SI 2008/2206, Sch 3 para 3(2).

14.   Concurrent registrations and transformation applications.   Certain provisions[1] apply in relation to (1) the effects of international registration[2] where a trade mark is also registered under the Trade Marks Act 1994; and (2) the transformation of an application for an international registration, or an international registration, into an application for registration of a trade mark under the 1994 Act[3].

A transformation application is an application to register a trade mark under the Trade Marks Act 1994 where (a) the mark was the subject of an international registration and the international registration was the subject of a request for extension[4]; and (b) the international registration was cancelled at the request of the office of origin[5].

However an application must only be treated as a transformation application where the goods and services cited in it are identical to some or all of the goods and services included in the international registration[6].

Any application made under the Trade Marks Act 1994 which is a transformation application must state that it is made by way of transformation[7]. Such an application may only be made before the end of the period of three months beginning immediately after the date on which the international registration was cancelled[8]. A transformation application may only be made by the person who was the holder of the international registration immediately before it was cancelled[9].

Where on or before the date the transformation application was made, the trade mark is protected as an international trade mark (UK)[10], the mark must be registered under the Trade Marks Act 1994; and it must have the date of filing of the cancelled international trade mark (UK)[11].

Where on that date the trade mark is not so protected, the transformation application is treated as an application to register under the 1994 Act and it has the date of filing of the request for extension relating to that mark[12].

Where in relation to the international registration a right of priority was claimed on the basis of a Convention application, the transformation application has the same right of priority[13].

The provisions below[14] apply where at the time protection is conferred on an international trade mark (UK) there is a concurrent registered trade mark[15]. A registration is concurrent where (i) the proprietor of the registered trade mark is the holder of the protected international trade mark (UK)[16]; (ii) the registered trade mark is the same as the protected international trade mark (UK); (iii) the goods and services in relation to which protection is conferred by the international trade mark (UK) include all those for which the registered trade mark is registered[17].

The protected international trade mark (UK) is treated as being registered under the Trade Marks Act 1994 as of the date of registration of the registered trade mark[18]. The priorities claimed in respect of the registered trade mark may also be claimed in respect of the international trade mark (UK)[19].

These provisions[20] continue to apply after the registered trade mark lapses or is surrendered, but cease to apply if or to the extent that it is revoked or declared invalid[21].

On the application of the holder of the protected international trade mark (UK) the registrar must note the international registration in the register against the registered trade mark[22].

1 Ie the provisions set out in the Trade Marks (International Registration) Order 2008, SI 2008/2206, art 5, Sch 4.
2 As to the meaning of 'international registration' see PARA 12 note 1.
3 Trade Marks (International Registration) Order 2008, SI 2008/2206, art 5.
4 As to the meaning of 'request for extension' see PARA 12 note 2.
5 Trade Marks (International Registration) Order 2008, SI 2008/2206, Sch 4 para 1(1). The reference in the text to a cancellation at the request of the office of origin is a reference to a cancellation at the request of the office of origin under the Madrid Protocol art 6(4): see PARA 8.
6 Trade Marks (International Registration) Order 2008, SI 2008/2206, Sch 4 para 1(2).
7 Trade Marks (International Registration) Order 2008, SI 2008/2206, Sch 4 para 1(3).
8 Trade Marks (International Registration) Order 2008, SI 2008/2206, Sch 4 para 1(4) (amended by SI 2013/445). As to calculation of time periods in regard to the Trade Marks (International Registration) Order 2008, SI 2008/2206, Sch 4 para 1(4) see Tribunal Practice Notice 1/2013, available from the Intellectual Property Office ('IPO') website, accessible at the date at which this volume states the law at www.ipo.gov.uk. As to the Intellectual Property Office (an operating name of the Patent Office) see PARA 16 note 2.
9 Trade Marks (International Registration) Order 2008, SI 2008/2206, Sch 4 para 1(5).
10 As to international trade marks (UK) see PARA 12.
11 Trade Marks (International Registration) Order 2008, SI 2008/2206, Sch 4 para 1(6).
12 Trade Marks (International Registration) Order 2008, SI 2008/2206, Sch 4 para 1(7).
13 Trade Marks (International Registration) Order 2008, SI 2008/2206, Sch 4 para 1(8). As to Convention applications see PARA 360.
14 Ie the provisions in the Trade Marks (International Registration) Order 2008, SI 2008/2206, Sch 4 para 2.
15 Trade Marks (International Registration) Order 2008, SI 2008/2206, Sch 4 para 2(1).
16 As to the meaning of 'protected international trade mark (UK)' see PARA 12 note 8.
17 Trade Marks (International Registration) Order 2008, SI 2008/2206, art 2, Sch 4 para 2(2).
18 Trade Marks (International Registration) Order 2008, SI 2008/2206, Sch 4 para 2(3).
19 Trade Marks (International Registration) Order 2008, SI 2008/2206, Sch 4 para 2(4).
20 Ie the provisions of the Trade Marks (International Registration) Order 2008, SI 2008/2206, Sch 4 para 2.
21 Trade Marks (International Registration) Order 2008, SI 2008/2206, Sch 4 para 2(5).
22 Trade Marks (International Registration) Order 2008, SI 2008/2206, Sch 4 para 2(6). As to the registrar and the register see PARAS 19, 21 et seq. For the purposes of Sch 4 para 2(6), the holder of the international trade mark (UK) must make an application to the registrar using Form TM28: Sch 4 para 2(7).

15.   Miscellaneous and general provisions; fees. There are a number of provisions[1] applicable in regard to miscellaneous and general matters[2]. Where the International Bureau[3] notifies the registrar[4] that it has corrected an international registration[5] and the correction either (1) substantially affects the identity of the trade mark[6]; or (2) alters the goods or services covered by the international registration[7], the registrar may treat the notification as a new request for extension[8].

A protected international trade mark (UK)[9] may only be assigned to an eligible person[10].

Judicial notice is taken of the following (a) the Madrid Protocol and the Common Regulations[11]; (b) copies issued by the International Bureau of entries in the International Register[12]; (c) copies of the periodical gazette published by the International Bureau[13]. Where in relation to the international registration a right of priority was claimed on the basis of a Convention application[14], the transformation application[15] has the same right of priority[16].

Where the protection of a protected international trade mark (UK) is revoked or declared invalid to any extent, the registrar must notify the International Bureau, and (i) in the case of a revocation, the rights of the proprietor are deemed to have ceased to exist to that extent as from the date of the application for revocation; or if the registrar or court is satisfied that the grounds for revocation existed at an earlier date, that date; (ii) in the case of a declaration of invalidity, the trade mark is to that extent deemed never to have been a protected international trade mark (UK)[17].

A request for information relating to a protected international trade mark (UK) must be made on the appropriate form[18].

Notwithstanding any other enactment or rule of law, the registrar may communicate to the International Bureau any information which the United Kingdom[19] is required to communicate by virtue of the Trade Marks (International Registration) Order 2008[20] or pursuant to the Madrid Protocol or Common Regulations[21].

The registrar may accept for transmission to the International Bureau fees payable to the International Bureau in respect of an application for international registration originating in the United Kingdom or a renewal of such an international registration, subject to such terms and conditions as the registrar may specify, either generally by published notice, or in any particular case by written notice to the applicant desiring to make payment by such means[22].

The fees to be paid in respect of any matters arising under the Trade Marks (International Registration) Order 2008[23] are those specified[24].

1   Ie the provisions in the Trade Marks (International Registration) Order 2008, SI 2008/2206, art 6, Sch 5.
2   Trade Marks (International Registration) Order 2008, SI 2008/2206, art 6.
3   As to the International Bureau see PARA 8.
4   As to the registrar see PARA 19.
5   As to the meaning of 'international registration' see PARA 12 note 1.
6   Where the Trade Marks (International Registration) Order 2008, SI 2008/2206, Sch 5 para (1)(a) (see head (1) in the text) applies, any earlier request for protection is deemed to have been withdrawn and any resulting protection granted to the international trade mark (UK) is be treated as having been declared invalid: Sch 5 para 1(2). As to international trade marks (UK) see PARA 12.
7   Where the Trade Marks (International Registration) Order 2008, SI 2008/2206, Sch 5 para (1)(b) (see head (2) in the text) applies and (1) the correction extends the goods and services covered by the request for extension, the new request for extension applies only to the additional goods and services; or (2) the correction restricts the goods and services covered by the international registration, to the extent it relates to goods and service outside the restriction,

an earlier request for protection is treated as having been withdrawn, and any resulting protection granted to the international trade mark (UK) is treated as having been declared invalid: Sch 5 para 1(3). As to the meaning of 'request for extension' see PARA 12 note 2.

8   Trade Marks (International Registration) Order 2008, SI 2008/2206, Sch 5 para 1(1).

9   As to the meaning of 'protected international trade mark (UK)' see PARA 12 note 8.

10   Trade Marks (International Registration) Order 2008, SI 2008/2206, Sch 5 para 2(1). An eligible person is (1) a national of any country which is a party to the Madrid Protocol (see PARA 8); (2) an individual domiciled in such a country; (3) a body incorporated under the law of such a country; and (4) a person who has a real and effective industrial or commercial establishment in such a country: Sch 5 para 2(2).

11   'Common Regulations' means the regulations adopted under the Madrid Protocol art 10 (see PARA 8) with effect from 1 April 1996 and as amended with effect from 1 April 2002: Trade Marks (International Registration) Order 2008, SI 2008/2206, art 2. More specifically they are the Common Regulations under the Madrid Agreement Concerning the International Registration of Mark and the Protocol Relating to that Agreement. They are divided into several chapters of rules as follows: Ch 1 (rr 1–7) General Provisions; Ch 2 (rr 8–13) International Applications; Ch 3 (rr 14–15) International Registrations; Ch 4 (rr 16–23) Facts in Contracting Parties Affecting International Registrations; Ch 5 (rr 24–28) Subsequent Designations; Changes; Ch 6 (rr 29–31) Renewals; Ch 7 (rr 32–33) Gazette and Data Base; Ch 8 (rr 34–38) Fees; and Ch 9 (rr 39–41) Miscellaneous. The text of the Common Regulations appears on the World Intellectual Property Organisation ('WIPO') website, accessible at the date at which this volume states the law at www.wipo.int.

12   Any document mentioned in the Trade Marks (International Registration) Order 2008, SI 2008/2206, Sch 5 para 3(1)(b) or (c) (see heads (b), (c) in the text) is admissible as evidence of any instrument or other act of the International Bureau so communicated: Sch 5 para 3(2).

13   Trade Marks (International Registration) Order 2008, SI 2008/2206, Sch 5 para 3(1). The reference in the text to publication is a reference to publication by the International Bureau under the Common Regulations r 32 (see note 11). See also note 12.

14   As to Convention applications see PARA 360.

15   As to transformation applications see PARA 14.

16   Trade Marks (International Registration) Order 2008, SI 2008/2206, Sch 5 para 3(3).

17   Trade Marks (International Registration) Order 2008, SI 2008/2206, Sch 5 para 4.

18   Trade Marks (International Registration) Order 2008, SI 2008/2206, Sch 5 para 5. The form is Form TM31M: see Sch 5 para 5. As to the use of forms see PARA 335.

19   As to the meaning of 'United Kingdom' see PARA 3 note 2.

20   Ie the Trade Marks (International Registration) Order 2008, SI 2008/2206.

21   Trade Marks (International Registration) Order 2008, SI 2008/2206, Sch 5 para 6.

22   Trade Marks (International Registration) Order 2008, SI 2008/2206, Sch 5 para 7.

23   See note 19.

24   Trade Marks (International Registration) Order 2008, SI 2008/2206, art 7. The reference in the text to specified fees is a reference to those fees specified in Sch 6 (amended by SI 2009/2464; SI 2010/32; and SI 2013/2237), the contents of which is not reproduced here.

(2) ADMINISTRATION

(i) The Secretary of State

16. Functions of the Secretary of State. The Secretary of State[1] is responsible for the Intellectual Property Office ('IPO')[2]. He appoints and supervises the Comptroller General of Patents, Designs and Trade Marks[3], who has the immediate control of the IPO[4] and is the Registrar of Trade Marks[5]. The Secretary of State may appoint and remove examiners and other officers and clerks for the IPO[6]. The Secretary of State has power to make rules[7] and to prescribe fees[8].

The Secretary of State no longer has any direct involvement in the administration of registered trade marks[9].

1   Ie one of Her Majesty's principal Secretaries of State: see the Interpretation Act 1978 s 5, Sch 1. As to the office of Secretary of State see CONSTITUTIONAL LAW AND HUMAN RIGHTS vol 8(2) (Reissue) PARA 355.

2 As to the Intellectual Property Office ('IPO'), its organisation and seal see PATENTS AND REGISTERED DESIGNS vol 79 (2008) PARAS 579–580. Note that the 'Intellectual Property Office' is an operating name of the Patent Office: see the Trade Marks Rules 2008, SI 2008/1797, r 2(1) (definition of 'the Office' substituted by SI 2009/2089). In relation to its functions as to trade marks it is generally called the Trade Marks Registry. Its address is Concept House, Cardiff Road, Newport, Gwent, NP10 8QQ; and its London office (as from 21 May 2012) is at 1st floor, 4 Abbey Orchard Street, London SW1P 2HT. The IPO's website is accessible at the date at which this volume states the law at www.ipo.gov.uk. As to the business hours and the business days of the IPO see PARA 334.

3 As to the Comptroller General of Patents, Designs and Trade Marks see PATENTS AND REGISTERED DESIGNS vol 79 (2008) PARA 577.

4 See the Patents and Designs Act 1907 s 62(2); and PATENTS AND REGISTERED DESIGNS vol 79 (2008) PARA 577.

5 See the Trade Marks Act 1994 s 62; and PARA 19.

6 Patents and Designs Act 1907 s 63(1) (amended by the Trade Marks Act 1994 Sch 4 para 2(1), (3)(a)).

7 See PARA 17.

8 See PARA 18.

9 His former function of supervision etc of certification trade marks (ie under the Trade Marks Act 1938 s 37 (repealed)) is now exercisable by the registrar (see the Trade Marks Act 1994 s 50, Sch 2; and PARA 148 et seq); and his former function of hearing appeals from the registrar (eg under the Trade Marks Act 1938 s 17(4) (repealed)) is now exercisable by a person appointed for the purpose (see the Trade Marks Act 1994 ss 76, 77; and PARAS 387–390).

17.   Power to make rules. The Secretary of State[1] may make rules:

(1)   for the purposes of any provision of the Trade Marks Act 1994 authorising the making of rules with respect to any matter; and

(2)   for prescribing anything authorised or required by any provision of that Act to be prescribed,

and generally for regulating practice and procedure under that Act[2].

Provision may in particular be made: (a) as to the manner of filing of applications and other documents; (b) requiring and regulating the translation of documents and the filing and authentication of any translation; (c) as to the service of documents; (d) authorising the rectification of irregularities of procedure; (e) prescribing time limits for anything required to be done in connection with any proceeding under the Trade Marks Act 1994; (f) providing for the extension of any time limit so prescribed, or specified by the registrar[3], whether or not it has already expired[4].

Rules under the Trade Marks Act 1994 must be made by statutory instrument which is subject to annulment in pursuance of a resolution of either House of Parliament[5].

1 As to the Secretary of State see PARA 16.

2 Trade Marks Act 1994 s 78(1). As to the rules that have been made see the Trade Marks Rules 2008, SI 2008/1797, which came into force on 1 October 2008 (see r 1). As to the revocation of previous rules and proceedings commenced under previous rules see the Trade Marks Act 1994 s 83, Sch 2. As to proceedings generally see PARA 334 et seq.

3 As to the registrar see PARA 19.

4 Trade Marks Act 1994 s 78(2).

5 Trade Marks Act 1994 s 78(3). In so far as the rules are procedural rules for the registrar (see PARA 340 et seq), the Secretary of State must consult with the Council on Tribunals before making them: see the Tribunals and Inquiries Act 1992 s 8(1) (prospectively repealed), Sch 1 Pt 1; and ADMINISTRATIVE LAW vol 1(1) (2001 Reissue) PARAS 56–57.

18.   Power to prescribe fees. There must be paid in respect of applications and registration[1] and other matters under the Trade Marks Act 1994 such fees as may be prescribed[2]; and provision may be made by rules as to the payment of a single fee in respect of two or more matters and as to the circumstances, if any, in which a fee may be repaid or remitted[3].

1   As to the requirements for registration see PARA 39 et seq; and as to the procedure on the application see PARA 334 et seq. As to the meaning of 'registration' see PARA 21 note 2.

2   Trade Marks Act 1994 s 79(1); Trade Marks Rules 2008, SI 2008/1797, r 4(1). Any form required to be filed with the registrar in respect of any specified matter is subject to the payment of the fee, if any, prescribed in respect of that matter by rules made under the Trade Marks Act 1994 s 79: Trade Marks Rules 2008, SI 2008/1797, r 4(2). As to the use of forms see PARA 335; and as to the registrar see PARA 19.

     As to the rules that have been made see the Trade Marks (Fees) Rules 2008, SI 2008/1958 (amended by SI 2009/2089; SI 2010/33; SI 2012/1003; and SI 2013/2236), which came into force on 1 October 2008 (Trade Marks (Fees) Rules 2008, SI 2008/1958, r 1(1)). The Trade Marks (Fees) Rules 2008, SI 2008/1958 are to be construed as one with the Trade Marks Rules 2008, SI 2008/1797: Trade Marks (Fees) Rules 2008, SI 2008/1958, r 1(2). The fees to be paid in respect of any matters arising under the Trade Marks Act 1994 and the Trade Marks Rules 2008, SI 2008/1797 are those specified in the Trade Marks (Fees) Rules 2008, SI 2008/1958, Schedule (amended by SI 2009/2089; SI 2010/33; SI 2012/1003; and SI 2013/2236): Trade Marks (Fees) Rules 2008, SI 2008/1958, r 2(1). In any case where a form specified in the Schedule as the corresponding form in relation to any matter is specified in the Trade Marks Rules 2008, SI 2008/1797, that form must be accompanied by the fee specified in respect of that matter (unless the Trade Marks Rules 2008, SI 2008/1797 otherwise provide): Trade Marks (Fees) Rules 2008, SI 2008/1958, r 2(2).

     All fees must be collected in money: see the Public Offices Fees (Patents, Designs and Trade Marks) Order 1964, SI 1964/45, art 1.

     It should be noted that the Trade Marks Act 1994 s 79 does not apply to international trade marks or requests for extension: see the Trade Marks (International Registration) Order 2008, SI 2008/2206, art 3(3), Sch 1 Pt 1; and PARA 12 note 10. For fees in relation to protected international trade marks (UK) see art 7, Sch 6; and PARA 15.

3   Trade Marks Act 1994 s 79(2). See note 2. Where the registrar (1) has received a request for expedited examination of an application for registration of a trade mark under the Trade Marks Rules 2008, SI 2008/1797, r 5(2) (see PARA 345); and (2) following the expiry of a period of ten business days (as specified in a direction given by the registrar under the Trade Marks Act 1994 s 80 (see PARA 334)) beginning on the business day after the date of filing of the application for registration, notifies the applicant, in accordance with Trade Marks Rules 2008, SI 2008/1797, r 15 (see PARA 345), whether or not it appears to the registrar that the requirements for registration are met, the registrar must repay the fee specified in the Trade Marks (Fees) Rules 2008, SI 2008/1958, Schedule in respect of a request for expedited examination: r 3(1). Where a fee has been paid in error, the registrar must repay the same; and where a fee is paid in excess of the amount specified, the registrar must remit the amount paid in excess: r 3(2).

(ii) The Registrar of Trade Marks

19.   General functions, reports and publications of the Registrar of Trade Marks. In the Trade Marks Act 1994, 'the registrar' means the Comptroller General of Patents, Designs and Trade Marks[1]. The register of trade marks[2] must be maintained by the registrar[3]. He has functions as to the registration of trade marks[4] and the rectification or correction of the register[5]. The registrar must include in his annual report as to patents and designs[6] a report on the execution of the Trade Marks Act 1994, including the discharge of his functions under the Madrid Protocol[7]; and that report must include an account of all money received and paid by him under or by virtue of the Act[8]. The registrar must also publish:

(1)   a journal, entitled 'the Trade Marks Journal', containing particulars of any application for the registration of a trade mark[9], including a representation of the mark, such information as is required to be published[10] and such other information relating to trade marks as the registrar thinks fit[11];

(2)   reports of cases relating to trade marks decided by him and of cases relating to trade marks decided by any court or body, whether in the United Kingdom[12] or elsewhere[13].

1   Trade Marks Act 1994 s 62. As to his appointment and supervision by the Secretary of State see PARA 16. As to the Comptroller General of Patents, Designs and Trade Marks generally see PATENTS AND REGISTERED DESIGNS vol 79 (2008) PARA 577. In practice the principal functions of the Registrar of Trade Marks are carried out by an officer having the rank of Assistant Comptroller; and that officer is often called 'the registrar'. Other functions are carried out by officers and clerks appointed by the Secretary of State: see PARA 16.
2   As to the register see PARA 21.
3   Trade Marks Act 1994 s 63(1). Section 63 applies to international trademarks (UK) but with modifications: see the Trade Marks (International Registration) Order 2008, SI 2008/2206, art 3, Sch 2 para 8; PARA 21 text and note 11; and PARA 12 note 15.
4   See PARA 334 et seq.
5   See PARAS 105, 378 et seq.
6   Ie under the Patents Act 1977 s 121: see PATENTS AND REGISTERED DESIGNS vol 79 (2008) PARA 578.
7   Trade Marks Act 1994 s 71(1). As to the Madrid Protocol see PARA 8 note 7.
8   Trade Marks Act 1994 s 71(2).
9   As to the meaning of 'trade mark' see PARA 41.
10   Ie under the Trade Marks Rules 2008, SI 2008/1797. For the purposes of the Trade Marks Act 1994, 'publish' means make available to the public; and references to publication in relation to an application for registration are to publication under s 38(1) (see PARA 365) and in relation to registration are to publication under s 40(4) (see PARA 370): s 103(1).
11   Trade Marks Act 1994 s 81; Trade Marks Rules 2008, SI 2008/1797, r 81.
12   As to the meaning of 'United Kingdom' see PARA 3 note 2.
13   See the Patents Act 1977 s 123(7); the Patents Rules 2007, SI 2007/3291, r 118; and PATENTS AND REGISTERED DESIGNS vol 79 (2008) PARA 580. Publication of the Reports of Patent, Design and Trade Mark Cases, commonly known as 'Reports of Patent Cases' (RPC), began in 1884.

20.   Exclusion of liability in respect of official acts. The registrar[1] is not to be taken to warrant the validity of the registration[2] of a trade mark[3] under the Trade Marks Act 1994 or under any treaty, convention, arrangement or engagement to which the United Kingdom[4] is a party[5].

The registrar is not subject to any liability by reason of, or in connection with, any examination required or authorised by the Act[6], or by the Trade Marks (International Registration) Order 2008[7], or any such treaty, convention, arrangement or engagement, or any report or other proceedings consequent on such examination[8].

No proceedings lie against an officer of the registrar in respect of any matter for which the registrar is not liable by virtue of the above provisions[9].

1   As to the registrar see PARA 19.
2   As to the meaning of 'registration' see PARA 21 note 2.
3   As to the meaning of 'trade mark' see PARA 41.
4   As to the meaning of 'United Kingdom' see PARA 3 note 2.
5   Trade Marks Act 1994 s 70(1).
6   See the Trade Marks Act 1994 s 37; and PARA 354.
7   Ie the Trade Marks (International Registration) Order 2008, SI 2008/2206.
8   Trade Marks Act 1994 s 70(2); and see the Trade Marks (International Registration) Order 2008, SI 2008/2206, art 3; and PARA 12.
9   Trade Marks Act 1994 s 70(3); and see the Trade Marks (International Registration) Order 2008, SI 2008/2206, art 3; and PARA 12.

(iii)   The Register of Trade Marks

21.   Maintenance of register. The registrar[1] must maintain a register of trade marks[2]; and there must be entered in the register in accordance with the Trade Marks Act 1994[3]:

(1)　registered trade marks[4];

(2)　such particulars as may be prescribed of registrable transactions[5] affecting a registered trade mark[6]; and

(3)　such other matters relating to registered trade marks as may be prescribed[7].

The register must be kept in such manner as may be prescribed[8] but need not be kept in documentary form[9].

The registrar must also maintain a supplementary register for the purpose of entering certain transactions[10] and disclaimers and limitations relating to international trade marks (UK)[11].

Existing registered marks[12] had to be transferred on 31 October 1994 to the register so kept and have effect[13] as if registered under the Act[14]; and existing registered marks registered as a series[15] had to be similarly registered in the new register[16]. In any other case notes indicating that existing registered marks were associated with other marks ceased to have effect on that date[17].

1　As to the registrar see PARA 19.

2　Trade Marks Act 1994 s 63(1). References in the Trade Marks Act 1994 to 'the register' are to the register so maintained by the registrar; and references to 'registration' (in particular, in the expression 'registered trade mark') are, unless the context otherwise requires, to registration in that register: s 63(1). As to the meaning of 'registered trade mark' see PARA 111. As to falsification of the register see PARA 130.

　　Section 63 applies to international trademarks (UK) but with modifications: see the Trade Marks (International Registration) Order 2008, SI 2008/2206, art 3, Sch 2 para 8; the text and note 11; and PARA 12 note 15.

　　For the purposes of the Trade Marks Act 1994 s 105, Sch 3 (transitional provisions) the Sheffield register kept under the Trade Marks Act 1938 Sch 2 (repealed) (see PARA 333) is to be treated as part of the register of trade marks kept under that Act: Trade Marks Act 1994 Sch 3 para 20(1). Applications made to the Cutlers' Company in accordance with the Trade Marks Act 1938 Sch 2 (repealed) which were pending on 31 October 1994 (ie the date on which the Trade Marks Act 1994 came into force: see the Trade Marks Act 1994 (Commencement) Order 1994, SI 1994/2550, art 2) must proceed after that date as if they had been made to the registrar: Trade Marks Act 1994 Sch 3 para 20(2).

　　There is no longer any requirement to maintain a copy in Manchester of copies of all entries in the register relating to textile goods as was formerly required under the Trade Marks Act 1938 s 39 (repealed): see PARA 332.

3　Trade Marks Act 1994 s 63(2). The Trade Marks Rules 2008, SI 2008/1797 are made under the Trade Marks Act 1994 s 63(2), (3): see the text and note 9. See note 2.

4　Trade Marks Act 1994 s 63(2)(a). See notes 2, 3. In practice the register includes details of pending applications for registration as well of registered trade marks.

5　As to the registrable transactions see PARA 114 et seq.

6　Trade Marks Act 1994 s 63(2)(b). As to the particulars so prescribed see PARA 24. See notes 2, 3.

7　Trade Marks Act 1994 s 63(2)(c). See notes 2, 3.

8　Trade Marks Act 1994 s 63(3). See notes 2, 3. Provision must in particular be made for public inspection of the register, and the supply of certified or uncertified copies, or extracts, of entries in the register: see s 63(3); and PARA 26.

9　Trade Marks Rules 2008, SI 2008/1797, r 46. In practice the register is now kept in the form of an electronic database which is publicly searchable via the Intellectual Property Office ('IPO') website, accessible at the date at which this volume states the law at www.ipo.gov.uk. As to the Intellectual Property Office (an operating name of the Patent Office) see PARA 16 note 2.

　　It should be noted that r 46 does not apply to international trade marks (UK) or requests for extension: see the Trade Marks (International Registration) Order 2008, SI 2008/2206, art 3, Sch 1 Pt 2; and PARA 12 note 13.

10　Ie transactions under the Trade Marks Act 1994 s 25(1) (as modified by the Trade Marks (International Registration) Order 2008, SI 2008/2206, Sch 2 para 1): see PARAS 12, 114.

11　Trade Marks Act 1994 s 63(1) (modified by the Trade Marks (International Registration) Order 2008, SI 2008/2206, art 3(3)(i), Sch 2 para 8(1), (2)). That register need not be kept in documentary form: Trade Marks Act 1994 s 63(3) (modified by the Trade Marks (International Registration) Order 2008, SI 2008/2206, Sch 2 para 8(1), (3)). Following notification from the International Bureau (see PARA 8 text and note 2) under the Common Regulations r 28(2) (see

PARA 11 note 5) the registrar may correct an error or omission in the information entered in the register required to be maintained under the Trade Marks Act 1994 s 63(1): see s 63(4) (modified by the Trade Marks (International Registration) Order 2008, SI 2008/2206, Sch 2 para 8(1), (4)). See also note 2. See also PARA 12 note 15.

12   Ie whether registered in Part A or Part B of the register kept under the Trade Marks Act 1938. 'As to the meaning of 'existing registered mark' see PARA 4 note 2.

13   Ie subject to the provisions of the Trade Marks Act 1994 Sch 3 (transitional provisions).

14   Trade Marks Act 1994 Sch 3 para 2(1). A condition entered on the former register in relation to an existing registered mark immediately before 31 October 1994 ceased to have effect on that date: Sch 3 para 3(1).

      Proceedings under the Trade Marks Act 1938 s 33 (repealed) (application to expunge or vary registration for breach of condition) which were pending on 31 October 1994 must be dealt with under the old law and any necessary alteration made to the new register: Trade Marks Act 1994 Sch 3 para 3(1). As to the meaning of 'the old law' see PARA 4 note 3.

      A disclaimer or limitation entered on the former register in relation to an existing registered mark immediately before 31 October 1994 had to be transferred to the new register and has effect as if entered on the register in pursuance of s 13 (see PARA 65): Sch 3 para 3(2).

15   Ie under the Trade Marks Act 1938 s 21(2) (repealed).

16   Trade Marks Act 1994 Sch 3 para 2(2). Provision may be made by rules for putting such entries in the same form as is required for entries under the Trade Marks Act 1994: Sch 3 para 2(2). At the date at which this volume states the law no such rules had been made.

17   Trade Marks Act 1994 Sch 3 para 2(3).

22. Registration of trade mark.

A trade mark is registered once the application for registration[1] has been accepted[2], either no notice of opposition[3] has been given within the prescribed time or all opposition proceedings have been withdrawn or decided in favour of the applicant, and any prescribed fee has been paid within the prescribed period[4].

1   As to the application procedure see PARAS 334 et seq.
2   As to acceptance see PARA 363.
3   As to opposition proceedings see PARA 366.
4   See the Trade Marks Act 1994 s 40(1), (2); and PARA 370.

23. Date of registration; retrospective effect.

A trade mark[1], when registered[2], is registered as of the date of filing of the application for registration[3]; and that date is deemed[4] to be the date of registration[5].

1   As to the meaning of 'trade mark' see PARA 41.
2   As to the meaning of 'registered' see PARA 21 note 2.
3   As to the meaning of 'the date of filing of an application for registration' see PARA 348. As to the requirements for registration see PARA 39 et seq; and as to the procedure on the application see PARA 334 et seq.
4   Ie for the purposes of the Trade Marks Act 1994.
5   Trade Marks Act 1994 s 40(3). The effect of registration is thus, for most purposes, retrospective to the date of application. As to actions for infringement and criminal proceedings, in respect of acts committed during the period after application is made for registration of a trade mark but before the date of actual registration, see PARA 67.

      It should be noted that s 40 does not apply to international trade marks (UK) or requests for extension: see the Trade Marks (International Registration) Order 2008, SI 2008/2206, art 3(3), Sch 1 Pt 1; and PARA 12 note 10.

24. Particulars of registered trade marks.

In addition to the entries in the register[1] of registered trade marks[2], there must be entered in the register in respect of each trade mark registered therein the following particulars[3]:

(1)   the date of registration[4], that is to say, the date of the filing of the application for registration[5];

(2)   the date of completion of the registration procedure[6];

(3) the priority date, if any, to be accorded pursuant to a claim to a right to priority[7];

(4) the name and address of the proprietor[8];

(5) the address for service, if any, as duly filed[9];

(6) any disclaimer or limitation of rights[10];

(7) any memorandum or statement of the effect of any memorandum relating to a trade mark of which the registrar has been notified on the appropriate form[11];

(8) the goods or services in respect of which the mark is registered[12];

(9) where the mark is a collective[13] or certification[14] mark, that fact[15];

(10) where the mark is registered[16] with the consent of the proprietor of an earlier trade mark or other earlier right, that fact[17];

(11) where the mark is registered pursuant to a transformation application[18], the number of the international registration[19], and either the priority date accorded to the international registration[20], or the date of recordal of the request for extension to the United Kingdom of the international registration[21]; and

(12) where the mark arises from the conversion of a Community trade mark or an application for a Community trade mark[22], the number of any other registered trade mark from which the Community trade mark or the application for a Community trade mark claimed seniority and the earliest seniority date[23].

1 As to the register see PARA 21.

2 Ie in addition to the entries in the register of registered trade marks required by the Trade Marks Act 1994 s 63(2)(a): see PARA 21 head (1). As to the meaning of 'registered trade mark' see PARA 111.

3 Trade Marks Rules 2008, SI 2008/1797, r 47. As to falsely representing a trade mark as registered see PARA 131.

4 Ie as determined in accordance with the Trade Marks Act 1994 s 40(3): see PARA 23.

5 Trade Marks Rules 2008, SI 2008/1797, r 47(a). As to the requirements for registration see PARA 39 et seq; and as to the procedure on the application see PARA 334 et seq.

It should be noted that r 47 does not apply to international trade marks (UK) or requests for extension: see the Trade Marks (International Registration) Order 2008, SI 2008/2206, art 3(3), Sch 1 Pt 2; and PARA 12 note 13.

6 Trade Marks Rules 2008, SI 2008/1797, r 47(b). See note 5. As to the date of registration see PARA 23.

7 Trade Marks Rules 2008, SI 2008/1797 r 47(c), which refers to claims made under the Trade Marks Act 1994 s 35 (see PARA 360) or s 36 (see PARA 361). See note 5.

8 Trade Marks Rules 2008, SI 2008/1797, r 47(d). See note 5.

9 Trade Marks Rules 2008, SI 2008/1797, r 47(e). See note 5. As to the address for service see r 11; and PARA 339.

10 Trade Marks Rules 2008, SI 2008/1797, r 47(f), which refers to disclaimers and limitations under the Trade Marks Act 1994 s 13(1)(a) or s 13(1)(b): see PARA 65 heads (1)–(2). See note 5.

11 Trade Marks Rules 2008, SI 2008/1797, r 47(g). See note 5. The appropriate form is Form TM24: r 47(g). As to the use of forms see PARA 335. As to the registrar see PARA 19.

12 Trade Marks Rules 2008, SI 2008/1797, r 47(h). See note 5.

13 As to collective marks see PARA 138 et seq.

14 As to certification marks see PARA 148 et seq.

15 Trade Marks Rules 2008, SI 2008/1797, r 47(i). See note 5.

16 Ie pursuant to the Trade Marks Act 1994 s 5(5): see PARA 62.

17 Trade Marks Rules 2008, SI 2008/1797, r 47(j). See note 5.

18 As to transformation applications see PARA 14.

19 As to international registrations see PARA 12.

20 Ie under the Madrid Protocol art 3(4): see PARA 8.

21 See the Trade Marks Rules 2008, SI 2008/1797, r 47(k). The reference in the text to the date of recordal is a reference to the date of recordal of the request for extension to the United Kingdom of the international registration under the Madrid Protocol art 3ter (see PARA 8). See note 5.

22 As to Community trade marks see PARA 159 et seq; and as to conversion of Community trade marks or Community trade mark applications see PARA 180 et seq.
23 Trade Marks Rules 2008, SI 2008/1797, r 47(l). See note 5.

25.   Trusts and equities. No notice of any trust (express, implied or constructive) may be entered in the register[1]; and the registrar[2] is not affected by any such notice[3].

Equities in respect of a registered trade mark may be enforced in like manner as in respect of other personal or movable property[4].

1 As to the register see PARA 21.
2 As to the registrar see PARA 19.
3 Trade Marks Act 1994 s 26(1). This does not prevent notice of agreements which affect the proprietorship of the registered trade mark, whether by creating trusts or otherwise, from being entered upon the register: *Re Casey's Patents* [1892] 1 Ch 104, (1891) 9 RPC 9, CA; *Kakkar v Szelke* [1989] FSR 225, (1988) Times, 18 October, CA. The provisions of the Trade Marks Act 1994 s 26 apply, with the necessary modifications, in relation to an application for the registration of a trade mark as in relation to a registered trade mark: s 27(1). As to the meaning of 'registered trade mark' see PARA 111. As to the requirements for registration see PARA 39 et seq; and as to the procedure on the application see PARA 334 et seq.
4 Trade Marks Act 1994 s 26(2). See also note 3.

26.   Inspection of the register; provision of copies and extracts. The register[1] must be open for inspection at the Intellectual Property Office ('IPO')[2] during its hours of business as duly[3] published[4]; and, where any portion of the register is kept otherwise than in documentary form, the right of inspection is a right to inspect the material on the register[5].

The registrar must supply a certified copy or extract or uncertified copy or extract, as requested on the appropriate form[6], of any entry in the register[7].

1 As to the register see PARA 21.
2 As to the Intellectual Property Office (an operating name of the Patent Office) see PARA 16 note 2.
3 Ie in accordance with the Trade Marks Rules 2008, SI 2008/1797, r 80: see PARA 334.
4 Trade Marks Act 1994 s 63(3)(a); Trade Marks Rules 2008, SI 2008/1797, r 50(1). See PARA 21 note 8. As to the meaning of 'publish' see PARA 19 note 10. In practice the register is now kept in the form of an electronic database which is publicly searchable via the IPO website, accessible at the date on which this volume states the law at www.ipo.gov.uk. See also note 2.
5 Trade Marks Act 1994 s 63(3)(a); Trade Marks Rules 2008, SI 2008/1797, r 50(2). See PARA 21 note 8.
6 The appropriate form is Form TM31R: Trade Marks Rules 2008, SI 2008/1797, r 51.
7 Trade Marks Act 1994 s 63(3)(b); Trade Marks Rules 2008, SI 2008/1797, r 51. See PARA 19 note 8. As to the use of forms see PARA 335.

27.   Inspection of documents. The registrar[1] must permit all documents filed[2] or kept at the Intellectual Property Office ('IPO') in relation to a registered mark or, where an application for the registration of a trade mark has been published[3], in relation to that application, to be inspected[4]. Corresponding provisions apply to an international trade mark[5]. The registrar is not, however, obliged to permit the inspection of any such document until he has completed any procedure, or the stage in the procedure which is relevant to the document in question, which he is required or permitted[6] to carry out[7].

Such right of inspection does not apply[8] to:

(1)   any document prepared in the IPO solely for use therein[9];

(2)   any document sent to the IPO, whether at its request or otherwise, for inspection and subsequent return to the sender[10];

(3)   any request for information[11];

(4)   any document issued by the IPO which the registrar considers should be treated as confidential[12];

(5)   any document in respect of which the registrar issues directions[13] that it be treated as confidential[14].

Nothing in the above provisions is to be construed as imposing on the registrar any duty of making available for public inspection[15]:

(a)   any document or part of a document which in his opinion disparages any person in a way likely to damage him[16];

(b)   any document or information filed at or sent to or by the IPO before 31 October 1994[17]; or

(c)   any document or information filed at or sent to or by the IPO after 31 October 1994 relating to an application for registration of a trade mark under the Trade Marks Act 1938[18].

No appeal lies from a decision of the registrar[19] not to make any document or part of a document available for public inspection[20].

1   As to the registrar see PARA 19.
2   For these purposes, references to the filing of any application, notice or other document are to be construed as references to its being delivered to the registrar at the Intellectual Property Office ('IPO'): see the Trade Marks Rules 2008, SI 2008/1797, r 2(3). As to the filing of documents by electronic means see PARA 336. As to the Intellectual Property Office (an operating name of the Patent Office) see PARA 16 note 2.
3   As to the meaning of 'publish' see PARA 19 note 10. As to publication of the application see PARA 365.
4   Trade Marks Rules 2008, SI 2008/1797, r 58(1), which is expressed to be subject to r 58(2), (3): see the text and notes 6–14.
5   See the Trade Marks (International Registration) Order 2008, SI 2008/2206, art 3; and PARA 12. See also generally PARA 11 et seq.
6   Ie under the Trade Marks Act 1994 or the Trade Marks Rules 2008, SI 2008/1797.
7   Trade Marks Rules 2008, SI 2008/1797, r 58(2). See also note 5.
8   Trade Marks Rules 2008, SI 2008/1797, r 58(3). See also note 5.
9   Trade Marks Rules 2008, SI 2008/1797, r 58(3)(a).
10   Trade Marks Rules 2008, SI 2008/1797, r 58(3)(b). For these purposes, unless the context otherwise requires, 'send' includes give: r 2(1).
11   Trade Marks Rules 2008, SI 2008/1797, r 58(3)(c), which refers to requests under r 56: see PARA 372.
12   Trade Marks Rules 2008, SI 2008/1797, r 58(3)(d).
13   Ie under the Trade Marks Rules 2008, SI 2008/1797, r 59: see PARA 28.
14   Trade Marks Rules 2008, SI 2008/1797, r 58(3)(e).
15   Trade Marks Rules 2008, SI 2008/1797, r 58(4). See also note 5.
16   Trade Marks Rules 2008, SI 2008/1797, r 58(4)(a).
17   Trade Marks Rules 2008, SI 2008/1797, r 58(4)(b).
18   Trade Marks Rules 2008, SI 2008/1797, r 58(4)(c). The Trade Marks Act 1938 is now repealed.
19   Ie under the Trade Marks Rules 2008, SI 2008/1797, r 58(4).
20   Trade Marks Rules 2008, SI 2008/1797, r 58(5). See also note 5.

28.   Confidential documents.   Where a document other than a form required by the registrar[1] and duly published[2] is filed[3] at the Intellectual Property Office ('IPO')[4] and the person filing it requests at the time of filing that it or a specified part of it be treated as confidential, giving his reasons for the request, the registrar may direct that it or part of it, as the case may be, be treated as confidential, and the document is not open to public inspection while the matter is being determined by the registrar[5].

Where such direction has been given and not withdrawn, nothing in these provisions is to be taken to authorise or require any person to be allowed to inspect the document or part of it to which the direction relates except by leave of the registrar[6]. The registrar must not withdraw any direction so given without prior consultation with the person at whose request the direction was given, unless the registrar is satisfied that such prior consultation is not reasonably practical[7].

The registrar may where he considers that any document issued by the IPO should be treated as confidential so direct; and upon such direction that document is not open to public inspection except by leave of the registrar[8].

Where a direction is given under the above provisions for a document to be treated as confidential, a record of the fact must be filed with the document[9].

1   As to the registrar see PARA 19.
2   Ie in accordance with the Trade Marks Rules 2008, SI 2008/1797, r 3: see PARA 335. As to the meaning of 'publish' see PARA 19 note 10.
3   As to the meaning of references to 'filing' see PARA 27 note 2. As to the filing of documents by electronic means see PARA 336.
4   As to the Intellectual Property Office (an operating name of the Patent Office) see PARA 16 note 2.
5   Trade Marks Rules 2008, SI 2008/1797, r 59(1). As to the principles applicable to a application to keep documents or parts thereof confidential see *Diamond Shamrock Technologies SA's Patent* [1987] RPC 91. As to the application to international trade marks see PARA 11 et seq.
6   Trade Marks Rules 2008, SI 2008/1797, r 59(2).
7   Trade Marks Rules 2008, SI 2008/1797, r 59(3).
8   Trade Marks Rules 2008, SI 2008/1797, r 59(4).
9   Trade Marks Rules 2008, SI 2008/1797, r 59(5).

29.   Request for change of name or address in the register.   The registrar[1] must, on a request made on the appropriate form[2] by the proprietor of a registered trade mark[3] or a licensee[4] or any person having an interest in or charge on a registered trade mark which has been duly registered[5], enter any change in his name or address as recorded in the register[6].

1   As to the registrar see PARA 19.
2   The appropriate form for changes of name, address or email is now Form TM21a and for change of details to an application it is Form TM21b: see generally the Trade Marks Rules 2008, SI 2008/1797, r 52. As to the use of forms see PARA 335.
3   As to the meaning of 'registered trade mark' see PARA 111.
4   As to the licensing of trade marks see PARAS 119–120.
5   Ie registered under the Trade Marks Rules 2008, SI 2008/1797, r 48: see PARA 115.
6   Trade Marks Act 1994 s 64(4); Trade Marks Rules 2008, SI 2008/1797, r 52. It should be noted that the Trade Marks Act 1994 s 64(4) does not apply to international trade marks (UK) or requests for extension: see the Trade Marks (International Registration) Order 2008, SI 2008/2206, art 3(3), Sch 1 Pt 1; and PARA 12 note 10.

30.   Registrar's power to remove matter from the register.   Where it appears to the registrar[1] that any matter in the register has ceased to have effect, he may remove that matter from the register[2]; but, before doing so:

(1)   he may publish[3] in the Trade Marks Journal the fact that it is intended to remove [4]; and

(2)   where any person appears to him to be affected by the removal, notice of the intended removal must be sent[5] to that person[6].

Within two months of the date on which the intention to remove the matter is published, or notice of the intended removal is sent, as the case may be[7]:

(a)   any person may file[8] notice of opposition to the removal on the appropriate form[9]; and

(b)   the person to whom a notice is sent under head (2) above may file, in writing, his objections, if any, to the removal, or a request to have his objections heard orally[10].

If, after considering any objections or opposition to the removal, the registrar is satisfied that the matter has not ceased to have effect, he must not remove it[11]. Where there has been no response to the registrar's notice, he may remove the matter; and, where representations objecting to the removal of the entry have been made, whether in writing or orally, the registrar may, if he is of the view after considering the objections that the entry or any part thereof has ceased to have effect, remove it or, as appropriate, the part thereof[12].

1   As to the registrar see PARA 19.
2   Trade Marks Act 1994 s 64(5); Trade Marks Rules 2008, SI 2008/1797, r 53(1). As to the register see PARA 21.
3   As to the meaning of 'publish' see PARA 19 note 10.
4   Trade Marks Rules 2008, SI 2008/1797, r 53(1)(a). As to the Trade Marks Journal see PARA 19.
5   As the meaning of 'send' see PARA 27 note 10.
6   Trade Marks Rules 2008, SI 2008/1797, r 53(1)(b).
7   Trade Marks Rules 2008, SI 2008/1797, r 53(2).
8   As to the meaning of references to 'filing' see PARA 27 note 2. As to the filing of documents by electronic means see PARA 336.
9   Trade Marks Rules 2008, SI 2008/1797, r 53(2)(a). See also note 10. The appropriate form is Form TM7: r 53(2)(a). As to the use of forms see PARA 335. See also Form TM7a (online only): notice of threatened opposition.
10 Trade Marks Rules 2008, SI 2008/1797, r 53(2)(b). Where opposition or objection is made under r 53(2)(a) or r 53(2)(b), r 63 (see PARA 340) applies: r 53(2).
11 Trade Marks Rules 2008, SI 2008/1797, r 53(3).
12 Trade Marks Rules 2008, SI 2008/1797, r 53(4).

31. Duration and renewal of registration. A trade mark[1] is registered[2] for a period of ten years from the date of registration[3]; but registration may be renewed[4] for further periods of ten years[5].

The registration of a trade mark may be renewed by the proprietor filing[6] a request for renewal on the appropriate form[7] at any time within the period of six months ending on the date of the expiration of the registration, subject to payment of a renewal fee[8]. At any time not earlier than six months nor later than one month before the expiration of the last registration of a trade mark, the registrar[9] must, except where renewal has already been duly effected[10], send[11] to the registered proprietor notice of the approaching expiration and inform him at the same time that the registration may be renewed[12]. If it appears to the registrar that a trade mark may be registered[13] at any time within six months before or at any time after the date on which renewal would be due, by reference to the date of application for registration, the registrar is to be taken to have complied with this obligation if he sends to the applicant notice to that effect within one month following the date of actual registration[14].

A request for renewal must be made, and the renewal fee paid, before the expiry of the registration[15]. If, on the expiration of the last registration of a trade mark, the renewal fee has not been paid, the registrar must publish[16] that fact[17], and, if within six months from the date of the expiration of the last registration the request for renewal is filed on the appropriate form[18] accompanied by the appropriate renewal fee and additional renewal fee, the registrar must renew the registration without removing the mark from the register[19].

Renewal takes effect from the expiry of the previous registration[20].

Where no request for renewal is filed, the registrar must remove the trade mark from the register[21], subject to his power[22] to restore the registration[23].

Where a mark is due to be registered after the date on which it is due for renewal, by reference to the date of application for registration, the request for renewal must be filed together with the renewal fee and additional renewal fee within six months after the date of actual registration[24].

The renewal or removal of any registration must be published on the Intellectual Property Office ('IPO') website[25].

1   As to the meaning of 'trade mark' see PARA 41.
2   As to the meaning of 'registered' see PARA 21 note 2. In the case of an international trade mark, the mark 'becomes protected': see PARA 11 et seq.
3   Trade Marks Act 1994 s 42(1). As to the meaning of 'date of registration' see PARA 23. Section 42(1) applies in relation to the registration of a mark in pursuance of an application made on or after 31 October 1994 (ie the date on which the Trade Marks Act 1994 came into force: see the Trade Marks Act 1994 (Commencement) Order 1994, SI 1994/2550, art 2); and the old law continues to apply in any other case: Trade Marks Act 1994 s 105, Sch 3 para 15(1). It is immaterial when the fee is paid: Sch 3 para 15(3). As to the meaning of 'the old law' see PARA 4 note 3.
      It should be noted that the Trade Marks Act 1994 ss 42, 43 do not apply to international trade marks (UK) or requests for extension: see the Trade Marks (International Registration) Order 2008, SI 2008/2206, art 3(3), Sch 1 Pt 1; and PARA 12 note 10.
4   Ie in accordance with the Trade Marks Act 1994 s 43: see the text and notes 6–25.
5   Trade Marks Act 1994 s 42(2). See note 3. This applies where the renewal falls due on or after 31 October 1994; and the old law applies in any other case: Sch 3 para 15(2). It is immaterial when the fee is paid: Sch 3 para 15(3).
6   As to the meaning of references to 'filing' see PARA 27 note 2. As to the filing of documents by electronic means see PARA 336.
7   The appropriate form is Form TM11: Trade Marks Rules 2008, SI 2008/1797, r 35. As to the use of forms see PARA 335.
8   Trade Marks Act 1994 s 43(1); Trade Marks Rules 2008, SI 2008/1797, r 35. See note 3. As to fees see PARA 18; and as to acts done by authorised agents see PARA 33. The Trade Marks Act 1994 s 43 applies where the renewal falls due on or after 31 October 1994; and the old law applies in any other case: Sch 3 para 15(2). It is immaterial when the fee is paid: Sch 3 para 15(3).
9   As to the registrar see PARA 19.
10   Ie under the Trade Marks Rules 2008, SI 2008/1797, r 35: see the text to notes 6–8.
11   As to the meaning of 'send' see PARA 27 note 10.
12   Trade Marks Act 1994 s 43(2); Trade Marks Rules 2008, SI 2008/1797, r 34(1). See notes 3, 8.
13   Ie under the Trade Marks Act 1994 s 40 (see PARA 370): Trade Marks Rules 2008, SI 2008/1797, r 34(2).
14   Trade Marks Rules 2008, SI 2008/1797, r 34(2).
15   Trade Marks Act 1994 s 43(3). See notes 3, 8.
16   As to the meaning of 'publish' see PARA 19 note 10.
17   Trade Marks Rules 2008, SI 2008/1797, r 36(1).
18   The appropriate form is Form TM11: Trade Marks Rules 2008, SI 2008/1797, r 36(2).
19   Trade Marks Act 1994 s 43(3); Trade Marks Rules 2008, SI 2008/1797, r 36(2). The periods specified in r 36 may only be extended in limited circumstances: see r 77, Sch 1; and PARA 338. See notes 3, 8.
20   Trade Marks Act 1994 s 43(4). See notes 3, 8.
21   As to the register see PARA 21.
22   Ie under the Trade Marks Rules 2008, SI 2008/1797, r 37: see PARA 32.
23   Trade Marks Act 1994 s 43(5); Trade Marks Rules 2008, SI 2008/1797, r 36(3). See notes 3, 8, 18. As to appeals from decisions of the registrar, including acts of the registrar in exercise of a discretion, see the Trade Marks Act 1994 ss 76, 77; and PARA 387 et seq.
24   Trade Marks Rules 2008, SI 2008/1797, r 36(4). See note 18.
25   Trade Marks Act 1994 s 43(6); Trade Marks Rules 2008, SI 2008/1797, r 36(5). See notes 3, 8, 18. As to the Intellectual Property Office (an operating name of the Patent Office) see PARA 16 note 2. The IPO website is accessible at the date at which this volume states the law at www.ipo.gov.uk.

32. Restoration to the register. Where the registrar[1] has removed the mark from the register for failure to renew its registration[2], he may, upon a request filed on the appropriate form[3] within six months of the date of the removal of the mark accompanied by the appropriate renewal fee and appropriate restoration fee, restore the mark to the register[4] and renew its registration if, having regard to the circumstances of the failure to renew, he is satisfied that it is just to do so[5]. The restoration of the registration, including the date of restoration, must be published on the Intellectual Property Office ('IPO') website[6].

1   As to the registrar see PARA 19.
2   Ie in accordance with the Trade Marks Rules 2008, SI 2008/1797, r 36: see PARA 31.
3   The appropriate form is Form TM13: Trade Marks Rules 2008, SI 2008/1797, r 37(1). As to the use of forms see PARA 335.
4   As to the register see PARA 21.
5   Trade Marks Act 1994 s 43(5); Trade Marks Rules 2008, SI 2008/1797, r 37(1). The periods specified in r 37 may only be extended in limited circumstances: see r 77, Sch 1; and PARA 338. As to fees see PARA 18. The Trade Marks Act 1994 s 43 applies where the renewal falls due on or after 31 October 1994; and the old law applies in any other case: Sch 3 para 15(2). As to the meaning of 'the old law' see PARA 4 note 3. In the absence of a challenge to the registrar's decision to restore a registration by way of judicial review, misconduct by the applicant for restoration (such as failure fully to disclose to the registrar all the relevant circumstances) cannot itself constitute grounds for a challenge to the restoration by way of rectification of the register, although it may be relevant to the exercise of any discretion by a tribunal hearing an application for rectification of the register on other grounds: *Second Sight Ltd v Novell UK Ltd and Novell Inc* [1995] RPC 423.
       It should be noted that the Trade Marks Act 1994 s 43 does not apply to international trade marks (UK) or requests for extension: see the Trade Marks (International Registration) Order 2008, SI 2008/2206, art 3(3), Sch 1 Pt 1; and PARA 12 note 10.
6   Trade Marks Act 1994 s 43(6); Trade Marks Rules 2008, SI 2008/1797, r 37(2). See note 5. As to the Intellectual Property Office (an operating name of the Patent Office) see PARA 16 note 2. The IPO website is accessible at the date at which this volume states the law at www.ipo.gov.uk.

(iv) Trade Mark Agents

A. IN GENERAL

33.   Recognition of agents.   Any act required or authorised by the Trade Marks Act 1994 to be done by or to a person in connection with the registration[1] of a trade mark[2], or any procedure relating to a registered trade mark[3], may be done[4] by or to an agent authorised by that person orally or in writing[5]. Where an agent has been so authorised, the registrar[6] may in any particular case require the personal signature or presence of the agent or the person authorising him to act as agent[7].

Where a person appoints an agent for the first time or appoints one agent in substitution for another, the newly appointed agent must file the appropriate form[8]. Where, after a person has become a party to proceedings before the registrar, he appoints an agent for the first time or appoints one agent in substitution for another, the newly appointed agent must file the appropriate form[9]; and any act required or authorised by the Trade Marks Act 1994 in connection with the registration of a trade mark or any procedure relating to a trade mark may not be done by or to the newly appointed agent until on or after the date on which he files the appropriate form[10].

The registrar may by notice in writing sent to an agent require him to produce evidence of his authority[11].

1   As to the meaning of 'registration' see PARA 21 note 2.
2   As to the meaning of 'trade mark' see PARA 41.
3   As to the meaning of 'registered trade mark' see PARA 111.

4 Ie except as otherwise provided by rules and subject to the Legal Services Act 2007. As to the making of rules generally see PARA 17. As to the Legal Services Act 2007 generally see LEGAL PROFESSIONS vol 65 (2008) PARA 301 et seq.

5 Trade Marks Act 1994 s 82 (amended by the Legal Services Act 2007 s 184(1), (2)). As to agency generally see AGENCY.

6 As to the registrar see PARA 19.

7 Trade Marks Rules 2008, SI 2008/1797, r 60(1).

8 Trade Marks Rules 2008, SI 2008/1797, r 60(2). The appropriate form is Form TM33: r 60(2). As to the use of forms see PARA 335.

9 Trade Marks Rules 2008, SI 2008/1797, r 60(3) The appropriate form is Form TM33P: r 60(3). See note 8.

10 Trade Marks Rules 2008, SI 2008/1797, r 60(4). The reference is to Form TM33 or Form TM33P as appropriate: r 60(4).

11 Trade Marks Rules 2008, SI 2008/1797, r 60(5).

34. Restrictions on practice. An individual who is not a registered trade mark attorney[1] may not[2]:

(1) carry on a business[3], otherwise than in partnership, under any name or other description which contains the words 'registered trade mark agent' or 'registered trade mark attorney'[4]; or

(2) in the course of a business otherwise describe or hold himself out, or permit himself to be described or held out, as a registered trade mark agent or a registered trade mark attorney[5].

A partnership or other unincorporated body must not[6]:

(a) carry on a business under any name or other description which contains the words 'registered trade mark agent' or 'registered trade mark attorney'[7]; or

(b) in the course of a business otherwise describe or hold itself out, or permit itself to be described or held out, as a firm of registered trade mark agents or registered trade mark attorneys[8],

unless the partnership or other body is registered in the register[9].

A body corporate must not:

(i) carry on a business, otherwise than in partnership, under any name or other description which contains the words 'registered trade mark agent' or 'registered trade mark attorney'[10]; or

(ii) in the course of a business otherwise describe or hold itself out, or permit itself to be described or held out, as a registered trade mark agent or a registered trade mark attorney[11],

unless all the body corporate is registered in the register[12].

A person who contravenes the above provisions commits an offence and is liable on conviction to a penalty[13]; and proceedings for such an offence may be begun at any time within a year from the date of the offence[14].

1 A 'registered trade mark attorney' means an individual whose name is entered in the register kept under the Trade Marks Act 1994 s 83 (see PARA 38): s 83(2) (s 83 substituted by the Legal Services Act 2007 s 184(1), (3)).

2 Trade Marks Act 1994 s 84(1) (amended by the Legal Services Act 2007 Sch 21 paras 109, 111(a)(i)).

3 For these purposes 'business' includes a trade or profession: Trade Marks Act 1994 s 103(1).

4 Trade Marks Act 1994 s 84(1)(a) (amended by the Legal Services Act 2007 Sch 21 paras 109, 111(a)(ii)).

5 Trade Marks Act 1994 s 84(1)(b) (amended by the Legal Services Act 2007 Sch 21 paras 109, 111(a)(iii)).

6 Trade Marks Act 1994 s 84(2) (amended by the Legal Services Act 2007 s 184(1), (4)(a)(i)).

7 Trade Marks Act 1994 s 84(2)(a) (amended by the Legal Services Act 2007 Sch 21 paras 109, 111(b)(i)).

8   Trade Marks Act 1994 s 84(2)(b) (amended by the Legal Services Act 2007 Sch 21 paras 109, 111(b)(ii)).
9   Trade Marks Act 1994 s 84(2) (amended by the Legal Services Act 2007 s 184(1), (4)(a)(i). The reference in the text to the register is a reference to the register kept under the Trade Marks Act 1994 s 83: see PARA 38.
10 Trade Marks Act 1994 s 84(3)(a) (amended by the Legal Services Act 2007 Sch 21 paras 109, 111(c)(i)).
11 Trade Marks Act 1994 s 84(3)(b) (amended by the Legal Services Act 2007 Sch 21 paras 109, 111(c)(ii)).
12 Trade Marks Act 1994 s 84(3) (amended by the Legal Services Act 2007 s 184(1), (4)(b)). The reference in the text to the register is a reference to the register kept under the Trade Marks Act 1994 s 83: see PARA 38.
13 Trade Marks Act 1994 s 84(4). The penalty on summary conviction is a fine not exceeding level 5 on the standard scale: s 84(4). As to the standard scale see SENTENCING AND DISPOSITION OF OFFENDERS vol 92 (2010) PARA 142. As to offences by partnerships and bodies corporate see PARA 122.
14 Trade Marks Act 1994 s 84(4).

35.   Privilege for communications with registered trade mark attorneys. As regards (1) communications as to any matter relating to the protection of any design or trade mark[1], or as to any matter involving passing off and (2) documents, material or information mentioned in head (1) above[2], where a trade mark attorney[3] so acts for a client[4] any such communication, document, material or information[5] is privileged from disclosure in like manner as if the trade mark attorney had at all material times been acting as the client's solicitor[6].

1   As to the meaning of 'trade mark' see PARA 41.
2   See the Trade Marks Act 1994 s 87(1) (amended by the Legal Services Act 2007 Sch 21 paras 109, 113). As to passing off see PARA 287 et seq.
3   For these purposes, 'trade mark attorney' means: (1) a registered trade mark attorney; or (2) a partnership entitled to describe itself as a firm of registered trade mark attorneys; or (3) a body corporate entitled to describe itself as a registered trade mark attorney: Trade Marks Act 1994 s 87(3) (amended by the Legal Services Act 2007 Sch 21 paras 109, 113(d)). As to the modification of this definition in relation to Community trade marks see PARA 179. As to the meaning of 'registered trade mark attorney' see PARA 34 note 1. As to partnerships entitled to describe themselves as firms of registered trade mark attorneys, and as to bodies corporate entitled to describe themselves as registered trade mark attorneys, see PARA 34.
4   Ie in relation to a matter mentioned in the Trade Marks Act 1994 s 87(1).
5   Ie any communication, document, material or information to which the Trade Marks Act 1994 s 87 applies.
6   Trade Marks Act 1994 s 87(2) (substituted by the Legal Services Act 2007 Sch 21 paras 109, 113(c)). As to legal professional privilege see LEGAL PROFESSIONS vol 66 (2009) PARAS 1032.

36.   Power of the registrar to refuse to deal with certain agents. The Secretary of State[1] may make rules authorising the registrar[2] to refuse to recognise as agent in respect of any business under the Trade Marks Act 1994[3]:

(1)   a person who has been convicted of the offence of describing himself as a registered trade mark agent or attorney when not entitled to do so[4];

(2)   a person whose name has been erased from and not restored to, or who is suspended from, the register of trade mark attorneys[5] on the ground of misconduct[6];

(3)   a person who is found by the Secretary of State to have been guilty of such conduct as would, in the case of a person registered in the register of trade mark attorneys, render the person liable to have the person's name erased from the register on the ground of misconduct[7];

(4)   a partnership or body corporate of which one of the partners or directors[8] is a person whom the registrar could refuse to recognise under head (1), head (2) or head (3) above[9].

The rules may contain such incidental and supplementary provisions as appear to the Secretary of State to be appropriate and may in particular prescribe circumstances in which a person is or is not to be taken to have been guilty of misconduct[10].

The registrar may accordingly refuse to recognise as agent in respect of any business under the Trade Marks Act 1994[11]:

(a)   a person who has been convicted of the offence of describing himself as a registered trade mark agent or attorney when not entitled to do so[12];

(b)   an individual whose name has been erased from and not restored to, or who is suspended from, the register of trade mark agents on the ground of misconduct[13];

(c)   a person who is found by the Secretary of State to have been guilty of such conduct as would, in the case of an individual registered in the register of trade mark attorneys, render him liable to have his name erased from the register on the ground of misconduct[14];

(d)   a partnership or body corporate of which one of the partners or directors is a person whom the registrar could refuse to recognise under head (a), head (b) or head (c) above[15].

1   As to the Secretary of State see PARA 16.
2   As to the registrar see PARA 19.
3   Trade Marks Act 1994 s 88(1). As to the making of rules generally see PARA 17.
4   Trade Marks Act 1994 s 88(1)(a). The offence referred to in the text is an offence under s 84: see PARA 34. As to the meaning of 'registered trade mark attorney' see PARA 34 note 1.
5   As to the register of trade mark attorneys see PARA 38.
6   Trade Marks Act 1994 s 88(1)(b) (amended by the Legal Services Act 2007 Sch 21 paras 109, 114(a)).
7   Trade Marks Act 1994 s 88(1)(c) (amended by the Legal Services Act 2007 Sch 21 paras 109, 114(b); and SI 2009/3348).
8   'Director', in relation to a body corporate whose affairs are managed by its members, means any member of the body: Trade Marks Act 1994 s 103(1).
9   Trade Marks Act 1994 s 88(1)(d).
10 Trade Marks Act 1994 s 88(2). The Trade Marks Rules 2008, SI 2008/1797 are made under the Trade Marks Act 1994 s 88(2): see the text and notes 11–15.
11 Trade Marks Rules 2008, SI 2008/1797, r 61.
12 Trade Marks Rules 2008, SI 2008/1797, r 61(a). The reference in the text to an offence is a reference to an offence under the Trade Marks Act 1994 s 84: see PARA 34.
13 Trade Marks Rules 2008, SI 2008/1797, r 61(b).
14 Trade Marks Rules 2008, SI 2008/1797, r 61(c).
15 Trade Marks Rules 2008, SI 2008/1797, r 61(d).

37.   Use of the term 'trade mark attorney'.   No offence is committed under the enactments restricting the use of certain expressions in reference to persons not qualified to act as solicitors[1] by the use of the term 'trade mark attorney' in reference to a registered trade mark attorney[2].

1   Ie under the Solicitors Act 1974 s 21 (see LEGAL PROFESSIONS vol 65 (2008) PARA 424), the Solicitors (Scotland) Act 1980 s 31 and the Solicitors (Northern Ireland) Order 1976, SI 1976/582, art 22.
2   Trade Marks Act 1994 s 86(1), (2) (s 86(1) amended by the Legal Services Act 2007 Sch 21 paras 109, 112). As to the meaning of 'registered trade mark attorney' see PARA 34 note 1.

B. THE REGISTER OF TRADE MARK ATTORNEYS; REGULATION

38.   General requirement to keep register; regulation of trade mark attorneys.   There is to continue to be a register of persons who act as agent for others for the purpose of applying for or obtaining the registration of trade marks[1]. An individual whose name is entered on this register is known as a registered trade mark attorney[2]. The register is to be kept by the Institute of Trade Mark Attorneys[3].

The person who keeps the register[4] may make regulations which regulate (1) the keeping of the register and the registration of persons; (2) the carrying on of trade mark agency work[5] by registered persons[6].

Those regulations may, amongst other things, make (a) provision as to the educational and training qualifications, and other requirements, which must be satisfied before an individual may be registered or for an individual to remain registered; (b) provision as to the requirements which must be met by a body (corporate or unincorporate) before it may be registered or for it to remain registered, including provision as to the management and control of the body; (c) provision as to the educational, training or other requirements to be met by regulated persons; (d) provision regulating the practice, conduct and discipline of registered persons or regulated persons; (e) provision authorising in such cases as may be specified in the regulations the erasure from the register of the name of any person registered in it, or the suspension of a person's registration; (f) provision requiring the payment of such fees as may be specified in or determined in accordance with the regulations; (g) provision about the provision to be made by registered persons in respect of complaints made against them; (h) provision about the keeping of records and accounts by registered persons or regulated persons; (i) provision for reviews of or appeals against decisions made under the regulations; (j) provision as to the indemnification of registered persons or regulated persons against losses arising from claims in respect of civil liability incurred by them[7].

1   Trade Marks Act 1994 s 83(1) (s 83 substituted by the Legal Services Act 2007 s 184(1), (3)). As to the meaning of 'registration' in relation to trade marks see PARA 21 note 2. As to the meaning of 'trade mark' see PARA 41.

2   See the Trade Marks Act 1994 s 83(2); and PARA 34 note 1.

3   Trade Marks Act 1994 s 83(3) (as substituted: see note 1). For more information about the Institute of Trade Mark Attorneys see the Institute's website accessible at the date this volume states the law at www.itma.org.uk. The Institute is the professional body responsible for the regulation of the trade mark attorney profession under the Legal Services Act 2007, and for representing the interests of the profession, nationally and internationally. The regulation of the profession has been delegated to a separate regulatory arm which operates at arm's length under the Intellectual Property Regulation Board (IPReg): see note 6.
    The Secretary of State, after consulting the Legal Services Board, may, by order, amend the Trade Marks Act 1994 s 83(3) so as to require the register to be kept by the person specified in the order: s 83(4), (5) (as so substituted). Such an order must be made by statutory instrument; but no such order may be made unless a draft of it has been laid before, and approved by a resolution of, each House of Parliament: s 83(6), (7) (as so substituted). As to the Secretary of State see PARA 16. As to the Legal Services Board see LEGAL PROFESSIONS vol 65 (2008) PARA 303 et seq. At the date at which this volume states the law no regulations had been made under s 83.

4   Ie under the Trade Marks Act 1994 s 83: see the text and notes 1–3.

5   For these purposes, 'trade mark agency work' means work done in the course of carrying on the business of acting as agent for others for the purpose of (1) applying for or obtaining the registration of trade marks in the United Kingdom or elsewhere; or (2) conducting proceedings before the Comptroller relating to applications for or otherwise in connection with the registration of trade marks: Trade Marks Act 1994 s 83A(7) (s 83A added by the Legal Services Act 2007 s 184(1), (3); and this definition amended by SI 2009/3339). As to the meaning of 'United Kingdom' see PARA 3 note 2. As to the Comptroller General of Patents, Designs and Trade Marks see PATENTS AND REGISTERED DESIGNS vol 79 (2008) PARA 577.

6   Trade Marks Act 1994 s 83A(1) (as added: see note 5). For these purposes, 'regulated person' means a person who is not a registered person but is a manager or employee of a body which is a registered person; 'registered person' means (1) a registered trade mark attorney; or (2) a body

(corporate or unincorporate) registered in the register kept under s 83 (see the text and notes 1–3); and 'manager', in relation to a body, has the same meaning as in the Legal Services Act 2007 (see s 207; and LEGAL PROFESSIONS vol 65 (2008) PARA 369 note 17): Trade Marks Act 1994 s 83A(7) (as so added).

Regulations under s 83A may make different provision for different purposes: s 83A(3) (as so added). Regulations under s 83A which are not regulatory arrangements within the meaning of the Legal Services Act 2007 (see LEGAL PROFESSIONS vol 65 (2008) PARA 377) are to be treated as such arrangements for the purposes of that Act: Trade Marks Act 1994 s 83A(4) (as so added). Before the appointed day, regulations under s 83A may be made only with the approval of the Secretary of State: s 83A(5) (as so added). For these purposes, 'appointed day' means the day appointed for the coming into force of the Legal Services Act 2007 Sch 4 para 1 (ie 1 January 2010): Trade Marks Act 1994 s 83A(7) (as so added). The powers conferred to make regulations under s 83A are not to be taken to prejudice (a) any other power which the person who keeps the register may have to make rules or regulations (however they may be described and whether they are made under an enactment or otherwise); (b) any rules or regulations made by that person under any such power: s 83A(6). At the date at which this volume states the law no regulations had been made under s 83A.

The Legal Services Act 2007 (see note 3) introduced the requirement that regulatory and representation bodies should be separate so the Intellectual Property Regulation Board was set up to oversee the regulation of trade make attorneys. For more information about the Intellectual Property Regulation Board see the Board's website accessible at the date this volume states the law at www.ipreg.org.uk. The Board has made a number of rules and regulations governing such matters as conduct, practice fees, examination, qualification, registration and rights to conduct litigation and advocacy and these are to be found on the website. See also note 3 in regard to the Institute of Trade Mark Attorneys.

7   Trade Marks Act 1994 s 83A(2)(a)–(j) (as added: see note 5). As to the meanings of 'regulated person' and 'registered person' see note 6.

(3) REQUIREMENTS FOR THE REGISTRATION OF UNITED KINGDOM TRADE MARKS AND FOR PROTECTION OF INTERNATIONAL MARKS

(i) Introduction

39. In general. Any sign[1] may be registered as a trade mark pursuant to a United Kingdom application unless one of a number of specified grounds for refusal exists; the registrar[2] has no discretion to refuse an application if none of these grounds applies[3]. The grounds for refusal are divided into two classes, described in the Trade Marks Act 1994 as 'absolute grounds for refusal'[4] and 'relative grounds for refusal'[5]. The absolute grounds for refusal are concerned with the intrinsic qualities of the trade mark itself, whereas the relative grounds for refusal are concerned with conflict with the prior rights of third parties. In addition, registration may, or in some cases must, be refused if the trade mark contains or consists of certain specially protected emblems[6]. The same grounds for refusal apply to the protection of an international registration[7] designating the United Kingdom, since such a registration is entitled to become protected if it satisfies the requirements for registration imposed on domestic applications[8].

Where grounds for refusal of registration exist in respect of only some of the goods or services for which the trade mark has been applied for, refusal of registration must cover those goods or services only[9].

1   As to the meaning of 'sign' see PARA 41 note 1.
2   As to the registrar see PARA 19.

3   *EUROLAMB Trade Mark* [1997] RPC 279, Appointed Person; *Procter & Gamble Ltd's Trade Mark Applications* [1999] RPC 673, CA; and see PARA 363. Cf the position on an application for revocation or a declaration of invalidity: see PARA 95.

4   See the Trade Marks Act 1994 s 3, marginal note. The same term is employed in Council
    Regulation (EC) 207/2009 (OJ L78, 24.3.2009, p 1) on the Community trade mark, art 7
    (formerly Council Regulation (EC) 40/94 (OJ L11, 14.1.94, p 1) art 7): see PARA 192 et seq. As
    to the effect of marginal notes see STATUTES AND LEGISLATIVE PROCESS vol 96 (2012) PARA 682.
    As to the absolute grounds for refusal of registration see PARA 42 et seq.
5   See the Trade Marks Act 1994 s 5, marginal note. The same term is employed in Council
    Regulation (EC) 207/2009 (OJ L78, 24.3.2009, p 1) on the Community trade mark, art 8
    (formerly Council Regulation (EC) 40/94 (OJ L11, 14.1.94, p 1) art 8): see PARA 201 et seq. As
    to the relative grounds for refusal of registration see PARA 54 et seq.
6   See the Trade Marks Act 1994 s 4; and PARA 50.
7   Ie from an application made to the International Bureau under the Madrid Protocol: see PARA
    11. As to the Madrid Protocol see PARA 8.
8   See the Trade Marks (International Registration) Order 2008, SI 2008/2206, art 3. The
    terminology used for international trade marks is different since they 'become protected' in the
    United Kingdom rather than being registered, but the substantive requirements which they need
    to satisfy are the same: see PARA 12. See also generally PARA 11 et seq.
9   See European Parliament and Council Directive (EC) 2008/95 (OJ L299, 8.11.2008, p 25) to
    approximate the laws of the member states relating to trade marks, art 13 (formerly Council
    Directive (EEC) 89/104 (OJ L40, 11.2.89, p 1) art 13); and PARA 363.

40. Date of assessment. Except where there is a valid claim to priority[1], when
considering whether a sign may be registered as a trade mark, the applicability of
both the absolute and the relevant grounds of refusal[2] must be considered as at
the date of filing of the application[3]. The same rule applies when considering
whether a registration should be declared invalid[4], except where the proprietor
relies upon distinctive character acquired by use as an answer to an objection
that the trade mark lacked distinctiveness[5].

1   Ie under the Trade Marks Act 1994 ss 35, 36. As to priority see PARA 360 et seq.
2   Ie under the Trade Marks Act 1994 ss 3, 5. As to meanings of 'absolute grounds of refusal' and
    'relative grounds of refusal' see PARA 39.
3   Case C-192/03 *Alcon Inc v Office for Harmonisation in the Internal Market (Trade Marks and
    Designs)* [2004] ECR I-8993, ECJ; Case C-542/07P *Imagination Technologies Ltd v Office for
    Harmonisation in the Internal Market (Trade Marks and Designs)* [2009] ECR I-4937, [2009]
    All ER (D) 219 (Jun), ECJ; *Bongrain SA's Trade Mark Application* [2004] EWCA Civ 1690,
    [2005] RPC 306, [2005] IP & T 563; *HOTPICKS Trade Mark* [2004] EWHC 689 (Ch), [2004]
    RPC 834. Nevertheless it is legitimate to take account of evidence from a later date if and in so
    far as it enables the drawing of conclusions as to the situation at the date of filing: Case
    C-192/03 *Alcon Inc v Office for Harmonisation in the Internal Market (Trade Marks and
    Designs)* above; cf Case C-259/02 *La Mer Technology Inc v Laboratories Goemar SA* [2004]
    ECR I-1159, ECJ. As to the date of filing see PARA 348.
4   Ie under the Trade Marks Act 1994 s 47: see PARA 102 et seq.
5   Ie by virtue of the proviso to the Trade Marks Act 1994 s 47(1): see PARA 102.

41. Meaning of 'trade mark'. For the purposes of the Trade Marks Act 1994,
'trade mark' means any sign[1] capable of being represented graphically[2] which is
capable of distinguishing goods or services of one undertaking from those of
other undertakings[3]. A trade mark may, in particular, consist of words (including
personal names), designs, letters, numerals or the shape of goods or their
packaging[4].

References in the Act to a trade mark include, unless the context otherwise
requires, references to a collective mark[5] or certification mark[6].

1   A sign is something which conveys a message: *Société des Produits Nestlé SA v Cadbury UK Ltd*
    [2013] EWCA Civ 1174 at [15(5)], [2013] All ER (D) 35 (Oct) at [15(5)] per Sir John
    Mummery. The subject matter of an application for trade mark registration which relates to all
    the conceivable shapes of a transparent bin or collection chamber forming part of the external
    surface of a vacuum cleaner is not a sign: Case C-321/03 *Dyson Ltd v Registrar of Trade Marks*
    [2007] ECR I-687, [2007] ETMR 34. Nor is a mark consisting of a three-dimensional
    ivory-coloured tile of any size on the top surface of which is shown any letter of the alphabet

and a numeral in the range 1 to 10 in any position: *J W Spear & Sons Ltd v Zynga Inc* [2012] EWHC 3345 (Ch), [2012] All ER (D) 326 (Nov) (affd [2013] EWCA Civ 1175, [2013] All ER (D) 39 (Oct)). Nor is a mark consisting of a particular colour being the 'predominant' colour applied to the whole visible surface of the packaging of the goods: *Société des Produits Nestlé SA v Cadbury UK Ltd* above. It has also been doubted whether an alignment of symbols on a fruit machine occurring on a (pseudo) random basis is a sign (*Electrocoin Automatics Ltd v Coinworld Ltd* [2004] EWHC 1498 (Ch) at [138], [2005] FSR 9 at [138], [2005] IP & T 132 at [138] per G Hobbs QC). See also the text and note 4.

2   To satisfy this requirement, the sign must be represented by graphical means, in particular images, lines or characters, and the representation must be clear, precise, self-contained, easily accessible, durable and objective: Case C-273/00 *Sieckmann v Deutsches Patent- und Markenamt* [2003] Ch 487, [2002] ECR I-11737, ECJ; Case C-104/01 *Libertel Groep BV v Benelux-Merkenbureau* [2004] Ch 83, [2003] ECR I-3793, ECJ; Case C-283/01 *Shield Mark BV v Kist (t/a Memex)* [2004] Ch 97, [2003] ECR I-14313, ECJ; Case C-49/02 *Heidelberger Bauchemie GmbH* [2004] ECR I-6129, [2004] All ER (D) 268 (Jun), ECJ. A representation which is contradictory does not satisfy this requirement: Case T-293/10 *Seven Towns Ltd v Office for Harmonisation in the Internal Market (Trade Marks and Designs)* [2012] ECR II-0000, CFI. Nor does a representation which covers a multitude of different combinations: *J W Spear & Sons Ltd v Zynga Inc* [2012] EWHC 3345 (Ch), [2012] All ER (D) 326 (Nov) (affd [2013] EWCA Civ 1175, [2013] All ER (D) 39 (Oct)).

A mere sample of colour does not satisfy this requirement, but a sample of a colour combined with a description in words of that colour may do so, as may a designation using an internationally recognised identification code: Case C-273/00 *Libertel Groep BV v Benelux-Merkenbureau* above. The mere juxtaposition of two colours, without shape or contours, does not satisfy this requirement, but a systematic arrangement of two colours in a predetermined and uniform way may do so: Case C-49/02 *Heidelberger Bauchemie GmbH* above. The specification of a mark as a particular colour being the 'predominant' colour applied to the whole visible surface of the packaging of the goods does not comply with this requirement: *Société des Produits Nestlé SA v Cadbury UK Ltd* [2013] EWCA Civ 1174, [2013] All ER (D) 35 (Oct).

A description of a sound in words or using onomatopoeia or by means of a sequence of musical notes without more does not satisfy this requirement, but full musical notation may do so: Case C-283/01 *Shield Mark BV v Kist (t/a Memex)* above. In the case of a spoken mark a sonogram has been held to comply with this requirement: Case R 295/2005-4 *Hexal AG's Application* (8 September 2005, unreported), OHIM Board of Appeal.

A representation of an odour by means of a chemical formula, a description in words or the deposit of a sample or all three does not satisfy this requirement: Case C-273/00 *Sieckmann v Deutsches Patent- und Markenamt* above; Case T-305/04 *Eden SARL v Office for Harmonisation in the Internal Market (Trade Marks and Designs)* [2005] ECR II-4705, [2006] ETMR 14, CFI (decision made under the equivalent provision of Council Regulation (EC) 40/94 (OJ L11, 14.1.94, p 1) on the Community trade mark, ie arts 4, 7(1)(a) (see now Council Regulation (EC) 207/2009 (OJ L78, 24.3.2009, p 1) arts 4, 7(1)(a)) (see PARAS 191, 193)). The same applies to a taste or flavour: Case R 120/2001-2 *Eli Lilly & Co's Application* [2004] ETMR 4, OHIM Board of Appeal (decision made under the equivalent provision of Council Regulation (EC) 40/94 (OJ L11, 14.1.94, p 1) on the Community trade mark, ie arts 4, 7(1)(a) (see now Council Regulation (EC) 207/2009 (OJ L78, 24.3.2009, p 1) arts 4, 7(1)(a)) (see PARAS 191, 193)).

In the case of a three-dimensional sign, it may be necessary for the applicant to present a clearly defined image of the sign; a mere description, even if conveying the clear and precise appearance of the sign, is not sufficient: Case R 156/1998-2 *Antoni and Alison's Application* [1998] ETMR 460, OHIM Board of Appeal (method of packing) (decision made under the equivalent provision of EC Council Regulation 40/94 (OJ L11, 14.1.94, p 1) on the Community trade mark, ie arts 4, 7(1)(a) (see now Council Regulation (EC) 207/2009 (OJ L78, 24.3.2009, p 1) arts 4, 7(1)(a)) (see PARAS 191, 193)); *Swizzels Matlow Ltd's Application* [1999] RPC 879, Appointed Person (shape of a sweet); and see Case C-321/03 *Dyson Ltd v Registrar of Trade Marks* [2007] ECR I-687 at [57]–[66], [2007] ETMR 34 at [57]–[66] per Léger Adv-Gen.

Trade marks which consist of moving images may be graphically represented by a sequence of stills combined with a description: Case R 443/2010-2 *Sony Ericsson Mobile Communications AB's Trade Mark Application* (23 September 2010, unreported), OHIM Board of Appeal.

Even if the representation satisfies this requirement, lack of precision in the representation may have adverse consequences for the distinctiveness of the trade mark: see *Nestlé SA's Trade Mark Application* [2004] EWCA Civ 1008, [2005] RPC 77, sub nom *Société des Produits*

Nestlé SA v Mars UK Ltd [2005] IP & T 551. On the other hand, evidence of distinctiveness does not prove that the trade mark complies with this requirement (or the requirement that it be a sign): *J W Spear & Sons Ltd v Zynga Inc* above.

As to whether an inadequate graphical representation filed initially can subsequently be rectified and the impact on the date of filing if this is done see PARAS 348, 357.

3   Trade Marks Act 1994 s 1(1) (derived from Council Directive (EEC) 89/104 (OJ L40, 11.2.89, p 1) to approximate the laws of the member states relating to trade marks, art 2 (see now European Parliament and Council Directive (EC) 2008/95 (OJ L299, 8.11.2008, p 25) art 2). Signs which do not satisfy the requirements of the Trade Marks Act 1994 s 1(1) may not be registered as trade marks: see s 3(1); and PARAS 43–44.

A sign is only incapable of distinguishing goods or services of one undertaking from those of other undertakings for this purpose if it is incapable of distinguishing the goods or services of the former from those of the latter irrespective of the goods or services in relation to which the sign may be used: Case C-363/99 *Koninklijke KPN Nederland NV v Benelux-Merkenbureau* [2006] Ch 1, [2004] ECR I-1619, ECJ; *Stichting BDO v BDO Unibank, Inc* [2013] EWHC 418 (Ch), [2013] All ER (D) 39 (Mar), [2013] ETMR 31.

A sign which consists of the shape of an article does not require any capricious addition, such as an embellishment which has no functional purpose, in order to be capable of distinguishing it for this purpose: Case C-299/99 *Koninklijke Philips Electronics NV v Remington Consumer Products Ltd* [2003] Ch 159, [2002] ECR I-5475, ECJ.

4   Trade Marks Act 1994 s 1(1). Trade marks may also consist of slogans: Case C-64/02P *Erpo Möbelwerk GbmH v Office for Harmonisation in the Internal Market (Trade Marks and Designs)* [2004] ECR I-10031, ECJ. Trade marks may also consist of colours, sounds and odours provided that the requirement for graphical representation is complied with: Case C-273/00 *Sieckmann v Deutsches Patent- und Markenamt* [2003] Ch 487, [2002] ECR I-11737, ECJ; Case C-104/01 *Libertel Groep BV v Benelux-Merkenbureau* [2004] Ch 83, [2003] ECR I-3793, ECJ; Case C-283/01 *Shield Mark BV v Kist (t/a Memex)* [2004] Ch 97, [2003] ECR I-14313, ECJ; Case C-49/02 *Heidelberger Bauchemie GmbH* [2004] ECR I-6129, [2004] All ER (D) 268 (Jun), ECJ. It appears that trade marks may also consist of moving images: see note 2.

5   As to collective marks see PARA 138 et seq. In relation to a collective mark the reference in the Trade Marks Act 1994 s 1(1) (see the text and notes 1–4) to distinguishing goods or services of one undertaking from those of other undertakings is to be construed as a reference to distinguishing goods or services of members of the association which is the proprietor of the mark from those of other undertakings: s 49(2), Sch 1 para 2.

6   Trade Marks Act 1994 s 1(2). As to certification marks see PARA 148 et seq. In relation to a certification mark the reference in s 1(1) (see the text and notes 1–4) to distinguishing goods or services of one undertaking from those of other undertakings is to be construed as a reference to distinguishing goods or services which are certified from those which are not: s 50(2), Sch 2 para 2.

(ii) Absolute Grounds for Refusal of Registration

42.   In general.   Each of the absolute grounds of refusal[1] is independent of the others and calls for separate examination[2]. This examination must be stringent and full in order to prevent trade marks from being improperly registered[3]. The registrar[4] must have regard to all the relevant facts and circumstances, as must the appointed person[5] or the court[6] on appeal from the registrar subject to the limits on their powers[7]. In assessing the applicability of the absolute grounds for refusal, the limits on the effects of the trade mark once registered[8] are immaterial[9]. Account may be taken of decisions in other member states to register the same trade mark in respect of the same goods or services, but such decisions cannot be regarded as decisive[10]. The same is true of previous decisions concerning other similar applications[11].

1   As to the meaning of 'absolute grounds of refusal' see PARA 39. As to the grounds of refusal see PARA 43 et seq.

2   Joined Cases C-53/01 and C-55/01 *Re Linde AG* [2003] ECR I-3161, sub nom *Linde AG v Deutsches Patent- und Markenamt* [2003] RPC 803, ECJ; Case C-363/99 *Koninklijke KPN Nederland NV v Benelux-Merkenbureau* [2006] Ch 1, [2004] ECR I-1619, ECJ; Case C-265/00 *Campina Melkunie BV v Benelux-Merkenbureau* [2004] ECR I-1699, [2004] IP & T 959, ECJ;

Joined Cases C-456/01P and C-457/01P *Henkel KGaA v Office for Harmonisation in the Internal Market (Trade Marks and Designs)* [2004] ECR I-5089, [2005] IP & T 1, ECJ; Case C-329/02P *SAT.1 Satelliten Fernsehen GmbH v Office for Harmonisation in the Internal Market (Trade Marks and Designs)* [2004] ECR I-8317, [2005] IP & T 943, ECJ; Case C-64/02P *Erpo Möbelwerk GbmH v Office for Harmonisation in the Internal Market (Trade Marks and Designs)* [2004] ECR I-10031, ECJ; Case C-37/03P *BioID AG v Office for Harmonisation in the Internal Market (Trade Marks and Designs)* [2005] ECR I-7975, [2005] All ER (D) 80 (Sep), ECJ.

3   Case C-104/01 *Libertel Groep BV v Benelux-Merkenbureau* [2004] Ch 83, [2003] ECR I-3793, ECJ; Case C-64/02P *Erpo Möbelwerk GbmH v Office for Harmonisation in the Internal Market (Trade Marks and Designs)* [2004] ECR I-10031, ECJ.

4   As to the registrar see PARA 19.

5   As to appeals to the appointed person see PARA 388 et seq.

6   As to appeals to the court see PARA 391 et seq.

7   Case C-363/99 *Koninklijke KPN Nederland NV v Benelux-Merkenbureau* [2006] Ch 1, [2004] ECR I-1619, ECJ; Case C-49/02 *Heidelberger Bauchemie GmbH* [2004] ECR I-6129, [2004] All ER (D) 268 (Jun), ECJ.

8   As to the limits on the effect of a trade mark once registered see the Trade Marks Act 1994 s 11; and PARA 76 et seq.

9   Case C-104/01 *Libertel Groep BV v Benelux-Merkenbureau* [2004] Ch 83, [2003] ECR I-3793, ECJ; Case C-404/02 *Nichols plc v Registrar of Trade Marks* [2005] All ER (EC) 1, [2004] ECR I-8499, ECJ.

10   Case C-218/01 *Henkel KGaA v Deutsches Patent- und Markenamt* [2004] ECR I-1725, ECJ.

11   Joined Cases C-39/08 and C-43/08 *Bild digital GmbH & Co KG v Präsident des Deutschen Patent- und Markenamts* [2009] ECR I-20, ECJ; Case C-51/10P *Agencja Wydawnicza Technopol sp zoo v Office for Harmonisation in the Internal Market (Trade Marks and Designs)* [2011] ECR I-1541, [2011] IP & T 948, ECJ; Case T-236/12 *Airbus SAS v Office for Harmonisation in the Internal Market (Trade Marks and Designs)* [2013] ECR II-0000, [2013] All ER (D) 156 (Jul), EGC; cf *British Sugar plc v James Robertson & Sons Ltd* [1996] RPC 281, [1996–97] ETMR 118.

43.   Signs which cannot constitute trade marks. Signs which do not satisfy the requirements of the statutory definition of a trade mark[1] may not be registered[2].

1   Ie signs which do not satisfy the requirements of the Trade Marks Act 1994 s 1(1): see PARA 41. There is no category of trade marks which is not excluded from registration by s 3(1)(b)–(d), (3) but which is nonetheless excluded from registration by s 3(1)(a): Case C-299/99 *Koninklijke Philips Electronics NV v Remington Consumer Products Ltd* [2003] Ch 159, [2002] ECR I-5475, ECJ. The goods or services for which a trade mark is sought to be registered must be identified by the applicant with sufficient clarity and precision to enable the competent authorities and competitors on that basis alone to determine the extent of protection conferred by the trade mark: Case C-307/10 *Chartered Institute of Patent Attorneys v Registrar of Trade Marks* [2013] RPC 313, [2012] IP & T 650, ECJ; Case T-571/11 *El Corte Inglés SA v Office for Harmonisation in the Internal Market (Trade Marks and Designs)* [2013] ETMR 30, EGC. However lack of clarity and precision in the specification of goods or services is not a ground of invalidity once a trade mark has been registered: *Stichting BDO v BDO Unibank, Inc* [2013] EWHC 418 (Ch), [2013] All ER (D) 39 (Mar), [2013] ETMR 31.

2   Trade Marks Act 1994 s 3(1)(a) (derived from Council Directive (ECC) 89/104 (OJ L40, 11.2.89, p 1) to approximate the laws of the member states relating to trade marks, art 3(1)(a) (see now European Parliament and Council Directive (EC) 2008/95 (OJ L299, 8.11.2008, p 25) art 3(1)(a))). As to the meaning of 'registered' see PARA 21 note 2. In the case of an international trade mark, the mark 'becomes protected': see PARAS 11 et seq, 39 note 8.

44.   Lack of distinctive character. The following must not be registered[1]:

(1)   trade marks[2] which are devoid of any distinctive character[3];

(2)   trade marks which consist exclusively of signs or indications which may serve, in trade[4], to designate the kind, quality, quantity, intended purpose, value, geographical origin, the time of production of goods or of rendering of services, or other characteristics of goods or services[5];

(3) trade marks which consist exclusively of signs or indications which have become customary in the current language or in the bona fide and established practices of the trade[6].

A trade mark must not, however, be refused registration by virtue of head (1), head (2) or head (3) above if, before the date of application for registration[7], it has in fact acquired a distinctive character as a result of the use[8] made of it[9].

1   Trade Marks Act 1994 s 3(1). As to the meaning of 'registered' see PARA 21 note 2. In the case of an international trade mark, the mark 'becomes protected': see PARAS 11 et seq, 39 note 8.
2   As to the meaning of 'trade mark' see PARA 41.
3   Trade Marks Act 1994 s 3(1)(b) (derived from Council Directive (EEC) 89/104 (OJ L40, 11.2.89, p 1) to approximate the laws of the member states relating to trade marks, art 3(1)(b) (see now European Parliament and Council Directive (EC) 2008/95 (OJ L299, 8.11.2008, p 25) art 3(1)(b))). Despite its position the Trade Marks Act 1994 s 3(1)(b) (see head (1) in the text) performs 'a residual or sweeping-up function' backing up s 3(1)(c), (d) (see heads (2), (3) in the text): *Proctor & Gamble Ltd's Trade Mark Application* [1999] RPC 673 at 679, CA, per Robert Walker LJ. This is because lack of distinctive character is the essence of any objection under the Trade Marks Act 1994 s 3(1)(b), (c) or (d): *West (t/a Eastenders) v Fuller Smith & Turner plc* [2003] EWCA Civ 48, [2003] FSR 816, [2003] IP & T 768. Thus a word mark which is descriptive of characteristics of the goods or services for the purposes of the Trade Marks Act 1994 s 3(1)(c) is necessarily devoid of distinctive character within s 3(1)(b): Case C-363/99 *Koninklijke KPN Nederland NV v Benelux-Merkenbureau* [2006] Ch 1, [2004] ECR I-1619, ECJ; Case C-265/00 *Campina Melkunie BV v Benelux-Merkenbureau* [2004] ECR I-1699, [2004] IP & T 959, ECJ. Conversely, a mark which is not descriptive may nevertheless be devoid of distinctive character: Joined Cases C-53/01 and C-55/01 *Re Linde AG* [2003] ECR I-3161, sub nom *Linde AG v Deutsches Patent- und Markenamt* [2003] RPC 803, ECJ; Case C-363/99 *Koninklijke KPN Nederland NV v Benelux-Merkenbureau* above.
    For a trade mark to possess distinctive character, it must serve to identify the goods or services in respect of which registration is applied for as originating from a particular undertaking and thus to distinguish the goods or services from those of other undertakings: Case C-299/99 *Koninklijke Philips Electronics NV v Remington Consumer Products Ltd* [2003] Ch 159, [2002] ECR I-5475, ECJ; Joined Cases C-53/01 and C-55/01 *Linde AG v Deutsches Patent- und Markenamt* above; Joined Cases C-456/01P and C-457/01P *Henkel KGaA v Office for Harmonisation in the Internal Market (Trade Marks and Designs)* [2004] ECR I-5089, [2005] IP & T 1, ECJ; Case C-136/02P *Mag Instrument Inc v Office for Harmonisation in the Internal Market (Trade Marks and Designs)* [2004] ECR I-9165, [2004] All ER (D) 75 (Oct), ECJ.
    The distinctive character of a mark must be assessed: (1) in relation to the goods or services in respect of which registration is applied for; and (2) according to the perception of the average consumer of those goods or services, who is deemed to be reasonably well-informed and reasonably observant and circumspect: Case C-299/99 *Koninklijke Philips Electronics v Remington Consumer Products* above; Joined Cases C-53/01 and C-55/01 *Linde AG v Deutsches Patent- und Markenamt* above; Case C-104/01 *Libertel Groep BV v Benelux-Merkenbureau* [2004] Ch 83, [2003] ECR I-3793, ECJ; Case C-218/01 *Henkel KGaA v Deutsches Patent- und Markenamt* [2004] ECR I-1725, ECJ; Case C-363/99 *Koninklijke KPN Nederland NV v Benelux-Merkenbureau* above; Joined Cases C-468/01P to C-472/01P *Procter & Gamble Co v Office for Harmonisation in the Internal Market (Trade Marks and Designs)* [2004] ECR I-5141, [2005] IP & T 1, ECJ; Case C-445/02P *Glaverbel SA v Office for Harmonisation in the Internal Market (Trade Marks and Designs)* [2004] ECR I-6267, ECJ; Joined Cases C-456/01P and C-457/01P *Henkel KGaA v Office for Harmonisation in the Internal Market (Trade Marks and Designs)* above. The fact that a sign is a capable of constituting a trade mark does not necessarily mean that the sign has distinctive character in relation to a specific product or service: Joined Cases C-456/01P and C-457/01P *Henkel KGaA v Office for Harmonisation in the Internal Market (Trade Marks and Designs)* above; Joined Cases C-468/01P to C-472/01P *Procter & Gamble Co v Office for Harmonisation in the Internal Market (Trade Marks and Designs)* above.
    The average consumer normally perceives a trade mark as a whole rather than analysing its details and therefore, in order to assess whether it has any distinctive character, the overall impression given by it must be considered; but it is legitimate for the competent authority first to examine each of the individual components of the mark: Case C-104/00P *DKV Deutsche Krankenversicherung AG v Office for Harmonisation in the Internal Market (Trade Marks and Designs)* [2002] ECR I-7561, [2002] All ER (D) 100 (Sep), ECJ; Joined Cases C-468/01P to

C-472/01P *Procter & Gamble Co v Office for Harmonisation in the Internal Market (Trade Marks and Designs)* above; Case C-329/02P *SAT.1 Satelliten Fernsehen GmbH v Office for Harmonisation in the Internal Market (Trade Marks and Designs)* [2004] ECR I-8317, [2005] IP & T 943, ECJ; Case C-136/02P *Mag Instrument Inc v Office for Harmonisation in the Internal Market (Trade Marks and Designs)* above; Case C-286/04P *Eurocermex SA v Office for Harmonisation in the Internal Market (Trade Marks and Designs)* [2005] ECR I-5797, [2005] IP & T 965, ECJ.

It is not necessary to establish distinctive character to show that the mark has a particular level of creativity or imagination or originality; but nor is it necessary to establish that the mark is devoid of distinctive character to show that the mark is commonly used or capable of being commonly used: Case C-329/02P *SAT.1 Satelliten Fernsehen GmbH v Office for Harmonisation in the Internal Market (Trade Marks and Designs)* above; Case 64/02P *Erpo Möbelwerk GbmH v Office for Harmonisation in the Internal Market (Trade Marks and Designs)* [2004] ECR I-10031, ECJ; Case C-37/03 *BioID AG v Office for Harmonisation in the Internal Market (Trade Marks and Designs)* [2005] ECR I-7975, [2005] All ER (D) 80 (Sep), ECJ.

The Court of First Instance (now the General Court) has consistently held that a minimum degree of distinctive character is sufficient to render this ground of refusal inapplicable: see eg Case T-34/00 *Eurocool Logistik GmbH v Office for Harmonisation in the Internal Market (Trade Marks and Designs)* [2002] ECR II-683, [2002] IP & T 756, CFI; Case T-79/00 *Rewe-Zentral AG v Office for Harmonisation in the Internal Market (Trade Marks and Designs)* [2002] ECR II-705, [2002] IP & T 533, CFI; Case T-128/01 *DaimlerChrysler Corpn v Office for Harmonisation in the Internal Market (Trade Marks and Designs)* [2003] ECR II-701, [2004] IP & T 150, CFI; Case T-305/02 *Nestlé Waters France v Office for Harmonisation in the Internal Market (Trade Marks and Designs)* [2003] ECR II-5207, [2004] IP & T 664, CFI; Case T-320/03 *Citicorp v Office for Harmonisation in the Internal Market (Trade Marks and Designs)* [2005] ECR II-3411, [2005] All ER (D) 81 (Sep), CFI. The European Court of Justice has held that it is not necessary to rule upon the possible dividing line between the concept of lack of distinctiveness and that of minimum distinctiveness: Case C-104/00P *Deutsche Krankenversicherung AG v Office for Harmonisation in the Internal Market (Trade Marks and Designs)* [2002] ECR I-7561, [2002] All ER (D) 100 (Sep), ECJ.

A trade mark can lose its distinctive character as a result of use by third parties: Case T-237/01 *Alcon Inc v Office for Harmonisation in the Internal Market (Trade Marks and Designs)* [2003] ECR II-411, CFI; *BACH and BACH FLOWER REMEDIES Trade Marks* [2000] RPC 513, sub nom *Bach Flower Remedies Ltd v Healing Herbs Ltd* [1999] IP & T 146, CA; *Rugby Football Union v Cotton Traders Ltd* [2002] EWHC 467 (Ch), [2002] IP & T 646, [2002] ETMR 76; *Score Draw Ltd v Finch* [2007] EWHC 462 (Ch), [2007] FSR 508, [2007] ETMR 54.

The criteria for assessment of distinctive character are the same for all categories of trade marks; but nevertheless the perception of the relevant public is not the same for all categories of trade marks and it may therefore be more difficult to establish distinctive character in relation to some categories (such as shapes, surface treatments, colours, personal names and advertising slogans) than others: Joined Cases C-53/01 and C-55/01 *Linde AG v Deutsches Patent- und Markenamt (Trade Marks and Designs)* above; Case C-104/01 *Libertel Groep BV v Benelux-Merkenbureau* above; Joined Cases C-456/01P and C-457/01P *Henkel KGaA v Office for Harmonisation in the Internal Market (Trade Marks and Designs)* above; Case C-445/02P *Glaverbel SA v Office for Harmonisation in the Internal Market (Trade Marks and Designs)* above; Case C-404/02 *Nichols plc v Registrar of Trade Marks* [2005] All ER (EC) 1, [2004] ECR I-8499, ECJ; Case C-136/02P *Mag Instrument Inc v Office for Harmonisation in the Internal Market (Trade Marks and Designs)* above; Case 64/02P *Office for Harmonisation in the Internal Market (Trade Marks and Designs) v Erpo Möbelwerk GbmH* above; Case C-447/02P *KWS Saat AG v Office for Harmonisation in the Internal Market (Trade Marks and Designs)* [2004] ECR I-10107, [2007] IP & T 314, [2004] All ER (D) 294 (Oct), ECJ. This does not mean that it is legitimate to assume that particular categories of marks, such as single letters, cannot have distinctive character: Case C-265/09P *BORCO-Marken-Import Matthiesen GmbH & Co KG v Office for Harmonisation in the Internal Market (Trade Marks and Designs)* [2010] ECR I-8265, [2011] IP & T 340, [2010] All ER (D) 54 (Sep), ECJ.

In the case of shapes, the more closely the shape for which registration is sought resembles the shape most likely to be taken by the product in question, the greater the likelihood of the shape being devoid of distinctive character; only a trade mark which departs significantly from the norms or customs of the sector and thereby fulfils its essential function of indicating origin is likely to possess distinctive character: Joined Cases C-456/01P and C-457/01P *Henkel KGaA v Office for Harmonisation in the Internal Market (Trade Marks and Designs)* above; Joined Cases C-468/01P to C-472/01P *Procter & Gamble Co v Office for Harmonisation in the*

Internal Market (Trade Marks and Designs) above; Case C-136/02P *Mag Instrument Inc v Office for Harmonisation in the Internal Market (Trade Marks and Designs)* above; Case C-24/05P *August Storck KG v Office for Harmonisation in the Internal Market (Trade Marks and Designs)* [2006] ECR I-5677, [2006] IP & T 946, ECJ; Case C-238/06P *Develey Holding GmbH v Office for Harmonisation in the Internal Market (Trade Marks and Designs)* [2007] ECR I-9375; [2007] All ER (D) 397 (Oct), [2008] ETMR 20, ECJ; Case T-460/05 *Bang & Olufson A/S v Office for Harmonisation in the Internal Market (Trade Marks and Designs)* [2007] ECR II-4207, [2007] All ER (D) 135 (Oct), CFI. The same approach applies to shapes consisting of the packaging of goods, such as liquids, which are packaged in trade for reasons linked to the very nature of the product: Joined Cases C-456/01P and C-457/01P *Henkel KGaA v Deutsches Patent- und Markenamt* above; Case C-173/04P *Deutsche SiSi-Werke GmbH & Co Betriebs KG v Office for Harmonisation in the Internal Market (Trade Marks and Designs)* [2006] ECR I-551, [2006] ETMR 41, ECJ. It also applies where the trade mark consists of the appearance of the surface of the packaging: Joined Cases C-344/10P and C-345/10P *Freixenet SA v Office for Harmonisation in the Internal Market (Trade Marks and Designs)* [2011] ECR I-0000, ECJ (frosted bottles). It is not enough to establish distinctive character that the shape is striking and unusual without more: *Bongrain SA's Trade Mark Application* [2004] EWCA Civ 1690, [2005] RPC 306, [2005] IP & T 563. Where, however, there is an established practice of using shapes to distinguish the trade origin of goods, the position is different: Case T-128/01 *DaimlerChrysler Corpn v Office for Harmonisation in the Internal Market (Trade Marks and Designs)* above (car radiator grilles). As to shape see also PARA 46.

In the case of colours, a single colour per se is very unlikely to be distinctive without use: Case C-104/01 *Libertel Groep BV v Benelux-Merkenbureau* above; Case C-447/02 *KWS Saat AG v Office for Harmonisation in the Internal Market (Trade Marks and Designs)* above.

In the case of personal names, it is not legitimate to assess distinctive character by applying general criteria such as the number of entries in telephone directories (*Nichols plc v Registrar of Trade Marks* above) but it is legitimate as part of a specific assessment of the distinctive character of the mark to take into account the commonness of the name and the extent to which personal names are used to designate commercial origin in the sector in question (*Oska's Ltd's Trade Mark Application* [2005] RPC 525, Appointed Person).

In the case of advertising slogans, the mere fact that a mark is perceived by the relevant public as a promotional formula and that, because of its laudatory nature, it could in principle be used by other undertakings, is not sufficient, in itself, to support the conclusion that the mark is devoid of distinctive character: Case C-398/08P *Audi AG v Office for Harmonisation in the Internal Market (Trade Marks and Designs)* [2010] ECR I-535, [2010] FSR 589, ECJ; Case C-311/11P *Smart Technologies ULC v Office for Harmonisation in the Internal Market (Trade Marks and Designs)* [2012] ETMR 49, [2012] All ER (D) 192 (Jul), ECJ. Nor can a slogan be required to be imaginative or display conceptual tension in order to be distinctive: Case 64/02P *Office for Harmonisation in the Internal Market (Trade Marks and Designs) v Erpo Möbelwerk GbmH* above; Case C-398/08P *Audi AG v Office for Harmonisation in the Internal Market (Trade Marks and Designs)* above; Case C-311/11P *Smart Technologies ULC v Office for Harmonisation in the Internal Market (Trade Marks and Designs)* above. The only question is whether the mark has distinctive character. Thus 'VORSPRUNG DURCH TECHNIK' (advance through technology) was held to have distinctive character (Case C-398/08P *Audi AG v Office for Harmonisation in the Internal Market (Trade Marks and Designs)* above), but not 'WIR MACHEN DAS BESONDERE EINFACH' (we make special things simple) (Case C-311/11P *Smart Technologies ULC v Office for Harmonisation in the Internal Market (Trade Marks and Designs)* above).

A term borrowed from the language of another member state, in which it is descriptive of the goods or services in question or otherwise devoid of distinctive character, is not precluded from registration by the Trade Marks Act 1994 s 3(1)(b) unless the relevant persons in the United Kingdom are capable of identifying the meaning of the term: Case C-421/04 *Matrazen Concorde AG v Hukla Germany SA* [2006] ECR I-2303, [2006] IP & T 483, [2006] ETMR 48, ECJ.

A mark may be devoid of distinctive character even if it is not exclusively descriptive, in particular because it includes graphical elements as well as descriptive words: see Case C-37/03 *BioID AG v Office for Harmonisation in the Internal Market (Trade Marks and Designs)* [2005] ECR I-7975, [2005] All ER (D) 80 (Sep), ECJ; Case C-92/10P *Media-Saturn-Holding GmbH v Office for Harmonisation in the Internal Market (Trade Marks and Designs)* [2011] ECR I-0002, ECJ; *Cycling IS ...Trade Mark Applications* [2002] RPC 729, Appointed Person; *QUICK WASH ACTION Trade Mark* (O/205/04), Appointed Person; *SUN RIPENED TOBACCO Trade Mark* (O/200/08), Appointed Person; *Starbucks (HK) Ltd v British Sky Broadcasting Group plc* [2012] EWHC 3074 (Ch), [2013] IP & T 251, [2012] All ER (D) 36 (Nov) (affd [2013] EWCA Civ 1465, [2013] All ER (D) 214 (Nov)).

In the case of device marks, even simple devices with descriptive connotations may have inherent distinctive character: *Koninklijke Philips NV v Remington Consumer Products Ltd* [2006] EWCA Civ 16, [2007] IP & T 206, [2006] FSR 537. On the other hand, devices which primarily serve a decorative purpose are devoid of distinctive character: Case C-307/11P *Deichmann SE v Office for Harmonisation in the Internal Market (Trade Marks and Designs)* [2012] ECR I-0000, ECJ; Case T-326/10 *V Fraas GmbH v Office for Harmonisation in the Internal Market (Trade Marks and Designs)* [2011] ECR II-0000, EGC.

4 'Trade' includes any business or profession: Trade Marks Act 1994 s 103(1).

5 Trade Marks Act 1994 s 3(1)(c) (derived from Council Directive (EEC) 89/104 (OJ L40, 11.2.89, p 1) art 3(1)(c) (see now European Parliament and Council Directive (EC) 2008/95 (OJ L299, 8.11.2008, p 25) art 3(1)(c))). This provision serves a public interest, which is to ensure that descriptive terms may be freely used by all and cannot be reserved to one undertaking by being registered as trade marks: Joined Cases C-108/97 and C-109/97 *Windsurfing Chiemsee Produktions- und Vertriebs GmbH v Boots- und Segelzubehör Walter Huber* [2000] Ch 523, [1999] ECR I-2779, [1999] ETMR 585, ECJ; Joined Cases C-53/01 and C-55/01 *Re Linde AG* [2003] ECR I-3161, sub nom *Linde AG v Deutsches Patent- und Markenamt* [2003] RPC 803, ECJ; Case C-104/01 *Libertel Groep BV v Benelux-Merkenbureau* [2004] Ch 83, [2003] ECR I-3793, ECJ; Case C-191/01P *Wm Wrigley Jr Co v Office for Harmonisation in the Internal Market (Trade Marks and Designs)* [2004] All ER (EC) 1040, sub nom *Office for Harmonisation in the Internal Market (Trade Marks and Designs) v Wm Wrigley Jr Co* [2003] ECR I-12447, ECJ; Case C-326/01P *Telefon & Buch VerlagsgmbH v Office for Harmonisation in the Internal Market (Trade Marks and Designs)* [2004] ECR I-1371, ECJ; Case C-150/02P *Streamserve Inc v Office for Harmonisation in the Internal Market (Trade Marks and Designs)* [2004] ECR I-1461, ECJ; Case C-363/99 *Koninklijke KPN Nederland NV v Benelux-Merkenbureau* [2006] Ch 1, [2004] ECR I-1619, ECJ; Case C-265/00 *Campina Melkunie BV v Benelux-Merkenbureau* [2004] ECR I-1699, [2004] IP & T 959, ECJ.

A mark must be refused registration under this provision if at least one of its possible meanings designates a characteristic of the goods or services concerned; it is not necessary that the mark actually be in use at the time of the application for registration in a way that is descriptive of goods or services such as those in relation to which the application is filed, or of characteristics of those goods or services; it is sufficient that it could be used for such purposes: Case C-191/01P *Office for Harmonisation in the Internal Market (Trade Marks and Designs) v Wm Wrigley Jr Co* above; Case C-363/99 *Koninklijke KPN Nederland NV v Benelux-Merkenbureau* above. It is not necessary for this provision to apply that the mark should be the only way of designating the characteristics of the goods or services in question; it is irrelevant whether there are other, more usual signs or indications for designating those characteristics: Case C-363/99 *Koninklijke KPN Nederland NV v Benelux-Merkenbureau* above; Case C-265/00 *Campina Melkunie BV v Benelux-Merkenbureau* above. It is also irrelevant whether the characteristics of the goods or services in question are commercially essential or merely ancillary: Case C-363/99 *Koninklijke KPN Nederland NV v Benelux-Merkenbureau* above. Where a sign is descriptive of a main product it will generally be descriptive of accessories and intermediates: Case T-171/11 *Hopf v Office for Harmonisation in the Internal Market (Trade Marks and Designs)* [2012] ECR II-0000, EGC. See also Case T-320/10 *Furstlich Castell'sches Domaenenamt Albrecht Furst zu Castell-Castell v Office for Harmonisation in the Internal Market (Trade Marks and Designs)* [2013] All ER (D) 171 (Sep), EGC where Case C-191/01P *Wm Wrigley Jr Co v Office for Harmonisation in the Internal Market (Trade Marks and Designs)* above was applied.

It is sufficient for this provision to apply that the mark has a descriptive meaning to specialists whether or not that meaning is known to the general public: Case T-367/02 *Wieland-Werke AG v Office for Harmonisation in the Internal Market (Trade Marks and Designs)* [2005] ECR II-47, [2005] All ER (D) 29 (Jan), CFI.

As a general rule, a mere combination of elements, each of which is descriptive of characteristics of the goods or services, without introducing any unusual variations, in particular as to syntax or meaning, will not result in anything other than a mark which designates characteristics of the goods or services; but such a combination may not be descriptive if it creates an overall impression which is sufficiently far removed from that produced by the elements themselves: Case C-363/99 *Koninklijke KPN Nederland NV v Benelux-Merkenbureau* above; Case C-265/00 *Campina Melkunie BV v Benelux-Merkenbureau* above (BIOMILD); and see also Case C-104/00P *DKV Deutsche Krankenversicherung AG v Office for Harmonisation in the Internal Market (Trade Marks and Designs)* [2002] ECR I-7561, [2002] All ER (D) 100 (Sep), ECJ (COMPANYLINE); Case C-326/01P *Telefon & Buch VerlagsgmbH v Office for Harmonisation in the Internal Market (Trade Marks and Designs)* above (UNIVERSALTELEFONBUCH); *Streamserve Inc v Office for Harmonisation in the Internal*

Market (Trade Marks and Designs) above (STREAMSERVE); Case C-273/05P *Office of Harmonisation in the Internal Market (Trade Marks and Designs) v Celltech R & D Ltd* [2007] ECR I-2883, [2007] ETMR 52,, ECJ (CELLTECH); Case C-408/08P *Lancôme Parfums et Beauté & Cie SNC v Office for Harmonisation in the Internal Market (Trade Marks and Designs)* [2010] ECR I-1347, ECJ (COLOR EDITION). If a phrase is descriptive, the addition of an acronym which is clearly derived from that phrase will not confer distinctive character on the mark considered as a whole: Joined Cases C-90/11 and C-91/11 *Alfred Strigl v Deutches Patent- und Markenamt* [2012] ECR I-0000, ECJ (MULTI MARKETS FUND MMF).

If the mark sought to be registered consists exclusively of a descriptive word, registration is precluded by the Trade Marks Act 1994 s 3(1)(c) even though the word is sought to be registered in a stylised script; it is otherwise if the mark includes graphical elements in addition to the word unless these are negligible: Case T-32/00 *Messe München GmbH v Office for Harmonisation in the Internal Market (Trade Marks and Designs)* [2000] ECR II-3829, [2001] IP & T 298, CFI; Case T-559/10 *Laboratoire Garnier et Cie v Office for Harmonisation in the Internal Market (Trade Marks and Designs)* [2012] ECR II-0000, [2012] All ER (D) 160 (Jul), EGC; *Hormel Foods Corpn v Antilles Landscape Investments NV* [2005] EWHC 13 (Ch), [2005] RPC 657, [2005] IP & T 822; *Starbucks (HK) Ltd v British Sky Broadcasting Group plc* [2012] EWHC 3074 (Ch), [2013] IP & T 251, [2012] All ER (D) 36 (Nov) (affd [2013] EWCA Civ 1465, [2013] All ER (D) 214 (Nov)); cf *O2 Holdings Ltd's Trade Mark Applications* (O/127/07), Appointed Person.

A term borrowed from the language of another member state, in which it is descriptive of the goods or services in question, is not precluded from registration by the Trade Marks Act 1994 s 3(1)(c) unless the relevant persons in the United Kingdom are capable of identifying the meaning of the term: Case C-421/04 *Matratzen Concord AG v Hukla Germany SA* [2006] ECR I-2303, [2006] IP & T 483, [2006] ETMR 48, ECJ; and see also Case T-569/10 *Bimbo SA v Office for Harmonisation in the Internal Market (Trade Marks and Designs)* [2012] All ER (D) 98 (Oct), [2013] ETMR 7, EGC.

In the case of geographical names, this provision is not confined to prohibiting the registration of geographical names as trade marks where they are already associated with the goods or services concerned in the mind of the relevant class of persons; but it does not preclude the registration of geographical names where the relevant class of persons would be unlikely to believe that such goods or services originated there: Joined Cases C-108/97 and C-109/97 *Windsurfing Chiemsee Produktions- und Vertriebs GmbH v Boots- und Segelzubehör Walter Huber* above. Compare Case T-295/01 *Nordmilch eG v Office for Harmonisation in the Internal Market (Trade Marks and Designs)* [2003] ECR II-4365, [2003] All ER (D) 244 (Oct), CFI (OLDENBURGER, Oldenburg being the name of two German towns, unregistrable for dairy products) with Case T-379/03 *Peek & Cloppenburg KG v Office for Harmonisation in the Internal Market (Trade Marks and Designs)* [2005] ECR II-4633, [2006] IP & T 167, [2006] ETMR 33, CFI (CLOPPENBURG, the name of a small German town, registrable for retail services). See also Case T-316/03 *Münchener Rückversicherungs-Gesellshaft AG v Office for Harmonisation in the Internal Market (Trade Marks and Designs)* [2005] ECR II-1951, [2006] ETMR 6, CFI (German equivalent of MUNICHFINANCIALSERVICES unregistrable for financial services); Decisions 621C/00207886/1 and 638C/00207866/2 *Think Promotions Ltd v All England Lawn Tennis Club (Wimbledon) Ltd* [2006] ETMR 36, OHIM Cancellation Division (WIMBLEDON registrable for variety of goods and services) (decision made under the equivalent provision of EC Council Regulation 40/94 (OJ L11, 14.1.94, p 1) on the Community trade mark, ie art 7(1)(c) (see PARA 194)); *Nordic Saunas Ltd's Trade Mark Application* [2002] ETMR 18, Appointed Person (NORDIC unregistrable for goods made of wood, but had acquired distinctiveness for saunas); *Tottenham Hotspur plc's Trade Mark Application* (O/024/03), Appointed Person (TOTTENHAM registrable for wide variety of goods and services).

Where a designation of origin or a geographical indication is registered under European Parliament and Council Regulation (EU) 1151/2012 (OJ L343, 14.12.2012, p 1), the registration of a trade mark the use of which would contravene the protections provided by that Regulation and which relates to a product of the same type must be refused if the application for registration of the trade mark is submitted after the date of submission of the registration application in respect of the designation of origin or the geographical indication to the European Commission; trade marks registered in breach of this provision are invalidated but (subject to certain conditions) there are exceptions for trade marks which have been applied for, registered or established by use in good faith within the territory of the EU before the date on which the application for protection of the designation of origin or geographical indication is submitted to the Commission, which may continue to be used and renewed for that product notwithstanding the registration of a designation of origin or geographical indication. See generally PARA 286. See also FOOD AND DRINK vol 51 (2013) PARA 815.

A collective or certification mark which consists of signs or indications which may designate the geographical origin of goods or services may, however, be registered: see the Trade Marks Act 1994 s 49(2), Sch 1 para 3 (collective marks: see PARA 139) and s 50(2), Sch 2 para 3 (certification marks: see PARA 149).

In principle there is nothing to prevent the application of this provision to an application to register a three-dimensional trade mark consisting of the shape of the goods: Joined Cases C-53/01 and C-55/01 *Linde AG v Deutsches Patent- und Markenamt* above. Similarly, in the case of three-dimensional trade marks consisting of packaging of goods which are packaged for reasons relating to the nature of the goods, the packaging may serve to designate characteristics of the goods within the meaning of this provision: Case C-218/01 *Henkel KGaA v Deutsches Patent- und Markenamt* [2004] ECR I-1725, ECJ.

The list of characteristics is not exhaustive: Case C-51/10P *Agencja Wydawnicza Technopol sp zoo v Office for Harmonisation in the Internal Market (Trade Marks and Designs)* [2011] ECR I-1541, [2011] IP & T 948, ECJ. In the case of names of performers and other celebrities, the name may designate a characteristic (ie the subject matter) of certain goods (particularly image carriers such as posters and figurines) and thus be unregistrable in respect of such goods by virtue of this provision: *Linkin Park LLC's Trade Mark Application* [2006] ETMR 74, Appointed Person.

6   Trade Marks Act 1994 s 3(1)(d) (derived from Council Directive (EEC) 89/104 (OJ L40, 11.2.89, p 1) art 3(1)(d) (see now European Parliament and Council Directive (EC) 2008/95 (OJ L299, 8.11.2008, p 25) art 3(1)(d))). This provision is to be interpreted as only precluding registration of a mark where the signs or indications of which the mark is exclusively composed had become customary in the current language or in the bona fide and established practices of the trade to designate the goods or services in respect of which registration of the mark is sought at the relevant date; it is immaterial for this purpose whether or not the mark is descriptive and whether or not the mark consists of an advertising slogan, indication of quality or incitement to purchase the goods or services: Case C-517/99 *Merz & Krell GmbH & Co v Deutsches Patent- und Markenamt* [2002] All ER (EC) 441, [2001] ECR I-6959, ECJ. In considering whether the mark has become customary in the current language it appears that the relevant circles principally consist of consumers and end users: Case T-322/03 *Telefon & Buch Verlagsgesellschaft gmbH v Office for Harmonisation in the Internal Market (Trade Marks and Designs)* [2006] ECR II-835, [2006] All ER (D) 231 (Mar), CFI; cf Case C-371/02 *Björnekulla Fruktindustrier AB v Procordia Food AB* [2004] ECR I-5791, [2004] RPC 912, ECJ. Thus the essence of the objection is that the sign is generic either amongst the general public or amongst the trade: *Hormel Foods Corpn v Antilles Landscape Investments NV* [2005] EWHC 13 (Ch), [2005] RPC 657, [2005] IP & T 822; *Stash Ltd's Trade Mark Application* (O/281/04), Appointed Person; and see Case C-192/03 *Alcon Inc v Office for Harmonisation in the Internal Market (Trade Marks and Designs)* [2004] ECR I-8993, ECJ (mark BSS generic in the relevant trade). In assessing the applicability of this objection it is legitimate to take into account materials published outside the relevant territory if these shed light on the position inside that territory: Case C-192/03 *Alcon Inc v Office for Harmonisation in the Internal Market (Trade Marks and Designs)* above. See also Case C-102/07 *Adidas AG v Marca Mode CV* [2006] ECR I-2439, [2009] IP & T 279, ECJ (issue as to distinctive character of figurative mark).

7   As to the meaning of 'the date of application for registration' see PARA 348 note 5.

8   For these purposes, references to 'use' (or any particular description of use) of a trade mark, or of a sign identical with, similar to, or likely to be mistaken for a trade mark, include use (or that description of use) otherwise than by means of a graphic representation: Trade Marks Act 1994 s 103(2).

9   Trade Marks Act 1994 s 3(1) proviso (derived from Council Directive (EEC) 89/104 (OJ L40, 11.2.89, p 1) art 3(3) (see now European Parliament and Council Directive (EC) 2008/95 (OJ L299, 8.11.2008, p 25) art 3(3))). As to acquiring distinctive character as a result of use see PARA 45.

45.   Distinctive character acquired as a result of use.

A trade mark[1] must not be refused registration on the grounds that it is devoid of distinctive character or descriptive or generic[2] if, before the date of application for registration, it has in fact acquired a distinctive character as a result of the use[3] made of it[4]. Similarly, where a trade mark was registered in breach of one of these grounds[5], it must not be declared invalid if, in consequence of the use which has been made of it, it has after registration acquired a distinctive character in relation to the goods or services for which it is registered[6]. It is not necessary to consider whether the mark has acquired a distinctive character, however, unless the applicant or proprietor has invoked the relevant provision[7].

In either case, what must be shown is that, through use[8], the trade mark has come to identify the goods or services in respect of which the trade mark is sought to be registered or is registered as originating from a particular undertaking and thus distinguishes the goods or services from those of other undertakings[9]. The competent authority must make an overall assessment of the relevant evidence[10]. Regard must be had to the inherent characteristics of the mark in question, such as whether it contains an element which is descriptive of the goods or services in question[11]; and the following may also be taken into account:

(1)   the market share held by goods bearing the mark;

(2)   how intensive, geographically widespread and longstanding the use of the mark has been;

(3)   the amount invested by the proprietor in promoting the mark;

(4)   the proportion of the relevant class of persons who, because of the mark, identify the goods or services as emanating from the proprietor;

(5)   evidence from trade and professional associations; and

(6)   (where the competent authority has particular difficulty in assessing the distinctive character) an opinion poll[12].

If the relevant class of persons, or at least a significant proportion of them, identifies goods or services as originating from a particular undertaking because of the trade mark, it has acquired a distinctive character; however, the circumstances in which that requirement may be regarded as satisfied cannot be shown to exist by reference to general, abstract data such as predetermined percentages[13].

Where a trader has been the only supplier of particular goods to the market, extensive use of a sign which consists of the shape of the goods may be sufficient to give the sign a distinctive character in circumstances where, as a result of that use, a substantial proportion of the relevant class of persons associates that shape with the trader and no other undertaking or believes that goods of that shape come from that trader; however, it is for the competent authority to verify that such circumstances exist on the basis of specific and reliable data and that such identification is as a result of the use of the sign as a trade mark[14].

1   As to the meaning of 'trade mark' see PARA 41.
2   Ie registration is precluded by the Trade Marks Act 1994 s 3(1)(b), (c) or (d): see PARA 44.
3   As to the meaning of 'use' see PARA 44 note 8. In order for the mark to have acquired distinctiveness it must have been used as a trade mark, that is to say, for the purposes of the identification, by the relevant class of person, of the goods or services as originating from a given undertaking: Case C-299/99 *Koninklijke Philips Electronics NV v Remington Consumer Products Ltd* [2003] Ch 159, [2002] ECR I-5475, ECJ; Case C-353/03 *Société des Produits Nestlé SA v Mars UK Ltd* [2006] All ER (EC) 348, [2005] ECR I-6135, [2006] IP & T 403, ECJ; C-24/05P *August Storck KG v Office for Harmonisation in the Internal Market (Trade Marks and Designs)* [2006] ECR I-5677, [2006] IP & T 946, ECJ; Case T117/06 *DeTeMedien v OHIM;* Case T-338/11 *Getty Images (US) Inc v Office for Harmonisation in the Internal Market (Trade Marks and Designs)* [2013] ETMR 19, EGC. Thus use of a mark as the name of goods (see eg *BACH and BACH FLOWER REMEDIES Trade Marks* [2000] RPC 513, sub nom *Bach Flower Remedies Ltd v Healing Herbs Ltd* [1999] IP & T 146, CA) or as the name of an ingredient of the goods (see eg *JERYL LYNN Trade Mark* [1999] FSR 491) will not result in the mark acquiring distinctive character. See also note 13.
4   Trade Marks Act 1994 s 3(1) proviso (derived from Council Directive (EEC) 89/104 (OJ L40, 11.2.89, p 1) to approximate the laws of the member states relating to trade marks, art 3(3) (see

now European Parliament and Council Directive (EC) 2008/95 (OJ L299, 8.11.2008, p 25) art 3(3))); and see PARA 44. This provision does not provide an independent right to have a trade mark registered, but is an exception to the relevant grounds of refusal: Case C-108/05 *Bovemij Verzekeringen NV v Benelux-Merkenbureau* [2006] ECR I-7605, [2007] ETMR 29, [2006] All ER (D) 46 (Sep), ECJ. The trade mark must have acquired distinctive character before the date of the application for registration in consequence of the use which had been made of it: Case C-542/07 *Imagination Technologies Ltd v Office for Harmonisation in the Internal Market (Trade Marks and Designs)* [2009] ECR I-4937, [2009] All ER (D) 219 (Jun), ECJ.

5   Ie registration should have been refused under the Trade Marks Act 1994 s 3(1)(b), (c) or (d): see PARA 44.

6   See the Trade Marks Act 1994 s 47(1) proviso; and see PARA 102.

7   Case C-136/02P *Mag Instrument Inc v Office for Harmonisation in the Internal Market (Trade Marks and Designs)* [2004] ECR I-9165, [2004] All ER (D) 75 (Oct), ECJ.

8   Such use may be as part of or in conjunction with a registered trade mark: Case C-353/03 *Société des Produits Nestlé SA v Mars UK Ltd* [2006] All ER (EC) 348, [2005] ECR I-6135, ECJ; Case C-24/05P *August Storck KG v Office for Harmonisation in the Internal Market (Trade Marks and Designs)* [2006] ECR I-5677, [2006] IP & T 946, [2006] All ER (D) 275 (Jun), ECJ; Case C-488/06P *L & D SA v Office for Harmonisation in the Internal Market (Trade Marks and Designs)* [2008] ECR I-5725, [2008] All ER (D) 260 (Jul), ECJ. Where a secondary mark is used together with a distinctive primary mark, however, it may be more difficult to show that the secondary mark has become distinctive: *Vibe Technologies Ltd's Trade Marks Application* [2009] ETMR 12, Appointed Person.

9   Joined Cases C-108/97 and 109/97 *Windsurfing Chiemsee Produktions und Vertriebs GmbH v Boots- und Segelzubehör Walter Huber* [2000] Ch 523, [1999] ECR I-2779, [1999] ETMR 585, ECJ; Case C-299/99 *Koninklijke Philips Electronics NV v Remington Consumer Products Ltd* [2003] Ch 159, [2002] ECR I-5475, ECJ. Registration of a trade mark can only be allowed on this basis if it is shown that the trade mark has acquired distinctive character through use throughout the territory of the member state and throughout the linguistic area in which there exists a ground for refusal: Case C-108/05 *Bovemij Verzekeringen NV v Benelux-Merkenbureau* [2006] ECR I-7605, [2007] ETMR 29, [2006] All ER (D) 46 (Sep), ECJ. It makes no difference if the market for the goods is confined to a particular region or locality: *Hull Daily Mail Publications Ltd's Application* [2009] RPC 199, Appointed Person.

10 Joined Cases C-108/97 and 109/97 *Windsurfing Chiemsee Produktions und Vertriebs GmbH v Boots- und Segelzubehör Walter Huber* [2000] Ch 523, [1999] ECR I-2779, [1999] ETMR 585, ECJ; Case C-342/97 *Lloyd Schuhfabrik Meyer & Co GmbH v Klijsen Handel BV* [1999] All ER (EC) 587, [1999] ECR I-3819, [2000] FSR 77, ECJ; Case C-104/01 *Libertel Groep BV v Benelux-Merkenbureau* [2004] Ch 83, [2003] ECR I-3793, ECJ; Case C-136/02P *Mag Instrument Inc v Office for Harmonisation in the Internal Market (Trade Marks and Designs)* [2004] ECR I-9165, [2004] All ER (D) 75 (Oct), ECJ. In assessing whether a trade mark has acquired distinctive character all the circumstances in which the relevant public may see that mark must be borne in mind including not only when the decision to purchase is made but also before that point, for example in advertising, and when the product is consumed: C-24/05P *August Storck KG v Office for Harmonisation in the Internal Market (Trade Marks and Designs)* [2006] ECR I-5677, [2006] IP & T 946, ECJ.

11 Joined Cases C-108/97 and 109/97 *Windsurfing Chiemsee Produktions und Vertriebs GmbH v Boots- und Segelzubehör Walter Huber* [2000] Ch 523, [1999] ECR I-2779, [1999] ETMR 585, ECJ; Case C-342/97 *Lloyd Schuhfabrik Meyer & Co GmbH v Klijsen Handel BV* [1999] All ER (EC) 587, [1999] ECR I-3819, [2000] FSR 77, ECJ. It follows that not all trade marks are equally lacking in distinctive character; and some will require more use than others before they acquire such character: see *Fine & Country Ltd v Okotoks Ltd* [2013] EWCA Civ 672, [2013] All ER (D) 137 (Jun).

12 Joined Cases C-108/97 and 109/97 *Windsurfing Chiemsee Produktions und Vertriebs GmbH v Boots- und Segelzubehör Walter Huber* [2000] Ch 523, [1999] ECR I-2779, [1999] ETMR 585, ECJ; Case C-342/97 *Lloyd Schuhfabrik Meyer & Co GmbH v Klijsen Handel BV* [1999] All ER (EC) 587, [1999] ECR I-3819, [2000] FSR 77, ECJ.

13 Joined Cases C-108/97 and 109/97 *Windsurfing Chiemsee Produktions und Vertriebs GmbH v Boots- und Segelzubehör Walter Huber* [2000] Ch 523, [1999] ECR I-2779, [1999] ETMR 585, ECJ; Case C-299/99 *Koninklijke Philips Electronics NV v Remington Consumer Products Ltd* [2003] Ch 159, [2002] ECR I-5475, ECJ.

14 Case C-299/99 *Koninklijke Philips Electronics NV v Remington Consumer Products Ltd* [2003] Ch 159, [2002] ECR I-5475, ECJ. Mere recognition of the sign by a substantial proportion of the relevant class of persons is not enough for this purpose: *Société des Produits Nestlé SA v Unilever Plc* [2002] EWHC 2709 (Ch), [2003] RPC 651; *Dyson Ltd v Registrar of Trade Marks*

[2003] EWHC 1062 (Ch), [2003] 1 WLR 2406; *Bongrain SA v Trade Mark Registry* [2004] EWCA Civ 1690, [2005] RPC 306. It appears that the same principle applies to other types of marks: see Case C-24/05P *August Storck KG v Office for Harmonisation in the Internal Market (Trade Marks and Designs)* [2006] ECR I-5677, [2006] IP & T 946, [2006] All ER (D) 275 (Jun), ECJ; *Vibe Technologies Ltd's Trade Marks Application* [2009] ETMR 12, Appointed Person. A two-dimensional depiction of a three-dimensional product on the surface of packaging of that product does not necessarily amount to use as a trade mark for this purpose: Case C-24/05P *August Storck KG v Office for Harmonisation in the Internal Market (Trade Marks and Designs)* above.

46.   Shape.   A sign must not be registered[1] as a trade mark[2] if it consists exclusively of[3]:

(1)   the shape which results from the nature of the goods themselves[4];

(2)   the shape of goods which is necessary to obtain a technical result[5]; or

(3)   the shape which gives substantial value to the goods[6].

1   As to the meaning of 'registered' see PARA 21 note 2. In the case of an international trade mark, the mark 'becomes protected': see PARAS 11 et seq, 39 note 8.

2   As to the meaning of 'trade mark' see PARA 41.

3   Trade Marks Act 1994 s 3(2) (derived from Council Directive (EEC) 89/104 (OJ L40, 11.2.89, p 1) to approximate the laws of the member states relating to trade marks, art 3(1)(e) (see now European Parliament and Council Directive (EC) 2008/95 (OJ L299, 8.11.2008, p 25) art 3(1)(e))).

These provisions serve a public interest, which is to ensure that shapes having the specified characteristics may be freely used by all and cannot be reserved to one undertaking by being registered as trade marks: Case C-299/99 *Koninklijke Philips Electronics NV v Remington Consumer Products Ltd* [2003] Ch 159, [2002] ECR I-5475, ECJ; Case C-104/01 *Libertel Groep BV v Benelux-Merkenbureau* [2004] Ch 83, [2003] ECR I-3793, ECJ; Case C-48/09P *Lego Juris A/S v Office for Harmonisation in the Internal Market (Trade Marks and Designs)* [2010] ECR I-8403, [2010] IP & T 1160, ECJ.

These provisions apply both to marks consisting strictly of the shape of the goods and to marks consisting of graphical representations of the shape of the goods: Case C-299/99 *Koninklijke Philips Electronics NV v Remington Consumer Products Ltd* above; Joined Cases T-331/10 and T-416/10 *Yoshida Metal Industry Co Ltd v Office for Harmonisation in the Internal Market (Trade Marks and Designs)* [2012] ECR I-0000, EGC.

A sign which is refused registration by virtue of these provisions cannot constitute a trade mark and cannot acquire a distinctive character by the use made of it: Case C-299/99 *Koninklijke Philips Electronics NV v Remington Consumer Products Ltd* above; Joined Cases C-53/01 and C-55/01 *Re Linde AG* [2003] ECR I-3161, sub nom *Linde AG v Deutsches Patent- und Markenamt* [2003] RPC 803, ECJ; Case C-218/01 *Henkel KGaA v Deutsches Patent- und Markenamt* [2004] ECR I-1725, ECJ; Case C-371/06 *Benetton Group SpA v G-Stae International BV* [2007] ECR I-7709, [2007], All ER (D) 118 (Sep), [2008] ETMR 8, ECJ. It follows that such an objection cannot be overcome by reliance upon opinion polls and similar evidence: Case C-48/09P *Lego Juris A/S v Office for Harmonisation in the Internal Market (Trade Marks and Designs)* above (decision made under the equivalent provision of EC Council Regulation 40/94 (OJ L11, 14.1.94, p 1) on the Community trade mark, ie art 7(1)(e) (see now Council Regulation (EC) 207/2009 (OJ L78, 24.3.2009, p 1) art 7(1)(e)) (see PARA 195)).

4   Trade Marks Act 1994 s 3(2)(a). 'Goods' refers to the goods in respect of which the trade mark is sought to be registered, and 'the nature of the goods' refers to their innate characteristics, for example the shape of a banana for bananas: *Philips Electronics BV v Remington Consumer Products Ltd* [1999] RPC 809 at 820, [1999] All ER (D) 465, CA, per Aldous LJ; referred to ECJ sub nom C-299/99 *Koninklijke Philips Electronics NV v Remington Consumer Products Ltd* [2003] Ch 159, [2002] ECR I-5475, ECJ. Thus the shape of a three-headed electric razor is not precluded from registration by this provision (*Philips Electronics BV v Remington Consumer Products Ltd* above), nor is the shape of an indented bar of soap (Case T-122/99 *Procter & Gamble Co v Office for Harmonisation in the Internal Market (Trade Marks and Designs)* [2000] ECR II-265, [2000] 2 CMLR 303, CFI).

5   Trade Marks Act 1994 s 3(2)(b). This provision must be interpreted to mean that a sign consisting exclusively of the shape of a product is unregistrable if it is established that the essential features of that shape are attributable only to the technical result; but this ground for refusal cannot be overcome by establishing that there are other shapes which allow the same technical result to be obtained: Case C-299/99 *Koninklijke Philips Electronics NV v Remington*

Consumer Products Ltd [2003] Ch 159, [2002] ECR I-5475, ECJ; Case C-48/09P *Lego Juris A/S v Office for Harmonisation in the Internal Market (Trade Marks and Designs)* [2010] ECR I-8403, [2010] IP & T 1160, ECJ. When assessing whether registration is precluded by this provision, the first step is to identify the essential characteristics or features of the shape of the goods judged by the impact on the eye of the average consumer; once they have been determined the second step is to determine whether the essential characteristics or features consisting solely of the shape of the goods are attributable only to the technical result: *Koninklijke Philips NV v Remington Consumer Products Ltd* [2006] EWCA Civ 16, [2007] IP & T 206, [2006] FSR 537; Case C-48/09P *Lego Juris A/S v Office for Harmonisation in the Internal Market (Trade Marks and Designs)* above. The fact that the shape was or is protected by a patent is not by itself a bar to the shape being registered as a trade mark, but it is strong evidence that the shape is functional: Case C-48/09P *Lego Juris A/S v Office for Harmonisation in the Internal Market (Trade Marks and Designs)* above (decision made under the equivalent provision of Council Regulation (EC) 40/94 (OJ L11, 14.1.94, p 1) on the Community trade mark, ie art 7(1)(e)(ii) (see now Council Regulation (EC) 207/2009 (OJ L78, 24.3.2009, p 1) art 7(1)(e)(ii)) (see PARA 195)); Case T-164/11 *Reddig GmbH v Office for Harmonisation in the Internal Market (Trade Marks and Designs)* [2013] IP & T 212, [2012] All ER (D) 108 (Sep), EGC. If the shape presented for registration is sufficiently stylised that the shape as a whole does not consist essentially of features attributable only to the technical result of using that shape, it is not precluded from registration by this provision: *Ekornes SA's Request for Protection* (O/017/06), Appointed Person.

6   Trade Marks Act 1994 s 3(2)(c). This provision excludes from registration shapes which add substantial value to the goods over other shapes, in the sense that they appeal to the eye: see *Philips Electronics BV v Remington Consumer Products Ltd* [1999] RPC 809 at 822, [1999] All ER (D) 465, CA, per Aldous LJ; referred to ECJ sub nom C-299/99 *Koninklijke Philips Electronics NV v Remington Consumer Products Ltd* [2003] Ch 159, [2002] ECR I-5475, ECJ. See also *Dualit Ltd's (Toaster Shapes) Trade Mark Applications* [1999] RPC 304, Trade Marks Registry; considered but not ruled upon on appeal [1999] RPC 890 at 903, [1999] All ER (D) 729 per Lloyd J. It is irrelevant that other characteristics of the goods, such as their technical quality, also add considerable value to the goods: Case T-508/08 *Bang & Olufson A/S v Office for Harmonisation in the Internal Market (Trade Marks and Designs)* [2011] ECR II-6975, [2012] ETMR 20, EGC.

47.   Public policy; immoral trade marks.   A trade mark[1] must not be registered[2] if it is contrary to public policy[3] or to accepted principles of morality[4].

1   As to the meaning of 'trade mark' see PARA 41.
2   As to the meaning of 'registered' see PARA 21 note 2. In the case of an international trade mark, the mark 'becomes protected': see PARAS 11 et seq, 39 note 8.
3   'Public policy' is a translation of the French expression 'ordre public': *Philips Electronics BV v Remington Consumer Products Ltd* [1998] RPC 283 at 310 per Jacob J (affd on other grounds [1999] RPC 809, [1999] All ER (D) 465, CA; referred to ECJ sub nom C-299/99 *Koninklijke Philips Electronics NV v Remington Consumer Products Ltd* [2003] Ch 159, [2002] ECR I-5475, ECJ); *FCUK Trade Mark* [2007] RPC 1, [2007] ETMR 8, Appointed Person. The concept of 'ordre public' covers the protection of public security, the physical integrity of individuals as part of society and the protection of the environment: Case T-356/93 *PLANT GENETIC SYSTEMS/Glutamine synthetase inhibitors* [1995] EPOR 357, EPO Board of Appeal.
4   Trade Marks Act 1994 s 3(3)(a) (derived from Council Directive (EEC) 89/104 (OJ L40, 11.2.89, p 1) to approximate the laws of the member states relating to trade marks, art 3(1)(f) (see now European Parliament and Council Directive (EC) 2008/95 (OJ L299, 8.11.2008, p 25) art 3(1)(f))). The applicability of this provision depends on the intrinsic qualities of the trade mark itself and not on circumstances relating to the conduct of the applicant: Case T-224/01 *Durferrit GmbH v Office for Harmonisation in the Internal Market (Trade Marks and Designs)* [2003] ECR II-1589, [2003] All ER (D) 136 (Apr), CFI; Case T-140/02 *Sportwetten GmbH Gera v Office for Harmonisation in the Internal Market (Trade Marks and Designs)* [2005] ECR II-3247, [2006] ETMR 15, CFI (in so far as they are relevant both cases were decided under the equivalent provision of EC Council Regulation 40/94 (OJ L11, 14.1.94, p 1) on the Community trade mark, ie art 7(1)(f) (see now Council Regulation (EC) 207/2009 (OJ L78, 24.3.2009, p 1) art 7(1)(f)) (see PARA 196)). This provision should be interpreted and applied consistently with the Convention for the Protection of Human Rights and Fundamental

Freedoms (Rome, 4 November 1950; TS 71 (1953); Cmd 8969) art 10 (ie the right to freedom of expression, which is now incorporated into United Kingdom law in the Human Rights Act 1998 s 1(3), Sch 1 art 10) (see RIGHTS AND FREEDOMS vol 88A (2013) PARAS 14, 398 et seq); it follows that registration should only be refused where this is justified by a pressing social need and is proportionate to the legitimate aim pursued: *Basic Trademark SA's Trade Mark Application* [2005] RPC 611, Appointed Person; Case R 495/2005-G *Kenneth's Application* [2007] ETMR 7, OHIM Enlarged Board of Appeal; Case T-232/10 *Couture Tech Ltd v Office for Harmonisation of the Internal Market (Trade Marks and Designs)* [2012] ETMR 5, ECJ; but see Case T-417/10 *Lopez v Office for Harmonisation in the Internal Market (Trade Marks and Designs)* [2012] ECR II-0000, EGC.

Marks which appear to glorify terrorism or offend the victims of terrorism will be refused under the first limb of this provision: Cases R 176/2004–2 and R 177/2004–2 *Falcon Sporting Goods AG's Application* (29 September 2004), OHIM Board of Appeal (BIN LADIN refused); Case R 495/2005-G *Kenneth's Application* above. Racist insults may be refused under both limbs: Case T-526/09 *PAKI Logistics GmbH v Office for Harmonisation in the Internal Market (Trade Marks and Designs)* [2011] ECR II-346, EGC (PAKI refused).

For the second limb of this provision to apply, use of the mark must contravene a generally accepted moral principle: *Ghazilian's Trade Mark Application* [2002] RPC 628, [2002] ETMR 631, Appointed Person; *FCUK Trade Mark* [2007] RPC 1, [2007] ETMR 8, Appointed Person. Mere offence to a section of the public, in the sense that that section of the public would consider the mark distasteful, is not enough for this provision to apply; but it does apply if use of the mark would justifiably cause outrage, or would be the subject of justifiable censure, amongst an identifiable section of the public as being likely to undermine significantly current religious, family or social values: *Ghazilian's Trade Mark Application* above; *Scranage's Trade Mark Application* (O/182/05), Appointed Person; *FCUK Trade Mark* above. In considering whether the mark is offensive the nature of the goods is relevant since it affects the context in which the mark is likely to be encountered: Case R 495/2005-G *Kenneth's Application* above (SCREW YOU acceptable for condoms and goods sold in sex shops but not for goods sold more widely). The slang meaning of a word may lead to an objection even if its normal meaning does not: Case R 111/2002–4 *Dick Lexic's Application* [2005] ETMR 99, OHIM Board of Appeal (decision made under the equivalent provision of Council Regulation (EC) 40/94 (OJ L11, 14.1.94, p 1), ie art 7(1)(f) (see now Council Regulation (EC) 207/2009 (OJ L78, 24.3.2009, p 1) art 7(1)(f)) (see PARA 196)). On the other hand a word which happens to be offensive in another Community language will not be objectionable if it is evident that this is inadvertent: Case R 558/2006–2 *Reva Electric Car Co (PVT) Ltd's Application* (18 July 2006, unreported), OHIM Board of Appeal (REVA offensive in Finnish but accompanying words THE ELECTRICITY CAR made it clear that this was accidental) (decision made under the equivalent provision of Council Regulation (EC) 40/94 (OJ L11, 14.1.94, p 1), ie art 7(1)(f) (see now Council Regulation (EC) 207/2009 (OJ L78, 24.3.2009, p 1) art 7(1)(f)) (see PARA 196)).

48. Deceptive trade marks. A trade mark[1] must not be registered[2] if it is of such a nature as to deceive the public, for instance as to the nature, quality or geographical origin of the goods or service[3].

1   As to the meaning of 'trade mark' see PARA 41.

2   As to the meaning of 'registered' see PARA 21 note 2. In the case of an international trade mark, the mark 'becomes protected': see PARAS 11 et seq, 39 note 8.

3   Trade Marks Act 1994 s 3(3)(b) (derived from Council Directive (EEC) 89/104 (OJ L40, 11.2.89, p 1) to approximate the laws of the member states relating to trade marks, art 3(1)(g) (see now European Parliament and Council Directive (EC) 2008/95 (OJ L299, 8.11.2008, p 25) art 3(1)(g))). This provision is concerned with deceptiveness which is inherent in the trade mark itself, as opposed to deception caused by the similarity of the trade mark to another trade mark (which may give rise to a relative ground of refusal: see PARA 54 et seq): see eg Case R-468/1999 *International Star Registry of Illinois Ltd's Application* (OJ OHIM 6/02, p 1185), OHIM Board of Appeal (INTERNATIONAL STAR REGISTRY likely to mislead consumers into believing that the organisation which used it was an authoritative body empowered to give names to stars) (decision made under the equivalent provision of Council Regulation (EC) 40/94 (OJ L11, 14.1.94, p 1) on the Community trade mark, ie art 7(1)(g) (see now Council Regulation (EC) 207/2009 (OJ L78, 24.3.2009, p 1) art 7(1)(g)) (see PARA 197)). In some cases a mark may be may be excluded from registration partly under this provision and partly for lack of distinctiveness: see eg Case R 246/1999–1 *Enotria Holdings Ltd's Application* (27 March 2000, unreported), OHIM Board of Appeal (ARCADIA descriptive for wine produced in Greece,

deceptive for wine produced in Italy) (decision made under the equivalent provision of Council Regulation (EC) 40/94 (OJ L11, 14.1.94, p 1), ie art 7(1)(g) (see now Council Regulation (EC) 207/2009 (OJ L78, 24.3.2009, p 1) art 7(1)(g)) (see PARA 197)); Decision 75C/000835728/1 *Beiersdorf AG's Trade Mark Application, Application for Cancellation by L'Oréal SA* [2001] ETMR 19, OHIM Cancellation Division (POUDRE LIBRE NATURELLE descriptive for cosmetics which were loose powders, deceptive for those which were not) (decision made under the equivalent provision of Council Regulation (EC) 40/94 (OJ L11, 14.1.94, p 1), ie art 7(1)(g) (see now Council Regulation (EC) 207/2009 (OJ L78, 24.3.2009, p 1) art 7(1)(g)) (see PARA 197)).

For registration to be refused there must be actual deceit or a serious risk that the consumer will be deceived: Case C-87/97 *Consorzio per la Tutela del Formaggio Gorgonzola v Käserei Champignon Hofmeister GmbH & Co KG and Eduard Bracharz GmbH* [1999] ECR I-1301, [1999] 1 CMLR 1203, ECJ; Case C-259/04 *Emanuel v Continental Shelf 128 Ltd* [2006] IP & T 887, sub nom *Elizabeth Florence Emanuel v Continental Shelf 128 Ltd* [2006] ETMR 56, ECJ. A trade mark corresponding to the name of the designer and first manufacturer of the goods bearing that mark may not, by reason of that feature alone, be refused registration on this ground even where the goodwill associated with that trade mark has been assigned, together with the business making the goods to which the mark relates, to another person: Case C-259/04 *Emanuel v Continental Shelf 128 Ltd* above.

The fact that a trade description is a trade mark, or part of a trade mark, does not prevent it from being a false trade description when applied to any goods, except when certain conditions are satisfied: see the Trade Descriptions Act 1968 s 34; and CONSUMER PROTECTION vol 21 (2011) PARA 513.

49. Illegal trade marks.

A trade mark[1] must not be registered[2] if or to the extent that its use[3] is prohibited in the United Kingdom[4] by any enactment or rule of law or by any provision of EU law[5].

1 As to the meaning of 'trade mark' see PARA 41.
2 As to the meaning of 'registered' see PARA 21 note 2. In the case of an international trade mark, the mark 'becomes protected': see PARAS 11 et seq, 39 note 8.
3 As to the meaning of 'use' see PARA 44 note 8.
4 As to the meaning of 'United Kingdom' see PARA 3 note 2.
5 Trade Marks Act 1994 s 3(4) (amended by SI 2011/1043) (Trade Marks Act 1994 s 3(4) originally derived from Council Directive (EEC) 89/104 (OJ L40, 11.2.89, p 1) to approximate the laws of the member states relating to trade marks, art 3(2)(a) (see now European Parliament and Council Directive (EC) 2008/95 (OJ L299, 8.11.2008, p 25) art 3(2)(a)), which makes it clear that the provision is concerned with laws other than trade mark laws). A trade mark application must be refused under this provision if use of the mark would contravene Council Regulation (EC) 1493/99 (OJ L179, 14.7.99, p 1) on the common organisation of the market in wine (see PARA 285 note 2): *MEZZACORONA Trade Mark* [2003] EWCA Civ 1861, [2004] RPC 537, sub nom *Miguel Torres SA v Cantine Mezzacorona SCARL* [2003] All ER (D) 407 (Dec) (held on the facts that there was no contravention).

50. Specially protected emblems.

A trade mark[1] which consists of or contains:

(1) the royal arms[2], or any of the principal armorial bearings of the royal arms, or any insignia or device so nearly resembling the royal arms or any such armorial bearing as to be likely to be mistaken for them or it[3];

(2) a representation of the royal crown or any of the royal flags[4];

(3) a representation of Her Majesty or any member of the royal family, or any colourable imitation thereof[5]; or

(4) words, letters or devices likely to lead persons to think that the applicant either has or recently has had royal patronage or authorisation[6],

must not be registered[7] unless it appears to the registrar[8] that consent has been given by or on behalf of Her Majesty or, as the case may be, the relevant member of the royal family[9].

A trade mark which consists of or contains a representation of:

(a)   the national flag of the United Kingdom (commonly known as the Union Jack)[10]; or

(b)   the flag of England, Wales, Scotland, Northern Ireland or the Isle of Man[11],

must not be registered if it appears to the registrar that the use of the trade mark[12] would be misleading or grossly offensive[13].

A trade mark must not be registered in the case of national emblems etc of Convention countries[14] or emblems etc[15] of certain international organisations[16].

Where a representation of:

(i)   any arms to which a person is entitled by virtue of a grant of arms by the Crown[17]; or

(ii)   any insignia so nearly resembling such arms as to be likely to be mistaken for them[18],

appears in a mark, the registrar must refuse to accept an application for the registration of the mark unless he is satisfied that the consent of the person entitled to the arms has been obtained[19]. Where such a mark is registered, nothing in the Trade Marks Act 1994 is to be construed as authorising its use in any way contrary to the laws of arms[20].

A trade mark which consists of or contains a controlled representation within the meaning of the Olympic Symbol etc (Protection) Act 1995[21] must not be registered unless it appears to the registrar that the application is made by the proprietor of the Olympics association right[22], or that consent has been given by or on behalf of the proprietor[23].

1   As to the meaning of 'trade mark' see PARA 41.
2   As to the royal arms see CROWN AND ROYAL FAMILY vol 12(1) (Reissue) PARAS 43–44; and as to the offence of unauthorised use of royal arms see PARA 468.
3   Trade Marks Act 1994 s 4(1)(a).
4   Trade Marks Act 1994 s 4(1)(b).
5   Trade Marks Act 1994 s 4(1)(c).
6   Trade Marks Act 1994 s 4(1)(d). In *QUEEN DIANA Trade Mark* [1991] RPC 395, Board of Trade, it was held that the mark was not caught by the corresponding rule made under the Trade Marks Act 1938 because there was no Queen Diana. The fact that a mark fell within the spirit of the rule was not sufficient to confer discretion to refuse to register.
7   As to the meaning of 'registered' see PARA 21 note 2. In the case of an international application, the mark 'becomes protected': see PARAS 11 et seq, 39 note 8.
8   As to the registrar see PARA 19.
9   Trade Marks Act 1994 ss 3(5), 4(1). Sections 3(5), 4 derive from Council Directive (EEC) 89/104 (OJ L40, 11.2.89, p 1) to approximate the laws of the member states relating to trade marks, art 3(2)(c) (see now European Parliament and Council Directive (EC) 2008/95 (OJ L299, 8.11.2008, p 25) art 3(2)(c)).
10   Trade Marks Act 1994 s 4(2)(a).
11   Trade Marks Act 1994 s 4(2)(b).
12   As to the meaning of 'use' see PARA 44 note 8.
13   Trade Marks Act 1994 ss 3(5), 4(2). See also note 9. Provision may be made by rules identifying the flags to which s 4(2)(b) (see head (b) in the text) applies: ss 3(5), 4(2). At the date at which this volume states the law no such rules had been made.
      As to appeals against any decision of the registrar see ss 76, 77; and PARA 387 et seq.
14   Ie the cases specified in the Trade Marks Act 1994 s 57: see PARA 51. As to the meaning of 'Convention country' see PARA 6 note 2.
15   Ie the cases specified in the Trade Marks Act 1994 s 58: see PARA 52.
16   Trade Marks Act 1994 ss 3(5), 4(3). See also note 9.
17   Trade Marks Act 1994 s 4(4)(a). See also note 9.
18   Trade Marks Act 1994 s 4(4)(b). See also note 9.
19   Trade Marks Act 1994 ss 3(5), 4(4); Trade Marks Rules 2008, SI 2008/1797, r 10. See also note 9.
20   Trade Marks Act 1994 ss 3(5), 4(4). See also note 9. As to the law of arms see PEERAGES AND DIGNITIES vol 79 (2008) PARA 870 et seq.

21 See PARA 464.
22 Ie the person for the time being appointed under the Olympic Symbol etc (Protection) Act 1995
    s 1(2): see PARA 472. As to the Olympics association right see PARA 472; and SPORTS LAW vol 96
    (2012) PARA 159 et seq.
23 Trade Marks Act 1994 ss 3(5), 4(5) (s 4(5) added by the Olympic Symbol etc (Protection)
    Act 1995 s 13(2), (3)). This provision has effect in relation to applications for registration made
    on or after 20 September 1995 (ie the date of commencement of the Olympic Symbol etc
    (Protection) Act 1995: s 13(3); Olympic Symbol etc (Protection) Act 1995 (Commencement)
    Order 1995, SI 1995/2472). See *Olympic Oils Ltd's Trade Mark Application* (O/081/00), Trade
    Marks Registry, where an application to register the word OLYMPIC alone and in combination
    with an Olympic torch device for oils and fats was refused on this ground.

51.   National emblems etc of Convention countries. A trade mark[1] which:

(1)   consists of or contains the flag of a Convention country[2] must not be
      registered[3] without the authorisation of the competent authorities of
      that country, unless it appears to the registrar[4] that use of the flag in the
      manner proposed is permitted without such authorisation[5];

(2)   consists of or contains the armorial bearings or any other state emblem
      of a Convention country which is protected under the Paris Convention
      or the WTO Agreement[6] must not be registered without the
      authorisation of the competent authorities of that country[7];

(3)   consists of or contains an official sign or hallmark adopted by a
      Convention country and indicating control and warranty must not,
      where the sign or hallmark is protected under the Paris Convention or
      the WTO Agreement, be registered in relation to goods or services of the
      same, or a similar kind, as those in relation to which it indicates control
      and warranty, without the authorisation of the competent authorities of
      the country concerned[8].

The above provisions as to national flags and other state emblems, and official
signs or hallmarks, apply equally to anything which from a heraldic point of
view imitates any such flag or other emblem, or sign or hallmark[9].

Nothing in the above provisions prevents the registration of a trade mark on
the application of a national of a country who is authorised to make use of a
state emblem, or official or hallmark, of that country, notwithstanding that it is
similar to that of another country[10].

For the above purposes, state emblems of a Convention country, other than
the national flag, and official signs or hallmarks, are regarded as protected under
the Paris Convention only if, or to the extent that[11]:

(a)   the country in question has notified[12] the United Kingdom[13] that it
      desires to protect that emblem, sign or hallmark[14];

(b)   the notification remains in force[15]; and

(c)   the United Kingdom has not objected to it[16] or any such objection has
      been withdrawn[17].

Such notification has effect only in relation to applications for registration
made more than two months after the receipt of the notification[18]. The registrar
must keep and make available for public inspection by any person, at all
reasonable hours and free of charge, a list of the state emblems and official signs
or hallmarks which are for the time being so protected[19].

1   As to the meaning of 'trade mark' see PARA 41.
2   As to the meaning of 'Convention country' see PARA 6 note 2.
3   As to the meaning of 'registered' see PARA 21 note 2. In the case of an international trade mark,
    the mark 'becomes protected': see PARAS 11 et seq, 39 note 8.
4   As to the registrar see PARA 19.

5   Trade Marks Act 1994 s 57(1). Sections 57, 59 derive from the Paris Convention art 6 ter and Council Directive (EEC) 89/104 (OJ L40, 11.2.89, p 1) to approximate the laws of the member states relating to trade marks, art 3(1)(h) (see now European Parliament and Council Directive (EC) 2008/95 (OJ L299, 8.11.2008, p 25) art 3(1)(h)). These provisions apply equally to trade marks for goods and for services: Joined Cases C-202/08P and C-208/08P *American Clothing Associates NV v Office for Harmonisation in the Internal Market (Trade Marks and Designs)* [2009] ECR I-6933, [2009] All ER (D) 61 (Sep), ECJ. As to the competent authorities' power to obtain an injunction restraining the use of the mark in the United Kingdom without their authorisation see the Trade Marks Act 1994 s 57(6); and PARA 470. As to the Paris Convention see PARA 6.

6   As to the meaning of 'the WTO Agreement' see PARA 7 note 1.

7   Trade Marks Act 1994 s 57(2) (s 57(2), (3) amended by SI 1999/1899). See also note 5.

8   Trade Marks Act 1994 s 57(3) (as amended: see note 7). See also note 5.

9   Trade Marks Act 1994 s 57(4). See also note 5. When making a comparison 'from a heraldic point of view' regard must be had to the heraldic description and not to any more detailed description: Case T-127/02 *Concept-Anlagen u Geräte nach 'GMP' für Produktion u Labour GmbH v Office for Harmonisation in the Internal Market (Trade Marks and Designs)* [2004] ECR II-1113, [2004] All ER (D) 175 (Apr), CFI (mark resembling emblem of Council of Europe with addition of letters ECA refused registration) (decided under the equivalent provision of Council Regulation (EC) 40/94 (OJ L11, 14.1.94, p 1) on the Community trade mark, ie art 7(1)(h) (see now Council Regulation (EC) 207/2009 (OJ L78, 24.3.2009, p 1) art 7(1)(h)) (see PARA 199)). Whether there is an imitation is to considered from the perspective of the average consumer, but this does not require a likelihood of confusion: Joined Cases C-202/08P and C-208/08P *American Clothing Associates NV v Office for Harmonisation in the Internal Market (Trade Marks and Designs)* [2009] ECR I-6933, [2009] All ER (D) 61 (Sep), ECJ.

10   Trade Marks Act 1994 s 57(5). See also note 5.

11   Trade Marks Act 1994 s 59(1). See also note 5.

12   Ie in accordance with the Paris Convention art 6 ter (3) as applied by the WTO Agreement.

13   As to the meaning of 'United Kingdom' see PARA 3 note 2.

14   Trade Marks Act 1994 s 59(1)(a).

15   Trade Marks Act 1994 s 59(1)(b).

16   Ie in accordance with the Paris Convention art 6 ter (4) as applied by the WTO Agreement: Trade Marks Act 1994 s 59(5) (added by SI 1999/1899).

17   Trade Marks Act 1994 s 59(1)(c).

18   Trade Marks Act 1994 s 59(3). See also note 5.

19   Trade Marks Act 1994 s 59(4). See also note 5.

52.   Emblems etc of certain international organisations. The following provisions apply to:

(1)   the armorial bearings, flags or other emblems; and

(2)   the abbreviations and names,

of international intergovernmental organisations of which one or more Convention countries[1] are members[2].

A trade mark[3] which consists of or contains any such emblem, abbreviation or name which is protected under the Paris Convention or the WTO Agreement[4] must not be registered[5] without the authorisation of the international organisation concerned, unless it appears to the registrar[6] that the use of the emblem, abbreviation or name in the manner proposed: (a) is not such as to suggest to the public that a connection exists between the organisation and the trade mark; or (b) is not likely to mislead the public as to the existence of a connection between the user and the organisation[7].

The above provisions as to emblems of an international organisation apply equally to anything which from a heraldic point of view imitates any such emblem[8].

Nothing in the above provisions affects the rights of a person whose bona fide use[9] of the trade mark in question began before 4 January 1962, when the relevant provisions of the Paris Convention entered into force in relation to the United Kingdom[10].

For the above purposes, the emblems, abbreviations and names of an international organisation are regarded as protected under the Paris Convention only if, or to the extent that[11]:

(i)   the organisation in question has notified[12] the United Kingdom that it desires to protect that emblem, abbreviation or name[13];

(ii)   the notification remains in force[14]; and

(iii)   the United Kingdom has not objected to it[15] or any such objection has been withdrawn[16].

Such notification has effect only in relation to applications for registration made more than two months after the receipt of the notification[17]. The registrar must keep and make available for public inspection by any person, at all reasonable hours and free of charge, a list of the emblems, abbreviations and names of international organisations which are for the time being so protected[18].

1   As to the meaning of 'Convention country' see PARA 6 note 2.
2   Trade Marks Act 1994 s 58(1). Sections 58, 59 derive from the Paris Convention art 6 ter and Council Directive (EEC) 89/104 (OJ L40, 11.2.89, p 1) to approximate the laws of the member states relating to trade marks, art 3(1)(h) (see now European Parliament and Council Directive (EC) 2008/95 (OJ L299, 8.11.2008, p 25) art 3(1)(h)). As to an international organisation's power to obtain an injunction restraining the use of the mark in the United Kingdom without its authorisation see the Trade Marks Act 1994 s 58(4); and PARA 471. As to the Paris Convention see PARA 6.
3   As to the meaning of 'trade mark' see PARA 41.
4   As to the meaning of 'the WTO Agreement' see PARA 7 note 1.
5   As to the meaning of 'registered' see PARA 21 note 2. In the case of an international trade mark, the mark 'becomes protected': see PARAS 11 et seq, 39 note 8.
6   As to the registrar see PARA 19.
7   Trade Marks Act 1994 s 58(2) (amended by SI 1999/1899). See also note 2.
8   Trade Marks Act 1994 s 58(3). See also note 2. As to the meaning of 'from a heraldic point of view' see PARA 51 note 9.
9   As to the meaning of 'use' see PARA 44 note 8.
10   Trade Marks Act 1994 s 58(5). See also note 2. As to the meaning of 'United Kingdom' see PARA 3 note 2.
11   Trade Marks Act 1994 s 59(2). See also note 2.
12   Ie in accordance with the Paris Convention art 6 ter (3) as applied by the WTO Agreement: Trade Marks Act 1994 s 59(5) (added by SI 1999/1899).
13   Trade Marks Act 1994 s 59(2)(a).
14   Trade Marks Act 1994 s 59(2)(b).
15   Ie in accordance with the Paris Convention art 6 ter (4) as applied by the WTO Agreement (see note 12).
16   Trade Marks Act 1994 s 59(2)(c).
17   Trade Marks Act 1994 s 59(3). See also note 2.
18   Trade Marks Act 1994 s 59(4). See also note 2.

53. Bad faith. A trade mark[1] must not be registered[2] if or to the extent that the application is made in bad faith[3].

The relevant date for assessing whether an application to register a trade mark was made in bad faith is the application date[4] although later evidence is relevant if it casts light on the position as at the application date[5].

A person is presumed to have acted in good faith unless the contrary is proved[6]. The standard of proof is the balance of probabilities, but cogent evidence is required due to the seriousness of the allegation. It is not enough to prove facts which are also consistent with good faith[7].

Bad faith includes not only dishonesty, but also some dealings which fall short of the standards of acceptable commercial behaviour observed by reasonable and experienced men in the particular area being examined[8]. In order to determine whether the applicant acted in bad faith, the tribunal must make an overall assessment, taking into account all the factors relevant to the particular case[9]. The tribunal must ascertain the defendant's knowledge of the matters in question and decide whether the defendant's conduct is dishonest, or otherwise falls short of the standards of acceptable commercial behaviour, judged by the ordinary standards of honest people[10]. Particular consideration must be given to the applicant's intention at the time when he files the application for registration[11].

1   As to the meaning of 'trade mark' see PARA 41.
2   As to the meaning of 'registered' see PARA 21 note 2. In the case of an international application, the mark 'becomes protected': see PARAS 11 et seq, 39 note 8.
3   Trade Marks Act 1994 s 3(6) (derived from Council Directive (EEC) 89/104 (OJ L40, 11.2.89, p 1) to approximate the laws of the member states relating to trade marks, art 3(2)(d) (see now European Parliament and Council Directive (EC) 2008/95 (OJ L299, 8.11.2008, p 25) art 3(2)(d))). The Trade Marks Act 1994 s 3(6) (and the equivalent provisions of Council Directive (EEC) 89/104 art 3(2)(d) and Council Regulation (EC) 207/2009 (OJ L78, 24.3.2009, p 1) art 52(1)(b)) are intended to prevent abuse of the trade mark system: see *Melly's Trade Mark Application* [2008] RPC 454, Appointed Person; Case R 633/2007–2 *CHOOSI Trade Mark* (29 February 2008, unreported), OHIM Board of Appeal. There are two main classes of abuse. The first concerns abuse vis-a-vis the relevant office; and the second concerns abuse vis-a-vis third parties: see *Hotel Cipriani Srl v Cipriani (Grosvenor Street) Ltd* [2008] EWHC 3032 (Ch), [2009] RPC 209 (affd [2010] EWCA Civ 110, [2010] Bus LR 1465, [2010] RPC 485). An example of the first kind of abuse is where a trade mark owner tries artificially to extend the grace period for non-use: see Case T-136/11 *Pelicantravel.com sro v Office for Harmonisation in the Internal Market (Trade Marks and Designs)* [2012] ECR II-0000, [2012] All ER (D) 258 (Dec), EGC. An example of the second kind of abuse is where the applicant is seeking to lay its hands on the trade mark of another party with whom it had contractual or quasi-contractual relations: see *BRUTT Trade Marks* [2007] RPC 462, Appointed Person and Case R1203/2005–1 *BRUTT Trade Mark* (30 July 2009, unreported), OHIM Board of Appeal. For a detailed discussion of the case law see *Red Bull GmbH v Sun Mark Ltd* [2012] EWHC 1929 (Ch) at [13], [2012] All ER (D) 186 (Jul) at [13] et seq per Arnold J.
4   Case C-529/07 *Chocoladenfabriken Lindt & Sprüngli AG v Franz Hauswirth GmbH* [2009] ECR I-4893, [2010] Bus LR 443, [2010] IP & T 367, ECJ.
5   *Hotel Cipriani Srl v Cipriani (Grosvenor Street) Ltd* [2008] EWHC 3032 (Ch), [2009] RPC 209 at 167 (affd [2010] EWCA Civ 110, [2010] Bus LR 1465, [2010] RPC 485); cf Case C-259/02 *La Mer Technology Inc v Laboratoires Goemar SA* [2004] ECR I-1159, [2004] FSR 785, ECJ and Case C-192/03 *Alcon Inc v OHIM* [2004] ECR I-8993, ECJ.
6   Case T-136/11 *Pelicantravel.com sro v Office for Harmonisation in the Internal Market (Trade Marks and Designs)* [2012] ECR II-0000, [2012] All ER (D) 258 (Dec), EGC.
7   *BRUTT Trade Marks* [2007] RPC 462, Appointed Person; Case R 336/20o7–2 *von Rossum v Heinrich Mack Nachf GmbH & Co KG* (13 November 2007, unreported), OHIM Board of Appeal; Case R 1621/2006–4 *Funke Kunststoffe GmbH v Astral Property Pty Ltd* (21 December 2009, unreported), OHIM Board of Appeal.
8   *Gromax Plasticulture Ltd v Don & Low Nonwovens Ltd* [1999] RPC 367; Case C000659037/1 *DAAWAT Trade Mark* (28 June 2004, unreported), OHIM Cancellation Division; *Harrison v Teton Valley Trading Co Ltd* [2004] EWCA Civ 1028, [2004] 1 WLR 2577, [2005] FSR 177.
9   Case C-529/07 *Chocoladenfabriken Lindt & Sprüngli AG v Franz Hauswirth GmbH* [2009] ECR I-4893 at 37, [2010] Bus LR 443, [2010] IP & T 367.
10 *AJIT WEEKLY Trade Mark* [2005] EWHC 1623 (Pat), [2006] RPC 25, Appointed Person; Case R 916/2004–1 *GERSON Trade Mark* (4 June 2009, unreported), OHIM Board of Appeal; *Campbell v Hughes* [2011] RPC 609, Appointed Person.
11 Case C-529/07 *Chocoladenfabriken Lindt & Sprüngli AG v Franz Hauswirth GmbH* [2009] ECR I-4893 at 42–45, [2010] Bus LR 443, [2010] IP & T 367 (the intention to prevent a third party from marketing a product or applying for registration of a sign without intending to use it may indicate bad faith on the part of the applicant); see also *Maslyukov v Diageo Distilling Ltd* [2010] EWHC 443 (Ch), [2010] RPC 641, [2010] All ER (D) 64 (May); *Frost Products Ltd v FC Frost Ltd* [2013] EWPCC 34, [2013] All ER (D) 323 (Jul). The fact that the applicant knew

or should have known that a third party was using a trade mark abroad which was liable to be confused with the mark applied for is not sufficient to demonstrate bad faith: Case C-320/12 *Malaysia Diary Industries Pte Ltd v Ankenaevnet For Patenter Og Varemaeker* [2013] ETMR 36, ECJ. If there is a commercial logic to the making of the application, it is unlikely to constitute bad faith: Case T-33/11 *Peeters Landbouwmachines BV v Office for Harmonisation in the Internal Market (Trade Marks and Designs)* [2012] ECR II-0000, EGC; Case T-291/09 *Carrols Corpn v Office for Harmonisation in the Internal Market (Trade Marks and Designs)* [2012] ECR II-0000, EGC (affd Case C-171/12P [2013] ECR I-0000, ECJ).

An applicant who does not have a bona fide intention to use the trade mark cannot honestly sign the declaration with regard to use required by the Trade Marks Act 1994 s 32(3) (see PARA 345); accordingly, 'bad faith' covers the case where a mark is applied for by an applicant who at the time had no intention of using the mark: *DEMON ALE Trade Mark* [2000] RPC 345, Appointed Person; *Ferrero SpA's Trade Marks* [2004] RPC 583, Appointed Person; and see *LABORATOIRE DE LA MER Trade Marks* [2002] FSR 790. To constitute bad faith, however, it is not enough for the applicant to have made a statement of intention to use the mark applied for that turns out to have been incorrect (eg because of a misunderstanding); it must be shown that the applicant knowingly made a false statement (or possibly made a statement with regardless disregard for whether it was true or false): *Robert McBride Ltd's Trade Mark Application* [2005] ETMR 85, Appointed Person. Furthermore, it is not necessarily bad faith if the applicant only has a possible or conditional intention to use the mark at some future date: *Knoll AG's Trade Mark* [2002] EWHC 899 (Ch), [2003] RPC 175, [2002] All ER (D) 133 (May); *32Red plc v WHG (International) Ltd* [2012] EWCA Civ 19, [2012] ETMR 14; *Red Bull GmbH v Sun Mark Ltd* [2012] EWHC 1929 (Ch) at [158], [2012] All ER (D) 186 (Jul).

By contrast, a lack of any intention to use a Community trade mark applied for does not in itself amount to bad faith under the equivalent provisions in Council Regulation (EC) 40/94 (OJ L11, 14.1.94, p 1) on the Community trade mark, ie art 51(1)(b) (see PARA 226): see Decision 34C/000053447/1 *Trillium Digital Systems Inc's Trade Mark* [2000] ETMR 1054, OHIM Cancellation Division; Decision 468C/00512632/1 *POTTERY BARN Trade Mark* [2005] ETMR 74, OHIM Cancellation Division; Decision 813C/001628395/1 *NAKED Trade Mark* (14 December 2004, unreported), OHIM Cancellation Division; Case T-507/08 *Psytech International Ltd v Office for Harmonisation in the Internal Market (Trade Marks and Designs)* [2011] ECR II-165, [2011] ETMR 46, EGC; Case T-136/11 *Pelicantravel.com sro v Office for Harmonisation in the Internal Market (Trade Marks and Designs)* [2012] ECR I-0000, [2012] All ER (D) 258 (Dec), EGC; but see Case C-529/07 *Chocoladenfabriken Lindt & Sprüngli AG v Franz Hauswirth GmbH* [2009] ECR I-4893, [2010] Bus LR 443, [2010] IP & T 367, ECJ; and Case C-569/08 *Internetportal und Marketing GmbH v Schlicht* [2010] ECR I-4871, [2011] Bus LR 726, ECJ.

It is debatable whether Council Directive (EEC) 89/104 (OJ L40, 11.2.89, p 1) does not permit the United Kingdom to require the applicant to verify his intention to use the mark in relation to the full width of the specification of goods or services set out in the application form and to conclude that he has acted in bad faith if he has no intention to use the mark in relation to some of those goods and services: see *Decon Laboratories Ltd v Fred Baker Scientific Ltd* [2001] RPC 293, (2001) Times, 28 February; *Knoll AG's Trade Mark* [2002] EWHC 899 (Ch), [2003] RPC 175, [2002] All ER (D) 133 (May); *Red Bull GmbH v Sun Mark Ltd* [2012] EWHC 1929 (Ch) at [158], [2012] All ER (D) 186 (Jul).

(iii) Relative Grounds for Refusal of Registration

54.   Meaning of 'earlier trade mark'. Many of the relative grounds for refusal of registration[1] depend upon the existence of an earlier trade mark[2]. An 'earlier trade mark' is:

(1)   a registered trade mark[3], international trade mark (UK)[4], Community trade mark[5] or international trade mark (EC)[6] which has a date of application for registration[7] earlier than that of the trade mark in question, taking account (where appropriate) of the priorities[8] claimed in respect of the trade marks[9];

(2)   a Community trade mark or international trade mark (EC) which has a valid claim to seniority[10] from an earlier registered trade mark or international trade mark (UK)[11];

(3)   a registered trade mark or international mark (UK) which has been

converted from a Community trade mark or international trade mark (EC) which itself had a valid claim to seniority within head (2) above from an earlier trade mark, and accordingly has the same claim to seniority[12]; or

(4)   a trade mark which, at the date of application for registration of the trade mark in question or, where appropriate, of the priority claimed in respect of the application, was entitled to protection under the Paris Convention or the WTO Agreement[13] as a well known trade mark[14].

References to an earlier trade mark include a trade mark in respect of which an application for registration has been made and which, if registered, would be an earlier trade mark by virtue of head (1) or head (2) above, subject to its being so registered[15].

A trade mark within head (1) or head (2) above whose registration expires[16] continues to be taken into account in determining the registrability of a later mark for a period of one year after the expiry unless the registrar[17] is satisfied that there was no bona fide use[18] of the mark during the two years immediately preceding the expiry[19].

1   As to the meaning of 'relative grounds for refusal' see PARA 39. As to the relative grounds of refusal see PARA 55 et seq.

2   The definition of 'earlier trade mark' in the Trade Marks Act 1994 s 6 (see the text and notes 3–19) is derived from Council Directive (EEC) 89/104 (OJ L40, 11.2.89, p 1) to approximate the laws of the member states relating to trade marks, art 4(2) (see now European Parliament and Council Directive (EC) 2008/95 (OJ L299, 8.11.2008, p 25) art 4(2)). The validity of an earlier trade mark may not be called into question in proceedings concerning the registration of a later trade mark, but only by way of a claim for revocation or a declaration of invalidity in the appropriate jurisdiction: Case T-6/01 *Matratzen Concord GmbH v Office for Harmonisation in the Internal Market (Trade Marks and Designs)* [2002] ECR II-4335, CFI (affd Case C-30/0P [2004] ECR I-3657, ECJ).

3   As to the meaning of 'registered trade mark' see PARA 111.

4   As to the meaning of 'international trade mark (UK)' see PARA 8 note 17.

5   As to the meaning of 'Community trade mark' see PARA 189.

6   As to the meaning of 'international trade mark (EC)' see PARA 8 note 17.

7   As to the meaning of 'the date of application for registration' in relation to a United Kingdom registered mark see PARA 348 note 5. In relation to an international trade mark, this is presumably the date of the international registration or, if later, the date when a request for extension of protection to the United Kingdom was made: see PARAS 23, 348.

8   As to claims to priority for registered trade marks of Convention applications and other relevant overseas applications see the Trade Marks Act 1994 ss 35, 36; and PARAS 360–361. As to claims to priority for Community trade marks of Convention applications and other relevant overseas applications see Council Regulation (EC) 40/94 (OJ L11, 14.1.94, p 1) on the Community trade mark, arts 29–31, 33 (see now Council Regulation (EC) 207/2009 (OJ L78, 24.3.2009, p 1) arts 29–31, 33); and PARA 267 et seq.

9   Trade Marks Act 1994 s 6(1)(a) (amended by SI 2004/2332).

10   As to seniority see PARAS 270–271.

11   Trade Marks Act 1994 s 6(1)(b) (substituted by SI 2004/2332).

12   Trade Marks Act 1994 s 6(1)(ba) (added by SI 2004/2332).

13   As to the meaning of 'well known trade mark entitled to protection under the Paris Convention or the WTO Agreement' see PARA 136. As to the Paris Convention see PARA 6. As to the meaning of the 'WTO Agreement' see PARA 7 note 1.

14   Trade Marks Act 1994 s 6(1)(c) (amended by SI 1999/1899). The Trade Marks Act 1994 s 6(1)(c) does not accurately reflect Council Directive (EEC) 89/104 (OJ L40, 11.2.89, p 1) to approximate the laws of the member states relating to trade marks, art 4(2)(d): see *Le Mans Autoparts Ltd's Trade Mark Application* (O/012/05), Appointed Person.

15   Trade Marks Act 1994 s 6(2).

16   As to the duration of a registered trade mark see PARA 31.

17   As to the registrar see PARA 19.

18   As to the meaning of 'use' see PARA 44 note 8. As to the revocation of the registration of a trade mark by reason of non-use see the Trade Marks Act 1994 s 46; and PARA 98 et seq.

19 Trade Marks Act 1994 s 6(3). Where, however, a trade mark which was on the register at the date of application has subsequently expired and can no longer be restored, it ceases to be an earlier trade mark (*TRANSPAY Trade Mark* [2001] RPC 191, Trade Marks Registry); and c f the position under Council Regulation (EC) 40/94 (OJ L11, 14.1.94, p 1) on the Community trade mark, art 8 (see now Council Regulation (EC) 207/2009 (OJ L78, 24.3.2009, p 1) art 8) (see PARA 201 note 10). As to appeals from decisions of the registrar, including acts of the registrar in exercise of a discretion, see the Trade Marks Act 1994 ss 76, 77; and PARA 387 et seq.

55.   Identical earlier mark for identical goods or services.   A trade mark[1] must not be registered[2] if it is identical[3] with an earlier trade mark[4] and the goods or services in relation to which the trade mark is applied for are identical[5] with the goods or services for which the earlier trade mark is protected[6].

1   As to the meaning of 'trade mark' see PARA 41.
2   As to the meaning of 'registered' see PARA 21 note 2. In the case of an international trade mark, the mark 'becomes protected': see PARAS 11 et seq, 39 note 8.
3   A trade mark is 'identical' with an earlier trade mark where it reproduces, without any modification or addition, all the elements constituting the trade mark or where, viewed as a whole, it contains differences so insignificant that they may go unnoticed by an average consumer: Case C-291/00 *LTJ Diffusion SA v Sadas Vertbaudet SA* [2003] ECR I-2799, [2003] IP & T 994, ECJ; and see *Reed Executive plc v Reed Business Information Ltd* [2004] EWCA Civ 159, [2004] RPC 767, [2004] IP & T 1049 (these two cases refer to infringement (see PARA 68), but the discussions of 'identical' trade marks are applicable for these purposes). See *International Business Machines Corpn v Web-Sphere Ltd* [2004] EWHC 529 (Ch), [2004] All ER (D) 328 (Mar), sub nom *WEBSPHERE Trade Mark* [2004] FSR 39, (decision made under the equivalent provision of Council (EC) Regulation 40/94 (OJ L11, 14.1.94, p 1) on the Community trade mark, ie art 9(1)(a) (see now Council Regulation (EC) 207/2009 (OJ L78, 24.3.2009, p 1) art 9(1)(a)) (see PARA 209)). Note that it is important to be clear as to the nature of the earlier trade mark: eg, if it is a word mark, then it will be identical to the same word presented in a particular script; but if it is a stylised word mark, then it may or may not be identical to the same word presented in a different script.
4   As to the meaning of 'earlier trade mark' see PARA 54.
5   There are 'identical' goods or services if the respective specifications overlap; there is no need for the specifications to co-extend: *GALILEO Trade Mark* [2005] RPC 569, Appointed Person (this case refers to infringement (see PARA 68), but the discussion of 'identical' goods and services is applicable for these purposes). If parts of the respective specifications overlap and parts do not, then this ground of refusal applies to the parts that overlap. Whether goods or services are 'identical' may depend on the construction of the specification. The correct approach to construction is that the words used in the specification should be given their natural and usual meaning; they should neither be given such a broad interpretation that the limits of the specification become fuzzy, nor strained to produce a narrow meaning: Case C-307/10 *Chartered Institute of Patent Attorneys v Registrar of Trade Marks* [2013] RPC 313, [2012] IP & T 650, ECJ; *Omega Engineering Inc v Omega SA* [2012] EWHC 3440 (Ch), [2012] All ER (D) 132 (Dec). In the case of services this involves identifying the core activity covered by the term used: *Avnet Ltd v Isoact Ltd* [1998] FSR 16 (provision of facility for customer to advertise on customer's own webpage not 'advertising and promotional services') (this case refers to infringement (see PARA 68), but the discussion of 'identical' goods and services is applicable for these purposes); *Reed Executive plc v Reed Business Information Ltd* [2004] EWCA Civ 159, [2004] RPC 767, [2004] IP & T 1049 (employment website did not provide 'employment agency services') (this case refers to infringement (see PARA 68), but the discussion of 'identical' goods and services is applicable for these purposes); and see also *Associated Newspapers Ltd v Express Newspapers* [2003] EWHC 1322 (Ch), [2003] FSR 909, [2004] IP & T 379 (free newspapers not identical to 'newspapers for sale in England and Wales' since not sold) (this case refers to infringement (see PARA 68), but the discussion of 'identical' goods and services is applicable for these purposes). The specification is to be construed as at the date of application: *Reed Executive plc v Reed Business Information Ltd* above.
6   Trade Marks Act 1994 s 5(1) (derived from Council Directive (EEC) 89/104 (OJ L40, 11.2.89, p 1) to approximate the laws of the member states relating to trade marks art 4(1)(a) (see now European Parliament and Council Directive (EC) 2008/95 (OJ L299, 8.11.2008, p 25) art 4(1)(a))). Cf the corresponding infringement provision: see the Trade Marks Act 1994 s 10(1); and PARAS 68, 69. The proprietor of an earlier trade mark cannot rely on this provision

to oppose, or have declared invalid, the registration of an identical later trade mark designating identical goods or services where there has been a long period of honest concurrent use of those two trade marks in circumstances such that that use neither has or is liable to have an adverse effect on the essential function of the trade mark of guaranteeing to consumers the origin of the goods or services: Case C-482/09 *Budejovicky Budvar np v Anheuser-Busch Inc* [2011] ECR I-8701, [2012] RPC 247, [2012] IP & T 160, ECJ; *Budejovicky Budvar np v Anheuser-Busch Inc* [2012] EWCA Civ 880, [2012] 3 All ER 1405, [2013] RPC 344. As to the position where the proprietor of the earlier trade mark consents to the registration see the Trade Marks Act 1994 s 5(5); and PARA 62.

56.   Identical earlier mark and similar goods or services; similar earlier mark and identical or similar goods or services.   A trade mark[1] must not be registered[2] if, because:

(1)   it is identical[3] with an earlier trade mark[4] and is to be registered for goods or services similar[5] to those for which the earlier trade mark is protected[6]; or

(2)   it is similar[7] to an earlier trade mark and is to be registered for goods or services identical[8] with or similar to those for which the earlier trade mark is protected[9],

there exists a likelihood of confusion on the part of the public, which includes the likelihood of association with the earlier trade mark[10].

1   As to the meaning of 'trade mark' see PARA 41.
2   As to the meaning of 'registered' see PARA 21 note 2. In the case of an international application, the mark 'becomes protected': see PARAS 11 et seq, 39 note 8.
3   As to the meaning of 'identical' in this context see PARA 55 note 3.
4   As to the meaning of 'earlier trade mark' see PARA 54.
5   As to the meaning of 'similar goods or services' see PARA 57.
6   Trade Marks Act 1994 s 5(2)(a).
7   There may be visual, aural and/or conceptual similarities between marks: see PARA 58 note 14. As to whether a threshold level of similarity is required see PARA 58 note 3.
8   As to the meaning of 'identical' in this context see PARA 55 note 5.
9   Trade Marks Act 1994 s 5(2)(b).
10 Trade Marks Act 1994 s 5(2) (derived from Council Directive (EEC) 89/104 (OJ L40, 11.2.89, p 1) to approximate the laws of the member states relating to trade marks, art 4(1)(b) (see now European Parliament and Council Directive (EC) 2008/95 (OJ L299, 8.11.2008, p 25) art 4(1)(b))). As to the likelihood of confusion see PARA 58; and as to the position where the proprietor of the earlier trade mark consents to the registration see the Trade Marks Act 1994 s 5(5); and PARA 62. As to the procedure for intervention see the Trade Marks Rules 2008, SI 2008/1797, r 21.

57.   Meaning of 'similar goods and services'.   The expression 'similar goods and services' is not defined[1]; the expression is not only important to refusal on one of the statutory relative grounds[2] but also to the statutory definition of infringement[3]. The purpose of the concept is to prevent marks from conflicting not only for the umbra of their respective actual goods or services, but for a penumbra also[4]. In some cases goods can be 'similar to' services.

In considering whether or not there is similarity, all factors relating to the goods or services must be taken into account[5]. These factors include: (1) the respective uses of the goods or services; (2) the respective users of the goods or services; (3) the physical nature of the goods or acts of service; (4) the respective trade channels through which the goods or services reach the market; (5) in the case of self-serve consumer items, where in practice they are respectively found or likely to be found in supermarkets, and in particular whether they are, or are likely to be, found on the same or different shelves; and (6) the extent to which the respective goods are in competition with each other[6]. Even if the goods are not in competition with each other, they may be similar if they are complementary[7]. However, the mere fact that a particular product is used as a component of another does not suffice in itself to show that the two are similar[8]. The nature of the marks being compared is irrelevant to the similarity or otherwise of the goods or services concerned; but when it comes to assessing the likelihood of confusion the two factors are interdependent[9].

1   Ie in either the Trade Marks Act 1994 or Council Directive (EEC) 89/104 (OJ L40, 11.2.89, p 1) to approximate the laws of the member states relating to trade marks (see now European Parliament and Council Directive (EC) 2008/95 (OJ L299, 8.11.2008, p 25)).

2   Ie the ground in the Trade Marks Act 1994 s 5(2): see PARA 56.

3   See the Trade Marks Act 1994 s 10(2); and PARA 70.

4   *H Young (Operations) Ltd v Medici Ltd* [2003] EWHC 1589 (Ch) at [20], sub nom *ANIMAL Trade Mark* [2004] FSR 383 at [20] per Jacob J.

5   Case C-39/97 *Canon Kabushiki Kaisha v Metro-Goldwyn-Mayer Inc (formerly Pathe Communications Corpn)* [1998] All ER (EC) 934, [1998] ECR I-5507, [1999] FSR 332, ECJ; Case C-416/04P *The Sunrider Corpn v Office for Harmonisation in the Internal Market (Trade Marks and Designs)* [2006] ECR I-4237, [2006] All ER (D) 178 (May), ECJ (decided under Council Regulation (EC) 40/94 (OJ L11, 14.1.94, p 1) on the Community trade mark (see now Council Regulation (EC) 207/2009 (OJ L78, 24.3.2009, p 1) (see PARA 159 et seq)); Case C-16/06P *Les Editions Albert René Sarl v Office for Harmonisation in the Internal Market (Trade Marks and Designs)* [2008] ECR I-10053, [2009] All ER (D) 44 (Jan), ECJ. As to the similarity of retail services with the goods retailed see Case T-116/06 *Oakley Inc v Office for Harmonisation in the Internal Market (Trade Marks and Designs)* [2008] ECR II-2455, EGC. There is a large body of case law from the General Court and the OHIM Boards of Appeal, not all of it consistent, as to similarity of goods and services; but most of the decisions are decisions on the facts of the individual case which do not raise any question of principle.

6   Case C-39/97 *Canon Kabushiki Kaisha v Metro-Goldwyn-Mayer Inc (formerly Pathe Communications Corpn)* [1998] All ER (EC) 934, [1998] ECR I-5507, [1999] FSR 332, ECJ; *British Sugar plc v James Robertson & Sons Ltd* [1996] RPC 281 at 296–297, [1996–97] ETMR 118 at 127 per Jacob J.

    The inquiry as to the extent to which the respective goods are competitive may take into account how those in the trade classify goods (e g whether market research companies, who act for the industry, put the goods or services in the same or different sectors): *British Sugar plc v James Robertson & Sons Ltd* above at 296–297 and 127 per Jacob J. However, the fact that the respective goods are in different classes for trade mark classification purposes does not necessarily mean that they are dissimilar: Case T-8/03 *El Corte Inglés SA v Office for Harmonisation in the Internal Market (Trade Marks and Designs)* [2004] ECR II-4297, CFI (decided under Council Regulation (EC) 40/94 (OJ L11, 14.1.94, p 1) on the Community trade mark (see now Council Regulation (EC) 207/2009 (OJ L78, 24.3.2009, p 1) (see PARA 159 et seq)); Case T-202/03 *Alecansan SL v Office for Harmonisation in the Internal Market (Trade Marks and Designs)* [2006] ECR II-19, [2006] IP & T 470, [2006] ETMR 93, CFI (decided under Council Regulation (EC) 40/94 (OJ L11, 14.1.94, p 1) on the Community trade mark (see now Council Regulation (EC) 207/2009 (OJ L78, 24.3.2009, p 1) (see PARA 159 et seq)).

7   Case C-39/97 *Canon Kabushiki Kaisha v Metro-Goldwyn-Mayer Inc (formerly Pathe Communications Corpn)* [1998] All ER (EC) 934, [1998] ECR I-5507, [1999] FSR 332, ECJ. Goods or services are complementary if there is a close connection between them, in the sense that one is indispensable or important for the use of the other in such a way that consumers may think that the responsibility for the production of those goods or the provision of those services lies with the same undertaking: Case T169/03 *Sergio Rossi SpA v Office for Harmonisation in the Internal Market (Trade Marks and Designs)* [2005] ECR II685, [2005] All ER (D) 18 (Mar), CFI (affd Case C-214/05P [2006] ECR I-7057), [2006] All ER (D) 286 (Jul), ECJ); Case T31/04 *Eurodrive Services and Distribution v Office for Harmonisation in the Internal Market (Trade Marks and Designs)* [2006] ECR II-37, CFI; Case T-420/03 *El Corte Inglés SA v Office for Harmonisation in the Internal Market (Trade Marks and Designs)* [2008] ECR I-837, CFI; Case T-325/06 *Boston Scientific Ltd v Office for Harmonisation in the Internal Market (Trade Marks and Designs)* [2008] ECR II-174, [2008] All ER (D) 52 (Sep), CFI; Case T-316/07 *Commercy AG v Office for Harmonisation in the Internal Market (Trade Marks and Designs)* [2009] ECR II-43, [2009] All ER (D) 193 (Jan), CFI; Case T-74/10 *Flaco-Geräte GmbH v Office for Harmonisation in the Internal Market (Trade Marks and Designs)* [2011] ECR II-130, EGC. The mere fact that one is important for the use of the other is not enough, however: see e g Case T-105/05 *Waterford Wedgwood plc v Office for Harmonisation in the Internal Market (Trade Marks and Designs)* [2007] ECR II-60, [2007] All ER (D) 102 (Jun), CFI (affd Case C-398/07P

[2009] ECR I-75, [2010] IP & T 65, ECJ) (wine and wineglasses). Nor is mere aesthetic complementarity: see eg *Sergio Rossi SpA v Office for Harmonisation in the Internal Market (Trade Marks and Designs)* above.

8   Case T-336/03 *Les Editions Albert René Sarl v Office for Harmonisation in the Internal Market (Trade Marks and Designs)* [2005] ECR II-4667, [2005] All ER (D) 322 (Oct), CFI (affd Case C-16/06P [2008] ECR I-10053, [2009] All ER (D) 44 (Jan), ECJ) (computer hardware and software not similar to telecommunications and other electronic products) (decided under Council Regulation (EC) 40/94 (OJ L11, 14.1.94, p 1) on the Community trade mark (see now Council Regulation (EC) 207/2009 (OJ L78, 24.3.2009, p 1) (see PARA 159 et seq)).

9   As to the likelihood of confusion see PARA 58.

58.   Likelihood of confusion.   The test of likelihood of confusion is used both for assessing the registrability of a trade mark[1] and as an ingredient of infringement[2]. The question in both situations is whether the combined effect of: (1) the identity or such similarity as there may be between the respective marks (or the mark and the sign); and (2) the identity or such similarity as there may be between the respective goods or services, is to give rise to a likelihood of confusion on the part of the public[3]. In the context of registration, the likelihood of confusion is to be judged assuming that both the mark applied for and the earlier mark, if registered, are in fair and normal use[4]. In the context of infringement, the court must assume that the registered trade mark[5] is used in a normal and fair manner in relation to all the goods or services for which it is registered[6]. It must next identify the sign which the defendant is using[7], and then assess the likelihood of confusion due to the use of that sign in relation to the goods or services in respect of which it is being used in the context in which it is being used[8].

The European Court of Justice has given guidance on the correct approach to the assessment of likelihood of confusion[9]:

(a)   the likelihood of confusion must be appreciated globally, taking account of all relevant factors[10];

(b)   the matter must be judged through the eyes of the average consumer of the goods or services in question[11], who is deemed to be reasonably well informed and reasonably circumspect and observant but who rarely has the chance to make direct comparisons between marks and must instead rely upon the imperfect picture of them he has kept in his mind, and whose attention varies according to the category of goods or services in question[12];

(c)   the average consumer normally perceives a mark as a whole and does not proceed to analyse its various details[13];

(d)   the visual, aural and conceptual similarities of the marks must therefore normally be assessed by reference to the overall impressions created by the marks bearing in mind their distinctive and dominant components[14];

(e)   the overall impression conveyed to the average consumer by a composite trade mark may, in certain circumstances, be dominated by one or more of its components[15], but it is only when all other components of a complex mark are negligible that it is permissible to make the comparison solely on the basis of the dominant elements[16];

(f)   and beyond the usual case, where the average consumer perceives a mark as a whole, it is possible that in a particular case an element in a composite sign corresponding to earlier trade mark may have an independent distinctive role in the composite sign without necessarily constituting the dominant element[17];

(g)   a lesser degree of similarity between the marks may be offset by a greater degree of similarity between the goods or services, and vice versa[18];

(h)   there is a greater likelihood of confusion where the earlier mark has a highly distinctive character, either per se or because of the use that has been made of it[19];

(i)   mere association, in the strict sense that the later mark brings the earlier mark to mind, is not sufficient[20];

(j)   the reputation of a mark does not give grounds for presuming a likelihood of confusion simply because of a likelihood of association in the strict sense[21];

(k)   the risk that the public might wrongly believe that the respective goods or services come from the same or economically linked undertakings constitutes a likelihood of confusion[22].

Both initial interest confusion[23] and post-sale confusion[24] can be relied upon to show that there is a likelihood of confusion.

Where there has been honest concurrent use[25] of the marks on a substantial scale for a substantial period of time without actual confusion, that may show that there is no likelihood of confusion provided that the circumstances of use of the later mark correspond to the circumstances relevant to the assessment of likelihood of confusion, for example regarding the goods or services in relation to which the mark has been used[26].

1   Ie under the Trade Marks Act 1994 s 5(2): see PARA 56.

2   Ie under the Trade Marks Act 1994 s 10(2): see PARA 70. The same interpretation must be applied to both provisions: Case C-425/98 *Marca Mode CV v Adidas AG* [2000] All ER (EC) 694, [2000] ECR I-4861, [2000] 2 CMLR 1061, [2000] ETMR 723, ECJ.

3   Generally speaking, this is a single composite question: see eg *European Ltd v Economist Newspaper Ltd* [1998] FSR 283, [1998] ETMR 536, CA; *BALMORAL Trade Mark* [1999] RPC 297, Appointed Person. In some cases, it may be possible to say that there is no similarity at all between the respective trade marks (or between the respective goods or services) and therefore conclude that there is no likelihood of confusion regardless of the reputation of the earlier trade mark or the identity of the goods or services: Case C-106/03P *Vedial SA v Office for Harmonisation in the Internal Market (Trade Marks and Designs)* [2004] ECR I-9573, [2005] ETMR 23, ECJ (decided under the equivalent provision of Council Regulation (EC) 40/94 (OJ L11, 14.1.94, p 1) on the Community trade mark, ie art 8(1)(b) (see now Council Regulation (EC) 207/2009 (OJ L78, 24.3.2009, p 1) art 8(1)(b)) (see PARA 203)); Case C-234/06P *Il Ponte Finanziara SpA v Office for Harmonisation of the Internal Market (Trade Marks and Designs)* [2007] ECR I-7333, [2008] ETMR 13, [2007] All ER (D) 77 (Sep), ECJ; Case C-57/08P *Gateway Inc v Office for Harmonisation of the Internal Market (Trade Marks and Designs)* [2008] ECR I-188, [2009] ETMR 32, ECJ; Case C-254/09P *Calvin Klein Trademark Trust v Office for Harmonisation of the Internal Market (Trade Marks and Designs)* [2010] ECR I-7989, [2011] ETMR 5, ECJ. This approach, however, can only safely be adopted in clear cases: Case C-235/05 *L'Oréal SA v Office of Harmonisation in the Internal Market (Trade Marks and Designs)* [2006] ECR I-57, ECJ; Case T-396/04 *Soffass SpA v Office for Harmonisation in the Internal Market (Trade Marks and Designs)* [2005] ECR II-4789, [2006] IP & T 272, CFI (affd Case C-92/06P [2006] ECR I-89, ECJ) (decided under the equivalent provision of Council Regulation (EC) 40/94 (OJ L11, 14.1.94, p 1), ie art 8(1)(b) (see now Council Regulation (EC) 207/2009 (OJ L78, 24.3.2009, p 1) art 8(1)(b)) (see PARA 203)); *esure Insurance Ltd v Direct Line Insurance plc* [2008] EWCA Civ 842, [2008] 2 FCR 269.

4   Case C-533/06 O2 *Holdings Ltd v Hutchison 3G UK Ltd* [2008] ECR I-4231, [2008] IP & T 1069, [2008] ETMR 55, ECJ.

5   As to the meaning of 'registered trade mark' see PARA 111.

6   *Compass Publishing BV v Compass Logistics Ltd* [2004] EWHC 520 (Ch), [2004] RPC 809, [2004] 17 LS Gaz R 32 (decided under the equivalent provision of Council Regulation (EC) 40/94 (OJ L11, 14.1.94, p 1) on the Community trade mark, ie art 9(1)(b) (see now Council Regulation (EC) 207/2009 (OJ L78, 24.3.2009, p 1) art 9(1)(b)) (see PARA 210)); *Hotel Cipriani Srl v Cipriani (Grosvenor Street) Ltd* [2008] EWHC 3032 (Ch), [2009] RPC 209 (affd [2010]

EWCA Civ 110, [2010] Bus LR 1465, [2010] RPC 485). The registered trade mark may not in fact be used in relation to all the goods or services for which it is registered or at all.

7   Case C-291/00 *LTJ Diffusion SA v Sadas Vertbaudet SA* [2003] ECR I-2799 at [49], [2003] IP & T 994 at [49] per Jacobs Adv-Gen; *Reed Executive plc v Reed Business Information Ltd* [2004] EWCA Civ 159, [2004] RPC 767, [2004] IP & T 1049; *Datacard Corporation v Eagle Technologies Ltd* [2011] EWHC 244 (Pat), [2012] Bus LR 160, [2011] RPC 443.

8   Case C-533/06 *O2 Holdings Ltd v Hutchison 3G UK Ltd* [2008] ECR I-4231, [2008] IP & T 1069, [2008] ETMR 55, ECJ; *Specsavers International Healthcare Ltd v Asda Stores Ltd* [2012] EWCA Civ 24, [2012] FSR 555. See also *JW Spear & Sons Ltd v Zynga Inc* [2013] EWHC 3348 (Ch), [2013] All ER (D) 22 (Nov) where *Specsavers International Healthcare Ltd v Asda Stores Ltd* above was applied.

9   The leading cases are Case C-251/95 *Sabel BV v Puma AG, Rudolf Dassler Sport* [1997] ECR I-6191, [1998] RPC 199, [1998] 1 CMLR 445, ECJ; Case C-342/97 *Lloyd Schuhfabrik Meyer & Co GmbH v Klijsen Handel BV* [1999] All ER (EC) 587, [1999] ECR I-3819, [2000] FSR 77, ECJ; Case C-39/97 *Canon Kabushiki Kaisha v Metro-Goldwyn-Mayer Inc (formerly Pathe Communications Corpn)* [1998] All ER (EC) 934, [1998] ECR I-5507, [1999] FSR 332, ECJ; Case C-425/98 *Marca Mode CV v Adidas AG* [2000] ECR I-4861, [2000] 2 CMLR 1061, [2000] ETMR 723, ECJ; Case C-3/03P *Matratzen Concord GmbH v Office for Harmonisation in the Internal Market (Trade Marks and Designs)* [2004] ECR I-3657, ECJ (decided under the equivalent provision of Council Regulation (EC) 40/94 (OJ L11, 14.1.94, p 1) on the Community trade mark, ie art 8(1)(b) (see now Council Regulation (EC) 207/2009 (OJ L78, 24.3.2009, p 1) (see PARA 203)); Case C-120/04 *Medion AG v Thomson Sales Germany & Austria GmbH* [2005] ECR I-8551, [2006] IP & T 150; Case C-334/05 *Office for Harmonisation in the Internal Market (Trade Marks and Designs) v Shaker de L Laudato & C SAS* [2007] ECR I-4529. There is a large body of case law from the ECJ and EGC as to likelihood of confusion; but many of the decisions are decisions on the facts of the individual case which do not raise any question of principle.

    The summary set out in heads (a)–(j) in the text is based on that adopted and applied by the trade marks registry, which was approved in *Specsavers International Healthcare Ltd v Asda Stores Ltd* [2012] EWCA Civ 24, [2012] FSR 555; but head (k) should read as set out in the text: *Interflora Inc v Marks & Spencer plc* [2013] EWHC 1291 (Ch), [2013] ETMR 35, [2013] All ER (D) 238 (May). Although this is a convenient summary, it is sometimes necessary to look in more detail at aspects of the European Court of Justice's case law: *Aveda Corpn v Dabur India Ltd* [2013] EWHC 589 (Ch), [2013] ETMR 33, [2013] All ER (D) 172 (Mar).

10 Case C-251/95 *Sabel BV v Puma AG, Rudolf Dassler Sport* [1997] ECR I-6191, [1998] 1 CMLR 445, [1998] RPC 199, ECJ.

11 Case C-251/95 *Sabel BV v Puma AG, Rudolf Dassler Sport* [1997] ECR I-6191, [1998] 1 CMLR 445, [1998] RPC 199, ECJ.

12 Case C-342/97 *Lloyd Schuhfabrik Meyer & Co GmbH v Klijsen Handel BV* [1999] All ER (EC) 587, [1999] ECR I-3819, [2000] FSR 77, ECJ. Some goods and services are consumed by the general public, others by a professional or specialised public. In the case of prescription pharmaceuticals, both publics must be considered: Case C-412/05P *Alcon Inc v Office for Harmonisation in the Internal Market (Trade Marks and Designs)* [2007] ECR I-3569, [2007] All ER (D) 238 (Apr), ECJ.

13 Case C-251/95 *Sabel BV v Puma AG, Rudolf Dassler Sport* [1997] ECR I-6191, [1998] 1 CMLR 445, [1998] RPC 199, ECJ.

14 Case C-251/95 *Sabel BV v Puma AG, Rudolf Dassler Sport* [1997] ECR I-6191, [1998] 1 CMLR 445, [1998] RPC 199, ECJ. A descriptive element will not constitute the distinctive and dominant component of a composite mark: see eg Case T-129/01 *Jose Alejandro SL v Office for Harmonisation in the Internal Market (Trade Marks and Designs)* [2003] ECR II-2251, CFI (decided under the equivalent provision of Council Regulation (EC) 40/94 (OJ L11, 14.1.94, p 1) on the Community trade mark, ie art 8(1)(b) (see now Council Regulation (EC) 207/2009 (OJ L78, 24.3.2009, p 1) art 8(1)(b)) (see PARA 203)); Joined Cases T-117/03 to T-119/03 *New Look Ltd v Office for Harmonisation in the International Market* [2004] ECR II-3471, CFI (decided under the equivalent provision of Council Regulation (EC) 40/94 (OJ L11, 14.1.94, p 1) on the Community trade mark, ie art 8(1)(b) (see now Council Regulation (EC) 207/2009 (OJ L78, 24.3.2009, p 1) art 8(1)(b)) (see PARA 203)); Case T-147/03 *Devinlec Developpement Innovation Leclerc SA v Office for Harmonisation in the Internal Market (Trade Marks and Designs)* [2006] ECR II-11, [2006] IP & T 436, CFI (affd Case C-171/06P [2007] ECR I-41, [2007] All ER (D) 278 (Mar), ECJ) (decided under the equivalent provision of Council Regulation (EC) 40/94 (OJ L11, 14.1.94, p 1) on the Community trade mark, ie art 8(1)(b) (see now Council Regulation (EC) 207/2009 (OJ L78, 24.3.2009, p 1) art 8(1)(b) (see PARA 203)); Case T-63/09 *Volkswagen AG v Office for Harmonisation in the Internal*

Market (Trade Marks and Designs) [2012] ECR II-0000, EGC; Case T-60/11 *Kraft Foods Global Brands LLC v Office for Harmonisation in the Internal Market (Trade Marks and Designs)* [2012] ECR II-0000, EGC. The same is true of a descriptive prefix or suffix forming part of a word mark: see eg Case T-202/04 *Madaus AG v Office for Harmonisation in the Internal Market (Trade Marks and Designs)* [2006] ECR II-1115, [2006] IP & T 591, [2006] ETMR 76, CFI (decided under the equivalent provision of Council Regulation (EC) 40/94 (OJ L11, 14.1.94, p 1) on the Community trade mark, ie art 8(1)(b) (see now Council Regulation (EC) 207/2009 (OJ L78, 24.3.2009, p 1) art 8(1)(b) (see PARA 203)); Case T-596/10 *Almunia Textil SA v Office for Harmonisation in the Internal Market (Trade Marks and Designs)* (2 February 2012), EGC. Considered as a whole, however, the earlier mark must be considered to have at least a certain degree of distinctiveness: Case C-196/11 *Formula One Licensing BV v Office for Harmonisation in the Internal Market (Trade Marks and Designs)* [2012] ECR I-0000, ECJ; Case T-109/11 *Apollo Tyres AG v Office for Harmonisation in the Internal Market (Trade Marks and Designs)* [2013] ECR II-0000, [2013] All ER (D) 75 (May), EGC.

Whether there is a likelihood of confusion depends on the net effect of the visual and/or aural and/or conceptual similarities in conjunction with the other factors. Thus mere conceptual similarity may be sufficient if the earlier mark has a particularly distinctive character (Case C-251/95 *Sabel BV v Puma AG, Rudolf Dassler Sport*); and mere aural similarity may also be sufficient (Case C-342/97 *Lloyd Schuhfabrik Meyer & Co GmbH v Klijsen Handel BV* [1999] All ER (EC) 587, [1999] ECR I-3819, [2000] FSR 77, ECJ). Conversely, in an appropriate case conceptual differences between the marks can counteract visual and aural similarities between them, leading to the conclusion that there is no likelihood of confusion: Case C-361/04P *Ruiz-Picasso v Office for Harmonisation in the International Market (Trade Marks and Designs)* [2006] ECR I-643, [2006] IP & T 283, ECJ (decided under the equivalent provision of Council Regulation (EC) 40/94 (OJ L11, 14.1.94, p 1) on the Community trade mark, ie art 8(1)(b) (see now Council Regulation (EC) 207/2009 (OJ L78, 24.3.2009, p 1) art 8(1)(b)) (see PARA 203)); Case C-16/06P *Les Editions Albert René Sarl v Office for Harmonisation in the Internal Market (Trade Marks and Designs)* [2008] ECR I-10053, [2009] All ER (D) 44 (Jan), ECJ. This is particularly so if there are visual differences as well: Case C-206/04P *Mühlens GmbH & Co KG v Office for Harmonisation in the International Market (Trade Marks and Designs)* [2006] IP & T 558, [2006] EMLR 57 (decided under the equivalent provision of EC Council Regulation 40/94 (OJ L11, 14.1.94, p 1), ie art 8(1)(b) (see PARA 203)). Aural similarity between the marks is less important in the case of goods which are marketed in such a way that the relevant public usually perceives the mark visually: Case T-292/01 *Phillips-Van Heusen Corpn v Office for Harmonisation in the International Market (Trade Marks and Designs)* [2003] ECR II-4335, [2003] All ER (D) 235 (Oct), CFI (decided under the equivalent provision of Council Regulation (EC) 40/94 (OJ L11, 14.1.94, p 1), ie art 8(1)(b) (see now Council Regulation (EC) 207/2009 (OJ L78, 24.3.2009, p 1) art 8(1)(b)) (see PARA 203)); Joined Cases T-117/03 to T/119/03 *New Look Ltd v Office for Harmonisation in the International Market (Trade Marks and Designs)* [2004] ECR II-3471, CFI (decided under the equivalent provision of Council Regulation (EC) 40/94 (OJ L11, 14.1.94, p 1) on the Community trade mark, ie art 8(1)(b) (see now Council Regulation (EC) 207/2009 (OJ L78, 24.3.2009, p 1) art 8(1)(b) (see PARA 203)); Case T-301/03 *Canali Ireland Ltd v Office for Harmonisation in the International Market (Trade Marks and Designs)* [2005] ECR II-2479, [2005] All ER (D) 317 (Jun), CFI (decided under the equivalent provision of Council Regulation (EC) 40/94 (OJ L11, 14.1.94, p 1) on the Community trade mark, ie art 8(1)(b) (see now Council Regulation (EC) 207/2009 (OJ L78, 24.3.2009, p 1) art 8(1)(b) (see PARA 203)).

The likelihood of confusion may be increased if the earlier trade mark forms part of a 'family' of trade marks having a common element provided that the marks have been used: Case C-234/06 *Il Ponte Finanziaria SpA v Office for Harmonisation in the Internal Market (Trade Marks and Designs)* [2007] ECR I-7333, [2008] ETMR 13, [2007] All ER (D) 77 (Sep), CFI (decided under the equivalent provision of Council Regulation (EC) 40/94 (OJ L11, 14.1.94, p 1) on the Community trade mark, ie art 8(1)(b) (see now Council Regulation (EC) 207/2009 (OJ L78, 24.3.2009, p 1) art 8(1)(b)) (see PARA 203)); Case C-16/06P *Les Editions Albert René Sarl v Office for Harmonisation in the Internal Market (Trade Marks and Designs)* above; Case T-301/09 *IG Communications Ltd v Office for Harmonisation in the Internal Market (Trade Marks and Designs)* [2012] ECR II-0000, [2012] All ER (D) 157 (Sep), EGC.

Where the trade mark is not registered in colour, but the proprietor has used it extensively in a particular colour or combination of colours with the result that it has become associated in the mind of a significant portion of the public with that colour or colours, the colour or colours which a third party uses in order to represent a sign alleged to infringe that trade mark are relevant to the global assessment of the likelihood of confusion: Case C-252/12 *Specsavers*

International Healthcare Ltd v Asda Stores Ltd [2013] ECR I-0000, [2013] ETMR 46, (2013) Times, 1 October, ECJ. Subject to that, normal and fair use of a trade mark registered in black and white will encompass all colours, and thus there may be likelihood of confusion with a sign whose colour is different to that used by the proprietor: *Phones4U Ltd v Phone4u.co.uk Internet Ltd* [2006] EWCA Civ 244, [2007] RPC 83, [2007] IP & T 439; *Mary Quant Cosmetics Japan v Able C&C Coc Ltd* [2011] RPC 156, Appointed Person; *La Chemise Lacoste SA v Baker Street Clothing Ltd* [2011] RPC 165, Appointed Person; *Specsavers International Healthcare Ltd v Asda Stores Ltd* [2012] EWCA Civ 24, [2012] FSR 555.

15 Case C-3/03P *Matratzen Concord GmbH v Office for Harmonisation in the Internal Market (Trade Marks and Designs)* [2004] ECR I-3657, ECJ (decided under the equivalent provision of Council Regulation (EC) 40/94 (OJ L11, 14.1.94, p 1) on the Community trade mark, i e art 8(1)(b) (see now Council Regulation (EC) 207/2009 (OJ L78, 24.3.2009, p 1) (see PARA 203)).

16 Case C-334/05P *Office of Harmonisation in the Internal Market (Trade Marks and Designs) v Shaker di L Laudato & C Sas* [2007] ECR I-4529, [2007] All ER (D) 91 (Jun), ECJ. See e g Case T-437/11 *Golden Balls Ltd v Office for Harmonisation in the Internal Market (Trade Marks and Designs)* [2013] All ER (D) 182 (Oct), EGC where Case C-334/05P *Office of Harmonisation in the Internal Market (Trade Marks and Designs) v Shaker di L Laudato & C Sas* above was applied.

17 Case C-120/04 *Medion AG v Thomson Multimedia Sales Germany & Austria GmbH* [2006] ECR I-8551, [2006] IP & T 150, [2006] ETMR 13, ECJ; see also Case C-3/03P *Matratzen Concord GmbH v Office for Harmonisation in the Internal Market (Trade Marks and Designs)* [2004] ECR I-3657, ECJ (decided under the equivalent provision of Council Regulation (EC) 40/94 (OJ L11, 14.1.94, p 1) on the Community trade mark, i e art 8(1)(b) (see now Council Regulation (EC) 207/2009 (OJ L78, 24.3.2009, p 1) (see PARA 203)). Thus there may be a likelihood of confusion where the contested sign is composed by juxtaposing the company name of another party and a registered trade mark which has normal distinctiveness and which, without alone determining the overall impression conveyed by the composite sign, still has an independent distinctive role therein: Case C-120/04 *Medion AG v Thomson Multimedia Sales Germany & Austria GmbH* above. This principle also applies where the contested sign is composed by juxtaposing the company name of another party and a sign which is similar to the registered trade mark: Case T-569/10 *Bimbo SA v Office for Harmonisation in the Internal Market (Trade Marks and Designs)* [2013] ETMR 7, EGC; *Aveda Corpn v Dabur India Ltd* [2013] EWHC 589 (Ch), [2013] ETMR 33. A surname does not retain an independent distinctive role in a composite mark simply because it is perceived as a surname; a sign made up of a forename and a surname may form a logical unit such that the surname is inseparable from the forename: Case C-51/09P *Becker v Harmon International Industries* [2010] ECR I-5805, ECJ; Case T-535/08 *Tuzzi Fashion GmbH v Office for Harmonisation in the Internal Market (Trade Marks and Designs)* [2012] ECR II-0000, EGC.

18 Case C-39/97 *Canon Kabushiki Kaisha v Metro-Goldwyn-Mayer Inc (formerly Pathe Communications Corpn)* [1998] All ER (EC) 934, [1998] ECR I-5507, [1999] FSR 332, ECJ; Case C-342/97 *Lloyd Schuhfabrik Meyer & Co GmbH v Klijsen Handel BV* [1999] All ER (EC) 587, [1999] ECR I-3819, [2000] FSR 77, ECJ; Case C-425/98 *Marca Mode CV v Adidas AG* [2000] All ER (EC) 694, [2000] ECR I-4861, [2000] 2 CMLR 1061, [2000] ETMR 723, ECJ.

19 Case C-251/95 *Sabel BV v Puma AG, Rudolf Dassler Sport* [1997] ECR I-6191, [1998] 1 CMLR 445, [1998] RPC 199, ECJ; Case C-39/97 *Canon Kabushiki Kaisha v Metro-Goldwyn-Mayer Inc (formerly Pathe Communications Corpn)* [1998] All ER (EC) 934, [1998] ECR I-5507, [1999] FSR 332, ECJ. In the infringement context, the distinctive character of the mark must be assessed as of the date when the defendant began to use the sign: Case C-145/05 *Levi Strauss & Co v Casucci Spa* [2006] ECR I-3703, [2007] FSR 170, [2006] ETMR 71, ECJ. If the defendant starts to use the sign in a materially different manner or context at a later date a fresh global assessment must be made: *Stichting BDO v BDO Unibank, Inc* [2013] EWHC 418 (Ch), [2013] ETMR 31, [2013] All ER (D) 39 (Mar). As to the assessment of distinctive character see PARAS 44–45.

20 Case C-251/95 *Sabel BV v Puma AG, Rudolf Dassler Sport* [1997] ECR I-6191, [1998] 1 CMLR 445, [1998] RPC 199, ECJ.

21 Case C-425/98 *Marca Mode CV v Adidas AG* [2000] All ER (EC) 694, [2000] ECR I-4861, [2000] 2 CMLR 1061, [2000] ETMR 723, ECJ.

22 Case C-39/97 *Canon Kabushiki Kaisha v Metro-Goldwyn-Mayer Inc (formerly Pathe Communications Corpn)* [1998] All ER (EC) 934, [1998] ECR I-5507, [1999] FSR 332, ECJ; Case C-342/97 *Lloyd Schuhfabrik Meyer & Co GmbH v Klijsen Handel BV* [1999] All ER (EC) 587, [1999] ECR I-3819, [2000] FSR 77, ECJ. The requirement to assess likelihood of confusion from the perspective of the average consumer does not mean that there is a single meaning rule;

accordingly, there is a likelihood of confusion if a significant section of the relevant public is likely to be confused: *Interflora Inc v Marks & Spencer plc* [2013] EWHC 1291 (Ch), [2013] ETMR 35, [2013] All ER (D) 238 (May).

23 *Och-Ziff Management Europe Ltd v Och Capital LLP* [2010] EWHC 2599 (Ch), [2011] Bus LR 632, [2011] FSR 289.

24 *Datacard Corpn v Eagle Technologies Ltd* [2011] EWHC 244 (Pat), [2012] Bus LR 160, [2011] RPC 443.

25 As to honest concurrent use see PARA 64 note 6.

26 In the registration context: Case C-498/07P *Aceites del Sur-Coosur SA v Koipe Corporación SL* [2009] ECR I-7371, [2009] All ER (D) 79 (Sep), ECJ; Case T-31/03 *Grupo Sada p a SA v Office for Harmonisation in the Internal Market (Trade Marks and Designs)* [2005] ECR II-1667, CFI (decided under the equivalent provision of Council Regulation (EC) 40/94 (OJ L11, 14.1.94, p 1) on the Community trade mark, i e art 8(1)(b) (see now Council Regulation (EC) 207/2009 (OJ L78, 24.3.2009, p 1) art 8(1)(b)) (see PARA 203)); Case T-29/04 *Castellblanch SA v Office for Harmonisation in the Internal Market (Trade Marks and Designs)* [2005] ECR II-5309, [2006] ETMR 61, CFI (decided under the equivalent provision of Council Regulation (EC) 40/94 (OJ L11, 14.1.94, p 1) on the Community trade mark, i e art 43(2), (3) (see now Council Regulation (EC) 207/2009 (OJ L78, 24.3.2009, p 1) art 42) (see PARA 265)); Case T-346/04 *Sadas SA v Office for Harmonisation in the Internal Market (Trade Marks and Designs)* [2005] ECR II-4891, [2006] IP & T 420, [2006] ETMR 27, CFI (decided under the equivalent provision of Council Regulation (EC) 40/94 (OJ L11, 14.1.94, p 1) on the Community trade mark, i e art 8(1)(b) (see now Council Regulation (EC) 207/2009 (OJ L78, 24.3.2009, p 1) art 8(1)(b)) (see PARA 203)); *Phones4U Ltd v Phone4u.co.uk Internet Ltd* [2006] EWCA Civ 244, [2007] RPC 83, [2007] IP & T 439; *Lunan Group Ltd v Edwin Co Ltd* [2006] EWHC 3284 (Ch), [2006] All ER (D) 214 (Dec), sub nom *FIORELLI Trade Mark* [2007] RPC 447. Co-existence on the register is not enough: Case R 360/2000–4 *Antas-Gestoa e Investimentos Lda v Magliera SL* (8 January 2002, unreported), OHIM Board of Appeal; Case R 1094/2009–2 *Independent Tobacco FZE v Rothmans of Pall Mall Ltd* (13 April 2010, unreported), OHIM Board of Appeal.

    In the infringement context see *Stichting BDO v BDO Unibank Inc* [2013] EWHC 418 (Ch), [2013] ETMR 31, [2013] All ER (D) 39 (Mar); cf *Compass Publishing BV Compass Logistics Ltd* [2004] EWHC 520 (Ch), [2004] RPC 809.

59.   Identical or similar mark taking unfair advantage of, or being detrimental to, distinctive character or repute of earlier mark. A trade mark[1] which is identical with or similar to an earlier trade mark[2] must not be registered[3] if, or to the extent that, the earlier trade mark has a reputation in the United Kingdom[4] (or, in the case of a Community trade mark[5] or international trade mark (EC)[6], in the European Union)[7] and the use[8] of the later mark without due cause[9] would take unfair advantage of, or be detrimental to, the distinctive character or the repute of the earlier trade mark[10].

1 As to the meaning of 'trade mark' see PARA 41.
2 As to the meaning of 'earlier trade mark' see PARA 54.
3 As to the meaning of 'registered' see PARA 21 note 2. In the case of an international trade mark, the mark 'becomes protected': see PARAS 11 et seq, 39 note 8.
4 As to the meaning of 'United Kingdom' see PARA 3 note 2.
5 As to the meaning of 'Community trade mark' see PARA 189.
6 As to the meaning of 'international trade mark (EC)' see PARA 8 note 17.
7 A trade mark has a reputation for this purpose if it is known to a significant part of the public concerned by the products or services covered by the trade mark, so that when confronted by a similar or identical mark, used even on dissimilar goods or services, they nevertheless make an association between the two marks: Case C-375/97 *General Motors Corpn v Yplon SA* [1999] All ER (EC) 865, [1999] ECR I-5421, [1999] 3 CMLR 427, [2000] RPC 572, ECJ. The stronger the registered trade mark's distinctive character and reputation, the easier it is to establish that unfair advantage will be taken of it or detriment will be caused to it: Case C-375/97 *General Motors Corpn v Yplon SA*; Case C-252/07 *Intel Corpn Inc v CPM United Kingdom Ltd* [2008] ECR I-8823, [2009] IP & T 559, ECJ.

    It is sufficient if the trade mark has acquired the necessary reputation in a substantial part of the United Kingdom: see Case C-375/97 *General Motors Corpn v Yplon SA* above (sufficient that trade mark had reputation in a substantial part of a member state). In the case of a

Community trade mark the mark must be known by a significant part of the relevant public in a substantial part of the territory of the European Union, but in an appropriate case the territory of a single Member State may suffice for this purpose: Case C-301/07 *PAGO International GmbH v Tirolmilch registrierte Genossenschaft mbH* [2009] ECR I-9429, [2009] All ER (D) 188 (Oct), ECJ.

8   As to the meaning of 'use' see PARA 44 note 8.

9   It is for the defendant to show that he has a 'due cause': Case C-252/07 *Intel Corpn Inc v CPM United Kingdom Ltd* [2008] ECR I-8823, [2009] IP & T 559, ECJ; *Pfizer Ltd v Eurofood Link (UK) Ltd* [2001] FSR 17, [2000] IP & T 280; *Premier Brands UK Ltd v Typhoon Europe Ltd* [2000] FSR 767, [2000] IP & T 218; *Societe Anonyme Des Bains De Mer Et Du Cercle Des Etrangers a Monaco v Anglofile International Ltd (t/a Monte Carlo Entertainment)* [2013] EWPCC 38, [2013] All ER (D) 89 (Sep). Mere honesty in adopting a trade mark is not enough; the defendant must show some sort of compulsion or right to use the mark or sign in question: *Premier Brands UK Ltd v Typhoon Europe Ltd* above. Where an advertisement displayed on the internet in response to a keyword corresponding to a trade mark with a reputation puts forward an alternative to the proprietor's goods or services without offering a mere imitation of those goods, without causing dilution or tarnishment and without adversely affecting the functions of the trade mark, such use falls, as a rule, within the ambit of fair competition in the sector for the goods or services concerned and is thus not without due cause: Case C-323/09 *Interflora Inc v Marks & Spencer plc* [2011] ECR I-8625, [2013] All ER (EC) 519, [2011] IP & T 888, ECJ; see also *Specsavers International Healthcare Ltd v Asda Stores Ltd* [2012] EWCA Civ 24, [2012] FSR 555. In an appropriate case the exercise of the right of freedom of expression may perhaps constitute due cause: cf *Laugh It Off Promotions CC v South African Breweries International (Finance) BV* 2005 (8) BCLR 743, SA CC.

10   Trade Marks Act 1994 s 5(3) (amended by SI 2004/946; SI 2004/2332; and SI 2011/1043). This provision is derived from Council Directive (EEC) 89/104 (OJ L40, 11.2.89, p 1) to approximate the laws of the member states relating to trade marks, art 4(3), (4)(a) (see now European Parliament and Council Directive (EC) 2008/95 (OJ L299, 8.11.2008, p 25) art 4(3), (4)(a)). The amendment made by the Trade Marks (Proof of Use, etc) Regulations 2004, SI 2004/946, gives effect to the rulings of the European Court of Justice that Council Directive (EEC) 89/104 (OJ L40, 11.2.89, p 1) art 4(4)(a) is to be interpreted as applying where the trade mark is sought to be registered for identical or similar goods or services to those in respect of which the earlier trade mark is registered as well as for goods or services which are not similar (Case C-292/00 *Davidoff & Cie SA v Gofkid Ltd* [2003] All ER (EC) 1029, [2003] ECR I-389, ECJ; Case C-408/01 *Adidas-Salomon AG v Fitnessworld Trading Ltd* [2004] Ch 120, [2003] ECR I-12537, ECJ), although the amendment was unnecessary (*Electrocoin Automatics Ltd v Coinworld Ltd* [2004] EWHC 1498 (Ch), [2005] FSR 79, [2005] IP & T 132). Cf the corresponding infringement provision: see the Trade Marks Act 1994 s 10(3); and PARA 71. As to the concepts of unfair advantage and detriment see PARA 60. As to the position where the proprietor of the earlier mark consents to the registration see the Trade Marks Act 1994 s 5(5); and PARA 62.

60.   Unfair advantage and detriment to earlier trade mark. The tests of taking unfair advantage of, and being detrimental to, the distinctive character or the repute of a mark are used both for assessing the registrability of a trade mark[1] and as an ingredient of infringement[2]. It must be shown that use[3] of the later trade mark would be likely to[4], or use of the sign does[5], take unfair advantage or cause detriment.

It is not necessary to prove confusion to establish an unfair advantage or detriment; it is sufficient for the degree of similarity between the trade mark applied for and the earlier trade mark to have the effect that the relevant section of the public establishes a link between them[6]. The existence of such a link must be appreciated globally taking into account all factors relevant to the circumstances of the case[7].

'Unfair advantage' (parasitism' or 'free riding') is taken where the use of the trade mark applied for would enable the applicant to exploit the distinctive character or repute of the earlier trade mark to market its goods or services, thereby taking the benefit of the promotional expenditure of the proprietor of the earlier trade mark and saving on its own investment in promotion[8].

Detriment to the repute of the earlier trade mark ('tarnishment' or 'degradation') is caused when the goods or services covered by the trade mark applied may be perceived by the public in such a way that the earlier trade mark's power of attraction is reduced, in particular where the goods or services covered by the trade mark applied for possess a characteristic or a quality which is liable to have a negative impact on the image of the earlier trade mark[9].

Detriment to the distinctive character of the earlier trade mark ('blurring' or 'dilution') is caused when the trade mark's ability to identify the goods or services for which it is registered is weakened, such as where the trade mark, which at one time aroused immediate association with the goods or services for which it is registered, is no longer capable of doing so[10].

1   Ie under the Trade Marks Act 1994 s 5(3) and under Council Regulation (EC) 207/2009 (OJ L78, 24.3.2009, p 1) on the Community trade mark, art 8(5) (formerly Council Regulation (EC) 40/94 (OJ L11, 14.1.94, p 1) art 8(5)): see PARAS 59, 204. As to the meaning of 'trade mark' see PARA 41.

2   Ie under the Trade Marks Act 1994 s 10(3) and under Council Regulation (EC) 207/2009 (OJ L78, 24.3.2009, p 1) art 9(1)(c) (formerly Council Regulation (EC) 40/94 (OJ L11, 14.1.94, p 1) art 9(1)(c)): see PARAS 71, 211.

3   As to the meaning of 'use' see PARA 44 note 8.

4   Case T-67/04 *SA Spa Monopole v Office for Harmonisation in the Internal Market (Trade Marks and Designs)* [2005] ECR II-1825, CFI (decision made under the equivalent provision of Council Regulation (EC) 40/94 (OJ L11, 14.1.94, p 1) on the Community trade mark, i e art 8(5) (see now Council Regulation (EC) 207/2009 (OJ L78, 24.3.2009, p 1) art 8(5)) (see PARA 204)).

5   *Mastercard International Inc v Hitachi Credit (UK) plc* [2004] EWHC 1623 (Ch), [2005] RPC 551, [2005] ETMR 10.

6   Case C-408/01 *Adidas-Salomon AG v Fitnessworld Trading Ltd* [2004] Ch 120, [2003] ECR I-12537, ECJ; and see also Case C-375/97 *General Motors Corpn v Yplon SA* [1999] All ER (EC) 865, [1999] ECR I-5421, [1999] 3 CMLR 427, [2000] RPC 572, ECJ. The existence of such a link is necessary, but not sufficient, to prove one of the requisite kinds of damage: Case C-252/07 *Intel Corpn Inc v CPM United Kingdom Ltd* [2008] ECR I-8823, [2009] IP & T 559, ECJ. The fact that the earlier mark is unique and has a huge reputation for certain specific types of goods or services, and that the later mark calls the earlier mark to mind, is not sufficient to establish that the use of the later mark takes or would take unfair advantage of, or is or would be detrimental to, the distinctive character or the repute of the earlier mark: Case C-252/07 *Intel Corpn Inc v CPM United Kingdom Ltd* above.

7   Case C-408/01 *Adidas-Salomon AG v Fitnessworld Trading Ltd* [2004] Ch 120, [2003] ECR I-12537, ECJ. The fact that the later trade mark would call the earlier trade mark to mind for the average consumer is tantamount to the existence of such a link: Case C-252/07 *Intel Corpn Inc v CPM United Kingdom Ltd* [2008] ECR I-8823, [2009] IP & T 559, ECJ. In the infringement context, the necessary link will not be established if the public views the sign purely as an embellishment: Case C-408/01 *Adidas-Salomon AG v Fitnessworld Trading Ltd* above.

8   Case C-487/07 *L'Oréal SA v Bellure NV* [2010] All ER (EC) 28, [2009] ECR I-5185, ECJ. See also Case C-408/01 *Adidas-Salomon AG v Fitnessworld Trading Ltd* [2004] Ch 120 at [37], [2003] ECR I-12537 at [39] per Jacobs Adv-Gen (opinion). The intention of the applicant or defendant is an important factor in determining whether there is unfair advantage: *Whirlpool Corpn v Kenwood Ltd* [2009] EWCA Civ 753, [2010] RPC 51, [2010] IP & T 203; *L'Oreal SA v Bellure NV* [2010] EWCA Civ 535, [2010] RPC 687, [2010] IP & T 1094; *Specsavers International Healthcare Ltd v Asda Stores Ltd* [2012] EWCA Civ 24, [2012] FSR 555. In essence, the court is required to make a judgment as to whether use of the mark applied for would amount, or the use of the sign does amount, to unfair competition: *Red Bull GmbH v Sun Mark Ltd* [2012] EWHC 1929 (Ch), [2012] All ER (D) 186 (Jul). In the registration context, it is sufficient for evidence to be produced of a real risk of unfair advantage in the future: Case C-197/07P *Aktieselskabet af 21 November 2001 v Office for Harmonisation in the Internal Market (Trade Marks and Designs)* [2008] ECR I-193, ECJ. Evidence of how the trade mark applied for has actually been used may be taken as indicating the probability of future unfair advantage: Case T-59/08 *Nute Partecipazioni SpA v Office for Harmonisation of the Internal Market (Trade Marks and Designs)* [2010] ECR II-5595, [2011] ETMR 19, EGC (advertisements creating impression that there was a connection between the respective trade

marks); Case T-332/10 *Viaguara SA v Office for Harmonisation in the Internal Market (Trade Marks and Designs)* [2012] ECR II-0000, EGC (advertisements for VIAGUARA beverages promoting association with male potency showed unfair advantage likely to be taken of repute of VIAGRA). The fact that the respective goods or services are in remote economic fields may be offset where the earlier trade mark has a high reputation: Case T-60/10 *Jackson International Trading Co Kurt D Brühl GmbH & Co, KG v Office for Harmonisation in the Internal Market (Trade Marks and Designs)* [2012] ECR II-0000, [2012] All ER (D) 2727 (Jul), EGC (ROYAL SHAKESPEARE for beverages and bar services would take unfair advantage of ROYAL SHAKESPEARE COMPANY).

9　　Case C-487/07 *L'Oréal SA v Bellure NV* [2010] All ER (EC) 28, [2009] ECR I-5185, ECJ. See also Case C-408/01 *Adidas-Salomon AG v Fitnessworld Trading Ltd* [2004] Ch 120 at [37], [2003] ECR I-12537 at [38] per Jacobs Adv-Gen (opinion). Detrimental effect occurs where the later mark is used for goods or services which provoke a reaction of annoyance or displeasure, whether through their intrinsic nature or because of the unpleasant mental association with the goods for which the earlier mark is reputed: Case R-1004/2000–1 *Ferrero SpA v Kindercare Learning Centers LLC* [2005] ETMR 6, OHIM Board of Appeal; Case T-357/09 *Emilio Pucci International BV v Office for Harmonisation in the Internal Market (Trade Marks and Designs)* [2012] ECR II-0000, EGC (use of EMIDIO TUCCI in respect of toilet paper likely to cause negative associations with earlier mark EMILIO PUCCI for luxury clothing, but not use in relation to firearms, explosives etc). If there is nothing in the later mark itself, or the goods or services in relation to which it is used, which has such a detrimental effect, it is immaterial that the later mark may be used in a context with which the proprietor of the earlier trade mark may not wish to be associated: *United Group plc v Unite the Union* (0/219/13), Appointed Person.

10　Case C-252/07 *Intel Corpn Inc v CPM United Kingdom Ltd* [2008] ECR I-8823, [2009] IP & T 559, ECJ; Case C-487/07 *L'Oréal SA v Bellure NV* [2010] All ER (EC) 28, [2009] ECR I-5185, ECJ. See also Case C-408/01 *Adidas-Salomon AG v Fitnessworld Trading Ltd* [2004] Ch 120 at [37], [2003] ECR I-12537 at [37] per Jacobs Adv-Gen (opinion). The more unique the earlier trade mark, the greater the likelihood that use of an identical or similar later mark will be detrimental to its distinctive character: Case C-252/07 *Intel Corpn Inc v CPM United Kingdom Ltd* above. Proof of detriment to the distinctive character of a trade mark requires evidence of a change in the economic behaviour of the average consumer consequent on the use of an offending mark, or a serious likelihood that such a change will occur in the future: Case C-252/07 *Intel Corpn Inc v CPM United Kingdom Ltd*. This does not mean that evidence of an actual change is required: Case C-100/11P *Helena Rubinstein SNC v Office for Harmonisation in the Internal Market (Trade Marks and Designs)* [2012] ECR II-0000, ECJ. See also Case C-383/12 P *Environmental Manufacturing LLP v Office for Harmonisation in the Internal Market (Trade Marks and Designs)* [2013] All ER(D) 196 (Nov), ECJ where it was said that the wording in Case C-252/07 *Intel Corpn Inc v CPM United Kingdom Ltd* above was explicit and that the concept of 'change in the economic behaviour of the average consumer' laid down an objective condition. That change could not be deduced solely from subjective elements like consumers' perceptions; evidence was not required to be adduced of actual detriment, but serious risk of such detriment allowing the use of logical deductions. Nonetheless, such deductions should not be the result of mere suppositions but had to be founded on 'an analysis of the probabilities and by taking account of the normal practice in the relevant commercial sector as well as all the other circumstances of the case'.

　　　For a general discussion of the concept of dilution see Schecter *The Rational Basis of Trademark Protection* (1926) 40 Harv L Rev 813; Martino *Trademark Dilution* (1st Edn, 1996); Mostert *Famous and Well-Known Marks* (2nd Edn, 2004).

61.　Refusal by virtue of an earlier right; meaning of 'earlier right'. A trade mark[1] must not be registered[2] if, or to the extent that, its use[3] in the United Kingdom[4] is liable to be prevented[5]:

(1)　by virtue of any rule of law (in particular, the law of passing off[6]) protecting an unregistered trade mark or other sign used in the course of trade[7]; or

(2)　by virtue of an earlier right[8], in particular by virtue of the law of copyright[9], design right[10] or registered designs[11].

A person thus entitled to prevent the use of a trade mark is referred to in the Trade Marks Act 1994 as the proprietor of an 'earlier right' in relation to the trade mark[12].

1   As to the meaning of 'trade mark' see PARA 41.
2   As to the meaning of 'registered' see PARA 21 note 2. In the case of an international trade mark, the mark 'becomes protected': see PARAS 11 et seq, 39 note 8.
3   As to the meaning of 'use' see PARA 44 note 8.
4   As to the meaning of 'United Kingdom' see PARA 3 note 2.
5   Trade Marks Act 1994 s 5(4). See also European Parliament and Council Directive (EC) 2008/95 (OJ L299, 8.11.2008, p 25) to approximate the laws of the member states relating to trade marks, art 4(4)(b), (c) (formerly Council Directive (EEC) 89/104 (OJ L40, 11.2.89, p 1) art 4(4)(b), (c)).
6   As to passing off see PARA 287 et seq. In this context the correct approach is to consider whether normal and fair use of the trade mark applied for would result in passing off: *WILD CHILD Trade Mark* [1998] RPC 455, Appointed Person; *CORGI Trade Mark* [1999] RPC 549, Appointed Person. This requires consideration of the effect upon the opponent's customers and potential customers, not upon the average consumer: Joined Cases T-114/07 and T-115/07 *Last Minute Network Ltd v Office for Harmonisation in the Internal Market (Trade Marks and Designs)* [2009] ECR II-1919, [2010] IP & T 77, [2010] ETMR 35, CFI; *Maier v ASOS plc* [2013] EWHC 2831 (Ch), [2013] All ER (D) 185 (Sep). Normally the issue must be determined as at the date of the filing of the application (Joined Cases T-114/07 and T-115/07 *Last Minute Network Ltd v Office for Harmonisation in the Internal Market (Trade Marks and Designs)* above; Case T-303/08 *Tresplain Investments Ltd v Office for Harmonisation in the Internal Market (Trade Marks and Designs)* [2010] ECR II-5659, EGC (affd Case C-76/11P [2011] ETMR 22, ECJ)); but if the mark applied for was in issue at that date, it would appear necessary to consider the position as at the date the use of the mark commenced: Case R 784/2010–2 *Sun Capital Partners, Inc v Sun Capital Partners Ltd* (14 December 2012) OHIM Board of Appeal; cf *Maier v ASOS plc* above; and see PARA 290. If the applicant is the senior user he should prevail, at least so far as the application corresponds to his earlier use: *Croom's Trade Mark Application* [2005] RPC 23, Appointed Person; *Taplanes Ltd's Trade Mark Application* (O/135/06), Appointed Person.
       It is sufficient for this purpose that use of the trade mark applied for would constitute extended passing off (see PARA 302): Case T-304/09 *Tilda Riceland Pte Ltd v Office for Harmonisation in the Internal Market (Trade Marks and Designs)* [2012] ETMR 15, EGC.
7   Trade Marks Act 1994 s 5(4)(a). As to the meaning of 'trade' see PARA 44 note 4.
8   Ie other than those referred to in the Trade Marks Act 1994 s 5(1)–(3) (see PARAS 55–56, 59) or s 5(4)(a) (see head (1) in the text).
9   As to copyright see COPYRIGHT vol 23 (2013) PARA 603 et seq.
10   As to design right see COPYRIGHT vol 23 (2013) PARAS 610, 1048 et seq.
11   Trade Marks Act 1994 s 5(4)(b). As to registered designs see PATENTS AND REGISTERED DESIGNS vol 79 (2008) PARA 681 et seq.
12   Trade Marks Act 1994 s 5(4). See also note 5. As to the position where the proprietor of the earlier mark consents to the registration see the Trade Marks Act 1994 s 5(5); and PARA 62.

62. Permission of the proprietor of an earlier trade mark or earlier right.

Nothing in the relative grounds for refusal of registration[1] prevents the registration of a trade mark[2] where the proprietor of the earlier trade mark[3] or other earlier right[4] consents to the registration[5].

1   Ie the Trade Marks Act 1994 s 5: see PARAS 55–61. As to the meaning of 'registration' see PARA 21 note 2.
2   As to the meaning of 'trade mark' see PARA 41.
3   As to the meaning of 'earlier trade mark' see PARA 54.
4   As to the meaning of 'earlier right' see PARA 61.
5   Trade Marks Act 1994 s 5(5). See also European Parliament and Council Directive (EC) 2008/95 (OJ L299, 8.11.2008, p 25) to approximate the laws of the member states relating to trade marks, art 4(5) (formerly Council Directive (EEC) 89/104 (OJ L40, 11.2.89, p 1) art 4(5)). An argument that the Trade Marks Act 1994 s 5(5) had been impliedly repealed by the Trade Marks (Relative Grounds) Order 2007, SI 2007/1976, was rejected in *Omega Engineering Inc v Omega SA (Omega AG) (Omega Ltd)* [2010] EWHC 1211 (Ch), [2010] ETMR 49 (affd [2011] EWCA Civ 645, [2011] All ER (D) 4 (Jun), [2011] ETMR 40). A coexistence agreement between the parties in which the proprietor of the earlier trade mark undertakes not to object to the registration of the trade mark applied for constitutes consent for this purpose: *Omega Engineering Inc v Omega SA (Omega AG) (Omega Ltd)*. It is not clear whether consent given after registration is sufficient. In relation to Community trade marks, consent may be given at

any time before the validity of the registration is challenged: see Council Regulation (EC) 207/2009 (OJ L78, 24.3.2009, p 1) on the Community trade mark, art 53(3); and PARA 227.

63. Raising of relative grounds in opposition proceedings in case of non-use. In opposition proceedings[1], where:

(1)   an application for registration of a trade mark[2] has been published[3];

(2)   there is an earlier trade mark of a certain kind[4] in relation to which the specified conditions[5] obtain; and

(3)   the registration procedure for the earlier trade mark was completed before the start of the period of five years ending with the date of publication[6],

the registrar[7] must not refuse to register the trade mark by reason of the earlier trade mark unless the 'use conditions' are met[8]. The 'use conditions' are met if:

(a)   within the period of five years ending with the date of publication of the application, the earlier trade mark has been put to genuine use[9] in the United Kingdom[10] by the proprietor or with his consent in relation to the goods or services for which it is registered[11]; or

(b)   the earlier trade mark has not been so used, but there are proper reasons[12] for non-use[13].

Where an earlier trade mark satisfies the use conditions in respect of some only of the goods or services for which it is registered, it must be treated for these purposes as if it were registered only in respect of those goods or services[14].

1   As to opposition proceedings see PARA 366 et seq.
2   As to the requirements for registration see PARA 39 et seq; and as to the procedure on the application see PARA 334 et seq. As to the meaning of 'trade mark' see PARA 41; and as to the meaning of 'registration' see PARA 21 note 2.
3   As to the meaning of 'publish' see PARA 19 note 10.
4   Ie an earlier trade mark of a kind falling within the Trade Marks Act 1994 s 6(1)(a), (b) or (ba): see PARA 54 heads (1)–(3)). As to the meaning of 'earlier trade mark' see PARA 54.
5   Ie the conditions specified in the Trade Marks Act 1994 s 5(1), (2) or (3): see PARAS 55–56, 59.
6   Cf the Trade Marks Act 1994 s 46(1)(a): see PARA 98.
7   As to the registrar see PARA 19.
8   Trade Marks Act 1994 s 6A(1), (2) (s 6A added by SI 2004/946; and the Trade Marks Act 1994 s 6A(1) amended by SI 2008/1067). See also European Parliament and Council Directive (EC) 2008/95 (OJ L299, 8.11.2008, p 25) to approximate the laws of the member states relating to trade marks, art 11(2) (formerly Council Directive (EEC) 89/104 (OJ L40, 11.2.89, p 1) art 11(2)). Nothing in the Trade Marks Act 1994 s 6A affects: (1) the refusal of the registration on the grounds mentioned in s 3 (absolute grounds for refusal: see PARA 42 et seq) or s 5(4) (refusal by virtue of an earlier right: see PARA 61); or (2) the making of an application for a declaration of invalidity under s 47(2) (application on relative grounds where no consent to registration: see PARA 103): s 6A(7) (as so added).
9   For these purposes, use of a trade mark includes use in a form differing in elements which do not alter the distinctive character of the mark in the form in which it was registered: Trade Marks Act 1994 s 6A(4)(a) (as added: see note 8). Cf s 46(2): see PARA 98.
       As to the meaning of 'genuine use' see PARA 98 note 6; and as to the meaning of 'use' generally see PARA 44 note 8.
10 For these purposes, use in the United Kingdom includes affixing the trade mark to goods or to the packaging of goods in the United Kingdom solely for export purposes: Trade Marks Act 1994 s 6A(4)(b) (as added: see note 8). Cf s 46(2): see PARA 98. In relation to a Community trade mark or an international trade mark (EC), any reference to the United Kingdom in s 6A(3), (4) must be construed as a reference to the European Union: s 6A(5) (as so added; and amended by SI 2008/1067; and SI 2011/1043). As to the meaning of 'United Kingdom' generally see PARA 3 note 2.
11 Trade Marks Act 1994 s 6A(3)(a) (as added: see note 8). See also note 10.
12 As to proper reasons see PARA 98 note 10.
13 Trade Marks Act 1994 s 6A(3)(b) (as added: see note 8). See also note 10.
14 Trade Marks Act 1994 s 6A(6) (as added: see note 8).

64. Power to require that relative grounds be raised in opposition proceedings. The Secretary of State[1] may by order provide that in any case a trade mark[2] must not be refused registration on relative grounds for refusal[3] unless objection on that ground is raised in opposition proceedings[4] by the proprietor of the earlier trade mark[5] or other earlier right[6]. The order may make such consequential provision as appears to the Secretary of State appropriate[7]:

(1)   with respect to the carrying out by the registrar[8] of searches of earlier trade marks[9]; and

(2)   as to the persons by whom an application for a declaration of invalidity may be made[10] on relative grounds[11].

Such an order must be made by statutory instrument; and no order may be made unless a draft of it has been laid before and approved by a resolution of each House of Parliament[12]. Such an order may contain such transitional provisions as appear to the Secretary of State to be appropriate[13].

1   As to the Secretary of State see PARA 16.
2   As to the meaning of 'trade mark' see PARA 41.
3   Ie a ground mentioned in the Trade Marks Act 1994 s 5: see PARAS 55–62.
4   As to opposition proceedings see PARA 366 et seq.
5   As to the meaning of 'earlier trade mark' see PARA 54.
6   Trade Marks Act 1994 s 8(1). The Trade Marks (Relative Grounds) Order 2007, SI 2007/1976, makes such provision: arts 1, 2. See PARA 382.
       As to the meaning of 'earlier right' see PARA 61. The Trade Marks Act 1994 s 7 (see further below) does not apply where there is an order in force under s 8: s 7(5).
       Where on an application for the registration of a trade mark it appears to the registrar: (1) that there is an earlier trade mark in relation to which the conditions specified in s 5(1), (2) or (3) (see PARAS 55–56, 59) obtain (s 7(1)(a)); or (2) that there is an earlier right in relation to which the condition set out in s 5(4) (see PARA 61) is satisfied (s 7(1)(b)), but the applicant shows to the satisfaction of the registrar that there has been honest concurrent use (see s 7(3) below) of the trade mark for which registration is sought (s 7(1)), the registrar must not refuse the application by reason of the earlier trade mark or other earlier right unless objection on that ground is raised in opposition proceedings by the proprietor of that earlier trade mark or other earlier right (s 7(2)). 'Honest concurrent use' means such use in the United Kingdom, by the applicant or with his consent, as would formerly have amounted to honest concurrent use for the purposes of the Trade Marks Act 1938: Trade Marks Act 1994 s 7(3). Nothing in s 7 affects: (a) the refusal of registration on the grounds mentioned in s 3 (absolute grounds for refusal: see PARA 42 et seq); or (b) the making of an application for a declaration of invalidity under s 47(2) (application on relative grounds where no consent to registration: see PARA 103): s 7(4). As to the requirements for registration see PARA 39 et seq; and as to the procedure on the application see PARA 334 et seq. As to the meaning of 'registration' see PARA 21 note 2. As to appeals from any decision of the registrar see ss 76, 77; and PARA 387 et seq. As to the meaning of 'United Kingdom' see PARA 3 note 2.
       There is no provision corresponding to the Trade Marks Act 1994 s 7 in Council Directive (EEC) 89/104 (OJ L40, 11.2.89, p 1) to approximate the laws of the member states relating to trade marks (see now European Parliament and Council Directive (EC) 2008/95 (OJ L299, 8.11.2008, p 25)).
7   Trade Marks Act 1994 s 8(2).
8   As to the registrar see PARA 19.
9   Trade Marks Act 1994 s 8(2)(a). An order making such provision as is mentioned in s 8(2)(a) may direct that so much of s 37 (see PARA 354) as requires a search to be carried out is to cease to have effect: s 8(3). The Trade Marks (Relative Grounds) Order 2007, SI 2007/1976, arts 3, 4 make such provision. See also PARA 354.
10   Ie made on the grounds specified in the Trade Marks Act 1994 s 47(2): see PARA 103.
11   Trade Marks Act 1994 s 8(2)(b). An order making such provision as is mentioned in s 8(2)(b) may provide that so much of s 47(3) (see PARAS 378, 441) as provides that any person may make an application for a declaration of invalidity is to have effect subject to the provisions of the order: s 8(4). The Trade Marks (Relative Grounds) Order 2007, SI 2007/1976, art 5 makes such provision: see PARA 103 notes 5, 8, and see also PARA 382.
12   Trade Marks Act 1994 s 8(5). No such draft of an order making such provision as is mentioned in s 8(1) (see the text and notes 1–6) may be laid before Parliament until after the end of the

period of ten years beginning with the day on which applications for Community trade marks may first be filed in pursuance of the Community Trade Mark Regulation: Trade Marks Act 1994 s 8(5). As to the meaning of 'Community trade mark' see PARA 189. The 'Community Trade Mark Regulation' means Council Regulation (EC) 40/94 of 20 December 1993 (OJ L11, 14.1.94, p 1), on the Community trade mark (see now Council Regulation (EC) 207/2009 (OJ L78, 24.3.2009, p 1) (see PARA 159): Trade Marks Act 1994 s 51.
13   Trade Marks Act 1994 s 8(6).

(iv) Registration subject to Disclaimer or Limitation

65. In general. An applicant for registration[1] of a trade mark[2], or the proprietor of a registered trade mark[3], may:

(1)   disclaim any right to the exclusive use[4] of any specified element of the trade mark[5]; or

(2)   agree that the rights conferred by the registration are to be subject to a specified territorial or other limitation[6].

Where the registration of a trade mark is subject to a disclaimer or limitation, the rights conferred by a registered trade mark[7] are restricted accordingly[8]. Disclaimers and limitations can similarly be made in relation to an international trade mark for which protection is sought or has been obtained in the United Kingdom[9].

Where the applicant for registration of a trade mark or the proprietor by notice in writing sent to the registrar disclaims any right to the exclusive use of any specified element of the trade mark or agrees that the rights conferred by the registrations are to be subject to a specified territorial or other limitation, the registrar must make the appropriate entry in the register and must publish[10] such disclaimer or limitation[11]. In the case of international trade marks, such entries are placed in the supplemental register[12].

There is no longer an explicit power in the registrar to call for a disclaimer or limitation[13]. Nevertheless it seems clear that, in determining the distinctiveness or otherwise of a mark, the registrar is able to take account of any offered disclaimer or limitation[14]. It is not certain whether or not the tribunal in proceedings for revocation or a declaration of invalidity of a registration could, as a matter of discretion, order that the relief be granted unless the proprietor made an appropriate disclaimer or limitation[15].

1   As to the meaning of 'registration' see PARA 21 note 2.
2   As to the meaning of 'trade mark' see PARA 41.
3   As to the meaning of 'registered trade mark' see PARA 111.
4   As to the meaning of 'use' see PARA 44 note 8.
5   Trade Marks Act 1994 s 13(1)(a).
6   Trade Marks Act 1994 s 13(1)(b). It is not possible to amend the trade mark itself under s 13(1)(b) since such amendments are only permissible under s 39 (see PARAS 356–357): *Nestlé SA's Trade Mark Application* [2004] EWCA Civ 1008, [2005] RPC 77, sub nom *Société des Produits Nestlé SA v Mars UK Ltd* [2005] IP & T 551 (in which it was held that it was not permissible to specify the colour and size of a shape mark under the Trade Marks Act 1994 s 13 or s 39). It may, however, be possible to specify more precisely a colour which has not been sufficiently clearly identified: *Ty Nant Spring Water Ltd's Trade Mark Application* [2000] RPC 55, [1999] ETMR 981, Appointed Person; *Robert McBride Ltd's Trade Mark Application* [2003] RPC 343, Appointed Person; and see PARA 348 note 6.
     It is not permissible to limit the goods or services in respect of which the trade mark is registered by reference to the absence of a particular characteristic: see PARA 345 note 7.
7   Ie the rights conferred by the Trade Marks Act 1994 s 9: see PARAS 66–67.
8   Trade Marks Act 1994 s 13(1); and see PARA 82. There is no reference to disclaimers or limitations in Council Directive (EEC) 89/104 (OJ L40, 11.2.89, p 1) to approximate the laws of the member states relating to trade marks (now European Parliament and Council Directive (EC) 2008/95 (OJ L299, 8.11.2008, p 25)).

Provision must be made by rules as to the publication and entry in the register of a disclaimer or limitation: Trade Marks Act 1994 s 13(2). In exercise of the power so conferred the Secretary of State has made the Trade Marks Rules 2008, SI 2008/1797, r 31: see the text and notes 10–11. As to the Secretary of State see PARA 16. As to the making of rules generally see PARA 17. As to the register see PARA 21.

     A disclaimer or limitation entered on the former register in relation to an existing registered mark immediately before 31 October 1994 had to be transferred to the new register and has effect as if entered on the register in pursuance of the Trade Marks Act 1994 s 13: s 105, Sch 3 para 3(2). As to the meaning of 'existing registered mark' see PARA 4 note 2. The system of conditions on registration is no longer continued: see Sch 3 para 3(1); and PARA 21.

9   See the Trade Marks (International Registration) Order 2008, SI 2008/2206, art 3; and PARA 12. See also generally PARA 11 et seq.

10   As to the meaning of 'publish' see PARA 19 note 10.

11   Trade Marks Rules 2008, SI 2008/1797, r 31.

12   See the Trade Marks (International Registration) Order 2008, SI 2008/2206, art 3; and PARA 21. See also generally PARA 11 et seq.

13   Ie as there was under the Trade Marks Act 1938 s 17(2) (repealed).

14   See *Nestlé SA's Trade Mark Application* [2004] EWCA Civ 1008, [2005] RPC 77, sub nom *Société des Produits Nestlé SA v Mars UK Ltd* [2005] IP & T 551.

15   Under the former law a disclaimer could be ordered: *Re Trade Marks Nos 39, 759 and 247, 273, J Wigfull & Sons Ltd v J Jackson & Son Ltd* [1916] 1 Ch 213, 33 RPC 97.

(4) INFRINGEMENT OF REGISTERED TRADE MARKS AND PROTECTED INTERNATIONAL TRADE MARKS (UK)

(i) Nature of Infringement

66. Rights conferred by registered trade mark. The proprietor of a registered trade mark[1] has exclusive rights in the trade mark which are infringed by use[2] of the trade mark in the United Kingdom[3] without his consent[4]. The same rights are enjoyed by the holder of a protected international trade mark (UK)[5].

1   As to the meaning of 'registered trade mark' see PARA 111.

2   As to the meaning of 'use' for the purposes of infringement see PARA 72; and as to the meaning of 'use' generally see PARA 44 note 8.

3   Use of a trade mark abroad may 'spill over' into the United Kingdom (eg where a person advertises on the internet or in publications which have international circulations: see *Euromarket Designs Inc v Peters* [2000] IP & T 1290, [2001] FSR 288). The test as to whether the use is use within the jurisdiction is the use is targeted at consumers within the jurisdiction: Case C-324/09 *L'Oréal SA v eBay International AG* [2012] All ER (EC) 501, [2011] ETMR 52, ECJ; *Euromarket Designs Inc v Peters*; *800-FLOWERS Trade Mark Application, 1–800 Flowers Inc v Phonenames Ltd* [2000] FSR 697, [2000] ETMR 369 (affd [2001] EWCA Civ 721, [2001] IP & T 839, [2002] FSR 191); *Stichting BDO v BDO Unibank Inc* [2013] EWHC 418 (Ch), [2013] All ER (D) 39 (Mar), [2013] ETMR 31. See also *Beautimatic International Ltd v Mitchell International Pharmaceuticals Ltd* [1999] IP & T 59, [2000] FSR 267 (manufacture of packaging in the United Kingdom for use on goods overseas). As to the meaning of 'United Kingdom' see PARA 3 note 2.

4   Trade Marks Act 1994 s 9(1) (part of which is derived from Council Directive (EEC) 89/104 (OJ L40, 11.2.89, p 1) to approximate the laws of the member states relating to trade marks, art 5(1), first sentence) (see now European Parliament and Council Directive (EC) 2008/95 (OJ L299, 8.11.2008, p 25) art 5(1))). The acts amounting to infringement, if done without the consent of the proprietor, are specified in the Trade Marks Act 1994 s 10 (see PARA 68 et seq): s 9(1). References in the Trade Marks Act 1994 to infringement of a registered trade mark are to any such infringement of the rights of the proprietor: s 9(2).

     Section 9(1) has been described as a 'chatty introduction' to the infringement provisions in s 10, adding no more than that the acts concerned must be done without consent: *British Sugar plc v James Robertson & Sons Ltd* [1996] RPC 281 at 291, [1996–97] ETMR 118 at 122 per Jacob J; and see also *Euromarket Designs Inc v Peters* [2000] IP & T 1290, [2001] FSR 288.

As to the meaning of references to doing anything with or without the consent of the proprietor of a registered trade mark see further the Trade Marks Act 1994 s 28(3); and PARA 119. As to what may constitute consent see PARA 84.

Where the registration of a trade mark is subject to a disclaimer or limitation, the rights conferred by the Trade Marks Act 1994 s 9 are restricted accordingly: see s 13(1); and PARA 82.

The exclusive rights conferred by s 9(1) do not override another's passing off rights: *Inter Lotto (UK) Ltd v Camelot Group plc* [2003] EWCA Civ 1132, [2003] 4 All ER 575, [2004] 1 WLR 955.

The Trade Marks Act 1994 s 9 applies in relation to an existing registered mark as from 31 October 1994, subject to s 105, Sch 3 para 4(2) (see PARA 81): Sch 3 para 4(1). The old law continues to apply in relation to infringements committed before that date: Sch 3 para 4(1). As to the meaning of 'existing registered mark' see PARA 4 note 2; and as to the meaning of 'the old law' see PARA 4 note 3.

As to the registrar's power to suspend trade mark rights of an enemy or enemy subject see PARA 92.

5　See the Trade Marks (International Registration) Order 2008, SI 2008/2206, art 3; and PARA 12. See also generally PARA 11 et seq.

67. Date from which rights run. The rights of the proprietor of a registered trade mark[1] have effect from the date of registration, that is to say[2], the date of filing of the application for registration[3], provided that:

(1)　no infringement proceedings[4] may be begun before the date on which the trade mark is in fact registered[5]; and

(2)　no offence of the unauthorised use of a trade mark etc in relation to goods[6] is committed by anything done before the date of publication of the registration[7].

1　As to the meaning of 'registered trade mark' see PARA 111. As to such rights see PARA 66.
2　Ie in accordance with the Trade Marks Act 1994 s 40(3): see PARA 23.
3　Trade Marks Act 1994 s 9(3). For transitional provisions see PARA 68 note 8. In relation to a protected international trade mark (UK) see the Trade Marks (International Registration) Order 2008, SI 2008/2206, art 3; and PARA 12. See also generally PARA 11 et seq.
4　For these purposes, 'infringement proceedings', in relation to a registered trade mark, includes proceedings under the Trade Marks Act 1994 s 16 (order for delivery up of infringing goods etc: see PARA 444): s 103(1).
5　Trade Marks Act 1994 s 9(3) proviso (a). As to procedure on application see PARA 334 et seq. See note 3.
6　Ie under the Trade Marks Act 1994 s 92: see PARAS 124–127.
7　Trade Marks Act 1994 s 9(3) proviso (b). See note 3.

68. Identical sign for identical goods or services. A person infringes a registered trade mark[1] if he uses[2] in the course of trade[3] a sign[4] which is identical[5] with the trade mark in relation to[6] goods or services which are identical[7] with those for which it is registered[8] provided that such use affects, or is liable to affect, one of the functions of the trade mark[9].

1　This also applies to a protected international trade mark (UK): see PARA 66. As to the meaning of 'registered trade mark' see PARA 111.
2　As to the meaning of 'use' for the purposes of infringement see PARA 72. In order to constitute infringement, the acts must be done without the consent of the proprietor: see the Trade Marks Act 1994 s 9(1); and PARA 66. As to the meaning of 'use' generally see PARA 44 note 8.
3　Use is 'in the course of trade' when it takes place in the context of commercial activity with a view to economic advantage and not as a private matter: Case C-206/01 *Arsenal Football Club plc v Reed* [2003] Ch 454, [2003] All ER (EC) 1, [2002] ECR I-10273, ECJ; Case C-48/05 *Adam Opel AG v Autec AG* [2007] ECR I-1017, [2007] IP & T 408, ECJ; Case C-17/06 *Céline SARL v Céline SA* [2007] ECR I-7041, [2008] IP & T 684, ECJ; Case C-533/06 *O2 Holdings Ltd v Hutchison 3G Ltd* [2008] ECR I-4231, [2008] IP & T 1069, ECJ; Joined Cases C-236/08, C-237/08 and C-238/08 *Google France SARL v Louis Vuitton Malletier SA; Google France SARL v Viaticum SA; Google France SARL v Centre national de recherche en relations humaines (CNRRH) SARL* [2011] All ER (EC) 411, [2010] ECR I-2417, ECJ. As to the

meaning of 'trade' see PARA 44 note 4. Use for political purposes is not use in the course of trade: *Unilever plc v Griffin* [2010] EWHC 899 (Ch), [2010] FSR 814 (use in party political television broadcast).

4   In order to decide whether the sign is identical or similar to the registered trade mark, the court must first ascertain what sign the defendant is using: Case C-291/00 *LTJ Diffusion SA v Sadas Vertbaudet SA* [2003] ECR I-2799 at [49], [2003] IP & T 994 at [49] per the opinion of Jacobs Adv-Gen; *Reed Executive plc v Reed Business Information Ltd* [2004] EWCA Civ 159, [2004] RPC 767, [2004] IP & T 1049. As to the meaning of 'sign' see PARA 41 note 1.

5   As to the meaning of 'identical' in this context see PARA 55 note 3.

6   Use of a sign 'in relation to' goods or services means use 'for the purposes of distinguishing' the goods or services in question, that is to say, as a trade mark as such: Case C-63/97 *Bayerische Motorenwerke AG v Deenik*[1999] All ER (EC) 235, [1999] ECR I-905, ECJ; Case C-245/02 *Anheuser-Busch Inc v Budejovicky Budvar np* [2004] ECR I-10989, [2007] IP & T 348, ECJ; Case C-17/06 *Céline SARL v Céline SA* [2007] ECR I-7041, [2008] IP & T 684, ECJ; and c f Case C-23/01 *Robelco NV v Robeco Groep NV* [2002] ECR I-10913, ECJ. This question is to be assessed from the perspective of the average consumer: *Schütz (UK) Ltd v Delta Containers UK Ltd* [2011] EWHC 1712 (Ch), [2011] All ER (D) 37 (Jul); *Red Bull GmbH v Sun Mark Ltd* [2012] EWHC 1929 (Ch) at [130], [2012] All ER (D) 186 (Jul). See also *British Sugar plc v James Robertson & Sons Ltd* [1996] RPC 281 at 293, [1996–97] ETMR 118 at 124 per Jacob J, explaining *Bravado Merchandising Services Ltd v Mainstream Publishing Ltd* [1996] FSR 205, 1996 SLT 597, Ct of Sess; *Trebor Bassett Ltd v Football Association* [1997] FSR 211 (trade mark on jersey of footballers not used in relation to photographs of those footballers); *Avnet Ltd v Isoact Ltd* [1998] FSR 16.

Use for purely descriptive purposes is not use 'in relation to' the goods or services because it is not use for the purposes of distinguishing those goods or services: Case C-2/00 *Hölterhoff v Freiesleben* [2002] All ER (EC) 665, [2002] ECR I-4187, ECJ. It would appear that the same is true of use for purely decorative purposes: Case C-102/07 *Adidas AG v Marca Mode CV* [2008] ECR I-2439, [2009] IP & T 279, ECJ. An alternative explanation of these cases is that the use does not adversely affect any of the functions of the trade mark: see PARA 69.

Use of a sign identical to the trade mark in comparative advertising amounts to use of that sign 'in relation to' the advertiser's goods or services as well the trade mark proprietor's goods or services: Case C-533/06 *O2 Holdings Ltd v Hutchison 3G Ltd* [2008] ECR I-4231, [2008] IP & T 1069, ECJ.

It should be noted that this issue does not arise in the registration context, where it is assumed that the trade mark applied for is to be used in relation to the specified goods or services, and the same assumption is made with respect to any earlier mark (subject to proof of use).

7   As to the meaning of 'identical' in this context see PARA 55 note 5.

8   Trade Marks Act 1994 s 10(1) (derived from Council Directive (EEC) 89/104 (OJ L40, 11.2.89, p 1) to approximate the laws of the member states relating to trade marks, art 5(1)(a) (see now European Parliament and Council Directive (EC) 2008/95 (OJ L299, 8.11.2008, p 25) art 5(1)(a))). Cf the corresponding relative ground of refusal: see the Trade Marks Act 1994 s 5(1); and PARA 55. As to the limits on the effect of a registered trade mark see PARA 74 et seq; and as to the exhaustion of rights conferred by a registered trade mark see PARA 87.

The Trade Marks Act 1994 s 10 applies in relation to an existing registered mark as from 31 October 1994, subject to s 105, Sch 3 para 4(2) (see PARA 81): Sch 3 para 4(1). The old law continues to apply in relation to infringements committed before that date: Sch 3 para 4(1). As to the meaning of 'existing registered mark' see PARA 4 note 2; and as to the meaning of 'the old law' see PARA 4 note 3.

9   See in particular Case C-206/01 *Arsenal Football plc v Reed* [2003] Ch 454, [2003] All ER (EC) 1, [2002] ECR I-10273 at 51, ECJ; Case C-245/02 *Anheuser-Busch Inc v Budejovicky Budvar np* [2004] ECR I-10989, [2007] IP & T 348, ECJ; Case C-48/05 *Adam Opel AG v Autec AG* [2007] ECR I-1017, [2007] IP & T 408, ECJ; Case C-17/06 *Céline SARL v Céline SA* [2007] ECR I-7041, [2008] IP & T 684, ECJ; Case C-62/08 *UDV North America Inc v Brandtraders NV* [2009] ECR I-1279, [2010] ETMR 25, ECJ; Case C-487/07 *L'Oréal SA v Bellure NV* [2010] All ER (EC) 28, [2009] ECR I-5185 at 58–64, [2010] Bus LR 303, ECJ; Joined Cases C-236/08, C-237/08 and C-238/08 *Google France SARL v Louis Vuitton Malletier SA; Google France SARL v Viaticum SA; Google France SARL v Centre national de recherche en relations humaines (CNRRH) SARL* [2011] All ER (EC) 411, [2010] ECR I-2417, ECJ; Case C-278/08 *Die BergSpechte Outdoor Reisen und Alpinschule Edi Koblmüller GmbH v Guni* [2010] ECR I-2517, [2010] All ER (D) 280 (Mar), ECJ; Case C-91/09 *Eis de GmbH v BBY Vertriebsgesellschaft mbH* [2010] ECR I-43, ECJ; Case C-558/08 *Portakabin Ltd v Primakabin BV* [2010] ECR I-6963, [2011] Bus LR 1339, ECJ; Case C-324/09 *L'Oréal SA v*

eBay International AG [2011] IP & T 819, [2012] All ER (EC) 501, ECJ; Case C-323/09 *Interflora Inc v Marks and Spencer plc* [2011] ECR I-8625, [2013] All ER (EC) 519, [2011] IP & T 888, ECJ. This case law establishes that the proprietor of a registered trade mark can only succeed in a claim a claim under Council Directive (EEC) 89/104 (OJ L40, 11.2.89, p 1) art 5(1)(a) (see now European Parliament and Council Directive (EC) 2008/95 (OJ L299, 8.11.2008, p 25) art 5(1)(a)), which is the equivalent provision to the Trade Marks Act 1994 s 10(1), if six conditions are satisfied: (1) there must be use of a sign by a third party within the relevant territory; (2) the use must be in the course of trade; (3) it must be without the consent of the proprietor of the trade mark; (4) it must be of a sign which is identical to the trade mark; (5) it must be in relation to goods or services which are identical to those for which the trade mark is registered; and (6) it must affect or be liable to affect one of the functions of the trade mark. The sixth condition does not appear on the face of the legislation, but has been read into it as a matter of interpretation: see *L'Oréal SA v eBay International AG* [2009] EWHC 1094 (Ch), [2009] RPC 693 at [288]–[306] per Arnold J; *Datacard Corpn v Eagle Technologies Ltd* [2011] EWHC 244 (Pat) at [244]–[272], [2012] Bus LR 160 at [244]–[272], [2011] RPC 443 at [244]–[272] per Arnold J; *Interflora Inc v Marks & Spencer plc* [2013] EWHC 1291 (Ch), [2013] ETMR 35, [2013] All ER (D) (May) at [177]–[179] per Arnold J. As to effect on the functions of the trade mark see PARA 69.

69.   Effect on the functions of the trade mark.   It is sufficient if the use of the sign affects or is liable to affect one of the functions of the trade mark[1]. The essential function of a trade mark is to guarantee the origin of the goods or services (the 'origin function'). There is an effect on the origin function where the use of the sign is such as to create the impression that there is a material link in course of trade between the goods concerned and the trade mark proprietor, contrary to the fact[2]. In the context of keyword advertising on the internet, there is an effect on the origin function if the advertisement does not enable reasonably well-informed and reasonably circumspect internet users, or enables them only with difficulty, to ascertain whether the goods or services referred to by the advertisement originate from the trade mark proprietor or an undertaking economically connected with it or, on the contrary, originate from a third party[3]. Use of the sign for purely descriptive purposes does not affect the origin function[4]. Nor does use purely as a company or trade name[5].

The European Court of Justice has so far recognised at least two other functions, the 'advertising function' and the 'investment function', although the distinction between these functions is not yet clear. The advertising function refers to the use of the trade mark as a factor in sales promotion or as an instrument in commercial strategy; but an increase in the trade mark proprietor's advertising costs in consequence of a competitor use of an identical sign in keyword advertising does not constitute an effect on the advertising function[6]. The investment function refers to the use of the trade mark to acquire or preserve a reputation capable of attracting consumers and retaining their loyalty, and is capable of being adversely affected by keyword advertising[7].

1   Case C-487/07 *L'Oréal SA v Bellure NV* [2010] All ER (EC) 28, [2009] ECR I-5185, [2010] Bus LR 303, ECJ.
2   Case C-206/01 *Arsenal Football plc v Reed* [2003] Ch 454, [2003] All ER (EC) 1, [2002] ECR I-10273, ECJ.
3   Joined Cases C-236/08, C-237/08 and C-238/08 *Google France SARL v Louis Vuitton Malletier SA; Google France SARL v Viaticum SA; Google France SARL v Centre national de recherche en relations humaines (CNRRH) SARL* [2011] All ER (EC) 411, [2010] ECR I-2417, ECJ; Case C-278/08 *Die BergSpechte Outdoor Reisen und Alpinschule Edi Koblmüller GmbH v Guni* [2010] ECR I-2517, [201] All ER (D) 280 (Mar), ECJ; Case C-91/09 *Eis.de GmbH v BBY Vertriebsgesellschaft mbH* [2010] ECR I-43, ECJ; Case C-558/08 *Portakabin Ltd v Primakabin BV* [2010] ECR I-6963, [2011] Bus LR 1339, ECJ; Case C-324/09 *L'Oréal SA v eBay International AG* [2012] All ER (EC) 501, [2011] IP & T 819, ECJ; Case C-323/09 *Interflora Inc v Marks and Spencer plc* [2011] ECR I-8625, [2013] All ER (EC) 519, [2011] IP & T 888, ECJ. It appears that this places an evidential onus on the advertiser to show that there

is no real risk of confusion: *Interflora Inc v Marks & Spencer plc* [2013] EWHC 1291 (Ch), [2013] ETMR 35, [2013] All ER (D) 238 (May). It also appears that the test is generally applicable and not just to keyword advertising: *Datacard Corpn v Eagle Technologies Ltd* [2011] EWHC 244 (Pat), [2012] Bus LR 160, [2011] RPC 443.

4   Case C-2/00 *Hölterhoff v Freiesleben* [2002] All ER (EC) 665, [2002] ECR I-4187, ECJ. It would appear that the same is true of use for purely decorative purposes: Case C-102/07 *Adidas AG v Marca Mode CV* [2008] ECR I-2439, [2009] IP & T 279, ECJ. An alternative explanation of these cases is that there is no use of the sign 'in relation' to the goods or services because it is not use for the purposes of distinguishing those goods or services: see PARA 68.

5   Case C-245/02 *Anheuser-Busch Inc v Budejovicky Budvar np* [2004] ECR I-10989, [2007] IP & T 348, ECJ. But it is otherwise where the company or trade name is used for the purpose of distinguishing goods or services; Case C-17/06 *Céline SARL v Céline SA* [2007] ECR I-7041, [2008] IP & T 684, ECJ.

6   Joined Cases C-236/08, C-237/08 and C-238/08 *Google France SARL v Louis Vuitton Malletier SA; Google France SARL v Viaticum SA; Google France SARL v Centre national de recherche en relations humaines (CNRRH) SARL* [2011] All ER (EC) 411, [2010] ECR I-2417, ECJ.

7   Case C-323/09 *Interflora Inc v Marks and Spencer plc* [2011] ECR I-8625, [2013] All ER (EC) 519, [2011] IP & T 888, ECJ. It appears that there will be an adverse effect where the image the trade mark conveys is damaged: *Interflora Inc v Marks & Spencer plc* [2013] EWHC 1291 (Ch), [2013] ETMR 35, [2013] All ER (D) 238 (May).

70. Identical sign for similar goods or services; similar sign for identical goods or services.

A person infringes a registered trade mark[1] if he uses[2] in the course of trade[3] a sign[4] where because:

(1)   the sign is identical with the trade mark and is used in relation to goods or services similar to those for which the trade mark is registered[5]; or

(2)   the sign is similar to the trade mark and is used in relation to goods or services identical with or similar to those for which the trade mark is registered[6],

there exists a likelihood of confusion on the part of the public, which includes the likelihood of association with the trade mark[7].

1   This also applies to a protected international trade mark (UK): see PARA 66. As to the meaning of 'registered trade mark' see PARA 111.

2   As to the meaning of 'use' for the purposes of infringement see PARA 89. In order to constitute infringement, the acts must be done without the consent of the proprietor: see the Trade Marks Act 1994 s 9(1); and PARA 66. As to the meaning of 'use' generally see PARA 44 note 8.

3   As to the meaning of 'in the course of trade' see PARA 68 note 3.

4   As to the sign see PARA 68 note 4. As to the meaning of 'sign' see PARA 41 note 1.

5   Trade Marks Act 1994 s 10(2)(a).

6   Trade Marks Act 1994 s 10(2)(b). As to the meaning of 'similar goods and services' see PARA 57.

7   Trade Marks Act 1994 s 10(2) (derived from Council Directive (EEC) 89/104 (OJ L40, 11.2.89, p 1) to approximate the laws of the member states relating to trade marks, art 5(1)(b) (see now European Parliament and Council Directive (EC) 2008/95 (OJ L299, 8.11.2008, p 25) art 5(1)(b))). Cf the corresponding relative ground for refusal of registration: see the Trade Marks Act 1994 s 5(2); and PARA 56. As to the likelihood of confusion see PARA 58. As to the limits on the effect of a registered trade mark see PARA 74 et seq; and as to the exhaustion of rights conferred by a registered trade mark see PARA 87. For transitional provisions see PARA 68 note 7.

As to the interpretation of Council Directive (EEC) 89/104 (OJ L40, 11.2.89, p 1) art 5(1) (see now European Parliament and Council Directive (EC) 2008/95 (OJ L299, 8.11.2008, p 25) art 5(1)) see PARA 68.

71. Identical or similar mark taking unfair advantage of, or being detrimental to, distinctive character or repute of earlier mark.

A person infringes a registered trade mark[1] if he uses[2] in the course of trade[3] in relation to goods or services a sign[4] which is identical with or similar to the trade mark where the trade mark has a reputation in the United Kingdom[5] and the use of the sign, being without due cause[6], takes unfair advantage of, or is detrimental to, the distinctive character or the repute of the trade mark[7].

1   This also applies to a protected international trade mark (UK): see PARA 66. As to the meaning of 'registered trade mark' see PARA 111.
2   As to the meaning of 'use' for the purposes of infringement see PARA 72. In order to constitute infringement, the acts must be done without the consent of the proprietor: see the Trade Marks Act 1994 s 9(1); and PARA 66. As to the meaning of 'use' generally see PARA 44 note 8.
3   As to the meaning of 'in the course of trade' see PARA 68 note 3.
4   As to the sign see PARA 68 note 4. As to the meaning of 'sign' see PARA 41 note 1.
5   As to the meaning of 'United Kingdom' see PARA 3 note 2.
6   As to the concept of use without due cause see PARA 59 note 9.
7   Trade Marks Act 1994 s 10(3) (amended by SI 2004/946) (derived from Council Directive (EEC) 89/104 (OJ L40, 11.2.89, p 1) to approximate the laws of the member states relating to trade marks, art 5(2) (see now European Parliament and Council Directive (EC) 2008/95 (OJ L299, 8.11.2008, p 25) art 5(2))). The amendment made by the Trade Marks (Proof of Use, etc) Regulations 2004, SI 2004/946, gives effect to the rulings of the European Court of Justice that Council Directive (EEC) 89/104 (OJ L40, 11.2.89, p 1) art 5(2) (see now European Parliament and Council Directive (EC) 2008/95 (OJ L299, 8.11.2008, p 25) art 5(2)) is to be interpreted as applying where the sign is used in relation to identical or similar goods or services to those in respect of which the earlier trade mark is registered as well as in relation to goods or services which are not similar (Case C-292/00 *Davidoff et Cie SA v Gofkid Ltd* [2003] All ER (EC) 1029, [2003] ECR I-389, ECJ; Case C-408/01 *Adidas-Salomon AG v Fitnessworld Trading Ltd* [2004] Ch 120, [2003] ECR I-12537, ECJ), although the amendment was unnecessary (*Electrocoin Automatics Ltd v Coinworld Ltd* [2004] EWHC 1498 (Ch), [2005] FSR 79, [2005] IP & T 132). Cf the corresponding relative ground of refusal: see the Trade Marks Act 1994 s 5(3); and PARA 59. As to the tests of unfair advantage and detriment see PARA 60. As to the limits on the effect of a registered trade mark see PARA 74 et seq; and as to the exhaustion of rights conferred by a registered trade mark see PARA 87. For transitional provisions see PARA 68 note 8.

72.   Meaning of 'use' for the purposes of infringement. For the purposes of the statutory provisions relating to the infringement of a registered trade mark[1], a person uses[2] a sign[3] if, in particular[4], he:

(1)   affixes it to goods or the packaging thereof[5];

(2)   offers or exposes goods for sale, puts them on the market or stocks them for those purposes under the sign, or offers or supplies services under the sign[6];

(3)   imports[7] or exports goods under the sign[8]; or

(4)   uses the sign on business[9] papers[10] or in advertising[11].

1   Ie for the purposes of the Trade Marks Act 1994 s 10 (see PARAS 68–71, 73): s 10(4) (derived from Council Directive (EEC) 89/104 (OJ L40, 11.2.89, p 1) to approximate the laws of the member states relating to trade marks, art 5(3) (see now European Parliament and Council Directive (EC) 2008/95 (OJ L299, 8.11.2008, p 25) art 5(3))). The provisions also apply to infringement of a protected international trade mark (UK): see PARA 66. As to the meaning of 'registered trade mark' see PARA 111.
2   Oral use of a sign can constitute 'use' for this purpose: Trade Marks Act 1994 s 103(2); *Jean Christian Perfumes Ltd v Thakrar* [2011] EWHC 1383 (Ch), [2011] FSR 812, [2011] All ER (D) 06 (Jun); and see PARA 44 note 8.
      It is not clear whether 'invisible' use of a sign, in particular in internet metatags, counts as use for this purpose: see *Reed Executive plc v Reed Business Information Ltd* [2004] EWCA Civ 159, [2004] RPC 767, [2004] IP & T 1049; cf *Road Tech Computer Systems Ltd v Mandata (Management and Data Services) Ltd* [2000] IP & T 1029.
3   As to the meaning of 'sign' see PARA 41 note 1.
4   This list is non-exhaustive: Case C-206/01 *Arsenal Football Club plc v Reed* [2003] Ch 454, [2003] All ER (EC) 1, [2002] ECR I-10273, ECJ; Case C-228/03 *Gillette Co v LA-Laboratories Ltd Oy* [2005] All ER (EC) 940, [2005] IP & T 1003, ECJ; Case C-48/05 *Adam Opel AG v Autec AG* [2007] ECR I-1017, [2007] IP & T 408, [2007] ETMR 33, ECJ; Joined Cases C-236/08, C-237/08 and C-238/08 *Google France SARL v Louis Vuitton Malletier*

SA; Google France SARL v Viaticum SA; Google France SARL v Centre national de recherche en relations humaines (CNRRH) SARL [2011] All ER (EC) 411, [2010] ECR I-2417, ECJ.

5   Trade Marks Act 1994 s 10(4)(a). The sign must be affixed to the goods in the United Kingdom to amount to an infringing use; it is not an infringement to order, manufacture or export packaging bearing the sign for the purposes of affixing it to the goods overseas: *Beautimatic International Ltd v Mitchell International Pharmaceuticals Ltd* [1999] IP & T 59, [2000] FSR 267. A person who fills cans to the order of another person to which the sign has already been applied by the other person does not thereby make use of the sign: Case C-119/10 *Frisdanken Industrie Winters BV v Red Bull GmbH* [2012] ETMR 16, ECJ.

6   Trade Marks Act 1994 s 10(4)(b). Offering and putting on the market include the offering and sale of goods bearing a trade mark and having the customs status of non-Community goods, when the offering and/or sale is effected while the goods are placed under the customs external transit procedure or the customs warehousing procedure if the offering or sale necessarily entails putting the goods on the market in the Community: Case C-405/03 *Class International BV v Colgate-Palmolive Co* [2006] Ch 154, sub nom *Class International BV v Unilever NV* [2005] ECR I-8735, ECJ. They also include the offering and sale within the European Union of goods currently located outside the European Union: Case C-324/09 *L'Oréal SA v eBay International AG* [2012] All ER (EC) 501, [2011] IP & T 819, ECJ.

A mark may be used notwithstanding that it is not visible to the consumer until after the sale (eg where the goods are sold over the internet); the obliteration of the mark before delivery does not mean that the mark has not been used: *Kabushiki Kaisha Sony Computer Entertainment v Nuplayer Ltd* [2005] EWHC 1522 (Ch), [2006] FSR 126, [2005] All ER (D) 188 (Jul).

7   Mere entry of goods into the United Kingdom under the external transit procedure or the customs warehousing procedure or the inward processing procedure is not sufficient to amount to importation so as to make this an infringement if the goods have not already been placed on the market in the European Economic Area by the trade mark proprietor or with his consent: Case C-115/02 *Administration des douanes et droits indirects v Rioglass SA* [2003] ECR I-12705, [2004] FSR 753, ECJ; Case C-405/03 *Class International BV v Colgate-Palmolive Co* [2006] Ch 154, sub nom *Class International BV v Unilever NV* [2005] ECR I-8735, ECJ. See also Case C-281/05 *Montex Holdings Ltd v Diesel SpA* [2006] ECR I-10881, [2007] IP & T 387, ECJ; *Eli Lilly and Co v 8PM Chemist Ltd* [2008] EWCA Civ 24, [2008] IP & T 730, [2008] FSR 313.

8   Trade Marks Act 1994 s 10(4)(c).

9   As to the meaning of 'business' see PARA 34 note 3.

10   Use in business papers includes use by a trade intermediary which is acting in its own name but on behalf of a vendor of goods: Case C-62/08 *UDV North America Inc v Brandtraders NV* [2009] ECR I-1279, [2010] ETMR 25, ECJ.

11   Trade Marks Act 1994 s 10(4)(d). For this purpose there must be use of the sign by the defendant in its own commercial communication; accordingly, an internet search engine provider does not 'use' signs selected by clients of its keyword advertising service: Joined Cases C-236/08, C-237/08 and C-238/08 *Google France SARL v Louis Vuitton Malletier SA; Google France SARL v Viaticum SA; Google France SARL v Centre national de recherche en relations humaines (CNRRH) SARL* [2011] All ER (EC) 411, [2010] ECR I-2417, ECJ. Advertising includes comparative advertising: see PARA 68 note 6. As to the limits on the effect of a registered trade mark see PARA 74 et seq; and as to the exhaustion of rights conferred by a registered trade mark see PARA 87. For transitional provisions see PARA 68 note 8.

73.   Application of mark to material for labelling or packaging. A person who applies a registered trade mark[1] to material intended to be used for labelling or packaging goods, as a business[2] paper, or for advertising goods or services, is to be treated as a party to any use[3] of the material which infringes the registered trade mark if, when he applied the mark, he knew or had reason to believe that the application of the mark was not duly authorised by the proprietor or a licensee[4].

1   This also applies to a protected international trade mark (UK): see PARA 66. As to the meaning of 'registered trade mark' see PARA 111.

2   As to the meaning of 'business' see PARA 34 note 3.

3   As to the meaning of 'use' for the purposes of infringement see PARA 72. In order to constitute infringement, the acts must be done without the consent of the proprietor: see the Trade Marks Act 1994 s 9(1); and PARA 66. As to the meaning of 'use' generally see PARA 44 note 8.

4   Trade Marks Act 1994 s 10(5). Cf the more restricted liability of printers etc under the common
     law in passing off: see *Paterson Zochonis & Co Ltd v Merfarken Packaging Ltd* [1986] 3 All ER
     522, [1983] FSR 273, CA (where a printer was not liable for the passing off achieved by his
     customer notwithstanding the suspicious circumstances in which printing was commissioned).
     As to knowing or having reason to believe see *LA Gear Inc v Hi-Tec Sports plc* [1992] FSR
     121, CA; and *ZYX Music GmbH v King* [1997] 2 All ER 129, [1997] EMLR 319, CA (which
     both deal with the concept in the context of the Copyright, Designs and Patents Act 1988: see
     COPYRIGHT vol 23 (2013) PARA 881). As to the granting of licences see PARAS 119–120. As to
     the rights of an exclusive licensee see the Trade Marks Act 1994 s 31(1), (2); and PARA 401. As
     to the limits on the effect of a registered trade mark see PARA 74 et seq; and as to the exhaustion
     of rights conferred by a registered trade mark see PARA 87. For transitional provisions see PARA
     68 note 8.
         Section 10(5) applies in relation to an authorised user of a registered collective mark or a
     registered certification mark as in relation to a licensee of a trade mark: see ss 49(2), 50(2),
     Sch 1 para 11(a), Sch 2 para 13(a); and PARAS 145, 156.

(ii) Limits on Effects of Registered Trade Marks

74.   Use for identifying goods or services of the proprietor or licensee.
Nothing in the statutory provisions relating to infringement of registered trade
marks[1] is to be construed as preventing the use[2] of a registered trade mark by
any person for the purpose of identifying goods or services as those of the
proprietor or a licensee[3]; but any such use otherwise than in accordance with
honest practices in industrial or commercial matters[4] is to be treated as infringing
the registered trade mark if the use without due cause[5] takes unfair advantage of,
or is detrimental to, the distinctive character or repute of the trade mark[6].

1   Ie the Trade Marks Act 1994 s 10(1)–(5): see PARAS 68–73. The same provisions apply to
     infringement of a protected international trade mark (UK): see PARA 66. As to the meaning of
     'registered trade mark' see PARA 111.
2   As to the meaning of 'use' for the purposes of infringement see PARA 72. As to the meaning of
     'use' generally see PARA 44 note 8.
3   As to the granting of licences see PARAS 119–120. As to the rights of an exclusive licensee see the
     Trade Marks Act 1994 s 31(1), (2); and PARA 401.
4   As to the meaning of 'honest practices' see PARA 80.
5   As to the concept of use without due cause see PARA 59 note 9.
6   Trade Marks Act 1994 s 10(6). This provision is not derived from Council Directive (EEC)
     89/104 (OJ L40, 11.2.89, p 1) to approximate the laws of the member states relating to trade
     marks. It has been suggested that it implements art 5(5) of the Directive, but art 5(5) permits
     member states to confer an additional right on trade mark proprietors to the rights conferred by
     art 5(1)–(4), not to provide additional defences to those provided by arts 6 and 7 (as to Council
     Directive (EEC) 89/104 (OJ L40, 11.2.89, p 1) arts 5–7 see now European Parliament and
     Council Directive (EC) 2008/95 (OJ L299, 8.11.2008, p 25) arts 5–7): see Case C-23/01
     Robelco NV v Robelco Groep NV [2002] ECR I-10913, [2002] All ER (D) 311 (Nov), ECJ. It
     is arguable that the Trade Marks Act 1994 s 10(6) is incompatible with Directive 89/104 since
     the European Court of Justice has ruled that arts 5–7 form a complete code and it is not open to
     national laws to provide other defences: Case C-355/96 *Silhouette International Schmied GmbH
     & Co KG v Hartlauer Handelsgesellschaft mbH* [1999] Ch 77, [1998] ECR I-4799, ECJ; Cases
     C-414/99 to C-416/99 *Zino Davidoff SA v A & G Imports Ltd* [2002] Ch 109, [2001] ECR
     I-8691, ECJ; Case C-244/00 *Van Doren + Q GmbH v Lifestyle sports + sportswear
     Handelgesellschaft mbH* [2004] All ER (EC) 912, [2003] ECR I-3051, ECJ; Case C-16/03 *Peak
     Holding AB v Axolin-Elinor AB* [2005] Ch 261, [2004] ECR I-11313, ECJ; *British Airways plc
     v Ryanair Ltd* [2001] IP & T 373, [2001] FSR 541; but see *Levi Strauss & Co v Tesco
     Stores Ltd* [2002] EWHC 1625 (Ch), [2003] RPC 319, [2003] IP & T 117 (the Trade Marks
     Act 1994 s 10(6) is not inconsistent if interpreted in the same way as s 11(2)(b) (see PARA 78)).
     For a discussion of the origins of this provision, and its defects, see *Barclays Bank plc v RBS
     Advanta* [1996] RPC 307 at 312–314, [1997] ETMR 199 at 204–206 per Laddie J. It has been
     said that it is a pointless provision which should be repealed: *O2 Holdings Ltd v Hutchison
     3G Ltd* [2006] EWCA Civ 1656 at [56], [2007] RPC 407 at [56], [2007] ETMR 19 at [56] per
     Jacob LJ.

So far as use of the trade mark in relation to the proprietor's own goods is concerned, the Trade Marks Act 1994 s 10(6) is probably unnecessary since such use is protected by s 12(1): see PARAS 86–87. It appears that s 12(1) should also be interpreted as applying to services.

The primary objective of the Trade Marks Act 1994 s 10(6) is to allow comparative advertising provided that it is honest: see *Barclays Bank plc v RBS Advanta* above at 312–313, 315, and at 204–205, 207–208 per Laddie J; *Vodafone Group plc v Orange Personal Communications Services Ltd* [1997] FSR 34, [1997] EMLR 84; *Cable & Wireless plc v British Telecommunications plc* [1998] FSR 383; *Emaco Ltd and Aktiebolaget Electrolux v Dyson Appliances Ltd* [1999] ETMR 903, (1999) Times, 8 February; *British Airways plc v Ryanair Ltd* above. However comparative advertising must now comply with Council Directive (EEC) 84/450 (OJ L250, 10.9.84, p 17) relating to the approximation of the laws, regulations and administrative provisions of the member states concerning misleading advertising, art 3a (added by Parliament and Council Directive (EEC) 97/55 (OJ L290, 6.10.97, p 18) art 1(4)) (see now European Parliament and Council Directive (EC) 2006/114 (OJ L376, 27.12.2006, p 21) art 4). Use of a trade mark (or a sign confusingly similar thereto) in comparative advertising which complies with Council Directive (EEC) 84/450 (OJ L250, 10.9.84, p 17) art 3a does not infringe, while use of a trade mark (or possibly a sign confusingly similar thereto) in comparative advertising which does not comply with art 3a does infringe: Case C-44/01 *Pippig Augenoptik GmbH v Hartlauer Handelsgesellschaft mbH* [2004] All ER (EC) 1156, [2003] ECR I-3095, ECJ; *O2 Holdings Ltd v Hutchison 3G Ltd* above; and see PARA 75. See also the caveat about earlier English cases on honest practices in the context of comparative advertising referred to in PARA 80 note 11.

For transitional provisions see PARA 68 note 8.

75. Comparative advertising. A registered trade mark[1] is not infringed by the use[2] of a sign which is identical or similar to the trade mark in comparative advertising[3] if the following conditions[4] are met[5]:

(1)   it is not misleading[6];

(2)   it compares goods or services meeting the same needs or intended for the same purpose;

(3)   it objectively compares one or more material, relevant, verifiable and representative features of those goods and services, which may include price;

(4)   it does not discredit or denigrate the trade marks, trade names, other distinguishing marks, goods, services, activities or circumstances of a competitor[7];

(5)   for products with designation of origin, it relates in each case to products with the same designation;

(6)   it does not take unfair advantage of the reputation of a trade mark, trade name or other distinguishing marks of a competitor or of the designation of origin of competing products[8];

(7)   it does not present goods or services as imitations or replicas of goods or services bearing a protected trade mark or trade name[9];

(8)   it does not create confusion among traders, between the advertiser and a competitor or between the advertiser's trade marks, trade names, other distinguishing marks, goods or services and those of a competitor[10].

1   This also applies to a protected international trade mark (UK): see PARA 66. As to the meaning of 'registered trade mark' see PARA 111.

2   As to the meaning of 'use' see PARA 44 note 8.

3   Comparative advertising means any advertising which explicitly or by implication identifies a competitor or goods or services offered by a competitor: European Parliament and Council Directive (EC) 2006/114 (OJ L376, 27.12.2006, p 21) concerning misleading and comparative advertising, art 2(c). This is a very broad definition: see Case C-112/99 *Toshiba Europe GmbH v Katun Germany GmbH* [2002] All ER (EC) 325, [2001] ECR I-7945, ECJ; Case C-44/01 *Pippig Augenoptik GmbH & Co KG v Hartlauer Handelsgesellschaft mbH* [2004] All ER (EC) 1156, [2003] ECR I-3095, ECJ; Case C-381/05 *De Landtsheer Emmanuel SA v Comité Interprofessionel du Vin de Champagne* [2008] All ER (EC) 1068, [2007] ECR I-3115, ECJ;

Case C-533/06 *O2 Holdings Ltd v Hutchison 3G UK Ltd* [2008] ECR I-4231, [2008] 3 CMLR 397, [2008] All ER (D) 155 (Jun), ECJ; *L'Oreal SA v Bellure NV* [2010] EWCA Civ 535, [2010] RPC 687, [2010] IP & T 1094.

4   Ie the conditions contained in European Parliament and Council Directive (EC) 2006/114 (OJ L376, 27.12.2006, p 21) art 4.

5   Case C-44/01 *Pippig Augenoptik GmbH v Hartlauer Handelsgesellschaft mbH* [2004] All ER (EC) 1156, [2003] ECR I-3095, ECJ; Case C-533/06 *O2 Holdings Ltd v Hutchison 3G UK Ltd* [2008] ECR I-4231, [2008] 3 CMLR 397, [2008] All ER (D) 155 (Jun), ECJ.

6   Ie within the meaning of European Parliament and Council Directive (EC) 2006/114 (OJ L376, 27.12.2006, p 21) arts 2(b), 3, 8(1) and European Parliament and Council Directive (EC) 2005/29 (OJ L149, 11.6.2005, p 22) concerning unfair business-to-consumer commercial practices in the internal market, arts 6, 7.

7   The advertisement complained of in *British Airways plc v Ryanair Ltd* [2001] IP & T 373, [2001] FSR 541 is an example of what might be regarded as denigration.

8   As to the concept of taking unfair advantage of the distinctive character or repute of a trade mark see PARA 60.

9   See Case C-487/07 *L'Oréal SA v Bellure NV* [2010] All ER (EC) 28, [2009] ECR I-5185, ECJ; and *L'Oreal SA v Bellure NV* [2010] EWCA Civ 535, [2010] RPC 687, [2010] IP & T 1094.

10 As to the concept of likelihood of confusion see PARA 58.

76.   Use of another registered trade mark. A registered trade mark[1] is not infringed by the use[2] of another registered trade mark in relation to goods or services for which the latter is registered[3]. Nor is it infringed by the use of a protected international trade mark (UK) in relation to goods or services within the scope of the protection conferred by that mark in the United Kingdom[4]. The defence relates only to use for which the defendant's mark is registered or protected[5]. A defendant may claim that the yet to be registered mark complained of could be validly registered and seek a stay of the action pending determination of his application for registration[6].

1   This also applies to a protected international trade mark (UK): see PARA 66. As to the meaning of 'registered trade mark' see PARA 111.

2   As to the meaning of 'use' see PARA 44 note 8.

3   Trade Marks Act 1994 s 11(1). This provision is not derived from Council Directive (EEC) 89/104 (OJ L40, 11.2.89, p 1) to approximate the laws of the member states relating to trade marks, and it is very doubtful that it is incompatible with the Directive for three reasons. First, the European Court of Justice has ruled that arts 5–7 (as to Council Directive (EEC) 89/104 (OJ L40, 11.2.89, p 1) arts 5–7 see now European Parliament and Council Directive (EC) 2008/95 (OJ L299, 8.11.2008, p 25) arts 5–7) form a complete code and it is not open to national laws to provide other defences: Case C-355/96 *Silhouette International Schmied GmbH & Co KG v Hartlauer Handelsgesellschaft mbH* [1999] Ch 77, [1998] ECR I-4799, ECJ; Cases C-414/99 to C-416/99 *Zino Davidoff SA v A & G Imports Ltd* [2002] Ch 109, [2001] ECR I-8691, ECJ; Case C-244/00 *Van Doren + Q GmbH v Lifestyle sports + sportswear Handelsgesellschaft mbH* [2004] All ER (EC) 912, [2003] ECR I-3051, ECJ; Case C-16/03 *Peak Holding AB u Axolin-Elinor AB* [2005] Ch 261, [2004] ECR I-11313, ECJ. Secondly, Council Regulation (EC) 40/94 (OJ L11, 14.1.94, p 1) on the Community trade mark contains no such provision, indeed art 106(1) implies the opposite. See *Intel Corpn Inc v CPM United Kingdom Ltd* [2007] EWCA Civ 431 at [6], [2007] RPC 846 at [6], [2007] IP & T 786 at [6] per Jacob LJ. Thirdly, the European Court of Justice has ruled that a Community trade mark proprietor can sue for infringement of the Community trade mark arising from the use of a later-registered Community trade mark without the need for the later mark to have been declared invalid beforehand: Case C-561/11 *Fédération Cynologique Internationale v Federación Canina Internacional de Perros de Pura Raza* [2013] Bus LR 693, ECJ. As to Community trade marks see PARA 159 et seq.
    The Trade Marks Act 1994 s 11(1) corresponds in general effect, though not in language, to the Trade Marks Act 1938 s 4(4) (repealed). See, however, the Trade Marks Act 1994 s 47(6) (effect of declaration of invalidity of registration); and PARA 96. Thus, if a defence of use of a registered trade mark is raised, it can be countered by a claim for a declaration that that mark is invalid.
    Section 11 applies in relation to an existing registered mark as from 31 October 1994, subject to s 105, Sch 3 para 4(2) (see PARA 81): Sch 3 para 4(1). The old law continues to apply

in relation to infringements committed before that date: Sch 3 para 4(1). As to the meaning of 'existing registered mark' see PARA 4 note 2; and as to the meaning of 'the old law' see PARA 4 note 3.

It would seem that, as under the Trade Marks Act 1938, the defendant's use must be of the mark as registered, not some variant: see *Eli Lilly & Co Ltd v Chelsea Drug Chemical Co Ltd* [1966] RPC 14.

4   See the Trade Marks (International Registration) Order 2008, SI 2008/2206, art 3; and PARA 12. See also generally PARA 11 et seq.

5   Ie only to goods and services falling within the specification for which the mark is registered, not to similar goods or services.

6   See PARA 405.

77.   Use of own name or address.   A registered trade mark[1] is not infringed by the use[2] by a person[3] of his own name[4] or address[5], provided the use is in accordance with honest practices in industrial or commercial matters[6].

1   This also applies to a protected international trade mark (UK): see PARA 66. As to the meaning of 'registered trade mark' see PARA 111.

2   As to the meaning of 'use' see PARA 44 note 8.

3   The 'own name' defence applies to corporations as well as natural persons: Case C-245/02 *Anheuser-Busch Inc v Budejovicky Budvar NP* [2004] ECR I-10989, [2007] IP & T 348, [2004] All ER (D) 271 (Nov), ECJ; Case C-17/06 *Céline SARL v Céline SA* [2007] ECR I-7041, [2008] IP & T 684, ECJ.

4   A person's 'own name' is the name that he is known by, so that it is not an infringement to use a name by which a person is commonly known: *Scandecor Development AB v Scandecor Marketing AB* [1998] FSR 500 at 521 per Lloyd J; revsd on other grounds [1999] FSR 26, CA; on appeal [2001] UKHL 21, [2001] IP & T 676, [2002] FSR 122 (questions referred to European Court of Justice but case settled prior to ruling). See also *Mercury Communications Ltd v Mercury Interactive (UK) Ltd* [1995] FSR 850 at 860–862 per Laddie J (a case under the Trade Marks Act 1938 s 8 (repealed)). Most commonly, this principle entitles companies to drop suffixes such as 'limited', 'plc' and so on (*Reed Executive plc v Reed Business Information Ltd* [2004] EWCA Civ 159, [2004] RPC 767, [2004] IP & T 1049; *Euromarket Designs Inc v Peters* [2000] IP & T 1290, [2001] FSR 288; *International Business Machines Corpn v Web-Sphere Ltd* [2004] EWHC 529 (Ch), [2004] All ER (D) 328 (Mar), sub nom *WEBSPHERE Trade Mark* [2004] FSR 39); but further abbreviations are not protected (*Premier Luggage and Bags Ltd v Premier Co (UK) Ltd* [2002] EWCA Civ 387, [2003] FSR 69). The principle also extends to the use of a company's trading name: *Hotel Cipriani Srl v Cipriani (Grosvenor Street) Ltd* [2010] EWCA Civ 110, [2010] Bus LR 1465, [2010] RPC 485.

5   Trade Marks Act 1994 s 11(2)(a) (derived from Council Directive (EEC) 89/104 (OJ L40, 11.2.89, p 1) to approximate the laws of the member states relating to trade marks, art 6(1)(a) (see now European Parliament and Council Directive (EC) 2008/95 (OJ L299, 8.11.2008, p 25) art 6(1)(a))). This provision extends to use of the name as a trade mark: *Reed Executive plc v Reed Business Information Ltd* [2004] EWCA Civ 159, [2004] RPC 767, [2004] IP & T 1049. For transitional provisions see PARA 76 note 3.

6   Trade Marks Act 1994 s 11(2) proviso (derived from Council Directive (EEC) 89/104 (OJ L40, 11.2.89, p 1) art 6(1) proviso (see now European Parliament and Council Directive (EC) 2008/95 (OJ L299, 8.11.2008, p 25) art 6(1) proviso)). As to the meaning of 'honest practices' see PARA 80.

78.   Use of descriptions.   A registered trade mark[1] is not infringed by the use[2] of indications concerning the kind, quality, quantity, intended purpose, value, geographical origin, the time of production of goods or of rendering of services, or other characteristics of goods or services[3], provided the use is in accordance with honest practices in industrial or commercial matters[4].

1   This also applies to a protected international trade mark (UK): see PARA 66. As to the meaning of 'registered trade mark' see PARA 111.

2   As to the meaning of 'use' see PARA 44 note 8.

3   Trade Marks Act 1994 s 11(2)(b) (derived from Council Directive (EEC) 89/104 (OJ L40, 11.2.89, p 1) to approximate the laws of the member states relating to trade marks, art 6(1)(b) (see now European Parliament and Council Directive (EC) 2008/95 (OJ L299, 8.11.2008, p 25)

art 6(1)(b))). This provision extends to use of the indication as a trade mark: Case C-100/02 *Gerolsteiner Brunnen GmbH & Co v Putsch GmbH* [2004] ECR I-691, [2004] RPC 761, ECJ (indication of geographical origin used as trade mark); Case C-245/02 *Anheuser-Busch Inc v Budejovicky Budvar np* [2004] ECR I-10989, [2007] IP & T 348, [2004] All ER (D) 271 (Nov), ECJ; *Fine & Country Ltd v Okotoks Ltd* [2013] EWCA Civ 672, [2013] All ER (D) 137 (Jun); see also *Reed Executive plc v Reed Business Information Ltd* [2004] EWCA Civ 159, [2004] RPC 767, [2004] IP & T 1049 (an 'own name' case).

In certain circumstances, purely descriptive use of a trade mark does not constitute infringing use at all and therefore it is not necessary to invoke this defence: Case C-2/00 *Hölterhoff v Freiesleben* [2002] All ER (EC) 665, [2002] ECR I-4187, ECJ; and see PARA 72.

As to the registration of marks consisting exclusively of indications etc see the Trade Marks Act 1994 s 3(1); and PARAS 43–44.

For transitional provisions see PARA 76 note 3.

4   Trade Marks Act 1994 s 11(2) proviso (derived from Council Directive (EEC) 89/104 (OJ L40, 11.2.89, p 1) art 6(1) proviso (see now European Parliament and Council Directive (EC) 2008/95 (OJ L299, 8.11.2008, p 25) art 6(1) proviso)). As to the meaning of 'honest practices' see PARA 80.

79.   Use necessary to indicate intended purpose, particularly accessories and spares.   A registered trade mark[1] is not infringed by the use[2] of the trade mark where it is necessary[3] to indicate the intended purpose of a product or service (in particular, as accessories or spare parts)[4], provided the use is in accordance with honest practices in industrial or commercial matters[5].

1   This also applies to a protected international trade mark (UK): see PARA 66. As to the meaning of 'registered trade mark' see PARA 111.
2   As to the meaning of 'use' see PARA 44 note 8.
3   In order to be necessary, the use must in practice constitute the only means of providing the public with comprehensible and complete information on the intended purpose in order to preserve the undistorted system of competition in the market for that product: Case C-228/03 *Gillette Co v LA-Laboratories Ltd Oy* [2005] All ER (EC) 940, [2005] IP & T 1003, ECJ. See also *Datacard Corpn v Eagle Technologies Ltd* [2011] EWHC 244 (Pat), [2012] Bus LR 160, [2011] RPC 443; *Bayerische Motoren Werke AG v Round & Metal Ltd* [2012] EWHC 2099 (Pat), [2012] All ER (D) 47 (Aug).
4   Trade Marks Act 1994 s 11(2)(c) (derived from Council Directive (EEC) 89/104 (OJ L40, 11.2.89, p 1) to approximate the laws of the member states relating to trade marks, art 6(1)(c) (see now European Parliament and Council Directive (EC) 2008/95 (OJ L299, 8.11.2008, p 25) art 6(1)(c))). The defence is not limited to accessories or spare parts: Case C-228/03 *Gillette Co v LA-Laboratories Ltd Oy* [2005] All ER (EC) 940, [2005] IP & T 1003, ECJ. For transitional provisions see PARA 76 note 3.
5   Trade Marks Act 1994 s 11(2) proviso (derived from Council Directive (EEC) 89/104 (OJ L40, 11.2.89, p 1) art 6(1) proviso (see now European Parliament and Council Directive (EC) 2008/95 (OJ L299, 8.11.2008, p 25) art 6(1) proviso)). As to the meaning of 'honest practices' see PARA 80.

80.   Honest practices in industrial and commercial matters.   Several of the statutory exemptions[1] from infringement[2] of a registered trade mark[3] are subject to the proviso that the use of the mark complained of must be 'in accordance with honest practices in industrial and commercial matters.' It is established that this is an objective test which constitutes in substance the expression of a duty to act fairly in relation to the legitimate interests of the trade mark proprietor[4]. The court must carry out an overall assessment of all the relevant circumstances, and in particular assess whether the defendant can be regarded as competing unfairly with the proprietor of the trade mark[5]. An important factor is whether the use of the sign complained of either gives rise to consumer deception or takes unfair advantage of, or is detrimental to, the distinctive character or repute of the trade mark; if it does, it is unlikely to qualify as being in accordance with honest practices[6]. A mere likelihood of confusion will not disqualify the use from being in accordance with honest practices if there is a good reason why such a likelihood of confusion should be tolerated[7].

The following factors, amongst others, may be treated as material[8]:

(1)   whether the defendant knew of the existence of the trade mark, and if not whether it would have been reasonable for it to conduct a search;

(2)   whether the defendant used the sign complained of in reliance on competent legal advice based on proper instructions;

(3)   the nature of the use complained of, and in particular the extent to which it is used as a trade mark for the defendant's goods or services[9];

(4)   whether the defendant knew that the trade mark owner objected to the use of the sign complained of, or at least should have appreciated that there was a likelihood that the owner would object;

(5)   whether the defendant knew, or should have appreciated, that there was a likelihood of confusion;

(6)   whether there has been actual confusion, and if so whether the defendant knew this;

(7)   whether the trade mark has a reputation, and if so whether the defendant knew this and whether the defendant knew, or at least should have appreciated, that the reputation of the trade mark would be adversely affected[10];

(8)   whether the defendant's use of the sign complained of interferes with the owner's ability to exploit the trade mark;

(9)   whether the defendant has a sufficient justification for using the sign complained of; and

(10)   the timing of the complaint from the trade mark owner.

Use of a trade mark will not be in accordance with honest practices if, for example[11]:

(a)   it is done in such a manner as to give the impression that there is a commercial connection between the third party and the trade mark owner[12];

(b)   it takes unfair advantage of the distinctive character or repute of the trade mark[13];

(c)   it entails the discrediting or denigration of the trade mark[14]; or

(d)   the third party presents its goods as imitations or replicas of the products bearing the trade mark[15].

1   Ie the Trade Marks Act 1994 s 10(6) (use for identifying goods or services of the proprietor: see PARA 74), s 11(2)(a) (use of own name or address: see PARA 77), s 11(2)(b) (use of specified descriptions: see PARA 78), s 11(2)(c) (use necessary to indicate intended purpose: see PARA 79). The concept of honest practices in industrial and commercial matters is also incorporated into several of the defences to infringement of the Olympics association right: see the Olympic Symbol etc (Protection) Act 1995 s 4; PARA 472; and SPORTS LAW vol 96 (2012) PARA 161.

2   As to the meaning of 'infringement' see PARA 66 note 4.

3   The same provisions apply to infringement of a protected international trade mark (UK): see PARA 66. As to the meaning of 'registered trade mark' see PARA 111.

4   Case C-63/97 *Bayersiche Motorenwerke AG v Deenik* [1999] 1 All ER (EC) 235, [1999] ECR I-905, ECJ; Case C-100/02 *Gerolsteiner Brunnen GmbH & Co v Putsch GmbH* [2004] ECR I-691, [2004] RPC 761, ECJ; Case C-245/02 *Anheuser-Busch Inc v Budejovicky Budvar NP* [2004] ECR I-10989, [2007] IP & T 348, [2004] All ER (D) 271 (Nov), ECJ; Case C-228/03 *Gillette Co v LA-Laboratories Ltd Oy* [2005] All ER (EC) 940, [2005] IP & T 1003, ECJ; Case C-17/06 *Céline SARL v Céline SA* [2007] ECR I-7041 at 33, [2008] IP & T 684.

5   Case C-100/02 *Gerolsteiner Brunnen GmbH & Co v Putsch GmbH* [2004] ECR I-691, [2004] RPC 761, ECJ; Case C-245/02 *Anheuser-Busch Inc v Budejovicky Budvar NP* [2004] ECR I-10989, [2007] IP & T 348, [2004] All ER (D) 271 (Nov), ECJ; Case C-17/06 *Céline SARL v Céline SA* [2007] ECR I-7041, [2008] IP & T 684.

6   Case C-228/03 *Gillette Co v LA-Laboratories Ltd Oy* [2005] All ER (EC) 940, [2005] IP & T
    1003, ECJ; Case C-245/02 *Anheuser-Busch Inc v Budejovicky Budvar NP* [2004] ECR I-10989,
    [2007] IP & T 348, [2004] All ER (D) 271 (Nov), ECJ; Case C-17/06 *Céline SARL v Céline SA*
    [2007] ECR I-7041, [2008] IP & T 684. Thus it appears that use which amounts to passing off
    will generally not be in accordance with honest practices: *Asprey & Garrard Ltd v WRA
    (Guns) Ltd* [2001] EWCA Civ 1499, [2002] IP & T 38, [2002] FSR 487; *Reed Executive plc v
    Reed Business Information Ltd* [2004] EWCA Civ 159, [2004] RPC 767, [2004] IP & T 1049.
    See, however, the text and note 12.
7   Case C-100/02 *Gerolsteiner Brunnen GmbH & Co v Putsch GmbH* [2004] ECR I-691, [2004]
    RPC 761, ECJ. It appears that the amount of confusion that can be tolerated before the defence
    is lost is a question of degree: *Reed Executive plc v Reed Business Information Ltd* [2004]
    EWCA Civ 159, [2004] RPC 767, [2004] IP & T 1049; *Fine & Country Ltd v Okotoks Ltd*
    [2013] EWCA Civ 672, [2013] All ER (D) 137 (Jun).
8   See *Samuel Smith Old Brewery (Tadcaster) v Lee (t/a Cropton Brewery)* [2011] EWHC 1879
    (Ch) at [118], [2011] All ER (D) 229 (Jul) at [118] per Arnold J (a case under European
    Parliament and Council Directive (EC) 2008/95 (OJ L299, 8.11.2008, p 25) art 6(1)(b) (see
    PARA 78)); applied in *Hotel Cipriani SRL v Fred 250 Ltd* [2013] EWHC 70 (Ch), [2013] All ER
    (D) 250 (Jan) and *Stichting BDO v BDO Unibank, Inc* [2013] EWHC 418 (Ch), [2013] All ER
    (D) 39 (Mar). It is irrelevant that the defendant has infringed, or acted in disregard of, third
    party intellectual property rights: *Samuel Smith Old Brewery (Tadcaster) v Lee (t/a Cropton
    Brewery)* above.
9   Case C-228/03 *Gillette Co v LA-Laboratories Ltd Oy* [2005] All ER (EC) 940, [2005] IP & T
    1003, ECJ.
10 Case C-245/02 *Anheuser-Busch Inc v Budejovicky Budvar NP* [2004] ECR I-10989, [2007] IP
    & T 348, [2004] All ER (D) 271 (Nov), ECJ; Case C-17/06 *Céline Sarl v Céline SA* [2007] ECR
    I-7041, [2008] IP & T 684, ECJ.
11 Case C-228/03 *Gillette Co v LA-Laboratories Ltd Oy* [2005] All ER (EC) 940 at [49], [2005] IP
    & T 1003 at [49], ECJ. These conditions are based on Council Directive (EEC) 84/450
    (OJ L250, 10.9.84, p 17) relating to the approximation of the laws, regulations and
    administrative provisions of the member states concerning misleading advertising,
    art 3a(1)(d)–(h) (added by Parliament and Council Directive (EEC) 97/55 (OJ L290, 6.10.97,
    p 18), art 1(4)) (see now European Parliament and Council Directive (EC) 2006/114 (OJ L376,
    27.12.2006, p 21) art 4): see *L'Oréal SA v Bellure NV* [2006] EWHC 2355 (Ch), [2007] RPC
    328, [2007] ETMR 1; and PARA 75. Earlier English cases on honest practices in the context of
    comparative advertising must now be viewed with considerable caution: see PARA 74 note 6.
12 Case C-63/97 *Bayersiche Motorenwerke AG v Deenik* [1999] 1 All ER (EC) 235, [1999] ECR
    I-905, ECJ; *Aktiebolaget Volvo v Heritage (Leicester) Ltd* [2000] FSR 253, [1999] All ER (D)
    478; *Hotel Cipriani Srl v Cipriani (Grosvenor Street) Ltd* [2010] EWCA Civ 110, [2010] Bus
    LR 1465, [2010] RPC 485; *Datacard Corpn v Eagle Technologies Ltd* [2011] EWHC 244 (Pat),
    [2012] Bus LR 160, [2011] RPC 443; *Bayerische Motoren Werke AG v Round & Metal Ltd*
    [2012] EWHC 2099 (Pat), [2012] All ER (D) 47 (Aug).
13 As to the concept of taking unfair advantage of the distinctive character or repute of a trade
    mark see PARA 60.
14 It is not clear whether, and if so how, this test differs from that of causing detriment to the
    distinctive character or repute of the trade mark (as to which see PARA 60). The advertisement
    complained of in *British Airways plc v Ryanair Ltd* [2001] IP & T 373, [2001] FSR 541 is an
    example of what might be regarded as denigration.
15 See Case C-487/07 *L'Oréal SA v Bellure NV* [2010] All ER (EC) 28, [2009] ECR I-5185, ECJ;
    and *L'Oreal SA v Bellure NV* [2010] EWCA Civ 535, [2010] RPC 687, [2010] IP & T 1094.

81.   Prior use; use lawful under the old law. A registered trade mark¹ is not
infringed by the use² in the course of trade³ in a particular locality of an earlier
right⁴ which applies only in that locality⁵.

It is not an infringement of an existing registered mark or a registered trade
mark of which the distinctive elements are the same or substantially the same as
those of an existing registered mark and which is registered for the same goods
or services to continue on and after 31 October 1994 any use⁶ which did not
amount to infringement of the existing registered mark under the old law⁷.

1   This also applies to a protected international trade mark (UK): see PARA 66. As to the meaning
    of 'registered trade mark' see PARA 111.

2   As to the meaning of 'use' see PARA 44 note 8.

3   As to the meaning of 'trade' see PARA 44 note 4.

4   For these purposes, an 'earlier right' means an unregistered trade mark or other sign continuously used in relation to goods or services by a person or a predecessor in title of his from a date prior to whichever is the earlier of: (1) the use of the first-mentioned trade mark in relation to those goods or services by the proprietor or a predecessor in title of his; or (2) the registration of the first-mentioned trade mark in respect of those goods or services in the name of the proprietor or a predecessor in title of his, and an earlier right is to be regarded as applying in a locality if, or to the extent that, its use in that locality is protected by virtue of any rule of law (in particular, the law of passing off): Trade Marks Act 1994 s 11(3). As to passing off see PARA 287 et seq.

5   Trade Marks Act 1994 s 11(3) (derived from Council Directive (EEC) 89/104 (OJ L40, 11.2.89, p 1) to approximate the laws of the member states relating to trade marks, art 6(2) (see now European Parliament and Council Directive (EC) 2008/95 (OJ L299, 8.11.2008, p 25) art 6(2))). What amounts to a 'particular locality' for this purpose is somewhat uncertain, in particular whether it could compass the whole of the United Kingdom or the whole of England and Wales: compare Council Regulation (EC) 40/94 (OJ L11, 14.1.94, p 1) on the Community trade mark, art 8(4) (see now Council Regulation (EC) 207/2009 (OJ L78, 24.3.2009, p 1) art 8(4)) and see PARA 205. It has been held that the county of Northamptonshire is a particular locality for this purpose: see *Redd Solicitors LLP v Red Legal Ltd* [2012] EWPCC 54, [2012] ETMR 13, [2012] All ER (D) 170 (Dec), PCC. For transitional provisions see PARA 76 note 3.

6   The use referred to in the text is use which would be regarded commercially as continued use: *Northern & Shell plc v Condé Nast & National Magazine Distributors Ltd* [1995] RPC 117.

7   Trade Marks Act 1994 s 105, Sch 3 para 4(2). This could be important eg where a competitor of the proprietor of a trade mark uses the same mark in relation to goods and services which are similar to, but do not fall within, the goods or services in respect of which a mark is registered. Such use could not amount to infringement of a registered trade mark under the Trade Marks Act 1938 but could, in the absence of the provisions of the Trade Marks Act 1994 Sch 3 para 4(2), amount to infringement of a registered trade mark under that Act: see PARAS 70–71. As to the meaning of 'the old law' see PARA 4 note 3.

82.   Acts within scope of a disclaimer or limitation. Where the registration of a trade mark[1] is subject to a disclaimer or limitation[2], the rights conferred by a registered trade mark[3] are restricted accordingly[4]. Disclaimers and limitations apply in the same way to protected international trade marks (UK)[5].

1   As to the meaning of 'registration' see PARA 21 note 2. As to the meaning of 'trade mark' see PARA 41.

2   As to registration subject to disclaimer or limitation see PARA 65.

3   As to the meaning of 'registered trade mark' see PARA 111.

4   Trade Marks Act 1994 s 13(1). There is no reference to disclaimers or limitations in Council Directive (EEC) 89/104 (OJ L40, 11.2.89, p 1) to approximate the laws of the member states relating to trade marks (see now European Parliament and Council Directive (EC) 2008/95 (OJ L299, 8.11.2008, p 25)).

    Where a trade mark is subject to a limitation, the mark cannot be infringed by use of a sign outside the field so limited: *Phones4U Ltd v Phone4u.co.uk Internet Ltd* [2006] EWCA Civ 244, [2007] RPC 83, [2007] IP & T 439 (mark limited as to colour not infringed by sign in different colour); and see also *Nestlé SA's Trade Mark Application* [2004] EWCA Civ 1008, [2005] RPC 77, sub nom *Société des Produits Nestlé SA v Mars UK Ltd* [2005] IP & T 551. A claim, such as a claim to a particular colour or combination of colours, is not a limitation: *L'Oréal SA v Bellure NV* [2006] EWHC 2355 (Ch), [2007] RPC 328, [2007] ETMR 1. For the European Court of Justice ruling in *L'Oréal SA v Bellure NV* above, see Case C-487/07 *L'Oréal SA v Bellure NV* [2010] All ER (EC) 28, [2009] ECR I-5185, ECJ, and for the application of the ECJ ruling, see *L'Oreal SA v Bellure NV* [2010] EWCA Civ 535, [2010] RPC 687, [2010] IP & T 1094.

    A contention by the proprietor that a word, which was disclaimed on its own, was the essential feature of the trade mark would lead to the very monopoly which he disclaimed, and will not therefore be accepted: *European Ltd v Economist Newspapers Ltd* [1998] FSR 283, [1998] ETMR 536, CA.

    Nothing in this provision affects the proprietor's rights in passing off: see the Trade Marks Act 1994 s 2(2); and PARA 398.

5   See the Trade Marks (International Registration) Order 2008, SI 2008/2206, art 3; and PARA 12.
     See also generally PARA 11 et seq. See PARA 65.

83.   Statutory acquiescence.   Where the proprietor of an earlier trade mark[1] or
other earlier right[2] has acquiesced[3] for a continuous period of five years in the
use[4] of a registered trade mark[5] in the United Kingdom[6], being aware of that use,
there ceases to be any entitlement on the basis of that earlier trade mark or other
right:

(1)   to apply for a declaration that the registration of the later trade mark is
       invalid; or

(2)   to oppose the use of the later trade mark in relation to the goods or
       services in relation to which it has been so used,

unless the registration of the later trade mark was applied for in bad faith[7].
    Where the above provisions apply, the proprietor of the later trade mark is not
entitled to oppose the use of the earlier trade mark or, as the case may be, the
exploitation of the earlier right, notwithstanding that the earlier trade mark or
right may no longer be invoked against his later trade mark[8].
    These provisions apply in the same way if the earlier trade mark, or the later
trade mark, or both, are protected international trade marks (UK) rather than
United Kingdom registered trade marks[9].

1   As to the meaning of 'earlier trade mark' see PARA 54. Registration of the earlier trade mark is
     not a prerequisite for the running of the five year period to commence: Case C-482/09
     Budejovocky Budvar, narodni podnik v Anheuser Busch Inc [2011] ECR I-8701, [2012] RPC
     247, [2011] All ER (D) 74 (Oct), ECJ.
2   As to the meaning of 'earlier right' see PARA 61.
3   Acquiescence is a concept of European Union law; and the proprietor of an earlier trade mark
     cannot be held to have acquiesced in the long and well-established honest use, of which he has
     long been aware, by a third party of a later trade mark if the proprietor was not in a position to
     oppose that use: Case C-482/09 *Budejovicky Budvar, narodni podnik v Anheuser Busch Inc*
     [2011] ECR I-8701, [2012] RPC 247, [2011] All ER (D) 74 (Oct), ECJ.
4   As to the meaning of 'use' see PARA 44 note 8.
5   As to the meaning of 'registered trade mark' see PARA 111.
6   As to the meaning of 'United Kingdom' see PARA 3 note 2.
7   Trade Marks Act 1994 s 48(1) (derived from Council Directive (EEC) 89/104 (OJ L40, 11.2.89,
     p 1) art 9(1), (2) (see now European Parliament and Council Directive (EC) 2008/95 (OJ L299,
     8.11.2008, p 25) art 9(1), (2))). Four conditions must be satisfied for the five-year period to start
     running: (1) the later trade mark must be registered; (2) the later trade mark must have been
     registered in good faith; (3) the later trade mark must be used by its proprietor; and (4) the
     proprietor of the earlier trade mark must be aware of the registration and use of the later trade
     mark: Case C-482/09 *Budejovicky Budvar, narodni podnik v Anheuser Busch Inc* [2011] ECR
     I-8701, [2012] RPC 247, [2011] All ER (D) 74 (Oct), ECJ; Case T-133/09 *I Marchi Italiani Srl
     v Office for Harmonisation in the Internal Market (Trade Marks and Designs)* [2012] All ER
     (D) 76 (Jul), EGC (affd Case C-381/12P [2013] ECR I-0000, ECJ).
     As to trade mark registrations applied for in bad faith see PARA 53.
8   Trade Marks Act 1994 s 48(2) (derived from Council Directive (EEC) 89/104 (OJ L40, 11.2.89,
     p 1) art 9(3) (see now European Parliament and Council Directive (EC) 2008/95 (OJ L299,
     8.11.2008, p 25) art 9(3))). It is not clear whether this would prevent a complaint based on
     passing off having regard to the Trade Marks Act 1994 s 2(2) (see PARA 398), although such a
     complaint might be barred by common law or equitable acquiescence.
9   See the Trade Marks (International Registration) Order 2008, SI 2008/2206, art 3; and PARA 12.
     See also generally PARA 11 et seq.

84.   Consent, acquiescence and delay.   A claimant's right of action for the
infringement of a trade mark may be barred by consent, acquiescence or
inordinate delay[1]. Clearly, consent to the use complained of is a bar to an
action[2]. Consent may be given formally pursuant to a licence[3] or informally[4].
The proprietor of a registered trade mark may invoke the rights conferred by

that trade mark against a licensee who contravenes any provision in his licensing contract with regard to its duration, the form covered by the registration in which the trade mark may be used, the scope of the goods or services for which the licence is granted, the territory in which the trade mark may be affixed, or the quality of the goods manufactured or of the services provided by the licensee[5]. Where there has been an express terminable licence, consent may be withdrawn by termination of the licence[6]. A gratuitous licence will normally be revocable upon reasonable notice[7]. Acquiescence may bar a claim where the proprietor has in some way allowed or encouraged the infringer to assume that no objection will be taken to the acts in question so that the subsequent enforcement of the right would be unconscionable[8]. Mere delay on the claimant's part, even with knowledge of the defendant's activities, does not amount to acquiescence[9]; but inordinate delay may give rise to a defence of laches if there are intervening acts which justify a refusal of relief[10]. Delay may also affect a claimant's right to damages[11] or delivery up[12] or other remedies[13].

1   As to acquiescence and delay generally see CIVIL PROCEDURE vol 11 (2009) PARAS 373–375; EQUITY vol 16(2) (Reissue) PARA 909 et seq.
2   This is in any event explicit: see the Trade Marks Act 1994 s 9(1); and PARA 66. In addition, no action will lie in relation to goods which have been put on the market in the European Economic Area with the proprietor's consent (which may be express or implied) unless there are legitimate reasons to oppose further commercialisation: see the Trade Marks Act 1994 s 12; and PARAS 87–88.
3   As to licensing of trade marks see PARAS 119–120.
4   Consent may in some cases be inferred: see PARA 91 text and notes 7, 8.
5   Council Directive (EEC) 89/104 (OJ L40, 11.2.89, p 1) art 8(2). This provision has not been transposed into the Trade Marks Act 1994, but ss 9(1) and 12(1) must be interpreted in accordance with it: see PARA 5 text and note 3. This provision is to be interpreted as meaning that the proprietor of a trade mark can invoke the rights conferred by that trade mark against a licensee who contravenes a provision in a licence agreement prohibiting, on grounds of the trade mark's prestige, sales to discount stores of goods such as the ones at issue in the main proceedings, provided it has been established that that contravention, by reason of the situation prevailing in the case in the main proceedings, damages the allure and prestigious image which bestows on those goods an aura of luxury: Case C-59/08 *Copad SA v Christian Dior Couture SA* [2009] ECR I-3421, [2011] IP & T 166, [2009] ETMR 40, ECJ.
6   See e g *Bostitch Trade Mark* [1963] RPC 183.
7   *Edwardes v Cotton* (1902) 19 TLR 34 (a copyright case); *Hart v Hyman* (1916) MacG Cop Cas (1911–16) 301 (a copyright case).
8   The extent to which acquiescence under English common law can be relied on as a defence in circumstances falling outside the new statutory acquiescence defence (see PARA 83) is not clear. For the common law see *Habib Bank Ltd v Habib Bank AG Zurich* [1981] 2 All ER 650, [1981] 1 WLR 1265, [1982] RPC 1, CA. The European Court of Justice has held that Council Directive (EEC) 89/104 (OJ L40, 11.2.89, p 1) art 5 precludes the proprietor of trade marks which, in a situation where there has been use shared with a third party, had consented to the use by that third party of signs which are identical to its marks in respect of certain goods in classes for which those marks are registered and which no longer consents to that use, from being deprived of any possibility of asserting the exclusive right conferred upon it by those marks against that third party and of itself exercising that exclusive right in respect of goods which are identical to those of that third party: Case C-661/11 *Martin Y Paz Diffusion SA v Depuydt* [2013] ECR I-0000, [2013] All ER (D) 208 (Sep), ECJ.
9   *Farmers Build Ltd v Carier Bulk Materials Handling Ltd* [1999] RPC 461, [2000] IP & T 49, CA (a design right case); *Jones v Stones* [1999] 1 WLR 1739, 78 P & CR 293, CA; *Re Loftus, Green v Gaul* [2006] EWCA Civ 1124, [2006] 4 All ER 1110, [2007] 1 WLR 591.
10   *Fisher v Brooker* [2009] UKHL 41, [2009] 4 All ER 789, [2009] 1 WLR 1764 (a copyright case). Normally detrimental reliance on the part of the defendant will be required: *Fisher v Brooker*.
11   See LIMITATION PERIODS vol 68 (2008) PARA 915 et seq.
12   See the Trade Marks Act 1994 s 18; and PARA 445.
13   Eg the claimant's right to an account: see PARAS 424, 426. As to injunctions see PARA 419 et seq.

85.   Effect of fraudulent trading or misrepresentation by the claimant.   Neither law nor equity assists a wholly fraudulent trade; both adopt the maxim 'ex turpi causa non oritur actio'[1]. Thus, if it is shown that the claimant's trade is of a fraudulent nature, he cannot succeed in any action for the use of his trade name or trade mark, or for passing off[2]. Normally, any fraudulent or deceptive use of his mark by a claimant will not only be a defence but will found an application for revocation of the registration[3]. Even where the claimant's trade is not wholly fraudulent, it seems that he is disentitled to equitable relief[4] if, in relation to the name or mark which he seeks to protect, he has been guilty of a material misrepresentation[5] calculated to mislead the public[6]. Whenever a mark is deceptive or used in a deceptive way, the modern practice is to dispute the validity of the registration, though these equitable defences would still, it seems, continue to be available[7]. Where the claimant is a company, it is not necessarily a defence that the claimant has failed to fulfil statutory requirements relating to the use of its name[8].

1   Ie no right of action arises from a bad cause: see EQUITY vol 16(2) (Reissue) PARA 560.
2   *Lee v Haley* (1869) 5 Ch App 155; *Ford v Foster* (1872) 7 Ch App 611 at 631; *Newman v Pinto* (1887) 4 RPC 508, CA; *Bile Bean Manufacturing Co v Davidson* (1906) 23 RPC 725, Ct of Sess; cf *California Fig Syrup Co v Taylor's Drug Co Ltd* (1897) 14 RPC 341 at 347 (on appeal 14 RPC 564, CA). There are difficulties in determining the scope of this principle: *Inter Lotto (UK) Ltd v Camelot Group plc* [2003] EWCA Civ 1132 at [33], [2003] 4 All ER 575 at [33], [2004] RPC 186 at [33] per Carnwath LJ. See also *Lilly Icos LLC v 8PM Chemists Ltd* [2009] EWHC 1905 (Ch), [2010] FSR 95; and *Les Laboratoires Servier v Apotex Inc* [2012] EWCA Civ 593, [2012] IP & T 925. In relation to passing off see also PARA 330. As to the prohibition of the registration of immoral, deceptive and illegal marks see PARAS 47–49.
3   Ie under the Trade Marks Act 1994 s 46(1)(d): see PARA 100.
4   The practice of the former Court of Chancery was not necessarily to refuse an injunction absolutely in a case where there had been misrepresentation but to refuse it unless and until the plaintiff had established a title at law: *Pidding v How* (1837) 8 Sim 477; *Perry v Truefitt* (1842) 6 Beav 66; *Flavel v Harrison* (1853) 10 Hare 467 at 473. It has been suggested that a misrepresentation which would be a good objection to affording equitable relief may not be an answer to a common law action for damages: *Jamieson & Co v Jamieson* (1898) 15 RPC 169 at 191, CA; and see *Wolff & Son v Nopitsch* (1900) 18 RPC 27 at 32, CA (possible distinction between action to enforce property right or right given by statute and action for passing off); cf *Ford v Foster* (1872) 7 Ch App 611 at 630 (explaining *Sykes v Sykes* (1824) 3 B & C 541).
5   Under the old law a representation that an article was such a misrepresentation (*Leather Cloth Co Ltd v American Leather Cloth Co Ltd* (1865) 11 HL Cas 523 at 543) if there had never been such a patent (*Flavel v Harrison* (1853) 10 Hare 467), or where the patent had expired (*Cheavin v Walker* (1877) 5 ChD 850 at 862, CA, overruling *Edelsten v Vick* (1853) 11 Hare 78). See also *Re A Boake, Roberts & Co Ltd's Trade Marks* (1909) 26 RPC 251. Where, however, 'patent' had become part of the name of the article, this rule would not apply: *Marshall v Ross* (1869) LR 8 Eq 651. See also *Gridley v Swimborne* (1888) 5 TLR 71, DC; *Cochrane v Macnish* [1896] AC 225, 13 RPC 100, PC. The same rule applied to a representation that a design (*Winser v Armstrong & Co* (1899) 16 RPC 167 at 172) or trade mark (*Lewis v Goodbody* (1892) 67 LT 194) was registered, but the use of 'Trade Mark' was not necessarily such a representation (*Sen Sen Co v Britten* [1899] 1 Ch 692, 16 RPC 137). Misrepresentations made by the plaintiff after the action was brought were not a bar to his right of action: *Siegert v Findlater* (1878) 7 ChD 801 at 811.
6   *Leather Cloth Co Ltd v American Leather Cloth Co Ltd* (1865) 11 HL Cas 523 at 542–543. Cf *Ford v Foster* (1872) 7 Ch App 611 (where a misrepresentation that the plaintiff was a patentee contained in invoices and advertisements was treated as a collateral misrepresentation not disentitling him to an injunction although affecting his right to an account). See also the cases cited in note 5. For further cases where misrepresentations have been held not to affect the plaintiff's rights see *Mrs Pomeroy Ltd v Scalé* (1906) 24 RPC 177 at 192 (representation that defendant was plaintiff's business manager after defendant had ceased to be such); *Plotzker v Lucas* (1907) 24 RPC 551 at 562, Ct of Sess (misrepresentation that plaintiffs were actual manufacturers).
7   It is not clear, however, whether to permit an equitable defence to a claim for infringement in circumstances where the trade mark was not liable to revocation would be consistent with

Council Directive (EEC) 89/104 (OJ L40, 11.2.89, p 1) to approximate the laws of the member states relating to trade marks (see now European Parliament and Council Directive (EC) 2008/95 (OJ L299, 8.11.2008, p 25)).

8 *Pearks, Gunston and Tee Ltd v Thompson, Talmey & Co* (1901) 18 RPC 185, CA; *HE Randall Ltd v British and American Shoe Co* [1902] 2 Ch 354 at 357, 19 RPC 393 at 402. See COMPANIES vol 14 (2009) PARA 220 et seq. Cf *Re Albert Baker & Co's Application* [1908] 2 Ch 86 at 103, 25 RPC 513 at 524; *Re Mann's Trade Marks* (1919) 36 RPC 189.

(iii) Exhaustion of Rights and Related Defences

86. Parallel trade; general position. A question of particular importance arises where the proprietor of a registered trade mark[1] in the United Kingdom[2], or a related party, markets goods under that trade mark, or another trade mark, in other countries: namely, in what circumstances other parties may, possibly in opposition to the wishes of the proprietor[3], acquire the proprietor's goods in one country and import them into another country (so-called 'parallel trade' or 'parallel importation'). This question can arise in the context both of importation to, and export from, the United Kingdom. Frequently there will be parallel trade mark rights in the two countries; and in current commercial conditions this question may be complicated by the fact that in practice it is quite likely that such parallel trade mark rights will be vested in different corporate entities within a multinational group of companies[4]. A further potential complication is that the trade mark rights in one or other or both of those countries may be exploited by a local licensee or distributor, rather than by the proprietor himself[5].

The position differs markedly, depending upon whether or not the countries of export and import are within the European Economic Area ('EEA')[6]. In the case of goods imported into the United Kingdom which were marketed in another country of the EEA, or vice versa, there is a wide-ranging statutory defence against infringement provided by the Trade Marks Act 1994[7]; and in addition there are defences arising under directly applicable provisions of the Treaty on the Functioning of the European Union[8]. In the case of importation of goods into the United Kingdom from a country outside the EEA importation is likely to be an infringement[9].

The export from the United Kingdom of goods placed on the market here by the proprietor of the trade mark will not in general amount to infringement of the trade mark registered in the United Kingdom, even if done without his consent or contrary to his express wishes[10], unless there exist legitimate reasons for the proprietor to oppose such export[11]. The export of goods in such circumstances may, however, result in liabilities arising from contravention of the laws of the country of importation[12].

In the context of parallel rights, the position under the law of passing off will also need to be considered[13].

1 This also applies to a protected international trade mark (UK) or a Community trade mark. As to the meaning of 'protected international trade mark (UK)' see PARA 12 note 8. See generally PARA 11 et seq. As to Community trade marks see PARA 159 et seq.
2 As to the meaning of 'United Kingdom' see PARA 3 note 2.
3 The proprietor may wish to prevent such cross-border trade for a variety of reasons: to maintain price differentials between national markets; to preserve good relations with distributors or retailers; or to prevent goods of differing qualities or characteristics from passing from one market to another.
4 See e g the complex company and trade mark ownership structure considered in *Revlon Inc v Cripps and Lee Ltd* [1980] FSR 85, 124 Sol Jo 184, CA.

5   The licensing of registered trade marks has in general become easier under the Trade Marks
    Act 1994, which explicitly countenances both exclusive and non-exclusive licences (see PARAS
    119–120), as compared with the position under the Trade Marks Act 1938.
6   The EEA was created by the Agreement on the European Economic Area (Oporto, 2 May 1992;
    Cm 2073; OJ L1, 3.1.94, p 3) (the 'EEA Agreement'). The EEA Agreement was between the
    European Community and its member states and the then states of the European Free Trade
    Association, namely Austria, Finland, Iceland, Liechtenstein, Norway, Switzerland and Sweden,
    and was intended to create an area of 19 countries throughout which the 'four freedoms' of the
    European Community (the free movement of goods, capital, services and people) would apply.
    The Protocol adjusting that Agreement (Brussels, 17 March 1993 OJ L1, 3.1.94, p 572) had the
    effect of excluding Switzerland, which chose on 1 December 1992 not to participate, and
    Liechtenstein; enabled the EEA Agreement to enter into force without being ratified by those
    two countries; and allowed for Liechtenstein to join the EEA Agreement at a future date: see 230
    HC Official Report (6th series), cols 414, 463. Austria, Finland and Sweden, who were member
    states of the EEA, moved on to become full members of the European Community on 1 January
    1995. In the same year Liechtenstein joined the EEA. At the date at which this volume states the
    law the EEA thus comprises the European Union (and Croatia once formally ratified) together
    with Iceland and Liechtenstein and Norway. The EEA Agreement was implemented in the
    United Kingdom by the European Economic Area Act 1993 which came into force on
    5 November 1993. As to the aims and provisions of the EEA Agreement see 539 HL Official
    Report (5th series), col 1315 et seq.
7   See the Trade Marks Act 1994 s 12(1); and PARA 87.
8   Ie the Treaty on the Functioning of the European Union (Rome, 25 March 1957; TS 1 (1973);
    Cmnd 5179) ('TFEU'). The Treaty was formerly known as the Treaty Establishing the European
    Community ('the EC Treaty'); it has been renamed and its provisions renumbered (see below).
        On 13 December 2007, the European Union (EU) member states signed the Treaty of Lisbon
    Amending the Treaty Establishing the European Union and the Treaty Establishing the European
    Community (Lisbon, 13 December 2007, ECS 13 (2007); Cm 7294) (OJ C306, 17.12.2007).
    The Treaty of Lisbon entered into force on 1 December 2009. The aim of the Treaty of Lisbon
    is to complete the process started by the Treaty of Amsterdam in 1997 and by the Treaty of Nice
    in 2001 with a view to enhancing the efficiency and democratic legitimacy of the Union and to
    improving the coherence of its action. In effect, the Treaty of Lisbon further amends and
    renumbers (1) the Treaty of Maastricht 1992 (also known as the Treaty Establishing the
    European Union, or the Treaty on the European Union, or 'TEU') (Maastricht, 7 February 1992;
    TS 12 (1994); Cm 2485); and (2) the Treaty of Rome 1957 (formerly known as the Treaty
    Establishing the European Community, or 'TEC', or the 'EC Treaty' (see above)). The Treaty of
    Lisbon also renames the Treaty Establishing the European Community: it is now named the
    Treaty on the Functioning of the European Union, or 'TFEU'. All references to the EC Treaty are
    now obsolete and have been renumbered by the TFEU. The name of the Treaty on the European
    Union remains unchanged.
        See PARAS 89–90.
9   See PARA 91.
10 Although the Trade Marks Act 1994 s 10(4)(c) (see PARA 72 head (3)) makes the export of
    goods under the trade mark an infringing use, that provision is subject to s 12(1) (see PARA 87).
    Once the goods have been placed on the market by the proprietor or with his consent within the
    EEA (which includes placing on the market within the United Kingdom itself), s 12(1) shields
    subsequent use of the trade mark in relation to those goods from being an infringement. It is not
    necessary, for s 12(1) to apply, that the goods should have crossed an intra-EEA frontier, and use
    of the mark by export (defined to amount to use by s 10(4)(c)) appears to be shielded by s 12(1)
    in the same way as would be use of the mark in the course of eg a resale of the goods internally
    within the United Kingdom.
11 See the Trade Marks Act 1994 s 12(2); and PARA 87. Such legitimate reasons include in
    particular where the condition of the goods has been changed or impaired after they have been
    put on the market: see s 12(2). Whether the desire of the proprietor of the trade mark not to
    undermine the market in the country to which the goods are being exported, or a difference in
    the quality of the goods sold there under the mark, could itself amount to a 'legitimate reason'
    in such a context is for the courts to decide. These would plainly not amount to legitimate
    reasons in an intra-EEA context: see PARA 87.
12 Whether any such liability would arise would depend upon the law of the country of
    importation. As to whether any action could be taken in the English courts in respect of the
    exporter's involvement in a possible infringement of the trade mark laws of the country of
    importation see CONFLICT OF LAWS. In the case of passing off, as distinct from statutory trade
    mark infringement, a trader in England can be sued in England for exporting goods to foreign

markets where the goods are calculated to be used as instruments of deception in that market, or for becoming a joint tortfeasor with persons abroad who use such goods or other materials for the purpose of passing off in foreign markets: see PARAS 314–315.

13   See PARA 329.

87.   Statutory exhaustion of rights where goods marketed within the European Economic Area.   A registered trade mark[1] is not infringed by the use[2] of the trade mark in relation to goods[3] which have been put on the market in the European Economic Area ('EEA')[4] under that trade mark[5] by the proprietor or with his consent[6]; but this provision does not apply where there exist legitimate reasons for the proprietor to oppose further dealings in the goods, in particular, where the condition of the goods has been changed or impaired after they have been put on the market[7]. Corresponding provisions apply to Community trade marks[8].

The above provision broadly corresponds to the position established under the case law of the European Court of Justice[9] in the context of trade between member states within the European Union. However, in some respects it may provide a defence in circumstances where the provisions of the Treaty on the Functioning of the European Union ('TFEU') would not do so[10]. There are in some circumstances defences other than 'exhaustion' available under the TFEU[11]; and there would seem to be no reason why the introduction of the above statutory defence should curtail the ambit of the defences under the TFEU in circumstances to which in the past they have been held to apply.

1   This also applies to a protected international trade mark (UK): see PARA 66. As to the meaning of 'registered trade mark' see PARA 111. As to the meaning of 'protected international trade mark (UK)' see PARA 12 note 8.

2   As to the meaning of 'use' see PARA 44 note 8.

3   Although on its face this provision only applies to goods, it is arguable that it should be interpreted as applying also to services in appropriate circumstances.

4   It is immaterial that the goods were manufactured in a non-EEA country if they have been put on the market in the EEA by the proprietor or with his consent: Case C-352/95 *Phytherion International SA v Jean Bourdon SA* [1997] ECR I-1729, [1997] FSR 936, ECJ. Importation of goods into the EEA does not amount to putting them on the market: Case C-296/00 *Prefetto Provincia di Cunea v Carbone* [2002] ECR I-4657, [2002] All ER (D) 480 (May), ECJ. Nor does offering goods for sale but not selling them; goods are put on the market in the EEA when they have been sold to an independent third party who acquires the right of disposal of the goods: Case C-16/03 *Peak Holding AB v Axolin-Elinor AB* [2005] Ch 261, [2004] ECR I-11313, ECJ. Where goods have been put on the market in the EEA, territorial restrictions on the purchaser's right to resell the goods do not preclude exhaustion of the proprietor's trade mark rights: Case C-16/03 *Peak Holding AB v Axolin-Elinor AB.* The sale of gas bottles precludes the exclusive licensee of trade marks affixed to the bottles from preventing the exchange of those bottles once empty for bottles filled with a competitor's gas (in the absence of a legitimate reason to oppose further commercialisation: Case C-46/10 *Viking Gas A/S v Kosan Gas A/S* [2011] ECR I-6161, [2011] ETMR 58, ECJ. Goods supplied to authorised distributors solely for demonstration purposes have not been put on the market with the proprietor's consent: Case C-127/09 *Coty Prestige Lancaster Group GmbH v Simex Trading AG* [2010] ECR I-4965, [2010] FSR 875, [2010] All ER (D) 82 (Jun), ECJ; Case C-324/09 *L'Oréal SA v eBay International AG* [2012] All ER (EC) 501, [2011] ETMR 52, ECJ. As to the EEA see PARA 86 note 6.

5   Where the goods are put on the market in a country other than the United Kingdom, it is immaterial whether or not the trade mark is registered in that country; all that matters is whether the goods are put on the market by or with the consent of the proprietor of the United Kingdom registration: cf Case C-187/80 *Merck & Co Inc v Stephar BV* [1981] ECR 2063, [1982] FSR 57, ECJ (a patent case). It seems likely that this provision will apply if the goods are put on the market under a sign which is 'identical' with the trade mark within the meaning of the Trade Marks Act 1994 s 10(1) (see PARAS 55 note 3, 68): cf Case C-313/94 *Fratelli Graffione SNC v Ditta Fransa* [1996] ECR I-6039, [1997] 1 CMLR 925, ECJ (COTONELLE/COTTONELLE).

6   Trade Marks Act 1994 s 12(1) (derived from Council Directive (EEC) 89/104 (OJ L40, 11.2.89, p 1) to approximate the laws of the member states relating to trade marks, art 7(1) (see now European Parliament and Council Directive (EC) 2008/95 (OJ L299, 8.11.2008, p 25) art 7(1))). As to the meaning of references to doing anything with or without the consent of the proprietor of a registered trade mark see the Trade Marks Act 1994 s 28(3); and PARA 119.
     For the purposes of s 12(1), marketing within the EEA by or with the consent of an economically-linked undertaking is deemed to be marketing by or with the consent of the proprietor: Case 9/93 *IHT Internationale Heiztechnik GmbH v Ideal Standard GmbH* [1994] ECR I-2789, [1995] FSR 59, ECJ. This principle does not apply to goods put on the market outside the EEA: *Roche Products Ltd v Kent Pharmaceuticals Ltd* [2006] EWCA Civ 1775, [2007] ETMR 27, [2006] All ER (D) 318 (Dec); and see *Mastercigars Direct Ltd v Hunters & Frankau Ltd* [2007] EWCA Civ 176, [2007] RPC 565, [2007] ETMR 44. It is not clear how far the concept of an 'economically-linked undertaking' extends for this purpose: see *Doncaster Pharmaceuticals Group Ltd v Bolton Pharmaceutical Co 100 Ltd* [2006] EWCA Civ 661, [2007] FSR 63.
     A licensee who puts goods bearing a trade mark on the market in disregard of a provision in a licence agreement does so without the consent of the proprietor of the trade mark where it is established that the provision in question is included in those listed in Council Directive (EEC) 89/104 (OJ L40, 11.2.89, p 1) art 8(2): Case C-59/08 *Copad SA v Christian Dior Couture SA* [2009] ECR I-3421, [2011] IP & T 166, [2009] ETMR 40, ECJ.
     The Trade Marks Act 1994 s 12 applies in relation to an existing registered mark as from 31 October 1994, subject to s 105, Sch 3 para 4(2) (see PARA 81): Sch 3 para 4(1). The old law continues to apply in relation to infringements committed before that date: Sch 3 para 4(1). As to the meaning of 'existing registered mark' see PARA 4 note 2; and as to the meaning of 'the old law' see PARA 4 note 3.
7   Trade Marks Act 1994 s 12(2) (derived from Council Directive (EEC) 89/104 (OJ L40, 11.2.89, p 1) art 7(2) (see now European Parliament and Council Directive (EC) 2008/95 (OJ L299, 8.11.2008, p 25) art 7(2))). As to what can amount to such legitimate reasons see PARA 88.
8   See Council Regulation (EC) 207/2009 (OJ L78, 24.3.2009, p 1) on the Community trade mark, art 13(1) (formerly Council Regulation (EC) 40/94 (OJ L11, 14.1.94, p 1) art 13(1)); and PARA 217.
9   Ie under the Treaty Establishing the European Community (Rome, 25 March 1957; TS 1 (1973); Cmnd 5179) (the 'EC Treaty') arts 28–30 (formerly arts 30–36; renumbered by virtue of the Treaty of Amsterdam: see *Treaty Citation (No 2) (Note)* [1999] All ER (EC) 646, ECJ) (and see now the Treaty on the Functioning of the European Union (Rome, 25 March 1957; TS 1 (1973); Cmnd 5179) ('TFEU') arts 34–36 (see PARA 86 note 8). As to the case law on free movement of goods see PARA 89.
10   Eg, unlike the defences under the TFEU, it appears to extend both to export from the United Kingdom to a non-EEA country (see PARA 86) and also to purely internal transactions within the United Kingdom which involve no inter-state trade element. All that is required for the Trade Marks Act 1994 s 12(1) to operate is that the goods shall have been placed on the market within the EEA, which on the face of it includes placing them on the market within the United Kingdom. As to the TFEU see note 9.
11   See PARA 89. See e g the case where the trade mark owner uses different trade marks in the different markets and the parallel importer substitutes one mark for the other (see PARA 89 text and note 5).

88. Legitimate reasons for the proprietor to oppose further dealings in the goods.

This exception to the statutory defence of exhaustion of rights under the Trade Marks Act 1994[1] is based upon[2] an exception to the rules on free movement of goods developed in the earlier case law[3] of the European Court of Justice. It was there established that the guarantee of origin provided by the presence of the trade mark means that the consumer or end user can be certain that the product has not been subject at a previous stage of marketing to interference by a third party, without the authorisation of the trade mark proprietor, in such a way as to affect the original condition of the product[4]. Accordingly, operations which interfere with or put at risk the original condition of the goods or which alter or interfere with their packaging may potentially give rise to legitimate reasons for the proprietor to oppose use of the mark on the affected goods[5].

A trade mark owner may legitimately oppose the further marketing of a pharmaceutical product where a third party has repackaged it and re-affixed the trade mark[6], unless the following five conditions are met[7]:

(1)   it is established that the enforcement of the trade mark rights by the owner would contribute to the artificial partitioning of the markets between the member states[8];

(2)   it is shown that the repackaging cannot adversely affect the original condition of the product inside the packaging[9];

(3)   the new packaging clearly states who repackaged the product and the name of the manufacturer[10];

(4)   the presentation of the repackaged product is not such as to be liable to damage the reputation of the trade mark and of its owner; and in particular the packaging must not be defective, of poor quality or untidy; and

(5)   the importer gives notice to the trade mark owner before the repackaged product is put on sale, and on demand supplies him with a specimen of the repackaged product[11].

The same conditions apply where the third party has affixed an additional external label[12].

Similar conditions apply to other types of goods[13]. Similar conditions also apply if, rather than repackaging the product, the parallel importer either removes and re-affixes or replaces labels bearing the trade mark[14].

In general, the reseller of trade marked goods must not act unfairly in relation to the legitimate interests of the trade mark owner, in particular in a way which damages the reputation of the trade mark[15]; however, the trade mark owner cannot object to the resale of his goods in a physically unaltered state merely because he objects to the 'down market' nature of the trade channels through which they are sold or the mode of advertising used in the sector of the retail trade concerned, unless it is established that, given the specific circumstances of the case, the use of the trade mark for this purpose damages the reputation of the trade mark[16]. Where a trade mark is used in advertising genuine goods of the trade mark owner in a way to which he takes objection, the considerations which relate to the question of whether the trade mark owner has legitimate reasons to oppose that use are very similar to those relating to the question of whether other permitted uses of a trade mark are in accordance with honest practices in industrial and commercial matters[17].

A number of situations have been recognised by the courts in the past where the marketing of genuine goods originating from the owner of a trade mark can nonetheless give rise to an action for passing off, for example where secondhand or used goods are sold as new, or where old deteriorated goods are sold as fresh, or where outmoded or superseded goods are sold as current production. In all these situations previously recognised by the law of passing off, it is likely that the courts will hold that the proprietor of a registered trade mark has legitimate reasons for opposing use of his trade mark in relation to the goods concerned[18].

The trade mark owner is not entitled to oppose the importation and resale of his goods unaltered from the state in which they were put on the market by him in one member state, because their quality differs from that of the goods sold by him under the mark in the market of importation[19].

1   Ie the exception contained in the Trade Marks Act 1994 s 12(2) to the defence against infringement provided by s 12(1), which provisions are in turn based upon Council Directive (EEC) 89/104 (OJ L40, 11.2.89, p 1) to approximate the laws of the member states relating to

trade marks, art 7 (see now European Parliament and Council Directive (EC) 2008/95 (OJ L299, 8.11.2008, p 25) art 7). As to this defence see PARA 87.

2   Joined Cases C-427/93, C-429/93 and C-436/93 *Bristol-Myers Squibb v Paranova A/S* [2003] Ch 75, [1996] ECR I-3457, ECJ. In this case, the court stated that Council Directive (EEC) 89/104 (OJ L40, 11.2.89, p 1) art 7 (see now European Parliament and Council Directive (EC) 2008/95 (OJ L299, 8.11.2008, p 25) art 7) reiterates the case law of the ECJ, and that it must be interpreted in the same way: see Joined Cases C-427/93, C-429/93 and C-436/93 *Bristol-Myers Squibb v Paranova A/S* at [31], [40].

3   Ie the rules on free movement of goods developed by the European Court of Justice under the Treaty Establishing the European Community (Rome, 25 March 1957; TS 1 (1973); Cmnd 5179) (the 'EC Treaty') arts 28–30 (formerly arts 30–36; renumbered by virtue of the Treaty of Amsterdam: see *Treaty Citation (No 2) (Note)* [1999] All ER (EC) 646, ECJ) (and see now the Treaty on the Functioning of the European Union (Rome, 25 March 1957; TS 1 (1973); Cmnd 5179) ('TFEU') arts 34–36 (see PARA 86 note 8): see PARA 89.

4   Case 102/77 *F Hoffman-La Roche & Co AG v Centrafarm Vertriebsgesellschaft Pharmazeutischer Erzeugnisse mbH* [1978] ECR 1139, [1978] 3 CMLR 217, ECJ; Case 1/81 *Pfizer Inc v Eurim-Pharm GmbH* [1981] ECR 2913, [1982] 1 CMLR 406, ECJ. This function of the guarantee of origin has been reiterated by the European Court of Justice as applicable in the context of Council Directive (EEC) 89/104 (OJ L40, 11.2.89, p 1) art 7 (see now European Parliament and Council Directive (EC) 2008/95 (OJ L299, 8.11.2008, p 25) art 7): see Joined Cases C-427/93, C-429/93 and C-436/93 *Bristol-Myers Squibb v Paranova A/S* [2003] Ch 75 at [47], [1996] ECR I-3457 at [47], ECJ; Case C-143/00 *Boehringer Ingelheim KG v Swingward Ltd* [2003] Ch 27 at [12], [2002] ECR I-3759 at [12], ECJ.

5   See Joined Cases C-427/93, C-429/93 and C-436/93 *Bristol-Myers Squibb v Paranova A/S* [1996] ECR I-3457, [1997] FSR 102, ECJ; Case C-379/97 *Pharmacia & Upjohn SA v Paranova A/S* [2000] Ch 571, [1999] All ER (EC) 880, [1999] ECR I-6927, ECJ; Case C-143/00 *Boehringer Ingelheim KG v Swingward Ltd* [2003] Ch 27, [2002] ECR I-3759, ECJ; Case C-348/04 *Boehringer Ingelheim KG v Swingward Ltd (No 2)* [2008] All ER (EC) 411, [2007] ECR I-3391, ECJ; Case C-276/05 *Wellcome Foundation Ltd v Paranova Pharmazeutika Handels GmbH* [2008] ECR I-10479, [2009] All ER (D) 106 (Jan), ECJ; *Speciality European Pharma Ltd v Doncaster Pharmaceuticals Group Ltd* [2013] EWHC 3624 (Ch), [2013] All ER (D) 291 (Nov).

6   The position is the same if the parallel importer repackages the product in new external packaging which does not bear the trade mark but leaves intact the original internal packaging to which the trade mark was affixed by the proprietor (or which contains tablets or capsules to which the trade mark was affixed by the proprietor ('partial debranding'); but it appears that the position is otherwise if the parallel importer repackages the product in a manner which removes all traces of the trade mark ('complete debranding'), in which case there is no infringement: *Boehringer Ingelheim KG and Boehringer Ingelheim Pharma GmbH v Swingward Ltd* [2004] EWCA Civ 757, [2004] IP & T 1026, [2004] ETMR 65; but see note 7.

7   Joined Cases C-427/93, C-429/93 and C-436/93 *Bristol-Myers Squibb v Paranova A/S* [2003] Ch 75 at [49], [1996] ECR I-3457 at [49], ECJ (restating the conditions stated in Case 102/77 *Hoffmann-La Roche & Co AG v Centrafarm* [1978] ECR 1139 at [7], ECJ). The conditions have been refined in the subsequent cases of Case C-379/97 *Pharmacia & Upjohn SA (formerly Upjohn SA) v Paranova A/S* [2000] Ch 571, [1999] All ER (EC) 880, [1999] ECR I-6927, [2000] FSR 621, ECJ; Case C-143/00 *Boehringer Ingelheim KG v Swingward Ltd* [2003] Ch 27, [2002] ECR I-3759, ECJ; Case C-348/04 *Boehringer Ingelheim KG v Swingward Ltd (No 2)* [2008] All ER (EC) 411, [2007] ECR I-3391, ECJ; Case C-276/05 *Wellcome Foundation Ltd v Paranova Pharmazeutika Handels GmbH* [2008] ECR I-10479, [2009] All ER (D) 106 (Jan), ECJ; *Speciality European Pharma Ltd v Doncaster Pharmaceuticals Group Ltd* [2013] EWHC 3624 (Ch), [2013] All ER (D) 291 (Nov) and see also Case E-3/02 *Paranova A/S v Merck & Co Inc* [2003] 3 CMLR 177, [2004] ETMR 1, EFTA Ct. The burden of proving compliance with conditions lies with the third party, but the burden with regard to conditions (2) and (4) in the text is only evidential: Case C-348/04 *Boehringer Ingelheim KG v Swingward Ltd (No 2)* above.

8   This condition does not mean that it must be established that the trade mark owner deliberately sought to partition markets between member states: Joined Cases C-427/93, C-429/93 and C-436/93 *Bristol-Myers Squibb v Paranova A/S* [2003] Ch 75, [1996] ECR I-3457, ECJ. Instead, it means that it must be objectively necessary to replace the trade mark; the condition of necessity is satisfied if the prohibition on replacing the trade mark hinders effective access to the markets of the importing member states. By contrast it is not satisfied if replacement of the trade mark is explicable solely by the parallel importer's desire to obtain a commercial advantage: Case C-379/97 *Pharmacia & Upjohn SA (formerly Upjohn SA) v Paranova A/S* [2000] Ch 571,

[1999] All ER (EC) 880, [1999] ECR I-6927, ECJ. Repackaging is objectively necessary if, without such repackaging, effective access to the market concerned, or a substantial part of that market, must be considered to be hindered as a result of strong resistance from a significant proportion of consumers to overstickered pharmaceutical products: Case C-143/00 *Boehringer Ingelheim KG v Swingward Ltd* [2003] Ch 27, [2002] ECR I-3759, ECJ. The condition that repackaging must be necessary is directed solely at the fact of repackaging, not the manner and style: Case C-348/04 *Boehringer Ingelheim KG v Swingward Ltd (No 2)* [2008] All ER (EC) 411, [2007] ECR I-3391, ECJ. The condition does not mean that the interference with the trade mark's proprietors rights should be the minimum necessary: Case C-348/04 *Boehringer Ingelheim KG v Swingward Ltd (No 2)*; Case C-276/05 *Wellcome Foundation Ltd v Paranova Pharmazeutika Handels GmbH* [2008] ECR I-10479, [2009] All ER (D) 106 (Jan), ECJ. The parallel importer must furnish the trade mark proprietor with the information which is necessary and sufficient to enable the latter to determine whether the repackaging of the product is necessary in order to market it in the Member State of importation: Case C-276/05 *Wellcome Foundation Ltd v Paranova Pharmazeutika Handels GmbH*. See also *Speciality European Pharma Ltd v Doncaster Pharmaceuticals Group Ltd* [2013] EWHC 3624 (Ch), [2013] All ER (D) 291 (Nov).

9   This is the case, in particular, where the importer has merely carried out operations involving no risk of the product being affected, eg the removal of blister packs, flasks, ampoules or inhalers from their original external packaging and their replacement in new external packaging, the fixing of stickers on the inner packaging, the addition of new user information or the insertion of an extra article; but the original condition of the product must not be indirectly affected, eg by the omission of important information or the provision of inaccurate information or by the fact that an extra article inserted by the parallel importer does not comply with the method of use and doses envisaged by the manufacturer: Joined Cases C-427/93, C-429/93 and C-436/93 *Bristol-Myers Squibb v Paranova A/S* [2003] Ch 75, [1996] ECR I-3457, ECJ. A trade mark is not damaged by its removal from the product; whether a trade mark is damaged by repackaging or relabelling is a matter of fact for the court: *Glaxo Group Ltd v Dowelhurst Ltd (Nos 2 and 3)* [2008] EWCA Civ 83, [2008] IP & T 806.

10   This information must be stated in print such that a person with normal eyesight, exercising a normal degree of attentiveness, would be in a position to understand; similarly the origin of any extra article from a source other than the trade mark owner must be indicated in such a way as to dispel any impression that the trade mark owner is responsible for it; but it is not necessary to indicate the repackaging was carried out without the authorisation of the trade mark owner: Joined Cases C-427/93, C-429/93 and C-436/93 *Bristol-Myers Squibb v Paranova A/S* [2003] Ch 75, [1996] ECR I-3457, ECJ. See also *Glaxo Group Ltd v Dowelhurst Ltd (Nos 2 and 3)* [2008] EWCA Civ 83, [2008] IP & T 806; and note 9. The trade mark proprietor cannot object on the ground that the new packaging indicates as the repackager not the undertaking which, on instructions, actually repackaged the product and holds an authorisation to do so, but the undertaking which holds the marketing authorisation for the product, on whose instructions the repackaging was carried out, and which assumes liability for the repackaging: Joined Cases C-400/09 and C/207/10 *Orifarm A/S v Merck Sharp & Dohme Corp* [2011] ECR I-7063, [2012] 1 CMLR 251, ECJ.

11   Notice must be given by the importer, it being immaterial whether the trade mark owner is aware of the repackaging by other means; the period of notice depends on the circumstances but in general 15 working days is a reasonable infringement; if notice is not given that alone is sufficient for the importation to be an infringement: Case C-143/00 *Boehringer Ingelheim KG v Swingward Ltd* [2003] Ch 27, [2002] All ER (EC) 581, [2002] ECR I-3759, ECJ. Where a parallel importer has failed to give notice, every subsequent importation infringes; damages for such infringements may be claimed on the same basis as if the goods were spurious depending on the extent of the damage to the trade mark proprietor and the principle of proportionality: Case C-348/04 *Boehringer Ingelheim KG v Swingward Ltd (No 2)* [2007] All ER (EC) 411, [2007] ECR I-3391, ECJ. See also *Glaxo Group Ltd v Dowelhurst Ltd (Nos 2 and 3)* [2008] EWCA Civ 83, [2008] IP & T 806. An account of profits is not a disproportionate remedy in such a case: *Hollister Inc v Medik Ostomy Supplies Ltd* [2012] EWCA Civ 1419, [2013] Bus LR 428, [2013] IP & T 577.

12   Case C-348/04 *Boehringer Ingelheim KG v Swingward Ltd (No 2)* [2008] All ER (EC) 411, [2007] ECR I-3391, ECJ; but cf Case C-352/95 *Phytherion International SA v Jean Bourdon SA* [1997] ECR I-1729, [1997] FSR 936, ECJ. See also *Glaxo Group Ltd v Dowelhurst Ltd (Nos 2 and 3)* [2008] EWCA Civ 83, [2008] IP & T 806; and note 9.

13   Case C-349/95 *Frits Loendersloot (t/a F Loendersloot Internationale Expeditie) v George Ballantine & Son Ltd* [1997] ECR I-6227, [1998] 1 CMLR 1015, ECJ; *Sony Computer Entertainments Inc v Tesco Stores Ltd* [2000] ETMR 102.

14　Case C-349/95 *Frits Loendersloot (t/a F Loendersloot Internationale Expeditie) v George Ballantine & Son Ltd* [1997] ECR I-6227, [1998] 1 CMLR 1015, ECJ. In such a case the person carrying out the relabelling must use the means which make parallel trade feasible while causing as little prejudice as possible to the 'specific subject matter' of the trade mark right; thus if the original labels comply with the rules on labelling in the member state of importation, but those rules require additional information to be given, relabelling is not necessary since the mere application of a sticker with the additional information will suffice: *Frits Loendersloot (t/a F Loendersloot Internationale Expeditie) v George Ballantine & Son Ltd* above.

15　Case C-337/95 *Parfums Christian Dior SA v Evora BV* [1997] ECR I-6013, [1998] 1 CMLR 737 at [45], ECJ. See Case C-59/08 *Copad SA v Christian Dior Couture SA* [2009] ECR I-3421, [2011] IP & T 166, ECJ. The trade mark proprietor may oppose the resale of goods on the ground that the reseller had removed the packaging where this has the consequence that essential information is missing or that the image of the product, and hence the reputation of the trade mark is damaged: Case C-324/09 *L'Oréal SA v eBay International AG* [2012] All ER (EC) 501, [2011] RPC 777, ECJ.

16　Case C-337/95 *Parfums Christian Dior SA v Evora BV* [1997] ECR I-6013, [1998] 1 CMLR 737 at [46]–[47], ECJ; Case C-59/08 *Copad SA v Christian Dior Couture SA* [2009] ECR I-3421, [2011] IP & T 166, ECJ.

17　Case C-228/03 *Gillette Co v LA-Laboratories Ltd Oy* [2005] All ER (EC) 940, [2005] IP & T 1003, ECJ. As to such permitted uses and what amounts to honest practices see PARAS 77–80.

18　For these situations under the law of passing off see PARA 300 heads (1), (3)–(7), together with the cases cited; but not PARA 300 head (2) (as to which see note 19).

19　Having chosen to put goods of different qualities out in different parts of the European Community single market, the trade mark owner must then face the consequence of goods of different qualities circulating round the market: Case 58/80 *Dansk Supermarked A/S v A/S Imerco* [1981] ECR 181, [1981] 3 CMLR 590, ECJ. See also Commission Decision (EC) 74/432 [1974] 2 CMLR D79 (*Re Advocaat Zwarte Kip*).

89.　Defence of free circulation of goods under the Treaty on the Functioning of the European Union.　Apart from the statutory defence of exhaustion of rights under the Trade Marks Act 1994[1], the case law of the European Court of Justice has established that, once goods bearing a particular trade mark have been placed on the market somewhere in the European Union with the proprietor's consent, he cannot use trade mark rights to prevent the free circulation in the single market of those goods under the trade mark applied to them[2]. This rule applies even where the quality of the goods sold by the proprietor under the trade mark differs between the national markets concerned[3]. It is legitimate for a third party to repackage or relabel the goods and to re-affix the trade mark in some circumstances[4]. Where the trade mark owner puts the same goods on the market in different member states under different trade marks, it is legitimate for the parallel importer to substitute the trade mark used in the state of importation in place of the trade mark which was applied to the goods by the trade mark owner in the country where they were placed on the market, if it is objectively necessary to replace the original trade mark in order that the product in question can be effectively marketed in that state by the parallel importer[5].

This defence has no application to cases where the same or similar trade marks are used by unconnected proprietors in different member states, notwithstanding that the existence of such national rights may result in the effective partitioning of the single market[6]. In such cases it is for the national court to apply its ordinary rules in assessing the question of confusing similarity between the marks; and the European Court of Justice cannot interfere with such findings of fact which are in the exclusive jurisdiction of the national court[7]. However, for the purposes of European Union law, different corporate entities within a group of companies are generally treated as part of a single undertaking, together with economically linked entities such as licensees. Thus the rules stated above regarding free movement of goods apply regardless of whether the trade mark rights in different member states are vested in the same corporate entity or in economically-linked undertakings[8]. It is permissible, however, to assign trade marks in some, but not all, member states to an economically unconnected undertaking and in those member states the assigned marks may be enforceable against goods of the assignor and vice versa[9]. The former rule that trade mark rights were unenforceable in respect of the use of the same mark upon goods imported from another member state where the mark on the imported goods had a common origin with that of the proprietor has been departed from by the European Court of Justice[10].

The rules stated above apply in general to the other member countries of the European Economic Area ('EEA')[11] in the same way as to countries of the European Union[12]. Those rules do not, however, apply in the same way to countries which merely have association agreements with the European Union[13], despite the fact that the wording of the relevant association agreement may be similar or identical to the provisions of the Treaty on the Functioning of the European Union mentioned above[14].

The rules stated above do not apply in relation to goods first marketed outside the European Community or the EEA[15].

1   Ie the Trade Marks Act 1994 s 12: see PARA 87.
2   Ie applying the Treaty Establishing the European Community (Rome, 25 March 1957; TS 1 (1973); Cmnd 5179) (the 'EC Treaty') arts 28–30 (formerly arts 30–36; renumbered by virtue of the Treaty of Amsterdam: see *Treaty Citation (No 2) (Note)* [1999] All ER (EC) 646, ECJ) (and see now the Treaty on the Functioning of the European Union (Rome, 25 March 1957; TS 1 (1973); Cmnd 5179) ('TFEU') arts 34–36 (see PARA 86 note 8)) on the free circulation of goods, which have direct effect within member states. See e g Case 119/75 *Terrapin (Overseas) Ltd v Terranova Industrie CA Kapferer & Co* [1976] ECR 1039 at 1061, [1976] 2 CMLR 482 at 505–506, ECJ (trade mark case); Case 187/80 *Merck & Co Inc v Stephar BV* [1981] ECR 2063, [1981] 3 CMLR 463, ECJ (a patent case).
3   See PARA 88 note 19.
4   He may need to do this e g to comply with different labelling or packaging regulations or different market expectations in the country of importation. As to the circumstances in which repackaging or relabelling and re-affixing of the trade mark may be undertaken see PARA 88.
5   Case C-379/97 *Pharmacia & Upjohn SA (formerly Upjohn SA) v Paranova A/S* [2000] Ch 571, [1999] All ER (EC) 880, [1999] ECR I-6927, ECJ; see PARA 88 note 8. This situation is outside the defence provided by the Trade Marks Act 1994 s 12 and (EEC) Council Directive 89/104 (OJ L40, 11.2.89, p 1) to approximate the laws of the member states relating to trade marks, art 7 (see now European Parliament and Council Directive (EC) 2008/95 (OJ L299, 8.11.2008, p 25) art 7), since those provisions only cover the further use (or re-affixing) of the same mark as that put on the goods by the trade mark owner, not the substitution of a different mark of the same owner: Case C-379/97 *Pharmacia & Upjohn SA (formerly Upjohn SA) v Paranova A/S* at [27]–[28]. For the statutory defence see PARAS 87–88.
6   Case 119/75 *Terrapin (Overseas) Ltd v Terranova Industrie CA Kapferer & Co* [1976] ECR 1039 at 1061, [1976] 2 CMLR 482 at 505–506, ECJ (trade mark case).
7   Case C-317/91 *Deutsche Renault AG v Audi AG* [1993] ECR I-6227, [1995] 1 CMLR 461, ECJ. However, such national rules have been harmonised by Council Directive (EEC) 89/104 (OJ L40, 11.2.89, p 1) art 5 (now Council Regulation (EC) 207/2009 (OJ L78, 24.3.2009, p 1) art 5) and the European Court of Justice does have jurisdiction to interpret this.
8   Case C-9/93 *IHT Internationale Heiztechnik GmbH v Ideal-Standard GmbH* [1994] ECR I-2789, [1994] 3 CMLR 857, ECJ.
9   Case C-9/93 *IHT Internationale Heiztechnik GmbH v Ideal-Standard GmbH* [1994] ECR I-2789, [1994] 3 CMLR 857, ECJ. It appears that a further reference to the European Court of Justice may be required to elucidate the dividing line between ownership of trade marks by economically-linked parties and ownership of trade marks by independent parties as a result of assignment: *Doncaster Pharmaceuticals Ltd v Bolton Pharmaceutical Co 100 Ltd* [2006] EWCA Civ 661, [2006] ETMR 65.
10   Case C-10/89 *SA CNL-Sucal NV v Hag GF AG* [1990] ECR I-3711, [1990] 3 CMLR 571, [1991] FSR 99, ECJ (overruling Case 192/73 *Van Zuylen Frères v Hag AG* [1974] ECR 731, [1974] 2 CMLR 127).

11 As to the EEA see PARA 86 note 6.
12 The Agreement on the European Economic Area (Oporto, 2 May 1992; Cm 2073; OJ L1, 3.1.94, p 3) (the 'EEA Agreement') arts 10–13 correspond to the EC Treaty arts 28–30 (formerly arts 30–36; as renumbered) (and see now the Treaty on the Functioning of the European Union (Rome, 25 March 1957; TS 1 (1973); Cmnd 5179) ('TFEU') arts 34–36 (see note 2)). The provisions of the EEA Agreement which correspond substantially to provisions of the EC Treaty (ie now the TFEU) are to be interpreted in conformity with the relevant rulings of the European Court of Justice given prior to 2 May 1992: Agreement on the European Economic Area art 6.
13 Eg Switzerland.
14 Case 270/80 *Polydor Ltd v Harlequin Record Shops Ltd* [1982] ECR 329, [1982] 1 CMLR 677, ECJ (where the association agreement between the European Community and Portugal was interpreted as not giving rise to a right to parallel import, despite the similarity of its wording with that of the EC Treaty arts 28, 30 (formerly arts 30, 36; as renumbered) (see now the Treaty on the Functioning of the European Union (Rome, 25 March 1957; TS 1 (1973); Cmnd 5179) ('TFEU') arts 34–36) (see note 2), having regard to the different objects and purposes of the association agreement from the EC Treaty).
15 Case 51/75 *EMI Records Ltd v CBS United Kingdom Ltd* [1976] ECR 811, [1976] 2 CMLR 235, ECJ. See PARA 91.

90. Other defences under the Treaty on the Functioning of the European Union. The enforcement of trade mark rights so as to discriminate between imports from different member states may not be permissible as amounting[1] to an 'arbitrary discrimination'[2]. A deliberate decision to use different trade marks in different member states so as to achieve a partition is probably a disguised restriction on trade between member states and the enforcement of the trade mark rights would not be permitted[3]. It is not permissible to use trade mark rights as a means to achieve market sharing or partitioning of the single market[4]. It is not clear whether any of the reasoning in the earlier cases[5] survives, though it is likely that an exclusive right may not be relied upon if it is connected with an agreement or practice in restraint of competition within the European Union[6].

1 Ie within the meaning of the Treaty Establishing the European Community (Rome, 25 March 1957; TS 1 (1973); Cmnd 5179) (the 'EC Treaty') art 30 (formerly art 36; renumbered by virtue of the Treaty of Amsterdam: see *Treaty Citation (No 2) (Note)* [1999] All ER (EC) 646, ECJ) (and see now the Treaty on the Functioning of the European Union (Rome, 25 March 1957; TS 1 (1973); Cmnd 5179) ('TFEU') art 36 (see PARA 86 note 8)).
2 Case 102/77 *Hoffmann-La Roche & Co AG v Centrafarm Vertriebsgesellschaft Pharmazeutischer Erzeugnisse mbH* [1978] ECR 1139, [1978] 3 CMLR 217, [1978] FSR 598, ECJ.
3 Case 3/78 *Centrafarm BV v American Home Products Corpn* [1978] ECR 1823, [1979] 1 CMLR 326, [1979] FSR 189, ECJ.
4 Case C-9/93 *IHT Internationale Heiztechnik GmbH v Ideal-Standard GmbH* [1994] ECR I-2789, [1994] 3 CMLR 857, ECJ (following the principles in Cases 56/64, 58/64 *Etablissements Consten Sarl and Grundig-Verkaufs-GmbH v EC Commission* [1966] ECR 299, [1966] CMLR 418, ECJ).
5 Ie cases based on the EC Treaty art 81 (formerly art 85; renumbered by virtue of the Treaty of Amsterdam: see *Treaty Citation (No 2) (Note)* [1999] All ER (EC) 646, ECJ) (and see now the Treaty on the Functioning of the European Union (Rome, 25 March 1957; TS 1 (1973); Cmnd 5179) ('TFEU') art 101) (see note 1)). See in particular Case 40/70 *Sirena Srl v Eda Srl* [1971] ECR 69, [1971] CMLR 260, ECJ (which may perhaps be explained as a case based on some sort of continued market sharing conduct: see Case 86/75 *EMI Records Ltd v CBS Grammofon A/S* [1976] ECR 871, [1976] 2 CMLR 235, ECJ).
6 Case 144/81 *Keurkoop BV v Nancy Kean Gifts BV* [1982] ECR 2853, [1983] 2 CMLR 47, [1983] FSR 381, ECJ.

91. Parallel imports from outside the European Union or the European Economic Area. The European Court of Justice has held that the Trade Marks Directive[1] cannot be interpreted as leaving it open to the member states to provide in their domestic law for exhaustion of the rights conferred by a trade mark in respect of products put on the market in non-member countries; and that such exhaustion occurs only where the products have been put on the market[2] in the European Economic Area ('EEA')[3] by the proprietor or with his consent[4]. That consent must be to the placing on the market of the goods concerned[5], not other similar goods of the trade mark owner[6]. Consent will normally be express, but it is conceivable that it may in some cases be inferred from facts and circumstances prior to, simultaneous with, or subsequent to, the placing of the goods on the market outside the EEA which unequivocally demonstrate that the proprietor has renounced his right to oppose the placing of the goods on the market within the EEA[7]. Consent cannot be inferred from:

(1)   the fact that the proprietor has not communicated to all subsequent purchasers of the goods placed on the market outside the EEA his opposition to marketing within the EEA;

(2)   the fact that the goods carry no warning of a prohibition on their being placed on the market within the EEA;

(3)   the fact that the proprietor has transferred the ownership of the goods bearing the trade mark without imposing any contractual restrictions and that, according to the law governing the contract, the property right transferred includes, in the absence of such reservations, an unlimited right of resale or, at the very least, a right to market the goods subsequently within the EEA[8].

It is consistent with the Trade Marks Directive for national law to provide that it is for the party relying upon the defence of exhaustion of rights to prove the conditions for such exhaustion[9]. Where, however, the defendant succeeds in establishing that there is a real risk of partitioning of national markets if he himself bears that burden of proof, particularly where the trade mark proprietor markets his products in the EEA using an exclusive distribution system, it is for the proprietor to establish that the products were initially placed on the market outside the EEA by him or with his consent; if such evidence is adduced, it is for the defendant to prove the consent of the trade mark proprietor to subsequent marketing of the products in the EEA[10].

1   Ie Council Directive (EEC) 89/104 (OJ L40, 11.2.89, p 1) to approximate the laws of the member states relating to trade marks (see now European Parliament and Council Directive (EC) 2008/95 (OJ L299, 8.11.2008, p 25)). See generally PARA 5.

2   As to the meaning of 'put on the market' see PARA 87 note 4.

3   As to the EEA see PARA 86 note 6.

4   Case C-355/96 *Silhouette International Schmied GmbH & Co KG v Hartlauer Handelsgellschaft mbH* [1999] Ch 77, [1998] All ER (EC) 769, [1998] ECR I-4799, ECJ. Consent by an economically-linked party is not sufficient for this purpose: *Honda Motor Co Ltd v Neesam* [2006] EWHC 1051 (Ch), [2006] All ER (D) 371 (Mar); and see *Mastercigars Direct Ltd v Hunters & Frankau Ltd* [2007] EWCA Civ 176, [2007] RPC 565, [2007] ETMR 44. The trade mark proprietor's enforcement of its right to first marketing of its trade marked goods in the EEA does not amount to an unlawful restriction on free movement of goods: *Oracle America Inc (formerly Sun Microsystems Inc) v M-Tech Data Ltd* [2012] UKSC 27, [2012] 4 All ER 338, [2012] IP & T 810. Nor does it amount to anti-competitive conduct under the Treaty on the Functioning of the European Union (TFEU) art 101 or an abuse of rights: *Oracle America Inc (formerly Sun Microsystems Inc) v M-Tech Data Ltd*. As to the TFEU see PARA 86 note 8.

5   Ie the actual parallel imported goods themselves.

6   Case C-173/98 *Sebago Inc v GB-Unic SA* [2000] Ch 558, [1999] All ER (EC) 575, [1999] ECR I-4103, ECJ; *Oracle America Inc (formerly Sun Microsystems Inc) v M-Tech Data Ltd* [2012] UKSC 27, [2012] 4 All ER 338, [2012] IP & T 810.

7   Joined Cases C-414/99 to C-416/99 *Zino Davidoff SA v A & G Imports Ltd* [2002] Ch 109, [2001] ECR I-8691, ECJ; C-324/08 *Makro Zelfbedieningsgroothandel CV v Diesel SpA* [2009] ECR I-10019, [2010] Bus LR 608, [2010] ETMR 2, ECJ. This is a high hurdle: see *Quiksilver*

        PTY Ltd v Charles Robertson (Developments) Ltd (t/a Trago Mills) [2004] EWHC 2010 (Ch), [2005] FSR 139; *Kabushiki Kaisha Sony Entertainment v Nuplayer Ltd* [2005] EWHC 1522 (Ch), [2006] FSR 126, [2005] All ER (D) 188 (Jul); *Hewlett-Packard Development Co LP v Expansys United Kingdom Ltd* [2005] EWHC 1495 (Ch), [2005] All ER (D) 170 (Jul); *Kabushiki Kaisha Sony Computer Entertainment v Electricbirdland Ltd* [2005] EWHC 2296 (Ch), [2005] All ER (D) 73 (Aug); *Sun Microsystems Inc v Amtec Computer Corpn Ltd* [2006] EWHC 62 (Ch), [2006] FSR 630; *Honda Motor Co Ltd v Neesam* [2006] EWHC 1051 (Ch), [2006] All ER (D) 371 (Mar); *Roche Products Ltd v Kent Pharmaceuticals Ltd* [2006] EWCA Civ 1775, [2007] ETMR 27, [2006] All ER (D) 318 (Dec); c f *Mastercigars Direct Ltd v Hunters & Frankau Ltd* [2007] EWCA Civ 176, [2007] RPC 565, [2007] ETMR 44.

 8   Joined Cases C-414/99 to C-416/99 *Zino Davidoff SA v A & G Imports Ltd* [2002] Ch 109, [2001] ECR I-8691, ECJ.

 9   Case C-244/00 *Van Doren + Q GmbH v Lifestyle sports + sportswear Handelgesellschaft mbH* [2004] All ER (EC) 912, [2003] ECR I-3051, ECJ.

10   Case C-244/00 *Van Doren + Q GmbH v Lifestyle sports + sportswear Handelgesellschaft mbH* [2004] All ER (EC) 912, [2003] ECR I-3051, ECJ.

(iv) Suspension of Trade Mark Rights of Enemy or Enemy Subject

92.   In general. Where, on application made by a person proposing to supply goods or services of any description, it is made to appear to the registrar[1]:

(1)   that it is difficult or impracticable to describe or refer to the goods or services without the use of a registered trade mark; and

(2)   that the proprietor of the registered trade mark, whether alone or jointly with another, is an enemy or an enemy subject,

the registrar may make an order suspending the rights given by the registered trade mark[2]. Such an order suspends those rights as regards the use of the trade mark:

(a)   by the applicant; and

(b)   by any person authorised by the applicant to do, for the purposes of or in connection with the supply by the applicant of the goods or services, things which would otherwise infringe the registered trade mark,

to such extent and for such period as the registrar considers necessary to enable the applicant to render well known and established some other means of describing or referring to the goods or services in question which does not involve the use of the trade mark[3].

    Where such an order has been made, no action for passing off[4] lies on the part of any person interested in the registered trade mark in respect of any use of it which by virtue of the order is not an infringement of the right conferred by it[5]. Such an order may be varied or revoked by a subsequent order made by the registrar[6].

1   As to the registrar see PARA 19.
2   Patents, Designs, Copyright and Trade Marks (Emergency) Act 1939 s 3(1) (s 3 substituted by the Trade Marks Act 1994 Sch 4 para 3(1), (2)); Patents, Designs, Copyright and Trade Marks (Emergency) Act 1939 s 10(1) (amended by the Trade Marks Act 1994 Sch 4 para 3(1), (3)(d)).
3   Patents, Designs, Copyright and Trade Marks (Emergency) Act 1939 s 3(2) (as substituted: see note 2); s 10(1) (as amended: see note 2).
4   As to passing off see PARA 287 et seq.
5   Patents, Designs, Copyright and Trade Marks (Emergency) Act 1939 s 3(3) (as substituted: see note 2).
6   Patents, Designs, Copyright and Trade Marks (Emergency) Act 1939 s 3(4) (as substituted: see note 2); s 10(1) (as amended: see note 2).

(5) SURRENDER, REVOCATION, INVALIDITY, ALTERATION AND RECTIFICATION

(i) Introduction

93. Modes of extinction or modification of registered trade marks and protected international trade marks (UK). The Trade Marks Act 1994 provides a number of ways in which the rights conferred by a registered trade mark may be cancelled or varied[1]. It uses the following terminology:

(1) 'surrender' for voluntary surrender by the proprietor[2];
(2) 'revocation' for removal of a registration on grounds which have arisen since registration[3];
(3) 'declaration of invalidity' for cases where the mark ought not to have been registered originally[4];
(4) 'rectification' for corrections concerning errors or omissions from the register other than matters concerned with validity[5];
(5) 'alteration'[6]; and
(6) 'disclaimer' and 'limitation'[7].

Except where proceedings concerning the trade mark in question are pending in the court[8], when the application must be made to the court, applications for revocation, declarations of invalidity or rectification may be made either to the registrar or to the court[9]. Applications for surrender, alteration, disclaimers or limitations can only be made to the registrar[10].

These provisions also apply to protected international trade marks (UK)[11] although in some respects the terminology differs[12].

1   Ie apart from lapse for failure to pay renewal fees: see PARA 31.
2   See PARAS 97, 377.
3   See PARAS 98–101, 380–381, 441.
4   See PARAS 102–104, 382, 441–442.
5   See PARAS 105, 383, 441.
6   See PARAS 106, 375.
7   See PARAS 65, 82, 376.
8   As to the meaning of 'the court' see PARA 331.
9   See the Trade Marks Act 1994 ss 46(4), 47(3), 64(2); and PARA 378. See also the Community Trade Mark Regulations 2006, SI 2006/1027, reg 3(1); and PARA 271.
10   As to surrender see the Trade Marks Act 1994 s 45(2); the Trade Marks Rules 2008, SI 2008/1797, r 33(1); and PARA 97. As to alteration see the Trade Marks Act 1994 s 44(2); and PARA 106. As to disclaimers or limitations see s 13(2); the Trade Marks Rules 2008, SI 2008/1797, r 31; and PARA 65.
11   As to the meaning of 'protected international trade mark (UK)' see PARA 12 note 8. See PARA 11 et seq.
12   See PARAS 65, 98 et seq.

94. Onus of proof; presumption of validity of original registration. Whenever a registered trade mark is under attack, then under normal principles the onus of proof will lie on the attacker[1]. In addition it is specifically provided that in all legal proceedings relating to a registered trade mark[2], including proceedings for rectification of the register, the registration[3] of a person as proprietor of a trade mark is prima facie evidence of the validity of the original registration and of any subsequent assignment or other transmission[4] of it[5].

In all legal proceedings relating to an international trade mark (UK)[6], the registration of a person as holder of an international trade mark (UK) is also prima facie evidence of the validity of the original international registration and of any subsequent assignment or other transaction of it[7].

1   Ie save for the exception that the onus of proof of use of a registered trade mark lies on the proprietor: see the Trade Marks Act 1994 s 100; and PARA 98 text and note 16.
2   As to the meaning of 'registered trade mark' see PARA 111.
3   As to the meaning of 'registration' see PARA 21 note 2.
4   As to assignment or other transmission of a registered trade mark see PARA 113 et seq.
5   Trade Marks Act 1994 s 72.
6   As to the meaning of 'international trade mark (UK)' see PARA 8 note 17.
7   See the Trade Marks (International Registration) Order 2008, SI 2008/2206, art 3; and PARA 12. As to the meaning of 'international register' see PARA 12 note 1. See also generally PARA 11 et seq.

95. Absence of discretion. By contrast with the position under the Trade Marks Act 1938[1], if an applicant for revocation of a trade mark (or, it would seem, for a declaration of invalidity[2] or for rectification) establishes that there are grounds for revocation (or invalidity or rectification) of the mark in whole or in part[3], the registrar or the court[4] has no discretion to refuse the order sought even though the relevant statutory provisions[5] use the word 'may'[6].

1   See *Re Magneta Time Co Ltd's Trade Mark* (1927) 44 RPC 169; cf *Re Somerlite Ltd's Trade Mark (No 520,004), Somerlite Ltd v Brown* (1934) 51 RPC 205, CA.
2   Mandatory words are used in Council Directive (EEC) 89/104 (OJ L40, 11.2.89, p 1) to approximate the laws of the member states relating to trade marks, arts 3, 4 (see now European Parliament and Council Directive (EC) 2008/95 (OJ L299, 8.11.2008, p 25) arts 3, 4) (from which the Trade Marks Act 1994 s 47 is derived). However, see also *Associated Newspapers Ltd v Express Newspapers* [2003] EWHC 1322 (Ch), [2004] IP & T 378, [2003] FSR 909.
3   As to the grounds for revocation generally see PARA 98 et seq; as to the grounds for a declaration of invalidity generally see PARA 102 et seq; and as to the grounds for rectification generally see PARA 105. As to the additional grounds for revocation or invalidity of a collective mark see PARAS 146–147; and as to the additional grounds for revocation or invalidity of a certification mark see PARAS 157–158.
4   As to the registrar see PARA 19. As to the meaning of 'the court' see PARA 331.
5   The relevant statutory provisions are the Trade Marks Act 1994 s 46(1) (see PARA 98), s 47(1), (2) (see PARA 102) and s 64(1) (see PARA 105).
6   *Premier Brands UK Ltd v Typhoon Europe Ltd* [2000] IP & T 218, [2000] FSR 767; *Scandecor Development AB v Scandecor Marketing AB* [2001] UKHL 21, [2001] IP & T 676, [2002] FSR 122 (question referred to European Court of Justice for ruling but case settled before ruling given). Cf the corresponding provision in Council Regulation (EC) 40/94 (OJ L11, 14.1.94, p 1) on the Community trade mark (the 'Community Trade Mark Regulation') (see now Council Regulation (EC) 207/2009 (OJ L78, 24.3.2009, p 1)): see PARA 221 note 2. The court does however does have discretion to suspend the grant of a declaration of invalidity pending an application for invalidity or revocation of a conflicting earlier trade mark: *Rousselon Freres et Cie v Horwood Homewares* [2008] EWHC 1660 (Ch), [2008] RPC 849, [2009] IP & T 625.

96. Effective date of revocation, declaration of invalidity or rectification. Where the registration of a trade mark is revoked to any extent[1], the rights of the proprietor are deemed to have ceased to that extent as from the date of the application for revocation[2] or, if the registrar or the court[3] is satisfied that the grounds for revocation existed at an earlier date, that date[4]. Where the protection of an international trade mark (UK)[5] is revoked, the rights of the proprietor are deemed to have ceased to exist as from the date on which the revocation is recorded in the international register[6].

Where the registration of a trade mark is declared invalid to any extent[7], the registration is to that extent deemed never to have been made; but this provision does not affect transactions past and closed[8]. The same obtains when the protection of an international trade mark (UK) is declared invalid[9].

Except where the registrar or the court directs otherwise, the effect of rectification of the register[10] is that the error or omission in question is deemed never to have been made[11].

1   As to the grounds for revocation generally see PARA 98 et seq; as to the additional grounds for revocation of a collective mark see PARA 146; and as to the additional grounds for revocation of a certification mark see PARA 157.
2   As to the meaning of 'registration' see PARA 21 note 2.
3   As to the registrar see PARA 19. As to the meaning of 'the court' see PARA 331.
4   Trade Marks Act 1994 s 46(6) (which has no antecedent in Council Directive (EEC) 89/104 (OJ L40, 11.2.89, p 1) to approximate the laws of the member states relating to trade marks (see now European Parliament and Council Directive (EC) 2008/95 (OJ L299, 8.11.2008, p 25)). It is not appropriate to grant an injunction prohibiting use of an infringing sign if the trade mark has been revoked: Case C-145/05 *Levi Strauss & Co v Casucci Spa* [2007] FSR 170, [2006] ETMR 71, ECJ. If the applicant for revocation seeks to revoke the trade mark from a date earlier than the application date he must plead the date as of which revocation is sought and explicitly allege that grounds for revocation existed at that date: see PARA 380 note 3.
5   As to the meaning of 'protected international trade mark (UK)' see PARA 12 note 8. See PARA 11 et seq.
6   See the Trade Marks (International Registration) Order 2008, SI 2008/2206, art 3; and PARA 12. As to the meaning of 'international register' see PARA 12 note 1. See also generally PARA 11 et seq.
7   As to the grounds for a declaration of invalidity see PARA 102 et seq; as to the additional grounds for invalidity of a collective mark see PARA 147; and as to the additional grounds for invalidity of a certification mark see PARA 158.
8   Trade Marks Act 1994 s 47(6) (which has no antecedent in Council Directive (EEC) 89/104 (OJ L40, 11.2.89, p 1) (see now European Parliament and Council Directive (EC) 2008/95 (OJ L299, 8.11.2008, p 25)).
9   See the Trade Marks (International Registration) Order 2008, SI 2008/2206, art 3; and PARA 12. See also generally PARA 11 et seq.
10 As to the grounds for rectification generally see PARA 105.
11 Trade Marks Act 1994 s 64(3).

(ii) Surrender

97.   In general.   A registered trade mark[1] may be surrendered by the proprietor in respect of some or all of the goods or services for which it is registered[2]. Surrender has effect from the date on which the registrar[3] makes and publishes the appropriate entry in the register[4].

The person in whose name an international trade mark registration stands may at any time remove protection in one or more contracting countries[5].

1   As to the meaning of 'registered trade mark' see PARA 111.
2   See the Trade Marks Act 1994 s 45; the Trade Marks Rules 2008, SI 2008/1797, r 33; and PARA 377.
3   As to the registrar see PARA 19.
4   In fact now the publication of the date of surrender is on the Intellectual Property Office ('IPO') website: see the Trade Marks Rules 2008, SI 2008/1797, r 33(3); and PARA 377. See also *RAPIER Trade Mark* (O/170/07), Appointed Person. Surrender does not render a pending application for revocation or invalidity moot or academic: see *RAPIER Trade Mark*. Cf the position in proceedings before the Office for Harmonisation in the Internal Market: see PARA 219 text and note 4. If notice of surrender is given during rectification proceedings affecting proprietorship, the registrar or the court will determine those first before considering whether to accept the surrender: *Skaga AB's Trade Mark Application* (O/134/03), Trade Marks Registry. As to the Intellectual Property Office (an operating name of the Patent Office) see PARA 16 note 2.
5   Madrid Agreement Concerning the International Registration of Marks (Madrid, 14 April 1891; TS 71 (1970); Cmnd 4437), as revised at Stockholm in 1967 and as amended in 1979, art 8 bis. As to the Madrid Agreement see PARA 8. A declaration is filed at the office in his home country for commutation to the International Bureau of the World Intellectual Property Organisation ('WIPO'), which in turn notifies the countries where protection has been removed. As to the International Bureau see PARA 8 text and note 2.

(iii)　Revocation

98.　Non-use.　The registration of a trade mark[1] may[2] be revoked on either of the following grounds[3]:

(1)　that within the period of five years[4] following the date of completion of the registration procedure[5] it has not been put to genuine[6] use[7] in the United Kingdom, by the proprietor or with his consent[8], in relation to the goods or services for which it is registered[9], and there are no proper reasons[10] for non-use[11];

(2)　that such use has been suspended for an uninterrupted period of five years, and there are no proper reasons for non-use[12].

These grounds also apply to the revocation of protection of a protected international trade mark (UK)[13].

The registration of a trade mark may not, however, be revoked on the grounds mentioned in head (1) or head (2) above if such use as is there referred to is commenced or resumed after the expiry of the five year period and before the application for revocation is made[14]; but any such commencement or resumption of use after the expiry of the five year period but within the period of three months before the making of the application is to be disregarded unless preparations for the commencement or resumption began before the proprietor became aware that the application might be made[15].

If in any civil proceedings under the Trade Marks Act 1994 a question arises as to the use to which a registered trade mark has been put, it is for the proprietor to show what use has been made of it[16].

1　As to the meaning of 'trade mark' see PARA 41.

2　As to the absence of discretion see PARA 95.

3　Trade Marks Act 1994 s 46(1).

4　The correct approach to calculating this period is that not less than five complete years must elapse during which the trade mark is registered but not genuinely used. It follows that the five year period cannot start until the day after the date on which the registration procedure is completed and must have ended not later than the day before the date on which the application is filed: *BSA BY R2 Trade Mark* [2008] RPC 496, Appointed Person; Tribunal Practice Notice 1/2007.

5　The date of completion of the registration procedure must be determined in accordance with national procedural rules: Case C-246/05 *Häupl v Lidl Stiftung & Co KG* [2007] ECR I-4673, [2007] All ER (D) 140 (Jun), ECJ; Case T-100/06 *Rajani v Office for Harmonisation in the Internal Market (Trade Marks and Designs)* [2008] ECR II-287, [2008] All ER (D) 262 (Nov), CFI (affd Case C-559/08P [2010] ECR I-110, ECJ). In the United Kingdom this is the date on which the registrar enters the registration on the register: see the Trade Marks Act 1994 s 40; the Trade Marks Rules 2008, SI 2008/1797, r 23; and PARA 370.

6　There is 'genuine use' of a trade mark where the trade mark is used in accordance with its essential function, which is to guarantee the identity of the origin of the goods or services for which it is registered, in order to create or preserve an outlet for those goods or services; genuine use does not include token use for the sole purpose of preserving the rights conferred by the mark: Case C-40/01 *Ansul BV v Ajax Brandbeveiliging BV* [2005] Ch 97, [2003] ECR I-2439, ECJ; Case C-259/02 *La Mer Technology Inc v Laboratoires Goemar SA* [2004] ECR I-1159, [2004] FSR 785, ECJ (and for the Court of Appeal decision implementing this ruling see *LABORATOIRE DE LA MER Trade Mark* [2005] EWCA Civ 978, [2006] FSR 41); Case C-416/04P *Sunrider Corpn v Office for Harmonisation in the Internal Market (Trade Marks and Designs)* [2006] ECR I-4237, [2006] All ER (D) 178 (May), ECJ. When assessing whether use of the trade mark is genuine, regard must be had to all the facts and circumstances relevant to establishing whether the commercial exploitation of the mark is real, particularly whether such use is viewed as warranted in the economic sector concerned to maintain or create a share in the market for the goods or services protected by the mark, the nature of those goods or services, the characteristics of the market and the scale and frequency of the use of the mark: Case C-40/01 *Ansul BV v Ajax Brandbeveiliging BV* above; Case C-259/02 *La Mer Technology Inc v Laboratoires Goemar SA* above. Classification of use of the mark as genuine use depends on consideration of the circumstances which pertain during the relevant period, but account may be taken of circumstances subsequent to that period which make it possible to better assess the extent to which the trade mark was used during that period and the real intentions of the proprietor during that period: Case C-259/02 *La Mer Technology Inc v Laboratoires Goemar SA* above.

Genuine use of the mark entails use on the market for the goods or services protected by that mark and not just internal use by the undertaking concerned; use of the mark must therefore relate to goods or services already marketed or about to be marketed and for which preparations by the undertaking to secure customers are underway, particularly in the form of advertising campaigns: Case C-40/01 *Ansul BV v Ajax Brandbeveiliging BV* above; Case C-259/02 *La Mer Technology Inc v Laboratoires Goemar SA* above; Case C-442/07 *Verein Radetzky-Orden v Bundesvereinigung Kameradschaft 'Feldmarschall Radetzky'* [2008] ECR I-9223, [2009] IP & T 676, [2009] ETMR 14, ECJ.

Use of the mark may in some cases be sufficient to establish genuine use even if that use is not quantitatively significant; even minimal use can therefore be sufficient to qualify as genuine; a de minimis rule cannot be laid down: Case C-259/02 *La Mer Technology Inc v Laboratoires Goemar SA* above; Case C-416/04P *Sunrider Corpn v Office for Harmonisation in the Internal Market (Trade Marks and Designs)* [2006] ECR I-4237, [2006] All ER (D) 178 (May), ECJ (this case considered the question of genuine use under the equivalent provision of Council Regulation (EC) 40/94 (OJ L11, 14.1.94, p 1) on the Community trade mark, i e art 43(2), (3) (see now Council Regulation (EC) 207/2009 (OJ L78, 24.3.2009, p 1) art 42) (see PARA 265)). Use of the mark by a single client which imports the products for which the mark is registered can be sufficient to demonstrate that such use is genuine, if it appears that the import operation has a genuine commercial justification for the proprietor of the mark: Case C-259/02 *La Mer Technology Inc v Laboratoires Goemar SA* above; *LABORATOIRE DE LA MER Trade Mark* above (held importation of small quantities of product by one importer was genuine use); Case C-416/04P *Sunrider Corpn v Office for Harmonisation in the Internal Market (Trade Marks and Designs)* above.

In assessing whether use is genuine the territorial extent of the use is a relevant factor: Case C-416/04P *Sunrider Corpn v Office for Harmonisation in the Internal Market (Trade Marks and Designs)* above; Case C-149/11 *Leno Merken BV v Hagelkruis Beheer BV* [2013] IP & T 295, [2013] ETMR 16, ECJ. Use of a trade mark on a foreign website is not sufficient to establish use in the United Kingdom: *CARTE BLEUE Trade Marks* [2002] RPC 599, Trade Marks Registry; and see PARA 66 note 3. The size of the proprietor's undertaking is also a relevant factor: *POLICE Trade Mark* [2004] RPC 693, Appointed Person.

There may be genuine use of a trade mark as a result of use of that mark as part of a composite mark or in conjunction with another mark, even if the latter mark is itself registered: Case C-12/12 *Colloseum Holding AG v Levi Strauss & Co* [2013] IP & T 705, [2013] ETMR 34, ECJ; Case C-252/12 *Specsavers International Healthcare Ltd v Asda Stores Ltd* [2013] ECR I-0000, [2013] ETMR 46, (2013) Times, 1 October, ECJ.

Use of the mark may be genuine even if the goods in respect of which it is registered are no longer available, e g if the proprietor makes use of the same mark for component parts of those goods or for goods and services directly connected with those goods: Case C-40/01 *Ansul BV v Ajax Brandbeveiliging BV* above.

Use need not be for profit-making purposes in order to be genuine; a charitable organisation can seek to create and preserve an outlet for its goods or services: Case C-442/07 *Verein Radetzky-Orden v Bundesvereinigung Kameradschaft 'Feldmarschall Radetzky'* [2008] ECR I-9223, [2009] IP & T 676, [2009] ETMR 14, ECJ.

Distribution of promotional items bearing the trade mark free of charge as a reward for the purchase of other goods and to encourage the sale of the latter does not constitute genuine use in relation to the promotional items: Case C-495/07 *Silberquelle GmbH v Maselli-Strickmode GmbH* [2009] ECR I-137, [2009] ETMR 28, ECJ.

In considering case law on genuine use, care needs to be taken with decisions of the CFI and EGC on cases arising under Council Regulation (EC) 40/94 (OJ L11, 14.1.94, p 1) art 43(2), (3) (see now Council Regulation (EC) 207/2009 (OJ L78, 24.3.2009, p 1) art 42) since Commission Regulation (EC) 2868/95 (OJ L303, 15.12.95, p 1) implementing Council Regulation (EC) No 40/94 on the Community trade mark, art 1 r 22 (as substituted by Commission Regulation (EC) 1041/2005 (OJ L172, 5.7.05, p 4)) specifies with some precision the nature and form of the evidence that the trade mark proprietor is required to furnish in such cases: see *EXTREME Trade Mark* [2008] RPC 2, Appointed Person; and PARA 265.

7   For these purposes (1) use of a trade mark includes use in a form differing in elements which do not alter the distinctive character of the mark in the form in which it was registered; and (2) use in the United Kingdom includes affixing the trade mark to goods or to the packaging of goods in

the United Kingdom solely for export purposes: Trade Marks Act 1994 s 46(2) (derived from Council Directive (EEC) 89/104 (OJ L40, 11.2.89, p 1) to approximate the laws of the member states relating to trade marks, art 10(2) (see now European Parliament and Council Directive (EC) 2008/95 (OJ L299, 8.11.2008, p 25) art 10(1), second subparagraph)). Head (1) above involves a two-stage inquiry: first, identify the differences between the mark as used and the mark as registered; and, second, assess whether they alter the distinctive character of the mark as registered, which should be assessed in the usual way through the perception of the average consumer of the goods or services in question (see PARA 44 note 3): *Anheuser-Busch Inc v Budejovicky Budvar Narodni Podnik* [2002] EWCA Civ 1534, sub nom *BUD and BUDWEISER BUDBRÄU Trade Marks* [2003] RPC 477. Changes to non-distinctive elements of a complex mark do not alter its distinctive character: Case T-135/04 *GfK AG v Office for Harmonisation in the Internal Market (Trade Marks and Designs)* [2005] ECR II-4865, [2006] ETMR 58, CFI (decided under the equivalent provision of Council Regulation (EC) 40/94 (OJ L11, 14.1.94, p 1) ie art 43(2), (3) (see now Council Regulation (EC) 207/2009 (OJ L78, 24.3.2009, p 1) art 42) (see PARA 265)); Case T-147/03 *Devinlec Developpement Innovation Leclerc SA v Office for Harmonisation in the Internal Market (Trade Marks and Designs)* [2006] ECR II-11, [2006] IP & T 436, CFI (affd Case C-171/06P [2007] ECR I-41, ECJ) (decided under the equivalent provision of Council Regulation (EC) 40/94 (OJ L11, 14.1.94, p 1) ie art 43(2), (3) (see now Council Regulation (EC) 207/2009 (OJ L78, 24.3.2009, p 1) art 42) (see PARA 265)); *NIRVANA Trade Mark* (O/262/06), Appointed Person. It is immaterial that the mark as used is itself the subject of a separate registration: Case C-553/11 *Rintisch v Eder* [2013] ETMR 5, ECJ; Case C-252/12 *Specsavers International Healthcare Ltd v Asda Stores Ltd* [2013] ECR I-0000, [2013] ETMR 46, (2013) Times, 1 October, ECJ. As to the meaning of 'use' generally see PARA 44 note 8; and as to the meaning of 'United Kingdom' see PARA 3 note 2.

8   It is immaterial for this purpose whether the proprietor imposes quality control on users of the mark, although this may be relevant to an objection under the Trade Marks Act 1994 s 46(1)(d) (see PARA 100): *SAFARI Trade Mark* [2002] RPC 497, Trade Marks Registry; *EINSTEIN Trade Mark* [2007] RPC 539, Appointed Person. Mere acquiescence by the proprietor in use by a third party does not constitute use with the proprietor's consent: *NIRVANA Trade Mark* (O/030/06), Trade Marks Registry (affd on other grounds (O/262/06), Appointed Person).

9   The trade mark is used 'in relation to' goods if it conveys to members of the public that the proprietor of the mark is in some way responsible for the quality of the goods, even if the goods are promotional items: *Premier Brands UK Ltd v Typhoon Europe Ltd* [2000] FSR 767, [2000] IP & T 218 (use of famous mark for tea on tea-towels, utensils etc); *DaimlerChrysler AG v Alavi (t/a Merc)* [2001] RPC 42, [2002] IP & T 496 (use of famous mark for cars on items of clothing); but see Case C-495/07 *Silberquelle GmbH v Maselli-Strickmode GmbH* [2009] ECR I-137, [2009] ETMR 28, ECJ. See also *ELLE Trade Marks* [1997] FSR 529, sub nom *Safeways Stores plc v Hachette Filipachi Presse* [1996–97] ETMR 552 (promotion of cosmetics in a magazine not use of name of magazine in relation to those goods); *Trebor Bassett Ltd v Football Association* [1997] FSR 211 (mark on jerseys of footballers not used in relation to photographs of those footballers).

10   Cf the Agreement on Trade-Related Aspects of Intellectual Property (TRIPs) (1994) (Cm 2557) art 19(1), which provides that circumstances arising independently of the will of the owner of the trademark which constitute an obstacle to the use of the trademark, such as import restrictions on or other governmental requirements for goods or services protected by the trademark, are to be recognised as valid reasons for non-use. As to TRIPs generally see PARA 7. Obstacles having a direct relationship with the trade mark which make its use impossible or unreasonable and which are independent of the will of the proprietor of the trade mark constitute proper reasons for non-use: Case C-246/05 *Häupl v Lidl Stiftung & Co KG* [2007] ECR I-4673, [2007] All ER (D) 140 (Jun), ECJ. National legislation which makes an exception to the requirement for use in the case of defensive marks cannot be relied on as constituting proper reasons for non-use: Case C-234/06P *Il Ponte Finanziaria SpA v Office for Harmonisation in the Internal Market (Trade Marks and Designs)* [2007] ECR I-7333 ECJ. In order to establish 'proper reasons' for non-use, it is necessary for the tribunal to be satisfied that in the absence of the suggested impediments to use there could and would have been genuine use of the trade mark during the relevant five year period: *CERNIVET Trade Mark* [2002] RPC 585, Appointed Person.

For examples of 'proper reasons' which have been accepted see *WORTH Trade Marks* [1998] RPC 875, Trade Marks Registry (revocation proceedings frustrated attempts to license the mark); *MAGIC BALL Trade Mark* [2000] RPC 439 (delays in developing a new manufacturing technique).

Factors which are or have become a normal condition of trade cannot constitute proper reasons for non-use: *Philosophy Inc v Ferretti Studio Srl* [2002] EWCA Civ 921, sub nom *PHILOSOPHY DI ALBERTA FERRETTI Trade Mark* [2003] RPC 287 (proprietor did nothing for most of five year period then encountered ordinary commercial delays in producing new product bearing mark); *INVERMONT Trade Mark* [1997] RPC 125, sub nom *Glen Catrine Bonded Warehouse Ltd's Application for Revocation* [1996–97] ETMR 56, Trade Marks Registry (difficult to introduce new brand to the relevant market); *CABANAS HABANA (Device) Trade Mark* [2000] RPC 26, Trade Marks Registry (US trade embargo of Cuba said to have prevented use of the mark); and see also *K-2 Trade Mark* [2000] RPC 413, Trade Marks Registry (proprietor could have complied with EC regulations).

11 Trade Marks Act 1994 s 46(1)(a) (derived from Council Directive (EEC) 89/104 (OJ L40, 11.2.89, p 1) arts 10(1), 12(1); and see now European Parliament and Council Directive (EC) 2008/95 (OJ L299, 8.11.2008, p 25) art 10(1), first subparagraph, art 12(1), first and second subparagraphs; and see 9th recital).

As to procedure on the application see PARA 378 et seq; as to the date from which revocation takes effect see PARA 96; as to the additional grounds for revocation of a collective mark see PARA 146; and as to the additional grounds for revocation of a certification mark see PARA 157.

An application under the Trade Marks Act 1938 s 26 (repealed) (removal from the register or imposition of a limitation on the ground of misuse) which was pending on 31 October 1994 must be dealt with under the old law and any necessary alteration made to the register: Trade Marks Act 1994 s 105, Sch 3 para 17(1). An application under s 46(1)(a) or s 46(1)(b) (see the text and note 10) may be made in relation to an existing registered mark at any time on or after 31 October 1994; but no such application for the revocation of the registration of an existing registered mark registered by virtue of the Trade Marks Act 1938 s 27 (repealed) (defensive registration of well known trade marks) may be made until more than five years after 31 October 1994: Trade Marks Act 1994 Sch 3 para 17(2). As to the register see PARA 21.

12 Trade Marks Act 1994 s 46(1)(b) (derived from Council Directive (EEC) 89/104 (OJ L40, 11.2.89, p 1) arts 10(1), 12(1) (see now European Parliament and Council Directive (EC) 2008/95 (OJ L299, 8.11.2008, p 25) art 10(1), first subparagraph, art 12(1), first and second subparagraphs)). See also note 9. As to procedure on the application see PARA 378 et seq; as to the date from which revocation takes effect see PARA 96; as to the additional grounds for revocation of a collective mark see PARA 146; and as to the additional grounds for revocation of a certification mark see PARA 157.

13 See the Trade Marks (International Registration) Order 2008, SI 2008/2206, art 3; and PARA 12. As to the meaning of 'protected international trade mark (UK)' see PARA 12 note 8. See also generally PARA 11 et seq. Note that the reference to the 'completion of the registration procedure' in the Trade Marks Act 1994 s 46(1)(a) is to be construed as a reference to the 'conferring of protection on an international registration in accordance with s 38B': see s 38B(3) (s 38B added as a modification by the Trade Marks (International Registration) Order 2008, SI 2008/2206, art 3(3)(i), Sch 2 para 6); and as to the Trade Marks Act 1994 s 38B see PARA 371, and see also PARA 12 note 15.

14 Trade Marks Act 1994 s 46(3) (derived from Council Directive (EEC) 89/104 (OJ L40, 11.2.89, p 1) art 12(1) (see now European Parliament and Council Directive (EC) 2008/95 (OJ L299, 8.11.2008, p 25) art 12(1), second subparagraph).

15 Trade Marks Act 1994 s 46(3) proviso (derived from Council Directive (EEC) 89/104 (OJ L40, 11.2.89, p 1) art 12(1) (see now European Parliament and Council Directive (EC) 2008/95 (OJ L299, 8.11.2008, p 25) art 12(1), third subparagraph). This provides a period for negotiation during which the proprietor cannot steal a march on his opponent by putting his mark into use. The applicant does not have to wait, however, and can bring the application as soon as the five year period has elapsed: *Philosophy Inc v Ferretti Studio Srl* [2002] EWCA Civ 921, sub nom *PHILOSOPHY DI ALBERTA FERRETTI Trade Mark* [2003] RPC 287.

16 Trade Marks Act 1994 s 100. This provision abolishes the artificial position under the Trade Marks Act 1938 whereby the applicant for revocation had to produce a prima facie case of non-use (by showing that he had made reasonable searches) before the proprietor had to respond. The same provision is made in relation to protected international trade marks (UK) by the Trade Marks (International Registration) Order 2008, SI 2008/2206, art 3. The effect is to place an evidential burden on the proprietor, while the legal burden of establishing the conditions for revocation lies on the applicant: *EXTREME Trade Mark* [2008] RPC 2, Appointed Person. The standard of proof is on the balance of probabilities, and the tribunal is not entitled to disregard unchallenged evidence of use: *EXTREME Trade Mark*. See also Case T-356/02 *Vitakraft-Werke Wührman & Sohn GmbH & Co KG v Office for Harmonisation in the Internal Market (Trade Marks and Designs)* [2004] ECR II-3445, [2004] All ER (D) 54 (Oct), CFI.

99.   Mark becoming common name.   The registration of a trade mark[1] may[2] be revoked on the ground that, in consequence[3] of acts[4] or inactivity[5] of the proprietor, it has become[6] the common name[7] in the trade[8] for a product or service for which it is registered[9].

This ground also applies to the revocation of the protection of a protected international trade mark (UK)[10].

1   As to the meaning of 'trade mark' see PARA 41.
2   As to the absence of discretion see PARA 95.
3   The acts or inactivity of the proprietor must be a cause of the mark becoming the common name, although they need not be the sole cause: *Hormel Foods Corpn v Antilles Landscape Investments NV* [2005] EWHC 13 (Ch), [2005] RPC 657, [2005] IP & T 822.
4   The acts concerned will clearly include descriptive use, including cases where the proprietor gives no name other than his trade mark to a new product. There is no longer any special provision concerning patented goods: cf the Trade Marks Act 1938 s 15(1)(b) (repealed).
5   The inactivity contemplated includes failure to take action against infringers: *Hormel Foods Corpn v Antilles Landscape Investments NV* [2005] EWHC 13 (Ch), [2005] RPC 657, [2005] IP & T 822.
6   Although the Trade Marks Act 1994 s 46(1)(c) is concerned with the situation where the mark has become generic after registration, the process may have started earlier.
7   It is sufficient for this purpose if the mark has become a common name; it does not have to be the only common name: *Hormel Foods Corpn v Antilles Landscape Investments NV* [2005] EWHC 13 (Ch), [2005] RPC 657, [2005] IP & T 822.
8   The relevant classes of person comprise principally consumers and end users, but depending on the product market concerned the influence of intermediaries on decisions to purchase, and thus their perception of the trade mark, must also be taken into consideration: Case C-371/02 *Björnekulla Fruktindustrier AB v Procordia Food AB* [2004] ECR I-5791, [2004] RPC 912, ECJ; Case C-409/12 *Backaldrin Österreich The Kornspitz Co Gmbh v Pfahnl Backmittel GmbH* [2013] ECR I-0000.
9   Trade Marks Act 1994 s 46(1)(c) (derived from Council Directive (EEC) 89/104 (OJ L40, 11.2.89, p 1) to approximate the laws of the member states relating to trade marks, art 12(2)(a) (see now European Parliament and Council Directive (EC) 2008/95 (OJ L299, 8.11.2008, p 25) art 12(2)(a))). As to procedure on the application see PARA 378 et seq; as to the date from which revocation takes effect see PARA 96; as to the additional grounds for revocation of a collective mark see PARA 146; and as to the additional grounds for revocation of a certification mark see PARA 157.
10 See the Trade Marks (International Registration) Order 2008, SI 2008/2206, art 3; and PARA 12. As to the meaning of 'protected international trade mark (UK)' see PARA 12 note 1. See also generally PARA 11 et seq.

100.   Liability to mislead in consequence of use.   The registration of a trade mark[1] may[2] be revoked on the ground that, in consequence[3] of the use[4] made of it by the proprietor or with his consent in relation to the goods or services for which it is registered, it is liable to mislead the public, particularly as to the nature, quality or geographical origin of those goods or services[5].

This ground also applies to the revocation of the protection of a protected international trade mark (UK)[6].

1   As to the meaning of 'trade mark' see PARA 41.
2   As to the absence of discretion see PARA 95.
3   It would appear that the use must be a cause of the mark becoming liable to mislead, although it need not be the sole cause: cf *Hormel Foods Corpn v Antilles Landscape Investments NV* [2005] EWHC 13 (Ch), [2005] RPC 657, [2005] IP & T 822.
4   As to the meaning of 'use' generally see PARA 44 note 8.
5   Trade Marks Act 1994 s 46(1)(d) (derived from Council Directive (EEC) 89/104 (OJ L40, 11.2.89, p 1) to approximate the laws of the member states relating to trade marks, art 12(2)(b) (see now European Parliament and Council Directive (EC) 2008/95 (OJ L299, 8.11.2008, p 25) art 12(2)(b))). This ground relates to events arising, as Council Directive (EEC) 89/104 (OJ L40, 11.2.89, p 1) (see now European Parliament and Council Directive (EC) 2008/95 (OJ L299, 8.11.2008, p 25) (see PARA 5)) says, 'after the date on which [the mark] was registered'. If the

mark was misleading at the time it was registered, it will be liable to be declared invalid pursuant to the Trade Marks Act 1994 s 47(1) (see PARA 102), which includes any of the provisions of s 3 (absolute grounds for refusal: see PARA 43 et seq), including therefore s 3(3)(b) (mark of such a nature as to deceive the public: see PARA 48). Otherwise, the conditions for revocation under s 46(1)(d) are the same as those for the refusal of registration under s 3(3)(b) (see PARA 48): Case C-259/04 *Emanuel v Continental Shelf 128 Ltd* [2006] IP & T 887, sub nom *Elizabeth Florence Emanuel v Continental Shelf 128 Ltd* [2006] ETMR 56, ECJ. A trade mark corresponding to the name of the designer and first manufacturer of the goods bearing that mark may not, by reason of that feature alone, be refused registration on this ground even where the goodwill associated with that trade mark has been assigned, together with the business making the goods to which the mark relates, to another person: Case C-259/04 *Emanuel v Continental Shelf 128 Ltd*.

It is unclear whether the Trade Marks Act 1994 s 46(1)(d) may be invoked where the proprietor allows another person to build up a goodwill in the mark so that the mark is liable to mislead the public as to trade origin: see *Scandecor Development AB v Scandecor Marketing AB* [1999] FSR 26, CA; on appeal [2001] UKHL 21, [2000] IP & T 676, [2002] FSR 122 (questions referred to European Court of Justice but case settled prior to ruling). However, the grant of a bare licence to use a trade mark (ie one with no quality control provisions), particularly if exclusive, will not, without more, render the trade mark deceptive: *EINSTEIN Trade Mark* [2007] RPC 539, Appointed Person.

As to procedure on the application see PARA 378 et seq; as to the date from which revocation takes effect see PARA 96; as to the additional grounds for revocation of a collective mark see PARA 146; and as to the additional grounds for revocation of a certification mark see PARA 157.

6   See the Trade Marks (International Registration) Order 2008, SI 2008/2206, art 3; and PARA 12. As to the meaning of 'protected international trade mark (UK)' see PARA 12 note 8. See also generally PARA 11 et seq.

101.   Partial revocation. Where grounds for revocation[1] exist in respect of only some of the goods or services for which the trade mark[2] is registered[3], revocation must relate to those goods or services only[4]. The same rule applies to the revocation of the protection in respect of part only of the goods and services in respect of which the international trade mark (UK) is protected[5].

1   As to the grounds for revocation see PARAS 98–100; as to the additional grounds for revocation of a collective mark see PARA 146; as to the additional grounds for revocation of a certification mark see PARA 157; and as to the date from which revocation takes effect see PARA 96.

2   As to the meaning of 'trade mark' see PARA 41.

3   As to the meaning of 'registered' see PARA 21 note 2.

4   Trade Marks Act 1994 s 46(5) (derived from Council Directive (EEC) 89/104 (OJ L40, 11.2.89, p 1) to approximate the laws of the member states relating to trade marks, art 13 (see now European Parliament and Council Directive (EC) 2008/95 (OJ L299, 8.11.2008, p 25) art 13)). This most commonly arises in the context of revocation for non-use, where it is often the case that the proprietor has used the mark in relation to only certain goods and services within the specification for which the mark is registered. Where the existing specification is worded in broad terms, it is not appropriate simply to apply a blue pencil test to the specification; rather the tribunal should re-word the specification to correspond to the use that has been made. To do this the tribunal must first find as a fact what goods or services the mark has been used in relation to and secondly arrive at a fair specification of goods or services having regard to the use made; for this purpose the tribunal should decide how the average consumer would describe such use. The aim is to arrive at a fair specification by identifying and defining not the particular examples of goods for which there has been genuine use, but the particular categories of use they should realistically be taken to exemplify: *Daimler AG v Sany Group Co Ltd* [2009] EWHC 1003 (Ch), [2009] ETMR 58, [2009] All ER (D) 128 (May); *Stichting BDO v BDO Unibank, Inc* [2013] EWHC 418 (Ch), [2013] ETMR 31, [2013] All ER (D) 39 (Mar). See also *Thomson Holidays Ltd v Norwegian Cruise Lines Ltd* [2002] EWCA Civ 1828, [2003] RPC 586, [2003] IP & T 299 ('arrangement of travel, tours and cruises' etc limited to 'all for package holidays'); see also *MINERVA Trade Mark* [2000] FSR 734 (registration for 'printed matter' limited to 'stationery'); *Decon Laboratories Ltd v Fred Baker Scientific Ltd* [2001] RPC 293, (2001) Times, 28 February ('cleaning and decontaminating substances and preparations' limited to 'all for non-domestic use'); *DaimlerChrysler AG v Alavi (t/a Merc)* [2001] RPC 42, [2002] IP & T 496 ('articles of clothing' limited to 'sweaters, anoraks, polo-shirts, scarves, T-shirts and baseball caps'); *West (t/a Eastenders) v Fuller Smith & Turner plc* [2003] EWCA Civ 48, [2003]

FSR 816, [2003] IP & T 768 ('beer' limited to 'bitter beer'); *Associated Newspapers Ltd v Express Newspapers* [2003] EWHC 1322 (Ch), [2004] IP & T 378, [2003] FSR 909 (mark registered for 'newspapers for sale in England and Wales only' not restricted even assuming only used for paid-for Sunday newspaper); *H Young (Operations) Ltd v Medici Ltd* [2003] EWHC 1589 (Ch), sub nom *ANIMAL Trade Mark* [2004] FSR 383 (mark registered for 'clothing' not restricted although only used for casual clothing of surfwear type); Case T-126/03 *Reckitt Benckiser (Espana) SL v Office for Harmonisation of the Internal Market (Trade Marks and Designs)* [2005] ECR II-2861, [2006] ETMR 50, [2005] All ER (D) 198 (Jul), CFI (mark registered for 'polish for metals' not restricted although only used for magic cotton); *WISI Trade Mark* [2006] RPC 580, [2006] ETMR 5, Appointed Person ('electrical and electronic apparatus and instruments' limited to 'apparatus and instruments for receiving, transmitting, amplifying, processing and measuring television signals etc'); *DATASPHERE Trade Mark* [2006] RPC 590, Appointed Person ('computer software and computer programmes' limited to 'all for use in or with banking or financial telecommunications systems'); Case T-256/04 *Mundipharma AG v Office for Harmonisation of the Internal Market (Trade Marks and Designs)* [2007] ECR II-449, [2007] All ER (D) 159 (Feb), CFI ('pharmaceutical and sanitary preparations; plasters restricted to 'therapeutic reparations for respiratory illnesses'); *EXTREME Trade Mark* [2008] RPC 2, Appointed Person (registration of 'luggage' maintained in view of use in relation to holdalls); *Maier v ASOS plc* [2013] EWHC 2831 (Ch), [2013] All ER (D) 185 (Sep) ('clothing footwear, 'headgear' restricted to 'specialist clothing for racing cyclists and casual wear including track-suits, t-shirts, polo shirts, caps and jackets').

　　As to procedure on the application see PARA 378 et seq; and as to the date from which revocation takes effect see PARA 96. Cf the similar provision relating to a partial declaration of invalidity: see the Trade Marks Act 1994 s 47(5) (derived from Council Directive (EEC) 89/104 (OJ L40, 11.2.89, p 1) art 13); and PARA 104.

5　See the Trade Marks (International Registration) Order 2008, SI 2008/2206, art 3; and PARA 12. As to the meaning of 'protected international trade mark (UK)' see PARA 12 note 8. See also generally PARA 11 et seq.

(iv) Declaration of Invalidity

102. Registration granted in breach of absolute grounds for refusal. The registration of a trade mark[1] may[2] be declared invalid on the ground that the trade mark was registered in breach of the absolute grounds[3] for refusal of registration[4]. The protection of a protected international trade mark (UK) must be declared invalid on the same ground[5].

Where the trade mark was registered even though it was devoid of any distinctive character[6] or consisted exclusively of signs or indications which might serve, in trade[7], to designate the kind etc of goods or services[8] or consisted exclusively of signs or indications which have become customary in the current language or in the bona fide and established practices of the trade[9], it must not be declared invalid if, in consequence of the use[10] which has been made of it, it has after registration acquired a distinctive character in relation to the goods or services for which it is registered[11].

1　As to the meaning of 'trade mark' see PARA 41.
2　As to the absence of discretion see PARA 95.
3　Ie on the ground that the trade mark was registered in breach of the Trade Marks Act 1994 s 3 (see PARA 43 et seq) or any of the provisions referred to therein.
4　Trade Marks Act 1994 s 47(1) (derived from Council Directive (EEC) 89/104 (OJ L40, 11.2.89, p 1) to approximate the laws of the member states relating to trade marks, art 3 (see now European Parliament and Council Directive (EC) 2008/95 (OJ L299, 8.11.2008, p 25) art 3)). As to the additional ground of invalidity of a collective mark see PARA 147; and as to the additional ground of invalidity of a certification mark see PARA 158.
5　See the Trade Marks (International Registration) Order 2008, SI 2008/2206, art 3; and PARA 12. As to the meaning of 'protected international trade mark (UK)' see PARA 12 note 8. See also generally PARA 11 et seq.
6　Ie in breach of the Trade Marks Act 1994 s 3(1)(b): see PARA 44 head (1).
7　As to the meaning of 'trade' see PARA 44 note 4.
8　Ie in breach of the Trade Marks Act 1994 s 3(1)(c): see PARA 44 head (2).

9   Ie in breach of the Trade Marks Act 1994 s 3(1)(d): see PARA 44 head (3).
10 As to the meaning of 'use' see PARA 44 note 8.
11 Trade Marks Act 1994 s 47(1) (derived from Council Directive (EEC) 89/104 (OJ L40, 11.2.89, p 1) art 3(3), second sentence (see now European Parliament and Council Directive (EC) 2008/95 (OJ L299, 8.11.2008, p 25) art 3(3))). As to acquiring distinctive character as a result of use see PARA 45.
    As to procedure on the application see PARA 378 et seq; and as to the effect of a declaration of invalidity see PARA 96. For the purposes of proceedings under the Trade Marks Act 1994 s 47, as it applies in relation to an existing registered mark, the provisions of the Trade Marks Act 1994 are deemed to have been in force at all material times; but no objection to the validity of the registration of an existing registered mark may be taken on the ground specified in s 5(3) (see PARA 59): s 105, Sch 3 para 18(2). As to the meaning of 'existing registered mark' see PARA 4 note 2.

103. Registration granted in breach of relative grounds for refusal.

The registration of a trade mark[1] may[2] be declared invalid on the ground:

(1)   that there is an earlier trade mark[3] in relation to which the specified conditions for refusal[4] obtain[5]; or

(2)   that there is an earlier right[6] in relation to which the specified condition for refusal[7] is satisfied[8],

unless the proprietor of that earlier trade mark or other earlier right has consented to the registration[9].

The registration of a trade mark may not be declared invalid on the ground that there is an earlier trade mark unless[10]:

(a)   the registration procedure for the earlier trade mark was completed within the period of five years ending with the date of the application for the declaration[11];

(d)   the registration procedure for the earlier trade mark was not completed before that date[12]; or

(c)   the 'use conditions' are met[13].

The use conditions are met if:

(i)   within the period of five years ending with the date of publication of the application the earlier trade mark has been put to genuine[14] use[15] in the United Kingdom[16] by the proprietor or with his consent in relation to the goods or services for which it is registered[17]; or

(ii)   the earlier trade mark has not been so used, but there are proper reasons[18] for non-use[19].

Where an earlier trade mark satisfies the use conditions in respect of some only of the goods or services for which it is registered, it must be treated for these purposes as if it were registered only in respect of those goods or services[20].

The protection of a protected international trade mark (UK) may be declared invalid on the same ground[21].

1   As to the meaning of 'trade mark' see PARA 41.
2   As to the absence of discretion see PARA 95.
3   As to the meaning of 'earlier trade mark' see PARA 54.
4   Ie the conditions set out in the Trade Marks Act 1994 s 5(1), (2) or (3): see PARAS 55–59.
5   Trade Marks Act 1994 s 47(2)(a). Only the proprietor or a licensee of the earlier trade mark or, in the case of an earlier collective mark or certification mark, the proprietor or an authorised user of such collective mark or certification mark may make an application for a declaration of invalidity on this ground: Trade Marks (Relative Grounds) Order 2007, SI 2007/1976, art 5(1), (2)(a).
6   As to the meaning of 'earlier right' see PARA 61.
7   Ie the condition set out in the Trade Marks Act 1994 s 5(4): see PARA 61.
8   Trade Marks Act 1994 s 47(2)(b). Only the proprietor of the earlier right may make an application for a declaration of invalidity on this ground: Trade Marks (Relative Grounds) Order 2007, SI 2007/1976, art 5(1), (2)(b).

9   Trade Marks Act 1994 s 47(2) (derived from Council Directive (EEC) 89/104 (OJ L40, 11.2.89, p 1) art 4 (see now European Parliament and Council Directive (EC) 2008/95 (OJ L299, 8.11.2008, p 25) art 4)). See also PARA 102 note 11. As to the date on which the proprietor must give such consent see PARA 62 text and note 5; as to procedure on the application see PARA 378 et seq; as to the effect of a declaration of invalidity see PARA 96; as to statutory acquiescence see PARA 83; as to the additional ground of invalidity of a collective mark see PARA 147; and as to the additional ground of invalidity of a certification mark see PARA 158.

10   Trade Marks Act 1994 s 47(2A) (s 47(2A)–(2E) added by SI 2004/946). The Trade Marks Act 1994 s 47(2A) (see heads (a)–(c) in the text) does not apply where the earlier trade mark is a trade mark within the Trade Marks Act 1994 s 6(1)(c) (see PARA 54 head (4)): s 47(2F) (added by SI 2008/1067).

11   Trade Marks Act 1994 s 47(2A)(a) (as added: see note 10). See note 10.

12   Trade Marks Act 1994 s 47(2A)(b) (as added: see note 10). See note 10.

13   Trade Marks Act 1994 s 47(2A)(c) (as added: see note 10). See note 10.

14   As to genuine use see PARA 98 note 6.

15   For these purposes, use of a trade mark includes use in a form differing in elements which do not alter the distinctive character of the mark in the form in which it was registered: Trade Marks Act 1994 s 47(2C)(a) (as added: see note 10). Cf the Trade Marks Act 1994 s 46(2): see PARA 98.

16   For these purposes, use in the United Kingdom includes affixing the trade mark to goods or to the packaging of goods in the United Kingdom solely for export purposes: Trade Marks Act 1994 s 47(2C)(b) (as added: see note 10). Cf s 46(2): see PARA 98. In relation to a Community trade mark or international trade mark (EC), reference to the United Kingdom must be construed as a reference to the European Union: s 47(2D) (as so added; and amended by SI 2008/1067; and SI 2011/1043). As to the meaning of 'United Kingdom' see PARA 3 note 2.

17   Trade Marks Act 1994 s 47(2B)(a) (as added: see note 10).

18   As to proper reasons see PARA 98 note 10.

19   Trade Marks Act 1994 s 47(2B)(b) (as added: see note 10).

20   Trade Marks Act 1994 s 47(2E) (as added: see note 10).

21   See the Trade Marks (International Registration) Order 2008, SI 2008/2206, art 3; and PARA 12. As to the meaning of 'protected international trade mark (UK)' see PARA 12 note 8. See also generally PARA 11 et seq.

104.   Partial declaration of invalidity.   Where the grounds of invalidity[1] exist in respect of only some of the goods or services for which the trade mark[2] is registered[3], the trade mark may be declared invalid as regards those goods or services only[4]. Likewise, a partial declaration of invalidity of the protection of a protected international trade mark (UK) may be made[5].

1   As to the grounds of invalidity see PARAS 102–103; as to the additional ground of invalidity of a collective mark see PARA 147; and as to the additional ground of invalidity of a certification mark see PARA 158.

2   As to the meaning of 'trade mark' see PARA 41.

3   As to the meaning of 'registered' see PARA 21 note 2.

4   Trade Marks Act 1994 s 47(5). It would appear that in appropriate circumstances the same approach should be applied under s 47(5) as under s 46(5) (see PARA 101 text and note 4). See also PARA 102 note 11. As to procedure on the application see PARA 378 et seq; and as to the effect of a declaration of invalidity see PARA 96.

5   See the Trade Marks (International Registration) Order 2008, SI 2008/2206, art 3; and PARA 12. As to the meaning of 'protected international trade mark (UK)' see PARA 12 note 8. See also generally PARA 11 et seq.

(v) Rectification of the Register

105.   In general.   Any person having a sufficient interest[1] may apply for the rectification of an error or omission in the register[2]; but an application for rectification may not be made in respect of a matter affecting the validity[3] of the registration[4] of a trade mark[5].

Except where the registrar[6] or the court[7] directs otherwise, the effect of rectification of the register is that the error or omission in question is deemed never to have been made[8].

1   Any person may apply; there is no need for the applicant to show that he is aggrieved by or otherwise interested in the registration: see PARA 378 text and note 3.
2   Trade Marks Act 1994 s 64(1) (which has no antecedent in Council Directive (EEC) 89/104 (OJ L40, 11.2.89, p 1) to approximate the laws of the member states relating to trade marks (see now European Parliament and Council Directive (EC) 2008/95 (OJ L299, 8.11.2008, p 25))). As to the register see PARA 21. An application under the Trade Marks Act 1938 s 32 (repealed) (rectification of register) or s 34 (repealed) (correction of register) which was pending on 31 October 1994 must be dealt with under the old law and any necessary alteration made to the new register: Trade Marks Act 1994 s 105, Sch 3 para 18(1). As to the meaning of 'the old law' see PARA 4 note 3.
3   A broadening of the specification of goods affects the validity of the registration: *Andreas Stihl AG & Co's Trade Mark Application* [2001] RPC 215, Appointed Person; cf Case T-128/99 *Signal Communications Ltd v Office for Harmonisation in the Internal Market (Trade Marks and Designs)* [2001] ECR II-3273, CFI (decided under Council Regulation (EC) 40/94 (OJ L11, 14.1.94, p 1) on the Community trade mark (see now Council Regulation (EC) 207/2009 (OJ L78, 24.3.2009, p 1)).
4   As to the meaning of 'registration' see PARA 21 note 2.
5   Trade Marks Act 1994 s 64(1) proviso. Rectification may be ordered where a purported assignment of the trade mark has been recorded but the assignment was made without authority: *Dasema Trading Ltd's Trade Mark* [2007] ETMR 15, Trade Marks Registry. Rectification may also be ordered where the registered proprietor has sold the trade mark to another party after registration: *Skaga AB's Trade Mark* (O/134/03), Trade Marks Registry. It is not clear whether rectification may be ordered on the ground that the registered proprietor was not the rightful proprietor at the time of the registration, or whether this is a ground which affects the validity of the registration, but the latter appears more likely. As to the meaning of 'trade mark' see PARA 41. As to procedure on the application see PARA 378 et seq; and as to the grounds on which a trade mark may be declared invalid see PARAS 102–103.
     The registration of a person as proprietor of a trade mark is prima facie evidence of the validity of the original registration: see the Trade Marks Act 1994 s 72; and PARA 94.
6   As to the registrar see PARA 19.
7   As to the meaning of 'the court' see PARA 331.
8   Trade Marks Act 1994 s 64(3).

(vi) Alteration of Registered Trade Mark

106.   In general.   A registered trade mark[1] may not be altered in the register[2] during the period of registration or on renewal[3]. Nevertheless the registrar[4] may, at the request of the proprietor, allow the alteration of a registered trade mark where the mark includes the proprietor's name or address and the alteration is limited to alteration of that name or address and does not substantially affect the identity[5] of the mark[6].

Where, upon the request of the proprietor, the registrar proposes to allow such alteration, he must publish[7] the mark as altered in the Trade Marks Journal[8].

1   As to the meaning of 'registered trade mark' see PARA 111.
2   As to the register see PARA 21.
3   Trade Marks Act 1994 s 44(1) (which has no antecedent in Council Directive (EEC) 89/104 (OJ L40, 11.2.89, p 1) to approximate the laws of the member states relating to trade marks (see now European Parliament and Council Directive (EC) 2008/95 (OJ L299, 8.11.2008, p 25)). This provision must be read subject to the Trade Marks Act 1994 s 13, which permits a disclaimer or limitation to be made to a registered trade mark: see PARA 65. An application under the Trade Marks Act 1938 s 35 (repealed) (alteration of registered trade mark) which was pending on 31 October 1994 must be dealt with under the old law and any necessary alteration made to the new register: Trade Marks Act 1994 s 105, Sch 3 para 16. As to the meaning of 'the old law' see PARA 4 note 3.

It should be noted that s 44 does not apply to international trade marks (UK) or requests for extension: see the Trade Marks (International Registration) Order 2008, SI 2008/2206, art 3(3), Sch 1 Pt 1; and PARA 12 note 10. See also generally PARA 11 et seq.

4   As to the registrar see PARA 19.

5   An alteration which affects the way a trade mark is or may be pronounced or its visual impact or the idea conveyed by the mark does substantially affect the identity of the mark: *Neutrogena Corpn v Golden Ltd* [1996] RPC 473 at 488–489, CA (a case under the Trade Marks Act 1938 s 30 (repealed)). See also the Trade Marks Act 1994 s 41(2) (in which the same expression appears); and PARA 346 note 2.

6   Trade Marks Act 1994 s 44(2). See note 3. As to procedure on the application see PARA 375.

7   As to the meaning of 'publish' see PARA 19 note 10.

8   Trade Marks Act 1994 s 44(3); Trade Marks Rules 2008, SI 2008/1797, r 32(2). See note 3. As to the Trade Marks Journal see PARA 19.

(6) GROUNDLESS THREATS OF INFRINGEMENT PROCEEDINGS

107.   In general.   Where a person threatens[1] another with proceedings for infringement[2] of a registered trade mark[3] other than:

(1)   the application of the mark to goods or their packaging[4];

(2)   the importation of goods to which, or to the packaging of which, the mark has been applied[5]; or

(3)   the supply of services under the mark[6],

any person aggrieved[7] may bring proceedings for relief[8].

The mere notification that a trade mark is registered, or that an application for registration has been made, does not constitute a threat of proceedings for the purposes of the above provisions[9]. Since there is no equivalent provision in respect of a threat of passing-off proceedings, it is possible to threaten anyone with such proceedings[10]; but caution will be required where such a threat is made along with a notification of the existence of a registered trade mark[11].

The same provisions apply to threats of infringement proceedings of a protected international trade mark (UK)[12].

1   The test for whether a communication constitutes a threat is whether a reasonable person, in the position of the recipient, would have understood it as a threat of proceedings: *Prince plc v Prince Sports plc* [1998] FSR 21; *L'Oréal (UK) Ltd v Johnson & Johnson* [2000] FSR 686, [2000] IP & T 789; *Best Buy Co Inc v Worldwide Sales Corpn España SL* [2011] EWCA Civ 618, [2011] Bus LR 1166, [2011] FSR 742, [2011] All ER (D) 238 (May). Accordingly, implied threats are threats for these purposes: *Scandecor Development AB v Scandecor Marketing AB* [1999] FSR 26, CA (on appeal [2001] UKHL 21, [2000] IP & T 676, [2002] FSR 122 (questions referred to European Court of Justice but case settled prior to ruling)), applying *Bowden Controls Ltd v Acco Cable Control Ltd* [1990] RPC 427 at 431 per Aldous J to the Trade Marks Act 1994 s 21. In relation to patents the courts have consistently held that any communication containing even a hint of legal action amounts to a threat: see PATENTS AND REGISTERED DESIGNS vol 79 (2008) PARA 559. The threat need not be communicated to the person threatened; accordingly, a threat made to manufacturer to sue the manufacturer's customers is actionable: *Sudarshan Chemical Industries Ltd v Clariant Produkte (Deutschland) GmbH* [2013] EWCA Civ 919, [2013] All ER (D) 41 (Aug) (a patent case). A statement which is not a threat cannot retrospectively constitute a threat as a result of subsequent events: *Prince plc v Prince Sports plc* above (cannot use later correspondence to construe alleged 'threat'). If the threat was made at a 'without prejudice' meeting or in a letter protected by the 'without prejudice' rule, it cannot be relied on and a claim based upon such a threat will be struck out as an abuse of process: *Unilever plc v Procter & Gamble Co* [2001] 1 All ER 783, [2000] 1 WLR 2436, CA (a patent case); but see *Best Buy Co Inc v Worldwide Sales Corpn España SL* above. A claim against a solicitor will not be permitted if it appears that the sole purpose of the claim is to create a conflict between the solicitor and his client: *Reckitt Benckiser (UK) v Home Pairfum Ltd* [2004] EWHC 302 (Pat), [2004] FSR 774.

2   As to the meaning of 'infringement proceedings' see PARA 67 note 4; and as to the meaning of 'infringement' see PARA 66 note 4. As to the acts which amount to infringement, if done without the consent of the proprietor, see the Trade Marks Act 1994 s 10; and PARA 68 et seq.

3   As to the meaning of 'registered trade mark' see PARA 111. It appears that a threat of proceedings made in relation to an application for a trade mark is actionable: cf *Brain v Ingledew Brown Benison & Garrett* [1996] FSR 341, CA (a patent case). As to justification in such a case see *Brain v Ingledew Brown Benison & Garrett (No 2)* [1997] FSR 271.

4   Trade Marks Act 1994 s 21(1)(a). A threat in relation to subsequent dealings is actionable even if the person threatened has applied the mark: *Prince plc v Prince Sports plc* [1998] FSR 21; cf *Cavity Trays Ltd v RMC Panel Products Ltd* [1996] RPC 361, CA (a patent case).

5   Trade Marks Act 1994 s 21(1)(b).

6   Trade Marks Act 1994 s 21(1)(c). Where a threat is made to a person who supplies services, it is a question of construction whether the threat relates purely to supplying services under the mark: *Prince plc v Prince Sports plc* [1998] FSR 21; cf *Brain v Ingledew Brown Benison & Garrett* [1996] FSR 341, CA (a patent case).

7   The expression 'person aggrieved' must be construed liberally. It includes the person to whom the threats are made: *Prince plc v Prince Sports plc* [1998] FSR 21. Cf the Patents Act 1977 s 70(1) (see PATENTS AND REGISTERED DESIGNS vol 79 (2008) PARA 557), where it is explicitly made clear that the right of action accrues to a person 'whether or not he is the person to whom the threats are made'; but even without that provision it would seem to be the same in relation to trade marks. It is sufficient for the claimant to show that his commercial interests have been adversely affected in a real, as opposed to a fanciful or minimal, way (*Brain v Ingledew Brown Benison & Garrett (No 3)* [1997] FSR 511); but if the claimant has not been adversely affected by the threat at all he is not a person aggrieved (*Samuel Smith Old Brewery (Tadcaster) v Lee (t/a Cropton Brewery)* [2011] EWHC 1879 (Ch), [2011] All ER (D) 229 (Jul)).

8   Trade Marks Act 1994 s 21(1). Section 21 contains a provision new in trade marks law but is based upon the equivalent provisions relating to patents (see the Patents Act 1977 s 70; and PATENTS AND REGISTERED DESIGNS vol 79 (2008) PARA 557 et seq) and registered designs (see the Registered Designs Act 1949 s 26; and PATENTS AND REGISTERED DESIGNS vol 79 (2008) PARA 772). As to justification of threats see PARA 108; and as to the relief obtainable see PARA 109.

9   Trade Marks Act 1994 s 21(4) (following the Patents Act 1977 s 70(5): see PATENTS AND REGISTERED DESIGNS vol 79 (2008) PARA 559).

10   Ie subject to the law of malicious falsehood (see DEFAMATION vol 32 (2012) PARA 776 et seq), for which it would, however, be necessary to prove that the person making the threat had no honest belief in his case.

11   See *Jaybeam Ltd v Abru Aluminium Ltd* [1976] RPC 308, [1975] FSR 334 (where a letter threatening proceedings for copyright infringement, and also mentioning the existence of a registered design, was held to contain an implicit threat to sue on the registered design).

12   See the Trade Marks (International Registration) Order, SI 2008/2206, art 3; and PARA 12. As to the meaning of 'protected international trade mark (UK)' see PARA 12 note 8. See also generally PARA 11 et seq.

108. Justification of threats.

The claimant is entitled to relief against groundless threats of infringement proceedings[1] unless the defendant shows that the acts in respect of which proceedings were threatened constitute (or, if done, would constitute) an infringement of the registered trade mark[2] concerned[3]. If that is shown by the defendant, the claimant is nevertheless entitled to relief if he shows that the registration of the trade mark is invalid[4] or liable to be revoked[5] in a relevant respect[6].

1   As to groundless threats of infringement proceedings see PARA 107; and as to the relief obtainable see PARA 109. As to the meaning of 'infringement proceedings' see PARA 67 note 4; and as to the meaning of 'infringement' see PARA 66 note 4. As to the acts which amount to infringement, if done without the consent of the proprietor, see the Trade Marks Act 1994 s 10; and PARA 68 et seq.

2   This provision also applies to a protected international trade mark (UK): see PARA 107 text and note 12. As to the meaning of 'registered trade mark' see PARA 111. As to the meaning of 'protected international trade mark (UK)' see PARA 12 note 8.

3   Trade Marks Act 1994 s 21(2).

4   Ie or that the protection of the protected international trade mark (UK) is invalid. As to the
     grounds for invalidity of registration see PARA 102 et seq.
5   As to the grounds for revocation of registration see PARA 98 et seq.
6   Trade Marks Act 1994 s 21(3).

109. Relief obtainable. The relief which may be applied for groundless
threats of infringement proceedings[1] is any of the following[2]:
(1)   a declaration that the threats are unjustifiable[3];
(2)   an injunction against the continuance of the threats[4];
(3)   damages in respect of any loss the claimant has sustained by the
       threats[5].

1   As to groundless threats of infringement proceedings see PARA 107; and as to justification of
     threats see PARA 108. As to the meaning of 'infringement proceedings' see PARA 67 note 4; and
     as to the meaning of 'infringement' see PARA 84 note 4. As to the acts which amount to
     infringement, if done without the consent of the proprietor, see the Trade Marks Act 1994 s 10;
     and PARA 68 et seq.
2   Trade Marks Act 1994 s 21(2). This includes an interim injunction: *Johnson Electric Industrial
     Manufactory Ltd v Mabuchi Motor KK* [1986] FSR 280 (a patent case).
3   Trade Marks Act 1994 s 21(2)(a). This encompasses a declaration of non-infringement: *L'Oréal
     (UK) Ltd v Johnson & Johnson* [2000] FSR 686, [2000] All ER (D) 290.
4   Trade Marks Act 1994 s 21(2)(b).
5   Trade Marks Act 1994 s 21(2)(c).

(7) REGISTERED TRADE MARKS AS OBJECTS OF PROPERTY; ASSIGNMENT AND LICENSING

(i) Introduction

110. In general. The Trade Marks Act 1994 contains substantially new
provisions relating to registered trade marks as objects of property, particularly
in relation to their assignment, transmission and licensing[1]. These provisions also
apply, with the necessary modifications, to applications for registration of trade
marks[2]. Most of these provisions also apply to protected international trade
marks (UK)[3].

The new provisions in the Trade Marks Act 1994 in all these respects give a
proprietor much greater freedom in principle than under the previous law[4]. It
remains the case, however, that he must not allow his mark to become deceptive
without risking revocation[5]. Subject to that, a registered trade mark has become
more assimilated to other incorporeal rights as regards the freedom of its owner
to deal with it[6].

1   Under the Trade Marks Act 1938 both assignment and licensing were closely controlled with a
     view to preventing marks from becoming deceptive: see the Trade Marks Act 1938 s 22
     (repealed) (assignment) and s 28 (repealed) (licensing).
        Even the provisions of that Act represented a liberalisation of the position obtaining before
     that Act was passed: see the Trade Marks Act 1905 s 22 (repealed), whereby a registered trade
     mark could only be assigned along with the business ie effectively with the business (see eg *Re
     John Sinclair Ltd's Trade Mark* [1932] 1 Ch 598, 49 RPC 123, CA). There was no provision in
     the Trade Marks Act 1905 permitting licensing at all. A history of these matters was provided in
     GE Trade Mark [1969] RPC 418 (revsd [1970] RPC 339, CA; affd [1973] RPC 297, HL).
2   Trade Marks Act 1994 s 27(1).
3   See the Trade Marks (International Registration) Order 2008, SI 2008/2206, art 3; and PARA 12.
     See also generally PARA 11 et seq.
4   Such was the intention: see the White Paper *Reform of Trade Marks Law* (Cm 1203)
     paras 4.34–4.39 (licensing), 4.44–4.47 (assignment).
5   See PARA 100.

6   See *Scandecor Development AB v Scandecor Marketing AB* [2001] UKHL 21, [2000] IP & T 676, [2002] FSR 122 (referred to European Court of Justice but case settled prior to ruling).

(ii) Registered Trade Marks and Protected International Trade Marks (UK) as Objects of Property

111. Registered trade mark is property. A registered trade mark is a property right obtained by the registration[1] of the trade mark under the Trade Marks Act 1994; and the proprietor of a registered trade mark has the rights[2] and remedies[3] provided by that Act[4]. A registered trade mark is personal property[5]. Equities in respect of a registered trade mark may be enforced[6] in like manner as in respect of other personal or movable property[7].

1   As to the meaning of 'registration' see PARA 21 note 2.
2   As to the rights see PARA 66.
3   As to the remedies see PARA 418 et seq.
4   Trade Marks Act 1994 s 2(1).
5   Trade Marks Act 1994 s 22. The provisions of s 22 and s 26 (see the text and notes 6–7) apply, with the necessary modifications, in relation to an application for the registration of a trade mark as in relation to a registered trade mark: s 27(1). If the applicant company is dissolved prior to registration the application vests bona vacantia: *Joe Cool (Manchester) Ltd's Trade Mark Application* [2000] RPC 926, Trade Marks Registry. These provisions also apply in relation to a protected international trade mark (UK): see the Trade Marks (International Registration) Order 2008, SI 2008/2206, art 3; and PARA 12. See also generally PARA 11 et seq. As to the requirements for registration see PARA 39 et seq; and as to the procedure on the application see PARA 334 et seq. As to the meaning of 'protected international trade mark (UK)' see PARA 12 note 8.
6   Ie subject to the provisions of the Trade Marks Act 1994.
7   Trade Marks Act 1994 s 26(2). See also note 5. As to trusts and equities generally see further PARA 25.

112. Co-ownership of registered trade mark. Where a registered trade mark[1] is granted to two or more persons jointly, each of them is entitled, subject to any agreement to the contrary, to an equal undivided share in the registered trade mark[2]. Where two or more persons are co-proprietors of a registered trade mark[3], the following provisions apply[4].

Subject to any agreement to the contrary, each co-proprietor is entitled, by himself or his agents, to do for his own benefit and without the consent[5] of or the need to account to the other or others, any act which would otherwise amount to an infringement[6] of the registered trade mark[7].

One co-proprietor may not, without the consent of the other or others, grant a licence[8] to use the registered trade mark or assign[9] or charge his share in the registered trade mark[10].

Infringement proceedings[11] may be brought by any co-proprietor, but he may not, without the leave of the court[12], proceed with the action unless the other, or each of the others, is either joined as a claimant or added as a defendant; a co-proprietor who is thus added as a defendant may not be made liable for any costs in the action unless he takes part in the proceedings[13].

Nothing in the above provisions affects the mutual rights and obligations of trustees or personal representatives, or their rights and obligations as such[14].

1   As to the meaning of 'registered trade mark' see PARA 111.
2   Trade Marks Act 1994 s 23(1). The provisions of s 23 apply, with the necessary modifications, in relation to an application for the registration of a trade mark as in relation to a registered trade mark: s 27(1). In s 23, as it applies in relation to an application for registration, the reference in s 23(1) to the granting of the registration is to be construed as a reference to the making of the application: s 27(2). These provisions also apply in relation to a protected

international trade mark (UK): see the Trade Marks (International Registration) Order 2008, SI 2008/1797, art 3; and PARA 11 et seq. As to the requirements for registration see PARA 39 et seq; and as to the procedure on the application see PARA 334 et seq. As to the meaning of 'protected international trade mark (UK)' see PARA 12 note 8.

The provisions of the Trade Marks Act 1994 s 23 apply as from 31 October 1994 to an existing registered mark of which two or more persons were immediately before that date registered as joint proprietors: s 105, Sch 3 para 7. So long as the relations between the joint proprietors remain such as are described in the Trade Marks Act 1938 s 63 (repealed) (joint ownership) there is, however, taken to be an agreement to exclude the operation of the Trade Marks Act 1994 s 23(1), (3): Sch 3 paras 1(1), 7. Where the relations between two or more persons interested in a trade mark was such that no one of them was entitled as between himself and the other or others to use it except either on behalf of both or all of them or in relation to an article with which both or all of them were connected in the course of trade, those persons might be registered as joint proprietors of the trade mark; and the Trade Marks Act 1938 had effect in relation to any rights to the use of the trade mark vested in those persons as if those rights had been vested in a single person: s 63(1) (repealed). Subject thereto, nothing in the Trade Marks Act 1938 authorised the registration as joint proprietors of two or more persons who used, or propose to used, a trade mark independently: s 63(2) (repealed). As to the meaning of 'trade' see PARA 44 note 4.

3　Ie whether by virtue of the Trade Marks Act 1994 s 23(1) (see the text to note 2) or otherwise.

4　Trade Marks Act 1994 s 23(2). See also note 2.

5　As to the meaning of 'consent' see the Trade Marks Act 1994 s 28(3); and PARA 119.

6　As to the meaning of 'infringement' see PARA 66 note 4. As to the acts which amount to infringement, if done without the consent of the proprietor, see the Trade Marks Act 1994 s 10; and PARA 68 et seq.

7　Trade Marks Act 1994 s 23(3). See also note 2. This represents a relaxation of the position under the Trade Marks Act 1938 s 63 (repealed) (cited in note 2).

8　As to the licensing of trade marks see PARAS 119–120.

9　As to assignment of a registered trade mark see PARA 113.

10　Trade Marks Act 1994 s 23(4). See also note 2.

11　As to the meaning of 'infringement proceedings' see PARA 67 note 4.

12　As to the meaning of 'the court' see PARA 331.

13　Trade Marks Act 1994 s 23(5). See also note 2. Nothing in s 23(5) affects the granting of interim relief on the application of a single co-proprietor: s 23(5).

14　Trade Marks Act 1994 s 23(6). See also note 2.

(iii) Assignment and Transmission

113.　In general. A registered trade mark[1] is transmissible by assignment[2], testamentary disposition or operation of law in the same way as other personal or movable property[3]. It is so transmissible either in connection with the goodwill of a business[4] or independently[5].

An assignment or other transmission of a registered trade mark or protected international trade mark (UK) may be partial, that is, limited so as to apply in relation to some but not all of the goods or services for which the trade mark is registered[6]; an assignment or other transmission of a registered trade mark (but not a protected international trade mark (UK)[7]) may be limited in relation to use[8] of the trade mark in a particular manner or a particular locality[9].

An assignment of a registered trade mark, or an assent relating to a registered trade mark, is not effective unless it is in writing signed by or on behalf of the assignor or, as the case may be, a personal representative; but, in a case where the assignor or personal representative is a body corporate, this requirement may be satisfied by the affixing of its seal[10].

The above provisions apply to assignment by way of security as in relation to any other assignment[11].

A registered trade mark may be the subject of a charge in the same way as other personal or movable property[12].

With the exception of a partial assignment limited by particular manner or locality of use, the above provisions apply in relation to a protected international trade mark (UK) in the same way as to registered trade marks[13].

Nothing in the Trade Marks Act 1994 is to be construed as affecting the assignment or other transmission of an unregistered trade mark as part of the goodwill of a business[14].

1   As to the meaning of 'registered trade mark' see PARA 111.
2   The assignment of a registered trade mark or any right in it is a registrable transaction: see the Trade Marks Act 1994 s 25(2); and PARA 114. The registration of a person as proprietor of a registered trade mark is prima facie evidence of the validity of any subsequent assignment or other transmission of it: see s 72; and PARA 94.
3   Trade Marks Act 1994 s 24(1). The provisions of s 24 apply, with the necessary modifications, in relation to an application for the registration of a trade mark as in relation to a registered trade mark: s 27(1). As to the requirements for registration see PARA 39 et seq; and as to the procedure on the application see PARA 334 et seq.
        Section 24 applies to transactions and events occurring on or after 31 October 1994 in relation to an existing registered mark; and the old law continues to apply in relation to transactions and events occurring before that date: s 105, Sch 3 para 8(1). As to the meaning of 'existing registered mark' see PARA 4 note 2; and as to the meaning of 'the old law' see PARA 4 note 3.
4   As to the meaning of 'business' see PARA 34 note 3.
5   Trade Marks Act 1994 s 24(1). As to the risk that an assignment without goodwill may render the trade mark deceptive see PARA 100.
6   Trade Marks Act 1994 s 24(2)(a); and see the Trade Marks (International Registration) Order 2008, SI 2008/2206, art 3; and PARA 12. As to the meaning of 'protected international trade mark (UK)' see PARA 12 note 8. See also generally PARA 11 et seq.
7   The Trade Marks (International Registration) Order 2008, SI 2008/2206 excludes the Trade Marks Act 1994 s 24(2)(b) (see the text and note 9) from applying to protected international trade marks (UK) or requests for extension: see the Trade Marks (International Registration) Order 2008, SI 2008/2206, art 3(3), Sch 1 Pt 1; and PARA 12 note 10.
8   As to the meaning of 'use' see PARA 44 note 8.
9   Trade Marks Act 1994 s 24(2)(b). A partial assignment may have dangers in respect of validity. For example, assignment for some goods with retention for closely similar goods could lead to confusion. Under the Trade Marks Act 1938 this was not allowed: see *Phantom Trade Mark* [1978] RPC 245, CA.
10   Trade Marks Act 1994 s 24(3).
11   Trade Marks Act 1994 s 24(4).
12   Trade Marks Act 1994 s 24(5).
13   See the Trade Marks (International Registration) Order 2008, SI 2008/2206, art 3; and PARA 11 et seq. See also notes 6, 7.
14   Trade Marks Act 1994 s 24(6). See also PARAS 297–298.

114. Registration of transactions affecting registered trade mark. On application being made to the registrar[1] by:

(1)   a person claiming to be entitled to an interest in or under a registered trade mark[2] by virtue of a registrable transaction[3]; or

(2)   any other person claiming to be affected by such a transaction[4],

the prescribed particulars[5] of the transaction must be entered in the register[6].

The following are registrable transactions:

(a)   an assignment of a registered trade mark or any right in it[7];

(b)   the grant of a licence under a registered trade mark[8];

(c)   the granting of any security interest, whether fixed or floating, over a registered trade mark or any right in or under it[9];

(d)   the making by personal representatives of an assent in relation to a registered trade mark or any right in or under it[10];

(e)   an order of a court or other competent authority transferring a registered trade mark or any right in or under it[11].

Until an application has been made for registration of the prescribed particulars of a registrable transaction: (i) the transaction is ineffective as against a person acquiring a conflicting interest in or under the registered trade mark in ignorance of it; and (ii) a person claiming to be a licensee[12] does not have the protection under the statutory provisions[13] relating to the rights and remedies of a licensee in relation to infringement[14].

Where a person becomes the proprietor or a licensee of a registered trade mark by virtue of a registrable transaction, and the mark is infringed before the prescribed particulars are registered, in proceedings for such an infringement the court[15] must not award him costs unless[16]:

(A)   an application for registration of the prescribed particulars of the transaction is made before the end of the period of six months beginning with its date[17]; or

(B)   the court is satisfied that it was not practicable for such an application to be made before the end of that period and that an application was made as soon as practicable thereafter[18].

The provisions above[19] apply to international trade marks (UK) but with modifications[20].

1   As to the registrar see PARA 19.
2   As to the meaning of 'registered trade mark' see PARA 111.
3   Trade Marks Act 1994 s 25(1)(a).
4   Trade Marks Act 1994 s 25(1)(b).
5   As to the prescribed particulars see PARA 115.
6   Trade Marks Act 1994 s 25(1). The provisions of s 25 apply, with the necessary modifications, in relation to an application for the registration of a trade mark as in relation to a registered trade mark: s 27(1). In s 25, as it applies in relation to a transaction affecting an application for the registration of a trade mark, the references to the entry of particulars in the register, and to the making of an application to register particulars, are to be construed as references to the giving of notice to the registrar of those particulars: s 27(3). As to the requirements for registration see PARA 39 et seq; as to the procedure on the application see PARA 334 et seq; and as to the register see PARA 21.
    As to the power to make rules for the amendment and removal of registered particulars see PARA 118.
    Existing entries under the Trade Marks Act 1938 s 25 (repealed) (registration of assignments and transmissions) had to be transferred on 31 October 1994 to the register kept under the Trade Marks Act 1994 and have effect as if made under s 25: s 105, Sch 3 para 8(2). Provision may be made by rules for putting such entries in the same form as is required for entries made under the Act: Sch 3 para 8(2).
    An application for registration under the Trade Marks Act 1938 s 25 (repealed) which was pending before the registrar on 31 October 1994 must be treated as an application for registration under the Trade Marks Act 1994 s 25 and must proceed accordingly; and the registrar may require the applicant to amend his application so as to conform with the requirements of that Act: Sch 3 para 8(3).
    An application under the Trade Marks Act 1938 s 25 (repealed) which has been determined by the registrar but not finally determined before 31 October 1994 must be dealt with under the old law; and the Trade Marks Act 1994 Sch 3 para 8(2) applies in relation to any resulting entry in the register: Sch 3 para 8(4). As to the meaning of 'the old law' see PARA 4 note 3.
    Where before 31 October 1994 a person has become entitled by assignment or transmission to an existing registered mark but has not registered his title, any application for registration on or after that date must be made under s 25: Sch 3 para 8(5). As to the meaning of 'existing registered mark' see PARA 4 note 2.
    In cases to which Sch 3 para 8(3) or Sch 3 para 8(5) applies, the Trade Marks Act 1938 s 25(3) (repealed) continues to apply (and the Trade Marks Act 1994 s 25(3), (4) does not apply) as regards the consequences of failing to register: Sch 3 para 8(6).
7   Trade Marks Act 1994 s 25(2)(a). As to assignments see PARA 113. An assignment by operation of law, particularly of the kind involved in universal succession following a merger, qualifies as an assignment for this purpose: *Thorn Security Ltd v Siemens Schweiz AG* [2008] EWCA Civ 1161, [2009] RPC 69, [2009] IP & T 67 (a patent case).

8   Trade Marks Act 1994 s 25(2)(b). As to the meaning of 'licence' see PARA 119 note 7.
9   Trade Marks Act 1994 s 25(2)(c).
10   Trade Marks Act 1994 s 25(2)(d).
11   Trade Marks Act 1994 s 25(2)(e).
12   As to the meaning of 'licensee' see PARA 119 note 7.
13   Ie the Trade Marks Act 1994 s 30 (see PARA 400) or s 31 (see PARA 401).
14   Trade Marks Act 1994 s 25(3).
15   As to the meaning of 'the court' see PARA 331.
16   Trade Marks Act 1994 s 25(4) (amended by SI 2006/1028). The Trade Marks Act 1994 s 25(4)
     follows the similar provision in the Patents Act 1977 s 68 (effect of non-registration on
     infringement proceedings: see PATENTS AND REGISTERED DESIGNS vol 79 (2008) PARA 553) with
     the important difference that it is the practicability of making the application for registration
     rather than the registration itself which matters: c f on the latter in relation to patents *Mölnlycke
     AB v Procter & Gamble Ltd (No 5)* [1994] RPC 49 at 110, CA. See also PARA 117 note 5. A
     party seeking to rely upon the Trade Marks Act 1994 s 25(4) must plead the relevant facts:
     Schütz (UK) Ltd v Werit (UK) Ltd [2013] UKSC 16, [2013] 2 All ER 177, [2013] RPC 395 (a
     patent case). The effect of this provision where two successive licences are granted to the same
     licensee and the licensee registers the first, but omits to register the second, is unclear: see *Schütz
     (UK) Ltd v Werit (UK) Ltd* above.
17   Trade Marks Act 1994 s 25(4)(a) (as amended: see note 16).
18   Trade Marks Act 1994 s 25(4)(b) (as amended: see note 16).
19   Ie the Trade Marks Act 1994 s 25, in particular s 25(1)(a), (2), (3), (4)(a).
20   See the Trade Marks (International Registration) Order 2008, SI 2008/2206, art 3(3)(i), Sch 2
     para 1; and PARA 12 note 15. See also generally PARA 11 et seq.

115.   Particulars of registrable transactions. Upon application made to the
registrar[1] by a person claiming to be entitled to an interest in or under a
registered trade mark by virtue of a registrable transaction or any other person
claiming to be affected by such a transaction[2], there must be entered in the
register[3] in respect of each trade mark the following particulars of registrable
transactions[4], that is to say:

(1)   in the case of an assignment[5] of a registered trade mark or any right in
      it: (a) the name and address of the assignee; (b) the date of the
      assignment; and (c) where the assignment is in respect of any right in the
      mark, a description of the right assigned[6];
(2)   in the case of the grant of a licence[7] under a registered trade mark: (a)
      the name and address of the licensee; (b) where the licence is an
      exclusive licence[8], that fact; (c) where the licence is limited[9], a
      description of the limitation; and (d) the duration of the licence if the
      same is or is ascertainable as a definite period[10];
(3)   in the case of the grant of any security interest over a registered trade
      mark or any right in or under it: (a) the name and address of the
      grantee; (b) the nature of the interest, whether fixed or floating; and (c)
      the extent of the security and the right in or under the mark secured[11];
(4)   in the case of the making by personal representatives of an assent in
      relation to a registered trade mark or any right in or under it: (a) the
      name and address of the person in whom the mark or any right in or
      under it vests by virtue of the assent; and (b) the date of the assent[12];
      and
(5)   in the case of a court or other competent authority transferring a
      registered trade mark or any right in or under it: (a) the name and
      address of the transferee; (b) the date of the order; and (c) where the
      transfer is in respect of a right in the mark, a description of the right
      transferred[13].

In each case, there must be entered the date on which the entry is made[14].

1   As to the registrar see PARA 19.
2   Ie any such person as is mentioned in the Trade Marks Act 1994 s 25(1)(a) or s 25(1)(b): see
    PARA 114 heads (1), (2).
3   As to the register see PARA 21.
4   Trade Marks Rules 2008, SI 2008/1797, r 48.
5   As to assignments see PARA 113.
6   Trade Marks Rules 2008, SI 2008/1797, r 48(a).
7   As to licences see PARAS 119–120.
8   As to exclusive licences see PARA 120.
9   As to limited licences see PARA 119.
10 Trade Marks Rules 2008, SI 2008/1797, r 48(b).
11 Trade Marks Rules 2008, SI 2008/1797, r 48(c).
12 Trade Marks Rules 2008, SI 2008/1797, r 48(d).
13 Trade Marks Rules 2008, SI 2008/1797, r 48(e).
14 Trade Marks Rules 2008, SI 2008/1797, r 48. As to the application to register or give notice of
    a transaction see PARA 116.

116.   Application to register or give notice of transaction.   An application to
register particulars of transactions affecting a registered trade mark[1] or to give
notice to the registrar of particulars affecting an application for registration of a
trade mark[2] must be made as follows[3]:

(1)   relating to an assignment[4] or transaction, other than a transaction
      referred to in heads (2) to (4) below, on Form TM16[5];

(2)   relating to the grant of a licence[6], on Form TM50[7];

(3)   relating to an amendment to, or termination of, a licence, on Form
      TM51[8];

(4)   relating to the grant, amendment or termination of any security interest,
      on Form TM24[9]; and

(5)   relating to the making by personal representatives of an assent or in
      relation to an order of a court or other competent authority, on Form
      TM24[10].

Any such application must:

(a)   where the transaction is an assignment, be signed by or on behalf of the
      parties to the assignment[11];

(b)   where the transaction falls within head (2), head (3) or head (4) above,
      be signed by or on behalf of the grantor of the licence or security
      interest[12],

or be accompanied by such documentary evidence as suffices to establish the
transaction[13].

Where an application to give notice to the registrar has been made of
particulars relating to an application for registration of a trade mark, upon
registration of the trade mark, the registrar must enter those particulars in the
register[14].

1   Ie a transaction to which the Trade Marks Act 1994 s 25 (see PARA 114) applies.
2   Ie a transaction to which the Trade Marks Act 1994 s 27(3) (see PARA 114 note 6) applies.
3   Trade Marks Rules 2008, SI 2008/1797, r 49(1), which is expressed to be subject to r 41(2) (see
    the text to notes 11–13).
4   As to assignments see PARA 113.
5   Trade Marks Rules 2008, SI 2008/1797, r 49(1)(a). As to the use of forms see PARA 335.
6   As to licences see PARAS 119–120.
7   Trade Marks Rules 2008, SI 2008/1797, r 49(1)(b).
8   Trade Marks Rules 2008, SI 2008/1797, r 49(1)(c).
9   Trade Marks Rules 2008, SI 2008/1797, r 49(1)(d).
10 Trade Marks Rules 2008, SI 2008/1797, r 49(1)(e).
11 Trade Marks Rules 2008, SI 2008/1797, r 49(2)(a).
12 Trade Marks Rules 2008, SI 2008/1797, r 49(2)(b).

13 Trade Marks Rules 2008, SI 2008/1797, r 49(2).
14 Trade Marks Rules 2008, SI 2008/1797, r 49(3).

117.   Sanctions for failure to register. The Trade Marks Act 1994 provides sanctions in the nature of deprivation of rights for failure to register any registrable transaction affecting a registered trade mark[1]. Thus, until an application has been made for registration of the prescribed particulars of a registrable transaction, the transaction is ineffective as against a person acquiring a conflicting interest in or under the registered trade mark in ignorance of it[2]; and a person claiming to be a licensee by virtue of the transaction does not have the protection of the provisions conferring rights and remedies on a licensee in relation to infringement[3]. Moreover, where a person becomes the proprietor or a licensee of a registered trade mark by virtue of a registrable transaction, and the mark is infringed before the prescribed particulars are registered, in proceedings for such an infringement the court[4] must not award him costs unless an application for registration of the prescribed particulars of the transaction is made before the end of the period of six months beginning with its date or the court is satisfied that it was not practicable for such an application to be made before the end of that period and that an application was made as soon as practicable thereafter[5].

1   The sanctions, so far as may be relevant, will also apply to failure to register or apply to register a registrable transaction in respect of a trade mark application (see the Trade Marks Act 1994 s 27(1)), and failure to apply to register or request recordal of relevant transactions in the supplementary register or the international register (as appropriate) in respect of international trade marks (UK) (see the Trade Marks (International Registration) Order 2008, SI 2008/2206, art 3, and also Sch 2 para 1; and PARAS 12, 114).
2   See the Trade Marks Act 1994 s 25(1)(a); and PARA 114.
3   See the Trade Marks Act 1994 s 25(3)(b); and PARA 114.
4   As to the meaning of 'the court' see PARA 331.
5   See the Trade Marks Act 1994 s 25(4); and PARA 114. See *Schütz (UK) Ltd v Werit (UK) Ltd* [2013] UKSC 16, [2013] 2 All ER 177, [2013] RPC 395; and PARA 114 note 16.

118.   Amendment and removal of registered particulars. Provision may be made by rules[1] as to:
(1)   the amendment of registered particulars[2] relating to a licence so as to reflect any alteration of the terms of the licence[3]; and
(2)   the removal of such particulars from the register[4]:
    (a)   where it appears from the registered particulars that the licence was granted for a fixed period and that period has expired[5]; or
    (b)   where no such period is indicated and, after such period as may be prescribed, the registrar[6] has notified the parties of his intention to remove the particulars from the register[7].
Provision may also be made by rules as to the amendment or removal from the register of particulars relating to a security interest on the application of, or with the consent of, the person entitled to the benefit of that interest[8].

1   Trade Marks Act 1994 s 25(5). The provisions of s 25 apply, with the necessary modifications, in relation to an application for the registration of a trade mark as in relation to a registered trade mark: s 27(1). See the Trade Marks Rules 2008, SI 2008/1797, r 49 (made partly under the Trade Marks Act 1994 s 25); and PARA 116. As to the requirements for registration see PARA 39 et seq; and as to the procedure on the application see PARA 334 et seq.
2   As to registered particulars see PARA 115.
3   Trade Marks Act 1994 s 25(5)(a). As to the licensing of trade marks see PARAS 119–120.
4   Trade Marks Act 1994 s 25(5)(b). As to the register see PARA 21. As to removal of matter from the register see the Trade Marks Rules 2008, SI 2008/1797, r 53; and PARA 30.
5   Trade Marks Act 1994 s 25(5)(b)(i).

6   As to the registrar see PARA 19.
7   Trade Marks Act 1994 s 25(5)(b)(ii).
8   Trade Marks Act 1994 s 25(6). See also note 1.

(iv) Licensing of Trade Marks

119. Freedom to license. A licence[1] to use a registered trade mark[2] may be general or limited[3].

A limited licence may, in particular, apply: (1) in relation to some but not all of the goods or services for which the trade mark is registered; or (2) in relation to use of the trade mark in a particular manner or a particular locality[4].

A licence is not effective unless it is in writing signed by or on behalf of the grantor; and, where the grantor is a body corporate, this requirement may be satisfied by the affixing of its seal[5].

Unless the licence provides otherwise, it is binding on a successor in title to the grantor's interest[6].

Where the licence so provides, a sub-licence may be granted by the licensee[7].

1   A licence to use a registered trade mark is a mere permission, and does not confer any proprietary right: *Northern & Shell plc v Condé Nast & National Magazines Distributors Ltd* [1995] RPC 117. The grant of a bare licence to use a trade mark (ie one with no quality control provisions), particularly if exclusive, will not, without more, render the trade mark deceptive: *EINSTEIN Trade Mark* [2007] RPC 539, Appointed Person; *Scandecor Development AB v Scandecor Marketing AB* [2001] UKHL 21, [2000] IP & T 676, [2002] FSR 122 (question referred to European Court of Justice for ruling but case settled before ruling given); cf Case C-9/93 *IHT Internationale Heiztechnik GmbH v Ideal Standard GmbH* [1994] ECR I-2789, [1995] FSR 59, ECJ; and see PARA 100.

2   The Trade Marks Act 1994 s 28 also applies with the necessary modifications in relation to a protected international trade mark (UK): see the Trade Marks (International Registration) Order 2008, SI 2008/2206, art 3; and PARA 12. As to the meaning of 'registered trade mark' see PARA 111. As to the meaning of 'protected international trade mark (UK)' see PARA 12 note 8. See also generally PARA 11 et seq.

3   Trade Marks Act 1994 s 28(1). The kind of licence here generally contemplated is a formal agreement rather than a mere informal consent to use the mark which suffices to provide the user with a defence to infringement (see PARA 66). As to the general rights of a licensee in the case of infringement see PARA 400; and as to the rights of an exclusive licensee see PARA 401. The grant of a licence under a registered trade mark is a registrable transaction: see s 25(2); and PARA 114. As to the amendment and removal of registered particulars see PARA 118.

Sections 28, 29(2) (see PARA 120) apply only in relation to licences granted on or after 31 October 1994; and the old law continues to apply in relation to licences granted before that date: s 105, Sch 3 para 9(1). As to the meaning of 'the old law' see PARA 4 note 3. For the former system of approved licensing see the Trade Marks Act 1938 s 28 (repealed), whereby so-called 'registered user agreements' were vetted by the registrar to ensure sufficient connection with the licensor.

Existing entries under s 28 (repealed) (registered users) had to be transferred on 31 October 1994 to the register kept under the Trade Marks Act 1994 and have effect as if made under s 25 (see PARA 114): Sch 3 para 9(2). Provision may be made by rules for putting such entries in the same form as is required under the Trade Marks Act 1994: Sch 3 para 9(2). At the date at which this volume states the law no such rules had been made.

An application for registration as a registered user which was pending before the registrar on 31 October 1994 must be treated as an application for registration of a licence under s 25(1) (see PARA 114) and must proceed accordingly: Sch 3 para 9(3). The registrar may require the applicant to amend his application so as to conform with the requirements of the Trade Marks Act 1994: Sch 3 para 9(3).

An application for registration as a registered user which has been determined by the registrar but not finally determined before 31 October 1994 is to be dealt with under the old law; and Sch 3 para 9(2) applies in relation to any resulting entry in the register: Sch 3 para 9(4).

Any proceedings pending on 31 October 1994 under the Trade Marks Act 1938 s 28(8) (repealed) or s 28(10) (repealed) (variation or cancellation of registration of registered user) is to be dealt with under the old law and any necessary alteration made to the new register: Trade Marks Act 1994 Sch 3 para 9(5).

4   Trade Marks Act 1994 s 28(1). This provision derives from Council Directive (EEC) 89/104 (OJ L40, 11.2.89, p 1) art 8(1) to approximate the laws of the member states (see now European Parliament and Council Directive (EC) 2008/95 (OJ L299, 8.11.2008, p 25) art 8(1)). See also note 3.
5   Trade Marks Act 1994 s 28(2). See also note 3.
6   Trade Marks Act 1994 s 28(3). References in the Trade Marks Act 1994 to doing anything with, or without, the consent of the proprietor of a registered trade mark is to be construed accordingly: s 28(3). See also note 3.
7   Trade Marks Act 1994 s 28(4). References in the Trade Marks Act 1994 to a licence or licensee include a sub-licence or sub-licensee: s 28(4). See also note 3.

120.   Exclusive licences.   An 'exclusive licence' means a licence[1], whether general or limited[2], authorising the licensee to the exclusion of all other persons, including the person granting the licence, to use[3] a registered trade mark[4] in the manner authorised by the licence; and the expression 'exclusive licensee' is to be construed accordingly[5].

An exclusive licensee has the same rights against a successor in title who is bound by the licence as he has against the person granting the licence[6].

Unless the licence provides otherwise, it is binding on a successor in title to the grantor's interest[7].

1   As to the meaning of 'licence' see PARA 119 note 7.
2   As to limited licences see PARA 119.
3   As to the meaning of 'use' see PARA 44 note 8. As to the burden of proving use of a registered trade mark see the Trade Marks Act 1994 s 100; and PARA 98.
4   The Trade Marks Act 1994 s 29 also applies with the necessary modifications in relation to a protected international trade mark (UK): see the Trade Marks (International Registration) Order 2008, SI 2008/2206, art 3; and PARA 12. See also generally PARA 11 et seq. As to the meaning of 'registered trade mark' see PARA 111.
5   Trade Marks Act 1994 s 29(1). As to the general rights of a licensee in the case of infringement see PARA 400; and as to the rights and remedies of an exclusive licensee see PARA 401.
6   Trade Marks Act 1994 s 29(2).
7   Trade Marks Act 1994 s 28(3).

(8)   OFFENCES

(i) Introduction

121.   In general.   The Trade Marks Act 1994 provides for a number of offences[1]. In addition a power of forfeiture of goods and materials relating to infringement is conferred upon a criminal court[2]. The offences under the Act relate to:

(1)   registered trade mark agents[3];
(2)   the unauthorised use of a registered trade mark[4];
(3)   falsification of the register[5];
(4)   falsely representing a trade mark as registered[6]; and
(5)   the unauthorised use of the royal arms[7].

The Olympic Symbol etc (Protection) Act 1995 provides for further offences relating to the unauthorised use of controlled representations[8].

1   For the application of these offences to Community trade marks see PARAS 251–252.
2   See the Trade Marks Act 1994 s 97; and PARA 123.
3   See the Trade Marks Act 1994 s 84; and PARA 34.

4　See the Trade Marks Act 1994 s 92; and PARAS 124–127.
5　See the Trade Marks Act 1994 s 94; and PARA 130.
6　See the Trade Marks Act 1994 s 95; and PARA 131.
7　See the Trade Marks Act 1994 s 99; and PARA 468.
8　See the Olympic Symbol etc (Protection) Act 1995 s 8; PARA 472; and SPORTS LAW vol 96 (2012) PARA 165. As to the meaning of 'controlled representation' see SPORTS LAW vol 96 (2012) PARA 160.

122.　Offences committed by partnerships and bodies corporate. Proceedings for an offence under the Trade Marks Act 1994 alleged to have been committed by a partnership must be brought against the partnership in the name of the firm and not in that of the partners[1]. A fine imposed on a partnership on its conviction in such proceedings must be paid out of the partnership assets[2].

Where a partnership is guilty of an offence under the Trade Marks Act 1994, every partner, other than a partner who is proved to have been ignorant of or to have attempted to prevent the commission of the offence, is also guilty of the offence and liable to be proceeded against and punished accordingly[3].

The following provisions apply for the purposes of proceedings under the Trade Marks Act 1994 against a partnership as in relation to a body corporate: (1) any rules of court relating to the service of documents; and (2) the statutory provisions[4] relating to procedure on charge of an offence[5].

Where an offence under the Trade Marks Act 1994 committed by a body corporate is proved to have been committed with the consent or connivance of a director[6], manager, secretary or other similar officer of the body, or a person purporting to act in any such capacity, he as well as the body corporate is guilty of the offence and liable to be proceeded against and punished accordingly[7].

1　Trade Marks Act 1994 s 101(1), which is expressed to be without prejudice to s 101(4) (see the text and note 3).
2　Trade Marks Act 1994 s 101(3).
3　Trade Marks Act 1994 s 101(4). It is not a requirement that the partnership has actually been convicted of the offence: *R v Wakefield and Purseglove* [2004] EWCA Crim 2278, 168 JP 505 (partnership dissolved by time of trial).
4　Ie the Magistrates' Courts Act 1980 s 46, Sch 3: see MAGISTRATES vol 71 (2013) PARA 513.
5　Trade Marks Act 1994 s 101(2).
6　As to the meaning of 'director' see PARA 36 note 8.
7　Trade Marks Act 1994 s 101(5).

123.　Forfeiture of counterfeit goods etc. Where there has come into the possession of any person[1] in connection with the investigation or prosecution of a relevant offence[2]:

(1)　goods which, or the packaging of which, bears a sign identical to or likely to be mistaken for a registered trade mark[3];

(2)　material bearing such a sign and intended to be used for labelling or packaging goods, as a business[4] paper in relation to goods, or for advertising goods[5]; or

(3)　articles specifically designed or adapted for making copies of such a sign[6],

that person may apply for an order for the forfeiture of the goods, material or articles[7].

Such an application may be made: (a) where proceedings have been brought in any court for a relevant offence relating to some or all of the goods, material or articles, to that court; (b) where no application for the forfeiture of the goods, material or articles has been made under head (a) above, by way of complaint to a magistrates' court[8].

On such an application the court must make an order for the forfeiture of any goods, material or articles only if it is satisfied that a relevant offence has been committed in relation to the goods, material or articles[9]. A court may infer for these purposes that such an offence has been committed in relation to any goods, material or articles if it is satisfied that such an offence has been committed in relation to goods, material or articles which are representative of them, whether by reason of being of the same design or part of the same consignment or batch or otherwise[10].

Any person aggrieved by an order so made by a magistrates' court, or by a decision of such a court not to make such an order, may appeal against that order or decision to the Crown Court; and an order so made may contain such provision as appears to the court to be appropriate for delaying the coming into force of the order pending the making and determination of any appeal, including any application[11] for a statement of case[12].

Where any goods, material or articles are so forfeited, they must be destroyed in accordance with such directions as the court may give[13]; but, on so making an order, the court may, if it considers it appropriate to do so, direct that the goods, material or articles to which the order relates must (instead of being destroyed) be released, to such person as the court may specify, on condition that that person causes the offending sign to be erased, removed or obliterated and complies with any order to pay costs which has been made against him in the proceedings for the order for forfeiture[14].

1   This includes a local weights and measures authority: see the Trade Marks Act 1994 s 93; and PARA 129.
2   For these purposes, a 'relevant offence' means (1) an offence under the Trade Marks Act 1994 s 92 (see PARAS 124–127); (2) an offence under the Trade Descriptions Act 1968 (see CONSUMER PROTECTION vol 21 (2011) PARA 510 et seq); (3) an offence under the Business Protection from Misleading Marketing Regulations 2008, SI 2008/1276 (see CONSUMER PROTECTION vol 21 (2011) PARA 500); (4) an offence under the Consumer Protection from Unfair Trading Regulations 2008, SI 2008/1277 (see CONSUMER PROTECTION vol 21 (2011) PARA 497 et seq); or (5) any offence involving dishonesty or deception: Trade Marks Act 1994 s 97(8) (amended by SI 2008/SI 1277).
3   Trade Marks Act 1994 s 97(1)(a). Section 97 also applies to protected international trade marks (UK): see the Trade Marks (International Registration) Order 2008, SI 2008/2206, art 3; and PARA 12. See also generally PARA 11 et seq. As to the application of this provision to Community trade marks see PARA 251. As to the meaning of 'registered trade mark' see PARA 111. As to the meaning of 'protected international trade mark (UK)' see PARA 12 note 8.
4   As to the meaning of 'business' see PARA 34 note 3.
5   Trade Marks Act 1994 s 97(1)(b).
6   Trade Marks Act 1994 s 97(1)(c).
7   Trade Marks Act 1994 s 97(1). Forfeiture proceedings are civil proceedings, and as such fall within the Convention on Jurisdiction and Enforcement of Judgments in Civil and Commercial matters (Brussels, 27 September 1968; Cmnd 7395) (see now Council Regulation (EC) 44/2001 on jurisdiction and the recognition and enforcement of judgments in civil and commercial matters (OJ L12, 16.1.2001, p. 1)) (see PARA 233; and CONFLICT OF LAWS vol 19 (2011) PARA 366): *R v Crown Court at Harrow, ex p UNIC Centre Sarl* [2000] 2 All ER 449, [2000] 1 WLR 2112, sub nom *Unic Centre Sarl v Brent & Harrow Trading Standards Office* [2000] FSR 667.
       As to the provisions permitting infringing goods, material or articles to be treated as prohibited goods see PARA 132.
8   Trade Marks Act 1994 s 97(2).
9   Trade Marks Act 1994 s 97(3).
10 Trade Marks Act 1994 s 97(4).
11 Ie under the Magistrates' Courts Act 1980 s 111: see MAGISTRATES vol 71 (2013) PARA 703 et seq.
12 Trade Marks Act 1994 s 97(5).
13 Trade Marks Act 1994 s 97(6).
14 Trade Marks Act 1994 s 97(7).

(ii) Unauthorised Use

124. Goods and packaging. A person commits an offence[1] who, with a view to[2] gain for himself or another, or with intent to cause loss to another, and without the consent of the proprietor[3]:

(1) applies to goods or their packaging a sign identical to, or likely to be mistaken for[4], a registered trade mark[5]; or

(2) sells or lets for hire, offers or exposes for sale or hire or distributes goods which bear, or the packaging of which bears, such a sign[6]; or

(3) has in his possession, custody or control in the course of a business[7] any such goods with a view to the doing of anything, by himself or another, which would be an offence under head (2) above[8].

A person guilty of an offence under head (1), head (2), or head (3) above is liable on conviction to imprisonment or a fine or both[9].

1 For an offence to be committed there must be civil infringement of the trade mark, and thus defences to infringement such as those under the Trade Marks Act 1994 s 11 (see PARAS 79–81) are also defences under s 92: *R v Johnstone* [2003] UKHL 28, [2003] 3 All ER 884, [2003] 1 WLR 1736. Furthermore, infringement and the commission of an offence requires use of the sign in question as a trade mark: *R v Johnstone*; *R v Isaac* [2004] EWCA Crim 1082, 168 JP 417 (jury must be directed that offence is committed only when as a first element the offending sign is used as an indication of trade origin). The test as to whether a sign has been used as an indication of trade origin is how the use of the sign would be perceived by the average consumer of the type of goods in question: *R v Thompson* [2006] EWCA Crim 3058, [2006] All ER (D) 223 (Nov).

2 The words 'with a view to' encompass something that the defendant had in contemplation, not necessarily something he wanted or intended to happen but something which might realistically occur; they are to be contrasted with 'with intent to': *R v Zaman* [2002] EWCA Crim 1862, [2003] FSR 230.

3 Trade Marks Act 1994 s 92(1).

4 'Applies' should be given its ordinary meaning of placing the sign on the goods or causing it to be so placed, and not extended to include the sale or exposure for sale of goods: *Nottinghamshire County Council v Woolworths plc* [2007] FSR 489.

   'Likely to be mistaken for' appears to be a narrower test than 'likelihood of confusion' under the Trade Marks Act 1994 s 10(2), since the latter compasses not only signs which the average consumer mistakes for a trade mark, but also those which he believes denote goods or services that come from the same or economically linked undertakings (see PARA 58). Nevertheless surrounding circumstances must equally be discounted, since otherwise a vendor of counterfeit goods could escape liability by making it clear that they were not genuine: see *Akhtar v Grout* (1998) 162 JP 714, DC.

5 Trade Marks Act 1994 s 92(1)(a). As to the meaning of 'registered trade mark' see PARA 127. This provision also applies to protected international trade marks (UK): see the Trade Marks (International Registration) Order 2008, SI 2008/2206, art 3; and PARA 12. See also generally PARA 11 et seq. As to the application of this provision to unauthorised use of a Community trade mark see PARA 251. As to the meaning of 'protected international trade mark (UK)' see PARA 12 note 8.

6 Trade Marks Act 1994 s 92(1)(b). Section 92(1)(b) is not limited to those cases where the other party to the immediate transaction would regard the sign as indicative of trade origin: *R v Morgan (Prosecution Appeal under s 58 of the Criminal Justice Act 2003)* [2006] EWCA Crim 1742, [2008] All ER (D) 120 (Mar).

7 As to the meaning of 'business' see PARA 34 note 3. As to the meaning of 'in the course of business' see PARA 449 note 1.

8 Trade Marks Act 1994 s 92(1)(c). Goods stored in the matrimonial home are not necessarily in the possession of both husband and wife: *R v Kousar* [2009] EWCA Crim 139, [2009] 2 Cr App Rep 88, [2009] All ER (D) 289 (Mar).

9 Trade Marks Act 1994 s 92(6). Such a person is liable on conviction on indictment to imprisonment for a term not exceeding ten years or to a fine or to both, or on summary conviction to imprisonment for a term not exceeding six months or to a fine not exceeding the statutory maximum or to both: see s 92(6). As to the statutory maximum see SENTENCING AND DISPOSITION OF OFFENDERS vol 92 (2010) PARA 140.

As to sentencing see *R v Gleeson* [2001] EWCA Crim 2023, [2002] 1 Cr App Rep (S) 485, [2001] All ER (D) 22 (Oct) (potential loss to music industry resulting from unauthorised use of trade marks on compact discs was factor relevant to level of sentence); *R v Woolridge* [2005] EWCA Crim 1086, [2006] 1 Cr App Rep (S) 72 (sentence has to reflect consequences of the offence and contain some element of deterrent); *R v Brayford* [2010] EWCA Crim 2329, [2011] 1 Cr App Rep (S) 638 (importation of large amount of counterfeit washing powder) (the professionalism of the enterprise and the actual or likely profit made from it are relevant factors in sentencing). A conviction under the Trade Marks Act 1994 s 92 can found a confiscation order under the Criminal Justice Act 1988 s 71 (repealed: see now the Proceeds of Crime Act 2002 s 6; and SENTENCING AND DISPOSITION OF OFFENDERS vol 92 (2010) PARA 390 et seq) even where the indictment did not allege selling or offering for sale the infringing goods: *R v Davies* [2003] EWCA Crim 3110, [2004] 2 All ER 706, [2004] FSR 486.

As to offences committed by partnerships and bodies corporate see PARA 122. For exceptions and defences see PARA 127. As to the power to issue search warrants see PARA 128.

125. Material for packaging etc. A person commits an offence[1] who with a view to[2] gain for himself or another, or with intent to cause loss to another, and without the consent of the proprietor[3]:

(1)   applies a sign identical to, or likely to be mistaken for[4], a registered trade mark[5] to material intended to be used for labelling or packaging goods, as a business[6] paper in relation to goods, or for advertising goods[7]; or

(2)   uses in the course of a business material bearing such a sign for labelling or packaging goods, as a business paper in relation to goods, or for advertising goods[8]; or

(3)   has in his possession, custody or control in the course of a business any such material with a view to the doing of anything, by himself or another, which would be an offence under head (2) above[9].

A person guilty of an offence under head (1), head (2), or head (3) above is liable on conviction to imprisonment or a fine or both[10].

1   As to committing an offence see PARA 124 note 1.
2   As to the meaning of 'with a view to' see PARA 124 note 2.
3   Trade Marks Act 1994 s 92(2).
4   As to the meaning of 'likely to be mistaken for' see PARA 124 note 4.
5   As to the meaning of 'registered trade mark' see PARA 111. This provision also applies to protected international trade marks (UK): see the Trade Marks (International Registration) Order 2008, SI 2008/2206, art 3; and PARA 12. See also generally PARA 11 et seq. As to the application of this provision to Community trade marks see PARA 251. As to the meaning of 'protected international trade mark (UK)' see PARA 12 note 8.
6   As to the meaning of 'business' see PARA 34 note 3.
7   Trade Marks Act 1994 s 92(2)(a).
8   Trade Marks Act 1994 s 92(2)(b).
9   Trade Marks Act 1994 s 92(2)(c).
10   Trade Marks Act 1994 s 92(6). Such a person is liable on conviction on indictment to imprisonment for a term not exceeding ten years or to a fine or to both, or on summary conviction to imprisonment for a term not exceeding six months or to a fine not exceeding the statutory maximum or to both: see s 92(6). As to the statutory maximum see SENTENCING AND DISPOSITION OF OFFENDERS vol 92 (2010) PARA 140. As to sentencing, see PARA 124 note 9. As to offences committed by partnerships and bodies corporate see PARA 122. For exceptions and defences see PARA 127. As to the power to issue search warrants see PARA 128.

126. Making and possessing copies of a sign. A person commits an offence[1] who with a view to gain[2] for himself or another, or with intent to cause loss to another, and without the consent of the proprietor[3]:

(1)   makes an article specifically designed or adapted for making copies of a sign identical to, or likely to be mistaken for[4], a registered trade mark[5]; or

(2)   has such an article in his possession, custody or control in the course of a business[6],

knowing or having reason to believe that it has been, or is to be, used to produce goods, or material for labelling or packaging goods, as a business paper in relation to goods, or for advertising goods[7].

A person guilty of an offence under head (1), head (2), or head (3) above is liable on conviction to imprisonment or a fine or both[8].

1   As to committing an offence see PARA 124 note 1.
2   As to the meaning of 'with a view to gain' see PARA 124 note 2.
3   Trade Marks Act 1994 s 92(3).
4   As to the meaning of 'likely to be mistaken for' see PARA 124 note 4.
5   Trade Marks Act 1994 s 92(3)(a). As to the meaning of 'registered trade mark' see PARA 111. This provision also applies to protected international trade marks (UK): see the Trade Marks (International Registration) Order 2008, SI 2008/2206, art 3; and PARA 12. See also generally PARA 11 et seq. As to the application of this provision to Community trade marks see PARA 251. As to the meaning of 'protected international trade mark (UK)' see PARA 12 note 8.
6   Trade Marks Act 1994 s 92(3)(b). As to the meaning of 'business' see PARA 34 note 3.
7   Trade Marks Act 1994 s 92(3).
8   Trade Marks Act 1994 s 92(6). Such a person is liable on conviction on indictment to imprisonment for a term not exceeding ten years or to a fine or to both, or on summary conviction to imprisonment for a term not exceeding six months or to a fine not exceeding the statutory maximum or to both: see s 92(6). As to the statutory maximum see SENTENCING AND DISPOSITION OF OFFENDERS vol 92 (2010) PARA 140. As to sentencing, see PARA 124 note 9. As to offences committed by partnerships and bodies corporate see PARA 122. For exceptions and defences see PARA 127. As to the power to issue search warrants see PARA 128.

127.   Exceptions and defences.   A person does not commit an offence of the unauthorised use of a trade mark etc in relation to goods[1] unless the goods are goods in respect of which the trade mark[2] is registered[3] or the trade mark has a reputation in the United Kingdom[4] and the use of the sign takes or would take unfair advantage of, or is or would be detrimental to, the distinctive character or the repute of the trade mark[5].

It is a defence for a person charged with any such offence to show that he believed on reasonable grounds that the use of the sign in the manner in which it was used, or was to be used, was not an infringement of the registered trade mark[6].

1   Ie an offence under the Trade Marks Act 1994 s 92(1)–(3): see PARAS 124–126. This provision also applies to protected international trade marks (UK): see the Trade Marks (International Registration) Order 2008, SI 2008/2206, art 3; and PARA 12. See also generally PARA 11 et seq. As to the application of this provision to Community trade marks see PARA 251. As to the meaning of 'protected international trade mark (UK)' see PARA 12 note 8.
2   As to the meaning of 'trade mark' see PARA 41.
3   As to the meaning of 'registered' see PARA 21 note 2.
4   As to the meaning of 'United Kingdom' see PARA 3 note 2.
5   Trade Marks Act 1994 s 92(4). As to tests of taking unfair advantage of, and detriment to, the distinctive character or repute of a trade see PARA 60.
6   Trade Marks Act 1994 s 92(5).The onus of proof is on the person charged, who bears a persuasive burden to prove the defence on the balance of probabilities: *R v Johnstone* [2003] UKHL 28, [2003] 3 All ER 884, [2003] 1 WLR 1736. The Trade Marks Act 1994 s 92(5) extends to an honest and reasonable belief that the mark concerned is not registered: *R v Johnstone*. This provision has been described as a broad general defence: *R v Keane* [2001] FSR 7 at [26] per Mance LJ; *R v Rhodes* [2002] EWCA Crim 1390, [2003] FSR 9. It does not extend to the contention that the defendant did not know what a registered trade mark was: *R v McCrudden* [2005] EWCA Crim 466, [2005] All ER (D) 309 (Feb).

128.   Search warrants.   Where a justice of the peace is satisfied by information on oath given by a constable that there are reasonable grounds for believing that an offence in relation to the unauthorised use of a trade mark in relation to goods[1] has been or is about to be committed in any premises[2], and that evidence that such an offence has been or is about to be committed is in those premises, he may issue a warrant authorising a constable to enter and search the premises, using such reasonable force as is necessary[3]. A warrant may authorise persons to accompany any constable executing the warrants, and remains in force for three months from the date of its issue[4]. In executing a warrant issued these provisions a constable may seize any article if he reasonably believes that it is evidence that an offence[5] has been or is about to be committed[6].

1   Ie an offence under the Trade Marks Act 1994 s 92: see PARAS 124–127.

2   'Premises' includes land, buildings, fixed or movable structures, vehicles, vessels, aircraft and hovercraft: Trade Marks Act 1994 s 92A(5) (s 92A added by the Copyright etc and Trade Marks Offences and Enforcement) Act 2002 s 6).

3   The Trade Marks Act 1994 s 92A(1) (as added: see note 2). The power conferred by s 92A(1) does not extend to authorising a search for certain classes of personal or confidential material contained in the Police and Criminal Evidence Act 1984 s 9(2) (see POLICE AND INVESTIGATORY POWERS vol 84A (2013) PARA 453): Trade Marks Act 1994 s 92A(2) (as so added).

4   Trade Marks Act 1994 s 92A(3) (as added (see note 2); and amended by the Serious Organised Crime and Police Act 2005 Sch 16 para 8).

5   Ie an offence under the Trade Marks Act 1994 s 92: see PARAS 124–127.

6   Trade Marks Act 1994 s 92A(4) (as added: see note 2).

129.   Enforcement function of local weights and measures authority.   It is the duty of every local weights and measures authority[1] to enforce within its area the statutory provisions[2] relating to the unauthorised use of a trade mark etc in relation to goods[3].

1   The local weights and measures authorities are: (1) in England: (a) for each non-metropolitan county, metropolitan district and London borough, the council of that county, district or borough; (b) for the City of London and the Inner and Middle Temples, the Common Council of the City of London; and (c) for the Isles of Scilly, the Council of the Isles of Scilly (Weights and Measures Act 1985 s 69(1)); and (2) in Wales: (a) for each county, the county council; and (b) for each county borough, the county borough council (s 69(2) (amended by the Local Government (Wales) Act 1994 Sch 16 para 75). As to the duties and functions of such authorities see the Weights and Measures Act 1985 Pt VI (ss 69–78); and WEIGHTS AND MEASURES vol 99 (2012) PARA 519 et seq.

2   Ie the Trade Marks Act 1994 s 92 (see PARAS 124–127), including such provisions in so far as they apply to Community trade marks (see PARA 251). This provision also applies to protected international trade marks (UK): see the Trade Marks (International Registration) Order 2008, SI 2008/2206, art 3; and PARA 12. See also generally PARA 11 et seq. As to the meaning of 'protected international trade mark (UK)' see PARA 12 note 8. The following provisions of the Trade Descriptions Act 1968 apply in relation to the enforcement of the Trade Marks Act 1994 s 92 as in relation to the enforcement of the Trade Descriptions Act 1968: s 27 (power to make test purchases), s 28 (power to enter premises and inspect and seize goods and documents), s 29 (obstruction of authorised officers), s 33 (compensation for the loss etc of goods seized) (see CONSUMER PROTECTION vol 21 (2011) PARA 523 et seq): Trade Marks Act 1994 s 93(2).

3   Trade Marks Act 1994 s 93(1). This provision does not, however, apply in relation to the enforcement of s 92 in Northern Ireland. As to enforcement in Northern Ireland see s 93(3). Nothing in s 93 is to be construed as authorising a local weights and measures authority to bring proceedings in Scotland for an offence: s 93(5).

   Any enactment which authorises the disclosure of information for the purpose of facilitating the enforcement of the Trade Descriptions Act 1968 applies as if the Trade Marks Act 1994 s 92 were contained in the Trade Descriptions Act 1968 and as if the functions of any person in relation to the enforcement of the Trade Marks Act 1994 s 92 were functions under the Trade Descriptions Act 1968: Trade Marks Act 1994 s 93(4).

(iii) Other Offences

130. Falsification of register etc. It is an offence for a person to make, or cause to be made, a false entry in the register of trade marks[1], knowing or having reason to believe that it is false[2].

It is also an offence for a person:

(1) to make or cause to be made anything falsely purporting to be a copy of an entry in the register; or

(2) to produce or tender or cause to be produced or tendered in evidence any such thing,

knowing or having reason to believe that it is false[3].

A person guilty of such an offence is liable on conviction to imprisonment or a fine or both[4].

1 As to the register see PARA 21. As to the meaning of 'trade mark' see PARA 41.
2 Trade Marks Act 1994 s 94(1). It should be noted that s 94 does not apply to international trade marks (UK) or requests for extension: see the Trade Marks (International Registration) Order 2008, SI 2008/2206, art 3(3), Sch 1 Pt 1; and PARA 12 note 10. See also generally PARA 11 et seq.
3 Trade Marks Act 1994 s 94(2). See note 2.
4 Trade Marks Act 1994 s 94(3). See note 2. Such a person is liable on conviction on indictment to imprisonment for a term not exceeding two years or to a fine or to both, or on summary conviction to imprisonment for a term not exceeding six months or to a fine not exceeding the statutory maximum or to both: see s 94(3). As to the statutory maximum see SENTENCING AND DISPOSITION OF OFFENDERS vol 92 (2010) PARA 140. As to offences committed by partnerships and bodies corporate see PARA 122.

131. Falsely representing trade mark as registered. It is an offence for a person:

(1) falsely to represent that a mark is a registered trade mark[1] or a protected international trade mark (UK)[2]; or

(2) to make a false representation as to the goods or services for which a trade mark is registered, or as to the goods or services covered by a protected international trade mark (UK),

knowing or having reason to believe that the representation is false[3]. A person guilty of such an offence is liable on conviction to a fine[4].

For these purposes, the use[5] in the United Kingdom[6] in relation to a trade mark of the word 'registered' or of any other word or symbol importing a reference, express or implied, to registration, is deemed to be a representation as to registration under the Trade Marks Act 1994 unless it is shown that the reference is to registration elsewhere than in the United Kingdom and that the trade mark is in fact so registered for the goods or services in question[7].

The use of the words 'trade mark' in respect of an unregistered trade mark does not necessarily constitute an offence under head (1) or head (2) above[8]. Where a false representation as to registration has been made, this may affect a claim in passing off[9] or a claim that a mark has become distinctive by use[10].

1 As to the meaning of 'registered trade mark' see PARA 111.
2 As to the meaning of 'protected international trade mark (UK)' see PARA 12 note 8. See note 3.
3 Trade Marks Act 1994 s 95(1). Section 95 applies to international trade marks (UK): see the Trade Marks (International Registration) Order 2008, SI 2008/2206, art 3; and PARA 12. See also generally PARA 11 et seq.
4 Trade Marks Act 1994 s 95(3). Such a person is liable on summary conviction to a fine not exceeding level 3 on the standard scale: see Trade Marks Act 1994 s 95(3). As to the standard scale see SENTENCING AND DISPOSITION OF OFFENDERS vol 92 (2010) PARA 142. As to offences committed by partnerships and bodies corporate see PARA 122.

5 As to the meaning of 'use' see PARA 44 note 8.
6 As to the meaning of 'United Kingdom' see PARA 3 note 2.
7 Trade Marks Act 1994 s 95(2). There is no express reference in the Trade Marks Act 1994 to the symbol ®, but s 95 will cover the use of it. It is sufficient for this purpose that the reference is consistent with registration outside the United Kingdom and that such registration exists: *Second Sight Ltd v Novell UK Ltd* [1995] RPC 423.
8 *Sen Sen Co v Britten* [1899] 1 Ch 692, 16 RPC 137.
9 As to passing off see PARA 287 et seq.
10 See PARA 85 note 5.

(9) IMPORTATION; POWERS OF THE COMMISSIONERS FOR HER MAJESTY'S REVENUE AND CUSTOMS

132. Infringing goods, material or articles to be treated as prohibited goods.
The proprietor of a registered trade mark[1], or a licensee[2], may give notice in writing to the Commissioners for Her Majesty's Revenue and Customs[3]:

(1)   that he is the proprietor or, as the case may be, a licensee of the registered trade mark[4];

(2)   that, at a time and place specified in the notice, goods which are, in relation to that registered trade mark, infringing goods[5], material[6] or articles[7] are expected to arrive in the United Kingdom[8] from outside the European Economic Area ('EEA')[9] or from within the EEA but not having been entered for free circulation[10]; and

(3)   that he requests the Commissioners to treat them as prohibited goods[11].

When such a notice is in force, the importation of the goods to which the notice relates, otherwise than by a person for his private and domestic use, is prohibited; but a person is not by reason of the prohibition liable to any penalty other than forfeiture of the goods[12].

The above provisions do not apply to goods placed in, or expected to be placed in, one of the following situations[13]:

(a)   when they are entered for release for free circulation, export or re-export;

(b)   when they are found during checks on goods entering or leaving the Community customs territory, placed under a suspensive procedure, in the process of being re-exported subject to notification or placed in a free zone or free warehouse,

in respect of which an application may be made under the European Union measures[14] laid down to prohibit the release of counterfeit and pirated goods[15].

1 As to the meaning of 'registered trade mark' see PARA 111. These provisions also apply to protected international trade marks (UK): see the Trade Marks (International Registration) Order 2008, SI 2008/2206, art 3; and PARA 12. See also generally PARA 11 et seq. As to the meaning of 'protected international trade mark (UK)' see PARA 12 note 8. As to the application of these provisions to Community trade marks see PARA 250.
2 As to licences see PARAS 119–120.
3 Trade Marks Act 1994 s 89(1) (amended by virtue of the Commissioners for Revenue and Customs Act 2005 s 50(1), (7)). As to the Commissioners for Her Majesty's Revenue and Customs see INCOME TAXATION vol 23(1) (Reissue) PARA 31 et seq. As to the form in which the notice is to be given see PARA 134. See generally HM Revenue and Customs Notice 34 *Intellectual Property Rights* (November 2012).
   The Trade Marks Act 1994 s 89(1) applies in relation to an authorised user of a registered collective mark or a registered certification mark as in relation to a licensee of a trade mark: see ss 49(2), 50(2), Sch 1 para 11(c), Sch 2 para 13(c); and PARAS 145, 156.
4 Trade Marks Act 1994 s 89(1)(a).
5 As to the meaning of 'infringing goods' see PARA 133.
6 As to the meaning of 'infringing material' see PARA 133.

7   As to the meaning of 'infringing articles' see PARA 133.
8   As to the meaning of 'United Kingdom' see PARA 3 note 2.
9   As to the EEA see PARA 86 note 6.
10 Trade Marks Act 1994 s 89(1)(b).
11 Trade Marks Act 1994 s 89(1)(c).
12 Trade Marks Act 1994 s 89(2).
13 Ie the situations referred to in Council Regulation (EC) 1383/2003 (OJ L196, 2.8.2003, p 7) concerning customs action against goods suspected of infringing certain intellectual property rights and the measures to be taken against goods found to have infringed such rights, art 1(1): Trade Marks Act 1994 s 89(3) (substituted by SI 2004/1473).

   See *Pointing v Customs and Excise Comrs* [1999] FSR 394 (customs officers may initiate a court action to determine whether the goods are counterfeit, but it is for the court to make the final decision).
14 Ie under Council Regulation (EC) 1383/2003 (OJ L196, 2.8.2003, p 7) art 5(1): Trade Marks Act 1994 s 89(3) (as substituted: see note 13). See *Pointing v Customs and Excise Comrs* [1999] FSR 394.
15 Trade Marks Act 1994 s 89(3) (as substituted: see note 13). Goods coming from a non-member state which are imitations of goods protected by a trade mark in the European Union cannot be classified as 'counterfeit goods' or 'pirated goods' within the meaning of those measures merely on the basis of the fact that they are brought into the customs territory of the European Union under a suspensive procedure; those goods may, on the other hand, infringe the right in question and therefore be classified as 'counterfeit goods' or 'pirated goods' where it is proven that they are intended to be put on sale in the European Union, such proof being provided, inter alia, where it turns that the goods have been sold to a customer in the European Union or offered for sale or advertised to consumers in the European Union, or where it is apparent from documents or correspondence concerning the goods that their diversion to European Union consumers is envisaged: Joined Cases C-446/09 and C-495/09 *Koninklijke Philips Electronics NV v Lucheng Meijing Industrial Co Ltd; Nokia Corpn v Revenue and Customs Comrs* [2012] Bus LR 1850, [2012] ETMR 13, ECJ.

133.   Meaning of 'infringing goods', 'infringing material' and 'infringing articles'. The expressions 'infringing goods', 'infringing material' and 'infringing articles' are to be construed as follows[1].

Goods are 'infringing goods', in relation to a registered trade mark[2], if they or their packaging bear a sign identical or similar to that mark[3] and:

(1)   the application of the sign to the goods or their packaging was an infringement[4] of the registered trade mark[5]; or

(2)   the goods are proposed to be imported into the United Kingdom[6] and the application of the sign in the United Kingdom to them or their packaging would be an infringement of the registered trade mark[7]; or

(3)   the sign has otherwise been used in relation to the goods in such a way as to infringe the registered trade mark[8].

Nothing in the above provisions is, however, to be construed as affecting the importation of goods which may lawfully be imported into the United Kingdom by virtue of an enforceable EU right[9].

Material is 'infringing material', in relation to a registered trade mark, if it bears a sign identical or similar to that mark[10] and either: (a) it is used for labelling or packaging goods, as a business[11] paper, or for advertising goods or services, in such a way as to infringe the registered trade mark[12]; or (b) it is intended to be so used and such use would infringe the registered trade mark[13].

'Infringing articles', in relation to a registered trade mark, means[14] articles: (i) which are specifically designed or adapted for making copies of a sign identical or similar to that mark[15]; and (ii) which a person has in his possession, custody or control, knowing or having reason to believe that they have been or are to be used to produce infringing goods or material[16].

1   Trade Marks Act 1994 s 17(1).

2 As to the meaning of 'registered trade mark' see PARA 111. As to protected international trade marks (UK) see the Trade Marks (International Registration) Order 2008, SI 2008/2206, art 3; and PARA 12. See also generally PARA 11 et seq. As to the meaning of 'protected international trademark (UK)' see PARA 12 note 8. As to the application of these provisions to Community trade marks see PARA 250.
3 Trade Marks Act 1994 s 17(2).
4 As to the meaning of 'infringement' see PARA 66 note 4. As to the acts which amount to infringement, if done without the consent of the proprietor, see the Trade Marks Act 1994 s 10; and PARA 68 et seq.
5 Trade Marks Act 1994 s 17(2)(a).
6 As to the meaning of 'United Kingdom' see PARA 3 note 2.
7 Trade Marks Act 1994 s 17(2)(b). See PARA 132 note 15.
8 Trade Marks Act 1994 s 17(2)(c).
9 Trade Marks Act 1994 s 17(3) (amended by SI 2011/1043). As to the meaning of 'enforceable EU right' see the European Communities Act 1972 s 2(1) (amended by the European Union (Amendment) Act 2008 Schedule Pt 1); and the Interpretation Act 1978 s 5, Sch 1 (amended by the European Union (Amendment) Act 2008 Schedule Pt 2). As to the prohibition of the importation of infringing goods, materials or articles see PARA 132.
10 Trade Marks Act 1994 s 17(4).
11 As to the meaning of 'business' see PARA 34 note 3.
12 Trade Marks Act 1994 s 17(4)(a).
13 Trade Marks Act 1994 s 17(4)(b).
14 Trade Marks Act 1994 s 17(5).
15 Trade Marks Act 1994 s 17(5)(a).
16 Trade Marks Act 1994 s 17(5)(b).

134.   Power of the Commissioners for Revenue and Customs to make regulations. The Commissioners for Her Majesty's Revenue and Customs[1] may make regulations prescribing the form in which notice is to be given requiring goods, materials or articles to be treated as prohibited goods[2] and requiring a person giving notice: (1) to furnish the Commissioners with such evidence as may be specified in the regulations, either on giving notice or when the goods are imported, or at both those times; and (2) to comply with such other conditions as may be specified in the regulations[3].

The regulations may, in particular, require a person giving such a notice: (a) to pay such fees in respect of the notice as may be specified by the regulations; (b) to give such security as may be so specified in respect of any liability or expense which the Commissioners may incur in consequence of the notice by reason of the detention of any goods or anything done to goods detained; (c) to indemnify the Commissioners against any such liability or expense, whether security has been given or not[4].

If notice is given[5] by the proprietor or licensee of a registered trade mark in respect of certain goods, it must be in the prescribed form[6] or a form to the like effect approved by the Commissioners; and separate notices must be given in respect each arrival of such goods[7]. A fee in respect of each notice must be paid to the Commissioners at the time it is given[8]. The person giving the notice must give to the Commissioners such security or further security within such time and in such manner, whether by deposit of a sum of money or guarantee, as the Commissioners may require, in respect of any liability or expense which they may incur in consequence of the notice by reason of the detention of any goods or anything done to goods so detained; and, if such security or further security is not given within the time specified by the Commissioners, the notice has no effect[9]. In every case, however, whether any security or further security is given or not, the person who has given the notice must keep the Commissioners indemnified against all such liability and expense[10].

The person giving the notice must, either on giving notice or when the goods are imported, furnish the Commissioners with the certificate of registration[11], or a copy of it, issued by the registrar[12] on the registration of the trade mark specified in the notice, together with evidence that such registration was duly renewed[13] at all such times as it may have expired[14]. If such a certificate or copy and, where applicable, evidence of renewal is not so furnished, the goods may not be detained or, if detained, must be released and any notice given in respect of them has no effect[15].

1   As to the Commissioners for Her Majesty's Revenue and Customs see INCOME TAXATION vol 23(1) (Reissue) PARA 31 et seq.
2   Ie notice under the Trade Marks Act 1994 s 89: see PARA 132.
3   Trade Marks Act 1994 s 90(1) (amended by virtue of the Commissioners for Revenue and Customs Act 2005 s 50(1), (7)). The regulations may make different provision as respects different classes of case to which they apply and may include such incidental and supplementary provisions as the Commissioners consider expedient: Trade Marks Act 1994 s 90(3). Any such regulations must be made by statutory instrument which is subject to annulment in pursuance of a resolution of either House of Parliament: s 90(4). As to the regulations that have been made see the Trade Marks (Customs) Regulations 1994, SI 1994/2625, which came into force on 31 October 1994 (see reg 1). See further the text and notes 5–15.
    These provisions also apply to protected international trade marks (UK): see the Trade Marks (International Registration) Order 2008, SI 2008/2206, art 3; and PARA 12. See also generally PARA 11 et seq. As to the meaning of 'protected international mark (UK)' see PARA 12 note 8. As to the application of these provisions to Community trade marks see PARA 250.
4   Trade Marks Act 1994 s 90(2).
5   Ie under the Trade Marks Act 1994 s 89(1): see PARA 132.
6   For the prescribed form of notice see the Trade Marks (Customs) Regulations 1994, SI 1994/2625, reg 2, Schedule.
7   Trade Marks (Customs) Regulations 1994, SI 1994/2625, reg 2.
8   Trade Marks (Customs) Regulations 1994, SI 1994/2625, reg 3. The fee is currently £30 plus VAT: reg 3.
9   Trade Marks (Customs) Regulations 1994, SI 1994/2625, reg 4, which is expressed to be without prejudice to the operation of reg 5 (see the text and note 10).
10 Trade Marks (Customs) Regulations 1994, SI 1994/2625, reg 5.
11 As to the issue of a certificate of registration see PARA 370.
12 As to the registrar see PARA 19.
13 As to renewal see PARA 31.
14 Trade Marks (Customs) Regulations 1994, SI 1994/2625, reg 6(1).
15 Trade Marks (Customs) Regulations 1994, SI 1994/2625, reg 6(2), which is expressed to be without prejudice to the operation of reg 5 (see the text and note 10).

135.   Power of the Commissioners for Revenue and Customs to disclose information. Where information relating to infringing goods[1], material[2] or articles[3] has been obtained or is held by the Commissioners for Her Majesty's Revenue and Customs[4] for the purposes of, or in connection with, the exercise of their functions in relation to imported goods, the Commissioners may authorise the disclosure of that information for the purpose of facilitating the exercise by any person of any function in connection with the investigation or prosecution of certain offences[5]. In civil proceedings the Commissioners may be ordered by a court to disclose information relating to the identity of an infringer pursuant to the court's powers to order disclosure from a party who, even if innocently, has become involved in wrongdoing[6].

1   As to the meaning of 'infringing goods' see PARA 133.
2   As to the meaning of 'infringing material' see PARA 133.
3   As to the meaning of 'infringing articles' see PARA 133.
4   As to the Commissioners for Her Majesty's Revenue and Customs see INCOME TAXATION vol 23(1) (Reissue) PARA 31 et seq.

5   Trade Marks Act 1994 s 91 (amended by the Commissioners for Revenue and Customs Act 2005 Sch 4 para 58; and SI 2008/1277). The offences referred to are those under: (1) the Trade Marks Act 1994 s 92 (see PARAS 124–127); (2) the Trade Descriptions Act 1968 (see CONSUMER PROTECTION vol 21 (2011) PARA 510 et seq); (3) the Business Protection from Misleading Marketing Regulations 2008, SI 2008/1276 (see CONSUMER PROTECTION vol 21 (2011) PARA 500); or (4) the Consumer Protection from Unfair Trading Regulations 2008, SI 2008/1277 (see CONSUMER PROTECTION vol 21 (2011) PARA 497 et seq): Trade Marks Act 1994 s 91 (as so amended).

     These provisions also apply to protected international trade marks (UK): see the Trade Marks (International Registration) Order 2008, SI 2008/2206, art 3; and PARA 12. See also generally PARA 11 et seq. As to the meaning of 'protected international trade mark (UK)' see PARA 12 note 8. As to the application of these provisions to Community trade marks see PARA 250.

6   See *Norwich Pharmacal Co v Customs and Excise Comrs* [1974] AC 133, [1973] 2 All ER 943, [1974] RPC 101, HL; but note the possible effect of the provisions of the Justice and Security Act 2013: see PARA 435.

(10) THE PARIS CONVENTION AND THE WTO AGREEMENT; SPECIAL PROVISIONS

136. Protection of well known trade marks. References in the Trade Marks Act 1994 to a trade mark[1] which is entitled to protection under the Paris Convention[2] or the WTO Agreement[3] as a well known trade mark are to a mark which is well known[4] in the United Kingdom[5] as being the mark of a person who:

(1)   is a national of a Convention country[6]; or

(2)   is domiciled[7] in, or has a real and effective industrial or commercial establishment in, a Convention country,

whether or not that person carries on business[8], or has any goodwill[9], in the United Kingdom; and references to the proprietor of such a mark are to be construed accordingly[10].

The proprietor of a trade mark which is entitled to protection under the Paris Convention or the WTO Agreement as a well known trade mark is entitled to restrain by injunction the use[11] in the United Kingdom of a trade mark which, or the essential part of which, is identical or similar[12] to his mark, in relation to identical or similar goods or services, where the use is likely to cause confusion[13].

1   As to the meaning of 'trade mark' see PARA 41.
2   As to the Paris Convention see PARA 6.
3   As to the WTO Agreement and its relationship to the Paris Convention see PARA 7.
4   The trade mark must be well known throughout the United Kingdom or a substantial part of it: Case C-328/06 *Nuño v Franquet* [2007] ECR I-10093, [2008] ETMR 12, [2007] All ER (D) 353 (Nov), ECJ. A trade mark can only be well known in respect of the goods or services in relation to which it had been used: *PACO/PACO LIFE IN COLOUR Trade Marks* [2000] RPC 451, Trade Marks Registry. In assessing whether a trade mark is well known it is appropriate to apply the criteria set out in the Joint Recommendation Concerning Provision on the Protection of Well Known Marks of the Paris Union and the World Intellectual Property Organisation (1999), art 2: *Hotel Cipriani Srl v Cipriani (Grosvenor Street) Ltd* [2008] EWHC 3032 (Ch), [2009] RPC 209 (affd [2010] EWCA Civ 110, [2010] Bus LR 1465, [2010] RPC 485).
5   As to the meaning of 'United Kingdom' see PARA 3 note 2.
6   As to the meaning of 'Convention country' see PARA 6 note 2. It has been held that the exclusion of the United Kingdom from the definition of 'Convention country' means that a person who is a national of, or domiciled or established in, the United Kingdom cannot invoke the Trade Marks Act 1994 s 56 (*CUTTY SARK Trade Mark* (O/285/01), Trade Marks Registry) but this may require reconsideration (*Imperial Tobacco Ltd v Berry Bros & Rudd Ltd* [2001] All ER (D) 447 (Oct)).
7   As to domicile see CONFLICT OF LAWS vol 19 (2011) PARA 336 et seq.
8   As to the meaning of 'business' see PARA 34 note 3.

9   As to goodwill see PERSONAL PROPERTY vol 80 (2013) PARA 807 et seq.

10 Trade Marks Act 1994 s 56(1) (s 56(1), (2) amended by SI 1999/1899). This provision
    implements the International Convention for the Protection of Industrial Property (Paris,
    20 March 1883) (the 'Paris Convention'), as revised (Stockholm, 14 July 1967 to 13 January
    1968; TS 61 (1970); Cmnd 4431), art 6 bis and the Agreement on Trade-Related Aspects of
    Intellectual Property Rights ('TRIPs') (1994) (Cm 2557) art 16(2). As to the Paris Convention
    see PARA 6; and as to TRIPs see PARA 7.
        The Trade Marks Act 1994 s 56 (now amended) overcomes the problem in passing off that
    certain marks, whilst they had a reputation in the United Kingdom, had no goodwill here
    because the proprietor had no trade in his goods or service here: see eg *Star Industrial Co Ltd v
    Yap Kwee Kor (t/a New Star Industrial Co)* [1976] FSR 256, PC; *Alain Bernardin & Cie v
    Pavilion Properties Ltd* [1967] RPC 581 ('Crazy Horse'). However, while the Trade Marks
    Act 1994 s 56 (now amended) removes the need for the proprietor to have a trade in the United
    Kingdom, he still needs to establish a likelihood of confusion to avail himself of the provision:
    Philips Electronics BV v Remington Consumer Products Ltd [1998] RPC 283 at 314 per
    Jacob J; affd [1999] RPC 809, [1999] All ER (D) 465, CA; referred to ECJ sub nom C-299/99
    Koninklijke Philips Electronics NV v Remington Consumer Products Ltd [2003] Ch 159,
    [2002] ECR I-5475, ECJ.
        As to the non-implementation of TRIPs art 16(3) see PARA 7 note 13.

11 As to the meaning of 'use' see PARA 44 note 8.

12 As to the requirement of similarity see PARA 7 note 11.

13 Trade Marks Act 1994 s 56(2) (as amended: see note 10). The right so conferred is subject to
    s 48 (effect of acquiescence by the proprietor of an earlier mark: see PARA 83): s 56(2) (as so
    amended). Nothing in s 56(2) affects the continuation of any bona fide use of a trade mark
    begun before 31 October 1994: s 56(3). See also note 10.

**137.   Attempts by agent or representative to register mark of principal; right of
principal to injunction.**   Where an application for registration[1] of a trade mark[2]
is made by a person who is an agent or representative[3] of a person who is the
proprietor of the mark in a Convention country[4], the following provisions
apply[5].

If the proprietor opposes the application, registration must be refused[6]. If the
application is granted, the proprietor may[7]:

(1)   apply for a declaration of the invalidity of the registration[8]; or

(2)   apply for the rectification of the register[9] so as to substitute his name as
       the proprietor of the registered trade mark[10].

The proprietor may, notwithstanding the rights conferred by the Trade Marks
Act 1994 in relation to a registered trade mark, by injunction restrain any use[11]
of the trade mark in the United Kingdom[12] which is not authorised by him[13].

The above provisions[14] do not apply if, or to the extent that, the agent or
representative justifies his action[15].

1   As to the requirements for registration see PARA 39 et seq; and as to the procedure on the
    application see PARA 334 et seq.

2   As to the meaning of 'trade mark' see PARA 41.

3   'Agent or representative' should be interpreted in the same manner as Council Regulation (EC)
    40/94 (OJ L11, 14.1.94, p 1) on the Community trade mark, art 8(3) (see now Council
    Regulation (EC) 207/2009 (OJ L78, 24.3.2009, p 1) art 8(3)): *Sribhan Jacob Co Ltd v Checker
    Leather Ltd* (O/066/08), Appointed Person. Accordingly, it is to be broadly construed as
    covering all kinds of relationships based on a contractual arrangement under which one party is
    representing the interests of the other, regardless of how the contractual relationship between the
    proprietor or principal on the one hand, and the applicant for the Community trade mark, on
    the other, is categorised: Case T-262/09 *Safariland LLC v Office for Harmonisation in the
    Internal Market (Trade Marks and Designs)* [2011] ETMR 47, EGC. Thus the expression
    includes licensees, franchisees, distributors and importers: see eg Decision 164C/000548644/1
    Promat Ltd v Pasture BV (19 December 2002, unreported), OHIM Cancellation Division;
    Case R 336/2001–2 *Sotorock Holding Ltd v Gordon* (7 July 2003, unreported), OHIM Board
    of Appeal; Decision 2486/2004 *Sybex Inc v Sybex-Verlag GmbH* (26 July 2004, unreported),

OHIM Opposition Division. The agency must relate to the United Kingdom: c f Decision 1131/2003 *NuScience Corpn v Basic Fashion Oy* (28 May 2003, unreported), OHIM Opposition Division.

4   As to the meaning of 'Convention country' see PARA 6 note 2.

5   Trade Marks Act 1994 s 60(1). Section 60 implements the International Convention for the Protection of Industrial Property (Paris, 20 March 1883) (the 'Paris Convention'), as revised (Stockholm, 14 July 1967 to 13 January 1968; TS 61 (1970); Cmnd 4431), art 6 (septies). As to the Paris Convention see PARA 6.

6   Trade Marks Act 1994 s 60(2). See also note 5.

7   Trade Marks Act 1994 s 60(3). See also note 5.

8   Trade Marks Act 1994 s 60(3)(a). As to the grounds for a declaration of invalidity of registration see PARA 102 et seq. See also note 5.

9   As to the register see PARA 21.

10 Trade Marks Act 1994 s 60(3)(b). See also note 5. An application under s 60(3)(a) or (b) (see heads (1), (2) in the text) must be made within three years of the proprietor becoming aware of the registration: s 60(6). As to the meaning of 'registered trade mark' see PARA 111.

11 As to the meaning of 'use' see PARA 44 note 8.

12 As to the meaning of 'United Kingdom' see PARA 3 note 2.

13 Trade Marks Act 1994 s 60(4). See also note 5. It would seem that the right so conferred is dependent upon the agent's having applied to register the trade mark himself.

    No injunction may be so granted in respect of a use in which the proprietor has acquiesced for a continuous period of three years or more: s 60(6).

14 Ie the Trade Marks Act 1994 s 60(2)–(4): see the text and notes 6–13.

15 Trade Marks Act 1994 s 60(5). It is presumed that consent by the proprietor would constitute justification: c f Council Regulation (EC) 207/2009 (OJ L78, 24.3.2009, p 1) on the Community trade mark, art 8(3) (formerly Council Regulation (EC) 40/94 (OJ L11, 14.1.94, p 1) art 8(3)); and PARA 206. Consent must be clear, specific and unconditional and must be valid on the day of application for registration: Case T-6/05 *DEF-TEC Defense Technology GmbH v Office for Harmonisation in the Internal Market (Trade Marks and Designs)* [2006] ECR II-2671, [2006] All ER (D) 23 (Sep), CFI; Joined Cases T-537/10 and T-538/10 *Adamowski v Office for Harmonisation in the Internal Market (Trade Marks and Designs)* [2012] ECR II-0000, EGC. The fact that the proprietor is unwilling to incur the expense of registering a trade mark does not justify an agent in registering it in his own name: Case R 336/2001–2 *Sotorock Holding Ltd v Gordon* (7 July 2003, unreported), OHIM Board of Appeal. It is doubtful whether ownership of the goodwill in the United Kingdom amounts to justification: *Sribhan Jacob Co Ltd v Checker Leather Ltd* (O/066/08), Appointed Person.

(11) COLLECTIVE MARKS

(i) In general

138. Nature of collective marks. A collective mark is a mark distinguishing the goods or services of members of the association which is the proprietor of the mark from those of other undertakings[1].

Subject to certain modifications[2], the provisions of the Trade Marks Act 1994 apply to collective marks[3].

1   Trade Marks Act 1994 s 49(1). A collective mark is a form of registered mark introduced by the Trade Marks Act 1994. It is essentially for trade associations, giving an indication that the goods or services are those of recognised members of the association which is proprietor. Collective marks were permitted by Council Directive (EEC) 89/104 (OJ L40, 11.2.89, p 1) to approximate the laws of the member states relating to trade marks, art 10 (see now European Parliament and Council Directive (EC) 2008/95 (OJ L299, 8.11.2008, p 25) art 10).

    In relation to a collective mark, the reference in the Trade Marks Act 1994 s 1(1) (signs of which a trade mark may consist: see PARA 41) to distinguishing goods or services of one undertaking from those of other undertakings is to be construed as a reference to distinguishing goods or services of members of the association which is the proprietor of the mark from those of other undertakings: s 49(2), Sch 1 para 2.

2   Ie subject to the provisions of the Trade Marks Act 1994 Sch 1: see note 1; and PARA 139 et seq.

3   Trade Marks Act 1994 Sch 1 para 1. Section 49, Sch 1 also apply with modifications to international trade marks (UK): see the Trade Marks (International Registration) Order 2008,

SI 2008/2206, art 3; and PARA 12. See also generally PARA 11 et seq. Accordingly, an application to register a collective mark has been refused pursuant to Trade Marks Act 1994 s 3(3)(b) (see PARAS 47, 48): *Chartered Insurance Institute v Association for Investment Management and Research* [2007] ETMR 76, Trade Marks Registry (CHARTERED FINANCIAL ANALYST misleading because consumers of financial services would be likely understand it offer a promise of quality assurance of the same kind as other professional designations granted by bodies with a Royal Charter but it did not).

139. Indication of geographical origin. A collective mark[1] may be registered[2] which consists of signs or indications which may serve, in trade[3], to designate the geographical origin of the goods or services[4]. The proprietor of such a mark is, however, not entitled to prohibit the use[5] of the signs or indications in accordance with honest practices in industrial or commercial matters (in particular, by a person who is entitled to use a geographical name)[6].

1   As to the meaning of 'collective mark' see PARA 138.
2   Ie notwithstanding the Trade Marks Act 1994 s 3(1)(c) (prohibition on registration of marks consisting of an indication of geographical origin): see PARA 44 head (2).
3   As to the meaning of 'trade' see PARA 44 note 4.
4   Trade Marks Act 1994 s 49(2), Sch 1 para 3(1).
5   As to the meaning of 'use' see PARA 44 note 8.
6   Trade Marks Act 1994 Sch 1 para 3(2).

140. Mark not to be misleading as to character or significance. A collective mark[1] may not be registered if the public is liable to be misled as regards the character or significance of the mark, in particular if it is likely to be taken to be something other than a collective mark[2]. The registrar[3] may accordingly require that a mark in respect of which application is made for registration[4] should include some indication that it is a collective mark[5]. An application may be amended[6] so as to comply with any such requirement[7].

1   As to the meaning of 'collective mark' see PARA 138.
2   Trade Marks Act 1994 s 49(2), Sch 1 para 4(1).
3   As to the registrar see PARA 19.
4   As to procedure on the application see PARA 334 et seq.
5   Trade Marks Act 1994 Sch 1 para 4(2).
6   Ie notwithstanding the Trade Marks Act 1994 s 39(2): see PARA 357.
7   Trade Marks Act 1994 Sch 1 para 4(2).

(ii) Regulations

141. Regulations governing use of collective mark. An applicant for registration of a collective mark[1] must file with the registrar[2] regulations governing the use[3] of the mark[4]. The regulations must specify the persons authorised to use the mark, the conditions of membership of the association and, where they exist, the conditions of use of the mark, including any sanctions against misuse[5]. Further requirements with which the regulations have to comply may be imposed by rules[6].

1   As to the meaning of 'collective mark' see PARA 138.
2   As to the registrar see PARA 19.
3   As to the meaning of 'use' see PARA 44 note 8.
4   Trade Marks Act 1994 s 49(2), Sch 1 para 5(1). As to approval of the regulations see PARA 142.
5   Trade Marks Act 1994 Sch 1 para 5(2).
6   Trade Marks Act 1994 Sch 1 para 5(2). At the date at which this volume states the law no such rules had been made.

142.   Approval of regulations. A collective mark[1] may not be registered unless the regulations governing the use of the mark[2] comply with the statutory requirements[3] and any further requirements imposed by rules[4] and are not contrary to public policy or to accepted principles of morality[5].

Within not less than three months of the date of the application for registration of a collective mark, the applicant must file the appropriate form[6] with the registrar[7] accompanied by a copy of the regulations governing the use of the mark and pay the prescribed fee[8]. If he does not do so, the application is deemed to be withdrawn[9].

The registrar must consider whether the above requirements[10] are met[11]. If it appears to the registrar that those requirements are not met, he must inform the applicant and give him an opportunity, within such period as the registrar may specify, to make representations or to file amended regulations[12]. If the applicant fails to satisfy the registrar that those requirements are met, or to file regulations amended so as to meet them, or to respond before the end of the specified period, the registrar must refuse the application[13]. If, however, it appears to the registrar that those requirements, and the other requirements for registration, are met, he must accept the application and must proceed[14] accordingly[15].

1   As to the meaning of 'collective mark' see PARA 138.
2   As to the regulations see PARA 141.
3   Ie the Trade Marks Act 1994 s 49(2), Sch 1 para 5(2): see PARA 141.
4   Ie rules made pursuant to the Trade Marks Act 1994 Sch 1 para 5(2): see PARA 141.
5   Trade Marks Act 1994 Sch 1 para 6(1). As to marks contrary to public policy or accepted principles of morality see PARA 47.
6   The appropriate form is Form TM35: Trade Marks Rules 2008, SI 2008/1797, r 29. As to the meaning of references to 'filing' see PARA 27 note 2. As to the filing of documents by electronic means see PARA 336.
7   As to the registrar see PARA 19.
8   Trade Marks Act 1994 Sch 1 para 6(2); Trade Marks Rules 2008, SI 2008/1797, r 29. The prescribed fee is currently £200: Trade Marks (Fees) Rules 2008, SI 2008/1958, r 2, Schedule. As to the use of forms see PARA 335; and as to fees see PARA 18.
9   Trade Marks Act 1994 Sch 1 para 6(2).
10 Ie the requirements mentioned in the Trade Marks Act 1994 Sch 1 para 6(1): see the text and notes 1–5.
11 Trade Marks Act 1994 Sch 1 para 7(1).
12 Trade Marks Act 1994 Sch 1 para 7(2). As to appeals from decisions of the registrar, including acts of the registrar in exercise of a discretion, see ss 76, 77; and PARA 387 et seq.
13 Trade Marks Act 1994 Sch 1 para 7(3).
14 Ie in accordance with the Trade Marks Act 1994 s 38: see PARAS 365–369.
15 Trade Marks Act 1994 Sch 1 para 7(4).

143.   Publication and inspection of regulations. The regulations[1] must be published[2] and notice of opposition may be given, and observations may be made, relating to the specified[3] matters[4]. This is in addition to any other grounds on which the application may be opposed or observations made[5].

The regulations governing the use of a registered collective mark[6] must be open to public inspection in the same way as the register[7].

1   As to the regulations see PARA 141.
2   As to the meaning of 'publish' see PARA 19 note 10.
3   Ie the matters specified in the Trade Marks Act 1994 s 49(2), Sch 1 para 6(1): see PARA 142.
4   Trade Marks Act 1994 Sch 1 para 8.
5   Trade Marks Act 1994 Sch 1 para 8.
6   As to the meaning of 'collective mark' see PARA 138.
7   Trade Marks Act 1994 Sch 1 para 9. As to the register being open to public inspection see s 63(3)(a); and PARA 26.

144.   Amendment of regulations.   An amendment of the regulations[1] governing the use of a registered collective mark[2] is not effective unless and until the amended regulations are filed[3] with the registrar[4] on the appropriate form[5] and accepted by him[6].

Before accepting any amended regulations the registrar may in any case where it appears to him expedient to do so cause them to be published[7]; and he must publish a notice indicating where copies of the amended regulations may be inspected[8]. If the registrar does so, any person may, within two months of the date of publication of the notice:

(1)   make observations to the registrar on the amendments relating to the specified matters[9] and the registrar must send[10] a copy thereof to the proprietor[11];

(2)   give notice to the registrar of opposition to the amendment on the appropriate form[12] which must include a statement of the grounds of opposition indicating why the amended regulations do not comply with the specified[13] requirements[14].

The registrar must send a copy of the appropriate form[15] to the proprietor; and thereafter the statutory provisions relating to opposition proceedings[16] apply to the proceedings as they apply to proceedings relating to opposition to an application for registration with certain modifications[17].

1   As to the regulations see PARA 141.
2   As to the meaning of 'collective mark' see PARA 138.
3   As to the meaning of references to 'filing' see PARA 27 note 2. As to the filing of documents by electronic means see PARA 336.
4   As to the registrar see PARA 19.
5   The appropriate form is Form TM36: Trade Marks Rules 2008, SI 2008/1797, r 30(1). As to the use of forms see PARA 335.
6   Trade Marks Act 1994 s 49(2), Sch 1 para 10(1); Trade Marks Rules 2008, SI 2008/1797, r 30(1).
7   As to the meaning of 'publish' see PARA 19 note 10.
8   Trade Marks Act 1994 Sch 1 para 10(2); Trade Marks Rules 2008, SI 2008/1797, r 30(2).
9   Ie the matters referred to in the Trade Marks Act 1994 Sch 1 para 6(1): see PARA 142.
10   As to the meaning of 'send' see PARA 27 note 10.
11   Trade Marks Act 1994 Sch 1 para 10(3); Trade Marks Rules 2008, SI 2008/1797, r 30(3).
12   The appropriate form is Form TM7: Trade Marks Rules 2008, SI 2008/1797, r 30(4).
13   Ie the requirements specified in the Trade Marks Act 1994 Sch 1 para 6(1): see PARA 142.
14   Trade Marks Act 1994 Sch 1 para 10(3); Trade Marks Rules 2008, SI 2008/1797, r 30(4).
15   The appropriate form is Form TM7: Trade Marks Rules 2008, SI 2008/1797, r 30(5).
16   Ie the Trade Marks Rules 2008, SI 2008/1797, rr 18, 20: see PARA 366.
17   Trade Marks Rules 2008, SI 2008/1797, r 30(5). As to those modifications see r 30(5)(a)–(c) (amended by SI 2013/444). As to calculation of time periods in regard to the Trade Marks Rules 2008, SI 2008/1797, r 30(5)(b) see Tribunal Practice Notice (TPN 1/2013), available from the Intellectual Property Office ('IPO') website, accessible at the date at which this volume states the law at www.ipo.gov.uk. As to the Intellectual Property Office (an operating name of the Patent Office) see PARA 16 note 2.

(iii) Infringement, Revocation and Invalidity

145.   Infringement; rights of authorised users.   The statutory provisions relating to:

(1)   the unauthorised application of a mark to certain material[1];

(2)   the adequacy of other remedies in relation to orders as to the disposal of infringing goods, material or articles[2]; and

(3)   the making of a request to the Commissioners for Her Majesty's

Revenue and Customs in relation to the prohibition of the importation of infringing goods, material or articles[3],

apply in relation to an authorised user of a registered collective mark[4] as in relation to a licensee[5] of a trade mark[6].

The following provisions[7] have effect as regards the rights of an authorised user in relation to infringement[8] of a registered collective mark[9].

An authorised user is entitled, subject to any agreement to the contrary between him and the proprietor, to call on the proprietor to take infringement proceedings[10] in respect of any matter which affects his interests[11]. If the proprietor refuses to do so or fails to do so within two months after being called upon, the authorised user may bring the proceedings in his own name as if he were the proprietor[12]. Where infringement proceedings are so brought, the authorised user may not, without the leave of the court[13], proceed with the action unless the proprietor is either joined as a claimant or added as a defendant; but this does not affect the granting of interim relief on an application by an authorised user alone[14]. A proprietor who is so added as a defendant may not be made liable for any costs in the action unless he takes part in the proceedings[15].

In infringement proceedings brought by the proprietor of a registered collective mark, any loss suffered or likely to be suffered by authorised users is to be taken into account; and the court may give such directions as it thinks fit as to the extent to which the claimant is to hold the proceeds of any pecuniary remedy on behalf of such users[16].

1 Ie the Trade Marks Act 1994 s 10(5): see PARA 73.
2 Ie the Trade Marks Act 1994 s 19(2): see PARA 446.
3 Ie the Trade Marks Act 1994 s 89: see PARA 132. As to the Commissioners for Her Majesty's Revenue and Customs see INCOME TAXATION vol 23(1) (Reissue) PARA 31 et seq.
4 As to the meaning of 'collective mark' see PARA 138.
5 As to the licensing of a registered trade mark see PARAS 119–120.
6 Trade Marks Act 1994 s 49(2), Sch 1 para 11 (amended by virtue of the Commissioners for Revenue and Customs Act 2005 s 50(1), (7)).
7 Ie the provisions of the Trade Marks Act 1994 Sch 1 para 12(2)–(6) (see the text and notes 10–16), which correspond to the provisions of s 30 (general provisions as to the rights of licensees in case of infringement: see PARA 400).
8 As to the meaning of 'infringement' see PARA 66 note 4. As to the acts which amount to infringement, if done without the consent of the proprietor, see the Trade Marks Act 1994 s 10; and PARA 68 et seq.
9 Trade Marks Act 1994 Sch 1 para 12(1).
10 As to the meaning of 'infringement proceedings' see PARA 67 note 4.
11 Trade Marks Act 1994 Sch 1 para 12(2).
12 Trade Marks Act 1994 Sch 1 para 12(3).
13 As to the meaning of 'the court' see PARA 331.
14 Trade Marks Act 1994 Sch 1 para 12(4).
15 Trade Marks Act 1994 Sch 1 para 12(5).
16 Trade Marks Act 1994 Sch 1 para 12(6).

146.   Grounds for revocation of registration.   Apart from the usual statutory grounds of revocation[1], the registration of a collective mark[2] may be revoked on the ground[3]:

(1)   that the manner in which the mark has been used[4] by the proprietor has caused it to become liable to mislead the public as regards the character or significance of the mark, in particular if it is likely to be taken to be something other than a collective mark[5]; or

(2)   that the proprietor has failed to observe, or to secure the observance of, the regulations[6] governing the use of the mark[7]; or

(3)   that an amendment of the regulations has been made so that the regulations no longer comply with the statutory requirements[8] and any further conditions imposed by rules[9] or are contrary to public policy or to accepted principles of morality[10].

1   Ie the grounds provided for in the Trade Marks Act 1994 s 46: see PARA 98 et seq.
2   As to the meaning of 'collective mark' see PARA 138.
3   Trade Marks Act 1994 s 49(2), Sch 1 para 13.
4   As to the meaning of 'use' see PARA 44 note 8.
5   Trade Marks Act 1994 Sch 1 para 13(a), which refers to Sch 1 para 4(1) (see PARA 140).
6   As to the regulations see PARA 141.
7   Trade Marks Act 1994 Sch 1 para 13(b).
8   Ie the Trade Marks Act 1994 Sch 1 para 5(2): see PARA 141.
9   Ie rules made under the Trade Marks Act 1994 Sch 1 para 5(2): see PARA 141.
10 Trade Marks Act 1994 Sch 1 para 13(c).

147.   Grounds for invalidity of registration.   Apart from the usual statutory grounds of invalidity[1], the registration of a collective mark[2] may be declared invalid on the ground that the mark was registered in breach of any of the statutory provisions relating to the prohibition on a mark being misleading as to character or significance[3] or the conditions subject to which a collective mark may be registered[4].

1   Ie the grounds provided for in the Trade Marks Act 1994 s 47: see PARA 102 et seq.
2   As to the meaning of 'collective mark' see PARA 138.
3   Ie the Trade Marks Act 1994 s 49(2), Sch 1 para 4(1): see PARA 140.
4   Trade Marks Act 1994 Sch 1 para 14. As to the conditions subject to which a collective mark may be registered see Sch 1 para 6(1); and PARA 142.
    In all legal proceedings relating to a registered trade mark, the registration of a person as proprietor of a trade mark is prima facie evidence of the validity of the original registration: see s 72; and PARA 94. As to the meaning of 'registered trade mark' see PARA 111. As to certificates of validity see PARA 429.

(12)   CERTIFICATION MARKS

(i)   In general

148.   Nature of certification marks.   A certification mark is a mark indicating that the goods or services in connection with which it is used are certified by the proprietor of the mark in respect of the origin, material, mode of manufacture of goods or performance of services, quality, accuracy or other characteristics[1].

Subject to certain modifications[2], the provisions of the Trade Marks Act 1994 apply to certification marks[3].

The assignment or other transmission of a registered certification mark is not effective without the consent of the registrar[4].

1   Trade Marks Act 1994 s 50(1). In general, certification marks were permitted by Council Directive (EEC) 89/104 (OJ L40, 11.2.89, p 1) to approximate the laws of the member states relating to trade marks, art 10 (see now European Parliament and Council Directive (EC) 2008/95 (OJ L299, 8.11.2008, p 25) art 10). Nevertheless it is arguable that the Trade Marks Act 1994 s 50 should not be interpreted as permitting the registration as certification marks of geographical designations or indications which are capable of being registered as protected designations of origin or protected geographical origins (as to which see PARA 285): see Joined Cases C-129/97 and C-130/97 *Re Chiciak and Fol* [1998] ECR I-3315, [1998] All ER (D) 253, ECJ; Case C-6/02 EC *Commission v France* [2003] ECR I-2389, [2003] All ER (D) 69 (Mar), ECJ. The definition in the Trade Marks Act 1994 s 50(1) corresponds to the definition in the Trade Marks Act 1938 s 37(1) (repealed). There was little litigation relating to certification marks under the Trade Marks Act 1938: see eg *Stilton Trade Mark* [1967] RPC 173

(certification by the Stilton Cheese Makers' Association that cheese came from a particular area and was made according to a particular recipe could be the subject of a registration); *Sea Island Cotton Certification Trade Marks* [1989] RPC 87 (which decided, as a matter of discretion, that a certification mark should not be expunged for minor breaches of the regulations).

Certification marks are normally registered by trade associations and the like (the British Standards Institution 'Kitemark' being a typical example), not to indicate membership of the association (for which collective marks cater: see PARA 138 et seq), but as a mark of quality.

In relation to a certification mark, the reference in the Trade Marks Act 1994 s 1(1) (signs of which a trade mark may consist: see PARA 41) to distinguishing goods or services of one undertaking from those of other undertakings is to be construed as a reference to distinguishing goods or services which are certified from those which are not: s 50(2), Sch 2 para 2. A certification mark may acquire a distinctive character through use: *Legal Aid Board v Comptroller General of Patents* [2000] All ER (D) 1246.

2 Ie subject to the provisions of the Trade Marks Act 1994 Sch 2: see note 1; and PARA 149 et seq.
3 Trade Marks Act 1994 Sch 2 para 1.
4 Trade Marks Act 1994 Sch 2 para 12. As to assignment and transmission see PARA 113 et seq; and as to the registrar see PARA 19. Section 20, Sch 2 also apply with modifications to international trade marks (UK): see the Trade Marks (International Registration) Order 2008, SI 2008/2206, art 3; and PARA 12. See also generally PARA 11 et seq.

149. Indication of geographical origin.

A certification mark[1] may be registered[2] which consists of signs or indications which may serve, in trade[3], to designate the geographical origin of the goods or services[4]. The proprietor of such a mark is, however, not entitled to prohibit the use[5] of the signs or indications in accordance with honest practices in industrial or commercial matters (in particular, by a person who is entitled to use a geographical name)[6].

1 As to the meaning of 'certification mark' see PARA 148.
2 Ie notwithstanding the Trade Marks Act 1994 s 3(1)(c) (prohibition on registration of marks consisting of an indication of geographical origin): see PARA 44 head (2).
3 As to the meaning of 'trade' see PARA 44 note 4.
4 Trade Marks Act 1994 s 50(2), Sch 2 para 3(1). See PARA 148 note 1.
5 As to the meaning of 'use' see PARA 44 note 8.
6 Trade Marks Act 1994 Sch 2 para 3(2).

150. Nature of proprietor's business.

A certification mark[1] may not be registered if the proprietor carries on a business[2] involving the supply of goods or services of the kind certified[3].

1 As to the meaning of 'certification mark' see PARA 148.
2 As to the meaning of 'business' see PARA 34 note 3.
3 Trade Marks Act 1994 s 50(2), Sch 2 para 4.

151. Mark not to be misleading as to character or significance.

A certification mark[1] may not be registered if the public is liable to be misled as regards the character or significance of the mark, in particular if it is likely to be taken to be something other than a certification mark[2]. The registrar[3] may accordingly require that a mark in respect of which application is made for registration[4] should include some indication that it is a certification mark[5]. An application may be amended[6] so as to comply with any such requirement[7].

1 As to the meaning of 'certification mark' see PARA 148.
2 Trade Marks Act 1994 s 50(2), Sch 2 para 5(1).
3 As to the registrar see PARA 19.
4 As to the procedure on the application see PARA 334 et seq.
5 Trade Marks Act 1994 Sch 2 para 5(2).
6 Ie notwithstanding the Trade Marks Act 1994 s 39(2): see PARA 357.
7 Trade Marks Act 1994 Sch 2 para 5(2).

(ii) Regulations

152. Regulations governing use of certification mark. An applicant for registration of a certification mark[1] must file with the registrar[2] regulations governing the use[3] of the mark[4]. The regulations must indicate who is authorised to use the mark, the characteristics to be certified by the mark, how the certifying body is to test those characteristics and to supervise the use of the mark, the fees, if any, to be paid in connection with the operation of the mark and the procedures for resolving disputes[5]. Further requirements with which the regulations have to comply may be imposed by rules[6].

1 As to the meaning of 'certification mark' see PARA 148.
2 As to the registrar see PARA 19.
3 As to the meaning of 'use' see PARA 44 note 8.
4 Trade Marks Act 1994 s 50(2), Sch 2 para 6(1). As to approval of the regulations see PARA 153.
    Regulations governing the use of an existing registered certification mark deposited at the Patent Office (now the Intellectual Property Office ('IPO')) in pursuance of the Trade Marks Act 1938 s 37 (repealed) are to be treated on and after 31 October 1994 as if filed under the Trade Marks Act 1994 Sch 2 para 6: s 105, Sch 3 para 19(1). Any request for amendment of the regulations which was pending on 31 October 1994 must be dealt with under the old law: Sch 3 para 19(2). As to the meaning of 'the old law' see PARA 4 note 3. As to the Intellectual Property Office (an operating name of the Patent Office) see PARA 16 note 2.
5 Trade Marks Act 1994 Sch 2 para 6(2). See also note 4.
6 Trade Marks Act 1994 Sch 2 para 6(2). See also note 4.

153. Approval of regulations etc. A certification mark[1] may not be registered unless:

(1) the regulations governing the use of the mark[2] comply with the statutory requirements[3] and any further requirements imposed by rules[4] and are not contrary to public policy or to accepted principles of morality[5]; and

(2) the applicant is competent to certify the goods or services for which the mark is to be registered[6].

Within not less than three months of the date of the application for registration of a certification mark, the applicant must file the appropriate form[7] with the registrar[8] accompanied by a copy of the regulations governing the use of the mark and pay the prescribed fee[9]. If he does not do so, the application is deemed to be withdrawn[10].

The registrar must consider whether the requirements of heads (1) and (2) above[11] are met[12]. If it appears to the registrar that those requirements are not met, he must inform the applicant and give him an opportunity, within such period as the registrar may specify, to make representations or to file amended regulations[13]. If the applicant fails to satisfy the registrar that those requirements are met, or to file regulations amended so as to meet them, or to respond before the end of the specified period, the registrar must refuse the application[14]. If, however, it appears to the registrar that those requirements, and the other requirements for registration, are met, he must accept the application and must proceed[15] accordingly[16].

1 As to the meaning of 'certification mark' see PARA 148.
2 As to the regulations see PARA 152.
3 Ie the Trade Marks Act 1994 s 50(2), Sch 2 para 6(2): see PARA 152.
4 Ie rules made pursuant to the Trade Marks Act 1994 Sch 2 para 6(2): see PARA 152.
5 Trade Marks Act 1994 Sch 2 para 7(1)(a). As to marks contrary to public policy or accepted principles of morality see PARA 47.
6 Trade Marks Act 1994 Sch 2 para 7(1)(b).

7   The appropriate form is Form TM35: Trade Marks Rules 2008, SI 2008/1797, r 29. As to the meaning of references to 'filing' see PARA 27 note 2. As to the filing of documents by electronic means see PARA 336.
8   As to the registrar see PARA 19.
9   Trade Marks Act 1994 Sch 2 para 7(2); Trade Marks Rules 2008, SI 2008/1797, r 29. The prescribed fee is currently £200: Trade Marks (Fees) Rules 2008, SI 2008/1958, r 2, Schedule. As to the use of forms see PARA 335; and as to fees see PARA 18.
10 Trade Marks Act 1994 Sch 2 para 7(2).
11 Ie the requirements mentioned in the Trade Marks Act 1994 Sch 2 para 7(1): see the text and notes 1–6.
12 Trade Marks Act 1994 Sch 2 para 8(1). As to appeals from decisions of the registrar, including acts of the registrar in exercise of a discretion, see ss 76, 77; and PARA 387 et seq.
13 Trade Marks Act 1994 Sch 2 para 8(2).
14 Trade Marks Act 1994 Sch 2 para 8(3).
15 Ie in accordance with the Trade Marks Act 1994 s 38: see PARAS 365–369.
16 Trade Marks Act 1994 Sch 2 para 8(4).

154.   Publication and inspection of regulations. The regulations[1] must be published[2] and notice of opposition may be given, and observations may be made, relating to the specified[3] matters[4]. This is in addition to any other grounds on which the application may be opposed or observations made[5].

The regulations governing the use of a registered certification mark[6] must be open to public inspection in the same way as the register[7].

1   As to the regulations see PARA 152.
2   As to the meaning of 'publish' see PARA 19 note 10.
3   Ie the matters specified in the Trade Marks Act 1994 s 50(2), Sch 2 para 7(1): see PARA 153.
4   Trade Marks Act 1994 Sch 2 para 9.
5   Trade Marks Act 1994 Sch 2 para 9.
6   As to the meaning of 'certification mark' see PARA 148.
7   Trade Marks Act 1994 Sch 2 para 10. As to the register being open to public inspection see s 63(3)(a); and PARA 26.

155.   Amendment of regulations. An amendment of the regulations[1] governing the use of a registered certification mark[2] is not effective unless and until the amended regulations are filed[3] with the registrar[4] on the appropriate form[5] and accepted by him[6].

Before accepting any amended regulations the registrar may in any case where it appears to him expedient to do so cause them to be published[7]; and he must publish a notice indicating where copies of the amended regulations may be inspected[8]. If the registrar does so, any person may, within two months of the date of publication of the notice:

(1)   make observations to the registrar on the amendments relating to the specified matters[9] and the registrar must send[10] a copy thereof to the proprietor[11];

(2)   give notice to the registrar of opposition to the amendment on the appropriate form[12] which must include a statement of the grounds of opposition indicating why the amended regulations do not comply with the specified[13] requirements[14].

The registrar must send a copy of the appropriate form[15] to the proprietor; and thereafter the statutory provisions relating to opposition proceedings[16] apply to the proceedings as they apply to proceedings relating to opposition to an application for registration with certain modifications[17].

1   As to the regulations see PARA 152.
2   As to the meaning of 'certification mark' see PARA 148.

3   As to the meaning of references to 'filing' see PARA 27 note 2. As to the filing of documents by
    electronic means see PARA 336.
4   As to the registrar see PARA 19.
5   The appropriate form is Form TM36: Trade Marks Rules 2008, SI 2008/1797, r 30(1). As to the
    use of forms see PARA 335.
6   Trade Marks Act 1994 s 50(2), Sch 2 para 11(1); Trade Marks Rules 2008, SI 2008/1797,
    r 30(1). See also PARA 152 note 4.
7   As to the meaning of 'publish' see PARA 19 note 10.
8   Trade Marks Act 1994 Sch 2 para 11(2); Trade Marks Rules 2008, SI 2008/1797, r 30(2).
9   Ie the matters referred to in the Trade Marks Act 1994 Sch 2 para 7(1): see PARA 153.
10 As to the meaning of 'send' see PARA 27 note 10.
11 Trade Marks Act 1994 Sch 2 para 11(3); Trade Marks Rules 2008, SI 2008/1797, r 30(3).
12 The appropriate form is Form TM7: Trade Marks Rules 2008, SI 2008/1707, r 30(4).
13 Ie the requirements specified in the Trade Marks Act 1994 Sch 2 para 7(1): see PARA 153.
14 Trade Marks Act 1994 Sch 2 para 11(3); Trade Marks Rules 2008, SI 2008/1797, r 30(4).
15 The appropriate form is Form TM7: Trade Marks Rules 2008, SI 2008/1797, r 30(5).
16 Ie the Trade Marks Rules 2008, SI 2008/1797, rr 18, 20: see PARA 366.
17 Trade Marks Rules 2008, SI 2008/1797, r 30(5). As to those modifications see r 30(5)(a)–(c)
    (amended by SI 2013/444).

(iii) Infringement, Revocation and Invalidity

156.   Infringement; rights of authorised users.   The statutory provisions
relating to:
   (1)   the unauthorised application of a mark to certain material[1];
   (2)   the adequacy of other remedies in relation to orders as to the disposal of
         infringing goods, material or articles[2]; and
   (3)   the making of a request to the Commissioners for Her Majesty's
         Revenue and Customs in relation to the prohibition of the importation
         of infringing goods, material or articles[3],
apply in relation to an authorised user of a registered certification mark[4] as in
relation to a licensee[5] of a trade mark[6].

   In infringement proceedings[7] brought by the proprietor of a registered
certification mark any loss suffered or likely to be suffered by authorised users
must be taken into account; and the court[8] may give such directions as it thinks
fit as to the extent to which the claimant is to hold the proceeds of any pecuniary
remedy on behalf of such users[9].

1   Ie the Trade Marks Act 1994 s 10(5): see PARA 73.
2   Ie the Trade Marks Act 1994 s 19(2): see PARA 446.
3   Ie the Trade Marks Act 1994 s 89: see PARA 132. As to the Commissioners for Her Majesty's
    Revenue and Customs see INCOME TAXATION vol 23(1) (Reissue) PARA 31 et seq.
4   As to the meaning of 'certification mark' see PARA 148.
5   As to the licensing of a registered trade mark see PARAS 119–120.
6   Trade Marks Act 1994 s 50(2), Sch 2 para 13. As to the meaning of 'trade mark' see PARA 41.
7   As to the meaning of 'infringement proceedings' see PARA 67 note 4.
8   As to the meaning of 'the court' see PARA 331.
9   Trade Marks Act 1994 Sch 2 para 14. This applies only in relation to infringements committed
    on or after 31 October 1994: s 105, Sch 3 para 6(2).

157.   Grounds for revocation of registration.   Apart from the usual statutory
grounds of revocation[1], the registration of a certification mark[2] may be revoked
on the ground[3]:
   (1)   that the proprietor has begun to carry on a business[4] involving the
         supply of goods or services of the kind certified[5];
   (2)   that the manner in which the mark has been used[6] by the proprietor has
         caused it to become liable to mislead the public as regards the character

or significance of the mark, in particular if it is likely to be taken to be something other than a certification mark[7];

(3)   that the proprietor has failed to observe, or to secure the observance of, the regulations[8] governing the use of the mark[9];

(4)   that an amendment of the regulations has been made so that the regulations no longer comply with the statutory requirements[10] and any further conditions imposed by rules[11] or are contrary to public policy or to accepted principles of morality[12]; or

(5)   that the proprietor is no longer competent to certify the goods or services for which the mark is registered[13].

1   Ie the grounds provided for in the Trade Marks Act 1994 s 46: see PARA 98 et seq.
2   As to the meaning of 'certification mark' see PARA 148.
3   Trade Marks Act 1994 s 50(2), Sch 2 para 15.
4   As to the meaning of 'business' see PARA 34 note 3.
5   Trade Marks Act 1994 Sch 2 para 15(a), which refers to such a business as is mentioned in Sch 2 para 4: see PARA 150.
6   As to the meaning of 'use' see PARA 44 note 8.
7   Trade Marks Act 1994 Sch 2 para 15(b). As to the manner referred to see Sch 2 para 5(1); and PARA 151.
8   Ie the Trade Marks Act 1994 Sch 2 para 6(2): see PARA 152.
9   Trade Marks Act 1994 Sch 2 para 15(c).
10   Ie the Trade Marks Act 1994 Sch 2 para 6(2): see PARA 152.
11   Ie rules made pursuant to the Trade Marks Act 1994 Sch 2 para 6(2): see PARA 152.
12   Trade Marks Act 1994 Sch 2 para 15(d).
13   Trade Marks Act 1994 Sch 2 para 15(e).

158. Grounds for invalidity of registration. Apart from the usual statutory grounds of invalidity[1], the registration of a certification mark[2] may be declared invalid on the ground that the mark was registered in breach of any of the statutory provisions relating to the nature of a proprietor's business[3], the prohibition on a mark being misleading as to character or significance[4] or the conditions[5] subject to which a certification mark may be registered[6].

1   Ie the grounds provided for in the Trade Marks Act 1994 s 47: see PARA 102 et seq.
2   As to the meaning of 'certification mark' see PARA 148.
3   Ie the Trade Marks Act 1994 s 50(2), Sch 2 para 4: see PARA 150.
4   Ie the Trade Marks Act 1994 Sch 2 para 5(1): see PARA 151.
5   Ie the Trade Marks Act 1994 Sch 2 para 7(1): see PARA 153.
6   Trade Marks Act 1994 Sch 2 para 16. In all legal proceedings relating to a registered trade mark, the registration of a person as proprietor of a trade mark is prima facie evidence of the validity of the original registration: see s 72; and PARA 94. As to the meaning of 'registered trade mark' see PARA 111. As to certificates of validity see PARA 429.

3. COMMUNITY TRADE MARKS

(1) INTRODUCTION

159. The Community Trade Mark Regulation. A system of registration of trade marks covering the whole of the European Union is provided for by the Community Trade Mark Regulation[1]. The Regulation provides for registration of a 'Community trade mark'[2] registered in accordance with the conditions contained in, and in the manner provided by, that Regulation[3].

A Community trade mark so registered has effect throughout the Community[4]. It is infringed by the performance of prohibited acts[5] anywhere in the Community[6]. Accordingly, a person wishing to protect a trade mark throughout the Community may register that mark in accordance with the Regulation: this can be an alternative to, or in addition to[7], registration in each of the member states[8].

The substantive law of Community trade marks[9], as provided for by the Regulation, closely mirrors the provisions of the Trade Marks Directive[10], and decisions as to the interpretation of identical or materially identical provisions of one are regarded as decisions on the interpretation of the other[11].

By virtue of the accession of the European Community to the Madrid Protocol[12], a Community trade mark can form the basis for an international application and an international registration can form the basis for an application for a Community trade mark[13].

1   Ie Council Regulation (EC) 207/2009 (OJ L78, 24.3.2009, p 1) on the Community trade mark (Codified version). It repeals and replaces in similar terms Council Regulation (EC) 40/94 (OJ L11, 14.1.94, p 1) on the Community trade mark and under Council Regulation (EC) 207/2009 (OJ L78, 24.3.2009, p 1) art 166 references to the repealed Regulation must be construed as references to the 2009 Regulation and read in accordance with the relevant correlation table. The Community Trade Mark Regulation does not prevent actions concerning a Community trade mark being brought under the law of member states relating in particular to civil liability and unfair competition: Council Regulation (EC) 207/2009 (OJ L78, 24.3.2009, p 1) art 14(2). Thus the Regulation does not affect the law of passing off in the United Kingdom: see PARA 287 et seq. The Regulation is referred to in the Trade Marks Act 1994 as 'the Community Trade Mark Regulation': s 51.

2   As to the meaning of 'Community trade mark' see Council Regulation (EC) 207/2009 (OJ L78, 24.3.2009, p 1) art 1(1); and PARA 189.

3   See Council Regulation (EC) 207/2009 (OJ L78, 24.3.2009, p 1) art 1(1); and PARA 189. For the requirements for registration as a Community trade mark see PARAS 188–206. As to the manner of registration see PARAS 261–266. The Community Trade Mark Regulation does not affect Council Regulation (EC) 510/2006 (OJ L93, 31.3.06, p 12) on the protection of geographical indications and designations of origin for agricultural products and foodstuffs, and in particular art 14 (see now European Parliament and Council Regulation (EU) 1151/2012) (OJ L343, 14.12.2012, p 1) art 14) (as to which see PARA 285, 286): Council Regulation (EC) 207/2009 (OJ L78, 24.3.2009, p 1) art 164.

4   Council Regulation (EC) 207/2009 (OJ L78, 24.3.2009, p 1) art 1(2); and see PARA 189. The Community Trade Mark Regulation also makes provision for the consequences of the enlargement of the Community: see art 165.

5   As to the prohibited acts which infringe a Community trade mark see Council Regulation (EC) 207/2009 (OJ L78, 24.3.2009, p 1) art 9; and PARA 207 et seq.

6   As to national proceedings for infringement of a Community trade mark see PARA 233 et seq. An action may be brought in a single court to restrain infringement throughout the European Union: see Council Regulation (EC) 207/2009 (OJ L78, 24.3.2009, p 1) art 98(1); and PARA 235.

7   There will of course be some circumstances in which it may be advantageous to register a trade mark in one or more of the member states. There are subtle differences in the requirements as to registration provided for by Council Regulation (EC) 207/2009 (OJ L78, 24.3.2009, p 1)

(formerly Council Regulation (EC) 40/94 (OJ L11, 14.1.94, p 1)) and by European Parliament and Council Directive (EC) 2008/95 (OJ L299, 8.11.2008, p 25) to approximate the laws of the member states relating to trade marks (formerly Council Directive (EEC) 89/104 (OJ L40, 11.2.89, p 1)) (which provides the requirements for registration in the member states: see PARA 5).

8 There will be many marks which are not registrable as Community trade marks but could be registered as national trade marks. In particular, where the requirements for registration as a Community trade mark are not met in any one member state, the trade mark may not be so registered: see Council Regulation (EC) 207/2009 (OJ L78, 24.3.2009, p 1) art 7(2); and PARA 192. However this would not prevent registration in those member states in which the requirements for registration provided for by European Parliament and Council Directive (EC) 2008/95 (OJ L299, 8.11.2008, p 25) were met.

A Community trade mark or an application for a Community trade mark may be converted into a national trade mark application if it ceases to have effect: see PARAS 180–186.

9 Ie in particular, the requirements for registration of a Community trade mark (cf the corresponding provisions under the Trade Marks Act 1994: see PARA 39 et seq), infringement (cf PARA 66 et seq) and revocation or invalidity (cf PARA 98 et seq).

10 Ie European Parliament and Council Directive (EC) 2008/95 (OJ L299, 8.11.2008, p 25) to approximate the laws of the member states relating to trade marks. See generally PARA 5.

11 See e g Case C-191/01P *Wm Wrigley Jr Co v Office for Harmonisation in the Internal Market (Trade Marks and Designs)* [2004] All ER (EC) 1040, sub nom *Office for Harmonisation in the Internal Market (Trade Marks and Designs) v Wm Wrigley Jr Co* [2003] ECR I-12447, ECJ. As to the law of registered trade marks in the United Kingdom see PARA 2 et seq.

However see also *Antoni and Alison's Application* [1998] ETMR 460, OHIM Board of Appeal (where it was said that is was not appropriate for the Board of Appeal to consider the interpretation of Council Directive (EEC) 89/104 (OJ L40, 11.2.89, p 1) by the member states); *Penny Makinson's (PI Associates') Application* [1999] ETMR 234, OHIM Board of Appeal.

12 See Council Regulation (EC) 1992/2003 (OJ L296, 14.11.03, p 1) on the Community trade mark to give effect to the accession of the European Community to the Protocol relating to the Madrid Agreement concerning the international registration of marks adopted at Madrid on 27 June 1989; and Council Decision (EC) 2003/793 (OJ L296, 14.11.03, p 20) approving the accession of the European Community to the Protocol relating to the Madrid Agreement concerning the international registration of marks, adopted at Madrid on 27 June 1989. As to the Madrid Agreement and the Protocol see PARA 8.

13 As to the international registration of marks under the Madrid Protocol see Council Regulation (EC) 207/2009 (OJ L78, 24.3.2009, p 1) arts 145–161. As to procedures concerning the international registration of marks see Commission Regulation (EC) 2868/95 (OJ L303, 15.12.95, p 1) implementing Council Regulation (EC) 40/94 on the Community trade mark, art 1 rr 102–126 (all added by Commission Regulation (EC) 782/2004 (OJ L123, 27.4.2004, p 88); and Commission Regulation (EC) 2868/95 (OJ L303, 15.12.95, p 1) rr 114, 122 amended by Commission Regulation (EC) 1041/2005 (OJ L172, 5.7.2005, p 4)). The details of these provisions are outside the scope of this work, but the system is comparable to that under the Trade Marks Act 1994 (see PARA 11 et seq).

A trade mark which is entitled to protection in the European Union by virtue of the Madrid Protocol is referred to in the Trade Marks Act 1994 as an 'international trade mark (EC)': see PARA 8 note 17.

160. Domestic implementation of the Community Trade Mark Regulation.

The Community Trade Mark Regulation[1] has general application. It is binding in its entirety and directly applicable in all member states[2]. Accordingly there is no Act of Parliament or secondary legislation which gives effect to the Regulation. The provisions of the Regulation have the force of law without such implementation[3].

The Secretary of State[4] may by regulations make such provision as he considers appropriate in connection with the operation of the Community Trade Mark Regulation[5]. Provision may in particular be made with respect to: (1) the making of applications for Community trade marks[6] by way of the Intellectual Property Office ('IPO')[7]; (2) the procedures for determining a posteriori the invalidity, or liability to revocation, of the registration of a trade mark from which a Community trade mark claims seniority; (3) the conversion of a

Community trade mark, or an application for a Community trade mark, into an application for registration under the Trade Marks Act 1994; (4) the designation of courts in the United Kingdom having jurisdiction over proceedings arising out of the Community Trade Mark Regulation[8].

Without prejudice to the generality of the above, provision may be made by regulations[9]: (a) applying in relation to a Community trade mark the statutory provisions relating to the remedy for groundless threats of infringement proceedings[10], the importation of infringing goods, material or articles[11], and offences[12]; and (b) making, in relation to the list of professional representatives[13] and persons on that list, provision corresponding to that made by, or capable of being made under, the statutory provisions[14] in relation to the register of trade mark attorneys and registered trade mark attorneys[15].

1   Ie Council Regulation (EC) 207/2009 (OJ L78, 24.3.2009, p 1) on the Community trade mark.

2   Treaty Establishing the European Community (Rome, 25 March 1957; TS1 (1973); Cmnd 5179) art 249 (formerly art 189; renumbered by virtue of the Treaty of Amsterdam: see *Treaty Citation (No 2) (Note)* [1999] All ER (EC) 646, ECJ) (and see now the Treaty on the Functioning of the European Union (Rome, 25 March 1957; TS 1 (1973); Cmnd 5179) ('TFEU') art 288 (see PARA 86 note 8); Council Regulation (EC) 40/94 (OJ L11, 14.1.94, p 1) art 160(4), 2nd para (amended by Council Regulation (EC) 1992/2003 (OJ L296, 14.11.03, p 1)).

3   It could, however, be said that the European Communities Act 1972 provides for the implementation of the Community Trade Mark Regulation: see the European Communities Act 1972 s 2(1) (amended by the European Union (Amendment) Act 2008 Schedule Pt 1).

4   As to the Secretary of State see PARA 16.

5   Trade Marks Act 1994 ss 51, 52(1). See note 8. References in the Trade Marks Act 1994 to an EU instrument include references to any instrument amending or replacing that instrument: s 103(3) (amended by SI 2011/1043).

6   For these purposes, 'Community trade marks' has the meaning given by Council Regulation (EC) 207/2009 (OJ L78, 24.3.2009, p 1) art 1(1) (see PARA 189): Trade Marks Act 1994 s 51. As to the meaning of 'United Kingdom' see PARA 3 note 2.

7   As to the Intellectual Property Office (an operating name of the Patent Office) see PARA 16 note 2.

8   Trade Marks Act 1994 ss 51, 52(2). Regulations under s 52 must be made by statutory instrument which is subject to annulment in pursuance of a resolution of either House of Parliament: s 52(4).

      The following regulations have been so made: (1) the Community Trade Mark (Fees) Regulations 1995, SI 1995/3175 (see PARA 261 note 6); (2) the Trade Marks (International Registrations Designating the European Community, etc) Regulations 2004, SI 2004/2332; (3) the Community Trade Mark Regulations 2006, SI 2006/1027 (see PARAS 179, 185, 233, 249–252, 271, 331).

      Many of the provisions of the Community Trade Mark Regulations 2006, SI 2006/1027, also apply to international trade marks (EC): reg 2(2). To that extent the regulations are better regarded as having been made pursuant to the Trade Marks Act 1994 s 54: see PARA 8.

9   As to the regulations see note 8.

10   Ie the Trade Marks Act 1994 s 21: see PARAS 107–109, 249.

11   Ie the Trade Marks Act 1994 ss 89–91: see PARAS 132–135, 250.

12   Ie the Trade Marks Act 1994 s 92 (see PARAS 124–127), s 93 (see PARA 129), s 95 (see PARA 131) and s 96 (supplementary provisions relating to summary proceedings in Scotland). See also PARA 251.

13   Ie the list maintained in pursuance of Council Regulation (EC) 207/2009 (OJ L78, 24.3.2009, p 1) art 93: see PARAS 177–178.

14   Ie the Trade Marks Act 1994 ss 84–88: see PARA 34 et seq.

15   Trade Marks Act 1994 s 52(3) (amended by the Legal Services Act 2007 Sch 21 para 110).

161. Community implementing provisions. The rules implementing the Community Trade Mark Regulation[1] must be adopted in an Implementing Regulation[2].

The Implementing Regulation[3] came into force on 22 December 1995[4], and it provides for the detailed operation of the Office for Harmonisation in the Internal Market[5] and for the procedures of the Office[6].

1   Ie Council Regulation (EC) 207/2009 (OJ L78, 24.3.2009, p 1) on the Community trade mark.

2   Council Regulation (EC) 207/2009 (OJ L78, 24.3.2009, p 1) art 162(1). See note 3.

3   The Implementing Regulation is Commission Regulation (EC) 2868/95 (OJ L303, 15.12.95, p 1) implementing Council Regulation (EC) 40/94 on the Community trade mark. The rules of procedure of the Boards of Appeal created by Council Regulation (EC) 40/94 (OJ L11, 14.1.94, p 1) (see now Council Regulation (EC) 207/2009 (OJ L78, 24.3.2009, p 1)) must be adopted and amended in accordance with the procedure laid down in art 163(2): art 162(3). The rules implementing Council Regulation (EC) 40/94 (OJ L11, 14.1.94, p 1) (now Council Regulation (EC) 207/2009 (OJ L78, 24.3.2009, p 1)) are provided by Commission Regulation (EC) 2868/95 (OJ L303, 15.12.95, p 1) art 1 (amended by Commission Regulation (EC) 782/2004 (OJ L123, 27.4.04, p 88); and Commission Regulation (EC) 1041/2005 (OJ L172. 5.7.05, p 4)); and transitional provisions are provided for by Commission Regulation (EC) 2868/95 (OJ L303, 15.12.95, p 1) art 2 (amended by Commission Regulation (EC) 355/2009 (OJ L109, 30.4.2009, p 3)).

4   Commission Regulation (EC) 2868/95 (OJ L303, 15.12.95, p 1) art 3.

5   As to the Office for Harmonisation in the Internal Market see PARA 163 et seq. For an outline of the procedure in the Office see PARA 260 et seq.

6   The detail of the rules laid down by Commission Regulation (EC) 2868/95 (OJ L303, 15.12.95, p 1) is beyond the scope of this work, although the content of those rules is summarised or referred to where appropriate.

162. Commencement and transitional provisions. The provisions of the Community Trade Mark Regulation[1] entered into force on 15 March 1994[2]. Applications for Community trade marks[3] were permitted to be filed at the Office for Harmonisation in the Internal Market[4] from 1 April 1996[5].

The member states were required to take the necessary measures[6] for the purpose of implementing the Regulation by 15 March 1997[7].

1   Ie Council Regulation (EC) 40/94 (OJ L11, 14.1.94, p 1) on the Community trade mark (now Council Regulation (EC) 207/2009 (OJ L78, 24.3.2009, p 1) on the Community trade mark).

2   Ie the date the original Regulation entered into force: see Council Regulation (EC) 40/94 (OJ L11, 14.1.94, p 1) art 160(1) (amended by Council Regulation (EC) 1992/2003 (OJ L296, 14.11.03, p 1)). The date mentioned in the text is the 60th day following that of the publication of the Regulation in the Official Journal of the European Communities: Council Regulation (EC) 40/94 (OJ L11, 14.1.94, p 1) art 160(1) (as so amended). As to the date of entry into force of Council Regulation (EC) 207/2009 (OJ L78, 24.3.2009, p 1) see art 167(1).

3   As to the meaning of 'Community trade mark' see PARA 189. As to applications for Community trade marks see PARAS 261–266.

4   As to the Office for Harmonisation in the Internal Market see PARA 163 et seq.

5   See Council Regulation (EC) 40/94 (OJ L11, 14.1.94, p 1) art 160(3) (amended by Council Regulation (EC) 1992/2003 (OJ L296, 14.11.03, p 1)). The date mentioned in the text is the date fixed by the Administrative Board of the Office pursuant to Council Regulation (EC) 40/94 (OJ L11, 14.1.94, p 1) art 160(3) (as so amended). Applications for Community trade marks filed within three months before that date are deemed to have been filed on that date: art 160(4), 1st para (amended by Council Regulation (EC) 1992/2003 (OJ L296, 14.11.03, p 1)).

6   Ie the necessary measures for the purpose of implementing what is now Council Regulation (EC) 207/2009 (OJ L78, 24.3.2009, p 1) art 95 (see PARA 233) and art 114 (see PARA 184). The United Kingdom measures are now contained in the Community Trade Mark Regulations 2006, SI 2006/1027: see PARA 160 note 8.

7   See Council Regulation (EC) 207/2009 (OJ L78, 24.3.2009, p 1) art 167(2).

(2) ADMINISTRATION

(i) The Office for Harmonisation in the Internal Market

163.   The Office for Harmonisation in the Internal Market. The Community Trade Mark Regulation[1] established the Office for Harmonisation in the Internal Market (Trade Marks and Designs), referred to in the Regulation as 'the Office'[2]. It has legal personality[3] and is represented and managed by its President[4]. The Office has its seat in Alicante, Spain[5].

The Protocol on the Privileges and Immunities of the European Communities[6] applies to the Office[7].

The contractual liability of the Office is governed by the law applicable to the contract in question[8]. In the case of non-contractual liability, the Office must, in accordance with the general principles common to the laws of the member states, make good any damage caused by its departments or by its servants in the performance of their duties[9].

The Office has also been entrusted with tasks related to the enforcement of intellectual property rights[10].

1   Ie Council Regulation (EC) 207/2009 (OJ L78, 24.3.2009, p 1) on the Community trade mark (formerly Council Regulation (EC) 40/94 (OJ L11, 14.1.94, p 1)).
2   Council Regulation (EC) 207/2009 (OJ L78, 24.3.2009, p 1) art 2. The Office is a body of the Community: art 115(1). The administration of the Office is provided for by arts 116, 118(5), 124–143. Those provisions are not within the scope of this work but are summarised in PARA 164 et seq.
3   Council Regulation (EC) 207/2009 (OJ L78, 24.3.2009, p 1) art 115(1). In each of the member states the Office enjoys the most extensive legal protection accorded to legal persons under their laws; it may in particular acquire or dispose of movable and immovable property and may be a party to legal proceedings: art 115(2).
4   Council Regulation (EC) 207/2009 (OJ L78, 24.3.2009, p 1) arts 115(3), 124(1). The particular functions of the President are laid down by art 124(2).
5   See the Statement by the Council and the Commission on the seat of the Office for Harmonisation in the Internal Market (Trade Marks and Designs) (OJ L11, 14.1.94, p 36).
6   Ie the Protocol on the Privileges and Immunities of the European Union (Brussels 8 April 1965; TS 1 (1973); Cmnd 5179): see INTERNATIONAL RELATIONS LAW vol 61 (2010) PARA 304 et seq.
7   Council Regulation (EC) 207/2009 (OJ L78, 24.3.2009, p 1) art 117.
8   Council Regulation (EC) 207/2009 (OJ L78, 24.3.2009, p 1) art 118(1). The European Court of Justice is competent to give judgment pursuant to any arbitration clause contained in a contract concluded by the Office: art 118(2).
9   Council Regulation (EC) 207/2009 (OJ L78, 24.3.2009, p 1) art 118(3). The European Court of Justice has jurisdiction in disputes relating to compensation for the damage referred to in this provision: art 118(4).
10 See European Parliament and Council Regulation (EU) 386/2012 (OJ L129, 16.5.2012, p 1) on entrusting the Office for Harmonisation in the Internal Market (Trade Marks and Designs) with tasks related to the enforcement of intellectual property rights, including the assembling of public and private sector representatives as a European Observatory on Infringements of Intellectual Property Rights.

164.   Staff and senior officials of the Office. The Community Trade Mark Regulation[1] makes provision for the employment of staff by the Office for Harmonisation in the Internal Market[2]. In general, the regulations[3] relating to staff of European Union bodies apply to the staff of the Office[4], and the powers conferred on those bodies by those regulations may be exercised by the Office in respect of its staff[5].

The President and any Vice-Presidents[6] of the Office are appointed by the European Council[7].

1   Ie Council Regulation (EC) 207/2009 (OJ L78, 24.3.2009, p 1) on the Community trade mark.

2   See Council Regulation (EC) 207/2009 (OJ L78, 24.3.2009, p 1) arts 116, 118(5). As to the establishment etc of the Office for Harmonisation in the Internal Market see PARA 163.

3   Ie the Staff Regulations of officials of the European Communities, the Conditions of Employment of other servants of the European Communities, and the rules adopted by agreement between the Institutions of the European Communities for giving effect to those Staff Regulations and Conditions of Employment apply to the staff of the Office.

4   Council Regulation (EC) 207/2009 (OJ L78, 24.3.2009, p 1) art 116(1).

5   Council Regulation (EC) 207/2009 (OJ L78, 24.3.2009, p 1) art 116(2).

6   As to Vice-Presidents see Council Regulation (EC) 207/2009 (OJ L78, 24.3.2009, p 1) art 124(3).

7   See Council Regulation (EC) 207/2009 (OJ L78, 24.3.2009, p 1) art 125, which lays down the procedure for and terms of their appointment.

165. Organs of the Office. The Community Trade Mark Regulation[1] makes provision for the following organs of the Office for Harmonisation in the Internal Market, in addition to the President and Vice-Presidents[2]:

(1)   the Administrative Board[3];

(2)   the Examiners[4];

(3)   the Opposition Divisions[5];

(4)   the Administration of Trade Marks and Designs and Legal Division[6];

(5)   the Cancellation Divisions[7];

(6)   the Boards of Appeal[8]; and

(7)   the Budget Committee[9].

1   Ie Council Regulation (EC) 207/2009 (OJ L78, 24.3.2009, p 1) on the Community trade mark.

2   As to the President and Vice-Presidents see PARAS 163–164. As to the establishment etc of the Office for Harmonisation in the Internal Market see PARA 163 et seq. The internal structure of the Office is regularly revised. As at the date at which this volume states the law, the structure is set out in Decision ADM-12–19 (11 September 2012).

3   The Administrative Board is set up by Council Regulation (EC) 207/2009 (OJ L78, 24.3.2009, p 1) art 126(1) and its powers, duties and organisation are governed by arts 126–129.

4   Examiners are competent to act pursuant to Council Regulation (EC) 207/2009 (OJ L78, 24.3.2009, p 1) art 130(a). An examiner is responsible for taking decisions on behalf of the Office in relation to an application for registration of a Community trade mark, including the matters referred to in art 36, art 38 and art 68 (see PARAS 262, 280): art 131. They are governed by art 137.

5   Opposition Divisions are competent to act pursuant to Council Regulation (EC) 207/2009 (OJ L78, 24.3.2009, p 1) art 130(b). They are responsible for taking decisions on an opposition to an application to register a Community trade mark (see PARA 265): art 132(1). As to their composition see arts 132(2), 137.

6   The Administration of Trade Marks and Designs and Legal Division is competent to act pursuant to Council Regulation (EC) 207/2009 (OJ L78, 24.3.2009, p 1) art 130(c). Its powers and duties are governed by arts 133, 137. No department of the Office with this name exists. As at the date at which this volume states the law, most of its functions are carried out by the Operations Support Department.

7   Cancellation Divisions are competent to act pursuant to Council Regulation (EC) 207/2009 (OJ L78, 24.3.2009, p 1) art 130(d). They are responsible for taking decisions in relation to an application for the revocation or declaration of invalidity of a Community trade mark (see PARAS 272–273): art 134(1). As to their composition see arts 134(2), 137.

8   The Boards of Appeal are competent to act pursuant to Council Regulation (EC) 207/2009 (OJ L78, 24.3.2009, p 1) art 130(e). They are responsible for deciding appeals from the decisions of Examiners, the Opposition Divisions, the Administration of Trade Marks and Legal Division and the Cancellation Divisions: art 135(1). As to their composition see arts 135(2), 136, 137. The Boards of Appeal form part of the administrative office responsible for registering trade marks and, although they enjoy a wide degree of independence while carrying out their duties, they are not to be classified as tribunals and the Convention for the Protection of Human Rights and Fundamental Freedoms (Rome, 4 November 1950; TS 71 (1953) Cmd 8969) ('the European Convention of Human Rights') art 6(1) (see RIGHTS AND FREEDOMS vol 88A (2013) PARAS 88, 243 et seq) does not apply: Case T-63/01 *Procter and Gamble v Office for Harmonisation in the Internal Market (Trade Marks and Designs)* [2002] ECR II-5255, (2002) Times, 28 December, CFI; Case T-273/01 *Krüger v Office for Harmonisation in the Internal*

Market (Trade Marks and Designs) [2005] ECR II-1271, [2005] All ER (D) 261 (Apr), CFI; Case T-284/11 *Metropolis Inmobiliarias y Restauraciones SL v Office for Harmonisation in the Internal Market (Trade Marks and Designs)* [2013] ECR II-0000, [2013] All ER (D) 91 (May), EGC; but cf *Lenzing AG's European Patent (UK)* [1997] RPC 245, sub nom *R v Comptroller of Patents, Designs and Trade Marks, ex p Lenzing AG* [1997] 9 LS Gaz R 31 (a patent case). As to appeals to a Board of Appeal see PARA 274 et seq.

There is provision for an Enlarged Board of Appeal (also known as the Grand Board of Appeal) chaired by the President of the Boards of Appeal to decide certain specific cases where the legal difficulty or the importance of the case or special circumstances justify it: Council Regulation (EC) 207/2009 (OJ L78, 24.3.2009, p 1) art 135(2)–(5). It is understood that the Enlarged Board of Appeal was created mainly to ensure consistency in the Office's case law, as with its counterpart the Enlarged Board of Appeal of the European Patent Office; but the need for this may be questioned given the appellate jurisdiction of the Court of First Instance (now the European General Court) and the European Court of Justice (see PARA 277). It may be noted that the economic importance of the case has already been regarded as sufficient justification for a reference to the Enlarged Board of Appeal: Case R 856/2004-G *Lego Juris A/S v Mega Brands Inc* [2007] ETMR 11, OHIM Enlarged Board of Appeal. The Enlarged Board of Appeal issued its first decision in Case R 495/2005-G *Application of Kenneth (t/a Screw You)* [2007] ETMR 7, OHIM Enlarged Board of Appeal.

9   As to the Budget Committee see PARA 166.

166. Budget and financial control. The Budget Committee[1] is responsible for the budget and financial control of the Office for Harmonisation in the Internal Market[2], in particular the adoption of the Office's budget[3]. An internal audit function must be set up within the Office, with an internal auditor appointed by the President responsible for verifying the proper operation of budget implementation systems and procedures of the Office[4]. The Budget Committee must also adopt internal financial provisions for the Office[5].

1   The Budget Committee is set up, attached to the Office for Harmonisation in the Internal Market, by Council Regulation (EC) 207/2009 (OJ L78, 24.3.2009, p 1) art 138(1). Its organisation is governed by arts 126(5), 127, 128, 129(1)–(4), (6), (7): art 138(2). The Budget Committee has the powers assigned to it by Council Regulation (EC) 207/2009 (OJ L78, 24.3.2009, p 1) on the Community trade mark, arts 38(4), 138–144: art 138(1). As to the establishment etc of the Office for Harmonisation in the Internal Market see PARA 163 et seq.

2   See Council Regulation (EC) 207/2009 (OJ L78, 24.3.2009, p 1) arts 138–143.

3   Council Regulation (EC) 207/2009 (OJ L78, 24.3.2009, p 1) art 140(3). As to the contents and preparation of the Office's budget see arts 139–140. In particular, the revenue and expenditure shown in the budget must balance: art 139(2).

4   Council Regulation (EC) 207/2009 (OJ L78, 24.3.2009, p 1) art 137. As to the President see PARAS 163–164.

5   See Council Regulation (EC) 207/2009 (OJ L78, 24.3.2009, p 1) art 143, which sets out the procedure for the adoption of such provisions.

167. Fees. Provision is made for fees regulations[1], which must determine the amounts of fees and the ways in which they are paid[2]. The amounts of the fees must be fixed at such a level as to ensure that the revenue in respect thereof is in principle sufficient for the budget of the Office for Harmonisation in the Internal Market[3] to be balanced[4].

Fees must be charged in particular in the cases listed below[5]:

(1)   late payment of the registration fee[6];

(2)   issue of a copy of the certificate of registration;

(3)   registration of a licence or another right in respect of a Community trade mark;

(4)   registration of a licence or another right in respect of an application for a Community trade mark;

(5)   cancellation of the registration of a licence or another right;

(6)   alteration of a registered Community trade mark[7];

(7)   issue of an extract from the register;
(8)   inspection of the files[8];
(9)   issue of copies of file documents;
(10) issue of certified copies of the application;
(11) communication of information in a file; and
(12) review of the determination of the procedural costs to be refunded.

1   See the Council Regulation (EC) 207/2009 (OJ L78, 24.3.2009, p 1) on the Community trade
    mark, art 144. The fees regulations must be adopted and amended in accordance with the
    procedure laid down in art 163(2): art 144(3). Commission Regulation (EC) 2869/95 (OJ L303,
    15.12.95, p 33) on the fees payable to the Office for Harmonisation in the Internal Market
    (Trade Marks and Designs) (amended by Commission Regulation (EC) 781/2004 (OJ L123,
    27.4.04, p 85); Commission Regulation (EC) 1042/2005 (OJ L172, 5.7.05, p 22); Commission
    Regulation (EC) 1687/2005 (OJ L271, 15.10.05, p 14); and Commission Regulation (EC)
    355/2009 (OJ L109, 30.4.2009, p 3)) was so adopted.
2   Council Regulation (EC) 207/2009 (OJ L78, 24.3.2009, p 1) art 144(1). Rights of the Office to
    the payment of a fee are extinguished after four years from the end of the calendar year in which
    the fee fell due (art 84(1)), and rights against the Office for the refunding of fees or sums of
    money paid in excess of a fee are extinguished after four years from the end of the calendar year
    in which the right arose (art 84(2)). That four year period is interrupted in the case covered by
    art 84(1) by a request for payment of the fee and in the case covered by art 84(2) by a reasoned
    claim in writing; on interruption it begins again immediately and ends at the latest six years after
    the end of the year in which it originally began, unless, in the meantime, judicial proceedings to
    enforce the right have begun; and in this case the period ends at the earliest one year after the
    judgment has acquired the authority of a final decision: art 84(3).
        The President of the Office may waive action for the enforced recovery of any sum due
    where the sum to be recovered is minimal or where such recovery is too uncertain: Commission
    Regulation (EC) 2868/95 (OJ L303, 15.12.95, p 1) implementing Council Regulation (EC)
    40/94 on the Community trade mark, art 1 r 74.
3   As to the establishment etc of the Office for Harmonisation in the Internal Market see PARA 163
    et seq.
4   Council Regulation (EC) 207/2009 (OJ L78, 24.3.2009, p 1) art 144(2). The Office is obliged to
    produce a balanced budget: see art 139(2); and PARA 166 note 3.
5   See Council Regulation (EC) 207/2009 (OJ L78, 24.3.2009, p 1) art 162(2).
6   As to registration of a licence or another right in respect of a Community trade mark see
    Council Regulation (EC) 207/2009 (OJ L78, 24.3.2009, p 1) arts 22(5), 23; and PARAS
    258–259.
7   As to alteration of a registered Community trade mark see Council Regulation (EC) 207/2009
    (OJ L78, 24.3.2009, p 1) art 48; and PARA 231.
8   As to the inspection of the Office's files see Council Regulation (EC) 207/2009 (OJ L78,
    24.3.2009, p 1) art 88; and PARA 172.

168.   Languages in the Office. The languages of the Office for Harmonisation
in the Internal Market are English, French, German, Italian and Spanish[1].
    An application for a Community trade mark[2] must be filed in one of the
official languages of the European Community[3]. The applicant must indicate a
second language, which must be a language of the Office, the use of which he
accepts as a possible language of proceedings for opposition, revocation or
invalidity proceedings[4]. Where the applicant for a Community trade mark is the
sole party to proceedings before the Office, the language of proceedings is the
language used for filing the application for a Community trade mark[5].
    The notice of opposition and an application for revocation or invalidity must
be filed in one of the languages of the Office[6]. If the language chosen[7] for the
notice of opposition or the application for revocation or invalidity is the
language of the application for a trade mark or the second language indicated
when the application was filed, that language will be the language of the
proceedings[8].

If the language chosen[9] for the notice of opposition or the application for revocation or invalidity is neither the language of the application for a trade mark nor the second language indicated when the application was filed, the opposing party or the party seeking revocation or invalidity is required to produce, at his own expense, a translation of his application either into the language of the application for a trade mark, provided that it is a language of the Office, or into the second language indicated when the application was filed[10]. The language into which the application has been translated will then become the language of the proceedings[11].

Parties to opposition, revocation, invalidity or appeal proceedings may agree that a different official language of the European Community is to be the language of the proceedings[12].

1   Council Regulation (EC) 207/2009 (OJ L78, 24.3.2009, p 1) on the Community trade mark, art 119(2). A challenge to the legality of the language regime established by what was then Council Regulation (EC) 40/94 (OJ L11, 14.1.94, p 1) art 115 on the ground that it was contrary to the Treaty Establishing the European Community (Rome, 25 March 1957; TS 1 (1973); Cmnd 5179) (the 'EC Treaty') art 6 (see now the Treaty on the Functioning of the European Union (Rome, 25 March 1957; TS 1 (1973); Cmnd 5179) ('TFEU') art 11 (see PARA 86 note 8)) was unsuccessful: Case C-361/01P *Kik v Office for Harmonisation in the Internal Market (Trade Marks and Designs)* [2003] ECR I-8283, [2004] IP & T 403, ECJ. Further provisions as to the use of languages in the Office are provided for by Commission Regulation (EC) 2868/95 (OJ L303, 15.12.95, p 1) implementing Council Regulation (EC) 40/94 on the Community trade mark (the 'Implementing Regulation') art 1 rr 16, 38, 95–99 (rr 16, 98 substituted, and r 38 amended, by Commission Regulation (EC) 1041/2005 (OJ L172, 5.7.05, p 4)). There is a body of case law of the Office for Harmonisation in the Internal Market Boards of Appeal and of the European General Court (formerly the Court of First Instance), not all of it consistent, on the interpretation and application of these provisions; for an example see Case T-6/05 *DEF-TEC Defense Technology GmbH v Office for Harmonisation in the Internal Market (Trade Marks and Designs)* [2006] ECR II-2671, [2006] All ER (D) 23 (Sep), CFI. As to the establishment etc of the Office for Harmonisation in the Internal Market see PARA 163 et seq. As to translation services required by the Office see Council Regulation (EC) 207/2009 (OJ L78, 24.3.2009, p 1) art 121.
2   As to the meaning of 'Community trade mark' see PARA 189. As to applications for Community trade marks see PARAS 261–266.
3   Council Regulation (EC) 207/2009 (OJ L78, 24.3.2009, p 1) art 119(1).
4   Council Regulation (EC) 207/2009 (OJ L78, 24.3.2009, p 1) art 119(3). If the application was filed in a language which is not one of the languages of the Office, the Office must arrange to have the application, as described in art 26(1) (see PARA 261), translated into the language indicated by the applicant: art 119(3).
5   Council Regulation (EC) 207/2009 (OJ L78, 24.3.2009, p 1) art 119(4). If the application was made in a language other than the languages of the Office, the Office may send written communications to the applicant in the second language indicated by the applicant in his application: art 119(4). Procedural documents must be drawn up by the Office in the language used for filing the application; the written communications which may be sent in the second language are any communications which from their content cannot be regarded as amounting to procedural documents: Case C-361/01P *Kik v Office for Harmonisation in the Internal Market (Trade Marks and Designs)* [2003] ECR I-8283, [2004] IP & T 403, ECJ.
6   Council Regulation (EC) 207/2009 (OJ L78, 24.3.2009, p 1) art 119(5).
7   Ie one of the languages of the Office, in accordance with Council Regulation (EC) 207/2009 (OJ L78, 24.3.2009, p 1) art 119(5): see the text and note 6.
8   Council Regulation (EC) 207/2009 (OJ L78, 24.3.2009, p 1) art 119(6).
9   See note 7.
10   Council Regulation (EC) 207/2009 (OJ L78, 24.3.2009, p 1) art 119(6). The translation must be produced within the period prescribed in the Implementing Regulation (see note 1): art 119(6).
11   Council Regulation (EC) 207/2009 (OJ L78, 24.3.2009, p 1) art 119(6).
12   Council Regulation (EC) 207/2009 (OJ L78, 24.3.2009, p 1) art 119(7).

169.   Control of legality.   The European Commission must check the legality of: (1) those acts of the President[1] of the Office for Harmonisation in the Internal

Market[2] in respect of which Community law does not provide for any check on legality by another body; and (2) acts of the Budget Committee[3] attached to the Office[4]. It must require that any such unlawful acts be altered or annulled[5].

Member states and any person directly and personally involved may refer to the Commission such an act, whether express or implied, for the Commission to examine the legality of that act. Such referral must be made within one month of the day on which the party concerned first became aware of the act in question. The Commission must take a decision within three months. If no decision has been taken within this period, the case is deemed to have been dismissed[6].

1   As to the President see PARAS 163–164.
2   As to the establishment etc of the Office for Harmonisation in the Internal Market see PARA 163 et seq.
3   As to the Budget Committee see PARA 166.
4   Council Regulation (EC) 207/2009 (OJ L78, 24.3.2009, p 1) on the Community trade mark, art 122(1). The Budget Committee is attached to the Office pursuant to art 138: art 122(1). As to the Budget Committee see PARA 166.
5   Council Regulation (EC) 207/2009 (OJ L78, 24.3.2009, p 1) art 122(2).
6   Council Regulation (EC) 207/2009 (OJ L78, 24.3.2009, p 1) art 122(3).

170.   Access to documents.   The provisions[1] regarding access to European Parliament, Council and Commission documents also apply to documents held by the Office for Harmonisation in the Internal Market[2].

1   Ie under Parliament and Council Regulation (EC) 1049/2001 (OJ L145, 31.5.01, p 43) regarding public access to European Parliament, Council and Commission documents.
2   Council Regulation (EC) 207/2009 (OJ L78, 24.3.2009, p 1) on the Community trade mark, art 123(1). The Administrative Board was required to adopt the practical arrangements for implementing these provisions: art 123(2). Decisions taken by the Office pursuant to Parliament and Council Regulation (EC) 1049/2001 (OJ L145, 31.5.01, p 43) art 8 may give rise to the lodging of a complaint to the Ombudsman or form the subject of an action before the Court of Justice under the conditions laid down in the Treaty Establishing the European Community (Rome, 25 March 1957; TS 1 (1973); Cmnd 5179) (the 'EC Treaty') arts 195, 230 respectively (see now the Treaty on the Functioning of the European Union (Rome, 25 March 1957; TS 1 (1973); Cmnd 5179) ('TFEU') arts 228, 263 respectively (see PARA 86 note 8)): Council Regulation (EC) 207/2009 (OJ L78, 24.3.2009, p 1) art 123(3). As to the establishment etc of the Office for Harmonisation in the Internal Market see PARA 163 et seq; and as to the Administrative Board see PARA 165 text and note 3.

(ii) Public Information

171.   The register of Community trade marks.   The Office for Harmonisation in the Internal Market[1] must keep a register, to be known as the register of Community trade marks, which must contain the prescribed particulars[2]; the register must be open to public inspection[3].

An application for a Community trade mark[4] and other prescribed information[5] must be published in all the official languages of the European Community[6].

1   As to the Office for Harmonisation in the Internal Market see PARA 163 et seq.
2   Ie those particulars the registration or inclusion of which is provided for by Council Regulation (EC) 207/2009 (OJ L78, 24.3.2009, p 1) on the Community trade mark (formerly Council Regulation (EC) 40/94 (OJ L11, 14.1.94, p 1)), or by Commission Regulation (EC) 2868/95 (OJ L303, 15.12.95, p 1) implementing Council Regulation (EC) 40/94 on the Community trade mark. Article 1 r 84 (amended by Commission Regulation (EC) 782/2004 (OJ L123, 27.4.04, p 88); and by Commission Regulation (EC) 1041/2005 (OJ L172, 5.7.05, p 4)) specifies precisely what the register must contain.

Perhaps the most important particular, the registration of which is provided for, is the registration of Community trade marks: see Council Regulation (EC) 207/2009 (OJ L78, 24.3.2009, p 1) art 45; and PARA 266.

The Office must also maintain an electronic data bank with the particulars of applications for registrations and entries in the register, which must be made available to the public: see Commission Regulation (EC) 2868/95 (OJ L303, 15.12.95, p 1) art 1 r 87.

3   Council Regulation (EC) 207/2009 (OJ L78, 24.3.2009, p 1) art 87.

4   As to the meaning of 'Community trade mark' see PARA 189. As to applications for Community trade marks see PARAS 261–266.

5   Ie all other information the publication of which is prescribed by Council Regulation (EC) 207/2009 (OJ L78, 24.3.2009, p 1) or Commission Regulation (EC) 2868/95 (OJ L303, 15.12.95, p 1).

6   Council Regulation (EC) 207/2009 (OJ L78, 24.3.2009, p 1) art 120(1). All entries in the register of Community trade marks must be made in all the official languages of the European Community: art 120(2). In cases of doubt, the text in the language of the Office in which the application for the Community trade mark was filed is authentic: art 120(3). If the application was filed in an official language of the European Community other than one of the languages of the Office, the text in the second language indicated by the applicant is authentic: art 120(3). As to the use of languages in the Office see PARA 168.

172.   Inspection of the Office's files.   The files relating to a Community trade mark[1] application[2] which have not yet been published[3] must not be made available for inspection without the consent of the applicant[4]. However, any person who can prove that the applicant for a Community trade mark has stated that, after the trade mark has been registered, he will invoke the rights under it against him, may obtain inspection of the files prior to the publication of that application and without the consent of the applicant[5].

Subsequent to the publication of the Community trade mark application, the files relating to the application and the resulting trade mark may be inspected on request[6].

However, where the files are inspected pursuant to the above provisions[7], certain documents in the file may be withheld from inspection[8].

1   As to the meaning of 'Community trade mark' see PARA 189.

2   As to applications for Community trade marks see PARAS 261–266.

3   As to publication see PARA 173.

4   Council Regulation (EC) 207/2009 (OJ L78, 24.3.2009, p 1) on the Community trade mark, art 88(1). Rules as to the keeping of files are provided for by Commission Regulation (EC) 2868/95 (OJ L303, 15.12.95, p 1) implementing Council Regulation (EC) 40/94 on the Community trade mark, art 1 r 91 (substituted by Commission Regulation (EC) 1041/2005 (OJ L172, 5.7.05, p 4)).

5   Council Regulation (EC) 207/2009 (OJ L78, 24.3.2009, p 1) art 88(2).

6   Council Regulation (EC) 207/2009 (OJ L78, 24.3.2009, p 1) art 88(3). The procedure for such inspection, and for communication of information in the files, is provided for by Commission Regulation (EC) 2868/95 (OJ L303, 15.12.95, p 1) art 1 rr 88–91 (r 89 amended by Commission Regulation (EC) 782/2004 (OJ L123, 27.4.04, p 88); and by Commission Regulation (EC) 1041/2005 (OJ L172, 5.7.05, p 4) and Commission Regulation (EC) 2868/95 (OJ L303, 15.12.95, p 1) r 91 as substituted (see note 4)).

7   Ie Council Regulation (EC) 207/2009 (OJ L78, 24.3.2009, p 1) art 88(2) or art 88(3).

8   Ie in accordance with the provisions of Commission Regulation (EC) 2868/95 (OJ L303, 15.12.95, p 1) (see PARA 161): Council Regulation (EC) 207/2009 (OJ L78, 24.3.2009, p 1) art 88(4).

The parts of the file which must be excluded from inspection pursuant to this provision are: (1) documents relating to exclusion or objection pursuant to art 132 (conflicts of interest of examiners or members of the Divisions of the Office for Harmonisation in the Internal Market); (2) draft decisions and opinions, and all other internal documents used for the preparation of decisions and opinions; and (3) parts of the file which the party concerned showed a special interest in keeping confidential before the application for inspection of the files was made, unless inspection of such part of the file is justified by overriding legitimate interests of the party seeking inspection: Commission Regulation (EC) 2868/95 (OJ L303, 15.12.95, p 1) art 1 r 88. As to the Office for Harmonisation in the Internal Market see PARA 163 et seq.

173. Periodical publications. The Office for Harmonisation in the Internal Market[1] must periodically publish:

(1)   a Community Trade Marks Bulletin containing entries made in the register of Community trade marks[2] as well as other prescribed particulars[3]; and

(2)   an Official Journal containing notices and information of a general character issued by the President of the Office, as well as any other information relevant to implementation of the Community Trade Mark Regulation[4].

In this way, applications for and registrations of Community trade marks are published by the Office[5].

1   As to the Office for Harmonisation in the Internal Market see PARA 163 et seq.
2   As to the register of Community trade marks see PARA 171.
3   Council Regulation (EC) 207/2009 (OJ L78, 24.3.2009, p 1) on the Community trade mark (the 'Community Trade Mark Regulation'), art 89(a). The particulars referred to are those the publication of which is prescribed by that regulation, or by Commission Regulation (EC) 2868/95 (OJ L303, 15.12.95, p 1) implementing Council Regulation (EC) 40/94 on the Community trade mark. Article 1 r 85 (amended by Commission Regulation (EC) 1041/2005 (OJ L172, 5.7.05, p 4)) makes further provision for the publication of the Community Trade Marks Bulletin.
4   Council Regulation (EC) 207/2009 (OJ L78, 24.3.2009, p 1) art 89(b). Commission Regulation (EC) 2868/95 (OJ L303, 15.12.95, p 1) art 1 r 86 makes further provision for the publication of the Official Journal of the Office. As to the President see PARAS 163–164.
5   Applications are required to be published by virtue of Council Regulation (EC) 207/2009 (OJ L78, 24.3.2009, p 1) art 39 (see PARA 262) and registrations must be registered by virtue of art 45 (see PARA 266).

174. Administrative co-operation and exchange of publications. Unless otherwise provided[1], the Office for Harmonisation in the Internal Market[2] and the courts or authorities of the member states must, on request, give assistance to each other by communicating information or opening files for inspection. Where the Office lays files open to inspection by courts, public prosecutors' offices or central industrial property offices, the inspection is not subject to the restrictions set down in the Community Trade Mark Regulation[3].

The Office and the central industrial property offices of the member states must despatch to each other on request and for their own use one or more copies of their respective publications free of charge[4].

The Office may conclude agreements relating to the exchange or supply of publications[5].

1   Ie in Council Regulation (EC) 207/2009 (OJ L78, 24.3.2009, p 1) on the Community trade mark (the 'Community Trade Mark Regulation'), or in national laws.
2   As to the Office for Harmonisation in the Internal Market see PARA 163 et seq.
3   Council Regulation (EC) 207/2009 (OJ L78, 24.3.2009, p 1) art 90. Further provision for co-operation between the Office and the authorities of the member states is provided for by Commission Regulation (EC) 2868/95 (OJ L303, 15.12.95, p 1) implementing Council Regulation (EC) 40/94 on the Community trade mark, art 1 rr 92–93.
    As to the inspection of the Office's files, and the restrictions thereon, see Council Regulation (EC) 207/2009 (OJ L78, 24.3.2009, p 1) art 88; and PARA 172.
4   Council Regulation (EC) 207/2009 (OJ L78, 24.3.2009, p 1) art 91(1).
5   Council Regulation (EC) 207/2009 (OJ L78, 24.3.2009, p 1) art 91(2).

(iii) Representation

175. Capacity to act. For the purpose of the Community Trade Mark Regulation[1], companies or firms and other legal bodies are regarded as legal persons if, under the terms of the law governing them, they have the capacity in their own name to have rights and obligations of all kinds, to make contracts or accomplish other legal acts and to sue and be sued[2].

1 Ie Council Regulation (EC) 207/2009 (OJ L78, 24.3.2009, p 1) on the Community trade mark.
2 Council Regulation (EC) 207/2009 (OJ L78, 24.3.2009, p 1) art 3. If a legal body has these capacities it qualifies as a legal person within the meaning of art 3 even if the law governing it does not grant it legal personality: Case R 195/1998–1 *Nauta Dutilh's Application* [2000] ETMR 90, OHIM Board of Appeal.

176. General principles of representation. Subject to the following[1], no person is compelled to be represented[2] before the Office for Harmonisation in the Internal Market[3]. The exceptions are:
(1) natural or legal persons not having either their domicile or their principal place of business or a real and effective industrial or commercial establishment in the Community must be professionally represented[4] before the Office in all proceedings[5], other than in filing an application for a Community trade mark[6];
(2) natural or legal persons having their domicile or principal place of business or a real and effective industrial or commercial establishment in the Community may be represented before the Office by an employee[7]; and an employee of a legal person to which this provision applies may also represent other legal persons which have economic connections with the first legal person, even if those other legal persons have neither their domicile nor their principal place of business nor a real and effective industrial or commercial establishment within the Community[8].

1 Ie subject to the provisions of Council Regulation (EC) 207/2009 (OJ L78, 24.3.2009, p 1) on the Community trade mark, art 90(2).
2 Ie professionally represented. For the provisions relating to professional representation see Council Regulation (EC) 207/2009 (OJ L78, 24.3.2009, p 1) art 93; and PARAS 177–178.
3 Council Regulation (EC) 207/2009 (OJ L78, 24.3.2009, p 1) art 92(1). As to the Office for Harmonisation in the Internal Market see PARA 163 et seq.
4 Ie represented in accordance with Council Regulation (EC) 207/2009 (OJ L78, 24.3.2009, p 1) art 93(1): see PARA 177.
5 Ie proceedings established by Council Regulation (EC) 207/2009 (OJ L78, 24.3.2009, p 1).
6 Council Regulation (EC) 207/2009 (OJ L78, 24.3.2009, p 1) art 92(2). An exception is provided for by art 92(3): see the text and note 8. See also Commission Regulation (EC) 2868/95 (OJ L303, 15.12.95, p 1) implementing Council Regulation (EC) 40/94 on the Community trade mark, which may permit other exceptions: Council Regulation (EC) 207/2009 (OJ L78, 24.3.2009, p 1) art 92(2).
7 Commission Regulation (EC) 2868/95 (OJ L303, 15.12.95, p 1) must specify whether and under what conditions an employee must file with the Office a signed authorisation for insertion on the file: Council Regulation (EC) 207/2009 (OJ L78, 24.3.2009, p 1) art 92(4). Commission Regulation (EC) 2868/95 (OJ L303, 15.12.95, p 1) requires that employees file with the Office a signed authorisation and sets out the applicable conditions: art 1 r 76(2)–(4) (added by Commission Regulation (EC) 1041/2005 (OJ L172, 5.7.05, p 4)).
8 Council Regulation (EC) 207/2009 (OJ L78, 24.3.2009, p 1) art 92(3).

177. Professional representation. Representatives acting before the Office for Harmonisation in the Internal Market[1] must file with it a signed authorisation for insertion on the files[2].

Representation of natural or legal persons before the Office may only be undertaken by:

(1)   any legal practitioner qualified in one of the member states and having his place of business within the Community, to the extent that he is entitled, within the said state, to act as a representative in trade mark matters[3]; or

(2)   professional representatives whose names appear on the list maintained for this purpose by the Office[4].

1   As to the Office for Harmonisation in the Internal Market see PARA 163 et seq.

2   Council Regulation (EC) 207/2009 (OJ L78, 24.3.2009, p 1) on the Community trade mark, art 93(1). The details of such authorisation are set out in Commission Regulation (EC) 2868/95 (OJ L303, 15.12.95, p 1) implementing Council Regulation (EC) 40/94 on the Community trade mark, art 1 r 76 (amended by Commission Regulation (EC) 1041/2005 (OJ L172, 5.7.05, p 4)). Further provisions on representations are provided for by Commission Regulation (EC) 2868/95 (OJ L303, 15.12.95, p 1) art 1 rr 75, 77.

3   Council Regulation (EC) 207/2009 (OJ L78, 24.3.2009, p 1) art 93(1)(a). As to the requirements to act as a representative in trade mark matters in the United Kingdom see PARA 33 et seq.

4   Council Regulation (EC) 207/2009 (OJ L78, 24.3.2009, p 1) art 93(1)(b). Commission Regulation (EC) 2868/95 (OJ L303, 15.12.95, p 1) must specify whether and under what conditions the representatives before the Office must file with the Office a signed authorisation for insertion on the file: Council Regulation (EC) 207/2009 (OJ L78, 24.3.2009, p 1) art 93(1)(b). Commission Regulation (EC) 2868/95 (OJ L303, 15.12.95, p 1) provides that professional representatives entered on the list maintained by the Office must file with the Office a signed authorisation for insertion in the file only if the Office expressly requires it or where there are a several parties to the proceedings in which the representative acts before the Office if the other party expressly asks for it: art 1 r 76(1) (amended by Commission Regulation (EC) 1041/2005 (OJ L172, 5.7.05, p 4)). As to the list of professional representatives see PARA 178.

178. The list of professional representatives. Any natural person who fulfils the following conditions may be entered on the list of professional representatives[1]:

(1)   he must be a national of one of the member states[2];

(2)   he must have his place of business or employment in the Community[3]; and

(3)   he must be entitled to represent natural or legal persons in trade mark matters before the central industrial property office of a member state[4].

Entry must be effected upon request, accompanied by a certificate furnished by the central industrial property office of the member state concerned indicating that the foregoing conditions[5] are fulfilled[6].

1   Council Regulation (EC) 207/2009 (OJ L78, 24.3.2009, p 1) on the Community trade mark, art 93(2).

     The conditions under which a person may be removed from the list of professional representatives are laid down in Commission Regulation (EC) 2868/95 (OJ L303, 15.12.95, p 1) implementing Council Regulation (EC) 40/94 on the Community trade mark: Council Regulation (EC) 207/2009 (OJ L78, 24.3.2009, p 1) art 93(5). Amendment of the list of representatives is provided for by Commission Regulation (EC) 2868/95 (OJ L303, 15.12.95, p 1) art 1 r 78.

2   Council Regulation (EC) 207/2009 (OJ L78, 24.3.2009, p 1) art 93(2)(a). The President of the Office for Harmonisation in the Internal Market may grant exemption from this requirement in special circumstances: art 93(4)(b). As to the President and the Office see PARAS 163–164.

3   Council Regulation (EC) 207/2009 (OJ L78, 24.3.2009, p 1) art 93(2)(b).

4   Council Regulation (EC) 207/2009 (OJ L78, 24.3.2009, p 1) art 93(2)(c). Where, in that member state, the entitlement is not conditional upon the requirement of special professional qualifications, persons applying to be entered on the list who act in trade mark matters before the central industrial property office of that state must have habitually so acted for at least five years. However, persons whose professional qualification to represent natural or legal persons in

trade mark matters before the central industrial property office of one of the member states is officially recognised in accordance with the regulations laid down by such state is not subject to the condition of having exercised the profession: art 93(2)(c). The President of the Office may grant exemption from the requirement that a person applying to be entered onto the list must have habitually acted in trade mark matters before the central industrial property office of the member state for at least five years: art 93(4)(a).

5   Ie the conditions laid down in Council Regulation (EC) 207/2009 (OJ L78, 24.3.2009, p 1) art 93(2): see heads (1)–(3) in the text.
6   Council Regulation (EC) 207/2009 (OJ L78, 24.3.2009, p 1) art 93(3).

179.   Privilege for communications with professional representatives. Any communication as to any matter relating to the protection of any trade mark or as to any matter involving passing off[1]:

(1)   between a person and his professional trade marks representative[2]; or

(2)   for the purpose of obtaining, or in response to a request for, information which a person is seeking for the purpose of instructing his professional trade marks representative[3],

is privileged from disclosure in legal proceedings in the same way as a communication between a person and his solicitor or a communication for the purpose of obtaining, or in response to a request for, information which a person is seeking for the purpose of instructing his solicitor[4].

1   Community Trade Marks Regulations 2006, SI 2006/1027, reg 11(1), (2). As to passing off see PARA 287 et seq.
2   Community Trade Marks Regulations 2006, SI 2006/1027, reg 11(2)(a). A person's 'professional trade marks representative' means a person who is retained by and is on the special list of professional representatives for trade marks matters referred to in Council Regulation (EC) 207/2009 (OJ L78, 24.3.2009, p 1) on the Community trade mark, art 93) (see PARAS 177–178): see the Community Trade Marks Regulations 2006, SI 2006/1027, reg 11(3).
3   Community Trade Marks Regulations 2006, SI 2006/1027, reg 11(2)(b).
4   Community Trade Marks Regulations 2006, SI 2006/1027, reg 11(2). Cf the Trade Marks Act 1994 s 87: see PARA 35. As to legal professional privilege see LEGAL PROFESSIONS vol 66 (2009) PARAS 1032, 1146.

(iv)   Conversion into a National Trade Mark Application

180.   Introduction. In some cases, a sign will satisfy the requirements for registration[1] as a Community trade mark[2] in some, but not all, member states[3]. In other cases, a mark may become liable to be revoked[4] or declared invalid[5] for reasons obtaining in some, but not all, member states[6]. However, a Community trade mark has equal effect throughout the Community[7]. It cannot be valid in respect of only part of the Community: therefore, if it is liable to be refused registration, declared invalid, or revoked[8] in one member state, it cannot continue to be registered at all.

In order to mitigate possible unfair consequences of this, a Community trade mark or a Community trade mark application[9] may be converted into a national trade mark application[10]. Accordingly, the applicant for or proprietor of a Community trade mark may request the conversion of his Community trade mark application or Community trade mark into a national trade mark application[11]:

(1)   to the extent that the Community trade mark application is refused, withdrawn, or deemed to be withdrawn[12]; or

(2)   to the extent that the Community trade mark ceases to have effect[13].

1   As to the requirements for registration as a Community trade mark see PARAS 188–206.
2   As to the meaning of 'Community trade mark' see PARA 189.

3   See PARA 192.

4   For the grounds of revocation see PARA 220 et seq.

5   For the grounds of invalidity see PARA 226 et seq.

6   Eg a Community trade mark would be liable to revocation if, in consequence of acts or inactivity of the proprietor, it has become the common name of the product in respect of which it is registered: see Council Regulation (EC) 207/2009 (OJ L78, 24.3.2009, p 1) on the Community trade mark, art 51(1)(b); and PARA 222.

7   See Council Regulation (EC) 207/2009 (OJ L78, 24.3.2009, p 1) art 1(2); and PARA 189.

8   As to whether a Community trade mark may be revoked for non-use if it is not used throughout the Community, or at least in a substantial part thereof, see PARAS 181 note 3, 220.

9   As to applications for Community trade marks see PARAS 261–266.

10   See Council Regulation (EC) 207/2009 (OJ L78, 24.3.2009, p 1) arts 112–114; the Community Trade Mark Regulations 2006, SI 2006/1027, reg 10; and PARAS 181–186.

11   Council Regulation (EC) 207/2009 (OJ L78, 24.3.2009, p 1) art 112(1).

12   Council Regulation (EC) 207/2009 (OJ L78, 24.3.2009, p 1) art 112(1)(a).

13   Council Regulation (EC) 207/2009 (OJ L78, 24.3.2009, p 1) art 112(1)(b).

181. Limitation of right to convert. Conversion cannot take place:

(1)   where the rights of the proprietor of the Community trade mark[1] have been revoked on the grounds of non-use[2], unless in the member state for which conversion is requested the Community trade mark has been put to use which would be considered to be genuine use under the laws of that member state[3]; or

(2)   for the purpose of protection in a member state in which, in accordance with the decision of the Office for Harmonisation in the Internal Market[4] or of the national court[5], grounds for refusal of registration or grounds for revocation or invalidity apply to the Community trade mark application or Community trade mark[6].

1   As to the meaning of 'Community trade mark' see PARA 189.

2   For revocation on the grounds of non-use see PARAS 220–221.

3   Council Regulation (EC) 207/2009 (OJ L78, 24.3.2009, p 1) on the Community trade mark, art 112(2)(a). This appears to imply that a Community trade mark may be revoked unless it is used in all member states or at least in a substantial part of the Community, contrary to the widely-held theory that use in one member state is sufficient to preserve a Community trade mark from revocation: see PARAS 220–221.

4   As to the Office for Harmonisation in the Internal Market see PARA 163 et seq.

5   See PARA 234 et seq.

6   Council Regulation (EC) 207/2009 (OJ L78, 24.3.2009, p 1) art 112(2)(b). It appears that this does not prevent conversion where the decision establishes conflict on relative grounds with an earlier Community trade mark, but only in some member states: Case C-514/06P *Armacell Enterprise GmbH v Office for Harmonisation in the Internal Market (Trade Marks and Designs)* [2008] ECR I-128, ECJ.

182. Time for filing a request for conversion. In cases where a Community trade mark application[1] is deemed to be withdrawn, the Office[2] must send to the applicant a communication fixing a period of three months from the date of that communication in which a request for conversion may be filed[3].

Where the Community trade mark application is withdrawn or the Community trade mark ceases to have effect as a result of a surrender being recorded[4] or of failure to renew the registration[5], the request for conversion must be filed within three months after the date on which the Community trade mark application has been withdrawn or on which the registration of the Community trade mark ceases to have effect[6].

Where the Community trade mark application is refused by decision of the Office or the Community trade mark ceases to have effect as a result of a decision of the Office or of a Community trade mark court, the request for conversion must be filed within three months after the date on which that decision acquired the authority of a final decision[7].

If the request is not filed within the period laid down, the Office will not transmit the request for conversion to the central industrial property offices of the relevant member states[8].

1   As to the meaning of 'Community trade mark' see PARA 189. As to applications for Community trade marks see PARAS 261–266.

2   As to the Office for Harmonisation in the Internal Market see PARA 163 et seq.

3   Council Regulation (EC) 207/2009 (OJ L78, 24.3.2009, p 1) on the Community trade mark, art 112(4).

4   As to surrender of a Community trade mark see Council Regulation (EC) 207/2009 (OJ L78, 24.3.2009, p 1) art 50; and PARA 219.

5   As to renewal of a Community trade mark see Council Regulation (EC) 207/2009 (OJ L78, 24.3.2009, p 1) art 47; and PARA 266.

6   Council Regulation (EC) 207/2009 (OJ L78, 24.3.2009, p 1) art 112(5).

7   Council Regulation (EC) 207/2009 (OJ L78, 24.3.2009, p 1) art 112(6).

8   See Council Regulation (EC) 207/2009 (OJ L78, 24.3.2009, p 1) art 113(3); and PARA 183. Further, the effect referred to in art 32 (date of filing of application equivalent to regular national filing: see PARA 261 note 23) lapses if the request is not filed in due time: art 112(7).

183.   Submission of a request for conversion. A request for conversion must be filed with the Office for Harmonisation in the Internal Market[1] and must specify the member states in which application of the procedure for registration of a national trade mark is desired[2].

If the Community trade mark application[3] has been published[4], receipt of any such request must be recorded in the register of Community trade marks[5] and the request for conversion must be published[6].

The Office must check whether conversion may be requested[7], whether the request has been filed within the prescribed period[8], whether the conversion fee has been paid[9] and whether the request fulfills the formal conditions[10]. If all these conditions are fulfilled, the Office must transmit the request to the central industrial property offices of the states specified therein[11].

1   As to the Office for Harmonisation in the Internal Market see PARA 163 et seq.

2   Council Regulation (EC) 207/2009 (OJ L78, 24.3.2009, p 1) on the Community trade mark, art 113(1). As to what the request must contain see Commission Regulation 2868/95 (EC) (OJ L303, 15.12.95, p 1) implementing Council Regulation (EC) 40/94 on the Community trade mark, art 1 r 44 (substituted by Commission Regulation (EC) 1041/2005 (OJ L172, 5.7.05, p 4)).

    The request will not be deemed to be filed until the conversion fee has been paid: Council Regulation (EC) 207/2009 (OJ L78, 24.3.2009, p 1) art 113(1). As to fees see PARA 167.

3   As to the meaning of 'Community trade mark' see PARA 189. As to applications for Community trade marks see PARAS 261–266.

4   As to publication see PARA 173.

5   As to the register of Community trade marks see PARA 171.

6   Council Regulation (EC) 207/2009 (OJ L78, 24.3.2009, p 1) art 113(2).

7   Ie in accordance with Council Regulation (EC) 207/2009 (OJ L78, 24.3.2009, p 1) art 112(1), (2): see PARAS 180–181.

8   Ie the period laid down in Council Regulation (EC) 207/2009 (OJ L78, 24.3.2009, p 1) art 112(4), (5), or (6), as the case may be: see PARA 182.

9   Ie in accordance with Council Regulation (EC) 207/2009 (OJ L78, 24.3.2009, p 1) 113(1): see the text and note 2.

10   Ie laid down in Commission Regulation (EC) 2868/95 (OJ L303, 15.12.95, p 1) art 1 r 44 (as substituted: see note 2).

11   Council Regulation (EC) 207/2009 (OJ L78, 24.3.2009, p 1) art 113(3). The procedure for examination, publication and transmission of the request is provided for by Commission Regulation (EC) 2868/95 (OJ L303, 15.12.95, p 1) art 1 rr 45–47 (rr 45, 47 substituted by Commission Regulation (EC) 1041/2005 (OJ L172, 5.7.05, p 4)).

184. Formal requirements for conversion. Any central industrial property office to which the request for conversion is transmitted may obtain from the Office for Harmonisation in the Internal Market[1] any additional information concerning the request enabling that office to make a decision regarding the national trade mark resulting from that conversion[2].

Any central industrial property office to which the request is transmitted may require that the applicant must, within not less than two months[3]:

(1) pay the national application fee[4];

(2) file a translation in one of the official languages of the state in question of the request and of the documents accompanying it[5];

(3) indicate an address for service in the state in question[6];

(4) supply a representation[7] of the trade mark in the number of copies specified by the state in question[8].

1 As to the Office for Harmonisation in the Internal Market see PARA 163 et seq.
2 Council Regulation (EC) 207/2009 (OJ L78, 24.3.2009, p 1) on the Community trade mark, art 114(1). A Community trade mark application or a Community trade mark transmitted in accordance with art 113 (see PARA 183) must not be subjected to formal requirements of national law which are different from or additional to those provided for in Council Regulation (EC) 207/2009 (OJ L78, 24.3.2009, p 1) or in Commission Regulation (EC) 2868/95 (OJ L303, 15.12.95, p 1) implementing Council Regulation (EC) 40/94 on the Community trade mark: Council Regulation (EC) 207/2009 (OJ L78, 24.3.2009, p 1) art 114(2).
   As to the procedure on receipt of such an application by the United Kingdom registrar see PARA 185.
3 Council Regulation (EC) 207/2009 (OJ L78, 24.3.2009, p 1) art 114(3).
4 Council Regulation (EC) 207/2009 (OJ L78, 24.3.2009, p 1) art 114(3)(a).
5 Council Regulation (EC) 207/2009 (OJ L78, 24.3.2009, p 1) art 114(3)(b).
6 Council Regulation (EC) 207/2009 (OJ L78, 24.3.2009, p 1) art 114(3)(c).
7 As to the requirements of a representation see PARA 261 note 10.
8 Council Regulation (EC) 207/2009 (OJ L78, 24.3.2009, p 1) art 114(3)(d).

185. Request for conversion to be treated as application under the Trade Marks Act 1994. Where pursuant to the relevant provisions[1] either:

(1) the applicant for or the proprietor of a Community trade mark[2] requests the conversion of his Community trade mark application or Community trade mark into an application for registration of a trade mark under the Trade Marks Act 1994[3]; or

(2) the holder of an international registration designating the European Union[4] requests[5] the conversion of that designation into an application for registration of a trade mark under the Trade Marks Act 1994[6], the following[7] applies[8].

Where the request has been transmitted to the registrar[9], it must be treated as an application for registration of a trade mark under the Trade Marks Act 1994[10].

1 Ie Council Regulation (EC) 207/2009 (OJ L78, 24.3.2009, p 1) on the Community trade mark, art 112: see PARAS 180–182.
2 As to the meaning of 'Community trade mark' see PARA 189.
3 Community Trade Mark Regulations 2006, SI 2006/1027, reg 10(1)(a). As to the meaning of 'registration' under the Trade Marks Act 1994 see PARA 21 note 2.
4 An 'international registration designating the European Union' means an international registration in relation to which a request has been made (either in the relevant international application or subsequently) for extension of protection to the European Community under the Madrid Protocol art 3 ter (1) or (2): Community Trade Mark Regulations 2006, SI 2006/1027, reg 2 (definition amended by SI 2011/1043). As to the Madrid Protocol see PARA 8. As to international registrations see PARA 11 et seq.

5   In accordance with Council Regulation (EC) 40/94 (OJ L11, 14.1.94, p 1) art 154(1)(a) (see now Council Regulation (EC) 207/2009 (OJ L78, 24.3.2009, p 1) art 159(1)(a)).

6   Community Trade Mark Regulations 2006, SI 2006/1027, reg 10(1)(b) (amended by SI 2011/1043).

7   Ie the Community Trade Mark Regulations 2006, SI 2006/1027, regs 2, 10(2), (3) (see the text and notes 9, 10).

8   Community Trade Mark Regulations 2006, SI 2006/1027, reg 10(1).

9   Ie under EC Council Regulation 40/94 (OJ L11, 14.1.94, p 1) art 109(3) (see now Council Regulation (EC) 207/2009 (OJ L78, 24.3.2009, p 1) art 113(3)): see PARA 183. As to the registrar see PARA 19.

10 Community Trade Mark Regulations 2006, SI 2006/1027, reg 10(2). It follows that the good faith of the applicant for a converted application must be judged by reference to the converted application and not the original Community trade mark application: *Rautaruukki Oyj v Ruukki Group Oyj* [2012] EWHC 2920 (Ch), [2012] All ER (D) 266 (Oct). A decision of the registrar in relation to the request must be treated as a decision of the registrar under the Trade Marks Act 1994: Community Trade Mark Regulations 2006, SI 2006/1027, reg 10(3). As to appeals from decisions of the registrar see PARA 386 et seq.

186.   Filing date, priority and seniority of converted application. The national trade mark application resulting from conversion of a Community trade mark[1] application or a Community trade mark enjoys in respect of the member states concerned the date of filing or the date of priority[2] of the Community application or trade mark[3]. Where seniority has been claimed[4] by the Community trade mark application from a national trade mark in the state concerned, the national converted application enjoys that claim to seniority[5].

1   As to the meaning of 'Community trade mark' see PARA 189.

2   As to priority see PARA 267 et seq.

3   Council Regulation (EC) 207/2009 (OJ L78, 24.3.2009, p 1) on the Community trade mark, art 112(3). This does not mean that a national trade mark resulting from conversion of a Community trade mark during the course of opposition proceedings founded on that Community trade mark may be relied upon as founding such proceedings: Case R 286/2002–3 *SFI Group plc v Sandhu* (12 June 2003, unreported), OHIM Board of Appeal.

4   Ie under Council Regulation (EC) 207/2009 (OJ L78, 24.3.2009, p 1) art 34 or art 35: see PARAS 270–271.

5   Council Regulation (EC) 207/2009 (OJ L78, 24.3.2009, p 1) art 112(3).

(v) Reciprocity

187.   In general. For the purposes of determining rights to priority[1], it is necessary for the Office for Harmonisation in the Internal Market[2] to establish whether a state which is not a party to the Paris Convention[3] or to the WTO Agreement[4] accords reciprocal treatment to first filings made at the Office.

If necessary, the President of the Office must request the EC Commission to inquire whether a state which is not a party to the Paris Convention or to the WTO Agreement accords reciprocal treatment within the meaning of the relevant provisions[5]. If the EC Commission determines that such reciprocal treatment is accorded, it must publish a communication to this effect in the Official Journal of the European Union[6].

The relevant provisions[7] take effect for the nationals of the states concerned from the date of publication in the Official Journal of the European Union of such a communication, unless the communication states an earlier date from which it is applicable. They cease to be effective from the date of publication in the Official Journal of the European Union of a communication to the effect that reciprocal treatment is no longer accorded, unless the communication states an earlier date from which it is applicable[8].

1   Ie under the provisions of Council Regulation (EC) 207/2009 (OJ L78, 24.3.2009, p 1) on the
    Community trade mark, art 29(5) (priority of certain applications: see PARA 267).
2   As to the Office for Harmonisation in the Internal Market see PARA 163 et seq.
3   As to the Paris Convention see PARA 6.
4   As to the WTO Agreement see PARA 7.
5   Commission Regulation (EC) 2868/95 (OJ L303, 15.12.95, p 1) implementing Council
    Regulation (EC) 40/94 on the Community trade mark, art 1 r 101(1) (art 1 r 101(1)–(3)
    substituted by Commission Regulation (EC) 1041/2005 (OJ L172, 5.7.05, p 4)). As to the
    relevant provisions see note 1. As to the President of the Office see PARA 163 text and note 4.
6   Commission Regulation (EC) 2868/95 (OJ L303, 15.12.95, p 1) art 1 r 101(2) (as substituted:
    see note 5). Any such communication must also be published in the Official Journal of the
    Office: art 1 r 101(4). As to the Official Journal of the Office see PARA 173.
7   See note 1.
8   Commission Regulation (EC) 2868/95 (OJ L303, 15.12.95, p 1) art 1 r 101(3) (as substituted:
    see note 5). Any such communication must also be published in the Official Journal of the
    Office: art 1 r 101(4).

(3) REQUIREMENTS FOR REGISTRATION

(i) Introduction

188.   In general.   Any sign[1] may be registered as a Community trade mark[2]
unless one of a number of specified grounds for refusal exists. The grounds for
refusal are divided into two classes, described in the Community Trade Mark
Regulation[3] as 'absolute grounds for refusal'[4] and 'relative grounds for refusal'[5].
This corresponds to the division under the Trade Marks Act 1994[6].

Where grounds for refusal of registration exist in respect of only some of the
goods or services for which a Community trade mark has been applied for,
refusal of registration must cover those goods or services only[7].

1   As to the meaning of 'sign' in the context of the Trade Marks Act 1994 see PARA 41 note 1.
2   As to the meaning of 'Community trade mark' see PARA 189.
3   Ie Council Regulation (EC) 207/2009 (OJ L78, 24.3.2009, p 1) on the Community trade mark.
4   See Council Regulation (EC) 207/2009 (OJ L78, 24.3.2009, p 1) art 7; and PARA 192 et seq.
5   See Council Regulation (EC) 207/2009 (OJ L78, 24.3.2009, p 1) art 8; and PARA 201 et seq.
6   See PARAS 39–64.
7   See Council Regulation (EC) 207/2009 (OJ L78, 24.3.2009, p 1) art 37(1) (see PARA 262),
    art 42(5) (see PARA 265), art 51(2) (see PARA 224), and arts 52(3), 53(5) (see PARA 229). Cf
    Council Directive (EEC) 89/104 (OJ L40, 11.2.89, p 1) to approximate the laws of the member
    states relating to trade marks, art 13 (see now European Parliament and Council Directive (EC)
    2008/95 (OJ L299, 8.11.2008, p 25) art 13).

189.   Meaning of 'Community trade mark'.   A Community trade mark is
defined as a trade mark[1] for goods or services which is registered[2] in accordance
with the conditions contained in the Community Trade Mark Regulation[3] and in
the manner there provided[4].

A Community trade mark has a unitary character. It has equal effect
throughout the Community. Thus it may not be registered, transferred or
surrendered, or be the subject of a decision revoking the rights of the proprietor
or declaring it invalid, nor may its use be prohibited, save in respect of the whole
Community[5].

1   'Trade mark' is not defined in Council Regulation (EC) 207/2009 (OJ L78, 24.3.2009, p 1) on
    the Community trade mark; but a sign which is not a trade mark within the meaning of the
    Trade Marks Act 1994 (see PARA 41) may not be registered as a Community trade mark:
    Council Regulation (EC) 207/2009 (OJ L78, 24.3.2009, p 1) arts 4, 7(1)(a); and see PARAS 191,
    193.
2   Ie under Council Regulation (EC) 207/2009 (OJ L78, 24.3.2009, p 1) art 45: see PARA 266.

3 Ie Council Regulation (EC) 207/2009 (OJ L78, 24.3.2009, p 1) on the Community trade mark.
4 Council Regulation (EC) 207/2009 (OJ L78, 24.3.2009, p 1) art 1(1). Thus a Community trade mark is obtained by registration: art 6. As to the conditions for registration see PARAS 192–206. As to the manner of registration see PARAS 261–266. Note that Community trade marks may now be obtained via an international application under the Madrid Protocol (see PARA 8): see PARA 159. Such trade marks are referred to in the Trade Marks Act 1994 as 'international trade marks (EC)': see PARA 8 note 17.
5 Council Regulation (EC) 207/2009 (OJ L78, 24.3.2009, p 1) art 1(2). This principle applies unless otherwise provided in the Regulation: art 1(2). Earlier national rights may be invoked to prohibit the use of Community trade marks only in certain circumstances: see art 110; and PARA 242.

190. Persons who can be proprietors of Community trade marks. Any natural or legal person[1], including authorities established under public law, may be the proprietor of a Community trade mark[2].

1 As to which bodies constitute legal persons for these purposes see PARA 175. The Office for Harmonisation in the Internal Market apparently considers that an English partnership can own a Community trade mark: see *Byford v Oliver* [2003] EWHC 295 (Ch), [2003] EMLR 416; *Michaels Foodmarket v Drinkstop Ltd* (O/168/05), Appointed Person.
2 Council Regulation (EC) 207/2009 (OJ L78, 24.3.2009, p 1) on the Community trade mark, art 5. As to the meaning of 'Community trade mark' see PARA 189.

191. Signs of which a Community trade mark may consist. A Community trade mark[1] may consist of any signs[2] capable of being represented graphically[3], particularly words, including personal names, designs, letters, numerals, the shape of goods or of their packaging, provided that such signs are capable of distinguishing[4] the goods or services of one undertaking from those of other undertakings[5].

1 As to the meaning of 'Community trade mark' see PARA 189.
2 As to the meaning of 'sign' in the context of the Trade Marks Act 1994 see PARA 41 note 1.
3 As to the requirement that the sign is capable of being represented graphically see PARA 41 note 2.
4 As to the requirement that signs are capable of distinguishing goods or services of one undertaking from other undertakings see PARA 41 note 3.
5 Council Regulation (EC) 207/2009 (OJ L78, 24.3.2009, p 1) on the Community trade mark, art 4. Signs which do not satisfy the requirements of art 4 may not be registered: see art 7(1)(a); and PARA 193.

(ii) Absolute Grounds for Refusal of Registration

192. In general. The absolute grounds for refusal of registration[1] of a Community trade mark[2] prohibit registration notwithstanding that the grounds of non-registrability[3] obtain in only a part of the Community[4].

1 Ie those set out in Council Regulation (EC) 207/2009 (OJ L78, 24.3.2009, p 1) on the Community trade mark, art 7(1). As to the absolute grounds generally see PARA 42.
2 As to the meaning of 'Community trade mark' see PARA 189.
3 As to the grounds of non-registrability see PARA 193 et seq.
4 Council Regulation (EC) 207/2009 (OJ L78, 24.3.2009, p 1) art 7(2); Case T-91/99 *Ford Motor Co v Office for Harmonisation in the Internal Market (Trade Marks and Designs)* [2000] ECR II-1925, [2000] 2 CMLR 276, CFI. Thus it is sufficient to render a trade mark ineligible for registration that the trade mark is descriptive (see Council Regulation (EC) 40/94 (OJ L11, 14.1.94, p 1) art 7(1)(c) (now Council Regulation (EC) 207/2009 (OJ L78, 24.3.2009, p 1) art 7(1)(c)); and PARA 194) or otherwise devoid of distinctive character (see Council Regulation (EC) 40/94 (OJ L11, 14.1.94, p 1) art 7(1)(b) (now Council Regulation (EC) 207/2009 (OJ L78, 24.3.2009, p 1) art 7(1)(b)); and PARA 194) in the language of one member state: see eg Case C-383/99P *Procter & Gamble Co v Office for Harmonisation in the Internal Market (Trade Marks and Designs)* [2002] Ch 82, [2002] All ER (EC) 29, [2001] ECR I-6251, ECJ. Similarly a

trade mark may be ineligible for registration on relative grounds (see PARA 201 et seq) due to the existence of an conflicting earlier trade mark or right in one member state: see e g Case C-3/03P *Matratzen Concord GmbH v Office for Harmonisation in the Internal Market (Trade Marks and Designs)* [2004] ECR I-3657, ECJ. As to the meaning of 'earlier trade mark' see PARA 201.

**193.	Signs which cannot constitute trade marks.** Signs which do not satisfy the requirements as to what a Community trade mark[1] may consist of[2] must not be registered[3].

1	As to the meaning of 'Community trade mark' see PARA 189.
2	Ie signs which do not satisfy the requirements of Council Regulation (EC) 207/2009 (OJ L78, 24.3.2009, p 1) on the Community trade mark, art 4: see PARA 191.
3	Council Regulation (EC) 207/2009 (OJ L78, 24.3.2009, p 1) art 7(1)(a). As to the meaning of 'registered' in this context see PARA 266 note 5.

**194.	Lack of distinctive character.** The following must not be registered[1] as Community trade marks[2]:

(1)	trade marks[3] which are devoid of any distinctive character[4];

(2)	trade marks which consist exclusively of signs or indications which may serve, in trade[5], to designate the kind, quality, quantity, intended purpose, value, geographical origin, time of production of the goods or of rendering of the service, or other characteristics of the goods or service[6];

(3)	trade marks which consist exclusively of signs or indications which have become customary in the current language or in the bona fide and established practices of the trade[7].

However, these prohibitions do not apply if the trade mark has become distinctive in relation to the goods or services for which registration is requested in consequence of the use which has been made of it[8].

1	As to the meaning of 'registered' in this context see PARA 266 note 5.
2	As to the meaning of 'Community trade mark' see PARA 189.
3	As to the meaning of 'trade mark' in this context see PARA 189 note 1.
4	Council Regulation (EC) 207/2009 (OJ L78, 24.3.2009, p 1) on the Community trade mark, art 7(1)(b). As to the meaning of 'devoid of distinctive character' see PARA 44 note 3.
5	'Trade' is not defined for the purposes of Council Regulation (EC) 207/2009 (OJ L78, 24.3.2009, p 1). For the purposes of the equivalent provision in the Trade Marks Act 1994, 'trade' includes any business or profession: see s 103(1); and PARA 44 note 4.
6	Council Regulation (EC) 207/2009 (OJ L78, 24.3.2009, p 1) art 7(1)(c). As to the meaning of this provision see further PARA 44 note 5. A Community collective mark which consists of signs or indications which may designate the geographical origin of goods or services may, however, be registered: see art 66(2); and PARA 279. As to Community collective marks see PARAS 278–284.
7	Council Regulation (EC) 207/2009 (OJ L78, 24.3.2009, p 1) art 7(1)(d). As to the meaning of this provision see further PARA 44 note 6.
8	Council Regulation (EC) 207/2009 (OJ L78, 24.3.2009, p 1) art 7(3). As to distinctive character acquired as a result of use see PARA 45. Such distinctive character through use must be acquired in the part of the Community in which the trade mark was devoid of distinctive character: Case T-91/99 *Ford Motor Co v Office for Harmonisation in the Internal Market (Trade Marks and Designs)* [2000] ECR II-1925, [2000] 2 CMLR 276, CFI; Case C-25/05 *August Storck KG v Office for Harmonisation in the Internal Market (Trade Marks and Designs)* [2006] ECR I-5719, [2006] IP & T 974, ECJ. It would be unreasonable, however, to require proof of such acquisition in each individual Member State: Case C-98/11P *Chocoladefabriken Lindt & Sprüngli AG v Office for Harmonisation in the Internal Market (Trade Marks and Designs)* [2012] ECR I-0000, ECJ. It is not necessary to consider whether the mark has acquired a distinctive character, however, unless the applicant or proprietor has invoked Council Regulation (EC) 40/94 (OJ L11, 14.1.94, p 1) art 7(3) (see now Council Regulation (EC) 207/2009 (OJ L78, 24.3.2009, p 1) art 7(3)): Case C-136/02P *Mag Instrument Inc v Office for Harmonisation in the Internal Market (Trade Marks and Designs)* [2004] ECR I-9165, [2004]

All ER (D) 75 (Oct), ECJ. An applicant may, however, invoke Council Regulation (EC) 40/94 (OJ L11, 14.1.94, p 1) art 7(3) (see now Council Regulation (EC) 207/2009 (OJ L78, 24.3.2009, p 1) art 7(3)) on appeal to the Board of Appeal even if he has not done so at first instance: Case T-163/98 *Procter & Gamble Co v Office for Harmonisation in the Internal Market (Trade Marks and Designs)* [1999] All ER (EC) 648, [1999] ECR II-2383, CFI; revsd on other grounds Case C-383/99P *Procter & Gamble Co v Office for Harmonisation in the Internal Market (Trade Marks and Designs)* [2002] Ch 82, [2002] All ER (EC) 29, [2001] ECR I-6251, ECJ. As to appeals to the Board of Appeal see PARAS 274–276.

195. Shape. A sign must not be registered as a Community trade mark[1], if it consists exclusively of[2]:

(1) the shape which results from the nature of the goods[3] themselves[4];

(2) the shape of goods which is necessary to obtain a technical result[5]; or

(3) the shape which gives substantial value to the goods[6].

1 As to the meaning of 'Community trade mark' see PARA 189.
2 Council Regulation (EC) 207/2009 (OJ L78, 24.3.2009, p 1) on the Community trade mark, art 7(1)(e). As to the purpose of these provisions see PARA 46 note 3. As to the meaning of 'registered' in this context see PARA 266 note 5.
3 As to the goods to be considered see PARA 46 note 3.
4 Council Regulation (EC) 207/2009 (OJ L78, 24.3.2009, p 1) art 7(1)(e)(i). As to the meaning of this provision see PARA 46 note 4. See Case T-28/08 *Mars, Inc v Office for Harmonisation in the Internal Market (Trade Marks and Designs)* [2009] ECR II-106, [2010] IP & T 578, CFI.
5 Council Regulation (EC) 207/2009 (OJ L78, 24.3.2009, p 1) art 7(1)(e)(ii). As to the meaning of this provision see PARA 46 note 5.
6 Council Regulation (EC) 207/2009 (OJ L78, 24.3.2009, p 1) art 7(1)(e)(iii). As to the meaning of this provision see PARA 46 note 6.

196. Public policy; immoral trade marks. A Community trade mark[1] must not be registered[2] if it is contrary to public policy[3] or to accepted principles of morality[4].

1 As to the meaning of 'Community trade mark' see PARA 189.
2 As to the meaning of 'registered' in this context see PARA 266 note 5.
3 As to the meaning of 'public policy' see PARA 47 note 3.
4 Council Regulation (EC) 207/2009 (OJ L78, 24.3.2009, p 1) on the Community trade mark, art 7(1)(f). As to the meaning of this provision see PARA 47 note 4.

197. Deceptive trade marks. A Community trade mark[1] must not be registered[2] if it is of such a nature as to deceive the public, for instance as to the nature, quality or geographical origin of the goods or service[3].

1 As to the meaning of 'Community trade mark' see PARA 189.
2 As to the meaning of 'registered' in this context see PARA 266 note 5.
3 Council Regulation (EC) 207/2009 (OJ L78, 24.3.2009, p 1) on the Community trade mark, art 7(1)(g). As to the meaning of this provision see further PARA 48 note 3.

198. State emblems etc protected under the Paris Convention. The Paris Convention[1] contains provisions prohibiting the registration of certain specially protected signs, which are incorporated by reference into the Community Trade Mark Regulation[2].

Under the Paris Convention, the signatories must:

(1) refuse or invalidate the registration, without authorisation of the competent authorities, either as trade marks or elements of trade marks, of armorial bearings, flags and other state emblems, of signatories to the Convention, official signs and hallmarks indicating control and warranty adopted by them[3], and any imitation from a heraldic point of view[4];

(2)   refuse or invalidate the registration, either as trade marks or elements of trade marks, of armorial bearings, flags and other emblems, abbreviations and names of international intergovernmental organisations of which one or more signatories to the Convention are members, with the exception of armorial bearings, flags and other emblems, abbreviations and names that are already the subject of international agreements in force, intended to ensure their protection[5].

In the case of state flags, the prohibition under head (1) above applies solely to marks registered after 6 November 1925[6]. In the case of all other signs under heads (1) and (2) above, the prohibition applies only to marks registered two or more months after receipt of a communication[7] that the signatory or international intergovernmental organisation wishes, wholly or within certain limits, to place the sign within the protection provided for by heads (1) and (2) above[8].

The above is subject to the provision that, in cases of bad faith, the signatories have the right to cancel even those marks incorporating state emblems, signs and hallmarks which were registered before 6 November 1925[9].

1   As to the Paris Convention see PARA 6.
2   See Council Regulation (EC) 207/2009 (OJ L78, 24.3.2009, p 1) on the Community trade mark, art 7(1)(h) (see PARA 199), which incorporates by reference the provisions of the Paris Convention art 6 ter. As to the manner in which the United Kingdom has incorporated these provision into domestic law see the Trade Marks Act 1994 ss 3(5), 4(3), 57–59; and PARAS 50–52.
3   Prohibition of the use (and, presumably, registration as a trade mark) of official signs and hallmarks indicating control and warranty apply solely in cases where the marks in which they are incorporated are intended to be used on goods of the same or similar kind: Paris Convention art 6 ter (2).
4   Paris Convention art 6 ter (1)(a). As to the meaning of this provision see PARA 51.
5   Paris Convention art 6 ter (1)(b). As to the meaning of this provision see PARA 52. Signatories to the Convention are not required to apply this provision: (1) to the prejudice of owners of rights acquired in good faith before the entry into force, in that country, of the Convention; or (2) when the registration is not of such a nature as to suggest to the public that a connection exists between the organisation concerned and the armorial bearings, flags, emblems, abbreviations and names, or if such registration is probably not of such a nature as to mislead the public as to the existence of a connection between the user and the organisation: art 6 ter (1)(c).
6   Paris Convention art 6 ter (5).
7   Ie in accordance with the Paris Convention art 6 ter (3).
8   Paris Convention art 6 ter (6).
9   Paris Convention art 6 ter (7).

199.   Prohibition on registration of state emblems etc as Community trade marks. The following must not be registered[1] as Community trade marks[2]:

(1)   trade marks which have not been authorised by the competent authorities and are to be refused pursuant to the Paris Convention[3]; or

(2)   trade marks which include badges, emblems or escutcheons other than those covered by head (1) above and which are of particular public interest, unless the consent of the appropriate authorities to their registration has been given[4].

1   As to the meaning of 'registered' in this context see PARA 266 note 5.
2   As to the meaning of 'Community trade mark' see PARA 189.
3   Council Regulation (EC) 207/2009 (OJ L78, 24.3.2009, p 1) on the Community trade mark, art 7(1)(h). The text refers to refusal pursuant to the Paris Convention art 6 ter: see PARA 198. As to the Paris Convention see PARA 6.
4   Council Regulation (EC) 207/2009 (OJ L78, 24.3.2009, p 1) art 7(1)(i). This provision is to be interpreted as conferring the same level of protection as Council Regulation (EC) 207/2009 (OJ L78, 24.3.2009, p 1) art 7(1)(h): Case T-3/12 *Kreyenberg v Office for Harmonisation in the*

Internal Market (Trade Marks and Designs) [2013] ECR II-0000, EGC ('MEMBER OF €E EURO EXPERTS' refused on ground that euro symbol was an emblem of particular public interest).

200.   Geographical indications and designations of origin.   The following must not be registered[1] as Community trade marks[2]:

(1)   trade marks for wines which contain or consist of a geographical indication identifying wines[3], or for spirits which contain or consist of a geographical indication identifying spirits with respect to such wines or spirits not having that origin[4];

(2)   trade marks which contain or consist of a protected designation of origin or a protected geographical indication[5] when they correspond to one of the protected situations[6] and regarding the same type of product, on condition that the application for registration of the trade mark has been submitted after the date of filing of the application for registration of the designation of origin or geographical indication[7].

1   As to the meaning of 'registered' in this context see PARA 266 note 5.

2   As to the meaning of 'Community trade mark' see PARA 189.

3   The expression 'geographical indication identifying wines' is not defined in Council Regulation (EC) 207/2009 (OJ L78, 24.3.2009, p 1) on the community trade mark and reference should be made to Council Regulation (EC) 1493/1999 (OJ L179, 14.7.99, p 1) on the common organisation of the market in wine: Case T-237/08 *Abadía Retuerta, SA v Office for Harmonisation in the Internal Market (Trade Marks and Designs)* [2010] ECR II-1583, EGC. If a geographical indication is protected under Council Regulation (EC) 1493/1999 (OJ L179, 14.7.99, p 1), it is immaterial that the list published by the Commission in the Official Journal, in accordance with art 54(5) of that regulation, does not refer to it: Case T-237/08 *Abadía Retuerta, SA v Office for Harmonisation in the Internal Market (Trade Marks and Designs)* above.

4   Council Regulation (EC) 207/2009 (OJ L78, 24.3.2009, p 1) on the Community trade mark, art 7(1)(j). This provision was added in order to give effect to the Agreement on Trade-Related Aspects of Intellectual Property Rights ('TRIPs') (1994) (Cm 2557) art 23(2): see Council Regulation (EC) 3288/94 (OJ L349, 31.12.94, p 83), 4th recital. As to TRIPs see PARA 7. Note that there is no corresponding provision in European Parliament and Council Directive (EC) 2008/95 (OJ L299, 8.11.2008, p 25) to approximate the laws of the Member States relating to trade marks or the Trade Marks Act 1994. For this ground of refusal to apply, it suffices that the mark contains or consists of elements which enable the geographical indication in question to be identified with certainty, whether or not the mark also includes a definite or indefinite article forming part of the indication, unless the geographical indication consists of a name of a place containing an article which is inseparable from that name and which gives that name its own, autonomous meaning: Case T-237/08 *Abadía Retuerta, SA v Office for Harmonisation in the Internal Market (Trade Marks and Designs)* [2010] ECR II-1583, EGC (CUVEE PALOMAR refused due to conflict with geographical indication EL PALOMAR).

5   Ie registered in accordance with Council Regulation (EC) 510/2006 (OJ L93, 31.3.06, p 12) on the protection of geographical indications and designations of origin for agricultural products and foodstuff (see now Council Regulation (EU) 1151/2012 (OJ L343, 14.12.2012, p 1) on quality schemes for agricultural products and foodstuffs). See further PARA 285 et seq.

6   Ie under Council Regulation (EC) 510/2006 (OJ L93, 31.3.06, p 12) art 13 (see now Council Regulation (EU) 1151/2012 (OJ L343, 14.12.2012, p 1) arts 13, 15).

7   Council Regulation (EC) 207/2009 (OJ L78, 24.3.2009, p 1) art 7(1)(k). Note that there is no corresponding provision in European Parliament and Council Directive (EC) 2008/95 (OJ L299, 8.11.2008, p 25) or the Trade Marks Act 1994. It appears that this provision would not prevent the registration of a generic word forming part of a protected designation of origin: see Case T-291/03 *Consorzio per la tutela del formaggio Grana Padano v Office for Harmonisation in the Internal Market (Trade Marks and Designs)* [2007] ECR II-3081, [2008] ETMR 3, [2007] All ER (D) 68 (Sep), CFI (registration of GRANA BIRAGHI invalid in light of PDO for GRANA PADANO; argument that GRANA generic failed on facts).

(iii) Relative Grounds for Refusal of Registration

201. Meaning of 'earlier trade mark'. For the purposes of the registration of a Community trade mark[1], an 'earlier trade mark' means:

(1) a Community trade mark, a trade mark registered in a member state, or, in the case of Belgium, the Netherlands or Luxembourg, at the Benelux Office for Intellectual Property or a trade mark registered under international arrangements which have effect either in a member state or in the Community[2], provided the mark has a date of application for registration[3] which is earlier than the date of registration of the Community trade mark, taking account (where appropriate) of the priorities[4] claimed in respect of those trade marks[5];

(2) applications for the trade marks referred to in head (1) above, subject to their registration[6]; and

(3) trade marks which, at the date of application for registration of the Community trade mark, or, where appropriate, of the priority claimed in respect of the application for registration of the Community trade mark, are well known[7] in a member state[8].

Most of the relative grounds for refusal of registration[9] depend upon the existence of an earlier trade mark[10].

1 As to the meaning of 'Community trade mark' see PARA 189.
2 Ie under the Madrid Agreement or Madrid Protocol: see PARA 8.
3 The date of application of the registration is the date of filing the application. As to the date of filing an application for a Community trade mark see PARA 261 note 23.
4 As to claims to priority of other applications see PARA 267 et seq.
5 Council Regulation (EC) 207/2009 (OJ L78, 24.3.2009, p 1) on the Community trade mark, art 8(2)(a). A national trade mark resulting from conversion of a Community trade mark application during the course of opposition does not constitute an 'earlier trade mark': Case R 286/2002–3 *SFI Group plc v Sandhu* (12 June 2003, unreported), OHIM Board of Appeal.
6 Council Regulation (EC) 207/2009 (OJ L78, 24.3.2009, p 1) art 8(2)(b).
7 Ie 'well known' within the meaning of the Paris Convention art 6 bis. See further PARA 136. As to the Paris Convention see PARA 6.
8 Council Regulation (EC) 207/2009 (OJ L78, 24.3.2009, p 1) art 8(2)(c).
9 See PARA 202 et seq.
10 The validity of an earlier trade mark may not be called into question in proceedings concerning the registration of a later trade mark, but only by way of a claim for revocation or a declaration of invalidity in the appropriate jurisdiction: Case T 6/01 *Matratzen Concord GmbH v Office for Harmonisation in the Internal Market (Trade Marks and Designs)* [2002] ECR II-4335, CFI (affd Case C-30/03P [2004] ECR I-3657, ECJ).
     If the earlier trade mark expires during the course of opposition proceedings it can no longer be relied upon: Case T-191/04 *MIP Metro Group Intellectual Property GmbH & Co KG v Office for Harmonisation in the Internal Market (Trade Marks and Designs)* [2006] ECR II-2855, [2006] All ER (D) 57 (Sep), CFI; and see also Case C-214/09P *Anheuser-Busch Inc v Office for Harmonisation of the Internal Market (Trade Marks and Designs)* [2010] ECR I-7665, [2010] ETMR 59, ECJ. Cf the position under the Trade Marks Act 1994 s 6: see PARA 54 note 19. By contrast, expiry of the earlier mark after the General Court has delivered its judgment on appeal from OHIM does not deprive that decision of its purpose or its effects: Case C-268/12P *Cadila Healthcare Ltd v Office for Harmonisation in the Internal Market (Trade Marks and Designs)* [2013] ECR I-0000, ECJ.

202. Identical earlier mark for identical goods or services. Upon opposition[1] by the proprietor of an earlier trade mark[2], a trade mark must not be registered[3], if it is identical[4] with the earlier trade mark and the goods or services for which registration is applied for are identical[5] with the goods or services for which the earlier trade mark is protected[6].

1　As to opposing an application for registration of a Community trade mark see Council Regulation (EC) 207/2009 (OJ L78, 24.3.2009, p 1) on the Community trade mark, arts 41–42; and PARA 265.
2　As to the meaning of 'earlier trade mark' see PARA 201.
3　As to the meaning of 'registered' in this context see PARA 266 note 5.
4　As to the meaning of 'identical' in this context see PARA 55 note 3.
5　As to the meaning of 'identical' in this context see PARA 55 note 5.
6　Council Regulation (EC) 207/2009 (OJ L78, 24.3.2009, p 1) art 8(1)(a). Cf the corresponding infringement provisions: see art 9(1)(a); and PARA 209.

203.　Identical earlier mark and similar goods or services; similar earlier mark and identical or similar goods or services. Upon opposition[1] by the proprietor of an earlier trade mark[2], a trade mark must not be registered[3], if because of its identity with or similarity to the earlier trade mark and the identity or similarity of the goods or services[4] covered by the trade mark there exists a likelihood of confusion on the part of the public in the territory in which the earlier trade mark is protected[5]. The likelihood of confusion includes the likelihood of association with the earlier trade mark[6].

1　As to opposing an application for registration of a Community trade mark see Council Regulation (EC) 207/2009 (OJ L78, 24.3.2009, p 1) on the Community trade mark, arts 41–42; and PARA 265.
2　As to the meaning of 'earlier trade mark' see PARA 201.
3　As to the meaning of 'registered' in this context see PARA 266 note 5.
4　As to the meaning of 'similarity of the goods or services' see PARA 57.
5　Council Regulation (EC) 207/2009 (OJ L78, 24.3.2009, p 1) art 8(1)(b). As to the likelihood of confusion see PARA 58 where there is detailed coverage of the relevant case law.
6　Council Regulation (EC) 207/2009 (OJ L78, 24.3.2009, p 1) art 8(1)(b). See also PARA 58.

204.　Identical or similar mark for dissimilar goods or services. Upon opposition[1] by the proprietor of an earlier trade mark[2], a trade mark must not be registered[3] where it is identical with or similar to the earlier trade mark and is to be registered for goods or services which are not similar[4] to those for which the earlier trade mark is registered, where:

(1)　in the case of an earlier Community trade mark[5], the trade mark has a reputation[6] in the Community; or

(2)　in the case of an earlier national trade mark[7], the trade mark has a reputation in the member state concerned,

and the use of a trade mark applied for without due cause[8] would take unfair advantage of, or be detrimental to, the distinctive character or the repute of the earlier trade mark[9].

1　As to opposing an application for registration of a Community trade mark see Council Regulation (EC) 207/2009 (OJ L78, 24.3.2009, p 1) on the Community trade mark, arts 41–42; and PARA 265.
2　As to the meaning of 'earlier trade mark' see PARA 201.
3　As to the meaning of 'registered' in this context see PARA 266 note 5.
4　This ground of objection can be invoked when the goods or services are identical or similar as well as when they are dissimilar: see PARA 59 note 10.
5　As to the meaning of 'Community trade mark' see PARA 189.
6　As to the meaning of 'reputation' see PARA 59 note 7.
7　Ie those trade marks (and applications for trade marks), other than Community trade marks, which are specified by Council Regulation (EC) 207/2009 (OJ L78, 24.3.2009, p 1) art 8(2). See PARA 201 head (1).
8　As to the meaning of 'without due cause' see PARA 59 note 9.
9　Council Regulation (EC) 207/2009 (OJ L78, 24.3.2009, p 1) art 8(5). As to the tests of unfair advantage and detriment see PARA 60.

205. Refusal by virtue of an earlier right. Upon opposition[1] by the proprietor[2] of a non-registered trade mark[3] or of another sign[4] used in the course of trade of more than mere local significance[5], a trade mark must not be registered as a Community trade mark[6] where and to the extent that, pursuant to the Community legislation or the law of the member state[7] governing that sign[8]:

(1) rights to the sign were acquired prior to the date of application for registration of the Community trade mark, or the date of priority[9] claimed for the application for registration of the Community trade mark[10]; and

(2) that sign confers on its proprietor the right to prohibit the use[11] of a subsequent trade mark[12].

1 As to opposing an application for registration of a Community trade mark see Council Regulation (EC) 207/2009 (OJ L78, 24.3.2009, p 1) on the Community trade mark, arts 41–42; and PARA 265.

2 'Proprietor' is not defined for the purposes of Council Regulation (EC) 207/2009 (OJ L78, 24.3.2009, p 1). In this context, it presumably means a person who is recognised by law as owning a right in respect of the trade mark, such as a right in passing off. As to ownership of goodwill at common law see PARA 296.

3 'Non-registered mark' is not defined for the purposes of Council Regulation (EC) 207/2009 (OJ L78, 24.3.2009, p 1). It would presumably include a trade mark protected by the law of passing off, even though, strictly speaking, the right protected by passing off is not a right in a non-registered trade mark, but in the goodwill of a business. See further PARA 289.

4 An appellation of origin can be a sign used in the course of trade within Council Regulation (EC) 40/94 (OJ L11, 14.1.94, p 1) art 8(4) (see now Council Regulation (EC) 207/2009 (OJ L78, 24.3.2009, p 1) art 8(4)): Joined Cases T-53/04 to T-56/04, T-58/04 and T-59/04 *Budejovicky Budvar np v Office for Harmonisation in the Internal Market (Trade Marks and Designs)* [2007] ECR II-57, [2007] All ER (D) 96 (June), CFI; Joined Cases T-57/04 and T-71/04 *Budejovicky Budvar np v Office for Harmonisation in the Internal Market (Trade Marks and Designs)* [2007] ECR II-1829, [2007] All ER (D) 98 (Jun), CFI. It is not clear whether the same is true of protected designations of origin and protected geographical indications (as to which see PARA 285): see Case C-96/09P *Anheuser-Busch Inc v Budejovicky Budvar np* [2011] ECR I-2131, [2011] ETMR 31, ECJ. Rights to a name or likeness in the nature of copyrights or personality rights cannot be relied upon under Council Regulation (EC) 40/94 (OJ L11, 14.1.94, p 1) art 8(4) (see now Council Regulation (EC) 207/2009 (OJ L78, 24.3.2009, p 1) art 8(4)) but must be invoked under Council Regulation (EC) 40/94 (OJ L11, 14.1.94, p 1) art 52(2) (see now Council Regulation (EC) 207/2009 (OJ L78, 24.3.2009, p 1) art 53(3)) (see PARA 228): Decision 506/2000 *EinStein Stadtcafé Verwaltungs- und Betriebsgesellschaft mbH's Application, Opposition of Hebrew University of Jerusalem* [2000] ETMR 952, OHIM Opposition Division.

5 In order to be of 'more than mere local significance' the sign must have a real presence on the relevant market and must be used in a substantial part of the relevant territory, taking account of the duration and intensity of the use of the sign, in particular in advertising and commercial correspondence: Case C-96/09P *Anheuser-Busch Inc v Office for Harmonisation in the Internal Market (Trade Marks and Designs)* [2011] ECR I-2131, [2011] ETMR 31, ECJ; *Frost Products Ltd v FC Frost Ltd* [2013] EWPCC 34, [2013] All ER (D) 323 (Jul).

6 As to the meaning of 'Community trade mark' see PARA 189.

7 Where national law is relied on, the opponent must provide particulars showing that he is entitled under the applicable national law to lay claim to the right in question, including particulars establishing the content of the national law: Case C-263/09P *Edwin Co Ltd v Office for Harmonisation in the Internal Market (Trade Marks and Designs)* [2011] ECR I-5853, ECJ; Case T-571/11 *El Corte Inglés SA v Office for Harmonisation in the Internal Market (Trade Marks and Designs)* [2013] ECR II-0000, [2013] ETMR 30, EGC; but where necessary the Office is obliged to inform itself of the relevant national law: Case T318/03 *Atomic Austria GmbH v Office for Harmonisation in the Internal Market (Trade Marks and Designs)* [2005] ECR II1319, [2005] All ER (D) 263 (Apr), CFI; Case T-303/08 *Tresplain Investments Ltd v Office for Harmonisation in the Internal Market (Trade Marks and Designs)* [2010] ECR II-5659, [2011] ETMR 44, EGC (affd Case C-76/11P [2012] ETMR 22, ECJ).

8 Council Regulation (EC) 207/2009 (OJ L78, 24.3.2009, p 1) art 8(4).

9 As to priority see PARA 267.

10 Council Regulation (EC) 207/2009 (OJ L78, 24.3.2009, p 1) art 8(4)(a).

11 'Use' in this context presumably means use in relation to the goods or services for which the application for the Community trade mark is made.

12 Council Regulation (EC) 207/2009 (OJ L78, 24.3.2009, p 1) art 8(4)(b). As to passing off see PARA 287 et seq.

206.   Attempts by agent or representative to register trade mark. Upon opposition[1] by the proprietor[2] of the trade mark, a Community trade mark[3] must not be registered[4] where an agent or representative[5] of the proprietor of the trade mark applies for registration of it in his own name without the proprietor's consent[6], unless the agent justifies his action[7].

1   As to opposing an application for registration of a Community trade mark see Council Regulation (EC) 207/2009 (OJ L78, 24.3.2009, p 1) on the Community trade mark, arts 41–42; and PARA 265.

2   As to the meaning of 'the proprietor' see PARA 205 note 2.

3   As to the meaning of 'Community trade mark' see PARA 189.

4   As to the meaning of 'registered' in this context see PARA 266 note 5.

5   As to the meaning of 'agent or representative' see PARA 137 note 3.

6   Such consent must be clear, specific and unconditional and must be valid on the day of application for registration: Case T-6/05 *DEF-TEC Defense Technology GmbH v Office for Harmonisation in the Internal Market (Trade Marks and Designs)* [2006] ECR II-2671, [2006] All ER (D) 23 (Sep), CFI ; Joined Cases T-537/10 and T-538/10 *Adamowski v Office for Harmonisation in the Internal Market (Trade Marks and Designs)* [2012] ECR II-0000, EGC.

7   Council Regulation (EC) 207/2009 (OJ L78, 24.3.2009, p 1) art 8(3). This implements the Paris Convention art 6 septies (1). As to the Paris Convention see PARA 6. As to justification see PARA 137 note 15.

(4)   EFFECTS OF COMMUNITY TRADE MARKS

207.   Rights conferred by registered trade mark. A Community trade mark[1] confers on the proprietor exclusive rights in it[2]. These rights are expressed as giving the proprietor the right to prevent all third parties not having his consent from doing certain acts[3].

The effects of Community trade marks are governed solely by Community legislation[4]; but in other respects, infringement of a Community trade mark is governed by the national law relating to infringement[5].

1   As to the meaning of 'Community trade mark' see PARA 189.

2   Council Regulation (EC) 207/2009 (OJ L78, 24.3.2009, p 1) on the Community trade mark, art 9(1).

3   Council Regulation (EC) 207/2009 (OJ L78, 24.3.2009, p 1) art 9(1). Although the acts set out in art 9(1) are not expressly described as amounting to an infringement of the Community trade mark, elsewhere the term infringement is often used interchangeably with a reference to the effects of a Community trade mark.
   As to infringement by use of a trade mark outside the jurisdiction see PARA 66 note 3; and as to the meaning of references to doing anything with or without the consent of the proprietor of a registered trade mark see PARA 259 note 4.

4   Ie Council Regulation (EC) 207/2009 (OJ L78, 24.3.2009, p 1).

5   Council Regulation (EC) 207/2009 (OJ L78, 24.3.2009, p 1) art 14(1). As to the bringing of an action for infringement see PARA 240 et seq.

208.   Date from which right runs. The rights conferred by a Community trade mark[1] prevail against third parties from the date of publication of registration of the trade mark[2].

However, reasonable compensation may be claimed in respect of matters arising after the date of publication of a Community trade mark application, which would, after publication of the registration of the trade mark, be prohibited[3] by virtue of the publication[4].

1   As to the meaning of 'Community trade mark' see PARA 189.
2   Council Regulation (EC) 207/2009 (OJ L78, 24.3.2009, p 1) on the Community trade mark, art 9(3). As to the publication of registration of a trade mark as a Community trade mark see PARA 173.
3   Ie the acts which the proprietor is or would be entitled to prevent under Council Regulation (EC) 207/2009 (OJ L78, 24.3.2009, p 1) arts 9(1), 11: see PARA 209 et seq.
4   Council Regulation (EC) 207/2009 (OJ L78, 24.3.2009, p 1) art 9(3). The court seized of the case may not decide on the merits until after the registration has been published: art 9(3).

209.   Identical mark for identical goods or services.   The proprietor of a Community trade mark[1] is entitled to prevent third parties not having his consent from using[2] in the course of trade[3] a sign which is identical[4] with the Community trade mark[5] in relation to goods or services which are identical[6] with those for which the Community trade mark is registered[7] provided that such use affects, or is liable to affect, one of the functions of the trade mark[8].

1   As to the meaning of 'Community trade mark' see PARA 189.
2   As to the meaning of 'use' see PARA 212.
3   As to the meaning of use 'in the course of trade' see PARA 68 note 3.
4   As to the meaning of 'identical' in this context see PARA 55 note 3.
5   As to the meaning of 'in relation to' in this context see PARA 68 note 6.
6   As to the meaning of 'identical' in this context see PARA 55 note 5.
7   Council Regulation (EC) 207/2009 (OJ L78, 24.3.2009, p 1) art 9(1)(a). As to the corresponding relative ground of refusal see art 8(1)(a); and PARA 202. As to the limits on the effect of a Community trade mark see PARAS 215–216; and as to the exhaustion of rights conferred by a Community trade mark see PARA 217.
8   See PARA 68 note 9; and PARA 69.

210.   Identical mark for similar goods or services; similar mark for identical goods or services.   The proprietor of a Community trade mark[1] is entitled to prevent third parties not having his consent from using[2] in the course of trade[3] any sign where because of its identity with or similarity to the Community trade mark and the identity or similarity of the goods or services[4] covered by the Community trade mark and the sign, there exists a likelihood of confusion on the part of the public. The likelihood of confusion includes the likelihood of association between the sign and the trade mark[5].

1   As to the meaning of 'Community trade mark' see PARA 189.
2   As to the meaning of 'use' see PARA 212.
3   As to the meaning of use 'in the course of trade' see PARA 68 note 3.
4   As to 'similarity of the goods or services' see PARA 57.
5   Council Regulation (EC) 207/2009 (OJ L78, 24.3.2009, p 1) on the Community trade mark, art 9(1)(b). As to the corresponding relative ground for refusal of registration see art 8(1)(b); and PARA 203. As to the likelihood of confusion see PARA 58; as to the limits on the effect of a Community trade mark see PARAS 215–216; and as to the exhaustion of rights conferred by a Community trade mark see PARA 217.

211.   Identical or similar mark for dissimilar goods or services.   The proprietor of a Community trade mark[1] is entitled to prevent third parties not having his consent from using[2] in the course of trade[3] any sign which is identical with or similar to the Community trade mark in relation to goods or services which are not similar[4] to those for which the Community trade mark is registered, where the latter has a reputation in the Community[5] and where the use of that sign without due cause[6] takes unfair advantage of, or is detrimental to, the distinctive character or repute of the Community trade mark[7].

1   As to the meaning of 'Community trade mark' see PARA 189.
2   As to the meaning of 'use' see PARA 212.

3 As to the meaning of use 'in the course of trade' see PARA 68 note 3.
4 This ground of objection can be invoked when the goods or services are identical or similar as well as when they are dissimilar: see PARA 71 note 7.
5 As to the meaning of 'reputation' see PARA 59 note 7.
6 As to the concept of use without due cause see PARA 59 note 9.
7 Council Regulation (EC) 207/2009 (OJ L78, 24.3.2009, p 1) on the Community trade mark, art 9(1)(c). Cf the corresponding relative ground for refusal of registration: see art 8(5); and PARA 204. As to the concept of unfair advantage or detriment to the distinctive character or repute of the Community trade mark see PARA 60.
   As to the limits on the effect of a Community trade mark see PARAS 215–216; and as to the exhaustion of rights conferred by a Community trade mark see PARA 217.

212. Meaning of 'use' for the purposes of infringement. The following inter alia[1] may be prohibited as infringing[2] a Community trade mark[3]:

(1) affixing the sign[4] to the goods or the packaging thereof[5];

(2) offering the goods, putting them on the market or stocking them for those purposes under that sign, or offering or supplying services thereunder[6];

(3) importing or exporting goods[7] under that sign[8]; or

(4) using the sign on business[9] papers[10] and in advertising[11].

1 This list is non-exhaustive: see PARA 72 note 4.
2 Ie prohibited under Council Regulation (EC) 207/2009 (OJ L78, 24.3.2009, p 1) on the Community trade mark, art 9(1): see PARAS 207–211.
3 As to the meaning of 'Community trade mark' see PARA 189. As to the limits on the effect of a Community trade mark see PARAS 215–216; and as to the exhaustion of rights conferred by a Community trade mark see PARA 217.
4 Ie the sign which the proprietor is entitled to prohibit others from using pursuant to Council Regulation (EC) 207/2009 (OJ L78, 24.3.2009, p 1) art 9(1). As to the manner in which the sign is used see PARA 72.
5 Council Regulation (EC) 207/2009 (OJ L78, 24.3.2009, p 1) art 9(2)(a). As to where the sign is applied to the goods or packaging outside the jurisdiction see PARA 72 note 5.
6 Council Regulation (EC) 207/2009 (OJ L78, 24.3.2009, p 1) art 9(2)(b). As to offering and putting goods on the market see PARA 72 note 6.
7 As to importing or exporting goods see PARA 72 note 7.
8 Council Regulation (EC) 207/2009 (OJ L78, 24.3.2009, p 1) art 9(2)(c).
9 'Business' is not defined for the purposes of Council Regulation (EC) 207/2009 (OJ L78, 24.3.2009, p 1). Cf the definition provided by the Trade Marks Act 1994: see PARA 34 note 3.
10 See PARA 72 note 10.
11 Council Regulation (EC) 207/2009 (OJ L78, 24.3.2009, p 1) art 9(2)(d). See PARA 72 note 11.

213. Reproduction of Community trade marks in dictionaries. If the reproduction of a Community trade mark[1] in a dictionary, encyclopaedia or similar reference work gives the impression that it constitutes the generic name of the goods or services for which the trade mark is registered, the publisher of the work must, at the request of the proprietor of the Community trade mark, ensure that the reproduction of the trade mark at the latest in the next edition of the publication is accompanied by an indication that it is a registered trade mark[2].

1 As to the meaning of 'Community trade mark' see PARA 189.
2 Council Regulation (EC) 207/2009 (OJ L78, 24.3.2009, p 1) on the Community trade mark, art 10. The conventional method of indicating that a mark is a registered trade mark is by the use of the ® sign in relation to it.
   The proprietor of a Community trade mark who does not enforce his rights under this provision risks his trade mark becoming the common name in the trade for the product or service in respect of which it is registered. If this happens, the mark may become liable to revocation pursuant to art 51(1)(b) on the grounds that this has occurred in consequence of his inactivity. See PARA 222.

214. Community trade mark registered in the name of an agent or representative. Where a Community trade mark[1] is registered in the name of the agent or representative of a person who is the proprietor[2] of that trade mark, without the proprietor's authorisation, the proprietor is entitled:

(1)   to oppose[3] the use[4] of his mark by his agent or representative if he has not authorised such use; and

(2)   to demand the assignment in his favour of the registration of the Community trade mark,

unless the agent or representative justifies his action[5].

1   As to the meaning of 'Community trade mark' see PARA 189.
2   It is presumed that 'proprietor' in this context has the same meaning as in Council Regulation (EC) 207/2009 (OJ L78, 24.3.2009, p 1) on the Community trade mark, art 8(3) (see PARAS 205 note 2, 206), since that provision and the provisions here are both derived from the Paris Convention art 6 septies. As to the Paris Convention see PARA 6.
3   It is presumed that 'oppose' in this context means that the proprietor of the trade mark is entitled to restrain the use of the trade mark by injunction. Cf the corresponding provisions under the Trade Marks Act 1994 s 60(4): see PARA 137.
4   As to the meaning of 'use' see PARA 212.
5   Council Regulation (EC) 207/2009 (OJ L78, 24.3.2009, p 1) arts 11, 18. Head (2) in the text also applies to applications for Community trade marks: art 24. See also note 2.

215. Limitation of the effects of a Community trade mark. A Community trade mark[1] does not entitle the proprietor to prohibit a third party from using[2] in the course of trade[3]:

(1)   his own name[4] or address[5];

(2)   indications concerning the kind, quality, quantity, intended purpose, value, geographical origin, time of production of the goods or of rendering of the service, or other characteristics of the goods or service[6]; or

(3)   the trade mark where it is necessary to indicate the intended purpose of a product or service, in particular as accessories or spare parts[7],

provided he uses them in accordance with honest practices in industrial or commercial matters[8].

1   As to the meaning of 'Community trade mark' see PARA 189.
2   As to the meaning of 'use' see PARA 212.
3   As to the meaning of 'trade' see PARA 194 note 5.
4   As to what constitutes a person's 'own name' and whether this defence is available to corporations see PARA 77 notes 3, 4.
5   See PARA 77 text and note 5.
6   See PARA 78 text and note 3.
7   See PARA 79.
8   Council Regulation (EC) 207/2009 (OJ L78, 24.3.2009, p 1) on the Community trade mark, art 12. As to the meaning of 'honest practices' see PARA 80.

216. Acquiescence. Where the proprietor of a Community trade mark[1] has acquiesced[2], for a period of five successive years, in the use[3] of a later Community trade mark in the Community while being aware of such use, he[4] is no longer entitled on the basis of the earlier trade mark either:

(1)   to apply for a declaration that the registration of the later trade mark is invalid; or

(2)   to oppose[5] the use of the later trade mark in relation to the goods or services in relation to which it has been so used,

unless the registration of the later trade mark was applied for in bad faith[6].

Where the proprietor of an earlier national trade mark[7] or other earlier sign[8] has acquiesced, for a continuous period of five successive years, in the use of a later Community trade mark in the member state in which the earlier trade mark or other earlier sign is protected while being aware of such use, he[9] is no longer entitled on the basis of the earlier trade mark either:

(a)   to apply for a declaration that the registration of the later trade mark is invalid; or

(b)   to oppose the use of the later trade mark in relation to the goods or services in relation to which it has been so used,

unless the registration of the later trade mark was applied for in bad faith[10].

In any such case[11], the proprietor of a later Community trade mark is not entitled to oppose the use of the earlier right, even though that right may no longer be invoked against the later Community trade mark[12].

1   As to the meaning of 'Community trade mark' see PARA 189.

2   As to the meaning of 'acquiesced' see PARA 83 note 3.

3   As to the meaning of 'use' see PARA 212.

4   It is not clear whether a third party would be prevented from applying for a declaration that the registration of the later trade mark is invalid by reason of this provision. It would be odd if the proprietor of the earlier trade mark or sign were so prevented but third parties were not, yet there is no explicit provision for this. Cf the Trade Marks Act 1994 s 48: see PARA 83.

5   As to the meaning of 'oppose' see PARA 214 note 3.

6   Council Regulation (EC) 207/2009 (OJ L78, 24.3.2009, p 1) art 54(1). As to the meaning of 'bad faith' see PARA 53 note 3.

7   Ie an 'earlier trade mark' within the meaning of Council Regulation (EC) 207/2009 (OJ L78, 24.3.2009, p 1) art 8(2), other than a Community trade mark: see PARA 201. Registration of the earlier trade mark is not a prerequisite for the running of the five year period to commence: see PARA 83 note 1.

8   Ie an earlier sign within the meaning of Council Regulation (EC) 207/2009 (OJ L78, 24.3.2009, p 1) art 8(4): see PARA 205.

9   See note 4.

10 Council Regulation (EC) 207/2009 (OJ L78, 24.3.2009, p 1) art 54(2). As to the conditions that must be satisfied before the period of limitation starts running see PARA 83 note 7.

11 Ie the cases referred to in Council Regulation (EC) 207/2009 (OJ L78, 24.3.2009, p 1) art 54(1), (2): see the text and notes 1–10.

12 Council Regulation (EC) 207/2009 (OJ L78, 24.3.2009, p 1) art 54(3).

217.   Exhaustion of rights.   A Community trade mark[1] does not entitle the proprietor to prohibit its use[2] in relation to goods which have been put on the market in the Community under that trade mark by the proprietor or with his consent[3]; but this provision does not apply where there exist legitimate reasons[4] for the proprietor to oppose further commercialisation of the goods, especially where the condition of the goods is changed or impaired after they have been put on the market[5].

Quite apart from this, the proprietor's right to enforce a Community trade mark may be restricted in some circumstances by the general rules under the Treaty on the Functioning of the European Union[6] relating to free movement of goods and competition law[7].

1   As to the meaning of 'Community trade mark' see PARA 189.

2   As to the meaning 'use' see PARA 212.

3   Council Regulation (EC) 207/2009 (OJ L78, 24.3.2009, p 1) on the Community trade mark, art 13(1). As to the effect of this provision see PARA 87. As to what may amount to the proprietor's consent see PARA 91.

4   As to what may amount to 'legitimate reasons' see PARA 88.

5   Council Regulation (EC) 207/2009 (OJ L78, 24.3.2009, p 1) art 13(2).

6   Ie Treaty on the Functioning of the European Union (Rome, 25 March 1957; TS 1 (1973); Cmnd 5179) ('TFEU') (formerly the Treaty Establishing the European Community (Rome, 25 March 1957; TS 1 (1973); Cmnd 5179) 'the EC Treaty'): see PARA 86 note 8.
7   See PARAS 89–90. The specific exhaustion defences under Council Regulation (EC) 207/2009 (OJ L78, 24.3.2009, p 1) and European Parliament and Council Directive (EC) 2008/95 (OJ L299, 8.11.2008, p 25) to approximate the laws of the member states relating to trade marks do not necessarily cover all the ground covered by the case law of the European Court of Justice interpreting the EC Treaty and the TFEU: see PARA 89 note 5.

(5) SURRENDER, REVOCATION, INVALIDITY, ALTERATION AND DIVISION

(i) Introduction

218.   Modes of extinction or modification of Community trade marks.   The Community Trade Mark Regulation[1] provides a number of ways in which the rights conferred by a Community trade mark[2] may be cancelled or varied[3]. It uses the following terminology:

(1)   'surrender' for voluntary surrender by the proprietor[4];
(2)   'revocation' for removal of a registration on grounds which have arisen since registration[5];
(3)   'declaration of invalidity' for cases where the mark ought not to have been registered originally[6];
(4)   'alteration' for minor corrections[7]; and
(5)   'division' for splitting a registration into two or more registrations[8].

1   Ie Council Regulation (EC) 207/2009 (OJ L78, 24.3.2009, p 1) on the Community trade mark.
2   As to the meaning of 'Community trade mark' see PARA 189.
3   Ie apart from lapse for failure to pay renewal fees: see PARA 266. Cf the position under the Trade Marks Act 1994: see PARA 93.
4   See PARA 219.
5   See PARA 220 et seq.
6   See PARA 226 et seq.
7   See PARA 231.
8   See PARA 232.

(ii) Surrender

219.   In general.   A Community trade mark[1] may be surrendered in respect of some or all of the goods or services for which it is registered[2]. Surrender can be entered only with the agreement of the proprietor of a right entered in the register[3].

The surrender must be declared to the Office for Harmonisation in the Internal Market in writing by the proprietor of the trade mark and does not have effect until it has been entered into the register[4].

1   As to the meaning of 'Community trade mark' see PARA 189.
2   Council Regulation (EC) 207/2009 (OJ L78, 24.3.2009, p 1) on the Community trade mark, art 50(1). As to the procedure for surrender see Commission Regulation (EC) 2868/95 (OJ L303, 15.12.95, p 1) implementing Council Regulation (EC) 40/94 on the Community trade mark, art 1 r 36 (amended by Commission Regulation (EC) 1041/2005 (OJ L172, 5.7.05, p 4)).
3   Council Regulation (EC) 207/2009 (OJ L78, 24.3.2009, p 1) art 50(3). If a licence has been registered, surrender can only be entered in the register if the proprietor of the trade mark proves that he has informed the licensee of his intention to surrender; this entry must be made on expiry of three months after the date on which the proprietor satisfies the Office for Harmonisation in the Internal Market that he has informed the licensee of his intention to

surrender the Community trade mark: art 50(3); Commission Regulation (EC) 2868/95 (OJ L303, 15.12.95) art 1 r 36(2). As to the Office for Harmonisation in the Internal Market see PARA 163 et seq.

4   Council Regulation (EC) 207/2009 (OJ L78, 24.3.2009, p 1) art 50(2). A Community trade mark which has been surrendered ceases to have effect only from the registration of the surrender: Case C-552/09 *Ferrero SpA v Office for Harmonisation of the Internal Market (Trade Marks and Designs)* [2011] ETMR 30, ECJ. If the proprietor applies to surrender a Community trade mark which is subject to an application for revocation or a declaration of invalidity the proceedings must continue: Decision 69C/000670042/1 *Lancôme Parfums et Beauté & Cie's Application* [2001] ETMR 89, OHIM Cancellation Division. The same is true if the proprietor surrenders a Community trade mark after a decision by the Board of Appeal: *Ferrero SpA v Office for Harmonisation of the Internal Market (Trade Marks and Designs)* above. Cf the position under the Trade Marks Act 1994 s 45: see PARA 97 note 5.and see also PARA 377.

(iii) Revocation

220. Use of Community trade marks. If, within the period of five years following registration[1] the proprietor has not put the Community trade mark[2] to genuine[3] use[4] in the Community[5], in connection with the goods or services for which it is registered, or if such use has been suspended for an uninterrupted period of five years, the Community trade mark is subject to the sanctions provided for[6], unless there are proper reasons[7] for non-use[8].

1   As to registration of a Community trade mark see PARA 266 note 5.
2   As to the meaning of 'Community trade mark' see PARA 189.
3   As to genuine use see PARA 98 note 6.
4   The following constitute use for these purposes: (1) use of the Community trade mark in a form differing in elements which do not alter the distinctive character of the mark in the form in which it was registered; and (2) affixing the Community trade mark to goods or to the packaging of goods in the Community solely for export purposes: Council Regulation (EC) 207/2009 (OJ L78, 24.3.2009, p 1) on the Community trade mark, art 15(1)(a), (b). See PARA 98 note 7. Use of the Community trade mark with the consent of the proprietor is deemed to constitute use by the proprietor: art 15(2). For the requirement of use as it applies to Community collective marks see PARA 283 note 1; and as to the meaning of references to 'use' generally see PARA 212.
5   The territorial borders of the member states must be disregarded in the assessment of whether a Community trade mark has been put to genuine use in the Community: Case C-149/11 *Leno Merken BV v Hagelkruis Beheer BV* [2013] IP & T 295, [2013] All ER (D) 53 (Jan), [2013] ETMR 16, ECJ.
6   Ie by Council Regulation (EC) 207/2009 (OJ L78, 24.3.2009, p 1): see art 51; and PARA 221.
7   As to the meaning of 'proper reasons' see PARA 98 note 10.
8   Council Regulation (EC) 207/2009 (OJ L78, 24.3.2009, p 1) art 15(1).

221. Non-use. The rights of the proprietor of the Community trade mark[1] must[2] be declared to be revoked on application to the Office for Harmonisation in the Internal Market[3] or on the basis of a counterclaim in infringement proceedings[4] if, within a continuous period of five years, the trade mark has not been put to genuine[5] use[6] in the Community[7] in connection with the goods or services for which it is registered, and there are no proper reasons[8] for non-use[9].

No person may claim that the proprietor's rights in a Community trade mark should be revoked where, during the interval between the expiry of the five-year period and the filing of the application or counterclaim, genuine use of the trade mark has been started or resumed. However, the commencement or resumption of use within a period of three months preceding the filing of the application or counterclaim which began at the earliest on expiry of the continuous period of five years of non-use is to be disregarded where preparations for the commencement or resumption occurred only after the proprietor became aware that the application or counterclaim may be filed[10].

1   As to the meaning of 'Community trade mark' see PARA 189.
2   Cf the corresponding provisions of the Trade Marks Act 1994 s 46: see PARAS 95, 98. In that Act, the permissive 'may' is used, but it has been held that there is no discretion not to revoke the mark. In Council Regulation (EC) 207/2009 (OJ L78, 24.3.2009, p 1) on the Community trade mark, art 51, the directive 'shall' is used, so it is clear there is no discretion in this provision.
3   As to the Office for Harmonisation in the Internal Market see PARA 163 et seq; and as to bringing an application for revocation in the Office see PARA 272 et seq.
4   As to the raising of a counterclaim for revocation in infringement proceedings see PARA 244 et seq.
5   As to genuine use see PARA 98 note 6.
6   As to the meaning of 'use' see PARA 220 note 4. In revocation proceedings for non-use the burden lies on the proprietor of the Community trade mark to prove genuine use within the relevant period or proper reasons for non-use: Decision 686C/000405555/1 *BARRICADE Trade Mark* (17 May 2004, unreported), OHIM Cancellation Division.
7   As to the requirement of genuine use in the Community see PARA 220.
8   As to the meaning of 'proper reasons' see PARA 98 note 10.
9   Council Regulation (EC) 207/2009 (OJ L78, 24.3.2009, p 1) art 51(1)(a).
10   Council Regulation (EC) 207/2009 (OJ L78, 24.3.2009, p 1) art 51(1)(a).

222.   Mark becoming common name. The rights of the proprietor of the Community trade mark[1] must[2] be declared to be revoked on application to the Office for Harmonisation in the Internal Market[3] or on the basis of a counterclaim in infringement proceedings[4] if, in consequence of acts or inactivity[5] of the proprietor, the trade mark has become the common name in the trade[6] for a product or service in respect of which it is registered[7].

1   As to the meaning of 'Community trade mark' see PARA 189.
2   See PARA 221 note 2.
3   As to the Office for Harmonisation in the Internal Market see PARA 163 et seq; and as to bringing an application for revocation in the Office see PARA 272 et seq.
4   As to the raising of a counterclaim for revocation in infringement proceedings see PARA 244 et seq.
5   As to the acts or inactivity of the proprietor see PARA 99. One mode of inactivity would be a failure to take action in relation to the reproduction of a Community trade mark in a dictionary etc: see PARA 213.
6   As to the meaning of 'common name in the trade' see PARA 99.
7   Council Regulation (EC) 207/2009 (OJ L78, 24.3.2009, p 1) on the Community trade mark, art 51(1)(b).

223.   Liability to mislead in consequence of use. The rights of the proprietor of the Community trade mark[1] must[2] be declared to be revoked on application to the Office for Harmonisation in the Internal Market[3] or on the basis of a counterclaim in infringement proceedings[4] if, in consequence of the use[5] made of it by the proprietor of the trade mark or with his consent in relation to the goods or services for which it is registered, it is liable to mislead the public, particularly as to the nature, quality or geographical origin of those goods or services[6].

1   As to the meaning of 'Community trade mark' see PARA 189.
2   See PARA 221 note 2.
3   As to the Office for Harmonisation in the Internal Market see PARA 163 et seq; and as to bringing an application for revocation in the Office see PARA 272 et seq.
4   As to the raising of a counterclaim for revocation in infringement proceedings see PARA 244 et seq.
5   As to the requirement for liability that the mark mislead in consequence of the use made of it see PARA 100 note 3. As to the meaning of 'use' see PARA 212.

6   Council Regulation (EC) 207/2009 (OJ L78, 24.3.2009, p 1) on the Community trade mark, art 51(1)(c). This ground relates to events arising after the registration date of the mark. If the mark was misleading as to its date of registration, it will be liable to be declared invalid pursuant to art 52(1) (see PARA 226), which includes any of the provisions of art 7 (absolute grounds for refusal: see PARA 192 et seq), including, therefore, art 7(1)(g) (mark of such a nature as to deceive the public: see PARA 197). As to the circumstances in which this ground may be invoked see PARA 100 note 5.

224.   Partial revocation. Where grounds for revocation[1] exist in respect of only some of the goods or services for which the Community trade mark[2] is registered[3], the rights of the proprietor must be declared to be revoked in respect of those goods or services only[4].

1   As to the grounds for revocation see PARAS 220–223; and as to the additional grounds for revocation of a Community collective mark see PARA 283.
2   As to the meaning of 'Community trade mark' see PARA 189.
3   As to the meaning of 'registered' see PARA 266 note 5.
4   Council Regulation (EC) 207/2009 (OJ L78, 24.3.2009, p 1) on the Community trade mark, art 51(2). As to narrowing the specification of goods or services in such circumstances see PARA 101 note 4; but note the slightly different approach of the Court of First Instance (now the European General Court) from that of the English courts in the cases cited.

225.   Date from which revocation takes effect. A Community trade mark[1] is deemed not to have had, as from the date of the application[2] for revocation[3] or of the counterclaim[4], the specified effects[5], to the extent that the rights of the proprietor have been revoked[6].

An earlier date, on which one of the grounds for revocation occurred, may be fixed in the decision[7] at the request of one of the parties[8].

Subject to certain national provisions[9], the retroactive effect of revocation of the trade mark does not affect the following[10]:

(1)   any decision on infringement which has acquired the authority of a final decision and has been enforced prior to the revocation decision[11]; or

(2)   any contract concluded prior to the revocation decision, in so far as it has been performed before that decision[12].

1   As to the meaning of 'Community trade mark' see PARA 189.

2   As to applications for revocation in the Office for Harmonisation in the Internal Market see PARA 272 et seq. As to the Office for Harmonisation in the Internal Market see PARA 163 et seq.

3   As to the grounds for revocation see PARAS 220–223. As to the additional grounds for revocation of a Community collective mark see PARA 283.

4   As to the raising of a counterclaim for revocation in infringement proceedings see PARA 244 et seq.

5   Ie the effects specified in Council Regulation (EC) 207/2009 (OJ L78, 24.3.2009, p 1) on the Community trade mark.

6   Council Regulation (EC) 207/2009 (OJ L78, 24.3.2009, p 1) art 55(1).

7   Ie the decision declaring the rights of the proprietor to be revoked.

8   Council Regulation (EC) 207/2009 (OJ L78, 24.3.2009, p 1) art 55(1).

9   Ie national provisions relating either to claims for compensation for damage caused by negligence or lack of good faith on the part of the proprietor of the trade mark, or unjust enrichment.

10 Council Regulation (EC) 207/2009 (OJ L78, 24.3.2009, p 1) art 55(3).

11 Council Regulation (EC) 207/2009 (OJ L78, 24.3.2009, p 1) art 55(3)(a).

12 Council Regulation (EC) 207/2009 (OJ L78, 24.3.2009, p 1) art 55(3)(b). However, repayment, to the extent justified by the circumstances, of sums paid under the relevant contract may be claimed on grounds of equity: art 55(3)(b).

(iv) Declaration of Invalidity

226. Registration granted in breach of absolute grounds for refusal. A Community trade mark[1] must be declared to be invalid on application to the Office for Harmonisation in the Internal Market[2] or on the basis of a counterclaim in infringement proceedings[3]:

(1) where the Community trade mark was registered in breach of the absolute grounds[4] for refusal of registration[5];

(2) where the applicant was acting in bad faith[6] when he filed the application for the trade mark[7].

Where the trade mark was registered even though it is devoid of any distinctive character[8] or consists exclusively of signs or indications which may serve, in trade[9], to designate the kind etc of goods or services[10] or consists exclusively of signs or indications which have become customary in the current language or in the bona fide and established practices of the trade[11], it may nevertheless not be declared invalid if, in consequence of the use[12] which has been made of it, it has after registration acquired a distinctive character in relation to the goods or services for which it is registered[13].

1   As to the meaning of 'Community trade mark' see PARA 189.
2   As to the Office for Harmonisation in the Internal Market see PARA 163 et seq; and as to bringing an application for a declaration of invalidity in the Office see PARA 272 et seq.
3   Council Regulation (EC) 207/2009 (OJ L78, 24.3.2009, p 1) on the Community trade mark, art 52(1) on the Community trade mark. As to the raising of a counterclaim for revocation in infringement proceedings see PARA 244 et seq.
4   Ie on the ground that the trade mark was registered contrary to the provisions of Council Regulation (EC) 207/2009 (OJ L78, 24.3.2009, p 1) art 7: see PARA 192 et seq.
5   Council Regulation (EC) 207/2009 (OJ L78, 24.3.2009, p 1) art 52(1)(a). The Cancellation Division is required to assess such an application on its merits and is not fettered by any decision during the application phase: Case R 766/2000–2 *Société France Cartes v Naipes Heraclio Fournier SA* [2002] ETMR 92, OHIM Board of Appeal (affd sub nom Joined Cases T-160/02 to T-162/02 *Naipes Heraclio Fournier SA v Office for Harmonisation in the Internal Market (Trade Marks and Designs)* [2005] ECR II-1643, [2005] All ER (D) 136 (May), CFI).
6   As to the meaning of 'bad faith' see PARA 53.
7   Council Regulation (EC) 207/2009 (OJ L78, 24.3.2009, p 1) art 52(1)(b). See note 6. As to the additional ground of invalidity of a Community collective mark see PARA 284.
8   Ie in breach of Council Regulation (EC) 207/2009 (OJ L78, 24.3.2009, p 1) art 7(1)(b): see PARA 194.
9   As to the meaning of 'trade' see PARA 194 note 5.
10   Ie in breach of Council Regulation (EC) 207/2009 (OJ L78, 24.3.2009, p 1) art 7(1)(c): see PARA 194.
11   Ie in breach of Council Regulation (EC) 207/2009 (OJ L78, 24.3.2009, p 1) art 7(1)(d): see PARA 194.
12   As to the meaning of 'use' see PARA 212.
13   Council Regulation (EC) 207/2009 (OJ L78, 24.3.2009, p 1) art 52(2). As to distinctive character acquired as a result of use see PARA 45.

227. Registration granted in breach of relative grounds for refusal. A Community trade mark[1] must be declared invalid on application to the Office for Harmonisation in the Internal Market[2] or on the basis of a counterclaim[3] in infringement proceedings[4]:

(1) where there is an earlier trade mark[5] in relation to which the specified conditions for refusal[6] are fulfilled[7];

(2) where the trade mark was registered in the name of the agent or representative of the proprietor thereof and the specified conditions[8] are fulfilled[9]; or

(3)   where there is an earlier right[10] in relation to which the specified condition for refusal[11] is fulfilled[12].

However, a Community trade mark may not be declared invalid where the proprietor of the earlier trade mark, trade mark or earlier right[13] (as the case may be) consents expressly to the registration of the Community trade mark before submission of the application for a declaration of invalidity or the counterclaim[14].

1   As to the meaning of 'Community trade mark' see PARA 189.
2   As to the Office for Harmonisation in the Internal Market see PARA 163 et seq; and as to bringing an application for a declaration of invalidity in the Office see PARA 272 et seq.
3   As to the raising of a counterclaim in infringement proceedings see PARA 244 et seq.
4   Council Regulation (EC) 207/2009 (OJ L78, 24.3.2009, p 1) on the Community trade mark, art 53(1).
5   Ie an earlier trade mark as referred to in Council Regulation (EC) 207/2009 (OJ L78, 24.3.2009, p 1) art 8(2): see PARA 201.
6   Ie the conditions set out in Council Regulation (EC) 207/2009 (OJ L78, 24.3.2009, p 1) art 8(1) or (5): see PARAS 202–204.
7   Council Regulation (EC) 207/2009 (OJ L78, 24.3.2009, p 1) art 53(1)(a).
8   Ie where there is a trade mark as referred to in Council Regulation (EC) 207/2009 (OJ L78, 24.3.2009, p 1) art 8(3) and the specified conditions are those set out in that provision: see PARA 206.
9   Council Regulation (EC) 207/2009 (OJ L78, 24.3.2009, p 1) art 53(1)(b).
10   Ie an earlier right as referred to in Council Regulation (EC) 207/2009 (OJ L78, 24.3.2009, p 1) art 8(4): see PARA 205.
11   Ie the condition set out in Council Regulation (EC) 207/2009 (OJ L78, 24.3.2009, p 1) art 8(4): see PARA 205.
12   Council Regulation (EC) 207/2009 (OJ L78, 24.3.2009, p 1) art 53(1)(c). Where the proprietor of such a right has previously applied for a declaration that the Community trade mark is invalid or made a counterclaim in infringement proceedings, he may not submit a new application for a declaration of invalidity or lodge a counterclaim on the basis of another of the rights referred to in art 53(1) or art 53(2) (see PARA 228) which he could have invoked in support of his first application or counterclaim: art 53(4). See Decision 793C/00192500/2 *Luis Cabellero SA v Scottish & Newcastle plc* (17 May 2004, unreported), OHIM Cancellation Division.
13   Ie the right referred to in EC Council Regulation 40/94 (OJ L11, 14.1.94, p 1) art 53(1): see the text and notes 1–12.
14   Council Regulation (EC) 207/2009 (OJ L78, 24.3.2009, p 1) art 53(3).

228.   Use of Community trade mark would infringe another earlier right.   A Community trade mark[1] must be declared invalid on application to the Office for Harmonisation in the Internal Market[2] or on the basis of a counterclaim in infringement proceedings[3] where the use of such trade mark may be prohibited pursuant to another earlier right[4], and in particular:

(1)   a right to a name[5];

(2)   a right of personal portrayal[6];

(3)   a copyright[7]; or

(4)   an industrial property right[8],

under the Community legislation or national law[9] governing the protection.

However, a Community trade mark may not be declared invalid where the proprietor of the earlier right[10] consents expressly to the registration of the Community trade mark before submission of the application for a declaration of invalidity or the counterclaim[11].

1   As to the meaning of 'Community trade mark' see PARA 189.
2   As to the Office for Harmonisation in the Internal Market see PARA 163 et seq; and as to bringing an application for a declaration of invalidity in the Office see PARA 272 et seq.
3   As to the raising of a counterclaim in infringement proceedings see PARA 244 et seq.

4   Council Regulation (EC) 207/2009 (OJ L78, 24.3.2009, p 1) on the Community trade mark, art 53(2). Where the proprietor of such a right has previously applied for a declaration that the Community trade mark is invalid or made a counterclaim in infringement proceedings, he may not submit a new application for a declaration of invalidity or lodge a counterclaim on the basis of another of the rights referred to in art 53(1) (see PARA 227) or art 53(2) which he could have invoked in support of his first application or counterclaim: art 53(4).

5   Council Regulation (EC) 207/2009 (OJ L78, 24.3.2009, p 1) art 53(2)(a). This provision is not restricted to situations where the registration of a Community trade mark conflicts with a right intended exclusively to protect a name as an attribute of the personality of the person concerned: Case C-263/09P *Edwin Co Ltd v Office for Harmonisation in the Internal Market (Trade Marks and Designs)* [2011] ECR I-5853, ECJ.

6   Council Regulation (EC) 207/2009 (OJ L78, 24.3.2009, p 1) art 53(2)(b).

7   Council Regulation (EC) 207/2009 (OJ L78, 24.3.2009, p 1) art 53(2)(c). As to copyright see COPYRIGHT vol 23 (2013) PARA 603 et seq.

8   Council Regulation (EC) 207/2009 (OJ L78, 24.3.2009, p 1) art 53(2)(d).

9   Where national law is relied on, the applicant for a declaration of invalidity must provide particulars showing that he is entitled under the applicable national law to lay claim to the right in question, including particulars establishing the content of the national law: Case C-263/09P *Edwin Co Ltd v Office for Harmonisation in the Internal Market (Trade Marks and Designs)* [2011] ECR I-5853, ECJ; but the Office is obliged to inform itself of the relevant national law: Case T-404/10 *National Lottery Commission v Office for Harmonisation in the Internal Market (Trade Marks and Designs)* [2012] IP & T 1011, [2012] All ER (D) 91 (Sep), EGC.

10   Ie the earlier right referred to in Council Regulation (EC) 207/2009 (OJ L78, 24.3.2009, p 1) art 53(2): see the text to notes 1–8.

11   Council Regulation (EC) 207/2009 (OJ L78, 24.3.2009, p 1) art 53(3).

229.   Partial declaration of invalidity.   Where the grounds of invalidity[1] exist in respect of only some of the goods or services for which the Community trade mark[2] is registered, the trade mark must be declared invalid as regards those goods or services only[3].

1   As to the grounds of invalidity see PARAS 226–228; and as to the additional ground of invalidity of a Community collective mark see PARA 284.

2   As to the meaning of 'Community trade mark' see PARA 189.

3   Council Regulation (EC) 207/2009 (OJ L78, 24.3.2009, p 1) on the Community trade mark, arts 52(3), 53(5). As to the effect of a declaration of invalidity see PARA 230. As to narrowing the specification of goods or services in such circumstances see PARA 104.

230.   Effect of declaration of invalidity.   A Community trade mark[1] is deemed not to have had, as from the outset, the specified effects[2], to the extent that the trade mark is declared invalid[3].

Subject to certain national provisions[4], the retroactive effect of invalidity of the trade mark does not affect the following[5]:

(1)   any decision on infringement which has acquired the authority of a final decision and has been enforced prior to the invalidity decision[6]; or

(2)   any contract concluded prior to the invalidity decision, in so far as it has been performed before that decision (although repayment, to the extent justified by the circumstances, of sums paid under the relevant contract may be claimed on grounds of equity)[7].

1   As to the meaning of 'Community trade mark' see PARA 189.

2   Ie the effects specified in Council Regulation (EC) 207/2009 (OJ L78, 24.3.2009, p 1) on the Community trade mark: see PARA 207 et seq.

3   Council Regulation (EC) 207/2009 (OJ L78, 24.3.2009, p 1) art 55(2). As to the grounds of invalidity see PARAS 226–228; and as to the additional ground of invalidity of a Community collective mark see PARA 284.

4   Ie national provisions relating either to claims for compensation for damage caused by negligence or lack of good faith on the part of the proprietor of the trade mark, or unjust enrichment.

5   Council Regulation (EC) 207/2009 (OJ L78, 24.3.2009, p 1) art 54(3).

6   Council Regulation (EC) 207/2009 (OJ L78, 24.3.2009, p 1) art 55(3)(a).
7   Council Regulation (EC) 207/2009 (OJ L78, 24.3.2009, p 1) art 55(3)(b).

(v) Alteration

231.   In general.   A Community trade mark[1] may not be altered in the register[2] during the period of registration or on renewal thereof[3]. Nevertheless, where the Community trade mark includes the name and address of the proprietor, an alteration not substantially affecting the identity of the trade mark as originally registered may be registered at the request of the proprietor[4].

The publication[5] of the registration of the alteration must contain a representation of the Community trade mark as altered; and third parties whose rights may be affected by the alteration may challenge its registration within a period of three months following publication[6].

1   As to the meaning of 'Community trade mark' see PARA 189.
2   As to the register of Community trade marks see PARA 188.
3   Council Regulation (EC) 207/2009 (OJ L78, 24.3.2009, p 1) on the Community trade mark, art 48(1).
4   Council Regulation (EC) 207/2009 (OJ L78, 24.3.2009, p 1) art 48(2). As to the procedure for alteration see Commission Regulation (EC) 2868/95 (OJ L303, 15.12.95, p 1) implementing Council Regulation (EC) 40/94 on the Community trade mark, art 1 rr 25–27 (rr 25, 26 amended by Commission Regulation (EC) 1041/2005 (OJ L172, 5.7.05, p 4)).
      As to the principles applied by the United Kingdom courts under the similar provision in the Trade Marks Act 1994 see PARA 106 note 5.
5   As to publication see PARA 173.
6   Council Regulation (EC) 207/2009 (OJ L78, 24.3.2009, p 1) art 48(3).

(vi) Division

232.   In general.   The proprietor of a Community trade mark[1] may divide the registration by declaring that some of the goods or services included in the original registration will be the subject of one or more divisional registrations[2]. The goods or services in the divisional registration must not overlap with the goods or services which remain in the original registration or those which are included in other divisional registrations[3].

Division is not permissible[4]:

(1)   if, where an application[5] for revocation of rights or for a declaration of invalidity has been entered against the original registration, a divisional declaration has the effect of introducing a division amongst the goods or services against which the application for revocation of rights or a declaration of invalidity is directed, until the decision of the Cancellation Division[6] has become final or the proceedings are finally terminated otherwise[7];

(2)   if, where a counterclaim[8] for revocation or for a declaration of invalidity has been entered in a case before a Community trade mark court[9], a divisional declaration has the effect of introducing a division amongst the goods or services against which the counterclaim is directed, until the mention of the Community trade mark court's judgment is recorded in the register[10].

1   As to the meaning of 'Community trade mark' see PARA 189.
2   Council Regulation (EC) 207/2009 (OJ L78, 24.3.2009, p 1) on the Community trade mark, art 49(1). The declaration must comply with the provisions set out in Commission Regulation (EC) 2868/95 (OJ L303, 15.12.95, p 1) implementing Council Regulation (EC) 40/94 on the Community trade mark: Council Regulation (EC) 207/2009 (OJ L78, 24.3.2009, p 1) art 49(3).

The declaration is subject to a fee and must be deemed not to have been made until the fee is paid: art 49(4). As to the procedure for the division of a registration see Commission Regulation (EC) 2868/95 (OJ L303, 15.12.95, p 1) art 1 r 25a (added by Commission Regulation (EC) 1041/2005 (OJ L172, 5.7.05, p 4)). The division will take effect on the date on which it is entered on the register: Council Regulation (EC) 207/2009 (OJ L78, 24.3.2009, p 1) art 49(5). As to the register of Community trade marks see PARA 171.

    All requests and applications submitted and all fees paid with regard to the original registration prior to the date on which the Office for Harmonisation in the Internal Market receives the declaration of division will be deemed to have been submitted or paid with regard to the divisional registration or registrations. The fees for the original registration which have been paid prior to the date on which the declaration of division is received will not be refunded: art 49(6). The divisional registration will preserve the filing date and any priority date and seniority date of the original registration: art 49(7). As to the Office for Harmonisation in the Internal Market see PARA 163 et seq.

    Division of an application to register a Community trade mark is also possible: see art 44(1); and PARA 264. Under the Trade Marks Act 1994 s 41(1) only division of an application, and not division of a registration, is permitted: see PARA 349.

3   Council Regulation (EC) 207/2009 (OJ L78, 24.3.2009, p 1) art 49(1).
4   Council Regulation (EC) 207/2009 (OJ L78, 24.3.2009, p 1) art 49(2).
5   As to bringing an application for revocation or a declaration of invalidity in the Office see PARA 272 et seq.
6   As to the Cancellation Division see PARA 165.
7   Council Regulation (EC) 207/2009 (OJ L78, 24.3.2009, p 1) art 49(2)(a).
8   As to the raising of a counterclaim in infringement proceedings see PARA 244 et seq.
9   As to Community trade mark courts see PARA 233.
10 Council Regulation (EC) 207/2009 (OJ L78, 24.3.2009, p 1) art 49(2)(b). The judgment is recorded pursuant to art 100(6): see PARA 247.

(6) NATIONAL ACTIONS RELATING TO COMMUNITY TRADE MARKS

(i) Introduction

233. In general. An action for infringement of a Community trade mark[1] must be brought in a court of one of the member states[2]. For that purpose, the member states must designate as limited a number as possible of national courts and tribunals[3] ('Community trade mark courts') which must perform the functions assigned to them[4]. For that purpose, in England and Wales the High Court and a number of county courts were designated as Community trade mark courts but now there is the Intellectual Property Enterprise Court[5].

    Given the unitary character of Community trade marks[6], it will often be the case that the courts of more than one member state could potentially exercise jurisdiction over an infringement action. In general[7], the Brussels Convention[8] applies to proceedings relating to Community trade marks and applications[9] for Community trade marks, as well as to proceedings relating to simultaneous and successive actions on the basis of Community trade marks and national trade marks[10].

1   As to the meaning of 'Community trade mark' see PARA 189.
2   See Council Regulation (EC) 207/2009 (OJ L78, 24.3.2009, p 1) on the Community trade mark, art 96; and PARA 234.
3   Ie courts and tribunals of first and second instance: see generally COURTS AND TRIBUNALS vol 24 (2010) PARA 601 et seq.
4   Council Regulation (EC) 207/2009 (OJ L78, 24.3.2009, p 1) art 95(1). Each member state was required to communicate to the EC Commission by 22 September 1995 a list of Community trade mark courts indicating their names and territorial jurisdiction: art 95(2). Any change made after communication of that list must be notified without delay by the member state concerned

to the Commission: art 95(3). This information must be notified by the Commission to the member states and published in the Official Journal of the European Communities: art 95(4).

As long as a member state has not communicated the list stipulated by art 95(2), jurisdiction for any proceedings resulting from an action or application in respect of which the Community trade mark courts have exclusive jurisdiction (ie which is covered by art 96: see PARA 234) and for which the courts of that state have jurisdiction (ie pursuant to art 97: see PARA 235) lies with the court of that state in question which would have jurisdiction ratione loci and ratione materiale in the case of proceedings relating to a national trade mark registered in that state: art 95(5).

5   Community Trade Mark Regulations 2006, SI 2006/1027, reg 12(1), (2). The county courts so designated were the county courts at Birmingham, Bristol, Cardiff, Leeds, Liverpool, Manchester and Newcastle upon Tyne: see reg 12(1), (2). For the purpose of hearing appeals from judgments of the designated first instance courts, the Court of Appeal was also designated as a Community trade mark court: reg 12(3). As from 1 October 2013 the Patents County Court, which was formerly designated as a Community trade mark court, was replaced by the Intellectual Property Enterprise Court, a specialist list of the Chancery Division of the High Court, as a result of the combined effect of the Crime and Courts Act 2013 s 17(5), 22, Sch 9 paras 21, 27, 30 and the Civil Procedure (Amendment No 7) Rules 2013, SI 2013/1974: see PARA 331; and generally CIVIL PROCEDURE; COURTS AND TRIBUNALS.

6   As to the unitary character of Community trade marks see PARA 189.

7   Ie unless otherwise specified in Council Regulation (EC) 207/2009 (OJ L78, 24.3.2009, p 1): see note 8.

8   Ie the Convention on Jurisdiction and Enforcement of Judgments in Civil and Commercial Matters (Brussels, 27 September 1968: Cmnd 7395), as amended by the Conventions on the Accession to that Convention of the states acceding to the European Communities. The Brussels Convention sets out (inter alia) the rules under which the courts of signatory states allocate jurisdiction between themselves. It has largely been superseded by Council Regulation (EC) 44/2001 (OJ L12, 16.1.01, p 1) on jurisdiction and the recognition and enforcement of judgments in civil and commercial matters (the 'Brussels I' Regulation), which is similar but not identical terms. Council Regulation (EC) 44/2001 is (prospectively) replaced by European Parliament and Council Regulation (EU) 1215/2012 (OJ L351, 20.12.2012, p 1) on jurisdiction and the recognition and enforcement of judgments in civil and commercial matters (with application, except for specified provisions, from 10 January 2015). See CONFLICT OF LAWS vol 19 (2011) PARA 366 et seq.

In the case of proceedings in respect of the actions or claims in respect of which the Community trade mark courts have exclusive jurisdiction (ie which are covered by Council Regulation (EC) 207/2009 (OJ L78, 24.3.2009, p 1) art 96: see PARA 234): (1) the Brussels Convention arts 2, 4, 5(1), (3), (4), (5) do not apply; (2) the Brussels Convention arts 17, 18 apply subject to the limitations in Council Regulation (EC) 207/2009 (OJ L78, 24.3.2009, p 1) art 97(4) (see PARA 235); and (3) the provisions of the Brussels Convention Title II which are applicable to persons domiciled in a member state are also applicable to persons who do not have a domicile in any member state but have an establishment therein: Council Regulation (EC) 207/2009 (OJ L78, 24.3.2009, p 1) art 94(2).

The provisions of the Brussels Convention which are rendered applicable by Council Regulation (EC) 207/2009 (OJ L78, 24.3.2009, p 1) have effect in respect of any member state solely in the text of the Convention which is in force in respect of that state at any given time: art 108.

As to the relationship between Council Regulation (EC) 40/94 (OJ L11, 14.1.94, p 1) (now Council Regulation (EC) 207/2009 (OJ L78, 24.3.2009, p 1)) and the Brussels Convention see *Prudential Assurance Co Ltd v Prudential Insurance Co of America* [2003] EWCA Civ 327, [2003] 1 WLR 2295, [2003] FSR 25.

9   As to an application for Community trade marks being an object of property see PARA 254 note 1.

10 Council Regulation (EC) 207/2009 (OJ L78, 24.3.2009, p 1) art 94(1).

(ii) Jurisdiction of National Courts

234.   Exclusive jurisdiction of Community trade mark courts. The Community trade mark courts[1] have exclusive jurisdiction:

(1)   for all infringement actions[2] and, if they are permitted under national law, actions in respect of threatened infringement[3] relating to Community trade marks[4];

(2)   for actions for declaration of non-infringement, if they are permitted under national law[5];

(3)   for all actions brought for reasonable compensation in respect of matters arising after the date of publication of the Community trade mark application, which matters would, after publication of the registration of the trade mark, be prohibited by virtue of that publication[6]; and

(4)   for counterclaims for revocation or for a declaration of invalidity of the Community trade mark[7].

1   As to the meaning of 'Community trade mark courts' see PARA 233.
2   As to infringement actions see PARA 240 et seq.
3   Actions for threatened infringement are permitted by the law of England and Wales: see PARA 398 note 1.
4   Council Regulation (EC) 207/2009 (OJ L78, 24.3.2009, p 1) on the Community trade mark, art 96(a). As to actions for groundless threats of infringement proceedings see PARA 249; cf PARAS 107–109. As to the meaning of 'Community trade mark' see PARA 189.
5   Council Regulation (EC) 207/2009 (OJ L78, 24.3.2009, p 1) art 96(b). Actions for a declaration of non-infringement are permitted by the law of England and Wales: see PARA 440.
6   Council Regulation (EC) 207/2009 (OJ L78, 24.3.2009, p 1) art 96(c), which refers to actions brought as a result of the acts referred to in art 9(3), second sentence (see PARA 208).
7   Council Regulation (EC) 207/2009 (OJ L78, 24.3.2009, p 1) art 96(d), which refers to counterclaims as pursuant to art 100 (see PARA 245 et seq). As to the grounds for revocation see PARAS 220–223; as to the additional grounds for revocation of a Community collective mark see PARA 283; as to the grounds of invalidity see PARAS 226–228; and as to the additional ground of invalidity of a Community collective mark see PARA 284.

235. International jurisdiction: exclusive jurisdiction of Community trade mark courts. The rules for determining which member state's Community trade mark courts[1] have jurisdiction over a dispute involving their exclusive jurisdiction[2] are as follows:

(1)   the general rule[3] is that proceedings in respect of which the Community trade mark courts have exclusive jurisdiction must be brought in the courts of the member state in which the defendant is domiciled or, if he is not domiciled in any of the member states, in which he has an establishment[4];

(2)   if head (1) above does not apply, such proceedings must be brought in the courts of the member state in which the claimant is domiciled or, if he is not domiciled in any of the member states, in which he has an establishment[5];

(3)   if neither head (1) nor head (2) above applies, such proceedings must be brought in the Spanish courts[6];

(4)   notwithstanding heads (1) to (3) above:

     (a)   if the parties agree that a different Community trade mark court will have jurisdiction over the dispute[7], that court will have exclusive jurisdiction[8];

     (b)   a Community trade mark court before whom a defendant enters an appearance will have jurisdiction, except where an appearance was entered solely to contest the jurisdiction[9];

(5)   such proceedings, with the exception of actions for a declaration of non-infringement of a Community trade mark, may also be brought in

the courts of the member state in which the act of infringement has been committed or threatened to be committed[10].

A Community trade mark court whose jurisdiction is based on heads (1) to (4) above has jurisdiction in respect of acts of infringement[11] committed or threatened within the territory of any of the member states[12]. Such a court has jurisdiction to grant provisional and protective measures which, subject to the appropriate procedure[13] are applicable in the territory of any member state; no other court has such jurisdiction[14].

A Community trade mark court whose jurisdiction is based on head (5) above has jurisdiction in respect of acts committed or threatened within the territory of the member state in which that court is situated[15].

1 As to the meaning of 'Community trade mark courts' see PARA 233.
2 Ie the actions and claims referred to in PARA 234.
3 Ie subject to the provisions of Council Regulation (EC) 207/2009 (OJ L78, 24.3.2009, p 1) on the Community trade mark, as well as any provisions of the Brussels Convention and Council Regulation (EC) 44/2001 (OJ L12, 16.1.01, p 1) on jurisdiction and the recognition and enforcement of judgments in civil and commercial matters, applicable by virtue of Council Regulation (EC) 207/2009 (OJ L78, 24.3.2009, p 1) art 94 (see PARA 233). As to the Brussels Convention see PARA 233 note 8. Council Regulation (EC) 44/2001 (OJ L12, 16.1.01, p 1) is (prospectively) replaced by European Parliament and Council Regulation (EU) 1215/2012 (OJ L351, 20.12.2012, p 1) on jurisdiction and the recognition and enforcement of judgments in civil and commercial matters (with application, except for specified provisions, from 10 January 2015).
4 Council Regulation (EC) 207/2009 (OJ L78, 24.3.2009, p 1) art 97(1). As to domicile for the purposes of the Brussels Convention see CONFLICT OF LAWS vol 19 (2011) PARA 380 et seq.
5 Council Regulation (EC) 207/2009 (OJ L78, 24.3.2009, p 1) art 97(2).
6 Council Regulation (EC) 207/2009 (OJ L78, 24.3.2009, p 1) art 97(3). Spain is the state where the Office for Harmonisation in the Internal Market has its seat: Statement by the Council and the Commission on the seat of the Office for Harmonisation in the Internal Market (Trade Marks and Designs) (OJ L11, 14.1.94, p 36). As to the Office for Harmonisation in the Internal Market see PARA 163 et seq.
7 Ie an agreement to which the Brussels Convention art 17 and Council Regulation (EC) 44/2001 (OJ L12, 16.1.01, p 1) art 23 apply: see CONFLICT OF LAWS vol 19 (2011) PARA 372. See note 3.
8 Ie the Brussels Convention art 17 and Council Regulation (EC) 44/2001 (OJ L12, 16.1.01, p 1) art 23 (see CONFLICT OF LAWS vol 19 (2011) PARA 390) apply in such a case: Council Regulation (EC) 207/2009 (OJ L78, 24.3.2009, p 1) art 97(4)(a). See also PARA 233 note 8. See note 3.
9 Ie the Brussels Convention art 18 and Council Regulation (EC) 44/2001 (OJ L12, 16.1.01, p 1) art 23 (see CONFLICT OF LAWS vol 19 (2011) PARA 391) apply in such a case: Council Regulation (EC) 207/2009 (OJ L78, 24.3.2009, p 1) art 97(4)(b). See also PARA 233 note 8. See note 3.
10 Council Regulation (EC) 207/2009 (OJ L78, 24.3.2009, p 1) art 97(5), which also applies to an act to which the second sentence of art 9(3) applies (see PARA 208).
11 Including acts to which the second sentence of Council Regulation (EC) 207/2009 (OJ L78, 24.3.2009, p 1) art 9(3) applies (see PARA 208).
12 Council Regulation (EC) 207/2009 (OJ L78, 24.3.2009, p 1) art 98(1). As to infringement actions see PARA 240 et seq.
13 Ie any necessary procedure pursuant to the Brussels Convention Title III: see CONFLICT OF LAWS vol 19 (2011) PARA 467 et seq.
14 Council Regulation (EC) 207/2009 (OJ L78, 24.3.2009, p 1) art 103(2). As to provisional and protective measures see PARA 241.
15 Council Regulation (EC) 207/2009 (OJ L78, 24.3.2009, p 1) art 98(2).

236. International jurisdiction: other cases. Within the member state whose courts have jurisdiction under the 'Brussels I' Regulation[1] or the Brussels Convention[2] as they apply to relevant proceedings[3], the courts which have jurisdiction for actions other than those in respect of which the Community trade mark courts[4] have exclusive jurisdiction[5] are those which would have jurisdiction ratione loci and ratione materiae in the case of actions relating to a national trade mark registered in that state[6].

Actions relating to a Community trade mark[7], other than those in respect of which the Community trade mark courts have exclusive jurisdiction, for which no court otherwise has jurisdiction[8], may be heard before the Spanish courts[9].

1   As to the 'Brussels I' Regulation see PARA 233 note 8.
2   As to the Brussels Convention see PARA 233 note 8.
3   Ie those mentioned in Council Regulation (EC) 207/2009 (OJ L78, 24.3.2009, p 1) on the Community trade mark, art 94(1) (see PARA 235). As to the application of the 'Brussels I' Regulation and the Brussels Convention to such proceedings see PARA 233.
4   As to the meaning of 'Community trade mark courts' see PARA 233.
5   Ie those referred to in Council Regulation (EC) 207/2009 (OJ L78, 24.3.2009, p 1) art 96: see PARA 234.
6   Council Regulation (EC) 207/2009 (OJ L78, 24.3.2009, p 1) art 106(1).
7   As to the meaning of 'Community trade mark' see PARA 189.
8   Ie under Council Regulation (EC) 207/2009 (OJ L78, 24.3.2009, p 1) art 94(1) or art 106(2).
9   Council Regulation (EC) 207/2009 (OJ L78, 24.3.2009, p 1) art 106(2); Statement by the Council and the Commission on the seat of the Office for Harmonisation in the Internal Market (Trade Marks and Designs) (OJ L11, 14.1.94, p 36). See PARA 235 note 6.

237.   Simultaneous and successive civil actions. Where actions for infringement[1] involving the same cause of action[2] and between the same parties are brought in the courts of different member states, one seized on the basis of a Community trade mark[3] and the other seized on the basis of a national trade mark, the following provisions[4] apply[5]:

(1)   the court other than the court first seized must of its own motion decline jurisdiction in favour of that court, where the trade marks concerned are identical and valid[6] for identical goods or services; and the court which would be required to decline jurisdiction may stay its proceedings if the jurisdiction of the other court is contested[7];

(2)   the court other than the court first seized may stay its proceedings where the trade marks concerned are identical and valid for similar goods or services[8] and where the trade marks concerned are similar and valid for identical or similar goods or services[9].

The court hearing an action for infringement on the basis of a Community trade mark must reject the action if a final judgment on the merits has been given on the same cause of action and between the same parties on the basis of an identical national trade mark valid for identical goods or services[10]. The court hearing an action for infringement on the basis of a national trade mark must reject the action if a final judgment on the merits has been given on the same cause of action and between the same parties on the basis of a Community trade mark valid for identical goods or services[11].

None of the above applies in respect of provisional, including protective, measures[12].

1   As to infringement actions see PARA 240 et seq.
2   The same cause of action means the same cause of action and the same subject matter: Case C-144/86 *Gubisch Maschinenfabrik KG v Palumbo* [1987] ECR 4861, ECJ; Case C-406/92 *Maciej Rataj, The Tatry (cargo owners) v Maciej Rataj* [1995] All ER (EC) 229, sub nom *The Tatry* [1994] ECR I-5439, ECJ. Whether the same cause of action is raised in the two actions is to be determined on the basis of the respective claims in each of the sets of proceedings, and not the defence which may be raised by a defendant: C-11/01 *Gantner Electronic GmbH v Basch Exploitatie Maatschapi* [2003] ECR I-4207, (2003) Times, 14 May, ECJ; *Kolden Holdings v Rodette Commerce Ltd* [2008] EWCA Civ 10, [2008] 3 All ER 612.
3   As to the meaning of 'Community trade mark' see PARA 189.
4   Ie the provisions described in the text and notes 6–9.
5   Council Regulation (EC) 207/2009 (OJ L78, 24.3.2009, p 1) on the Community trade mark, art 109(1).

6   'Valid' should be construed as meaning registered or in force: *Prudential Assurance Co Ltd v Prudential Insurance Co of America* [2002] EWHC 534 (Ch) at [76], [2003] FSR 97 at [76], [2002] IP & T 781 at [76] per Laddie J (affd on other grounds [2003] EWCA Civ 327, [2003] 1 WLR 2295, [2003] IP & T 1070).

7   Council Regulation (EC) 207/2009 (OJ L78, 24.3.2009, p 1) art 109(1)(a).

8   As to the meaning of 'similar goods or services' see PARA 57.

9   Council Regulation (EC) 207/2009 (OJ L78, 24.3.2009, p 1) art 109(1)(b).

10 Council Regulation (EC) 207/2009 (OJ L78, 24.3.2009, p 1) art 109(2). This provision (actually its predecessor Council Regulation (EC) 40/94 (OJ L11, 14.1.94, p 1) art 105(2)) and Council Regulation (EC) 207/2009 (OJ L78, 24.3.2009, p 1) art 109(3) (see the text and note 11) (actually its predecessor Council Regulation (EC) 40/94 (OJ L11, 14.1.94, p 1) art 105(3)) only apply where a final judgment has been given by a court seized on the basis of an identical trade mark valid for identical goods or services; they do not apply where there is no such dual identity: *Prudential Assurance Co Ltd v Prudential Insurance Co of America* [2003] EWCA Civ 327, [2003] 1 WLR 2295, [2003] IP & T 1070. It is not clear whether they apply only where both the earlier proceedings and the later proceedings are proceedings for infringement or whether they apply where the earlier proceedings are concerned with validity: *Prudential Assurance Co Ltd v Prudential Insurance Co of America* (above).

11 Council Regulation (EC) 207/2009 (OJ L78, 24.3.2009, p 1) art 109(3). See note 10.

12 Council Regulation (EC) 207/2009 (OJ L78, 24.3.2009, p 1) art 109(4).

238.   Related actions. A Community trade mark court[1] hearing one of the following types of action:

(1)   an infringement action[2];

(2)   an action in respect of threatened infringement relating to Community trade marks[3];

(3)   an action brought for reasonable compensation in respect of matters arising after the date of publication of the Community trade mark application, which matters would, after publication of the registration of the trade mark, be prohibited by virtue of that publication[4]; or

(4)   a counterclaim for revocation or for a declaration of invalidity of the Community trade mark[5],

must, unless there are special grounds for continuing the hearing, of its own motion after hearing the parties or at the request of one of the parties and after hearing the parties, stay the proceedings if the validity of the Community trade mark is already in issue before another Community trade mark court on account of a counterclaim or where an application for revocation or for a declaration of invalidity has already been filed at the Office for Harmonisation in the Internal Market[6].

The Office, when hearing an application for revocation or for a declaration of invalidity must, unless there are special grounds for continuing the hearing, of its own motion after hearing the parties or at the request of one of the parties and after hearing the parties, stay the proceedings if the validity of the Community trade mark is already in issue on account of a counterclaim before another Community trade mark court. However, if one of the parties so requests, the court may, after hearing the other parties to those proceedings, stay the proceedings; the Office must in this instance continue the proceedings pending before it[7].

In any such case, where the Community trade mark court stays proceedings it may order provisional and protective measures for the duration of the stay[8].

1   As to the meaning of 'Community trade mark courts' see PARA 233.

2   As to infringement actions see PARA 240 et seq.

3   As to actions for groundless threats of infringement proceedings see PARA 249; cf PARAS 107–109. As to the meaning of 'Community trade mark' see PARA 189.

4   Ie an action brought as a result of the acts referred to in Council Regulation (EC) 207/2009
    (OJ L78, 24.3.2009, p 1) on the Community trade mark, art 9(3), second sentence (see PARA
    208).
5   Ie an action referred to in Council Regulation (EC) 207/2009 (OJ L78, 24.3.2009, p 1) art 96
    (see PARA 234), other than an action for a declaration of non-infringement. As to bringing a
    counterclaim for revocation or for a declaration of invalidity of the Community trade mark see
    PARA 244 et seq; as to the grounds for revocation see PARAS 220–223; and as to the grounds for
    a declaration of invalidity see PARAS 226–228.
6   Council Regulation (EC) 207/2009 (OJ L78, 24.3.2009, p 1) art 104(1). The presumption in
    favour of a stay is a strong one and it will be an exceptional case where there are special grounds
    justifying refusal of a stay; it is not relevant that the application to the Office was made in
    reaction to a threat of infringement proceedings, but specific facts giving to particular urgency
    may constitute special grounds: *Starbucks (HK) Ltd v British Sky Broadcasting Group plc; EMI
    (IP) Ltd v British Sky Broadcasting Group plc* [2012] EWCA Civ 1201, [2013] IP & T 222,
    [2012] All ER (D) 93 (Sep). See also *Regents University v Regent's University London* [2013]
    EWPCC 39, [2013] All ER (D) 50 (Sep) where *Starbucks (HK) Ltd v British Sky Broadcasting
    Group plc; EMI (IP) Ltd v British Sky Broadcasting Group plc* above was applied. As to the
    Office for Harmonisation in the Internal Market see PARA 163 et seq; and as to bringing an
    application for revocation in the Office see PARA 272 et seq.
7   Council Regulation (EC) 207/2009 (OJ L78, 24.3.2009, p 1) art 104(2). The court's discretion is
    unfettered: see *Kitfix Swallow Group Ltd v Great Gizmos Ltd* [2007] EWHC 2668 (Ch), [2008]
    Bus LR 465, [2008] FSR 244 (no stay of domestic proceedings where subsequent proceedings
    before Office had been stayed and then resumed).
8   Council Regulation (EC) 207/2009 (OJ L78, 24.3.2009, p 1) art 104(3). As to provisional and
    protective measures see PARA 241.

239.   Jurisdiction of appeal courts.   An appeal to the Community trade mark
courts of second instance[1] lies from judgments of the Community trade mark
courts in respect of proceedings in respect of which the Community trade mark
courts have exclusive jurisdiction[2]. The conditions under which an appeal may
be lodged with a Community trade mark court of second instance must be
determined by the national law of the member state in which the court is
located[3]; and the national rules concerning further appeal are applicable in
respect of judgments of Community trade mark courts of second instance[4].

1   As to the meaning of 'Community trade mark court' see PARA 233. As to the duty of member
    states to appoint Community trade mark courts of first and second instance see PARA 233.
2   Council Regulation (EC) 207/2009 (OJ L78, 24.3.2009, p 1) on the Community trade mark,
    art 105(1). For the proceedings in respect of which the Community trade mark courts have
    exclusive jurisdiction see PARA 234.
3   Council Regulation (EC) 207/2009 (OJ L78, 24.3.2009, p 1) art 105(2).
4   Council Regulation (EC) 207/2009 (OJ L78, 24.3.2009, p 1) art 105(3).

(iii)   Proceedings for Infringement of Community Trade Marks

240.   In general.   The principle underlying the enforcement of Community
trade marks[1], and the other rights relating thereto[2], is that the courts of the
member states must apply the provisions of Community law[3]; and any aspect not
covered by Community law, in particular procedural provisions, should be
governed by that member state's national law[4].

   Thus the Community trade mark courts[5] must apply the provisions of
Community law[6]; but on all other matters not covered by it, such a court must
apply its national law, including its private international law[7]. Unless otherwise
provided[8], a Community trade mark court must apply the rules of procedure
governing the same type of action relating to a national trade mark in the
member state where it has its seat[9].

1   As to the meaning of 'Community trade mark' see PARA 189.

2   Eg the rights created by Council Regulation (EC) 207/2009 (OJ L78, 24.3.2009, p 1) on the Community trade mark, arts 11, 18: see PARA 214.

3   Ie Council Regulation (EC) 207/2009 (OJ L78, 24.3.2009, p 1).

4   See Council Regulation (EC) 207/2009 (OJ L78, 24.3.2009, p 1) art 101 (see the text and notes 5–9) and art 102(2) (see PARA 241).

5   As to the meaning of 'Community trade mark courts' see PARA 233.

6   Council Regulation (EC) 207/2009 (OJ L78, 24.3.2009, p 1) art 101(1). See note 3.

7   Council Regulation (EC) 207/2009 (OJ L78, 24.3.2009, p 1) art 101(2).

8   Ie by Council Regulation (EC) 207/2009 (OJ L78, 24.3.2009, p 1).

9   Council Regulation (EC) 207/2009 (OJ L78, 24.3.2009, p 1) art 101(3). For the procedure in the High Court see PARA 398 et seq. For a situation where a court of one member state must apply the law of another member state see art 102(2); and PARA 241 text and note 6.

241. Remedies for infringement; provisional and protective measures. Where a Community trade mark court[1] finds that the defendant has infringed or threatened to infringe a Community trade mark[2], it must, unless there are special reasons for not doing so[3], issue an order prohibiting the defendant from proceeding with the acts which infringed or would infringe the Community trade mark[4]. It must also take such measures in accordance with its national law as are aimed at ensuring that this prohibition is complied with[5].

In all other respects the Community trade mark court must apply the law of the member state in which the acts of infringement or threatened infringement were committed, including the private international law[6]. Thus remedies are a matter for national law[7].

Application may be made to the courts of a member state, including the Community trade mark courts[8], for such provisional, including protective, measures in respect of a Community trade mark or Community trade mark application[9] as may be available under the law of that state in respect of a national trade mark[10], even if a Community trade mark court of another member state has jurisdiction[11] as to the substance of the matter[12].

1   As to the meaning of 'Community trade mark court' see PARA 233.

2   As to the meaning of 'Community trade mark' see PARA 189; and as to the acts which infringe a Community trade mark see PARA 207 et seq.

3   The mere fact that the risk of further infringement or threatened infringement of a Community trade mark is not obvious or is otherwise merely limited does not constitute a special reason for a Community trade mark court not to issue an order prohibiting the defendant from proceeding with those acts: Case C-316/05 *Nokia Corpn v Wärdell* [2006] ECR I-12083, [2007] IP & T 499, ECJ. Nor does the fact that the national law includes a general prohibition of the infringement of Community trade marks and provides for the possibility of penalising further infringement or threatened infringement, whether intentional or due to gross negligence, does not constitute a special reason for a Community trade mark court not to issue an order prohibiting the defendant from proceeding with those acts: Case C-316/05 *Nokia Corp v Wärdell* (above).

4   Council Regulation (EC) 207/2009 (OJ L78, 24.3.2009, p 1) on the Community trade mark, art 102(1). A prohibition against further infringement or threatened infringement of a Community trade mark must, as a rule, extend to the entire area of the European Union; but if the court finds that the acts of infringement or threatened infringement are limited to a single Member State or to part of the territory of the European Union, in particular because the claimant has restricted the territorial scope of its action or because the defendant proves that the use of the sign at issue does not affect or is not liable to affect the functions of the trade mark, for example on linguistic grounds, the court must limit the territorial scope of the prohibition which it issues: Case-235/09 *DHL Express France SAS v Chronopost SA* [2011] ECR I-2801, [2011] FSR 857, [2011] IP & T 403, ECJ; *Interflora Inc v Marks & Spencer plc* [2013] EWHC 1484 (Ch), [2013] All ER (D) 95 (Jun).

5   Council Regulation (EC) 207/2009 (OJ L78, 24.3.2009, p 1) on the Community trade mark, art 102(1). See Case C-316/05 *Nokia Corpn v Wärdell* [2006] ECR I-12083, [2007] IP & T 499, ECJ.

6   Council Regulation (EC) 207/2009 (OJ L78, 24.3.2009, p 1) art 102(2). Thus a Community trade mark court which has jurisdiction in respect of acts committed or threatened in any member state (ie pursuant to art 97(1), (2), (3) or (4): see PARA 235) must apply the law of the member state or states in which the acts of infringement or threatened infringement were committed, including the private international law, rather than its own domestic law.

7   Save that, as provided for by Council Regulation (EC) 207/2009 (OJ L78, 24.3.2009, p 1) art 102(2) (see the text and note 6), effective injunctive relief must be available. As to the remedies for infringement of a Community trade mark in the English courts see PARA 418 et seq.

8   The use of the words 'including the Community trade mark courts' in this provision suggests that courts of the member states other than Community trade mark courts also have jurisdiction to make such provisional orders.

9   As to a Community trade mark application being an object of property see PARA 253 et seq.

10 Where judicial authorities are called upon to apply national rules with a view to ordering provisional measures for the protection of Community trade marks, they are required to do so as far as possible in the light of the wording and purpose of the Agreement on Trade-Related Aspects of Intellectual Property ('TRIPs') (1994) (Cm 2557) art 50: Joined Cases C-300/98 and C-392/98 *Parfums Christian Dior SA v TUK Consultancy BV* [2000] ECR I-11307, ECJ; Case C-89/99 *Schieving-Nijstad VOF v Groenefeld* [2001] ECR I-5851, [2002] IP & T 353, ECJ; and see also Case C-53/96 *Hermès International v FHT Marketing Choice* [1998] ECR I-3603, [1999] RPC 107, ECJ. As to interim measures available under English law see PARA 432 et seq. As to TRIPs see PARA 7.

11 Ie under Council Regulation (EC) 207/2009 (OJ L78, 24.3.2009, p 1).

12 Council Regulation (EC) 207/2009 (OJ L78, 24.3.2009, p 1) art 103(1).

242. Prohibition of use of Community trade marks. The Community Trade Mark Regulation[1] does not, unless otherwise provided for, affect the following:

(1)   the right existing under the laws of the member states to invoke claims for infringement of earlier rights[2] in relation to the use of a later Community trade mark[3]; however, claims for infringement of certain such rights[4] may no longer be invoked if the proprietor of the earlier right can no longer, due to his acquiescence, apply for a declaration that the Community trade mark is invalid[5];

(2)   the right to bring proceedings under the civil, administrative or criminal law of a member state or under provisions of Community law for the purpose of prohibiting the use of a Community trade mark to the extent that the use of a national trade mark may be prohibited under the law of that member state or under Community law[6].

1   Ie Council Regulation (EC) 207/2009 (OJ L78, 24.3.2009, p 1) on the Community trade mark.

2   Ie earlier rights within the meaning of Council Regulation (EC) 207/2009 (OJ L78, 24.3.2009, p 1) art 8 (see PARA 205) or art 53(2) (see PARA 228).

3   As to the meaning of 'Community trade mark' see PARA 189.

4   Ie those earlier rights within the meaning of Council Regulation (EC) 207/2009 (OJ L78, 24.3.2009, p 1) art 8(2), (4) (see PARAS 201, 205).

5   Council Regulation (EC) 207/2009 (OJ L78, 24.3.2009, p 1) art 110(1). As to the loss of the proprietor's entitlement to make an application in such circumstances see art 54(2); and PARA 216.

6   Council Regulation (EC) 207/2009 (OJ L78, 24.3.2009, p 1) art 110(2).

243. Prior rights applicable to particular localities. The proprietor of an earlier right which only applies to a particular locality[1] may oppose[2] the use[3] of the Community trade mark[4] in the territory where his right is protected in so far as the law of the member state concerned so permits[5]. This ceases to apply if the proprietor of the earlier right has acquiesced[6] in the use of the Community trade mark in the territory where his right is protected for a period of five successive years, being aware of such use, unless the Community trade mark was applied for in bad faith[7]. However, the proprietor of the Community trade mark is not entitled to oppose the use of that earlier right even though that right may no longer be invoked against the Community trade mark[8].

1   As to the meaning of an 'earlier right which only applies to a particular locality' see PARAS 81 text and notes 4, 5, 205 note 5.
2   As to the meaning of 'oppose' see PARA 214 note 3.
3   As to the meaning of 'use' see PARA 212.
4   As to the meaning of 'Community trade mark' see PARA 189.
5   Council Regulation (EC) 207/2009 (OJ L78, 24.3.2009, p 1) on the Community trade mark, art 111(1).
6   As to the meaning of 'acquiesce' see PARA 83 note 3.
7   Council Regulation (EC) 207/2009 (OJ L78, 24.3.2009, p 1) art 111(2). As to the meaning of 'bad faith' see PARA 53.
8   Council Regulation (EC) 207/2009 (OJ L78, 24.3.2009, p 1) art 111(3). This provision gives the owner of the earlier right protection against being sued by the owner of a subsequently acquired Community trade mark: *Compass Publishing BV v Compass Logistics Ltd* [2004] EWHC 520 (Ch), [2004] RPC 809, [2004] 17 LS Gaz R 32.

(iv) Challenging Validity of Community Trade Marks in National Courts

244. Presumption of validity; procedures for challenge to validity. A national court which is dealing with an action relating to a Community trade mark[1], other than one in respect of which the Community trade mark courts[2] have exclusive jurisdiction[3], must treat the trade mark as valid[4]. Further, the Community trade mark courts must treat a Community trade mark as valid unless its validity is put in issue by the defendant with a counterclaim[5] for revocation or declaration of invalidity[6], or by challenging it (to the limited extent possible) in an action for threats of infringement proceedings[7].

Thus a person cannot challenge the validity or apply for revocation of a Community trade mark in a national court unless he is threatened with, or sued for, infringement of that Community trade mark[8]. If he wishes to challenge its validity or apply for revocation of his own motion, he must apply to the Office for Harmonisation in the Internal Market[9] to do so[10].

1   As to the meaning of 'Community trade mark' see PARA 189.
2   As to the meaning of 'Community trade mark courts' see PARA 233.
3   As to exclusive jurisdiction see Council Regulation (EC) 207/2009 (OJ L78, 24.3.2009, p 1) on the Community trade mark, art 96; and PARA 234.
4   Council Regulation (EC) 207/2009 (OJ L78, 24.3.2009, p 1) art 107.
5   In certain proceedings (ie actions referred to in Council Regulation (EC) 207/2009 (OJ L78, 24.3.2009, p 1) art 96(a), (c): see PARA 234), a plea relating to revocation or invalidity of the Community trade mark submitted otherwise than by way of a counterclaim is admissible in so far as the defendant claims that the rights of the proprietor of the community trade mark could be declared invalid on account of an earlier right of the defendant: art 99(3).
6   Council Regulation (EC) 207/2009 (OJ L78, 24.3.2009, p 1) art 99(1).
7   Ie in accordance with Council Regulation (EC) 207/2009 (OJ L78, 24.3.2009, p 1) art 99(3): see note 5. The validity of a Community trade mark may not be put in issue in an action for a declaration of non-infringement: art 99(2).
8   Furthermore, the defendant to a claim for infringement is not entitled to raise a counterclaim for revocation or declaration of invalidity which does not provide a defence to the claim for infringement: *Adobe Systems Inc v Netcom Distributors Ltd* [2012] EWHC 1087 (Ch), [2013] FSR 81.
9   As to the Office for Harmonisation in the Internal Market see PARA 163 et seq.
10 As to challenging the validity of a Community trade mark or applying for revocation in the Office see PARAS 272–273; as to the grounds for revocation see PARAS 220–223; as to the additional grounds for revocation of a Community collective mark see PARA 283; as to the grounds of invalidity see PARAS 226–228; and as to the additional ground of invalidity of a Community collective mark see PARA 284.

245.   Bringing of a counterclaim.   A counterclaim[1] for revocation or for a declaration of invalidity may only be made on the grounds for revocation[2] or invalidity[3] prescribed[4].

The Community trade mark court[5] with which a counterclaim for revocation or for a declaration of invalidity of the Community trade mark[6] has been filed must inform the Office for Harmonisation in the Internal Market[7] of the date on which the counterclaim was filed[8]. A Community trade mark court must reject a counterclaim if a decision taken by the Office relating to the same subject matter and cause of action involving the same parties has already become final[9].

If the counterclaim is brought in a legal action to which the proprietor of the trade mark is not already a party, he must be informed thereof[10] and may be joined as a party to the action in accordance with the conditions set out in national law[11].

1   As to the requirement that the application be brought by way of counterclaim see also Council Regulation (EC) 207/2009 (OJ L78, 24.3.2009, p 1) on the Community trade mark, art 99(3); and PARA 244 note 5.
2   As to the grounds for revocation see PARAS 220–223. As to the additional grounds for revocation of a Community collective mark see PARA 283.
3   As to the grounds of invalidity see PARAS 226–228; and as to the additional ground of invalidity of a Community collective mark see PARA 284.
4   Council Regulation (EC) 207/2009 (OJ L78, 24.3.2009, p 1) art 100(1). As to the grounds for invalidity see PARAS 226–228. See also PARA 244 note 8.
5   As to the meaning of 'Community trade mark court' see PARA 233.
6   As to the meaning of 'Community trade mark' see PARA 189.
7   As to the Office for Harmonisation in the Internal Market see PARA 163 et seq.
8   Council Regulation (EC) 207/2009 (OJ L78, 24.3.2009, p 1) art 100(4). The Office must record this fact in the register of Community trade marks: art 100(4). The Office may, if it thinks fit, invite the parties to make a friendly settlement: arts 57(4), 100(5). As to the register see PARA 171.
9   Council Regulation (EC) 207/2009 (OJ L78, 24.3.2009, p 1) art 100(2). As to the meaning of 'the same cause of action' see PARA 237 note 2.
10   It is not clear who must inform the proprietor that his Community trade mark is under attack. The most appropriate procedure would be to serve the counterclaim on the proprietor.
11   Council Regulation (EC) 207/2009 (OJ L78, 24.3.2009, p 1) art 100(3).

246.   Proof of use of earlier Community and national trade marks on a counterclaim.   If the proprietor of the Community trade mark[1] so requests, the proprietor of an earlier Community or national trade mark[2], being a party to the invalidity proceedings, must furnish proof that, during the period of five years preceding the date of the application for a declaration of invalidity, the earlier Community or national trade mark has been put to genuine use in the relevant member state in connection with the goods or services in respect of which it is registered and which he cites as justification for his application, or that there are proper reasons for non-use, provided the earlier Community or national trade mark has at that date been registered for not less than five years[3].

If, at the date on which the Community trade mark application was published, the earlier Community trade mark had been registered for not less than five years, the proprietor of the earlier Community trade mark must furnish proof that, in addition, the prescribed conditions[4] were satisfied at that date[5].

In the absence of proof to this effect the application for a declaration of invalidity must be rejected. If the earlier Community trade mark has been used in relation to part only of the goods or services for which it is registered it must, for the purpose of the examination of the application for a declaration of invalidity, be deemed to be registered in respect only of that part of the goods or services[6].

1   As to the meaning of 'Community trade mark' see PARA 189.
2   Ie an earlier Community or national trade mark referred to in Council Regulation (EC)
    207/2009 (OJ L78, 24.3.2009, p 1) on the Community trade mark, art 8(2)(a): see PARA 201.
3   Council Regulation (EC) 207/2009 (OJ L78, 24.3.2009, p 1) arts 57(2), (3), 100(5).
4   Ie that during the period of five years preceding the date of publication of the Community trade
    mark application, the earlier Community trade mark was put to genuine use in the Community
    in connection with the goods or services in respect of which it is registered and which the
    proprietor cites as justification for the counterclaim, or that there are proper reasons for
    non-use: see Council Regulation (EC) 207/2009 (OJ L78, 24.3.2009, p 1) art 42(2); and PARA
    265. As to what constitutes use see PARA 220. As to genuine use see PARA 98 note 6. As to
    proper reasons for non-use see PARA 98 note 10.
5   Council Regulation (EC) 207/2009 (OJ L78, 24.3.2009, p 1) arts 57(2), (3), 100(5).
6   Council Regulation (EC) 207/2009 (OJ L78, 24.3.2009, p 1) arts 57(2), (3), 100(5). Cf PARA
    101.

247.   Decision on the merits of a counterclaim. If the examination of the
application for revocation of rights[1] or for a declaration of invalidity[2] reveals
that the trade mark should not have been registered[3] in respect of some or all of
the goods or services for which it is registered, the rights of the proprietor of the
Community trade mark[4] must be revoked or the trade mark must be declared
invalid in respect of those goods or services; otherwise the application for
revocation of rights or for a declaration of invalidity must be rejected[5].

   Where a Community trade mark court[6] has given judgment which has become
final on a counterclaim for revocation or for invalidity of a Community trade
mark, a copy of the judgment must be sent to the Office for Harmonisation in
the Internal Market[7].

1   As to the grounds for revocation see PARAS 220–223; and as to the additional grounds for
    revocation of a Community collective mark see PARA 283.
2   As to the grounds of invalidity see PARAS 226–228; and as to the additional ground of invalidity
    of a Community collective mark see PARA 284.
3   It is presumed that there should be read into this part of Council Regulation (EC) 207/2009
    (OJ L78, 24.3.2009, p 1) on the Community trade mark, art 57(5) words to the effect of 'or that
    the trade mark should be revoked', since revocation relates to events which occur after a
    registration: ex hypothesi, the trade mark was rightly registered but should now be revoked. See
    PARAS 218, 220 et seq.
4   As to the meaning of 'Community trade mark' see PARA 189.
5   Council Regulation (EC) 207/2009 (OJ L78, 24.3.2009, p 1) arts 57(5), 100(5).
6   As to the meaning of 'Community trade mark court' see PARA 233.
7   Council Regulation (EC) 207/2009 (OJ L78, 24.3.2009, p 1) art 100(6). Any party may request
    information about such a transmission (art 100(6)) but it is not clear from whom. The Office
    must mention the judgment in the register of Community trade marks in accordance with the
    provisions of Commission Regulation (EC) 2868/95 (OJ L303, 15.12.95, p 1) implementing
    Council Regulation (EC) 40/94 on the Community trade mark: Council Regulation (EC)
    207/2009 (OJ L78, 24.3.2009, p 1) art 100(6). As to the Office for Harmonisation in the
    Internal Market see PARA 163 et seq. As to the register of Community trade marks see PARA 171.

248.   Request that counterclaim proceed by way of application to the Office.
The Community trade mark court[1] hearing a counterclaim for revocation[2] or for
a declaration of invalidity[3] may stay the proceedings on application by the
proprietor of the Community trade mark[4] and after hearing the other parties,
and may request the defendant to submit an application for revocation or for a
declaration of invalidity to the Office for Harmonisation in the Internal Market[5]
within a time limit which it must determine[6].

   If such an application is not made within the time limit, the proceedings must
continue; and the counterclaim is deemed withdrawn[7].

   Where the Community trade mark court stays the proceedings it may order
provisional and protective measures for the duration of the stay[8].

1   As to the meaning of 'Community trade mark court' see PARA 233.
2   As to the grounds for revocation see PARAS 220–223; and as to the additional grounds for revocation of a Community collective mark see PARA 283.
3   As to the grounds of invalidity see PARAS 226–228; and as to the additional ground of invalidity of a Community collective mark see PARA 284.
4   As to the meaning of 'Community trade mark' see PARA 189.
5   As to the Office for Harmonisation in the Internal Market see PARA 163 et seq; and as to applying for revocation or for a declaration of invalidity to the Office see PARAS 272–273.
6   Council Regulation (EC) 207/2009 (OJ L78, 24.3.2009, p 1) on the Community trade mark, art 100(7).
7   Council Regulation (EC) 207/2009 (OJ L78, 24.3.2009, p 1) art 100(7).
8   Council Regulation (EC) 207/2009 (OJ L78, 24.3.2009, p 1) arts 100(7), 104(3). As to provisional and protective measures see PARA 241.

(v) Miscellaneous Proceedings

249.   Groundless threats of infringement proceedings. The statutory provisions[1] relating to groundless threats of infringement proceedings apply in relation to a Community trade mark[2] as in relation to a registered trade mark[3].

1   Ie the Trade Marks Act 1994 s 21: see PARAS 107–109.
2   As to the meaning of 'Community trade mark' see PARA 189.
3   Community Trade Mark Regulations 2006, SI 2006/1027, regs 2, 6(1). The provisions relating to threats also apply with minor modifications to an international trade mark (EC): regs 2(2), 6(2) (reg 6(2) amended by SI 2011/1043). As to the meaning of 'international trade mark (EC)' see PARA 8 note 17. As to the meaning of 'registered trade mark' see PARA 111.

250.   Importation of infringing goods, materials or articles. The statutory provisions[1] providing that infringing goods[2], material[3] or articles[4] may be treated as prohibited goods, and relating to the power of the Commissioners for Her Majesty's Revenue and Customs[5] to disclose information, apply in relation to a Community trade mark[6] as they apply in relation to a registered trade mark[7].

1   Ie the Trade Marks Act 1994 ss 89, 90, 91: see PARAS 132, 134–135.
2   As to the meaning of 'infringing goods' see PARA 133.
3   As to the meaning of 'infringing material' see PARA 133.
4   As to the meaning of 'infringing articles' see PARA 133.
5   As to the Commissioners for Her Majesty's Revenue and Customs see INCOME TAXATION vol 23(1) (Reissue) PARA 31 et seq.
6   As to the meaning of 'Community trade mark' see PARA 189.
7   Community Trade Mark Regulations 2006, SI 2006/1027, regs 2, 7(1) (amended by virtue of the Commissioners for Revenue and Customs Act 2005 s 50(1), (7)). The Trade Marks (Customs) Regulations 1994, SI 1994/2625 (see PARA 134) apply in relation to notices given under the provisions of the Trade Marks Act 1994 s 89 as so applied: Community Trade Mark Regulations 2006, SI 2006/1027, reg 7(2). These provisions also apply to international trade marks (EC): reg 2(2). As to the meaning of 'international trade mark (EC)' see PARA 8 note 17. As to the meaning of 'registered trade mark' see PARA 111.

251.   Offences and forfeiture. The statutory provisions[1] relating to unauthorised use of a trade mark etc in relation to goods, search warrants, the enforcement function of local weights and measures authorities[2] and forfeiture apply in relation to a Community trade mark[3] as they apply in relation to a registered trade mark[4].

1   Ie the Trade Marks Act 1994 s 92 (unauthorised use of a trade mark etc in relation to goods: see PARAS 124–127), s 92A (search warrants: see PARA 128), s 93 (enforcement function of local weights and measures authorities: see PARA 129), s 97 (forfeiture: see PARA 123).
2   As to local weights and measures authorities see PARA 129 note 1.
3   As to the meaning of 'Community trade mark' see PARA 189.

4 Community Trade Mark Regulations 2006, SI 2006/1027, regs 2, 8(1). For the purposes of the provisions mentioned in the text and note 1, references to goods in respect of which a trade mark is registered include goods in respect of which an international trade mark (EC) confers protection in the European Union: reg 8(2) (amended by SI 2011/1043). These provisions also apply to international trade marks (EC): Community Trade Mark Regulations 2006, SI 2006/1027, reg 2(2). As to the meaning of 'international trade mark (EC)' see PARA 8 note 17. As to the meaning of 'registered trade mark' see PARA 111.

252. Falsely representing trade mark as a Community trade mark. It is an offence for a person:

(1) falsely to represent that a mark is a Community trade mark[1]; or

(2) to make false representations as to the goods or services for which a Community trade mark is registered,

knowing or having reason to believe that the representation is false[2].

1 As to the meaning of 'Community trade mark' see PARA 189. Cf the similar provision relating to registered trade marks provided by the Trade Marks Act 1994 s 95: see PARA 131.
2 Community Trade Mark Regulations 2006, SI 2006/1027, reg 9(1). A person guilty of an offence under this regulation is liable on summary conviction to a fine not exceeding level 3 on the standard scale: reg 9(2). As to the standard scale see SENTENCING AND DISPOSITION OF OFFENDERS vol 92 (2010) PARA 142. These provisions also apply to international trade marks (EC): reg 2(2). As to the meaning of 'international trade mark (EC)' see PARA 8 note 17.

(7) COMMUNITY TRADE MARKS AS OBJECTS OF PROPERTY; ASSIGNMENT AND LICENSING

253. In general. Community trade marks[1], like trade marks registered under the Trade Marks Act 1994[2], may be assigned and licensed without substantial restrictions. The proprietor must not allow his mark to become deceptive without risking revocation[3]. Subject to that, a Community trade mark is treated in a similar way to other incorporeal rights as regards the freedom of its owner to deal with it.

1 As to the meaning of 'Community trade mark' see PARA 189.
2 As to registered trade marks as objects of property, and as to assignment and licensing of the same, see PARA 110 et seq.
3 See PARA 223.

254. Community trade marks as objects of property. A Community trade mark[1] is to be regarded as an object of property which exists separately from the undertaking whose goods or services are designated by it[2].

Thus a Community trade mark may, independently of the undertaking, be given as security or be the subject of rights in rem[3] and it may be levied in execution[4].

1 As to the meaning of 'Community trade mark' see PARA 189. Council Regulation (EC) 207/2009 (OJ L78, 24.3.2009, p 1) on the Community trade mark, art 24 provides that the provisions relating to Community trade marks as objects of property (ie arts 16–23) apply to applications for Community trade marks. Therefore, such applications are similarly to be regarded as objects of property. As to the making of an application for a Community trade mark see PARAS 261–266.
2 Council Regulation (EC) 207/2009 (OJ L78, 24.3.2009, p 1) 11th recital.
3 Council Regulation (EC) 207/2009 (OJ L78, 24.3.2009, p 1) art 19(1). At the request of one of the parties, the rights mentioned in art 19(1) must be entered into the register (see PARA 171) and published: art 19(2). As to the consequences of failing to register such rights see art 23; and PARA 259.
4 Council Regulation (EC) 207/2009 (OJ L78, 24.3.2009, p 1) art 20(1). As regards the procedure for levy of execution in respect of a Community trade mark, the courts and authorities of the

member states determined in accordance with art 16 (see PARA 255) have exclusive jurisdiction: art 20(2). On request of one of the parties, levy of execution must be entered into the register and published: art 20(3). The effects vis-à-vis third parties of the levy of execution are governed by the law of the member state determined in accordance with art 16 (see PARA 255): art 23(3).

255. Dealing with Community trade marks as national trade marks. Unless otherwise provided[1], a Community trade mark[2] as an object of property[3] must be dealt with in its entirety, and for the whole area of the Community, as a national trade mark[4] registered in:

(1)   the member state in which, according to the register of Community trade marks, the proprietor has his seat or his domicile on the relevant date[5];

(2)   if head (1) above does not apply, the member state in which, according to the register of Community trade marks, the proprietor has an establishment on the relevant date[6]; or

(3)   in cases which are not provided for by head (1) or head (2) above, Spain[7].

1   Ie under Council Regulation (EC) 207/2009 (OJ L78, 24.3.2009, p 1) on the Community trade mark, arts 17–24 (see PARAS 214, 254, 256–259).
2   As to the meaning of 'Community trade mark' see PARA 189.
3   As to applications for Community trade marks as objects of property see PARA 254 note 1.
4   Council Regulation (EC) 207/2009 (OJ L78, 24.3.2009, p 1) art 16(1).
5   Council Regulation (EC) 207/2009 (OJ L78, 24.3.2009, p 1) art 16(1)(a).
6   Council Regulation (EC) 207/2009 (OJ L78, 24.3.2009, p 1) art 16(1)(b).
7   Council Regulation (EC) 207/2009 (OJ L78, 24.3.2009, p 1) art 16(2). Spain is the state where the Office for Harmonisation in the Internal Market has its seat: see art 16(2); Statement by the Council and the Commission on the seat of the Office for Harmonisation in the Internal Market (Trade Marks and Designs) (OJ L11, 14.1.94, p 36).
     If two or more persons are mentioned in the register of Community trade marks (see PARA 171) as joint proprietors, Council Regulation (EC) 207/2009 (OJ L78, 24.3.2009, p 1) art 16(1) applies to the joint proprietor first mentioned; failing this it applies to the subsequent joint proprietors in the order in which they are mentioned; and where art 16(1) does not apply to any of the joint proprietors, art 16(2) applies: art 16(3).

256. Insolvency proceedings. The only insolvency proceedings in which a Community trade mark[1] may be involved are those opened in the member state in the territory of which the debtor has his centre of main interests[2]. However, where the debtor is an insurance undertaking or a credit institution[3], the only insolvency proceedings in which a Community trade mark may be involved are those opened in the member state where that undertaking or institution has been authorised[4]. In the case of joint proprietorship of a Community trade mark, these provisions apply to the share of the joint proprietor[5]. Where a Community trade mark is involved in insolvency proceedings, on request of the competent national authority an entry to this effect must be made in the register[6] and published in the Community Trade Marks Bulletin[7].

1   As to the meaning of 'Community trade mark' see PARA 189; and as to the application of these provisions to applications for Community trade marks see PARA 254 note 1.
2   Council Regulation (EC) 207/2009 (OJ L78, 24.3.2009, p 1) on the Community trade mark, art 21(1). As to the meaning of 'centre of main interests' see COMPANY AND PARTNERSHIP INSOLVENCY vol 16 (2011) PARA 59 note 6.
3   Ie as defined in Parliament and Council Directive (EC) 2001/17 (OJ L110, 20.4.01, p 28) on the re-organisation and winding up of insurance undertakings and in Parliament and Council Directive (EC) 2001/24 (OJ 125, 5.5.01, p 15) on the re-organisation and winding up of credit institutions respectively.
4   Council Regulation (EC) 207/2009 (OJ L78, 24.3.2009, p 1) art 21(1).
5   Council Regulation (EC) 207/2009 (OJ L78, 24.3.2009, p 1) art 21(2).

6   As to the register see PARA 171.
7   Council Regulation (EC) 207/2009 (OJ L78, 24.3.2009, p 1) art 21(3). As to the Community
Trade Marks Bulletin see PARA 173.

257.   Transfer of Community trade marks.   In general[1], an assignment of the
Community trade mark[2] must be made in writing and requires the signature of
the parties to the contract, except when it is a result of a judgment; otherwise it
is void[3].

A Community trade mark may be transferred, separately from any transfer of
the undertaking, in respect of some or all of the goods or services for which it is
registered[4].

On request of one of the parties a transfer must be entered in the register[5] and
published[6]. As long as the transfer has not been entered in the register, the
successor in title may not invoke the rights arising from the registration of the
Community trade mark[7].

1   Ie without prejudice to Council Regulation (EC) 207/2009 (OJ L78, 24.3.2009, p 1) on the
Community trade mark, art 17(2) (which provides that a transfer of the whole of the
undertaking includes the transfer of the Community trade mark except where, in accordance
with the law governing the transfer, there is agreement to the contrary or circumstances clearly
dictate otherwise). Article 17(2) applies to the contractual obligation to transfer the
undertaking: art 17(2). The word 'whole' in art 17(2) (in fact an earlier similar version of the
provision) must be interpreted in a common sense manner, and it is immaterial if the transfer is
subject to one or two express exceptions or if the parties transferred the beneficial ownership of
parallel UK trade marks but failed to transfer the bare legal title: *My Fotostop Ltd v Fotostop
Group Ltd* [2006] EWHC 2729 (Ch), [2007] FSR 453.
2   As to the meaning of 'Community trade mark' see PARA 189; and as to the application of these
provisions to applications for Community trade marks see PARA 254 note 1.
3   Council Regulation (EC) 207/2009 (OJ L78, 24.3.2009, p 1) art 17(3).
4   Council Regulation (EC) 207/2009 (OJ L78, 24.3.2009, p 1) art 17(1). All documents which
require notification to the proprietor of the Community trade mark in accordance with art 79
(see PARA 260) must be addressed to the person registered as proprietor: art 17(8).
5   As to the register see PARA 171.
6   Council Regulation (EC) 207/2009 (OJ L78, 24.3.2009, p 1) art 17(5). As to the procedure see
Commission Regulation (EC) 2868/95 (OJ L303, 15.12.95, p 1) implementing Council
Regulation (EC) 40/94 on the Community trade mark, art 1 rr 31–32, 35 (all amended by
Commission Regulation (EC) 1041/2005 (OJ L172, 5.7.05, p 4)). As to the consequences of
failing to register a transfer see Council Regulation (EC) 207/2009 (OJ L78, 24.3.2009, p 1)
art 17(6) (see the text and note 7) and art 23 (see PARA 259).
        Where it is clear from the transfer documents that because of the transfer the Community
trade mark is likely to mislead the public concerning the nature, quality or geographical origin
of the goods or services in respect of which it is registered, the Office for Harmonisation in the
Internal Market must not register the transfer unless the successor agrees to limit registration of
the Community trade mark to goods or services in respect of which it is not likely to mislead:
art 17(4). As to the Office for Harmonisation in the Internal Market see PARA 163 et seq.
7   Council Regulation (EC) 207/2009 (OJ L78, 24.3.2009, p 1) art 17(6). Where there are time
limits to be observed vis-à-vis the Office, the successor in title may make the corresponding
statements to the Office once the request for registration of the transfer has been received by the
Office: art 17(7).

258.   Licensing of Community trade marks.   A Community trade mark[1] may
be licensed for some or all of the goods or services for which it is registered and
for the whole or part of the Community[2]. A licence may be exclusive or
non-exclusive[3]. On request of one of the parties the grant or transfer of a licence
in respect of a Community trade mark must be entered in the register[4] and
published[5].

Without prejudice to the provisions of the licensing contract, the licensee may
bring proceedings for infringement[6] of a Community trade mark only if its

proprietor consents to it[7]. However, the holder of an exclusive licence may bring such proceedings if the proprietor of the trade mark, after formal notice, does not himself bring infringement proceedings within an appropriate period[8].

For the purpose of obtaining compensation for damage suffered by him, a licensee is entitled to intervene in infringement proceedings brought by the proprietor of the Community trade mark[9].

1　As to the meaning of 'Community trade mark' see PARA 189.
2　Council Regulation (EC) 207/2009 (OJ L78, 24.3.2009, p 1) on the Community trade mark, art 22(1). See PARA 119. As to the dangers of licensing in this way see PARA 113 note 9. The proprietor of a Community trade mark may invoke the rights conferred by that trade mark against a licensee who contravenes any provision in his licensing contract with regard to (1) its duration; (2) the form covered by the registration in which the trade mark may be used; (3) the scope of the goods or services for which the licence is granted; (4) the territory in which the trade mark may be affixed; or (5) the quality of the goods manufactured or of the services provided by the licensee: art 22(2). See PARA 84 note 5.
3　Council Regulation (EC) 207/2009 (OJ L78, 24.3.2009, p 1) art 22(1). The Regulation contains no definition of an exclusive licence: cf the Trade Marks Act 1994 s 29(1); and PARA 120.
4　As to the register see PARA 171.
5　Council Regulation (EC) 207/2009 (OJ L78, 24.3.2009, p 1) art 22(5). As to the procedure see Commission Regulation (EC) 2868/95 (OJ L303, 15.12.95, p 1) implementing Council Regulation (EC) 40/94 on the Community trade mark, art 1 rr 33–35 (rr 33, 35 amended, and r 34 substituted, by Commission Regulation (EC) 1041/2005 (OJ L172, 5.7.05, p 4)). As to the consequences of failing to register a licence see Council Regulation (EC) 207/2009 (OJ L78, 24.3.2009, p 1) art 23; and PARA 259.
6　As to infringement proceedings see PARA 240 et seq; and as to the grounds on which such proceedings may be brought see PARA 207 et seq.
7　Council Regulation (EC) 207/2009 (OJ L78, 24.3.2009, p 1) art 22(3).
8　Council Regulation (EC) 207/2009 (OJ L78, 24.3.2009, p 1) art 22(3).
9　Council Regulation (EC) 207/2009 (OJ L78, 24.3.2009, p 1) art 22(4).

259. Effects of dealings in Community trade marks vis-à-vis third parties. Certain legal acts[1] concerning a Community trade mark[2] only have effects vis-à-vis third parties in all the member states after entry in the register[3]. Nevertheless, such an act, before it is so entered, has effect vis-à-vis third parties who have acquired rights in the trade mark after the date of that act but who knew of the act at the date on which the rights were acquired[4].

The above provisions[5] do not apply in the case of a person who acquires the Community trade mark or a right concerning the Community trade mark by way of transfer of the whole of the undertaking or by any other universal succession[6].

1　Ie the legal acts referred to in Council Regulation (EC) 207/2009 (OJ L78, 24.3.2009, p 1) on the Community trade mark, art 17 (transfer of Community trade marks: see PARA 257), art 19 (security and rights in rem: see PARA 254) and art 22 (licensing of Community trade marks: see PARA 258).
2　As to the meaning of 'Community trade mark' see PARA 189; and as to the application of these provisions to applications for Community trade marks see PARA 254 note 1.
3　Council Regulation (EC) 207/2009 (OJ L78, 24.3.2009, p 1) art 23(1). As to the register see PARA 171.
4　Council Regulation (EC) 207/2009 (OJ L78, 24.3.2009, p 1) art 23(1). The effect of these provisions is that a successor in title to a Community trade mark or right in it is bound by a licence already granted if: (1) the licence was registered; (2) he has notice of it; or (3) he acquired the Community trade mark by way of transfer of the whole of the undertaking or by any other universal succession. Accordingly, where Council Regulation (EC) 207/2009 (OJ L78, 24.3.2009, p 1) refers to the 'consent' of the proprietor, this should be read as including a case where the proprietor is bound by a licence under these provisions. Such a position is expressly provided for by the Trade Marks Act 1994 s 28(3): see PARA 119 notes 3, 6.
　　As to the effects of levy of execution of a Community trade mark see Council Regulation (EC) 207/2009 (OJ L78, 24.3.2009, p 1) art 23(3); and PARA 254 note 4.

Until such time as common rules for the member states in the field of bankruptcy enter into force, the effects vis-à-vis third parties of bankruptcy or like proceedings are governed by the law of the member state in which such proceedings are first brought within the meaning of national law or of conventions applicable in this field: see art 23(4).

5　Ie Council Regulation (EC) 207/2009 (OJ L78, 24.3.2009, p 1) art 23(1).
6　Council Regulation (EC) 207/2009 (OJ L78, 24.3.2009, p 1) art 23(2). See also note 4.

(8) PROCEDURE IN THE OFFICE FOR HARMONISATION IN THE INTERNAL MARKET

(i) In general

260. Introduction. The Community Trade Mark Regulation[1] and the Implementing Regulation[2] provide for detailed rules of procedure for proceedings in the Office for Harmonisation in the Internal Market[3], relating to applications[4] for Community trade marks[5], opposition proceedings[6], applications for revocation or a declaration of invalidity[7] and appeals[8]. The detail of these procedures is beyond the scope of this work, but a summary follows.

1　Ie Council Regulation (EC) 207/2009 (OJ L78, 24.3.2009, p 1) on the Community trade mark.
2　Ie Commission Regulation (EC) 2868/95 (OJ L303, 15.12.95, p 1) implementing Council Regulation (EC) 40/94 on the Community trade mark. See PARA 161.
3　As to the Office for Harmonisation in the Internal Market see PARA 163 et seq. General rules of procedure are set out in Council Regulation (EC) 207/2009 (OJ L78, 24.3.2009, p 1) arts 75–82. They provide for the statement of reasons on which decisions are based: art 75. There is considerable case law of the European Court of Justice, the Court of First Instance and the European General Court as to the extent of the reasons required. The decision may only be based on reasons or evidence on which the parties concerned have had an opportunity to present their comments: see Case C447/02P *KWS Saat AG v Office for Harmonisation in the Internal Market (Trade Marks and Designs)* [2004] ECR I10107, [2007] IP & T 314, ECJ; Case T-79/00 *Rewe Zentral AG v Office for Harmonisation in the Internal Market (Trade Marks and Designs)* [2002] ECR II-705, [2002] IP & T 533, CFI; Case T-36/01 *Glasverbal v Office for Harmonisation in the Internal Market (Trade Marks and Designs)* [2002] ECR II-3887, [2002] IP & T 684, CFI; but cf Case T-303/03 *Lidl Stiftung & Co KG v Office for Harmonisation in the Internal Market (Trade Marks and Designs)* [2005] ECR II-1917, CFI; Case T-273/02 *Krüger GmbH & Co KG v Office for Harmonisation in the Internal Market (Trade Marks and Designs)* [2005] ECR II-1271, [2005] All ER (D) 261 (Apr), CFI; Case T242/02 *Sunrider Corpn v Office for Harmonisation in the Internal Market (Trade Marks and Designs)* [2005] ECR II2793, CFI; Case T168/04 *L & D SA v Office for Harmonisation in the Internal Market (Trade Marks and Designs)* [2006] ECR II2699, CFI (affd Case C-488/06P [2008] ECR I-5725, [2008] All ER (D) 260 (Jul), ECJ); and Case T-279/09 *Aiello v Office for Harmonisation in the Internal Market (Trade Marks and Designs)* [2012] All ER (D) 158 (Jul), EGC. They also provide for the examination of the facts by the Office of its own motion except in proceedings relating to relative grounds for refusal (Council Regulation (EC) 207/2009 (OJ L78, 24.3.2009, p 1) art 76(1)); for the Office to have a discretion to disregard facts or evidence not submitted in due time (art 76(2); and see Case C-29/05P *Office for Harmonisation in the Internal Market (Trade Marks and Designs) v Kaul GmbH* [2007] ECR I-2213, [2007] IP & T 1008, ECJ; cf Case T-86/05 *K & L Ruppert Stiftung & Co Handels-KG v Office for Harmonisation in the Internal Market (Trade Marks and Designs)* [2007] ECR II-4923 (affd Case C-90/08 [2009] ECR I-26, ECJ)); for oral proceedings and the taking of evidence (Council Regulation (EC) 207/2009 (OJ L78, 24.3.2009, p 1) arts 77–78; and see Case C-370/10P *Ravensberger AG v Office for Harmonisation in the Internal Market (Trade Marks and Designs)* [2011] ECR I-27, ECJ concerning the Office's discretion as to whether to hold oral proceedings); for notification (Council Regulation (EC) 207/2009 (OJ L78, 24.3.2009, p 1) art 79); for revocation of decisions where the Office has made an obvious procedural error (art 80; and see Case C-402/11P *Jaeger & Polacek GmbH v Office for Harmonisation in the Internal Market (Trade Marks and Designs)* [2012] All ER (D) 345 (Oct), ECJ); and for the re-establishment of rights or the continuation of proceedings in the event of missed time limits (Council Regulation (EC) 207/2009 (OJ L78, 24.3.2009, p 1) arts 81–82; and see Case C-479/09 *Evets Corpn v Office for*

Harmonisation in the Internal Market (Trade Marks and Designs) [2010] ECR I-117, ECJ; Case T-136/08 *Aurelia Finance SA v Office for Harmonisation in the Internal Market (Trade Marks and Designs)* [2009] ECR II-1361, [2009] All ER (D) 166 (May), CFI; Case T-271/09 *Prinz Sobieski zu Schwarzenberg v Office for Harmonisation of the Internal Market (Trade Marks and Designs)* [2011] ECR II-288, EGC; and Case T-236/11 *Brainlab AG v Office for Harmonisation of the Internal Market (Trade Marks and Designs)* [2012] ETMR 34, EGC). Time limits directly fixed by the legislation, as opposed to those set by the Office, are in principle non-extendible: Case T-232/00 *Chef Revival USA Inc v Office for Harmonisation in the Internal Market (Trade Marks and Designs)* [2002] ECR II-2749, [2002] All ER (D) 60 (Jun), CFI; Case T-388/00 *Institut für Lernsysteme GmbH v Office for Harmonisation in the Internal Market (Trade Marks and Designs)* [2002] ECR II-4301, [2002] All ER (D) 340 (Oct), CFI; but see Case T-163/98 *Procter & Gamble Co v Office for Harmonisation in the Internal Market (Trade Marks and Designs)* [1999] ECR II-2383, [1999] All ER (EC) 648 (revsd on other grounds Case C-383/99P *Procter & Gamble Co v Office for Harmonisation in the Internal Market (Trade Marks and Designs)* [2002] Ch 82, [2001] ECR I-6521, ECJ); Case T-308/01 *Henkel KGgA v Office for Harmonisation in the Internal Market (Trade Marks and Designs)* [2003] ECR II-3253, [2003] All ER (D) 155 (Sep), CFI; Case T-164/02 *Kaul GmbH v Office for Harmonisation in the Internal Market (Trade Marks and Designs)* [2004] ECR II-3807, [2005] IP & T 392, CFI) (revsd on other grounds Case C-29/05P *Office for Harmonisation in the Internal Market (Trade Marks and Designs) v Kaul GmbH* [2007] ECR II-2213, [2007] IP & T 1008, ECJ); and see also Case T-136/08 *Aurelia Finance SA v Office for Harmonisation in the Internal Market (Trade Marks and Designs)* [2009] ECR II-1361, [2009] All ER (D) 166 (May), CFI (in light of Council Regulation (EC) 40/94 (OJ L11, 14.1.94, p 1) art 78 (now Council Regulation (EC) 207/2009 (OJ L78, 24.3.2009, p 1) art 81), clear that restitutio in integrum was subject to two requirements, first that the party had exercised all due care required by the circumstances, and second that non-observance by the party had direct consequence of causing loss of any right or means of redress); and Case C-402/11P *Jaeger & Polacek GmbH v Office for Harmonisation in the Internal Market (Trade Marks and Designs)* [2012] All ER (D) 345 (Oct), ECJ (purported reversal of decision that opposition to registration of mark inadmissible). Provisions relating to costs are provided for in Council Regulation (EC) 207/2009 (OJ L78, 24.3.2009, p 1) arts 85–86; and Commission Regulation (EC) 2868/95 (OJ L303, 15.12.95, p 1) art 1 r 94 (amended by Commission Regulation (EC) 1041/2005 (OJ L172, 5.7.05, p 4)). Further procedural matters are provided for by Commission Regulation (EC) 2868/95 (OJ L303, 15.12.95, p 1) art 1 rr 52–60, 70–73 (rr 53, 59, 72 amended, r 60 substituted, and r 53a added, by Commission Regulation (EC) 1041/2005 (OJ L172, 5.7.05, p 4)).

Detailed provision as to notification by the Office is made by Commission Regulation (EC) 2868/95 (OJ L303, 15.12.95, p 1) art 1 rr 61–69 (rr 61, 62, 65, 66 amended by Commission Regulation (EC) 1041/2005 (OJ L172, 5.7.05, p 4)); and provision as to other communications with the Office are provided for by Commission Regulation (EC) 2868/95 (OJ L303, 15.12.95, p 1) art 1 rr 79–80, 82–83 (rr 79–80, 82 amended, and r 83 substituted, by Commission Regulation (EC) 1041/2005 (OJ L172, 5.7.05, p 4)).

In the absence of procedural provisions in Council Regulation (EC) 207/2009 (OJ L78, 24.3.2009, p 1), Commission Regulation (EC) 2868/95 (OJ L303, 15.12.95, p 1), Commission Regulation (EC) 2869/95 (OJ L303, 15.12.95, p 33) on the fees payable to the Office for Harmonisation in the Internal Market (Trade Marks and Designs), or the rules of procedure of the Boards of Appeal, the Office must take into account the principles of procedural law generally recognised in the member states: Council Regulation (EC) 207/2009 (OJ L78, 24.3.2009, p 1) art 83.

4   The procedure relating to applications for Community trade marks is provided for by Council Regulation (EC) 207/2009 (OJ L78, 24.3.2009, p 1) arts 25–28, art 36, arts 37–40, arts 43, 44 and art 45: see PARA 261 et seq.

5   As to the meaning of 'Community trade mark' see PARA 189.

6   The procedure relating to opposition proceedings is provided for by Council Regulation (EC) 207/2009 (OJ L78, 24.3.2009, p 1) arts 41–42: see PARA 265.

7   The procedure relating to applications for revocation or a declaration of invalidity is provided for by Council Regulation (EC) 207/2009 (OJ L78, 24.3.2009, p 1) arts 56–57: see PARAS 272–273.

8   The procedure relating to appeals is provided for by Council Regulation (EC) 207/2009 (OJ L78, 24.3.2009, p 1) arts 58–65: see PARAS 274–277.

(ii) Applications for a Community Trade Mark

261. Filing of applications. An application for a Community trade mark[1] must be filed, at the choice of the applicant:

(1) at the Office for Harmonisation in the Internal Market[2]; or

(2) at the central industrial property office of a member state or, in the case of Belgium, the Netherlands or Luxembourg, at the Benelux Trade Mark Office[3].

Where the application is filed as mentioned in head (2) above, the office mentioned there must take all steps to forward the application to the Office for Harmonisation in the Internal Market within two weeks[4] after filing[5].

An application[6] for a Community trade mark must contain:

(a) a request for the registration of a Community trade mark[7];

(b) information identifying the applicant[8];

(c) a list of the goods or services in respect of which the registration is requested[9];

(d) a representation of the trade mark[10];

(e) if the applicant has appointed a representative[11], his name and the address of his place of business[12];

(f) where the priority of a previous application is claimed[13], a declaration to that effect, stating the date on which and the country in or for which the previous application was filed[14];

(g) where exhibition priority is claimed[15], a declaration to that effect, stating the name of the exhibition and the date of the first display of the goods or services[16];

(h) where the seniority of one or more earlier trade marks[17] is claimed[18], a declaration to that effect, stating the member state or member states in or for which the relevant registration was effective, the number of the relevant registration, and the goods or services for which the mark is registered[19];

(i) where applicable, a statement that the application is for registration of a Community collective mark[20];

(j) specification of languages in which the application has been filed, and the second language[21];

(k) the signature of the applicant or his representative in accordance with the relevant rule[22]; and

(l) where applicable, the request of a search report[23].

1   As to the meaning of 'Community trade mark' see PARA 189.

2   As to the Office for Harmonisation in the Internal Market see PARA 163 et seq.

3   Council Regulation (EC) 207/2009 (OJ L78, 24.3.2009, p 1) on the Community trade mark, art 25(1)(a), (b). An application filed at the central industrial property office of a member state or, in the case of Belgium, the Netherlands or Luxembourg, at the Benelux Trade Mark Office has the same effect as if it had been filed on the same date at the Office for Harmonisation in the Internal Market: art 25(1)(b).

4   Such applications which reach the Office more than two months after filing are deemed to have been filed on the date on which the application reached the Office: Council Regulation (EC) 207/2009 (OJ L78, 24.3.2009, p 1) art 25(3).

5   Council Regulation (EC) 207/2009 (OJ L78, 24.3.2009, p 1) art 25(2). The central industrial property office or, in the case of Belgium, the Netherlands or Luxembourg, the Benelux Trade Mark Office may charge the applicant a fee which must not exceed the administrative costs of receiving and forwarding the application: art 25(2).

6   The application for a Community trade mark is subject to the payment of the application fee and, when appropriate, of one or more class fees: Council Regulation (EC) 207/2009 (OJ L78,

    24.3.2009, p 1) art 26(2). The application fee in the United Kingdom is currently set at £15.00: Community Trade Mark (Fees) Regulations 1995, SI 1995/3175, reg 2.

7   Council Regulation (EC) 207/2009 (OJ L78, 24.3.2009, p 1) art 26(1)(a), (3); Commission Regulation (EC) 2868/95 (OJ L303, 15.12.95, p 1) art 1 r 1(1)(a). If the applicant is applying for a Community collective mark, then the application must indicate this: see Council Regulation (EC) 207/2009 (OJ L78, 24.3.2009, p 1) art 66(1); and PARA 278.

8   Council Regulation (EC) 207/2009 (OJ L78, 24.3.2009, p 1) art 26(1)(b). The application must contain the name, address and nationality of the applicant and the state in which he is domiciled or has his seat or an establishment. Names of natural persons must be indicated by the person's family name and given name or names. Names of legal entities, as well as bodies falling under art 3 (capacity to act: see PARA 175) must be indicated by their official designation and include the legal form of the entity, which may be abbreviated in a customary manner. The telephone numbers, fax numbers, electronic mail address and details of other data communications links under which the applicant accepts to receive communications may be given. Only one address may, in principle, be indicated for each applicant; where several addresses are indicated, only the address mentioned first will be taken into account, except where the applicant designates one of the addresses as an address for service: Commission Regulation 2868/95 (EC) (OJ L303, 15.12.95, p 1) art 1 r 1(1)(b) (substituted by Commission Regulation (EC) 1041/2005 (OJ L172, 5.7.05, p 4)).

9   Council Regulation (EC) 207/2009 (OJ L78, 24.3.2009, p 1) art 26(1)(c). This requirement may be fulfilled by a reference to the list of goods or services of a previous Community trade mark application: Commission Regulation (EC) 2868/95 (OJ L303, 15.12.95, p 1) art 1 r 1(1)(c) (amended by Commission Regulation (EC) 1041/2005 (OJ L172, 5.7.05, p 4)). Goods and services in respect of which Community trade marks are applied for must be classified in conformity with the system of classification provided by the Nice Agreement concerning the International Classification of Goods and Services for the purposes of the Registration of Marks of 15 June 1957 (as revised on 13 May 1977) (Cmnd 6898), as revised and amended: Council Regulation (EC) 207/2009 (OJ L78, 24.3.2009, p 1) art 28; Commission Regulation (EC) 2868/95 (OJ L303, 15.12.95, p 1) art 1 r 2(1). As to the Nice Classification see PARA 352. As to the use of the general indications in the class headings of the Nice Classification see PARA 345 note 7. The Office's practice is not to accept descriptions such as 'All goods/services in Class X', but it formerly treated descriptions comprising all the general indications in the class headings of the Nice Classification as covering all goods or services comprised within the relevant class or classes: see Communication 4/03 of the President of the Office; and see Case T-66/11 *Present-Service Ullrich GmbH v Office for Harmonisation in the Internal Market (Trade Marks and Designs)* [2013] ETMR 29, [2013] All ER (D) 263 (Feb) (treating applicant as having so intended by virtue of Communication 4/03). At the date at which this volume states the law, the Office's practice is only to treat such descriptions in that manner if the applicant expressly specifies that that it is the applicant's intention: see Communication 2/12 of the President of the Office.

10 Council Regulation (EC) 207/2009 (OJ L78, 24.3.2009, p 1) art 26(1)(d); Commission Regulation (EC) 2868/95 (OJ L303, 15.12.95, p 1) art 1 r 1(1)(d). As to the requirement of graphical representation of the trade mark see PARA 41 note 2. As to the method of representing the mark see Commission Regulation (EC) 2868/95 (OJ L303, 15.12.95, p 1) art 1 r 3 (amended by Commission Regulation (EC) 1041/2005 (OJ L172, 5.7.05, p 4)). For example, an application for a three-dimensional mark must contain an indication to that effect and must depict the mark graphically or photographically with no more than six different perspectives (Commission Regulation (EC) 2868/95 (OJ L303, 15.12.95, p 1) art 1 r 3(4)); similarly, an application for a coloured mark must include a colour representation of the mark and the colours making up the mark must be indicated in words and may include a reference to a recognised colour code (art 1 r 3(5) (as so amended)).

11 As to representation see PARA 175 et seq.

12 Commission Regulation (EC) 2868/95 (OJ L303, 15.12.95, p 1) art 1 r 1(1)(e). The address of his place of business must be in accordance with art 1 r 1(1)(b): see note 8. If the representative has more than one business address or if there are two or more representatives with different business addresses, the application must indicate which address is the address for service; where such an indication is not made, only the first-mentioned address will be taken into account as an address for service: art 1 r 1(1)(e).

13 Ie pursuant to Council Regulation (EC) 207/2009 (OJ L78, 24.3.2009, p 1) art 30: see PARA 267.

14 Commission Regulation (EC) 2868/95 (OJ L303, 15.12.95, p 1) art 1 r 1(1)(f).

15 Ie pursuant to Council Regulation (EC) 207/2009 (OJ L78, 24.3.2009, p 1) art 33: see PARA 268.

16　Commission Regulation (EC) 2868/95 (OJ L303, 15.12.95, p 1) art 1 r 1(1)(g).
17　Ie trade marks registered in a member state, including a trade mark registered in the Benelux countries or registered under international arrangements having effect in a member state.
18　Ie pursuant to Council Regulation (EC) 207/2009 (OJ L78, 24.3.2009, p 1) art 34: see PARA 270.
19　Commission Regulation (EC) 2868/95 (OJ L303, 15.12.95, p 1) art 1 r 1(1)(h).
20　Commission Regulation (EC) 2868/95 (OJ L303, 15.12.95, p 1) art 1 r 1(1)(i). As to Community collective marks see PARA 278 et seq.
21　Commission Regulation (EC) 2868/95 (OJ L303, 15.12.95, p 1) art 1 r 1(1)(j). As to languages see PARA 168.
22　Commission Regulation (EC) 2868/95 (OJ L303, 15.12.95, p 1) art 1 r 1(1)(k) (substituted by Commission Regulation (EC) 1041/2005 (OJ L172, 5.7.05, p 4)). The relevant rule is Commission Regulation (EC) 2868/95 (OJ L303, 15.12.95, p 1) art 1 r 79: see PARA 260.
23　Commission Regulation (EC) 2868/95 (OJ L303, 15.12.95, p 1) art 1 r 1(1)(l) (added by Commission Regulation (EC) 1041/2005 (OJ L172, 5.7.05, p 4)). The search report is referred to in Council Regulation (EC) 207/2009 (OJ L78, 24.3.2009, p 1) art 38(2): see PARA 262. The search reports must be prepared using a standard form which contains at least the following information: (1) the name of the central industrial property offices that carried out the search; (2) the number of the trademark applications or registrations mentioned in the search report; (3) the date of application and, if applicable, the date of priority of the trademark applications or registrations mentioned in the search report; (4) the date of registration of the trademarks mentioned in the search report; (5) the name and contact address of the holder of the trademarks applications or registrations mentioned in the search report; (6) a representation of the trademarks applied for or registered mentioned in the search report; and (7) an indication of the classes, according to the Nice Classification, for which the earlier national trademarks are applied for or registered or of the goods and services for which the trademarks mentioned in the search report are either applied for or registered: Commission Regulation (EC) 2868/95 (OJ L303, 15.12.95, p 1) art 1 r 5a (added by Commission Regulation (EC) 1041/2005 (OJ L172, 5.7.05, p 4)).
　　The date of filing of a Community trade mark application is the date on which documents containing the information specified in Council Regulation (EC) 207/2009 (OJ L78, 24.3.2009, p 1) art 26(1) (see heads (a)–(d) in the text) are filed with the Office by the applicant or, if the application has been filed with the central office of a member state or with the Benelux Trade Mark Office, with that office, subject to payment of the application fee within a period of one month of filing such documents: art 27; Commission Regulation (EC) 2868/95 (OJ L303, 15.12.95, p 1) art 1 r 5. Council Regulation (EC) 207/2009 (OJ L78, 24.3.2009, p 1) art 27 precludes account being taken not only of the day but also of the hour and minute of filing of an application for a Community trade mark with OHIM for the purposes of establishing that trade mark's priority over a national trade mark filed on the same day, where, according to the national legislation, the hour and minute of filing are relevant: Case C-190/10 *Génesis Seguros Generales Sociedad Anónima de Seguros y Reaseguros (Génesis) v Boys Toys SA* [2012] ECR I–0000, [2012] ETMR 25, ECJ.
　　A Community trade mark application which has been accorded a date of filing is, in the member states, equivalent to a regular national filing, where appropriate with the priority claimed for the Community trade mark application: Council Regulation (EC) 207/2009 (OJ L78, 24.3.2009, p 1) art 32.

262.　Consideration of the application. The Office for Harmonisation in the Internal Market[1] must examine whether the Community trade mark[2] application satisfies the prescribed[3] requirements[4]; and provision is made for the correction of deficiencies which can be corrected[5].

Once the Office has accorded a date of filing to the application[6], it must draw up a Community search[7] report citing those earlier Community trade marks or Community trade mark applications discovered which may be invoked[8] against the registration of the Community trade mark applied for[9].

Thereafter, the application must be published to the extent that it is not refused[10], and third parties may comment upon the application[11].

Where a trade mark is ineligible for registration[12] in respect of some or all of the goods or services covered by the Community trade mark application, the application must be refused as regards those goods or services[13].

1   As to the Office for Harmonisation in the Internal Market see PARA 163 et seq.

2   As to the meaning of 'Community trade mark' see PARA 189.

3   Ie (1) the requirements for the accordance of a date of filing in accordance with Council Regulation (EC) 207/2009 (OJ L78, 24.3.2009, p 1) on the Community trade mark, art 27 (see PARA 261 note 23); (2) the conditions laid down in Council Regulation (EC) 207/2009 (OJ L78, 24.3.2009, p 1) and in Commission Regulation (EC) 2868/95 (OJ L303, 15.12.95, p 1) implementing Council Regulation (EC) 40/94 on the Community trade mark; and (3) where appropriate, the payment of the class fees within the prescribed period: Council Regulation (EC) 207/2009 (OJ L78, 24.3.2009, p 1) art 36(1).

4   Council Regulation (EC) 207/2009 (OJ L78, 24.3.2009, p 1) art 36(1).

5   See Council Regulation (EC) 207/2009 (OJ L78, 24.3.2009, p 1) art 36(2)–(7). As to the general procedural provisions for proceedings in the Office see PARA 260 note 3. Examination is undertaken by the examiners: see PARA 165.

6   Ie in accordance with Council Regulation (EC) 207/2009 (OJ L78, 24.3.2009, p 1) art 27: see PARA 261 note 23. A decision to grant a filing date cannot be revoked (except, perhaps, under Council Regulation (EC) 207/2009 (OJ L78, 24.3.2009, p 1) art 80: see PARA 260 note 3): Case R 78/1998–1 *Notetry Ltd's Application* [1999] ETMR 435, OHIM Board of Appeal; Case R 157/1998–3 *Chemisphere UK Inc's Application* [1999] ETMR 999, OHIM Board of Appeal. A refusal to grant a filing date may be challenged on appeal: Case R 227/1998–3 *Beta-Film GmbH & Co's Application* (30 April 1999, unreported), OHIM Board of Appeal; Case R 143/1998–1 *Vitabiotics Ltd's Application* (OJ OHIM 01/00 p 144), OHIM Board of Appeal.

7   Provision for searching is made in Council Regulation (EC) 207/2009 (OJ L78, 24.3.2009, p 1) art 38(3)–(7).

8   Ie under Council Regulation (EC) 207/2009 (OJ L78, 24.3.2009, p 1) art 8: see PARA 202 et seq.

9   Council Regulation (EC) 207/2009 (OJ L78, 24.3.2009, p 1) art 38(1).

    Where, at the time of filing a Community trade mark application, the applicant requests that a search report also be prepared by the central industrial property offices of the member states and where the appropriate search fee has been paid within the time limit for the payment of the filing fee, the Office must, as soon as the Community trade mark application has been accorded a date of filing, transmit a copy thereof to the central industrial property office of each member state which has informed the Office of its decision to operate a search in its own register of trade marks in respect of Community trade mark applications: art 38(2).

10 If the conditions which the application for a Community trade mark must satisfy have been fulfilled and if the period referred to in Council Regulation (EC) 207/2009 (OJ L78, 24.3.2009, p 1) art 38(7) has expired, the application must be published to the extent that it has not been refused pursuant to art 37 (see the text and notes 12–13): art 39(1). Where, after publication, the application is refused under art 37, the decision that it has been refused must be published upon becoming final: art 39(2). As to publication of the application see Commission Regulation (EC) 2868/95 (OJ L303, 15.12.95, p 1) art 1 r 12 (amended by Commission Regulation (EC) 1041/2005 (OJ L172, 5.7.05, p 4)).

11 Council Regulation (EC) 207/2009 (OJ L78, 24.3.2009, p 1) provides that following the publication of the Community trade mark application, any natural or legal person and any group or body representing manufacturers, producers, suppliers of services, traders or consumers may submit to the Office written observations, explaining on which grounds under art 7 (absolute grounds for refusal of registration: see PARA 192 et seq), in particular, the trade mark must not be registered ex officio: art 40(1). Such persons must not be parties to the proceedings before the Office: art 40(1); and accordingly they have no right of appeal if the Office disagrees with the observations: Case R1071/2010–1 *Consejo Regulador de la Denominación de Origen Protegida 'Jamón de Huelva''s Appeal* (4 November 2010, unreported), OHIM Board of Appeal. The observations mentioned above must be communicated to the applicant, who may comment on them: Council Regulation (EC) 207/2009 (OJ L78, 24.3.2009, p 1) art 40(2). This is an important procedure, because it is the only way in which third parties can raise absolute grounds for refusal against an application (which cannot be raised in opposition proceedings: see PARA 265).

12 Ie under Council Regulation (EC) 207/2009 (OJ L78, 24.3.2009, p 1) art 7: see PARA 192 et seq.

    Where the trade mark contains an element which is not distinctive, and where the inclusion of the said element in the trade mark could give rise to doubts as to the scope of protection of the trade mark, the Office may request, as a condition for registration of the said trade mark, that the applicant state that he disclaims any exclusive right to such element; and any disclaimer must be published together with the application or the registration of the Community trade mark, as the case may be: Council Regulation (EC) 207/2009 (OJ L78, 24.3.2009, p 1) art 37(2). Disclaimers are not common in Office practice; cf disclaimers under the Trade Marks Act 1994 s 13: see PARA 65.

The Office is not bound to follow decisions by member states on the absolute grounds prohibiting registrability (see PARA 192 et seq), and must in each case make its own assessment as to the existence of such grounds. However such decisions may be taken into account: see PARA 42 text and note 10. Nor is the Office bound to follow its own earlier decisions: see PARA 42 text and note 11.

13   Council Regulation (EC) 207/2009 (OJ L78, 24.3.2009, p 1) art 37(1). However, the application may not be refused before the applicant has been given the opportunity of withdrawing or amending his application or submitting his observations: art 37(3).

263.   Withdrawal, restriction and amendment of the application.   The applicant may at any time[1] withdraw[2] his Community trade mark[3] application or restrict[4] the list of goods or services[5] contained in it. Where the application has already been published, the withdrawal or restriction must also be published[6].

In other respects, a Community trade mark application may be amended, upon request of the applicant, only by correcting the name and address of the applicant, errors of wording or of copying, or obvious mistakes, provided that such correction does not substantially change the trade mark or extend the list of goods or services[7]. Where the amendments affect the representation of the trade mark or the list of goods or services and are made after publication of the application, the trade mark application must be published as amended[8].

1   Restrictions and amendments may be made on appeal: Case T-289/02 *Telepharmacy Solutions Inc v Office for Harmonisation in the Internal Market (Trade Marks and Designs)* [2004] ECR II-2851, [2004] All ER (D) 122 (Jul), CFI; Case R 544/2002–1 *EarthLink Network Inc v Stamer Musikanlagen GmbH* (17 December 2003, unreported), OHIM Board of Appeal.

2   The withdrawal of an application for a Community trade mark must be made expressly and unconditionally by the applicant: Case T-219/00 *Ellos v Office for Harmonisation in the Internal Market (Trade Marks and Designs)* [2002] ECR II-753, [2002] IP & T 384, CFI; Joined Cases T-466/04 and T-467/04 *Dami v Office for Harmonisation in the Internal Market (Trade Marks and Designs)* [2006] ECR II-183, [2006] All ER (D) 09 (Feb), CFI.

3   As to the meaning of 'Community trade mark' see PARA 189.

4   Whether an amendment restricts the list of goods or services is a question of substance not form: see Case R-517/2001–1 *Financial Interactive Inc's Application* (OJ OHIM 01/03 p 33), OHIM Board of Appeal.

5   As to the list of goods or services see Council Regulation (EC) 207/2009 (OJ L78, 24.3.2009, p 1) on the Community trade mark, art 28; Commission Regulation (EC) 2868/95 (OJ L303, 15.12.95, p 1) art 1 r 2(1); and PARA 261 note 9.

6   Council Regulation (EC) 207/2009 (OJ L78, 24.3.2009, p 1) art 43(1). The procedure for such amendment is provided for by Commission Regulation (EC) 2868/95 (OJ L303, 15.12.95, p 1) art 1 r 13 (amended by Commission Regulation (EC) 1041/2005 (OJ L172, 5.7.05, p 4)). A request to amend the application to restrict the list of goods or services must be made expressly and unconditionally: Case T-219/00 *Ellos v Office for Harmonisation in the Internal Market (Trade Marks and Designs)* [2002] ECR II-753, [2002] IP & T 384, CFI; Case T-396/02 *August Storck KG v Office for Harmonisation in the Internal Market (Trade Marks and Designs)* [2004] ECR II-3821, [2004] All ER (D) 157 (Nov), CFI; Case C-412/05 *Alcon Inc v Office for Harmonisation in the Internal Market (Trade Marks and Designs)* [2007] ECR I-3569, [2007] ETMR 68, [2007] All ER (D) 238 (Apr), ECJ. A request is not unconditional if it is made subject to a prior finding that the applicant's contested goods and services are similar to the opponent's goods and services: Case T-48/06 *Astex Therapeutics Ltd v Office for Harmonisation in the Internal Market (Trade Marks and Designs)* [2008] ECR II-161, [2008] All ER (D) 51 (Sep), CFI. On appeal to the EGC, such a restriction is possible only if the applicant confines itself to withdrawing one or more goods or services from the specification, one or more categories of goods or services which were included, as such, in that specification; Case T-458/05 *Tegometall International AG v Office for Harmonisation in the Internal Market (Trade Marks and Designs)*

[2007] ECR II-4721, [2007] All ER (D) 307 (Nov), CFI; Case T-304/06 *Paul Reber GmbH & Co. KG v Office for Harmonisation in the Internal Market (Trade Marks and Designs)* [2008] ECR II-1927, CFI.

7   As to the circumstances in which a typographical error in the trade mark applied for may be corrected see Case T-128/99 *Signal Communications Ltd v Office for Harmonisation in the Internal Market (Trade Marks and Designs)* [2001] ECR II-3273, CFI (TELEYE amended to TELEEYE). Cf the approach under the Trade Marks Act 1994 s 39: see PARA 357.

8   Council Regulation (EC) 207/2009 (OJ L78, 24.3.2009, p 1) art 43(2). As to the procedure for such amendment see Commission Regulation (EC) 2868/95 (OJ L303, 15.12.95, p 1) art 1 r 14. As to publication see PARA 173.

264. Division of the application. The applicant may divide the application by declaring that some of the goods or services included in the original application will be the subject of one or more divisional applications[1]. The goods or services in the divisional application must not overlap with the goods or services which remain in the original application or those which are included in other divisional applications[2].

Division is not permissible:

(1)   if, where an opposition[3] has been entered against the original application, such a divisional declaration has the effect of introducing a division amongst the goods or services against which the opposition has been directed, until the decision of the Opposition Division[4] has become final or the opposition proceedings are finally terminated otherwise[5];

(2)   during the periods laid down in the Implementing Regulation[6].

1   Council Regulation (EC) 207/2009 (OJ L78, 24.3.2009, p 1) on the Community trade mark, art 44(1). The declaration must comply with the provisions set out in Commission Regulation (EC) 2868/95 (OJ L303, 15.12.95, p 1) implementing Council Regulation (EC) 40/94 on the Community trade mark (the 'Implementing Regulation'): Council Regulation (EC) 207/2009 (OJ L78, 24.3.2009, p 1) art 44(3). The declaration is subject to a fee and must be deemed not to have been made until the fee is paid: art 44(4).

    The division must take effect on the date on which it is recorded in the files kept by the Office concerning the original application: art 44(5). All requests and applications submitted and all fees paid with regard to the original application prior to the date on which the Office for Harmonisation in the Internal Market receives the declaration of division are deemed also to have been submitted or paid with regard to the divisional application or applications; the fees for the original application which have been duly paid prior to the date on which the declaration of division is received must not be refunded: art 44(6). The divisional application must preserve the filing date and any priority date and seniority date of the original application: art 44(7). As to the Office for Harmonisation in the Internal Market see PARA 163 et seq.

    As to the procedure for the division of an application see Commission Regulation (EC) 2868/95 (OJ L303, 15.12.95, p 1) art 1 r 13a (added by Commission Regulation (EC) 1041/2005 (OJ L172, 5.7.05, p 4); and amended by Commission Regulation (EC) 355/2009 (OJ L109, 30.4.2009, p 3)).

    Division of a Community trade mark registration is also possible: see Council Regulation (EC) 207/2009 (OJ L78, 24.3.2009, p 1) art 49; and PARA 232. Under the Trade Marks Act 1994 s 41(1) only division of an application, and not division of a registration, is permitted: see PARA 349.

2   Council Regulation (EC) 207/2009 (OJ L78, 24.3.2009, p 1) art 44(1).

3   As to oppositions see PARA 265.

4   As to the Opposition Division see PARA 165.

5   Council Regulation (EC) 207/2009 (OJ L78, 24.3.2009, p 1) art 44(2)(a).

6   Council Regulation (EC) 207/2009 (OJ L78, 24.3.2009, p 1) art 44(2)(b). As to the Implementing Regulation see note 1.

265. Opposition. Within a period of three months following the publication[1] of a Community trade mark[2] application[3], notice of opposition to registration of the trade mark may be given on the grounds that it may not be registered by reason of one of the relative grounds for refusal of registration[4]:

(1)   by the proprietors of earlier trade marks[5], as well as licensees authorised by the proprietors of those trade marks, in respect of the relevant grounds[6];

(2)   by the proprietors of trade marks, whose agents or representatives have applied to register the trade mark in their own names[7];

(3)   by the proprietors of earlier marks or signs[8] and by persons authorised under the relevant national law to exercise such rights[9].

Opposition must be expressed in writing and must specify the grounds on which it is made[10].

If the applicant so requests,[11] the proprietor of an earlier Community trade mark or an earlier national trade mark who has given notice of opposition must furnish proof that, during the period of five years preceding the date of publication of the Community trade mark application, the earlier trade mark had been put to genuine use[12] in the Community[13] or in the member state in question, as the case may be, in connection with goods or services in respect of which it is registered and which he cites as justification for his opposition, or that there are proper reasons[14] for non-use, provided that the earlier trade mark has been registered for not less than five years[15]. In absence of proof to that effect, the opposition must be rejected[16]. If the earlier trade mark has been used in relation to part only of the goods or services for which it is registered it is, for the purposes of the examination of the opposition, deemed to be registered in respect of only that part of the goods or services[17].

The Office for Harmonisation in the Internal Market may, if it thinks fit, invite the parties to an opposition to make a friendly settlement[18]; otherwise it must consider and rule upon the opposition[19]. If examination of the opposition reveals that the trade mark may not be registered in respect of some or all of the goods or services for which the Community trade mark application has been made, the application must be refused in respect of those goods or services; otherwise, the opposition must be rejected[20].

1   As to publication of Community trade mark applications see PARA 262 note 11.

2   As to the meaning of 'Community trade mark' see PARA 189.

3   Notice of opposition to registration of the trade mark may also be given, subject to the same conditions, in the event of the publication of an amended application in accordance with Council Regulation (EC) 207/2009 (OJ L78, 24.3.2009, p 1) on the Community trade mark, art 43(2): see PARA 263 text and note 8.

4   Council Regulation (EC) 207/2009 (OJ L78, 24.3.2009, p 1) art 41(1). As to the relative grounds of refusal see art 8; and PARA 201 et seq. Absolute grounds for refusal (ie under art 7: see PARA 192 et seq) cannot be raised in opposition proceedings, instead they must be raised by way of third party observations under art 40: see PARA 262 note 11.

5   Ie trade marks referred to in Council Regulation (EC) 207/2009 (OJ L78, 24.3.2009, p 1) art 8(2): see PARA 201. An earlier trade mark is presumed to be valid, and it is not open to the applicant to argue that the earlier trade mark is invalid eg by virtue of other national rights in the member state concerned: Case R 723/2001–2 Barocco Roma Srl v Moda Nuova Fashion AB (16 December 2003, unreported), OHIM Board of Appeal.

6   Council Regulation (EC) 207/2009 (OJ L78, 24.3.2009, p 1) art 41(1)(a). The relevant grounds are those under art 8(1) (see PARAS 202–203) and art 8(5) (see PARA 204): art 41(1)(a).

7   Council Regulation (EC) 207/2009 (OJ L78, 24.3.2009, p 1) art 41(1)(b). The trade marks concerned are those referred to in art 8(3) (see PARA 206): art 41(1)(b).

8   Ie earlier marks or signs referred to in Council Regulation (EC) 207/2009 (OJ L78, 24.3.2009, p 1) art 8(4): see PARA 205. The validity of an earlier trade mark may not be called into question in proceedings concerning the registration of a later trade mark, but only by way of a claim for revocation or a declaration of invalidity in the appropriate jurisdiction: Case T-6/01 Matratzen Concord GmbH v Office for Harmonisation in the Internal Market (Trade Marks and Designs) [2002] ECR II-4335 (affd Case C-30/0P [2004] ECR I-3657). Similarly, an earlier right such as an appellation of origin relied upon by the opponent must be presumed to be valid unless it has

been declared invalid by a judgment of a competent court that has become final: Case C-96/09P *Anheuser-Busch Inc v Budejovicky Budvar np* [2011] ECR I-2131, [2011] ETMR 31, ECJ.

9 Council Regulation (EC) 207/2009 (OJ L78, 24.3.2009, p 1) art 41(1)(c). As to the form and contents of the notice of opposition see further Commission Regulation (EC) 2868/95 (OJ L303, 15.12.95, p 1) implementing Council Regulation (EC) 40/94 on the Community trade mark, art 1 r 15 (substituted by Commission Regulation (EC) 1041/2005 (OJ L172, 5.7.05, p 4)). An earlier trade mark is sufficiently identified in the notice of opposition if the notice states the registration number and the member state in which it is registered: Case T-186/04 *Spa Monopole, compagnie fermière de Spa SA/NV v Office for Harmonisation in the Internal Market (Trade Marks and Designs)* [2005] ECR II-2333, [2005] All ER (D) 143 (Jun), CFI. As to particulars of earlier rights claimed under national law see PARA 205 note 7. As to the Office for Harmonisation in the Internal Market see PARA 163 et seq.

10 Council Regulation (EC) 207/2009 (OJ L78, 24.3.2009, p 1) art 41(3). It must not be treated as duly entered until the opposition fee has been paid: art 41(3). Within a period fixed by the Office, the opponent may submit in support of his case facts, evidence and arguments: art 41(3). The notice of opposition must state the grounds on which opposition is based, whereas the submission of facts, evidence and arguments is, at this stage, merely optional: Case T-232/00 *Chef Revival USA Inc v Office for Harmonisation in the Internal Market (Trade Marks and Designs)* [2002] ECR II-2749, [2002] All ER (D) 60 (Jun), CFI; Case T-53/05 *Calavo Growers Inc v Office for Harmonisation in the Internal Market (Trade Marks and Designs)* [2007] ECR II-37, [2007] All ER (D) 80 (Jan), CFI. It is sufficient for this purpose to state 'the opposition is based on a likelihood of confusion' or to tick the relevant box on the official form: Case T-53/05 *Calavo Growers Inc v Office for Harmonisation in the Internal Market (Trade Marks and Designs)*. Where black and white copies of notices of opposition were transmitted to the Office by fax before the expiry of the opposition period and colour originals were sent by post promptly thereafter, the oppositions were in time even though the originals arrived after the expiry of the period: Joined Cases T-239/05, T-240/05, T-245/05 to T-247/05, T-255/05, T-274/05 to T-280/05 *Black & Decker Corpn v Office for Harmonisation in the Internal Market (Trade Marks and Designs)* [2007] ECR II-43, [2007] All ER (D) 221 (May), CFI.

In the examination of the opposition the Office must invite the parties, as often as necessary, to file observations within a period set them by the Office, on communications issued by the other parties or issued by itself: Council Regulation (EC) 207/2009 (OJ L78, 24.3.2009, p 1) art 42(1). Failure by the applicant to file observations may not be interpreted as an implied withdrawal of the application: Case T-171/06 *Laytoncrest Ltd v Office for Harmonisation in the Internal Market (Trade Marks and Designs)* [2009] ECR II-547, [2009] All ER (D) 168 (Mar), CFI. The Office is not obliged to inform the opponent that its evidence as to the existence of the earlier right relied on is inadequate and give it an opportunity to remedy the deficiency: Case T-420/03 *El Corte Inglés SA v Office for Harmonisation in the Internal Market (Trade Marks and Designs)* [2008] ECR II-837, [2008] All ER (D) 195 (Jun), CFI.

11 The applicant must make any such request within the period specified by the Office for filing his observations on the opposition: Commission Regulation (EC) 2868/95 (OJ L303, 15.12.95, p 1) art 1 r 22(1) (art 1 r 22 substituted by Commission Regulation (EC) 1041/2005 (OJ L172, 5.7.05, p 4)). See also Case T-112/03 *L'Oréal SA v Office for Harmonisation in the Internal Market (Trade Marks and Designs)* [2005] ECR II-949, [2005] All ER (D) 267 (Mar), CFI; affd on other grounds Case C-235/05P *L'Oréal SA v Office for Harmonisation in the Internal Market (Trade Marks and Designs)* [2006] ECR I-57, ECJ.

There is no requirement for an absence of bad faith on the part of the applicant in making any such request: Case T-298/10 *Gross v Office for Harmonisation of the Internal Market (Trade Marks and Designs)* [2012] ETMR 29, EGC.

12 As to genuine use see PARA 98 note 6.

13 As to the meaning of 'in the Community' see PARA 220 note 5.

14 As to the meaning of 'proper reasons' see PARA 98 note 10.

15 Council Regulation (EC) 207/2009 (OJ L78, 24.3.2009, p 1) art 42(2), (3). The obligation to prove use of a national trade mark in the relevant member state is unaffected by a bilateral agreement between that member state and another country whereby use in the latter is tantamount to use in the former: Case T-170/11 *Rivella International AG v Office for Harmonisation in the Internal Market (Trade Marks and Designs)* [2012] ECR II-0000, EGC. As to the procedure to be followed in the event of a request for proof of use, and the nature and form that evidence of use must take, see Commission Regulation (EC) 2868/95 (OJ L303, 15.12.95, p 1) art 1 r 22 (as substituted: see note 11). These provisions are of some practical importance and there are a considerable number of decisions of the Court of First Instance and the European General Court interpreting them: see in particular e g Case T-334/01 *MFE Marienfelde Gmbh v Office for Harmonisation in the Internal Market (Trade Marks and*

Designs) [2004] ECR II-2787, [2004] All ER (D) 125 (Jul), CFI; Case T-203/02 *Sunrider Corpn v Office for Harmonisation in the Internal Market (Trade Marks and Designs)* [2004] ECR II-2811, [2004] All ER (D) 129 (Jul), CFI (affd Case C-416/04P *Sunrider Corpn v Office for Harmonisation in the Internal Market (Trade Marks and Designs)* [2006] ECR I-4267, [2006] All ER (D) 178 (May), ECJ); Case T-356/02 *Vitakraft-Werke Wuhrmann & Sohn GmbH & Co KG v Office for Harmonisation in the Internal Market (Trade Marks and Designs)* [2004] ECR II-3445, [2004] All ER (D) 54 (Oct), CFI; Case T-303/03 *Lidl Stiftung & Co KG v Office for Harmonisation in the Internal Market (Trade Marks and Designs)* [2005] ECR II-1917, CFI. It should be noted that the Office takes a very exacting view of what is required to prove use of a trade mark, and in particular that it considers that evidence in the form of an affidavit or witness statement by a representative of the proprietor is of little weight unless corroborated by independent evidence: see e g Case R 1075/2005–2 *Rodcraft Pneumatic Tools GmbH & Co KG v Rolson Tools Ltd* (8 June 2006, unreported), OHIM Board of Appeal; and cf *Rolson Tools Ltd's Trade Mark Application* (O/011/06), Appointed Person. The EGC has held that in order to assess the evidential value of such a document, regard should be had first and foremost to the credibility of the account it contains; it is then necessary to take account, in particular, of the person from whom the document originates, the circumstances in which it came into being, the person to whom it was addressed and whether, on its face, the document appears sound and reliable: Case T303/03 *Lidl Stiftung & Co KG v Office for Harmonisation in the Internal Market (Trade Marks and Designs)* [2005] ECR II1917, CFI; Case T86/07 *DeichmannSchuhe v Office for Harmonisation in the Internal Market (Trade Marks and Designs)* [2008] ECR II-321, CFI; Case T-214/08 *Paul Alfons Rehbein (GmbH & Co.) KG v Office for Harmonisation in the Internal Market (Trade Marks and Designs)* [2012] ECR II-0000, EGC.

16 Council Regulation (EC) 207/2009 (OJ L78, 24.3.2009, p 1) art 42(2), (3).

17 Council Regulation (EC) 207/2009 (OJ L78, 24.3.2009, p 1) art 42(2), (3).

18 Council Regulation (EC) 207/2009 (OJ L78, 24.3.2009, p 1) art 42(4).

19 Procedural provisions for oppositions are provided for by Commission Regulation (EC) 2868/95 (OJ L303, 15.12.95, p 1) art 1 rr 16–22 (rr 16–20, 22 substituted by Commission Regulation (EC) 1041/2005 (OJ L172, 5.7.05, p 4)). These provide inter alia for a two month 'cooling off period' once the opposition has been ascertained to be admissible: Commission Regulation (EC) 2868/95 (OJ L303, 15.12.95, p 1) art 1 r 19 (as so substituted). Oppositions are the responsibility of the Opposition Divisions of the Office: see PARA 165. As to the general procedural provisions for proceedings in the Office see PARA 260 note 3. The opposition division is not obliged to reject an opposition as unfounded where the opponent's grounds of opposition contain the essential information for assessing its objection, even if the explanation of those grounds has not been translated into the correct language: Case T-53/05 *Calavo Growers Inc v Office for Harmonisation in the Internal Market (Trade Marks and Designs)* [2007] ECR II-37, [2007] All ER (D) 80 (Jan), CFI.

20 Council Regulation (EC) 207/2009 (OJ L78, 24.3.2009, p 1) art 42(5). The decision refusing the application must be published upon becoming final: art 42(6). If an opposition based upon several earlier trade marks or rights is upheld with regard to one such trade mark or right, the Office is not required to rule upon the remaining trade marks or rights: Case T-342/02 *Metro-Goldwyn-Mayer Lion Corpn v Office for Harmonisation in the Internal Market (Trade Marks and Designs)* [2004] ECR II-3191, [2004] All ER (D) 113 (Sep), CFI; Case T-194/05 *TeleTech Holdings Inc v Office for Harmonisation in the Internal Market (Trade Marks and Designs)* [2006] ECR II-1367, CFI.

266.   Registration and renewal. Where an application meets the prescribed requirements[1] and where no notice of opposition[2] has been given within the prescribed period[3], or where opposition has been rejected by a definitive decision[4], the trade mark must be registered[5] as a Community trade mark[6].

Community trade marks are registered for a period of ten years from the date of filing[7] of the application; and registration may be renewed[8] for further periods of ten years[9].

1 Ie the requirements of Council Regulation (EC) 207/2009 (OJ L78, 24.3.2009, p 1) on the Community trade mark.

2 As to the notice of opposition see Council Regulation (EC) 207/2009 (OJ L78, 24.3.2009, p 1) art 41; and PARA 265.

3 Ie the period referred to in Council Regulation (EC) 207/2009 (OJ L78, 24.3.2009, p 1) art 41(1): see PARA 265.

4   As to the examination of the opposition see Council Regulation (EC) 207/2009 (OJ L78, 24.3.2009, p 1) art 42; and PARA 265 text and note 15.
5   No definition of 'registered' is provided for by Council Regulation (EC) 207/2009 (OJ L78, 24.3.2009, p 1), although that term is used extensively (cf the Trade Marks Act 1994 s 63(1): see PARA 21 note 2). 'Registered' in the context of a Community trade mark must therefore mean registered in accordance with these provisions, in particular Council Regulation (EC) 207/2009 (OJ L78, 24.3.2009, p 1) art 45. As to the register of Community trade marks see PARA 171.
6   Council Regulation (EC) 207/2009 (OJ L78, 24.3.2009, p 1) art 45. The trade mark will only be registered provided that the registration fee has been paid within the period prescribed; if the fee is not paid within this period the application is deemed to be withdrawn: art 45. Further provision for registration is provided for by Commission Regulation (EC) 2868/95 (OJ L303, 15.12.95, p 1)) implementing Council Regulation (EC) 40/94 on the Community trade mark, art 1 rr 23–24 (r 24 amended by Commission Regulation (EC) 1041/2005 (OJ L172, 5.7.2005, p 4)). As to the meaning of 'Community trade mark' see PARA 189.
7   As to the date of filing see PARA 261 note 23.
8   Ie in accordance with the following provisions: Council Regulation (EC) 207/2009 (OJ L78, 24.3.2009, p 1) art 46. The Office for Harmonisation in the Internal Market must inform the proprietor of the Community trade mark, and any person having a registered right in respect of the Community trade mark, of the expiry of the registration in good time before the said expiry; but failure to give such information does not involve the responsibility of the Office: art 47(2). Registration of the Community trade mark must be renewed at the request of the proprietor of the trade mark or any person expressly authorised by him, provided that the fees have been paid: art 47(1). Renewal takes effect from the day following the date on which the existing registration expires; and the renewal must be registered: art 47(5). As to the Office for Harmonisation in the Internal Market see PARA 163 et seq.

    The request for renewal must be submitted within a period of six months ending on the last day of the month in which protection ends; the fees must also be paid within this period; failing this, the request may be submitted and the fees paid within a further period of six months following the last day of the month in which protection ends, provided that an additional fee is paid within this further period: art 47(3). Where the request is submitted or the fees paid in respect of only some of the goods or services for which the Community trade mark is registered, registration must be renewed for those goods or services only: art 47(4).

    Further procedural rules relating to notification of expiry and renewal are provided for by Commission Regulation (EC) 2868/95 (OJ L303, 15.12.95, p 1) art 1 rr 29, 30 (r 30 substituted by Commission Regulation (EC) 1041/2005 (OJ L172, 5.7.2005, p 4)).
9   Council Regulation (EC) 207/2009 (OJ L78, 24.3.2009, p 1) art 46.

(iii) Priority and Seniority

267. Right of priority. A person who has duly filed an application for a trade mark in or for any state party to the Paris Convention[1] or to the WTO Agreement[2], or his successors in title, enjoys, for the purpose of filing a Community trade mark[3] application for the same trade mark in respect of goods or services which are identical with or contained within those for which the application has been filed, a right of priority[4] during a period of six months from the date of filing of the first application[5].

Every filing that is equivalent to a regular national filing[6] under the national law of the state where it was made or under bilateral or multilateral agreements must be recognised as giving rise to a right of priority[7].

If the first filing has been made in a state which is not a party to the Paris Convention or the WTO Agreement, the provisions described above[8] apply only in so far as that state, according to published findings[9], grants, on the basis of a first filing made at the Office for Harmonisation in the Internal Market[10] and subject to equivalent conditions[11], a right of priority having equivalent effect[12].

An applicant desiring to take advantage of the priority of a previous application must file a declaration of priority and a copy of the previous application[13].

1   As to the Paris Convention see PARA 6.
2   As to the WTO Agreement see PARA 7.
3   As to the meaning of 'Community trade mark' see PARA 189.
4   As to the effect of the priority right see PARA 269.
5   Council Regulation (EC) 207/2009 (OJ L78, 24.3.2009, p 1) on the Community trade mark, art 29(1). A subsequent application for a trade mark which was the subject of a previous first application in respect of the same goods or services, and which is filed in or in respect of the same state must be considered as the first application for the purposes of determining priority, provided that, at the date of filing of the subsequent application, the previous application has been withdrawn, abandoned or refused, without being open to public inspection and without leaving any rights outstanding, and has not served as a basis for claiming a right of priority; and the previous application may not thereafter serve as a basis for claiming a right of priority: art 29(4).
6   A regular national filing means any filing that is sufficient to establish the date on which the application was filed, whatever may be the outcome of the application: Council Regulation (EC) 207/2009 (OJ L78, 24.3.2009, p 1) art 29(3). As to filing an application under the Trade Marks Act 1994 see PARA 345 et seq.
7   Council Regulation (EC) 207/2009 (OJ L78, 24.3.2009, p 1) art 29(2).
8   Ie Council Regulation (EC) 207/2009 (OJ L78, 24.3.2009, p 1) art 29(1)–(4).
9   As to the publication of such findings see PARA 187.
10   As to the Office for Harmonisation in the Internal Market see PARA 163 et seq.
11   Ie conditions equivalent to those laid down in Council Regulation (EC) 207/2009 (OJ L78, 24.3.2009, p 1).
12   Council Regulation (EC) 207/2009 (OJ L78, 24.3.2009, p 1) art 29(5).
13   Council Regulation (EC) 207/2009 (OJ L78, 24.3.2009, p 1) art 30. If the language of the latter is not one of the languages of the Office, the applicant must file a translation of the previous application in one of those languages: art 30. As to the languages of the Office see PARA 168. Further procedural requirements are laid down in Commission Regulation (EC) 2868/95 (OJ L303, 15.12.95, p 1) implementing Council Regulation (EC) 40/94 on the Community trade mark, art 1 r 6 (amended by Commission Regulation (EC) 1041/2005 (OJ L172, 5.7.05, p 4)).

268. Exhibition priority. If an applicant for a Community trade mark[1] has displayed goods or services under the mark applied for, at a recognised international exhibition[2], he may, if he files the application within a period of six months from the date of the first display of the goods or services under the mark applied for, claim a right of priority[3] from that date[4].

1   As to the meaning of 'Community trade mark' see PARA 189.
2   Ie an official or officially recognised international exhibition: (1) falling within the terms of the Convention relating to International Exhibitions (Paris, 22 November 1928; TS 9 (1931); Cmd 3776), as amended and supplemented by any Protocol to that Convention which is in force; or (2) falling within the terms of any subsequent treaty or convention replacing that Convention: see the Patents Act 1977 s 130(1). The Convention has been supplemented by Protocols, all signed at Paris, dated 10 May 1948 (TS 57 (1951); Cmd 8311), 16 November 1966 (TS 14 (1968); Cmnd 3557), and 30 November 1972 (Misc 14 (1973); Cmnd 5317).
3   As to the effect of a right of priority see PARA 269.
4   Council Regulation (EC) 207/2009 (OJ L78, 24.3.2009, p 1) on the Community trade mark, art 33(1). The reference is to claiming a right of priority from that date within the meaning of art 31 (see PARA 269): art 33(1). Further procedural requirements are laid down in Commission Regulation (EC) 2868/95 (OJ L303, 15.12.95, p 1) implementing Council Regulation (EC) 40/94 on the Community trade mark, art 1 r 7. An applicant who wishes to claim priority pursuant to this provision must file evidence of the display of goods or services under the mark applied for under the conditions laid down in Commission Regulation (EC) 2868/95 (OJ L303, 15.12.95, p 1): Council Regulation (EC) 207/2009 (OJ L78, 24.3.2009, p 1) art 33(2).
    An exhibition priority granted in a member state or in a third country does not extend the period of priority laid down in art 29 (see PARA 267): art 33(3).

269. Effect of priority right. The right of priority[1] has the effect that the date of priority counts as the date of filing of the Community trade mark application for the purposes of establishing which rights take precedence[2].

1 As to the claiming of a right of priority see Council Regulation (EC) 207/2009 (OJ L78, 24.3.2009, p 1) on the Community trade mark, arts 29–30 (see PARA 267), art 33 (see PARA 268).

2 Council Regulation (EC) 207/2009 (OJ L78, 24.3.2009, p 1) art 31. It is necessary to establish rights to priority for the purpose of resolving conflicts with other applications or with conflicting national rights such as those mentioned in art 8: see PARA 201 et seq.

270. Claiming the seniority of a national trade mark. The proprietor[1] of an earlier trade mark[2] registered in a member state[3], or registered under international arrangements having effect in a member state[4], who applies for an identical trade mark for registration as a Community trade mark[5] for goods or services which are identical with or contained within those for which the earlier trade mark has been registered, may claim for the Community trade mark the seniority[6] of the earlier trade mark in respect of the member state in or for which it is registered[7].

The proprietor of a Community trade mark who is the proprietor of an earlier identical[8] trade mark registered in a member state[9] or of an earlier identical trade mark with an international registration effective in a member state[10] for goods or services which are identical with those for which the earlier trade mark has been registered or contained within them may claim the seniority of the earlier trade mark in respect of the member state in or for which it is registered[11].

1 In this context the proprietor is the legal owner of the senior mark, whether or not he is also the registered proprietor: Case R 5/97–1 *BatMark Inc's Application* [1998] ETMR 448, OHIM Board of Appeal.

2 As to the meaning of 'earlier trade mark' see PARA 201.

3 Ie including a trade mark registered in the Benelux countries, ie Belgium, the Netherlands or Luxembourg.

4 Ie such as international trade marks which are protected in member states pursuant to the Madrid Agreement or Madrid Protocol: see PARA 8.

5 As to the meaning of 'Community trade mark' see PARA 189.

6 For the effect of seniority see PARA 271.

7 Council Regulation (EC) 207/2009 (OJ L78, 24.3.2009, p 1) on the Community trade mark, art 34(1). As to the procedure for the claiming of seniority see Commission Regulation (EC) 2868/95 (OJ L303, 15.12.95, p 1) implementing Council Regulation (EC) 40/94 on the Community trade mark, art 1 rr 8, 28 (both amended by Commission Regulation (EC) 1041/2005 (OJ L172, 5.7.05, p 4)).

8 In Case R-10/1998–2 *International Business Machines Corpn's Application* [1998] ETMR 642, OHIM Board of Appeal, it was held that THINKPAD was identical to THINK PAD for this purpose. This is consistent with the subsequent jurisprudence of the European Court of Justice as to the meaning of 'identical': see PARA 55 note 3.

9 See note 3.

10 See note 4.

11 Council Regulation (EC) 207/2009 (OJ L78, 24.3.2009, p 1) art 35(1). Thus seniority may be claimed either when the Community trade mark is applied for (ie under art 34(1): see the text and notes 1–7) or at any time after registration (ie under art 35(1)). The right to claim the seniority of an earlier national trade mark continues to exist, without limitation of time, after the registration of the mark: see Case R 5/97–1 *BatMark Inc's Application* [1998] ETMR 448, OHIM Board of Appeal.

271. Effect of seniority. Seniority[1] has the sole effect that, where the proprietor of the Community trade mark[2] surrenders the earlier trade mark[3] or allows it to lapse, he is deemed to continue to have the same rights as he would have had if the earlier trade mark had continued to be registered[4].

Where the proprietor of a Community trade mark claims the seniority of a registered trade mark[5] which has been removed from the register[6] or has been surrendered[7], application may be made to the registrar[8] or to the court[9] by any person for a declaration that, if the registered trade mark had not been so removed or surrendered, it would have been liable to be revoked[10] or declared[11] invalid[12].

The seniority claimed for the Community trade mark lapses if the earlier trade mark the seniority of which is claimed is declared to have been revoked or to be invalid or if it is surrendered prior to the registration of the Community trade mark[13].

1 As to claiming seniority see PARA 270.
2 As to the meaning of 'Community trade mark' see PARA 189.
3 Ie the trade mark upon which seniority is based: see PARA 270.
4 Council Regulation (EC) 207/2009 (OJ L78, 24.3.2009, p 1) on the Community trade mark, arts 34(2), 35(2). See also Case R1219/2000-3 *Sara Lee/DE Espana SA v Health Products Ltd* (17 October 2001, unreported), OHIM Board of Appeal; *RAPIER Trade Mark* (O/170/07), Appointed Person.
5 Ie a trade mark registered under the Trade Marks Act 1994. As to the meaning of 'registered trade mark' see PARA 111.
6 Ie under the Trade Marks Act 1994 s 43: see PARA 31. As to the register (ie the register maintained pursuant to s 63) see PARA 21.
7 Ie pursuant to the Trade Marks Act 1994 s 45: see PARA 377.
8 As to the registrar see PARA 19.
9 As to the meaning of 'the court' see PARA 331.
10 Ie under the Trade Marks Act 1994 s 46: see PARA 98 et seq.
11 Ie under the Trade Marks Act 1994 s 47: see PARA 102 et seq.
12 Community Trade Mark Regulations 2006, SI 2006/1027, reg 3(1), (3). Application may likewise be made where such a proprietor claims the seniority of an international trade mark (UK) (see PARA 8 note 17): reg 3(2). Where a registered trade mark has been surrendered in respect of some only of the goods or services for which it is registered, these provisions apply in relation to those goods or services: reg 3(5). An address for service (see PARA 339) must be filed by the person making the application and by the proprietor of the Community trade mark unless the registrar otherwise directs: reg 3(4). The Trade Mark Rules 2008, SI 2008/1797, rr 38–43, 45, 62–79, 82 (see PARAS 336 et seq, 380 et seq) apply to such proceedings before the registrar with the necessary modifications: Community Trade Mark Regulations 2006, SI 2006/1027, reg 4(2) (amended by SI 2008/1959).
13 Council Regulation (EC) 207/2009 (OJ L78, 24.3.2009, p 1) arts 34(3), 35(2).

(iv) Proceedings relating to Revocation or Invalidity

272. Application for revocation or for a declaration of invalidity. An application for revocation[1] of the rights of the proprietor of a Community trade mark[2] or for a declaration that the trade mark is invalid[3] may be submitted[4] to the Office for Harmonisation in the Internal Market[5] by the following persons[6]:

(1) where the application is for revocation[7] or for a declaration of invalidity on absolute grounds[8], by any natural or legal person and any group or body set up for the purpose of representing the interests of manufacturers, producers, suppliers of services, traders or consumers, which under the terms of the law governing it has the capacity in its own name to sue and be sued[9];

(2) where the application is for a declaration of invalidity on relative grounds relating to an earlier trade mark or protected sign[10], by the relevant persons[11];

(3) where the application is for a declaration of invalidity on relative grounds relating to some other earlier right[12], by the owners of the earlier rights or by the persons who are entitled under the law of the member state concerned to exercise the rights in question[13].

The application must be filed in a written reasoned statement[14].

1   As to the grounds for revocation see PARAS 220–223; and as to the additional grounds for revocation of a Community collective mark see PARA 283.
2   As to the meaning of 'Community trade mark' see PARA 189.
3   As to the grounds of invalidity see PARAS 226–228; and as to the additional ground of invalidity of a Community collective mark see PARA 284.
4   An application for a declaration of invalidity may only be submitted after the Community trade mark has been entered on the register: Decision 89C/000317701/1 *Avensa AG v Mikkelson* (6 July 2000, unreported), OHIM Cancellation Division.
5   Council Regulation (EC) 207/2009 (OJ L78, 24.3.2009, p 1) on the Community trade mark, art 56(1). As to the Office for Harmonisation in the Internal Market see PARA 163 et seq. As to the procedure on such an application see PARA 273.
6   The list in the text is not exhaustive, because it does not indicate who may make an application for revocation of a Community collective mark on the additional ground specified in Council Regulation (EC) 207/2009 (OJ L78, 24.3.2009, p 1) art 73 (see PARA 283) or an application for a declaration of invalidity of a Community collective mark on the additional ground specified in art 74 (see PARA 284). Article 73 is similar in concept to art 51(1)(c) (mark liable to mislead in consequence of use: see PARA 223), while art 74 is similar in concept to art 52 (registration granted in breach of absolute grounds: see PARA 226); so perhaps they should both fall within head (1) in the text. An alternative view is that there is no restriction on who may bring an application under arts 73, 74.
7   Ie where Council Regulation (EC) 207/2009 (OJ L78, 24.3.2009, p 1) art 51 applies: see PARA 221 et seq.
8   Ie where Council Regulation (EC) 207/2009 (OJ L78, 24.3.2009, p 1) art 52 applies: see PARA 226.
9   Council Regulation (EC) 207/2009 (OJ L78, 24.3.2009, p 1) art 56(1)(a). By contrast with heads (2) and (3) in the text, under head (1) the applicant is not required to show any interest in bringing the proceedings: Case C-408/08P *Lancôme Parfums et Beauté & Cie SNC v Office for Harmonisation in the Internal Market (Trade Marks and Designs)* [2010] ECR I-1347, ECJ. Accordingly, there can be no question of an abuse of rights by an applicant for a declaration of invalidity arising out of the applicant's motives for bringing the application: Case T-396/11 *Ultra Air GmbH v Office for Harmonisation in the Internal Market (Trade Marks and Designs)* [2013] ECR II-0000, EGC. Nor is the right of application restricted to nationals of EU member states: Case T-223/08 *Iranian Tobacco Co v Office for Harmonisation in the Internal Market (Trade Marks and Designs)* [2009] ECR II-229, EGC.
10   Ie where Council Regulation (EC) 207/2009 (OJ L78, 24.3.2009, p 1) art 53(1) applies: see PARA 227.
11   Council Regulation (EC) 207/2009 (OJ L78, 24.3.2009, p 1) art 56(1)(b). The relevant persons are those referred to in art 41(1) (see PARA 265): art 56(1)(b). An earlier decision of the Office in opposition proceedings does not preclude a later application for a declaration of invalidity by the same person based on the same earlier trade marks or rights: Case T-140/08 *Ferrero SpA v Office for Harmonisation in the Internal Market (Trade Marks and Designs)* [2009] ECR II-3941, [2010] Bus LR D70, CFI. As to the position where the earlier trade mark relied upon falls due for renewal during the cancellation proceedings, see PARA 201 note 10.
12   Ie where Council Regulation (EC) 207/2009 (OJ L78, 24.3.2009, p 1) art 53(2) applies: see PARA 228.
13   Council Regulation (EC) 207/2009 (OJ L78, 24.3.2009, p 1) art 56(1)(c).
14   Council Regulation (EC) 207/2009 (OJ L78, 24.3.2009, p 1) art 56(2). The application is not deemed to have been filed until the fee has been paid: art 56(2). An application for revocation or for a declaration of invalidity is inadmissible if an application relating to the same subject matter and cause of action, and involving the same parties, has been adjudicated on by a court in a member state and has acquired the authority of a final decision: art 56(3).

273.   Examination of the application. The Office for Harmonisation in the Internal Market[1] may, if it thinks fit, invite the parties to make a friendly settlement[2]; otherwise it must examine and adjudicate upon the application[3].

If the proprietor of the Community trade mark[4] so requests[5], the proprietor of an earlier Community trade mark or an earlier national trade mark[6] who is party to the proceedings must furnish proof that, during the period of five years preceding the date of an application for a declaration of invalidity[7], the earlier trade mark had been put to genuine use[8] in the Community[9] or in the member state in question, as the case may be, in connection with goods or services in respect of which it is registered and which he cites as justification for his application, or that there are proper reasons[10] for non-use, provided that the earlier trade mark has been registered for not less than five years[11]. If, at the date on which the Community trade mark application was published[12], the earlier trade mark had been registered for not less than five years, the proprietor of the earlier trade mark must furnish proof that, in addition, the specified conditions[13] were satisfied at that date[14]. In the absence of proof to that effect, the application must be rejected[15]. If the earlier trade mark has been used in relation to part only of the goods or services for which it is registered it is, for the purposes of the examination of the application, deemed to be registered in respect of only that part of the goods or services[16].

If the examination of the application for revocation of rights[17] or for a declaration of invalidity[18] reveals that the trade mark should not have been registered in respect of some or all of the goods or services for which it is registered[19], the rights of the proprietor of the Community trade mark must be revoked[20] or it must be declared invalid[21] in respect of those goods or services; otherwise the application for revocation of rights or for a declaration of invalidity must be rejected[22]. A record of the Office's decision on the application for revocation of rights or for a declaration of invalidity must be entered in the register[23] once it has become final[24].

1   As to the Office for Harmonisation in the Internal Market see PARA 163 et seq.
2   Council Regulation (EC) 207/2009 (OJ L78, 24.3.2009, p 1) on the Community trade mark, art 57(4).
3   Provision for examination of the application is made by Council Regulation (EC) 207/2009 (OJ L78, 24.3.2009, p 1) art 57; and by Commission Regulation (EC) 2868/95 (OJ L303, 15.12.95, p 1) implementing Council Regulation (EC) 40/94 on the Community trade mark, art 1 rr 37–41 (r 38 amended, and r 39 substituted, by Commission Regulation (EC) 1041/2005 (OJ L172, 5.7.05, p 4)). As to the general procedural provisions for proceedings in the Office see PARA 260 note 3. Applications for revocation or for a declaration of invalidity are the responsibility of the Cancellation Divisions: see PARA 165. If the application is withdrawn the proceedings will be terminated; there is no basis for the Office to consider the application ex officio: Decision 55C/000142158/1 *Groupe Sepcon SA v Ziff Davis Publishing Holdings Inc* (5 November 2001, unreported), OHIM Cancellation Division. If, however, the proprietor applies to surrender the Community trade mark, the proceedings must continue: Decision 69C/000670042/1 *Lancôme Parfums et Beauté & Cie's Application* [2001] ETMR 89, OHIM Cancellation Division.
4   As to the meaning of 'Community trade mark' see PARA 189.
5   It is presumed that the proprietor must make any such request within the period specified by the Office for making observations on the application: cf Case T-112/03 *L'Oréal SA v Office for Harmonisation in the Internal Market (Trade Marks and Designs)* [2005] ECR II-949, [2005] All ER (D) 267 (Mar), CFI; affd on other grounds Case C-235/05P *L'Oréal SA v Office for Harmonisation in the Internal Market (Trade Marks and Designs)* [2006] ECR I-57, ECJ.
6   This includes national trade marks which do not have to be used under national law because they are defensive registrations: Case C-234/06P *Il Ponte Finanziaria SpA v Office for Harmonisation in the Internal Market (Trade Marks and Designs)* [2007] ECR I-7333, [2007] Bus LR D121, ECJ. In the United Kingdom defensive registrations were abolished by the Trade Marks Act 1994 s 46(1)(a) (see PARA 98 head (1)), and it is questionable whether they are consistent with Council Directive (EEC) 89/104 (OJ L40, 11.2.89, p 1) to approximate the law of the member states relating to trade marks (now European Parliament and Council Directive (EC) 2008/95 (OJ L299, 8.11.2008, p 25)).
7   Ie where the application is based on relative grounds (as to which see PARA 201 et seq).
8   As to genuine use see PARA 98 note 6.
9   As to the meaning of 'in the Community' see PARA 220 note 5.
10 As to the meaning of 'proper reasons' see PARA 98 note 10.
11 Council Regulation (EC) 207/2009 (OJ L78, 24.3.2009, p 1) art 57(2). Use does not have to be proved if the five year period expires during the course of the cancellation proceedings: Decision 336C/000633214/1 *Parfums Givenchy SA v Flotique NV* (27 October 2003, unreported), OHIM Cancellation Division. As to the procedure to be followed in the event of a request for

proof of use, and the nature and form that evidence of use must take, see Commission Regulation (EC) 2868/95 (OJ L303, 15.12.95, p 1) art 1 rr 22(3), (4), 40(6) (all substituted by Commission Regulation (EC) 1041/2005 (OJ L172, 5.7.05, p 4)). See also PARA 265 note 15.

12 As to publication see PARA 173.

13 Ie those in Council Regulation (EC) 207/2009 (OJ L78, 24.3.2009, p 1) art 42(2): see PARA 265.

14 Council Regulation (EC) 207/2009 (OJ L78, 24.3.2009, p 1) art 57(2). In such a case the applicant must prove use in both periods: Decision 332C/000208686/1 *Gorina & Sauquet SA v Performance Sailcraft Europe Ltd* (11 November 2003, unreported), OHIM Cancellation Division; Case R 627/2003–2 *McDonald's International Property Co Ltd v Andros Food SA* (5 July 2004, unreported), OHIM Board of Appeal.

15 Council Regulation (EC) 207/2009 (OJ L78, 24.3.2009, p 1) art 57(2).

16 Council Regulation (EC) 207/2009 (OJ L78, 24.3.2009, p 1) art 57(2).

17 As to the grounds for revocation see PARAS 220–223; and as to the additional grounds for revocation of a Community collective mark see PARA 283.

18 As to the grounds of invalidity see PARAS 226–228; and as to the additional ground of invalidity of a Community collective mark see PARA 284.

19 Presumably there should be read into this part of Council Regulation (EC) 207/2009 (OJ L78, 24.3.2009, p 1) art 57(5) words to the effect of 'or that the trade mark should be revoked', since revocation relates to events which occur after a registration: ex hypothesi, the trade mark was rightly registered but should now be revoked. See PARAS 218, 220 et seq.

20 As to the date from which revocation takes effect see PARA 225.

21 As to the effect of a declaration of invalidity see PARA 230.

22 Council Regulation (EC) 207/2009 (OJ L78, 24.3.2009, p 1) art 57(5).

23 As to the register see PARA 171.

24 Council Regulation (EC) 207/2009 (OJ L78, 24.3.2009, p 1) art 57(6).

(v) Appeals

274. Appeals to the Board of Appeal. An appeal lies from decisions[1] of the examiners[2], the Opposition Divisions[3], the Administration of Trade Marks and Designs and Legal Division[4], and the Cancellation Divisions[5]. It has suspensive effect[6].

Any party to proceedings adversely affected by a decision may appeal; and any other parties to the proceedings are parties to the appeal proceedings as of right[7].

Notice of appeal must be filed in writing at the Office for Harmonisation in the Internal Market[8] within two months after the date of notification of the decision appealed from[9]. Within four months after the date of notification of the decision, a written statement setting out the grounds of appeal must be filed[10].

1 A decision which does not terminate proceedings as regards one of the parties can only be appealed together with the final decision, unless the decision allows separate appeal: Council Regulation (EC) 207/2009 (OJ L78, 24.3.2009, p 1) on the Community trade mark, art 58(2).

2 As to the examiners see PARA 165.

3 As to the Opposition Divisions see PARA 165.

4 As to the Administration of Trade Marks and Designs and Legal Division see PARA 165.

5 Council Regulation (EC) 207/2009 (OJ L78, 24.3.2009, p 1) art 58(1). As to the Cancellation Divisions see PARA 165.

6 Council Regulation (EC) 207/2009 (OJ L78, 24.3.2009, p 1) art 58(1).

7 Council Regulation (EC) 207/2009 (OJ L78, 24.3.2009, p 1) art 59.

8 As to the Office for Harmonisation in the Internal Market see PARA 163 et seq.

9 Council Regulation (EC) 207/2009 (OJ L78, 24.3.2009, p 1) art 60. As to the form and content of a notice of appeal see Commission Regulation (EC) 2868/95 (OJ L303, 15.12.95, p 1) implementing Council Regulation (EC) 40/94 on the Community trade mark, art 1 r 48; and see Case T-225/09 *Claro SA v Office for Harmonisation of the Internal Market (Trade Marks and Designs)* [2010] ECR II-72, EGC (affd Case C-349/10P [2011] ECR I-17, ECJ).

The notice is deemed to have been filed only when the fee for appeal has been paid: Council Regulation (EC) 207/2009 (OJ L78, 24.3.2009, p 1) art 60. As to fees see PARA 167.

10 Council Regulation (EC) 207/2009 (OJ L78, 24.3.2009, p 1) art 60. Failure to file a written statement of grounds of appeal is fatal to the admissibility of the appeal: Case T-71/02 *Classen*

Holding KG v Office for Harmonisation of the Internal Market (Trade Marks and Designs) [2003] ECR II-3181, [2003] All ER (D) 109 (Sep), CFI. If there has been assignment of the earlier trade mark or earlier right which was not taken into account during proceedings before the Opposition Division, the assignee must adduce the necessary proof that he is the owner in order to establish locus standi to appeal within the four month period: Case C-53/11P *Office for Harmonisation of the Internal Market (Trade Marks and Designs) v Nike International Ltd* [2012] ETMR 32, ECJ.

275. Revision of decisions. If the party which has lodged the appeal is the sole party to the proceedings, and if the department whose decision is contested considers the appeal to be admissible and well founded, the department must rectify its decision[1]. If the decision is not rectified within one month after receipt of the statement of grounds, the appeal must be remitted to the Board of Appeal[2] without delay and without comment as to its merit[3].

Where the party which had lodged the appeal is opposed by another party and if the department whose decision is contested considers the appeal to be admissible and well founded, the department must rectify its decision[4]. The decision may only be rectified if the department whose decision is contested notifies the other party of its intention to rectify it and that party accepts it within two months of the date on which it received the notification[5]. If within two months of receiving such notification the other party does not accept that the contested decision is to be rectified and makes a declaration to that effect or does not make any declaration within the period laid down, the appeal must be remitted to the Board of Appeal without delay and without comment as to its merit[6]. If the department whose decision is contested does not consider the appeal to be admissible and well founded within one month after receipt of the statement of grounds, it must[7] remit the appeal to the Board of Appeal without delay and without comment as to its merit[8].

1   Council Regulation (EC) 207/2009 (OJ L78, 24.3.2009, p 1) on the Community trade mark, art 61(1). These provisions provide for a system of so-called 'interlocutory revision' similar to that operated by the European Patent Office which enables first instance departments to change their minds, thereby short-circuiting an appeal.
2   As to appeals to the Board of Appeal see PARA 274.
3   Council Regulation (EC) 207/2009 (OJ L78, 24.3.2009, p 1) art 61(2).
4   Council Regulation (EC) 207/2009 (OJ L78, 24.3.2009, p 1) art 62(1).
5   Council Regulation (EC) 207/2009 (OJ L78, 24.3.2009, p 1) art 62(2).
6   Council Regulation (EC) 207/2009 (OJ L78, 24.3.2009, p 1) art 62(3).
7   Ie instead of taking the measures provided for in Council Regulation (EC) 207/2009 (OJ L78, 24.3.2009, p 1) art 62(2), (3): see the text and notes 5, 6.
8   Council Regulation (EC) 207/2009 (OJ L78, 24.3.2009, p 1) art 62(4).

276. Examination of, and decisions in respect of, appeals. Provision is made for the consideration of and adjudication upon appeals by the Board of Appeal[1]. There is also a further regulation laying down the rules of procedure of the Boards of Appeal[2].

1   Ie in Council Regulation (EC) 207/2009 (OJ L78, 24.3.2009, p 1) on the Community trade mark, arts 63, 64; Commission Regulation (EC) 2868/95 (OJ L303, 15.12.95, p 1) implementing Council Regulation (EC) 40/94 on the Community trade mark, art 1 rr 49–51 (r 50 amended, and r 51 substituted, by Commission Regulation (EC) 1041/2005 (OJ L172, 5.7.05, p 4)).
    As to the Board of Appeal see PARA 165; and as to the general procedural provisions for proceedings in the Office see PARA 260 note 3.
    There is a continuity of function between the first instance departments and the Boards of Appeal and therefore the Board of Appeal must re-examine the first instance decision: Case C-29/05P *Office for Harmonisation in the Internal Market (Trade Marks and Designs) v Kaul GmbH* [2007] ECR I-2213, [2007] IP & T 1008, ECJ; Case T-163/98 *Procter &*

Gamble Co v Office for Harmonisation in the Internal Market (Trade Marks and Designs) [1999] All ER (EC) 648, [1999] ECR II-2383 (revsd on other grounds Case C-383/99P *Procter & Gamble Co v Office for Harmonisation in the Internal Market (Trade Marks and Designs)* [2002] Ch 82, [2001] ECR I-6251, ECJ); Case T-63/01 *Procter and Gamble v Office for Harmonisation in the Internal Market (Trade Marks and Designs)* [2002] ECR II-5255, (2002) Times, 28 December, CFI; Case T-308/01 *Henkel KGaA v Office for Harmonisation in the Internal Market (Trade Marks and Designs)* [2003] ECR II-3253, [2003] All ER (D) 155 (Sep), CFI (affd on other grounds Joined Cases C-456/01P and C-457/01P *Henkel KGaA v Office for Harmonisation in the Internal Market (Trade Marks and Designs)* [2004] ECR I-5089, [2005] IP & T 1, ECJ). The Board of Appeal has a discretion as to whether or not to take into account facts or evidence which have not been submitted at first instance: Case C-29/05P *Office for Harmonisation in the Internal Market (Trade Marks and Designs) v Kaul GmbH* above. The Board of Appeal must consider all the appellant's arguments, even if not raised below: Case T-163/98 *Procter & Gamble Co v Office for Harmonisation in the Internal Market* above. The Board of Appeal must also consider of its own motion all relevant matters of law and fact even if not raised by a specific ground of appeal: Case T-308/01 *Henkel KGaA v Office for Harmonisation in the Internal Market* above. On an appeal from the examiner the Board of Appeal is entitled to raise a ground of refusal which had not been raised at first instance: Case T-122/99 *Procter and Gamble v Office for Harmonisation in the Internal Market (Trade Marks and Designs)* [2000] ECR II-265, [2000] 2 CMLR 303, CFI. Where the appellant has missed a time limit at first instance, the Board of Appeal is entitled, but not obliged, to dismiss the appeal on the same ground: Case T-112/03 *L'Oréal SA v Office for Harmonisation in the Internal Market (Trade Marks and Designs)* [2005] ECR II-949, [2005] All ER (D) 267 (Mar), CFI; affd on other grounds Case C-235/05P *L'Oréal SA v Office for Harmonisation in the Internal Market (Trade Marks and Designs)* [2006] ECR I-57, ECJ.

2   See Commission Regulation (EC) 216/96 (OJ L28, 6.2.1996, p 11) laying down the rules of procedure of the Boards of Appeal of the Office for Harmonisation in the Internal Market (amended by Commission Regulation (EC) 2082/2004 (OJ L360, 7.12.2004, p 8). Where an OHIM Board of Appeal includes a member of an earlier Board of Appeal whose decision has been annulled by the European General Court contrary to Commission Regulation (EC) 216/96 (OJ L28, 6.2.1996, p 11) art 1(d)(2) the decision of the later Board is invalid: Case T-106/12 *Cytochroma Development Inc v Office for Harmonisation in the Internal Market* [2013] All ER (D) 113 (Jul), EGC.

277.   Appeals to the European General Court and European Court of Justice.

Actions may be brought[1] before the European Court of Justice against decisions of the Boards of Appeal[2] on appeals[3]. Such actions are brought in the European General Court (EGC) (formerly the Court of First Instance) which is attached to the Court of Justice[4]. A further appeal lies from the General Court to the Court of Justice itself on points of law[5].

The action may be brought on grounds of lack of competence, infringement of an essential procedural requirement, infringement of the Treaty[6], of the Community Trade Mark Regulation or of any rule of law relating to their application or misuse of power[7].

The General Court or the Court of Justice has jurisdiction to annul or to alter the contested decision[8].

1   The action is open to any party to proceedings before the Board of Appeal adversely affected by its decision: Council Regulation (EC) 207/2009 (OJ L78, 24.3.2009, p 1) on the Community trade mark (the 'Community Trade Mark Regulation') art 65(4). Where the applicant is appealing against a decision of the Board of Appeal the primary defendant is the Office for Harmonisation in the Internal Market even in inter partes disputes, although the other party may intervene to support the Board of Appeal's decision. As to the Office for Harmonisation in the Internal Market see PARA 163 et seq.

2   As to the Board of Appeal see PARA 165.

3   Council Regulation (EC) 207/2009 (OJ L78, 24.3.2009, p 1) art 65(1). As to appeals to the Board of Appeal see PARA 274. The action must be brought before the European Court of Justice within two months of the date of notification of the decision of the Board of Appeal: art 65(5).

4   Treaty on the Functioning of the European Union (Rome, 25 March 1957; TS 1 (1973); Cmnd 5179) ('TFEU') art 256 (see PARA 86 note 8) (formerly the Treaty Establishing the

European Community (Rome, 25 March 1957; TS 1 (1973); Cmnd 5179) (the 'EC Treaty') art 225 (formerly art 168a; renumbered by virtue of the Treaty of Amsterdam: see *Treaty Citation (No 2) (Note)* [1999] All ER (EC) 646, ECJ)). See also EEC/ECSC/Euratom Council Decision 88/591 (OJ L319, 25.11.88, p 1) establishing a Court of First Instance of the European Communities, art 5. However by virtue of the ESC Treaty art 97, the ECSC Treaty has expired and since 24 July 2002, the sectors previously covered by this Treaty, and the procedural rules and other secondary legislation derived from it, have been subject to the rules of the EC Treaty (now TFEU) (see above) as well as the procedural rules and other secondary legislation derived from the EC Treaty (now TFEU).

The rules of procedure of the Court of First Instance (now the European General Court) (OJ L136, 30.5.91, p 1) were amended to make provision for proceedings arising from the Office for Harmonisation in the Internal Market (OJ L172, 22.7.95, p 3), adding arts 130–136. Only independent lawyers authorised to practise before the court of a member state may represent parties before the Court of First Instance (now the European General Court) and European Court of Justice: Case T-79/99 *Euro-lex European Law Expertise GmbH v Office for Harmonisation in the Internal Market (Trade Marks and Designs)* [1999] ECR II-3555, CFI; Case T-315/03 *Wilfer v Office for Harmonisation in the Internal Market (Trade Marks and Designs)* [2005] ECR II-1981, CFI; Case T-123/04 *Cargo Partner AG v Office for Harmonisation in the Internal Market (Trade Marks and Designs)* [2005] ECR II-3979, [2006] ETMR 35, CFI.

5   TFEU art 256(1) (formerly the EC Treaty art 225(1): see note 4). Since the Court of First Instance (now the European General Court) has exclusive jurisdiction to assess the evidence and find the facts, these matters do not form a point of law subject to review by the Court of Justice unless the Court of First Instance has distorted the evidence: Case C-104/00 *DKV Deutsche Krankenversicherung AG v Office for Harmonisation in the Internal Market* [2002] ECR I-7561, [2002] All ER (D) 100 (Sep), ECJ; Case C-37/03P *BioID AG v Office for Harmonisation in the Internal Market (Trade Marks and Designs)* [2005] ECR I-7975, ECJ; Case C-214/05P *Sergio Rossi SpA v Office for Harmonisation in the Internal Market (Trade Marks and Designs)* [2006] ECR I-7057, ECJ.

6   Ie the TFEU (formerly the EC Treaty): see note 4.

7   Council Regulation (EC) 207/2009 (OJ L78, 24.3.2009, p 1) art 65(2). The Court of First Instance (now the European General Court) may annul or alter a decision of the Board of Appeal only if, at the time the decision was adopted, it was vitiated by one of these grounds; it may not annul or alter a decision on grounds which come into existence subsequently: Case C-416/04P *Sunrider Corpn v Office for Harmonisation in the Internal Market (Trade Marks and Designs)* [2006] ECR I-4237, [2006] All ER (D) 178 (May), ECJ; Case C-29/05P *Office for Harmonisation in the Internal Market (Trade Marks and Designs) v Kaul GmbH* [2007] ECR I-2213, [2007] IP & T 1008, ECJ. The purpose of appeals to the Court of First Instance (now the European General Court) is to review the legality of decisions of the Boards of Appeal, and not to re-examine the facts in the light of documents produced for the first time before it; accordingly new evidence is not admissible on such appeals: Case C-214/05P *Sergio Rossi SpA v Office for Harmonisation in the Internal Market (Trade Marks and Designs)* [2006] ECR I-7057, ECJ; Case C-29/05P *Office for Harmonisation in the Internal Market (Trade Marks and Designs) v Kaul GmbH* above. On appeal to the Court of First Instance (now the European General Court), the Office for Harmonisation in the Internal Market is not obliged to defend the Board of Appeal's decision, but it cannot seek forms of order annulling or altering the decision of the Board of Appeal on a point not raised by the appeal or put forward pleas not raised in the appeal: Case C-106/03 *Vedial SA v Office for Harmonisation in the Internal Market (Trade Marks and Designs)* [2005] ECR I-9573, ECJ; Case T-107/02 *GE Betz Inc v Office for Harmonisation in the Internal Market (Trade Marks and Designs)* [2004] ECR II-1845, [2004] All ER (D) 360 (Jun), CFI; Case T-379/03 *Peek & Cloppenburg KG v Office for Harmonisation in the Internal Market (Trade Marks and Designs)* [2006] ECR II-4633, sub nom *Peek & Cloppenburg's Application* [2006] ETMR 33, CFI. The Office for Harmonisation in the Internal Market is entitled to depart from the reasoning of the Board of Appeal provided that its arguments do not amount to new grounds for annulment of the decision: Case T-6/05 *DEF-TEC Defense Technology GmbH v Office for Harmonisation in the Internal Market (Trade Marks and Designs)* [2006] ECR II-2671, [2006] All ER (D) 23 (Sep), CFI.

8   Council Regulation (EC) 207/2009 (OJ L78, 24.3.2009, p 1) art 65(3). The Office for Harmonisation in the Internal Market must take the necessary measures to comply with the judgment of the General Court or the European Court of Justice: art 65(6); and see Case T-163/98 *Procter & Gamble Co v Office for Harmonisation in the Internal Market (Trade Marks and Designs)* [1999] ECR II-2383, [1999] ETMR 767, CFI. The appellant or intervener cannot request the court to, for example, direct the Office for Harmonisation in the Internal

Market to declare the trade mark in suit invalid: Case T-331/99 *Mitsubishi HiTec Paper Bielefeld GmbH v Office for Harmonisation in the Internal Market (Trade Marks and Designs)* [2001] ECR II-433, [2001] IP & T 459, CFI; Case T-34/00 *Eurocool Logistik GmbH v Office for Harmonisation in the Internal Market (Trade Marks and Designs)* [2002] ECR II-683, [2002] IP & T 756, CFI; Case T-129/01 *Alejandro v Office for Harmonisation in the Internal Market (Trade Marks and Designs)* [2003] ECR II-2251, CFI; Joined Cases T-160/02 to T-162/02 *Naipes Heraclio Fournier SA v Office for Harmonisation in the Internal Market (Trade Marks and Designs)* [2005] ECR II-1634, [2005] All ER (D) 136 (May), CFI.

(9) COMMUNITY COLLECTIVE MARKS

(i) In general

278. Introduction. A Community collective mark is a Community trade mark[1] which is described as such when the mark is applied for[2] and is capable of distinguishing the goods or services of the members of the association which is the proprietor of the mark from those of other undertakings[3].

Associations of manufacturers, producers, suppliers of services, or traders which, under the terms of the law governing them, have the capacity in their own name to have rights and obligations of all kinds, to make contracts or accomplish other legal acts and to sue and be sued, as well as legal persons governed by public law, may apply for Community collective marks[4].

The provisions of the Community Trade Mark Regulation[5] apply to Community collective marks, unless it provides[6] otherwise[7].

1 As to the meaning of 'Community trade mark' see PARA 189.
2 As to applications for Community trade marks see PARAS 261–266.
3 Council Regulation (EC) 207/2009 (OJ L78, 24.3.2009, p 1) on the Community trade mark, art 66(1). The rules contained in Commission Regulation (EC) 2868/95 (OJ L303, 15.12.95, p 1) implementing Council Regulation (EC) 40/94 on the Community trade mark, art 1, apply to Community collective marks, subject to art 1 r 43 (see PARA 281 note 4).
4 Council Regulation (EC) 207/2009 (OJ L78, 24.3.2009, p 1) art 66(1).
5 Ie Council Regulation (EC) 207/2009 (OJ L78, 24.3.2009, p 1) (OJ L11, 14.1.94, p 1).
6 Ie by Council Regulation (EC) 207/2009 (OJ L78, 24.3.2009, p 1) arts 67–74: see PARA 280 et seq.
7 Council Regulation (EC) 207/2009 (OJ L78, 24.3.2009, p 1) art 66(3).

279. Geographical indications. In derogation from the relevant provision[1], signs or indications which may serve, in trade, to designate the geographical origin of the goods or services may constitute Community collective marks[2].

A collective mark does not entitle the proprietor to prohibit a third party from using in the course of trade such signs or indications, provided he uses them in accordance with honest practices in industrial or commercial matters[3]; in particular, such a mark may not be invoked against a third party who is entitled to use a geographical name[4].

1 Ie Council Regulation (EC) 207/2009 (OJ L78, 24.3.2009, p 1) on the Community trade mark, art 7(1)(c): see PARA 194.
2 Council Regulation (EC) 207/2009 (OJ L78, 24.3.2009, p 1) art 66(2). In the case of such a mark, the regulations governing use (see PARA 281) must authorise any person whose goods or services originate in the geographical area concerned to become a member of the association which is the proprietor of the mark: see art 67(2); and PARA 281 note 3. As to the meaning of 'Community collective mark' see PARA 278. As to protected designations of origin, protected geographical indications and traditional specialities guaranteed see PARA 285.
3 As to the meaning of 'honest practices in industrial or commercial matters' see PARA 80.
4 Council Regulation (EC) 207/2009 (OJ L78, 24.3.2009, p 1) art 66(2).

280.   Application for a Community collective mark. In addition to the grounds provided for refusal of a Community trade mark application[1], an application for a Community collective mark[2] must be refused:

(1)   where the additional provisions relating to Community collective marks[3] are not satisfied[4];

(2)   where the regulations governing use[5] are contrary to public policy or to accepted principles of morality[6]; or

(3)   if the public is liable to be misled as regards the character or the significance of the mark, in particular if it is likely to be taken to be something other than a collective mark[7].

Apart from the general rules on observations by third parties[8], any person, group or body referred to in those general rules may submit to the Office for Harmonisation in the Internal Market[9] written observations based on the particular grounds on which the application for a Community collective mark should be refused[10].

1   Ie Council Regulation (EC) 207/2009 (OJ L78, 24.3.2009, p 1) on the Community trade mark, arts 36, 37: see PARA 262.

2   As to the meaning of 'Community collective mark' see PARA 278.

3   Ie Council Regulation (EC) 207/2009 (OJ L78, 24.3.2009, p 1) art 66 (see PARAS 278–279) or art 67 (see PARA 281).

4   Council Regulation (EC) 207/2009 (OJ L78, 24.3.2009, p 1) art 68(1).

5   As to the regulations governing the use of a Community collective mark see PARA 281.

6   Council Regulation (EC) 207/2009 (OJ L78, 24.3.2009, p 1) art 68(1).

7   Council Regulation (EC) 207/2009 (OJ L78, 24.3.2009, p 1) art 68(2). An application must not be refused if the applicant, as a result of amendment of the regulations governing use, meets the requirements of art 68(1), (2): art 68(3).

8   Ie the cases mentioned in Council Regulation (EC) 207/2009 (OJ L78, 24.3.2009, p 1) art 40: see PARA 262.

9   As to the Office for Harmonisation in the Internal Market see PARA 163 et seq.

10   Council Regulation (EC) 207/2009 (OJ L78, 24.3.2009, p 1) art 69. Such refusal would be under the terms of art 68.

(ii) Regulations

281.   Regulations governing use of a Community collective mark. An applicant for a Community collective mark[1] must submit regulations governing its use within the prescribed period[2]. Such regulations must specify: (1) the persons authorised to use the mark; (2) the conditions of membership of the association[3]; and (3) where they exist, the conditions of use of the mark including sanctions[4].

The proprietor of a Community collective mark must submit to the Office for Harmonisation in the Internal Market[5] any amended regulations governing use[6]. The amendment must not be mentioned in the register[7] if the amended regulations do not satisfy the relevant[8] requirements[9].

For these purposes[10], amendments to the regulations governing use take effect only from the date of entry of the mention of the amendment in the register[11].

1   As to the meaning of 'Community collective mark' see PARA 278.

2   Council Regulation (EC) 207/2009 (OJ L78, 24.3.2009, p 1) on the Community trade mark, art 67(1).

3   The regulations governing use of a mark as a sign or indication which may serve, in trade, to designate the geographical origin of the goods or services (ie a mark referred to in Council Regulation (EC) 207/2009 (OJ L78, 24.3.2009, p 1) art 66(2): see PARA 279) must authorise any person whose goods or services originate in the geographical area concerned to become a member of the association which is the proprietor of the mark: art 67(2).

4   Council Regulation (EC) 207/2009 (OJ L78, 24.3.2009, p 1) art 67(2). As to what the regulations must specify see Commission Regulation (EC) 2868/95 (OJ L303, 15.12.95, p 1) implementing Council Regulation (EC) 40/94 on the Community trade mark, art 1 r 43.

5   As to the Office for Harmonisation in the Internal Market see PARA 163 et seq.

6   Council Regulation (EC) 207/2009 (OJ L78, 24.3.2009, p 1) art 71(1). The provisions permitting observations by third parties (ie art 69: see PARA 280) apply to amended regulations governing use: art 71(3).

7   As to the register see PARA 171.

8   Ie the requirements of Council Regulation (EC) 207/2009 (OJ L78, 24.3.2009, p 1) art 67 (see the text and notes 1–4) or the grounds for refusal referred to in art 66 (see PARA 280).

9   Council Regulation (EC) 207/2009 (OJ L78, 24.3.2009, p 1) art 71(2).

10 Ie for the purposes of applying Council Regulation (EC) 207/2009 (OJ L78, 24.3.2009, p 1).

11 Council Regulation (EC) 207/2009 (OJ L78, 24.3.2009, p 1) art 71(4).

(iii) Infringement, Revocation and Invalidity

282. Persons who are entitled to bring an action for infringement of a Community collective mark. The provisions concerning the rights of licensees[1] apply to every person who has authority to use a Community collective mark[2]. The proprietor of a Community collective mark is entitled to claim compensation on behalf of persons who have authority to use the mark where they have sustained damage in consequence of unauthorised use of the mark[3].

1   Ie Council Regulation (EC) 207/2009 (OJ L78, 24.3.2009, p 1) on the Community trade mark, art 22(3), (4): see PARA 258.

2   Council Regulation (EC) 207/2009 (OJ L78, 24.3.2009, p 1) art 72(1). As to the meaning of 'Community collective mark' see PARA 278.

3   Council Regulation (EC) 207/2009 (OJ L78, 24.3.2009, p 1) art 72(2). For the grounds on which an infringement action may be brought see PARA 207 et seq. As to the procedural and jurisdictional issues concerning infringement actions see PARA 233 et seq.

283. Revocation of a Community collective mark. Apart from the grounds provided for revocation[1], the rights of the proprietor of a Community collective mark[2] must be revoked[3] on application to the Office for Harmonisation in the Internal Market[4] or on the basis of a counterclaim[5] in infringement proceedings[6], if:

(1)   the proprietor does not take reasonable steps to prevent the mark being used in a manner incompatible with the conditions of use, where these exist, laid down in the regulations governing use[7], amendments to which have, where appropriate, been mentioned in the register[8];

(2)   the manner in which the mark has been used by the proprietor has caused it to become liable to mislead the public[9];

(3)   an amendment to the regulations governing use of the mark has been mentioned in the register in breach of the relevant provisions[10], unless the proprietor of the mark, by further amending the regulations governing use, complies with the requirements of those provisions[11].

1   Ie in Council Regulation (EC) 207/2009 (OJ L78, 24.3.2009, p 1) on the Community trade mark, art 51: see PARA 220 et seq. One of the grounds provided for revocation of a Community trade mark is non-use: see art 51(1)(a); and PARA 221. It is provided that use of a Community collective mark by any person who has authority to use it satisfies the requirements of Council Regulation (EC) 207/2009 (OJ L78, 24.3.2009, p 1), provided that the other conditions imposed with regard to the use of Community trade marks are fulfilled: art 70.

2   As to the meaning of 'Community collective mark' see PARA 278.

3   As to the date from which revocation takes effect see PARA 225.

4   As to the Office for Harmonisation in the Internal Market see PARA 163 et seq. As to bringing an application for revocation in the Office see PARAS 272–273.

5   As to bringing an application for revocation by way of counterclaim see PARA 244 et seq.

6	Council Regulation (EC) 207/2009 (OJ L78, 24.3.2009, p 1) art 73.
7	As to the regulations governing use see PARA 281.
8	Council Regulation (EC) 207/2009 (OJ L78, 24.3.2009, p 1) art 73(a). As to the register see PARA 171.
9	Council Regulation (EC) 207/2009 (OJ L78, 24.3.2009, p 1) art 73(b), which refers to art 68(2): see PARA 280. Head (2) in the text will overlap with the ground for revocation provided for by art 51(1)(c) (see PARA 223).
10	Ie Council Regulation (EC) 207/2009 (OJ L78, 24.3.2009, p 1) art 71(2): see PARA 281.
11	Council Regulation (EC) 207/2009 (OJ L78, 24.3.2009, p 1) art 73(c).

**284.	Invalidity of a Community collective mark.** Apart from the grounds provided for a declaration of invalidity[1], a Community collective mark[2] which is registered in breach of the requirements for registration as a Community collective mark[3] must be declared invalid[4] on application to the Office for Harmonisation in the Internal Market[5] or on the basis of a counterclaim[6] in infringement proceedings, unless the proprietor of the mark, by amending the regulations governing use[7], complies with the requirements of those provisions[8].

1	Ie in Council Regulation (EC) 207/2009 (OJ L78, 24.3.2009, p 1) on the Community trade mark, arts 52, 53: see PARA 226 et seq.
2	As to the meaning of 'Community collective mark' see PARA 278.
3	Ie Council Regulation (EC) 207/2009 (OJ L78, 24.3.2009, p 1) art 68: see PARA 280.
4	As to the effect of a declaration of invalidity see PARA 230.
5	As to the Office for Harmonisation in the Internal Market see PARA 163 et seq. As to bringing an application for a declaration of invalidity in the Office see PARAS 272–273.
6	As to bringing an application for a declaration of invalidity by way of counterclaim see PARA 244 et seq.
7	As to the regulations governing use see PARA 281.
8	Council Regulation (EC) 207/2009 (OJ L78, 24.3.2009, p 1) art 74.

# (10)	PROTECTED DESIGNATIONS OF ORIGIN, PROTECTED GEOGRAPHICAL INDICATIONS AND TRADITIONAL SPECIALITIES GUARANTEED

**285.	In general.** There is no provision for Community certification marks as distinct from Community collective marks[1]. Instead, European Union law provides for three types of protection[2] for the names of foods and agricultural products which denote foods and agricultural products made in a particular region or in a traditional way, namely:

(1)	a protected designation of origin ('PDO')[3];
(2)	a protected geographical indication ('PGI')[4]; and
(3)	a traditional speciality guaranteed ('TSG'), formerly known as a certificate of specific character ('CSC')[5].

These forms of protection are distinct from trade marks[6] although there are certain similarities[7].

1	By contrast the Trade Marks Act 1994 provides for both collective marks (see PARA 138 et seq) and certification marks (see PARA 148 et seq). As to the meaning of 'Community collective mark' see PARA 278. Signs which may serve in trade to designate the geographical origin of the goods or services may constitute Community collective marks: see PARA 279.
2	In addition to these three general types of protection, there are various regimes for the protection of names of specific products: see e g Council Regulation (EC) 1493/99 (OJ L179, 14.7.99, p 1) on the common organisation of the market in wine, arts 47–53, Annex VII (amended by Council Regulation (EC) 2585/2001 (OJ L345, 29.12.01, p 10); and by Council Regulation (EC) 2165/2005 (OJ L345, 28.12.05, p 1)) and Council Regulation (EC) 1493/99 (OJ L179, 14.7.99, p 1) Annex VIII (amended by Council Regulation (EC) 2165/2005 (OJ L345, 28.12.05, p 1)), which implement the Agreement on Trade-Related Aspects of

Intellectual Property ('TRIPs') (1994) (Cm 2557) art 23. As to TRIPs see PARA 7. Such legislation may require certain names to be used as well as prohibiting others: see *Antonio Munoz Y Cia SA v Frumar Ltd* [1999] 3 CMLR 684, [1999] FSR 872 (grape varieties). As to the relationship between trade marks and such legislation see Case C-303/97 *Verbraucherschutzverein EV v Sektkellerei GC Kessler GmbH & Co* [1999] ECR I-513, [1999] 1 CMLR 756, ECJ; *MEZZACORONA Trade Mark* [2003] EWCA Civ 1861, [2004] RPC 537, sub nom *Miguel Torres SA v Cantine Mezzacorona SCARL* [2003] All ER (D) 407 (Dec).

3   See Council Regulation (EC) 510/2006 (OJ L93, 31.3.06, p 12) on the protection of geographical indications and designations of origin for agricultural products and foodstuffs (see further below), which implemented TRIPs arts 22, 24. Since the Regulation (as well as its successor) has direct effect it creates rights which individuals may rely upon against other individuals before national courts, subject to the requirement of legal certainty: C-108/01 *Consorzio del Prosciutto di Parma v Asda Stores Ltd* [2003] ECR I-5121, [2003] 2 CMLR 639, ECJ. The Regulation is exhaustive in nature, with the result that it precludes the application of a system of protection laid down by a bilateral agreement between two member states which confers on a designation, which is recognised under the law of one member state as constituting a designation of origin, protection in another member state where that protection is actually claimed, despite the fact that no application for registration of that designation of origin has been made in accordance with the Regulation: Case C-478/07 *Budejovicky Budvar np v Rudolf Ammersin GmbH* [2009] ECR I-7721, [2009] ETMR 65, ECJ. Council Regulation (EC) 510/2006 (OJ L93, 31.3.06, p 12) and Council Regulation (EC) 509/2006 (OJ L93, 31.3.06, p 1) (see the text and note 5) have been replaced by Council Regulation (EU) 1151/2012 (OJ L343, 14.12.2012, p 1) on quality schemes for agricultural products and foodstuffs which has correlation tables with the replaced regulations: see art 58(2). Council Regulation (EU) 1151/2012 (OJ L343, 14.12.2012, p 1) also introduces a fourth tier of protection, namely an optional quality term: see arts 27–34.

4   See Council Regulation (EC) 510/2006 (OJ L93, 31.3.06, p 12); and see note 3.

5   See Council Regulation (EC) 509/2006 (OJ L93, 31.3.06, p 1) on agricultural products and foodstuffs as traditional specialities guaranteed; and see note 3.

6   As to these forms of protection see FOOD AND DRINK vol 51 (2013) PARA 814 et seq.

7   PDOs and PGIs fall within the definition of 'industrial property' in the Paris Convention art 1 and the ECJ has held that they constitute 'industrial and commercial property' (ie intellectual property) rights when analysing the compatibility of the legislation with the Treaty Establishing the European Community (Rome, 25 March 1957; TS 1 (1973); Cmnd 5179) (the 'EC Treaty') art 29 (now the Treaty on the Functioning of the European Union (Rome, 25 March 1957; TS 1 (1973); Cmnd 5179) ('TFEU') art 35 (and see PARA 86 note 8): Case C-388/95 *Belgium v Spain* [2000] ECR I-3123, [2002] 1 CMLR 755, ECJ; Case C-469/00 *Ravil SARL v Bellon Import SARL* [2003] ECR I-5053, [2003] All ER (D) 296 (May), ECJ; C-108/01 *Consorzio del Prosciutto di Parma v Asda Stores Ltd* [2003] ECR I-5121, [2003] 2 CMLR 639, ECJ. As to the Paris Convention see PARA 6.

286. Relationship between trade marks, designations of origin and geographical indications.

A name proposed for registration as a designation of origin or geographical indication must not be registered[1] where, in the light of a trade mark's reputation and renown and the length of time it has been used, registration of the name proposed as the designation of origin or geographical indication would be liable to mislead the consumer as to the true identity of the product[2].

A reasoned statement of opposition to registration of a designation of origin or geographical indication is admissible if it is received in time and shows that the registration of the name proposed would jeopardise the existence of an entirely or partly identical name or of a trade mark or the existence of products which have been legally on the market for at least five years preceding the publication of the application for registration[3].

Where a designation of origin or a geographical indication is registered, the registration of a trade mark the use of which would contravene the provision on protected situations[4] and which relates to a product of the same type must be refused if the application for registration of the trade mark is submitted after the date of submission of the registration application in respect of the designation of origin or the geographical indication[5]. Trade marks registered in breach of this provision must be invalidated[6].

A trade mark the use of which corresponds to one of the protected situations[7] which has been applied for, registered or established by use, if that possibility is provided for by the legislation concerned[8], in good faith[9] within the territory of the European Union before the date on which the application for protection of the designation of origin or geographical indication is submitted may continue to be used and renewed for that product notwithstanding the registration of a designation of origin or geographical indication provided that no grounds for its invalidity or revocation exist as specified by the Trade Marks Directive[10] or the Community Trade Mark Regulation[11]. In such cases, the use of the protected designation of origin or protected geographical indication must be permitted as well as use of the relevant trade marks[12].

1   Ie under Council Regulation (EU) 1151/2012 (OJ L343, 14.12.2012, p 1) on quality schemes for agricultural products and foodstuffs (which replaces Council Regulation (EC) 510/2006 (OJ L93, 31.3.06, p 12) on the protection of geographical indications and designations of origin for agricultural products and foodstuffs): see PARA 285 note 3.

2   Council Regulation (EU) 1151/2012 (OJ L343, 14.12.2012, p 1) art 6(4). This is confined to the possibility of a mistake on the part of the consumer as to the true identity of the product as a result of registration of the name at issue having regard to the trade mark's reputation and renown and the length of time it has been used: Case C-343/07 *Bavaria NV v Bayerischer Brauerbund EV* [2009] ECR I-5491, [2009] All ER (D) 101 (Sep), [2009] ETMR 61, ECJ.

3   Council Regulation (EU) 1151/2012 (OJ L343, 14.12.2012, p 1) art 10(c). As to publication see art 50.

4   Ie under Council Regulation (EU) 1151/2012 (OJ L343, 14.12.2012, p 1) art 13. Registered names are protected against: (1) any direct or indirect commercial use of a registered name in respect of products not covered by the registration where those products are comparable to the products registered under that name or where using the name exploits the reputation of the protected name, including when those products are used as an ingredient; (2) any misuse, imitation or evocation, even if the true origin of the products or services is indicated or if the protected name is translated or accompanied by an expression such as 'style', 'type', 'method', 'as produced in', 'imitation' or similar, including when those products are used as an ingredient; (3) any other false or misleading indication as to the provenance, origin, nature or essential qualities of the product that is used on the inner or outer packaging, advertising material or documents relating to the product concerned, and the packing of the product in a container liable to convey a false impression as to its origin; (4) any other practice liable to mislead the consumer as to the true origin of the product: art 13(1). Where a protected designation of origin or a protected geographical indication contains within it the name of a product which is considered to be generic, the use of that generic name is not to be considered to be contrary to heads (1) or (2) above: art 13(1).
     'Evocation' of a protected designation within head (2) above covers a situation where the term used to designate a product incorporates part of a protected designation, so that when a consumer is confronted with the name of the product, the image triggered in his mind is that of the product whose designation is protected; it is possible for a protected designation to be evoked where there is no likelihood of confusion between the products concerned: Case C-87/97 *Consorzio per la Tutela del Formaggio Gorgonzola v Käserei Champignon Hofmeister GmbH & Co KG* [1999] ECR I-1301, [1999] 1 CMLR 1203, ECJ (CAMBOZOLA for a soft blue cheese evoked GORGONZOLA); and see also Case C-132/05 *EC Commission v Germany* [2009] All ER (EC) 58, [2008] ECR I-957, [2008] ETMR 32, ECJ (PARMESAN infringed PARMIGIANO REGGIANO)

5   Council Regulation (EU) 1151/2012 (OJ L343, 14.12.2012, p 1) art 14(1). See also PARA 200.

6   Council Regulation (EU) 1151/2012 (OJ L343, 14.12.2012, p 1) art 14(1).

7   See Council Regulation (EU) 1151/2012 (OJ L343, 14.12.2012, p 1) art 13; and note 4.

8   It would appear that this would cover the law of passing off, which is provided for by the Trade Marks Act 1994 s 2(2): see PARA 398. As to passing off see PARA 287 et seq.

9   The concept of good faith must be viewed in the light of the entire body of legislation, both national and international, in force at the time when the application for registration of the trade mark was lodged; in principle the proprietor of the trade mark cannot benefit from a

presumption of good faith if the legislation in force at the material time clearly precluded acceptance of his registration: Case C-87/97 *Consorzio per la Tutela del Formaggio Gorgonzola v Käserei Champignon Hofmeister GmbH & Co KG* [1999] ECR I-1301, [1999] 1 CMLR 1203, ECJ; and see also Case C-343/07 *Bavaria NV v Bayerischer Brauerbund EV* [2009] ECR I-5491, [2009] All ER (D) 101 (Sep), [2009] ETMR 61, ECJ.

10 Ie Council Regulation (EC) 207/2009 (OJ L78, 24.3.2009, p 1) to approximate the laws of the member states relating to trade marks (formerly Council Directive (EC) 89/104 (OJ L40, 11.2.89, p 1)). As to the grounds of invalidity or revocation under the provisions of the Trade Marks Act 1994 corresponding to the relevant provisions of the Trade Marks Directive see PARA 98 et seq.

11 Council Regulation (EU) 1151/2012 (OJ L343, 14.12.2012, p 1) art 14(2). The Community Trade Mark Regulation is European Parliament and Council Directive (EC) 2008/95 (OJ L299, 8.11.2008, p 25) on the Community trade mark (formerly Council Regulation (EC) 40/94 (OJ L11, 14.1.94, p 1). As to the grounds of invalidity or revocation under the Community Trade Mark Regulation see PARA 220 et seq.

12 Council Regulation (EU) 1151/2012 (OJ L343, 14.12.2012, p 1) art 14(2).

4. PASSING OFF

(1) THE ELEMENTS OF PASSING OFF

(i) Introduction

287.   Elements of the action for passing off. The necessary elements of the action for passing off have been restated by the House of Lords as being three[1] in number:

(1)   that the claimant's goods or services have acquired a goodwill in the market and are known by some distinguishing name, mark or other indicium;

(2)   that there is a misrepresentation by the defendant (whether or not intentional) leading or likely to lead the public to believe that goods or services offered by the defendant are goods or services of the claimant; and

(3)   that the claimant has suffered or is likely to suffer damage as a result of the erroneous belief engendered by the defendant's misrepresentation[2].

The restatement of the elements of passing off in the form of this classical trinity[3] has been preferred as providing greater assistance in analysis and decision than the formulation of the elements of the action previously expressed by the House[4]. This latest statement, like the House's previous statements[4], should not, however, be treated as akin to a statutory definition or as if the words used by the House constitute an exhaustive, literal definition of 'passing off'[5], and in particular should not be used to exclude from the ambit of the tort recognised forms of the action for passing off which were not under consideration on the facts before the House[6].

1   See note 3.
2   *Reckitt & Colman Products Ltd v Borden Inc* [1990] 1 All ER 873 at 880, [1990] 1 WLR 491 at 499, [1990] RPC 341 at 406, HL, per Lord Oliver of Aylmerton, and at 889, 510 and 417 per Lord Jauncey of Tullichettle ('Jif Lemon'). See e g *Bocacina Ltd v Boca Cafes Ltd* [2013] EWHC 3090 (IPEC), [2013] All ER (D) 152 (Oct) where *Reckitt & Colman Products Ltd v Borden Inc* above was applied. As to the Intellectual Property Enterprise Court (IPEC) see PARAS 233 note 5, 331.
3   They were described as the 'classical trinity' in *Consorzio del Prosciutto di Parma v Marks & Spencer plc* [1991] RPC 351 at 368–369, CA, per Nourse LJ ('Parma ham'). See also *County Sound plc v Ocean Sound plc* [1991] FSR 367 at 372, CA, per Nourse LJ.
4   Ie in *Erven Warnink BV v J Townend & Sons (Hull) Ltd* [1979] AC 731, [1979] 2 All ER 927, [1980] RPC 31, HL ('Advocaat'), where Lord Diplock at 742, 932–933 and 93 and Lord Fraser of Tullybelton at 755–756, 943–944 and 105–106 each formulated the elements of the action in markedly differing terms, with the remaining three members of the House agreeing with both Lord Diplock and Lord Fraser of Tullybelton.
5   *My Kinda Bones Ltd v Dr Pepper's Stove Co Ltd* [1984] FSR 289. As to the dangers of treating speeches in the House of Lords as if they were statutory definitions see *Cassell & Co Ltd v Broome* [1972] AC 1027 at 1085, [1972] 1 All ER 801 at 836, HL, per Lord Reid.
6   *Bristol Conservatories Ltd v Conservatories Custom Built Ltd* [1989] RPC 455 at 466, CA, per Ralph Gibson LJ (a case of 'reverse' passing off: see PARA 303); *Chelsea Man Menswear Ltd v Chelsea Girl Ltd* [1987] RPC 189 at 206, CA, per Slade LJ (where the misrepresentation was to suppliers rather than to customers).

288.   History and legal nature of the action for passing off. The action for passing off may have been recognised at common law as long ago as during the reign of Elizabeth I[1]. It seems that the action for passing off at common law originally grew out of the action for deceit, and, like the action for deceit, required a false representation made fraudulently, but differed from it in that the persons deceived were the plaintiff's customers rather than the plaintiff himself[2]. The action at common law was extended to cases where the defendant's customers were not themselves deceived but the defendant sold fraudulently marked goods to retail dealers with the express purpose of the goods being resold to ultimate purchasers as the plaintiff's goods[3]. Although at first equity followed the common law in requiring fraudulent intent on the part of the defendant[4], it was later accepted that an injunction could be granted in equity in the absence of intention to deceive if the defendant's actions would in fact result in deception[5]. It was soon accepted, both at law[6] and in equity[7], that it was unnecessary that the goods passed off had to be inferior to the plaintiff's[8].

Equity's willingness to protect the exclusive right to use a trade name or mark even in the absence of fraud was recognised as being based on a right of property, by contrast with the purely personal right to relief at law based on fraud[9]. Equity came to recognise and develop an exclusive property in a trade mark applied to goods acquired by first public use of the mark, which was distinct from the action for passing off founded on misrepresentation; these so-called 'unregistered trade marks' have been superseded by the statutory registration of trade marks and can no longer be enforced, but this does not affect rights of action for passing off[10]. The common law courts maintained the requirement that fraudulent intent had to be proved in an action for passing off until the fusion of the courts of common law and equity[11], and subsequent judicial observations have maintained that passing off in the absence of fraudulent intent is actionable in equity only[12]. Although the practical consequences of this distinction have diminished[13] and it has on occasion been overlooked[14], the equitable principles underlying the grant of injunctions in passing off cases may still be of significance in some circumstances[15].

Passing off is a form of unfair competition, but English law does not recognise a general tort of unfair competition[16].

1 An unreported case was mentioned in the judgment of Doderidge J in *Southern v How* (1618) Poph 143 at 144, where a defendant fraudulently counterfeited the mark of a clothier from Gloucester; but another report says that the plaintiff was the deceived customer rather than the owner of the mark (Cro Jac 468 at 471), and another that Doderidge J did not make clear which of them was the plaintiff (2 Roll Rep 26 at 28).
2 *Singer Manufacturing Co v Wilson* (1876) 2 ChD 434 at 453, CA, per Mellish LJ.
3 *Sykes v Sykes* (1824) 3 B & C 541.
4 *Blanchard v Hill* (1742) 2 Atk 484 at 485 per Lord Hardwicke LC. See also *Motley v Downman* (1837) 3 My & Cr 1 at 10 (argument) and at 14 per Lord Cottenham LC.
5 *Millington v Fox* (1838) 3 My & Cr 338.
6 *Blofeld v Payne* (1833) 4 B & Ad 410.
7 *Edelsten v Edelsten* (1863) 1 De GJ & Sm 185.
8 See *Singer Manufacturing Co v Loog* (1882) 8 App Cas 15 at 30, HL, per Lord Blackburn.
9 *Hall v Barrows* (1863) 4 De GJ & Sm 150 at 158 per Lord Westbury LC.
10 Trade Marks Act 1994 s 2(2). As to the statutory registration of trade marks see PARA 2 et seq.
11 *Crawshay v Thompson* (1842) 4 Man & G 357; *Rodgers v Nowill* (1847) 5 CB 109; and see *Dixon v Fawcus* (1861) 3 E & E 537. For a summary of the development of passing off at law and in equity see *Singer Manufacturing Co v Wilson* (1876) 2 ChD 434 at 453–455, CA, per Mellish LJ.
12 *Singer Manufacturing Co v Wilson* (1876) 2 ChD 434, CA; *Birmingham Small Arms Co Ltd v Webb & Co* (1906) 24 RPC 27 at 31 per Parker J; *AG Spalding & Bros v AW Gamage Ltd* (1915) 32 RPC 273 at 283, HL, per Lord Parker of Waddington; *Marengo v Daily Sketch and Sunday Graphic Ltd* [1948] 1 All ER 406, (1948) 65 RPC 242 at 253, HL, per Lord du Parcq.
13 *Habib Bank Ltd v Habib Bank AG Zurich* [1981] 2 All ER 650 at 666, [1981] 1 WLR 1265 at 1284–1285, [1982] RPC 1 at 36, CA, where it was said that it is irrelevant whether the cause of action arises at law or in equity for the purposes of the defences of estoppel or acquiescence. As to whether damages or accounts of profits are recoverable in the absence of fraudulent intent see PARA 424 et seq.

14 See *HP Bulmer Ltd and Showerings Ltd v J Bollinger SA and Champagne Lanson Père et Fils* [1978] RPC 79 at 135, CA.
15 *Elida Gibbs Ltd v Colgate-Palmolive Ltd* [1983] FSR 95 at 100. As to the use of a trader's own name and concurrent use see PARA 326 et seq.
16 *L'Oreal SA v Bellure NV* [2007] EWCA Civ 968, [2007] RPC 196. See also PARA 306.

(ii) Goodwill

289. Nature of goodwill. An action for passing off is now recognised as being a remedy for the invasion of a right of property[1], the property being in the goodwill likely to be injured by the misrepresentation rather than in the mark, name or get-up improperly used[2]. 'Goodwill' has been defined as the benefit and advantage of the good name, reputation and connection of a business, the attractive force which brings in custom, and the one thing which distinguishes an old-established business from a new business at its first start[3]. Although goodwill usually runs hand in hand with reputation, goodwill and reputation are not identical concepts[4].

1 As to the development by the courts of equity of the concept that passing off, in the absence of fraudulent intent, could be restrained as an interference with a right of property, by contrast with the personal action at common law based on the intentional fraud of the defendant, see PARA 288.
2 *Frank Reddaway & Co Ltd v George Banham & Co Ltd* [1896] AC 199, 13 RPC 218, HL, per Lord Herschell; *AG Spalding & Bros v AW Gamage Ltd* (1915) 32 RPC 273 at 284, HL, per Lord Parker of Waddington; *Star Industrial Co Ltd v Yap Kwee Kor (t/a New Star Industrial Co)* [1976] FSR 256 at 269, PC; *Erven Warnink BV v J Townend & Sons (Hull) Ltd* [1979] AC 731 at 740–741, [1979] 2 All ER 927 at 931–932, [1980] RPC 31 at 92, HL, per Lord Diplock; *Harrods Ltd v Harrodian School Ltd* [1996] RPC 697 at 711, CA, per Millet LJ; *Dawnay Day & Co Ltd v Cantor Fitzgerald International* [2000] RPC 669 at 701, CA, per Scott V-C; *Premier Luggage & Bags Ltd v Premier Co (UK) Ltd* [2002] EWCA Civ 387 at [37], [2003] FSR 69 at [37] per Chadwick LJ; *Phones 4U Ltd v Phone4u.co.uk Internet Ltd* [2006] EWCA Civ 244 at [9], [2007] RPC 83 at [9] per Jacob LJ. The concept of future goodwill is not helpful for this purpose: *Teleworks Ltd v Telework Group plc* [2002] RPC 535.
3 *IRC v Muller & Co's Margarine Ltd* [1901] AC 217 at 223–224, HL, per Lord Macnaghten. As to goodwill generally see PERSONAL PROPERTY vol 80 (2013) PARA 807 et seq.
4 Thus it may be possible for a trade mark to have a reputation in the United Kingdom but for the proprietor of the trade mark not to own any goodwill here because he does not have any trade or business here: see PARA 295.

290. Required proof and extent of goodwill etc. For there to be goodwill and reputation under a name, mark or other indicium there must be customers or prospective customers who recognise the name, mark or other indicium as distinctive of the claimant's goods or services[1]. Thus the key evidence for proof of goodwill is to show the court what was actually done to publicise the name or badge relied on; the amount spent on advertising and promotion is not of great significance[2].

An action for passing off can be maintained by a small trader with a limited clientele provided that he has built up sufficient goodwill that he will suffer substantial damage by reason of the misrepresentation complained of[3]. If the geographical extent of the goodwill is confined, then the claimant's ability to maintain a claim may be similarly confined[4].

Goodwill can in some circumstances be generated in respect of a service which is provided free to the consumer[5].

In order to succeed in a claim for passing off, the claimant must have established a goodwill under the relevant name, mark or indicium as at the date the defendant commenced the activities complained of[6].

1   See *Reckitt & Colman Products Ltd v Borden Inc* [1990] 1 All ER 873 at 880, [1990] 1 WLR
     491 at 499, [1990] RPC 341 at 406, HL, per Lord Oliver of Aylmerton. The test for proving
     goodwill in a passing off action is not the same as that for proving that an inherently descriptive
     trade mark has acquired a distinctive character: *Phones 4U Ltd v Phone4u.co.uk Internet Ltd*
     [2006] EWCA Civ 244 at [25]–[26], [32]–[34], [2007] RPC 83 at [25]–[26], [32]–[34] per
     Jacob LJ.
2   *Phones 4U Ltd v Phone4u.co.uk Internet Ltd* [2006] EWCA Civ 244 at [6] and [33], [2007]
     RPC 83 at [6] and [33] per Jacob LJ. By contrast turnover figures are highly pertinent.
3   See *Stannard v Reay* [1967] RPC 589 (fish and chip van); *Chelsea Man Menswear Ltd v Chelsea
     Girl Ltd* [1985] FSR 567 (affd [1987] RPC 189, CA) (small clothing business); *Sutherland v V2
     Music Ltd* [2002] EWHC 14 (Ch), [2002] IP & T 904 (band with no recording contract); *IN
     Newman Ltd v Adlem* [2005] EWCA Civ 741, [2006] FSR 253 (village funeral directors
     business); and c f *Hart v Relentless Records Ltd* [2002] EWHC 1984 (Ch), [2003] FSR 647
     (goodwill too small for any likelihood of damage).
4   This is particularly so in cases involving the supply of services: *Clock Ltd v Clock House
     Hotel Ltd* (1936) 53 RPC 269; *Stannard v Reay* [1967] RPC 589. Cf *Chelsea Man
     Menswear Ltd v Chelsea Girl Ltd* [1985] FSR 567 (affd [1987] RPC 189, CA) (nationwide
     injunction granted although plaintiff's trade in clothing geographically restricted).
5   *Plentyoffish Media Inc v Plenty More LLP* [2011] EWHC 2568 (Ch), [2012] RPC 89, [2011]
     All ER (D) 92 (Oct); *Starbucks (HK) Ltd v British Sky Broadcasting Group plc* [2012] EWHC
     3074 (Ch), [2013] IP & T 251, [2012] All ER (D) 36 (Nov) (affd [2013] EWCA Civ 1465,
     [2013] All ER (D) 214 (Nov)).
6   *Cadbury Schweppes Pty Ltd v Pub Squash Co Pty Ltd* [1981] 1 All ER 213, [1981] 1 WLR 193,
     [1981] RPC 429, PC; *Anheuser-Busch Inc v Budejovicky Budvar Narodni Podnik* [1984] FSR
     413, CA; *Inter Lotto (UK) Ltd v Camelot Group plc* [2003] EWCA Civ 1132, [2003] 4 All ER
     575, [2004] 1 WLR 955. It is arguable that this is the date on which the defendant starts
     actually using the name or mark in issue rather than eg the date upon which he registers a
     domain name incorporating that name or mark: *Phones 4U Ltd v Phone4u.co.uk Internet Ltd*
     [2006] EWCA Civ 244 at [15], [2007] RPC 83 at [15] per Jacob LJ.

291.   Whether actual trade need have commenced.   An action for passing off
can be sustained prior to the actual commencement of trading by the claimant. A
claimant may acquire a substantial reputation prior to making sales of a product
or service because of advance advertising and press publicity and, in such a case,
may sue others who seek to trade on the reputation which he has acquired[1]. A
company may in some circumstances acquire a reputation and goodwill that is
able to be protected even before its formal incorporation and within hours of the
announcement of its intended formation[2]. Where a claimant has incurred
considerable expense making preparations for the launch of a product which will
rapidly acquire a reputation once launched, a defendant who commences
advertising before the claimant with the intention of defeating the claimant's
acquisition of an exclusive right to the mark concerned may be restrained by a
quia timet injunction[3].

1   *WH Allen & Co v Brown Watson Ltd* [1965] RPC 191; *BBC v Talbot Motor Co Ltd* [1981]
     FSR 228; *Turner v General Motors (Australia) Pty Ltd* (1929) 42 CLR 352 (Aus); *Starbucks
     (HK) Ltd v British Sky Broadcasting Group plc* [2012] EWHC 3074 (Ch), [2013] IP & T 251,
     [2012] All ER (D) 36 (Nov) (affd [2013] EWCA Civ 1465, [2013] All ER (D) 214 (Nov));
     c f *S Chivers & Sons v S Chivers & Co Ltd* (1900) 17 RPC 420 at 431 per Farwell J; *Athletes
     Foot Marketing Associates Inc v Cobra Sports Ltd* [1980] RPC 343 at 357 per Walton J. See
     also *My Kinda Bones Ltd v Dr Pepper's Stove Co Ltd* [1984] FSR 289 per Slade J (where an
     application to strike out an action where the claimant relied only on pre-launch publicity was
     dismissed).
2   See *Fletcher Challenge Ltd v Fletcher Challenge Pty Ltd* [1982] FSR 1 (where the announcement
     of an intended merger of Challenge Corpn Ltd and Fletcher Holdings Ltd under the name
     'Fletcher Challenge' gave rise to sufficient reputation to restrain the defendants who adopted
     that name the day after the announcement); *Glaxo plc v Glaxowellcome Ltd* [1996] FSR 388
     (where the announcement of an intended merger of Glaxo plc and Wellcome plc under the name
     gave rise to sufficient reputation to restrain the defendants who adopted the name
     'Glaxowellcome' the day after the announcement). In each of these cases, however, the goodwill

and reputation of each of the antecedent entities would have sufficed to found a claim for passing off on the basis that the name being used by the defendant misrepresented that it was the product of a merger between that entity and the other.

3   *Elida Gibbs Ltd v Colgate-Palmolive Ltd* [1983] FSR 95 (where it was shown that, had the defendant's advertisements continued after the launch of the plaintiff's product, there would have been confusion and, in placing the advertisements, the defendant company had no motive of promoting an existing trade of its own).

292.   Cessation or suspension of trade.   The cessation or suspension of trade, or of the use of a name, mark or other indicium in a trade, will often leave a residual reputation and goodwill in the public mind which the trader may sue to protect, particularly if it is intended to resume the trade after a temporary interruption[1]. Whether sufficient residual reputation still exists to maintain an action for passing off is a question of fact[2]. Cessation of production of goods or provision of services does not necessarily mean that there has been a cessation of business capable of sustaining goodwill, still a less a destruction of the existing goodwill[3]. An action cannot be maintained, however, when the goodwill is positively abandoned by the breaking up of the business[4]; nor can an action be maintained by the former trader when the goodwill is assigned to another person[5].

1   *Poiret v Jules Poiret Ltd* (1920) 37 RPC 177 (where the plaintiff was called up for military service and his dressmaking establishment was converted into a shirt factory for the French army); *Music Corpn of America v Music Corpn (Great Britain) Ltd* (1946) 64 RPC 41 (where the plaintiff found it impracticable to continue the business during the war but fully intended to revive it as soon as conditions allowed); *Berkeley Hotel Co Ltd v Berkeley International (Mayfair) Ltd* [1972] RPC 237 (where the plaintiff's hotel had been sold and demolished but the plaintiffs were in the course of rebuilding on another site); *Ad-Lib Club Ltd v Granville* [1971] 2 All ER 300, [1972] RPC 673 (where the plaintiff's club had been forced to close by a noise-nuisance injunction but the plaintiffs were looking for alternative premises); *Levey v Henderson–Kenton (Holdings) Ltd* [1974] RPC 617 (where the plaintiff's department store was closed after a fire and other premises belonging to him were compulsorily acquired); *Thermawear Ltd v Vedonis Ltd* [1982] RPC 44 (plaintiff still had goodwill five years after ceasing to use mark on its goods); and see also *Sutherland v V2 Music Ltd* [2002] EWHC 14 (Ch), [2002] IP & T 904 (band which achieved limited success in 1993 still in existence and had some goodwill in 2001).

2   *Norman Kark Publications Ltd v Odhams Press Ltd* [1962] 1 All ER 636, [1962] 1 WLR 380, [1962] RPC 163 (where it was held that an intention not to abandon the goodwill is insufficient if the reputation of the plaintiff's mark has in fact dwindled); *Minimax GmbH & Co KG v Chubb Fire Ltd* [2008] EWHC 1960 (Pat), [2008] All ER (D) 385 (Jul).

3   *Maslyukov v Diageo Distilling Ltd* [2010] EWHC 443 (Ch), [2010] Bus LR D135, [2010] RPC 641 (continued sales of malt whisky by third parties sustained goodwill after closure of distilleries).

4   *Pink v JA Sharwood & Co Ltd* (1913) 30 RPC 725 (where the business was broken up and the plant and assets sold by the plaintiff's receiver in lunacy); *Ultraframe (UK) Ltd v Fielding* [2005] EWHC 1638 (Ch), [2005] All ER (D) 397 (Jul) (company in liquidation); *WS Foster & Son Ltd v Brooks Brothers UK Ltd* [2013] EWPCC 18, [2013] All ER (D) 232 (Mar) (boot making business discontinued); cf *Second Sight Ltd v Novell UK Ltd and Novell Inc* [1995] RPC 423.

5   *Star Industrial Co Ltd v Yap Kwee Kor (t/a New Star Industrial Co)* [1976] FSR 256, PC.

293.   Meaning of 'trader'; actions by non-traders.   The action for passing off concerns business or trading activities, so actions by non-traders for misrepresentations damaging to them[1] do not in general fall within the scope of passing off[2]. 'Trader' is, however, very widely interpreted and includes persons engaged in professional, literary and artistic occupations[3]. Actions for passing off may also be sustained by professional associations[4] and non-profit trade associations or chambers of commerce[5]. The courts have been willing to extend protection to claimants who are not engaged in trading activities in the ordinary sense of the word, such as charitable bodies[6], whether incorporated or unincorporated[7], and political organisations[8]. There have been cases where an individual has been entitled to restrain the use of his name in a business in a way which might potentially expose him to liability, apparently without regard to whether or not he is himself engaged in a trading activity[9].

1   Other causes of action, such as injurious falsehood or defamation, may be applicable in some circumstances: see generally DEFAMATION.
2   *Day v Brownrigg* (1878) 10 ChD 294, CA (where it was held that there could be no action by a private individual to prevent a neighbour adopting the same name for his house); *Earl Cowley v Countess Cowley* [1901] AC 450, HL (where no action lay to restrain continued use of a title by the former wife of a peer after her remarriage); *Kean v McGivan* [1982] FSR 119, CA (where one political party had no right of action to prevent a new party adopting the same name).
3   See eg *Lord Byron v Johnston* (1816) 2 Mer 29 (author's name); *Hines v Winnick* [1947] Ch 708, [1947] 2 All ER 517, 64 RPC 113 (musician's assumed name); *Marengo v Daily Sketch and Sunday Graphic Ltd* [1948] 1 All ER 406, 65 RPC 242, HL (cartoonist's nom de plume); *Clark v Associated Newspapers Ltd* [1998] 1 All ER 959, [1998] RPC 261 (false attribution of authorship). Authors, artists and composers may also be protected by the statutory right of a person to sue in respect of a false attribution to him of the authorship of a literary, dramatic, musical or artistic work: see the Copyright, Designs and Patents Act 1988 s 84; and COPYRIGHT vol 23 (2013) PARA 1018 et seq.
4   *Society of Accountants in Edinburgh v Corpn of Accountants Ltd* (1893) 20 R 750, Ct of Sess; *Society of Accountants and Auditors v Goodway and London Association of Accountants Ltd* [1907] 1 Ch 489; *Institute of Chartered Accountants of England and Wales v Hardwick* (1919) 35 TLR 342, CA; *Society of Incorporated Accountants v Vincent* (1954) 71 RPC 325; *British Association of Aesthetic Plastic Surgeons v Cambright Ltd* [1987] RPC 549; *Law Society of England & Wales v Society of Lawyers* [1996] FSR 739; cf *Society of Architects v Kendrick* (1910) 26 TLR 433. See also *British Medical Association v Marsh* (1931) 48 RPC 565 (chemist held himself out as being a branch of the association). Under the Trade Marks Act 1994 statutory protection is now afforded to trade associations by the registration of collective marks: see PARA 138 et seq.
5   *Lagos Chamber of Commerce Inc v Registrar of Companies and Association of Merchants and Industrialists* (1955) 72 RPC 263, PC.
      However, a trade association cannot maintain an action in a representative capacity on behalf of its members who use a particular descriptive appellation (see PARA 302), because if the trade association does not itself use that appellation it has no goodwill to protect and thus does not have the same interest as its members: *Chocosuisse Union des Fabricants Suisses de Chocolat v Cadbury Ltd* [1999] RPC 826, CA; *Scotch Whisky Association v JD Vintners Ltd* [1997] Eu LR 446. See, however, *Artistic Upholstery Ltd v Art Forma (Furniture) Ltd* [1999] 4 All ER 277, [2000] FSR 311, where a trade association was held able to own, through its members, goodwill which could found an action for passing off.
6   *British Legion v British Legion Club (Street) Ltd* (1931) 48 RPC 555; *Re Dr Barnardo's Homes, National Incorporated Association v Barnardo Amalgamated Industries Ltd and Benardout* (1949) 66 RPC 103; *Old Apostolic Church Of Africa v Non-white Old Apostolic Church of Africa* [1975] (2) SA 684, SAHC; *Holy Apostolic and Catholic Church of the East (Assyrian) Australia NSW Parish Association v A-G* (1986) 16 IPR 619, NSWCA; *British Diabetic Association v Diabetic Society* [1995] 4 All ER 812, [1996] FSR 1.
7   *British Legion v British Legion Club (Street) Ltd* (1931) 48 RPC 555 at 562–563.
8   *Burge v Haycock* [2001] EWCA Civ 900, [2002] RPC 553, [2002] IP & T 213 (holding that *Kean v McGivan* [1982] FSR 119, CA (in which relief was refused) was a case on its own facts).
9   *Routh v Webster* (1847) 10 Beav 561 (where the unauthorised use of an individual's name in the promotion of a joint stock company was restrained). See also *Gray v Smith* (1889) 43 ChD 208, CA (where a successor to a partnership's business was held not entitled to use the name of a retired partner in a way which might expose him to continuing liabilities). It is not clear whether these actions are a species of passing off or a separate type of action.

294. Shared reputations. In order to maintain an action for passing off a claimant need not be the only person entitled to make use of a particular mark or name[1]. Thus where the goodwill connected with the use of a trade name originally used in a single business is divided between different persons, each of those persons has an independent right to sue a third person for passing off by use of the trade name[2]. The same result may follow where different traders independently build up goodwill under the same name[3].

Where the claimant is one of a class of persons involved in trading in goods under a descriptive name, he can maintain an action for passing off against a defendant misusing the name if his business or goodwill is likely to suffer more than minimal damage as a result of the defendant's activities[4]. The nature of the reputation and goodwill in this instance is different in kind from that enjoyed where the reputation in a trade name has been divided, for example a descriptive name, such as 'advocaat', which is non-proprietary in nature can be used by any trader to describe his goods which possess its qualities[5], whereas the trade name indicates the origin of the goods rather than any particular standard of quality and can be used only by the persons who share the reputation[6].

Where two or more parties share reputation in a mark, one may be restrained from making a misrepresentation which damages the goodwill owned by the other or others[7].

1   As to concurrent rights of use see PARA 328.
2   *Dent v Turpin, Tucker v Turpin* (1861) 2 John & H 139; *Southorn v Reynolds* (1865) 12 LT 75.
3   *Parker & Son (Reading) Ltd v Parker* [1965] RPC 323; *Byford v Oliver* [2003] EWHC 295 (Ch), sub nom *SAXON Trade Mark* [2003] FSR 704, [2003] EMLR 416. See also *Sutherland v V2 Music Ltd* [2002] EWHC 14 (Ch), [2002] IP & T 904. By contrast, an goodwill generated by an 'alliance' of persons may be owned by the members of the group for the time and devolve by succession upon continuing members of the alliance: *Williams and Williams v Canaries Seaschool SLU (Club Sail Trade Marks)* [2010] RPC 826, Appointed Person.
4   *Erven Warnink BV v J Townend & Sons (Hull) Ltd* [1979] AC 731 at 748, [1979] 2 All ER 927 at 937, [1980] RPC 31 at 98, HL. See also PARA 302.
5   See *Erven Warnink BV v J Townend & Sons (Hull) Ltd* [1979] AC 731 at 747, [1979] 2 All ER 927 at 937, [1980] RPC 31 at 97, HL.
6   As to assignment and transmission see PARA 297.
7   *Sir Robert McAlpine Ltd v Alfred McAlpine plc* [2004] EWHC 630 (Ch), [2004] RPC 711.

295.   Ownership of goodwill by foreign traders.   A number of considerations arise when a claimant seeks to restrain the use in the United Kingdom of a name, mark or other indicium under which he has carried on business abroad[1]. A claimant in any case of passing off must prove a reputation extending to the geographical area in which the defendant's use of the name, mark or other indicium complained of is taking place[2], whether this is in another part of the country in which the claimant trades or in a different country, because, if he has no reputation in that area, the defendant's use of a similar name or mark cannot involve any misrepresentation[3]. If the claimant can establish that a substantial number of persons with whom the defendant intends to trade in the United Kingdom know of the claimant and will believe that the defendant's business is a branch of or connected with the claimant's business, so that the element of misrepresentation is established, the claimant must further show, as in any action for passing off, that the misrepresentation poses a real and tangible risk of injury to his business or goodwill[4].

It is unclear, however, whether there is an additional requirement that the claimant must carry on business in, or at least have a trade extending to, the country in which he seeks to restrain the defendant from using the mark or name, or whether the geographical separation of the claimant's business from the defendant's is a factual element which merely makes it difficult, but not impossible in all circumstances, for a claimant to show that the defendant's activities are likely to cause him substantial damage. What is clear is that a claimant who has no place of business in the United Kingdom and does not directly trade there, but whose goods are imported either by consumers or by intermediaries, can acquire[5] a reputation and goodwill that is able to be protected[6]. A business carried on abroad but taking bookings from customers in the United Kingdom can likewise acquire a reputation and goodwill able to be protected[7]. On the other hand, a business which has no customers in the United Kingdom has no goodwill to support a passing off action even if it has a reputation here[8].

It is more doubtful whether passing off can be established where the claimant's goods or services are neither marketed in the United Kingdom nor purchased by customers in the United Kingdom, but his customers who have come across his goods or services abroad reside in or come to the United Kingdom. It has, however, been held[9] that a claimant whose establishment in Paris had been advertised in England through travel agents, and who had some customers in England who had visited Paris, could not maintain an action for passing off in England against a defendant who had adopted the name of the claimant's establishment and used similar advertising with the intent of exploiting the claimant's reputation, because goodwill could not be acquired without actual user in England[10]. This decision has been criticised as wrongly decided[11], and tenuous user in the United Kingdom has been treated as justification for protection of a reputation primarily acquired by trade abroad[12], but the case has been cited with approval by the Court of Appeal[13].

The extent to which a reputation acquired by trading abroad may be protected in the United Kingdom may depend to some extent upon whether a trader is to be treated as a matter of law as having a separate goodwill in each country in which he trades[14] or whether the confining of goodwill to a particular country or area is a question of fact depending on the trading patterns and circumstances involved[15]. If goodwill is to be treated as a matter of law as stopping at frontiers, there may still be cases where the defendant's activities are likely to cause damage to the claimant's business in the country or countries where he trades[16]. However, even if the claimant has no protectable goodwill in the United Kingdom for the purpose of founding an action for passing off, he may have a statutory right to restrain by injunction the use in the United Kingdom of a mark protected as a well known trade mark under the Paris Convention[17]. There may also be a statutory right where a foreign trader's mark is misappropriated by an agent or representative of his in the United Kingdom[18].

1   As to passing off by the use of a name or mark see PARA 309 et seq; and as to passing off by similarity of get-up or shape of goods see PARA 321 et seq.

2   This is not necessarily the same country or area as that in which the defendant carries on business, in cases where the defendant applies a deceptive mark to goods for sale to ultimate purchasers in a different area or country: see PARA 290. As to enabling passing off by others see PARA 314.

3   *Cellular Clothing Co Ltd v Maxton and Murray* [1899] AC 326, 16 RPC 397, HL, per Lord Shand; *Lee v Haley* (1869) 5 Ch App 155 (where the injunction was limited to a single street); *Barber v Manico* (1893) 10 RPC 93; *George Outram & Co Ltd v London Evening Newspapers Co Ltd* (1911) 28 RPC 308; *Brestian v Try* [1958] RPC 161, CA.

4   As to the requirement to show damage see PARA 316.

5   In some circumstances the importer, rather than the foreign manufacturer, may acquire ownership of the goodwill: see PARA 296. There is, however, nothing to prevent the defendant's own acts, in importing the claimant's goods, from creating a protectable goodwill in the United Kingdom belonging to the claimant which then entitles the claimant to sue the defendant (or others) for passing off: *Nishika Corpn v Goodchild* [1990] FSR 371.

6   *Collins Co v Brown* (1857) 3 K & J 423 (where the basis of the decision was that the defendant's fraud gave rise to a personal cause of action based on property); *SA des Anciens Etablissements Panhard et Levassor v Panhard Levassor Motor Co Ltd* [1901] 2 Ch 513,

18 RPC 405 (approved in *Anheuser-Busch Inc v Budejovicky Budvar Narodni Podnik* [1984] FSR 413, CA); *Poiret v Jules Poiret Ltd* (1920) 37 RPC 177 (where the plaintiff had no place of business in England but he or his agents had made visits to sell dresses and had given a display at 10 Downing Street); *Roberts Numbering Machine Co v Davis* (1935) 53 RPC 79 (where the plaintiff had never had a business in England or an agency in the strict sense of the word but had sold to a sole importer); *Nishika Corpn v Goodchild* [1990] FSR 371 (where the defendant had imported the plaintiff's goods); *Jian Tools for Sale Inc v Roderick Manhattan Group Ltd* [1995] FSR 924 (where the American plaintiff had sold goods to customers in the United Kingdom through magazines circulating there); *Mecklermedia Corpn v DC Congress GmbH* [1998] Ch 40, [1998] 1 All ER 148, [1997] FSR 627 (where the plaintiff had organised trade shows in the United Kingdom); and see *IRC v Muller & Co's Margarine Ltd* [1901] AC 217 at 233, HL, per Lord Robertson. In *Starbucks (HK) Ltd v British Sky Broadcasting Group plc* [2012] EWHC 3074 (Ch), [2013] IP & T 251, [2012] All ER (D) 36 (Nov) (affd [2013] EWCA Civ 1465, [2013] All ER (D) 214 (Nov)) the claimants were considered to have goodwill in Hong Kong but not in the United Kingdom sufficiently to found passing off; the universal presence and accessibility of the internet, which enabled access to be gained in the United Kingdom to television programmes emanating from Hong Kong, was not considered a sufficiently close market link to establish an identifiable goodwill with a customer base in the United Kingdom.

7 *Grant (t/a Globe Furnishing Co) v Levitt* (1901) 18 RPC 361 (where the plaintiff carried on business in Liverpool and corresponded with customers in Ireland); *Sheraton Corpn of America v Sheraton Motels Ltd* [1964] RPC 202 (where the owners of an international chain of hotels took bookings for their hotels abroad through an office established in London); *Pete Waterman Ltd v CBS United Kingdom Ltd* [1993] EMLR 27 (where the defendant operated a recording studio in New York which was booked by, and which rendered invoices to, United Kingdom customers); *Hotel Cipriani Srl v Cipriani (Grosvenor Street) Ltd* [2010] EWCA Civ 110, [2010] Bus LR 1465, [2010] RPC 485 (where a hotel in Venice took bookings from United Kingdom customers).

8 *Plentyoffish Media Inc v Plenty More LLP* [2011] EWHC 2568 (Ch), [2012] RPC 89, [2011] All ER (D) 92 (Oct); *Starbucks (HK) Ltd v British Sky Broadcasting Group plc* [2012] EWHC 3074 (Ch), [2013] IP & T 251, [2012] All ER (D) 36 (Nov) (affd [2013] EWCA Civ 1465, [2013] All ER (D) 214 (Nov)).

9 Ie in *Alain Bernardin & Cie v Pavilion Properties Ltd* [1967] RPC 581.

10 *Alain Bernardin & Cie v Pavilion Properties Ltd* [1967] RPC 581 at 584, based principally on a dictum of Jenkins LJ in *T Oertli AG v EJ Bowman (London) Ltd* [1957] RPC 388 at 397, CA (affd [1959] RPC 1, HL), and on an extract from the speech of Lord Macnaghten in *IRC v Muller & Co's Margarine Ltd* [1901] AC 217 at 223–224, HL.

11 See *Maxim's Ltd v Dye* [1978] 2 All ER 55 at 58, [1977] 1 WLR 1155 at 1158, [1977] FSR 364 at 367 per Graham J (not following *Alain Bernardin & Cie v Pavilion Properties Ltd* [1967] RPC 581; but explaining *IRC v Muller & Co's Margarine Ltd* [1901] AC 217, HL; and applying *Baskin-Robbins Ice Cream Co v Gutman* [1976] FSR 545 at 548 per Graham J); *Pete Waterman Ltd v CBS United Kingdom Ltd* [1993] EMLR 27 at 53 per Browne-Wilkinson V-C. See also *C and A Modes v C and A (Waterford) Ltd* [1978] FSR 126, Ir CA; *Orkin Exterminating Co Inc v Pestco of Canada Ltd* (1985) 19 DLR 90, Ont CA; *Dominion Rent A Car Ltd v Budget Rent A Car Systems (1970) Ltd* [1987] 2 NZLR 395, NZ CA; *ConAgra Inc v McCain Foods (Aust) Pty Ltd* (1992) 23 IPR 193, Aust HC; *Calvin Klein Inc v International Apparel Syndicate* [1995] FSR 515, Calcutta HC; *Yahoo Inc v Akash Akora* [1999] FSR 931, Delhi HC. In *Metric Resources Corpn v Leasemetrix Ltd* [1979] FSR 571, Megarry V-C considered that the correctness of the decision in *Alain Bernardin & Cie v Pavilion Properties Ltd* above was a difficult point of law fully arguable on either side; and in *Athletes Foot Marketing Associates Inc v Cobra Sports Ltd* [1980] RPC 343, Walton J adopted the intermediate position that it was sufficient for a plaintiff to have some customers in the United Kingdom but insufficient to have a reputation but no customers, a position which was followed in *Pete Waterman Ltd v CBS United Kingdom Ltd* above.

12 *Globelegance BV v Sarkissian* [1974] RPC 603. See also *JC Penney Co Inc v Punjabi Nick* [1979] FSR 26, Hong Kong SC; *Tan-Ichi Co v Jancar Ltd* [1990] FSR 151, Hong Kong SC (commenting on changes in modern day trading conditions resulting from increased numbers of travellers and tourists); but see *Hotel Cipriani Srl v Cipriani (Grosvenor Street) Ltd* [2010] EWCA Civ 110, [2010] Bus LR 1465, [2010] RPC 485.

13 *Anheuser-Busch Inc v Budejovicky Budvar Narodni Podnik* [1984] FSR 413, CA (where the plaintiffs had some reputation, but no trade, in the United Kingdom except that they made considerable sales to American personnel through United States service stores, and it was held that the sale of the defendants' beer on the general market would cause the plaintiffs no damage as they had no trade in that market to be interfered with).

14 See *Star Industrial Co Ltd v Yap Kwee Kor (t/a New Star Industrial Co)* [1976] FSR 256 at 269,
    PC; *Erven Warnink BV v J Townend & Sons (Hull) Ltd* [1979] AC 731 at 752, [1979] 2 All ER
    927 at 941, [1980] RPC 31 at 102, HL, per Lord Fraser of Tullybelton, citing *Star
    Industrial Co Ltd v Yap Kwee Kor (t/a New Star Industrial Co)* above. In *Metric Resources
    Corpn v Leasemetrix Ltd* [1979] FSR 571 at 579, Megarry V-C considered that in no sense was
    Star Industrial Co Ltd v Yap Kwee Kor (t/a New Star Industrial Co) above a decision that the
    owner of a business carried on outside the jurisdiction could not establish goodwill capable of
    protection within the jurisdiction before beginning to trade there, although literal application of
    what was said in that case provided support for that proposition.

15 See *IRC v Muller & Co's Margarine Ltd* [1901] AC 217 at 224, HL, per Lord Macnaghten, at
    228 per Lord James of Hereford and at 233–234 per Lord Robertson, who considered that, if
    the trade of the German margarine factory had been diffused over several countries, the question
    of the location of the goodwill would have been more complex, and c f Lord Lindley at 235 who
    considered that goodwill was located at the place where the business was carried on;
    Lacteosote Ltd v Alberman [1927] 2 Ch 117, 44 RPC 211 (where the French and British
    markets were supplied from a single factory in France and the goodwill in the United Kingdom
    was held not severable from that of the French business); *Ingenohl v Wing On & Co
    (Shanghai) Ltd* (1927) 44 RPC 343, PC (where expropriation of the goodwill of part of a
    business in the Philippines was held to carry with it the right to use the marks of the business in
    other countries in competition with the original owner); *Maxim's Ltd v Dye* [1978] 2 All ER 55
    at 59, [1977] 1 WLR 1155 at 1159–1160, [1977] FSR 364 at 368 per Graham J; *C and A
    Modes v C and A (Waterford) Ltd* [1978] FSR 126 at 138, Ir CA, per Henchy J (where the
    plaintiff's business in Northern Ireland had many customers from the Republic of Ireland);
    Anheuser-Busch Inc v Budejovicky Budvar Narodni Podnik [1984] FSR 413, CA (where
    goodwill attached to the plaintiff's trade in United States service bases in the United Kingdom
    was treated as an extension of the plaintiff's American goodwill); *Pete Waterman Ltd v CBS
    United Kingdom Ltd* [1993] EMLR 27 at 53–58 per Browne-Wilkinson V-C, who questioned
    the need for a severable goodwill locally situate within the jurisdiction.

16 See e g *Sheraton Corpn of America v Sheraton Motels Ltd* [1964] RPC 202 (cited in note 7). In
    an appropriate case it may be possible for the claimant to sue the defendant in England for a
    wrong actionable under the law of the country in question by virtue of the Private International
    Law (Miscellaneous Provisions) Act 1995 Pt III (ss 9–15A) (see CONFLICT OF LAWS vol 19
    (2011) PARA 662 et seq). It should be noted that the Private International Law (Miscellaneous
    Provisions) Act 1995 Pt III (see above) is superseded by European Parliament and Council
    Regulation (EC) 864/2007 (OJ L199, 31.7.2007, p 40) on the law applicable to contractual
    obligations ('the Rome II Regulation'), with effect from 11 January 2009, in cases where that
    Regulation applies. Accordingly, it is necessary for choice of law purposes to distinguish
    between those claims which will continue to be governed by the rules of the common law and
    those which will be governed by the 1995 Act or by the Rome II Regulation: see CONFLICT OF
    LAWS vol 19 (2011) PARA 647 et seq.

17 See PARA 136. As to the Paris Convention see PARA 6.

18 See PARA 137.

296.   Ownership of goodwill attached to names, marks etc.   Questions often
arise as to the ownership of the goodwill attached to names, marks and other
indicia used in relation to goods or services with which two or more persons
have been connected in different capacities[1].

Thus, when goods made by a foreign manufacturer are imported by a dealer,
the goodwill in the name or mark applied to them may belong, depending on the
circumstances[2], either to the manufacturer[3] or to the dealer[4]. Where the foreign
manufacturer is from a country which belongs to the Paris Convention[5], he may
have a statutory right to restrain the unauthorised use by an agent or
representative of his in the United Kingdom of a trade mark of which he is
proprietor in his own country[6]. A name or mark initially belonging to and
denoting goods of the manufacturer can become distinctive of the dealer if he is
allowed over a sufficient period to sell goods made by himself or acquired from
other sources under the name or mark[7]. Where the mark is the manufacturer's
mark, an importer cannot maintain an action against a third person for the
passing off of goods as those of the manufacturer by the use of the mark, even

though he has by contract with the manufacturer the exclusive right to import the goods and suffers pecuniary damage as a result of the passing off[8]. Although by contract the dealer and manufacturer may regulate the ownership of a name or mark as between themselves, their contractual arrangements will not necessarily bind a third person, so that, if the name or mark in fact denotes goods of a foreign manufacturer, the purported assignment of the goodwill attached to the mark in the United Kingdom to the importer will not prevent a third person from importing goods to which the manufacturer has applied the name or mark[9]. Similarly, a purported assignment of goodwill in a mark to the manufacturer may not give him good title to sue a third person if the mark in fact denotes goods originating from the business of the dealer[10].

Similar questions arise as to the ownership of goodwill in names and marks as between licensors and licensees of patented and other manufacturing processes, where it seems essential in order for the licensor to retain ownership of the goodwill that he should exercise sufficient control over the manufacture and sale of products by the licensee[11].

Questions as to the ownership of the goodwill in a name can arise between employer and employee where the employee's name, either real or assumed, is used in the course of the employer's business. It is possible for the employee's name to be so used in the course of the employer's business that it becomes distinctive of the employer rather than of the employee[12].

The nom de plume of a writer or the assumed name of a performer or musician prima facie belongs to the individual concerned[13].

Where various members of a group of companies use trading styles which embody a common element distinctive of the group, or are associated in various capacities with goods bearing trade marks used by the group, the ownership of the goodwill attached to the names or marks as between members of the group may be uncertain[14]. It would appear that, in the absence of contrary agreement, a subsidiary or associated company which is permitted by the group to build up a business acquires an interest in the goodwill sufficient to enable it to continue to trade under the same style after its connection with the group is severed[15]. Where an international group of companies trades in a particular country through a particular company, the goodwill enjoyed in that country may belong to that company in the sense that the company is the appropriate claimant in an action for passing off, but nevertheless the goodwill and reputation may remain that of the international group so that other members of the group can also trade in that country without transfer of the goodwill or licence, express or implied[16].

1   Similar questions arose under the old law relating to registered trade marks, and the cases are still of relevance in connection with ownership of goodwill in an action for passing off, since only the person entitled to ownership of the goodwill attached to the mark was entitled to register it: *Re Apollinaris Co's Trade Marks* [1891] 2 Ch 186 at 226, 8 RPC 137 at 160–161, CA, per Fry LJ. The question of ownership often arose as between importers and overseas manufacturers: see *European Blair Camera Co's Trade Mark* (1896) 13 RPC 600; *Re New Atlas Rubber Co Ltd's Trade Mark* (1918) 35 RPC 269 ('Talisman'); *Re Warschauer's Application* (1925) 43 RPC 46 ('Obermeier'); *Re Elaine Inescourt's Trade Mark* (1928) 46 RPC 13; *Re Lesquendieu Trade Marks* (1934) 51 RPC 273. See also *Re Wood's Trade Mark* (1886) 32 ChD 247, 3 RPC 81, CA; *Walker & Sons Ltd v Kego* (1921) 38 RPC 25; *Re Impex Electrical Ltd's Trade Marks, Impex Electrical Ltd v Weinbaum* (1927) 44 RPC 405; *JH Coles Pty Ltd v Need* [1934] AC 82, 50 RPC 379, PC; *Re Kidax (Shirts) Ltd's Applications* [1960] RPC 117 at 124, CA; *Re Diehl KG's Application* [1969] 3 All ER 338, [1970] 2 WLR 944, [1970] RPC 435.

2   The issue of ownership of goodwill always turns on the facts on the case, such that reference to previous decisions is unlikely to be helpful: *Scandecor Development AB v Scandecor Marketing AB* [1999] FSR 26, CA; on appeal [2001] UKHL 21, [2001] IP & T 676.

3 *Richards v Butcher* [1891] 2 Ch 522, 7 RPC 288 (affd [1891] 2 Ch 522 at 540, 8 RPC 249, CA); *Van Zeller v Mason, Cattley & Co* (1907) 25 RPC 37; *Dental Manufacturing Co Ltd v C De Trey & Co* [1912] 3 KB 76, 29 RPC 617, CA; *Imperial Tobacco Co of India Ltd v Bonnan* [1924] AC 755, 41 RPC 441, PC; *Edison Storage Battery Co v Britannia Batteries Ltd* (1931) 48 RPC 350; *Roberts Numbering Machine Co v Davis* (1935) 53 RPC 79; *A/B Helsingfors Manus v RJ Fullwood & Bland Ltd* [1949] Ch 208, [1949] 1 All ER 205, CA.

4 See eg *J Defries & Sons Ltd and Helios Manufacturing Co v Electric and Ordnance Accessories Co Ltd* (1906) 23 RPC 341 (where the name was chosen by the dealer and the articles were made up by the manufacturer to the dealer's order and it was held that the dealer was entitled to restrain the manufacturer from applying the mark to other goods); *Ullman & Co v Cesar Leuba* [1908] AC 443, 25 RPC 673, PC; *DIEHL Trade Mark* [1969] 3 All ER 335, [1970] RPC 435; *MedGen Inc v Passion for Life Products Ltd* [2001] FSR 496 (product developed in the United States by claimant but exclusively marketed in the United Kingdom by defendant).

5 As to the Paris Convention see PARA 6.

6 See the Trade Marks Act 1994 s 60(1), (4); and PARA 137.

7 *Jaeger v Jaeger & Co Ltd* (1927) 44 RPC 437, CA; *Sturtevant Engineering Co Ltd v Sturtevant Mill Co of USA Ltd* [1936] 3 All ER 137, 53 RPC 430; *Adrema Ltd v Adrema-Werke GmbH and BEM Business Efficiency Machines Ltd* [1958] RPC 323; *Scandecor Development AB v Scandecor Marketing AB* [1999] FSR 26, CA (on appeal [2001] UKHL 21, [2001] IP & T 676). See also *T Oertli AG v EJ Bowman (London) Ltd* [1959] RPC 1, HL. Cf *Gromax Plasticulture Ltd v Don & Low Nonwovens Ltd* [1999] RPC 367 (where a distributor had sold a supplier's goods for a number of years in co-operation with the supplier it was held that goodwill in the mark was jointly owned).

8 *Richards v Butcher* [1891] 2 Ch 522 at 540, 8 RPC 249, CA; *Dental Manufacturing Co Ltd v C De Trey & Co* [1912] 3 KB 76, 29 RPC 617, CA. There is some doubt as to how rigid this rule is after the decision in *Erven Warnink BV v J Townend & Sons (Hull) Ltd* [1979] AC 731, [1979] 2 All ER 927, [1980] RPC 31, HL. See PARA 302.

9 It is not clear whether the basis of this rule is that the purported assignment of goodwill is altogether ineffective because there is no assignment of the goodwill in the business (ie the manufacturing business) to which the mark in fact relates (see *Lacteosote Ltd v Alberman* [1927] 2 Ch 117, 44 RPC 211), or whether the importer would have good title to sue for true piracy but cannot restrain importation of goods bearing the manufacturer's mark because that use of the mark involves no misrepresentation (see *Imperial Tobacco Co of India Ltd v Bonnan* [1924] AC 755 at 762, 41 RPC 441 at 448, PC). As to parallel imports generally see PARA 329.

10 *Ullman & Co v Cesar Leuba* [1908] AC 443, 25 RPC 673, PC.

11 *T Oertli AG v EJ Bowman (London) Ltd* [1959] RPC 1 at 7, HL, per Lord Reid; and see *Freeman Bros v Sharpe Bros & Co Ltd* (1899) 16 RPC 205; cf *JH Coles Pty Ltd v Need* [1934] AC 82, 50 RPC 379, PC. As to the ownership of goodwill as between franchisor and franchisee see PARA 299 note 1.

12 *Birmingham Vinegar Brewery Co v Liverpool Vinegar Co and Holbrook* (1888) 4 TLR 613 (where an employer was held entitled to restrain an ex-employee and persons to whom the employee purported to assign the right to sell sauce bearing the ex-employee's name); cf *Franke v Chappell* (1887) 3 TLR 524 (where the name 'Richter concerts' was held to be associated with the conductor Richter and not with the person who had first organised concerts with Richter under that name, so that he could not prevent others from announcing concerts by Richter as 'Richter concerts').

13 See *Landa v Greenberg* (1908) 24 TLR 441; *Hines v Winnick* [1947] Ch 708 at 713, [1947] 2 All ER 517 at 520, 64 RPC 113 at 117 per Vaisey J; *Modern Fiction Ltd v Fawcett* (1949) 66 RPC 230; *Forbes v Kemsley Newspapers Ltd* (1951) 68 RPC 183; *Sykes v John Fairfax & Sons Ltd* [1978] FSR 312.

14 It is rarely of practical importance in actions for passing off against third persons whether the goodwill is owned by the parent company, its subsidiaries or is shared between them, since the general practice when in doubt is to join as claimants the parent and all relevant subsidiaries in order to prevent the defendant from taking a technical point on title to sue.

15 *Habib Bank Ltd v Habib Bank AG Zurich* [1981] 2 All ER 650, [1981] 1 WLR 1265, [1982] RPC 1, CA; and see also *Dawnay Day & Co Ltd v Cantor Fitzgerald International* [2000] RPC 669, CA (where the agreement was that the subsidiary could use the name 'Dawnay Day' only for so long as it remained a company in the Dawnay Day group). Cf *Anderson & Lembke Ltd v Anderson & Lembke Inc* [1989] RPC 124 (United Kingdom branch of foreign corporation which had common origin to separate United Kingdom company entitled to state its affiliation on notepaper and business cards; but it had adopted a different trading style).

16	*Habib Bank Ltd v Habib Bank AG Zurich* [1981] 2 All ER 650 at 661, [1981] 1 WLR 1265 at 1278, [1982] RPC 1 at 30, CA, per Oliver LJ. See also *Revlon Inc v Cripps and Lee Ltd* [1980] FSR 85, CA; *Imperial Tobacco Co of India Ltd v Bonnan* [1924] AC 755 at 762, 41 RPC 441 at 448, PC.

297. Assignment and transmission of goodwill and rights in marks, names etc. The goodwill[1] of a business, and with it the appendant right to restrain others from using names, marks or other indicia confusingly similar to those used in the business, generally passes by devolution upon death[2], by operation of law[3] or by assignment[4]. Some names or marks, for example an artist's name, may so denote a particular individual and his personal skills as to be incapable of assignment[5]. However, the courts generally consider that names, marks and other indicia, even if originally derived from an individual's name used in a business, may come to denote goods or services originating from that business without being a representation as to the persons by whom the business is from time to time carried on, so that a successor to the business is entitled to continue to represent by the use of such names or marks that his goods or services come from that business, and to restrain a stranger from using them in a way which will lead to deception[6]. However, it follows from this that a mere right to use a name or mark cannot be validly assigned so as to confer rights against the public[7] without the goodwill of the business concerned[8] or at least of a severed or severable part of it[9]. Goodwill in distinct geographical areas is in general divisible[10], but in some circumstances the goodwill in one country cannot be severed from that of the business as a whole[11].

By statute, registered trade marks may now be assigned without the goodwill of the business to which they relate[12]. When a registered trade mark is assigned, it is not clear whether or to what extent the common law rights attaching to the mark, or the rights to an unregistered mark used in the same business in relation to the same goods, may be assigned with it without the goodwill of the business[13].

1	As to goodwill see PARA 289 et seq.
2	*Croft v Day* (1843) 7 Beav 84.
3	Eg upon the bankruptcy of an individual the goodwill vests in his trustee in bankruptcy: see BANKRUPTCY AND INDIVIDUAL INSOLVENCY vol 5 (2013) PARAS 437–438.
4	*Churton v Douglas* (1859) John 174; *Hall v Barrows* (1863) 4 De GJ & Sm 150; *Levy v Walker* (1879) 10 ChD 436, CA. See also *Harrods Ltd v Harrods (Buenos Aires) Ltd* [1999] FSR 187, CA (English retailer giving South American company irrevocable permission to use the name 'Harrods' in South America); *Tin Tin Yat Pao (International) Ltd v Tin Tin Publication Development Ltd* [2000] 3 HKC 1, [2000] IP & T 1109, HK CFA (licence to carry on licensor's business for a limited period akin to assignment and reversion back).
5	See *Leather Cloth Co Ltd v American Leather Cloth Co Ltd* (1865) 11 HL Cas 523 at 545 per Lord Kingsdown; *Thorneloe v Hill* [1894] 1 Ch 569 at 575, 11 RPC 61 at 70 per Romer J. The statutory right of a person to sue in respect of a false attribution of ownership of a literary, dramatic, musical or artistic work under the Copyright, Designs and Patents Act 1988 s 84 appears to be a personal right exercisable by the individual concerned, or by his personal representatives up to 20 years after his death: see s 86(2); and COPYRIGHT vol 23 (2013) PARA 1027.
6	*Leather Cloth Co Ltd v American Leather Cloth Co Ltd* (1865) 11 HL Cas 523 at 534 per Lord Cranworth, who said that the question in every such case must be whether the purchaser in continuing the use of the original trade mark would, according to the ordinary usages of trade, be understood as saying more than that he was carrying on the same business as had been formerly carried on by the person whose name constituted the trade mark; *Thorneloe v Hill* [1894] 1 Ch 569 at 575, 11 RPC 61 at 70 per Romer J; *Rickerby v Reay* (1903) 20 RPC 380.
7	A purported assignment may be effective between the parties to it.
8	This is because the successor's use of the name or mark, in falsely passing off his goods and services as coming from the source from which the public is accustomed to receive them, is itself

deceptive, and he has no better right than a stranger to restrain the use of such name or mark by a third person: *Thorneloe v Hill* [1894] 1 Ch 569, 11 RPC 61. This was also the old position in relation to registered trade marks, although that law has now been radically altered by statute to facilitate assignments of registered marks with or without the goodwill of the business: see the Trade Marks Act 1994 s 24(1); and PARA 113. The old cases relating to assignments of registered marks are, however, still relevant in the context of assignment of common law goodwill. Any assignment of trade marks in gross, ie dissociated from the goodwill of their business of origin, was invalid: *Pinto v Badman* (1891) 8 RPC 181, CA. A mark could not be assigned for parts of a wholesale business or for selling rights without manufacturing rights: *Lacteosote Ltd v Alberman* [1927] 2 Ch 117, 44 RPC 211; *Re John Sinclair Ltd's Trade Mark* [1932] 1 Ch 598, 49 RPC 123, CA; *Re Dobie & Sons Ltd's Trade Mark* (1935) 52 RPC 333. See also *Re Berna Commercial Motors Ltd* [1915] 1 Ch 414, 32 RPC 113; *Re GH Mumm & Co's Applications* (1922) 39 RPC 379; *Re Cranbux Ltd's Application* [1928] Ch 829, 45 RPC 281. A mark which in fact never had been used was not assignable: see *Re Ducker's Trade Mark* [1929] 1 Ch 113, 45 RPC 397, CA.

9   *Thorneloe v Hill* [1894] 1 Ch 569 at 577, 11 RPC 61 at 72.
10   *Star Industrial Co Ltd v Yap Kwee Kor (t/a New Star Industrial Co)* [1976] FSR 256, PC.
11   *Lacteosote Ltd v Alberman* [1927] 2 Ch 117, 44 RPC 211 (where French and British markets were supplied from a single factory in France and it was held that the goodwill in Britain was not separately assignable). See also *Ingenohl v Wing On & Co (Shanghai) Ltd* (1927) 44 RPC 343, PC.
12   See the Trade Marks Act 1994 s 24(1); and PARA 113.
13   The provisions of the Trade Marks Act 1938 s 22(3) (repealed), which explicitly authorised the conveyance of rights to an unregistered mark without the goodwill of the business when assigned together with a registered mark, have not been replaced. The Trade Marks Act 1994 s 24(6) (see PARA 113) merely states that the Act does not affect the assignment of an unregistered trade mark as part of the goodwill of the business.

298. Effect of transfer of goodwill. The transfer of the goodwill of a business generally gives to the successor the right, as against the predecessor, to use the name, marks[1] and other indicia of the business, even if the name of the business includes the predecessor's own name[2]. However, there may be some circumstances in which, because continued use of the name under which the business was previously carried out could amount to a misrepresentation[3], continued use of the name can be restrained by the predecessor in title or other parties formerly associated with the business[4].

Generally, following a transfer of goodwill, the predecessor is not entitled to represent by the use of the name or marks of the firm, or otherwise, that he is carrying on the same business as before[5], although in the absence of a contractual restriction he is entitled to continue in the same line of business in the same area[6], and to make plain his former connection with the business[7].

If the name of the business concerned is the personal name of the transferor, the transfer of the goodwill does not of itself deprive him of the right enjoyed by any other person of trading under his own name[8], although it seems that in such circumstances there may be a positive obligation upon the transferor to make plain in advertisements or by other means that his connection with the former business has ceased[9]. Goodwill and the appendant rights to use names or marks are usually assigned expressly, but may be conveyed by implication in the sale of the assets of a business as a going concern[10].

1   The rights to trade marks, whether registered or unregistered, generally pass with the goodwill of a business in the absence of an express stipulation to the contrary: *William Currie & Co v Currie* (1898) 15 RPC 339. See also PARA 297.
2   *Churton v Douglas* (1859) John 174; *Melrose-Drover Ltd v Heddle* (1901) 4 F (Ct of Sess) 1120; *Wood v Hall* (1915) 33 RPC 16. See also *Levy v Walker* (1879) 10 ChD 436, CA. In using the name or mark the successor is, however, not entitled to use the predecessor's name in such a way as to represent that the predecessor is still carrying on the business: *Thynne v Shove* (1890) 45 ChD 577. As to goodwill generally see PERSONAL PROPERTY vol 80 (2013) PARA 807 et seq.

3   Eg that the defendant is part of the corporate group who previously carried on that business.
4   Eg a former parent company once the connection with it implied by the name of the subsidiary
    has ceased: *Dawnay Day & Co Ltd v Cantor Fitzgerald International* [2000] RPC 669, CA.
5   *Churton v Douglas* (1859) John 174; *Mrs Pomeroy Ltd v Scalé* (1906) 24 RPC 177 at 181 per
    Buckley J; *May v May* (1914) 31 RPC 325, DC; *IN Newman Ltd v Adlem* [2005] EWCA Civ
    741, [2006] FSR 253.
6   *Hall v Barrows* (1863) 4 De GJ & Sm 150; *Labouchere v Dawson* (1872) LR 13 Eq 322.
7   *Trego v Hunt* [1896] AC 7 at 27, HL, per Lord Davey; *Anderson & Lembke Ltd v Anderson &
    Lembke Inc* [1989] RPC 124; *Dawnay Day & Co Ltd v Cantor Fitzgerald International* [2000]
    RPC 669, CA. See also *Leather Cloth Co Ltd v American Leather Cloth Co Ltd* (1865) 11 HL
    Cas 523 at 540–541.
8   *Mrs Pomeroy Ltd v Scalé* (1906) 24 RPC 177 at 181 per Buckley J, and at 188 per Parker J. As
    to the right of an individual to trade under his own name, notwithstanding that confusion may
    result, see PARA 326.
9   *Mrs Pomeroy Ltd v Scalé* (1906) 24 RPC 177 at 192 per Parker J; *May v May* (1914) 31 RPC
    325, DC; *IN Newman Ltd v Adlem* [2005] EWCA Civ 741, [2006] FSR 253. In this respect the
    transferor may be under a slightly higher duty than a third person in the same situation by virtue
    of an implied contractual duty arising between a vendor and purchaser of goodwill. A person
    who voluntarily sells the goodwill of a business may also have an implied duty to the purchaser
    not to solicit his former customers: *Trego v Hunt* [1896] AC 7, HL. No such duty can be
    implied where goodwill has been transferred compulsorily, eg by a sale by a trustee in
    bankruptcy of part of a bankrupt's assets: *Walker v Mottram* (1881) 19 ChD 355, CA.
10 *Rickerby v Reay* (1903) 20 RPC 380.

299. Licensing of goodwill and rights in marks, names etc.

The use of names, marks and other indications of origin of goods or services may be licensed to others[1] but, as in relation to assignments[2], a person who licenses or purports to license the use of a name or mark in gross, namely without exercising quality control over, or otherwise retaining sufficient connection with, the goods or business concerned[3], may lose the right to sue third persons for passing off since the names or marks will have ceased in fact to denote the claimant's goods or business[4].

The Trade Marks Act 1994 has greatly liberalised the rights of the proprietor of a registered trade mark to license his mark as compared with the more restrictive registered user requirements under the Trade Marks Act 1938[5]. The provisions of the Trade Marks Act 1938 which deemed use by a registered user to be use by the proprietor for the purposes of both that Act and the common law[6] have, however, not been replaced in the Trade Marks Act 1994, thereby rendering it unclear whether licensing in gross of a registered trade mark will cause loss of the proprietor's concurrent common law right to sue for passing off[7].

1   An increasingly common form of licence of goodwill is a franchise agreement. Such an
    agreement is best regarded as a lease of goodwill by the franchisee to the franchisor, which
    reverts back to the franchisor (hopefully enhanced by the activities of the franchisee) at the end
    of the period of the franchise: *Kall Kwik Printing (UK) Ltd v Rush* [1996] FSR 114;
    Dyno-Rod plc v Reeve [1999] FSR 148. See also *Tin Tin Yat Pao (International) Ltd v Tin Tin
    Publication Development Ltd* [2000] 3 HKC 1, [2000] IP & T 1109, HK CFA,. A franchisor
    has title to sue for passing off since its ability to attract fees to itself is goodwill: *Fine &
    Country Ltd v Okotoks Ltd* [2013] EWCA Civ 672, [2013] All ER (D) 137 (Jun).
2   As to the assignment of rights in marks and names see PARA 297.
3   See *T Oertli AG v EJ Bowman (London) Ltd* [1959] RPC 1 at 7, HL, per Lord Reid. Cf *JH
    Coles Pty Ltd v Need* [1934] AC 82, 50 RPC 379, PC (where the franchising of the name of the
    plaintiff's store to the defendant on condition that the defendant acquired his goods from the
    plaintiff did not prevent the trade name from remaining distinctive of the plaintiff); *Tin Tin Yat
    Pao (International) Ltd v Tin Tin Publication Development Ltd* [2003] 3 HKC 1, [2000] IP & T
    1109, HK CFA (where the licensor licensed the licensee to carry on the very business formerly
    carried on by the licensor for a limited period, the mark under which the mark was conducted

remained distinctive of that business; in any event the licence contained an implied negative covenant that the licensee would not operate the business after the expiry of the licence).

4   *Thorneloe v Hill* [1894] 1 Ch 569, 11 RPC 61. See also *Star Industrial Co Ltd v Yap Kwee Kor (t/a New Star Industrial Co)* [1976] FSR 256 at 271, PC (criticising *Warwick Tyre Co Ltd v New Motor and General Rubber Co Ltd* [1910] 1 Ch 248, 27 RPC 161).

The law relating to the licensing of registered trade marks has now been relaxed freely to permit licensing (see PARA 119) and this will not generally render the trade mark deceptive (see PARA 100), but the old cases relating to invalidity of registered trade marks through licensing are still relevant to passing off. Before the Trade Marks Act 1938 the grant of a licence to use a trade mark for goods other than those of the proprietor invalidated a registered trade mark: *Bowden Wire Co Ltd v Bowden Brake Co Ltd* (1913) 30 RPC 580 (affd (1914) 31 RPC 385, HL). Cf *Manus Akt v RJ Fullwood and Bland Ltd* [1949] Ch 208, [1949] 1 All ER 205, 66 RPC 71, CA (where it was held that a clause in a patent licence requiring the defendants to use the registered mark did not invalidate the mark). See also *Somerlite Ltd v Brown* (1934) 51 RPC 205 at 224, CA. Such licensing was held to be deceptive in the same way as an assignment divorced from the goodwill of the business was considered deceptive: *Bowden Wire Co Ltd v Bowden Brake Co Ltd* (1914) 31 RPC 385 at 392, HL, per Lord Loreburn. In other words, a licence of a trade mark was thought to be contrary to the very purpose of such a mark, namely to denote the trade origin of goods. After the passage of the Trade Marks Act 1938, however, it was held that the exercise of effective quality control was generally sufficient to save a licensed mark from invalidity: *Bostitch Trade Mark* [1963] RPC 183 at 195–197 (where there was a licence of design and know-how together with a trade mark licence and the trade mark was held valid), referred to with apparent approval in *Re American Greetings Corpn's Application* [1984] 1 All ER 426, [1984] 1 WLR 189, HL. Cf *Weston Trade Mark* [1968] RPC 167 (where the trade connection had long been destroyed and the mark denoted the goods of an ex-licensee); *British Petroleum Co Ltd v European Petroleum Distributors Ltd* [1968] RPC 54 (where the fact that a licence to a wholly-owned subsidiary was unregistered was held to be irrelevant); *GE Trade Mark* [1969] RPC 418 at 457, 459 per Graham J (on appeal [1970] RPC 339 at 372, CA, per Salmon LJ, and at 391–395 per Cross LJ) (where a joint venture company was subject to the quality control of the registered proprietor); and *McGREGOR Trade Mark* [1979] RPC 36 (where the trade mark was revoked because it had been licensed without any quality control). As to the position under the Trade Marks Act 1994 see *Scandecor Development AB v Scandecor Marketing AB* [1999] FSR 26, [1998] All ER (D) 370, CA; on appeal [2001] UKHL 21, [2001] IP & T 676.

5   See PARA 119.
6   Ie the Trade Marks Act 1938 s 28(2) (repealed).
7   It is not clear whether the registered trade mark would be rendered invalid for this reason: see PARA 100.

(iii) Misrepresentation

300.   Nature of the misrepresentation. The earliest recognised type of misrepresentation in an action for passing off is a false representation that the defendant's goods are the claimant's[1]. The action also embraces a wide range of more subtle misrepresentations[2], such as:

(1)   that the claimant's goods of one class or quality are of another class or quality[3];

(2)   that the claimant's goods of a type or quality sold abroad which is different from the type or quality of the claimant's goods normally sold in the home market are goods of the type or quality normally sold in the home market[4];

(3)   that secondhand or used goods of the claimant are new[5];

(4)   that seconds or rejects of the claimant's manufacture to which the claimant has chosen not to apply his mark are goods of the claimant's ordinary manufacture[6];

(5)   that stale or deteriorated goods are in the state of freshness in which purchasers would ordinarily receive the claimant's goods[7];

(6) that outmoded or superseded goods are the claimant's current production[8];

(7) that altered or adulterated goods are goods of the claimant's original manufacture[9];

(8) that goods are covered by the claimant's guarantee when they are not so covered[10]; or

(9) that the defendant's goods belong to a class of goods with a discrete reputation, when they do not[11].

The same principles as apply to goods apply to misrepresentations relating to businesses or services, so that the misrepresentation may be that the defendant's business is the business of the claimant[12], or is a branch or department or subsidiary company of the claimant[13], or that the defendant is authorised to act as agent for[14] the claimant or is a member of[15], or has some special relationship with, the claimant, such as that of authorised dealer[16].

A mere representation that the defendant is sponsored by the claimant or that the claimant provides financial support to the defendant is not sufficient to found an action for passing off, where there is no likelihood of persons to whom the representation has been made relying upon the exercise by the claimant of control over the defendant's trading standards or the quality of the defendant's goods or services[17]. On the other hand, a misrepresentation that a celebrity has endorsed the defendant's goods or services is actionable[18]. So too is a misrepresentation that a celebrity has authorised the use of her image on the defendant's goods[19].

1   *Frank Reddaway & Co Ltd v George Banham & Co Ltd* [1896] AC 199 at 204, 13 RPC 218 at 224, HL, per Lord Halsbury. It is unnecessary for this purpose that purchasers should be aware of the actual identity of the claimant so long as they are induced to believe that the defendant's goods are from a source which they recognise and which is in fact the claimant: see PARA 301. As to misrepresentation generally see MISREPRESENTATION.

2   However, a false representation cannot found an action in passing off unless it relates to the claimant's goods: *Schulke & Mayr (UK) Ltd v Alkapharm (UK) Ltd* [1999] FSR 161; and see PARA 302 note 12.

3   *Teacher v Levy* (1905) 23 RPC 117; *AG Spalding & Bros v AW Gamage Ltd* (1915) 32 RPC 273, HL.

4   *Champagne Heidsieck & Cie v Scotto and Bishop* (1926) 43 RPC 101 (labels on the plaintiff's continental quality champagne bottles were replaced with imitations of the labels on the plaintiff's English quality champagne). It has been held that a defendant can make an implied representation to this effect even when he does no more than import goods and sell them under the marks and labels which the claimant himself has applied to them, if the claimant sells differing qualities of goods under similar labels in territorially distinct markets: *Colgate-Palmolive Ltd v Markwell Finance Ltd* [1989] RPC 497, CA; *Microsoft Corpn v Computer Future Distribution Ltd* [1998] All ER (D) 78; cf *Revlon Inc v Cripps and Lee Ltd* [1980] FSR 85 at 112, CA (where Templeman LJ held that there could be no passing off when products manufactured, named, labelled and put into circulation by a member of the plaintiff's group of companies were sold by the defendants without any alteration to the contents, name or label). As to parallel imports see PARA 329.

5   *Gillette Safety Razor Co and Gillette Safety Razor Ltd v Franks* (1924) 41 RPC 499; *Morris Motors Ltd v Lilley (t/a G and L Motors)* [1959] 3 All ER 737, [1959] 1 WLR 1184. The circumstances in which goods are sold, such as the nature of the trade outlet, and the appearance of the goods themselves, may, however, mean that customers would realise the goods were secondhand, in which case there is no passing off: *General Electric Co Ltd v Pryce's Stores* (1933) 50 RPC 232.

6   *Britains Ltd v M Morris & Co (London) Ltd* [1961] RPC 217. This extends to excess or unauthorised goods manufactured by a contractor which the trade mark owner has not adopted as his own: *Primark Stores Ltd v Lollypop Clothing Ltd* [2001] FSR 637, [2000] All ER (D) 2099.

7   *Wilts United Dairies Ltd v Thomas Robinson Sons & Co Ltd* [1958] RPC 94, CA.

8 See *Harris v Warren and Philips* (1918) 35 RPC 217; *Paquin Ltd v John Barker & Co Ltd* (1934) 51 RPC 431 (where such a misrepresentation was held to be not made out on the facts).
9 *Westinghouse Brake and Saxby Signal Co Ltd v Varsity Eliminator Co Ltd* (1935) 52 RPC 295; *Rolls-Royce Motors Ltd v Zanelli* [1979] RPC 148 (revsd [1979] RPC 152, CA).
10 *Morris Motors Ltd v Lilley (t/a G and L Motors)* [1959] 3 All ER 737, [1959] 1 WLR 1184; *Sony KK v Saray Electronics (London) Ltd* [1983] FSR 302, CA.
11 See PARA 302.
12 *Joseph Rodgers & Sons Ltd v WN Rodgers & Co* (1924) 41 RPC 277 at 291; *Law Society of England and Wales v Griffiths* [1995] RPC 16.
13 *Walter v Ashton* [1902] 2 Ch 282; *Lloyd's v Lloyd's (Southampton) Ltd* (1912) 29 RPC 433, CA; *Ewing v Buttercup Margarine Co Ltd* [1917] 2 Ch 1, 34 RPC 232, CA; *FW Woolworth & Co Ltd v Woolworths (Australasia) Ltd* (1930) 47 RPC 337 (subsidiary); *Kimberley-Clark v Fort Sterling Ltd* [1997] FSR 877; *Dawnay Day & Co Ltd v Cantor Fitzgerald International* [2000] RPC 669 at 701, CA (member of corporate group).
14 *Wheeler and Wilson Manufacturing Co v Shakespear* (1869) 39 LJ Ch 36.
15 *Society of Accountants and Auditors v Goodway and London Association of Accountants Ltd* [1907] 1 Ch 489.
16 *Morris Motors Ltd v Lilley (t/a G and L Motors)* [1959] 3 All ER 737, [1959] 1 WLR 1184; *Sony KK v Saray Electronics (London) Ltd* [1983] FSR 302, CA.
17 *Harrods Ltd v Harrodian School Ltd* [1996] RPC 697, CA; cf *Tavener Rutledge Ltd v Trexapalm Ltd* [1977] RPC 275 at 280 per Walton J.
18 *Irvine v TalkSport Ltd* [2003] EWCA Civ 423, [2003] 2 All ER 881, [2003] FSR 619. As to merchandising of names etc see PARA 323.
19 *Fenty v Arcadia Group Brands Ltd* [2013] EWHC 2310 (Ch), [2013] All ER (D) 410 (Jul).

301. Claimant's identity need not be known. There is no necessity in an action for passing off that the persons deceived should be aware of the claimant's identity, so long as they are accustomed to the claimant's goods or services and are induced by the defendant's misrepresentation to believe that the defendant's goods or services come from the accustomed source[1].

1 *Birmingham Vinegar Brewery Co Ltd v Powell* [1897] AC 710, 14 RPC 720, HL; *William Edge & Sons Ltd v William Niccolls & Sons Ltd* [1911] AC 693 at 705, 28 RPC 582 at 593–594, HL; *T Oertli AG v EJ Bowman (London) Ltd* [1957] RPC 388 at 397, CA, per Jenkins LJ (affd [1959] RPC 1, HL); *F Hoffmann-La Roche & Co AG v DDSA Pharmaceuticals Ltd* [1972] RPC 1, CA (coloured drug capsules); *United Biscuits (UK) Ltd) v Asda Stores Ltd* [1997] RPC 513 at 533 per Robert Walker J. See also *Copydex Ltd v Noso Products Ltd* (1952) 69 RPC 38 (where a rival glue was advertised 'as shown on television', referring to a programme in which the plaintiff's product had been used but the plaintiff's name not mentioned). See also 'reverse' passing off; and PARA 303. As to misrepresentation generally see MISREPRESENTATION.

302. Misuse of descriptive terms: 'extended' passing off. It was long considered essential in an action for passing off that the misrepresentation should relate specifically to the claimant[1], in the sense of representing that the goods or business concerned were his goods or business, or at least in some way connected with or guaranteed by him[2], as opposed to being a misrepresentation about the nature or quality of the defendant's goods or services which did not imply that the claimant was in any way responsible for them or for the defendant[3]. Thus no action lay where the defendant falsely asserted that his goods were as good as or better than those of the claimant[4], or misapplied a descriptive term to his own goods which was genuinely descriptive of the claimant's goods[5].

It has, however, been decided by the House of Lords[6] that a defendant who falsely applies to his goods a descriptive appellation to which they are not entitled is liable to an action for passing off at the suit of persons whose business or goodwill will be damaged by the misuse of the descriptive appellation concerned (so-called 'extended' passing off)[7]. In such cases the claimant must show that the appellation has a sufficiently definite meaning[8], which denotes a particular group of products, and that those products have a discrete reputation as a group[9], such that the appellation has a significance greater than its literal, descriptive[10] meaning[11]. Thus it remains the law that a representation which does not relate to the claimant's goods or services, even in this extended sense of relating to them as part of such a group with a discrete reputation, cannot found an action in passing off[12].

In the classic form of passing off action, the only person entitled to bring the action is the person to whom the name, mark or other indicium misused by the defendant refers, so that other persons legitimately trading in goods bearing that name or mark, such as exclusive importers or distributors, cannot maintain an action for passing off even though the defendant's activities cause damage to their trade[13]. Where, however, there is passing off of a product which has a character intrinsic to and inseparable from its descriptive name, for example 'advocaat'[14], such a limitation seems inappropriate in view of the non-proprietary nature of the name or mark misused, and it appears that any person manufacturing or dealing in the genuine product whose business or goodwill will suffer more than minimal damage as a result of the defendant's activities may maintain an action[15]. Indeed, the decision of the House of Lords in the 'advocaat' case[16] may open the way for persons other than the proprietor of the goodwill attached to a mark or name to sue in respect of a misuse of the mark or name which is damaging to them[17].

1   This was required whether or not his actual identity was known: see PARA 301. As to misrepresentation generally see MISREPRESENTATION.

2   As to the nature of the misrepresentation see PARA 300.

3   *Native Guano Co Ltd v Sewage Manure Co* (1889) 8 RPC 125, HL. What mattered was that goods were accepted on the faith of the plaintiff's reputation: see *HP Bulmer Ltd and Showerings Ltd v J Bollinger SA and Champagne Lanson Père et Fils* [1978] RPC 79 at 117, CA, per Goff LJ. Cases such as *AG Spalding & Bros v AW Gamage Ltd* (1915) 32 RPC 273, HL (passing off one quality of the plaintiff's own goods as another) and *Wilts United Dairies Ltd v Thomas Robinson Sons & Co Ltd* [1958] RPC 94, CA (passing off old goods of the plaintiffs as fresh) did not represent a departure from this general principle, since, in effect, the defendant was attributing to or placing in the mouth of the plaintiff a statement, express or implied, as to the origin, class or quality of goods.

4   *White v Mellin* [1895] AC 154, HL; *Hubbuck & Sons Ltd v Wilkinson, Heywod and Clark Ltd* [1899] 1 QB 86, CA; cf *Masson Seeley & Co Ltd v Embosotype Manufacturing Co* (1924) 41 RPC 160. See also *Irving's Yeast-Vite Ltd v Horsenail* (1934) 51 RPC 110, HL. An action for trade libel may, however, lie where the defendant falsely and maliciously disparages the claimant's goods in a way likely to result in pecuniary damage: see DEFAMATION vol 32 (2012) PARA 776 et seq.

5   *Canham v Jones* (1813) 2 Ves & B 218; *Native Guano Co Ltd v Sewage Manure Co* (1889) 8 RPC 125, HL.

6   Ie in *Erven Warnink BV v J Townend & Sons (Hull) Ltd* [1979] AC 731, [1979] 2 All ER 927, [1980] RPC 31, HL.

7   *Erven Warnink BV v J Townend & Sons (Hull) Ltd* [1979] AC 731, [1979] 2 All ER 927, [1980] RPC 31, HL (approving *Bollinger v Costa Brava Wine Co Ltd* [1960] Ch 262, [1959] 3 All ER 800, [1960] RPC 16 (champagne); *Vine Products Ltd v Mackenzie & Co Ltd* [1969] RPC 1 (sherry); *John Walker & Sons Ltd v Henry Ost & Co Ltd* [1970] 2 All ER 106, [1970] 1 WLR 917, [1970] RPC 489 (whisky)). It is not necessary for this purpose that the product has a particular cachet in terms of being a luxury or premium brand: *Diageo North America Inc v Intercontinental Brands (ICB) Ltd* [2010] EWCA Civ 920, [2011] 1 All ER 242, CA (vodka). See also *Scotch Whisky Association v JD Vintners Ltd* [1997] Eu LR 446 (Scotch whisky); *Chocosuisse Union des Fabricants Suisses de Chocolat v Cadbury Ltd* [1999] RPC 826, CA (Swiss chocolate); *Matthew Gloag & Son Ltd v Welsh Distillers Ltd* [1998] FSR 718, [1998] ETMR 504 (arguable application of 'Welsh Whisky' to Scotch whisky could be restrained as reverse passing off (see PARA 303); claim succeeded in relation to low-strength vodka); *Fage*

UK Ltd v Chobani UK Ltd [2013] EWHC 630 (Ch), [2013] All ER (D) 267 (Mar) ('Greek yoghurt'). As to descriptive names see also PARA 319.

8 *Erven Warnink BV v J Townend & Sons (Hull) Ltd* [1979] AC 731 at 739, 754, [1979] 2 All ER 927 at 930, 942, [1980] RPC 31 at 91, 104, HL; *Consorzio del Prosciutto di Parma v Marks & Spencer plc* [1991] RPC 351 at 364, CA ('Parma ham') (where it was alleged that Parma ham pre-sliced and packaged would deteriorate to an extent that it could no longer be classed as genuine Parma ham; allegation struck out); *Chocosuisse Union des Fabricants Suisses de Chocolat v Cadbury Ltd* [1998] RPC 117 at 129 per Laddie J (affd [1999] RPC 826 at 832, CA, per Chadwick LJ). See also *Lang Bros Ltd v Goldwell Ltd* [1977] FSR 353, Ct of Sess (where the meaning implied by a Scottish-looking get-up of a drink consisting of Scotch whisky mixed with English ginger wine was insufficiently definite).

9 The necessary reputation involves some perceived quality; it does not matter if there are other goods outside the class which have identical characteristics or have the same or higher quality: *Chocosuisse Union des Fabricants Suisses de Chocolat v Cadbury Ltd* [1998] RPC 117 at 128 per Laddie J (affd [1999] RPC 826, CA).

10 Thus in the case of geographical appellations, if the description means no more than that the goods come from that place, there is no reputation to protect: see *Chocosuisse Union des Fabricants Suisses de Chocolat v Cadbury Ltd* [1998] RPC 117 at 129 per Laddie J (giving the example of English pencils or French ball-bearings) (affd [1999] RPC 826, CA). The converse of this is that it would be passing off to use the appellation which, although true in its geographical sense, falsely suggested that the goods were of the class in question (eg it would be passing off to call wine 'champagne' even if from the Champagne region, if it was not made in accordance with the traditional recipe).

11 *Chocosuisse Union des Fabricants Suisses de Chocolat v Cadbury Ltd* [1998] RPC 117 at 129 per Laddie J (affd [1999] RPC 826 at 832, CA, per Chadwick LJ). See also *Erven Warnink BV v J Townend & Sons (Hull) Ltd* [1979] AC 731 at 742, [1979] 2 All ER 927 at 933, [1980] RPC 31 at 93, HL, per Lord Diplock (for reasons of policy the action for passing off is not necessarily available in all types of misrepresentation in the course of trade which may cause damage to the business or goodwill of rival traders).

The status of cases such as *Combe International Ltd v Scholl (UK) Ltd* [1980] RPC 1 (where it was held arguable that a misrepresentation that the defendant's goods were the same as the claimant's could give the claimant a cause of action) is now unclear. See also note 12.

12 *Schulke & Mayr (UK) Ltd v Alkapharm (UK) Ltd* [1999] FSR 161 (no cause of action based on misrepresentation that the defendant's goods have some quality that they do not in fact possess). It follows that previous decisions that false claims to medals, testimonials or praise in fact belonging to the claimant did not give rise to an action for passing off, unless the claims led to the defendant's goods or business being taken as the claimant's, may remain good law: see *Batty v Hill* (1863) 1 Hem & M 264 (claim to Prize Medal from 1862 Exhibition); *National Starch Manufacturing Co v Munn's Patent Maizena and Starch Co* [1894] AC 275, 11 RPC 281, PC; *Tallerman v Dowsing Radiant Heat Co* [1900] 1 Ch 1, CA (where a commendation in a medical journal of the plaintiff's system of treatment was falsely applied to the defendant's); *Adolph Frankau & Co Ltd v Pflueger* (1910) 28 RPC 130; *Accumulator Industries Ltd v CA Vandervell & Co* (1912) 29 RPC 391; *Cambridge University Press v University Tutorial Press* (1928) 45 RPC 335 (where a false representation that the defendant's book was prescribed for university examinations was not actionable as passing off). See, however, *SDS Biotech UK Ltd v Power Agrichemicals Ltd* (1989) [1995] FSR 797; *Hodge Clemco Ltd v Airblast Ltd* [1995] FSR 806 (both holding it arguable that a misrepresentation that the defendant had the approval of a regulatory body could found an action for passing off).

13 *Richards v Butcher* (1890) 7 RPC 288 (importers of Heidsieck champagne not entitled to maintain an action); *Dental Manufacturing Co Ltd v C De Trey & Co* [1912] 3 KB 76, 29 RPC 617, CA.

14 Ie the type of passing off exemplified by the facts of *Erven Warnink BV v Townend & Sons (Hull) Ltd* [1979] AC 731, [1979] 2 All ER 927, [1980] RPC 31, HL.

15 *Erven Warnink BV v J Townend & Sons (Hull) Ltd* [1979] AC 731 at 748, [1979] 2 All ER 927 at 937, [1980] RPC 31 at 98, HL, per Lord Diplock.

16 Ie *Erven Warnink BV v Townend & Sons (Hull) Ltd* [1979] AC 731, [1979] 2 All ER 927, [1980] RPC 31, HL.

17 There appears to be little difference in principle between a class of traders who deal in goods originating from a particular manufacturer and bearing his trade mark, whose business and goodwill may suffer from a third person falsely applying the mark to goods not originating from that manufacturer, and a class of traders dealing in goods under a name which describes their geographical origin or qualities. As to the bringing of actions by trade associations see PARA 293 note 5; and as to descriptive and geographical names see PARA 319.

303. 'Reverse' passing off. So-called 'reverse' passing off occurs when a defendant passes off the claimant's goods or services as his own[1]. Such a misrepresentation normally requires more than the mere application of the defendant's trade marks to the claimant's goods, since dealers in the ordinary course of trade apply their marks to goods made by others and merely doing so does not of itself imply that those goods are manufactured by the dealer. Where such a misrepresentation is made, it may be doubtful whether it falls within the scope of the action for passing off, and, if so, it is actionable, if at all, only as a malicious falsehood[2]. A case which at first sight appears to be reverse passing off may, however, in fact be a subtle form of ordinary passing off. This can occur when the defendant represents that goods made by the claimant were made by himself in order to pass off his business as a dealer as a branch of a well known business which manufactures the parts in which he deals[3]. Alternatively, the defendant may represent that some of the claimant's goods are made by himself in order to gain credit for other goods made by himself[4], in effect passing off his own goods as coming from the same manufacturing source as the claimant's goods, even though the claimant's connection with those goods is not known[5]. In such a case the defendant's own activities in showing to his customers the claimant's goods (or photographs of them) may create for the claimant a goodwill which he is entitled to protect as the true, although unidentified, manufacturer of the goods[6].

1 See *Henderson & Son v Munro & Co* (1905) 7 F 636, Ct of Sess (where the issue of a trade circular likely to induce the belief that work in fact done by the plaintiff was done by the defendant was restrained). Reverse passing off may also be committed when the defendant applies a false, descriptive appellation to goods which ought to bear the appellation which the claimant is entitled to protect under the principles laid down in *Erven Warnink BV v J Townend & Sons (Hull) Ltd* [1979] AC 731, [1979] 2 All ER 927, [1980] RPC 31, HL (see PARA 302): see *Matthew Gloag & Son Ltd v Welsh Distillers Ltd* [1998] FSR 718, [1998] ETMR 504 (arguable that Scotch whisky could be passed off as 'Welsh whisky'). As to misrepresentation generally see MISREPRESENTATION.
2 See DEFAMATION vol 32 (2012) PARA 776 et seq.
3 *AGS Manufacturing Co Ltd v Aeroplane General Sundries Co Ltd* (1918) 35 RPC 127, CA (where the defendants advertised that the letters AGS by which the plaintiff's parts were known stood for their own name).
4 Eg by using the claimant's goods as a sample to sell his own goods.
5 See *William Edge & Sons Ltd v William Niccolls & Sons Ltd* [1911] AC 693 at 705, 709, 28 RPC 582 at 594, 596, HL (where the defendants applied a label bearing their name to goods identical in get-up to the plaintiff's goods which were sold with no name on them, causing the public to believe that the defendants were the manufacturers of the goods which had long been on the market and that they had only now disclosed their name). See also *Copydex Ltd v Noso Products Ltd* (1952) 69 RPC 38 (where a rival glue was advertised 'as shown on television', referring to a programme in which the plaintiff's product had been used but the plaintiff's name not mentioned). It is generally not necessary that the identity of the claimant is known in order for him to sustain an action for passing off: see PARA 301.
6 *British Conservatories Ltd v Conservatories Custom Built Ltd* [1989] RPC 455, CA (where the defendant showed to customers photographs of the conservatories in fact built by the claimant, claiming that they were samples of work done by the defendant). For a similar case see *Plomien Fuel Economiser Co Ltd v National School of Salesmanship Ltd* (1943) 60 RPC 209 at 213, CA.

304. Manner in which the misrepresentation may be effected. The misrepresentation in an action for passing off may be effected by an express statement[1], but more commonly it is implied in the defendant's use of a mark, trade name or get-up with which the goods or business of another are associated in the minds of the relevant class of the trade or public[2]. Misrepresentation by the use of similar get-up has a wide ambit, extending sometimes to the shape of goods themselves[3] or to the use of similar decorations for premises[4], similar livery for vehicles and employees[5], similar advertising slogans or themes[6], similar telephone numbers[7] or sound effects[8].

Other ways in which the misrepresentation may be effected are by substituting other goods in response to an order for the claimant's goods in circumstances when it is not obvious to the customer receiving the goods that substitution has taken place[9], or by physically annexing or associating the defendant's goods to or with the claimant's goods[10], or by substituting a service or process employing other materials or machinery in response to a demand for the claimant's service or process[11], or by an agent who has been selling his principal's goods or services introducing new lines of goods or services of his own in such a way as to represent that they are from the same source[12].

Implied misrepresentations may in some circumstances arise simply by customers assuming, in the absence of any indication to the contrary, that goods have passed through the normal channels of trade[13], or that goods are new, unadulterated or unaltered[14].

Where a trader who has made no misrepresentation to his intended customer realises from something the customer said or did that the customer is under a self-induced misapprehension that the trader is, or is connected with, a competitor, failure to correct that misapprehension amounts to misrepresentation[15].

It is important to note that the misrepresentation in an action for passing off may be, and often is, effected indirectly, where the defendant places into the hands of others goods or articles calculated to deceive ultimate purchasers of those goods, even where no misrepresentation is made to the persons with whom the defendant immediately deals[16].

1　Eg a statement that goods are made by a named claimant. As to misrepresentation generally see MISREPRESENTATION.

2　*Birmingham Vinegar Brewery Co Ltd v Powell* [1897] AC 710 at 711–712, 14 RPC 720 at 727–728, HL, per Lord Halsbury LC; *AG Spalding & Bros v AW Gamage Ltd* (1915) 32 RPC 273 at 284, HL, per Lord Parker. Members of the relevant trade or public who are familiar with the claimant's use of a name, mark or get-up will infer from the defendant's use of a name, mark or get-up which is the same or similar that the goods or business concerned are the same or connected, and in this sense the representation is implied rather than express. Since this kind of misrepresentation arises by association with the claimant's mark or other indicium, it is unnecessary that the persons deceived should know the actual identity of the claimant with whose use of the name, mark or get-up they have been familiar: see PARA 283. However, it is necessary to establish that persons who are familiar with the claimant's mark will be deceived: *HFC Bank plc v Midland Bank plc* [2000] FSR 176. See also *Antec International Ltd v South Western Chicks (Warren) Ltd* [1998] FSR 738.

3　As to passing off by similarity of get-up or shape of goods see PARA 321.

4　See *Laraine Day Ltd v Kennedy* (1952) 70 RPC 19.

5　*Knott v Morgan* (1836) 2 Keen 213 (imitation of the green livery and gold hatbands of the plaintiff's omnibus coachmen and conductors restrained); *W and G Du Cros Ltd v Gold* (1912) 30 RPC 117 (get-up of taxis).

6　*Cadbury Schweppes Pty Ltd v Pub Squash Co Pty Ltd* [1981] 1 All ER 213, [1981] 1 WLR 193, [1981] RPC 429, PC.

7　*Law Society of England and Wales v Griffiths* [1995] RPC 16.

8　*BBC v TalkSport Ltd* [2001] FSR 53 (claim that defendant broadcaster was misrepresenting itself as broadcasting 'live' from sports events by use of sound effects compromised on appeal by giving of undertakings).

9　*Bovril Ltd v Bodega Co Ltd* (1916) 33 RPC 153; *Pearson Bros v Valentine & Co* (1917) 34 RPC 267 (where the defendants supplied mackintoshes bearing their own label in response to orders for the plaintiff's mackintoshes and it was held that it was not sufficient to leave it to the customer to examine the goods with care); *Thomas French & Sons Ltd v John Rhind & Sons Ltd* [1958] RPC 82; *Showerings Ltd v Blackpool Tower Co Ltd* [1975] FSR 40 (substitute drinks served in bar); *Havana Cigar and Tobacco Factories Ltd v Oddenino* [1924] 1 Ch 179, 41 RPC 47, CA (where it was held that as 'Corona cigar' had an ambiguous meaning, the defendant was under a duty to inquire whether a purchaser wanted the plaintiffs' cigar or a cigar of corona type). See also *Showerings Ltd v Entam Ltd* [1975] FSR 45. Where it is immediately obvious to the customer on receipt of a product that a substitution has occurred, it seems that there is no passing off as the necessary element of misrepresentation is not present, whatever may be the contractual remedies as between customer and supplier: *Lever Bros Ltd v Masbro' Equitable Pioneers Society Ltd* (1912) 29 RPC 225 at 232–233, CA, per Fletcher Moulton LJ; cf *Purefoy Engineering Co Ltd v Sykes Boxall & Co Ltd* (1955) 72 RPC 89 at 93, CA (where it appears to be suggested that it would have made no difference if catalogues accompanying parts supplied in response to orders for the plaintiff's part numbers had made it clear that the parts were not the plaintiffs' because the damage to the plaintiffs would by then have been done). It is, however, hard to see what, if any, misrepresentation is involved and therefore what the cause of action is, even if the claimants suffer damage.

10 *Illustrated Newspapers Ltd v Publicity Services (London) Ltd* [1938] Ch 414, [1938] 1 All ER 321, 55 RPC 172; *Mail Newspapers plc v Insert Media Ltd* [1987] RPC 521 (both cases where the defendant's advertising supplement was inserted into the plaintiff's magazines); *Morny Ltd v Ball and Rogers (1975) Ltd* [1978] FSR 91 (where other goods were included in a gift package with the plaintiff's goods).

11 *Sales Affiliates Ltd v Le Jean Ltd* [1947] Ch 295, [1947] 1 All ER 287, 64 RPC 103 (hair-waving process).

12 *International Scientific Communications Inc v Pattison* [1979] FSR 429.

13 *Sony KK v Saray Electronics (London) Ltd* [1983] FSR 302, CA. See also *Seiko Time Canada Ltd v Consumers Distributing Co Ltd* (1980) 112 DLR (3d) 500. The sale of the goods of a particular manufacturer does not, however, of itself normally carry with it a representation that the goods have passed through a particular trade channel, such as a sole distributor: *Dental Manufacturing Co Ltd v C De Trey & Co* [1912] 3 KB 76 at 87, 29 RPC 617 at 625, CA, per Fletcher Moulton LJ.

14 See the cases cited in the notes to PARA 300.

15 *British Sky Broadcasting Group plc v Sky Home Services Ltd* [2006] EWHC 3165 (Ch), [2007] 3 All ER 1066, [2007] FSR 321.

16 See PARA 314.

305.   Misrepresentation must be material.   The misrepresentation must be material, in the sense of being likely to influence the actions of the persons to whom it is made[1]. A misrepresentation as to the origin of goods is generally sufficient even though the defendant's goods are not in fact inferior to the claimant's[2]. A mere representation that the claimant sponsors or financially supports the defendant, without any belief by the public that it can rely on quality control exercised by the claimant, is not material[3]. On the other hand, a misrepresentation that a celebrity has endorsed or authorised the defendant's goods or services is actionable[4].

1 *Reckitt & Colman Products Ltd v Borden Inc* [1990] 1 All ER 873 at 889, [1990] 1 WLR 491 at 510, [1990] RPC 341 at 417, HL, per Lord Jauncey of Tullichettle ('Jif Lemon'); *Hodgkinson and Corby Ltd v Wards Mobility Services Ltd* [1994] 1 WLR 1564, [1995] FSR 169. Any confusion must be more than momentary and inconsequential: *Clark v Associated Newspapers Ltd* [1998] 1 All ER 959 at 966, [1998] RPC 261 at 271 per Lightman J; *HFC Bank plc v Midland Bank plc* [2000] FSR 176. A misrepresentation may be actionable even though the customer has ceased to be misled by the time that the transaction is concluded (so called 'initial interest confusion'): *Och-Ziff Management Europe Ltd v Och Capital LLP* [2010] EWHC 2599 (Ch), [2011] Bus LR 632, [2011] FSR 289. As to the nature of the misrepresentation see PARA 300; and as to the persons to whom it is made see PARA 308. As to misrepresentation generally see MISREPRESENTATION.

2 *Singer Manufacturing Co v Loog* (1882) 8 App Cas 15 at 29–30, HL, per Lord Blackburn. This has been justified on the basis that the customer is likely to rely upon the assurance of quality given to him by the claimant's connection with the goods.

3 *Harrods Ltd v Harrodian School Ltd* [1996] RPC 697, CA; and see also *Tavener Rutledge Ltd v Trexapalm Ltd* [1977] RPC 275 at 280 per Walton J.

4   *Irvine v TalkSport Ltd* [2002] EWHC 367 (Ch), [2002] 2 All ER 414, [2002] EMLR 679 (affd [2003] EWCA Civ 423, [2003] 2 All ER 881, [2003] EMLR 538); *Fenty v Arcadia Group Brands Ltd* [2013] EWHC 2310 (Ch), [2013] All ER (D) 410 (Jul). As to merchandising of names generally see PARA 323.

306. Misrepresentation is an essential element. The existence of a misrepresentation is an essential element of the action for passing off, so that activities which in some sense can be regarded as taking advantage of the claimant's trading reputation and goodwill, such as copying the claimant's goods of a novel character[1] or copying his novel system of advertising[2], or selling goods or services by reference to him or his goods or services by saying that they are similar or a substitute for them[3], or an accessory to be used in conjunction with them[4], are not actionable in English law in the absence of a misrepresentation, even if such conduct might in other jurisdictions be actionable as unfair competition[5].

Representations to the effect that the defendant's goods or services are equivalent to or a substitute for the claimant's are often made, not expressly, but by the adoption of a similar get-up[6] or similar advertising methods or slogans[7], and this is not actionable so long as the goods are sufficiently distinguished by other means.

The use of a similar name or get-up in order to satirise or disparage the claimant or his goods or business is not actionable as passing off[8] in the absence of a misrepresentation that the defendant's goods or business are those of the claimant even if such conduct is likely to be damaging or hurtful to the claimant[9].

1   *Hodgkinson and Corby Ltd v Wards Mobility Services Ltd* [1994] 1 WLR 1564, [1995] FSR 169 (there is no tort of copying, nor of taking a rival's market or customers, neither being susceptible of ownership). As to misrepresentation generally see MISREPRESENTATION.
2   *Wertheimer v Stewart, Cooper & Co* (1906) 23 RPC 481.
3   *Leather Cloth Co Ltd v American Leather Cloth Co Ltd* (1865) 11 HL Cas 523 at 540–541; *Singer Manufacturing Co v Loog* (1882) 8 App Cas 15, HL ('Singer system' sewing machines); *Apollinaris Co Ltd v Duckworth & Co* (1906) 23 RPC 540, CA (salts for making up simulated mineral waters).
4   *GH Gledhill & Sons Ltd v British Perforated Toilet Paper Co* (1911) 28 RPC 429; on appeal 28 RPC 714, CA.
5   See *Cadbury Schweppes Pty Ltd v Pub Squash Co Pty Ltd* [1981] 1 All ER 213, [1981] 1 WLR 193, [1981] RPC 429, PC; *L'Oreal SA v Bellure NV* [2007] EWCA Civ 936, [2008] FSR 208, [2007] All ER (D) 122 (Oct), CA; but cf *Arsenal Football Club plc v Reed* [2003] EWCA Civ 696 at [70]–[71], [2003] 3 All ER 865 at [70]–[71], [2003] RPC 696 at [70]–[71] per Aldous LJ (obiter).
6   See *Fisons Ltd v EJ Godwin (Peat Industries) Ltd* [1976] RPC 653; *Tetrosyl Ltd v Silver Paint & Lacquer Co Ltd* [1980] FSR 68, CA.
7   *Cadbury Schweppes Pty Ltd v Pub Squash Co Pty Ltd* [1981] 1 All ER 213, [1981] 1 WLR 193, [1981] RPC 429, PC.
8   In some circumstances this may be actionable as a trade libel, or, if defamatory, as libel or slander: see DEFAMATION vol 32 (2012) PARAS 555, 776 et seq.
9   *Miss World (Jersey) Ltd v James Street Productions Ltd* [1981] FSR 309, CA ('Miss Alternative World' ugliness competition); cf *New Zealand Olympic and Commonwealth Games Association Inc v Telecom New Zealand Ltd* [1996] FSR 757, NZ HC (defendant's advertisement contained a play on the Olympic symbol). As to the protection of the Olympic symbol in the United Kingdom see PARA 472.

307. Confusion without any misrepresentation. An actionable misrepresentation normally entails confusion or the likelihood of confusion on the part of a relevant section of the trade or public[1]. The existence of such confusion arising from the defendant's activities does not, however, necessarily mean that there is an actionable misrepresentation[2]. For example, when a new retail shop is set up close to an existing shop in the same line of business, some confusion is likely to be caused by that very fact, but confusion arising from that cause alone is to be disregarded for the purpose of determining whether there is a misrepresentation[3]. Similarly, where the public is familiar with the claimant's goods or services of a particular kind, substantial numbers of persons may assume that competing goods or services offered by a newcomer are the goods or services of the claimant with whom they have hitherto been familiar, but confusion arising merely from this cause is to be disregarded[4]. Cases of this kind often arise when the claimant has been the first to introduce to the market goods or services of a novel character[5]. In such circumstances the claimant may have used and adopted words descriptive of his goods or services which, while he is the sole manufacturer or supplier, must necessarily denote these goods or services, but this of itself does not make the defendant's use of the words in a descriptive manner a misrepresentation even if a degree of confusion results[6]. It may be necessary to distinguish confusion which arises because the defendant adopts utilitarian features of the claimant's goods or services, as opposed to features which are a capricious addition to the article concerned[7], although there is no absolute rule that a claimant cannot rely on confusion arising from the adoption of utilitarian features if he can discharge the heavy factual burden of showing that the public regards those features as an indication of trade origin and is moved to purchase the defendant's goods because of the erroneous belief engendered by the defendant's adoption of those features[8]. Confusion can also arise, without there being a misrepresentation, where a defendant has a special right to use a name either by reason of its being his own name[9] or by reason of established concurrent use[10]. In cases of this kind the courts have proceeded on the basis that the defendant is doing no more than making a truthful statement of fact which he has a legitimate interest in making[11], and the fact that it is misapprehended by some persons is not the defendant's responsibility unless he does something additional to increase the risk of confusion[12]; but these cases have been explained on the basis that there is a misrepresentation but the defendant has a special privilege to make it[13].

1   As to the elements of the action for passing off see PARA 287. As to misrepresentation generally see MISREPRESENTATION.
2   See *My Kinda Town Ltd v Soll* [1983] RPC 407 at 418, CA, per Oliver LJ; *Barnsley Brewery Co Ltd v RBNB* [1997] FSR 462 at 467 per Robert Walker J; *HFC Bank plc v Midland Bank plc* [2000] FSR 176 at 182–183, 201 per Lloyd J; *Premier Luggage & Bags Ltd v Premier Company (UK) Ltd* [2002] EWCA Civ 387 at [37], [2003] FSR 69 at [37] per Chadwick LJ. The distinction between confusion and deception is elusive: *Reed Executive plc v Reed Business Information Ltd* [2004] EWCA Civ 159 at [91], [111], [2004] RPC 767 at [91], [111], [2004] IP & T 1049 at [91], [111] per Jacob LJ. The difference is that deception is really likely to damage the claimant's goodwill: *Phones 4U Ltd v Phone4u.co.uk Internet Ltd* [2006] EWCA Civ 244 at [19], [2007] RPC 83 at [19] per Jacob LJ.
3   *Laraine Day Ltd v Kennedy* (1952) 70 RPC 19 at 22.
4   *Jones Bros Ltd v Anglo-American Optical Co* (1912) 24 RPC 361 at 369, CA (where Fletcher Moulton LJ said that to establish a misrepresentation it must be shown that some aspect of the name, style, get-up etc adopted by the defendant, over and above the mere similarity of the goods, is likely to influence purchasers). See, however, *Reckitt & Colman Products Ltd v Borden Inc* [1990] 1 All ER 873, [1990] 1 WLR 491, [1990] RPC 341, HL ('Jif Lemon') (where it was considered that the fact that the plaintiff had enjoyed a de facto monopoly for many years in small lemon-shaped containers for lemon juice imposed a greater duty on newcomers to that market to take steps to distinguish their goods from those of the plaintiff); *British Sky Broadcasting Group plc v Sky Home Services Ltd* [2006] EWHC 3165 (Ch), [2007] 3 All ER 1066, [2007] FSR 321 (which held that where a de facto monopoly existed the competitor was not subjected to a free-standing duty to distinguish his product from any connection with the

monopoly, but he was obliged to take such care as would prevent his chosen marketing method from conveying a misrepresentation to the effect that there was such a connection). As to passing off by similarity of get-up or of the articles themselves see PARA 321.

5   See *Compatibility Research Ltd v Computer Psyche Co Ltd* [1967] RPC 201 at 206 (a case which concerned a computer dating bureau, where Stamp J said that a trader who sets up a new trade has no monopoly of that trade or of the manner of carrying it on, and he cannot stop a rival trader copying his ideas, notwithstanding that confusion will be caused); *My Kinda Town Ltd v Soll* [1983] RPC 407, CA.

6   See *Cellular Clothing Co Ltd v Maxton and Murray* [1899] AC 326, HL; *British Vacuum Cleaner Co Ltd v New Vacuum Cleaner Co Ltd* [1907] 2 Ch 312, 24 RPC 641; *My Kinda Town Ltd v Soll* [1983] RPC 407 at 420, CA, per Oliver LJ. As to special considerations applying where what is complained of is the use of descriptive words, or words which a claimant has invented as a name for a new product or service, see PARA 320.

7   *JB Williams Co v H Bronnley & Co Ltd* (1909) 26 RPC 765 at 773, CA, per Fletcher Moulton LJ. Such an addition is much more likely to be taken and relied upon as a badge of trade origin than is a utilitarian feature.

8   *Reckitt & Colman Products Ltd v Borden Inc* [1990] 1 All ER 873, [1990] 1 WLR 491, [1990] RPC 341, HL ('Jif Lemon'); *Hodgkinson and Corby Ltd v Wards Mobility Services Ltd* [1994] 1 WLR 1564, [1995] FSR 169.

9   *Turton v Turton* (1889) 42 ChD 128, CA. As to the right of a person to make use of his own name see PARA 326.

10 *Habib Bank Ltd v Habib Bank AG Zurich* [1981] 2 All ER 650, [1981] 1 WLR 1265, [1982] RPC 1, CA. As to concurrent use see PARA 328.

11 Eg that a man named John Turton is carrying on business with his two sons as partners: see *Turton v Turton* (1889) 42 ChD 128 at 135 per Lord Esher MR.

12 *Marengo v Daily Sketch and Daily Graphic Ltd* (1946) [1992] FSR 1 at 2, CA, per Lord Greene MR ('No one is entitled to be protected against confusion as such. Confusion may result from one collision of two independent rights or liberties, and where this is the case, neither party can complain; they must put up with the results of the confusion as one of the misfortunes which occur in life'); revsd on the facts sub nom *Marengo v Daily Sketch and Sunday Graphic Ltd* [1948] 1 All ER 406, 65 RPC 242, HL. However, once a substantial number of people are misled there is passing off: *Reed Executive plc v Reed Business Information Ltd* [2004] EWCA Civ 159 at [111], [2004] RPC 767 at [111], [2004] IP & T 1049 at [111] per Jacob LJ.

13 See *Joseph Rodgers & Sons Ltd v WN Rodgers & Co* (1924) 41 RPC 277 at 291 per Romer J. Cf *Phones 4U Ltd v Phone4u.co.uk Internet Ltd* [2006] EWCA Civ 244 at [21], [2007] RPC 83 at [21] per Jacob LJ (referring to cases of honest concurrent use and very descriptive marks as not being cases of mere confusion but rather 'cases of tolerated deception or a tolerated level of deception').

308.   Persons to whom the misrepresentation is made.

Normally the misrepresentation in an action for passing off is made to customers of the claimant or to ultimate consumers of goods or services supplied by him[1]. The misrepresentation may, however, be made to other persons, such as other members of the trade or the claimant's suppliers[2]. For example, the defendant's financial failure or bad behaviour as a customer might cause damage to the claimant's credit and reputation among his suppliers if the defendant were thought to be associated with him[3].

1   Consumers of the claimant's services may comprise more than one category of person: *Fine & Country Ltd v Okotoks Ltd* [2013] EWCA Civ 672, [2013] All ER (D) 137 (Jun) (consumers of estate agency services included buyers as well as sellers of houses). As to the elements of the action for passing of see PARA 287. As to misrepresentation generally see MISREPRESENTATION.

2   *Chelsea Man Menswear Ltd v Chelsea Girl Ltd* [1987] RPC 189 at 206, CA (expressly rejecting the argument that the reference to customers in the formulation (now superseded) of the requirements of passing off in *Erven Warnink BV v J Townend & Sons (Hull) Ltd* [1979] AC 731, [1979] 2 All ER 927, [1980] RPC 31, HL (see PARA 287) should be read literally as excluding from the ambit of the action cases of misrepresentations to suppliers). See also *R and J Pullman Ltd v Pullman* (1919) 36 RPC 240; *FW Woolworth & Co Ltd v Woolworths (Australasia) Ltd* (1930) 47 RPC 337; *Brestian v Try* [1958] RPC 161, CA.

3   See *JC Penney Co Inc v Penneys Ltd* [1979] FSR 29 (Hong Kong), in which it appears that
     R and J Pullman Ltd v Pullman (1919) 36 RPC 240 and *FW Woolworth & Co Ltd v
     Woolworths (Australasia) Ltd* (1930) 47 RPC 337 were not cited. There seems to be no reason
     in principle why misrepresentations to bankers, investors etc which have the effect of damaging
     the claimant's trading reputation and credit amongst them should not equally be actionable.

309. Establishing misrepresentation. To establish a likelihood of deception in
an action for passing off where there has been no misrepresentation[1] generally
requires the presence of two factual elements:

(1)   that a name, mark or other distinctive indicium used by the claimant has
       acquired a reputation[2] among a relevant class of persons; and

(2)   that members of that class will mistakenly infer from the defendant's use
       of a name, mark or other indicium which is the same or sufficiently
       similar that the defendant's goods or business are from the same source[3]
       or are connected.

While it is helpful to think of these two factual elements as two successive
hurdles which the claimant must surmount, consideration of these two aspects
cannot be completely separated from each other[4].

The question whether deception is likely is one for the court[5], which will have
regard to:

(a)   the nature and extent of the reputation relied upon[6];

(b)   the closeness or otherwise of the respective fields of activity in which the
       claimant and the defendant carry on business[7];

(c)   the similarity of the mark, name etc used by the defendant to that of the
       claimant[8];

(d)   the manner in which the defendant makes use of the name, mark etc
       complained of and collateral factors[9]; and

(e)   the manner in which the particular trade is carried on, the class of
       persons who it is alleged is likely to be deceived and all other
       surrounding circumstances[10].

In assessing whether deception is likely, the court attaches importance to the
question whether the defendant can be shown to have acted with a fraudulent
intent, although a fraudulent intent is not a necessary part of the cause of
action[11].

The evidence which is admissible on the question of likelihood of deception,
and the way in which the court assesses it, including the significance to be
attached to the presence or absence of actual instances of deception, are
discussed elsewhere in this title in relation to both passing off and infringement
of trade marks[12].

1   Eg an express statement that the defendant's goods or services are goods or services of the
     claimant: see PARA 304. As to misrepresentation as an essential element of the action see PARA
     306. As to misrepresentation generally see MISREPRESENTATION.

2   See *Tavener Rutledge Ltd v Specters Ltd* [1959] RPC 355 at 362, CA, per Lord Evershed MR,
     and at 364 per Harman LJ.

3   This will be the inference drawn in the classic case of a defendant passing off his goods or
     business as the claimant's; the nature of the inference drawn will vary depending upon which of
     the many different forms of passing off is occurring: see PARA 300.

4   *Magnolia Metal Co v Tandem Smelting Syndicate Ltd* (1900) 17 RPC 477 at 486, HL, per
     Lord Halsbury.

5   See PARA 413.

6   See PARA 310.

7   See PARA 311.

8   The factors to be taken into account in assessing whether or not names, marks etc are
     deceptively similar for the purposes of passing off are similar to those to be taken into account

in assessing the likelihood of confusion in registered trade mark actions (see PARA 58): see *Reed Executive plc v Reed Business Information Ltd* [2004] EWCA Civ 159 at [78]–[79], [2004] RPC 767 at [78]–[79], [2004] IP & T 1049 at [78]–[79] per Jacob LJ. In particular, it is equally relevant in passing off cases to consider the visual, aural and conceptual similarities between the respective names or marks and the possibility of imperfect recollection. Care should, however, be taken when applying registered trade mark cases in actions for passing off, because in trade mark actions the question to be decided is the narrower and more artificial one of whether the defendant's mark is confusingly similar to the registered mark, and some factors are not relevant which are relevant in actions for passing off, e g factors which are collateral to the defendant's use of the mark complained of. Equally the principle developed by the European Court of Justice that trade marks with a highly distinctive character are entitled to broader protection does not apply to passing off, although there is some truth in the opposite proposition: *Reed Executive plc v Reed Business Information Ltd* [2004] EWCA Civ 159 at [83]–[86], [2004] RPC 767 at [83]–[86], [2004] IP & T 1049 at [83]–[86] per Jacob LJ. See also *Interflora Inc v Marks and Spencer plc* [2013] EWCA Civ 319 at [26]–[34], [2013] All ER (D) 14 (Apr) at [26]–[34] per Lewison LJ; and *Fine & Country Ltd v Okotoks Ltd* [2013] EWCA Civ 672 at [72] and [82], [2013] All ER (D) 137 (Jun) at [72] and [82] per Lewison LJ.

9   Eg the similarity or dissimilarity of get-up or secondary indicia, such as label wordings or business addresses, or the use of express words of disclaimer sufficient to prevent deception which might otherwise arise.

10   See PARA 312.

11   See PARA 313.

12   See PARA 412 et seq.

310. Reputation as an element of establishing deception.

Normally the reputation required to be established by the claimant in an action for passing off is that the name, mark or other indicium has by use come to be regarded as identifying goods or services from a particular source known or unknown[1], or, where there is passing off of a product which has a character intrinsic to its descriptive name, as denoting goods or services of a particular composition, standard, quality or geographical origin[2]. The fact that only the claimant has in the past made use of the name, mark or other feature concerned is not conclusive that it has come to be regarded as distinctive[3], but distinctiveness will readily be inferred when the name, mark or other feature is invented or fancy and has no direct relation to the character or quality of the goods[4].

1   *T Oertli AG v EJ Bowman (London) Ltd* [1959] RPC 1 at 4, HL, per Viscount Simonds. As to misrepresentation generally see MISREPRESENTATION.

2   In this type of passing off the name or mark denotes not the goods or services of a particular person but goods or services of a particular standard or quality (e g advocaat or champagne): see PARA 302.

3   *Payton & Co Ltd v Snelling, Lampard & Co Ltd* (1899) 17 RPC 48, CA (affd [1901] AC 308, 17 RPC 628, HL); *White, Tomkins and Courage Ltd v United Confectionery Co Ltd* (1914) 31 RPC 286.

4   *Cellular Clothing Co Ltd v Maxton and Murray* [1899] AC 326 at 339, 16 RPC 397 at 406–407, HL, per Lord Shand. Special considerations apply when a claimant seeks to prove that he has established a reputation in words which are recognised as descriptive of his goods or services: see PARA 319.

311. Common field of activity and likelihood of deception.

It is not a requirement for success in a passing off action that the claimant and the defendant be engaged in a common field of activity[1]. The presence or absence of a common field of activity in which the claimant and the defendant are engaged is a factor to be taken into account in considering whether it is likely that persons coming across the defendant's use of the name, mark etc complained of will assume[2] that he and the claimant are connected[3]. Such a factor may also be significant in deciding, even assuming that a misrepresentation is established, whether the claimant is likely to suffer any substantial damage as a result of the defendant's activities[4].

Where the defendant's activities, although not in an area of business in which the claimant is engaged, are in an area of business which might be assumed to be a natural extension of the claimant's business, likelihood of deception will readily be inferred[5]. However, even where the fields of activity in which the claimant and the defendant are engaged are remote from each other, it is possible for deception to occur if the name or mark used is highly distinctive[6], or if the claimant's mark or name is well known and is closely copied with regard to style, lettering etc[7].

Deception may also occur where the defendant falsely represents that a celebrity has endorsed his goods or services even if the goods and services are remote from the celebrity's field of endeavour[8].

1   *Harrods Ltd v Harrodian School Ltd* [1996] RPC 697 at 714, CA, per Millet LJ (disapproving *McCulloch v May* (1948) 65 RPC 58); *Irvine v TalkSport Ltd* [2002] EWHC 367 (Ch) at [24]–[29], [2002] 2 All ER 414 at [24]–[29], [2002] EMLR 679 at [24]–[29] per Laddie J (affd [2003] EWCA Civ 423, [2003] 2 All ER 881, [2003] EMLR 538).

2   As to this implied misrepresentation see PARA 304; and as to misrepresentation as an essential element of the action for passing off see PARA 306.

3   *Annabel's (Berkeley Square) Ltd v Schock (t/a Annabel's Escort Agency)* [1972] RPC 838 at 844, CA, per Russell LJ; *Harrods Ltd v Harrodian School Ltd* [1996] RPC 697 at 714, CA, per Millet LJ.

4   As to a common field of activity and damage see PARA 317.

5   *Dunlop Pneumatic Tyre Co Ltd v Dunlop Lubricant Co* (1898) 16 RPC 12 at 15; *Ames Crosta Ltd v Pionex International Ltd* [1977] FSR 46; *NAD Electronics Inc v NAD Computer Systems Ltd* [1997] FSR 380.

6   *Lego System A/S v Lego M Lemelstrich Ltd* [1983] FSR 155 (garden sprinklers sold under the same name as well known toy bricks).

7   *Walter v Ashton* [1902] 2 Ch 282 (bicycle shop passed off as being a branch of 'The Times' newspaper).

8   *Irvine v TalkSport Ltd* [2002] EWHC 367 (Ch), [2002] 2 All ER 414, [2002] EMLR 679 (affd [2003] EWCA Civ 423, [2003] 2 All ER 881, [2003] EMLR 538).

312.   Factors and circumstances to be considered in assessing the likelihood of deception. In deciding whether deception sufficient to sustain an action for passing off[1] has occurred or is likely, all the circumstances must be considered[2]. The degree of similarity of the name, mark or other feature concerned[3] is important but not necessarily decisive, so that an action for infringement of a registered trade mark may succeed on the same facts where an action for passing off fails[4] or vice versa[5]. The circumstances in which the defendant's name, mark or get-up is likely to come to the attention of persons who might be confused must be considered, so that in sales to retail customers it is relevant to take into account that the customer does not always have the opportunity of carefully examining the goods and may not be able to see the claimant's and defendant's goods side by side[6] and may in any case have an imperfect recollection of the claimant's goods or mark[7]. Trade customers may be less susceptible to deception than retail customers, so that the use of marks or names in advertisements or circulars, or in relation to goods or services, directed to the trade may create no danger of deception even though retail customers would be deceived if the marks or names were used in advertisements to them or attached to goods so as to come to their attention[8]. The fact that the persons who might be deceived are illiterate, badly educated or unable to understand the language or script in which distinguishing words or names are written is to be taken into account as potentially increasing the likelihood of deception[9].

For a misrepresentation to be established, it is generally not essential to show that all members of the relevant class of persons will be deceived, but merely that a majority[10] or a substantial proportion[11] is likely to be. It is not sufficient, however, that only careless or indifferent persons[12], or ignorant persons with little or no knowledge of the trade concerned[13], are likely to be deceived, nor is it sufficient to show that persons will be deceived who have such an imperfect or insufficient recollection of the claimant's mark that they cannot fairly be said to fall within the class of persons amongst whom the claimant has goodwill[14].

1 As to the requirement that the claimant must suffer damage see PARAS 316–318.

2 *Burberrys v JC Cording & Co Ltd* (1909) 26 RPC 693 at 701 per Parker J.

3 As to factors to be taken into account in assessing the similarity of marks, names etc see PARA 309 note 8.

4 *Saville Perfumery Ltd v June Perfect Ltd and FW Woolworth & Co Ltd* (1941) 58 RPC 147 at 174, HL (decided under the Trade Marks Act 1938, but the position is likely to be the same under the Trade Marks Act 1994). This is because the question to be decided on infringement of registered trade marks is the rather narrower and more artificial question of whether the defendant's mark is confusingly similar to the registered mark. Some factors which are relevant in an action for passing off, eg that the defendant is using the mark in conjunction with other matter which makes confusion either more or less likely, are not relevant to infringement of registered trade marks. As to the infringement of registered trade marks see PARA 66 et seq.

5 *Re Joule's Trade Marks, Thompson v Montgomery* (1889) 41 ChD 35, 6 RPC 404, CA (affd [1891] AC 217, 8 RPC 361, HL). See eg *United Biscuits (UK) Ltd v Asda Stores Ltd* [1997] RPC 513 (where passing off was established, but trade mark infringement was not proved because the appropriate comparison was with the trade mark as registered, and not with the mark in actual use). See also the examples given in *Phones 4U Ltd v Phone4u.co.uk Internet Ltd* [2006] EWCA Civ 244 at [25], [2007] RPC 83 at [25] per Jacob LJ.

6 *Packham & Co Ltd v Sturgess & Co* (1898) 15 RPC 669 at 673, CA, per Chitty LJ.

7 *Seixo v Provezende* (1866) 1 Ch App 192; *Thomas Hubbuck & Son Ltd v William Brown Sons & Co* (1900) 17 RPC 638 at 645, CA; *Wright, Crossley & Co v Blezard* (1910) 27 RPC 299; *Ravenhead Brick Co Ltd v Ruabon Brick and Terra Cotta Co Ltd* (1937) 54 RPC 341 at 349 per Simonds J. It is possible to carry the doctrine of imperfect recollection too far: *Chappie Ltd v Spratt's Patent Ltd* (1954) 71 RPC 455. The fact that the products are sold in different industries or market segments will reduce the likelihood of deception: *Lumos Skincare Ltd v Sweet Squared Ltd* [2012] EWPCC 22, [2012] All ER (D) 265 (May); revsd [2013] EWCA Civ 590, [2013] All ER (D) 42 (Jun) (sufficient for claimant to show the likelihood of deception by inference).

8 *Ford v Foster* (1872) 7 Ch App 611 at 627 per James LJ; *Singer Manufacturing Co v Loog* (1882) 8 App Cas 15 at 20, HL, per Lord Selborne LC; *Star Cycle Co Ltd v Frankenburgs* (1907) 24 RPC 405, CA; *Claudius Ash Son & Co Ltd v Invicta Manufacturing Co Ltd* (1912) 29 RPC 465, HL.

9 *R Johnston & Co v Archibald Orr Ewing & Co* (1882) 7 App Cas 219, HL; *Wilkinson v Griffith* (1891) 8 RPC 370; *Saville Perfumery Ltd v June Perfect Ltd and FW Woolworth & Co Ltd* (1941) 58 RPC 147 at 176, HL. See also *Topps Co Inc v Top Hannah Agencies Ltd* (2000) Times, 14 February, where the Court of Session suggested that where goods were sold to children the impression on a child had to be considered.

10 *Havana Cigar and Tobacco Factories Ltd v Oddenino* [1924] 1 Ch 179, 41 RPC 47, CA.

11 *Saville Perfumery Ltd v June Perfect Ltd and FW Woolworth & Co Ltd* (1941) 58 RPC 147 at 176, HL; *Neutrogena Corpn v Golden Ltd* [1996] RPC 473 at 493–494, CA, per Morritt LJ; *Clark v Associated Newspapers Ltd* [1998] 1 All ER 959 at 966, [1998] RPC 261 at 271 per Lightman J. See also *Singer Manufacturing Co v Loog* (1882) 8 App Cas 15 at 18, HL (where Lord Selborne LC said that the imitation of another's trade mark, in a manner liable to mislead the unwary, cannot be justified by showing either that the device or inscription upon the imitated mark is ambiguous and capable of being understood by different persons in different ways, or that a person who carefully and intelligently examined and studied it might not be misled).

12 *Norman Kark Publications Ltd v Odhams Press Ltd* [1962] 1 All ER 636, [1962] 1 WLR 380, [1962] RPC 163; *Morning Star Co-operative Society Ltd v Express Newspapers Ltd* [1979] FSR 113 at 117 (where Foster J said that the two newspapers were so different that only 'a moron in a hurry' would be misled).

13 *Payton & Co Ltd v Snelling, Lampard & Co Ltd* (1899) 17 RPC 48 at 57 per Romer LJ (affd
    [1901] AC 308, 17 RPC 628, HL) (where the customers confused were those who had no
    knowledge of the characteristics of coffee tins which were in fact common to the trade);
    Starbucks (HK) Ltd v British Sky Broadcasting Group plc [2012] EWHC 3074 (Ch), [2013] IP
    & T 251, [2012] All ER (D) 36 (Nov) (affd [2013] EWCA Civ 1465, [2013] All ER (D) 214
    (Nov)).

14 *HFC Bank plc v HSBC Bank plc (formerly Midland Bank plc)* [2000] FSR 176 (where it was
    considered essential that the claimant should demonstrate that it had achieved 'brand name
    recognition' to show it had goodwill, and the relevant test of deception related to its customers
    as regards whom it had achieved such recognition).

313. Effect of fraudulent intention. Although proof of a fraudulent intention
on the defendant's part is not a necessary element of the cause of action for
passing off[1], a fraudulent intention, if established, is a fact from which the court
will readily infer that the defendant has succeeded in achieving his object of
inducing deception[2]; but an intention to deceive is not conclusive that deception
is in fact likely to occur[3]. Where a fraudulent intention is relied upon by the
claimant, it must be pleaded expressly and proved by evidence[4]. Differing views
have been expressed as to the relevance of a conscious decision on the part of the
defendant to live dangerously if there is no fraudulent intention[5].

Some of the commonest ways in which a fraudulent intention on the
defendant's part may be inferred are from the lack of any adequate explanation
or convincing reason for the adoption by the defendant of the name, mark or
other indicium in question[6], and from such matters as the garnishing of the
defendant's name so as to increase the chance that it will be mistaken for the
claimant's name[7], the adoption of laudatory epithets which are used by the
claimant but which are incorrect when used to describe the defendant's goods or
services[8], a false representation that a business is long-established in a way likely
to lead persons to connect that business with the claimant's longer established
business[9], a false representation that the defendant has an office in a place where
the claimant has one[10], the adoption of the claimant's advertising slogans[11], or
the deliberate imitation of the claimant's trade forms[12] or get-up[13]. A request for
an excessively large sum of money to desist may be regarded as evidence of a
fraudulent intention[14]. An inference of fraudulent intention can also be drawn
from the employment in a nominal capacity of a person with a particular
surname in order to make use of his name in the business or the purported
purchase or licensing from such a person of a right to make use of his name
when he has no genuine business goodwill to convey[15].

1 This is true at least of the cause of action in equity. As to the history of the distinction between
   passing off as a cause of action at common law and in equity see PARA 288.

2 *Slazenger & Sons v Feltham & Co* (1889) 6 RPC 531 at 538, CA (where Lindley LJ said 'Why
   should we be astute to say that the defendant cannot succeed in doing that which he is straining
   every nerve to do?'); *Payton & Co Ltd v Snelling, Lampard & Co Ltd* (1899) 17 RPC 48 at
   56, CA (affd [1901] AC 308, 17 RPC 628, HL) (where Romer LJ said 'you may well infer ...
   that a man who was going to do a scoundrelly action for his own benefit would take care to do
   it effectually'); *Office Cleaning Services Ltd v Westminster Window and General Cleaners Ltd*
   (1946) 63 RPC 39 at 42, HL (where Lord Simonds said 'But if the intention to deceive is found,
   it will be readily inferred that deception will result. Who knows better than the trader the
   mysteries of his trade?'). See also *A & E Television Networks LLC v Discovery
   Communications Europe Ltd* [2013] EWHC 109 (Ch), [2013] All ER (D) 03 (Feb), where
   Office Cleaning Services Ltd v Westminster Window and General Cleaners Ltd above was
   applied.
      To be relevant the intention must, however, be to mislead. A mere underestimate of a degree
   of initial confusion is not enough: *Reckitt & Colman Products Ltd v Borden Inc* [1990] RPC

341   at 385–389, CA, per Slade LJ (the point not being argued in the subsequent appeal to the
      House of Lords: see *Reckitt & Colman Products Ltd v Borden Inc* [1990] 1 All ER 873, [1990]
      1 WLR 491, HL).
3   *Claudius Ash Son & Co Ltd v Invicta Manufacturing Co Ltd* (1912) 29 RPC 465 at 475, HL,
      per Lord Loreburn LC.
4   *Claudius Ash Son & Co Ltd v Invicta Manufacturing Co Ltd* (1912) 29 RPC 465 at 475, HL,
      per Lord Loreburn LC.
5   In *United Biscuits (UK) Ltd v Asda Stores Ltd* [1997] RPC 513 at 530 Robert Walker J said that
      'the court was not bound to disregard' 'a conscious decision to live dangerously'. See also *HP
      Bulmer Ltd v J Bollinger SA* [1978] RPC 79 at 122, CA, per Goff LJ; *Sodastream Ltd v Thorn
      Cascade Co Ltd* [1982] RPC 459 at 466, CA, per Kerr LJ; *Harrods Ltd v Harrodian School Ltd*
      [1996] RPC 697 at 706, CA, per Millett LJ. In *Specsavers International Healthcare Ltd v Asda
      Stores Ltd* [2012] EWCA Civ 24, [2012] FSR 555 at [115] Kitchin LJ said that 'it is important
      to distinguish between a defendant who takes a conscious decision to live dangerously and one
      who intends to cause deception' (but *HP Bulmer Ltd v J Bollinger SA* above, *Sodastream Ltd v
      Thorn Cascade Co Ltd* above and *Harrods Ltd v Harrodian School Ltd* above were not cited).
6   *Poiret v Jules Poiret Ltd and Nash* (1920) 37 RPC 177.
7   *Turton v Turton* (1889) 42 ChD 128 at 134, CA.
8   *Mappin and Webb Ltd v Leapman* (1905) 22 RPC 398; *Joseph Rodgers & Sons Ltd v
      Hearnshaw and Hearnshaw* (1906) 23 RPC 349.
9   *Mallan v Davis* (1886) 3 TLR 221; *William Coulson & Sons v James Coulson & Sons* (1887) 3
      TLR 740; *J Lyons & Co Ltd v Lyons* (1931) 49 RPC 188; *Dagenham Girl Pipers Ltd v Vishnu
      Pather* (1951) 69 RPC 1.
10   *Van Oppen & Co Ltd v Van Oppen* (1903) 20 RPC 617 at 619.
11   *Harrods Ltd v R Harrod Ltd* (1923) 41 RPC 74, CA.
12   *Van Oppen & Co Ltd v Van Oppen* (1903) 20 RPC 617.
13   *Price's Patent Candle Co Ltd v Ogston and Tennant Ltd* (1909) 26 RPC 797; *W and G Du
      Cros Ltd v Gold* (1912) 30 RPC 117; *Parker & Son (Reading) Ltd v Parker* [1965] RPC 323.
14   Ie because it implies an act of extortion backed up with a threat to deliberately pass off if the
      amount requested is not paid: see *Glaxo plc v Glaxowellcome Ltd* [1996] FSR 388 (offer to sell
      company incorporated under name of proposed merged business); *British
      Telecommunications plc v One in a Million Ltd* [1998] 4 All ER 476, [1999] FSR 1, CA (offer
      to sell internet domain name).
15   See the cases of fraud cited in connection with the right of an individual to make use of his own
      name in PARA 326.

314.   Passing off where misrepresentation is made indirectly.   A trader is not
permitted to use any mark, device or other means[1] whereby, although he does
not make a false representation to a direct purchaser of his goods, he enables
such a purchaser to make a false representation to ultimate purchasers of those
goods[2].
   Where goods are sold to trade customers who are not themselves deceived but
the goods are so marked or got up as to be calculated[3] to deceive ultimate
purchasers, the claimant's cause of action for passing off is regarded as complete,
both at law[4] and in equity[5], as soon as the goods are disposed of to the trade
customers. Any such goods calculated to deceive are regarded as instruments of
deception, and the court has jurisdiction to grant injunctive relief where a
defendant is equipped with or is intending to equip another with an instrument
of deception[6]. It is not enough that the goods are merely capable of being used
by dealers to perpetrate frauds on their customers; the goods, or leaflets or other
material supplied with them, must be intended or of such a nature as to suggest,
or readily or easily lend themselves to, such passing off, as otherwise the
consequence is too remote to be attributed to the supplier of the goods[7]. The fact
that some middlemen have chosen to pass off goods which are capable of being
sold in a perfectly lawful manner does not mean that the supplier has caused or
enabled the passing off[8]. Goods may be regarded as calculated to deceive when
they are marked with a distinctive feature by which the claimant's goods have
become known in the market which enables dealers to supply them in response

to requests for the claimant's goods[9]. It is unnecessary that the goods should actually be marked deceptively when they are supplied to middlemen if the goods, packaging or labels are supplied in component form for the purpose of final assembly into products which will be deceptive[10]. The supply of goods in the United Kingdom for export to a country where they are calculated to deceive amounts to passing off[11], at least where the trader in the United Kingdom has sufficient knowledge that the sale of the goods abroad will be deceptive[12].

Similarly, indirect misrepresentations may be made in connection with the passing off of services or businesses, although such a misrepresentation occurs more rarely than in connection with the passing off of goods[13].

1   As to passing off by use of a name or mark see PARA 309 et seq; and as to passing off by similarity of get-up or shape of goods see PARA 321 et seq.
2   *Singer Manufacturing Co v Loog* (1880) 18 ChD 395 at 412, CA, per James LJ (affd (1882) 8 App Cas 15, HL); *Frank Reddaway & Co Ltd v George Banham & Co Ltd* [1896] AC 199 at 216, 13 RPC 218 at 231, HL, per Lord Macnaghten.
3   For these purposes, 'calculated' means that it is the reasonably foreseeable consequence that ultimate purchasers will be deceived; it does not have to be the intended consequence: *Erven Warnink BV v J Townend & Sons (Hull) Ltd* [1979] AC 731 at 742, [1979] 2 All ER 927 at 933, [1980] RPC 31 at 93, HL.
4   *Sykes v Sykes* (1824) 3 B & C 541. Damage (which is an essential ingredient of the action) is inferred from the threat that a quantity of deceptive goods is likely to be resold at any moment: *Draper v Trist* [1939] 3 All ER 513 at 522–523, 56 RPC 429 at 436, CA, per Sir Wilfrid Greene MR.
5   *Lever v Goodwin* (1887) 36 ChD 1, 4 RPC 492, CA (where an account of profits was awarded in respect of all the deceptive goods sold to middlemen, not just the proportion passed off to customers as the claimant's goods).
6   *British Telecommunications plc v One in a Million Ltd* [1998] 4 All ER 476, [1999] FSR 1, CA. It appears from this that a mere intention to equip oneself with an instrument of fraud, even without any intention to use it, may be restrained. It seems that eg a company which is formed with an inherently deceptive name, or the registration of an inherently deceptive domain name is to be treated as analogous to goods which are instruments of deception. As to domain names as instruments of deception see PARA 325.
7   *Singer Manufacturing Co v Loog* (1882) 8 App Cas 15 at 21, HL, per Lord Selborne LC; *Payton & Co Ltd v Snelling, Lampard & Co Ltd* [1901] AC 308 at 311, 17 RPC 628 at 635, HL, per Lord Macnaghten; *John Brinsmead & Sons Ltd v Brinsmead* (1913) 30 RPC 493 at 509, 511–512, CA, per Buckley LJ (who said that a defendant was not liable where a 'little additional lever' of falsehood applied by the dealer was needed to pass the goods off as the plaintiffs'); *Cadbury Ltd v Ulmer GmbH* [1988] FSR 385 ('Flakes') (where a defendant supplying chocolate bars the same shape as Cadbury's Flakes to ice-cream vendors was held not liable for acts of passing off committed by the vendors).
8   *Apollinaris Co Ltd v Duckworth & Co* (1906) 23 RPC 540 at 548, CA, per Warrington J (where salts prepared by the defendants, according to the analysis of the plaintiffs' mineral water, were reconstituted by a customer and sold as genuine mineral water). As to assisting passing off by others see also PARA 315.
9   *R Johnstone & Co v Archibald Orr Ewing & Co* (1882) 7 App Cas 219, HL; *Lee Kar Choo (t/a Yeen Thye Co) v Lee Lian Choon (t/a Chuan Lee Co)* [1967] 1 AC 602, [1966] 3 All ER 1000, PC; cf *Boord & Son Inc v Bagots, Hutton & Co Ltd* [1916] 2 AC 382, 33 RPC 357, HL.
10 *John Walker & Sons Ltd v Henry Ost & Co Ltd* [1970] 2 All ER 106, [1970] 1 WLR 917, [1970] RPC 489 (where bulk whisky was supplied together with bottles and deceptive labels); *John Walker & Sons Ltd v Douglas McGibbon & Co Ltd* [1975] RPC 506, Ct of Sess. In *John Walker & Sons Ltd v Henry Ost & Co Ltd* above at 115, 928 and 504, in relation to one of the two types of labels involved, it was said that it does not make the defendant any the less culpable if, instead of supplying the deceptive labels, he merely supplies the product knowing and intending that deceptive labels will be applied; and in *White Horse Distillers Ltd v Gregson Associates Ltd* [1984] RPC 61, bulk whisky supplied without labels was described as an 'inchoate instrument of deception' where the supplier knew of and participated in its marketing with deceptive labels in Uruguay. Liability in these circumstances is better explained on the basis that the defendant is liable for facilitating the passing off or cognate tort which occurs abroad (see PARA 315) rather than on the basis that the supply of unmarked goods not inherently deceptive is itself an act of passing off.

11 *R Johnston & Co v Archibald Orr Ewing & Co* (1882) 7 App Cas 219, HL.
12 *John Walker & Sons Ltd v Henry Ost & Co Ltd* [1970] 2 All ER 106 at 120, [1970] 1 WLR 917 at 933, [1970] RPC 489 at 508–509.
13 See e g *Society of Accountants and Auditors v Goodway and London Association of Accountants Ltd* [1907] 1 Ch 489, where the defendant association conferred upon its members the right to use the title 'incorporated accountant', so causing deception. As to the use of internet domain names to pass off see PARA 325.

315. Assisting or being involved in passing off by others. The liability of a person who enables or assists others to pass off their goods as the claimant's goods by supplying packaging or materials[1] is to be decided on principles more restricted than those which apply to a person who actually supplies goods, whether made up or in component form, so labelled or got up as to be calculated to deceive[2]. Negligence on the part of a printer who supplies deceptive packaging but fails to make sufficient inquiry is not enough to found liability[3], nor is mere negligence on the part of a person who supplies unlabelled bulk material without knowledge of and participation in the application of deceptive labels by his customer[4]. It may be that knowingly to supply materials for the purpose of enabling goods to be passed off would give rise to liability in negligence or an analogous cause of action[5], but the supply of materials which some customers may use for the purpose of passing off does not give rise to liability if the materials can also be used lawfully[6].

Under a head of liability distinct from that of liability for enabling passing off by others, persons who supply materials or who otherwise assist or are involved in the commission of passing off may incur liability as joint wrongdoers. To do so they must satisfy the requirement of being parties to a common design in the course of which the passing off occurs[7]; and under this head persons who make themselves parties to acts of passing off or cognate torts occurring abroad can be sued in the United Kingdom in respect of those acts[8]. Similarly, promoters involved in the formation of companies with deceptive names[9], or directors and managers of companies which engage in passing off[10], may incur liability.

Persons who facilitate passing off by others in circumstances where they do not themselves become wrongdoers may nevertheless, under the protective jurisdiction of equity, be restrained by injunction from parting with deceptive goods which have come under their control[11], or be ordered to disclose information as to the identity of their correspondents to enable the claimants to take proceedings against the wrongdoers[12].

1 As to passing off by similarity of get-up see PARA 321 et seq.
2 See *John Walker & Sons Ltd Henry Ost & Co Ltd* [1970] 2 All ER 106, [1970] 1 WLR 917, [1970] RPC 489. As to indirect passing off where the goods supplied are calculated to deceive see PARA 314.
3 *Paterson Zochonis Ltd v Merfarken Packaging Ltd* [1986] 3 All ER 522, [1983] FSR 273, CA.
4 *White Horse Distillers Ltd v Gregson Associates Ltd* [1984] RPC 61.
5 *Paterson Zochonis Ltd v Merfarken Packaging Ltd* [1983] FSR 273 at 283, CA, per Oliver LJ, at 289 per Fox LJ, and at 301 per Robert Goff LJ.
6 *Apollinaris Co Ltd v Duckworth & Co* (1906) 23 RPC 540 at 548, CA, per Warrington J (where mineral water salts were used for making up into mineral water which was passed off as genuine). See also *CBS Inc v Ames Records and Tapes Ltd* [1982] Ch 91, [1981] 2 All ER 812, [1981] RPC 407 (where blank tapes were used by customers for infringing copyright), and the cases there cited.
7 *CBS Songs Ltd v Amstrad Consumer Electronics plc* [1988] AC 1013, [1988] 2 All ER 484, [1988] RPC 567, HL (no common design between the suppliers of home taping equipment and home tapers to infringe copyright); *Unilever plc v Gillette (UK) Ltd* [1989] RPC 583, CA; *Credit Lyonnais Bank Nederland NV v Export Credit Guarantee Department* [1998] 1 Lloyd's Rep 19, CA. See also *Cadbury Ltd v Ulmer GmbH* [1988] FSR 385 ('Flakes') (where a

defendant supplying chocolate bars the same shape as Cadbury's Flakes to ice-cream vendors was held not liable for acts of passing off committed by the vendors).

8	*John Walker & Sons Ltd v Henry Ost & Co Ltd* [1970] 2 All ER 106, [1970] 1 WLR 917, [1970] RPC 489 (where in Ecuador whisky mixed with local spirit was passed off as a Scotch whisky, and liability for the passing off in Ecuador was treated as distinct from the defendants' liability for passing off by the act of supplying the whisky with labels calculated to deceive). The power of the court to grant relief in respect of the defendants' participation in the passing off occurring abroad formerly arose from the general rule that a court in England or Wales will grant relief against a defendant over whom it has personal jurisdiction in respect of an act done in a foreign country which is actionable according to English law and which is not justifiable according to the law of the country concerned: see *John Walker & Sons Ltd v Henry Ost & Co Ltd* at 120, 933 and 509. See also *Alfred Dunhill Ltd v Sunoptic SA* [1979] FSR 337, CA (where an injunction was granted extending to the United Kingdom and Switzerland, with liberty to the plaintiffs to apply to extend the injunction to other countries on proof of passing off there and of the local law). Now such conduct may be actionable in England by virtue of the Private International Law (Miscellaneous Provisions) Act 1995 Pt III (ss 9–15A) (see CONFLICT OF LAWS vol 19 (2011) PARA 662); but it seems clear that this involves proof that the conduct is tortious under local law rather than by virtue of the English law of passing off. In order to advance such a claim the relevant propositions of foreign law should be pleaded: *Mother Bertha Music Ltd v Bourne Music Ltd* [1997] ELMR 457; *Global Multimedia International Ltd v ARA Media Services* [2006] EWHC 3107 (Ch), [2007] 1 All ER (Comm) 1160; *HG Investment Managers Ltd v HIG European Capital Partners LLP* [2009] FSR 947.

It should be noted that the Private International Law (Miscellaneous Provisions) Act 1995 Pt III (see above) is superseded by European Parliament and Council Regulation (EC) 864/2007 (OJ L199, 31.7.2007, p 40) on the law applicable to contractual obligations ('the Rome II Regulation'), with effect from 11 January 2009, in cases where that Regulation applies. Accordingly, it is necessary for choice of law purposes to distinguish between those claims which will continue to be governed by the rules of the common law and those which will be governed by the 1995 Act or by the Rome II Regulation: see CONFLICT OF LAWS vol 19 (2011) PARA 647 et seq.

9	*SA des Anciens Etablissements Panhard and Levassor v Panhard Levassor Motor Co Ltd* [1901] 2 Ch 513, 18 RPC 405; cf *Allen v Original Samuel Allen & Sons Ltd* (1915) 32 RPC 33.

10	*MCA Records Inc v Charly Records Ltd* [2001] EWCA Civ 1441, [2002] FSR 401, [2002] EMLR 1.

11	See PARA 436.

12	See PARA 435.

(iv) Damage

316. Types of damage. It is essential to an action for passing off that the defendant's activities cause substantial damage to the claimant's business or goodwill, or are likely to do so if continued[1]. Where the defendant's goods or services compete with the claimant's, it is likely that the claimant will suffer loss of profits as a result of purchasers buying the defendant's goods or services in place of the claimant's[2]. Damage may occur despite the fact that the defendant's goods or services are not inferior to the claimant's[3], although, if they are inferior, the claimant may suffer additional damage to the reputation of his goods or services. Damage may also occur even if the consumer had ceased to be misled by the time the transaction is concluded[4].

Where the claimant and the defendant do not compete and so the defendant's activities cannot lead directly to loss of sales by the claimant, the claimant may nevertheless suffer damage by being associated in the minds of the relevant traders or the public with the defendant or his business, goods or services[5]. The quality of the defendant's goods or services, the kind of business he does and the credit which he enjoys are all matters which may injure a claimant who is assumed wrongly to be associated with him[6]. Damage is likely to occur if the defendant[7] or his business[8] is unsavoury in character, and, if the defendant has adopted a name similar to the claimant's with fraudulent intent, the court will readily infer the probability of tangible injury to the claimant's trade reputation[9]. Even where there is no reason to suppose that there is anything concerning the defendant or his business which would adversely affect the claimant in the immediate future, the fact that the claimant's reputation is placed at the mercy of an entity over which the claimant has no control and which might get into difficulties in the future[10] may be sufficient to justify the grant of a permanent injunction at the trial[11], provided that the degree to which the claimant and the defendant may be associated by the public is sufficiently great[12]. In some cases the risk that the claimant may be exposed to litigation if the public assumes that he is responsible for the defendant's business has been held to give rise to a tangible risk of damage to the claimant[13].

1   *Reckitt & Colman Products Ltd v Borden Inc* [1990] 1 All ER 873, [1990] 1 WLR 491, [1990] RPC 341, HL, per Lord Oliver of Aylmerton ('Jif Lemon'). While confusion which is quickly corrected, so that it does not give rise to any damage, will not found an action in passing off (see PARA 318), it is open to question whether damage of the relevant sort is sustained where persons are led to the defendant by means of a misrepresentation, and are then disabused before transacting business which would otherwise have gone to the claimant: see *HFC Bank plc v Midland Bank plc* [2000] FSR 176 at 186, 202 per Lloyd J.

2   *Draper v Trist* [1939] 3 All ER 513, 56 RPC 429, CA (where it was held that, if the defendant puts a quantity of goods on the market which are calculated to be taken as the claimant's, the court will generally infer that this will lead to some loss of sales by the claimant without necessarily requiring proof of individual transactions in which this can be shown to have taken place). See also *Procea Products Ltd v Evans & Sons Ltd* (1951) 68 RPC 210; *McDonald's Hamburgers Ltd v Burgerking (UK) Ltd* [1987] FSR 112, CA; *Kimberley-Clark Ltd v Fort Sterling Ltd* [1997] FSR 877 (plaintiff entitled to protection not only from loss of sales but also from commercial damage caused by a competitor taking the benefit of his reputation); *Clark v Associated Newspapers Ltd* [1998] 1 All ER 959, [1998] RPC 261 (damage may be presumed in a case of false attribution of authorship).

3   *Blofeld v Payne* (1833) 4 B & Ad 410; *Edelsten v Edelsten* (1863) 1 De GJ & Sm 185. See also *Singer Manufacturing Co v Loog* (1882) 8 App Cas 15 at 30, HL, per Lord Blackburn.

4   *Och-Ziff Management Europe Ltd v Och Capital LLP* [2010] EWHC 2599 (Ch), [2011] Bus LR 632, [2011] FSR 289 ('initial interest confusion').

5   This may extend to dilution or erosion of the claimant's goodwill through loss of distinctiveness of the mark in question: *Taittinger SA v Allbev Ltd* [1994] 4 All ER 75, [1993] FSR 641, CA ('elderflower champagne'; damage through the erosion of the uniqueness which attends the word 'champagne'). See also *British Telecommunications plc v One in a Million Ltd* [1998] 4 All ER 476, [1999] FSR 1, CA; *Irvine v TalkSport Ltd* [2002] EWHC 367 (Ch) at [34]–[38], [2002] 2 All ER 414 at [34]–[38], [2002] EMLR 679 at [34]–[38] per Laddie J (affd [2003] EWCA Civ 423, [2003] 2 All ER 881, [2003] EMLR 538); but see *Harrods Ltd v Harrodian School Ltd* [1996] RPC 697 at 715–716, CA, per Millet LJ.

6   *Ewing v Buttercup Margarine Co Ltd* [1917] 2 Ch 1 at 13, 34 RPC 232 at 239, CA, per Warrington LJ; *Chelsea Man Menswear Ltd v Chelsea Girl Ltd* [1987] RPC 189 at 202, CA, per Slade LJ; *Phones 4U Ltd v Phone4u.co.uk Internet Ltd* [2006] EWCA Civ 244 at [14], [2007] RPC 83 at [14] per Jacob LJ.

7   *Harrods Ltd v R Harrod Ltd* (1923) 41 RPC 74, CA (where a moneylender fraudulently passed himself off as a branch of the well known store).

8   *Annabel's (Berkeley Square) Ltd v Schock (t/a Annabel's Escort Agency)* [1972] RPC 838, CA (where an escort agency was restrained from trading under the same name as the well known night club). Cf *McCulloch v Lewis A May (Produce Distributors) Ltd* [1947] 2 All ER 845 at 851, 65 RPC 58 at 67 (where the opinion of some witnesses that the plaintiff would lower himself by allowing his name to be attached to breakfast cereals was held not to give rise to a tangible risk of injury to his professional reputation); *Stringfellow v McCain Foods (GB) Ltd* [1984] RPC 501, [1984] FSR 175 (revsd [1984] RPC 501 at 525, CA).

9   *Lloyd's v Lloyd's (Southampton) Ltd* (1912) 29 RPC 433, CA; *Harrods Ltd v R Harrod Ltd* (1923) 41 RPC 74, CA.

10 *FW Woolworth & Co Ltd v Woolworths (Australasia) Ltd* (1930) 47 RPC 337; *British Legion v British Legion Club (Street) Ltd* (1931) 48 RPC 555 at 564.

11 This risk of damage in the long term does not justify the grant of an interim injunction, for which the likelihood of damage to the claimant's business or his trading reputation must be

much more direct and immediate, eg arising from the poor quality of the defendant's goods: see *Lyons Maid Ltd v Trebor Ltd* [1967] RPC 222.

12 See *Society of Motor Manufacturers and Traders Ltd v Motor Manufacturers' and Traders' Mutual Insurance Co Ltd* [1925] Ch 675 at 692, 42 RPC 307 at 319, CA, per Warrington LJ (who said that, even if a certain number of persons were to think that the defendants were connected with the plaintiffs, in the circumstances there was no tangible risk of loss or damage to the plaintiffs).

13 *Walter v Ashton* [1902] 2 Ch 282 (bicycle shop passed off as being a branch of 'The Times' newspaper); *Illustrated Newspapers Ltd v Publicity Services (London) Ltd* [1938] Ch 414, [1938] 1 All ER 321, 55 RPC 172.

317. Common field of activity and damage. The similarity of the fields of activity in which the claimant and the defendant are engaged is highly relevant to the question of whether or not the defendant's use of the name, mark or other indicium complained of amounts to a misrepresentation, since the more disparate the fields, whether geographically or in terms of the type of business carried on, the less likely it is that the defendant will be assumed to be connected with the claimant[1]. However, even though substantial numbers of persons assume that the claimant and the defendant are connected, if the claimant and the defendant are not engaged in the same or associated fields of activity, it may be that there is no real and tangible risk that the claimant will suffer damage, and accordingly his action for passing off will not succeed[2]. Where the fields of activity of the claimant and the defendant are different, the question whether a connection is likely to be assumed between the claimant and the defendant, and the question whether such association gives rise to a real and tangible risk of damage, are not always clearly distinguished[3].

In considering whether there is a likelihood of damage to the claimant's business, the court may have regard not only to the present state of affairs but also to the fact that natural expansion of the claimant's business or of the defendant's business may bring the claimant and the defendant into competition in the future[4]. It has been held that the use of the claimant's reputation to promote the sale of goods which he is not engaged in selling can be regarded as causing damage to him even in the absence of any present or reasonably imminent intention on his part of selling or licensing the sale of such goods himself, the damage being the appropriation of the claimant's reputation in that field and the potential of exploiting it, and the loss of the fee which he would have been able to secure from the defendant for the use of his name and reputation[5]. Where, however, the claimant's and the defendant's fields of activity are far removed, even if certain uninformed members of the public or persons with special connections with the claimant were to believe mistakenly that there is a connection between them, a court should not readily infer the likelihood of consequential damage to the claimant, especially against an innocent defendant[6]. The attitude of the courts as to what constitutes sufficient likelihood of damage has changed over the years so that some of the older cases where the likelihood of damage to the claimant was held to be insufficient would now not necessarily be followed[7].

1 *Annabel's (Berkeley Square) Ltd v Schock (t/a Annabel's Escort Agency)* [1972] RPC 838 at 844, CA, per Russell LJ. As to a common field of activity and likelihood of deception see PARA 311.

2 *Ormond Engineering Co Ltd v Knopf* (1932) 49 RPC 634 (where a false representation that the defendant's goods were licensed under the plaintiff's patent was not actionable as the plaintiffs were not themselves selling competing goods); *McCulloch v Lewis A May (Produce Distributors) Ltd* [1947] 2 All ER 845, 65 RPC 58 (where breakfast cereal was sold under the name of a well known children's broadcaster but it was held that there was no likelihood of

damage to the plaintiff in his profession). See also *Sim v HJ Heinz Co Ltd* [1959] 1 All ER 547, [1959] 1 WLR 313, [1959] RPC 75, CA (where there was imitation of an actor's voice in an advertisement); *Anheuser-Busch Inc v Budejovicky Budvar Narodni Podnik* [1984] FSR 413, CA (where sales of the defendants' beer in the general market in the United Kingdom was held not likely to damage the plaintiff's business of selling beer abroad and to American service bases in the United Kingdom); *Harrods Ltd v Harrodian School Ltd* [1996] RPC 697, CA (where a school was run under a name similar to the well-known store, it was held unlikely that the store's goodwill would be damaged by anything which happened at the school).

3   See eg *Albion Motor Car Co Ltd v Albion Carriage and Motor Body Works Ltd* (1917) 34 RPC 257. The two questions cannot be considered in isolation, as the question whether the defendant's activities pose a real and tangible risk of injury to the claimant's business or goodwill depends among other things on the degree to which the claimant and the defendant are likely to be associated, so that a high risk of association justifies an injunction even when there is only a remote risk of damage (see *FW Woolworth & Co Ltd v Woolworths (Australasia) Ltd* (1930) 47 RPC 337), but a low risk of confusion does not justify an injunction unless the probability of damage is much more real (see *Society of Motor Manufacturers and Traders Ltd v Motor Manufacturers' and Traders' Mutual Insurance Co Ltd* [1925] Ch 675 at 692, 42 RPC 307 at 319, CA).

4   *Dunlop Pneumatic Tyre Co Ltd v Dunlop Lubricant Co* (1898) 16 RPC 12 at 15 (plaintiff's business); *Crystalate Gramophone Record Manufacturing Co Ltd v British Crystalite Co Ltd* (1934) 51 RPC 315 at 322 (defendant's business).

5   See *Henderson v Radio Corpn Pty Ltd* [1969] RPC 218 at 236, 244 (where a photograph of ballroom dancers was placed on a record sleeve in such a way as to suggest that the dancers had sponsored or recommended the music); *Lego System A/S v Lego M Lemelstrich Ltd* [1983] FSR 155 (where garden sprinklers were sold under the same name as well known toy bricks); *Anheuser-Busch Inc v Budejovicky Budvar Narodni Podnik* [1984] FSR 413, CA (where the defendant's entry into the general market in the United Kingdom where the plaintiffs had a reputation unconnected with ability or willingness to supply the goods was held not to give rise to potential damage to the plaintiffs); *Irvine v TalkSport Ltd* [2003] EWCA Civ 423, [2003] 2 All ER 881, [2003] EMLR 538 (where the claimant racing driver succeeded in a claim for passing off by misrepresentation of endorsement against the defendant radio station and recovered as damages the fee he could have charged). See also *WWF-World Wide Fund for Nature v World Wrestling Federation Entertainment Inc* [2007] EWCA Civ 286, [2008] 1 All ER 74, [2008] 1 WLR 445 (damages for breach of covenant not to use trade mark). As to merchandising see also PARA 323.

6   *Stringfellow v McCain Foods (GB) Ltd* [1984] RPC 501 at 525, CA (where the defendant marketed long, thin potato chips as 'Stringfellows', the name of a night club proprietor, and the court refused to conclude that substantial damage was likely even though there was a degree of misrepresentation).

7   See eg *Clark v Freeman* (1848) 11 Beav 112 (commented on in *Walter v Ashton* [1902] 2 Ch 282 at 293) (where an eminent physician was refused an injunction to prevent the fraudulent sale of quack medicine under his name); *Borthwick v Evening Post* (1888) 37 ChD 449, CA (where it was held that the assumption by the public that a new evening newspaper was connected with an existing morning newspaper was not likely to prejudice the publishers of the morning newspaper).

318.   Confusion without damage.   In some circumstances where one business is confused with another, there may be, nevertheless, no damage of a kind which will sustain an action for passing off[1]. This is so even where the claimant and the defendant are in directly competing fields of business if the confusion is likely to be rapidly put right or if it causes clerical and administrative errors which lead to misdirected letters and telephone calls but which are likely to be put right because of the way in which the business is conducted without resulting in any loss to or diversion of business from the claimant[2]. Similarly, confusion and inconvenience caused by the adoption of the same telegraphic address[3], or the claimant's failure to take extra precautions in identifying himself to persons with whom he corresponds[4], have been held insufficient to sustain an action.

1   As to damage as an essential of the action for passing off see PARAS 316–318.

2   *Meikle v Williamson* (1909) 26 RPC 775; *John Hayter Motor Underwriting Agencies Ltd v RBHS Agencies Ltd* [1977] FSR 285, CA; *Pasterfield v Denham* [1999] FSR 168, Plymouth County Court. See also PARA 316 text and note 1.

3   *Street v Union Bank of Spain and England* (1885) 30 ChD 156; *George Outram & Co Ltd v London Evening Newspapers Co Ltd* (1911) 28 RPC 308 at 312.

4   *George Outram & Co Ltd v London Evening Newspapers Co* Ltd (1911) 28 RPC 308. See also *Newsweek Inc v BBC* [1979] RPC 441, CA.

(2) PARTICULAR CASES OF PASSING OFF

(i) Descriptive, Generic and Geographical Names

319. Descriptive and geographical names. Special considerations apply where the claimant seeks to restrain as passing off the use of words or phrases which are descriptive of the goods or services concerned or of their geographical origin[1].

It is possible for a word or phrase which is wholly descriptive of the goods or services concerned to become so associated with the goods or services of a particular trader that its use by another trader is capable of amounting to a representation that his goods or services are those of the first trader[2]. In these circumstances it is sometimes said that, although the primary meaning of the words is descriptive, they have acquired a secondary meaning as indicating the products of a particular trader and no other[3]. However, a trader who seeks to prove that words which are prima facie descriptive have acquired such a secondary meaning faces a heavy burden[4], and the fact that such words, if used on their own without differentiation or explanation, will deceive does not mean that they cannot fairly be used with distinguishing words[5] or in a context where their meaning is descriptive[6]. Where the similarity between the trade marks or names of the claimant and defendant lies in descriptive words, the court will generally accept that small differences will be sufficient to distinguish them, at any rate in the absence of fraudulent intent[7], even if some degree of confusion arises between the claimant and the defendant as a result, as to do otherwise would allow the claimant unfairly to monopolise words in common use in the English language[8]. Descriptiveness is a matter of degree, and words which have some reference to the goods or services concerned are not necessarily to be treated in the same way as if they were the natural or usual description of those goods or services[9].

Similar principles apply to geographical names, so that it is difficult for a claimant to establish that a word having prima facie a geographical significance will indicate, when used by a defendant, the claimant's goods or services rather than goods or services from or connected with the geographical area concerned, especially where the goods are a natural product of the area rather than a manufactured article which could be made anywhere[10]. However, even though it might be possible for a geographical name to be used with adequate distinction in a way which is not deceptive, a name originally purely geographical in its significance may become so associated with the claimant's goods or services that its use on its own as a trade mark or name without adequate distinction will amount to passing off[11], especially if it is used in conjunction with get-up or other indicia similar to that used by the claimant[12]. Formerly the misapplication of a geographical name to goods was not actionable at the suit of a trader who legitimately made use of that name, unless by doing so the defendant represented that his goods were goods of the claimant[13], but this is no longer the law[14].

1 As to misuse of descriptive terms see PARA 302.

2 *Frank Reddaway & Co Ltd v George Banham & Co Ltd* [1896] AC 199, 13 RPC 218, HL (where it was held unlawful to apply to the goods a description which is literally true, but which is intended to and does convey to a purchaser that they are the claimant's goods). See also *Barnsley Brewery Co Ltd v RBNB* [1997] FSR 462 (where the plaintiff failed to show that 'Barnsley Bitter' had acquired a secondary meaning in fact); *Antec International Ltd v South Western Chicks (Warren) Ltd* [1998] FSR 738.

3 See e g *Cellular Clothing Co Ltd v Maxton and Murray* [1899] AC 326 at 333, 339, 343, 16 RPC 397 at 403, 406, 409, HL.

4 See *Cellular Clothing Co Ltd v Maxton and Murray* [1899] AC 326, 16 RPC 397, HL. Cf the strange facts of *Frank Reddaway & Co Ltd v George Banham & Co Ltd* [1896] AC 199, 13 RPC 218, HL (where it was not known in the trade that the phrase 'camel hair' was descriptive of the plaintiff's belting, and the defendant used it with intent to pass off his goods as the plaintiff's).

5 *Frank Reddaway & Co Ltd v George Banham & Co Ltd* [1896] AC 199 at 210, 222, 13 RPC 218 at 228, 234, HL.

6 *Burberrys v JC Cording & Co Ltd* (1909) 26 RPC 693.

7 *Aerators Ltd v Tollitt* [1902] 2 Ch 319, 19 RPC 418; *Office Cleaning Services Ltd v Westminster Window and General Cleaners Ltd* (1946) 63 RPC 39, HL; *World Athletics and Sporting Publications Ltd v ACM Webb (Publishing) Co Ltd* [1981] FSR 27, CA ('Athletics Weekly' and 'Athletics Monthly' magazines). Cf *Mothercare Ltd v Robson Books Ltd* [1979] FSR 466.

8 See *Cellular Clothing Co Ltd v Maxton and Murray* [1899] AC 326 at 339–340, 16 RPC 397 at 407, HL, per Lord Shand; *British Vacuum Cleaner Co Ltd v New Vacuum Cleaner Co Ltd* [1907] 2 Ch 312 at 328–329, 24 RPC 641 at 655 per Parker J; *Motor Manufacturers and Traders' Society Ltd v Motor Manufacturers and Traders' Mutual Insurance Co Ltd* [1925] Ch 675 at 689–690, 42 RPC 307 at 318–319, CA, per Lawrence J and at 692 and 320 per Sargent LJ; *Office Cleaning Services Ltd v Westminster Window and General Cleaners Ltd* (1946) 63 RPC 39 at 43, HL, per Lord Simonds; *Phones 4U Ltd v Phone4u.co.uk Internet Ltd* [2006] EWCA Civ 244 at [23], [2007] RPC 83 at [23], per Jacob LJ. It appears that the courts are influenced by the consideration that a claimant who adopts as a mark or trading style words which are wholly descriptive of his goods or services is himself partly responsible for confusion which arises from the fair use by others of those descriptive words. See *Mothercare UK Ltd v Penguin Books Ltd* [1988] RPC 113, CA (where the well known stores group was held not entitled to restrain the publication of a book about caring for children entitled 'Mother Care/Other Care').

9 *Music Corpn of America v Music Corpn (Great Britain) Ltd* (1946) 64 RPC 41 at 44; *Legal and General Assurance Society Ltd v Daniel* [1968] RPC 253, CA; *Pickwick International Inc (GB) Ltd v Multiple Sound Distributors Ltd* [1972] 3 All ER 384, [1972] 1 WLR 1213, [1972] RPC 786; *Computervision Corpn v Computer Vision Ltd* [1975] RPC 171. Cf *Newsweek Inc v BBC* [1979] RPC 441, CA (television programme called 'Newsweek'). By analogy, fancy packaging which cleverly refers to the characteristics of the goods themselves is not to be equated with a description of the goods: *Reckitt & Colman Products Ltd v Borden Inc* [1990] 1 All ER 873, [1990] 1 WLR 491, [1990] RPC 341, HL ('Jif Lemon').

10 *Rugby Portland Cement Co Ltd v Rugby and Newbold Portland Cement Co Ltd* (1891) 9 RPC 46, CA; *Grand Hotel Co of Caledonia Springs Ltd v Wilson* [1904] AC 103, 21 RPC 117, PC (where competitors were legitimately entitled to use the name 'Caledonia' in order to gain advantage from the fame acquired by the plaintiffs' mineral water from the same locality); *Hopton Wood Stone Firms Ltd v Gething* (1910) 27 RPC 605. See also *Tigon Mining and Finance Corpn Ltd v South Tigon Mining Co Ltd* (1931) 48 RPC 526 (where a name belonging originally to the plaintiff company became so associated with an area where it conducted mining operations that it could be used by the defendant without deception as a geographical word).

11 *Seixo v Provezende* (1866) 1 Ch App 192; *Montgomery v Thompson* [1891] AC 217, 8 RPC 361, HL; *North Cheshire and Manchester Brewery Co Ltd v Manchester Brewery Co Ltd* [1899] AC 83, HL; *Worcester Royal Porcelain Co Ltd v Locke & Co* (1902) 19 RPC 479; *Berkeley Hotel Co Ltd v Berkeley International (Mayfair) Ltd* [1972] RPC 237.

12 *Price's Patent Candle Co Ltd v Ogston and Tennant Ltd* (1909) 26 RPC 797. See also *Wotherspoon v Currie* (1872) LR 5 HL 508 (where the defendant set up premises in Glenfield for the purpose of enabling him to pass off his starch as the plaintiff's which was sold under the name 'Glenfield Starch').

13 *California Fig Syrup Co v Taylor's Drug Co Ltd* (1897) 14 RPC 564, CA.

14 *Erven Warnink BV v J Townend & Sons (Hull) Ltd* [1979] AC 731, [1979] 2 All ER 927, [1980] RPC 31. See also PARA 302.

320. Invented name, or the name of the introducer or patentee, for novel goods or services. Special considerations may apply where a claimant introduces a new product and has for a period of time, either because of a patent or because of practical or commercial considerations, a monopoly in supplying it[1]. The courts are reluctant to permit a claimant under the guise of an action for passing off to seek to hamper competition by preventing competitors from making use of a name which is apt to describe the product, even if the name was invented and given to the product by the claimant[2].

In such circumstances a claimant faces an evidential difficulty, in that it is to be expected that, while his product enjoys a de facto monopoly, it will be referred to or asked for by its descriptive name alone, but it does not follow from evidence of such practice that the public will still regard the descriptive name as denoting the goods of a particular manufacturer once there is a competitor on the market[3], and it does not matter for this purpose that the words, although apt in common usage to describe the product, are, if strictly or scientifically construed, inaccurate[4]. A further difficulty may arise in that confusion may be inevitable when a new competitor enters a market which has hitherto been supplied by one trader, simply as a result of the similarity of the goods or services concerned[5]. In order to succeed in an action for passing off, the claimant must show that confusion is created or increased by some misrepresentation on the defendant's part, and it may be difficult to show that the particular use made by the defendant of inherently descriptive words is an operative misrepresentation causing confusion in addition to that arising simply from the similarity of the goods or services themselves[6]. Furthermore, a court may consider that, where a claimant trades under or uses as a trade mark words which are inherently descriptive of the goods or services without further distinguishing them, he brings on himself the risk of confusion arising from other traders' fair use of such descriptive terms[7].

It is possible for the name of the first inventor or introducer of a novel article to come to indicate not the goods made by or under the licence of that particular individual but goods of that type made by any person, in which case the name of the inventor or introducer is said to have become publici juris or generic[8], although this is far less prone to happen than in the case of words which are inherently descriptive[9]. More common is the situation where the name of the introducer or inventor can be used in a context where it signifies products of the general type[10] but where the use of the name in relation to the goods without sufficient distinction or qualification is likely to mislead and will be restrained[11].

1 See *Cellular Clothing Co Ltd v Maxton and Murray* [1899] AC 326 at 344, 16 RPC 397 at 409, HL.
2 *McCain International Ltd v Country Fair Foods Ltd* [1981] RPC 69, CA (where it was held that the name 'oven chips' was descriptive of the product). See also *eFax.com Inc v Oglesby* [2000] IP & T 992, (2000) Times, 16 March (prefixing a word with an established meaning with the letter 'e' is descriptive of internet services).
3 *Siegert v Findlater* (1878) 7 ChD 801 at 813 ('Angostura Bitters'); *Parsons v Gillespie* [1898] AC 239 at 245, 15 RPC 57 at 62, PC ('Flaked Oatmeal'); *Cellular Clothing Co Ltd v Maxton and Murray* [1899] AC 326 at 344, 16 RPC 397 at 409, HL, per Lord Davey; *Linoleum Manufacturing Co v Nairn* (1878) 7 ChD 834 (where 'linoleum' was held to be descriptive); *McCain International Ltd v Country Fair Foods Ltd* [1981] RPC 69, CA. See also the comments of the members of the House of Lords on the 'monopoly assumption' in *Reckitt & Colman Products Ltd v Borden Inc* [1990] 1 All ER 873, [1990] 1 WLR 491, [1990] RPC 341, HL ('Jif Lemon').
4 *Parsons v Gillespie* [1898] AC 239 at 245, 15 RPC 57 at 62, PC; *Horlick's Malted Milk Co v Summerskill* (1916) 33 RPC 108 at 114, CA (affd 34 RPC 63, HL); *McCain International Ltd v Country Fair Foods Ltd* [1981] RPC 69 at 74, CA.

5 As to confusion without any misrepresentation see PARA 307.
6 *My Kinda Town Ltd v Soll* [1983] RPC 407 at 420, CA, per Oliver LJ, and at 434 per Robert Goff LJ. Similar considerations arise where passing off is alleged to occur as a result of the similarity of features of goods which are of benefit in use: see PARA 321.
7 *British Vacuum Cleaner Co Ltd v New Vacuum Cleaner Co Ltd* [1907] 2 Ch 312 at 328–329, 24 RPC 641 at 655 per Parker J.
8 *Canham v Jones* (1813) 2 Ves & B 218 ('Velno's Vegetable Extract'); *Liebig's Extract of Meat Co Ltd v Hanbury* (1867) 17 LT 298; *Ford v Foster* (1872) 7 Ch App 611 at 628 per Mellish LJ.
9 See e g *Burberrys v Raper and Pulleyn* (1906) 23 RPC 170.
10 See e g *Singer Manufacturing Co v Loog* (1882) 8 App Cas 15, HL ('Singer system' sewing machines).
11 *Singer Machine Manufacturers v Wilson* (1877) 3 App Cas 376, HL; *AV Roe & Co Ltd v Aircraft Disposal Co Ltd* (1920) 37 RPC 249.

(ii) Get-up and Shape of Goods

321. Passing off by similarity of get-up or shape of goods. Passing off may occur, not only by reason of any similarity of trade marks or names[1], but because of the similarity of the general appearance or get-up of goods, or the premises in which business is conducted, or the advertising materials and other documents used in connection with the defendant's goods or services[2].

The similarity of get-up may be such that passing off is likely to occur even though the trade marks or names are wholly different[3], especially where the goods are likely to be bought by illiterate or uneducated persons[4], but similarity or dissimilarity[5] of get-up is only one of the factors to be taken into account in deciding whether in all the circumstances there is a likelihood of deception, and a dissimilar name or mark, if given prominence, may negate the similarity of get-up[6]. A competing trader may adopt a get-up similar to that of the claimant's product, not in order to pass off his goods as the claimant's but in order impliedly to represent to the public that his goods are similar to or a substitute for the claimant's, thus competing in and taking advantage of a market created by the claimant's efforts; this is legitimate so long as he does not thereby represent his product as the claimant's or connected with it[7].

In assessing whether or not the get-up of the defendant's goods is deceptively similar to the claimant's, characteristics which are common to the trade should be disregarded[8], but the use in combination of a number of features which are individually used by others in the trade can amount to passing off[9]. Thus where the defendant adopts a feature used by the claimant which is also used by others in the trade, so that its use as such is unobjectionable, the defendant may nevertheless have to take greater care not to copy other features of the get-up of the claimant's goods[10]. Further, where the general appearance of the goods is necessarily similar, a defendant needs to take greater care to avoid adopting those features which are distinctive to the get-up of the claimant's goods[11]. It appears that a trader who is the first to import goods cannot monopolise features which are common to the trade in those goods in their country of origin, at least if no dishonesty is involved in the competing importation[12].

It is possible for passing off to occur by reason of the similarity of the shape, nature or other characteristics of the goods themselves, as opposed to features of their packaging or marks applied to them[13]. Where, however, what is sought to be restrained is the copying of features of the claimant's goods which have value in use, as opposed to capricious attributes of shape or colour, the courts are reluctant to allow a claimant to secure a monopoly in a new type or design of goods under the guise of an action for passing off[14], and in this regard the principles applied are closely parallel to those which apply where the claimant seeks to restrain as passing off the use of words or phrases which are descriptive of the goods or services concerned[15]. It is more difficult to establish as a matter of fact that purchasers will assume merely from attributes which have utility that the defendant's goods are the claimant's, particularly because they may buy those goods because of their utility or because of their visual appeal without caring or giving thought to who makes them[16]. Moreover, confusion which arises simply as a result of a new competitor selling a type of goods or services which previously have only been sold by the claimant is not regarded in law as arising from a representation made by the defendant[17], and there is some authority that a defendant who simply copies attributes of the claimant's goods which give some benefit in use is not to be treated in law as thereby making a representation[18].

1	As to passing off by use of a name or mark see PARA 309 et seq.

2	As to misrepresentation as an essential element of the action see PARA 306.

3	*Reckitt & Colman Products Ltd v Borden Inc* [1990] 1 All ER 873, [1990] 1 WLR 491, [1990] RPC 341, HL ('Jif Lemon') (where differing trade names and labels were held insufficient on the facts to prevent confusion arising from the adoption by the defendant of a lemon-shaped plastic container for lemon juice); *Tavener Rutledge Ltd v Specters Ltd* [1959] RPC 355, CA (see the photographs of tins at [1959] RPC 83); *United Biscuits (UK) Ltd v Asda Stores Ltd* [1997] RPC 513 (where similarities in packaging of 'Puffin' biscuits to packaging of 'Penguin' biscuits resulted in passing off whereas the name alone did not).

4	*Lever v Godwin* (1887) 36 ChD 1 at 5, 4 RPC 492 at 504, CA; *Lee Kar Choo (t/a Yeen Thye Co) v Lee Lian Choon (t/a Chuan Lee Co)* [1967] 1 AC 602, [1966] 3 All ER 1000, PC.

5	See eg *Coleman & Co Ltd v John Brown & Co* (1899) 16 RPC 619, CA.

6	*Schweppes Ltd v Gibbens* (1905) 22 RPC 601 at 606–607, HL (where Lord Halsbury LC expressed the view that persons who are so careless that they do not treat the label fairly but take the goods without sufficient consideration and without reading what is written plainly on them cannot be said to be deceived because they do not care what they are getting); *Fisons Ltd v EJ Godwin (Peat Industries) Ltd* [1976] RPC 653; *Tetrosyl Ltd v Silver Paint and Lacquer Co Ltd* [1980] FSR 68, CA.

7	*F King & Co Ltd v Gillard & Co* [1905] 2 Ch 7, 22 RPC 327, CA; *Cadbury Schweppes Pty Ltd v Pub Squash Co Pty Ltd* [1981] 1 All ER 213 at 218–219, [1981] 1 WLR 193 at 200, [1981] RPC 429 at 491, PC. See also PARA 306.

8	*Hennessy (James) & Co v Keating* (1908) 25 RPC 361, 52 Sol Jo 455, 24 TLR 534, HL; *JB Williams Co v H Bronnley & Co Ltd* (1909) 26 RPC 765, CA. The evidence of customers who have little knowledge of the goods on the market, and so do not know which features of the claimant's goods are common to the trade and which are distinguishing characteristics, should be disregarded by the court: *Payton & Co Ltd v Snelling, Lampard & Co Ltd* (1899) 17 RPC 48 at 57, CA, per Romer LJ (affd [1901] AC 308, 17 RPC 628, HL).

9	*Lever v Goodwin* (1887) 36 ChD 1, 4 RPC 492, CA.

10	*W and G Du Cros Ltd v Gold* (1912) 30 RPC 117 at 126.

11	*Cordes v R Addis & Son* (1923) 40 RPC 133 at 139.

12	*Boord & Son Inc v Bagots, Hutton & Co Ltd* [1916] 2 AC 382 at 393, sub nom *Re Bagots, Hutton & Co Ltd's Application* 33 RPC 357, HL, per Lord Loreburn.

13	See *Hodgkinson and Corby Ltd v Wards Mobility Services Ltd* [1994] 1 WLR 1564, [1995] FSR 169; *RJ Elliott & Co Ltd v Hodgson* (1902) 19 RPC 518 (imitation of specially shaped cigars restrained); *F Hoffman–La Roche & Co AG v DDSA Pharmaceuticals Ltd* [1972] RPC 1, CA (coloured drug capsules); cf *Roche Products Ltd v Berk Pharmaceuticals Ltd* [1973] RPC 473, CA.

14	*William Edge & Sons Ltd v William Niccolls & Sons Ltd* [1911] AC 693, HL (where the plaintiffs had for many years been the only firm to sell laundry blue in bags to which a stick was attached, thus allowing the bags to be dipped in the water without staining the user's hands, and the defendants were restrained from imitating the shape of the plaintiff's stick but not from using any stick). As to the statutory policy reflected in the restrictions on the registrability of the shape of goods as trade marks see PARA 46.

15	As to the use of descriptive names see PARA 319.

16	*Blundell v Sidney Margolis Ltd* (1951) 68 RPC 71 (bubble gum in the shape of teeth); *Hawkins and Tipson Ltd (Proprietors of Green Bros) v Fludes Carpets Ltd and British Floorcloth Co Ltd*

[1957] RPC 8 (pattern on coconut floor matting); *British American Glass Co Ltd v Winton Products (Blackpool) Ltd* [1962] RPC 230 (ornamental dogs); *Gordon Fraser Gallery Ltd v Tatt* [1966] RPC 505 (style of greetings cards); *Jarman and Platt Ltd v I Barget Ltd* [1977] FSR 260, CA (style of furniture); *Lyngstad v Anabas Products Ltd* [1977] FSR 62 (where it was held that badges depicting popular musicians were bought for their own sake rather than because buyers assumed that the sale of the goods was connected with the persons depicted); *Politechnika Ipari Szovetkezet v Dallas Print Transfers Ltd* [1982] FSR 529 ('Rubik' puzzle cubes).

17 For circumstances where confusion arises as a result of the defendant's activities, but not as a result of any misrepresentation on his part, see PARA 307.

18 *Benchairs Ltd v Chair Centre Ltd* [1974] RPC 429 at 435–436 per Graham J (revsd on another point [1974] RPC 429, CA), applying a dictum of Fletcher Moulton LJ in *JB Williams Co v H Bronnley & Co Ltd* (1909) 26 RPC 765 at 773, CA. See also *Jones Bros Ltd v Anglo-American Optical Co* (1912) 29 RPC 361, CA. Cf *Children's Television Workshop Inc v Woolworths (NSW) Ltd* [1981] RPC 187, NSW SC. That this is a rule of law, as distinct from a factual circumstance giving rise to greater difficulties of proof on the part of the claimant, was, however, doubted in *Reckitt & Colman Products Ltd v Borden Inc* [1990] 1 All ER 873, [1990] 1 WLR 491, [1990] RPC 341, HL ('Jif Lemon').

(iii) Titles

322. Titles. In general the title of an individual book does not function as a trade mark[1], and it would therefore seem doubtful whether such a title can be protected by an action for passing off, quite apart from the difficulty that it is commonplace for two or more books to be published with the same or similar titles. In principle the title of an individual play or film stands in the same position. Nevertheless there is some authority suggesting that a distinctive title can be protected[2].

Periodicals and other serials, including books published in successive editions, sequels and radio and television programmes, stand in a different position. It is clear that in principle the title of periodicals and serials may be protected[3], but often such claims fail because the title is descriptive and small differences in the title and/or other differences in the publication suffice to distinguish it[4].

In addition, the author of a book or play may have a remedy for the passing off of a film or the like as an adaptation of his book or play if that is not the case[5].

1 *SCIENCE AND HEALTH Trade Mark* [1968] RPC 402. See also *Games Workshop Ltd v Transworld Publishers Ltd* [1993] FSR 705, CA.

2 *Mathieson v Sir Isaac Pitman & Sons Ltd* (1930) 47 RPC 541 (claim in respect of 'How to Appeal against Your Rates' failed because it was descriptive and had not acquired a secondary meaning); *WH Allen & Co v Brown Watson* [1965] RPC 191 (passing off expurgated edition of book as unexpurgated edition); *Hexagon Pty Ltd v Australian Broadcasting Commission* [1976] RPC 628, NSW SC. See also *20th Century Fox Film Corpn v Gala Film Distributors Ltd* [1957] RPC 105.

3 See e g *Walter v Emmott* (1885) 54 LJ Ch 1059, CA; *Reed v O'Meara* (1904) 21 LR Ir 216; *Blacklock v Bradshaw* (1926) 43 RPC 97; *Morgan-Grampian plc v Training Personnel Ltd* [1992] FSR 267; *Games Workshop Ltd v Transworld Publishers Ltd* [1993] FSR 705, CA; *Associated Newspapers Ltd v Express Newspapers* [2003] EWHC 1322 (Ch), [2003] FSR 909; *Local Sunday Newspapers Ltd v Johnstone Press plc* [2001] All ER (D) 183 (Jun). See also *Marcus Publishing plc v Hutton-Wild Communications Ltd* [1990] RPC 576, CA.

4 See e g *Borthwick v The Evening Post* (1888) 37 ChD 449, CA; *George Outram & Co Ltd v London Evening Newspapers Co* (1911) 28 RPC 308; *Ridgway Co v Amalgamated Press Ltd* (1912) 29 RPC 130; *William Stevens Ltd v Cassell & Co Ltd* (1913) 30 RPC 199; *Ridgway Co v Hutchinson* (1923) 40 RPC 335; *Rubber & Technical Press Ltd v Maclaren & Sons Ltd* [1961] RPC 264; *Baylis & Co (Maidenhead Advertiser) Ltd v Darlenko Ltd* [1974] FSR 284; *DC Thomson & Co Ltd v Kent Messenger Ltd* [1975] RPC 191; *Morning Star Co-operative Society Ltd v Express Newspapers Lt*d [1979] FSR 113; *Newsweek Inc v BBC* [1979] RPC 441, CA; *World Athletics and Sporting Publications Ltd v ACM Webb (Publishing) Co Ltd*

[1981] FSR 27, CA; *Advance Magazine Publishing Inc v Redwood Publishing Ltd* [1993] FSR 449; *County Sound plc v Ocean Sound Ltd* [1991] FSR 367, CA; *Tamworth Herald Co Ltd v Thomson Free Newspapers Ltd* [1991] FSR 337; *Evegate Publishing Ltd v Newsquest Media (Southern) Ltd* [2013] EWHC 1975 (Ch), [2013] All ER (D) 132 (Jul).

5   *Raleigh v Kinematograph Trading Co Ltd* (1914) 31 RPC 143; *Samuelson v Producers Distributing Co Ltd* [1932] 1 Ch 201, CA; cf *Houghton v Film Booking* (1931) 48 RPC 329; *Loew's Inc v Littler* (1955) 72 RPC 166.

(iv) Personality and Character Merchandising

323. Merchandising and passing off. 'Merchandising' is the practice which has been growing very common over recent years of licensing the use of a name or mark, or of the representation or attributes of a real or fictional person or character, in connection with goods or services. In certain circumstances the law of passing off will restrain the unauthorised use by third persons of such names, marks, representations or other attributes[1].

Where a trade mark or trade name is licensed to licensees or franchisees, rather than used directly by the owner of the mark or name, then, provided that the licensor exercises sufficient control over, or otherwise maintains sufficient connection with, the goods or services so as to make the use of the name or mark distinctive of him, he can generally restrain the unauthorised use of the name or mark in the same way as if he had built up the goodwill and reputation attached to the mark by his own trade rather than through licensees[2].

It is more difficult to prevent the use of a name or mark in relation to goods or services which the owner of the name or mark has not yet marketed, whether directly or through licensees[3]. In such circumstances, the claimant must first establish that, notwithstanding the difference between the fields of activity in which the claimant and the defendant are engaged, the public will assume a connection with the claimant and accordingly the use of the name or mark will be a misrepresentation[4], and secondly that the misrepresentation creates a real and tangible risk of damage to the claimant[5]. Where the name is an individual's name and the defendant has expressly or implicitly represented[6] that the individual has licensed or endorsed the goods or services, it may be easier to succeed where the goods or services are in some way associated with the capacity in which the individual has become famous, so that the public can be expected to rely on his skill and judgment[7], than when the individual's professional capacities or attributes are totally unconnected with the goods or services concerned[8].

1   Other rights which are potentially applicable are those as to registered trade marks (see PARA 39 et seq), and, especially where representations of fictional characters are concerned, copyright: see *King Features Syndicate Inc v O and M Kleeman Ltd* [1941] AC 417, [1941] 2 All ER 403, 58 RPC 207, HL; and COPYRIGHT vol 23 (2013) PARAS 863–864.

2   *JH Coles Pty Ltd v Need* [1934] AC 82, 50 RPC 379, PC. As to licensing generally see PARA 299.

3   The use of trade marks which are famous as applied to one kind of goods, particularly luxury goods, to promote the sale of unrelated goods is increasingly common: see e g *Alfred Dunhill Ltd v Sunoptic SA* [1979] FSR 337, CA (where a mark originally used for pipes and tobacco was applied to jewellery, leather goods, watches, glassware and other diverse goods). See also *News Group Newspapers Ltd v Rocket Record Co Ltd* [1981] FSR 89 (where newspaper publishers marketed a range of goods under the mark 'Page 3' and were able to restrain the release by the defendants of a single record entitled 'Page Three').

4   As to a common field of activity and the likelihood of deception see PARA 311.

5   As to the requirement of damage see PARA 317.

6   The mere use of an individual's name or likeness does not necessarily imply that he has authorised the goods or services concerned: *Lyngstad v Anabas Products Ltd* [1977] FSR 62 (badges depicting popular musicians); cf *Elvis Presley Trade Marks* [1999] RPC 567, CA (memorabilia depicting deceased popular musician).

7   See *Henderson v Radio Corpn Pty Ltd* [1969] RPC 218 at 236, 244 (where a photograph of
    ballroom dancers was placed on a record sleeve in such a way as to suggest that they had
    endorsed or recommended the music); *Irvine v TalkSport Ltd* [2002] EWHC 367 (Ch), [2002]
    2 All ER 414, [2002] EMLR 679 (affd [2003] EWCA Civ 423, [2003] 2 All ER 881, [2003]
    EMLR 538) (where advertisement contained doctored photograph of claimant racing driver
    suggesting that he was listening to defendant radio station and thus endorsing it); *Fenty v
    Arcadia Group Brands Ltd* [2013] EWHC 2310 (Ch), [2013] All ER (D) 410 (Jul) (t-shirts
    bearing image of claimant singer).

8   *McCulloch v Lewis A May (Produce Distributors) Ltd* [1947] 2 All ER 845, 65 RPC 58 (where
    breakfast cereal was sold under the name of a well known children's broadcaster but it was held
    that there was no likelihood of damage to the plaintiff in his profession); but the requirement for
    a common field of activity laid down in this case has been disapproved by the Court of Appeal
    (see PARA 311). It would appear that where the claimant has a reputation for endorsing goods
    and services, or if his celebrity is such that members of the public would think that he was
    endorsing the defendant's product or service despite its nature, a claim may lie in respect of
    goods or services fairly remote from his own field: *Irvine v TalkSport Ltd* [2002] EWHC 367
    (Ch), [2002] 2 All ER 414, [2002] EMLR 679 (affd [2003] EWCA Civ 423, [2003] 2 All ER
    881, [2003] EMLR 538).
        In very special circumstances unauthorised representation of endorsement by an individual
    may give rise to an action for defamation: see *Tolley v JS Fry & Sons Ltd* [1931] AC 333, HL
    (where a caricature of an amateur golfer used as an advertisement was held capable of implying
    that the golfer had prostituted his amateur status by taking money for endorsing chocolate). See
    also DEFAMATION vol 32 (2012) PARAS 511–512.

324.   Fictional characters from books, films and television series.   To restrain a
defendant from making use of the names, likenesses or other incidents of
fictional characters or stories[1], a series of propositions must be established.

First, it must be shown that the public will assume from the way in which
reference is made to the character or story that the defendant's goods or services
are connected with or licensed by the claimant[2]. This is more difficult to establish
if the use of the character or story is of inherent value to the goods or services
marketed, so that members of the public buy the goods or services for their own
sake and not because the use of the character or story implies a connection with
the claimant[3]. It has been argued that the practice of licensing the use of
characters and other matter from films and television productions has become so
widespread that the public will now assume that licensing has taken place[4].

Secondly, the assumption on the part of the public that the claimant is
connected with the defendant's goods or services must arise from a
misrepresentation made by the defendant, and, if the defendant has merely
adopted features of the claimant's character or story which have intrinsic value in
relation to the intended use of the goods or services concerned, it may be more
difficult to attribute the assumptions made by the public to any
misrepresentation on the part of the defendant[5].

Thirdly, the claimant must establish that the misrepresentation is material and
a mere supposition on the part of the public that the claimant is receiving a
licence fee without any reliance on the reputation of the claimant as a guarantee
of the quality or origin of the goods concerned may not be sufficient[6].

Fourthly, the claimant must establish the likelihood of damage to his business
or goodwill as a result of the defendant's misrepresentation[7]. Even if the
likelihood of long-term damage can be established such as would justify the
grant of a permanent injunction at the trial, a claimant may have difficulty in
obtaining an interim injunction if he is engaged in a licensing operation and his
damage pending trial can be adequately compensated by money damages[8].

1   As to the practice of merchandising see PARA 323.

2   *BBC Worldwide Ltd v Pally Screen Printing Ltd* [1998] FSR 665. See also *Conan Doyle v London Mystery Magazine Ltd* (1949) 66 RPC 312 (where references to Sherlock Holmes and the use of his fictitious address by a magazine did not imply a connection with the author of the Sherlock Holmes detective stories); *Wombles Ltd v Wombles Skips Ltd* [1977] RPC 99 (where a skip company adopted the name of mythical creatures inhabiting Wimbledon Common); *Grundy Television Pty Ltd v Startrain Ltd* [1988] FSR 581 ('Neighbours') (where publication of a magazine about characters in the claimant's fictional television series did not imply a representation that the magazine was an official publication by the producers of the television series). The use of a fictional character may, however, be capable of implying a connection: see *Shaw Bros (Hong Kong) Ltd v Golden Harvest (UK) Ltd* [1972] RPC 559 (Hong Kong) ('One Armed Swordsman'); *Hexagon Pty Ltd v Australian Broadcasting Commission* [1976] RPC 628 ('Alvin Purple').

3   See *Lyngstad v Anabas Products Ltd* [1977] FSR 62 at 68 ('ABBA') (where it was held that badges depicting popular musicians satisfied a popular demand among teenagers for effigies of their idols and did not imply that the musicians had authorised them); and cf *Elvis Presley Trade Marks* [1999] RPC 567, CA.

4   This was not established by the plaintiffs in *Lyngstad v Anabas Products Ltd* [1977] FSR 62; *Tavener Rutledge Ltd v Trexapalm Ltd* [1977] RPC 275 ('Kojakpops'); or *Lorimar Productions Inc v Sterling Clothing Manufacturers Ltd* [1982] RPC 395, SA SC. The assumption was held arguable in *IPC Magazines Ltd v Black and White Music Corpn* [1983] FSR 348 ('Judge Dredd') (interlocutory injunction refused). It was successfully argued in *Mirage Studios v Counter-Feat Clothing Co Ltd* [1991] FSR 145 ('Ninja Turtles') (interlocutory injunction granted).

5   See *JB Williams Co v H Bronnley & Co Ltd* (1909) 26 RPC 765 at 773, CA, per Fletcher-Moulton LJ; and PARA 307. Cf *Children's Television Workshop Inc v Woolworths (NSW) Ltd* [1981] RPC 187, NSW SC ('Muppets'). See also *Tarzan Trade Mark* [1970] RPC 450, CA (where an application to register 'Tarzan' in respect of games, clothes and playthings was refused on the grounds that it had direct reference to the character and quality of goods which portrayed or related to the well-known fictional character).

6   *Tavener Rutledge Ltd v Trexapalm Ltd* [1977] RPC 275 at 280–281 per Walton J ('Kojakpops'). See also PARA 305. A dictum in *Mirage Studios v Counter-Feat Clothing Co Ltd* [1991] FSR 145 at 159 ('Ninja Turtles'), that there is no requirement that the public should rely on the defendant's misrepresentation, is difficult to reconcile with *Reckitt & Colman Products Ltd v Borden Inc* [1990] 1 All ER 873 at 889, [1990] 1 WLR 491 at 510, [1990] RPC 341 at 417, HL, per Lord Jauncey of Tullichettle ('Jif Lemon') and with *Harrods Ltd v Harrodian School Ltd* [1996] RPC 697 at 712–713, CA, per Millet LJ. See also *Hodgkinson and Corby Ltd v Wards Mobility Services Ltd* [1994] 1 WLR 1564, [1995] FSR 169.

7   See PARA 317.

8   *IPC Magazines Ltd v Black & White Music Corpn* [1983] FSR 348.

(v) Internet Domain Names

325. Domain names as an instrument of fraud; registration of domain names. A recent problem thrown up by the widespread use of the internet is the registration of domain names comprising famous names and marks of others, a practice often referred to as 'cybersquatting'. Historically, the courts have had little hesitation in restraining the registration of company names comprising famous names and marks, and a similar approach is adopted with respect to domain names. Mere registration of a distinctive domain name can amount to passing off. These and other internet-related issues are considered elsewhere[1].

1   As to the use of domain names as an instrument of fraud see INFORMATION TECHNOLOGY LAW vol 57 (2012) PARA 584. As to registration of domain names see INFORMATION TECHNOLOGY LAW vol 57 (2012) PARA 585. As to trade marks and internet society service provider liability see INFORMATION TECHNOLOGY LAW vol 57 (2012) PARA 586. See also generally INFORMATION TECHNOLOGY LAW vol 57 (2012) PARA 583.

(3) SPECIAL DEFENCES

(i) Use of Trader's Own Name

326. Use by an individual of his own name. An individual has certain rights to make use of his own name in the course of trade where the use of that name by another person would amount to passing off[1]. The original justification for this rule was that, as regards passing off at common law where fraudulent intent was a necessary ingredient of the cause of action[2], the legitimate use by a trader of his own name would not, without more, give rise to the inference of fraudulent intent which would be inferred from the use of that name by a third person who had no legitimate reason for using it[3]. As regards the action in equity, even though the defendant's use of his own name gave rise to misapprehension among the claimant's customers and caused injury to the claimant, there was no equity to restrain the defendant from making a statement of fact, namely that the business was carried on by a person with that name, made honestly in the usual manner in which such statements are made in the course of business and which the defendant had a legitimate interest in making[4].

More recently the appellate courts have adopted a more restrictive attitude to the right of a trader to use his own name[5], and the precise extent of the right is now not altogether clear[6]. This more restrictive approach may owe much to the fact that under modern trading conditions it is less essential than it used to be for a trader to use his personal name in carrying on a business[7].

Whatever the exact scope of a trader's right to use his own name, it is clear that a fraudulent intent will vitiate the right, and there are numerous cases where unsuccessful attempts have been made to pass off by getting individuals with little or no real connection with a business to lend their name to it[8]. Similarly, the unwarranted garnishing of the defendant's name with labelling, style of script or get-up similar to the styles used by the claimant can amount to fraud and can be restrained[9]. Even in the absence of fraud, the writing of the defendant's name in an unclear way[10], or the abbreviating of his name[11] in such a way as to increase the risk of deception, may be restrained, although there is some authority for the proposition that a trader using his own name is not under a positive obligation to take extra precautions to distinguish himself from his established rival[12].

The right of an individual to use his own name extends also to the adoption of a firm name which fairly describes the individuals making up the partnership[13]. The right also extends to assumed names which have been acquired by reputation[14] and to a name which has become familiar to the public as the defendant's fancy name[15], but not to the adoption as a trading style of a mere personal nickname[16].

The balance of authority favours the proposition that, whatever the nature and scope of the right of an individual to use his name as a trading name, it does not extend to a right to mark his goods if deception is thereby caused[17].

1   As to the scope of the action for passing off, and the meaning of 'trader', see PARA 293.
2   As to the history of the action for passing off see PARA 288.
3   See *Burgess v Burgess* (1853) 3 De GM & G 896 at 905 per Turner LJ.
4   *Turton v Turton* (1889) 42 ChD 128 at 147, CA, per Fry LJ.
5   *Parker-Knoll Ltd v Knoll International Ltd* [1962] RPC 265, HL, where the majority of the House of Lords (Lord Morris of Borth-y-Gest at 279, Lord Hodson at 283, and Lord Guest at 287 agreeing with Lord Hodson) adopted the test that, if the plaintiff's name or mark is proved to have acquired a secondary meaning, so as to denote goods made by a particular person and not goods made by any other person even though such other person may have the same name,

then a person may, even by using his own name innocently, be making a representation which is untrue and which may be restrained by an action for passing off. See also *John Brinsmead & Sons Ltd v Brinsmead* (1913) 30 RPC 493 at 507–509, CA, per Buckley LJ; *Baume & Co Ltd v AH Moore Ltd* [1958] Ch 907, [1958] 2 All ER 113, [1958] RPC 226, CA.

6   If, as some of the judgments in the cases cited in note 5 suggest, a trader can only make use of his own name if to do so will not lead to deception, it is difficult to see what advantage is given by the law to a trader using his own name over a person adopting it arbitrarily. However, in *Parker-Knoll Ltd v Knoll International Ltd* [1962] RPC 265, HL, the majority of the House of Lords approved an injunction containing a proviso that the restraint was not to interfere with any use in good faith by the defendants of their full name, implying that some use could legitimately be made of the name but not making clear what use. In *Marengo v Daily Sketch and Sunday Graphic Ltd* [1948] 1 All ER 406, (1948) 65 RPC 242 at 251, HL, Lord Simonds considered that a person may carry on business honestly under his own name notwithstanding that confusion arises. In *Reed Executive plc v Reed Business Information Ltd* [2004] EWCA Civ 159 at [111], [2004] RPC 767 at [111], [2004] IP & T 1049 at [111] and in *IN Newman Ltd v Adlem* [2005] EWCA Civ 714 at [46]–[47], [2006] FSR 253 at [46]–[47], Jacob LJ held that there was a defence if use of the name only caused non-damaging confusion but that there was passing off if a substantial number of people were misled. See also *Taylor Bros Ltd v Taylors Group Ltd* [1988] 2 NZLR 1, NZ HC (to the same effect).

In *Hotel Cipriani Srl v Cipriani (Grosvenor Street) Ltd* [2010] EWCA Civ 110, [2010] Bus LR 1465, [2010] RPC 485 the Court of Appeal clarified the scope of the own name defence in registered trade mark law, holding that a limited company could also rely on a trading name under which it operated as its 'own name', the defence not being limited to the use of a limited company's registered name; the same approach might apply to the use of the defence in cases of passing off.

7   See *Parker-Knoll Ltd v Knoll International Ltd* [1962] RPC 265 at 289, HL, per Lord Devlin, who considered it no grave hardship for a trader to pick another name if he enters a market in which his surname has already been appropriated by another trader. The attitude of the courts may be less restrictive in fields, eg the professions, where it is still usual for individuals to trade under their own names: see eg *Parker & Son (Reading) Ltd v Parker* [1965] RPC 323 at 326 per Plowman J (estate agents). See also the judgment of Didcott J in *Boswell-Wilkie Circus (Pty) Ltd v Brian Boswell Circus (Pty) Ltd* [1985] FSR 434, SA SC (which extensively reviews the progressive narrowing in English and Commonwealth authorities of the extent of the right of a trade to use his own name) (affd on appeal [1986] FSR 479, SA SC).

8   *Croft v Day* (1843) 7 Beav 84; *Southorn v Reynolds* (1865) 12 LT 75; *Massam v Thorley's Cattle Food Co* (1880) 14 ChD 748, CA; *Joseph Rodgers & Sons Ltd v WN Rodgers & Co* (1924) 41 RPC 277; *Alfred Dunhill Ltd v Sunoptic SA* [1979] FSR 337, CA. A number of cases involve attempts by a scion of a famous family to cash in on the family name: *Alfred Dunhill Ltd v Sunoptic SA*; *Guccio Gucci SpA v Gucci* [1991] FSR 89; *Asprey & Garrard Ltd v WRA (Guns) Ltd* [2001] EWCA Civ 1499, [2002] FSR 487, [2002] IP & T 38. See also PARA 313.

9   *Croft v Day* (1843) 7 Beav 84 at 89; *J Lyons & Co Ltd v Lyons* (1931) 49 RPC 188; *Parker & Son (Reading) Ltd v Parker* [1965] RPC 323.

10 *Marengo v Daily Sketch and Sunday Graphic Ltd* [1948] 1 All ER 406, 65 RPC 242, HL (where in passing off involving cartoonists 'Kim' and 'Kem', the 'i' of 'Kim' was written in such a way that it could be mistaken for an 'e').

11 *Wright, Layman and Umney Ltd v Wright* (1949) 66 RPC 149, CA; *Taylor Bros Ltd v Taylors Group Ltd* [1988] 2 NZLR 1, NZ HC.

12 *Jamieson & Co v Jamieson* (1898) 15 RPC 169 at 183, CA, per Lindley MR. It is doubtful how far this would now be followed in view of the more restrictive attitude of the courts. See also *Wright, Layman and Umney Ltd v Wright* (1949) 66 RPC 149, CA (where a qualified injunction was granted restraining the defendant from using the name 'Wright' or 'Wrights' without clearly distinguishing his goods from those of the plaintiff).

13 *Turton v Turton* (1889) 42 ChD 128, CA (where Thomas Turton & Sons Ltd sued in respect of confusion caused when the first defendant, on taking his two sons into partnership, changed the firm name from John Turton & Co to John Turton & Sons); cf *Joseph Rodgers & Sons Ltd v WN Rodgers & Co* (1924) 41 RPC 277 (where a man called Muller took a young man called WN Rodgers into partnership and adopted the firm name 'WN Rodgers & Co' for the purpose of trading on the plaintiff's reputation; passages in the judgment which suggest that the right of a trader to use his name is restricted to the use of his full forenames and surname must be read subject to *Turton v Turton* above).

14 *Jay's Ltd v Jacobi* [1933] Ch 411, 50 RPC 132.

15 *Marengo v Daily Sketch and Daily Graphic Ltd* (1946) [1992] FSR 1, CA; revsd on the facts sub
     nom *Marengo v Daily Sketch and Sunday Graphic Ltd* [1948] 1 All ER 406, 65 RPC 242, HL.
16 *Biba Group Ltd v Biba Boutique* [1980] RPC 413; *NAD Electronics Ltd v NAD Computer
     Systems Ltd* [1997] FSR 380.
17 The distinction was first drawn in *Joseph Rodgers & Sons Ltd v WN Rodgers & Co* (1924)
     41 RPC 277 at 292 per Romer J, and, although inconsistent with previous authority (see
     Burgess v Burgess (1853) 3 De GM & G 896, CA; *Jamieson & Co v Jamieson* (1898) 15 RPC
     169, CA; *John Brinsmead & Sons Ltd v Brinsmead* (1913) 30 RPC 493, CA, all of which
     involved marking the defendant's name on goods), was subsequently approved in *Baume
     & Co Ltd v AH Moore Ltd* [1958] Ch 907 at 916, [1958] 2 All ER 113 at 116, [1958] RPC 266
     at 268, CA, per Romer LJ. In *Parker-Knoll Ltd v Knoll International Ltd* [1962] RPC 265, HL,
     the distinction was approved by Lord Morris of Borth-y-Gest at 279, by Lord Hodson at 284
     and by Lord Guest (concurring) at 287, but was criticised as illogical by Lord Denning
     (dissenting) at 277. See also *Marengo v Daily Sketch and Sunday Graphic Ltd* [1948] 1 All ER
     406, (1948) 65 RPC 242, HL, which was treated as a case of use of trading name, rather than of
     application of a mark to goods, even though the signature complained of was applied to copies
     of cartoons circulated in a newspaper. In *Reed Executive plc v Reed Business Information Ltd*
     [2004] EWCA Civ 159 at [110]–[112], [2004] RPC 767 at [110]–[112], [2004] IP & T 1049
     at [110]–[112] per Jacob LJ, the distinction was treated as settled law; but it was held that there
     was passing off if a substantial number of people were misled even in the case of use of the name
     as the name of the business.

327.   Use by corporation of its own name. On coming into existence a
corporation has its name chosen by its promoters, and it does not have the same
natural right to use its name as an individual has[1], but an established company
may have such a right even when it enters a market in which it has not previously
traded[2]. A newly-formed company may in general take the name under which
the business which is formed to take over has previously been lawfully carried
on, but an individual who has no existing business or goodwill to transfer cannot
confer upon a new company a special right to use his name[3].

1 *Hendriks v Montagu* (1881) 17 ChD 638. See also *Turton v Turton* (1889) 42 ChD 128 at 146,
    148, CA; *Fine Cotton Spinners and Doublers' Association Ltd and John Cash & Sons Ltd v
    Harwood Cash & Co Ltd* [1907] 2 Ch 184 at 190, 24 RPC 533 at 538 per Joyce J; *Asprey &
    Garrard Ltd v WRA (Guns) Ltd* [2001] EWCA Civ 1499, [2002] FSR 487, [2002] IP & T 38.
2 *Saunders v Sun Life Assurance Co of Canada* [1894] 1 Ch 537; cf *Adrema Ltd v
    Adrema-Werke GmbH and BEM Business Efficiency Machines Ltd* [1958] RPC 323; but see
    Taylor Bros Ltd v Taylors Group Ltd [1988] 2 NZLR 1, NZ HC. See PARA 326 note 6.
3 *Massam v Thorley's Cattle Food Co* (1880) 14 ChD 748, CA; *Tussaud v Tussaud* (1890) 44
    ChD 678; *Fine Cotton Spinners and Doublers' Association Ltd and John Cash & Sons Ltd v
    Harwood Cash & Co Ltd* [1907] 2 Ch 184, 24 RPC 533; *Kingston, Miller & Co Ltd v Thomas
    Kingston & Co Ltd* [1912] 1 Ch 575, 29 RPC 289.

(ii) Concurrent Rights

328.   Concurrent use and shared reputation. In certain circumstances two or
more traders may acquire independent rights to carry on trade side by side using
the same or similar names or marks, when the use of such names or marks by a
third person without any such special right would undoubtedly constitute
passing off[1]. These rights are to be distinguished from cases where descriptive[2] or
fancy terms are common to the trade as a whole so that any new entrant is
entitled to make use of them provided that he does so fairly[3]. Concurrent rights
to use proprietary, as opposed to descriptive, names or marks can arise by
division between different persons of the goodwill of a business which was
initially a single business[4], by attainment of independence by a subsidiary or
associated company from its group[5], by natural expansion of businesses using
marks of independent origin into areas in which they come into conflict[6], or by
continuing use by small local users in good faith after a mark has become

generally identified with the products of a particular large manufacturer[7]. A claimant's acquiescence in a defendant's use of a name or mark can result in the defendant's acquiring goodwill of his own in the name or mark so that it becomes unconscionable to allow the claimant to bar the defendant's continued use of that name or mark in an action for passing off[8].

Neither party with a concurrent right to use a name or mark can prevent the other from continuing to use it[9] but the vested right of property of traders in marks which they have honestly adopted and which by public use have attracted valuable goodwill must be accommodated with the interest of the public in not being deceived about the origin of goods[10]. A concurrent right of use does not, however, justify the use, whether intentionally or not, of a name or mark with attributes which increase the risk of confusion[11].

Another source of concurrent rights of use can arise from the rules of the European Union as to free movement of goods and as to competition[12].

1   Each of the traders may sue a third person without the concurrence of the other if his own business will suffer some damage as a result of the third person's passing off: see PARA 294.

2   Eg the term 'advocaat': see *Erven Warnink BV v J Townend & Sons (Hull) Ltd* [1979] AC 731, [1979] 2 All ER 927, [1980] RPC 31, HL.

3   See PARA 302.

4   *Dent v Turpin, Tucker v Turpin* (1861) 2 John & H 139; *Southorn v Reynolds* (1865) 12 LT 75; *Sir Robert McAlpine Ltd v Alfred McAlpine plc* [2004] EWHC 630 (Ch), [2004] RPC 711. Concurrent rights can also arise where part of a business is compulsorily severed, e g by the wartime expropriation of the part of a business in one country giving rise to a concurrent right of the original owner and the owner of the expropriated business to use the marks in a third country: see *Ingenohl v Wing On & Co (Shanghai) Ltd* (1927) 44 RPC 343, PC.

5   *Habib Bank Ltd v Habib Bank AG Zurich* [1981] 2 All ER 650, [1981] 1 WLR 1265, [1982] RPC 1, CA; *Anderson & Lembke Ltd v Anderson & Lembke Inc* [1989] RPC 124.

6   *General Electric Co v General Electric Co Ltd* [1972] 2 All ER 507 at 519, [1972] 1 WLR 729 at 743, [1973] RPC 297 at 326, HL, per Lord Diplock; and see *City Link Travel Holdings Ltd v Lakin* [1979] FSR 653; *Pete Waterman Ltd v CBS United Kingdom Ltd* [1993] EMLR 27. See also *Anheuser-Busch Inc v Budejovicky Budvar Narodni Podnik* [1984] FSR 413, CA, which might be regarded as such a case (and was at first instance by Whitford J) although the ground of decision in the Court of Appeal was that the plaintiff had no goodwill in the United Kingdom. A defence of honest concurrent use cannot succeed where the defendant had not acquired a protectable goodwill at the time that it commenced the acts complained of: *WS Foster & Son Ltd v Brooks Brothers UK Ltd* [2013] EWPCC 18, [2013] All ER (D) 232 (Mar).

7   *Star Cycle Co Ltd v Frankenburgs* (1907) 24 RPC 405 at 414, CA, per Fletcher Moulton LJ.

8   *Habib Bank Ltd v Habib Bank AG Zurich* [1981] 2 All ER 650, [1981] 1 WLR 1265, [1982] RPC 1, CA; cf *Poiret v Jules Poiret Ltd* (1920) 37 RPC 177 (where it did not avail the defendants that they had carried on business for several years after the plaintiff had been called up to the war, as they had adopted his name fraudulently). See also *Byford v Oliver* [2003] EWHC 295 (Ch), [2003] EMLR 416.

9   *Edge & Sons Ltd v Gallon & Son* (1900) 17 RPC 557, HL; *Marengo v Daily Sketch and Daily Graphic Ltd* (1946) [1992] FSR 1 at 2, CA, per Lord Greene MR ('Confusion may result from the collision of two independent rights or liberties, and where that is the case neither party can complain; they must put up with the results of the confusion as one of the misfortunes which occur in life') (revsd on the facts sub nom *Marengo v Daily Sketch and Sunday Graphic Ltd* [1948] 1 All ER 406, 65 RPC 242, HL).

10   See *General Electric Co v General Electric Co Ltd* [1972] 2 All ER 507 at 519, [1972] 1 WLR 729 at 743, [1973] RPC 297 at 326, HL, per Lord Diplock. See also *Phones 4U Ltd v Phone4u.co.uk Internet Ltd* [2006] EWCA Civ 244 at [21], [2007] RPC 83 at [21] per Jacob LJ.

11   *Marengo v Daily Sketch and Sunday Graphic Ltd* [1948] 1 All ER 406, 65 RPC 242, HL; *Sir Robert McAlpine Ltd v Alfred McAlpine plc* [2004] EWHC 630 (Ch), [2004] RPC 711 (defendant not entitled to call itself 'McAlpine' simpliciter).

12   See the Treaty on the Functioning of the European Union (Rome, 25 March 1957; TS 1 (1973); Cmnd 5179) ('TFEU') arts 34–36 (see PARA 86 note 8) (formerly the Treaty Establishing the European Community (Rome, 25 March 1957; TS 1 (1973); Cmnd 5179) (the 'EC Treaty') arts 28–30). See also PARA 89.

(iii) Parallel Imports

329. Parallel imports and passing off. 'Parallel imports' means strictly the importation and sale by others of goods originating from the owner of industrial property rights in parallel with his own importation of such goods, whether carried out by himself or through authorised agents[1], but is used more generally to describe the importation and sale by third persons of goods obtained in another country which originate from an internationally known company or group irrespective of whether the company or group satisfies the market in the United Kingdom by imports from that country[2].

The importation and sale in the United Kingdom of the claimant's goods bearing the marks under which the claimant has allowed them to be sold in a foreign country does not generally amount to passing off[3], since no misrepresentation is involved as to the origin of the goods[4]. Attempts by a claimant to argue that the sale of goods bearing a manufacturer's mark impliedly represents that the goods have passed through the accustomed channels of supply have been rejected by the courts[5], as has an attempt to sever and assign the goodwill of the business of importing the goods into the United Kingdom from the goodwill of the business carried on in the country of origin[6]. It generally makes no difference that the imported goods originate not from the same legal person who supplies the goods to the market in the United Kingdom but from another member of the same group of companies, since in modern trading conditions customers will usually neither know nor care which company within a group is responsible for manufacture or sale of the goods, the commercial origin of which is indicated by marks used by the group as a whole[7]. Even if the goodwill in the United Kingdom attached to the marks is owned by a particular member of the group so that the particular company is the appropriate claimant in an action against passing off by third persons, this does not permit the company to sue in respect of goods originating from another member of the same group if the element of misrepresentation is lacking[8]. It is probable that goods which are manufactured and to which the marks are applied under licence stand in the same position as goods actually made by a member of the group of companies[9].

The importation and sale by the defendant of the claimant's goods of one quality not marketed by the claimant in the United Kingdom can amount to passing off those goods as goods of another quality sold by the claimant in the United Kingdom even where the defendant sells the goods in the packaging in which the claimant, or the claimant's associated or subsidiary company, marketed them in another country[10].

Actionable passing off occurs when the importer alters the labelling on the foreign quality goods to the labelling used by the claimant for his goods of the quality sold on the English market[11]. If the labelling on the foreign goods is different from that on the English goods, it may be difficult for the claimant to establish that the public will assume them to be of the same quality[12].

Where the goods are imported from another member state of the European Union or the European Economic Area ('EEA'), regard should also be had to the overriding effect of the rules of European Union law as to free movement of goods and competition[13].

1 See e g *Imperial Tobacco Co of India Ltd v Bonnan* [1924] AC 755, 41 RPC 411, PC.
2 See e g *Revlon Inc v Cripps and Lee Ltd* [1980] FSR 85, CA.
3 As to the position with regard to registered trade marks see PARA 91.
4 *Imperial Tobacco Co of India Ltd v Bonnan* [1924] AC 755, 41 RPC 441, PC.

5 *Dental Manufacturing Co Ltd v C De Trey & Co* [1912] 3 KB 76, 29 RPC 517, CA; *Imperial Tobacco Co of India Ltd v Bonnan* [1924] AC 755, 41 RPC 441, PC. Cf *Sony KK v Saray Electronics (London) Ltd* [1983] FSR 302, CA; *Seiko Time Canada Ltd v Consumers Distributing Co Ltd* (1980) 112 DLR (3d) 500.
6 *Lacteosote Ltd v Alberman* [1927] 2 Ch 117, 44 RPC 211.
7 *Revlon Inc v Cripps and Lee Ltd* [1980] FSR 85, CA.
8 *Imperial Tobacco Co of India Ltd v Bonnan* [1924] AC 755 at 763, 41 RPC 441 at 448, PC. See also *Habib Bank Ltd v Habib Bank AG Zurich* [1981] 2 All ER 650 at 661–662, [1981] 1 WLR 1265 at 1278–1279, [1982] RPC 1 at 30, CA, per Oliver LJ.
9 For consideration by a foreign court of the general principles involved see Case IZR 85/71 *Francesco Cinzano & Cie GmbH v Java Kaffeegeschäfte GmbH & Co* [1974] 2 CMLR 21, German SC.
10 *Colgate-Palmolive Ltd v Markwell Finance Ltd* [1989] RPC 497, CA (inferior Colgate toothpaste for the Brazilian market imported in the United Kingdom). See, however, *Revlon Inc v Cripps and Lee Ltd* [1980] FSR 85 at 112, CA, where Templeman LJ held that there could be no passing off when products manufactured, named, labelled and put into circulation by a member of the plaintiff's group of companies were sold by the defendants without any alteration to the contents, name or label.
11 *Champagne Heidsieck & Cie v Scotto and Bishop* (1926) 43 RPC 101.
12 See *Champagne Heidsieck & Cie Monopole SA v Buxton* [1930] 1 Ch 330, 47 RPC 28; *Revlon Inc v Cripps and Lee Ltd* [1980] FSR 85, CA.
13 As to registered trade marks see PARAS 86–90. In general the same European Union law defences apply to passing off as apply to registered trade marks in respect of goods circulating within the EEA, even though the statutory 'exhaustion' defence does not apply; however, in relation to goods imported from outside the EEA the position under the law of passing off is radically different to registered trade marks: see PARA 91. As to the EEA see PARA 86 note 6.

(iv) Name, Mark or Trade of Claimant Fraudulent or Deceptive

330. Claimant disentitled to protection. A claimant may be disentitled to protection in an action for passing off if the trade which he carries on is as a whole fraudulent[1], or if the name or mark which he seeks to protect is fraudulent or deceptive[2], although the making of some collateral misrepresentations in the course of his trade which do not make the trade as a whole a fraud will not disentitle the claimant to relief[3]. The claimant may be guilty of deception as to the origin of goods if he allows goods with which he has no connection to be sold under his name or mark, but allowing this to happen without fraudulent intent for a time because of temporary difficulties need not disentitle him to protection[4].

1 *Lee v Haley* (1869) 5 Ch App 155 at 159; *Bile Bean Manufacturing Co Ltd v Davidson* (1906) 22 RPC 553 (on appeal 23 RPC 725).
2 *Leather Cloth Co Ltd v American Leather Cloth Co Ltd* (1865) 11 HL Cas 523 at 542. As to the position relating to registered trade marks see PARA 85.
3 *Ford v Foster* (1872) 7 Ch App 611 (false statements made in advertisements that the plaintiff's goods were patented). In *Sykes v Sykes* (1824) 3 B & C 541, the use of the word 'patent' in a trade mark where a patent had expired long ago was held unobjectionable, as it had become part of the description of the article.
4 *JH Coles Pty Ltd v Need* [1934] AC 82, 50 RPC 379, PC. The assignment or licensing of names or marks in gross may render them deceptive and incapable of protection: see PARAS 297, 299.

5. PROCEDURE RELATING TO TRADE MARKS AND PASSING OFF

(1) INTRODUCTION

331. Jurisdiction of the registrar, of the Office for Harmonisation in the Internal Market and of the courts. Applications to register a United Kingdom trade mark[1] or to protect an international trade mark in the United Kingdom[2], and oppositions[3] to such applications, must be made to the registrar[4]. Applications to register Community trade marks[5], and oppositions[6] to such applications, must be made to the Office for Harmonisation in the Internal Market (Trade Marks and Designs)[7]. The courts have no original jurisdiction to entertain such applications and oppositions.

In the Trade Marks Act 1994, unless the context otherwise requires, 'the court' means in England and Wales the High Court or a designated county court[8]. As from 1 October 2013 the Patents County Court is replaced by the Intellectual Property Enterprise Court within the Chancery Division of the High Court[9]. Proceedings for infringement of United Kingdom registered trade marks, protected international trade marks (UK) and Community trade marks may be brought there[10]. The registrar has no jurisdiction over such proceedings.

In proceedings for revocation, for a declaration of invalidity or for rectification of United Kingdom registered trade marks or protected international trade marks (UK), the applicant may opt to make his application either to the registrar or to the court[11]. In proceedings for infringement of a Community trade mark, the defendant may counterclaim for revocation or a declaration of invalidity[12]. Otherwise revocation or a declaration of invalidity of a Community trade mark may only be sought in the Office for Harmonisation in the Internal Market[13].

Proceedings for passing off[14] may mostly be brought in the High Court[15]. The registrar has no jurisdiction over passing off proceedings.

Where there are concurrent proceedings before the registrar and the court involving the same or similar issues, the registrar may stay the registry proceedings and, if he does not, the court may do so[16].

All procedure in the Trade Marks Registry is governed by the Trade Marks Rules 2008[17]. The Civil Procedure Rules 1998[18] do not apply to proceedings in the Registry, but in so far as the registrar has a discretion it will generally be exercised in accordance with the overriding objective[19]. An appeal lies from any decision of the registrar under the Trade Marks Act 1994, including any act of the registrar in exercise of a discretion vested in him by or under that Act, except as otherwise expressly provided by rules[20]. In general, appeals from decisions of the registrar lie, at the option of the appellant, either to the High Court or to a person appointed by the Lord Chancellor[21].

Appeals from decisions of the Office for Harmonisation in the Internal Market lie to the European General Court (formerly the Court of First Instance) and thence to the Court of Justice of the European Union on a point of law[22].

1   As to the requirements for registration see PARA 39 et seq; and as to the procedure on the application see PARA 334 et seq.
2   As to protected international trade marks (UK) see PARA 12.
3   As to opposition proceedings see PARAS 366–368.
4   As to the registrar see PARA 19; and as to proceedings in the Registry see PARA 334 et seq.
5   As to the meaning of 'Community trade mark' see PARA 189.

6   As to oppositions to Community trade mark applications see PARA 265.
7   As to the Office for Harmonisation in the Internal Market see PARA 163 et seq.
8   Trade Marks Act 1994 s 75(a) (amended by SI 2005/587). The reference actually is to a county
    court having jurisdiction by virtue of an order under the Courts and Legal Services Act 1990 s 1
    (see COURTS AND TRIBUNALS vol 24 (2010) PARA 863). As from a day to be appointed, the
    wording is revised so that instead of 'or a county court having jurisdiction' it reads ', or the
    county court where it has jurisdiction': Trade Marks Act 1994 s 75(a) (prospectively amended
    by the Crime and Courts Act 2013 Sch 9 Pt 3 para 134). At the date at which this volume states
    the law no such appointment has been made. The county courts so designated were the county
    courts at Birmingham, Bristol, Cardiff, Leeds, Liverpool, Manchester and Newcastle upon Tyne:
    High Court and County Courts Jurisdiction Order 1991, SI 1991/724, art 2(7A), (7B) (added by
    SI 2005/587). See note 9.
9   As from 1 October 2013 the Patents County Court was replaced by the Intellectual Property
    Enterprise Court as a result of the combined effect of the Crime and Courts Act 2013 ss 17(5),
    22, Sch 9 paras 21, 27, 30 and the Civil Procedure (Amendment No 7) Rules 2013,
    SI 2013/1974: see generally CIVIL PROCEDURE; COURTS AND TRIBUNALS. 'Intellectual Property
    Enterprise Court' means a specialist list within the Chancery Division of the High Court:
    CPR r 63.1(2)(g).
10 County Courts Act 1984 s 15(1) (amended by SI 1991/724); High Court and County Courts
    Jurisdiction Order 1991, SI 1991/724, art 2(7A), (7B) (as added: see note 8); Community Trade
    Marks Regulations 2006, SI 2006/1027, reg 12. As from a day to be appointed, the precise
    wording of the County Courts Act 1984 s 15(1) is revised slightly to refer to 'the county court'
    rather than 'a county court': s 15(1) (prospectively amended by the Crime and Courts Act 2013
    Sch 9 Pt 1 paras 1, 10(1)(b)). At the date at which this volume states the law no such
    appointment has been made.
       Claims relating to matters arising out of the Trade Marks Act 1994 and other intellectual
    property rights set out in Practice Direction 63 must be started in (1) the Chancery Division of
    the High Court; (2) the Intellectual Property Enterprise Court; or (3) save as set out in Practice
    Direction 63, a county court where there is also a Chancery District Registry: see CPR 63.13,
    Practice Direction—Intellectual Property Claims PD63 para 16.1.
11 See the Trade Marks Act 1995 ss 46(4), 47(3), 64(2); and PARA 378.
12 See Council Regulation (EC) 207/2009 (OJ L78, 24.3.2009, p 1) on the Community mark,
    arts 96(d), 100; and PARAS 234, 245.
13 See Council Regulation (EC) 207/2009 (OJ L78, 24.3.2009, p 1) art 56; and PARA 272.
14 As to passing off see PARA 287 et seq.
15 High Court proceedings for passing off must generally be brought in the Chancery Division of
    the High Court or the Intellectual Property Enterprise Court: see CPR 63.13, *Practice
    Direction—Intellectual Property Claims* PD63 para 16.1; and note 10.
16 *Sears plc v Sears Roebuck & Co* [1993] RPC 385 (affd CA, 26 November 1993, unreported);
    Philips Electronics NV v Remington Consumer Products Ltd (No 2) [1999] ETMR 835, [1999]
    All ER (D) 351; *GENIUS Trade Mark* [1999] RPC 741, Trade Mark Registry; *Jules Rimet
    Cup Ltd v Football Association Ltd* [2006] EWHC 2415 (Ch), [2006] All ER (D) 65 (Aug).
17 Ie the Trade Marks Rules 2008, SI 2008/1797.
18 Ie the Civil Procedure Rules 2008, SI 2008/3132 ('CPR'): see generally CIVIL PROCEDURE.
19 Ie under CPR 1.1: Tribunal Practice Notice (TPN 1/2000) [2000] RPC 587. Tribunal Practice
    Notices are available from the Intellectual Property Office ('IPO') or on its website, accessible at
    the date at which this volume states the law at www.ipo.gov.uk. As to the Intellectual Property
    Office (an operating name of the Patent Office) see PARA 16 note 2.
20 See the Trade Marks Act 1994 s 76(1); and PARA 387. The right of appeal so conferred is much
    wider than the right of appeal conferred by the Trade Marks Act 1938. As to the limitations on
    the right of appeal under the Trade Marks Act 1938 see *PREDATOR Trade Mark* [1982] RPC
    387. Judicial review was formerly the only means of challenging a decision by the registrar in
    cases where no appeal was provided for by the Trade Marks Act 1938 or the rules made under
    it: see *Adidas Sarl's Trade Mark* [1983] RPC 262.
21 See PARA 387 et seq.
22 See Council Regulation (EC) 207/2009 (OJ L78, 24.3.2009, p 1) art 65; and PARA 277.

332.   Trade marks for textile goods. Under the Trade Marks Act 1938 a
record ('the Manchester record') had to be kept at the Manchester branch of the
Trade Marks Registry and in that record had to be entered copies of all entries in

the general register relating to trade marks registered in respect of textile goods[1]. There is no requirement under the Trade Marks Act 1994 to maintain the Manchester record.

1 See the Trade Marks Act 1938 s 39 (repealed).

333. Sheffield marks for metal goods. Under the Trade Marks Act 1938[1] a register had to be kept by the Cutlers' Company[2] at Sheffield in which were entered marks for metal goods, if the applicant carried on business in Hallamshire or within six miles of it. The Sheffield register formed part of the general register, and marks entered on it had also to be entered in London[3]. By virtue of the Trade Marks Act 1994 the Sheffield register is to be treated as part of the register kept under the Trade Marks Act 1938; and applications made to the Cutlers' Company which were pending on 31 October 1994 must proceed on and after that date as if they had been made to the registrar[4].

1 See the Trade Marks Act 1938 s 30, Sch 2 (repealed).
2 'The Cutlers' Company' means the Master, Wardens, Searchers, Assistants and Commonalty of the Company of Cutlers in Hallamshire in the county of York: Trade Marks Act 1938 s 38 (repealed). The company was incorporated in 1623 by 21 Jac 1 c 31 (Hallamshire Cutlers) (1623). The Lordship and Liberty of Hallamshire is one of the manors comprised in the old borough of Sheffield.
3 See the Trade Marks Act 1938 s 30, Sch 2 (repealed).
4 See the Trade Marks Act 1994 s 105, Sch 3 para 20; and PARA 21 note 2. As to the registrar see PARA 19.

(2) PROCEDURE ON APPLICATION FOR REGISTRATION OF TRADE MARK OR PROTECTION OF INTERNATIONAL MARK

(i) In general

334. Business hours and business days. The registrar[1] may give directions specifying the hours of business of the Intellectual Property Office ('IPO')[2] for the purpose of the transaction by the public of business under the Trade Marks Act 1994 and the days which are business days for that purpose[3]. Any directions so given must be published[4] on the IPO website[5]. The IPO is be open at all times for the filing[6] of applications in respect of which no declaration as to priority[7] is made; the IPO is open at all times on Monday to Friday for the purpose of filing applications, forms and documents[8]; and the IPO is open on Monday to Friday between 9:00 am and 5:00 pm for all other types of business not detailed above[9]. The following are non-business days for all purposes under the 1994 Act[10]: (1) all Saturdays and Sundays; (2) Good Friday and Christmas Day; (3) a day which is specified or proclaimed to be a bank holiday[11].

Business done on any day after the specified hours of business, or on a day which is not a business day, is deemed to have been done on the next business day; and, where the time for doing anything under the Trade Marks Act 1994 expires on a day which is not a business day, that time is extended to the next business day[12].

1 As to the registrar see PARA 19.
2 As to the Intellectual Property Office (an operating name of the Patent Office) see PARA 16 note 2.
3 Trade Marks Act 1994 s 80(1). Directions so given may make different provision for different classes of business and must be published in the prescribed manner: s 80(3).

4 As to the meaning of 'publish' see PARA 19 note 10.
5 Trade Marks Rules 2008, SI 2008/1797, r 80. The IPO's website is accessible at the date at which this volume states the law at www.ipo.gov.uk.
6 As to the meaning of references to 'filing' see PARA 27 note 2; and as to the filing of documents by electronic means see PARA 336.
7 Ie for the purposes of the Trade Marks Act 1994 s 35 (see PARA 360) or s 36 (see PARA 361).
8 Ie except applications in respect of which no declaration for the purpose of the Trade Marks Act 1994 s 35 (see PARA 360) or s 36 (see PARA 361) is made.
9 Statement by the Comptroller-General of Patents, Designs and Trade Marks, July 2011: see www.ipo.gov.uk.
10 Ie except for the filing of applications in respect of which no declaration for the purpose of the Trade Marks Act 1994 s 35 (see PARA 360) or s 36 (see PARA 361) is made.
11 See note 9. Such specification or proclamation is under the Banking and Financial Dealings Act 1971 s 1: see TIME vol 97 (2010) PARA 321.
12 Trade Marks Act 1994 s 80(2).

335.   Use of forms. The registrar[1] may require the use of such forms as he may direct for any purpose relating to the registration of a trade mark[2] or any other proceeding before him under the Trade Marks Act 1994[3]. Any forms required by the registrar to be used for the purpose of registration of a trade mark or any other proceedings before him[4] and any directions with respect to their use must be published[5] and any amendment or modification of a form or of the directions with respect to its use must be published[6]. A requirement to use a form as published is satisfied by the use either of a replica of that form or of a form which is acceptable to the registrar and contains the information required by the form as published and complies with any directions as to the use of such a form[7]. If the form used is not a replica, it must preserve the essential features of the prescribed form. The registrar cannot exempt anyone from the obligation to use an acceptable form as and when required by the Trade Marks Act 1994 and the Trade Marks Rules 2008[8], but is able to decide whether departures from the prescribed forms are acceptable[9].

1 As to the registrar see PARA 19.
2 As to the meaning of 'trade mark' see PARA 41.
3 Trade Marks Act 1994 s 66(1). Any form required to be filed with the registrar in respect of any specified matter is subject to the payment of the fee, if any, prescribed in respect of that matter by rules made under s 79 (see PARA 18): Trade Marks Rules 2008, SI 2008/1797, r 4(2). As to the meaning of references to 'filing' see PARA 27 note 2; and as to the filing of documents by electronic means see PARA 336. As to fees see PARA 18.
4 Ie pursuant to the Trade Marks Act 1994 s 66.
5 As to the meaning of 'publish' see PARA 19 note 10.
6 Trade Marks Act 1994 s 66(2); Trade Marks Rules 2008, SI 2008/1797, r 3(1). The forms required to be used under the Trade Marks Act 1994 and the Trade Marks Rules 2008, SI 2008/1797, are published on the Intellectual Property Office ('IPO') website, accessible at the date at which this volume states the law at www.ipo.gov.uk. As to the Intellectual Property Office (an operating name of the Patent Office) see PARA 16 note 2.
7 Trade Marks Rules 2008, SI 2008/1797, r 3(2). This is except in relation to Forms TM6 and TM7A.
8 Ie the Trade Marks Rules 2008, SI 2008/1797.
9 *Re M's Application* [1985] RPC 249, CA; *KML Invest AB's Trade Mark Application* [2004] RPC 972, Appointed Person.

336.   Filing of documents by electronic means and electronic communications. The registrar[1] may, at his discretion, permit as an alternative to sending by post or delivery of the application, notice or other document in legible form the filing[2] of the application, notice or other document by electronic means subject to such terms or conditions as he may specify either generally by published[3] notice or in any particular case by written notice to the person desiring to file any such documents by such means[4].

The delivery using electronic communications[5] to any person by the registrar of any document is deemed to be effected, unless the registrar has otherwise specified, by transmitting an electronic communication containing the document to an address provided or made available to the registrar by that person as an address of his for the receipt of electronic communications[6]. Unless the contrary is provided such delivery is deemed to be effected immediately upon the transmission of the communication[7].

1 As to the registrar see PARA 19.
2 For the general meaning of references to 'filing' see PARA 27 note 2.
3 As to the meaning of 'publish' see PARA 19 note 10.
4 Trade Marks Rules 2000, SI 2008/1797, r 78. It is now possible to file a trade mark application online via the Intellectual Property Office ('IPO') website, accessible at the date at which this volume states the law at www.ipo.gov.uk. As to the Intellectual Property Office (an operating name of the Patent Office) see PARA 16 note 2.
5 Ie electronic communications within the meaning of the Electronic Communications Act 2000 (see CIVIL PROCEDURE vol 11 (2009) PARA 947): Trade Marks Rules 2008, SI 2008/1797, r 79(2).
6 Trade Marks Rules 2008, SI 2008/1797, r 79(1).
7 Trade Marks Rules 2008, SI 2008/1797, r 79(1).

337.   Translations. Where any document or part thereof which is in a language other than English is filed[1] or sent[2] to the registrar[3], the registrar may require that there be furnished a translation into English of the document or that part, verified to the satisfaction of the registrar as corresponding to the original text[4]. The registrar may, however, refuse to accept any translation which he considers inaccurate; and thereupon another translation of the document in question verified to the satisfaction of the registrar as corresponding to the original text must be furnished[5].

1 As to the meaning of references to 'filing' see PARA 27 note 2. As to the filing of documents by electronic means see PARA 336.
2 Ie in pursuance of the Trade Marks Act 1994 or the Trade Marks Rules 2008, SI 2008/1797.
3 As to the registrar see PARA 19.
4 Trade Marks Rules 2008, SI 2008/1797, r 82(1).
5 Trade Marks Rules 2008, SI 2008/1797, r 82(2).

338.   Calculation of times and periods; alteration of time limits. The registrar[1] may certify any day as an interrupted day[2] where (1) there is an event or circumstance causing an interruption in the normal operation of the Intellectual Property Office ('IPO')[3]; or (2) there is a general interruption or subsequent dislocation in the postal services of the United Kingdom[4].

Any such certificate of the registrar must be displayed in the IPO and published on the IPO website[5]. Where the time for doing anything under the Trade Marks Rules 2008[6] expires on an interrupted day, the registrar must extend that time to the next following day not being an interrupted day (or an excluded day)[7].

The registrar must extend any time limit in the Trade Marks Rules 2008 where he is satisfied that the failure to do something under those rules was wholly or mainly attributed to a delay in, or failure of, a communication service[8]. Any such extension is to be made after giving the parties such notice, and subject to such conditions, as the registrar may direct[9].

Subject to important exceptions[10], the registrar may, at the request of the person or party concerned or at the registrar's own initiative extend a time or period prescribed by the Trade Marks Rules 2008 or a time or period specified by the registrar for doing any act and any such extension[11] must be made subject to such conditions as the registrar may direct[12].

Such a request for extension[13] may be made before or after the time or period in question has expired and must be made (a) where the application for registration has not been published and the request for an extension relates to a time or period other than one specified in relation to deficiencies in a trade mark application[14] and is made before the time or period in question has expired, in writing[15]; and (b) in any other case, on Form TM9[16].

Where such an extension[17] is requested in relation to proceedings before the registrar[18], the party seeking the extension must send a copy of the request to every other person who is a party to the proceedings[19].

1   As to the registrar see PARA 19.
2   For these purposes, 'interrupted day' means a day certified by the registrar under the Trade Marks Rules 2008, SI 2008/1797, r 75(1): r 75(4).
3   Trade Marks Rules 2008, SI 2008/1797, r 75(1)(a). As to the Intellectual Property Office (an operating name of the Patent Office) see PARA 16 note 2.
4   Trade Marks Rules 2008, SI 2008/1797, r 75(1)(b). As to the meaning of 'United Kingdom' see PARA 3 note 2.
5   Trade Marks Rules 2008, SI 2008/1797, r 75(2). The IPO's website is accessible at the date at which this volume states the law at www.ipo.gov.uk.
6   Ie the Trade Marks Rules 2008, SI 2008/1797.
7   Trade Marks Rules 2008, SI 2008/1797, r 75(3). An 'excluded day' is a day which is not a business day as specified in a direction given by the registrar under the Trade Marks Act 1994 s 80 (see PARA 334): Trade Marks Rules 2008, SI 2008/1797, r 75(4).
8   Trade Marks Rules 2008, SI 2008/1797, r 76(1). A communication service is a service by which documents may be sent and delivered, and includes post, facsimile, email and courier: r 76(3).
9   Trade Marks Rules 2008, SI 2008/1797, r 76(2).
10 The exceptions are specified in the Trade Marks Rules 2008, SI 2008/1797, r 77(4), (5) (see below).
       The registrar must extend a flexible time limit, except a time or period which applies in relation to proceedings before the registrar or the filing of an appeal to the Appointed Person under r 71 (see PARA 389), where (1) the request for extension is made before the end of the period of two months beginning immediately after the date the relevant time or period expired; and (2) no previous request has been made under r 77(4): r 77(4) (amended by SI 2013/444). For these purposes, 'flexible time limit' means (a) a time or period prescribed by the Trade Marks Rules 2008, SI 2008/1797, except a time or period prescribed by the rules listed in Sch 1 (see below); or (b) a time or period specified by the registrar for doing any act or taking any proceedings; and 'proceedings before the registrar' means any dispute between two or more parties relating to a matter before the registrar in connection with a trade mark: r 77(6). As to calculation of time periods see Tribunal Practice Notice (TPN 1/2013), available from the IPO website (see note 5).
       A time limit listed in the Trade Marks Rules 2008, SI 2008/1797, Sch 1 (see below) (whether it has already expired or not) may be extended under r 77(1) if, and only if (i) the irregularity or prospective irregularity is attributable, wholly or in part, to a default, omission or other error by the registrar, the IPO or the International Bureau; and (ii) it appears to the registrar that the irregularity should be rectified: r 77(5). As to the International Bureau see PARA 8 text and note 2.
       The time limits in Sch 1 are those in r 17(2) (filing notice of opposition) (see PARA 366); r 17(3) (filing notice of opposition: request for extension of time) (see PARA 366); r 18(1) (counter-statement in opposition proceedings) (see PARA 366); r 19(4) (responding to preliminary indication) (see PARA 366); r 25(2) (opposition to amendment after publication) (see PARA 357); r 30(4) (opposition to amendment of regulations of collective and certification marks) (see PARA 144); r 32(3) (opposition to alteration of mark) (see PARA 375); r 35 (renewal of registration) (see PARA 31); r 36(2) (delayed renewal) (see PARA 31); r 37(1) (restoration of registration) (see PARA 32); r 38(3) (counter-statement for revocation on grounds of non-use) (see PARA 380); r 39(3) (counter-statement for revocation on grounds other than non-use) (see

PARA 381); r 41(6) (counter-statement for invalidity) (see PARA 382); 43(2) (setting aside cancellation of application or revocation or invalidation of registration) (see PARA 385); r 53(2) (opposition to removal of matter from register) (see PARA 30); r 55(1) (opposition to proposals for change of classification) (see PARA 374); and r 77(4) (period for making a retrospective request to extend a flexible time period) (see above).

11 Ie under the Trade Marks Rules 2008, SI 2008/1797, r 77(1).
12 Trade Marks Rules 2008, SI 2008/1797, r 77(1). Rule 74 (see PARA 343) is subject to s 77.
13 Ie under the Trade Marks Rules 2008, SI 2008/1797, r 77.
14 Ie other than one specified in the Trade Marks Rules 2008, SI 2008/1797, r 13: see PARA 345.
15 Trade Marks Rules 2008, SI 2008/1797, r 77(2)(a) (amended by SI 2009/2089).
16 Trade Marks Rules 2008, SI 2008/1797, r 77(2)(b).
17 See note 11.
18 See note 10.
19 Trade Marks Rules 2008, SI 2008/1797, r 77(3).

339.   Address for service.   For the purposes of any proceedings under the Trade Marks Act 1994 or the Trade Marks Rules 2008[1], an address for service must be filed by:

(1)   an applicant for the registration of a trade mark[2];

(2)   any person who opposes the registration of a trade mark in opposition proceedings[3];

(3)   any person who applies for revocation[4], a declaration of invalidity[5] or rectification[6] under the Act[7];

(4)   the proprietor of the registered trade mark who opposes such an application[8].

The proprietor of a registered trade mark, or any person who has registered an interest in a registered trade mark, may file an address for service on the appropriate form or, in the case of an assignment of a registered trade mark, on the appropriate form[9]. Where a person has provided an address for service, he may substitute a new address for service by notifying the registrar on the appropriate form[10].

An address for service filed under this provision[11] must be an address in the United Kingdom[12], another EEA state[13] or the Channel Islands[14].

Where a person had failed to file an address for service as required[15] and the registrar has sufficient information enabling him to contact that person, the registrar must direct that person to file an address for service[16]. Where such a direction has been given, the person directed must file an address for service before the end of the period of one month beginning immediately after the date of the direction[17]. Where such a direction was given and the period prescribed has expired or the registrar has insufficient information to give such a direction[18], then:

(a)   in the case of an applicant for the registration of a trade mark, the application will be treated as withdrawn[19];

(b)   in the case of a person opposing the registration of a trade mark, his opposition will be treated as withdrawn[20];

(c)   in the case of a person applying for revocation, a declaration of invalidity or rectification, his application will be treated as withdrawn[21]; and

(d)   in the case of a proprietor opposing such an application, he will be deemed to have withdrawn from the proceedings[22].

Of the above provisions, only head (a) above[23] does not apply to international trade marks[24].

1   Ie the Trade Marks Rules 2008, SI 2008/1797.

2 Trade Marks Rules 2008, SI 2008/1797, r 11(1)(a). As to the requirements for registration see PARA 39 et seq; and as to the procedure on the application see PARA 345 et seq.
3 Trade Marks Rules 2008, SI 2008/1797, r 11(1)(b). As to opposition proceedings see PARAS 366–368.
4 As to revocation see PARAS 98 et seq, 378 et seq.
5 As to a declaration of invalidity see PARAS 102 et seq, 378 et seq.
6 As to rectification see PARAS 105, 378 et seq.
7 Trade Marks Rules 2008, SI 2008/1797, r 11(1)(c).
8 Trade Marks Rules 2008, SI 2008/1797, r 11(1)(d).
9 Trade Marks Rules 2008, SI 2008/1797, r 11(2). The appropriate form is Form TM33 or Form TM16 respectively: r 11(2). As to the use of forms see PARA 335.
10 Trade Marks Rules 2008, SI 2008/1797, r 11(3). The appropriate form is Form TM33: r 11(3). It is the responsibility of the person concerned to notify any change of address for service to the registrar, and the registrar is under no duty to verify the currency of the address for service when sending documents: *OIOI Trade Mark* (O/340/04), Appointed Person.
11 Ie under the Trade Marks Rules 2008, SI 2008/1797, r 11.
12 As to the meaning of 'United Kingdom' see PARA 3 note 2.
13 As to the EEA see PARA 86 note 6.
14 Trade Marks Rules 2008, SI 2008/17 97, r 11(4).
15 Ie under the Trade Marks Rules 2008, SI 2008/1797, r 11(1).
16 Trade Marks Rules 2008, SI 2008/1797, r 12(1).
17 Trade Marks Rules 2008, SI 2008/1797, r 12(2) (amended by SI 2013/444). As to calculation of time periods see Tribunal Practice Notice (TPN 1/2013), available from the Intellectual Property Office ('IPO') website, accessible at the date at which this volume states the law at www.ipo.gov.uk. As to the Intellectual Property Office (an operating name of the Patent Office) see PARA 16 note 2.
18 Trade Marks Rules 2008, SI 2008/1797, r 12(3).
19 Trade Marks Rules 2008, SI 2008/1797, r 12(4)(a). It should be noted that r 12(4)(a) does not apply to international trade marks (UK) or requests for extension: see the Trade Marks (International Registration) Order 2008, SI 2008/2206, art 3(3), Sch 1 Pt 2; and PARA 12 note 13.
20 Trade Marks Rules 2008, SI 2008/1797, r 12(4)(b).
21 Trade Marks Rules 2008, SI 2008/1797, r 12(4)(c).
22 Trade Marks Rules 2008, SI 2008/1797, r 12(4)(d).
23 Ie the Trade Marks Rules 2008, SI 2008/1797, r 12(4)(a): see the text and note 19.
24 See the Trade Marks (International Registration) Order 2008, SI 2008/2206, art 3(3), Sch 1 Pt 2; and PARA 12 note 13. See generally PARA 11 et seq.

(ii) Procedural Powers of the Registrar

340. In general. Without prejudice to any provisions of the trade marks legislation[1] requiring the registrar[2] to hear any party to proceedings under that legislation[3], or to give such party an opportunity to be heard, the registrar must, before taking any decision on any matter which is or may be adverse to any party to any proceedings before him, give that party an opportunity to be heard[4]. The registrar must give that party at least 14 days' notice, beginning on the day on which notice is sent, of the time when he may be heard unless that party consents to shorter notice[5].

In relation to the examination of witnesses on oath and the disclosure and production of documents, the registrar has all the powers of an official referee of the Senior Courts or the Court of Judicature[6]; and the rules applicable to the attendance of witnesses before such a referee apply in relation to the attendance of witnesses in proceedings before the registrar[7].

The Intellectual Property Office ('IPO') has issued general guidance as to the practice which will be followed in exercise of the registrar's powers of case management, pre-hearing review and generally when the registrar is acting as a tribunal[8].

The hearing before the registrar of any dispute between two or more parties relating to any matter in connection with an application for the registration of a mark or a registered mark must be in public unless the registrar, after consultation with those parties who appear in person or are represented at the hearing, otherwise directs[9].

1   Ie any provisions of the Trade Marks Act 1994 or the Trade Marks Rules 2008, SI 2008/1797.
2   As to the registrar see PARA 19.
3   Ie proceedings under the Trade Marks Act 1994 or the Trade Marks Rules 2008, SI 2008/1797.
4   Trade Marks Rules 2008, SI 2008/1797, r 63(1). Rule 63 does not apply to fast track opposition proceedings (see PARA 366 text and notes 6, 7): r 63(3) (added by SI 2013/2235).
     Tribunal Practice Notice (TPN 5/2000) [2001] RPC 253 sets out the registrar's practice with regard to hearings under the Trade Marks Rules 2000, SI 2000/136, r 54 (now the Trade Marks Rules 2008, SI 2008/1797, r 63). Tribunal Practice Notices are available from the Intellectual Property Office ('IPO') or on its website, accessible at the date at which this volume states the law at www.ipo.gov.uk. As to the Intellectual Property Office (an operating name of the Patent Office) see PARA 16 note 2.
     The right to a hearing is a fundamental right under the Convention for the Protection of Human Rights and Fundamental Freedoms (Rome, 4 November 1950; TS 71 (1953); Cmd 8969) art 6 (see RIGHTS AND FREEDOMS vol 88A (2013) PARAS 88, 243 et seq), and the denial of a hearing will normally constitute a serious irregularity in procedure: *Gracey's Trade Mark Application* (O/375/01), Appointed Person; *MOVIESTAR Trade Mark* [2005] RPC 623, Appointed Person. Where a decision is taken in breach of the Trade Marks Rules 2000, SI 2000/136, r 54 (see now the Trade Marks Rules 2008, SI 2008/1797, r 63), the affected party is entitled to challenge the decision under the Trade Marks Rules 2000, SI 2000/136, r 66 (see now the Trade Marks Rules 2008, SI 2008/1797, r 74) (see PARA 343): *RAPIER Trade Mark* (O/170/07), Appointed Person.
5   Trade Marks Rules 2008, SI 2008/1797, r 63(2). See note 4. As to calculation of time periods see Tribunal Practice Notice (TPN 1/2013), available from the IPO website (see note 4).
6   Trade Marks Act 1994 s 69(b) (amended by the Constitutional Reform Act 2005 Sch 11 Pt 4 para 31); Trade Marks Rules 2008, SI 2008/1797, r 65.
     The power to order disclosure (formerly referred to as discovery) of documents should be exercised only in respect of documents which are relevant to the matter in dispute and disclosure of which is necessary to dispose fairly of the proceedings: *LIFESAVERS Trade Mark* [1997] RPC 563; and see also *Merrell Dow Pharmaceuticals Inc's (Terfenidine) Patent* [1991] RPC 221.
7   Trade Marks Act 1994 s 69(c); Trade Marks Rules 2008, SI 2008/1797, r 65.
8   Tribunal Practice Notice (TPN 1/2000) [2000] RPC 587. The Tribunal Practice Notice relates generally to proceedings relating to patents, trade marks and designs, and applies to proceedings where there are two or more parties in front of the registrar as well as proceedings where only one party and the registrar are involved.
9   Trade Marks Rules 2008, SI 2008/1797, r 66(1). As to the registrar's decisions see PARA 386.

341.   Evidence; proceedings generally. The Trade Marks Rules 2008[1] may make provision as to the giving of evidence in proceedings before the registrar[2] under the Trade Marks Act 1994[3]. Evidence filed[4] in any proceedings may be given by witness statement, affidavit, statutory declaration; or in any other form which would be admissible as evidence in proceedings before the court[5].

A witness statement[6] may only be given in evidence if it includes a statement of truth[7]. The general rule is that evidence at hearings is to be by witness statement unless the registrar or any enactment requires otherwise[8].

Except where the Trade Marks Act 1994 or the Trade Marks Rules 2008 otherwise provide, the registrar may give such directions as to the management of any proceedings as the registrar thinks fit, and in particular may: (1) require a document, information or evidence to be filed within such period as the registrar may specify[9]; (2) require a translation of any document[10]; (3) require a party or a party's legal representative to attend a hearing[11]; (4) hold a hearing by telephone or by using any other method of direct oral communication[12]; (5) allow a statement of case to be amended, subject to a proviso[13]; (6) stay the whole, or any part, of the proceedings either generally or until a specified date or event[14]; (7) consolidate proceedings, subject to a proviso[15]; (8) direct that part of any proceedings be dealt with as separate proceedings[16]; (9) exclude any evidence which the registrar considers to be inadmissible[17]; (10) direct that with effect from the date specified in the direction opposition proceedings which have been commenced on Form TM7F as a fast track opposition but which do not satisfy the criteria for a fast track opposition may continue as if the opposition proceedings were an opposition to the registration commenced[18] on Form TM7[19].

The registrar may control the evidence by giving directions as to (a) the issues on which evidence is required; and (b) the way in which the evidence is to be placed before the registrar[20].

When the registrar gives directions under any provision of the Trade Marks Rules 2008, the registrar may (i) make them subject to conditions; and (ii) specify the consequences of failure to comply with the directions or a condition[21].

The registrar may at any stage of any proceedings direct that the parties to the proceedings attend a case management conference or pre-hearing review[22].

In the case of a fast track opposition (A) proceedings must be held orally only if the Intellectual Property Office ('IPO') requests it or if either party to the proceedings requests it and the registrar considers that oral proceedings are necessary to deal with the case justly and at proportionate cost; and (B) the parties must be given at least 14 days' notice beginning on the date on which the notice is sent, of the time when the oral proceedings are to take place unless each party to the proceedings consents to shorter notice[23].

In the case of a fast track opposition, where no oral hearing is held, the registrar must give the parties the opportunity to provide arguments in writing before reaching a decision that is adverse to either party[24].

1   Ie the Trade Marks Rules 2008, SI 2008/1797.

2   As to the registrar see PARA 19.

3   Trade Marks Act 1994 s 69(a).

4   As to the meaning of references to 'filing' see PARA 27 note 2. As to the filing of documents by electronic means see PARA 336. Under the Trade Marks Rules 2008, SI 2008/1797, evidence is only considered filed when (1) it has been received by the registrar; and (2) it has been sent to all other parties to the proceedings: r 64(6).

5   See the Trade Marks Rules 2008, SI 2008/1797, r 64(1). This is subject to r 62(2) (see the text and note 18) and r 64(2)–(6) (see the text and notes 4, 6–8).
     If a party desires to test the evidence given by affidavit, statutory declaration or witness statement, then prima facie and within reason he should be allowed to do so: *Alliance & Leicester plc's Trade Mark Application* [2002] RPC 573; *Hokko Chemical Industry Co Ltd v Hokochemie GmbH* (O/158/08), Appointed Person. The registrar usually requires reasonable written notice to be given of any desire to cross-examine a witness: see Tribunal Practice Notice 3/210. Tribunal Practice Notices are available from the Intellectual Property Office ('IPO') or on its website, accessible at the date at which this volume states the law at www.ipo.gov.uk. As to the Intellectual Property Office (an operating name of the Patent Office) see PARA 16 note 2.
     In the absence of cross-examination or other proper challenge it is not open to the registrar to disbelieve evidence which is not obviously incredible: *EXTREME Trade Mark* [2008] RPC 2, Appointed Person. This does not mean that it is not possible for the registrar to make a finding of bad faith in the absence of cross-examination: *BRUTT Trade Marks* [2007] RPC 341, Appointed Person. See also Tribunal Practice Notice 5/2007.
     As to hearsay evidence in registry proceedings see *Practice Notice* [1999] RPC 294; *DUCCIO Trade Mark* (O/343/09), Appointed Person; Tribunal Practice Direction 5/2009.

6   In the Trade Marks Rules 2008, SI 2008/1797, a witness statement is a written statement signed by a person that contains the evidence which that person would be allowed to give orally: r 64(5).

7   Trade Marks Rules 2008, SI 2008/1797, r 64(2). For the purposes of the Trade Marks Rules 2008, SI 2008/1797, a statement of truth (1) means a statement that the person making the statement believes that the facts stated in a particular document are true; and (2) must be dated and signed by (a) in the case of a witness statement, the maker of the statement; (b) in any other case, the party or legal representative of such party: r 64(4).

8   Trade Marks Rules 2008, SI 2008/1797, r 64(3).

9   Trade Marks Rules 2008, SI 2008/1797, r 62(1)(a).

10   Trade Marks Rules 2008, SI 2008/1797, r 62(1)(b). As to translations see PARA 337.

11   Trade Marks Rules 2008, SI 2008/1797, r 62(1)(c).

12   Trade Marks Rules 2008, SI 2008/1797, r 62(1)(d).

13   Trade Marks Rules 2008, SI 2008/1797, r 62(1)(e) (substituted by SI 2013/2235). This is provided that: (1) where an application is made to add grounds of opposition other than under the Trade Marks Act 1994 s 5(1) (see PARA 55) or s 5(2) (see PARA 56), the application must be made on Form TM7G; and (2) in the case of fast track oppositions (see PARA 366 text and notes 6, 7) the registrar may only permit a statement of case to be amended to add additional or alternative earlier registered or protected trade marks as additional grounds of opposition under the Trade Marks Act 1994 s 5(1) or s 5(2), provided that the total number of earlier trade marks relied upon may not exceed three: Trade Marks Rules 2008, SI 2008/1797, r 62(1)(e) (as so substituted). As to the meaning of 'fast track opposition' see PARA 366 note 6.

14   Trade Marks Rules 2008, SI 2008/1797, r 62(1)(f). In particular, the registrar may, where appropriate, stay the proceedings pending the determination of an application for revocation or a declaration of invalidity of an earlier trade mark, including a Community trade mark, relied upon by the opponent or applicant for a declaration of invalidity: see *American Home Products Corp v Knoll AG* [2002] EWHC 828 (Ch), [2002] All ER (D) 169 (Mar); *Croom's Trade Mark Application* [2005] RPC 23, Appointed Person; *JUICY DIAMONDS Trade Mark* (O/231/07), *KULTUN MADRAN Trade Mark* (0/124/11), Appointed Person; *Sensormatic Electronics LLC v Anglo Design Holdings plc* (O/203/13), Appointed Person.

15   Trade Marks Rules 2008, SI 2008/1797, r 62(1)(g) (substituted by SI 2013/2235). This is provided that where a fast track opposition (see PARA 366 text and notes 6, 7) is consolidated with other non-fast track proceedings, it must no longer be treated as a fast track opposition: Trade Marks Rules 2008, SI 2008/1797, r 62(1)(g) (as so substituted).

16   Trade Marks Rules 2008, SI 2008/1797, r 62(1)(h).

17   Trade Marks Rules 2008, SI 2008/1797, r 62(1)(i).

18   Ie under the Trade Marks Rules 2008, SI 2008/1797, r 17: see PARA 366.

19   Trade Marks Rules 2008, SI 2008/1797, r 62(1)(j) (added by SI 2013/2235).

20   Trade Marks Rules 2008, SI 2008/1797, r 62(2).

21   Trade Marks Rules 2008, SI 2008/1797, r 62(3).

22   Trade Marks Rules 2008, SI 2008/1797, r 62(4).

23   Trade Marks Rules 2008, SI 2008/1797, r 62(5) (added by SI 2013/2235). As to guidance on oral hearings versus written submissions see Tribunal Practice Notice (TPN 2/2013) on Fast Track Oppositions, available from the IPO website (see note 5).

24   Trade Marks Rules 2008, SI 2008/1797, r 62(6) (added by SI 2013/2235).

342. Costs and security for costs. The registrar[1] may in any proceedings before him, under the Trade Marks Act 1994 or the Trade Marks Rules 2008[2], by order award any party such costs as he may consider reasonable; and he may direct how and by what parties they are to be paid[3]. Any such order of the registrar may be enforced in the same way as an order of the High Court[4].

The registrar may require any person who is a party in any proceedings before him, under the Trade Marks Act 1994 or the Trade Marks Rules 2008, to give security for costs in relation to those proceedings; and he may require security for the costs of any appeal from his decision[5]. In default of such security being given, the registrar, in the case of proceedings before him, or the person duly appointed[6], in the case of an appeal, may treat the party in default as having withdrawn his application, opposition, objection or intervention, as the case may be[7].

1   As to the registrar see PARA 19.

2   Ie the Trade Marks Rules 2000, SI 2008/1797.

3   Trade Marks Act 1994 s 68(1); Trade Marks Rules 2008, SI 2008/1797, r 67. The registrar's
     normal practice is to make modest awards of costs on a scale, but he has a discretion to order
     compensatory costs: *Rizla Ltd's Application* [1993] RPC 365. An award of costs should not
     exceed the costs incurred, and a litigant in person should not be in any more favourable position
     in proceedings before the registrar than in the High Court under CPR r 48.6 (now r. 46.5): *Inbev
     SA v Air Parts Europe Ltd* (O/160/08), Appointed Person. The Intellectual Property Office
     ('IPO') has issued guidance as to the practice in exercising powers to award costs in, inter alia,
     trade mark matters: Tribunal Practice Notice 6/2008. Tribunal Practice Notices are available
     from the IPO or on its website, accessible at the date at which this volume states the law at
     www.ipo.gov.uk. As to the Intellectual Property Office (an operating name of the Patent Office)
     see PARA 16 note 2.
4   Trade Marks Act 1994 s 68(2)(a).
5   Trade Marks Act 1994 s 68(3); Trade Marks Rules 2008, SI 2000/1797, r 68(1).
6   Ie appointed under the Trade Marks Act 1994 s 76: see PARA 387 et seq.
7   Trade Marks Act 1994 s 68(3); Trade Marks Rules 2008, SI 2008/1797, r 68(2).

343.   Correction of irregularities of procedure. Subject to the provision on
alteration of time limits[1], the registrar[2] may authorise the rectification of any
irregularity in procedure[3] (including the rectification of any document filed)
connected with any proceeding or other matter before the registrar or the
Intellectual Property Office ('IPO')[4]. Any such rectification[5] must be made after
giving the parties such notice and subject to such conditions as the registrar may
direct[6].

1   Ie subject to the Trade Marks Rules 2008, SI 2008/1797, r 77: see PARA 338.
         The registrar's powers under the Trade Marks Rules 2000, SI 2000/136, r 66 (see now the
     Trade Marks Rules 2008, SI 2008/1797, r 74) cannot be used in a manner contrary to other
     provisions of the Trade Marks Act 1994 or the Trade Marks Rules 2000, SI 2000/136 (see now
     the Trade Marks Rules 2008, SI 2008/1797), and accordingly cannot be used to extend time
     limits which are inextensible by virtue of the Trade Marks Rules 2000, SI 2000/136, r 68(3) (see
     now the Trade Marks Rules 2008, SI 2008/1797, r 77): *E's Applications* [1983] RPC 231, HL;
     KML Invest AB's Trade Mark Application [2004] RPC 972, Appointed Person. The registrar
     has power under the Trade Marks Rules 2000, SI 2000/136, r 66 (see now the Trade Marks
     Rules 2008, SI 2008/1797, r 74) to withdraw the registration of a trade mark if the registration
     was procedurally irregular: see *Andreas Stihl AG & Co's Trade Mark Application* [2001] RPC
     215, Appointed Person; *BAT OUT OF HELL Trade Mark* (O/398/02), Appointed Person.
2   As to the registrar see PARA 19.
3   An irregularity in procedure is simply a failure to observe procedural rules, whatever the cause
     of the failure may be: *E's Applications* [1983] RPC 231 at 250, HL, per Lord Diplock. An
     attempt by a solicitor to file a notice of opposition on the last day which failed because he
     attempted to use an out of date fax number, when the current fax numbers of the Patent Office
     (see note 4) were published weekly in the Trade Marks Journal, did not amount to an
     irregularity in the Patent Office and so there was no power to extend time: *MONSTER
     MUNCH Trade Mark* [1997] RPC 721, Trade Marks Registry. As to the Trade Marks Journal
     see PARA 19.
4   Trade Marks Rules 2008, SI 2008/1797, r 74(1). As to the Intellectual Property Office (an
     operating name of the Patent Office) see PARA 16 note 2.
5   Ie under the Trade Marks Rules 2008, SI 2008/1797, r 74(1).
6   Trade Marks Rules 2008, SI 2008/1797, r 74(2).

344.   Registrar's inherent jurisdiction. The registrar[1] has an inherent
jurisdiction to regulate procedure before him provided that he neither creates a
substantial jurisdiction where none existed nor exercises that power in a manner
inconsistent with the express provisions conferring jurisdiction upon him[2]. It
appears that it is pursuant to this inherent jurisdiction that the registrar grants or
refuses parties to proceedings before him permission to amend their statements
of case[3].

1   As to the registrar see PARA 19.

2   *Pharmedica GmbH's Trade Mark Application* [2000] RPC 536, [2000] All ER (D) 28; *ACADEMY Trade Mark* [2000] RPC 35, Appointed Person; *Hyde's Trade Mark Applications (No 2)* (O/333/05), Appointed Person.

3   See *COFFEEMIX Trade Mark* [1998] RPC 717, Appointed Person; and cf *BSA BY R2 Trade Mark* (O/144/07), Appointed Person.

(iii) Application for Registration

345. Application relating to United Kingdom registered marks. An application for registration[1] of a trade mark[2] must be made to the registrar[3] and must be filed[4] on the appropriate form[5]. The application must contain: (1) a request for registration of a trade mark; (2) the name and address of the applicant[6]; (3) a statement of the goods or services in relation to which it is sought to register the trade mark[7]; and (4) a representation[8] of the trade mark[9]. The application must also specify the class or classes to which it relates[10]. The application must state that the trade mark is being used[11], by the applicant or with his consent, in relation to those goods or services, or that he has a bona fide intention that it should be so used[12].

The application is subject to the payment of the application fee and such class fees as may be appropriate[13].

Where an application is filed on Form TM3 (a 'standard application') the application is subject to the payment of the standard application fee and such class and series fees as may be appropriate[14]. Where an application is filed on Form e-TM3 (an 'electronic application') the application is subject to the payment of the e-filed application fee and such class and series fees as may be appropriate, which are payable at the time the electronic application is made and if they are not so paid the application is subject to the payment of the standard application fee[15] and such class and series fees as may be appropriate[16].

Where an application is for the registration of a single trade mark, an applicant may request the registrar to undertake an expedited examination of the application[17]. A request for expedited examination[18] must be made on Form e-TM3 and is subject to payment of the prescribed fee[19]. Where an applicant makes a request for expedited examination, the application fee and any class fees payable in respect of the application are payable at the time the application is made[20].

Where the registrar receives a request for expedited examination as above[21], the date on which the registrar is deemed to have notified the applicant whether or not it appears to the registrar that the requirements for registration are met is the date on which notice is sent to the applicant[22].

Where an application for registration of a trade mark does not satisfy the statutory requirements[23], the registrar must send[24] notice thereof to the applicant to remedy the deficiencies or, as the case may be, default of payment[25]. Such a notice must specify a period, of not less than 14 days, within which the applicant must remedy the deficiencies or the default of payment[26].

Where, before the expiry of the above period[27] the applicant:

(a)   fails to remedy any deficiency relating to the contents of the application notified to him[28], the application is deemed never to have been made[29]; or

(b)   fails to remedy any other deficiency[30] notified to him or fails to make payment[31], the application is treated as abandoned[32].

1   As to the meaning of 'registration' see PARA 21 note 2.
2   As to the meaning of 'trade mark' see PARA 41.

3   As to the registrar see PARA 19.
4   As to the meaning of references to 'filing' see PARA 27 note 2. As to the filing of documents by
     electronic means see PARA 336.
5   Trade Marks Act 1994 s 32(1); Trade Marks Rules 2008, SI 2008/1797, r 5(1) (substituted by
     SI 2009/2089). An application for the registration of a trade mark (other than a transformation
     application (see PARA 14), which must be filed on Form TM4) must be filed on Form TM3 or,
     where the application is filed in electronic form using the filing system provided on the
     Intellectual Property Office ('IPO') website, on Form e-TM3: Trade Marks Rules 2008,
     SI 2008/1797, r 5(1) (as so substituted). The IPO website is accessible at the date at which this
     volume states the law at www.ipo.gov.uk. As to the Intellectual Property Office (an operating
     name of the Patent Office) see PARA 16 note 2. As to the use of forms see PARA 335.
         An application for registration of a mark under the Trade Marks Act 1938 which was
     pending on 31 October 1994 must be dealt with under the old law and, if registered, the mark
     must be treated as an existing registered mark: Trade Marks Act 1994 s 105, Sch 3 para 10(1).
     The power of the Secretary of State under s 78 (see PARA 17) to make rules regulating practice
     and procedure, and as to the matters mentioned in s 78(2), is exercisable in relation to such an
     application; and different provision may be made for such applications from that made for other
     applications: Sch 3 para 10(2). As to the Secretary of State see PARA 16. The Trade Marks
     Act 1938 s 23 (repealed) (provisions as to associated trade marks) must be disregarded in
     dealing on and after 31 October 1994 with an application for registration: Trade Marks
     Act 1994 Sch 3 para 10(3). As to the meaning of 'the old law' see PARA 4 note 3; and as to the
     meaning of 'existing registered mark' see PARA 4 note 2.
         In the case of a pending application for registration which had not been advertised under the
     Trade Marks Act 1938 s 18 (repealed) before 31 October 1994, the applicant might give notice
     to the registrar claiming to have the registrability of the mark determined in accordance with the
     provisions of the Trade Marks Act 1994: Sch 3 para 11(1). Notice duly given was irrevocable
     and had the effect that the application was treated as if made immediately after 31 October
     1994: Sch 3 para 11(3).
         It should be noted that the Trade Marks Act 1994 s 32(1), (2), (4) does not apply to
     protected international trade marks (UK) or requests for extension: see the Trade Marks
     (International Registration) Order 2008, SI 2008/2206, art 3, Sch 1 Pt 1; and PARA 12 note 10.
     See also PARA 347.
6   An application by a partnership may now be made in the name of the partnership, rather than in
     the names of the individual partners as formerly: Practice Amendment Notice PAN 2/04; but see
     Drinkstop Ltd v Michaels Foodmarket (O/168/05), Appointed Person.
7   The goods and services for which the protection of the trade mark is sought must be identified
     by the applicant with sufficient clarity and precision to enable the competent authorities and
     economic operators, on that basis alone, to determine the extent of the protection conferred by
     the trade mark: Case C-307/10 *Chartered Institute of Patent Attorneys v Registrar of Trade
     Marks* [2012] ECR I-000, [2012] IP & T 650, [2013] RPC 313, ECJ. This does not preclude the
     use of the general indications of the class headings of the Nice Classification provided that such
     identification is sufficiently clear and precise: Case C-307/10 *Chartered Institute of Patent
     Attorneys v Registrar of Trade Marks*. An applicant for a trade mark who uses all the general
     indications of a particular class heading of the Nice Classification to identify the goods or
     services for which the protection of the trade mark is sought must specify whether its
     application for registration is intended to cover all the goods or services included in the
     alphabetical list of that class or only some of those goods or services. If the application concerns
     only some of those goods or services, the applicant is required to specify which of the goods or
     services in that class are intended to be covered: Case C-307/10 *Chartered Institute of Patent
     Attorneys v Registrar of Trade Marks*; and see also *Chartered Institute of Patent Attorneys v
     Registrar of Trade Marks* [2013] RPC 20, Appointed Person; Practice Amendment Notice
     03/13; but see Case T-66/11 *Present-Service Ullrich GmbH & Co KG v Office for
     Harmonisation in the Internal Market (Trade Marks and Designs)* [2013] All ER (D) 263 (Feb),
     EGC. As to the Nice Classification see PARA 352.
         It is not permissible to specify the goods or services by means of a statement that the goods
     or services in question do not possess a particular characteristic: Case C-363/99 *Koninklijke
     KPN Nederland NV v Benelux-Merkenbureau* [2006] Ch 1, [2004] ECR I-1619, ECJ; *Croom's
     Trade Mark Application* [2005] RPC 23, Appointed Person (limitation to clothing 'none being
     items of haute couture' not allowed); *Oska's Ltd's Trade Mark Application* [2005] RPC 525,
     Appointed Person (limitation to clothing for sale to particular market not allowed); *Monsoon
     Accessorize Ltd v Agatha Diffusion* (O/024/10), Appointed Person (exclusion of 'charm or
     novelty earrings and novelty cufflinks' not allowed); Case T-458/05 *Tegometall International
     AG v Office for Harmonisation in the Internal Market (Trade Marks and Designs)* [2007] ECR

II-4721, [2007] All ER (D) 307 (Nov), CFI (limitation to 'not of imitation wood' not allowed); Case R 1509/2008–2 *Couture Tech Ltd's Application* [2010] ETMR 45, OHIM Board of Appeal (limitation 'to be used exclusive in trade and which are moral [sic]' not allowed). A restriction on the scope of the goods or services is, however, permissible even if framed in negative terms: *SVM Asset Management Ltd's Trade Mark Application* (O/043/05), Appointed Person (limitation to financial services 'not including the provision of venture capital' and 'not including the provision of any such services to the pharmaceutical biotechnological and bioscientific sectors' both allowed). Such a restriction may be expressed by reference to the function of the goods: *Omega Engineering Inc v Omega SA (Omega AG) (Omega Ltd)* [2012] EWHC 3440 (Ch), [2012] All ER (D) 132 (Dec) (limitation of 'period timers … for industrial and/or scientific purposes' to 'period timers intended for a scientific or industrial application in measuring, signalling, checking, displaying or recording heat or temperature (including such having provision to record heat or temperature over a period of time and/or to display the time of day)' acceptable).

8 A trade mark must be capable of being represented graphically: see the Trade Marks Act 1994 s 1(1); and PARA 41. The registrar's current practice in relation to marks incorporating or consisting of colours is set out in Practice Amendment Notice 2/07.

9 Trade Marks Act 1994 s 32(2). See note 5.

10 See the Trade Marks Rules 2008, SI 2008/1797, r 8(2)(a), (3); and PARA 353. As to the classification of goods and services see PARA 351 et seq.

11 As to the meaning of 'use' see PARA 44 note 8.

12 Trade Marks Act 1994 s 32(3). If the applicant does not intend to use the mark, the application may be objectionable as made in bad faith: see PARA 53.

13 Trade Marks Act 1994 s 32(4); Trade Marks Rules 2008, SI 2008/1797, r 5(1) (as substituted: see note 5). As to fees see PARA 18. See also note 5.

14 Trade Marks Rules 2008, SI 2008/1797, r 5(1A) (r 5(1A), (1B) added by SI 2009/2089).

15 Ie referred to in the Trade Marks Rules 2008, SI 2008/1797, r 5(1A).

16 Trade Marks Rules 2008, SI 2008/1797, r 5(1B) (as added: see note 14).

17 Trade Marks Rules 2008, SI 2008/1797, r 5(2). This is subject to r 5(6). Where it appears to the registrar that the period (the 'routine period') within which applicants are routinely notified of the outcome of an examination under the Trade Marks Act 1994 s 37 (see PARAS 354, 363) is equal to or less than the period specified in the Trade Marks Rules 2008, SI 2008/1797, r 5(5) (see note 18), the registrar may suspend the right of applicants to file a request for expedited examination until such time as the routine period exceeds the period specified in r 5(5) and the registrar must, in each case, publish a notice on the Office website to this effect: r 5(6) (added by SI 2009/2089).

18 In the Trade Marks Rules 2008, SI 2008/1797, rr 5, 15 a 'request for expedited examination' means a request that, following an examination under the Trade Marks Act 1994 s 37 (see PARAS 354, 363), the registrar notify the applicant within a period of ten business days (as specified in a direction given by the registrar under s 80 (see PARA 334)) beginning on the business day after the date of filing of the application for registration whether or not it appears to the registrar that the requirements for registration are met: Trade Marks Rules 2008, SI 2008/1797, r 5(5). As to calculation of time periods in regard to r 5(5) see Tribunal Practice Notice (TPN 1/2013), available from the IPO website (see note 5).

19 Trade Marks Rules 2008, SI 2008/1797, r 5(3) (amended by SI 2009/2089).

20 Trade Marks Rules 2008, SI 2008/1797, r 5(4). Accordingly r 13 (see the text and notes 23–32) does not apply insofar as it relates to the failure of an application to satisfy the requirements of the Trade Marks Act 1994 s 32(4) (see the text and note 13): Trade Marks Rules 2008, SI 2008/1797, r 5(4).

21 Ie under the Trade Marks Rules 2008, SI 2008/1797, r 5.

22 Trade Marks Rules 2008, SI 2008/1797, r 15.

23 Ie the requirements of the Trade Marks Act 1994 s 32(2), (3) or (4) (see the text and notes 1–13); or the Trade Marks Rules 2008, SI 2008/1797, r 5(1) (see the text and notes 1–13).

24 As to the meaning of 'send' see PARA 27 note 10.

25 Trade Marks Rules 2008, SI 2008/1797, r 13(1). The reference in the text to default of payment is to such default in the case of the Trade Marks Act 1994 s 32(4): see the text and note 13.
    It should be noted that the Trade Marks Rules 2008, SI 2008/1797, r 13 does not apply to international trade marks (UK) or requests for extension: see the Trade Marks (International Registration) Order 2008, SI 2008/2206, art 3(3), Sch 1 Pt 2; and PARA 12 note 13.

26 Trade Marks Rules 2008, SI 2008/1797, r 13(2) (amended by SI 2009/2089). See note 25.

27 Ie under the Trade Marks Rules 2008, SI 2008/1797, r 13(2). As to extension of time limits see r 77; and PARA 338.

28 Ie any deficiency notified to him in respect of the Trade Marks Act 1994 s 32(2): see the text and notes 6–9.
29 Trade Marks Rules 2008, SI 2008/1797, r 13(3)(a). See note 25.
30 Ie any deficiency notified to him in respect of the Trade Marks Act 1994 s 32(3) (see the text to notes 11–12) or the Trade Marks Rules 2008, SI 2008/1797, r 5(1) (see the text and notes 1–13).
31 Ie as required by the Trade Marks Act 1994 s 32(4): see the text and note 13.
32 Trade Marks Rules 2008, SI 2008/136, r 13(3)(b). See note 25.

346.   Series of trade marks.   An application may be made[1] for the registration of a series of trade marks[2] in a single registration provided that the series comprises of no more than six trade marks[3]. Where an application for registration of a series of trade marks comprises three or more trade marks, the application is subject to the payment of the prescribed fee for each trade mark in excess of two trade marks[4].

Following such an application[5], if the registrar[6] is satisfied that the marks constitute a series, he must accept the application[7].

At any time the applicant for registration of a series of trade marks or the proprietor of a registered series of trade marks may request the deletion of a mark in that series and, following such request, the registrar must delete the mark[8]. Where[9] the registrar deletes a trade mark from an application, the application in so far as it relates to the deleted mark is to be treated as withdrawn[10].

1 Ie in accordance with the Trade Marks Rules 2008, SI 2008/1797, r 5 (see PARA 345) and on the appropriate form (TM12): see r 28. As to the use of forms see PARA 335.
2 For these purposes, a 'series of trade marks' means a number of trade marks which resemble each other as to their material particulars and differ only as to matters of a non-distinctive character not substantially affecting the identity of the trade mark: Trade Marks Act 1994 s 41(2). For trade marks to qualify as a series the differences between them must be sufficiently insignificant that the average consumer would be unlikely to notice the differences: *Sony Ericsson Mobile Communications AB's Trade Mark Application* (O/138/06), Appointed Person. As to the meaning of 'trade mark' see PARA 41.
   It should be noted that the Trade Marks Act 1994 s 41 does not apply to international trade marks (UK) or requests for extension: see the Trade Marks (International Registration) Order 2008, SI 2008/2206, art 3(3), Sch 1 Pt 1; and PARA 12 note 10.
3 Trade Marks Act 1994 s 41(1)(c), (3); Trade Marks Rules 2008, SI 2008/1797, r 28(1) (substituted by SI 2009/2089).
4 Trade Marks Rules 2008, SI 2008/1797, r 28(1A) (added by SI 2009/2089). As to fees see PARA 18.
5 Ie under the Trade Marks Rules 2008, SI 2008/1797, r 28(1).
6 As to the registrar see PARA 19.
7 Trade Marks Rules 2008, SI 2008/1797, r 28(2).
8 Trade Marks Rules 2008, SI 2008/1797, r 28(5).
9 Ie under the Trade Marks Rules 2008, SI 2008/1797, r 28(5).
10 Trade Marks Rules 2008, SI 2008/1797, r 28(6).

347.   Protection for international registrations.   The procedure by which an international registration[1] becomes protected in the United Kingdom is initiated in a different way from an application for registration of a United Kingdom trade mark, but thereafter follows a similar procedure and it is subject to the same substantive requirements[2] for achieving protection in the United Kingdom as for the registrability of a registered mark[3]. A person desiring to secure protection for a trade mark in the United Kingdom via this route must make a request to extend the protection of his international registration to the United Kingdom; such a request may be included in his original international application, or extension to the United Kingdom may be requested subsequently to the initial international registration[4]. The International Bureau[5] notifies the British registrar after receiving a request for the extension of protection of an international registration to the United Kingdom[6]. The incoming international registration is not subject to the requirements of the Trade Marks Act 1994 or rules requiring the filing of the application in the Intellectual Property Office ('IPO') or pertaining to its form[7]. There are, however, corresponding and broadly similar requirements relating to the application for international registration[8]. Apart from these exceptions, there are provisions applying in relation to the making of applications for international registration by way of the IPO as office of origin[9]; and also provisions applying in relation to the effects of international registration where a trade mark is also registered under the Trade Marks Act 1994 and the transformation of an application for an international registration, or an international registration, into an application for registration of a trade mark under the Trade Marks Act 1994[10].

1 Ie an international trade mark registration on the international register operated under the Madrid Protocol: see PARA 11 et seq. As to the Madrid Protocol see PARA 8.
2 Ie including any requirements imposed by the Trade Marks Act 1994, the Trade Marks (Relative Grounds) Order 2007, SI 2007/1976 and the Trade Marks Rules 2008, SI 2008/1797: see Trade Marks (International Registration) Order 2008, SI 2008/2206, art 3; and PARA 12.
3 See PARA 39.
4 Applications for international registration are filed through the home trade mark office of the applicant. For an outline of the procedure followed under the Madrid Protocol see PARA 11 et seq.
5 As to the International Bureau see PARA 8 text and note 2.
6 Madrid Protocol art 3 (ter).
7 Ie the Trade Marks Act 1994 ss 32–34; and the Trade Marks Rules 2008, SI 2008/1797, rr 5–9, 11, 13 (see PARAS 345, 348, 351, 352–353, 360). Those provisions of the 1994 Act and some of the 2008 Rules (ie rr 6, 8, 9, 13) are excluded from applying to international registrations by the Trade Marks (International Registration) Order 2008, SI 2008/2206, art 3(3), Sch 1 Pt 1, Pt 2: see PARA 12 notes 10, 13, and see generally PARA 11 et seq. As to the Intellectual Property Office (an operating name of the Patent Office) see PARA 16 note 2.
8 See the Madrid Protocol art 3(1)–(3); and the Madrid Common Regulations r 9. A detailed description of these provisions which form part of the international regime established under the Madrid Agreement and Protocol is outside the scope of this work. As to the Madrid Protocol see PARA 8.
9 See the Trade Marks (International Registration) Order 2008, SI 2008/2206, art 4, Sch 3; and PARA 13.
10 See the Trade Marks (International Registration) Order 2008, SI 2008/2206, art 5, Sch 4; and PARA 14.

348. Date of filing. The date of filing of an application for registration[1] of a trade mark[2] is the date on which documents containing everything required to be contained in the application[3] are furnished to the registrar[4] by the applicant[5]. If, however, documents are furnished on different days, the date of filing is the last of those days[6].

For an international registration[7], the equivalent of the date of filing of a domestic trade mark application is the date of the international registration with certain exceptions[8]. In the case of a request for extension of protection it is the date when a request is recorded in the international register[9]. The date of the international registration is normally the date when the international application was received in the office of origin[10].

1 As to the meaning of references to 'registration' see PARA 21 note 2.
2 As to the meaning of 'trade mark' see PARA 41.
3 Ie required by the Trade Marks Act 1994 s 32(2): see PARA 345.
4 As to the registrar see PARA 19.

5   Trade Marks Act 1994 s 33(1). References in the Trade Marks Act 1994 to the date of
     application for registration are to the date of filing of the application: s 33(2). The date of filing
     is important because: (1) it may be critical in the event of conflicting applications for the same or
     similar marks (see PARA 54); and (2) once registration is granted, many of the rights conferred by
     the mark date back to the date of application (see PARAS 23, 67).
          The Trade Marks (International Registration) Order 2008, SI 2008/2206 excludes the Trade
     Marks Act 1994 s 33(1) from applying to protected international trade marks (UK) or requests
     for extension: see the Trade Marks (International Registration) Order 2008, SI 2008/2206,
     art 3, Sch 1 Pt 1; and PARA 12 note 10. See also PARA 347.
6   Trade Marks Act 1994 s 33(1). Thus if the application does not contain an adequate
     representation of the mark sought to be registered, e g because it does not identify a colour
     unambiguously, it will only be accorded a date of filing when the uncertainty has been resolved
     (*Ty Nant Spring Water Ltd's Trade Mark Application* [2000] RPC 55, [1999] ETMR 981,
     Appointed Person; *Robert McBride Ltd's Trade Mark Application* [2003] RPC 343, Appointed
     Person) if it is permissible at all (see *Nestlé SA's Trade Mark Application* [2004] EWCA Civ
     1008, [2005] RPC 77, sub nom *Société des Produits Nestlé SA v Mars UK Ltd* [2005] IP & T
     551). See note 5.
7   As to international registrations see PARAS 8, 11 et seq.
8   See the Trade Marks (International Registration) Order 2008, SI 2008/2206, art 3(3), Sch 1
     Pt 1, art 3(3)(i), Sch 2 para 2; and 12 notes 10, 13.
9   See the Trade Marks Act 1994 s 33(1) (substituted as a modification by the Trade Marks
     (International Registration) Order 2008, SI 2008/2206, art 3(3)(i), Sch 2 para 2). See note 8.
10   Madrid Protocol art 3(4). As to the Madrid Protocol see PARA 8.

349.   Division of application.   At any time before registration[1] an applicant
may send[2] to the registrar[3] a request[4] to divide the specification[5] of his
application for registration (the 'original application') into two or more separate
applications ('divisional applications'), indicating for each division the
specification of goods or services[6]; each divisional application is be treated as a
separate application for registration with the same filing date[7] as the original
application[8].
     Where the request to divide an application is sent after publication of the
application[9], any objections in respect of, or opposition to, the original
application are to be taken to apply to each divisional application and must be
proceeded with accordingly[10].
     Upon division of an original application in respect of which notice has been
given to the registrar of particulars relating to the grant of a licence, or a security
interest or any right in or under it, the notice and the particulars are deemed to
apply in relation to each of the applications into which the original application
has been divided[11].

1   In context this must mean at any time before registration or refusal of the application:
     Sensornet Ltd's Trade Mark Application [2007] RPC 185, Appointed Person. The registrar has
     power to permit the division of an application during the pendency of an appeal against a
     decision to refuse the application since the registrar's practice is to treat appeals as being of
     suspensory effect: *Sensornet Ltd's Trade Mark Application*; *Aggregate Industries Ltd's Trade
     Mark Application* (O/178/06), Appointed Person. As to the meaning of 'registration' see PARA
     21 note 2.
2   As to the meaning of 'send' see PARA 27 note 10.
3   As to the registrar see PARA 19.
4   The request must be sent on Form TM12. As to the use of forms see PARA 335.
5   As to the meaning of 'specification' see PARA 351 note 1.
6   Trade Marks Act 1994 s 41(1)(a); Trade Marks Rules 2008, SI 2008/1797, r 26(1). These
     provisions (or their equivalents) do not permit an application for a series of marks to be divided
     into an application for each of those marks (or combinations thereof); such a division is
     provided for by the Trade Marks Rules 2000, SI 2000/136, r 21 (see now the Trade Marks
     Rules 2008, SI 2008/1797, r 28) (see PARA 346): *Dualit Ltd's (Toaster Shapes) Trade Mark
     Applications* [1999] RPC 890, [1999] All ER (D) 729.

It should be noted that the Trade Marks Act 1994 s 41 does not apply to international trade marks (UK) or requests for extension: see the Trade Marks (International Registration) Order 2008, SI 2008/2206, art 3(3), Sch 1 Pt 1; and PARA 12 note 10.

7   As to the meaning of 'date of filing' see PARA 348.
8   Trade Marks Rules 2008, SI 2008/1797, r 26(2).
9   As to the publication of the application see PARA 365.
10   Trade Marks Rules 2008, SI 2008/1797, r 26(3).
11   Trade Marks Rules 2008, SI 2008/1797, r 26(4).

350. Merger of separate applications. Provision may be made by rules as to the merging of separate applications[1]. However the Trade Marks Rules 2008[2] make no such provision[3].

1   Trade Marks Act 1994 s 41(1)(b).
     It should be noted that the Trade Marks Act 1994 s 41 does not apply to international trade marks (UK) or requests for extension: see the Trade Marks (International Registration) Order 2008, SI 2008/2206, art 3(3), Sch 1 Pt 1; and PARA 12 note 10.
2   Ie the Trade Marks Rules 2008, SI 2008/1797.
3   The Trade Marks Rules 2008, SI 2008/1797, r 27 has provisions as to the merging of separate registrations (see PARA 373) but the provisions as to merging of separate applications have been revoked.

(iv) Classification of Goods and Services

351. Classification of goods and services. Every application must specify[1] the class of goods or services[2] to which it relates[3]. Goods and services must be classified for the purposes of the registration of trade marks[4] according to the Nice Classification[5]. When a trade mark is registered it must be classified according to the version of the Nice Classification that had effect on the date of application for registration[6]. Any question arising as to the class within which any goods or services fall must be determined by the registrar, whose decision is final[7].

It is important which goods or services a mark is registered for[8], and care must accordingly be taken to ensure that the application covers all the goods or services with which an applicant may be concerned.

There is a guide listing most goods alphabetically with an indication of the appropriate class for those goods. That guide is an indication of practice and not a decision on questions of classification[9].

These provisions do not apply to international registrations[10] but there are corresponding international provisions relating to classification[11].

1   For these purposes, 'specification' means the statement of goods or services in respect of which a trade mark is registered or proposed to be registered: Trade Marks Rules 2008, SI 2008/1797, r 2(1).
2   Ie under the 'Nice Classification': see note 5.
3   Trade Marks Rules 2008, SI 2008/1797, r 8(2)(a). An application may relate to more than one class: see PARA 353.
4   As to the meaning of 'trade mark' see PARA 41.
5   Trade Marks Act 1994 s 34(1): Trade Marks Rules 2008, SI 2008/1797, r 7(1). The 'Nice Classification' means the system of classification under the Nice Agreement: r 2(1). The 'Nice Agreement' means the Nice Agreement Concerning the International Classification of Goods and Services for the Purposes of the Registration of Marks of 15 June 1957, which was last amended on 28 September 1979: Trade Marks Rules 2008, SI 2008/1797, r 2(1). See further PARAS 10, 352.
     The purpose of classification is primarily administrative but registration by reference to a particular class of goods or services may affect substantive rights: see e g *Re AA Byrd & Co Ltd's Application* (1953) 70 RPC 212; *CAL-U-TEST Trade Mark* [1967] FSR 39; *GE Trade Mark* [1969] RPC 418 at 458–459 (on appeal [1970] RPC 339, CA; revsd sub nom

General Electric Co v General Electric Co Ltd [1972] 2 All ER 507, [1972] 1 WLR 729, [1973] RPC 297, HL); *TORNADO Trade Mark* [1979] RPC 155, Trade Marks Registry; *British Sugar plc v James Robertson & Sons Ltd* [1996] RPC 281; *Avnet Inc v Isoact Ltd* [1998] FSR 16; *Altecnic Ltd's Trade Mark Application* [2001] EWCA Civ 1928, [2002] RPC 639; but cf *Carless, Capel & Leonard v F Pilmore-Bedford & Sons* (1928) 45 RPC 205; *Ofrex Ltd v Rapesco Ltd* [1963] RPC 169. See also *Omega Engineering Inc v Omega SA (Omega AG) (Omega Ltd)* [2010] EWHC 1211 (Ch), [2010] FSR 625, [2010] ETMR 49 (affd [2011] EWCA Civ 645, [2011] ETMR 40, [2011] All ER (D) 4 (Jun)).

    In some circumstances goods may be classified in more than one class: *Omega Engineering Inc v Omega SA* above.

    The registrar may exercise the powers conferred by rules under the Trade Marks Act 1994 s 65 (adaptation of entries to new classification: see PARA 374) to secure that any existing registered marks which do not conform to the system of classification prescribed under s 34 are brought into conformity with that system: s 105, Sch 3 para 12. As to the registrar see PARA 19.

6   Trade Marks Rules 2008, SI 2008/1797, r 7(2).

7   Trade Marks Act 1994 s 34(2). This provision only applies to determinations made by the registrar with regard to questions of classification in proceedings within the exclusive competence of the registrar: *Red Bull GmbH v Potters Ltd* [2013] RPC 385, Appointed Person. This provision does not empower the registrar to permit an applicant to transfer an application from one class to another in circumstances falling outside the Trade marks Act 1994 s 39(2) (see PARA 357): *Altecnic Ltd's Trade Mark Application* [2001] EWCA Civ 1928, [2002] RPC 639.

8   The position is, however, not as crucial under the Trade Marks Act 1994 as it was under the Trade Marks Act 1938 s 4(1) (repealed) (where it was essential in the case of infringement that the confusingly similar mark should be used on goods or services falling within the specification of goods of the registered mark; similarity of goods or services to those registered was not enough).

9   See *GE Trade Mark* [1969] RPC 418 at 458–459; on appeal [1970] RPC 339, CA; revsd sub nom *General Electric Co v General Electric Co Ltd* [1972] 2 All ER 507, [1972] 1 WLR 729, [1973] RPC 297, HL.

10   See the Trade Marks (International Registration) Order 2008, SI 2008/2206, art 3(3), Sch 1 Pt 1; and PARA 12 note 10. As to the meaning of 'international registration' see PARA 12 note 1. See also PARA 347.

11   Madrid Protocol art 3(2). The indication of classes given by the applicant is subject to control by the International Bureau, which exercises that control in association with the office of origin of the international application. As to the International Bureau see PARA 8. As to the Madrid Protocol see PARA 8. See also PARA 347.

352. The Nice Classification. When a trade mark is registered it must be classified according to the version of the Nice Classification[1] that had effect on the date of application for registration[2]. The current edition[3] of the Nice Classification classifies goods[4] and services[5] as follows[6]:

(1)   Class 1: chemicals used in industry, science and photography, as well as in agriculture, horticulture and forestry; unprocessed artificial resins, unprocessed plastics; manures; fire extinguishing compositions; tempering and soldering preparations; chemical substances for preserving foodstuffs; tanning substances; adhesives used in industry.

(2)   Class 2: paints, varnishes, lacquers; preservatives against rust and against deterioration of wood; colorants; mordants; raw natural resins; metals in foil and powder form for painters, decorators, printers and artists.

(3)   Class 3: bleaching preparations and other substances for laundry use; cleaning, polishing, scouring and abrasive preparations; soaps; perfumery, essential oils, cosmetics, hair lotions; dentifrices.

(4)   Class 4: industrial oils and greases; lubricants; dust absorbing, wetting and binding compositions; fuels (including motor spirit) and illuminants; candles and wicks for lighting.

(5)   Class 5: pharmaceutical and veterinary preparations; sanitary preparations for medical purposes; dietetic food and substances adapted

for medical or veterinary use, food for babies; dietary supplements for humans and animals; plasters, materials for dressings; material for stopping teeth, dental wax; disinfectants; preparations for destroying vermin; fungicides, herbicides.

(6)   Class 6: common metals and their alloys; metal building materials; transportable buildings of metal; materials of metal for railway tracks; non-electric cables and wires of common metal; ironmongery, small items of metal hardware; pipes and tubes of metal; safes; goods of common metal not included in other classes; ores.

(7)   Class 7: machines and machine tools; motors and engines (except for land vehicles); machine coupling and transmission components (except for land vehicles); agricultural implements other than hand-operated; incubators for eggs; automatic vending machines.

(8)   Class 8: hand tools and implements (hand-operated); cutlery; side arms; razors.

(9)   Class 9: scientific, nautical, surveying, photographic, cinematographic, optical, weighing, measuring, signalling, checking (supervision), life-saving and teaching apparatus and instruments; apparatus and instruments for conducting, switching, transforming, accumulating, regulating or controlling electricity; apparatus for recording, transmission or reproduction of sound or images; magnetic data carriers, recording discs; compact discs, DVDs and other digital recording media; mechanisms for coin-operated apparatus; cash registers, calculating machines, data processing equipment, computers; computer software; fire-extinguishing apparatus.

(10) Class 10: surgical, medical, dental and veterinary apparatus and instruments, artificial limbs, eyes and teeth; orthopedic articles; suture materials.

(11) Class 11: apparatus for lighting, heating, steam generating, cooking, refrigerating, drying, ventilating, water supply and sanitary purposes.

(12) Class 12: vehicles; apparatus for locomotion by land, air or water.

(13) Class 13: firearms; ammunition and projectiles; explosives; fireworks.

(14) Class 14: precious metals and their alloys and goods in precious metals or coated therewith, not included in other classes; jewellery, precious stones; horological and chronometric instruments.

(15) Class 15: musical instruments.

(16) Class 16: paper, cardboard and goods made from these materials, not included in other classes; printed matter; bookbinding material; photographs; stationery; adhesives for stationery or household purposes; artists' materials; paint brushes; typewriters and office requisites (except furniture); instructional and teaching material (except apparatus); plastic materials for packaging (not included in other classes); printers' type; printing blocks.

(17) Class 17: rubber, gutta-percha, gum, asbestos, mica and goods made from these materials and not included in other classes; plastics in extruded form for use in manufacture; packing, stopping and insulating materials; flexible pipes, not of metal.

(18) Class 18: leather and imitations of leather, and goods made of these materials and not included in other classes; animal skins, hides; trunks and travelling bags; umbrellas, parasols and walking sticks; whips, harness and saddlery.

(19) Class 19: building materials (non-metallic); non-metallic rigid pipes for building; asphalt, pitch and bitumen; non-metallic transportable buildings; monuments, not of metal.

(20) Class 20: furniture, mirrors, picture frames; goods (not included in other classes) of wood, cork, reed, cane, wicker, horn, bone, ivory, whalebone, shell, amber, mother-of-pearl, meerschaum and substitutes for all these materials, or of plastics.

(21) Class 21: household or kitchen utensils and containers; combs and sponges; brushes (except paint brushes); brush-making materials; articles for cleaning purposes; steelwool; unworked or semi-worked glass (except glass used in building); glassware, porcelain and earthenware not included in other classes.

(22) Class 22: ropes, string, nets, tents, awnings, tarpaulins, sails, sacks and bags (not included in other classes); padding and stuffing materials (except of rubber or plastics); raw fibrous textile materials.

(23) Class 23: yarns and threads, for textile use.

(24) Class 24: textiles and textile goods, not included in other classes; bed and table covers.

(25) Class 25: clothing, footwear, headgear.

(26) Class 26: lace and embroidery, ribbons and braid; buttons, hooks and eyes, pins and needles; artificial flowers.

(27) Class 27: carpets, rugs, mats and matting, linoleum and other materials for covering existing floors; wall hangings (non-textile).

(28) Class 28: games and playthings; gymnastic and sporting articles not included in other classes; decorations for Christmas trees.

(29) Class 29: meat, fish, poultry and game; meat extracts; preserved, frozen, dried and cooked fruits and vegetables; jellies, jams, compotes; eggs, milk and milk products; edible oils and fats.

(30) Class 30: coffee; tea, cocoa and artificial coffee; rice; tapioca and sago; flour and preparations made from cereals; bread, pastry and confectionery; ices; sugar, honey, treacle; yeast, baking-powder; salt, mustard; vinegar, sauces (condiments); spices; ice.

(31) Class 31: grains and agricultural, horticultural and forestry products not included in other classes; live animals; fresh fruits and vegetables; seeds, natural plants and flowers; foodstuffs for animals, malt.

(32) Class 32: beers; mineral and aerated waters and other non-alcoholic beverages; fruit beverages and fruit juices; syrups and other preparations for making beverages.

(33) Class 33: alcoholic beverages (except beers).

(34) Class 34: tobacco; smokers' articles; matches.

(35) Class 35: advertising[7]; business management; business administration; office functions[8].

(36) Class 36: insurance; financial affairs; monetary affairs; real estate affairs.

(37) Class 37: building construction; repair; installation services.

(38) Class 38: telecommunications.

(39) Class 39: transport; packaging and storage of goods; travel arrangement.

(40) Class 40: treatment of materials.

(41) Class 41: education; providing of training; entertainment; sporting and cultural activities.

(42) Class 42: scientific and technological services and research and design relating thereto; industrial analysis and research services; design and development of computer hardware and software.

(43) Class 43: services for providing food and drink; temporary accommodation.

(44) Class 44: medical services; veterinary services; hygienic and beauty care for human beings or animals; agriculture, horticulture and forestry services.

(45) Class 45: legal services; security services for the protection of property and individuals; personal and social services rendered by others to meet the needs of individuals.

1   As to the meaning of the 'Nice Classification' see PARA 351 note 5.
2   Trade Marks Rules 2008, SI 2008/1797, r 7(2).
3   Ie the tenth edition, in force from 1 January 2013. The 2013 version is available online from the World Intellectual Property Organisation's website, accessible at the date at which this volume states the law at www.wipo.int. The paper publication has been discontinued, the tenth edition published in 2011 being the last printed edition. The annual versions of each edition of the Nice Classification are available in the authentic languages only, ie in English and in French. At the request of interested national trademark offices, the International Bureau will publish official texts in other languages for the new editions only. As at the date that this volume states the law, the next, eleventh edition, is likely to be published in 2016. An application may relate to more than one class: see PARA 353.
4   Classes 1–34 (see heads (1)–(34) in the text) relate to goods.
5   Classes 35–45 (see heads (35)–(45) in the text) relate to services.
6   Formerly the Trade Marks Rules 2000, SI 2000/136, Sch 2 (revoked by SI 2001/3832) set out the classification of goods for registrations dated before 27 July 1938 (when the Trade Marks Act 1938 came into force) except where a specification had been converted to the classification set out in Sch 3 (revoked by SI 2006/3039) whether under the old law (see PARA 17 note 2) or under the provisions relating to reclassification. By the end of 2001 all remaining registrations dated before 27 July 1938 had been reclassified. The Trade Marks Rules 2000, SI 2000/136, Schs 3, 4 (revoked by SI 2006/3039) set out the classification of goods for registrations dated before 1 January 2002, and 1 January 2007 respectively, based on the Nice Classifications that were then current. The Nice Classifications are no longer set out in detail in United Kingdom statutory instruments. See also note 3.
7   The provision of support services to customers to enable them to carry their own advertisements on their own websites is apparently not an advertising or promotional service falling within Class 35: *Avnet Inc v Isoact Ltd* [1998] FSR 16.
8   Services provided in connection with retail trade may be the subject of a trade mark registration provided that details are provided with regard to the goods or type of goods to which those services relate: Case C-418/02 *Praktiker Bau- und Heimwerkermarkte AG* [2006] Ch 144, [2005] ECR I-5873, ECJ. The registrar's practice is to classify such services in Class 35: Practice Amendment Notice 6/05. Shopping centre services may also be the subject of a trade mark application provided that they are sufficiently clearly specified: *Land Securities plc v Registrar of Trade Marks* [2008] EWHC 1744 (Pat), [2009] RPC 159, [2010] IP & T 248; and see Practice Amendment Notice 01/09.

353. Application may relate to more than one class.   An application may be made for registration in more than one class[1] of goods or services[2]. Every application must specify the class[3] to which it relates and the goods or services which are appropriate to that class[4]. The goods or services must be described in such as way as to indicate clearly the nature of those goods or services and to allow them to be classified in the classes[5]. If the application relates to more than one class, the specification[6] contained in it must set out the classes in consecutive numerical order and the specification of the goods or services must be grouped accordingly[7]. If the specification contained in the application lists items by reference to a class in which they do not fall, the applicant may request, by filing the appropriate form[8], that his application be amended to include the appropriate class for those items; and, upon the payment of such class fee as may be appropriate, the registrar must amend his application accordingly[9]. Where the application does not satisfy the requirements as to specification of the classes and goods or services[10], the registrar must send[11] notice of this to the applicant[12]. The notice must specify a period, of not less than one month, within which the applicant must satisfy those requirements[13]. Where the applicant fails to satisfy the above requirements[14] before the expiry of the period, his application for registration, in so far as it relates to any goods or services which failed that requirement, must be treated as abandoned[15]. Where the applicant fails to satisfy the latter requirements[16] before the expiry of the period, the application for registration must be treated as abandoned[17].

1 Ie more than one class in the Nice Classification: see PARA 352.
2 Trade Marks Rules 2008, SI 2008/1797, r 8(1). As to the registrar's duty to notify the applicant of any deficiency under r 8 see PARA 345. As to the registrar see PARA 19.
   It should be noted that rr 8, 9 do not apply to international trade marks (UK) or requests for extension: see the Trade Marks (International Registration) Order 2008, SI 2008/2206, art 3(3), Sch 1 Pt 2; and PARA 12 note 13.
3 Ie the class in the Nice Classification: see PARAS 351–352.
4 Trade Marks Rules 2008, SI 2008/1797, r 8(2). See note 2. The applicant should exercise care in specifying the class of the goods or services, since it may not be possible to change this by a subsequent amendment: see *Altecnic Ltd's Trade Mark Application* [2001] EWCA Civ 1928, [2002] RPC 639; and PARA 357. See also *Omega Engineering Inc v Omega SA* [2010] EWHC 1211 (Ch), [2010] FSR 625, [2010] ETMR 49 (affd [2011] EWCA Civ 645, [2011] All ER (D) 4 (Jun), [2011] ETMR 40).
5 Trade Marks Rules 2008, SI 2008/1797, r 8(2). The classes referred to are those in the Nice Classification: see PARAS 351–352. See note 2.
6 As to the meaning of 'specification' see PARA 351 note 1.
7 Trade Marks Rules 2008, SI 2008/1797, r 8(3). See note 2.
8 The appropriate form is Form TM3A. As to the use of forms see PARA 335. As to the meaning of references to 'filing' see PARA 27 note 2. As to the filing of documents by electronic means see PARA 336.
9 Trade Marks Rules 2008, SI 2008/1797, r 8(4). See note 2. It would appear that such an amendment is permissible under the Trade Marks Act 1994 s 39(2) (see PARA 357) on the basis that it is an obvious mistake: *Altecnic Ltd's Trade Mark Application* [2001] EWCA Civ 1928, [2002] RPC 639; *Aunty G Ltd's Trade Mark Application* (O/083/04), Appointed Person. As to fees see PARA 18.
10 Ie the requirements in the Trade Marks Rules 2008, SI 2008/1797, r 8(2)(b), (3) (see the text and notes 4, 7).
11 As to the meaning of 'send' see PARA 27 note 10.
12 Trade Marks Rules 2008, SI 2008/1797, r 9(1). See note 2.
13 Trade Marks Rules 2008, SI 2008/1797, r 9(2). See note 2.
14 Ie the requirements of the Trade Marks Rules 2008, SI 2008/1797, r 9(2).
15 Trade Marks Rules 2008, SI 2008/1797, r 9(3). See note 2.
16 Ie the requirements of the Trade Marks Rules 2008, SI 2008/1797, r 9(3).
17 Trade Marks Rules 2008, SI 2008/1797, r 9(4). See note 2.

(v) Examination of Application

354. Applications for registration of United Kingdom trade marks. The registrar[1] must examine whether an application for registration[2] of a trade mark[3] satisfies the requirements of the Trade Marks Act 1994, including any requirements imposed by rules[4]. In connection with such an examination the registrar may carry out a search of earlier trade marks[5] for the purpose of notifying the applicant and other persons about the existence of earlier trade marks that might be relevant to the proposed registration[6].

In practice, following receipt of the application, if the registrar considers that objections exist, he writes to the applicant indicating what these are. Sometimes such objections can be settled by correspondence. The applicant may ask for a hearing[7]. The nature of the objection may be such[8] that it can be overcome by evidence[9].

1 As to the registrar see PARA 19.
2 As to the requirements for registration see PARA 39 et seq; and as to the procedure on the application see PARAS 334 et seq, 356 et seq.
3 As to the meaning of 'trade mark' see PARA 41.
4 Trade Marks Act 1994 s 37(1). As to the formal requirements to be satisfied by the applicant see PARA 345; as to the substantive requirements for registrability see PARA 39 et seq; and as to the making of rules generally see PARA 17.
   The registrar is not subject to any liability by reason of, or in connection with, any examination required or authorised by the Trade Marks Act 1994: see s 70(2); and PARA 20.
5 As to the meaning of 'earlier trade mark' see PARA 54.
6 See the Trade Marks Act 1994 s 8(2)(a), (3); the Trade Marks (Relative Grounds) Order 2007, SI 2007/1976, arts 3, 4; and PARA 64. The primary purpose of the search is to identify potentially conflicting earlier rights: see PARA 54 et seq. As to notifying the results of a search under the Trade Marks (Relative Grounds) Order 2007, SI 2007/1976, art 4 see the Trade Marks Rules 2008, SI 2008/1797, r 14 (amended by SI 2012/1003). As to calculation of time periods see Tribunal Practice Notice (TPN 1/2013), available from the Intellectual Property Office ('IPO') website, accessible at the date at which this volume states the law at www.ipo.gov.uk. As to the Intellectual Property Office (an operating name of the Patent Office) see PARA 16 note 2.
7 See the Trade Marks Rules 2008, SI 2008/1797, r 63; and PARA 340.
8 Eg based on the requirement for distinctiveness: see PARA 44.
9 As to the registrar's power to direct the filing of documents, information and evidence see PARA 340; and as to evidence see PARA 341.

355. Applications for protection of international registrations. Upon receiving from the International Bureau[1] notification of an international registration[2] designating the United Kingdom, the registrar[3] must examine whether it satisfies the requirements of the Trade Marks Act 1994, including any requirements imposed by rules as they apply to international registrations[4]. If it appears to the registrar that the requirements for registration are not met, he must give notice of provisional refusal[5] to the International Bureau[6]. Where the International Bureau notifies the registrar or the registrar considers that a particular term used to indicate any of the goods and services included in the international registration is too vague for the purpose of classification or is incomprehensible or is linguistically incorrect the registrar may give notice of provisional refusal to the International Bureau in respect of that term[7]. In either case, the notice of provisional refusal must specify a period within which the holder of the international registration may then make representations to the registrar or amend the request for extension by limiting the goods and services[8].

1 As to the International Bureau see PARAS 8.
2 As to the meaning of 'international registration' see PARA 12 note 1.
3 As to the registrar see PARA 19.
4 See the Trade Marks (International Registration) Order 2008, SI 2008/2206, art 3; and PARA 12. See also the Trade Marks Act 1994 s 37(1); and PARA 354.
5 Notices of provisional refusal must set out the matters required by the Madrid Protocol art 5 and the Common Regulations r 17: see the Trade Marks Act 1994 ss 38A, 38B (modified by way of insertion by the Trade Marks (International Registration) Order 2008, SI 2008/2206, art 3(3)(i), Sch 2 para 6); and PARA 12 note 15 and see also PARAS 366, 371. As to the Madrid Protocol see PARA 8; and as to the Common Regulations see PARA 11 note 5.
6 See the Trade Marks Act 1994 s 37(3) (s 37 modified by the Trade Marks (International Registration) Order 2008, SI 2008/2206, Sch 2 para 4); and PARA 12 note 15.
7 See the Trade marks Act 1994 s 37(4) (as modified: see note 6); and PARA 12 note 15.
8 See the Trade Marks Act 1994 s 37(5) (as modified: see note 6); and PARA 12 note 15.

356.   Withdrawal or restriction of application.   The applicant may at any time withdraw his application for registration of a trade mark or restrict the goods or services covered by the application[1]. If the application has been published[2], the withdrawal or restriction must also be published[3].

In regard to international trade marks (UK) the goods and services covered by a request for extension may be restricted at any time by the applicant provided that if the request for extension has been published, the restriction must also be published in the Trade Marks Journal[4].

1   Trade Marks Act 1994 s 39(1). As to the meaning of 'trade mark' see PARA 41. As to whether the applicant may offer a restriction conditionally or must do so unconditionally see *Sensornet Ltd's Trade Mark Application* [2007] RPC 185, Appointed Person. Cf the following decisions made under Council Regulation (EC) 40/94 (OJ L1, 14.1.94, p 1) on the Community trade mark, art 44(1) (see now Council Regulation (EC) 207/2009 (OJ L78, 24.3.2009, p 1) art 43(1)) (see PARA 263): Case T-219/00 *Ellos v Office for Harmonisation in the Internal Market (Trade Marks and Designs)* [2002] ECR II-753, [2002] IP & T 384, CFI; Case T-396/02 *August Storck KG v Office for Harmonisation in the Internal Market (Trade Marks and Designs)* [2004] ECR II-3821, [2004] All ER (D) 157 (Nov), CFI; Case C-412/05P *Alcon Inc v Office for Harmonisation in the Internal Market (Trade Marks and Designs)* [2007] ECR I-3569, [2007] All ER (D) 238 (Apr), ECJ.
2   As to the meaning of 'publish' see PARA 19 note 10.
3   Trade Marks Act 1994 s 39(1). See also the Trade Marks Rules 2008, SI 2008/1797, r 25(1); and PARA 357.
4   See the Trade Marks Act 1994 s 39(1) (modified by the Trade Marks (International Registration) Order 2008, SI 2008/2206, art 3(3)(i), Sch 2 para 7); and PARA 12 note 15. As to the Trade Marks Journal see PARA 19.

357.   Correction and amendment of application.   Apart from amendments restricting the scope of goods or services covered by an application for registration of a trade mark[1], in other respects an application may be amended, at the request of the applicant, only by correcting:

(1)   the name or address of the applicant;

(2)   errors of wording or of copying; or

(3)   obvious mistakes,

and then only where the correction does not substantially affect the identity of the trade mark[2] or extend the goods or services covered by the application[3]. A request for an amendment of an application to correct an error or to change the name or address of the applicant or in respect of any amendment requested after publication of the application must be made on the appropriate form[4].

Where a request is made for amendment of an application[5] which has been published in the Trade Marks Journal and the amendment affects the representation of the trade mark or the goods or services covered by the application, the amendment or a statement of the effect of the amendment must also be so published[6].

Any person claiming to be affected by the amendment may, within one month of the date on which the amendment or a statement of the effect of the amendment was published[7], give notice to the registrar of opposition to the amendment[8]. Such notice must include a statement of the grounds of objection which must, in particular, indicate why the amendment would not be permissible[9].

1   Ie pursuant to the Trade Marks Act 1994 s 39(1): see PARA 356.
2   A correction does not substantially affect the identity of the trade mark if the differences are sufficiently insignificant that they are likely to go unnoticed by the average consumer: see *Sony Ericsson Mobile Communications AB's Trade Mark Applications* (O/138/06), Appointed

Person; but cf Case T-128/99 *Signal Communications Ltd v Office for Harmonisation in the Internal Market (Trade Marks and Designs)* [2001] ECR II-3273, CFI.

3 Trade Marks Act 1994 s 39(2). This restriction is designed to prevent an applicant stealing a march on a rival in a case of conflicting rights where the identity of a mark applied for or the scope of goods and services covered by an application filed on a particular date may be crucial. It is always open to an applicant to file an additional new application with the changed mark or the extra goods or services which he wishes to cover, but the new application will have a later date. Thus an amendment to the application to change the class of the goods specified is not permissible under s 39(2) unless the class originally stated was an obvious mistake (*Altecnic Ltd's Trade Mark Application* [2001] EWCA Civ 1928, [2002] RPC 639); nor are amendments to limit the colour and specify the size of a shape mark permissible under the Trade Marks Act 1994 s 39(2) (*Nestlé SA's Trade Mark Application* [2004] EWCA Civ 1008, [2005] RPC 77, sub nom *Société des Produits Nestlé SA v Mars UK Ltd* [2005] IP & T 551).

It should be noted that the Trade Marks Act 1994 s 39(2) does not apply to international trade marks (UK) or requests for extension: see the Trade Marks (International Registration) Order 2008, SI 2008/2206, art 3(3), Sch 1 Pt 1; and PARA 12 note 10.

4 Trade Marks Rules 2008, SI 2008/1797, r 24. The appropriate form is Form TM21: r 24. As to the use of forms see PARA 335.

5 Ie pursuant to the Trade Marks Act 1994 s 39: see the text and notes 1–3; and PARA 356.

6 Trade Marks Act 1994 s 39(3); Trade Marks Rules 2008, SI 2008/1797, r 25(1). As to the meaning of 'publish' see PARA 19 note 10. As to the Trade Marks Journal see r 81; and PARA 19.

7 Ie under the Trade Marks Rules 2008, SI 2008/1797, r 25(1): see the text and notes 5–6.

8 Trade Marks Rules 2008, SI 2008/1797, r 25(2). The notice must be given on Form TM7: r 25(2).

9 Trade Marks Rules 2008, SI 2008/1797, r 25(2). The reference in the text to why the amendment would not be permissible is a reference to why the amendment would not fall within the Trade Marks Act 1994 s 39(2): see the text and notes 1–3. The registrar must send a copy of the Form TM7 to the applicant, and the provisions of the Trade Marks Rules 2008, SI 2008/1797, rr 17, 18, 20 (see PARAS 366–367) apply to proceedings relating to the opposition to the amendment of the application as they apply to proceedings relating to opposition to the registration of a trade mark with certain modifications: see r 25(3) (amended by SI 2013/444). As to calculation of time periods see Tribunal Practice Notice (TPN 1/2013), available from the Intellectual Property Office ('IPO') website, accessible at the date at which this volume states the law at www.ipo.gov.uk. As to the Intellectual Property Office (an operating name of the Patent Office) see PARA 16 note 2.

358.   Disclaimer or limitation of application.   An applicant for registration[1] of a trade mark[2] may[3]:

(1)   disclaim any right to the exclusive use[4] of any specified element of the trade mark[5]; or

(2)   agree that the rights conferred by the registration are to be subject to a specified territorial or other limitation[6].

Disclaimers and limitations can similarly be made in relation to an international trade mark for which protection is sought in the United Kingdom[7].

1 As to the meaning of 'registration' see PARA 21 note 2.
2 As to the meaning of 'trade mark' see PARA 41.
3 Trade Marks Act 1994 s 13(1). The proprietor of a registered trade mark may also make disclaimers and limitations: see PARA 376. As to the making of such disclaimers and limitations see PARA 65. As to the effect of such disclaimers and limitations on the proprietor's rights see PARA 82.
4 As to the meaning of 'use' see PARA 44 note 8.
5 Trade Marks Act 1994 s 13(1)(a).
6 Trade Marks Act 1994 s 13(1)(b).
7 See the Trade Marks (International Registration) Order 2008, SI 2008/2206, art 3; and PARA 12.

359.   Correction of international registrations.   Where the International Bureau[1] notifies[2] the registrar[3] that it has corrected an international registration designating the United Kingdom[4], and the correction either substantially affects the identity of the trade mark[5] or reduces or extends the goods or services comprised in the international registration, the registrar may treat such a notification of correction as a new request for extension[6].

1 As to the International Bureau see PARA 8 text and note 2.
2 Ie pursuant to the Common Regulations r 28. As to the Common Regulations see PARA 11 note 5.
3 As to the registrar see PARA 19.
4 As to the meaning of 'international registration designating the United Kingdom' see PARA 13.
5 As to corrections which substantially affect the identity of a trade mark see PARA 357 note 2.
6 Trade Marks (International Registration) Order 2008, SI 2008/2206, art 6, Sch 5 para 1(1). As to the meaning of 'request for extension' see PARA 12 note 2. Where the registrar does so the provisions of Sch 5 para 1(2), (3) apply.

(vi) Priority of Convention and Overseas Applications

360. Claim to priority of Convention application. A person who has duly filed an application for protection of a trade mark[1] in a Convention country[2] (a 'Convention application'), or his successor in title, has a right to priority[3], for the purposes of registering the same trade mark under the Trade Marks Act 1994 for some or all of the same goods or services, for a period of six months from the date of filing[4] of the first such application[5]. If the application for registration under the Act is made within that six month period[6]:

(1)   the relevant date for the purpose of establishing which rights take precedence is the date of filing of the first Convention application[7]; and

(2)   the registrability of the trade mark is not affected by any use[8] of the mark in the United Kingdom[9] in the period between that date and the date of the application under the Act[10].

Any filing which in a Convention country is equivalent to a regular national filing[11], under its domestic legislation or an international agreement, is treated as giving rise to the right of priority[12].

A subsequent application[13] concerning the same subject as the first Convention application, filed in the same Convention country, is considered the first Convention application (of which the filing date is the starting date of the period of priority), if at the time of the subsequent application (a) the previous application has been withdrawn, abandoned or refused, without having been laid open to public inspection and without leaving any rights outstanding; and (b) it has not yet served as a basis for claiming a right of priority[14]. The previous application may not thereafter serve as a basis for claiming a right of priority[15].

Where a right to priority is claimed by reason of an application for protection of a trade mark duly filed in a Convention country[16] or in another country or territory[17] (an 'overseas application'), the application for registration[18] must specify (i) the number accorded to the overseas application by the registering or other competent authority of the relevant country; (ii) the country in which the overseas application was filed; and (iii) the date of filing[19]. The registrar may, in any particular case, by notice require the applicant to file, within such period of not less than one month as the notice may specify, such documentary evidence as the registrar may require certifying, or verifying to the satisfaction of the registrar, the date of the filing of the overseas application, the country or registering or competent authority, the representation of the mark and the goods or services covered by the overseas application[20].

A right to priority arising as a result of a Convention application may be assigned or otherwise transmitted, either with the application or independently[21].

The above provisions apply so as to confer a right of priority in relation to protection of an international registration[22] designating the United Kingdom as they apply in relation to registering a trade mark under the Trade Marks Act 1994, but the manner of claiming priority is determined in accordance with the Madrid Protocol and Common Regulations instead of following the procedure under the Trade Marks Act 1994[23].

1   As to the meaning of 'trade mark' see PARA 41.
2   As to the meaning of 'Convention country' see PARA 6 note 2.
3   The effect of a right to priority is that the application enjoys the date of filing in the Convention country rather than the later date of filing in the United Kingdom, for the purposes of resolving conflicts with other applications or with conflicting common law rights based on use: see PARAS 54, 61.
4   As to the meaning of 'date of filing' see PARA 348.
5   Trade Marks Act 1994 s 35(1). See also note 21. Section 35 applies to an application for registration under the Trade Marks Act 1994 made on or after 31 October 1994 notwithstanding that the Convention was made before that date: Trade Marks Act 1994 s 105, Sch 3 para 13.
6   Trade Marks Act 1994 s 35(2).
7   Trade Marks Act 1994 s 35(2)(a).
8   As to the meaning of 'use' see PARA 44 note 8. As to the burden of proving use of a trade mark see the Trade Marks Act 1994 s 100; and PARA 98.
9   As to the meaning of 'United Kingdom' see PARA 3 note 2.
10 Trade Marks Act 1994 s 35(2)(b). See also note 5.
11 For these purposes, a 'regular national filing' means a filing which is adequate to establish the date on which the application was filed in that country, whatever may be the subsequent fate of the application: Trade Marks Act 1994 s 35(3). The requirement for a 'regular national filing' is satisfied by evidence of a procedurally regular filing in the relevant Convention country: *FSS Trade Mark* [2001] RPC 763, Appointed Person.
12 Trade Marks Act 1994 s 35(3). See also note 5.
13 Ie presumably a subsequent application by the same applicant or a successor in title to him, although the Trade Marks Act 1994 s 35(4) does not expressly say so.
14 Trade Marks Act 1994 s 35(4). See also note 5.
15 Trade Marks Act 1994 s 35(4).
16 Ie under the Trade Marks Act 1994 s 35.
17 Ie in respect of which provision corresponding to that made in the Trade Marks Act 1994 s 35 is made under s 36 (see PARA 361).
18 Ie under the Trade Marks Rules 2008, SI 2008/1797, r 5: see PARA 345.
19 Trade Marks Act 1994 s 35(5); Trade Marks Rules 2008, SI 2008/1797, r 6(1). See also note 5. It should be noted that r 6 does not apply to international trade marks (UK) or requests for extension: see the Trade Marks (International Registration) Order 2008, SI 2008/2206, art 3(3), Sch 1 Pt 2; and PARA 12 note 13. See note 23.
20 Trade Marks Act 1994 s 35(5); Trade Marks Rules 2008, SI 2008/1797, r 6(2). See also note 5.
21 Trade Marks Act 1994 s 35(6). The reference in s 35(1) (see the text to notes 1–5) to the applicant's successor in title is to be construed accordingly: s 35(6). See also note 5.
22 The effect of a valid claim to priority is that the international registration enjoys in the United Kingdom a date earlier than its date of registration in the event of coming into conflict with other applications or marks. For the date of the international registration, which is normally the date of filing of the international application in the office of origin, see PARAS 23, 348. As to the meaning of 'international registration' see PARA 12 note 1.
23 See the Trade Marks Act 1994 s 35(5) (modified by the Trade Marks (International Registration) Order 2008, SI 2008/2206, art 3(3(i); Sch 2 para 3); and PARA 12 note 15. As to the Madrid Protocol see PARA 8; and as to the Common Regulations see PARA 11 note 5.

361.   Claim to priority from other relevant overseas application; new applications. Her Majesty may by Order in Council make provision for conferring on a person who has duly filed an application for protection of a trade mark[1] in:

(1)   any of the Channel Islands or a colony; or

(2)   a country or territory in relation to which Her Majesty's government in the United Kingdom has entered into a treaty, convention, arrangement or engagement for the reciprocal protection of trade marks,

a right to priority, for the purpose of registering the same trade mark under the Trade Marks Act 1994 for some or all of the same goods or services, for a specified period from the date of filing[2] of that application[3].

A person who has duly filed[4] an application for the protection of a trade mark in a relevant country[5] has a right to priority, for the purpose of registering the same trade mark under the Trade Marks Act 1994 for some or all of the same goods or services, for a period of six months from the date of filing of the application in that country[6]. Where the application for registration under the Act is made within that period of six months: (a) the relevant date for the purpose of establishing which rights take precedence is the date of the filing of the application in the relevant country; and (b) the registrability of the trade mark is not affected by any use of the mark in the United Kingdom[7] in the period between that date and the date of the application under the Trade Marks Act 1994[8].

A subsequent application concerning the same subject as the first application, duly filed in the same relevant country, is considered the first application to be filed in that country (of which the filing date is the starting date of the period of priority) if at the time of the subsequent application: (i) the previous application has been withdrawn, abandoned or refused, without having been laid open to public inspection and without leaving any rights outstanding; and (ii) it has not yet served as a basis for claiming right of priority[9].

A previous application may not, however, serve as a basis for claiming a right of priority where a subsequent application is so considered as the first application to be filed[10].

A right to priority so conferred vests in the person filing the application or his successors in title, unless otherwise stated in the application, and may be assigned or otherwise transmitted, either with the application or independently[11].

Where a right to priority is claimed by reason of such an application, particulars of that claim must be included in the application for registration filed under the Trade Marks Act 1994; and unless a certificate[12] is filed with the application, such particulars must include the relevant country and the date of filing[13]. There must be filed within three months of the filing of the application for registration under the Act a certificate by the registering or other competent authority of the relevant country certifying, or verifying to the satisfaction of the registrar: (A) the date of the filing of the application; (B) the relevant country or registering or competent authority; (C) the representation of the mark; and (D) the goods or services covered by the application[14].

1   As to the meaning of 'trade mark' see PARA 41.
2   As to the meaning of 'date of filing' see PARA 348.
3   Trade Marks Act 1994 s 36(1). Any such Order in Council may make provision corresponding to that made by s 35 (see PARA 360) in relation to Convention countries or such other provision as appear to Her Majesty to be appropriate: s 36(2). A statutory instrument containing any such Order in Council is subject to annulment in pursuance of a resolution of either House of Parliament: s 36(3). As to the meaning of 'Convention country' see PARA 6 note 2.
      As to the order that has been made see the Trade Marks (Claims to Priority from Relevant Countries) Order 1994, SI 1994/2803 (amended by SI 1995/2997). The order, as originally enacted, came into force on 5 December 1994: Trade Marks (Claims to Priority from Relevant Countries) Order 1994, SI 1994/2803, art 1.
4   For these purposes, 'duly filed' means a filing which is adequate to establish the date on which the application was filed in the relevant country in question, whatever may be the subsequent fate of the application: Trade Marks (Claims to Priority from Relevant Countries) Order 1994, SI 1994/2803, art 2.
5   For these purposes, 'relevant country' means Antigua and Barbuda, Bahrain, Belize, Bolivia, Botswana, Brunei Darussalam, Colombia, Djibouti, Dominica, Ecuador, Guatemala, Hong

Kong, India, Jamaica, Kuwait, Macau, Maldives, Mozambique, Myanmar, Namibia, Nicaragua, Pakistan, Sierra Leone, Thailand: Trade Marks (Claims to Priority from Relevant Countries) Order 1994, SI 1994/2803, art 2, Schedule (substituted by SI 1995/2997).
6   Trade Marks (Claims to Priority from Relevant Countries) Order 1994, SI 1994/2803, art 3.
7   As to the meaning of 'United Kingdom' see PARA 3 note 2.
8   Trade Marks (Claims to Priority from Relevant Countries) Order 1994, SI 1994/2803, art 4.
9   Trade Marks (Claims to Priority from Relevant Countries) Order 1994, SI 1994/2803, art 5.
10 Trade Marks (Claims to Priority from Relevant Countries) Order 1994, SI 1994/2803, art 6.
11 Trade Marks (Claims to Priority from Relevant Countries) Order 1994, SI 1994/2803, art 7.
12 Ie a certificate as is referred to in the Trade Marks (Claims to Priority from Relevant Countries) Order 1994, SI 1994/2803, art 8(2): see the text and note 14.
13 Trade Marks (Claims to Priority from Relevant Countries) Order 1994, SI 1994/2803, art 8(1).
14 Trade Marks (Claims to Priority from Relevant Countries) Order 1994, SI 1994/2803, art 8(2).

362. Claim to priority from other relevant overseas application; old applications. Where before 31 October 1994 a person duly filed an application for protection of a trade mark[1] in a relevant country[2] which is not a Convention country (a 'relevant overseas application'), he, or his successor in title, has a right to priority, for the purposes of registering the same trade mark under the Trade Marks Act 1994 for some or all of the same goods or services, for a period of six months from the date of filing of the relevant overseas application[3].

If the application for registration under the Act is made within that six month period: (1) the relevant date for the purposes of establishing which rights take precedence is the date of filing of the relevant overseas application; and (2) the registrability of the trade mark is not affected by any use of the mark in the United Kingdom[4] in the period between that date and the date of the application under the Act[5].

Any filing which in a relevant country is equivalent to a regular national filing[6], under its domestic legislation or an international agreement, is treated as giving rise to the right of priority[7].

A subsequent application concerning the same subject as the relevant overseas application, filed in the same country, is considered the relevant overseas application (of which the filing date is the starting date of the period of priority), if at the time of the subsequent application:

(a)   the previous application has been withdrawn, abandoned or refused, without having been laid open to public inspection and without leaving any rights outstanding; and

(b)   it has not yet served as a basis for claiming a right of priority[8].

The previous application may not thereafter serve as a basis for claiming a right of priority[9].

A right to priority arising as a result of a relevant overseas application may be assigned or otherwise transmitted, either with the application or independently[10].

1   As to the meaning of 'trade mark' see PARA 41.
2   'Relevant country' meant a country which was specified in an Order in Council under the Trade Marks Act 1938 s 39A at the time of the application under s 38A or such other time as might be specified in the Order in Council: s 39A(10) (added by the Patents, Designs and Marks Act 1986 Sch 2 para 5). The Trade Marks Act 1938 was repealed by the Trade Marks Act 1994 s 106(2), Sch 5. The Order in Council so made was the Trade Marks and Service Marks (Relevant Countries) Order 1986, SI 1986/1303 (amended by SI 1986/1890; SI 1986/2236; SI 1987/170; SI 1988/1856; SI 1990/2593; SI 1992/2672; and SI 1993/1258).
3   Trade Marks Act 1994 s 105, Sch 3 para 14(1). See also note 9. Nothing in Sch 3 para 14 affects proceedings on an application for registration under the Trade Marks Act 1938 made before 31 October 1994 (see the Trade Marks Act 1994 Sch 3 para 10; and PARA 345): Sch 3 para 14(7).

Provision may be made by rules as to the manner of claiming a right to priority on the basis of a relevant overseas application: Sch 3 para 14(5). At the date at which this volume states the law no such rules had been made.

4 As to the meaning of 'United Kingdom' see PARA 3 note 2.

5 Trade Marks Act 1994 Sch 3 para 14(2).

6 For these purposes, a 'regular national filing' means a filing which is adequate to establish the date on which the application was filed in that country, whatever may be the subsequent fate of the application: Trade Marks Act 1994 Sch 3 para 14(3).

7 Trade Marks Act 1994 Sch 3 para 14(3).

8 Trade Marks Act 1994 Sch 3 para 14(4).

9 Trade Marks Act 1994 Sch 3 para 14(4).

10 Trade Marks Act 1994 Sch 3 para 14(6). The reference in Sch 3 para 14(1) (see the text and notes 1–3) to the applicant's 'successor in title' is to be construed accordingly: Sch 3 para 14(6).

(vii) Acceptance or Refusal of Application or of International Registration

363. Acceptance or refusal of application for a registered trade mark. If it appears to the registrar[1] that the requirements for registration[2] are not met, he must inform the applicant and give him an opportunity, within such period as the registrar may specify, to make representations or to amend the application[3]. If the applicant fails to satisfy the registrar that those requirements are met, or to amend the application so as to meet them, or fails to respond before the end of the specified period[4], the registrar must refuse to accept the application[5]. Although there is no longer any statutory power under which the registrar may accept applications subject to amendments, disclaimers or limitations[6], in practice the registrar continues to indicate to applicants cases where objection could be overcome by an appropriate amendment, disclaimer or limitation[7]. If, however, it appears to the registrar that the requirements for registration are met, he must accept the application[8].

Where grounds for refusal of registration exist in respect of only some of the goods or services for which the trade mark has been applied for, refusal must cover those goods or services only[9]; and accordingly the registrar must accept the application so far as it relates to goods or services in respect of which grounds for refusal do not exist[10].

1 As to the registrar see PARA 19.

2 As to the requirements for registration see PARA 39 et seq.

3 Trade Marks Act 1994 s 37(3).

4 If there is a failure to respond before the end of the specified period, then refusal is mandatory: *POSTPERFECT Trade Mark* [1998] RPC 255, Appointed Person.

5 Trade Marks Act 1994 s 37(4). By contrast with a decision following opposition proceedings (see PARA 367), there is no specific requirement for the registrar to notify the applicant of a decision under this provision stating his reasons. Instead the general rule that the registrar must send the applicant written notice of the decision applies, and the applicant may then request a statement of the reasons for the decision: see the Trade Mark Rules 2008, SI 2008/1797, r 69; and PARA 386. When refusing registration of a trade mark, the registrar is required to state in his decision his conclusion for each of the individual goods and services specified in the application, regardless of the manner in which that application was formulated; nevertheless, where the same ground of refusal is given for a category or group of goods or services, the registrar may use general reasoning for all of the goods or services: Case C-239/05 *BVBA Management, Training en Consultancy v Benelux Merkenbureau* [2007] ECR I-1455, [2007] ETMR 35, ECJ. As to appeals from decisions of the registrar see PARA 387 et seq.

6 Ie as there was under the Trade Marks Act 1938 s 17(2) (repealed). As to disclaimers and limitations see PARA 65.

7 Eg a disclaimer of an element of the mark applied for, or a territorial limitation might overcome an objection of lack of distinctiveness: see PARA 65.

8 Trade Marks Act 1994 s 37(5); *EUROLAMB Trade Mark* [1997] RPC 279, Appointed Person; *Procter & Gamble Ltd's Trade Mark Applications* [1999] RPC 673, [1999] ETMR 816, CA;

and see further PARA 39. In this respect the Trade Marks Act 1994 differs from the Trade Marks Act 1938, which gave the registrar a residual discretion to refuse registration of a mark even if it met the statutory requirements.

9 European Parliament and Council Directive (EC) 2008/95 (OJ L299, 8.11.2008, p 25) to approximate the laws of the member states relating to trade marks, art 13 (formerly Council Directive (EEC) 89/104 (OJ L40, 11.2.89, p 1) art 13). These provisions have no counterpart in the Trade Marks Act 1994 s 37 (cf s 46(5) (see PARA 101) and s 47(5) (see PARA 104), but nevertheless they are binding upon the registrar: *MISTER LONG Trade Mark* [1998] RPC 401, Appointed Person; *Nettec Solutions Ltd's Trade Mark Application* [2003] RPC 308, Appointed Person; *Sensornet Ltd's Trade Mark Application* [2007] RPC 185, Appointed Person.

10 *Sensornet Ltd's Trade Mark Application* [2007] RPC 185, Appointed Person; *CITYBOND Trade Mark* [2007] RPC 301, Appointed Person; *Giorgio Armani SpA v Sunrich Clothing Ltd* [2010] EWHC 2939 (Ch), [2011] RPC 392; *NMSI Trading Ltd's Trade Mark Application* [2012] RPC 149, Appointed Person; *Advanced Perimeter Systems Ltd v Keycorp Ltd* [2012] RPC 336, 359, Appointed Person; *Rautaruukki Oyj v Ruukki Group Oyj* [2012] EWHC 2920 (Ch), [2012] All ER (D) 266 (Oct); *YouView TV Ltd v Total Ltd* [2012] EWHC 3158 (Ch), [2012] All ER (D) 123 (Nov). See also *Stichting BDO v BDO Unibank, Inc* [2013] EWHC 418 (Ch), [2013] ETMR 31 [2013] All ER (D) 39 (Mar). As these authorities demonstrate, this requirement can raise issues of procedural efficiency and fairness. The registrar's current practice is set out in Tribunal Practice Note 1/2012.

364.   Decision as to whether to uphold notice of provisional refusal of protection for international registration. Where the registrar[1] has given notice of provisional refusal[2] to the International Bureau[3], the registrar must notify the International Bureau accordingly as to the final decision[4] on whether the refusal should be upheld[5].

1 As to the registrar see PARA 19.
2 Ie notice of provisional refusal pursuant to the Trade Marks Act 1994 s 37(3), (4) or s 38(2) (modified by the Trade Marks (International Registration) Order 2008, SI 2008/2206, art 3(3)(i), Sch 2 paras 4, 5) (see PARAS 355, 366). See also PARA 12 note 15.
3 As to the International Bureau see PARA 8 note 2.
4 Ie a decision from which no appeal may be brought: Trade Marks Act 1994 s 38A(4) (added as modification by the Trade Marks (International Registration) Order 2008, SI 2008/2206, art 3(3)(i), Sch 2 para 6) (see PARA 366). See also PARA 12 note 15.
5 Ie in the light of the representations made by the holder (if any) (see PARA 354) or in the light of the parties' evidence and argument in opposition proceedings (see PARA 366): Trade Marks Act 1994 s 38A(4) (as added: see note 4).

365.   Publication of applications. When an application for registration of a trade mark[1] has been accepted, the registrar[2] must publish[3] the application[4]. If the essential features of the mark are not clearly depicted, the registrar ought to re-publish the application in correct form and the opposition period will start from the date of re-publication[5].

These provisions apply similarly in regard an application for protection of an international registration[6], and if it appears to the registrar that the application is entitled to protection[7] in relation to all or some of the goods or services specified in the international registration, the registrar must publish a notice specifying particulars of the international registration and the goods and services for which protection is to be conferred[8].

1 As to the requirements for registration see PARA 39 et seq; and as to the procedure on the application see the text and notes 2–5; and PARAS 334 et seq, 366 et seq. As to the meaning of 'trade mark' see PARA 41.
2 As to the registrar see PARA 19.
3 As to the meaning of 'publish' see PARA 19 note 10. Such publication is in the Trade Marks Journal. As to the Trade Marks Journal see the Trade Marks Rules 2008, SI 2008/1797, r 81; and PARA 19.
4 Trade Marks Act 1994 s 38(1); Trade Marks Rules 2008, SI 2008/1797, r 16.

5   *CREOLA Trade Mark* [1997] RPC 507; *Andreas Stihl AG & Co's Trade Mark Application* [2001] RPC 215, Appointed Person. As to opposition see PARA 366 et seq.
6   As to the meaning of 'international registration' see PARA 12 note 1.
7   Ie that it satisfies the requirements of the Trade Marks Act 1994, including any requirements imposed by rules, as they apply to international registrations: see PARA 355.
8   See the Trade Marks (International Registration) Order 2008, SI 2008/2206, art 3; and PARA 12.

(viii) Opposition Proceedings

366. Opposition proceedings. Any person[1] may, within the prescribed time from the date of the publication of the application[2], give notice to the registrar[3] of opposition to the registration of a trade mark[4]; the notice must be given in writing in the prescribed manner, and must include a statement of the grounds of opposition[5].

Subject to the provision on the filing of notice of fast track opposition[6] and Form 7F[7], any notice to the registrar of opposition to the registration, including the statement of the grounds of opposition, must be filed on Form TM7[8]. Unless the following applies[9], the time prescribed for these purposes[10] is the period of two months beginning immediately after the date on which the application was published[11]. Where a request for an extension of time for the filing of Form TM7 has been made on Form TM7A, before the expiry of the above period[12] and where this provision applies, the time prescribed for the above purposes[13] in relation to any person having filed a Form TM7A (or, in the case of a company, any subsidiary[14] or holding company[15] of that company or any other subsidiary of that holding company) is the period of three months beginning immediately after the date on which the application was published[16]. Where a person makes a request for such an extension of time[17], Form TM7A must be filed electronically using the filing system provided on the Intellectual Property Office ('IPO') website or by such other means as the registrar may permit[18].

Where the opposition is based on a trade mark which has been registered, there must be included in the statement of the grounds of opposition a representation of that mark and (1) the details of the authority with which the mark is registered; (2) the registration number of that mark; (3) the goods and services in respect of which that mark is registered, and the opposition is based; and (4) where the registration procedure for the mark was completed before the start of the period of five years ending with the date of publication, a statement detailing whether during the period[19] the mark has been put to genuine use in relation to each of the goods and services in respect of which the opposition is based or whether there are proper reasons for non-use (the 'statement of use')[20].

Where the opposition is based on a trade mark in respect of which an application for registration has been made, there must be included in the statement of the grounds of opposition a representation of that mark and those matters set out in heads (1) to (3) above, with references to registration being construed as references to the application for registration[21].

Where the opposition is based on an unregistered trade mark or other sign which the person opposing the application claims to be protected by virtue of any rule of law (in particular, the law of passing off)[22], there must be included in the statement of the grounds of opposition a representation of that mark or sign and the goods and services in respect of which such protection is claimed[23].

The registrar must send a copy of Form TM7 to the applicant and the date upon which this is sent is for these purposes[24], the 'notification date'[25].

The applicant must, within the relevant period[26], file a Form TM8, which must include a counter-statement[27].

Where the applicant fails to file a Form TM8 or counter-statement within the relevant period, the application for registration, insofar as it relates to the goods and services in respect of which the opposition is directed, must, unless the registrar otherwise directs, be treated as abandoned[28]. The registrar must send a copy of Form TM8 to the person opposing the registration[29].

If the opposition or part of it is based on the relative grounds of refusal[30]; and the registrar has not indicated to the parties that the registrar thinks that it is inappropriate for this provision to apply, the following applies[31].

After considering the statement of the grounds of opposition and the counter-statement the registrar must send notice to the parties ('the preliminary indication') stating whether it appears to the registrar that registration of the mark should not be refused in respect of all or any of the goods and services listed in the application on the grounds set out[32]; or registration of the mark should be refused in respect of all or any of the goods and services listed in the application on the grounds so set out[33]. The date upon which the preliminary indication is sent is the 'indication date'[34].

Where it appeared to the registrar[35] that registration of the mark should not be refused in respect of all or any of the goods or services listed in the application on the grounds set out[36], the person opposing the registration must, within one month of the indication date, file a notice of intention to proceed with the opposition based on those grounds by filing a Form TM53, otherwise that person's opposition to the registration of the mark in relation to those goods or services on the grounds set out[37] is deemed to have been withdrawn[38].

Where it appeared to the registrar[39] that registration of the mark should be refused in respect of all or any of the goods or services listed in the application on the grounds set out[40], the applicant must, within one month of the indication date, file a notice of intention to proceed on Form TM53, otherwise the applicant is deemed to have withdrawn the request to register the mark in respect of the goods or services for which the registrar indicated registration should be refused[41].

A person who files a Form TM53 must, at the same time, send a copy to all other parties to the proceedings[42]. The registrar need not give reasons for the preliminary indication nor is the preliminary indication subject to appeal[43].

Where (a) Form TM53 has been filed by either party; (b) the opposition or part of it is based on grounds other than those set out[44] and the applicant has filed a Form TM8; or (c) the registrar has indicated to the parties that it is inappropriate for the provision on preliminary indication[45] to apply, the registrar must specify the periods within which evidence and submissions may be filed by the parties[46].

Where (i) the opposition is based on an earlier trade mark[47]; or (ii) the opposition or part of it is based on grounds other than those set out[48]; or (iii) the truth of a matter set out in the statement of use is either denied or not admitted by the applicant, the person opposing the registration ('the opposer') must file evidence supporting the opposition[49].

Where the opposer files no such evidence[50], the opposer is deemed to have withdrawn the opposition to the registration to the extent that it is based on (A) the matters in head (i) or head (ii) above; or (B) an earlier trade mark which has been registered and which is the subject of the statement of use referred to in head (iii) above[51].

The registrar may, at any time, give leave to either party to file evidence upon such terms as the registrar thinks fit[52].

In regard to protected international trade marks (UK)[53] any person may, within the prescribed time from the date of the publication of the application, give notice to the registrar of opposition to the registration in which event the registrar must give notice of provisional refusal to the International Bureau[54]; and the notice to the registrar must be given in writing in the prescribed manner, and must similarly include a statement of the grounds of opposition[55].

A notice of provisional refusal must set out certain matters[56]. Except as provided below[57], a notice of provisional refusal may not be given after the expiry of the relevant period[58].

Where before the expiry of the relevant period the registrar has given notice to the International Bureau that the period prescribed[59] expires after the end of the relevant period; or that the period prescribed[60] expires less than one month before the end of the relevant period, a notice of provisional refusal may be given after the expiry of the relevant period provided that it is given before the end of the period of one month beginning immediately after the period prescribed[61].

Where the registrar sends the International Bureau a notice of provisional refusal, the registrar must notify the International Bureau as to the final decision (meaning a decision from which no appeal may be brought) on whether the refusal should be upheld[62].

1　The opponent does not have to show that he is aggrieved by, or otherwise interested in, the application: *Pharmedica GmbH's Trade Mark Application* [2000] RPC 536, [2000] All ER (D) 28; cf *Oystertec plc's Patent* [2002] EWHC 2324 (Pat), [2003] RPC 559, sub nom *Oystertec plc v Edward Evans Barker* [2003] IP & T 1015. When an opponent transfers to another person the interest which he is seeking to protect by means of the opposition, e g upon sale of the relevant business or earlier trade mark, the registrar has a discretion to permit the substitution of that person as opponent, even in the absence of any explicit statutory power under the Trade Marks Act 1994 or rules authorising such a substitution: *Pharmedica GmbH's Trade Mark Application* above. See notes 20, 22.

2　Ie publication under the Trade Marks Rules 2008, SI 2008/1797, r 16: see PARA 365. As to the meaning of 'publish' see PARA 19 note 10.

3　As to the registrar see PARA 19.

4　As to the meaning of 'trade mark' see PARA 41.

5　Trade Marks Act 1994 s 38(2). The statement of grounds should properly plead and particularise the material facts upon which an allegation is based; and the previous practice that led to pleadings before the Trade Marks Registry often failing to identify the issues should not continue: *Julian Higgins' Trade Mark Application* [2000] RPC 321; *CLUB EUROPE Trade Mark* [2000] RPC 329, [1999] All ER (D) 686; *DEMON ALE Trade Mark* [2000] RPC 345, Appointed Person. The Trade Marks Registry has published a Tribunal Practice Notice 1/2000, [2000] RPC 587 setting out the matters which should be contained in pleadings. See also Tribunal Practice Notice 1/2010. Tribunal Practice Notices are available from the Intellectual Property Office ('IPO') or on its website, accessible at the date at which this volume states the law at www.ipo.gov.uk. As to the Intellectual Property Office (an operating name of the Patent Office) see PARA 16 note 2. As to the procedural powers of the registrar see further PARA 340.

6　'Fast track opposition' means an opposition (1) brought solely on grounds under the Trade Marks Act 1994 s 5(1) (see PARA 55) or s 5(2) (see PARA 56); (2) based on no more than three earlier trade marks, each of which is registered in the UK or in the EU, or is protected in one or another of those territories as an international trade mark (UK) or (EU); (3) where proof of use of the earlier marks can be provided with the notice of opposition; and (4) which the opponent considers may be determined without the need for further evidence and without an oral hearing: Trade Marks Rules 2008, SI 2008/1797, r 2(1) (definition added by SI 2013/2235). As to the meaning of 'earlier trade mark' see PARA 54. As to the meanings of 'international trade mark (UK)' and 'international trade mark (EU)' see PARA 8 note 17.

7　Ie subject to the Trade Marks Rules 2008, SI 2008/1797, r 17A (see below). As to the use of forms see PARA 335.
　　A notice to the registrar of fast track opposition to the registration, including the statement of the grounds of opposition, may be filed on Form TM7F: r 17A(1) (r 17A added by SI 2013/2235). As to guidance on the use of Form TM7F see Tribunal Practice Notice (TPN 2/2013) on Fast Track Oppositions, available from the IPO website (see note 5). A notice of fast

track opposition to the registration filed on Form TM7F and a notice of opposition to the registration filed on Form TM7 (see note 8) must constitute alternatives and an opponent must not maintain more than one opposition against the same trade mark application: Trade Marks Rules 2008, SI 2008/1797, r 17A(2) (as so added). Unless r 17A(4) (see below) applies, the time prescribed for the purposes of the Trade Marks Act 1994 s 38(2) (see the text and notes 1–5) is the period of two months beginning immediately after the date on which the application was published: Trade Marks Rules 2008, SI 2008/1797, r 17A(3) (as so added). This provision applies where a request for an extension of time for the filing of Form TM7 or TM7F (see the text and note 8) has been made on Form TM7A, before the expiry of the period referred to in r 17A(3) (see above) and where this provision applies, the time prescribed for the purposes of the Trade Marks Act 1994 s 38(2) in relation to any person having filed a Form TM7A (or, in the case of a company, any subsidiary or holding company of that company or any other subsidiary of that holding company) is the period of three months beginning immediately after the date on which the application was published: Trade Marks Rules 2008, SI 2008/1797, r 17A(4) (as so added). Forms TM7F and TM7A must be filed electronically using the filing system provided on the IPO website or by such other means as the registrar may permit: r 17A(5) (as so added). There must be included in the statement of the grounds of opposition a representation of that mark and (1) the details of the authority with which the mark is registered or protected; (2) the registration number of that mark; (3) the goods and services in respect of which (a) that mark is registered; and (b) the opposition is based; (4) the date of completion of the registration procedure or of granting protection to an international trade mark (UK) or (EU); and (5) where the registration or protection procedure for the mark was completed before the start of the period of five years ending with the date of publication, a statement detailing whether during the period referred to in the Trade Marks Act 1994 s 6A(3)(a) (see PARA 63) the mark has been put to genuine use in relation to each of the goods and services in respect of which the opposition is based: Trade Marks Rules 2008, SI 2008/1797, r 17A(6) (as so added). Where the earlier mark is subject to proof of use under the Trade Marks Act 1994 s 6A (see PARA 63), the proof of use that the opponent wishes to rely upon must be provided with the notice of fast track opposition: Trade Marks Rules 2008, SI 2008/1797, r 17A)(7) (as so added). The registrar must send a copy of Form TM7F to the applicant and the date upon which this is sent is, for the purposes of r 18 (see the text and notes 26–29), the 'notification date': r 17A(8) (as so added). For these purposes 'subsidiary' and 'holding company' have the same meaning as in the Companies Act 2006 (see COMPANIES vol 14 (2009) PARA 25): Trade Marks Rules 2008, SI 2008/1797, r 17A(9) (as so added).

8   Trade Marks Rules 2008, SI 2008/1797, r 17(1).
     The notice must correctly identify the trade mark application sought to be opposed and the registrar has no power to put right an error made in identifying the application after the application has become registered: *DUCATI Trade Mark* [1998] RPC 227, Trade Marks Registry; c f *Andreas Stihl AG & Co's Trade Mark Application* [2001] RPC 215, Appointed Person; *BAT OUT OF HELL Trade Mark* (O/398/02), Appointed Person.
9   Ie unless the Trade Marks Rules 2008, SI 2008/1797, r 17(3) (see the text and notes 12–16) applies.
10   Ie for the purposes of the Trade Marks Act 1994 s 38(2): see the text and notes 1–5.
11   Trade Marks Rules 2008, SI 2008/1797, r 17(2) (amended by SI 2013/444). As to calculation of time periods in regard to the Trade Marks Rules 2008, SI 2008/1797, rr 17(2), (3), 18(3), (4), (5), (6) see Tribunal Practice Notice (TPN 1/2013), available from the IPO website (see note 5).
12   Ie the period referred to in the Trade Marks Rules 2008, SI 2008/1797, r 17(2).
13   See note 10.
14   For these purposes, 'subsidiary' and 'holding company' have the same meaning as in the Companies Act 2006 (see COMPANIES vol 14 (2009) PARA 25): Trade Marks Rules 2008, SI 2008/1797, r 17(9).
15   See note 12.
16   Trade Marks Rules 2008, SI 2008/1797, r 17(3) (amended by SI 2013/444). See note 11.
17   Ie under the Trade Marks Rules 2008, SI 2008/1797, s 17(3).
18   Trade Marks Rules 2008, SI 2008/1797, r 17(4). As to the website see note 5.
19   Ie the period referred to in the Trade Marks Act 1994 s 6A(3)(a): see PARA 63 head (a).
20   Trade Marks Rules 2008, SI 2008/1797, r 17(5). For the purposes of r 20 (see the text and notes 44–52) head (4) is the 'statement of use': r 17(5). The opponent must be the proprietor of the earlier trade mark: see the Trade Marks Act 1994 s 8(1), the Trade Marks (Relative Grounds) Order 2007, SI 2007/1976, art 2; and PARA 64.
21   Trade Marks Rules 2008, SI 2008/1797, r 17(6)
22   As to reliance upon such earlier rights see PARA 61. The opponent must be the proprietor of the earlier right: see the Trade Marks Act 1994 s 8(1), the Trade Marks (Relative Grounds)

Order 2007, SI 2007/1976, art 2; and PARA 64. Where the opponent relies on extended passing off, it is sufficient that it is a member of the class of traders who can claim ownership of the goodwill: Case T-304/09 *Tilda Riceland Pte Ltd v Office for Harmonisation in the Internal Market (Trade Marks and Designs)* [2012] ECR II-0000, [2012] ETMR 15, EGC. As to passing off see PARA 287 et seq.

23 Trade Marks Rules 2008, SI 2008/1797, r 17(7).

24 Ie for the purposes of the Trade Marks Rules 2008, SI 2008/1797, r 18: see the text and notes 26–29.

25 Trade Marks Rules 2008, SI 2008/1797, r 17(8).

26 Unless the Trade Marks Rules 2008, SI 2008/1797, r 18(4), (5) or (6) (see below) applies, the relevant period is the period of two months beginning immediately after the notification date: r 18(3) (amended by SI 2013/444). As to the 'notification date' see the text and note 25. See note 11.

The Trade Marks Rules 2008, SI 2008/1797, r 18(4) applies where (1) the applicant and the person opposing the registration agree to an extension of time for the filing of Form TM8; (2) within the period of two months beginning immediately after the notification date, either party files Form TM9c requesting an extension of time for the filing of Form TM8; and (3) during the period beginning on the date Form TM9c was filed and ending nine months after the notification date, no notice to continue on Form TM9t is filed by the person opposing the registration and no request for a further extension of time for the filing of Form TM8 is filed on Form TM9e, and where r 18(4) applies the relevant period is the period of nine months beginning immediately after the notification date: r 18(4) (amended by SI 2013/444). See note 11.

The Trade Marks Rules 2008, SI 2008/1797, r 18(5) applies where (a) a request for an extension of time for the filing of Form TM8 has been filed on Form TM9c in accordance with r 18(4)(b) (see head (2) above); (b) during the period referred to r 18(4)(c) (see head (3) above), either party files Form TM9e requesting a further extension of time for the filing of Form TM8 which request includes a statement confirming that the parties are seeking to negotiate a settlement of the opposition proceedings; and (c) the other party agrees to the further extension of time for the filing of Form TM8, and where r 18(5) applies the relevant period is the period of eighteen months beginning immediately after the notification date: r 18(5) (amended by SI 2013/444). See note 11.

The Trade Marks Rules 2008, SI 2008/1797, r 18(6) applies where (i) a request for an extension of time for the filing of Form TM8 has been filed on Form TM9c in accordance with r 18(4)(b) (see head (2) above); and (ii) the person opposing the registration has filed a notice to continue on Form TM9t,and where r 18(6) applies the relevant period begins on the notification date and ends one month after the date on which Form TM9t was filed or two months beginning immediately after the notification date, whichever is the later: r 18(6) (amended by SI 2013/444). See note 11.

27 Trade Marks Rules 2008, SI 2008/1797, r 18(1).

28 Trade Marks Rules 2008, SI 2008/1797, r 18(2).

29 Trade Marks Rules 2008, SI 2008/1797, r 18(7).

30 Ie as set out in the Trade Marks Act 1994 s 5(1) (see PARA 55) or s 5(2) (see PARA 56).

31 Trade Marks Rules 2008, SI 2008/1797, r 19(1). Note that r 19 does not apply to fast track oppositions (see the text and notes 6, 7): r 19(1A) (added by SI 2013/2235).

32 See note 30.

33 Trade Marks Rules 2008, SI 2008/1797, r 19(2). See notes 30, 31.

34 Trade Marks Rules 2008, SI 2008/1797, r 19(3). See note 31.

35 Ie under the Trade Marks Rules 2008, SI 2008/1797, r 19(2).

36 See note 30.

37 See note 30.

38 Trade Marks Rules 2008, SI 2008/1797, r 19(4). See note 31.

39 See note 35.

40 See note 30.

41 Trade Marks Rules 2008, SI 2008/1797, r 19(5). See note 31.

42 Trade Marks Rules 2008, SI 2008/1797, r 19(6). See note 31.

43 Trade Marks Rules 2008, SI 2008/1797, r 19(7). See note 31.

44 See note 30.

45 Ie the Trade Marks Rules 2008, SI 2008/1797, r 19: see the text and notes 30–42.

46 Trade Marks Rules 2008, SI 2008/1797, r 20(1). See note 52.

47 Ie of a kind falling within the Trade Marks Act 1994 s 6(1)(c): see PARA 54 head (4).

48 See note 30.

49 Trade Marks Rules 2008, SI 2008/1797, r 20(2). See note 52.

50 Ie under the Trade Marks Rules 2008, SI 2008/1797, r 20(2).
51 Trade Marks Rules 2008, SI 2008/1797, r 20(3). See note 52.
52 Trade Marks Rules 2008, SI 2008/1797, r 20(4). Note that r 20(1)–(3) does not apply to fast
    track oppositions (see the text and notes 6, 7) but r 20(4) does: r 20(5) (added by SI 2013/2235).
    As to further evidence under the Trade Marks Rules 2008, SI 2008/1797, r 20(4) see Tribunal
    Practice Notice (TPN 2/2013) on Fast Track Oppositions, available from the IPO website (see
    note 5).
53 As to the meanings of 'protected international trade mark (UK)' and 'protected' and protection'
    see PARA 12 note 8.
54 As to the International Bureau see PARA 8 text and note 2.
55 Trade Marks Act 1994 s 38(2) (as modified by the Trade Marks (International Registration)
    Order 2008, SI 2008/2206, art 3(3)(i), Sch 2 para 5). See PARA 12 note 15. See also generally
    art 3; and PARA 12. See also the text and notes 56–61.
56 Trade Marks Act 1994 s 38A(1) (s 38A added as a modification by the Trade Marks
    (International Registration) Order 2008, SI 2008/2206, art 3(3)(i), Sch 2 para 6): see PARA 12
    note 15. The reference in the text to certain matters is a reference to the matters required by the
    Madrid Protocol art 5 and the Common Regulations r 17. As to the Madrid Protocol see PARA
    8; and as to the Common Regulations see PARA 11 note 5. See also PARA 12 note 15.
57 Ie in the Trade Marks Act 1994 s 38A(3).
58 Trade Marks Act 1994 s 38A(2) (as added: see note 56). For these purposes, the 'relevant
    period' is the period of 18 months beginning immediately after the date the International Bureau
    sent the registrar the request for extension: s 38A(5) (as so added). As to the meaning of 'request
    for extension' see PARA 12 note 2.
59 Ie prescribed for the purposes of the Trade Marks Act 1994 s 38(2): see the text and notes 1–5.
60 See note 59.
61 Trade Marks Act 1994 s 38A(3) (as added: see note 56). See note 59.
62 Trade Marks Act 1994 s 38A(4) (as added: see note 56).

367.   Registrar's decision. The registrar[1] must send to each party to the
proceedings written notice of any decision made in any proceedings before the
registrar stating the reasons for that decision and for the purposes of any appeal
against that decision[2] the date on which the notice is sent is taken to be the date
of the decision[3].
Similar provisions apply to international trade marks (UK)[4].

1   As to the registrar see PARA 19.
2   Ie subject to the Trade Marks Rules 2008, SI 2008/1797, r 69(2): see note 3.
3   Trade Marks Rules 2008, SI 2008/1797, r 69(1). Where a statement of the reasons for the
    decision is not included in the notice sent under r 69(1), any party may, within one month of the
    date on which the notice was sent to that party, request the registrar on Form TM5 to send a
    statement of the reasons for the decision and upon such request the registrar must send such a
    statement, and the date on which that statement is sent is deemed to be the date of the registrar's
    decision for the purpose of any appeal against it: r 69(2).
4   See the Trade Marks (International Registration) Order 2008, SI 2008/2206, art 3; and PARA 12.
    As to notification of a decision on whether a notice of provisional refusal is upheld see PARA 366
    text and note 56.

368.   Res judicata. If an opponent is successful, and a fresh application is
made and he opposes again, the matter may or may not be res judicata
depending in particular on whether the different application date and any
differences in the trade marks applied for affect the causes of action and/or the
issues raised[1]. Lack of success will not preclude the opponent from subsequently
challenging the validity of the registration unless the particular circumstances of
the later challenge mean that it is an abuse of process[2].

1   *Re William Hunt & Sons, The Brades Ltd's Application* (1911) 28 RPC 302; *Re Massachusetts
    Saw Works' Application* (1918) 35 RPC 137; c f *Unilever Ltd's (Striped Toothpaste No 2) Trade
    Marks* [1987] RPC 13; *Philips Electronics NV v Remington Consumer Products Ltd (No 2)*
    [1999] ETMR 835, [1999] All ER (D) 351; *Hormel Foods Corpn v Antilles Landscape
    Investments NV* [2005] EWHC 13 (Ch), [2005] RPC 657, [2005] IP & T 822.

2   *Special Effects Ltd v L'Oréal SA* [2007] EWCA Civ 1, [2007] RPC 380, [2007] All ER (D) 29
    (Jan). This decision reflects the position regarding successive proceedings before the Office for
    Harmonisation in the Internal Market: see PARA 272 note 11. As to the Office for
    Harmonisation in the Internal Market see PARA 163 et seq. Cf *Evans v Focal Point Fires plc*
    [2009] EWHC 2784 (Ch), [2011] IP & T 120, [2011] All ER (D) 130 (Nov) (defendant
    company had no reasonable prospect of defending claim for passing off as trade mark had
    previously been declared invalid by trade marks registry). See also *Virgin Atlantic Airways Ltd v
    Zodiac Seats UK Ltd (formerly Contour Aerospace Ltd)* [2013] UKSC 46, [2013] 4 All ER 715,
    [2013] RPC 747.

(ix) Observations on Registrability

369.   In general. Where an application for registration of a trade mark has
been published[1], any person may, at any time before the registration[2] of the trade
mark[3], make observations in writing to the registrar[4] as to whether the trade
mark should be registered[5]. Similarly, where a notice has been published that
protection in the United Kingdom will be conferred on an international
registration[6], any person may, at any time before the trade mark becomes
protected, make observations in writing to the registrar as to whether the trade
mark should be protected[7]. A person who makes observations does not thereby
become a party to the proceedings on the application or international
registration[8].

The registrar must send[9] to the applicant for a United Kingdom trade mark a
copy of any documents containing any such observations[10].

1   As to publication of the application see PARA 365.
2   As to the meaning of 'registration' see PARA 21 note 2.
3   As to the meaning of 'trade mark' see PARA 41.
4   As to the registrar see PARA 19.
5   Trade Marks Act 1994 s 38(3).
6   As to the meaning of 'international registration' see PARA 12 note 1. As to the meaning of
    'United Kingdom' see PARA 3 note 2.
7   See the Trade Marks (International Registration) Order 2008, SI 2008/2206, art 3; and PARA 12.
8   Trade Marks Act 1994 s 38(3); and see the Trade Marks (International Registration)
    Order 2008, SI 2008/2206, art 3; and PARA 12.
9   As to the meaning of 'send' see PARA 27 note 10.
10 Trade Marks Rules 2008, SI 2008/1797, r 22.

(x) Registration

370.   Registration of trade mark. Where an application has been accepted
and:

(1)   no notice of opposition[1] is given within the specified period[2]; or
(2)   all opposition proceedings are withdrawn or decided in favour of the
       applicant[3],

the registrar[4] must register the trade mark unless it appears to him, having regard
to matters coming to his notice since he accepted the application[5], that the
registration requirements (other than the relative grounds for refusal[6]) were not
met at that time[7]. A trade mark may not, however, be so registered unless any fee
prescribed for the registration is paid within the prescribed period; if the fee is
not paid within that period, the application is deemed to be withdrawn[8].

On the registration of a trade mark the registrar must publish[9] the registration
on the Intellectual Property Office ('IPO') website[10], specifying the date upon
which the trade mark was entered in the register[11] and issue to the applicant a
certificate of registration[12].

1   As to opposition proceedings see PARAS 366–368.
2   Trade Marks Act 1994 s 40(1)(a). The specified period is the period referred to in s 38(2) (see
    PARA 366): s 40(1)(a).
        It should be noted that s 40 does not apply to international trade marks (UK) or requests for
    extension: see the Trade Marks (International Registration) Order 2008, SI 2008/2206, art 3(3),
    Sch 1 Pt 1; and PARA 12 note 10.
3   Trade Marks Act 1994 s 40(1)(b). See note 2.
4   As to the registrar see PARA 19.
5   Eg as a result of third party observations (as to which see PARA 369).
6   Ie under the Trade Marks Act 1994 s 5(1)–(3): see PARA 54 et seq.
7   Trade Marks Act 1994 s 40(1) (amended by SI 2004/946). See note 2. Once the relevant time
    limits have expired the registrar is obliged to take timely steps to enter the trade mark on the
    register: *CREOLA Trade Mark* [1997] RPC 507. The registrar has power to withdraw a
    registration if it is subsequently discovered that the registration was procedurally irregular: see
    Andreas Stihl AG & Co's Trade Mark Application [2001] RPC 215, Appointed Person; *BAT
    OUT OF HELL Trade Mark* (O/398/02), Appointed Person; and PARA 343.
8   Trade Marks Act 1994 s 40(2). As to fees see PARA 18.
9   As to the meaning of 'publish' see PARA 19 note 10.
10 The IPO's website is accessible at the date at which this volume states the law at
    www.ipo.gov.uk. As to the Intellectual Property Office (an operating name of the Patent Office)
    see PARA 16 note 2.
11 Ie the date of filing of the application for registration: Trade Marks Act 1994 s 40(3): see PARA
    23.
12 Trade Marks Act 1994 s 40(4); Trade Marks Rules 2008, SI 2008/1797, r 23. See note 2.

371.   Conferring of protection on an international registration. Where no
notice of provisional refusal is given to the International Bureau[1] following
publication[2], the international registration[3] which is the subject of the request for
extension is protected as a protected international trade mark (UK)[4] with effect
from the first day immediately following the end of the period prescribed[5].

Where notice of provisional refusal is given following publication[6], the
international registration which is the subject of the request for extension is
protected as a protected international trade mark (UK) with effect from the date
on which the registrar notifies the International Bureau that the final decision is
that the provisional refusal should not be upheld[7].

When an international registration becomes protected as a protected
international trade mark (UK), the registrar must:

(1)   notify the International Bureau that the international registration is
      protected in the United Kingdom[8]; and

(2)   publish a notice specifying the number of the international registration
      in respect of that trade mark, the date on which protection is conferred
      and the date and place of publication of the request for extension[9] in
      relation to that trade mark[10].

1   As to the International Bureau see PARA 8 text and note 2.
2   Ie under the Trade Marks Act 1994 s 38(1): see PARA 365.
3   As to the meaning of 'international registration' see PARA 12 note 1.
4   As to the meanings of 'protected international trade mark (UK)', 'protected' and 'protection' see
    PARA 12 note 8.
5   Trade Marks Act 1994 s 38B(1) (s 38B added as a modification by the Trade Marks
    (International Registration) Order 2008, SI 2008/2206, art 3(3)(i), Sch 2 para 6). See also PARA
    12 note 15. The reference in the text to the end of the period prescribed is a reference to the end
    of the period prescribed for the purposes of the Trade Marks Act 1994 s 38(2): see PARA 366
    text and notes 1–5.
6   See note 2.
7   Trade Marks Act 1994 s 38B(2) (as added: see note 5). The reference in the text to the
    provisional refusal not being upheld is a reference to the provisional refusal not being upheld
    under s 38A(4): see PARA 366 text and note 62.
8   As to the meaning of 'United Kingdom' see PARA 3 note 2.

9   See note 2.
10 Trade Marks Act 1994 s 38B(4) (as added: see note 5). The reference to the 'completion of the
    registration procedure' in s 46(1) (see PARA 98) is to be construed as a reference to the conferring
    of protection on an international registration in accordance with s 38B: s 38B(3) (as so added).

(xi) Supply of Information

372. Information about applications and registered trade marks. After
publication of an application for registration of a trade mark[1], the registrar[2]
must on request provide a person with such information and permit him to
inspect such documents relating to the application, or to any registered trade
mark resulting from it, as may be specified in the request, subject, however, to
any prescribed restrictions[3]. Any request must be made on the appropriate form[4]
and must be accompanied by the appropriate fee, if any[5].

Before publication of an application for registration of a trade mark,
documents or information constituting or relating to the application must not be
published by the registrar or communicated by him to any person except (1) in
such cases and to such extent as may be prescribed[6]; or (2) with the consent of
the applicant, but subject as follows[7]. Where a person has been notified that an
application for registration of a trade mark has been made, and that the
applicant will, if the application is granted, bring proceedings against him in
respect of acts done after publication of the application, he may make a request
for information[8] notwithstanding that the application has not been published[9].

The above provisions apply similarly to information in the possession of the
registrar relating to international registrations[10] in respect of which protection is
sought in the United Kingdom, before and after the registrar has published a
notice that protection will be conferred[11].

1   As to the publication of the application see PARA 365. As to the meaning of 'trade mark' see
    PARA 41; and as to the meaning of 'publish' see PARA 19 note 10.
2   As to the registrar see PARA 19.
3   Trade Marks Act 1994 s 67(1). As to the restrictions see PARAS 27–28.
4   Ie Form TM31C. As to the use of forms see PARA 335.
5   Trade Marks Act 1994 s 67(1); Trade Marks Rules 2008, SI 2008/1797, r 56. As to fees see
    PARA 18.
        It should be noted that r 56 does not apply to international trade marks (UK) or requests for
    extension: see the Trade Marks (International Registration) Order 2008, SI 2008/2206, art 3(3),
    Sch 1 Pt 2; and PARA 12 note 13.
6   Before publication of an application for registration the registrar must make available for
    inspection by the public the application and any amendments made to it and any particulars
    contained in a notice given to the registrar under the Trade Marks Rules 2008, SI 2008/1797,
    r 49 (see PARA 116): r 57(1).
7   Trade Marks Act 1994 s 67(2). Nothing in s 67(2) relating to publication of information may be
    construed as preventing the publication of decisions on cases relating to trade marks decided by
    the registrar: Trade Marks Rules 2008, SI 2008/1797, r 57(2).
8   Ie under the Trade Marks Act 1994 s 67(1): see the text to notes 1–5.
9   Trade Marks Act 1994 s 67(3).
10 As to the meaning of 'international registration' see PARA 12 note 1.
11 See the Trade Marks (International Registration) Order 2008, SI 2008/2206, art 3; and PARA 12.
    Note in particular that for this purpose the Trade Marks Act 1994 s 67(2)(a) (see head (1) in the
    text) is modified so that the words 'any information recorded in the International Register or'
    appear after the words 'in such cases': see the Trade Marks (International Registration)
    Order 2008, SI 2008/2206, art 3(3((i), Sch 2 para 9. See also PARA 12 note 15.

(3) OTHER PROCEEDINGS IN THE TRADE MARKS REGISTRY

(i) Merger, Reclassification and Alteration

373. Merger of separate registrations. The proprietor of two or more registrations of a trade mark[2], the applications relating to which were filed[1] on the same date, may request the registrar[3] to merge them into a single registration; and the registrar must, if satisfied that the registrations are in respect of the same trade mark, merge them into a single registration[4]. Where any registration of a trade mark to be so merged is subject to a disclaimer or limitation, the merged registration is also restricted accordingly[5]. Where any registration of a trade mark to be so merged has had registered in relation to it particulars relating to the grant of a licence or a security interest or any right in or under it, or of any memorandum or statement of the effect of a memorandum, the registrar must enter in the register the same particulars in relation to the merged registration[6]. The date of registration of the merged registration is, where the separate registrations bear different dates of registration, the latest of those dates[7].

1   As to the meaning of 'trade mark' see PARA 41.
2   As to the meaning of 'file' see PARA 27 note 2.
3   As to the registrar see PARA 19. The request must be made on Form TM17. As to the use of forms see PARA 335.
4   Trade Marks Act 1994 s 41(1)(b); Trade Marks Rules 2008, SI 2008/1797, r 27(3) (amended by SI 2012/1003).
     No application under the Trade Marks Rules 2008, SI 2008/1797, r 27(3) may be granted in respect of the registration of a trade mark which (1) is the subject of proceedings for its revocation or invalidation; or (2) is the subject of an international registration within the meaning of the Trade Marks (International Registration) Order 2008, SI 2008/2206, art 2 (see PARA 12 note 1) which has not become independent of the trade mark as provided for in accordance with the Madrid Protocol art 6: Trade Marks Rules 2008, SI 2008/1797, r 27(3A) (added by SI 2012/1003).
     It should also be noted that the Trade Marks Act 1994 s 41 does not apply to international trade marks (UK) or requests for extension: see the Trade Marks (International Registration) Order 2008, SI 2008/2206, art 3(3), Sch 1 Pt 1; and PARA 12 note 10.
5   Trade Marks Rules 2008, SI 2008/1797, r 27(4).
6   Trade Marks Rules 2008, SI 2008/1797, r 27(5).
7   Trade Marks Rules 2008, SI 2008/1797, r 27(6).

374. Reclassification; opposition to proposals. The registrar[1] may at any time amend an entry in the register[2] which relates to the classification of a registered trade mark so that it accords with the current Nice Classification[3]. This power may not be exercised so as to extend the rights conferred by the registration, except where it appears to the registrar that compliance with this requirement would involve undue complexity and that any extension would not be substantial and would not adversely affect the rights of any person[4].

Before making any such amendment to the register, the registrar must give the proprietor of the mark written notice of his proposals for amendment[5] and must at the same time advise the proprietor that:

(1)   he may make written objections to the proposals, within two months of the date of the notice, stating the grounds of his objections[6]; and

(2)   if no written objections are received within the period specified, the registrar must publish[7] the proposals and he will not be entitled to make any objections thereto upon such publication[8].

If the proprietor makes no written objections within the period specified in head (1) above or at any time before the expiration of that period decides not to make any objections, the registrar must as soon as practicable after the expiration of that period or upon receipt of the notice publish the proposals in the Trade Marks Journal[9]. Where the proprietor makes written objections within the period specified in head (2) above, the registrar must, as soon as possible after having considered the objections, publish the proposals in the Journal or, where he has amended the proposals, publish the proposals as amended in the Journal; and the registrar's decision is final and not subject to appeal[10].

Any person may, within two months of the date on which the proposals were published[11], give notice to the registrar of opposition to the proposals[12] and such notice must include a statement of the grounds of opposition which must, in particular, indicate why the proposed amendments would be contrary[13] to the statutory provisions[14]. If no notice of opposition is so filed within the time specified, or where any opposition has been determined, the registrar must make the amendments as proposed and must enter in the register the date when they were made; and his decision is final and not subject to appeal[15].

1   As to the registrar see PARA 19.
2   As to the register see PARA 21.
3   Trade Marks Rules 2008, SI 2008/1797, r 54(1). As to classification of goods and services see PARA 351; and as to the 'Nice Classification' see PARA 352.
    The Secretary of State may make provision by rules (see the text and notes 5–15) empowering the registrar to do such things as he considers necessary to implement any amended or substituted classification of goods or services for the purposes of the registration of trade marks: Trade Marks Act 1994 s 65(1). Provision may in particular be made for the amendment of existing entries on the register to accord with the new classification: s 65(2). The rules may empower the registrar: (1) to require the proprietor of a registered trade mark, within such time as may be prescribed, to file a proposal for amendment of the register; and (2) to cancel or refuse to renew the registration of the trade mark in the event of his failing to do so: s 65(4). Any such proposal must be advertised, and may be opposed, in such manner as may be prescribed: s 65(5). As to the Secretary of State see PARA 16 et seq; and as to the making of rules generally see PARA 17.
    It should be noted that s 65 does not apply to international trade marks (UK) or requests for extension: see the Trade Marks (International Registration) Order 2008, SI 2008/2206, art 3(3), Sch 1 Pt 1; and PARA 12 note 10. See also generally PARA 11 et seq.
4   Trade Marks Act 1994 s 65(3). See note 3.
5   Trade Marks Rules 2008, SI 2008/1797, r 54(2).
6   Trade Marks Rules 2008, SI 2008/1797, r 54(2)(a).
7   As to the meaning of 'publish' see PARA 19 note 10.
8   Trade Marks Rules 2008, SI 2008/1797, r 54(2)(b).
9   Trade Marks Rules 2008, SI 2008/1797, r 54(3). As to the Trade Marks Journal see PARA 19.
10 Trade Marks Rules 2008, SI 2008/1797, r 54(4).
11 Ie under the Trade Marks Rules 2008, SI 2008/1797, r 54: see the text to notes 1–10.
12 Notice must be given on Form TM7. As to the use of forms see PARA 335.
13 Ie how the proposed amendments would be contrary to the Trade Marks Act 1994 s 65(3): see the text and note 3.
14 Trade Marks Rules 2008, SI 2008/1797, r 55(1).
15 Trade Marks Rules 2008, SI 2008/1797, r 55(2).

375.   Alteration of registered trade mark at proprietor's request.   A registered trade mark[1] may not be altered in the register[2] during the period of registration or on renewal[3]. Nevertheless the registrar[4] may, at the request of the proprietor, allow the alteration of a registered trade mark where the mark includes the proprietor's name or address and the alteration is limited to alteration of that name or address and does not substantially affect the identity[5] of the mark[6].

The proprietor may request the registrar[7] for such alteration of his registered trade mark as is permitted under the above provisions; and the registrar may require evidence by statutory declaration or otherwise as to the circumstances in which the application is made[8].

Where, upon the request of the proprietor, the registrar proposes to allow such alteration, he must publish[9] the mark as altered in the Trade Marks Journal[10].

Any person claiming to be affected by the alteration may, within two months of the date of publication of the mark as altered give notice to the registrar of objection to the alteration[11] which must include a statement of the grounds of objection[12]. The registrar must send a copy of objection to the alteration[13] to the proprietor; and thereafter the procedure relating to opposition proceedings[14] applies with consequent modifications[15].

1   As to the meaning of 'registered trade mark' see PARA 111.
2   As to the register see PARA 21.
3   Trade Marks Act 1994 s 44(1). An application under the Trade Marks Act 1938 s 35 (repealed) (alteration of registered trade mark) which was pending on 31 October 1994 must be dealt with under the old law and any necessary alteration made to the new register: Trade Marks Act 1994 s 105, Sch 3 para 16. As to the meaning of 'the old law' see PARA 4 note 3.
4   As to the registrar see PARA 19.
5   As to the expression 'not substantially affecting its identity' see PARA 357 note 2.
6   Trade Marks Act 1994 s 44(2) (which has no counterpart in Council Directive (EEC) 89/104 (OJ L40, 11.2.89, p 1) to approximate the laws of the member states relating to trade marks (see now European Parliament and Council Directive (EC) 2008/95 (OJ L299, 8.11.2008, p 25)).
7   Ie on Form TM25. As to the use of forms see PARA 335.
8   Trade Marks Act 1994 s 44(3); Trade Marks Rules 2008, SI 2008/1797, r 32(1).
9   As to the meaning of 'publish' see PARA 19 note 10.
10   Trade Marks Act 1994 s 44(3); Trade Marks Rules 2000, SI 2008/1797, r 32(2). As to the Trade Marks Journal see PARA 19.
11   Ie on Form TM7.
12   Trade Marks Act 1994 s 44(3); Trade Marks Rules 2008, SI 2008/1797, r 32(3).
13   Ie on Form TM7.
14   As to the procedure relating to opposition proceedings (in particular under the Trade Marks Rules 2008, SI 2008/1797, rr 18, 20 see PARA 366.
15   See the Trade Marks Act 1994 s 44(3); and the Trade Marks Rules 2008, SI 2008/1797, r 32(4) (amended by SI 2013/444). As to calculation of time periods see Tribunal Practice Notice (TPN 1/2013), available from the Intellectual Property Office ('IPO') website, accessible at the date at which this volume states the law at www.ipo.gov.uk. As to the Intellectual Property Office (an operating name of the Patent Office) see PARA 16 note 2.

376. Disclaimer or limitation of registered trade mark. The proprietor of a registered trade mark[1] may[2]:

(1)   disclaim any right to the exclusive use[3] of any specified element of the trade mark[4]; or

(2)   agree that the rights conferred by the registration are to be subject to a specified territorial or other limitation[5].

Disclaimers and limitations can similarly be made in relation to an international trade mark for which protection has been obtained in the United Kingdom[6].

1   As to the meaning of 'registered trade mark' see PARA 111.
2   Trade Marks Act 1994 s 13(1). The applicant for registration of a trade mark may also make disclaimers and limitations: see PARA 358. As to the making of such disclaimers and limitations see PARA 65. As to the effect of such disclaimers and limitations on the proprietor's rights see PARA 82.
3   As to the meaning of 'use' see PARA 44 note 8.
4   Trade Marks Act 1994 s 13(1)(a).

5 Trade Marks Act 1994 s 13(1)(b).
6 See the Trade Marks (International Registration) Order 2008, SI 2008/2206, art 3; and PARA 12. As to the meaning of 'United Kingdom' see PARA 3 note 2. See also PARA 11 et seq.

(ii) Surrender

377. Procedure. The proprietor may surrender a registered trade mark[1] in respect of some or all of the goods or services for which it is registered by sending[2] notice to the registrar[3]: (1) in respect of all the goods or services for which it is registered[4]; or (2) in respect of only those goods or services specified by him in the notice[5].

Any such notice is, however, of no effect unless the proprietor in that notice: (a) gives the name and address of any person having a registered interest in the mark; and (b) certifies that any such person has been sent not less than three months' notice of the proprietor's intention to surrender the mark or is not affected or, if affected, consents to the surrender[6].

Upon the surrender taking effect, the registrar must make the appropriate entry in the register[7] and must publish[8] the date of the surrender on the Intellectual Property Office ('IPO') website[9].

1 As to the meaning of 'registered trade mark' see PARA 111.
2 As to the meaning of 'send' see PARA 27 note 10.
3 As to the registrar see PARA 19.
4 Trade Marks Act 1994 s 45(1), (2); Trade Marks Rules 2008, SI 2008/1797, r 33(1)(a). Notice under these circumstances must be sent on Form TM22: r 33(1)(a). As to the use of forms see PARA 335.
   It should be noted that the Trade Marks Act 1994 s 45 does not apply to international trade marks (UK) or requests for extension: see the Trade Marks (International Registration) Order 2008, SI 2008/2206, art 3(3), Sch 1 Pt 1; and PARA 12 note 10. See also generally PARA 11 et seq.
5 Trade Marks Act 1994 s 45(1), (2); Trade Marks Rules 2008, SI 2008/1797, r 33(1)(b). Notice under these circumstances must be sent on Form TM23: r 33(1)(b). See note 4.
6 Trade Marks Act 1994 s 45(2); Trade Marks Rules 2008, SI 2008/1797, r 33(2). See note 4.
7 As to the register see PARA 21.
8 As to the meaning of 'publish' see PARA 19 note 10.
9 Trade Marks Act 1994 s 45(2); Trade Marks Rules 2008, SI 2008/1797, r 33(3). See note 4. As to when surrender takes effect see PARA 97. As to the use of forms see PARA 335. The IPO website is accessible at the date at which this volume states the law at www.ipo.gov.uk. As to the Intellectual Property Office (an operating name of the Patent Office) see PARA 16 note 2.

(iii) Revocation, Declaration of Invalidity and Rectification

378. Choice of forum. An application for revocation, for a declaration of invalidity or for rectification of the register[1] in relation to a United Kingdom registered trade mark, or an application for revocation or a declaration of invalidity of the protection of a protected international trade mark (UK)[2], may be made by any person[3], and may be made either to the registrar[4] or to the court[5] except that:

(1) if proceedings concerning the trade mark in question are pending in the court, the application must be made to the court[6]; and

(2) if in any other case the application is made to the registrar, he may at any stage of the proceedings refer the application to the court[7].

An applicant must take certain considerations into account in deciding whether to make his application to the registrar or to the court. The procedure before the registrar is significantly cheaper but often slower, not only because registry procedure is relatively relaxed but because the option to appeal as of right makes the possibility of delay greater. In practice disclosure is infrequently sought before the registrar and, where sought, limited. Furthermore, cross-examination is uncommon and, where it does occur, less intense and wide-ranging than in the court. In general, therefore, registry proceedings are appropriate where an amicable settlement is envisaged or where the parties are more or less friendly but desirous of having the position clarified, or where costs are the overriding concern.

1 As to these applications and the circumstances in which they are appropriate see PARAS 98–105; as to the additional grounds for revocation or invalidity of a collective mark see PARAS 146–147; and as to the additional grounds for revocation or invalidity of a certification mark see PARAS 157–158.

2 See the Trade Marks (International Registration) Order 2008, SI 2008/2206, art 3 (see PARA 12) which applies generally the grounds and procedures relating to revocation and declaration of invalidity of United Kingdom registered trade marks to protected international trade marks (UK). In particular it applies to them the Trade Marks Act 1994 ss 46, 47 (see PARA 98 et seq), and the Trade Marks Rules 2008, SI 2008/1797, rr 38–42) (see PARA 380 et seq). As to the meaning of 'protected international trade mark (UK)' see PARA 12 note 8.

3 The applicant does not have to show that he is aggrieved by, or otherwise interested in, the registration: *Pharmedica GmbH's Trade Mark Application* [2000] RPC 536, [2000] All ER (D) 28; cf *Oystertec plc's Patent* [2002] EWHC 2324 (Pat), [2003] RPC 559, sub nom *Oystertec plc v Edward Evans Barker* [2003] IP & T 1015.

4 As to the registrar see PARA 19. As to procedure on the application before the registrar see PARA 378 et seq.

5 Trade Marks Act 1994 s 46(4) (revocation), s 47(3) (declaration of invalidity), s 64(2) (rectification). So much of s 47(3) as provides that any person may make an application for a declaration of invalidity has effect subject to the Trade Marks (Relative Grounds) Order 2007, SI 2007/1976, art 5 (see PARA 103, note 5, 8): art 5(3). See also the Community Trade Mark Regulations 2006, SI 2006/1027, reg 3(1); and PARA 271. As to the meaning of 'the court' see PARA 331.

6 Trade Marks Act 1994 ss 46(4)(a), 47(3)(a), 64(2)(a).

7 Trade Marks Act 1994 ss 46(4)(b), 47(3)(b), 64(2)(b). In practice the registrar seldom exercises the power to refer to the court. If, within 14 days of receiving notification of the decision to refer, the applicant does not make to the court the appropriate application, he is deemed to have abandoned the application: see *Practice Direction—Intellectual Property Claims* PD63 para 18.3. This period may be extended by the registrar or the court: see para 18.4.

379. 'No challenge' clauses; res judicata. It is not uncommon for parties to enter into agreements which prohibit the making of a challenge to the validity of other parties' trade marks either as terms of trade mark licences[1] or of trade mark delimitation agreements. Whether such an agreement prevents the making of an application for revocation as distinct from an application for a declaration of invalidity depends on the true construction of the agreement[2]. Such agreements may or may not be unenforceable under European Union competition law or under domestic restraint of trade law, depending on the circumstances[3].

If an unsuccessful application for a declaration of invalidity is made the applicant will be precluded by res judicata from making a further application on different grounds, but will not be precluded from applying to revoke the registration; an application for revocation may or may not be an abuse of process depending on the circumstances[4].

1 As to licences see PARAS 119–120.

2 *Fenchurch Environmental Group Ltd v Ad Tech Holdings Ltd* (O/236/05), Appointed Person.

3 See Case 35/83 *BAT Cigaretten-Fabriken GmbH v EC Commission* [1985] ECR 363, [1985] 2 CMLR 470, ECJ; *Apple Corpn Ltd v Apple Computer Inc* [1991] 3 CMLR 49; *WWF – World Wildlife Fund for Nature v World Wrestling Federation Entertainment Inc* [2002] EWCA Civ

196, [2003] IP & T 98; *Fenchurch Environmental Group Ltd v Ad Tech Holdings Ltd* (O/236/05), Appointed Person; *Fenchurch Environmental Group Ltd v Bactiguard AB* (O/095/07), Trade Marks Registry.

4   *Hormel Foods Corpn v Antilles Landscape Investments NV* [2005] EWHC 13 (Ch), [2005] RPC 657, [2005] IP & T 822. Cf *Evans v Focal Point Fires plc* [2009] EWHC 2784 (Ch), [2011] IP & T 120, [2011] All ER (D) 130 (Nov) (defendant company had no reasonable prospect of defending claim for passing off as trade mark had previously been declared invalid by trade marks registry). See also *Virgin Atlantic Airways Ltd v Zodiac Seats UK Ltd (formerly Contour Aerospace Ltd)* [2013] UKSC 46, [2013] 4 All ER 715, [2013] RPC 747.

380.   Revocation for non-use. An application to the registrar[1] for revocation for non-use of a trade mark[2] must be made on the appropriate form[3]. The registrar must send[4] a copy of that form[5] to the proprietor[6]. Within two months of the date on which he was sent a copy of the form[7] by the registrar, the proprietor must file his own form[8] which must include a counter-statement[9].

Where the proprietor fails to file evidence of use of the mark or evidence supporting the reasons for non-use of the mark within the above period[10] the registrar must specify a further period of not less than two months within which the evidence must be filed[11].

The registrar must send a copy of the form[12] and any evidence of use, or evidence supporting reasons for non-use, filed by the proprietor to the applicant[13].

Where the proprietor fails to file the form[14] within that period[15] the registration of the mark must, unless the registrar directs otherwise, be revoked[16]. Where the proprietor fails to file evidence within that period[17] or any further period[18], the registrar may treat the proprietor as not opposing the application and the registration of the mark must, unless the registrar directs otherwise, be revoked[19].

The registrar may, at any time, give leave to either party to file evidence upon such terms as the registrar thinks fit[20].

1   As to the registrar see PARA 19.
2   Ie under the Trade Marks Act 1994 s 46(1)(a) or (b): see PARAS 98, 378.
3   Trade Marks Rules 2008, SI 2008/1797, r 38(1). The appropriate form is Form TM26(N). As to the use of forms see PARA 335. Where the applicant seeks to revoke the registration from a date earlier than the date of the application for revocation, he must set out in the statement of grounds the date as of which revocation is sought and then explicitly allege that grounds for revocation existed at that date: *Omega SA v Omega Engineering Inc* [2003] EWHC 1334 (Ch), [2003] FSR 893. Where the applicant fails to plead his case correctly (e g because he specifies a date for revocation which the registrar has no power to order) the registrar has power in an appropriate case to permit him to amend his statement of grounds without re-commencing the procedure: *BSA BY R2 Trade Mark* (O/144/07), Appointed Person.
4   As to the meaning of 'send' see PARA 27 note 10.
5   Ie Form TM26(N).
6   Trade Marks Rules 2008, SI 2008/1797, r 38(2).
7   Ie Form TM26(N).
8   Ie Form TM8(N). As to the meaning of references to 'filing' see PARA 27 note 2. As to the filing of documents by electronic means see PARA 336.
9   Trade Marks Rules 2008, SI 2008/1797, r 38(3). As to extension of the time limit see r 77, Sch 1; and PARA 338. The proprietor may comply with the Trade Marks Rules 2000, SI 2000/136, r 31(3) (an earlier version of the Trade Marks Rules 2008, SI 2008/1797, r 38(3)) if he files evidence within the time limit even if it is technically inadmissible for failure to comply with the Trade Marks Rules 2000, SI 2000/136, r 55 (see now the Trade Marks Rules 2008, SI 2008/1797, r 62) (see PARA 341): *Argentum Ltd v Middlesex Silver Co Ltd* [2005] EWHC 2992 (Ch), sub nom *ARGENTUM Trade Mark* [2006] RPC 509. The proprietor cannot satisfy the Trade Marks Rules 2000, SI 2000/136, r 31(3) (see now the Trade Marks Rules 2008, SI 2008/1797, r 38(3)) by filing evidence consisting of a bare assertion of use of the mark; the evidence must provide a sufficient explanation of how the mark has been used to enable the

registrar to conclude that the proprietor has an arguable defence to the application for revocation. The evidence does not, however, have to be so persuasive that, if unanswered, it would necessarily discharge the burden of proof lying on the proprietor: *Almighty Marketing Ltd v Milk Link Ltd* [2005] EWHC 2584 (Ch), sub nom *MOO JUICE Trade Mark* [2006] RPC 501; *BSA BY R2 Trade Mark* (O/144/07) Appointed Person.

10 Ie within the period specified in the Trade Marks Rules 2008, SI 2008/1797, r 38(3).
11 Trade Marks Rules 2008, SI 2008/1797, r 38(4).
12 Ie Form TM8(N).
13 Trade Marks Rules 2008, SI 2008/1797, r 38(5).
14 Ie Form TM8(N).
15 See note 10.
16 Trade Marks Rules 2008, SI 2008/1797, r 38(6).
17 See note 10.
18 Ie specified under the Trade Marks Rules 2008, SI 2008/1797, r 38(4).
19 Trade Marks Rules 2008, SI 2008/1797, r 38(7). As to the exercise of the registrar's discretion if the proprietor files the documents late see *Lowden v Lowden Guitar Co Ltd* [2004] EWHC 2531 (Ch), sub nom *LOWDEN Trade Mark* [2005] RPC 377; *Music Choice Ltd v Target Brands Inc* [2005] EWHC 3323 (Ch), sub nom *Music Choice Ltd's Trade Mark* [2006] RPC 358; *Argentum Ltd v Middlesex Silver Co Ltd* [2005] EWHC 2992 (Ch), sub nom *ARGENTUM Trade Mark* [2006] RPC 509. The registrar must give the proprietor a hearing as required by the Trade Marks Rules 2000, SI 2000/136, r 54 (see now Trade Marks Rules 2008, SI 2008/1797, r 63) (see PARA 340) before exercising his discretion: *MOVIESTAR Trade Mark* [2005] RPC 623, Appointed Person.
20 Trade Marks Rules 2008, SI 2008/1797, r 38(8).

381.   Revocation for grounds other than non-use.   An application to the registrar[1] for revocation on grounds other than non-use[2] must be made on the appropriate form[3] and must include a statement of the grounds on which the application is made and be accompanied by a statement of truth[4]. The registrar must send[5] a copy of the form[6] and the statement of grounds on which the application is made to the proprietor[7]. Within two months of the date on which he was sent a copy of the form[8] and the statement by the registrar, the proprietor must file his own form[9] including a counter-statement, otherwise the registrar may treat the proprietor as not opposing the application and the registration of the mark must, unless the registrar directs otherwise, be revoked[10]. The registrar must send a copy of the form[11] to the applicant[12].

Where the proprietor has filed the above form[13], the registrar must specify the periods within which further evidence may be filed by the parties[14].

Where the applicant files no further evidence in support of the application the applicant, must, unless the registrar otherwise directs, be deemed to have withdrawn the application[15]. The registrar must notify the proprietor of any such direction[16].

The registrar may, at any time give leave to either party to file evidence upon such terms as the registrar thinks fit[17].

1   As to the registrar see PARA 19.
2   Ie under the Trade Marks Act 1994 s 46(1)(c) or s 46(1)(d): see PARAS 99–100, 378.
3   Ie Form TM26(O). As to the use of forms see PARA 335.
4   Trade Marks Rules 2008, SI 2008/1797, r 39(1).
5   As to the meaning of 'send' see PARA 27 note 10.
6   Ie Form TM26(O).
7   Trade Marks Rules 2000, SI 2008/1797, r 39(2).
8   Ie Form TM26(O).
9   Ie Form TM8. As to the meaning of references to 'filing' see PARA 27 note 2. As to the filing of documents by electronic means see PARA 336.
10 Trade Marks Rules 2008, SI 2008/136, r 39(3). As to extension of the time limit see r 77, Sch 1; and PARA 338.
11 Ie Form TM8.

12 Trade Marks Rules 2000, SI 2008/1797, r 39(4). As to the exercise of the registrar's discretion if the proprietor files the documents late see PARA 380 note 19.
13 Ie Form TM8.
14 Trade Marks Rules 2000, SI 2008/1797, r 40(1) (amended by SI 2008/2300).
15 Trade Marks Rules 2000, SI 2008/1797, r 40(2).
16 Trade Marks Rules 2000, SI 2008/1797, r 40(3). The reference in the text to any such direction is a reference to any direction under r 40(2).
17 Trade Marks Rules 2000, SI 2008/1797, r 40(4).

382. Application for declaration of invalidity. An application to the registrar[1] for a declaration of invalidity[2] must be filed[3] on the appropriate form[4] and must include a statement of the grounds on which the application is made and must be accompanied by a statement of truth[5]. Where the application is based on an earlier trade mark[6] which has been registered or in respect of which an application for registration has been made, there must be included in the statement of the grounds a representation of that mark and (1) details of the authority with which that mark is registered or has been applied for; (2) the registration or application number of that mark; (3) the goods and services[7] in respect of which that mark is registered or has been applied for, and the application is based; and (4) where neither of the relevant conditions applies[8] to the mark, a statement detailing whether during the relevant period[9] it has been put to genuine use in relation to each of the goods and services in respect of which the application is based or whether there are proper reasons for non-use[10] (the 'statement of use')[11].

Where the application is based on an unregistered trade mark or other sign which the opponent claims to be protected by virtue of any rule of law (in particular the law of passing off)[12], there must be included in the statement of grounds on which the application is made a representation of that mark or sign and the goods or services in respect of which such protection is claimed[13].

The registrar must send[14] a copy of the form[15] and the statement of the grounds on which the application is made to the proprietor[16].

The proprietor must, within two months of the date on which a copy of the form[17] and the statement was sent by the registrar, file his own form[18], which must include a counter-statement, otherwise the registrar may treat the proprietor as not opposing the application and registration of the mark must, unless the registrar otherwise directs, be declared invalid[19].

The registrar must send a copy of the form[20] to the applicant[21].

Where the proprietor has filed his form[22], the registrar must send notice to the applicant inviting the applicant to file evidence in support of the grounds on which the application is made and any submissions and to send a copy to all the other parties[23]. The registrar must specify the periods within which evidence and submissions may be filed by the parties[24].

Where (a) the application is based on an earlier trade mark entitled to protection as a well known trade mark[25]; or (b) the application or part of it is based on certain grounds[26]; or (c) the truth of a matter set out in the statement of use is either denied or not admitted by the proprietor, the applicant must file evidence supporting the application[27].

Where the applicant files no evidence as above[28], the applicant is deemed to have withdrawn the application to the extent that it is based on (i) the matters in heads (a) or (b) above; or (ii) an earlier trade mark which has been registered and is the subject of the statement of use referred to in head (c) above[29].

The registrar may, at any time give leave to either party to file evidence upon such terms as the registrar thinks fit[30].

1   As to the registrar see PARA 19.
2   Ie under the Trade Marks Act 1994 s 47: see PARAS 102, 378.
3   As to the meaning of references to 'filing' see PARA 27 note 2. As to the filing of documents by electronic means see PARA 336.
4   Ie on Form TM26(I). As to the use of forms see PARA 335.
5   Trade Marks Rules 2008, SI 2008/1797, r 41(1)..
6   As to the meaning of 'earlier trade mark' see PARA 54. The applicant must be the proprietor or a licensee of the earlier trade mark relied upon or the proprietor or an authorised user of an earlier collective mark or certification mark: see the Trade Marks Act 1994 s 8(1), the Trade Marks (Relative Grounds) Order 2007, SI 2007/1976, art 5(2)(a); and PARA 64. If it is registered the earlier trade mark must be presumed to be validly registered unless the applicant brings separate proceedings to challenge that registration: see the Trade Marks Act 1994 s 72; and PARA 94.
7   As to classification of goods and services see PARA 351 et seq. Lack of clarity of the specification of the goods and services is not a ground of invalidity: see *Stichting BDO v BDO Unibank, Inc* [2013] EWHC 418 (Ch), [2013] NLJR 291, [2013] All ER (D) 39 (Mar).
8   Ie the conditions specified in the Trade Marks Act 1994 s 47(2A)(a) or s 47(2A)(b): see PARA 103.
9   Ie the period referred to in the Trade Marks Act 1994 s 47(2B)(a): see PARA 103.
10 As to genuine use and proper reasons for non-use see PARA 98.
11 Trade Marks Rules 2008, SI 2008/1797, r 41(2)(a)–(d), (3). Note that head (4) in the text is the 'statement of use' for the purposes of r 42: see the text and notes 22–30.
12 As to reliance upon such earlier rights see PARA 61. The opponent must be the proprietor of the earlier right: see the Trade Marks Act 1994 s 8(1), the Trade Marks (Relative Grounds) Order 2007, SI 2007/1976, art 5(2)(b); and PARA 64.
13 Trade Marks Rules 2008, SI 2008/1797, r 41(4).
14 As to the meaning of 'send' see PARA 27 note 10.
15 Ie Form TM26(I).
16 Trade Marks Rules 2008, SI 2008/1797, s 41(5)
17 Ie Form TM26(I).
18 Ie Form TM8.
19 Trade Marks Rules 2008, SI 2008/1797, r 41(6). As to the exercise of the registrar's discretion if the proprietor files the documents late see PARA 380 note 19.
20 Ie Form TM8.
21 Trade Marks Rules 2008, SI 2008/1797, r 41(7).
22 Ie Form YM8.
23 Trade Marks Rules 2008, SI 2008/1797, r 42(1).
24 Trade Marks Rules 2008, SI 2008/1797, r 42(2).
25 Ie of an earlier trade mark of a kind falling within the Trade Marks Act 1994 s 6(1)(c): see PARA 54.
26 Ie grounds other than those set out in the Trade Marks Act 1994 s 5(1) (see PARA 55) or s 5(2) (see PARA 56).
27 Trade Marks Rules 2008, SI 2008/1797, r 42(3).
28 Ie under the Trade Marks Rules 2008, SI 2008/1797, r 42(3).
29 Trade Marks Rules 2008, SI 2008/1797, r 42(4).
30 Trade Marks Rules 2008, SI 2008/1797, r 42(5).

383. Application for rectification of the register. An application to the registrar[1] for rectification of an error or omission in the register[2] must be made on the appropriate form[3] together with a statement of the grounds on which the application is made and any evidence in support of those grounds[4]. Where the application is made by a person other than the proprietor of the registered trade mark, the registrar must send[5] a copy of the application and the statement, together with any evidence filed, to the proprietor, and may give such direction with regard to the filing of subsequent evidence upon such terms as he thinks fit[6].

1   As to the registrar see PARA 19.
2   Ie under the Trade Marks Act 1994 s 64(1): see PARA 105.
3   Ie Form TM26(R). As to the use of forms see PARA 335.
4   Trade Marks Rules 2008, SI 2008/1797, r 44(1).

5   As to the meaning of 'send' see PARA 27 note 10.
6   Trade Marks Rules 2008, SI 2008/1797, r 44(2).

384.   Interveners.   Any person, other than the registered proprietor, claiming to have an interest[1] in proceedings on an application to the registrar[2] for revocation[3] or for a declaration of invalidity[4] or for rectification[5] may file an application to the registrar[6] for leave to intervene, stating the nature of his interest; and the registrar may, after hearing the parties concerned if so they request a hearing, refuse such leave or grant leave upon such terms and conditions, including any undertaking as to costs, as he thinks fit[7].

1   See *Gardinol Chemical Co Ltd's Application* (1948) 65 RPC 455; *Silexine Paints Ltd's Application* (1953) 71 RPC 91.
2   As to the registrar see PARA 19.
3   Ie an application under the Trade Marks Rules 2008, SI 2008/1797, r 38 (see PARA 380) or r 39 (see PARA 381).
4   Ie an application under the Trade Marks Rules 2008, SI 2008/1797, r 41: see PARA 382.
5   Ie an application under the Trade Marks Rules 2008, SI 2008/1797, r 44: see PARA 383.
6   Ie on Form TM27. As to the use of forms see PARA 335. As to the meaning of references to 'filing' see PARA 27 note 2. As to the filing of documents by electronic means see PARA 336.
7   Trade Marks Rules 2008, SI 2008/1797, r 45(1). Any person granted leave to intervene ('the intervener') is treated, subject to the terms and conditions imposed in respect of the intervention, as a party to the proceedings for the purposes of the application of the provisions of rr 38–40, r 41 and r 42 or r 44 as appropriate (see PARAS 380–383) and rr 62–73 (see PARAS 340–342, 367, 386, 389, 390): r 45(2).

385.   Setting aside cancellation of application or revocation or invalidation of registration.   This provision[1] applies where (1) an application for registration is treated as abandoned[2]; (2) the registration of a mark is revoked[3]; or (3) the registration of a mark is declared invalid[4], and the applicant or the proprietor (as the case may be) claims that the decision of the registrar[5] to treat the application as abandoned or revoke the registration of the mark or declare the mark invalid (as the case may be) ('the original decision') should be set aside on certain grounds[6]. For this purpose the matters to which the registrar must have regard include whether the person seeking to set aside the decision made an application to do so promptly upon becoming aware of the original decision and any prejudice which may be caused to the other party to the original proceedings if the original decision were to be set aside[7].

Where this provision applies, the applicant or the proprietor must, within a period of six months beginning immediately after the date that the application was refused or the register was amended to reflect the revocation or the declaration of invalidity (as the case may be), file an application on the appropriate form[8] to set aside the decision of the registrar and must include evidence in support of the application and must copy the form and the evidence to the other party to the original proceedings under the relevant provisions[9].

Where the applicant or the proprietor demonstrates to the reasonable satisfaction of the registrar that the failure to file the required relevant form[10] within the period specified in the relevant provisions[11] was due to a failure to receive other required forms[12], the original decision may be set aside on such terms and conditions as the registrar thinks fit[13].

1   Ie the Trade Marks Rules 2008, SI 2008/1797, r 43.
2   Ie under the Trade Marks Rules 2008, SI 2008/1797, r 18(2): see PARA 366.
3   Ie under the Trade Marks Rules 2008, SI 2008/1797, r 38(6) (see PARA 380) or r 39(3) (see PARA 381).
4   Ie under the Trade Marks Rules 2008, SI 2008/1797, r 41(6): see PARA 382.

5   As to the registrar see PARA 19.
6   Trade Marks Rules 2008, SI 2008/1797, r 43(1). The grounds are those set out in r 43(4).
7   Trade Marks Rules 2008, SI 2008/1797, r 43(4).
8   Ie on Form TM29.
9   Trade Marks Rules 2008, SI 2008/1797, r 43(2) (amended by SI 2013/444). The reference in the text to relevant provisions is a reference to the rules referred to in the Trade Marks Rules 2008, SI 2008/1797, r 43(1): see the text and notes 2–4. As to calculation of time periods in regard to the Trade Marks Rules 2008, SI 2008/1797, r 43(2) see Tribunal Practice Notice (TPN 1/2013), available from the Intellectual Property Office ('IPO') website, accessible at the date at which this volume states the law at www.ipo.gov.uk. As to the Intellectual Property Office (an operating name of the Patent Office) see PARA 16 note 2.
10 Ie Form TM8.
11 See note 9.
12 Ie Form TM7, Form TM26(N), Form TM26(O) or Form TM26(I) (as the case may be).
13 Trade Marks Rules 2008, SI 2008/1797, r 43(3).

(4) APPEALS FROM THE REGISTRAR

(i) Right of Appeal

386. Registrar's decision. When, in any proceedings before him[1], the registrar[2] has made a decision, he must send[3] notice of his decision in writing to each party to the proceedings; and, for the purpose of any appeal against the registrar's decision, the date of the decision is the date when the notice is sent[4]. Where, however, a statement of the reasons for the decision is not included in the notice so sent, any party may, within one month of the date on which the notice was sent to him, request the registrar[5] to send him a statement of the reasons for the decision and upon such request the registrar must send such a statement; and the date on which that statement is sent is deemed to be the date of the registrar's decision for the purpose of any appeal against it[6].

1   As to the procedural powers of the registrar see PARA 340 et seq.
2   As to the registrar see PARA 19.
3   As to the meaning of 'send' see PARA 27 note 10.
4   Trade Marks Rules 2008, SI 2008/1797, r 69(1). Where the registrar has issued a reasoned decision the decision is final and the registrar has no power to reconsider it save in exceptional circumstances: *Andreas Stihl AG & Co's Trade Mark Application* [2001] RPC 215, Appointed Person; *Hyde's Trade Mark Application (No 2)* (O/333/05), Appointed Person.
5   Ie on Form TM5. As to the use of forms see PARA 335.
6   Trade Mark Rules 2008, SI 2008/1797, r 69(2). As to appeals from decisions of the registrar, including acts of the registrar in exercise of a discretion, see PARA 387 et seq. The registrar's practice is to give interim decisions orally and/or by letter. Even if these contain outline reasons, the registrar will issue a formal decision containing full reasons upon receipt of Form TM5. It is not clear whether the registrar has power to reconsider his decision between giving notice of the decision and giving his full reasons.

387. Choice of forum. An appeal lies from any decision[1] of the registrar under the Trade Marks Act 1994, except as otherwise expressly provided by rules[2]. The registrar's practice is to treat the filing of an appeal as suspensive of the decision under appeal[3].

Any such appeal may be brought either to an appointed person[4] or to the court[5]. Subject only to the appointed person's power to refer the appeal to the court[6], the appellant may bring the appeal before the tribunal of his choice. The appointed person is a specialist tribunal which is intended to provide a more informal, speedier and cheaper forum[7]. Thus there are no restrictions on rights of audience and the usual practice of the appointed persons is not to award costs in ex parte appeals[8] and, like the registrar[9], only to make modest awards of costs in inter partes appeals. On an appeal to the court there is a further right of appeal in the ordinary way[10]. Where an appeal is made to an appointed person and he does not refer it to the court, he must hear and determine the appeal and his decision is final[11]. However, such a decision will doubtless be open to attack by way of judicial review in case of error of law[12].

1   For these purposes, 'decision' includes any act of the registrar in exercise of a discretion vested in him by or under the Trade Marks Act 1994: s 76(1). As to the registrar see PARA 19; and as to his decision see PARA 386.

2   Trade Marks Act 1994 s 76(1). The only matters in respect of which the Trade Marks Rules 2008, SI 2008/1797 exclude appeals and render the decision of the registrar final are matters involving a change of classification (see rr 54(4), 55(2); and PARA 374) which are consistent with the Trade Marks Act 1994 s 34(2) (see PARA 351) and a decision to make a filed document or part of it confidential (see the Trade Marks Rules 2008, SI 2008/1797, r 58(5); and PARA 27).

    Except as otherwise expressly provided by the 2008 Rules an appeal lies from any decision of the registrar made under the 2008 Rules relating to a dispute between two or more parties in connection with a trade mark, including a decision which terminates the proceedings as regards one of the parties or a decision awarding costs to any party ('a final decision') or a decision which is made at any point in the proceedings prior to a final decision ('an interim decision'): r 70(1). An interim decision (including a decision refusing leave to appeal under r 70) may only be appealed against independently of any appeal against a final decision with the leave of the registrar: r 70(2).

3   *Nettec Solutions Ltd's Trade Mark Application* [2003] RPC 308, Appointed Person.

4   As to the meaning of 'appointed person' see PARA 388. As to the procedure on appeals to the appointed person see PARA 389. The provisions of the Trade Marks Act 1994 s 76 in effect widen the former system under which essentially only certain disputes between a party and the registrar could optionally be appealed to the Secretary of State (see e g the Trade Marks Act 1938 s 17(4) (repealed)). As to the Secretary of State see PARA 16.

5   Trade Marks Act 1994 s 76(2). For the purposes of appeals in England and Wales 'the court' means the High Court: s 76(6) (added by SI 2005/587).

6   See the Trade Marks Act 1994 s 76(3): and PARA 390.

7   See *AJ & MA Levy's Trade Mark (No 2)* [1999] RPC 358, Appointed Person; *ACADEMY Trade Mark* [2000] RPC 35, Appointed Person. The European Court of Justice has accepted that the appointed person is a court or tribunal for the purposes of references under the Treaty Establishing the European Community (Rome, 25 March 1957; TS 1 (1973); Cmnd 5179) (the 'EC Treaty') art 234 (see now the Treaty on the Functioning of the European Union (Rome, 25 March 1957; TS 1 (1973); Cmnd 5179) ('TFEU') art 267) (see generally PARA 86 note 8)): Case C-259/04 *Emanuel v Continental Shelf 128 Ltd* [2006] ECR I-3089, ECJ.

8   *AD2000 Trade Mark* [1997] RPC 168, Appointed Person; cf *SM Jaleel & Co Ltd's Trade Mark Application* [2000] RPC 471, Appointed Person. Ex parte appeals are those in disputes between an applicant and the registrar.

9   See PARA 342.

10 As to appeals to the Court of Appeal generally see CIVIL PROCEDURE vol 12 (2009) PARA 1701 et seq.

11 See the Trade Marks Act 1994 s 76(4); and PARA 389.

12 *Hyde's Trade Mark Application (No 2)* (O/333/05), Appointed Person.

(ii) Appeals to the Appointed Person

388. Persons appointed to hear and determine appeals. An 'appointed person' means[1] a person appointed by the Lord Chancellor to hear and decide appeals under the Trade Marks Act 1994[2]. A person is not eligible for such appointment unless: (1) he satisfies the judicial-appointment eligibility condition on a five-year basis[3]; (2) he is an advocate or solicitor in Scotland of at least five years' standing[4]; (3) he is a member of the Bar of Northern Ireland or solicitor of the Court of Judicature of Northern Ireland of at least five years' standing[5]; or (4) he has held judicial office[6].

An appointed person holds and must vacate office in accordance with his terms of appointment, subject to the following[7]:

(a)   there must be paid to him such remuneration (whether by way of salary or fees), and such allowances, as the Secretary of State[8] with the approval of the Treasury may determine[9];

(b)   he may resign his office by notice in writing to the Lord Chancellor[10];

(c)   the Lord Chancellor may by notice in writing remove him from office if he has become bankrupt or a debt relief order[11] has been made in respect of him or he made an arrangement with his creditors or, in Scotland, his estate has been sequestrated or he has executed a trust deed for his creditors or entered into a composition contract; or if he is incapacitated by physical or mental illness; or if he is in the opinion of the Lord Chancellor otherwise unable or unfit to perform his duties as an appointed person[12].

The Lord Chancellor must consult the Secretary of State before exercising his powers under the above provisions[13]. He may only remove an appointed person from office with the concurrence of the appropriate senior judge[14].

1   Ie for the purposes of the Trade Marks Act 1994 s 76: see PARAS 387, 389–390.
2   Trade Marks Act 1994 s 77(1). A person so appointed is disqualified for membership of the House of Commons: see the House of Commons Disqualification Act 1975 s 1(1)(f), Sch 1 Pt III (amended by the Trade Marks Act 1994 Sch 4 para 6). In practice the persons so appointed are selected from lawyers experienced in trade mark matters. As to the Lord Chancellor see CONSTITUTIONAL LAW AND HUMAN RIGHTS vol 8(2) (Reissue) PARA 477 et seq.
3   Trade Marks Act 1994 s 77(2)(a) (substituted by the Tribunals, Courts and Enforcement Act 2007 Sch 10 Pt 1 para 25(1), (2)). As to the condition see the Trade Marks Act 1994 s 50; and LEGAL PROFESSIONS vol 65 (2008) PARA 645.
4   Trade Marks Act 1994 s 77(2)(b) (amended by the Tribunals, Courts and Enforcement Act 2007 Sch 10 Pt 1 paras 25(1), (3)).
5   Trade Marks Act 1994 s 77(2)(c) (amended by the Constitutional Reform Act 2005 Sch 11 Pt 3 para 5; and the Tribunals, Courts and Enforcement Act 2007 Sch 10 Pt 1 para 25(1), (3)).
6   Trade Marks Act 1994 s 77(2)(d).
7   Trade Marks Act 1994 s 77(3).
8   As to the Secretary of State see PARA 16.
9   Trade Marks Act 1994 s 77(3)(a). As to the Treasury see CONSTITUTIONAL LAW AND HUMAN RIGHTS vol 8(2) (Reissue) PARA 512 et seq.
10   Trade Marks Act 1994 s 77(3)(b).
11   Ie under the Insolvency Act 1986 Pt VIIA (ss 251A–251X): see BANKRUPTCY AND INDIVIDUAL INSOLVENCY vol 5 (2013) PARA 91.
12   Trade Marks Act 1994 s 77(3)(c) (amended by SI 2012/2404).
13   Trade Marks Act 1994 s 77(4) (amended by virtue of SI 1999/678).
14   Trade Marks Act 1994 s 77(5) (s 77(5), (6) added by the Constitutional Reform Act 2005 s 15(1), Sch 4 para 238). The appropriate senior judge is the Lord Chief Justice of England and Wales unless the person to be removed exercises functions wholly or mainly in Scotland (in which case it is the Lord President of the Court of Session) or in Northern Ireland (in which case it is the Lord Chief Justice of Northern Ireland): Trade Marks Act 1994 s 77(6) (as so added).

389.   Procedure on appeal to appointed person.   Notice of appeal to the appointed person[1] must be filed on the appropriate form[2] which must include the appellant's grounds of appeal and his case in support of the appeal[3]. The notice must be filed with the registrar[4] within the period of 28 days beginning immediately after the date of the registrar's decision[5] which is the subject of the appeal ('the original decision')[6]. The registrar must send[7] the notice and statement to the appointed person[8]. Where any person other than the appellant was a party to the proceedings before the registrar in which the original decision was made, the registrar must send to that person a copy of the notice and the statement and the respondent may, within the period of 21 days beginning immediately after the date on which the notice and statement was sent, file a notice responding to the notice of appeal[9]. The respondent's notice must specify any grounds on which the respondent considers the original decision should be maintained where these differ from or are additional to the grounds given by the registrar in the original decision[10]. The registrar must send a copy of the respondent's notice to the person appointed and a copy to the appellant[11].

Where an appeal is made to an appointed person and he does not refer it to the court[12], he must send written notice of the time and place appointed for the oral hearing of the appeal[13]:

(1) where no person other than the appellant was a party to the proceedings in which the decision appealed against was made, to the registrar and to the appellant[14]; and

(2) in any other case, to the registrar[15] and to each person who was a party to those proceedings[16].

The notice must be sent at least 14 days before time appointed for the oral hearing[17].

If all the persons notified inform the appointed person that they do not wish to make oral representations, the appointed person may hear and determine the case on the basis of any written representations and the time and place for the oral hearing may be vacated[18].

The appointed person has the same powers in relation to costs, security for costs and evidence as the registrar[19]. He also has an inherent power to regulate procedure before him[20]; and this includes power to allow amendment to the grounds of appeal before him, even at a late stage[21].

The appointed person must hear and determine the appeal[22], and his decision is final[23]. He must send a copy of his decision, with a statement of his reasons for it, to the registrar and to each person who was a party to the proceedings before him[24].

1 Ie the person appointed under the Trade Marks Act 1994 s 76: see PARA 387. As to the meaning of 'appointed person' see PARA 388.

2 Ie Form TM55. See note 3. As to the use of forms see PARA 335. As to the meaning of references to 'filing' see PARA 27 note 2. As to the filing of documents by electronic means see PARA 336.

3 Trade Marks Rules 2008, SI 2008/1797, r 71(1) (amended by SI 2013/2235). The Trade Marks Rules 2008, SI 2008/1797, r 71(1) is subject to r 71(1A) (see below): r 71(1) (as so amended). Where the appeal arises in proceedings between two or more parties, notice of appeal to the person appointed under the Trade Marks Act 1994 s 76 (see PARA 387) must be filed on Form TM55P, which must include the appellant's grounds of appeal and his case in support of the appeal: Trade Marks Rules 2008, SI 2008/1797, r 71(1A) (added by SI 2013/2235).

    Neither prolixity nor formality are required in the statement of case; it should outline each of the grounds of appeal relied upon and state the case relied upon in support of those grounds. It is not acceptable to reserve the right to elaborate further unidentified arguments at the hearing of the appeal: *COFFEEMIX Trade Mark* [1998] RPC 717, Appointed Person. An interim decision may only be appealed against independently of any appeal against a final decision with the leave of the registrar: see the Trade Marks Rules 2008, SI 2008/1797, r 70(2) and PARA 387 note 2.

4 As to the registrar see PARA 19.

5 As to the registrar's decision see PARA 386.

6 Trade Marks Rules 2008, SI 2008/1797, r 71(2) (substituted by SI 2013/2235). The notice is Form TM55 or Form TM55P: see notes 2, 3. As to calculation of time periods in regard to the Trade Marks Rules 2008, SI 2008/1797, r 71(2), (4) see Tribunal Practice Notice 1/2013, available from the Intellectual Property Office ('IPO') website, accessible at the date at which this volume states the law at www.ipo.gov.uk. As to the Intellectual Property Office (an operating name of the Patent Office) see PARA 16 note 2.

7 As to the meaning of 'send' see PARA 27 note 10.

8 Trade Marks Rules 2008, SI 2008/1797, r 71(3).

9   Trade Marks Rules 2008, SI 2008/1797, r 71(4) (amended by SI 2013/444). See note 6. It is unclear whether the respondent may cross-appeal by way of respondent's notice: cf *EXTREME Trade Mark* (O/161/07), Appointed Person.

10 Trade Marks Rules 2008, SI 2008/1797, r 71(5).

11 Trade Marks Rules 2008, SI 2008/1797, r 71(6).

12 As to the referral of questions to the court see the Trade Marks Act 1994 s 76(3); and PARA 390. As to the meaning of 'the court' see PARA 387 note 5.

13 Trade Marks Rules 2008, SI 2008/1797, r 73(1).

14 Trade Marks Rules 2008, SI 2008/1797, r 73(1)(a).

15 This enables the registrar to appear if he so wishes in appeals which involve parties opposed to each other. He appears not so much as an adversary to the appellant but with a view to commenting on matters of trade mark law and other matters affecting the registry: *CORGI Trade Mark* [1999] RPC 549, Appointed Person.

16 Trade Marks Rules 2008, SI 2008/1797, r 73(1)(b).

17 Trade Marks Rules 2008, SI 2008/1797, r 73(2).

18 Trade Marks Rules 2008, SI 2008/1797, r 73(3).

19 Trade Marks Act 1994 s 76(5), applying ss 68–69 (see PARAS 340–342). The Trade Marks Rules 2008, SI 2008/1797, r 62 (see PARA 341), r 65 (see PARA 340), r 67 (see PARA 342) and r 68 (see PARA 342) apply to the appointed person and to proceedings before him as they apply to the registrar and to proceedings before the registrar: r 73(4). If there is an oral hearing of the appeal r 66 (see PARA 340) applies to the person appointed and to proceedings before the person appointed as it applies to the registrar and to proceedings before the registrar: r 73(5).

20 *ACADEMY Trade Mark* [2000] RPC 35, Appointed Person; *Pharmedica GmbH's Trade Mark Application* [2000] RPC 536, [2000] All ER (D) 28.

21 *COFFEEMIX Trade Mark* [1998] RPC 717, Appointed Person.

22 CPR 52.11 does not apply to appeals to the appointed person, but the appointed person adopts the same approach of treating appeals as limited to a review of the registrar's decision unless justice requires a re-hearing: *ROYAL ENFIELD Trade Marks* [2002] RPC 508, Appointed Person; *Vibe Technologies Ltd's Application* [2009] ETMR 12, Appointed Person. Accordingly, the appointed person applies the same principles as the court (as to which see PARA 396). See also PARA 391 et seq.

23 Trade Marks Act 1994 s 76(4). The appointed person may only re-consider his decision in exceptional circumstances: *Hyde's Trade Mark Application (No 2)* (O/333/05), Appointed Person. It appears that in principle the appointed person is amenable to judicial review.

24 Trade Marks Rules 2008, SI 2008/1797, r 73(6).

390. Transfer to the court of an appeal to appointed person. Where an appeal is made to an appointed person[1], he may refer the appeal to the court[2] if:

(1)   it appears to him that a point of general legal importance is involved[3];

(2)   the registrar[4] requests that it be so referred[5]; or

(3)   such a request is made by any party to the proceedings before the registrar in which the decision appealed against was made[6].

Before doing so the appointed person must give the appellant and any other party to the appeal an opportunity to make representations as to whether the appeal should be referred to the court[7].

In any case where it appears to the appointed person that a point of general legal importance is involved in the appeal, he must send[8] to the registrar and to every party to the proceedings in which the decision appealed against was made notice to that effect[9]; and, within 28 days of the date on which a notice is so sent, the person to whom it was sent may make representations as to whether the appeal should be referred to the court[10].

Any request made under head (2) or head (3) above must be made within 28 days of the date on which the notice of appeal is sent[11] by the registrar[12]; and a request under head (3) above must be sent to the registrar who must send it to the appointed person and send a copy of the request to any other party to the proceedings[13]. Where the registrar so requests that the appeal be referred to the court, he must send a copy of the request to each party to the proceedings[14].

Within 28 days of the date on which a copy of a request is sent[15] by the registrar, the person to whom it is sent may make representations as to whether the appeal should be referred to the court[16].

The appellant must file a claim form seeking the court's determination of the appeal within 14 days of receiving notification of the decision to refer[17].

1 As to the meaning of 'appointed person' see PARA 388.
2 Trade Marks Act 1994 s 76(3). The power to refer appeals to the High Court should be used sparingly and in the absence of a point of legal importance should be very rare. In addition to points of legal importance, considerations to be taken into account are the views of the parties, the expense involved and the public interest: *ACADEMY Trade Mark* [2000] RPC 35, Appointed Person. The fact that the parties agree upon a referral is not determinative: *Tom Parker Ltd v Parker Intangibles* (0/065/09), Appointed Person. The need for authoritative guidance on a point of law, particularly if a request for referral is supported by the registrar and one of the parties, can outweigh the additional expense: *AJ & MA Levy's Trade Mark (No 2)* [1999] RPC 358, Appointed Person. As to the meaning of 'the court' in this context see PARA 387 note 5.
3 Trade Marks Act 1994 s 76(3)(a). See also note 2.
4 As to the registrar see PARA 19.
5 Trade Marks Act 1994 s 76(3)(b).
6 Trade Marks Act 1994 s 76(3)(c).
7 Trade Marks Act 1994 s 76(3). See also note 2.
8 As to the meaning of 'send' see PARA 27 note 10.
9 Trade Marks Rules 2008, SI 2008/1797, r 72(5). See also note 2.
10 Trade Marks Rules 2008, SI 2008/1797, r 72(6). See also note 2.
11 Ie under the Trade Marks Rules 2008, SI 2008/1797, r 71(4): see PARA 389.
12 Trade Marks Rules 2008, SI 2008/1797, r 72(1).
13 Trade Marks Rules 2008, SI 2008/1797, r 72(3).
14 Trade Marks Rules 2008, SI 2008/1797, r 72(2).
15 Ie under the Trade Marks Rules 2008, SI 2008/1797, r 72(2) or r 72(3): see the text and notes 13–14.
16 Trade Marks Rules 2008, SI 2008/1797, r 72(4).
17 *Practice Direction—Intellectual Property Claims* PD63 para 25.2.

(iii) Appeals to the High Court

A. BRINGING OF APPEAL

391. In general. In England and Wales appeals to the court[1] are assigned to the Chancery Division of the High Court[2]. Such appeals are subject to the ordinary procedural rules applying to appeals[3]. Where they require a document to be served, it must also be served on the registrar[4]. Unless the court orders otherwise, an appellant's notice must be served on each respondent as soon as practicable; and in any event not later than seven days, after it is filed[5].

1 As to the meaning of 'the court' in this context see PARA 387 note 5.
2 CPR 63.16(2).
3 Ie those under CPR Pt 52: CPR 63.16(1).
4 CPR 63.16(3).
5 See CPR 52.4(3). See also Tribunal Practice Notice 1/2003. Tribunal Practice Notices are available from the Intellectual Property Office ('IPO') or on its website, accessible at the date at which this volume states the law at www.ipo.gov.uk. As to the Intellectual Property Office (an operating name of the Patent Office) see PARA 16 note 2.

392. The registrar's role in appeals. In the case of an appeal from an ex parte decision of the registrar (for example, a refusal of an application to register a mark), the registrar is the respondent and normally appears by counsel. In the case of an appeal from a inter partes matter (for example, opposition, revocation, invalidity or rectification), the registrar is not the respondent, but in certain cases he is entitled to appear and may be directed to appear by the court[1]. Even when the registrar is entitled to appear, however, he normally does not do so unless a matter of public interest or registry practice arises[2]. If the case is one in which the registrar is not entitled to appear as of right, he may seek permission to intervene if a matter of public interest or registry practice arises[3]. Even if the registrar does not appear (or submit a written statement in lieu of an appearance[4]), the court may request him to provide information as to his practice[5].

1 See the Trade Marks Act 1994 s 74(1); and PARA 443.
2 In such circumstances the registrar asks by letter to be informed if any order other than that asked for or a refusal of the application is to be made, and to be given an opportunity to comment on any such order.
3 See e g *Altecnic Ltd's Trade Mark Application* [2001] EWCA Civ 1928, [2002] RPC 639.
4 As to the registrar's power to submit to the court a written statement instead of appearing see the Trade Marks Act 1994 s 74(2); and PARA 443.
5 See e g *Phones4U Ltd v Phone4u.co.uk Ltd* [2006] EWCA Civ 244, [2007] RPC 83.

B. CONDUCT OF APPEAL

393. Further steps. The proceedings on an appeal from the registrar to the High Court are regulated by the general provisions dealing with appeals to the High Court from lower courts or tribunals[1]. After being served with the appellant's notice, the respondent may within 14 days serve a respondent's notice, and must do so if he wishes to ask the High Court to uphold the order of the registrar for reasons different from or additional to those given by the registrar[2]. There is no longer any specific statutory prohibition on fresh grounds of objection (not taken below) being raised on appeal[3] and so the matter will be governed by general principles[4].

1 Ie by CPR Pt 52, and practice directions made thereunder. As to CPR Pt 52 see CIVIL PROCEDURE vol 12 (2009) PARA 1657 et seq.
2 CPR 52.5(2)(b), (4)(b).
3 Cf the Trade Marks Act 1938 ss 17(6), 18(9) (both repealed).
4 As to amendment of the grounds of appeal see CPR 52.8. As to admission of fresh evidence see CPR 52.11(2); and PARA 394.

394. Fresh evidence; cross-examination on appeal. There is no express mention in the Trade Marks Act 1994 or the rules made under it of any power in the court to admit fresh evidence[1]. The general rule in relation to appeals which by or under any enactment lie to the High Court from any tribunal or person is that such evidence is not admissible unless the court orders otherwise[2]. The discretion to admit fresh evidence is exercised on essentially the same principles as those applicable to any appeal, but there are certain factors which are peculiar to trade mark cases[3]. It may be appropriate for the admissibility of fresh evidence to be heard as a preliminary issue on the appeal[4].

Under the Trade Marks Act 1938 there was a practice whereby the court allowed on appeal cross-examination of deponents to statutory declarations used before the registrar[5]. This practice has not been adopted under the Trade Marks Act 1994[6] because the registrar is now given power to order disclosure and all the powers of an official referee[7], thus equating proceedings in the Trade Marks Registry with proceedings in the Intellectual Property Office ('IPO') under which cross-examination had to be sought in the tribunal of first instance, namely the IPO[8].

1 There was in some but not all circumstances such a power under the Trade Marks Act 1938: see eg s 18(8) (repealed).
2 See CPR 52.11(2); and CIVIL PROCEDURE vol 12 (2009) PARA 1672.
3 See *EI Du Pont De Nemours & Co v ST Dupont* [2003] EWCA Civ 1368, [2006] 1 WLR 2793, sub nom *DU PONT Trade Mark* [2004] FSR 293 (in which the earlier authorities are reviewed); *Ladd v Marshall* [1954] 3 All ER 745, [1954] 1 WLR 1489, CA (in which the basic factors are set out). Additional factors which may be relevant are the nature of the mark and the objections to it, the desirability of avoiding multiplicity of proceedings and the public interest in not admitting invalid trade marks onto the register.
4 *EI Du Pont De Nemours & Co v ST Dupont* [2003] EWCA Civ 1368, [2006] 1 WLR 2793, sub nom *DU PONT Trade Mark* [2004] FSR 293.
5 See *Re Kidax Ltd's Application* [1959] RPC 167, CA. Justification for this included the fact that the registrar under the Trade Marks Act 1938 had limited powers e g he had no power to order disclosure.
6 See *Alliance & Leicester plc's Trade Mark Application* [2002] RPC 573.
7 See the Trade Marks Rules 2008, SI 2008/1797, r 65; and PARA 340.
8 *J Sainsbury Ltd's Application* [1981] FSR 406, CA. Cf PATENTS AND REGISTERED DESIGNS vol 79 (2008) PARA 595. As to the Intellectual Property Office (an operating name of the Patent Office) see PARA 16 note 2.

395. Costs of appeals. In appeals to the High Court under the Trade Marks Act 1994 costs normally follow the event in accordance with the general practice[1]. There is no longer any express statutory provision as to the registrar's costs[2] so they are in the discretion of the court in the normal way. The general rule is, however, likely to remain unchanged, namely that, where the registrar appears to defend his own decision and loses, he will be ordered to pay the costs[3]. Where he appears primarily to assist the court, no order as to his costs will normally be made[4], but he nevertheless may be ordered to pay costs[5]. Where rights in a pending application are assigned while proceedings are pending, an order for costs may be made in favour of both assignor and assignee[6].

1 As to costs generally see PARA 431; and CIVIL PROCEDURE vol 12 (2009) PARA 1672.
2 Ie as there was under the Trade Marks Act 1938 s 48 (repealed).
3 See *Svenska AB Gasaccumulator's Application* [1962] 1 All ER 886 at 896, [1962] 1 WLR 657n at 671n, [1962] RPC 106 at 117, CA; *STILTON Trade Mark* [1967] RPC 173.
4 See eg *PHANTOM Trade Mark* [1978] RPC 245, CA.
5 See *PNEUVEYOR Trade Mark* [1967] FSR 542 (where administrative errors caused the dispute between the parties, and the registrar was ordered to pay both the applicant's and the respondent's costs of rectification proceedings).
6 *Re Marly Laboratory Ltd's Application* [1952] 1 All ER 1057, 69 RPC 156, CA.

C. THE COURT'S POWERS

396. The court's power to review the registrar's decision. An appeal to the High Court from the registrar is limited to a review of the decision below unless the court considers that in the circumstances of an individual appeal it would be in the interests of justice to hold a re-hearing[1]. Unlike under the Trade Marks Act 1938[2], the court has no power to exercise its own discretion as opposed to reviewing the registrar's exercise of discretion[3]. This is mainly relevant to case management issues, since the registrar has no discretion to refuse to register a trade mark which satisfies the requirements for registration[4].

Neither the Trade Marks Act 1994 nor the Trade Marks Rules 2008[5] provide for the court's powers on an appeal. Accordingly the court has all the powers of the registrar[6].

The court has power to suspend a declaration of invalidity made on relative grounds pending an application by the owner of the impugned trade mark for revocation or a declaration of invalidity of the earlier trade mark[7].

1   See CPR 52.11(1). As to CPR Pt 52 see CIVIL PROCEDURE vol 12 (2009) PARA 1657 et seq. See
    also *EI Du Pont De Nemours & Co v ST Dupont* [2003] EWCA Civ 1368, [2006] 1 WLR
    2793, sub nom *DU PONT Trade Mark* [2004] FSR 293. This applies even in the case of an
    appeal from an ex parte decision of the registrar: *Dyson Ltd v Registrar of Trade Marks* [2003]
    EWHC 1062 (Ch), [2003] 1 WLR 2406, sub nom *Dyson Ltd's Trade Mark Application* [2003]
    RPC 821. As to the correct approach to a review of the registrar's decision see *South Cone Inc
    v Bessant (t/a Reef)* [2002] EWCA Civ 763, sub nom *REEF Trade Mark* [2003] RPC 101; *EI
    Du Pont De Nemours & Co v ST Dupont*, sub nom *DU PONT Trade Mark* above.

2   Trade Marks Act 1938 s 52 (repealed).
3   See the Trade Marks Act 1994 s 76(1); and PARA 387.
4   See PARA 95.
5   Ie the Trade Marks Rules 2008, SI 2008/1797.
6   See CPR 52.10(1).
7   *Rousselon Frères et Cie v Horwood Homewares Ltd* [2008] EWHC 1660 (Ch), [2008] RPC
    849, [2009] IP & T 625.

D. REGISTRATION AFTER APPEAL AND OF COURT ORDERS

397.   Registration. If the court on appeal decides in favour of registration,
then, unless the court otherwise orders, the mark is registered at once, even
though the registrar or opponent appeals further[1]. There is no longer any express
provision in the Trade Marks Act 1994 or the rules made thereunder governing
the registration of orders of the court[2]. Such orders are normally registered all
the same.

1   *Re Dubonnet SA's Application* (1915) 32 RPC 241, CA; *Re F Reddaway & Co Ltd's
    Application* [1925] Ch 693, 42 RPC 397, CA.
2   As to the matters required to be entered in the register see PARA 24.

(5) ACTIONS FOR INFRINGEMENT AND PASSING OFF

(i) Bringing of Proceedings

398.   In general. An infringement[1] of a registered trade mark[2] or of a
protected international trade mark (UK)[3] is actionable by the proprietor[4] of the
trade mark[5].

No proceedings lie to prevent or recover damages for the infringement of an
unregistered trade mark as such; but nothing in the Trade Marks Act 1994
affects the law of passing off[6].

Actions for infringement of a registered trade mark or a protected
international trade mark (UK) may generally be brought in the Chancery
Division of the High Court or more specifically in the Intellectual Property
Enterprise Court; and the same is true of actions for passing off[7]. Such actions
are, therefore, subject to the Civil Procedure Rules generally, there being no
special rules relating to passing off, and only limited special provisions[8] relating
to infringement of trade marks. Actions are often brought for both infringement
and passing off; and for procedural purposes it is convenient to discuss them
together, although they are distinct causes of action.

The jurisdiction of the courts, and of the courts of other member states, in
relation to actions for infringement of a Community trade mark is dealt with
elsewhere in this title[9].

1   As to the meaning of 'infringement' see PARA 66 note 4. As to the acts which amount to
    infringement, if done without the consent of the proprietor, see the Trade Marks Act 1994 s 10;

and PARA 68 et seq. An action in respect of a threatened act of infringement may be brought on the quia timet basis on ordinary principles: see CIVIL PROCEDURE vol 11 (2009) PARAS 362, 365, 367; EQUITY vol 16(2) (Reissue) PARA 484.

2   As to the meaning of 'registered trade mark' see PARA 111.

3   As to protected international trade marks (UK) see PARA 12.

4   As to the meaning of references to the proprietor of a registered trade mark in the provisions relating to infringement see the Trade Marks Act 1994 s 31(1), (2); and PARA 401 note 5.

5   Trade Marks Act 1994 s 14(1). In an action for infringement all such relief by way of damages, injunctions, accounts or otherwise is available to the proprietor as is available in respect of the infringement of any other property right: s 14(2). As to infringement proceedings by a co-proprietor see s 23(5); and PARA 112.
     Section 14 applies in relation to infringement of an existing registered mark committed on or after 31 October 1994, subject to s 105, Sch 3 para 4(2) (see PARA 81), and the old law continues to apply in relation to infringements committed before that date: Sch 3 para 4(1). As to the meaning of 'existing registered mark' see PARA 4 note 2; and as to the meaning of 'the old law' see PARA 4 note 3.

6   Trade Marks Act 1994 s 2(2). See *Inter Lotto (UK) Ltd v Camelot Group plc* [2003] EWCA Civ 1132, [2003] 4 All ER 575, [2004] RPC 186. As to passing off see PARA 287 et seq.

7   See PARA 331 note 1.

8   Ie CPR 63.13; and *Practice Direction—Intellectual Property Claims* PD63 paras 16.1–24.1.

9   See PARAS 240 et seq, 331. Note, however, that where the legislation providing for the Community trade mark does not cover a specific matter, the court must apply the rules applicable in national proceedings: see PARA 240.

399.   Parties.   The claimant in an action for infringement of a registered trade mark[1] is usually the registered proprietor. Nevertheless it seems probable that, as under previous Acts[2], the assignee of a mark may commence proceedings even though his title has not yet been registered[3]. Licensees[4] and exclusive licensees[5] and authorised users of a registered collective mark[6] or a registered certification mark[7] are provided for separately. Civil proceedings lie against the Crown for an infringement committed by a servant or agent of the Crown, with the authority of the Crown, of a registered trade mark[8].

In an action for passing off the proper claimant is the trader whose goodwill has been or is likely to be injured by the passing off[9].

All persons may be joined as defendants against whom the right to any relief is alleged to exist, whether jointly, severally or in the alternative[10]. Vicarious[11] and joint[12] liability may be asserted on ordinary principles.

1   As to the meaning of 'registered trade mark' see PARA 111.

2   See *Ihlee v Henshaw* (1886) 31 ChD 323; *Magnolia Metal Co v Atlas Metal Co* (1897) 14 RPC 389, CA.

3   See, by way of further illustration, the Trade Marks Act 1994 s 9 (see PARAS 66–67), s 10 (see PARA 68 et seq) and s 14 (see PARA 398), which refer to 'the proprietor' not 'the registered proprietor'. Doubtless the registered proprietor would have to be joined in the action as either claimant or defendant; and the assignee ought to register his assignment as soon as possible, particularly since by virtue of s 25(4) (see PARA 114), he loses his rights to financial compensation. Cf the similar position of an assignee of a patent: see PATENTS AND REGISTERED DESIGNS vol 79 (2008) PARA 521.

4   See PARA 400.

5   See PARA 401.

6   See PARA 145.

7   See PARA 156.

8   Crown Proceedings Act 1947 s 3(1)(b) (s 3(1) substituted by the Copyright, Designs and Patents Act 1988 Sch 7 para 4(1); and amended by the Trade Marks Act 1994 Sch 4 para 1(1), (2)). Save as so provided, no proceedings lie against the Crown by virtue of the Crown Proceedings Act 1947 in respect of an infringement of a registered trade mark: s 3(1) (as so substituted and amended).

9   It is common to join a number of claimants where there is some doubt as to which owns the relevant goodwill. As to the right of one of several traders entitled to a shared reputation to sue see PARA 294. A trade association does not have locus to sue in a passing off action to protect

the goodwill of the businesses of its members, but in some circumstances it may be entitled to sue to protect its own goodwill: see PARA 293 text and notes 4–5.

10 See e g *A Macaulay (Tweeds) Ltd v Hepworths Ltd* [1961] RPC 184 (where, in an action for passing off concerning the use of label 'Harris Tweed' on goods, a Scottish trade association and Scottish manufacturers were properly joined as defendants).

11 See e g *Grierson, Oldham & Co Ltd v Birmingham Hotel & Restaurant Co Ltd* (1901) 18 RPC 158; *E Cusenier et Fils, Ainé, et Compagnie and George Idle Chapman & Co Ltd v Gaiety Bars & Restaurant Co Ltd* (1902) 19 RPC 357; *Havana Cigar Factories Ltd v Tiffin (1905) Ltd* (1909) 26 RPC 473, CA.

12 See *CBS Songs Ltd v Amstrad Consumer Electronics plc* [1988] AC 1013, [1988] RPC 567, HL; *Unilever plc v Gillette (UK) Ltd* [1989] RPC 583, CA; *Credit Lyonnais Bank Nederland NV v Export Credit Guarantee Department* [1998] 1 Lloyd's Rep 19, [1997] 34 LS Gaz R 29, CA; *MCA Records Inc v Charly Records Ltd* [2001] EWCA Civ 1441, [2002] EMLR 1.

400. General provisions as to rights of licensees in case of infringement. On general principles a licensee of a trade mark has no proprietary right in the mark; any right of action in such a licensee is, therefore, merely that conferred by the Trade Marks Act 1994[1].

The following provisions have effect with respect to the rights of a licensee[2] in relation to infringement[3] of a registered trade mark[4]; but they do not apply where or to the extent that the licensee has a right[5] to bring proceedings in his own name[6].

A licensee is entitled, unless his licence[7], or any licence through which his interest is derived, provides otherwise, to call on the proprietor of the registered trade mark to take infringement proceedings[8] in respect of any matter which affects his interests[9]. If the proprietor refuses to do so or fails to do so within two months after being called upon, the licensee may bring the proceedings in his own name as if he were the proprietor[10].

Where infringement proceedings are so brought by a licensee[11], the licensee may not, without the leave of the court[12], proceed with the action unless the proprietor is either joined as a claimant or added as a defendant; but this does not affect the granting of interim relief on an application by a licensee alone[13]. A proprietor who is so added as a defendant may not be made liable for any costs in the action unless he takes part in the proceedings[14].

In infringement proceedings brought by the proprietor of a registered trade mark any loss suffered or likely to be suffered by licensees must be taken into account, and the court may give such directions as it thinks fit as to the extent to which the claimant is to hold the proceeds of any pecuniary remedy on behalf of licensees[15].

The above provisions apply in relation to an exclusive licensee[16] if or to the extent that he has[17] the rights and remedies of an assignee as if he were the proprietor of the registered trade mark[18].

1 *Northern & Shell plc v Condé Nast & National Magazine Distributors Ltd and Penthouse Publications Ltd* [1995] RPC 117.
2 As to the meaning of 'licensee' see PARA 119 note 7. As to licences see PARAS 119–120.
3 As to the meaning of 'infringement' see PARA 66 note 4.
4 As to the meaning of 'registered trade mark' see PARA 111.
5 Ie by virtue of the Trade Marks Act 1994 s 31(1): see PARA 401.
6 Trade Marks Act 1994 s 30(1). Section 30 applies to licences granted before 31 October 1994, but only in relation to infringements committed on or after that date: s 105, Sch 3 para 6(1). For provisions in relation to authorised users of collective marks corresponding to the provisions of s 30 see s 49(2), Sch 1 para 12; and PARA 145. As to authorised users of certification marks see s 50(2), Sch 2 para 14; and PARA 156.
7 As to the meaning of 'licence' see PARA 119 note 7.
8 As to the meaning of 'infringement proceedings' see PARA 67 note 4.
9 Trade Marks Act 1994 s 30(2). See also note 6.

10 Trade Marks Act 1994 s 30(3). See also note 6. Section 30(3) is similar to the Trade Marks
    Act 1938 s 28(3) (repealed), which was held to be a complete code so that the licensee (then
    called a registered user) had no entitlement to sue apart from that provision: *Levi Strauss & Co
    v French Connection Ltd* [1982] FSR 443. The same reasoning would lead to the same result
    under the Trade Marks Act 1994 s 30(3).
11 Ie by virtue of the Trade Marks Act 1994 s 30.
12 As to the meaning of 'the court' see PARA 331.
13 Trade Marks Act 1994 s 30(4). See also note 6. Success on such an application might be
    prejudiced by the licensee's enforced two months' wait, though probably not if he gave the
    defendant due warning.
14 Trade Marks Act 1994 s 30(5). See also note 6.
15 Trade Marks Act 1994 s 30(6). See also note 6.
16 As to the meaning of 'exclusive licensee' see PARA 120.
17 Ie by virtue of the Trade Marks Act 1994 s 31(1): see PARA 401.
18 Trade Marks Act 1994 s 30(7). Thus his licensees have the right to take action and so on. See
    also note 6.

401. Exclusive licensee having rights and remedies of assignee. An exclusive
licence[1] may provide that the licensee[2] is to have, to such extent as may be
provided by the licence, the same rights and remedies in respect of matters
occurring after the grant of the licence as if the licence had been an assignment[3].
Where or to the extent that such provision is made, the licensee is entitled,
subject to the provisions of the licence and to the following provisions, to bring
infringement proceedings[4], against any person other than the proprietor[5], in his
own name[6].

Any such rights and remedies of an exclusive licensee[7] are concurrent with
those of the proprietor of the registered trade mark[8].

In an action so brought by an exclusive licensee a defendant may avail himself
of any defence which would have been available to him if the action had been
brought by the proprietor of the registered trade mark[9].

Where proceedings for infringement of a registered trade mark brought by the
proprietor or an exclusive licensee relate wholly or partly to an infringement in
respect of which they have concurrent rights of action, the proprietor or, as the
case may be, the exclusive licensee may not, without the leave of the court[10] and
subject to any agreement to the contrary between the exclusive licensee and the
proprietor, proceed with the action unless the other is either joined as a claimant
or added as a defendant; but this does not affect the granting of interim relief on
an application by a proprietor or exclusive licensee alone[11]. A person who is so
added as a defendant may not be made liable, subject to any agreement to the
contrary between the exclusive licensee and the proprietor, for any costs in the
action unless he takes part in the proceedings[12].

Subject to any agreement to the contrary between the exclusive licensee and
the proprietor, where an action for infringement of a registered trade mark is
brought which relates wholly or partly to an infringement in respect of which the
proprietor and an exclusive licensee have or had concurrent rights of action[13]:

(1)   the court must, in assessing damages, take into account the terms of the
       licence and any pecuniary remedy already awarded or available to either
       of them in respect of the infringement[14];

(2)   no account of profits may be directed if an award of damages has been
       made, or an account of profits has been directed, in favour of the other
       of them in respect of the infringement[15]; and

(3)   the court must, if an account of profits is directed, apportion the profits
       between them as the court considers just, subject to any agreement
       between them[16].

The proprietor of a registered trade mark must, subject to any agreement to the contrary between the exclusive licensee and the proprietor, notify any exclusive licensee who has a concurrent right of action before applying for an order for delivery up[17]; and the court may on the application of the licensee make such order as it thinks fit having regard to the terms of the licence[18].

1   As to the meaning of 'exclusive licence' see PARA 120.
2   As to the meaning of 'licensee' see PARA 119 note 7.
3   Trade Marks Act 1994 s 31(1). As to assignment of registered trade marks see PARA 113 et seq.
4   As to the meaning of 'infringement proceedings' see PARA 67 note 4; and as to the meaning of 'infringement' see PARA 66 note 4. As to the acts which amount to infringement, if done without the consent of the proprietor, see the Trade Marks Act 1994 s 10; and PARA 68 et seq.
5   References to the proprietor of a registered trade mark in the provisions of the Trade Marks Act 1994 relating to infringement are to be construed accordingly: s 31(2). As to the meaning of 'registered trade mark' see PARA 111. An action against the proprietor would have to be for breach of contract. The exclusive licensee would not have any remedies under the Trade Marks Act 1994 against the proprietor.
6   Trade Marks Act 1994 s 31(1).
7   As to the meaning of 'exclusive licensee' see PARA 120.
8   Trade Marks Act 1994 s 31(2).
9   Trade Marks Act 1994 s 31(3). This would seem to prevent a successful action in trade mark infringement by the exclusive licensee in respect of goods of his licensor made abroad (either by the licensor or his licensee). See *Northern & Shell plc v Condé Nast & National Magazine Distributors Ltd and Penthouse Publications Ltd* [1995] RPC 117; but see more generally the cases relating to parallel imports cited at PARA 91.
10 As to the meaning of 'the court' see PARA 331.
11 Trade Marks Act 1994 s 31(4), (8).
12 Trade Marks Act 1994 s 31(5), (8).
13 Trade Marks Act 1994 s 31(6), (8). The provisions of s 31(6) apply whether or not the proprietor and the exclusive licensee are both parties to the action; and, if they are not both parties, the court may give such directions as it thinks fit as to the extent to which the party to the proceedings is to hold the proceeds of any pecuniary remedy on behalf of the other: s 31(6).
14 Trade Marks Act 1994 s 31(6)(a), (8). See also note 13.
15 Trade Marks Act 1994 s 31(6)(b), (8). See also note 13.
16 Trade Marks Act 1994 s 31(6)(c), (8). See also note 13.
17 Ie an order under the Trade Marks Act 1994 s 16: see PARA 444.
18 Trade Marks Act 1994 s 31(7), (8).

402.   Claim.   In an action for infringement of a registered trade mark[1] the claimant need only assert his registered title[2] and allege the facts constituting infringement. Those facts will depend upon the type of infringement alleged[3]. The mark must actually be registered, or have become protected, at the date of commencement of the action. It is not enough that registration has been applied for but not yet granted, even though it will date back to the date of application if granted[4].

In a claim for passing off, whether alone or in conjunction with a claim for infringement, the claimant must allege the facts on which the claim to goodwill in the name or the mark is based, and this applies also where he is complaining of confusion likely to be caused by the trading name of some other person[5]. If he alleges fraudulent intent, he must plead it specifically[6].

Particulars must be given sufficient to identify any individual instances of infringement or passing off as to which the claimant proposes to give evidence at the trial[7]. Where an account or inquiry as to damages is claimed[8], it is not necessary that more than a few instances should be given. Without alleging individual sales or deception of named persons, the claimant may rely on the similarity of a name or mark as in itself establishing probability of confusion[9].

1   As to the meaning of 'registered trade mark' see PARA 111.

2   *La Radiotechnique v Weinbaum* [1928] Ch 1, 44 RPC 361. As to evidence of registration see
    PARA 410. In the case of a protected international trade mark (UK), the proprietor will rely upon
    his registration as holder of the mark on the international register, which is prima facie evidence
    of the validity of the original international registration and of any subsequent assignment or
    other transmission of it: see PARA 110. However, there is no statutory presumption of the
    validity of its protected status in the United Kingdom although such a presumption would
    appear to arise on general principles of the presumption of validity of official acts following the
    publication by the registrar of particulars stating the date upon which, and the goods or services
    in respect of which, protection is conferred (see the Trade Marks Act 1994 s 38B (added as a
    modification by the Trade Marks (International Registration) Order 2008, SI 2008/2206,
    art 3(3)(i), Sch 2 para 6); and PARA 371). As to the meaning of 'protected international trade
    mark (UK)' see PARA 12 note 8. As to the meaning of 'international register' see PARA 12 note 1.
3   See the Trade Marks Act 1994 s 10; and PARA 68 et seq.
4   See the Trade Marks Act 1994 s 9(3) (see PARA 67) and s 40(3) (see PARA 23). Similarly, it is not
    enough if an international registration designating the United Kingdom has not yet achieved
    protected status: see PARA 371. As to the meaning of 'international registration' see PARA 12
    note 1.
5   As to the burden of proof in actions for passing off see PARA 290 et seq.
6   *Claudius Ash, Son & Co Ltd v Invicta Manufacturing Co Ltd* (1912) 29 RPC 465 at 475, HL;
    HP Bulmer Ltd and Showerings Ltd v J Bollinger SA and Champagne Lanson Père et Fils
    [1978] RPC 79 at 121, CA. The relevant intention must be to deceive, a mere knowledge that
    the acts concerned will do so not being sufficient. See PARA 313. See also *India Rubber, Gutta
    Percha and Telegraph Works Ltd v County Golf Co* (1925) 42 RPC 225 (amendment of claim
    alleging fraud).
7   See the cases cited at PARA 414 note 1.
8   See PARAS 424–426.
9   *Reddaway v Bentham Hemp-Spinning Co* [1892] 2 QB 639, 9 RPC 503, CA.

(ii) Defences

**403.   Defences to proceedings for infringement; counterclaims or applications
for revocation, invalidity or rectification.**   Apart from traversing the facts
alleged, a defendant in an infringement action may plead that what he is doing
does not come within the statutory meaning of 'infringement'[1], or that he comes
within one of the statutory or other exemptions from infringement[2]. He may also
deny the claimant's title or allege that the registration is invalid or should be
revoked. If so, he may put in issue the validity of the trade mark in his defence or
may apply by counterclaim[3] for an order for revocation of the registration or for
a declaration of invalidity of the registration or for rectification of the register, or
he may do all of those things[4].

1   See the Trade Marks Act 1994 ss 9, 10; and PARA 66 et seq.
2   See PARA 80 et seq.
3   Ie under CPR Pt 20: see CIVIL PROCEDURE vol 11 (2009) PARA 618 et seq.
4   As to claims for revocation, declaration of invalidity or rectification see PARA 441.

404.   Defences in actions for passing off.   A defendant in an action for passing
off may deny the claimant's claim that the name or get-up is distinctive of the
claimant's goods or services[1], or he may allege fraud[2] or acquiescence or a licence
disentitling the claimant to succeed[3]. He may also plead that there was no real
and tangible danger of deception arising by the use of the mark or indicium
complained of[4]. The defendant may allege that he has an independent or
concurrent right to use the mark, name or get-up[5]. Where the defendant merely
traverses the claimant's allegation that a name or mark is distinctive of the
claimant's goods, the defendant will not be ordered to serve particulars of use of
the name or mark by others[6].

1   Cf PARAS 300 et seq, 321 et seq.

2   See PARA 313.
3   See PARA 299.
4   See PARA 309 et seq.
5   See PARA 328.

6   *La Radiotechnique v Weinbaum* [1928] Ch 1, 44 RPC 361. If, however, the defendant pleads affirmatively that the name or mark has been in common use, particulars identifying any prior user may be ordered to be given: *Aquascutum Ltd v Moore and Scantlebury* (1903) 20 RPC 640; *Schweppes Ltd v Gibbens* (1905) 22 RPC 113, CA.

405.   Stay pending application for registration by defendant. It is a defence to an action for infringement of a registered trade mark or of a protected international trade mark (UK) that the defendant is himself using a validly registered mark[1]. Occasions arise when a defendant is sued in respect of the use of a mark which is itself the subject of an application by the defendant to register. A registration, if effected, will date back to the date of the application[2], the success of that application would provide a complete defence to the action. Accordingly, it is possible for a defendant, in such circumstances, to apply for a stay of the action against him[3] or even a stay of a final injunction[4]. A defendant who is the holder of an international registration for which protection has been requested in the United Kingdom may similarly apply for a stay until the procedure leading to the mark becoming protected has been completed[5]. A stay will be granted only where the interests of justice (taking into account the claims of both parties) so require[6]. It will be relevant if the action and defendant's application before the registrar raise essentially the same issues. Where this is so, a stay of the action will not normally be granted because as a general rule a claimant has a right of choice of tribunal[7].

1   See the Trade Marks Act 1994 s 11(1); and PARA 76. As to the meaning of 'registered trade mark' see PARA 111; and as to protected international trade marks (UK) see PARA 12.
2   See the Trade Marks Act 1994 s 40(3); and PARA 23.
3   See eg *JU James & Sons Ltd v Wafer Razor Co Ltd* (1932) 49 RPC 597, CA. As to stay of proceedings generally see CIVIL PROCEDURE vol 11 (2009) PARA 529 et seq.
4   See *Electrolux Ltd v Electrix Ltd* (1953) 70 RPC 127; on appeal (1954) 71 RPC 23, CA (stay of an injunction granted because of the defendant's long concurrent use). However, the application to register ultimately failed: see *Electrix Ltd v Electrolux Ltd* [1960] AC 722, [1959] 3 All ER 170, [1959] RPC 283, HL.
5   Once the mark becomes protected, its effect will date back to the date of the international registration: see PARA 23.
6   See *Berlei (UK) Ltd v Bali Brassiere Co Inc* [1970] RPC 469 (stay refused). The final injunction permitted the defendants to continue their application for concurrent registration: see [1972] RPC 568. See also *JU James & Sons Ltd v Wafer Razor Co Ltd* (1932) 49 RPC 597, CA; *Flowerdale Ltd v Hale Electric Co Ltd* (1949) 66 RPC 333, CA (stay refused because the infringement action raised essentially the same issues as the registry proceedings, which were themselves stayed (see (1949) 66 RPC 86)); *Agfa AG v Ilford Ltd* [1960] RPC 108 (stay refused); *Second Sight Ltd v Novell UK Ltd* [1995] RPC 423 (stay granted).
7   *Flowerdale Ltd v Hale Electric Co Ltd* (1949) 66 RPC 333, CA; *Ravenhead Brick Co Ltd v Ruabon Brick and Terra Cotta Co Ltd* (1937) 54 RPC 341; *Colibri Lighters Ltd v Markt & Co (London) Ltd* [1959] RPC 8.

406.   Stay of proceedings by way of settlement. In accordance with general principles it is possible for an action to be compromised on agreed terms, the action being stayed except for the purposes of enforcing the agreed terms[1]. Where an undertaking to inform the registrar of any proposed order has been given[2], he should be informed of the proposed order. Such an order, if not observed, can be enforced by the grant of an injunction and an inquiry as to damages[3]. Settlements in passing off and trade mark cases often contain undertakings to the court (as to non-use of a mark complained of) in addition to such agreed terms.

1 Ie by a so-called 'Tomlin' order: see CIVIL PROCEDURE vol 12 (2009) PARA 1141.
2 See PARA 392.
3 *Hyatt Roller Bearing Co and Delco Remy and Hyatt Ltd v Frederick Pollard & Co (Bearings) Ltd* (1934) 52 RPC 115.

407. Discontinuance. The discontinuance of an action for infringement of a trade mark or for passing off is governed by the ordinary rules[1]. Normally the court will require the claimant to undertake not to bring any future action in respect of any such act as was alleged in the action concerned to be wrongful, whenever that act was committed[2].

1 See CPR Pt 38; and CIVIL PROCEDURE vol 11 (2009) PARA 723 et seq.
2 See *American International Group Inc v London American International Corpn Ltd* [1982] FSR 441.

408. Effect of beginning proceedings on right to give warning against infringement while proceedings are pending. When proceedings relating to the validity of a registered trade mark, or proceedings against the proprietor of the mark for passing off, are pending, the sending by or on behalf of the proprietor of a warning letter to a trade journal or to a member of the trade against the consequences of infringing the mark does not in itself amount to contempt of court, even though no mention is made of the pending proceedings, unless the letter is likely to harm the other party to the proceedings in the preparation and presentation of his case by tending to discourage people from giving evidence on his behalf[1].

Apart from any question of contempt when there are pending proceedings, the proprietor of a trade mark must be careful not to expose himself to proceedings in respect of groundless threats of trade mark proceedings[2].

1 *Carl-Zeiss-Stiftung v Rayner & Keeler Ltd, Re Trade Mark No 249,457* [1960] 3 All ER 289, [1960] 1 WLR 1145, [1961] RPC 1. See also *Thorley's Cattle Food Co v Massam* (1880) 14 ChD 763, CA; cf *J and P Coats v Chadwick* [1894] 1 Ch 347 (where a circular issued to the trade while an action for infringement was pending did not amount to a mere warning but libelled the defendants, and was calculated to create bias in the minds of recipients and to deter them from coming forward as witnesses for the defendants). Cf PATENTS AND REGISTERED DESIGNS vol 79 (2008) PARA 526. It has been said in relation to advertisements of proceedings concerning the infringement of patents that the claimant must not state that his success is certain or that the defendant has infringed: see PATENTS AND REGISTERED DESIGNS vol 79 (2008) PARA 526. Cf *Carl-Zeiss-Stiftung v Rayner & Keeler Ltd, Re Trade Mark No 249,457* above at 294, 301, at 1153, 1162, and at 9, 16 (criticising a dictum in *Goulard and Gibbs v Lindsay & Co Ltd and Ferranti* (1887) 4 RPC 189 at 190; and commenting on *Mullard Radio Valve Co Ltd v Rothermel Corpn Ltd* (1933) 51 RPC 1). As to contempt of court by comment on pending proceedings generally see CONTEMPT OF COURT vol 22 (2012) PARA 17 et seq.
2 See the Trade Marks Act 1994 s 21; and PARAS 107–109.

(iii) Disclosure

409. Disclosure. The normal rules as to disclosure apply to actions for infringement and for passing off[1]. It is normal for the claimant to seek an inquiry as to damages or an account of profits, and therefore disclosure in these actions before trial has usually been limited to those matters relevant to the issue of liability, as distinct from matters relevant to quantum[2]. The latter arise only if the claimant succeeds; the courts have been reluctant to compel the defendant to disclose, for example, the names of his customers to a trade rival until the claimant's rights have been established[3]. Once liability has been established, however, the claimant is entitled to certain disclosure to enable him to elect between an inquiry as to damages and an account of profits[4]. For the purposes of an account of profits or an inquiry as to damages all necessary disclosure must be given[5].

The normal rules as to privilege apply in relation to these classes of action. In addition, communications as to any matter relating to the protection of any design or trade mark, or as to any matter involving passing off, with trade mark agents and patent agents, attracts legal professional privilege in the same way as communications with a solicitor[6].

1   See CPR Pt 31; and CIVIL PROCEDURE vol 11 (2009) PARA 538 et seq. In an appropriate case disclosure may be obtained from a non-party: see CPR 31.17; and *American Home Products Corpn v Novartis Pharmaceuticals UK Ltd (No 2)* [2001] EWCA Civ 165, [2001] FSR 784, [2001] IP & T 752.
2   See *Baldock v Addison* [1995] 3 All ER 437, [1995] 1 WLR 158.
3   *Carver v Pinto Leite* (1871) 7 Ch App 90; *Fennessy v Clark* (1887) 37 ChD 184, CA; *Re Wills' Trade Marks* [1892] 3 Ch 201, 9 RPC 346, CA. Cf *Howe v M'Kernan* (1862) 30 Beav 547; *Aubanel and Alabaster Ltd v Aubanel* (1950) 67 RPC 222, CA. As to the position where actual deception is alleged see PARA 414 note 1.
4   *Island Records Ltd v Tring International plc* [1995] 3 All ER 444, [1996] 1 WLR 1256; *Brugger v Medicaid* [1996] FSR 362.
5   See *Leather Cloth Co Ltd v Hirschfeld* (1863) 1 Hem & M 295; *Powell v Birmingham Vinegar Brewery Co Ltd* (1896) 14 RPC 1, CA (names and addresses of customers); *Manus Akt v RJ Fullwood and Bland Ltd* [1949] Ch 208, [1949] 1 All ER 205, 66 RPC 71, CA. Cf PATENTS AND REGISTERED DESIGNS vol 79 (2008) PARA 535.
6   See the Trade Marks Act 1994 s 87 (trade mark agents: see PARA 35); and the Copyright, Designs and Patents Act 1988 s 280 (patent agents: see PATENTS AND REGISTERED DESIGNS vol 79 (2008) PARA 618).

(iv) Evidence

410.   Evidence of registration.   In all legal proceedings relating to a registered trade mark[1], including proceedings for rectification of the register[2], the registration of a person as proprietor of a trade mark is prima facie evidence of the validity of the original registration and of any subsequent assignment or other transmission of it[3]. Similar provisions apply in relation to protected international trade marks (UK)[4].

Entries in the register are provable by the original certificate of registration[5] or by a certified copy of the entry[6]. Judicial notice must be taken of copies issued by the International Bureau of entries in the international register and copies of the gazette published by the International Bureau, and they are admissible as evidence of any instrument or other act thereby communicated of the International Bureau[7].

A statement in writing submitted to the court by the registrar, when he is not directed by the court to appear, is deemed to form part of the evidence in proceedings for revocation, declaration of invalidity or rectification[8].

1   As to the meaning of 'registered trade mark' see PARA 111.
2   As to proceedings for rectification of the register see PARA 378 et seq. As to the register see PARA 21.
3   See the Trade Marks Act 1994 s 72; and PARA 94.
4   See PARA 94.
5   Ie the certificate issued under the Trade Marks Act 1994 s 40(2): see PARA 370. The certificate of registration is the legal and proper proof of registration: *Re William Crawford & Sons' Application* (1917) 34 RPC 97.

6   As to the supply of certified copies of entries in the register see PARA 26. Whenever legal proceedings concerning a registered trade mark arise, such a certified copy should be requested. Often, especially at the interim relief stage, evidence of registration is given by producing a photocopy of the advertisement of the mark concerned in the relevant Trade Marks Journal together with evidence as to the state of the register revealed by an inspection. As to the International Bureau see PARA 8 text and note 2.

7   See the Trade Marks (International Registration) Order 2008, SI 2008/2206, art 3; and PARA 12.

8   See the Trade Marks Act 1994 s 74(2); and PARA 443.

411.   Evidence as to other registrations. Evidence as to other trade marks that have been registered is in principle irrelevant when considering whether a particular mark satisfies the requirements for registration[1]. The same applies when considering whether the use of one mark infringes another[2]. If the marks have been used concurrently, however, evidence of this is relevant and admissible[3].

1   See PARA 42 text and note 11. As to the requirements for registration see PARA 39 et seq.

2   *Neutrogena Corpn v Golden Ltd* [1996] RPC 473 at 502–503, CA, per Jacob J (a case under the Trade Marks Act 1938 s 30 (repealed)).

3   See PARA 414.

412.   Evidence as to trade usage etc. In any action relating to a trade mark or trade name under the provisions of the Trade Marks Act 1938, evidence had to be admitted as to the usages of the trade concerned and of any relevant trade mark or trade name or get-up legitimately used by other persons[1]. Notwithstanding the repeal of that provision by, and its not being re-enacted in, the Trade Marks Act 1994, it is clear that such evidence is admissible on general principles; it is relevant probative matter[2].

1   See the Trade Marks Act 1938 s 49 (repealed).

2   Thus such evidence has routinely been admitted in passing off actions for many years. Cf *Mitchell v Henry* (1880) 15 ChD 181, CA. References to trade papers are admissible for this purpose: see *Singer Manufacturing Co v Loog* (1882) 8 App Cas 15 at 24, HL; *Daimler Motor Car Co Ltd v British Motor Traction Co Ltd* (1901) 18 RPC 465. Interrogatories might be served on this point: *Perry & Co Ltd v Hessin & Co* (1910) 28 RPC 108. Interrogatories have now been replaced by requests for further information: see CPR Pt 18; and CIVIL PROCEDURE vol 11 (2009) PARA 611 et seq.

413.   Similarity a question of fact for the court; admissibility of evidence. It is for the court or other tribunal concerned to decide whether the similarity of the mark, name or get-up complained of to that registered or employed by the claimant is such as (in combination with the similarity of goods or services) to give rise to a likelihood of confusion or to be calculated to deceive (depending on the nature of the proceedings). The tribunal is entitled to make a decision based on its own experience even in the absence of evidence[1]. It is not proper for witnesses to be asked whether in their opinion confusion or deception is likely[2]. Witnesses may, however, be properly called to show the custom of the trade as to the use of names or matters of get-up[3], the circumstances in which the articles are sold[4] and the method in which the claimant's name etc is used[5], and any other matters necessary to instruct the court and enable it to arrive at a decision on this point[6], and the court should decide in view of this evidence and not merely on an inspection of the objects[7]. The court may refer to dictionaries as to the meaning of a word and the use to which it is put[8]. A witness may be asked if he himself would be deceived; an expert witness may legitimately give evidence that, according to his experience of the conduct of the business concerned, traders or customers will adopt certain practices[9].

What degree of similarity is likely to deceive or cause confusion in any instance is incapable of definition a priori[10]; and the observations of judges upon other and quite different facts are usually of little help[11].

1   *North Cheshire and Manchester Brewery Co Ltd v Manchester Brewery Co Ltd* [1899] AC 83, HL; *Tokalon Ltd v Davidson & Co* (1914) 31 RPC 74, Ct of Sess (affd 32 RPC 133, CA); *AG Spalding & Bros v AW Gamage Ltd and Benetfink & Co Ltd* (1915) 32 RPC 273, HL; *Tavener Rutledge Ltd v Specters Ltd* [1959] RPC 355, CA; *Neutrogena Corpn v Golden Ltd* · [1996] RPC 473, CA; *BACH and BACH FLOWER REMEDIES TRADE MARKS* [2000] RPC 513, sub nom *Bach Flower Remedies Ltd v Healing Herbs Ltd* [1999] IP & T 146, [1999] All ER (D) 1142, CA; *Premier Luggage and Bags Ltd v Premier Co (UK) Ltd* [2002] EWCA Civ 387, [2003] FSR 69; *Interflora Inc v Marks and Spencer plc* [2013] EWCA Civ 319, [2013] All ER (D) 14 (Apr).

2   *Mothercare UK Ltd v Penguin Books Ltd* [1988] RPC 113 at 116, CA; *Island Trading Co v Anchor Brewing Co* [1989] RPC 287; *Payton & Co Ltd v Snelling, Lampard & Co Ltd* [1901] AC 308 at 312, 17 RPC 628 at 635, HL; *AG Spalding & Bros v AW Gamage Ltd* (1915) 32 RPC 273 at 286, 290, HL. See also *North Cheshire and Manchester Brewery Co Ltd v Manchester Brewery Co Ltd* [1899] AC 83 at 85, HL; *Claudius Ash, Son & Co Ltd v Invicta Manufacturing Co Ltd* (1912) 29 RPC 465 at 476, HL; *Re Spiller Ltd's Application* (1952) 69 RPC 327 (on appeal (1953) 70 RPC 51, CA; affd (1954) 71 RPC 234, HL); *Harker Stagg Ltd's Trade Mark* (1954) 71 RPC 136 at 140, CA; *Tavener Rutledge Ltd v Specters Ltd* [1959] RPC 355 at 360–361, CA. See also note 9.

3   See e g *George Ballantine & Son Ltd v Ballantyne Stewart & Co Ltd* [1959] RPC 273 at 279–280, CA (tendency to abbreviate composite name).

4   These circumstances include the class of purchasers (*R Johnston & Co v Archibald Orr Ewing & Co* (1882) 7 App Cas 219, HL; *Wilkinson v Griffith* (1891) 8 RPC 370), their likely reactions and behaviour (*Guccio Gucci SpA v Paolo Gucci* [1991] FSR 89), the manner in which articles are asked for *(Imperial Tobacco Co (of Great Britain and Ireland) Ltd v Purnell & Co* (1904) 21 RPC 598, CA; *Havana Cigar and Tobacco Factories Ltd v Oddenino* (1923) 40 RPC 229 at 241; *John Jaques & Sons Ltd v Chess* [1940] 2 All ER 285, 57 RPC 77, CA; *GB Delavelle Ltd v Stanley* (1946) 63 RPC 103 at 109; *Sales Affiliates Ltd v Le Jean Ltd* [1947] Ch 295 at 301–302, [1947] 1 All ER 287 at 290–291, 64 RPC 103 at 110), and the features to which customers attach importance (*Perry & Co Ltd v T Hessin & Co* (1912) 29 RPC 509 at 533, CA; *Dunhill v Bartlett and Bickley* (1922) 39 RPC 426). See generally *BACH and BACH FLOWER REMEDIES TRADE MARKS* [2000] RPC 513, sub nom *Bach Flower Remedies Ltd v Healing Herbs Ltd* [1999] IP & T 146, CA; *Interflora Inc v Marks and Spencer plc* [2013] EWCA Civ 319, [2013] All ER (D) 14 (Apr).

5   *Daimler Motor Car Co Ltd v British Motor Traction Co Ltd* (1901) 18 RPC 465; *Standard Bank of South Africa Ltd v Standard Bank Ltd* (1909) 26 RPC 310.

6   As to evidence generally in passing off cases see *North Cheshire and Manchester Brewery Co Ltd v Manchester Brewery Co Ltd* [1899] AC 83, HL. In *Wilkinson v Griffith* (1891) 8 RPC 370 at 372, the court admitted evidence of increase in the defendant's sales after the adoption of the label complained of as showing that this had caused the goods to be bought as the plaintiff's goods.

7   See e g *Reckitt & Colman Products Ltd v Borden Inc* [1990] 1 All ER 873, [1990] 1 WLR 491, [1990] RPC 341 at 397, HL ('Jif Lemon'). See also *London General Omnibus Co Ltd v Lavell* [1901] 1 Ch 135 at 138, 18 RPC 74 at 79, CA.

8   *Coca-Cola Co of Canada Ltd v Pepsi-Cola of Canada Ltd* [1942] 1 All ER 615, (1942) 59 RPC 127; *Broadhead's Application* (1950) 67 RPC 209, CA; *Colgate-Palmolive Co's Application* [1957] RPC 25; *Textron Inc and Textron Ltd v Henry C Stevens Ltd and Blick Office Equipment Ltd* [1977] RPC 283 (where the court had regard to a letter from the publishers of the Oxford English Dictionary as to the meaning of a word not yet in the dictionary); *Hormel Foods Corpn v Antilles Landscape Investments NV* [2005] EWHC 13 (Ch), [2005] RPC 657, [2005] IP & T 822; *Universal Music MGB LA LLC v Hicks* (O/431/12), Appointed Person.

9   *Claudius Ash, Son & Co Ltd v Invicta Manufacturing Co Ltd* (1912) 29 RPC 465, HL; *Royal Warrant Holders' Association v Edward Deane and Beal Ltd* [1912] 1 Ch 10, 28 RPC 721; *Perry & Co Ltd v T Hessin & Co* (1912) 29 RPC 509, CA; *Harrods Ltd v R Harrod Ltd* (1923) 41 RPC 74, CA; *George Ballantine & Son Ltd v Ballantyne, Stewart & Co Ltd* [1959] RPC 273 at 280, CA. In cases concerned with ordinary consumer goods or services, however, expert evidence is of no value: *esure Insurance Ltd v Direct Line Insurance plc* [2008] EWCA Civ 842, [2009] IP & T 706; *Hasbro Inc v 123 Nahrmittel GmbH* [2011] EWHC 199 (Ch), [2011] FSR 539, [2011] ETMR 25. It has been suggested (on motion) that trade witnesses could give

evidence of direct opinion as to the probability of deception (*Sodastream Ltd v Thorn Cascade Co Ltd* [1982] Com LR 64, [1982] RPC 459, CA); and that in an area which requires specialised knowledge it was admissible for trade witnesses to give evidence as to whether their customers would be confused (*Guccio Gucci SpA v Paolo Gucci* [1991] FSR 89). However it has also been held that such experts are not experts as to the likelihood of confusion: *European Ltd v Economist Newspaper Ltd* [1998] FSR 283, [1998] ETMR 536, CA.

10   *Seixo v Provezende* (1866) 1 Ch App 192 at 196 per Lord Cranworth, cited in *Re Rysta Ltd's Application, Re Aristoc Ltd's Opposition* [1943] 1 All ER 400 at 406, 60 RPC 87 at 108, CA, per Luxmoore LJ.

11   *R Johnston & Co v Archibald Orr Ewing & Co* (1882) 7 App Cas 219 at 219–220, HL, per Lord Watson. Citing previous decisions on a question of fact is neither a useful nor a proper exercise: *Mölnlycke AB v Procter & Gamble Co (No 5)* [1994] RPC 49 at 114, CA; *Oska's Ltd's Trade Mark Application* [2005] RPC 525, Appointed Person. Accordingly, many decided cases involving comparison of two or more marks have not been cited in this title.

414.   Evidence of actual deception. Evidence may be given as to cases of actual deception, where persons have traded with the defendant under the impression that they were trading with the claimants, or have bought the infringing goods under the impression that they were the goods of the claimants[1]. If such instances relate to direct dealing with the defendants or their agents, they may constitute part of the cause of action, but, even if they do not, they are still available as evidence to show that the similarity is such as is likely to deceive[2]. The absence of actual deception may also be relevant, depending upon the extent and nature of the use of the parties' respective marks[3].

Evidence may also be given of persons having asked for goods by the claimant's trade name and having been given the wrong goods, whether in fact such persons were deceived or not[4]. The court attaches importance to evidence that both marks have actually been in use for a long time, or that goods bearing the marks have been sold through the same outlets to the public, without any instances of confusion having arisen[5]. Such absence of confusion may, however, be capable of explanation[6].

1   Note that evidence of actual confusion does not necessarily show that anyone has been deceived by a misrepresentation as is required for a case in passing off: *Premier Luggage and Bags Ltd v Premier Co (UK) Ltd* [2002] EWCA Civ 387, [2003] FSR 69. Where actual deception is alleged, the names and addresses of the persons deceived have been ordered to be disclosed: *Humphries & Co v Taylor Drug Co* (1888) 39 ChD 693, 5 RPC 687; cf *Duke & Sons v Wisden & Co* (1897) 77 LT 67, CA. In practice, now that witness statements of evidence in chief are supplied in advance of trial, this may no longer be necessary. Where the defendant seeks to show that the wrong goods were given inadvertently in these cases, other instances may be proved by the claimant to rebut this defence: *Parozone Co Ltd v Johnston Gibson* (1904) 21 RPC 317, Ct of Sess.

2   *John Brinsmead & Sons Ltd v Brinsmead* (1913) 30 RPC 137 at 146. Where the defendants pleaded that, if any salesman of theirs had made such representations as were alleged by the plaintiffs, he had acted contrary to the defendants' express instructions, particulars were ordered to be given of the instructions: *Boston Marine Patents Co Ltd v Wheeler and Thomson* (1954) 71 RPC 432.

3   Compare e g *HP Bulmer Ltd and Showerings Ltd v J Bollinger SA and Champagne Lanson Père et Fils* [1978] RPC 79, CA, with *Portakabin Ltd v Powerblast Ltd* [1990] RPC 471. If absence of confusion is to be relied upon, it must first be shown that there has been an opportunity for confusion to occur: *Phones4U Ltd v Phone4u.co.uk Ltd* [2006] EWCA Civ 244, [2007] RPC 83.

4   See PARA 415 note 2.

5   *HP Bulmer Ltd and Showerings Ltd v J Bollinger SA and Champagne Lanson Père et Fils* [1978] RPC 79, CA. See also *Re White Rose Application* (1885) 30 ChD 505; *Re Lambert's Trade Mark* (1889) 6 RPC 344, CA; *Re Talbot's Trade Mark* (1894) 11 RPC 77 at 81; *Re Holbrook's Ltd's Application* (1909) 26 RPC 791; *Re Carborundum Co's Application* (1909) 26 RPC 504; *Kidax (Shirts) Ltd's Applications* [1959] RPC 295 at 308 (approved on appeal [1960] RPC 117, CA); *Re Helena Rubenstein Ltd's Application* [1960] RPC 229.

6 *Berlei (UK) Ltd v Bali Brassiere Co Inc* [1969] 2 All ER 812, [1969] 1 WLR 1306, [1969] RPC 472, HL. See also *Schweppes Ltd v Gibbens* (1905) 22 RPC 113, CA (on appeal 22 RPC 601, HL); *AG Spalding & Bros v AW Gamage Ltd* (1915) 32 RPC 273 at 286, HL; *Electrolux Ltd v Electrix Ltd* (1953) 70 RPC 127 at 132 (on appeal (1954) 71 RPC 23, CA).

415. Trap orders. The claimant may rely on 'trap orders', or orders given for the claimant's goods by persons sent for that purpose[1] to shops where it is expected that in response to an order for the claimant's goods the infringing goods will be supplied. Although recognising the necessity for this class of evidence, the court scrutinises very closely all the circumstances surrounding the trap orders and insists that the evidence show that the order was given in a perfectly clear manner, so that the defendant or his employees fully realised what was being asked for[2]. Unless the defendants have been informed promptly that the claimants propose to rely on particular sales after they have occurred, they may be unfairly handicapped, as a shop assistant cannot be expected to remember the details of every sale effected[3]. It is not sufficient to send a trap order to a person who is known to stock only an alleged infringing article, in a form which implies that the goods required are stocked, nor will deception necessarily be inferred from the fact of supplying the infringing article in response to orders for the claimant's goods if this is negatived by the get-up of the goods[4].

1 It is permissible for such a person to be a solicitor even if he conceals his qualification, and whether or not he may offend against the rules of professional conduct is irrelevant: *Marie Claire Album SA v Hartstone Hosiery Ltd* [1993] FSR 692.

2 *Stillitz v Jones and Higgins Ltd* (1942) 60 RPC 15 at 17. Where possible, it is preferable that the orders should be in writing: *Cart & Sons v Crisp & Co Ltd* (1902) 19 RPC 497 at 500; *Smith's Potato Crisps Ltd v Paige's Potato Crisps Ltd* (1928) 45 RPC 132, CA; *Cellular Clothing Co Ltd v G White & Co Ltd* (1952) 70 RPC 9. Evidence based on trap orders was treated as unsatisfactory in *Natural Chemicals Ltd and Veno's Drug Co Ltd and Irving's Yeast-Vite Ltd (Consolidated) v Amblins (Chemists) Ltd* (1940) 57 RPC 323; *Cellular Clothing Co Ltd v G White & Co Ltd* above; but such evidence was accepted in *Showerings Ltd v Cheltenham and Hereford Breweries Ltd* [1958] RPC 446; *Thomas French & Sons Ltd v John Rhind & Sons Ltd* [1958] RPC 82; *Showerings Ltd v Blackpool Tower Co Ltd* [1975] FSR 40.

3 *Ripley v Griffiths* (1902) 19 RPC 590 at 597; *HP Truefitt Ltd and Truefitt v Edney* (1903) 20 RPC 321; *Re Burroughs, Wellcome & Co's Trade Marks, Wellcome v Thompson and Capper* (1904) as reported in 21 RPC 69 at 84; *Lever Bros Ltd v Masbro' Equitable Pioneer Society Ltd* (1912) 29 RPC 225 at 235, CA; *Cellular Clothing Co Ltd v G White & Co Ltd* (1952) 70 RPC 9. See also *John Knight & Sons Ltd v Crisp & Co Ltd* (1904) 21 RPC 670 at 673; *CC Wakefield & Co Ltd v Board* (1928) 45 RPC 261; *FW Hampshire & Co (1927) Ltd v General Kaputine Syndicate Ltd* (1930) 47 RPC 437; *Fox's Glacier Mints Ltd v Joblings* (1932) 49 RPC 352; *Broads & Co v Cast Iron Drainage* [1970] FSR 363; *Diageo North America Inc v Intercontinental Brands (ICB) Ltd* [2010] EWHC 17(Ch), [2010] 3 All ER 147.

4 *Re Registered Trade Marks, Fitchetts Ltd v Loubet & Co Ltd* (1919) 36 RPC 296 at 304; cf *Showerings Ltd v Blackpool Tower Co Ltd* [1975] FSR 40.

416. Survey evidence. Attempts have been made in a number of cases to ascertain the opinions of members of the public by means of market research techniques involving a survey. The polls have varied in degree of sophistication[1]. In general, these surveys have had little effect on the case concerned[2], and the courts have generally accepted them as corroborative evidence only. Where they have been successful, a number of persons polled have given direct evidence[3].

There are two distinct problems associated with such surveys. First, it is a difficult task to frame questions which are totally fair and not open to criticism[4]. The mere fact of asking a question may often have an effect invalidating the result[5]. Secondly, there is the problem of getting the evidence properly before the court. It is clear that full information as to the whole survey must be given, including details as to how the respondents were chosen, as otherwise the survey will be rejected as valueless. Such information can be provided by giving evidence as to how the survey was conducted and making available to the opposite party all the answers received[6].

It has been held that a properly conducted poll does not constitute hearsay evidence because it is evidence of an external fact, namely public opinion[7]. Differing views have been expressed as to whether the evidence of market researchers reporting the results of surveys constitutes expert evidence[8].

In deciding whether to give permission to admit evidence from a survey in a trade mark case (as opposed to a passing off case), the court needs to consider whether the survey evidence is of real value in enabling the court to assess the reactions of the reasonably well-informed and reasonably observant average consumer, and that the value of the survey justifies its cost[9].

1 For an example of an inexact poll see *Treasure Cot Co Ltd v Hamleys Bros Ltd* (1950) 67 RPC 89 at 93. More statistically valid surveys were carried out in *Coca-Cola Co v William Struthers & Sons Ltd* [1968] RPC 231, Ct of Sess; *GE Trade Mark* [1969] RPC 418 at 446 per Graham J (on appeal [1970] RPC 339, CA; revsd [1973] RPC 297 at 321, HL); *Customglass Boats Ltd v Salthouse Bros Ltd* [1976] RPC 589 (NZ); *Tetrosyl Ltd v Silver Paint and Lacquer Co Ltd* [1980] FSR 68, CA; *Lego System A/S v Lego M Lemelstrich Ltd* [1983] FSR 155.

2 See *Interflora Inc v Marks and Spencer plc* [2013] EWCA Civ 319 at [77]–[134], [2013] All ER (D) 14 (Apr), at [77]–[134] per Lewison LJ. *Reckitt & Colman Products Ltd v Borden Inc* [1990] 1 All ER 873, [1990] 1 WLR 491, [1990] RPC 341, HL ('Jif Lemon'), is a notable exception. For a summary of the surveys see *Reckitt & Colman Products Ltd v Borden Inc* at 350 per Walton J. Even in that case there was, however, one 'experiment' which was not really a survey at all: the reactions of members of the public were tested in supermarkets after they had put the defendants' 'lemon' in their shopping baskets with a genuine view to purchase.

3 Eg *McDonald's Hamburgers Ltd v Burgerking (UK) Ltd* [1986] FSR 45; *Reckitt & Colman Products Ltd v Borden Inc* [1990] 1 All ER 873, [1990] 1 WLR 491, [1990] RPC 341, HL ('Jif Lemon'); *Neutrogena Corpn v Golden Ltd* [1996] RPC 473, CA. In recent years surveys have increasingly been used as a means to obtain witnesses rather than as evidence in their own right. The courts have placed limits on the number of such witnesses that can be called: see *BACH and BACH FLOWER REMEDIES TRADE MARKS* [2000] RPC 513, sub nom *Bach Flower Remedies Ltd v Healing Herbs Ltd* [1999] IP & T 146, CA.

4 *Scott Ltd v Nice-Pak Products Ltd* [1989] FSR 100, CA. See also the cases cited in note 1; and *Re Hack's Application* (1940) 58 RPC 91 at 110; *United Biscuits (UK) Ltd v Burtons Biscuits Ltd* [1992] FSR 14 (another case where a poll was held to be of no value); *Stringfellow v McCain Foods (GB) Ltd* [1984] RPC 501, [1984] FSR 175 (revsd [1984] RPC 501 at 525, CA). Nor is it acceptable to conduct a survey which excludes a relevant class of persons: *Dualit Ltd's (Toaster Shapes) Trade Mark Applications* [1999] RPC 890.

5 *Imperial Group plc v Phillip Morris Ltd* [1984] RPC 293 at 303; *Reed Executive plc v Reed Business Information Ltd* [2004] EWCA Civ 159, [2004] RPC 767, [2004] IP & T 1049; *Interflora Inc v Marks and Spencer plc* [2013] EWCA Civ 319, [2013] All ER (D) 14 (Apr); Case T-22/11 *Sogepi Consulting y Publicidad SL v Office for Harmonisation in the Internal Market (Trade Marks and Designs)* [2012] ECR II-0000, EGC.

6 *A Baily & Co Ltd v Clark, Son and Morland* [1938] AC 557, 55 RPC 253, sub nom *Re Clark, Son and Morland's Trade Mark* [1938] 2 All ER 377, HL.

7 See *Lego System A/S v Lego M Lemelstrich Ltd* [1983] FSR 155. Whether this view would be universally accepted remains to be seen. If the view is correct, then it means that there is no opportunity of testing that opinion by cross-examination, a result which seems hardly consistent with normal principles of litigation.

8 *Reckitt & Colman Products Ltd v Borden Inc (No 2)* [1987] FSR 407 (which held that it did not); *O2 Holdings Ltd and O2 (UK) Ltd v Hutchinson 3G Ltd (No 2)* [2006] EWHC 601 (Ch), [2006] RPC 766, [2006] ETMR 55 (which held that it did).

9 See *Interflora Inc v Marks and Spencer plc* [2013] EWCA Civ 319, [2013] All ER (D) 14 (Apr).

417. Evaluation of likelihood of confusion on appeal. An appellate court will be reluctant to interfere with the first instance tribunal's evaluation of the likelihood of confusion in the absence of an error of principle[1].

1   *South Cone Inc v Bessant (t/a Reef)* [2002] EWCA Civ 763, sub nom *REEF Trade Mark* [2003] RPC 101; *EI Du Pont De Nemours & Co v ST Dupont* [2003] EWCA Civ 1368, [2006] 1 WLR 2793, sub nom *DU PONT Trade Mark* [2004] FSR 293; *Fine & Country Ltd v Okotoks Ltd* [2013] EWCA Civ 672, [2013] All ER (D) 137 (Jun).

(v) Relief

A. IN GENERAL

418. Types of relief available. Following judgment at trial for a claimant in an action for infringement of a registered trade mark or a protected international trade mark (UK)[1], or for passing off[2], the types of relief available are those generally available in respect of the infringement of a property right[3]. These include a permanent injunction[4], a declaration[5], an inquiry as to damages[6] or an account of profits[7], an order for delivery up, erasure or destruction[8], a certificate of contested validity of a registered trade mark[9], and costs[10]. In relation to registered trade marks the statutory remedies of erasure[11] and delivery up[12] are also available. In addition the court may order appropriate measures for the dissemination and publication of the judgment to be taken at the defendant's expense[13].

Following judgment at trial for a claimant in an action for infringement of a Community trade mark[14], the court must, unless there are special reasons for not doing so, grant a permanent injunction[15]; otherwise it must give the same relief as for infringement of a registered trade mark[16].

Interim remedies are of particular importance in infringement and passing off cases[17]. These remedies include interim injunctions[18], search orders[19], orders for immediate disclosure[20], freezing injunctions[21] and, on occasions, certain orders under the protective jurisdiction of equity against non-infringers (for example, disclosure of names of infringers and interim preservation)[22]. Summary judgment[23] is also available in suitable cases[24]. Applications for interim relief should be considered in all cases, as a successful application almost always results in an early termination of the infringement and also a considerable saving in time and costs.

1   As to actions for infringement see PARA 66 et seq. As to the meaning of 'registered trade mark' see PARA 111. As to protected international trade marks (UK) see PARA 12.
2   As to passing off see PARA 287 et seq.
3   This is explicit in relation to registered trade marks (see the Trade Marks Act 1994 s 14(2); and PARA 416); but in relation to passing off it follows under the general law.
4   See PARAS 419–422.
5   See PARA 423.
6   See PARA 425.
7   See PARA 426.
8   See PARA 427.
9   See PARA 429.
10   See PARA 431.
11   See PARA 428.
12   See PARAS 444–446.
13   European Parliament and Council Directive (EC) 2004/48 (OJ L157, 30.4.2004, p 45) on the enforcement of intellectual property rights, art 15; *Practice Direction—Intellectual Property Claims* PD63 para 26(2). In the case of a successful right owner, such order should normally only be made where it will serve one of the two purposes identified in recital (27) of Directive 2004/48: *Samsung Electronics (UK) Ltd v Apple Inc* [2012] EWCA Civ 1339, [2013] IP & T 15. In an appropriate case the court has jurisdiction under the Senior Courts Act 1981 s 37(1) to make an order in favour of a successful defendant: *Samsung Electronics (UK) Ltd v Apple Inc* above.

14 As to the bringing of an action for infringement of a Community trade mark see PARA 233 et seq.

15 See Council Regulation (EC) 207/2009 (OJ L78, 24.3.2009, p 1) on the Community trade mark, art 102(1); and PARA 241. See also Case C-316/05 *Nokia Corpn v Wärdell* [2007] 1 CMLR 1167, [2007] IP & T 499. The practical effect of this requirement is similar to the English practice as to the grant of injunctions: see PARAS 419–422.

16 Ie if the acts of infringement were committed or threatened to be committed in the United Kingdom. See Council Regulation (EC) 207/2009 (OJ L78, 24.3.2009, p 1) on the Community trade mark, art 102(2) (which provides that, as regards sanctions for infringement, the court must apply the law of the member state in which the acts of infringement were committed); and PARA 241.

17 'The very life of a trade mark depends upon the promptitude with which it is vindicated': see *Orr Ewing & Co v Johnston & Co* (1880) 13 ChD 434 at 464, CA, per James LJ; approved (1882) 7 App Cas 219, HL. As a general proposition this statement remains as true today as when it was said: *Phones4U Ltd v Phone4u.co.uk Ltd* [2006] EWCA Civ 244, [2007] RPC 83.

18 See PARAS 432–433.

19 These were formerly known as Anton Piller orders. See PARA 434.

20 See PARA 435.

21 These were formerly known as Mareva injunctions. See PARA 438.

22 See PARAS 435–436.

23 Ie under CPR Pt 24: see CIVIL PROCEDURE vol 11 (2009) PARA 524 et seq.

24 See PARA 439.

B. INJUNCTION AND DECLARATION

419. Permanent injunction. An infringement of a registered or protected international trade mark, or the passing off of goods or services, gives generally[1] the right to an injunction to restrain its continuance[2]; but, where it is clear that the defendant has no intention of continuing the wrongful acts, a declaration may be granted in lieu of an injunction, together with liberty to apply for an injunction[3]. Where the act is an isolated and innocent act[4] or where the acts were inadvertent[5], particularly if the defendant has promptly admitted the claimant's rights[6], an injunction may not be granted. Where, however, there was evidence of the act having been done by mistake but the defendant refused to give an apology or to offer any undertaking, an injunction has been granted[7]. Similarly, where a defendant insists on a claim of right to do certain things, it is no ground for refusing an injunction to restrain him from doing them to prove that he has not yet done them in fact[8]. An application by the defendant for the registration of a trade mark is a sufficient threat to use the mark[9]. Even if the defendant offers an undertaking, the claimant may well be entitled (as, for example, where publicity is desirable) to an order in open court if the infringement was deliberate[10].

If an offer made after the commencement of proceedings is to deny the claimant an injunction, it must be an offer that would give the claimant all to which he is entitled[11]. Offers can be made without prejudice except on the question of costs[12]. Where such an offer is made, the subsequent costs of continuing proceedings to obtain an order in open court may not be recoverable[13].

1 In proceedings against the Crown the court may not grant an injunction but may make an order declaratory of the parties' rights: see the Crown Proceedings Act 1947 s 21; and CROWN PROCEEDINGS AND CROWN PRACTICE vol 12(1) (Reissue) PARA 134. See, however, *Re M* [1994] 1 AC 377, sub nom *M v Home Office* [1993] 3 All ER 537, HL (court has jurisdiction in proceedings for judicial review to grant an injunction against a Minister of the Crown).

2 *Edelsten v Edelsten* (1863) 1 De GJ & Sm 185 at 199 (non-statutory mark); *Upmann v Forester* (1883) 24 ChD 231 (non-statutory mark); *Slazenger & Sons v Spalding & Bros* [1910] 1 Ch 257, 27 RPC 20 (registered trade mark); *Forth and Clyde and Sunnyside Iron Cos Ltd v*

William Sugg & Co Ltd (1928) 45 RPC 382. As to the need to allege and show an intention to continue the wrongful acts see *Cellular Clothing Co Ltd v G White & Co Ltd* (1952) 70 RPC 9; and as to the enforcement by injunction of an order staying proceedings on agreed terms (a 'Tomlin' order) see PARA 406.

3 *Treasure Cot Co Ltd v Hamley Bros Ltd* (1950) 67 RPC 89; *Sterwin AG v Brocades (Great Britain) Ltd* [1979] RPC 481; *Numatic International Ltd v Qualtex Ltd (No 2)* [2010] EWHC 1797 (Pat), [2010] RPC 736. There is no power to make an interim declaration: see note 1.

4 *Leahy, Kelly and Leahy v Glover* (1893) 10 RPC 141 (act of employee without principal's knowledge); *Burberrys v Watkinson* (1906) 23 RPC 141 (isolated mistake); *Kodak Ltd v Grenville* (1908) 25 RPC 416 (honest isolated act); *John Knight & Sons Ltd v Crisp & Co Ltd* (1904) 21 RPC 670 (single instance of passing off with no intention of continuance and no proof of damage). Cf *Société Française Radio-Electrique v West Central Wireless Supplies* (1928) 45 RPC 276 (single sale of article, but article previously publicly exhibited under plaintiff's trade mark; plaintiff entitled to injunction or undertaking, but order drafted to make clear that infringement was innocent, so that this fact might appear if order advertised).

5 *Wayne V Myers Co Ltd v LE Fields Auto Services Ltd* (1954) 71 RPC 435 (infringement of trade mark and passing off).

6 *Upmann v Elkan* (1871) 7 Ch App 130.

7 *Steiner Products Ltd v Stevens* [1957] RPC 439.

8 *Havana Cigar and Tobacco Factories Ltd v Oddenino* [1924] 1 Ch 179 at 190, 41 RPC 47 at 54, CA.

9 *Ravenhead Brick Co Ltd v Ruabon Brick and Terra Cotta Co Ltd* (1937) 54 RPC 341. See also the Trade Marks Act 1994 s 32(3); and PARA 345.

10 *Gandy Belt Manufacturing Co Ltd v Fleming, Birkby and Goodall Ltd* (1901) 18 RPC 276 (followed in *JT Smith and JE Jones Ltd v Service, Reeve & Co Ltd* [1914] 2 Ch 576, 31 RPC 319); *Fox v Luke* (1925) 43 RPC 37; *Kodak Ltd v T Illingworth & Co Ltd* (1925) 43 RPC 33; and see PARA 418.

11 See *Colgate-Palmolive Ltd v Markwell Finance Ltd* [1989] RPC 497, CA; *Brugger v Medicaid* [1996] FSR 362; *Experience Hendrix LLC v Times Newspapers Ltd* [2008] EWHC 458 (Ch), [2008] All ER (D) 146 (Mar); cf *Roache v News Group Newspapers Ltd* (1992) Times, 23 November, [1998] EMLR 161; *AB v CD* [2011] EWHC 602 (Ch), [2011] IP & T 504. Thus the offer should include costs: *Société Française Radio-Electrique v West Central Wireless Supplies* (1928) 45 RPC 276. See also *AG Spalding & Bros v AW Gamage Ltd* (1915) 32 RPC 273 at 287, HL; and *Illustrated Newspapers Ltd v Publicity Services (London) Ltd* [1938] Ch 414 at 424, [1938] 1 All ER 321 at 329, 55 RPC 172 at 183.

12 These are now known as 'Part 36 offers': see CPR Pt 36, codifying the procedure approved in *Calderbank v Calderbank* [1976] Fam 93, [1975] 3 All ER 333, CA, extended to all cases by *Cutts v Head* [1984] Ch 290, [1984] 1 All ER 597, CA. See CIVIL PROCEDURE vol 11 (2009) PARA 729 et seq. Where such an offer is made, the fact that such an offer has been made must not be communicated to the judge until the case has been decided: CPR 36.13(2).

13 See *Slazenger v Pigott* (1895) 12 RPC 439; *Winkle & Co Ltd v Gent & Son* (1914) 31 RPC 473; *Rippingilles Albion Lamp Co Ltd v Clarke's Syphon Stove Co Ltd* (1917) 34 RPC 365.

420. Form of permanent injunction. The form of injunction varies according to the acts to be restrained[1]. In an action for infringement of a registered trade mark, the injunction restrains the infringement of the mark generally[2]. In an action for passing off, the injunction may relate to the use of a trading name or to the use of a mark or name on goods[3]. A passing off injunction relating to the use of a mark or name on goods may restrain user of the mark or name without clearly distinguishing the goods from the claimant's[4], but it is difficult to comply with such an injunction[5]. An injunction may be granted restraining user calculated to deceive[6], or imitation of get-up[7], or sale under a name or mark so closely resembling the claimant's as to be calculated to pass off or enable others to pass off goods as his[8], or the sale of goods other than the claimant's goods under a particular name unless it is first ascertained that the claimant's goods are not required[9]. In other passing off cases, the order may not give the defendant the opportunity to distinguish his goods from the claimants'[10]. In special cases, the order may permit sales under a mark only if certain labelling precautions are taken[11]. In general a passing off injunction will extend to the whole of England

and Wales, even though the claimant has established a reputation in a limited area only[12]. A mandatory injunction requiring a company to change its name may be ordered[13].

1	In practice, an injunction is not granted in a form so qualified that it might be said subsequently to have amounted to the court laying down a course of conduct which the defendant might pursue: see *Kerfoot v RA Cooper Ltd* (1908) 25 RPC 508. An undertaking agreed between the parties may, however, be in such a form: see *Twentieth Century Fox Film Corpn v Gala Film Distributors Ltd* [1957] RPC 105. For the apt words restraining acts by agents etc see *Marengo v Daily Sketch and Sunday Graphic Ltd* [1948] 1 All ER 406, 65 RPC 242, HL.

2	See eg *Dunlop Rubber Co Ltd v AA Booth & Co Ltd* (1926) 43 RPC 139; *Forth and Clyde and Sunnyside Iron Cos Ltd v William Sugg & Co Ltd* (1928) 45 RPC 382; *Reynolds v Laffeaty's Ltd* [1958] RPC 387 at 396; *Interflora Inc v Marks and Spencer plc* [2013] EWHC 1484 (Ch), [2013] All ER (D) 95 (Jun); cf *Coflexip SA v Stolt Comex Seaway MS Ltd* [2001] 1 All ER 952, [2001] RPC 182, CA (a patents case). Occasionally the injunction contains a reference to the specific infringing mark complained of. It may contain a saving corresponding to the terms of the Trade Marks Act 1994 s 11(2)(a) (see PARA 77) for the defendant to use his own name in accordance with honest practices: *Parker-Knoll (Textiles) Ltd's Trade Mark, Parker-Knoll Ltd v Knoll International Ltd* [1961] RPC 346 at 373, CA (affd [1962] RPC 265, HL). A qualified injunction may be granted in some circumstances: *Microsoft Corpn v Plato Technology Ltd* [1999] IP & T 1, CA (restricted injunction granted where defendant infringed claimant's rights only in a relatively minor and unintended way and no evidence of intention of repeating infringements); *Glaxo Group Ltd v Dowelhurst Ltd* [2004] EWCA Civ 290, [2004] IP & T 1035, [2005] ETMR 104 (qualified injunction granted in parallel import case where it was difficult for defendant to tell whether goods were in free circulation or not); *Sun Microsystems Inc v Amtec Computer Corpn Ltd* [2006] EWHC 62 (Ch), [2006] FSR 630 (differently qualified injunction granted in parallel import case). See also *Oracle America Inc (formerly Sun Microsystems Inc) v M-Tech Data Ltd* [2012] UKSC 27, [2012] 4 All ER 338, [2012] IP & T 810. For a case where the court granted a full injunction, and refused the qualification sought by the defendant on the ground that to include it could involve the court in deciding management and commercial questions, see *British Telecommunications plc v Nextcall Telecom plc* [2000] FSR 679. In *Interflora Inc v Marks and Spencer plc* above it was held that the court's normal practice of granting a general injunction was not contrary to Parliament and Council Directive (EC) 2004/48 (OJ L157 30.4.04, p 45) on the enforcement of intellectual property rights, art 3(2).

3	As to the restraint of the use of a trader's own name see PARA 326.

4	See eg *R Johnston & Co v Archibald Orr Ewing & Co* (1882) 7 App Cas 219 at 234, HL: *Frank Reddaway & Co Ltd v George Banham & Co Ltd* [1896] AC 199 at 221, HL; *Re Teofani & Co's Trade Mark, Teofani & Co Ltd v Teofani* [1913] 2 Ch 545, 30 RPC 446; *Brittain Publishing Co (London) Ltd and London and Local Newspapers Ltd v Trade and Commercial Press Ltd* [1957] RPC 134; *Parker-Knoll (Textiles) Ltd's Trade Mark, Parker-Knoll Ltd v Knoll International Ltd* [1961] RPC 346 at 373, CA (affd [1962] RPC 265, HL).

5	As to the problems involved see eg *Parker-Knoll Ltd v Knoll International Ltd* [1962] RPC 243, CA (proceedings for infringement), although the defendants did ultimately succeed in distinguishing (see *Parker-Knoll plc v Knoll Overseas Ltd* [1985] FSR 349).

6	See eg *Ideal General Supply Co Ltd v Louis Edelson and Bette Edelson (t/a the Ideal Clothing Co)* [1957] RPC 252 at 259; *Siegert v Findlater* (1878) 7 ChD 801 at 814.

7	*William Edge & Sons Ltd v William Niccolls & Sons Ltd* [1911] AC 693, 28 RPC 582, HL; *Biro Swan Ltd v Tallon Ltd* [1961] RPC 326.

8	See *Adrema Ltd v Adrema-Werke GmbH and BEM Business Efficiency Machines Ltd* [1958] RPC 323 at 332.

9	*Havana Cigar and Tobacco Factories Ltd v Oddenino* [1924] 1 Ch 179, 41 RPC 47, CA; *Goddard v Watford Co-operative Society* (1924) 41 RPC 218; and see *Treasure Cot Co Ltd v Hamley Bros Ltd* (1950) 67 RPC 89 at 94 (declaration granted in lieu of an injunction). Such an injunction will not be qualified by a proviso excusing the defendant if he uses his best endeavours to comply: *Showerings Ltd v Entam* [1975] FSR 45.

10	See *Montgomery v Thompson* [1891] AC 217, 8 RPC 361, HL (where it was not thought practicable to allow the defendant to distinguish).

11	See *Sony KK v Saray Electronics (London) Ltd* [1983] FSR 302, CA (disclaiming labels required).

12	*Chelsea Man Menswear Ltd v Chelsea Girl Ltd* [1987] RPC 189, CA.

13 *Glaxo plc v Glaxowellcome Ltd, Cullen and MacDonald* [1996] FSR 388. If the company refuses or neglects to change its name it appears that an order should be sought against the members of the company requiring them to pass the appropriate special resolution: *Halifax plc v Halifax Repossessions Ltd* [2004] EWCA Civ 331, [2004] FSR 903, [2004] IP & T 905.

421.   Stay of permanent injunction. A stay of a permanent injunction may be granted in accordance with general principles[1]. In particular, a stay may be granted to give the defendant sufficient time to comply with the injunction[2]. Where a stay pending appeal is sought, the claimant will now normally be required to give a cross-undertaking in damages if the stay is to be refused[3]. If a cross-undertaking in damages is offered, the grant or refusal of a stay pending appeal will depend on the balance of the risk of injustice[4].

1   See CIVIL PROCEDURE vol 12 (2009) PARA 1357 et seq.
2   Eg where it would involve re-labelling or a change of company name: see e g *Saville Perfumery Ltd v June Perfect Ltd and FW Woolworth & Co Ltd* (1941) 58 RPC 147 at 169, HL.
3   See *Minnesota Mining and Manufacturing Co v Johnson and Johnson Ltd* [1976] RPC 671, CA (a patent case).
4   *Novartis AG v Hospira UK Ltd* [2013] EWHC 1285 (Pat), [2013] All ER (D) 117 (May); revd [2013] EWCA Civ 583 (a patent case). A stay pending appeal on terms that the defendant paid 10% of its gross proceeds of sale into a joint account was granted in *CPC (United Kingdom) Ltd v Keenan* [1986] FSR 527 ('Oxbridge' marmalade). This was an interlocutory appeal but the same sort of consideration may arise after full trial.

422.   Enforcement of injunction. An injunction or undertaking is enforced in the usual way, for example by committal[1] as against an individual, or by sequestration[2] as against a body corporate or, possibly, its directors. Personal service of the order must have normally been effected on the directors if the order is to be so enforced against them[3]. If contempt is alleged, the court must decide the matter even if it means deciding a question of liability in a pending action[4]. If breach of a final order is alleged, the court must determine any issues which are not res judicata as a result of the previous judgment[5]. Costs on a successful application are normally awarded on an indemnity basis[6].

1   See now CPR Pt 81; and see generally CONTEMPT OF COURT vol 22 (2012) PARA 95 et seq. See also CIVIL PROCEDURE vol 12 (2009) PARA 1514 et seq.
2   See *Edward Grey Ltd v Greys (Midlands) Ltd* (1952) 70 RPC 25; *C Alexander & Co Ltd v Devon Cold Wave Co Ltd* [1957] RPC 331; *English Rose Ltd v Daintifyt Brassiere Co Ltd* [1958] RPC 359 (affd [1959] RPC 41, CA) (cases where no order was made save for payment of the plaintiff's costs as between solicitor and client); *Brittain Publishing Co (London) Ltd v Trade and Commercial Press Ltd* [1957] RPC 271 (no order made); *General Radio Co v General Radio Co (Westminster) Ltd* [1958] RPC 68 (no order except that costs of motion should be plaintiff's costs in action). See also CIVIL PROCEDURE vol 12 (2009) PARAS 1245, 1249, 1269, 1380 et seq. Leave for withdrawing sequestration proceedings is needed: see *Showerings Ltd v Fern Vale Brewery Co Ltd* [1958] RPC 462. A clear breach must be shown if sequestration is to be granted: *Redwing Ltd v Redwing Forest Products Ltd* (1947) 64 RPC 67.
3   See now CPR Pt 81 Section 2 (rr 81.4–81.11); and see generally CONTEMPT OF COURT vol 22 (2012) PARA 95 et seq. See also CIVIL PROCEDURE vol 12 (2009) PARA 1249. See also *Redwing Ltd v Redwing Forest Products Ltd* (1947) 64 RPC 67.
4   *Chanel Ltd v FGM Cosmetics Ltd* [1981] FSR 471. See, however, *Spectravest Inc v Aperknit Ltd* [1988] FSR 161, where Millett J held that, in the case of an interlocutory injunction not to infringe the plaintiff's copyright, the injunction meant the copyright claimed by the plaintiff and that the subsistence and ownership of the copyright was to be assumed. Cf *Staver Co Inc v Digitext Display Ltd* [1985] FSR 512, where Scott J took the view that such a form of injunction required the plaintiff to prove his case in full to succeed on a contempt motion. It is always better to frame an interim injunction by reference to precise acts only and omitting any reference to a legal right.
5   *Hotel Cipriani SRL v Fred 250 Ltd* [2013] EWHC 70 (Ch), [2013] ETMR 18, [2013] All ER (D) 250 (Jan).

6   As to the indemnity basis see CPR 44.4(1). Assessment of costs is now generally either on the
     standard basis or on the indemnity basis: see CPR 44.4; and CIVIL PROCEDURE vol 12 (2009)
     PARA 1747.

423. Declaration. Normally a declaration that a defendant has infringed a
trade mark is unnecessary because the grant of the injunction speaks for itself.
Occasionally an injunction is not awarded, as being unnecessary in the
circumstances[1]. A declaration may be granted that certain acts did or did not
contravene an injunction or that certain proposed acts would or would not
contravene the injunction[2].

1   See eg *Treasure Cot Co Ltd v Hamley Bros Ltd* (1950) 67 RPC 89; *Sterwin AG v Brocades
     (Great Britain) Ltd* [1979] RPC 481; and PARA 419. Normally a declaration would be the
     appropriate remedy against the Crown: see PARA 419 note 1.
2   *Hotel Cipriani SRL v Fred 250 Ltd* [2013] EWHC 70 (Ch), [2013] ETMR 18, [2013] All ER
     (D) 250 (Jan).

C. PECUNIARY REMEDIES

424. Damages or account of profits. The two pecuniary remedies of an
inquiry as to damages or account of profits are alternatives. Following judgment
on the question of liability[1] the claimant is given an election as to which he
prefers[2]. It is possible for the court to refuse either remedy and instead to award
nominal damages only, but it will do so only where it is very clear that there is no
actual damage[3]. An account of profits is an equitable remedy and on general
principles[4] may be refused or limited where the claimant is at fault in some way[5]
or where the defendant is blameless[6].

1   It is the usual practice in trade mark and passing off cases for the claimant to claim an inquiry as
     to damages or an account of profits at his election and for there to be a split trial between
     liability and quantum. This is particularly convenient in this class of case where the primary
     remedy is an injunction and where quantifying damages or profits may be difficult. If a case
     were to arise where it was sensible to deal with the claim for pecuniary relief at the same time as
     trial, the claimant would have to elect between damages or an account at an earlier stage.
2   See *Weingarten Bros v Bayer & Co* (1905) 22 RPC 341 at 351, 92 LT 511 at 513, HL. An
     inquiry as to damages or an account of profits is a remedy additional to an injunction:
     Weingarten Bros v Bayer & Co. It seems usually to have been left to the option of the claimant
     whether an inquiry as to damages or an account of profits should be granted (see *Weingarten
     Bros v Bayer & Co*; *Saxlehner v Apollinaris Co* [1897] 1 Ch 893 at 902, 14 RPC 645 at 656),
     but in *Van Zeller v Mason, Cattley & Co* (1907) 25 RPC 37 at 41, Joyce J treated the matter as
     one for the discretion of the court. As to disclosure to enable the claimant to make his election
     see PARA 409. As to damages generally see DAMAGES vol 12(1) (Reissue) PARA 801 et seq. As
     account of profits see EQUITY vol 16(2) (Reissue) PARAS 553, 691 et seq.
3   *McDonald's Hamburgers Ltd v Burgerking (UK) Ltd* [1987] FSR 112 at 122, CA, per Kerr LJ.
     For earlier cases see *Sanitas Co Ltd v Condy* (1886) 4 RPC 195; *Magnolia Metal Co v Atlas
     Metal Co* (1897) 14 RPC 389, CA. The costs of an inquiry are in the discretion of the court so
     that, if the claimant fails to prove damage (or to overtop a payment into court), he will be
     ordered to pay the costs of the inquiry.
4   See EQUITY vol 16(2) (Reissue) PARAS 553, 558–560.
5   See eg *Lever Bros, Port Sunlight Ltd v Sunniwite Products Ltd* (1949) 66 RPC 84 at 102
     (account only from date of letter before action because plaintiff had delayed).
6   See eg *AG Spalding & Bros v AW Gamage Ltd* (1915) 32 RPC 273 at 283, HL, per
     Lord Parker. See also *Henry Heath Ltd v Frederick Gorringe Ltd* (1924) 41 RPC 457.

425. Inquiry as to damages. Where in an action for infringement of an
intellectual property right the defendant knew, or had reasonable grounds to
know, that he engaged in infringing activity, the damages awarded to the
claimant must be appropriate to the actual prejudice he suffered as a result of the

infringing activity[1]. When awarding such damages, all appropriate aspects must be taken into account, including in particular[2]:

(1)   the negative economic consequences, including any lost profits, that the claimant has suffered and any unfair profits made by the defendant; and

(2)   elements other than economic factors, including the moral prejudice caused to the claimant by the infringement.

Where appropriate, such damages may be awarded on the basis of the royalties or fees which would have been due had the defendant obtained a licence[3].

Except to the extent that they are inconsistent with these provisions[4], substantially the same principles govern inquiries as to damages and the measure of damages in actions for the infringement of trade marks as in actions for passing off[5]. The claimant can recover only in respect of such damage as he can be shown to have in fact sustained or as must be presumed to flow from the acts proved to have been committed by the defendant[6]. It is no defence to a claim for more than nominal damages[7] that the defendant acted innocently[8]. An inquiry as to damages may be refused if there is no evidence of such damage[9] or a payment into court has been made sufficient to cover any damage[10]. Such an inquiry is normally granted at the risk of the claimant as to costs[11]. An inquiry as to damages may be ordered against both a company and individuals who have been responsible for the company's tortious acts[12]. The form of an order for inquiry as to damages should indicate that the inquiry is to be limited to damage suffered by the claimant through the defendant's wrongful acts as distinct from damage caused by mere trade competition[13].

The measure of damages recoverable is largely a question of fact to be determined in the light of the evidence by the tribunal in the way in which a jury would estimate damages[14]. In general the claimant is entitled to damages for all loss actually sustained by him as the natural and direct consequence of the defendant's wrongful acts, including any loss of trade sustained either directly from those acts or properly attributable to the injury to the claimant's reputation and goodwill caused by the acts[15]. It will not be assumed in the absence of evidence that, where the defendant has sold deceptive articles, every one of the sales would, but for the deception, have necessarily been obtained by the claimant[16]. The court will, however, presume that the presence on the market of a large quantity of deceptive goods will have an adverse effect on the claimant's business; and where such goods have been sold to a middleman, it is not necessary for the claimant to prove that there has been a fraudulent resale by the middleman[17]. Where the claimant cannot prove diversion of trade or any specific damage to goodwill, he may be able to claim damages assessed on a reasonable royalty basis[18]. In assessing a reasonable royalty, it is relevant to consider both comparable licences and non-infringing alternatives[19]. The costs of putting innocent third parties on notice are recoverable as damages[20], as are the costs of a prior legal action for disclosure to find out the name of the defendant[21].

Where damages will fall to be included by the claimant in his statement of profits, no account should be taken of income tax in assessing them[22]. VAT may be payable on a sum of damages received by way of settlement[23].

Damages can be recovered only in respect of an act which has taken place within the six years preceding the issue of the writ[24], unless concealed fraud is established[25]. Damages have been refused on the ground of delay[26].

1   Intellectual Property (Enforcement, etc) Regulations 2006, SI 2006/1028, reg 3(1).

2   Intellectual Property (Enforcement, etc) Regulations 2006, SI 2006/1028, reg 3(2)(a). Regulation 3 is derived from Parliament and Council Directive (EC) 2004/48 (OJ L157 30.4.04, p 45) art 13.

3 Intellectual Property (Enforcement, etc) Regulations 2006, SI 2006/1028, reg 3(2)(b).

4 Intellectual Property (Enforcement, etc) Regulations 2006, SI 2006/1028, reg 3(3).

5 Cf *Manus Akt v RJ Fullwood and Bland Ltd* (1954) 71 RPC 243 (damages for infringement and passing off assessed together).

6 See *Draper v Trist* [1939] 3 All ER 513, 56 RPC 429, CA; *Ideal General Supply Co Ltd v Louis Edelson and Bette Edelson (t/a the Ideal Clothing Co)* [1957] RPC 252 at 258. As to the assessment of damages in tort generally see DAMAGES vol 12(1) (Reissue) PARA 851 et seq.

7 As to entitlement to nominal damages see *AG Spalding & Bros v AW Gamage Ltd* (1915) 32 RPC 273, HL; *Draper v Trist* [1939] 3 All ER 513 at 518, 56 RPC 429 at 435, CA. Nominal damages have, however, been refused where the plaintiff had promptly put an end to the wrongful act of the defendant and had not shown that it had suffered any loss: *Ideal General Supply Co Ltd v Louis Edelson and Bette Edelson (t/a the Ideal Clothing Co)* [1957] RPC 252 at 258.

8 *Gillette UK Ltd v Edenwest Ltd* [1994] RPC 279.

9 See PARA 424 note 2.

10 *Samuelson v Producers Distributing Co Ltd* (1931) as reported in 48 RPC 580 at 590.

11 *AG Spalding & Bros v AW Gamage Ltd* (1915) 32 RPC 273, HL. See also e g *Draper v Trist* (1939) as reported in 56 RPC 429 (claim put forward for £48,000; £2,000 recovered; plaintiffs awarded half their costs); *Manus Akt v RJ Fullwood and Bland Ltd* (1954) 71 RPC 243 (claim for between £67,000 and £76,000, but £10,000 was awarded; plaintiff awarded costs of inquiry).

12 *Middlemas and Wood v Moliver & Co Ltd* (1921) 38 RPC 97; *Oertli AG V EJ Bowman (London) Ltd* [1956] RPC 282 (where it was said that a director would not be liable for any new passing off which occurred after he ceased to be a director).

13 *Baume & Co Ltd v AH Moore Ltd* [1958] RPC 319, CA (where the defendants withdrew an objection to an order referring to sale under any name 'calculated' to pass off the goods as the plaintiffs'). See also *Singer Manufacturing Co v British Empire Manufacturing Co Ltd* (1903) 20 RPC 313 at 320. As to disclosure in relation to an inquiry as to damages see PARA 409.

14 See *Alexander & Co v Henry & Co, Mitchell and Waller & Co* (1895) 12 RPC 360; *Ledger Sons & Co v J Munro & Co Ltd* (1916) 33 RPC 53, Ct of Sess; *Juggi Lal-Kamlapat and Juggilal-Kamlapat Mills Co of Cawnpore v Swadeshi Co Ltd* (1928) 46 RPC 74, PC; *Manus Akt v RJ Fullwood and Bland Ltd* (1954) 71 RPC 243 at 250; and see generally *General Tire and Rubber Co v Firestone Tyre and Rubber Co Ltd* [1975] 2 All ER 173, [1975] 1 WLR 819, [1976] RPC 197, HL.

15 *AG Spalding & Bros v AW Gamage Ltd* (1918) 35 RPC 101, CA. Such damages may include the cost of advertisements to counteract the effect of the defendant's conduct.

16 *Leather Cloth Co Ltd v Hirschfield* (1865) LR 1 Eq 299; *Alexander & Co v Henry & Co, Mitchell and Waller & Co* (1895) 12 RPC 360; *Magnolia Metal Co v Atlas Metal Co* (1897) 14 RPC 389, CA; *Ledger Sons & Co v J Munro & Son Ltd* (1916) 33 RPC 53 at 59, Ct of Sess; *Draper v Trist* [1939] 3 All ER 513 at 520, 56 RPC 429 at 437, CA; *PC Products Ltd v Dalton* [1957] RPC 199 at 202, Ct of Sess.

17 *Draper v Trist* [1939] 3 All ER 513, 56 RPC 429, CA.

18 *32Red plc v WHG (Gibraltar) Ltd* [2013] EWHC 815 (Ch), [2013] All ER (D) 93 (Apr); *National Guild of Removers & Storers Ltd v Silveria* [2010] EWPCC 15, [2011] FSR 250. This is an application of the 'user principle': see also *Stoke on Trent City Council v W & J Wass Ltd* [1988] 3 All ER 394, [1988] 1 WLR 1406, CA; *Inverugie Investments Ltd v Hackett* [1995] 3 All ER 841. [1995] 1 WLR 713, PC; *A-G v Blake* [2001] 1 AC 268, [2000] 4 All ER 385, HL. The user principle is well-established in relation to other intellectual property rights: see *Meters v Metropolitan Gas Meters Ltd* (1911) 28 RPC 157, 104 LT 113, CA (patents); *Stovin-Bradford v Volpoint Properties Ltd* [1971] Ch 1007, [1971] 3 All ER 570, CA (copyright); *Michael O'Mara Books Ltd v Express Newspapers plc* [1998] EMLR 383, [1999] FSR 49 (copyright); *Blayney (t/a Aardvark Jewelry) v Clogau St David's Gold Mines Ltd* [2002] EWCA Civ 1007, [2003] FSR 360, CA (copyright); *Seager v Copydex Ltd (No 2)* [1969] 2 All ER 718, [1969] 1 WLR 809, CA (confidential information); *Dowson & Mason Ltd v Potter* [1986] 2 All ER 418, [1986] 1 WLR 1419, CA (confidential information); *Force India Formula One Team Ltd v Aerolab SRL* [2013] EWCA Civ 780, [2013] All ER (D) 39 (Jul) (confidential information). However, it has been doubted whether the user principle is always applicable to trade mark cases: *Reed Executive plc v Reed Business Information Ltd* [2004] EWCA Civ 159, [2004] RPC 767, [2004] IP & T 1049.

19 *32Red plc v WHG (Gibraltar) Ltd* [2013] EWHC 815 (Ch), [2013] All ER (D) 93 (Apr).

20 *Dormeuil Frères SA v Feraglow Ltd* [1990] RPC 449.

21 *Morton-Norwich Products Inc v Intercen Ltd (No 2)* [1981] FSR 337.

22 *PC Products Ltd v Dalton* [1957] RPC 199 at 202, Ct of Sess.

23 *Cooper Chasney Ltd v Customs and Excise Comrs* [1992] FSR 298.
24 See the Limitation Act 1980 s 2 (actions founded on tort); and LIMITATION PERIODS vol 68 (2008) PARA 979 et seq.
25 See the Limitation Act 1980 s 32; and LIMITATION PERIODS vol 68 (2008) PARA 1220 et seq.
26 *F Reddaway & Co Ltd v Stevenson & Bro Ltd and Stevenson* (1902) 20 RPC 276; *GH Gledhill & Sons Ltd v British Perforated Toilet Paper Co* (1911) 28 RPC 429. It is difficult to see the justification for this, unless delay is such as to debar the entire cause of action or there has been such delay in pursuing an inquiry that it is struck out for want of prosecution. As to the effect of delay and acquiescence generally see PARA 83.

426.   Account of profits. The court may grant an account of profits[1] where one party knowingly marks his goods with the trade mark of the claimant or passes off his goods as those of the claimant[2]. An account may also be granted where one party owes a duty to another; the person to whom the duty is owed is entitled to recover from the other party every benefit which that other party has received by virtue of his fiduciary position, if in fact he has obtained it without the knowledge or consent of the party to whom he owes the duty[3]. An account is normally refused if the defendant was ignorant of the claimant's rights, and is limited to the period, if any, during which the defendant had knowledge of the claimant's rights[4]. An account cannot be granted in respect of any matter which arose more than six years before the commencement of the action[5], except in a case of concealed fraud[6]. Where the claimant has without excuse failed for a considerable period to take proceedings after he has become aware that an infringement of his rights has taken place, an account may be granted of profits only up to the time when he became aware of his rights[7], or may be dated only from the time when he complained to the defendants[8], or may be refused except as regards the period since the commencement of proceedings[9]. The costs of taking an account are normally reserved.

In taking an account of profits, which is an equitable relief, the damage which the claimant has suffered is totally immaterial, the object of the account being to give the claimant the actual profits which the defendant has made and of which equity strips him as soon as it is established that the profits were improperly made[10]. The claimant is, however, only entitled to an account of such profits as ought to be treated as having been improperly made by the defendant[11]. Accordingly, on the sale of goods by the defendant to a middleman, the profit for which the defendant must account is the profit which he has made by the sale of the goods in fraudulent dress to the middleman and it is immaterial whether the middleman sells the goods to retailers fraudulently or not[12].

1 An account of profits and an inquiry as to damages are alternative remedies: see PARA 424. As to the remedy of account generally see EQUITY vol 16(2) (Reissue) PARAS 553, 691 et seq; as to accounts as ancillary to injunctions see CIVIL PROCEDURE vol 11 (2009) PARA 335; and as to disclosure in relation to an account of profits see PARA 409.
2 *AG Spalding & Bros v AW Gamage Ltd* (1915) 32 RPC 273 at 283, HL, per Lord Parker.
3 *Electrolux Ltd v Electrix Ltd* (1953) 70 RPC 158 at 159. As to the disability of a person in a fiduciary position to make a profit from that position generally see EQUITY vol 16(2) (Reissue) PARAS 856–858; TRUSTS AND POWERS vol 98 (2013) PARA 366 et seq.
4 *Edelsten v Edelsten* (1863) 1 DeGJ & Sm 185 at 199; *Ellen v Slack* (1880) 24 Sol Jo 290; *Slazenger & Sons v Spalding & Bros* [1910] 1 Ch 257, 27 RPC 20.
5 See the Limitation Act 1980 s 23, applying the time limit applicable to the claim which is the basis of the duty to account. See also s 2 (actions founded on tort); and LIMITATION PERIODS vol 68 (2008) PARA 1008.
6 See the Limitation Act 1980 s 32; and LIMITATION PERIODS vol 68 (2008) PARA 1220 et seq.
7 See *Electrolux Ltd v Electrix Ltd* (1953) 70 RPC 158 at 159 (order made that the plaintiffs should be entitled to recover any damages proved); *Edward Young & Co Ltd v Holt* (1947) 65 RPC 25 at 31 (plaintiff's delay held justified).
8 *Lever Bros, Port Sunlight Ltd v Sunniwite Products Ltd* (1949) 66 RPC 84 at 102.

9   *Harrison v Taylor* (1865) 12 LT 339; *Ford v Foster* (1872) 7 Ch App 611. As to the effect of delay or acquiescence on the right of action see PARA 84.

10 *Draper v Trist* [1939] 3 All ER 513 at 522, 56 RPC 429 at 439, CA. See also *Hollister Incorporated v Medik Ostomy Supplies Ltd* [2012] EWCA Civ 1419, [2013] IP & T 577, [2012] All ER (D) 114 (Nov).

11 See *Hollister Inc v Medik Ostomy Supplies Ltd* [2012] EWCA Civ 1419, [2013] FSR 24, [2013] IP & T 577, [2012] All ER (D) 114 (Nov) (trade mark proprietor entitled to all profits from infringing parallel imports where notice not given; defendant not entitled to deduct a proportion of its general overheads without evidence that such overheads were properly attributable to dealings in infringing products). See also *My Kinda Town Ltd v Soll* [1983] RPC 15, CA (where the principles of an account in a passing off case are discussed).

12 *Lever v Goodwin* (1887) 36 ChD 1 at 7; cited in *Draper v Trist* [1939] 3 All ER 513 at 523, 56 RPC 429 at 439, CA. As to the presumption of damage arising from sales of deceptive goods to a middleman when an inquiry has been ordered as to damages see PARA 425.

D. NON-PECUNIARY REMEDIES

427. Delivery up of infringing articles or erasure of mark. An order may be made for the delivery up of infringing articles or labels or the erasure of an infringing mark[1]. Where the mark can be erased, the order will be for erasure only[2]. Delivery up is an equitable remedy ancillary to an injunction[3]. It is routine for the order to be accompanied by an order for verification upon oath that erasure or delivery up has been effected. Where the court makes an order for delivery up or destruction of infringing goods, or articles designed or adapted to make such goods, the person against whom the order is made must pay the costs of complying with that order unless the court orders otherwise[4].

1   *Farina v Silverlock* (1858) 4 K & J 650; *Edelsten v Edelsten* (1863) 1 DeGJ & Sm 185 at 189, 196; *Slazenger & Sons v Feltham & Co* (1889) 6 RPC 531 at 538, CA; cf *Lissen Ltd v Mutton* (1928) 46 RPC 10 (order for delivery up refused in action for passing off). See also *Warwick Tyre Co Ltd v New Motor and General Rubber Co Ltd* [1910] 1 Ch 248, 27 RPC 161.

2   See the cases cited in note 1. See also *County Chemical Co Ltd v Frankenburg* (1904) 21 RPC 722 (no order for delivery up made because the articles could be used legitimately in other ways and because of the plaintiff's delay in beginning the action).

3   As to the statutory power to order the erasure etc of an offending sign see PARA 428; and as to the statutory power to order delivery up of infringing goods etc see PARAS 444–446.

4   *Practice Direction—Intellectual Property Claims* PD63 para 26.1.

428. Statutory power to make order for erasure etc of offending sign. Where a person is found to have infringed[1] a registered trade mark[2], the court[3] may make an order[4] requiring him:

(1)   to cause the offending sign to be erased, removed or obliterated from any infringing goods[5], material[6] or articles[7] in his possession, custody or control[8]; or

(2)   if it is not reasonably practicable for the offending sign to be erased, removed or obliterated, to secure the destruction of the infringing goods, material or articles in question[9].

If any such order is not complied with, or it appears to the court likely that such an order would not be complied with, the court may order that the infringing goods, material or articles be delivered to such person as the court may direct for erasure, removal or obliteration of the sign, or for destruction, as the case may be[10].

1   As to the meaning of 'infringement' see PARA 66 note 4. As to the acts which amount to infringement, if done without the consent of the proprietor, see the Trade Marks Act 1994 s 10; and PARA 68 et seq.

2   As to the meaning of 'registered trade mark' see PARA 111.

3   As to the meaning of 'the court' see PARA 331.
4   Trade Marks Act 1994 s 15(1).
5   As to the meaning of 'infringing goods' see PARA 133.
6   As to the meaning of 'infringing material' see PARA 133.
7   As to the meaning of 'infringing articles' see PARA 133.
8   Trade Marks Act 1994 s 15(1)(a).
9   Trade Marks Act 1994 s 15(1)(b).
10 Trade Marks Act 1994 s 15(2).

429.   Certificate of validity of contested registration.   If in proceedings before the court[1] the validity of the registration[2] of a trade mark[3] is contested and it is found by the court that the trade mark is validly registered[4], the court may give a certificate to that effect[5]. If the court gives such a certificate, and in subsequent proceedings[6]:

(1)   the validity of the registration is again questioned; and

(2)   the proprietor obtains a final order or judgment in his favour,

he is entitled to his costs as between solicitor and client[7] unless the court directs otherwise; but this provision does not extend to the costs of an appeal in any such proceedings[8].

1   As to the meaning of 'the court' see PARA 331.
2   As to the grounds on which the registration of a trade mark may be declared invalid see PARA 102 et seq.
3   As to the meaning of 'trade mark' see PARA 41. This provision also applies if the validity of the protection of a protected international trade mark (UK) is contested: see the Trade Marks (International Registration) Order 2008, SI 2008/2206, art 3; and PARA 12. As to the meaning of 'protected international trade mark (UK)' see PARA 12 note 8.
4   As to the meaning of 'registered' see PARA 21 note 2.
5   Trade Marks Act 1994 s 73(1). There is no longer any express procedure whereby the proprietor can ask the registrar to add to the entry in the register a note that the certificate of validity has been granted in the course of the proceedings. It is, however, likely that in practice an entry would be made. A certificate given before 31 October 1994 under the Trade Marks Act 1938 s 47 (repealed) (certificate of validity of contested registration) has effect as if given under the Trade Marks Act 1994 s 73(1): s 105, Sch 3 para 21. As to the registrar see PARA 19.
6   Under earlier legislation it was held that 'subsequent proceedings' meant proceedings started after the certificate had been given: *Automatic Weighing Machine Co v International Hygienic Society* (1889) 6 RPC 475 at 480; *Saccharin Corpn Ltd v Anglo-Continental Chemical Works* [1901] 1 Ch 414, 17 RPC 307. That is, however, unlikely to be so held in respect of a certificate issued under the Trade Marks Act 1994 s 73; cf the corresponding position in relation to patents (see *Mölnlyke AB v Procter & Gamble Ltd (No 5)* [1994] RPC 49 at 139, CA). Under previous legislation it was held that there was no appeal against the grant of such a certificate per se: *Haslam Foundry and Engineering Co Ltd v Hall* (1888) 20 QBD 491, 5 RPC 144, CA. The grant is purely discretionary: *Re Impex Electrical Ltd's Trade Marks, Impex Electrical Ltd v Weinbaum* (1927) 44 RPC 405 at 411. It is unlikely that a certificate will be given where the registration is attacked only on the ground of alleged non-use: *Lever Bros, Port Sunlight Ltd v Sunniwite Products Ltd* (1949) 66 RPC 84 at 102.
7   'Solicitor and own client' costs no longer exist as a basis for assessment of costs (formerly known as taxation of costs). Assessment of costs is now either on the standard basis or on the indemnity basis: see CPR Pt 44; and CIVIL PROCEDURE vol 12 (2009) PARA 1734 et seq. It is possible to argue that the reference in the Trade Marks Act 1994 s 73(2) to 'costs as between solicitor and client' is meant to refer to some higher standard but the better view is probably that it simply re-enacts the old provision and that the reference is to be taken to be the nearest equivalent to what was taxation on solicitor and own client basis (ie on the indemnity basis).
8   Trade Marks Act 1994 s 73(2).

430.   Notification of court order to registrar.   Where any order of the court affects the validity of an entry in the register, the court and the party in whose favour the order is made must serve a copy on the registrar within 14 days[1]. Where the order is made in favour of more than one party, a copy must be served by such party as the court directs[2].

1   *Practice Direction—Intellectual Property Claims* PD63 para 20.1, applying para 14.1.
2   *Practice Direction—Intellectual Property Claims* PD63 para 20.1, applying para 14.2.

E. COSTS

431. Costs. Subject to the statutory provision as to the effect of a certificate of validity[1], the costs of proceedings for infringement or passing off are in the discretion of the court and the same general principles apply in determining by whom costs are to be payable as in the case of other actions[2].

A successful party will generally be awarded costs[3]; but under the Civil Procedure Rules 2008[4] costs orders should generally reflect the level of success which he has achieved[5]. Thus where a successful claimant has claimed too widely or has made allegations which he has failed to prove, he may be wholly or partly deprived of costs[6], or may be given the general costs of the action or the costs of claims or issues on which he has succeeded, but ordered to pay the costs of claims or issues on which he has failed[7]. A claimant has been disallowed the costs of unnecessary evidence[8]. Where a claimant has brought an action for infringement and passing off and has succeeded as to one ground of action but failed as to the other, he has been awarded the general costs of the action, but the defendant has been awarded costs on the issue on which the claimant failed and the costs have been set off[9]. Where an offer giving the claimant all to which he is entitled is made by the defendant during proceedings, the costs of continuing proceedings may not be recoverable[10]. The costs of putting innocent third parties on notice are recoverable as damages[11], as are the costs of a prior legal action for disclosure to find out the name of the defendant[12].

A successful defendant may be refused his costs where, for example, he has made unfounded charges of fraud[13], or has by his conduct brought the action on himself[14].

Misrepresentations by the defendant, even if they are not of such a nature as to give the claimant a cause of action, have in many cases led to the defendant's being deprived of costs[15], but this is not a proper course where the misrepresentations have reference to a collateral matter and have nothing to do with the claimant's case[16].

The costs of three counsel have sometimes been allowed[17].

1   See the Trade Marks Act 1994 s 73; and PARA 429.
2   As to costs generally see CPR Pt 44; and CIVIL PROCEDURE vol 12 (2009) PARA 1734 et seq. CPR 44.3 gives the court a very broad discretion as to the orders it may make in relation to costs. Costs are normally assessed on the standard basis: see CPR 44.4(1); and CIVIL PROCEDURE vol 12 (2009) PARA 1747.
3   See CPR 44.3(2)(a); and CIVIL PROCEDURE vol 12 (2009) PARA 1738. Where a retail trader innocently purchased and dealt with a small quantity of goods which turned out to be an infringement of a trade mark, the court made no order as to costs: *American Tobacco Co v Guest* [1892] 1 Ch 630. As to the costs of the registrar appearing where the relief sought includes revocation, a declaration of invalidity or rectification see PARA 395.
4   Ie the Civil Procedure Rules 2008, SI 2008/3132 ('CPR'): see generally CIVIL PROCEDURE.
5   *Phonographic Performance Ltd v AEI Rediffusion Music Ltd* [1999] 2 All ER 299, sub nom *AEI Rediffusion Music Ltd v Phonographic Performance Ltd (No 2)* [1999] 1 WLR 1507, CA.
6   See CPR 44.3(4), (5); and CIVIL PROCEDURE vol 12 (2009) PARA 1739. Cf *Moet v Couston* (1864) 33 Beav 578; *Standish v Whitwell* (1866) 14 WR 512; *Metzler v Wood* (1877) 8 ChD 606; *Findlater, Mackie, Todd & Co Ltd v Henry Newman & Co* (1902) 19 RPC 235; *Montgomerie & Co Ltd v Young Bros* (1903) 20 RPC 781; *OT Ltd v Cumming & Co* (1914)

32 RPC 69, Ct of Sess; *Fram Manufacturing Co Ltd v Eric Morton & Co* (1922) 40 RPC 33, CA; *Joseph Rodgers & Sons Ltd v WN Rodgers & Co* (1924) 41 RPC 277; *John Jaques & Sons Ltd v Chess* [1939] 3 All ER 227, 56 RPC 415 (on appeal [1940] 2 All ER 285, 57 RPC 77, CA). Cf *Jay v Ladler* (1888) 40 ChD 649, 6 RPC 136; *Rowland v Mitchell* (1896) 13 RPC 457; *Hodgson and Simpson v Kynoch* (1898) 15 RPC 465. See, however, notes 2–3.

7   See CPR 44.3(4); *Pierce v Franks* (1846) 15 LJ Ch 122; *Saxlehner v Apollinaris Co* [1897] 1 Ch 893, 14 RPC 645; *GF Hipkins & Sons v Plant* (1898) 15 RPC 294; *Pneumatic Rubber Stamp Co v Lindler* (1898) 15 RPC 525. See, however, notes 2–3.

8   *Daimler Motor Co (1904) Ltd v London Daimler Co Ltd* (1907) 24 RPC 379, CA (half costs of evidence allowed).

9   *Lever Bros Ltd v Bedingfield* (1898) 15 RPC 453; on appeal (1899) 16 RPC 3, CA (where judgment on the issue on which the plaintiff had succeeded in the court below was given for the defendant with costs of the appeal but not of the action); *Natural Chemicals Ltd and Veno's Drug Co Ltd and Irving's Yeast-Vite Ltd (Consolidated) v Amblins (Chemists) Ltd* (1940) 57 RPC 323. See, however, notes 2–3.

10   See PARA 437 text and notes 11–13. Cf *Colgate-Palmolive Ltd v Markwell Finance Ltd* [1989] RPC 497, CA (where a 'Calderbank' offer was insufficient so the plaintiff recovered its costs).

11   *Dormeuil Frères SA v Feraglow Ltd* [1990] RPC 449.

12   *Morton-Norwich Products Inc v Intercen Ltd (No 2)* [1981] FSR 337.

13   *Baker v Rawson* (1890) 45 ChD 519, 8 RPC 89; *Hargreave v Freeman* [1891] 3 Ch 39, 8 RPC 237. See notes 2–3.

14   *Lambert and Butler Ltd v Goodbody* (1902) 19 RPC 377; and see *Lever Bros Ltd v Bedingfield* (1899) 16 RPC 3, CA; *Claudius Ash Sons & Co v Invicta Manufacturing Co Ltd* (1912) 29 RPC 465, HL. See notes 2–3.

15   *Estcourt v Estcourt Hop Essence Co* (1875) 10 Ch App 276; *Newman v Pinto* (1887) 4 RPC 508, CA; *Thorneloe v Hill* [1894] 1 Ch 569 at 578, 11 RPC 61 at 72; *Lever Bros Ltd v Bedingfield* (1899) 16 RPC 3, CA; *Valentine Meat Juice Co v Valentine Extract Co Ltd* (1899) 17 RPC 1 at 13; *Winser v Armstrong & Co* (1899) 16 RPC 167 at 172; *B Warsop & Sons Ltd v Warsop* (1904) 21 RPC 481; *Cambridge University Press v University Tutorial Press* (1928) 45 RPC 335. See, however, notes 2–3.

16   *F King & Co Ltd v Gillard & Co* [1905] 2 Ch 7, 22 RPC 327, CA. Probably this rule would not apply to such cases as *Estcourt v Estcourt Hop Essence Co* (1875) 10 Ch App 276; *Newman v Pinto* (1887) 4 RPC 508, CA, in each of which the plaintiff had a cause of action, but failed because of fraud of which the defendant was equally guilty. See notes 2–3.

17   Such costs were granted in *Re Burroughs, Wellcome & Co's Trade Mark* (1905) 22 RPC 164; *Re Crosfield & Sons Ltd's Application* (1910) 27 RPC 433; *Adrema Ltd v Adrema-Werke GmbH and BEM Business Efficiency Machines Ltd* [1958] RPC 323. They were, however, refused in *Mercedes Daimler Motor Co Ltd v FIAT Motor Cab Co Ltd* (1913) 31 RPC 8; *Bentley Motors (1931) Ltd v Lagonda Ltd and Bentley, Re Bentley (1931) Ltd's Trade Mark No 528,124* (1947) 64 RPC 33. See also LEGAL PROFESSIONS vol 66 (2009) PARA 1316. See notes 2–3.

F. INTERIM AND SUMMARY REMEDIES

432.   Interim injunction. The general principles as to the grant of interim injunctions are discussed elsewhere in this work[1]. However, in actions for passing off or for infringement of a registered trade mark the prospects of the claimant's success[2] are often bound up with the question of whether damages are an adequate remedy. Thus where the claimant alleges that the defendant's mark is confusingly similar to his own, the question whether damages are an adequate remedy to the claimant will depend largely upon the court's assessment of whether there will be significant confusion pending trial, and this is a key question in assessing liability itself[3]. Further, it seems likely, at least in trade mark and passing off cases, that in the absence of a serious conflict of evidence relating to primary facts the court will pay greater attention to the claimant's prospects of success than it might otherwise pay[4], as in that type of case the result of the application is likely to be determinative of the action[5]. Where damages are not an adequate remedy to either party, the court must choose the course which appears to involve the least risk of causing injustice[6]. There are cases where it would be inappropriate to grant an interim injunction unless the claimant accepts a similar restraint[7].

Where the claimant seeks to restrain a competitor from comparative advertising on the ground of trade mark infringement, no interim injunction should be granted unless the court is satisfied that the claimant is more likely than not to succeed on trial[8].

Delay in seeking an interim injunction normally affects the status quo of the parties but is not always fatal[9], although it is hard to convince a court that a claimant who has delayed is really suffering serious and irreparable damage[10]. The claimant is required to give a cross-undertaking in damages if he is to be awarded an interim injunction[11].

The terms of an interim injunction should normally be limited to what is necessary to protect the claimant pending trial[12]; and the injunction should be drafted so as to define what the defendant may not do without a dependence upon the legal right, as otherwise enforcement will require proof of infringement or passing off on a contempt motion[13].

Applications for interim injunctions are sometimes resolved by the defendant's giving an undertaking to the court[14]. Where this is done, the claimant may not normally seek a wider injunction on a subsequent occasion pending trial[15], nor may a defendant who has given such an undertaking withdraw it merely because he gave the undertaking on a mistaken view of the law[16]. Applications for interim injunctions often result in orders for a speedy trial[17].

1 See CIVIL PROCEDURE vol 11 (2009) PARAS 316, 383 et seq. See, in particular, *American Cyanamid Co v Ethicon Ltd* [1975] AC 396, [1975] 1 All ER 504, [1975] RPC 513, HL (a patent infringement case), where the general principles as to the grant of interim injunctions were recast. The principles of *American Cyanmid Co v Ethicon Ltd* apply also to actions for passing off: *County Sound plc v Ocean Sound Ltd* [1991] FSR 367, CA.

2 'The court must be satisfied that the claim is not frivolous or vexatious, in other words that there is a serious question to be tried': *American Cyanamid Co v Ethicon Ltd* [1975] AC 396 at 408, [1975] 1 All ER 504 at 510, [1975] RPC 513 at 541, HL, per Lord Diplock. As to the meaning of 'frivolous or vexatious' and 'serious question to be tried' in the context of interim injunctions see further *Mothercare Ltd v Robson Books Ltd* [1979] FSR 466 (passing off).

3 See *Sirdar Ltd v Les Fils de Louis Mulliez and Orsay Knitting Wools Ltd* [1975] FSR 309 at 312–313 per Graham J. Once the claimant has established an arguable case, it is likely, however, that damages will not be an adequate remedy. There will be the substantial difficulty of establishing the extent of confusion and damage, and quantification of that: see e g *Morgan-Grampian plc v Training Personnel Ltd* [1992] FSR 267; *Antec International Ltd v South Western Chicks (Warren) Ltd* [1997] FSR 278. If, however, the risk of deception is not great so that the consequences to the claimant are not likely to be severe, an injunction may be refused: *Management Publications Ltd v Blenheim Exhibitions Group plc* [1991] FSR 348 (affd [1991] FSR 550, CA); *Financial Times Ltd v Evening Standard Co Ltd* [1991] FSR 7; *Stacey v 2020 Communications plc* [1991] FSR 49.

4 See *Newsweek Inc v British Broadcasting Corpn* [1979] RPC 441, CA; *Alfred Dunhill Ltd v Sunoptic SA* [1979] FSR 337, CA; *County Sound plc v Ocean Sound Ltd* [1991] FSR 367, CA; *Tamworth Herald Co Ltd v Thomson Free Newspapers Ltd* [1991] FSR 337; *United Biscuits (UK) Ltd v Burton Biscuits Ltd* [1992] FSR 14; *Advance Magazine Publishing Inc v Redwood Publishing Ltd* [1993] FSR 449.

5 See *British Broadcasting Corpn v Talbot Motor Co Ltd* [1981] FSR 228; *Parmass/Pelly Ltd v Hodges* [1982] FSR 329. This is especially so if the injunction is to be granted, for then the defendant will have to change to another name or mark pending trial and is unlikely, having established that name or mark, to change back if he is successful at the trial. Other cases where this factor was taken into account include *Boots Co Ltd v Approved Prescription Services Ltd* [1988] FSR 45, CA; *Post Office v Interlink Express Parcels Ltd* [1989] FSR 369; *Stacey v 2020 Communications plc* [1991] FSR 49; *Gala of London Ltd v Chandler Ltd* [1991] FSR 294; *Management Publications Ltd v Blenheim Exhibitions Group plc* [1991] FSR 348 (affd [1991]

FSR 550, CA); *Blazer plc v Yardley & Co Ltd* [1992] FSR 501. In all these cases the claimant, though having an 'arguable' case, did not have a strong one.

6   *NWL Ltd v Woods, The Nawala* [1979] 3 All ER 614, [1979] 1 WLR 1294, HL; *Cayne v Global Natural Resources plc* [1984] 1 All ER 225, CA.

7   See e g *Nationwide Building Society v Nationwide Estate Agents Ltd* [1987] FSR 579 (where both parties were trying to establish the word 'Nationwide' for an estate agency business and the court took the view that the plaintiff might establish an unfair commercial advantage by way of building up a reputation pending trial if the defendant alone were restrained).

8   *Boehringer Ingelheim Ltd v Vetplus Ltd* [2007] EWCA Civ 583, [2007] FSR 737, [2007] All ER (D) 221 (Jun). See the Human Rights Act 1998 s 12(3); and CONFIDENCE AND INFORMATIONAL PRIVACY vol 19 (2011) PARA 84. When the urgency of the matter does not permit full consideration of the merits, a lesser probability of success will suffice: *Red Dot Technologies Ltd v Apollo Fire Detectors Ltd* [2007] EWHC 1166 (Ch). The rule against prior restraint established in *Bonnard v Perryman* [1891] 2 Ch 269 (in the interests of freedom of speech, the courts will not restrain the publication of a defamatory statement, whether a trade libel or a personal one, where the defendant says he is going to justify it at the trial of the action, except where the statement is obviously untruthful and libellous) does not apply to trade mark or passing off cases: *Boehringer Ingelheim Ltd v Vetplus Ltd* above.

9   See e g *CPC (United Kingdom) Ltd v Keenan* [1986] FSR 527 ('Oxbridge' marmalade); *Cavendish House (Cheltenham) Ltd v Cavendish Woodhouse Ltd* [1970] RPC 234, CA.

10   See e g *Gala of London Ltd v Chandler Ltd* [1991] FSR 294.

11   See CIVIL PROCEDURE vol 11 (2009) PARA 419 et seq. It is not fatal to the claimant's case if he cannot show sufficient assets to be good for the cross-undertaking, but that is a factor to be taken into account: *Allen v Jambo Holdings Ltd* [1980] 2 All ER 502, [1980] 1 WLR 1252, CA. Where the claimant is abroad, the undertaking in damages can be given by a solvent party within the jurisdiction: see e g *Hobart Manufacturing Co v Cannon Industries Ltd* [1959] RPC 269.

12   See e g *Biro Swan Ltd v Tallon Ltd* [1961] RPC 326. See also CIVIL PROCEDURE vol 11 (2009) PARAS 395–395.

13   See PARA 422.

14   See *Showerings Ltd v Mecca Ltd* [1957] RPC 217; *Copydex Ltd v Noso Products Ltd* (1952) 69 RPC 38; *Coca Cola Co v AG Barr & Co Ltd* [1961] RPC 387, Ct of Sess. If a perpetual undertaking is offered on the hearing of an interim injunction, this should be recited in the order: *Stillitz v Jones and Higgins Ltd* (1942) 60 RPC 15.

15   *GCT (Management) Ltd v Laurie Marsh Group Ltd* [1973] RPC 432.

16   *Chanel Ltd v FW Woolworth & Co Ltd* [1981] 1 All ER 745, [1981] 1 WLR 485, CA.

17   For this reason interim injunctions are much less common than was formerly the case. In some cases trials have taken place within two or three months of proceedings being commenced. This means that the balance of convenience is quite different to a situation where the trial will not take place for a year or more.

433. Without notice interim injunctions. Interim injunctions, like other interim remedies, may be granted on application without notice if it appears to the court that there are good reasons for not giving notice[1]. This would be the case if the matter is so urgent that there is not time to give notice, or if the giving of notice would frustrate the purpose of the application. Normally, particularly where the defendant has been given no informal notice, such injunctions are confined to cases of fraud or near fraud. Without notice interim injunctions are often awarded together with search orders and similar relief against counterfeiters and dealers in counterfeit goods[2].

1   CPR 25.3(1). If an application is made without notice, the evidence in support must state the reasons for not giving notice: CPR 25.3(3).

2   As to search orders see PARA 434.

434. Search orders and interim delivery-up orders. On the application of the claimant without notice[1], the court has power to order a defendant to permit the search of the defendant's premises for articles and documents relating to the alleged wrongdoing[2]. This power is exercised only where the claimant shows a strong prima facie case[3]. In relation to actions for passing off or infringement of a registered trade mark, this form of order is normally made only in cases of counterfeiting, as it is only in those cases that the court can be convinced of the need for the exercise of this powerful remedy[4]. Alternatively, a lesser form of order may be made requiring immediate delivery up but stopping short of requiring the defendant to permit a search[5].

1   As to the making of applications without notice see PARA 433 text and note 1.
2   CPR 25.1(1)(h). Such orders were formerly known as 'Anton Piller' orders, after *Anton Piller KG v Manufacturing Processes Ltd* [1976] Ch 55, [1976] 1 All ER 779, [1976] RPC 719, CA. They are now called search orders and are regulated by the Civil Procedure Act 1997 s 7(1); and *Practice Direction—Interim Injunctions* PD25A paras 7.1–7.11. The practice direction also specifies the normal form of the search order and makes provision for its execution to be supervised by a 'supervising solicitor' of requisite experience who acts as an officer of the court and is independent of the claimants' solicitors. Normally, the application is heard in private, as any kind of advance warning would defeat the purpose of the order.
3   See CIVIL PROCEDURE vol 11 (2009) PARA 403. As to search orders generally see CIVIL PROCEDURE vol 11 (2009) PARA 402 et seq.
4   It is in the public interest to suppress as soon as possible the fraud on the public involved in the public sale of counterfeit product; and although enforcement of the order is a matter of discretion, the principle of the rule of law requires that the court should not be deflected from requiring disclosure by allegations that the person concerned will be subjected to violence if he complies: *Coca Cola Co v Gilbey* [1996] FSR 23, CA.
5   See *Universal City Studios Inc v Mukhtar & Sons* [1976] 2 All ER 330, [1976] 1 WLR 568.

435.   Disclosure of names of infringers.   By interim procedures[1], a claimant can compel a defendant, and also an innocent person who, through no fault of his own and whether voluntarily or not, has become mixed up in wrongful conduct, to give disclosure of the name of the infringer or other wrongdoers[2]; where a defendant is himself the primary alleged wrongdoer, disclosure of his customers' names may be given at the interim stage[3], but this is unlikely in cases where liability is in doubt[4]. Such disclosure is, however, routinely given in cases of counterfeiting, and may be given without notice[5]. The claimant will normally have to pay the costs of the innocent person, but can recover them from the wrongdoer[6].

Where the purpose of the application for disclosure is to enable the claimant to discover the name of the infringer, it is not necessary to seek the leave of the court to use the information obtained for that purpose[7]. If, however, the claimant wishes to use the information obtained for some other purpose, for example to take proceedings abroad, then he may need the leave of the court[8].

1   See *RCA Corpn v Reddingtons Rare Records* [1975] 1 All ER 38, [1974] 1 WLR 1445, [1975] RPC 95.
2   See *Norwich Pharmacal Co v Customs and Excise Comrs* [1974] AC 133, [1973] 2 All ER 943, [1974] RPC 101, HL; *X Ltd v Morgan Grampian (Publishers) Ltd* [1991] 1 AC 1, [1990] 2 All ER 1, HL; *Ashworth Hospital Authority v MGN Ltd* [2002] UKHL 29, [2002] 4 All ER 193, HL; *Interbrew SA v Financial Times Ltd* [2002] EWCA Civ 274, [2002] 2 Lloyd's Rep 229, [2002] EMLR 446, CA; *Rugby Football Union v Consolidated Information Systems Ltd* [2012] UKSC 55, [2013] 1 All ER 928, [2012] 1 WLR 3333. Disclosure may also be obtained of the identities of persons who are not wrongdoers: *CHC Software Care Ltd v Hopkins & Wood* [1993] FSR 241; *P v T* [1997] 4 All ER 200, [1997] 1 WLR 1309. As to the availability of the remedy of interim disclosure see CPR 25.1(1)(i), (j); and CIVIL PROCEDURE vol 11 (2009) PARA 315. As to the principles of applying for disclosure before proceedings have commenced, or against a person who is not party to proceedings, see CPR 31.16–31.18; and CIVIL PROCEDURE vol 11 (2009) PARAS 112, 550. In some circumstances the provisions of the Justice and Security Act 2013 may be relevant. Certain courts hearing civil proceedings may make a declaration that the case is one in which a closed material application may be made in relation to specific pieces of material where disclosures would be damaging to the interests of national security: see ss 6–11; and CIVIL PROCEDURE.
3   See *Intelsec Systems Ltd v Grech-Cini* [1999] 4 All ER 11, [2000] 1 WLR 1190.

4 *Freedman v Hillingdon Shirts Co Ltd* [1975] FSR 449.
5 See *EMI Ltd v Sarwar and Haidar* [1977] FSR 146, CA (where the order for discovery was given in conjunction with an Anton Piller order (as to which see PARA 434)). As to the making of applications without notice see PARA 433 text and note 1.
6 *Totalise plc v The Motley Fool Ltd* [2001] EWCA Civ 1897, [2003] 2 All ER 972, [2002] 1 WLR 1233.
7 *Sony Corpn v Anand* [1981] FSR 398; *Roberts v Jump Knitwear Ltd* [1981] FSR 527.
8 See e g *Crest Homes plc v Marks* [1987] AC 829, [1987] 2 All ER 1074, HL; and CIVIL PROCEDURE vol 11 (2009) PARAS 402, 404.

436. Protective injunction against non-infringer. If a person has in his possession or control goods the dissemination of which, whether in the way of trade or, possibly, merely by way of gifts[1], will infringe another's trade mark[2], then, as soon as he is aware of this fact, he becomes subject to an equitable duty not to allow those goods to pass out of his possession or control, at any rate in circumstances in which the proprietor of the mark might be injured by an ensuing infringement. The person having the goods in his possession or control must not aid the infringement by letting the goods get into the hands of those who may use them or deal with them in a way which will invade the proprietor's rights, as, even though by doing so he might not himself infringe the trade mark, he would be in dereliction of his duty to the proprietor. This duty is one which will, if necessary, be enforced in equity by way of injunction[3].

The claimant will normally have to pay the costs of the innocent person, but can recover them from the wrongdoer[4]. This kind of injunction may be especially useful in putting a stop to infringement while the true infringer is located or identified.

1 See *Upmann v Forester* (1883) 24 ChD 231.
2 Or, it would seem, result in passing off, at least where the goods constitute instruments of deception: see PARA 314.
3 See *Norwich Pharmacal Co v Customs and Excise Comrs* [1974] AC 133 at 146, [1972] 3 All ER 813 at 823, [1972] RPC 743 at 771, CA, per Buckley LJ; revsd on other grounds [1974] AC 133, [1973] 2 All ER 943, [1974] RPC 101, HL. See also *L'Oréal SA v eBay International AG* [2009] EWHC 1094 (Ch) at [452]–[453], [2009] RPC 693 at [452]–[453] per Arnold J.
4 *Smith Kline and French Laboratories Ltd v RD Harbottle (Mercantile) Ltd* [1980] RPC 363; *Morton-Norwich Products Inc v Intercen Ltd (No 2)* [1981] FSR 337; c f *Miller Brewing Co v Mersey Docks and Harbour Co* [2003] EWHC 1606 (Ch), [2004] IP & T 542, [2004] FSR 81.

437. Injunctions against intermediaries. Member states of the European Union are required to ensure that rightholders are in a position to apply for an injunction against intermediaries whose services are used by a third party to infringe an intellectual property right[1].

The above provision has been interpreted as requiring the member states to ensure that the national courts with jurisdiction in relation to the protection of intellectual property rights are able to order the operator of an online marketplace to take measures which contribute, not only to bringing to an end infringements of those rights by users of that marketplace, but also to preventing further infringements of that kind; such injunctions must be effective, proportionate, dissuasive and must not create barriers to legitimate trade[2].

1 See Parliament and Council Directive (EC) 2004/48 (OJ L157 30.4.04, p 45) on the enforcement of intellectual property rights, art 11, third sentence.
2 Case C-324/09 *L'Oréal SA v eBay International AG* [2012] All ER (EC) 501, [2011] RPC 777, [2011] IP & T 819, ECJ. See also *L'Oréal SA v eBay International AG* [2009] EWHC 1094 (Ch) at [444]–[454], [2009] RPC 693 at [444]–[454] per Arnold J; and *Twentieth Century Fox Film*

Corpn v British Telecommunications plc [2011] EWHC 1981 (Ch) at [150]–[156], [2012] 1 All ER 806 at [150]–[156], [2012] Bus LR 1461 at [150]–[156] per Arnold J.

438. Freezing injunctions. In certain circumstances the court may grant an injunction, on application without notice[1], restraining the defendant from removing his assets from the jurisdiction or otherwise dealing with them in such a way that they would no longer be available to satisfy the claimant's judgment[2]. Such an injunction may be of particular importance in cases of counterfeiting, where defendants seldom voluntarily pay damages. A freezing injunction is often sought together with a search order[3] and a disclosure order[4].

1　As to the making of applications without notice see PARA 433 text and note 1.
2　CPR 25.1(1)(f). Such injunctions are known as 'freezing injunctions'; they were formerly known as 'Mareva' injunctions, after *Mareva Compania Naviera SA v International Bulkcarriers SA, The Mareva* [1980] 1 All ER 213n, [1975] 2 Lloyd's Rep 509, CA, but now fall within the scope of CPR Pt 25. A party may also be directed to provide information about relevant property or assets which are or may be the subject of an application for a freezing injunction: CPR 25.1(1)(g). For forms of the freezing injunction see *Practice Direction—Interim Injunctions* PD25A. As to CPR Pt 25 see CIVIL PROCEDURE vol 11 (2009) PARA 315 et seq.
3　As to search orders see PARA 434.
4　As to disclosure orders see PARA 435.

439. Summary judgment. Summary judgment is available in cases involving passing off and infringement of a registered trade mark in accordance with general principles[1]. In general it will be easier to show that there is no real prospect of success in a case of infringement than in a case of passing off, as in most infringement cases the claimant's title will be effectively beyond challenge and there may be little dispute about the nature of the defendant's acts[2].

1　See CPR Pt 24; and CIVIL PROCEDURE vol 11 (2009) PARA 524 et seq.
2　See *Sony Corpn v Anand (No 2)* [1982] FSR 200 (where the plaintiff was content to take an inquiry as to damages for infringement, leaving his other monetary claims (for passing off and infringement of copyright) until after the trial of the main action). For an example of summary judgment in a trade mark case see *Origin Natural Resources Inc v Origin Clothing Ltd* [1995] FSR 280; but see *Bolton Pharmaceutical Co 100 Ltd v Doncaster Pharmaceuticals Group Ltd* [2006] EWCA Civ 661, [2006] All ER (D) 289 (May), sub nom *Doncaster Pharmaceuticals Group Ltd v Bolton Pharmaceutical Co 100 Ltd* [2007] FSR 63 (summary judgment must be confined to appropriate cases).

(6) OTHER COURT CLAIMS

(i) Claims for a Declaration of Non-infringement and in Respect of Groundless Threats

440. In general. A claim may be brought for a declaration of non-infringement of a registered trade mark under the court's inherent jurisdiction where the defendant has asserted a contrary right or formulated an adverse claim[1]. There are no special procedural rules applicable to such claims, which are essentially claims for infringement in reverse[2].

A claim may also be brought in relation to groundless threats of infringement proceedings seeking a declaration that the threats are unjustifiable, an injunction against the continuance of the threats, and damages in respect of any loss sustained as a result of the threats[3]. There are no special procedural rules applicable to such claims[4].

1　See *L'Oréal (UK) Ltd v Johnson & Johnson* [2000] FSR 686, [2000] IP & T 789.

2   Since the burden of proof is on the claimant, however, the claimant may fail for want of proof that his acts do not infringe: see *Point Solutions Ltd v Focus Business Solutions Ltd* [2007] EWCA Civ 14, [2007] All ER (D) 160 (Jan) (a copyright case).

3   Ie under the Trade Marks Act 1994 s 21: see PARAS 107–109.

4   Note, however, that once the claimant proves a threat, the burden of justifying that threat by showing that the claimant has or would infringe falls on the defendant: see the Trade Marks Act 1994 s 21(3); and PARA 108.

(ii) Claims for Revocation, Declaration of Invalidity and Rectification

441. In general. An application for revocation, for a declaration of invalidity or for rectification of the register[1] in relation to a United Kingdom registered trade mark, or an application for revocation or a declaration of invalidity of the protection of a protected international trade mark (UK)[2], may be made to the court[3] by any person[4]. A claim form relating to such a claim may be served on the proprietor:

(1)   at the address for service[5] given in the United Kingdom register, provided that the address is within the jurisdiction[6]; or

(2)   in accordance with the relevant rules[7] at the address for service given in the United Kingdom register or the register of the Office for Harmonisation in the Internal Market[8].

Where a claim is made for any of these remedies which would affect an entry in the register, the claimant must at the same time as serving the other parties serve a copy of the claim form and any accompanying documents on the registrar[9].

The normal rules as to disclosure and evidence apply to claims for revocation, declarations of invalidity and rectification.

Where an order of the court affects the validity of an entry in the register, the court and the party in whose favour the order is made must serve a copy of the order on the registrar within 14 days[10]. Where the order is made is favour of more than one party, a copy must be served on such party as the court directs[11].

1   As to these applications and the circumstances in which they are appropriate see PARAS 98–105; as to the additional grounds for revocation or of invalidity of a collective mark see PARAS 146–147; and as to the additional grounds for revocation or invalidity of a certification mark see PARAS 157–158.

2   See the Trade Marks (International Registration) Order 2008, SI 2008/2206, art 3; and PARAS 12, 98–101, 103, 378. As to the meaning of 'protected international trade mark (UK)' see PARA 12 note 8.

3   As to the meaning of 'the court' see PARA 331.

4   Trade Marks Act 1994 s 46(4) (revocation), s 47(3) (declaration of invalidity), s 64(2) (rectification). Except in certain circumstances, the applicant may also bring the claim before the registrar: see PARA 378. As from 1 October 2007, so much of s 47(3) as provides that any person may make an application for a declaration of invalidity has effect subject to the Trade Marks (Relative Grounds) Order 2007, SI 2007/1976, art 5 (see PARA 103, notes 5, 8): art 5(3). As to the meaning of 'any person' see PARA 378 text and note 3.

5   As to the provision of an address for service see PARA 339.

6   See CPR 63.14(2)(a).

7   Ie CPR 6.32(1), CPR 6.33(1) or CPR 6.33(2).

8   See CPR 63.14(2)(b). As to the Office for Harmonisation in the Internal Market see PARA 163 et seq.

9   See CPR 63.14(3). As to the registrar's appearance in such proceedings see PARA 443. As to the registrar see PARA 19.

10   *Practice Direction—Intellectual Property Claims* PD63 para 20.1, applying para 14.1.

11   *Practice Direction—Intellectual Property Claims* PD63 para 20.1, applying para 14.2.

442.   Registrar's power to apply for declaration of invalidity.   In the case of bad faith in the registration of a trade mark[1], the registrar[2] may himself apply to the court[3] for a declaration of invalidity of the registration[4].

1   As to the requirements for registration see PARA 39 et seq; as to bad faith see PARA 53; and as to the procedure on the application see PARA 334 et seq. As to the meaning of 'trade mark' see PARA 41.
2   As to the registrar see PARA 19.
3   As to the meaning of 'the court' see PARA 331.
4   Trade Marks Act 1994 s 47(4). There seems to be no express power of the registrar to apply for rectification in relation to other matters affecting the register. Under the Trade Marks Act 1938 s 32(3) (repealed) the registrar's power to apply in case of fraud extended not only to registration but also to assignment and transmission. As to the meaning of 'registration' see PARA 21 note 2.

443.   Registrar's appearance in proceedings involving the register.   In proceedings before the court[1] involving an application for:

(1)   the revocation of the registration of a trade mark[2];
(2)   a declaration of the invalidity of the registration of a trade mark[3]; or
(3)   the rectification of the register[4],

the registrar[5] is entitled to appear and be heard, and must appear if so directed by the court[6].

Unless otherwise directed by the court, the registrar may instead of appearing submit to the court a statement in writing signed by him, giving particulars of:

(a)   any proceedings before him in relation to the matter in issue;
(b)   the grounds of any decision given by him affecting it;
(c)   the practice of the Intellectual Property Office ('IPO')[7] in like cases; or
(d)   such matters relevant to the issues and within his knowledge as registrar as he thinks fit,

and the statement is deemed to form part of the evidence in the proceedings[8].

Anything which the registrar is or may be authorised or required to do under the above provisions may be done on his behalf by a duly authorised officer[9].

1   As to the meaning of 'the court' see PARA 331.
2   As to the revocation of the registration of a trade mark see PARAS 98 et seq, 378 et seq; as to the additional grounds for revocation of a collective mark see PARA 146; and as to the additional grounds for revocation of a certification mark see PARA 157.
3   As to the invalidity of the registration of a trade mark see PARAS 102 et seq, 378 et seq; as to the additional ground of invalidity of a collective mark see PARA 147; and as to the additional ground of invalidity of a certification mark see PARA 158.
4   As to rectification of the register see PARAS 105, 378 et seq.
5   As to the registrar see PARA 19.
6   Trade Marks Act 1994 s 74(1).
7   As to the Intellectual Property Office (an operating name of the Patent Office) see PARA 16 note 2.
8   Trade Marks Act 1994 s 74(2).
9   Trade Marks Act 1994 s 74(3).

(iii)   Claims for Delivery Up and Disposal

444.   Statutory power to order delivery up of infringing goods etc.   The proprietor of a registered trade mark[1] may apply to the court[2] for an order for the delivery up to him, or such other person as the court may direct, of any infringing goods[3], material[4] or articles[5] which a person has in his possession, custody or control in the course of a business[6]. An application may not, however, be made after the end of the period after which the remedy of delivery up is not available[7]; and no order may be made unless the court also makes, or it appears to the court that there are grounds for making, an order[8] as to the disposal of infringing goods etc[9].

A person to whom any infringing goods, material or articles are delivered up in pursuance of an order under these provisions[10] must, if an order as to the disposal of infringing goods etc[11] is not made, retain them pending the making of such an order, or the decision not to make such an order[12].

Nothing in the above provisions affects any other power of the court[13].

1   As to the meaning of references to the proprietor of a registered trade mark in the provisions relating to infringement see the Trade Marks Act 1994 s 31(1), (2); and PARA 401 text and note 5. As to the meaning of 'registered trade mark' see PARA 111. These provisions equally apply to protected international trade marks (UK): see the Trade Marks (International Registration) Order 2008, SI 2008/2206, art 3; and PARA 12.
2   As to the meaning of 'the court' see PARA 331.
3   As to the meaning of 'infringing goods' see PARA 133.
4   As to the meaning of 'infringing material' see PARA 133.
5   As to the meaning of 'infringing articles' see PARA 133.
6   Trade Marks Act 1994 s 16(1). As to the meaning of 'business' see PARA 34 note 3. As to the period after which the remedy of delivery up is not available see PARA 445; and as to disposal of infringing goods etc see PARA 446. The proprietor of a registered trade mark must notify any exclusive licensee before applying for an order under s 16: see s 31(7); and PARA 401.
    Section 16 applies to infringing goods, material or articles whether made before, on or after 31 October 1994: s 105, Sch 3 para 5.
    There is no specific requirement in s 16(1) that the person against whom an application is made is an infringer. It is possession, custody or control of infringing goods in the course of a business which suffices. Thus a carrier or warehouseman, for example, could be made the subject of an application under s 16. An application under s 16 may be made at the same time as an application under s 19 (see PARA 446): *Miller Brewing Co v Mersey Docks and Harbour Co* [2003] EWHC 1606 (Ch), [2004] IP & T 542, [2004] FSR 81.
7   Ie the end of the period specified in the Trade Marks Act 1994 s 18: see PARA 445.
8   Ie an order under the Trade Marks Act 1994 s 19: see PARA 446.
9   Trade Marks Act 1994 s 16(2). See also note 6.
10 Ie an order under the Trade Marks Act 1994 s 16.
11 See note 8.
12 Trade Marks Act 1994 s 16(3). See also note 6.
13 Trade Marks Act 1994 s 16(4). See also note 6.

445.   Period after which statutory remedy of delivery up not available.   An application for an order for delivery up of infringing goods, material or articles[1] may not be made after the end of the period of six years from:

(1)   in the case of infringing goods[2], the date on which the trade mark[3] was applied to the goods or their packaging[4];

(2)   in the case of infringing material[5], the date on which the trade mark was applied to the material[6]; or

(3)   in the case of infringing articles[7], the date on which they were made[8],

except as mentioned in the provisions described below[9].

If during the whole or part of that period the proprietor of the registered trade mark[10] is under a disability[11] or is prevented by fraud or concealment from discovering the facts entitling him to apply for an order, an application may be made at any time before the end of the period of six years from the date on which he ceased to be under a disability or, as the case may be, could with reasonable diligence have discovered those facts[12].

1   Ie an order under the Trade Marks Act 1994 s 16: see PARA 444.
2   As to the meaning of 'infringing goods' see PARA 133.
3   As to the meaning of 'trade mark' see PARA 41.
4   Trade Marks Act 1994 s 18(1)(a).

5   As to the meaning of 'infringing material' see PARA 133.
6   Trade Marks Act 1994 s 18(1)(b).
7   As to the meaning of 'infringing articles' see PARA 133.
8   Trade Marks Act 1994 s 18(1)(c).
9   Trade Marks Act 1994 s 18(1). See the text and notes 10–12. As to disposal of infringing goods etc see PARA 446.
10 As to the meaning of references to the proprietor of a registered trade mark in the provisions relating to infringement see the Trade Marks Act 1994 s 31(1), (2); and PARA 401 note 5. As to the meaning of 'registered trade mark' see PARA 111.
11 For these purposes, 'disability' has the same meaning as in the Limitation Act 1980 (see s 38(2); and LIMITATION PERIODS vol 68 (2008) PARA 1170): Trade Marks Act 1994 s 18(3).
12 Trade Marks Act 1994 s 18(2).

446.   Order as to disposal of infringing goods etc. Where infringing goods[1], material[2] or articles[3] have been delivered up in pursuance of an order for delivery up[4], an application may be made to the court[5]:

(1)   for an order that they be destroyed or forfeited to such person as the court may think fit[6]; or

(2)   for a decision that no such order should be made[7].

In considering what order, if any, should be made, the court must consider whether other remedies available in an action for infringement[8] of the registered trade mark[9] would be adequate to compensate the proprietor[10] and any licensee[11] and protect their interests[12].

Provision must be made by rules of court as to the service of notice on persons having an interest in the goods, material or articles[13], and any such person is entitled:

(a)   to appear in proceedings for a disposal order, whether or not he was served with notice; and

(b)   to appeal against any order made, whether or not he appeared,

and an order does not take effect until the end of the period within which notice of an appeal may be given or, if before the end of that period notice of appeal is duly given, until the final determination or abandonment of the proceedings on the appeal[14].

Where there is more than one person interested in the goods, material or articles, the court must make such order as it thinks just[15].

If the court decides that no disposal order should be made, the person in whose possession, custody or control the goods, material or articles were before being delivered up is entitled to their return[16].

1   As to the meaning of 'infringing goods' see PARA 133.
2   As to the meaning of 'infringing material' see PARA 133.
3   As to the meaning of 'infringing articles' see PARA 133.
4   Ie an order under the Trade Marks Act 1994 s 16: see PARA 444.
5   Trade Marks Act 1994 s 19(1). As to the meaning of 'the court' see PARA 331.
6   Trade Marks Act 1994 s 19(1)(a).
7   Trade Marks Act 1994 s 19(1)(b).
8   As to the meaning of 'infringement' see PARA 66 note 4. As to the acts which amount to infringement, if done without the consent of the proprietor, see the Trade Marks Act 1994 s 10; and PARA 68 et seq.
9   As to the meaning of 'registered trade mark' see PARA 111.
10 As to the meaning of references to the proprietor of a registered trade mark in the provisions relating to infringement see the Trade Marks Act 1994 s 31(1), (2); and PARA 401 text and note 5.
11 As to the meaning of 'licensee' see PARA 119 note 7. As to licences see PARAS 119–120.
12 Trade Marks Act 1994 s 19(2). Section 19(2) applies in relation to an authorised user of a registered collective mark or a registered certification mark as in relation to a licensee of a trade mark: see ss 49(2), 50(2), Sch 1 para 11(b), Sch 2 para 13(b); and PARAS 145, 156.

13 For these purposes, references to a person having an interest in goods, material or articles include any person in whose favour an order could be made under the Trade Marks Act 1994 s 19; the Registered Designs Act 1949 s 24D (see PATENTS AND REGISTERED DESIGNS vol 79 (2008) PARA 767); the Copyright, Designs and Patents Act 1988 s 114, s 204 or s 231 (see COPYRIGHT vol 23 (2013) PARAS 969, 1082, 1259); or the Community Designs Regulations 2005, SI 2005/2339, reg 1C (see PATENTS AND REGISTERED DESIGNS vol 79 (2008) PARA 779): Trade Marks Act 1994 s 19(6) (amended by SI 2006/1028).

14 Trade Marks Act 1994 s 19(3). Where an application is made under s 19, the applicant must serve the claim form or application notice on all identifiable persons having an interest in the goods, materials or articles within the meaning of s 19 (see note 13): see *Practice Direction—Intellectual Property Claims* PD63 para 19.1.

15 Trade Marks Act 1994 s 19(4).

16 Trade Marks Act 1994 s 19(5).

6. HALLMARKS, ARMS, EMBLEMS AND BUSINESS NAMES

(1) HALLMARKING

(i) The Legislation

447. History. From a very early date the standard and marking of gold and silver plate have been enforced by statute[1]. In 1300 it was ordained that no goldsmith of England or in the King's dominion should make any vessel, jewel or anything of gold or silver except of a certain alloy[2] and should not part with possession until it was assayed and marked by the wardens of the goldsmith craft in London[3]. The marks commonly known as hallmarks consist of the maker's or sponsor's mark and the assay marks denoting the standard, place and year of assay[4].

1 The earliest statute is an ordinance of 22 Hen 3 ('De auro fabricando in Civitate Londoniarum') (1238): see the Report of the Departmental Committee on Hallmarking (Cmnd 663) (1959) para 22.
2 The ordinance 28 Edw 1 c 20 (Vessels of gold, assaying etc) (1300) (repealed) laid down 'the touch of Paris' (ie 19½ carats) as the standard for gold, and the sterling standard (ie 925 parts per 1,000) as the standard for silver. For a summary of the history of the legislation of hallmarking see the Report of the Departmental Committee on Hallmarking (Cmnd 663) (1959) para 20 et seq. See also *Westwood v Cann* [1952] 2 QB 887, [1952] 2 All ER 349, CA.
3 See 28 Edw 1 c 20 (Vessels of gold, assaying etc) (1300) (repealed).
4 See the Report of the Departmental Committee on Hallmarking (Cmnd 663) (1959) paras 104–110. As to sponsor's marks see PARA 460; and as to assay marks see PARA 450 note 13.

448. Current legislation. Following the Report of the Departmental Committee on Hallmarking[1] the substantial body of old statutes concerned with hallmarking were repealed and replaced by a new code contained in the Hallmarking Act 1973. That Act and the orders made under it form the current legislation[2]. That Act expressly relates only to the hallmarking of articles of gold, silver or platinum[3]; but has additionally been applied by order to palladium[4].

A number of the enforcement provisions of the Trade Descriptions Act 1968[5] are applied in relation to the enforcement of the Hallmarking Act 1973[6]. In addition the Hallmarking Act 1973 may be enforced under the Enterprise Act 2002 in certain circumstances[7].

Any local statutory provision[8] which was inconsistent with any provision of the Hallmarking Act 1973 ceased to have effect[9].

Provision is made for the Secretary of State to make regulations and orders for purposes under the Hallmarking Act 1973[10].

1 Ie the Report of the Departmental Committee on Hallmarking (Cmnd 663) (1959).
2 The Hallmarking Act 1973 came into operation on 1 January 1975 except for s 13, Sch 4 (see PARA 464) which came into operation on 1 January 1974: s 24(2). Certain functions under the Hallmarking Act 1973 are 'relevant functions' for the purposes of the Regulatory Enforcement and Sanctions Act 2008 s 4, Sch 3: see LOCAL GOVERNMENT vol 69 (2009) PARA 733. Certain persons or indorsements mentioned in the Hallmarking Act 1973 are specified for the purposes of Regulatory Enforcement and Sanctions Act 2008 s 37, Schs 5, 6 (meaning of 'regulator' for the purposes of imposing civil sanctions): see ADMINISTRATIVE LAW.
3 As to the meaning of 'precious metal' see Hallmarking Act 1973 s 22(1); and PARA 450 note 9.
  The Secretary of State may by order, on the application of the British Hallmarking Council or of his own volition after consultation with the Council, apply provisions of the Hallmarking Act 1973 to any other metal and subject to amendments and adaptations: see s 17(1), (2); and for an order made under this provision see text and note 4.
  As to the Secretary of State see PARA 16. As to the British Hallmarking Council see PARA 464.

The Secretary of State may cause a local inquiry to be held in connection with the discharge of his functions under the Hallmarking Act 1973 or in any case where it appears to him to be expedient in connection with any matter arising under that Act or any of the functions of assay offices or the British Hallmarking Council: ss 20(1), 22(1). In relation to any inquiry so held the provisions of the Local Government Act 1972 s 250(2)–(5) (evidence and costs at local inquiries: see LOCAL GOVERNMENT vol 69 (2009) PARA 105) apply as if the inquiry were held in pursuance of s 250(1) save that s 250(4) (costs of department) applies only in a case where the Secretary of State so directs: Hallmarking Act 1973 s 20(1)(a). The person appointed to hold such an inquiry must report in writing to the Secretary of State, who must publish the report together with such observations, if any, as he thinks fit: see s 20(2). For these purposes, 'functions' includes powers and duties: s 22(1). As to the meaning of 'assay office' see PARA 451.

A local inquiry held under s 20(1) is designated for the purposes of the Tribunals and Inquiries Act 1992 s 16(2) (see ADMINISTRATIVE LAW vol 1(1) (2001 Reissue) PARA 15): see the Tribunals and Inquiries (Discretionary Inquiries) Order 1975, SI 1975/1379, art 3, Schedule Pt II para 104.

4 Hallmarking Act 1973 (Application to Palladium) Order 2009, SI 2009/2040, art 2.

5 As to the Trade Descriptions Act 1968 generally see CONSUMER PROTECTION vol 21 (2011) PARA 510 et seq.

6 See the Hallmarking Act 1973 s 9; and PARa 465.

7 See PARA 465.

8 For these purposes, 'local statutory provision' means a provision of a local Act, including an Act confirming a provisional order, or a provision of a public general Act passed with respect only to any particular locality, or a provision of an instrument made under any such local or public general Act or of an instrument in the nature of a local enactment made under any other Act, or a provision of a charter or franchise: Hallmarking Act 1973 s 22(1).

9 Hallmarking Act 1973 s 18(1). The Secretary of State may on the application of an assay office or of his own volition, by order repeal or amend any local statutory provision where it appears to him that that provision is inconsistent with, or has become unnecessary in consequence of, any provision of the Hallmarking Act 1973: s 18(2). Before making such an order the Secretary of State must consult with any person or body representative of persons who appear to him to be concerned: s 18(3). Such an order may contain such transitional, supplemental or incidental provisions as appear to the Secretary of State to be expedient: s 18(4). At the date at which this volume states the law no such order had been made.

10 See the Hallmarking Act 1973 s 21(1)–(4). An order may not be made under s 16 (see PARA 452) unless a draft of the order has been approved by a resolution of each House of Parliament (s 21(5)); and any statutory instrument containing an order under s 14 (see PARA 464) is subject to annulment in pursuance of a resolution of either House of Parliament (s 21(6)).

(ii) Hallmarks and Assay Offices

449. Prohibited descriptions of unhallmarked articles. Any person who, in the course of a trade or business[1]:

(1) applies[2] to an unhallmarked article[3] a description[4] indicating that it is wholly or partly made of gold, silver, platinum or palladium[5]; or

(2) supplies, or offers to supply[6], an unhallmarked article to which such a description is applied[7],

is guilty of an offence[8] unless, in the case of a description, it is a permitted description[9] or, in the case of an article, it is exempt[10].

In any proceedings for such an offence it is a defence for the person charged to prove that, in reliance on information supplied by another person, he believed that the article concerned was one which was exempt from hallmarking[11] and that he could not with reasonable diligence have ascertained that it was not such an article[12].

1 'In the course of trade or business' is defined neither in the Hallmarking Act 1973 nor in the Trade Descriptions Act 1968 to which many of the provisions of the Hallmarking Act 1973 refer. Cf the Fair Trading Act 1973 s 137(2) and the Enterprise Act 2002 s 183(1) ('business' includes a professional practice and includes any other undertaking which is carried on for gain or reward or which is an undertaking in the course of which goods or services are supplied otherwise than free of charge: COMPETITION vol 18 (2009) PARA 314). Clearly the trade or

business need not be retail, nor need the offender's trade or business be that of conducting the particular transaction concerned: *Havering London Borough Council v Stevenson* [1970] 3 All ER 609, [1970] 1 WLR 1375, DC (car hire firm selling its used cars held to be doing so in the course of its trade or business as a car hire firm); cf *Davies v Sumner* [1984] 1 WLR 405, DC (affd [1984] 3 All ER 831, [1984] 1 WLR 1301, HL) (false representation by a self-employed courier as to the mileage of a car sold by him held not to be a false trade description). The trade or business need not be full-time: cf *Stevenson v Beverley Bentinck Ltd* [1976] 2 All ER 606, [1976] 1 WLR 483, CA (meaning of 'private purchaser' in the Hire-Purchase Act 1964); *Re Griffin, ex p Board of Trade* (1890) 60 LJQB 235 at 237, CA, per Lord Esher MR; *Abernethie v AM and J Kleiman Ltd* [1970] 1 QB 10, [1969] 2 All ER 790, CA (meaning of 'business' in the Landlord and Tenant Act 1954 Pt II (ss 23–46): see LANDLORD AND TENANT vol 63 (2012) PARA 823). On the other hand some degree of regularity is required (*Davies v Sumner* above); cf *R & B Customs Brokers Co Ltd v United Dominions Trust Ltd* [1988] 1 All ER 847, [1988] 1 WLR 321, CA (meaning of 'in the course of a business' in the Unfair Contract Terms Act 1977 s 12: see CONSUMER PROTECTION vol 21 (2011) PARA 431); *Pensher Security Door Co Ltd v Sunderland City Council* [2000] RPC 249, CA (meaning of 'in the course of business' in the Copyright, Patents and Designs Act 1988 s 23: see COPYRIGHT vol 23 (2013) PARA 877); but see *Stevenson v Rogers* [1999] QB 1028, [1999] 1 All ER 613, CA ('in the course of business' in the Sale of Goods Act 1979 s 14(2) (see SALE OF GOODS AND SUPPLY OF SERVICES vol 91 (2012) PARA 79) covered any sale by a business). The words cover the business of buying as well as that of selling (*Fletcher v Budgen* [1974] 2 All ER 1243, [1974] 1 WLR 1056, DC) and are to be treated as wide in scope (*Fletcher v Budgen*; and see *Fletcher v Sledmore* [1973] RTR 371, DC). They do not, however, cover cases where false trade descriptions are applied to goods otherwise than in association with a contract for the sale or supply of goods (*Wickens Motors (Gloucester) Ltd v Hall* [1972] 3 All ER 759, sub nom *Hall v Wickens Motors (Gloucester) Ltd* [1972] 1 WLR 1418, DC (false trade description applied well after sale held not to be applied in the course of a trade or business)), but it is not necessary that the description is applied by a directly contracting party (*Fletcher v Sledmore* above).

2   The Trade Descriptions Act 1968 s 4 (meaning of 'applies' in relation to the applying of a trade description: see CONSUMER PROTECTION vol 21 (2011) PARA 515) applies for the purposes of the Hallmarking Act 1973 s 1: s 1(7)(b). A trade description or statement published in any newspaper, book or periodical or in any film or sound or television broadcast or in any programme included in any programme service within the meaning of the Broadcasting Act 1990 (see BROADCASTING vol 4 (2011) PARA 507), other than a sound or television broadcasting service is not deemed to be a description applied in the course of a trade or business unless it is or forms part of an advertisement: Trade Descriptions Act 1968 s 39(2) (amended by the Broadcasting Act 1990 Sch 20 para 11); applied by the Hallmarking Act 1973 s 1(9) (saved in respect of that application by SI 2008/1277, which in other respects repealed the Trade Descriptions Act 1968 s 39(2)). 'Advertisement' includes a catalogue, a circular and a price list: Hallmarking Act 1973 s 1(7)(a). As to advertisements see also note 8.

3   As to the meaning of 'unhallmarked article' see PARA 456.

4   Where a description relates to the fineness of gold or silver, the Hallmarking Act 1973 Sch 1 Pt III (paras 1–3) (use of the words 'carats', 'sterling' and 'Britannia': see PARA 459) applies for construing that description: s 1(5). As to the meaning of 'fineness' see PARA 450.

5   Hallmarking Act 1973 s 1(1)(a) (amended by SI 2009/2040).

6   For these purposes, a person exposing articles for supply, or having articles in his possession for supply, 'offers to supply' them: Hallmarking Act 1973 s 1(7)(c).

7   Hallmarking Act 1973 s 1(1)(b).

8   Hallmarking Act 1973 s 1(1). The offence under s 1(1)(b) (see head (2) in the text) does not require proof of mens rea: see *Chilvers v Rayner* [1984] 1 All ER 843, [1984] 1 WLR 328, DC. As to offences generally see PARA 466. The Secretary of State may by order: (1) prescribe any cases or circumstances in which the Hallmarking Act 1973 s 1(1) is, or is not, to apply; and (2) add to, amend or repeal all or any of the provisions of Sch 1 Pt I (paras 1, 2) (see PARA 457), Sch 1 Pt II (paras 1–18) (see PARA 458) or Sch 1 Pt III (paras 1–3) (see PARA 459); and (3) make any consequential amendments in s 1: see Sch 1 Pt IV para 1(1), (2). As to the orders made, and as to the articles thus exempted, see PARA 458; and as to the making of orders generally see PARA 448. As to the Secretary of State see PARA 16.

    Where in an advertisement a description is used in relation to any class of articles, the description is to be taken as referring to all articles of the class, whether or not in existence at the time the advertisement is published: (1) for the purpose of determining whether an offence has been committed under s 1(1)(a) (see head (1) in the text); and (2) where articles of the class are supplied or offered to be supplied by a person publishing or displaying the advertisement, also for the purpose of determining whether an offence has been committed under s 1(1)(b) (see head (2) in the text): s 1(8)(a), (b). In determining whether any goods are of a class to which a trade description used in an advertisement relates, regard is to be had not only to the form and content of the advertisement but also to the time, place, manner and frequency of its publication and all other matters making it likely or unlikely that a person to whom the goods are supplied would think of the goods as belonging to the class in relation to which the trade description is used in the advertisement: Trade Descriptions Act 1968 s 5(3); applied by the Hallmarking Act 1973 s 1(8).

In proceedings for an offence under the Hallmarking Act 1973 committed by the publication of an advertisement, it is a defence for the person charged to prove that he is a person whose business it is to publish or arrange for the publication of advertisements and that he received the advertisement for publication in the ordinary course of business and did not know and had no reason to suspect that its publication would amount to an offence under that Act: s 8, Sch 3 para 5.

9   Hallmarking Act 1973 s 1(2). See Sch 1 Pt I; and PARA 457.
10   Hallmarking Act 1973 s 1(3). See Sch 1 Pt II; and PARA 458.
11   Ie by virtue of the Hallmarking Act 1973 Sch 1 Pt II: see PARA 458.
12   Hallmarking Act 1973 Sch 3 para 6.

450.   Approved hallmarks. 'Approved hallmarks' means:

(1)   marks struck by an assay office[1] in the United Kingdom[2], whether before, on or after 1 January 1975, under the law for the time being in force[3];

(2)   marks struck outside the United Kingdom by an assay office[4];

(3)   marks struck by the Wardens and Commonalty of Goldsmiths of the City of Dublin before 1 April 1923[5];

(4)   convention hallmarks[6]; or

(5)   EEA hallmarks[7].

Subject to the relevant statutory provisions[8], any article of precious metal[9] which is submitted to an assay office for hallmarking and which upon assay is found in all its parts to be of a standard of fineness[10] not less than the minimum fineness[11] for that precious metal must[12] be struck by that assay office with the approved hallmarks[13]. Hallmarking is not permitted, however, unless the assay office is of opinion that the use of any solder or adhesive in the article is not excessive and that solder complies with the specified requirements[14]. An article comprised of more than one precious metal part must be struck with the approved hallmarks only if the assay office is of the opinion that a person will be able to determine, when the article is hallmarked, which part is made of which precious metal[15].

If an assay office has refused to hallmark an article submitted to it for hallmarking and the person submitting the article has referred the matter to the British Hallmarking Council in writing, the Council must consider the case, and, if it is of the opinion that the assay office was acting unreasonably in refusing to hallmark the article, it must direct the assay office to strike the article with the approved hallmarks[16].

After consulting the Council and such other persons as he thinks fit[17], the Secretary of State may make regulations wholly or partly varying, supplementing or replacing the statutory provisions as to approved hallmarks and the procedures relating to them[18].

Any dealer[19] must keep exhibited at all times, in a conspicuous position in a part of his premises to which those with whom he deals are commonly admitted, a notice in terms approved and in a form supplied by the Council describing such approved hallmarks and including such explanatory matter as the Council thinks fit[20]. It is an offence for any dealer to fail to exhibit or keep exhibited a notice required to be so exhibited[21].

1   As to the meaning of 'assay office' see PARA 451.
2   As to the meaning of 'United Kingdom' see PARA 3 note 2.
3   Hallmarking Act 1973 s 2(1)(a).
4   Hallmarking Act 1973 s 2(1)(aa) (added by SI 2013/251). Certain modifications are made of provisions of the Hallmarking Act 1973 s 4, Sch 2 and Sch 5 in order to enable assay offices to strike hallmarks outside the United Kingdom and for such hallmarks to be treated as if they were had been struck in the United Kingdom: see s 4A (added by SI 2013/251).
5   Hallmarking Act 1973 s 2(1)(b).
6   Hallmarking Act 1973 s 2(1)(c), (2). As to the meaning of 'convention hallmarks' see PARA 454.
7   Hallmarking Act 1973 s 2(1)(d), (2) (s 2(1)(d) added, and s 2(2) amended, by SI 1998/2978). As to the meaning of 'EEA hallmarks' see PARA 455.
8   Ie subject to the Hallmarking Act 1973 s 4, Sch 2: see note 11.
9   For these purposes, 'precious metal', in relation to any article, means gold, silver or platinum, or any other metal to which the provisions of the Hallmarking Act 1973 are applied by an order under s 17: s 22(1). The Act has been applied additionally to palladium: see PARA 448.
10 For these purposes, 'fineness', in relation to any precious metal, means the number of parts by weight of that fine metal in 1,000 parts by weight of alloy: Hallmarking Act 1973 s 22(1). 'Standard of fineness' means any one of the standards of fineness specified in Sch 2 Pt I para 2 col 2 (see note 13); and reference to an article as being of one of those standards means that the article is of a fineness in all its parts of not less than that standard: s 22(1).
11 For these purposes, 'minimum fineness', in relation to any precious metal, means the lowest standard of fineness specified for a precious metal, namely for gold the standard of 375, for silver the standard of 800, for platinum the standard of 850, and for palladium the standard of 500: Hallmarking Act 1973 s 22(1) (definition amended by SI 1998/2978; and SI 2009/2040). See also PARA 459.
12 In relation to business carried on outside the United Kingdom by an assay office (see note 4) 'must' should be read as 'may': Hallmarking Act 1973 s 4(1) modified by s 4A(2) (s 4A added by SI 2013/251).
13 Hallmarking Act 1973 s 4(1). As respects articles comprised of a single precious metal, the marks to be struck are the assay office mark, the standard mark, the pictorial mark, the date letter and any additional mark directed under Sch 2: see s 4(1)(a) (amended by SI 1998/2978). In relation to business carried on outside the United Kingdom by an assay office (see note 4) the reference to an assay office mark is to be taken as a reference to the mark approved by the British Hallmarking Council for such use: Hallmarking Act 1973 s 4(1)(a) modified by s 4A(2) (s 4A added by SI 2013/251).
    The pictorial mark, the date letter and the optional additional mark may be struck only if a request to that effect is made by the person who submits the article to the assay office, but the absence of such mark does not in itself render the article unhallmarked: Hallmarking Act 1973 s 4(2) (substituted by SI 1998/2978). See also Case C-293/93 *Straffesag v Houtwipper* [1995] All ER (EC) 163, [1994] ECR I-4249, ECJ; and PARA 455.
    The details of these marks are set out in the Hallmarking Act 1973 Sch 2 Pt I (paras 1–5) (substituted by SI 1998/2978), and are as follows:
    (1)   The assay office mark. This is a leopard's head for the London assay office; a castle for the Edinburgh assay office; an anchor for the Birmingham assay office; and a rose for the Sheffield assay office (see the Hallmarking Act 1973 Sch 2 Pt I para 1 (as so substituted)). This does not apply in relation to business carried on outside the United Kingdom by an assay office (see note 4): s 4A(3)(a) (as so added).
    (2)   The standard mark. This depends on the standard of fineness and is: (a) in relation to gold: (i) 375 for a standard of fineness of 375; (ii) 585 for a standard of fineness of 585; (iii) 750 for a standard of fineness of 750; (iv) 916 for a standard of fineness of 916.6; (v) 990 for a standard of fineness of 990; and (vi) 999 for a standard of fineness of 999; (b) in relation to silver: (i) 800 for a standard of fineness of 800; (ii) 925 for a standard of fineness of 925; (iii) 958 for a standard of fineness of 958.4; and (iv) 999 for a standard of fineness of 999; (c) in relation to platinum: (i) 850 for a standard of fineness of 850; (ii) 900 for a standard of fineness of 900; (iii) 950 for a standard of fineness of 950; and (iv) 999 for a standard of fineness of 999; and (d) in relation to palladium: (i) 500 for a standard of fineness of 500; (ii) 950 for a standard of fineness of 950; and (iii) 999 for a standard of fineness of 999; (see Sch 2 Pt I para 2 (Sch 2 Pt I as so substituted; and paras 2, 3 further amended by SI 2009/2040)).
    (3)   The optional pictorial mark. This is: (a) a crown for gold; (b) a lion passant or, in relation to the Edinburgh assay office, a lion rampant for silver, or in the alternative the figure of Britannia for silver with a standard of fineness of 925, 958.4 or 999; (c) an orb

surmounted by a cross for platinum; (d) the head of Pallas Athene for palladium (see Sch 2 Pt I para 3 (as so substituted and amended)).

(4)   Optional date letter. Such distinct variable letter of the alphabet to denote the year in which the article is marked as may be for the time being directed in writing by the Council (Sch 2 Pt I para 4 (as so substituted)).

(5)   Optional additional mark. Such mark (if any) as may be for the time being directed in writing by the Council (Sch 2 Pt I para 5 (as so substituted)).

As respects articles comprised of two or more precious metals, marks are struck in accordance with Sch 2 Pt II (paras 6–15) (substituted by SI 2007/872): Hallmarking Act 1973 s 4(1)(b); and as respects articles comprised of precious metal and other materials marks are struck in accordance with Sch 2 Pt III (paras 16–19) (as so substituted): s 4(1)(c). Certain of those provisions are modified in relation to business carried on outside the United Kingdom by an assay office: see s 4A(3) (as so added).

As respects all such articles, marks must be struck in compliance with any directions given by the British Hallmarking Council pursuant to Sch 2 Pt IV para 20 (renumbered by SI 2007/872) with respect to any shield or other border by which any approved hallmark is to be enclosed: Hallmarking Act 1973 s 4(1). As to the British Hallmarking Council see PARA 464. As to the meaning of 'assay office' see PARA 451.

14   Hallmarking Act 1973 s 4(3)(a), (b) (amended by SI 1986/1757). No article may be struck with the approved hallmarks unless: (1) except in a case where the assay office otherwise permits, any solder used in an article of: (a) gold, is gold of a fineness not less than the standard of fineness of the article, save that solder used in any article (i) of a standard of fineness of 916.6 or above may be of a fineness not less than 750; and (ii) of filigree work or being a watch case and in either case of a standard of fineness of 750 may be of a fineness not less than 740; and (iii) of white gold of a standard of fineness of not less than 585 and not more than 750 may be of a fineness not less than 500; (b) silver, is silver of a fineness not less than 650; (c) platinum, is gold, silver, platinum or palladium or a combination of two or more thereof and is of a fineness or, as the case may be, of a combined fineness not less than the standard of fineness of the article; (d) palladium, is gold, solver, platinum or palladium or a combination of two or more thereof and is of a fineness or, as the case may be, of a combined fineness not less than the standard of fineness of the article; and (2) solder of a fineness less than the standard of fineness of the article or adhesive is used in a quantity not more than is necessary for joining parts of the article and is not used for strengthening, weighting, filling or otherwise: Hallmarking Act 1973 s 4(3)(b) (amended by SI 1986/1757; SI 1998/2978; and SI 2009/2040).

15   Hallmarking Act 1973 s 4(3A) (added by SI 2007/872).

16   Hallmarking Act 1973 s 4(5). It is the duty of an assay office to which such a direction has been given to comply with the direction: s 4(6).

17   As to the holding of a local inquiry see PARA 448.

18   See the Hallmarking Act 1973 s 4(7)(a), (b). As to the making of regulations generally see PARA 448.

At the date at which this volume states the law the Hallmarking (Approved Hallmarks) Regulations 1986, SI 1986/1757; the Hallmarking (Hallmarking Act Amendment) Regulations 1998, SI 1998/2978; and the Hallmarking Act 1973 (Amendment) Regulations 2007, SI 2007/872 (see the text and notes 1–14) had been made. As to the Secretary of State see PARA 16.

19   For these purposes, 'dealer' means a person engaged in the business of making, supplying, selling (including selling by auction) or exchanging articles of precious metal or in other dealings in such articles: Hallmarking Act 1973 s 22(1).

20   Hallmarking Act 1973 s 11(1). The Council may make a reasonable charge for the supply of any copy of a notice required to be exhibited: s 11(2).

21   Hallmarking Act 1973 s 11(1). As to offences see PARA 466.

451.   The assay offices.   'Assay office' means each of the following bodies[1]:

(1)   the Wardens and Commonalty of the Mystery of Goldsmiths of the City of London ('the London Assay Office');

(2)   the Incorporation of Goldsmiths of the City of Edinburgh ('the Edinburgh Assay Office');

(3)   the Guardians of the Standard of Wrought Plate in Birmingham ('the Birmingham Assay Office');

(4)   the Guardians of the Standard of Wrought Plate within the town of Sheffield ('the Sheffield Assay Office'),

and any other body duly authorised under any enactment, order, charter or franchise[2] for the assaying and hallmarking of precious metals[3].

The powers and duties of assay offices are prescribed by statute[4].

Nothing contained in the Hallmarking Act 1973 renders any assay office liable as respects any damage caused by it to any article in the reasonable exercise or, as the case may be, discharge of any of the powers and duties conferred or imposed upon it by that Act[5].

Her Majesty's Mint[6] may at any time and from time to time as thought fit in normal office hours visit any assay office for the purpose of inspecting the assay department of that office and of ascertaining and assessing the accuracy and efficiency of its methods and procedures of assay; and a report on the assay department of each assay office must be prepared once in every period of 14 months by the Queen's Assay Master and presented to the Deputy Master of Her Majesty's Mint, copies of such reports having first been sent to the British Hallmarking Council and the assay office concerned[7].

Every assay office has power to make charges for assaying and hallmarking articles of precious metals not exceeding, in the case of articles manufactured in, or intended for sale or supply in, the United Kingdom[8], such charges as are for the time being directed in writing by the British Hallmarking Council[9].

It is the duty of an assay office to comply with directions and regulations issued by the British Hallmarking Council[10].

1　Hallmarking Act 1973 s 22(1). References in the Hallmarking Act 1973 to an assay office include, as respects an assay office which is engaged in the business of an assay office and which carries on any other activity, reference to so much only of the undertaking of that assay office as relates wholly to its business as such an assay office and as may be certified in that behalf by that assay office: s 22(2).

2　This includes a body for the time being established under the Hallmarking Act 1973 s 16(1)(a) (see PARA 452 head (1)) and also, where the context so admits, a body which, whilst it has been so authorised at any time before or after the passing of the Hallmarking Act 1973, has since being so authorised been dissolved or has ceased business in such assaying and hallmarking: s 22(1). As to the meaning of 'precious metal' see PARA 450 note 9.

3　Hallmarking Act 1973 s 22(1).

4　See the text and notes 5–10; and PARAS 452–453.

5　Hallmarking Act 1973 s 15(2).

6　As to Her Majesty's Mint see FINANCIAL SERVICES AND INSTITUTIONS vol 49 (2008) PARA 1281.

7　Hallmarking Act 1973 s 15(1), Sch 5 para 3(1). If such assay methods, in the opinion of Her Majesty's Mint, are not of such a standard as will enable that assay office to report accurately on the fineness of any article, or articles, of precious metal, then Her Majesty's Mint must notify the British Hallmarking Council and the assay office forthwith and make to each of them such recommendations as appear requisite in relation to such assay methods; and the Council must consult with the assay office as to the action to be taken upon each such recommendation: Sch 5 para 3(2). As to the meaning of 'fineness' see PARA 450 note 10. As to the British Hallmarking Council see PARA 464.

　　Her Majesty's Mint is entitled to make a reasonable charge to each assay office in respect of the performance of its functions under Sch 5 para 3: Sch 5 para 3(3). As to the meaning of 'functions' see PARA 448 note 3.

8　As to the meaning of 'United Kingdom' see PARA 3 note 2.

9　Hallmarking Act 1973 s 12(1). The Secretary of State may, however, from time to time give to the Council and to assay offices such directions as he considers expedient in relation to charges made under s 12(1): s 12(1) proviso. Subject to s 12(1), every assay office has power to make for services and facilities provided by it such charges as it from time to time thinks fit: s 12(2). As to the power of the Council to set maximum charges which may be made by assay offices see PARA 464. As to the Secretary of State see PARA 16.

10　See the Hallmarking Act 1973 s 13(3); and PARA 464.

452.　Orders constituting, dissolving etc or conferring powers on assay offices.

The Secretary of State[1] may at any time by order[2]:

(1) on the application of the British Hallmarking Council[3], provide for the constitution of an assay office[4] at such place as may be specified in the order[5]; or

(2) on the application of the Council, provide for the closure and dissolution of any assay office or its amalgamation with another assay office[6]; or

(3) on the application of the London Assay Office, confer, vary or abolish duties or powers imposed or conferred on the assay office under any local statutory provision affecting its undertaking, and for that purpose repeal or amend any such provision[7];

(4) on the application of any of the Edinburgh, Birmingham or Sheffield Assay Offices vary or abolish duties or powers imposed or conferred on the assay office by any local statutory provision affecting its undertaking, and for that purpose repeal or amend any such provision or, on such an application, impose new duties on or confer new powers on, or make alterations or additions to or omissions from the constitution of, the assay office[8].

Provision is made as to the detailed procedure concerning consultation, submission of draft orders, publication, and the handling of objections to orders proposed to be made under the provisions described above[9].

1   As to the Secretary of State see PARA 16.
2   As to the procedure for making orders under this provision see the Hallmarking Act 1973 s 21(5). Any order so made may contain incidental, consequential and supplementary provisions: see s 16(3). As to the making of orders generally see PARA 448.
3   As to the British Hallmarking Council see PARA 464.
4   As to the meaning of 'assay office' see PARA 451.
5   Hallmarking Act 1973 s 16(1)(a).
6   Hallmarking Act 1973 s 16(1)(b).
7   Hallmarking Act 1973 s 16(1)(c).
8   Hallmarking Act 1973 s 16(1)(c) (retrospectively amended in its application to the Birmingham, Edinburgh and Sheffield Assay Offices by the Birmingham Assay Office Act 1995; the Edinburgh Assay Office Order Confirmation Act 1995; and the Sheffield Assay Office Act 1995). In exercise of the power so conferred the Secretary of State has made the Sheffield Assay Office Order 1978, SI 1978/639 (amended by SI 1991/1997; and SI 2008/948); the Edinburgh Assay Office Order 1979, SI 1979/1587 (amended by SI 1989/992; SI 1991/1997; SI 1993/2135; and SI 2008/948); and the Birmingham Assay Office Order 1989, SI 1989/900 (amended by SI 1991/1997; and SI 2008/948).
9   See the Hallmarking Act 1973 s 16(4), Sch 6 Pts I, II.

453.   Powers and duties of assay offices. An assay office[1] may refuse to assay or mark any new ware[2] if it is submitted at a stage of its manufacture which is unreasonable for assaying of and striking of marks on the new ware[3].

Upon receipt of any article submitted to an assay office for assay and hallmarking, the assay office must[4] examine the same to ascertain whether it is in its opinion sufficiently advanced in workmanship and, if composed of one or more parts, whether all the parts are present, and also whether the article complies with the conditions of the Hallmarking Act 1973 so as to permit it to be struck with the approved hallmarks[5]; and, if the assay office is dissatisfied as respects any of such matters, it must return the article without making an assay thereof[6].

If, upon receipt and view of any article submitted to an assay office for assay and hallmarking, the assay office suspects that other materials than precious metal[7] of not less than the minimum fineness[8] therefor have been introduced or concealed in any such article, the assay office may cause the same to be cut[9]; and, if upon cutting:

(1)   any such other materials are found therein, the article must be broken and defaced and it, or the value thereof, is forfeited to the assay office and applied towards its general expenses[10];

(2)   no such other materials are found therein, the assay office, but not any other person, is liable in damages to any person interested in the article[11].

An assay office may[12] cause to be drawn, scraped, cut or otherwise removed from an article submitted to it such quantity of precious metal or take such other sample or do such other thing as may be necessary to enable an accurate assay to be made of the article and may retain the quantity so removed and apply it, or the value thereof, towards its general expenses[13].

In the event of any part of any article or any sample from any article being found to be of a fineness:

(a)   less than the minimum fineness for the precious metal of that article, the article the subject of the assay must be returned to the person submitting the same after payment of the prescribed charge; and, if the article is a new ware, the assay office has power, before so returning the article, to break it and any other articles which were submitted with it in the same parcel of work[14];

(b)   not less than such minimum fineness, the article must be struck with the approved hallmarks and delivered to the person submitting the same after payment of the prescribed charge[15].

If an assay office is satisfied where two or more articles being new wares are submitted to it in one parcel of work for assay and hallmarking that all the articles so submitted are intended to assay to a single standard of fineness, the assay office may[16] carry out a single assay in respect of some or all of the articles contained in such parcel[17].

Each assay office is responsible both for the safe custody of the dies to be used by that assay office for the purpose of striking articles with the approved hallmarks and other marks and for the disposal of such dies as and when the same are no longer required[18].

1   As to the meaning of 'assay office' see PARA 451.
2   For these purposes, 'new ware' means: (1) any article which is a substantially complete manufacture and which has not as such been supplied on a sale by retail; and (2) any article which has been the subject of an improper alteration: Hallmarking Act 1973 s 22(1). 'Improper alteration' means an addition, alteration or repair which has been made to an article bearing approved hallmarks and which: (a) contravened s 5 (see PARA 461); or (b) was made before 1 January 1975 and would have required the consent of an assay office if s 5 had been in force; or (c) in the case of an article which bears a convention hallmark or an EEA hallmark, would have required that consent if the addition, alteration or repair had been made in the United Kingdom: ss 2(5), 22(1) (s 2(5)(c) amended by SI 1998/2978). Heads (b), (c) above do not apply, however, if, after the making of the addition, alteration or repair, the article has been re-assayed and struck with any further approved hallmark: Hallmarking Act 1973 s 2(5) proviso. As to the meaning of 'convention hallmark' see PARA 454; as to the meaning of 'EEA hallmark' see PARA 455; and as to the meaning of 'United Kingdom' see PARA 3 note 2.
3   Hallmarking Act 1973 s 15(1), Sch 5 para 1.
4   In relation to business outside the United Kingdom carried on by an assay office, 'must' should be read as 'may': Hallmarking Act 1973 s 15(1), Sch 5 para 2(1) (modified by s 4A(4) (added by SI 2013/251)).
5   As to the meaning of 'approved hallmarks' see PARA 450.
6   Hallmarking Act 1973 Sch 5 para 2(1).

7	As to the meaning of 'precious metal' see PARA 450 note 9.
8	As to the meaning of 'minimum fineness' see PARA 450 note 11; and as to the meaning of 'fineness' see PARA 450 note 10.
9	Hallmarking Act 1973 Sch 5 para 2(2).
10	Hallmarking Act 1973 Sch 5 para 2(2)(a).
11	Hallmarking Act 1973 Sch 5 para 2(2)(b).
12	Ie subject to the Hallmarking Act 1973 Sch 5 para 2(1), (2) (see the text and notes 6–11) and Sch 5 para 2(5) (see the text and note 17).
13	Hallmarking Act 1973 Sch 5 para 2(3).
14	Hallmarking Act 1973 Sch 5 para 2(4)(a).
15	Hallmarking Act 1973 Sch 5 para 2(4)(b).
16	Ie notwithstanding anything in the Hallmarking Act 1973 Sch 5 para 2(3): see the text and note 13.
17	Hallmarking Act 1973 Sch 5 para 2(5).
18	Hallmarking Act 1973 Sch 5 para 4(1). After consultation with all the assay offices the British Hallmarking Council may make regulations in or in connection with the discharge by assay offices of the duty imposed upon them by Sch 5 para 4(1) and as to the manner in which any such die is to be made or used and generally in relation thereto: Sch 5 para 4(2). As to the British Hallmarking Council see PARA 464.

454. Convention hallmarks. 'Convention hallmarks' means marks struck by an assay office[1] under the law of a country outside the United Kingdom[2], being marks designated for this purpose by order of the Secretary of State[3] as marks recognised pursuant to any international convention or treaty to which Her Majesty's government in the United Kingdom is a party[4]. The Secretary of State may make such provision by order as appears to him appropriate for enabling articles submitted to an assay office in the United Kingdom to be struck with marks which, pursuant to any such convention or treaty, will, or will with other marks, be accorded recognition under the law of any other country[5].

1	As to the meaning of 'assay office' see PARA 451.
2	As to the meaning of 'United Kingdom' see PARA 3 note 2.
3	As the Secretary of State see PARA 16.
4	Hallmarking Act 1973 ss 2(1)(c), (2), 22(1). The effect of these provisions is to enable the United Kingdom government to comply with the Convention on the Control and Marking of Articles of Precious Metals 1972 (Vienna, 15 November 1972; TS 53 (1978); Cmnd 7219). As to the relevant orders see note 5.
5	Hallmarking Act 1973 s 2(3) (amended by SI 1998/2978). Such an order may contain consequential or incidental provisions, including provision for excluding or modifying any of the provisions of the Hallmarking Act 1973: s 2(3). In exercise of the power so conferred the Secretary of State has made the Hallmarking (International Convention) Order 2002, SI 2002/506 (amended by SI 2011/3039), which: (1) recognises certain foreign hallmarks and sponsors' marks, with the result that articles bearing such marks are to be treated as hallmarked for the purposes of the Hallmarking Act 1973 and may therefore be described in the United Kingdom as being of the precious metal of which they are made; and (2) provides for the application in the United Kingdom of similar marks which are to be recognised in other Convention countries. As to the making of orders generally see PARA 448.

455. EEA hallmarks and free movement of goods under EU law. 'EEA hallmarks' means marks struck in an EEA state[1] other than the United Kingdom[2], being marks which have been struck by an independent body in accordance with the law of that state, and provide information which is equivalent to the information provided by the assay office marks and standard marks[3], and which is intelligible to consumers in the United Kingdom[4]. The provisions relating to EEA hallmarks were inserted[5] in the Hallmarking Act 1973 in consequence of a decision of the European Court of Justice interpreting and applying the rules on free movement of goods under the EU Treaty[6]. In accordance with that decision, the rules on free movement of goods require member states to permit the marketing of articles of precious metal hallmarked by an independent body in the member state of exportation[7], so long as that hallmark contains information which is equivalent to that provided by the hallmarks required by the member state of importation and which is intelligible to consumers in that state[8]. Thus member states may not require the application of hallmarks denoting a particular standard of fineness in parts per thousand or the application of a sponsor's mark registered in the country of importation or an approved national or convention hallmark where those articles have been lawfully marketed in another member state bearing hallmarks which convey equivalent information such as hallmarks indicating the standard of fineness in parts per thousand[9]. National rules which prohibit the marketing of articles of precious metal which do not indicate their date of manufacture cannot be enforced, where those articles have been lawfully marketed in another member state from which they have been imported[10].

In accordance with general principles of EU law, the domestic provisions relating to EEA hallmarks are to be interpreted as far as possible in conformity with the provisions of EU law[11] to which they give effect[12]. Further, the EU rules on free movement of goods have direct effect and national provisions relating inter alia to hallmarking requirements cannot be enforced to the extent that they conflict with those rules. Accordingly, it is possible if the statutory provisions relating to EEA hallmarks do not go far enough that the EU rules on free movement of goods could directly provide a defence to a person marketing hallmarked articles from other member states.

1   'EEA state', in relation to any time, means a state which at that time is a member state, or any other state which at that time is a party to the EEA agreement: Hallmarking Act 1973 s 2(2A) (added by SI 1998/2978; and substituted by SI 2007/872); Interpretation Act 1978 s 5, Sch 1 (definition added by the Legislative and Regulatory Reform Act 2006 s 26(1)). As to the EEA and the EEA agreement see PARA 86 note 6.

2   As to the meaning of 'United Kingdom' see PARA 3 note 2.

3   Ie the information provided by marks under the Hallmarking Act 1973 s 4(1)(a)(i), (ii): see PARA 450 note 13.

4   Hallmarking Act 1973 ss 2(1)(d), (2), 22(1) (s 2(1)(d) and the definition in s 22(1) added, and s 2(2) amended, by SI 1998/2978).

5   Ie by the Hallmarking (Hallmarking Act Amendment) Regulations 1998, SI 1998/2978. The parts of these Regulations making provision for EEA hallmarks were made under the powers conferred by the European Communities Act 1972 s 2(2), to amend domestic laws in order to give effect to EU obligations of the United Kingdom.

6   Case C-293/93 *Straffesag v Houtwipper* [1994] ECR 1–4249, [1995] All ER (EC) 163, ECJ. The rules on free movement of goods are contained in what is now the Treaty on the Functioning of the European Union ('TFEU') (see note 11; and PARAS 86 note 8, 89). See generally CUSTOMS AND EXCISE vol 30 (2012) PARA 3 et seq.

7   Case C-293/93 *Straffesag v Houtwipper* [1994] ECR 1–4249, [1995] All ER (EC) 163, ECJ (Answer 2 to the questions of the national court). See also Case C-30/99 *Commission of the European Communities v Ireland (United Kingdom intervening)* [2001] ECR I-4619, sub nom *EC Commission v Ireland (United Kingdom intervening)* [2001] 3 CMLR 573, ECJ. It is for the national court to examine whether the articles of precious metal have been hallmarked by an independent body in the member state of exportation: *Straffesag v Houtwipper* above (Answer 3).

8   Case C-293/93 *Straffesag v Houtwipper* [1994] ECR 1–4249, [1995] All ER (EC) 163, ECJ (Answer 1 to the questions of the national court). See also Case C-30/99 *Commission of the European Communities v Ireland (United Kingdom intervening)* [2001] ECR I-4619, sub nom *EC Commission v Ireland (United Kingdom intervening)* [2001] 3 CMLR 573, ECJ. It is a matter for the national court to determine as a question of fact the equivalence of information provided by the hallmark: *Straffesag v Houtwipper* above (Answer 3).

9   Case C-30/99 *Commission of the European Communities v Ireland (United Kingdom intervening)* [2001] ECR I-4619, sub nom *EC Commission v Ireland (United Kingdom intervening)* [2001] 3 CMLR 573, ECJ.

10 Case C-293/93 *Straffesag v Houtwipper* [1995] All ER (EC) 163, [1994] ECR 1–4249, ECJ (Answer 4).
11 Ie the Treaty Establishing the European Community (Rome, 25 March 1957; TS 1 (1973); Cmnd 5179) (the 'EC Treaty') arts 28–30 (formerly arts 30–36; renumbered by virtue of the Treaty of Amsterdam: see *Treaty Citation (No 2) (Note)* [1999] All ER (EC) 646, ECJ) (and see now the Treaty on the Functioning of the European Union (Rome, 25 March 1957; TS 1 (1973); Cmnd 5179) ('TFEU') arts 34–36 (see PARAS 86 note 8, 89))), as interpreted by the decision of the European Court of Justice in Case C-293/93 *Straffesag v Houtwipper* [1995] All ER (EC) 163, [1994] ECR 1–4249, ECJ and in Case C-30/99 *EC Commission v Ireland (United Kingdom intervening)* [2001] ECR I-4619, [2001] 3 CMLR 573, ECJ.
12 See PARA 5 text and note 3.

456.   Meaning of 'unhallmarked article'.   An article is unhallmarked if it does not bear the approved hallmarks[1] and the sponsor's mark[2], or if the article has been the subject of any improper alteration[3].

1   As to the meaning of 'approved hallmarks' see PARA 450. As to the approved hallmarks whose absence does not render an article unhallmarked see the Hallmarking Act 1973 s 4(2); and PARA 450 note 13.
2   As to the meaning of 'sponsor's mark' see PARA 460.
3   Hallmarking Act 1973 ss 2(4), 22(1). As to the meaning of 'improper alteration' see PARA 453 note 2.

457.   Permissible descriptions.   Certain descriptions of unhallmarked articles[1] are permitted notwithstanding the general prohibition[2]. The description 'gold' is permissible if qualified by the word 'plated' or 'rolled'; the description 'silver' 'platinum' or 'palladium' is permissible if qualified by the word 'plated'[3].

This does not apply, however, if the description is false or is applied to an article for which the description is inappropriate[4].

If the description is in writing, the lettering of 'plated' or 'rolled' is to be at least as large as any other lettering in the description[5].

A description is also permissible if it is implicitly or in express terms confined to the colour of the article[6].

1   As to the meaning of 'unhallmarked article' see PARA 456.
2   See the Hallmarking Act 1973 s 1(2), Sch 1 Pt I. As to the general prohibition see s 1(1); and PARA 449.
3   Hallmarking Act 1973 Sch 1 Pt I para 1(1) (amended by SI 2009/2040).
4   Hallmarking Act 1973 Sch 1 Pt I para 1(3).
5   Hallmarking Act 1973 Sch 1 Pt I para 1(2).
6   Hallmarking Act 1973 Sch 1 Pt I para 2.

458.   Exempted articles.   Certain unhallmarked articles[1] are exempted from the general prohibition[2] on the application of 'gold', 'silver', 'platinum' or 'palladium' descriptions to such articles[3]. The exemptions fall into three classes:
(1)   articles exempted generally[4];
(2)   articles exempt if of minimum fineness[5]; and
(3)   articles manufactured or exempted before 1 January 1975[6].

1   As to the meaning of 'unhallmarked article' see PARA 456.
2   Ie under the Hallmarking Act 1973 s 1(1): see PARA 449.
3   See Hallmarking Act 1973 Sch 1 Pt II (paras 1–18) (amended by SI 1975/1883; SI 1982/256; SI 1986/1758; SI 2007/880; SI 2007/2493; and SI 2009/2040).
      The Hallmarking (Exempted Articles) Order 1982, SI 1982/256, was made to overcome the criticism in *Barge v Graham Brown (Oasis Trading) Ltd* [1981] 3 All ER 360, DC.
4   The articles so exempted are:
      (1)   an article which is intended for dispatch to a destination outside the United Kingdom (Hallmarking Act 1973 Sch 1 Pt II para 1);

(2) an article which is outside the United Kingdom, or which is in course of consignment from outside the United Kingdom to an assay office in the United Kingdom (Sch 1 Pt II para 2);

(3) any coin which is, or was formerly at any time, a current coin of the United Kingdom or of any other territory (Sch 1 Pt II para 3);

(4) any article which has been used, or is intended to be used, for medical, dental, veterinary, scientific or industrial purposes (Sch 1 Pt II para 4);

(5) any battered article fit only to be re-manufactured (Sch 1 Pt II para 5 (substituted by SI 1975/1883));

(6) any article of gold, silver or palladium thread (Hallmarking Act 1973 Sch 1 Pt II para 6 (amended by SI 2009/2040));

(7) any raw material (including any bar, plate, sheet, foil, rod, wire, strip or tube) or bullion (Hallmarking Act 1973 Sch 1 Pt II para 7);

(8) any manufactured article which is not substantially complete, and which is intended for further manufacture (Sch 1 Pt II para 8);

(9) any article which is wholly or mainly of platinum and which was manufactured before 1 January 1975 (Sch 1 Pt II para 9);

(10) any article which is wholly or mainly of palladium and which was manufactured before 1 January 2010 (Sch 1 Pt II para 9A (added by SI 2009/2040)).

As to the meaning of 'United Kingdom' see PARA 3 note 2.

5　As to the meaning of 'minimum fineness' see PARA 450 note 11. The articles so exempt if of minimum fineness are:

(1) any article which: (a) is wholly or mainly of gold or of silver or of gold and silver assaying in all its gold parts not less than 375 parts per 1,000 and in all its silver parts not less than 800 parts per 1,000; and (b) was manufactured before the year 1950 and has not since the beginning of that year been the subject of any alteration which would be an improper alteration if the article had previously borne approved hallmarks (Hallmarking Act 1973 Sch 1 Pt II para 10 (substituted by SI 1975/1883; and amended by SI 2007/880));

(2) any musical instrument, where the description is applied to the mouthpiece, and the mouthpiece is of minimum fineness (Hallmarking Act 1973 Sch 1 Pt II para 11 (amended by SI 1986/1758));

(3) any article containing only one precious metal, being a metal of minimum fineness and of a weight less than the specified weight (ie for gold 1 gram, for silver 7.78 grams, for platinum 0.5 gram) and for palladium 1 gram, but not including any article manufactured on or after 1 January 2008 or containing materials other than precious metal unless the article satisfies the conditions for hallmarking of the Hallmarking Act 1973 Sch 2 Pt III (see PARA 450 note 13) (Sch 1 Pt II para 12(1), (2) (substituted by SI 1982/256; and amended by SI 2007/2493));

(4) any article which contains silver, gold, platinum or palladium of minimum fineness, in which the total weight of the metal is less than 7.78 grams, 1 gram, 0.5 gram or 1 gram respectively, subject to certain exceptions (see the Hallmarking Act 1973 Sch 1 Pt II paras 12A—12D (paras 12A—12C added by SI 2007/2493; the Hallmarking Act 1973 Sch 1 Pt II para 12C further amended by SI 2009/2040; and the Hallmarking Act 1973 Sch 1 Pt II para 12D added by SI 2009/2040)).

(5) any article, except an article made of chainwork, which is wholly of one or more precious metals of minimum fineness and which is so small or thin that it cannot be hallmarked (Hallmarking Act 1973 Sch 1 Pt II para 13 (substituted by SI 1975/1883; and amended by SI 1986/1758));

(6) any article which is of minimum fineness and which is imported temporarily (whether as a trade sample, or as intended for exhibition or otherwise) and for the time being remains under the control of the Commissioners for Her Majesty's Revenue and Customs (see CUSTOMS AND EXCISE vol 31 (2012) PARA 921) (Hallmarking Act 1973 Sch 1 Pt II para 14 (amended by SI 1986/1758; and by virtue of the Commissioners for Revenue and Customs Act 2005 s 50(1), (7)));

(7) any article, any precious metal in which is of minimum fineness, and which either: (a) contains gold and platinum but not silver, and the weight of the gold parts of which exceeds 50% of the total weight of the precious metals in the article, that total weight being less than 1 gram; or (b) contains silver and either gold or platinum or both gold and platinum, and the weight of the silver parts of which exceeds 50% of the total weight of the precious metals in the article, that total weight being less than 7.78 grams, but not including any article manufactured on or after 1 January 2008 or which contains materials other than precious metal unless the article satisfies the conditions

for hallmarking of the Hallmarking Act 1973 Sch 2 Pt III (see PARA 450 note 13) (Sch 1 Pt II para 14A(1), (2) (s 14A added by SI 1982/256; and amended by SI 2007/2493)). Heads (2)–(7) above do not apply to any article in which solder containing precious metal is used unless the solder is of a standard of fineness equivalent to that which would be required under the Hallmarking Act 1973 s 4(3) (see PARA 450) if the article were submitted to an assay office for hallmarking: Sch 1 Pt II para 14AA (added by SI 1986/1758) As to the meaning of 'precious metal' see PARA 450 note 9; as to the meaning of 'improper alteration' see PARA 453 note 2; and as to the meaning of 'assay office' see PARA 451.

6   The following articles of gold are exempt, if manufactured before 1 January 1975, and (except in the case of articles mentioned in head (4) below) of minimum fineness:

    (1)   rings, except wedding rings, pencil cases, lockets, watch chains and thimbles (Hallmarking Act 1973 Sch 1 Pt II para 15(a));

    (2)   articles consisting entirely of filigree work (Sch 1 Pt II para 15(b));

    (3)   articles so heavily engraved or set with stones that it is impossible to mark them without damage (Sch 1 Pt II para 15(c));

    (4)   jewellers works, i e the actual setting only in which stones or other jewels are set, and jointed sleeper earrings (Sch 1 Pt II para 15(d)).

The following articles of silver are exempt, if manufactured before 1 January 1975, and (except in the case of articles mentioned in head (e) below) of minimum fineness:

    (a)   lockets, watch chains and stamped medals (Sch 1 Pt II para 16(1)(a));

    (b)   mounts the weight of which is less than 15.55 grams (Sch 1 Pt II para 16(1)(b));

    (c)   articles consisting entirely of filigree work (Sch 1 Pt II para 16(1)(c));

    (d)   silver articles the weight of which is less than 7.78 grams (Sch 1 Pt II para 16(1)(d));

    (e)   jewellers works, i e the actual setting only in which stones or other jewels are set (Sch 1 Pt II para 16(1)(e)).

The following articles are not, however, so exempt: necks and collars for bottles on cruet stands; buttons and studs, seals, wine labels, shoe clasps, buckles or patch boxes; salt spoons, shovels or ladles, teaspoons, tea strainers, caddy ladles or spoons; ornaments for cabinets, knife cases, tea caddies, bridles, stands or frames: Sch 1 Pt II para 16(2).

Articles of gold or silver manufactured before 1 January 1975, other than articles mentioned in Sch 1 Pt II para 15 or Sch 1 Pt II para 16, and being of such descriptions as, under any enactment in force immediately before 25 July 1973, to be specifically exempt from hallmarking, are exempt: Sch 1 Pt II para 17.

Where an exemption depends on the date of manufacture, or the date of any alteration, the manufacture or alteration is presumed to be after that date until the contrary is proved: Sch 1 Pt II para 18.

459.   Descriptions relating to fineness.   A description indicating that an article, or the metal in an article, is of so many carats, is to be presumed to be an indication that the article or metal is of gold, and that its fineness[1] is that specified[2] for that number of carats[3].

A description of an article, or of the metal in an article, as 'sterling' or (except in the phrase 'Britannia metal') 'Britannia' is to be presumed to be an indication that the article, or the metal, is of silver[4].

These provisions also apply for the purposes of legislation relating to protection from misleading marketing and unfair trading[5].

1   As to the meaning of 'fineness' see PARA 450 note 10.

2   Ie 9 carats indicates gold of a standard of fineness of 375 parts per thousand; 12 carats indicates gold of a standard of fineness of 500 parts per thousand; 14 carats indicates gold of a standard of fineness of 585 parts per thousand; 15 carats indicates gold of a standard of fineness of 625 parts per thousand; 18 carats indicates gold of a standard of fineness of 750 parts per thousand; 22 carats indicates gold of a standard of fineness of 916.6 parts per thousand; and so in proportion for any other number of carats: Hallmarking Act 1973 s 1(5), Sch 1 Pt III para 2.

3   Hallmarking Act 1973 Sch 1 Pt III paras 1, 2(1). Schedule 1 Pt III para 2 does not apply, however, if (as in a case where the article is a precious stone) the word 'carat' is used as a measure of weight for precious stones and not as a measure of fineness: Sch 1 Pt III para 2(2).

4   Hallmarking Act 1973 Sch 1 Pt III paras 1, 3(1). If 'sterling' is the word used, the description is to be presumed to be an indication that the silver is of a standard of fineness of 925: Sch 1 Pt III para 3(2). If the word used is 'Britannia', the description is to be presumed to be an indication that the silver is of a standard of fineness of 958.4: Sch 1 Pt III para 3(3).

5 Hallmarking Act 1973 Sch 1 Pt III para 1 (amended by SI 2008/1277). The legislation mentioned is the Business Protection from Misleading Marketing Regulations 2008, SI 2008/1276 (see COMPETITION), and the Consumer Protection from Unfair Trading Regulations 2008, SI 2008/1277 (see CONSUMER PROTECTION vol 21 (2011) PARA 497).

In any case where the giving of a description of the fineness (whether in parts per thousand or otherwise) of any precious metal constitutes advertising within the meaning of the Business Protection from Misleading Marketing Regulations 2008, SI 2008/1276 or a commercial practice within the meaning of the Consumer Protection from Unfair Trading Regulations 2008, SI 2008/1277 and the description is false to any extent or degree (except by understating the fineness), the giving of the description is to be treated as satisfying the requirements of those Regulations (requirements for advertising to be misleading, or for a commercial practice to be a misleading action): see Hallmarking Act 1973 s 1(4A)—(4D) (added by SI 2008/1277). As to the meaning of 'precious metal' see PARA 450 note 9.

460. Sponsors' marks. 'Sponsor's mark' means:

(1) a mark struck on an article and indicative of the manufacturer or sponsor[1]; or

(2) a mark designated as a sponsor's mark by order of the Secretary of State[2] as a mark recognised pursuant to any international convention or treaty to which Her Majesty's government in the United Kingdom[3] is a party and as a sponsor's mark for the purposes of the Hallmarking Act 1973[4]; or

(3) a mark struck on an article in an EEA state[5] which indicates the manufacturer or sponsor of the article[6].

Before an article is submitted to an assay office[7] to be struck with the approved hallmarks[8], there must be struck on the article a sponsor's mark[9]. A sponsor's mark must be authorised by registration with an assay office by which the article is intended to be so struck[10].

Any person who without authority strikes an article with a mark purporting to be an authorised sponsor's mark is guilty of an offence[11].

1 Hallmarking Act 1973 ss 3(1), 22(1). 'Sponsor's mark' includes a mark applied under the corresponding provisions of earlier legislation: see s 22(1).
2 As to the Secretary of State see PARA 16.
3 As to the meaning of 'United Kingdom' see PARA 3 note 2.
4 Hallmarking Act 1973 s 22(1). For the orders made for this purpose see PARA 454 note 5.
5 As to the meaning of 'EEA state' see PARA 455 note 1.
6 Hallmarking Act 1973 s 22(1) (amended by SI 1998/2978).
7 As to the meaning of 'assay office' see PARA 451.
8 As to the meaning of 'approved hallmark' see PARA 450.
9 Hallmarking Act 1973 s 3(1). The assay office and the manufacturer or sponsor of an article may, however, make arrangements for the sponsor's mark to be struck by that assay office upon submission of the article to be struck with the approved hallmarks: Hallmarking Act 1973 s 3(1) proviso.
10 See the Hallmarking At 1973 s 3(2). An assay office must maintain a register of sponsor's marks for the time being registered and approved by it: s 3(3)(b). A registered sponsor's mark, other than one registered on or before 31 December 1975, must be of such design as may be approved by an assay office: see s 3(3)(a) (amended by SI 2013/251). Registration fees are to be paid, and punches and other equipment approved, in accordance with regulations made by the British Hallmarking Council: see the Hallmarking Act 1973 s 3(4), (5). Any assay office may register its own sponsor's mark, of such design as may be approved by the Council, and strike it on an article submitted to it where it would not be justified in requiring the applicant to register his own sponsor's mark: see s 3(6). The registration of a sponsor's mark ceases to have effect after the expiration of the period of ten years following registration, but without prejudice to the making of any application for renewal: s 3(7). As to the British Hallmarking Council see PARA 464.
11 Hallmarking Act 1973 s 3(8). As to offences see PARA 466.

461. Alterations to hallmarked articles. It is an offence for any person to make an addition, alteration or repair to an article bearing approved hallmarks[1], except in accordance with the written consent of an assay office[2]. It is also an offence for any person to remove, alter or deface any mark[3] struck on an article, except in accordance with the written consent of an assay office[4]. In giving any consent for these purposes an assay office may make it a condition of the consent that the article concerned, or any addition made to it, be further assayed and struck with the appropriate marks[5].

It is not an offence under the provisions described above[6], however, to batter an article so as to render it fit only for re-manufacture[7]; nor is it an offence[8] to make an addition to an article which is not a new ware[9] if the character of the article, and the purposes for which it can be used, remain unaltered and the metal added satisfies the specified conditions[10]. In certain circumstances it is not an offence to add a coating of silver, gold, platinum, palladium or rhodium to an article[11].

1 As to the meaning of 'approved hallmarks' see PARA 450.
2 Hallmarking Act 1973 s 5(1). As to the meaning of 'assay office' see PARA 451. As to offences see PARA 466.
3 For these purposes, 'mark' means a sponsor's mark, any approved hallmark, the word 'filled', the word 'metal' or any other word for the time being prescribed by or under the Hallmarking Act 1973 s 4 or Sch 2 (see PARA 450): s 5(2). As to the meaning of 'sponsor's mark' see PARA 460.
4 Hallmarking Act 1973 s 5(2).
5 Hallmarking Act 1973 s 5(6). For these purposes, the appropriate marks are the sponsor's mark and such of the approved hallmarks as may be specified in directions issued by the British Hallmarking Council or, in the absence of any such directions, such of the approved hallmarks as may be determined by the assay office: s 5(6)(a), (b). As to the British Hallmarking Council see PARA 464.
   If an application for consent under s 5(1) or s 5(2) has been refused and the applicant has referred the matter in writing to the Council, the Council must consider the case and, if of the opinion that the assay office was acting unreasonably in withholding the consent applied for, must direct the assay office to grant the consent (s 5(7)), and, without prejudice to s 5(6), it is the duty of an assay office to which a direction has been given to comply with such a direction (s 5(8)).
6 Ie under the Hallmarking Act 1973 s 5(1) or (2): see the text and notes 1–4.
7 Hallmarking Act 1973 s 5(3).
8 Ie under the Hallmarking Act 1973 s 5(1): see the text and notes 1–2.
9 As to the meaning of 'new ware' see PARA 453 note 2.
10 Hallmarking Act 1973 s 5(4). The conditions so specified are that: (1) the addition must be of the same precious metal as that of the article; (2) the metal added to the article must be of a fineness not less than the standard of fineness of the article; and (3) the amount of metal added must not exceed the lesser of: (a) 1 gram of gold, 5 grams of silver, 0.5 gram of platinum or 1 gram of palladium, as the case may be; and (b) 50% of the weight of the article immediately before the addition was made: s 5(4) (amended by SI 2009/2040). As to the meaning of 'precious metal' see PARA 450 note 9; and as to the meanings of 'fineness' and 'standard of fineness' see PARA 450 note 10.
11 See the Hallmarking Act 1973 s 5(5) (amended by SI 2009/2040; and SI 2013/251), which provides that it is not an offence to add a coating of a thickness not exceeding two micrometres at any point to the whole or any part of:
   (1) an article of gold, if the coating (a) is of gold of a fineness not less than the standard of fineness of the article, or (b) is of platinum of not less than the minimum fineness; or
   (2) an article of silver, if the coating (a) is of silver of a fineness not less than the standard of fineness of the article, or (b) is of gold, platinum or palladium of not less than the minimum fineness;
   (3) an article of palladium, if the coating (a) is of palladium of not less than the standard of fineness of the article, or (b) is of gold or platinum of not less than the minimum fineness;
   (4) an article of platinum, if the coating is of platinum of not less than the standard of fineness of the article; or

(5)   an article of gold, silver, platinum or platinum, if the coating is of rhodium.
As to the meaning of 'minimum fineness' see PARA 450 note 11.

462.   Treatment of unauthorised marks.   At its discretion an assay office[1] may cancel or obliterate any mark of the character of a hallmark, whether the mark appears to be an approved hallmark[2] or to be a mark which in the opinion of the assay office is likely to be confused with such a hallmark, which an article coming into its custody or possession bears, and which it is satisfied has not been struck on the article by an assay office according to law or is not a true description because the article appears to have been the subject of an improper alteration[3]. If it is proved that an assay office has:

(1)   cancelled or obliterated any such mark[4] which has been struck by an assay office according to law on an article which has not been the subject of an improper alteration; or

(2)   obliterated any ancient mark upon an article,

the assay office (but not any other person) is liable in damages to any person interested in the article[5].

It is an offence for any person knowingly or for any dealer[6] to supply or offer to supply any article bearing any mark of the character of a hallmark and which may, if the article is in the possession of an assay office, be cancelled, obliterated or defaced[7], unless the article has been first submitted to an assay office to enable it at its discretion to cancel, obliterate or deface that mark[8].

1   As to the meaning of 'assay office' see PARA 451.
2   As to the meaning of 'approved hallmarks' see PARA 450.
3   Hallmarking Act 1973 s 7(1). As to the meaning of 'improper alteration' see PARA 453 note 2.
    Notwithstanding anything in any enactment, an assay office may not, otherwise than by leave of the owner or other person appearing to have the control of any article, obliterate any ancient mark but must cancel it in a manner authorised by the British Hallmarking Council: s 7(2). The Council may issue directions to assay offices as to the manner in which an ancient mark may be so cancelled: s 7(3). For these purposes, 'ancient mark' means a mark of the character of a hallmark appearing to an assay office to have been struck or incorporated before 22 December 1854, whether or not by an assay office according to law at the time of its marking or incorporation, upon or into an article which has not since been the subject of an improper alteration: s 7(7). As to the British Hallmarking Council see PARA 464.
4   Ie any mark as described in the Hallmarking Act 1973 s 7(1): see the text to notes 1–3.
5   Hallmarking Act 1973 s 7(4). In any action brought against an assay office in pursuance of s 7(4) it is a defence for it to prove that it had reasonable cause to believe that the circumstances specified respectively in s 7(4)(a) or s 7(4)(b) (see heads (1) and (2) in the text) did not exist: s 7(5).
6   As to the meaning of 'dealer' see PARA 450 note 19.
7   Ie under the Hallmarking Act 1973 s 7(1): see the text to notes 1–3.
8   Hallmarking Act 1973 s 7(6). As to offences see PARA 466.

463.   Counterfeiting.   Any person who:

(1)   with intent to defraud or deceive[1], makes a counterfeit of any die[2] or mark[3]; or

(2)   removes any mark from an article of precious metal[4] with intent to transpose it to any other article, whether of precious metal or not, or affixes to any article whether of precious metal or not, any mark which has been removed from an article of precious metal[5]; or

(3)   utters[6] any counterfeit of a die or any article bearing a counterfeit of a mark[7]; or

(4)   without lawful authority or excuse has in his custody or under his control anything which is, and which he knows or believes to be, a

counterfeit of a die or an article, whether of precious metal or not, which bears a counterfeit of any mark[8],

is guilty of an offence[9].

Facts giving rise to an offence of counterfeiting under these provisions may also give rise to offences under other Acts[10].

1　Cf *R v Heron* [1982] 1 All ER 993, [1982] 1 WLR, 451, HL.
2　For these purposes, 'die' means the whole or part of any plate, tool or instrument by means of which any mark of the nature of a sponsor's mark or a hallmark is struck on any metal: Hallmarking Act 1973 s 6(2). As to the meaning of 'sponsor's mark' see PARA 460.
3　Hallmarking Act 1973 s 6(1)(a). For these purposes, 'mark' means any mark of the nature of a sponsor's mark or hallmark: s 6(2).
4　As to the meaning of 'precious metal' see PARA 460 note 9.
5　Hallmarking Act 1973 s 6(1)(b).
6　For these purposes, a person utters any counterfeit die or article bearing a counterfeit mark if, knowing or believing the die or mark, as the case may be, to be a counterfeit, he supplies, offers to supply or delivers the die or article: Hallmarking Act 1973 s 6(3). See *Selby v DPP* [1972] AC 515, sub nom *R v Selby* [1971] 3 All ER 810, HL (offence of uttering counterfeit coins under the Coinage Offences Act 1936 supposed an intent to pass them off as genuine); *R v Walmsley, De Reya and Jackson* (1977) 67 Cr App Rep 30, CA. For counterfeiting offences under the Forgery and Counterfeiting Act 1981 see CRIMINAL LAW vol 26 (2010) PARA 476 et seq.
7　Hallmarking Act 1973 s 6(1)(c).
8　Hallmarking Act 1973 s 6(1)(d).
9　Hallmarking Act 1973 s 6(1) (amended by the Magistrates' Courts Act 1980 s 32(2)). Such a person is liable on conviction on indictment to imprisonment for a term not exceeding ten years or a fine, or on summary conviction to a fine not exceeding the prescribed sum: see the Hallmarking Act 1973 s 6(1) (as so amended). As to the prescribed sum see SENTENCING AND DISPOSITION OF OFFENDERS vol 92 (2010) PARA 141. As to offences under the Hallmarking Act 1973 generally see PARA 466.
10　Eg under the Theft Act 1968 (see CRIMINAL LAW vol 25 (2010) PARA 278 et seq), the Forgery and Counterfeiting Act 1981 (see CRIMINAL LAW vol 25 (2010) PARA 339 et seq) or the Trade Descriptions Act 1968 or other legislation intended to protect against unfair commercial practices (see CONSUMER PROTECTION vol 21 (2011) PARA 497 et seq).

(iii)　The British Hallmarking Council

464.　The British Hallmarking Council.　The British Hallmarking Council[1] is charged with the duty of ensuring that adequate facilities for the assaying and hallmarking of articles of precious metal[2] are available as from time to time required in the United Kingdom[3], of supervising the activities of assay offices[4] in that behalf, of taking all steps appearing to be open to it for ensuring the enforcement of the law with respect to hallmarking and of advising the Secretary of State[5] with respect to all matters concerning the due execution of the Hallmarking Act 1973 including any matter which may be referred to the Council by the Secretary of State[6].

In addition to the functions[7] specifically conferred on it by or under any other provisions of the Hallmarking Act 1973, the Council has the following functions[8]:

(1)　to advise the Secretary of State as it thinks fit with respect to the making of orders and regulations under the Hallmarking Act 1973 and with respect to the amendment of the law as it affects, whether directly or indirectly, the hallmarking of articles of precious metal, including advice as to the application of some or all of the provisions of the Act to any metal other than gold, silver and platinum[9];

(2)　subject to any directions in that behalf given by the Secretary of State, to fix the maximum charges for the time being to be charged by assay offices for assaying and hallmarking articles of precious metal manufactured in or intended for sale in the United Kingdom[10];

(3)   to advise the Secretary of State upon any need appearing to the Council from time to time for the establishment of any further assay office or for the closure of any assay office or for its amalgamation with another assay office[11];

(4)   to assist, by the provision of such technical and other services of the Council as may be available, all authorities and persons concerned in the enforcement of the Hallmarking Act 1973, to appoint such officers as the Council considers appropriate to act as inspectors and otherwise for the detecting of offences and enforcing the Hallmarking Act 1973 by or on behalf of the Council and to institute proceedings in that behalf[12];

(5)   to authorise any assay office to carry on its business in whole or in part, subject to any conditions which may be specified by the Council in so authorising, in such place (whether in the United Kingdom or elsewhere) as may be specified by the Council additional to the place at which the assay office is otherwise authorised[13];

(6)   to make temporary or permanent arrangements by directions, or to authorise the making of such arrangements between assay offices, whereby, notwithstanding anything in any enactment, facilities specified in any case by the Council need not be afforded at an assay office but are afforded at another or others[14];

(7)   to issue directions or regulations to all assay offices or, as the case may require, to an assay office in particular, as to the equipment and procedures to be provided and adopted by them or it in the assaying and hallmarking of precious metals and as to all other matters upon which such directions or regulations may be issued by the Council under the provisions of the Hallmarking Act 1973[15]; and

(8)   subject to such provisions of the Hallmarking Act 1973 as confer powers in particular on the Council, to do anything which in its opinion is calculated to facilitate the proper discharge of any or all of its functions[16].

It is the duty of an assay office to comply with directions and regulations issued by the Council pursuant to head (6) or head (7) above[17]. Any assay office which is aggrieved by any such direction or regulation may, however, make written representation in that behalf to the Secretary of State who may determine all issues which may be raised upon any such representation; and it is the duty of the Council to comply with any determination so made by the Secretary of State[18].

All directions, regulations, authorities, notices or other instruments given or made by the Council under or in pursuance of any provision of the Hallmarking Act 1973 must be in writing and may be given or made under the hand of the secretary or other officer of the Council authorised in that behalf[19].

The Council must submit an annual report to the Secretary of State[20].

1   The British Hallmarking Council came into existence on 1 January 1974; and it has performed the functions assigned to it by or under the Hallmarking Act 1973 since 1 January 1975: see s 13(1)(b).
    Detailed provision is made as to the composition and operation of the Council, governing: number, qualifications and appointment of members; tenure of office; election of chairman; attendance of non-members; appointment of a technical committee and other committees; voting; procedure; incorporation; expenses and accounts; remuneration and payments to the chairman and other members; and officers and servants of the Council: s 13(1)(c), Sch 4 (amended by SI 1991/1997; SI 2003/1326; and SI 2008/948).

Provision is also made for the amendment of the Hallmarking Act 1973 Sch 4, having regard to the establishment of a new assay office, the dissolution of any assay office or its amalgamation with another assay office, or other substantial changes in the functions, administration or activities of any assay office, or any other considerations: see s 14.

As to the British Hallmarking Council generally, including directions and regulations, reference should be had to its website, accessible at the date at which this volume states the law at www.gov.uk/government/organisations/british-hallmarking-council.

2   As to the meaning of 'precious metal' see PARA 450 note 9.
3   As to the meaning of 'United Kingdom' see PARA 3 note 2.
4   As to the meaning of 'assay office' see PARA 451.
5   As to the Secretary of State see PARA 16.
6   Hallmarking Act 1973 s 13(1)(a).
7   As to the meaning of 'functions' see PARA 448 note 3.
8   Hallmarking Act 1973 s 13(2), which is expressed to be without prejudice to s 13(1): see the text and notes 1–6.
9   Hallmarking Act 1973 s 13(2)(a). As to the application of the Act to palladium, and the making of orders and regulations generally, see PARA 448.
10 Hallmarking Act 1973 s 13(2)(b). As to the power of assay offices to make charges see PARA 451.
11 Hallmarking Act 1973 s 13(2)(c). As to the establishment and closure of assay offices see PARA 452.
12 Hallmarking Act 1973 s 13(2)(d).
13 Hallmarking Act 1973 s 13(2)(e) (amended by SI 2013/251).
14 Hallmarking Act 1973 s 13(2)(f).
15 Hallmarking Act 1973 s 13(2)(g).
16 Hallmarking Act 1973 s 13(2)(h).
17 Hallmarking Act 1973 s 13(3). As to powers and duties of assay offices generally see PARA 451.
18 Hallmarking Act 1973 s 13(3) proviso.
19 Hallmarking Act 1973 s 13(4).
20 See the Hallmarking Act 1973 s 19(1)–(3). Any person, on application to the Council, is entitled to be furnished with copies of such reports and of statements summarising the Council's accounts, on payment of such reasonable sums as the Council may determine: see s 19(4).

(iv) Enforcement of the Statutory Provisions

465. Enforcing authorities. It is the duty of every local weights and measures authority[1] to enforce the provisions of the Hallmarking Act 1973 within its area[2]. The British Hallmarking Council[3] and the assay offices[4] may also enforce the provisions of that Act[5]. Certain provisions of the Descriptions Act 1968[6] apply in relation to the enforcement of the Hallmarking Act 1973[7]. In addition the Hallmarking Act 1973 may be enforced under Part 8 of the Enterprise Act 2002[8] in certain circumstances[9].

1   As to the meaning of 'local weights and measures authority' see PARA 129 note 1.
2   Hallmarking Act 1973 s 9(1). The Trade Descriptions Act 1968 s 26 (enforcing authorities: see CONSUMER PROTECTION vol 21 (2011) PARA 523) applies in relation to the enforcement of the Hallmarking Act 1973 by a local weights and measures authority as it applies in relation to the enforcement of the Trade Descriptions Act 1968: Hallmarking Act 1973 s 9(1).
3   As to the British Hallmarking Council see PARA 464.
4   As to the meaning of 'assay office' see PARA 451.
5   Hallmarking Act 1973 s 9(2).
6   Ie the Trade Descriptions Act 1968 s 27 (power to make test purchases), s 28 (power to enter premises and inspect and seize goods and documents), s 29 (obstruction of authorised officers), s 30 (notice of test and intended prosecution), s 31 (evidence by certificate) and s 33 (compensation for loss etc of goods seized): see CONSUMER PROTECTION vol 21 (2011) PARA 523 et seq. Any reference in those provisions to a local weights and measures authority and a duly authorised officer of such an authority is to be construed, in relation to the enforcement of the Hallmarking Act 1973, as including respectively a reference to the Council and an assay office and a duly authorised officer of the Council and of an assay office: Hallmarking Act 1973 s 9(4). Section 9(4) excludes from its operation the Trade Descriptions Act 1968 s 30(2), (4), but those provisions are, however, repealed.

7   Hallmarking Act 1973 s 9(3).
8   Ie the Enterprise Act 2002 Pt 8 (ss 210–236): see COMPETITION vol 18 (2009) PARA 339 et seq.
9   See the Enterprise Act 2002 (Part 8 Domestic Infringements) Order 2003, SI 2003/1593; and the
     Enterprise Act 2002 (Part 8 Notice to OFT of Intended Prosecution Specified Enactments,
     Revocation and Transition Provision) Order 2003, SI 2003/1376. A public authority holding
     information to which the Enterprise Act 2002 s 237 applies may disclose that information to
     any person for the purpose of facilitating the exercise of any function that person has by virtue
     of the Hallmarking Act 1973: see the Enterprise Act 2002 s 241, Sch 15; and COMPETITION
     vol 18 (2009) PARA 330.

466. Offences. The Hallmarking Act 1973 makes provision as to the penalty
that may be imposed for an offence under the Act where no other penalty is
specified[1]. No prosecution for an offence under the Act may be commenced after
the expiration of three years from the commission of the offence or one year
from its discovery by the prosecutor, whichever is the earlier[2].

Where the commission by any person of such an offence is due to the act or
default of some other person, that other person is guilty of the offence; and a
person may be charged with and convicted of the offence by virtue of this
provision whether or not proceedings are taken against the first-mentioned
person[3].

Where an offence which has been committed by a body corporate is proved to
have been committed with the consent and connivance of, or to be attributable
to any neglect on the part of, any director[4], manager, secretary or other similar
officer of the body corporate, or any person who was purporting to act in any
such capacity, he as well as the body corporate is guilty of that offence and is
liable to be proceeded against and punished accordingly[5].

Upon the conviction of any person of such an offence, the court may order
any article that is the subject of the proceedings to be delivered to an assay
office[6] which, subject to the order, may exercise the like powers in relation to the
article as if it had been submitted to it for hallmarking[7].

1   A person guilty of such an offence is liable on conviction on indictment to imprisonment for a
     term not exceeding two years or a fine or both, or on summary conviction to a fine not
     exceeding the prescribed sum: see the Hallmarking Act 1973 s 8, Sch 3 para 1 (amended by the
     Magistrates' Courts Act 1980 s 32(2)). As to the prescribed sum see SENTENCING AND
     DISPOSITION OF OFFENDERS vol 92 (2010) PARA 141.
2   Hallmarking Act 1973 Sch 3 para 2(1).
3   Hallmarking Act 1973 Sch 3 para 4. As to the defences available in proceedings for an offence
     under s 1 see Sch 3 para 6; and PARA 449. As to the defence of innocent publication of an
     advertisement see Sch 3 para 5; and PARA 449 note 8.
4   In relation to any body corporate established by or under any enactment for the purpose of
     carrying on under national ownership any industry or part of an industry or undertaking, being
     a body corporate whose affairs are managed by its members, 'director' means a member of that
     body corporate: Hallmarking Act 1973 s 3 para 3(2). As to bodies corporate see generally
     COMPANIES vol 14 (2009) PARA 1; CORPORATIONS.
5   Hallmarking Act 1973 s 3 para 3(1).
6   As to the meaning of 'assay office' see PARA 451.
7   Hallmarking Act 1973 s 10(1). Any article delivered to an assay office pursuant to such an order
     must be returned to the person entitled to it: s 10(2). As to the powers of an assay office in
     relation to goods delivered to it for hallmarking see PARAS 451–453.

(2) PROOF AND MARKING OF GUN BARRELS

467. Summary of the legislation. Under the Gun Barrel Proof Acts 1868 to
1978[1], the Worshipful Company of the Gunmakers of the City of London Proof
House and the Guardians of the Birmingham Proof House are required to
maintain proof houses in or near London and Birmingham respectively and may

provide branch proof houses in any convenient place[2]. All commercially produced gun barrels[3] are required to be proved by one or other of those two companies, which also maintain a register of foreign proof marks[4]. Penalties are imposed for offences in relation to the stamping and marking of barrels and for dealing with small arms not duly proved[5]. The Secretary of State[6] exercises certain supervisory functions[7].

1   The Gun Barrel Proof Act 1868, the Gun Barrel Proof Act 1950 (both of which are private Acts) and the Gun Barrel Proof Act 1978 may be cited together as the Gun Barrel Proof Acts 1868 to 1978: Gun Barrel Proof Act 1978 s 9(2). The Gun Barrel Proof Act 1978 amends earlier legislation to enable the United Kingdom to accede to the Convention for the Reciprocal Recognition of Proof Marks of Small-arms (Brussels, 1 July 1969; TS 84 (1980); Cmnd 8063). Nearly all countries which manufacture and export sporting weapons and other small arms are signatories to this convention. As to the meaning of 'United Kingdom' see PARA 3 note 2.

2   See the Gun Barrel Proof Act 1868 s 4 (amended by the Gun Barrel Proof Act 1978 Sch 3; and the Statute Law (Repeals) Act 1993); and the Gun Barrel Proof Act 1978 s 3.

3   The Gun Barrel Proof Acts 1868 to 1978 do not apply to government firearms: see the Gun Barrel Proof Act 1868 s 119 (amended by the Gun Barrel Proof Act 1978 Sch 3 para 9).

4   As to the register of foreign proof marks held by the Permanent International Commission for the Proof of Small Arms ('convention proof marks') see the Gun Barrel Proof Act 1868 s 129 (substituted by the Gun Barrel Proof Act 1978 Sch 1). As to charges for proving and marking barrels see the Gun Barrel Proof Act 1868 s 118 (amended by SI 1996/1576, so as to remove restrictions on maxima which may be charged). As to exemption of firearms which bear convention proof marks see the Gun Barrel Proof Act 1868 s 130 (substituted by the Gun Barrel Proof Act 1978 Sch 1).

5   See the Gun Barrel Proof Act 1868 ss 122, 143; the Gun Barrel Proof Act 1978 s 2; and CRIMINAL LAW vol 25 (2010) PARA 347. As to offences in relation to convention proof marks see the Gun Barrel Proof Act 1868 s 131 (substituted by the Gun Barrel Proof Act 1978 Sch 1).

6   Administrative functions under the Gun Barrel Proof Acts 1868 to 1950 had by 1966 devolved on to the Board of Trade and are therefore now exercisable by the Secretary of State. As to the Secretary of State see PARA 16.

7   See the Gun Barrel Proof Act 1868 s 117 (amended by the Gun Barrel Proof Act 1978 s 5, Sch 3).

(3) USE OF ROYAL ARMS

468. Restrictions on use of royal arms. A person may not without the authority of Her Majesty use in connection with any business the royal arms (or arms so closely resembling the royal arms as to be calculated to deceive) in such manner as to be calculated to lead to the belief that he is duly authorised to use the royal arms[1]. Nor may a person without the authority of Her Majesty or of a member of the royal family use in connection with any business any device, emblem or title in such a manner as to be calculated to lead to the belief that he is employed by, or supplies goods or services to, Her Majesty or that member of the royal family[2].

A person who contravenes the above provisions commits an offence and is liable on summary conviction to a fine[3].

Contravention of the above provisions may be restrained by injunction in proceedings brought by any person who is authorised to use the arms, device, emblem or title in question or any person authorised by the Lord Chamberlain to take such proceedings[4].

Nothing in the above provisions affects any right of the proprietor of a trade mark containing any such arms, device, emblem or title to use that trade mark[5].

If any person, in the course of any trade or business, gives, by whatever means, any false indication, direct or indirect, that any goods or services supplied by him or any methods adopted by him are or are of a kind supplied to or approved by Her Majesty or any member of the royal family, he is guilty of an offence[6].

If any person, in the course of any trade or business, uses, without the authority of Her Majesty, any device or emblem signifying the Queen's Award to Industry or anything so nearly resembling such a device or emblem as to be likely to deceive, he is guilty of an offence[7].

1   Trade Marks Act 1994 s 99(1). A royal warrant is an intimation from the proper authority representing the Crown that a particular trader has had dealings with the Crown, and is not an exercise of the royal prerogative: *Re Imperial Tobacco Co of Great Britain and Ireland's Trade Marks* [1915] 2 Ch 27, 32 RPC 40 (affd [1915] 2 Ch 27 at 41, 32 RPC 361, CA). As to the licensing of the use of the Royal Arms see CROWN AND ROYAL FAMILY vol 12(1) (Reissue) PARA 44.

2   Trade Marks Act 1994 s 99(2).

3   Trade Marks Act 1994 s 99(3). The fine must not exceed level 2 on the standard scale: see s 99(3). As to the standard scale see SENTENCING AND DISPOSITION OF OFFENDERS vol 92 (2010) PARA 142.

4   Trade Marks Act 1994 s 99(4).

5   Trade Marks Act 1994 s 99(5). Some trade marks may be lawful, even though they contain the royal arms or devices, emblems or titles within s 99: *Re Imperial Tobacco Co of Great Britain and Ireland's Trade Marks* [1915] 2 Ch 27 at 45, 32 RPC 361 at 369, CA. See also *Royal McBee Corpn's Applications* [1961] RPC 84.

6   See the Trade Descriptions Act 1968 s 12(1); and CONSUMER PROTECTION vol 21 (2011) PARA 518.

7   See the Trade Descriptions Act 1968 s 12(2); and CONSUMER PROTECTION vol 21 (2011) PARA 518.

(4) USE OF ARMORIAL BEARINGS

469.   The Court of Chivalry. Complaints relating to the usurpation of armorial bearings[1] are dealt with by the Court of Chivalry, which has jurisdiction in matters of dignity and arms as far as they are not cognisable by the ordinary courts[2].

1   As to armorial bearings generally see PEERAGES AND DIGNITIES vol 79 (2008) PARA 870 et seq. See also the Trade Marks Act 1994 s 99(5); and PARA 468.

2   See *Manchester Corpn v Manchester Palace of Varieties Ltd* [1955] P 133 at 149, [1955] 1 All ER 387 at 393, Court of Chivalry, per Lord Goddard, Surrogate; and PEERAGES AND DIGNITIES vol 79 (2008) PARA 874.

(5) USE OF NATIONAL EMBLEMS AND EMBLEMS OF INTERNATIONAL ORGANISATIONS

470.   National emblems of Convention countries. Where the authorisation of the competent authorities of a Convention country[1] is or would be required for the registration of a trade mark[2], those authorities are entitled to restrain by injunction[3] any use of the mark in the United Kingdom[4] without their authorisation[5].

1   As to the meaning of 'Convention country' see PARA 6 note 2.

2   Ie by virtue of the Trade Marks Act 1994 s 57: see PARA 51. As to the meaning of 'trade mark' see PARA 41.

3   As to enforcement by injunction under the Trade Marks Act 1994 generally see PARA 419 et seq.

4   As to the meaning of 'United Kingdom' see PARA 3 note 2.

5 Trade Marks Act 1994 s 57(6). Nothing in s 57 prevents the registration of a trade mark on the application of a national of a country who is authorised to make use of a state emblem, or official sign or hallmark, of that country, notwithstanding that it is similar to that of another country: see s 57(5); and PARA 34.

471. Emblems of international organisations. Where the authorisation of an international organisation is or would be required for the registration of a trade mark[1], that organisation is entitled to restrain by injunction[2] any use of the mark in the United Kingdom[3] without its authorisation[4].

1 Ie by virtue of the Trade Marks Act 1994 s 58: see PARA 52. As to the meaning of 'trade mark' see PARA 41.
2 As to enforcement by injunction under the Trade Marks Act 1994 generally see PARA 419 et seq.
3 As to the meaning of 'United Kingdom' see PARA 3 note 2.
4 Trade Marks Act 1994 s 58(4). Nothing in s 58 affects the rights of a person whose bona fide use of the trade mark in question began before 4 January 1962 (when the relevant provisions of the Paris Convention entered into force in relation to the United Kingdom): see the Trade Marks Act 1994 s 58(5); and PARA 52. As to the Paris Convention see PARA 6.

(6) THE OLYMPICS ASSOCIATION RIGHT, THE PARALYMPICS ASSOCIATION RIGHT AND THE LONDON OLYMPICS ASSOCIATION RIGHT

472. The Olympics Association Right, The Paralympics Association Right and The London Olympics Association Right. Provision is made for the creation of the Olympics association right and the Paralympics association right[1]. Those rights operate for the protection of the Olympic and Paralympic symbols, mottos and protected words[2]. They govern the use or authorisation of those controlled representations[3] by proprietors appointed by the Secretary of State, and define those usages of controlled representations which without the consent of the proprietors will or will not constitute infringement of the right[4]. Applying a controlled representation to goods, or distributing goods which bear a controlled representation, and various defined activities associated therewith, without the consent of the proprietor, is an offence[5].

Comparable provision was also made for the creation of a London Olympics Association Right, to restrict association between any goods and services and the London 2012 Olympics and Paralympics without the consent of the proprietor[6]. That right expired on 31 December 2012[7].

1 See the Olympic Symbol etc (Protection) Act 1995 ss 1, 5A; and SPORTS LAW vol 96 (2012) PARA 159 et seq. The various amendments to the Olympic Symbol etc (Protection) Act 1995 required to create and apply its provisions to the Paralympic association right were made by the London Olympic Games and Paralympic Games Act 2006.
2 As to those protected matters see SPORTS LAW vol 96 (2012) PARA 160.
3 As to the meaning of 'controlled representation' see SPORTS LAW vol 96 (2012) PARA 160.
4 See the Olympic Symbol etc (Protection) Act 1995 ss 2–4; and SPORTS LAW vol 96 (2012) PARAS 160–161. As to proceedings and remedies for infringement see SPORTS LAW vol 96 (2012) PARAS 162–163; as to groundless threats of action for infringement see SPORTS LAW vol 96 (2012) PARA 164.
5 See the Olympic Symbol etc (Protection) Act 1995 s 8; and SPORTS LAW vol 96 (2012) PARA 165.
6 See the London Olympic Games and Paralympic Games Act 2006 Sch 4; and SPORTS LAW vol 96 (2012) PARAS 166–170.
7 See the London Olympic Games and Paralympic Games Act 2006 s 40(8); and SPORTS LAW vol 96 (2012) PARA 166.

(7) USE OF RED CROSS AND MILITARY EMBLEMS

473. Restrictions on use of Red Cross and associated emblems. It is not lawful for any person, without the authority of the Secretary of State[1], to use for any purpose whatsoever any of the following emblems or designations[2]:

(1)   the emblem of a red cross with vertical and horizontal arms of the same length on, and completely surrounded by, a white ground, or the designation 'Red Cross' or 'Geneva Cross'[3];

(2)   the emblem of a red crescent moon on, and completely surrounded by, a white ground, or the designation 'Red Crescent'[4];

(3)   the following emblem in red on, and completely surrounded by, a white ground, that is to say, a lion passing from right to left of, and with its face turned towards, the observer, holding erect in its raised right forepaw a scimitar, with, appearing above the lion's back, the upper half of the sun shooting forth rays, or the designation 'Red Lion and Sun'[5];

(4)   the sign of an equilateral blue triangle on, and completely surrounded by, an orange ground, being the international distinctive sign of civil defence[6];

(5)   any of the distinctive symbols specified in Chapter III of Annex I to the first protocol to the Geneva Convention[7], being the signals of identification for medical units and transports[8];

(6)   the emblem of a red frame in the shape of a square on edge on a white ground conforming to the illustration prescribed in the third protocol to the Geneva Convention (and whether or not incorporating another emblem, or a combination of emblems), or the designation 'Red Crystal' or 'third Protocol emblem'[9].

Nor is it lawful for any person, without the authority of the Secretary of State, to use for any purpose whatsoever[10]:

(a)   any design consisting of a white or silver cross with vertical and horizontal arms of the same length on, and completely surrounded by, a red ground, being the heraldic emblem of the Swiss Confederation, or any other design so nearly resembling that design as to be capable of being mistaken for that heraldic emblem[11];

(b)   any design or wording so nearly resembling any of the emblems or designations specified in heads (1) to (3) above as to be capable of being mistaken for, or, as the case may be, understood as referring to, one of those emblems[12];

(c)   any design so nearly resembling the sign specified in head (4) above as to be capable of being mistaken for that sign[13];

(d)   any signal so nearly resembling any of the signals referred to in head (5) above as to be capable of being mistaken for one of those signals[14].

If any person contravenes the above provisions, he is guilty of an offence and liable on summary conviction to a fine[15] and to forfeit any goods or other article upon or in connection with which the emblem, designation, sign, signal, design or wording was used[16].

In the case of a trade mark registered before the specified date[17] the above provisions do not apply by reason only of its consisting of or containing a design or wording which reproduces or resembles an emblem or designation specified in head (2) or head (3) above, or a design reproducing or resembling the sign referred to in head (4) above[18], or a design or wording reproducing or resembling the emblem or a designation specified in head (6) above[19]; and, where a person is charged with using such a design or wording for any purpose and it is proved that he used it otherwise than as, or as part of, a trade mark so registered, it is a defence for him to prove[20]:

(i)   that he lawfully used that design or wording for that purpose before the specified date[21]; or

(ii)   in a case where he is charged with using the design or wording upon goods, that the design or wording had been applied to the goods before he acquired them by some other person who had manufactured or dealt with the goods in the course of trade and who lawfully used the design or wording upon similar goods before that date[22].

The above provisions extend to the use in or outside the United Kingdom[23] of any such emblem, designation, design, wording, sign or signal as is referred to in heads (1) to (5) above or heads (a) to (d) above on any British ship[24] or any British-controlled aircraft or hovercraft[25].

Any of the above provisions may be extended by order to the Channel Islands, the Isle of Man or any colony[26].

1   Ie the Secretary of State as successor to the Board of Trade. As to the Secretary of State see PARA 16.

2   Geneva Conventions Act 1957 s 6(1) (amended by the Geneva Conventions (Amendment) Act 1995 ss 2(2)(a), 5(a)(i)). As to the distinctive emblems of the Red Cross see ARMED CONFLICT AND EMERGENCY vol 3 (2011) PARA 29.

     As to the power of the Secretary of State to make regulations authorising specified uses and people for the purposes of the Geneva Conventions Act 1957 s 6(1), (2) see s 6A (added by the Geneva Conventions (Amendment) Act 1995 s 3; and amended by the Geneva Conventions and United Nations Personnel (Protocols) Act 2009 s 1(1), (6)).

3   Geneva Conventions Act 1957 s 6(1)(a).

4   Geneva Conventions Act 1957 s 6(1)(b).

5   Geneva Conventions Act 1957 s 6(1)(c).

6   Geneva Conventions Act 1957 s 6(1)(d) (s 6(1)(d), (e) added by the Geneva Conventions (Amendment) Act 1995 s 2(2)(b)).

7   Ie the Protocol, additional to the Geneva Conventions of 12 August 1949, and relating to the Protection of Victims of International Armed Conflicts done on 10 June 1977 (Geneva, 12 December 1977; Cmnd 6927) (the 'Geneva Conventions 1949 Protocol I') Annex I Ch III arts 6–9. The Protocol is set out in the Geneva Conventions Act 1957 Sch 5 (added by the Geneva Conventions (Amendment) Act 1995 Schedule). See ARMED CONFLICT AND EMERGENCY vol 3 (2011) PARA 18.

8   Geneva Conventions Act 1957 s 6(1)(e) (as added: see note 6).

9   See the Geneva Conventions Act 1957 s 6(1)(f) (added by the Geneva Conventions and United Nations Personnel (Protocols) Act 2009 s 1(4)). The third protocol is the Protocol, additional to the Geneva Conventions of 12 August 1949, and relating to the Adoption of an Additional Distinctive Emblem done on 8 December 2005 (Geneva, 8 December 2005; Misc 8 (2006); Cm 6917) (Geneva Conventions 1949 Protocol III). Protocol III has been implemented into English law by the Geneva Conventions and United Nations Personnel (Protocols) Act 2009, and is set out in the Geneva Conventions Act 1957 Sch 7; see ARMED CONFLICT AND EMERGENCY vol 3 (2011) PARAS 18, 29.

10 Geneva Conventions Act 1957 s 6(2) (amended by the Geneva Conventions (Amendment) Act 1995 s 2(3)(a)).

11 Geneva Conventions Act 1957 s 6(2)(a).

12 Geneva Conventions Act 1957 s 6(2)(b).

13 Geneva Conventions Act 1957 s 6(2)(c) (s 6(2)(c), (d) added by the Geneva Conventions (Amendment) Act 1995 s 2(3)(b)).

14 Geneva Conventions Act 1957 s 6(2)(d) (as added: see note 13).

15 Ie a fine not exceeding level 5 on the standard scale: see the Geneva Conventions Act 1957 s 6(3) (amended by the Geneva Conventions (Amendment) Act 1995 s 2(4)(a)–(c); and by virtue of the Criminal Justice Act 1982 ss 37, 38, 46). As to the standard scale see SENTENCING AND DISPOSITION OF OFFENDERS vol 92 (2010) PARA 142.

16 Geneva Conventions Act 1957 s 6(3) (as amended: see note 15). Proceedings under s 6 may not be instituted in England except by or on behalf of the Director of Public Prosecutions: s 6(7)

(amended by the Geneva Conventions (Amendment) Act 1995 s 2(7)). As to the Director of Public Prosecutions see CRIMINAL PROCEDURE vol 27 (2010) PARA 23.

As to the commission of such an offence by a body corporate see the Geneva Conventions Act 1957 s 6(5). As to bodies corporate see generally COMPANIES vol 14 (2009) PARA 1; CORPORATIONS.

17 Ie generally 31 July 1957, the date of the passing of the Geneva Conventions Act 1957.

In relation to head (4) in the text, this date is to be read as 19 July 1995 (ie the date of the passing of the Geneva Conventions (Amendment) Act 1995).

In relation to head (6) in the text, this date is to be read as 2 July 2009 (ie the date of the passing of the Geneva Conventions and United Nations Personnel (Protocols) Act 2009).

18 See the Geneva Conventions Act 1957 s 6(4A) (added by the Geneva Conventions (Amendment) Act 1995 s 2(5)). In relation to head (4) in the text the reference to 31 July 1957 is to be read as a reference to 19 July 1995: Geneva Conventions Act 1957 s 6(4A) (as so added). See note 17.

19 See the Geneva Conventions Act 1957 s 6(4B) (s 6(4B)–(4D) added by the Geneva Conventions and United Nations Personnel (Protocols) Act 2009 s 1(1), (5)). In relation to head (4) in the text the reference to 31 July 1957 is to be read as a reference to 2 July 2009: Geneva Conventions Act 1957 s 6(4D) (as so added).

However, s 6(4B) does not apply where the use of the design or wording concerned is such as would appear, in time of armed conflict, to confer the protection of the Geneva conventions and, where applicable, the first protocol and the second protocol: Geneva Conventions Act 1957 s 6(4C) (as so added). As to those conventions and protocols see ARMED CONFLICT AND EMERGENCY vol 3 (2011) PARA 18.

20 Geneva Conventions Act 1957 s 6(4).

21 Geneva Conventions Act 1957 s 6(4)(a). As to the specified date see note 17.

22 Geneva Conventions Act 1957 s 6(4)(b).

23 As to the meaning of 'United Kingdom' see PARA 3 note 2.

24 Ie within the meaning of what is now the Merchant Shipping Act 1995: see SHIPPING AND MARITIME LAW vol 93 (2008) PARA 230.

25 Geneva Conventions Act 1957 s 6(6) (amended by the Geneva Conventions (Amendment) Act 1995 s 2(6)). As to British-controlled aircraft or hovercraft see the Civil Aviation Act 1982 s 92, or s 92 as applied to hovercraft by virtue of any provision made under the Hovercraft Act 1968; and AIR LAW vol 2 (2008) PARA 619.

26 See the Geneva Conventions Act 1957 s 8(2) (amended by the Geneva Conventions (Amendment) Act 1995 s 5(b)); and the Geneva Conventions (Amendment) Act 1995 s 7(4); and the Geneva Conventions and United Nations Personnel (Protocols) Act 2009 s 3(3). As to orders extending those Acts see the Geneva Conventions Act (Guernsey) Order 1966, SI 1966/948 (amended by SI 2010/2965); the Geneva Conventions Act (Jersey) Order 1966, SI 1966/949; the Geneva Conventions Act (Guernsey) Order 1999, SI 1999/1316 (amended by SI 2010/2965); the Geneva Conventions (Overseas Territories) Order 2010, SI 2010/2963; the Geneva Conventions Act (Isle of Man) Order 2010, SI 2010/2964; and the Geneva Conventions Act (Jersey) Order 2012, SI 2012/2589.

474.   Restrictions on use of the word 'Anzac'. It is unlawful to use in connection with any trade, business, calling or profession the word 'Anzac'[1], or any word closely resembling that word, without the authority of a Secretary of State[2] given on the request of the government of Australia or New Zealand, notwithstanding that such word forms part of any trade mark, or of the name of any company or society or other body, which was registered before 15 December 1916[3].

If any person acts in contravention of the above provisions, he is guilty of an offence and liable on summary conviction to a fine[4].

1 'Anzac' is an abbreviation for 'Australian and New Zealand Army Corps'.

2 Ie one of Her Majesty's principal Secretaries of State: see PARA 16 note 1.

3 'Anzac' (Restriction on Trade Use of Word) Act 1916 s 1(1) (amended by the Statute Law Revision Act 1927).

4 'Anzac' (Restriction on Trade Use of Word) Act 1916 s 1(2) (amended by virtue of the Criminal Justice Act 1982 ss 35, 37, 38, 46). The fine must not exceed level 3 on the standard scale: see the 'Anzac' (Restriction on Trade Use of Word) Act 1916 s 1(2) (as so amended). As to the standard scale see SENTENCING AND DISPOSITION OF OFFENDERS vol 92 (2010) PARA 142.

When a company or society is guilty of any such contravention, without prejudice to the liability of the company or society, every director, manager, secretary or other officer of the company who is knowingly a party to the contravention is guilty of an offence and liable to the like penalty: s 1(2).

(8) USE OF INDICIA OF CHARTERED ASSOCIATIONS

475. Restrictions on use of indicia of chartered associations. The Chartered Associations (Protection of Names and Uniforms) Act 1926 restricts the use of the name, designation, uniform or badge of any association incorporated by Royal Charter (not being an association representative of any profession or business) protected by an order made under the Act[1].

1   See CORPORATIONS vol 24 (2010) PARA 322.

(9) CONTROLS OVER BUSINESS AND COMPANY NAMES

476. Business and company names. The Companies Act 2006 imposes controls on the use of certain descriptions and terms in business names[1]. The Act prohibits the use, without the approval of the Secretary of State, of: (1) a name which would be likely to give the impression that the business is connected with Her Majesty's Government, with the Welsh Assembly Government, with any part of the Scottish administration, with any local authority or with any public authority specified in regulations made under the Act[2]; (2) a name including a word or expression specified in regulations made under the Act[3]; (3) a name including a word or expression or other indication that is associated with a particular type of company or form of organisation specified in regulations made under the Act[4]; or (4) a name that gives so misleading an indication of the of the nature of the activities of the business as to be likely to cause harm to the public[5].

In the case of individuals and partnerships[6], specified details are required to appear on business letters, orders, invoices, receipts and demands for payments of debts[7]. A notice must be displayed in any premises where the business is carried on and to which customers have access[8]. Failure to comply with these requirements is an offence[9]. Breach of these requirements may give other parties a defence to a claim for breach of contract in certain circumstances[10].

Provision is made by the Companies Act 2006 restricting and regulating the names by which companies may be registered under the Act[11] and on the names used by overseas companies for business purposes in the United Kingdom[12].

1   See the Companies Act 2006 ss 1192–1199; and COMPANIES vol 14 (2009) PARA 223 et seq.
2   See the Companies Act 2006 s 1193. In connection with an application for the approval of the Secretary of State under ss 1193, 1194 regulations may be made under those provisions requiring an applicant to seek the view of a specified government department or other body: see s 1195. Approval given for the purposes of ss 1993, 1194 may be withdrawn: see s 1196.
3   See the Companies Act 2006 s 1194.
4   See the Companies Act 2006 s 1197.
5   See the Companies Act 2006 s 1198.
6   See PARTNERSHIP vol 79 (2008) PARA 9.
7   See the Companies Act 2006 s 1202.
8   See the Companies Act 2006 s 1204.
9   See the Companies Act 2006 s 1205.
10   See the Companies Act 2006 s 1206.
11   See the Companies Act 2006 Pt 5 (ss 53–85); and COMPANIES vol 14 (2009) PARA 196 et seq.
12   See the Companies Act 2006 ss 1047, 1048; and COMPANIES vol 15 (2009) PARA 1827.

INDEX

Trade Marks and Trade Names

References are to paragraph numbers; superior figures refer to notes

References are to paragraph numbers; superior figures refer to notes

References are to paragraph numbers; superior figures refer to notes

LONDON OLYMPICS ASSOCIATION
RIGHT
creation of, 472
MISREPRESENTATION
sponsorship, as to, 300
passing off action. *See* PASSING OFF
NATIONAL EMBLEMS
emblems, use of, 470
OFFENCES
bodies corporate, committed by, 122
Community trade mark, powers
applying in relation to, 251
counterfeit goods or packaging,
forfeiture of, 123
false representation of trade mark as
registered, 131
hallmarking, 466
partnership, committed by, 122
register, falsification of, 130
Trade Marks Act 1994, under, 121
unauthorised use—
defences, 127
exceptions, 127
goods and packaging, of, 124
making and possessing copies of
sign, 126
materials for packaging, signs on,
125
search warrant, issue of, 128
weights and measures authorities,
enforcement function of, 129
OFFICE FOR HARMONISATION IN
THE INTERNAL MARKET
administrative co-operation, 174
appeals from—
Board of Appeal, to, 274
decisions, 276
European Court of Justice, to, 277
European General Court, to, 331
European General Court, to, 277
examination of, 276
revision of decisions, 275
application for Community trade
mark—
amendment, 263
consideration of, 262
contents of, 261
division, 264
examination, 262
filing, 261
filing date, 262
jurisdiction, 331
languages of, 168, 171
opposition to, 265
priority—
effect of right, 269

OFFICE FOR HARMONISATION IN
THE INTERNAL
MARKET—*continued*
application for Community trade
mark—*continued*
priority—*continued*
exhibition, 268
right of, 267
publication, 262
registration, 266
restriction of, 263
seniority of national mark—
claiming, 270
effect of, 271
withdrawal, 263
budget, 166
contractual liability, 163
documents, access to, 170
establishment of, 163
exchange of publications, 174
fees, 167
files, inspection of, 172
financial control, 166
functions of, 163
invalidity, declaration of—
application for, 272
examination of application, 273
languages, 168
legality, control of, 169
organs of, 165
periodical publications, 173
proceedings in, rules, 260
register of Community trade marks,
maintenance of, 171
representation before—
capacity to act, 175
general principles of, 176
professional representatives—
communications with, privileged,
179
generally, 177
list of, 178
revocation—
application for, 272
examination of application, 273
seat, 163
senior officials, 164
staff, 164

OLYMPIC ASSOCIATION RIGHT
creation of, 472

OLYMPIC SYMBOL
special protection, 50

PARALLEL IMPORTS
meaning, 329
passing off, and, 329

References are to paragraph numbers; superior figures refer to notes

References are to paragraph numbers; superior figures refer to notes

Words and Phrases

Words in parentheses indicate the context in which the word or phrase is used

References are to paragraph numbers; superior figures refer to notes